THE CAMBRIDGE HISTORY OF
CANADIAN LITERATURE

From Aboriginal writing to Margaret Atwood, this is a complete English-language history of Canadian writing in English and French from its beginnings. The multi-authored volume pays special attention to works from the 1960s and after, to multicultural and Indigenous writing, popular literature, and the interaction of anglophone and francophone cultures throughout Canadian history. Established genres such as fiction, drama, and poetry are discussed alongside forms of writing which have traditionally received less attention, such as the essay, nature-writing, life-writing, journalism, and comics, and also writing in which the conventional separation between genres has broken down, such as the poetic novel. Written by an international team of distinguished scholars, the volume includes a separate, substantial section discussing major genres in French, as well as a detailed chronology of historical and literary / cultural events, and an extensive bibliography covering criticism in English and French.

CORAL ANN HOWELLS is Professor Emerita at the University of Reading and is currently Associate Fellow, Institute of English Studies, University of London. She has published widely on the topic of Canadian literature, especially on contemporary Canadian women writers including Margaret Atwood and Alice Munro. Editor of *The Cambridge Companion to Margaret Atwood* (Cambridge, 2006), she has twice been the recipient of the Margaret Atwood Society Best Book Prize, in 1997 and 2006. She is a Fellow of the Royal Society of Canada.

EVA-MARIE KROLLER is Professor in the Department of English at the University of British Columbia, Vancouver. Her numerous publications on Canadian literature include *Canadian Travellers in Europe, 1851–1900* (1987), *George Bowering: Bright Circles of Colour* (1992), and *The Cambridge Companion to Canadian Literature* (2004). She was editor of *Canadian Literature* (1995–2003) and she is a Fellow of the Royal Society of Canada.

THE CAMBRIDGE
HISTORY OF
CANADIAN LITERATURE

*

Edited by
CORAL ANN HOWELLS
and
EVA-MARIE KRÖLLER

CAMBRIDGE
UNIVERSITY PRESS

University Printing House, Cambridge CB2 8BS, United Kingdom

Published in the United States of America by Cambridge University Press, New York

Cambridge University Press is part of the University of Cambridge.

It furthers the University's mission by disseminating knowledge in the pursuit of education, learning and research at the highest international levels of excellence.

www.cambridge.org
Information on this title: www.cambridge.org/9781107646193

© Cambridge University Press 2009

This publication is in copyright. Subject to statutory exception and to the provisions of relevant collective licensing agreements, no reproduction of any part may take place without the written permission of Cambridge University Press.

First published 2009
First paperback edition 2014

A catalogue record for this publication is available from the British Library

ISBN 978-0-521-86876-1 Hardback
ISBN 978-1-107-64619-3 Paperback

Cambridge University Press has no responsibility for the persistence or accuracy of URLs for external or third-party internet websites referred to in this publication, and does not guarantee that any content on such websites is, or will remain, accurate or appropriate.

Contents

List of plates   page ix
List of maps   xi
List of contributors   xii
Acknowledgments   xiii
Chronology   xiv

Introduction
CORAL ANN HOWELLS AND EVA-MARIE KRÖLLER   1

PART ONE
OLD AND NEW WORLD, LA NOUVELLE-FRANCE,
THE CANADAS, DOMINION OF CANADA   7

1 · Native societies and French colonization   9
BARBARA BELYEA

2 · Reports from la Nouvelle-France: the Jesuit *Relations*, Marie de l'Incarnation, and Élisabeth Bégon   29
E. D. BLODGETT

3 · Migrations, multiple allegiances, and satirical traditions: from Frances Brooke to Thomas Chandler Haliburton   47
MARTA DVOŘÁK

4 · Writing in the Northwest: narratives, journals, letters, 1700–1870   67
BRUCE GREENFIELD

Contents

5 · Literature of settlement   87
CAROLE GERSON

6 · History in English and French, 1832–1898   104
E. D. BLODGETT

PART TWO
THE POST-CONFEDERATION PERIOD   125

7 · Post-Confederation poetry   127
D. M. R. BENTLEY

8 · Writing by Victorian naturalists   144
CHRISTOPH IRMSCHER

9 · Short fiction   166
GERALD LYNCH

10 · Bestselling authors, magazines, and the international market   185
MICHAEL PETERMAN

11 · Textual and social experiment in women's genres   204
JANICE FIAMENGO

12 · Canada and the Great War   224
SUSAN FISHER

PART THREE
MODELS OF MODERNITY,
POST-FIRST WORLD WAR   245

13 · Staging personalities in modernism and realism   247
IRENE GAMMEL

14 · E. J. Pratt and the McGill poets   272
ADRIAN FOWLER

Contents

15 · The 1940s and 1950s: signs of cultural change   289
CORAL ANN HOWELLS

16 · The Centennial   312
EVA-MARIE KRÖLLER

17 · Forms of non-fiction: Innis, McLuhan, Frye, and Grant   335
DAVID STAINES

PART FOUR
AESTHETIC EXPERIMENTS, 1960 AND AFTER   355

18 · Quartet: Atwood, Gallant, Munro, Shields   357
ROBERT THACKER

19 · The short story   381
W. H. NEW

20 · Canadian drama: performing communities   402
ANNE NOTHOF

21 · Poetry   422
KEVIN McNEILLY

22 · Poetry, drama, and the postmodern novel   441
IAN RAE

23 · Comic art and *bande dessinée*: from the funnies to graphic novels   460
JEAN-PAUL GABILLIET

24 · "Ghost stories": fictions of history and myth   478
TERESA GIBERT

25 · Indigenous writing: poetry and prose   499
LALLY GRAUER AND ARMAND GARNET RUFFO

26 · Contemporary Aboriginal theater   518
HELEN GILBERT

Contents

27 · Transcultural life-writing 536
ALFRED HORNUNG

28 · Multiculturalism and globalization 556
NEIL TEN KORTENAAR

PART FIVE
WRITING IN FRENCH 581

29 · Poetry 583
ROBERT YERGEAU

30 · Drama 605
JANE MOSS

31 · Fiction 629
RÉJEAN BEAUDOIN AND ANDRÉ LAMONTAGNE

Bibliography 652
Index 706

List of plates

1. Louis Nicolas, "Capitaine de la nation illinois. Il est armé de sa pipe et de son dard." ("Chief of the Illinois nation. He is armed with his pipe and his spear.") *Codex canadiensis* (*c.* 1700). Gilcrease Museum, Tulsa, OK. — *page* 21
2. "Carte dressée sur le rapport du nommé Onouatary, Sauvage Oneyoutte, établi, à la Présentation le 13 février 1756, dans Journal de la campagne d'hiver de Gaspard-Joseph Chaussegros de Léry, 1756." ("Map drawn up from the account of the aforesaid Onouatary, an Oneida Savage, recorded, at the presentation of 13 February 1756, in Gaspard-Joseph Chaussegros de Léry's journal of the winter campaign, 1756.") Musée de la civilisation, collection du Séminaire de Québec, fonds Viger-Verreau. P32/O-94D/L-71. — 22
3. Eric Gill, "The Martyrdom of Jean de Brébeuf," in *The Travels and Sufferings of Father Jean de Brébeuf Among the Hurons of Canada as Described by Himself*, ed. and tr. Theodore Besterman (London: Golden Cockerel Press, 1938). Bruce Peel Special Collections Library, University of Alberta. — 36
4. a) and b) Gospel of St. Mark in English and Mohawk, tr. Joseph Brant, 1787. British Library Board. All Rights Reserved 222.h.17 Rare Books. — 56
5. Thomas Chandler Haliburton, *The Clockmaker* (London: Richard Bentley, 1839). Koerner Library, the University of British Columbia. — 63
6. Plate III from Catharine Parr Traill and Agnes Fitzgibbon, *Canadian Wildflowers* (1868): "Yellow Adder's Tongue (*Erythronium Americanum*), Large White Trillium (*Trillium Grandiflorum*), Wild Columbine (*Aquilegia Canadensis*)." Reproduced from the Rare Book Collection of the Canadian Museum of Nature, Ottawa, Ontario. — 149
7. "Prairie Hen (*Cupidonia Cupio*)," chromolithograph from W. Ross King, *The Sportsman and Naturalist in Canada* (1866). Courtesy the Lilly Library, Indiana University, Bloomington. — 155
8. F. E. S. (i.e. Evvy Smith), "Princess Louise or Woolverton. For the Canadian Horticulturalist," from *The Canadian Horticulturalist* 11.9 (1888), frontispiece facing [p. 193]. Author's collection. — 160
9. "Pear Tree, Showing Pendulous Habit Caused by Weight of Fruit," illustration from photograph in J. T. Bealby, *Fruit Ranching in British Columbia*, 2nd edn. (1911), facing p. 192. Author's collection. — 161
10. Baroness Elsa von Freytag-Loringhoven in Costume, *c.* 1920. George Grantham Bain Collection, Library of Congress, Washington, DC. — 250

List of plates

11. F. P. Grove and Family, Lake Winnipeg, 1923. Leonard and Mary Grove, Toronto, Ontario. — 254
12. Cover image, Robert J. Stead's *Grain* (1926). George H. Doran Company. — 258
13. L. M. Montgomery, "Myself in 1902," self-portrait photograph taken in her bedroom in Cavendish. L. M. Montgomery Collection, Archival and Special Collections, University of Guelph Archives. *L. M. Montgomery* is a trademark of Heirs of L. M. Montgomery Inc. — 266
14. Graeme Taylor, John Glassco, and Robert McAlmon on the beach at Nice, c. 1928. PA 188182. Library and Archives of Canada. Courtesy of William Toye, literary executor for the estate of John Glassco. — 270
15. "Nelvana of the Northern Lights," drawn by Adrian Dingle, front cover Triumph-Adventure Comics, c. 1945. Copyright Nelvana Limited. Used with permission. All rights reserved. Copyright Library and Archives Canada. Reproduced with the permission of the Minister of Public Works and Government Services Canada (2008). — 465
16. Steven Keewatin Sanderson, *Darkness Calls*. Healthy Aboriginal Network, Vancouver, 2006. — 466
17. Margaret Atwood, "Survivalwoman." Copyright Margaret Atwood, *This Magazine*, 1975. — 470

List of maps

1. Canada *page* xlvi
2. Tribal distributions in and near Canada at time of contact xlvii

List of contributors

RÉJEAN BEAUDOIN University of British Columbia
BARBARA BELYEA University of Calgary
D. M. R. BENTLEY University of Western Ontario
E. D. BLODGETT University of Alberta
MARTA DVOŘÁK Sorbonne Nouvelle
JANICE FIAMENGO University of Ottawa
SUSAN FISHER University of the Fraser Valley
ADRIAN FOWLER Sir Wilfred Grenfell College, Memorial University of Newfoundland
JEAN-PAUL GABILLIET Université de Bordeaux
IRENE GAMMEL Ryerson University
CAROLE GERSON Simon Fraser University
TERESA GIBERT Universidad Nacional de Educación a Distancia, Madrid
HELEN GILBERT Royal Holloway College, University of London
LALLY GRAUER University of British Columbia Okanagan
BRUCE GREENFIELD Dalhousie University
ALFRED HORNUNG Johannes-Gutenberg-Universität
CORAL ANN HOWELLS University of Reading / University of London
CHRISTOPH IRMSCHER Indiana University
NEIL TEN KORTENAAR University of Toronto
EVA-MARIE KRÖLLER University of British Columbia
ANDRÉ LAMONTAGNE University of British Columbia
GERALD LYNCH University of Ottawa
KEVIN MCNEILLY University of British Columbia
JANE MOSS Colby College / Duke University
WILLIAM H. NEW University of British Columbia
ANNE NOTHOF Athabasca University
MICHAEL PETERMAN Trent University
IAN RAE King's University College at The University of Western Ontario
ARMAND GARNET RUFFO Carleton University
DAVID STAINES University of Ottawa
ROBERT THACKER St. Lawrence University
ROBERT YERGEAU University of Ottawa

Acknowledgments

We thank the contributors for their fine work and collegiality, the University of British Columbia and the Foundation for Canadian Studies in the United Kingdom for financial support, Laura Potter and Melanie Sanderson for excellent research assistance, Dominique Yupangco and Miranda Clifford for expert technical help, and Patricia Lackie and Carol Wong for efficient clerical support. Robin Howells, David Staines, André Lamontagne, Réjean Beaudoin, Lally Grauer, and Gordon Bölling gave generous scholarly advice. We also thank the individuals who assisted us with the illustrations, and acknowledge especially Robert Desmarais of the Bruce Peel Special Collections Library at the University of Alberta and Sean Muir of the Healthy Aboriginal Network, as well as Tim Ford for his work on the illustrations in Christoph Irmscher's chapter. We thank Rebecca Jones and Rosina Di Marzo at Cambridge University Press, and our copy editor, David Watson. Sarah Stanton was, as always, an inspiring editor.

Chronology

Year	Historical	Literary and Cultural
c. 12,000 BCE	Asiatic migrants cross land bridge in the Bering Sea to North America	
c. 11,000 BCE	Bluefish Caves (Yukon): earliest evidence of human habitation in North America currently recorded	
10,000–8000 BCE	Cordilleran and Laurentian ice sheets retreat	
	Fluted Point and Early Microblade cultures spread across North America	
8000–4000 BCE	Plano people: first recorded cremation burial	
4000–1000 BCE	Maritime Archaic people: use toggling harpoon and large watercraft; construct burial mounds containing funereal gifts; Laurentian Archaic and Shield Archaic people: leave gifts, some elaborately crafted, with the dead	
1000 BCE–CE 500	Point Peninsula / Meadowood / Saugeen people: earth-mound burial; silver ornaments	
	Middle Northwest Coast people: development of elaborate artifacts	
	Late Palaeo-Eskimo: bone and ivory carvings	

Chronology

Year	Historical	Literary and Cultural
CE 500–European contact	Northern Algonquin (including Beothuk) and Late Nesikep: rock art	
985/986	First European sighting of Baffin Island ("Helluland"), Labrador ("Markland"), and the Gulf of St. Lawrence ("Vinland"), as recounted in Bjarno Harjulfsen's *Graenlendinga Saga*	
1000	Viking Settlement in Newfoundland	
1390–1450	Iroquois Confederacy	
1497	John Cabot sails to Newfoundland	
1545		Jacques Cartier, *Bref récit et succincte narration de la navigation faite en MDXXXV et MDXXXVI par le Capitaine Jacques Cartier aux îles de Canada, Hochelaga, Saguenay et autres*
1534	Jacques Cartier sails to the Gulf of St. Lawrence	
1556	First map of New France, by Giacomo Gastaldi, published in Giovanni Ramusio's *Navigationi e viaggi*, an account of Cartier's 1534 voyage	
1576, 1577, 1578	Martin Frobisher's Arctic expeditions	
1605	Founding of Port Royal	
1606		Marc Lescarbot's *Le Théâtre de Neptune* performed in Port Royal harbor
1608	Quebec founded by Samuel de Champlain	
1610	Henry Hudson sails to Hudson Bay	Jesuit *Relations* (published 1632–73) begin with Pierre Biard's letters from Acadia
1613		*Les Voyages du Sieur de Champlain Xaintongeois*

Chronology

Year	Historical	Literary and Cultural
1624	First written treaty (Algonquin–French–Mohawk Peace)	
1627	Creation of the Compagnie des cent associés	
1632		Gabriel Sagard, *Le Grand Voyage du pays des Hurons*; Marie de l'Incarnation begins her *Écrits spirituels* (1632–1654)
1642	Ville Marie (Montreal) founded	
1639	Marie de l'Incarnation sails for Quebec	
1659	Pierre-Esprit Radisson and Médard Chouart de Groseilliers travel to Lake Superior and Michigan	
1664	François du Creux, in *Historiae canadiensis, seu Nova-Franciae*, describes an "immensity of woods and prairies"	Pierre Boucher, *Histoire véritable et naturelle des mœurs et productions du pays de la Nouvelle-France*
1670	Hudson's Bay Company begins operations	
1680	Death of Kateri Tekakwitha (beatified in 1980)	
1694		L'Affaire *Tartuffe*
1697		Louis Hennepin's *Nouvelle découverte d'un très grand pays* features the first published illustration of Niagara Falls
1701	Peace of Montreal	
1703		Louis-Armand de Lahontan, *Nouveaux voyages de M. le baron de Lahontan dans l'Amérique septentrionale*; *Mémoires de l'Amérique septentrionale* (1703); *Supplément aux voyages du Baron de Lahontan* (1704)
1713	Treaty of Utrecht	
1744		Pierre-François Xavier de Charlevoix, *Histoire et description générale de la Nouvelle France*
1748		Marie-Elisabeth Bégon (1696–1755) writes letters to

Chronology

Year	Historical	Literary and Cultural
		her son-in-law, published as *Lettres au cher fils* (ed. Nicole Deschamps) in 1972
1751	First printing press in Nova Scotia	
1753		Peter Kalm's *Travels* published in Sweden (English version: 1770)
1755	Deportation of the Acadians	
1756	Seven Years' War begins (1756–63)	
1759	Battle of the Plains of Abraham	
1763	Treaty of Paris	
1764	First printing press in Quebec: *La Gazette de Québec* begins publication	
1769		Frances Brooke, *The History of Emily Montague*
1775	American War of Independence begins (1775–83)	
1776	American Declaration of Independence	
1778	James Cook in Nootka Sound	*Gazette littéraire de Montréal* begins publication (1778–9)
1792	Captains George Vancouver and Dionisio Alcalà Galiano on the West Coast	
1783	An estimated 40,000 Loyalists emigrate from the United States to Maritimes and Canada	
1789	French Revolution; Alexander Mackenzie travels to Beaufort Sea (1793 expedition from Canada to Pacific, arriving at the Bella Coola River)	
1812	War of 1812; Selkirk Settlement on Red River founded	
1819–22	First Franklin overland expedition	
1821	Completion of Lachine Canal	Thomas McCulloch, *Letters of Mephibosheth Stepsure*; Julia

Chronology

Year	Historical	Literary and Cultural
		Hart, *St. Ursula's Convent; or, The Nun of Canada*
1825		Oliver Goldsmith, *The Rising Village*
1829	Shanawdithit (known as Nancy or Nance April), the last known Beothuk, dies	
1832		John Richardson, *Wacousta; or, The Prophecy*
1833	First Canadian steamship, the *Royal William*, crosses the Atlantic	
1836		Catharine Parr Traill, *The Backwoods of Canada*; Thomas Chandler Haliburton, *The Clockmaker, or The Sayings and Doings of Samuel Slick of Slickville*
1837	Rebellion, Upper Canada, Lower Canada	Aubert de Gaspé fils, *L'Influence d'un livre*
1838		*Literary Garland* (1838–51); Anna Jameson, *Winter Studies and Summer Rambles in Canada*
1839	Lord Durham's Report	
1841	Act of Union (Upper and Lower Canada)	
1844	Institut canadien founded; Toronto *Globe* established	Antoine Gérin-Lajoie, "Un Canadien errant: le proscrit"
1845		François-Xavier Garneau, *Histoire du Canada depuis sa découverte jusqu'à nos jours* begins publication: 4 vols. (1845–8)
1845	Last sighting, in July, of Sir John Franklin's second overland expedition in Baffin Bay; Franklin's disappearance triggers some forty-two expeditions into the Arctic North between 1847 and 1879	
1846		Patrice Lacombe, *La Terre paternelle*
1847		Henry Wadsworth Longfellow, *Evangeline, a Tale of Acadie*

Chronology

Year	Historical	Literary and Cultural
1848		James Huston, *Le Répertoire national, ou Recueil de littérature canadienne*; Pierre Boucher de Boucherville, *Une de perdue, deux de trouvées*
1852		Susanna Moodie, *Roughing it in the Bush*
1853		Moodie, *Life in the Clearings*; Olivier Chauveau, *Charles Guérin*
1854	Seigneurial system abolished; Reciprocity Treaty between Canada and the United States (the first international free trade agreement)	
1856		Charles Sangster, *The St. Lawrence and the Saguenay*
1857	Ottawa named capital of Canada; Palliser and Hind-Dawson expeditions to Northwest	
1862		Octave Crémazie, "Promenade de trois morts"; Gérin-Lajoie, *Jean Rivard, le défricheur canadien*
1863		Aubert de Gaspé père, *Les Anciens Canadiens*; Goldwin Smith, *The Empire*
1864		Rosanna Leprohon, *Antoinette de Mirecourt*; Antoine Gérin-Lajoie, *Jean Rivard, économiste*; Arthur Buies, *Lettres sur le Canada*; Charles Taché, *Forestiers et voyageurs*; *Revue canadienne* begins publication (1864–1922)
1865		Ernest Gagnon, *Chansons populaires du Canada*
1866		Napoléon Bourassa, *Jacques et Marie*
1867	British North America Act; Confederation; Constitution Act recognizes English and French as official languages in	

Chronology

Year	Historical	Literary and Cultural
	Parliament and Canadian courts; Sir John Macdonald Prime Minister (1867–73; 1878–91)	
1868	Canada First Movement founded	Catharine Parr Traill and Agnes Moodie Fitzgibbon, *Canadian Wild Flowers*
1869	Red River Rebellion (led by Louis Riel)	*Canadian Illustrated News* begins publication (1869–83)
1870	Manitoba and Northwest Territories join Confederation	
1871	British Columbia joins Confederation	
1872	Creation of the Public Archives of Canada	
1873	Prince Edward Island joins Confederation	
1875		Honoré Beaugrand, *Jeanne la Fileuse* begins publication in *La République*
1876	Indian Act	
1877		William Kirby, *The Golden Dog: A Legend of Quebec*
1880	Calixa Lavallée composes "O Canada" (words Adolphe-Basile Routhier)	Ch. G. D. Roberts, *Orion and Other Poems*
1882	Royal Society of Canada founded by the Marquis de Lorne, Governor-General of Canada	
1884	Standard Time Zone system introduced; potlatch ceremony prohibited; Riel Rebellion (1884–5)	Laure Conan, *Angéline de Montbrun*; Isabella Valancy Crawford, *Old Spookses' Pass, Malcolm's Katie and Other Poems*
1885	Canadian Pacific Railway completed; Chinese Immigration Act	
1887		Louis Fréchette, *La Légende d'un peuple*; *Saturday Night* magazine begins publication (1887–2001)

Chronology

Year	Historical	Literary and Cultural
1888		Archibald Lampman, *Among the Millet*; James de Mille, *A Strange Manuscript Found in a Copper Cylinder*; *The Week* begins publication (1888–95)
1889		William D. Lighthall, *Songs of the Great Dominion*
1890	Manitoba Schools Act	
1892		Louis Fréchette, *Originaux et détraqués*
1893		*Canadian Magazine* (combined earlier *Massey's Magazine* and *Canadian Magazine of Politics, Science, Art and Literature*) begins publication (1893–1937)
1895		L'École littéraire de Montréal founded; Jules-Paul Tardivel, *Pour la Patrie*
1896	Sir Wilfrid Laurier Prime Minister (1896–1911)	Gilbert Parker, *The Seats of the Mighty*; Ch. G. D. Roberts, *Earth's Enigmas*; *Maclean's Magazine* begins publication; Edmond de Nevers, *L'Avenir du peuple canadien-français*
1897	Women's Institute established	William Drummond, *The Habitant and Other French Canadian Poems*
1898	Yukon Territory formed	Ernest Thompson Seton, *Wild Animals I Have Known*
1899–1902	Boer War causes divisiveness between English and French Canadians	
1901		Ralph Connor, *The Man from Glengarry*
1904		Sara Jeannette Duncan, *The Imperialist*; *Émile Nelligan et son œuvre*, ed. Louis Dantin; Rodolphe Girard, *Marie Calumet*; Charles ab der Halden, *Études de littérature canadienne-française*; Pamphile Le May, *Les Gouttelettes*

Chronology

Year	Historical	Literary and Cultural
1905	Alberta and Saskatchewan become provinces	
1906		Camille Roy gives his first course in Canadian literature; Alfred Garneau, *Poésies*
1907		Robert Service, *Songs of a Sourdough*; Albert Lozeau, *L'Âme solitaire*; Camille Roy, *Essais sur la littérature canadienne*; *Tableau de l'histoire de la littérature canadienne-française*
1908		L. M. Montgomery, *Anne of Green Gables*; Nellie McClung, *Sowing Seeds in Danny*; Martin Allerdale Grainger, *Woodsmen of the West*
1909	Canadian Commission of Conservation established	
1911		Pauline Johnson, *Legends of Vancouver*; "Lettres de Fadette" begin in *Le Devoir*; Paul Morin, *Le Paon d'émail*
1912	Public Archives Act	Stephen Leacock, *Sunshine Sketches of a Little Town*
1913	National Gallery of Canada Act	Marjorie Pickthall, *The Drift of Pinions*; Blanche Lamontagne-Beauregard, *Visions gaspésiennes*
1914	First World War begins; War Measures Act; Komagata Maru Incident	Adjutor Rivard, *Chez nous*; Arsène Bessette, *Le Débutant*; film: Edward Curtis, *In the Land of the Head Hunters*
1915		John McCrae's "In Flanders Fields" published in *Punch* magazine
1916	Voting rights to women in Manitoba, Saskatchewan, Alberta	Louis Hémon, *Maria Chapdelaine*, serialized in *Le Temps* (France), 1914; Marcel Dugas, *Psyché au cinéma*
1917	Halifax Explosion; Conscription Crisis; Battle of Vimy Ridge	

Chronology

Year	Historical	Literary and Cultural
1918	First World War ends	Albert Laberge, *La Scouine*; *Le Nigog* founded (twelve issues); Camille Roy, *Manuel d'histoire de la littérature canadienne-française*
1919	Winnipeg General Strike; Immigration Amendment Act	Lionel Groulx, *La Naissance d'une race*; Marie-Victorin, *Récits laurentiens*; *Canadian Bookman* begins publication (1919–39)
1920		Group of Seven founded; Ray Palmer Baker, *A History of English Canadian Literature to Confederation*; Jean-Aubert Loranger, *Les Atmosphères*
1921	Mackenzie King Prime Minister (1921–6, 1926–30, 1935–48)	Canadian Authors' Association founded; Léon Petitjean and Henri Rollin, *Aurore, l'enfant martyre*
1922		Prix Athanase-David founded
1923	Chinese Exclusion Act	
1924		Lionel Groulx, *Notre maître le passé*
1925		F. P. Grove, *Settlers of the Marsh*; Martha Ostenso, *Wild Geese*; *McGill Fortnightly Review* begins publication (1925–7); Robert Choquette, *À travers les vents*
1927	Old Age Pensions Act	F. P. Grove, *A Search for America*; Mazo de la Roche, *Jalna*
1928		*Chatelaine* begins publication
1929	Persons Case; Wall Street Crash	Alfred Desrochers, *À l'ombre de l'Orford*
1931	Statute of Westminster	Jovette Bernier, *La Chair décevante*; Albert Pelletier, *Carquois*
1933		Claude Henri Grignon, *Un homme et son péché* (radio serial 1939–62); Alain Grandbois, *Né à Québec*; Charles G. D. Roberts, *Eyes of the Wilderness*

Chronology

Year	Historical	Literary and Cultural
1932		Jean Narrache, *Quand j'parl' tout seul*
1934	Archibald Belaney (Grey Owl), *Pilgrims in the Wild*	Morley Callaghan, *Such Is My Beloved*; Jean-Charles Harvey, *Les Demi-Civilisés*; Alain Grandbois, *Poèmes*; Médje Vézina, *Chaque heure a son visage*; Simone Routier, *La Tentation*
1935	John Buchan (Lord Tweedsmuir) Governor-General (1935–40)	
1936	Canadian Broadcasting Corporation established as independent Crown corporation; Trans-Canada Airlines (changed to Air Canada 1965)	First Governor General's Literary Awards; Morley Callaghan, *Now That April's Here and Other Stories*; A. J. M. Smith et al., *New Provinces*
1937		Donald Creighton, *The Commercial Empire of the St. Lawrence, 1760–1850*; Hector de Saint-Denys Garneau, *Regards et jeux dans l'espace*; Félix-Antoine Savard, *Menaud, maître-draveur*; Gratien Gélinas, *Fridolinades*
1938		Ringuet, *Trente arpents*
1939	Canada enters the Second World War	National Film Board founded; Anne Marriott, *The Wind Our Enemy*; Irene Baird, *Waste Heritage*; Léo-Paul Desrosiers, *Les Engagés du Grand Portage*
1940	Unemployment Insurance Act; voting rights granted to women in Quebec (the last province to do so)	A. M. Klein, *Hath Not a Jew*; E. J. Pratt, *Brébeuf and His Brethren*
1941	Pearl Harbor	Emily Carr, *Klee Wyck*; Sinclair Ross, *As For Me and My House*; Hugh MacLennan, *Barometer Rising*
1942	Dominion Plebiscite Act; Conscription Crisis; Internment of Japanese Canadians	Earle Birney, *David and Other Poems*

Chronology

Year	Historical	Literary and Cultural
1943		A. J. M. Smith, *News of the Phoenix*; *Book of Canadian Poetry: A Critical and Historical Anthology*; E. K. Brown, *On Canadian Poetry*; Félix Leclerc, *Adagio*
1944		Donald Creighton, *Dominion of the North*; Gwethalyn Graham, *Earth and High Heaven*; Roger Lemelin, *Au pied de la pente douce*; Yves Thériault, *Contes pour un homme seul*; Alain Grandbois, *Les Îles de la nuit*
1945	Germany capitulates; nuclear bombs dropped on Hiroshima and Nagasaki; Japan capitulates	Gabrielle Roy, *Bonheur d'occasion* (1947 Prix Fémina); Hector de Saint-Denys Garneau, *Journal*; Germaine Guèvremont, *Le Survenant*; Hugh MacLennan, *Two Solitudes*; Elizabeth Smart, *By Grand Central Station I Sat Down and Wept*
1946	Canadian Citizenship Act	Félix Leclerc, *Pieds nus dans l'aube*; Gilles Hénault, *Théâtre en plein air*; Berthelot Brunet, *Histoire de la littérature canadienne-française*; Lionel Groulx founds the Institut d'histoire de l'Amérique française
1947	Chinese Exclusion Act revoked; GATT (General Agreement on Tariffs and Trade)	John Sutherland, *Other Canadians*; Malcolm Lowry, *Under the Volcano*; W. O. Mitchell, *Who Has Seen the Wind*; Rina Lasnier, *Le Chant de la montée*; Clément Marchand, *Les Soirs rouges*; Robert Charbonneau, *La France et nous*
1948	Japanese Canadians (as last Asian Canadians) acquire the right to vote; Universal	Paul-Émile Borduas et al., *Refus global*; Gratien Gélinas, *Tit-Coq*; Roger Lemelin, *Les*

Chronology

Year	Historical	Literary and Cultural
	Declaration of Human Rights, United Nations	*Plouffe*; Paul-Marie Lapointe, *Le Vierge incendié*
1949	Asbestos Strike in Quebec; Newfoundland enters Confederation	Françoise Loranger, *Mathieu*; Robert Giguère, *Faire naître*; Paul Borduas, *Projections libérantes*; Hector de Saint-Denys Garneau, *Poésies complètes*
1950		Pierre Trudeau and Gérard Pelletier found *Cité libre*; Anne Hébert, *Le Torrent*; Harold Innis, *Empire and Communications*; Dorothy Livesay, *Call My People Home*; John Coulter, *Riel*; Gabrielle Roy, *La Petite Poule d'eau*; Robert Elie, *La Fin des songes*; Lionel Groulx, *Histoire du Canada français depuis la découverte*, 4 vols.
1951	Indian Act; Report of the Royal Commission on National Development in the Arts, Letters and Sciences (the Massey Report)	A. M. Klein, *The Second Scroll*; Marshall McLuhan, *The Mechanical Bride*
1952	Vincent Massey first Canadian Governor-General; National Library Act; Universal Copyright Act	Ernest Buckler, *The Mountain and the Valley*; E. J. Pratt, *Towards the Last Spike*; Marcel Dubé, *De l'autre côté du mur*; Emile Nelligan, *Poésies complètes, 1896–1899*, ed. Luc Lacourcière; Ernest Gagnon, *L'Homme d'ici*
1953	Historic Sites and Monuments Act	Anne Hébert, *Le Tombeau des rois*; Marcel Dubé, *Zone*; André Langevin, *Poussière sur la ville*
1954		Ethel Wilson, *Swamp Angel*; Mordecai Richler, *The Acrobats*; Hector de Saint-Denys Garneau, *Journal*; Yves Thériault, *Aaron*

Chronology

Year	Historical	Literary and Cultural
1954–75	Vietnam War; Canada receives more than 125,000 draft evaders from the US	Margaret Laurence, *A Tree for Poverty*
1955		Gabrielle Roy, *Rue Deschambault*; music: Glenn Gould records Bach's *Goldberg Variations*; Félix Leclerc records "Moi, mes souliers"
1956	Avro Arrow production cancelled	Leonard Cohen, *Let Us Compare Mythologies*; Adele Wiseman, *The Sacrifice*; Sam Selvon, *The Lonely Londoners*
1957	Lester Pearson receives the Nobel Peace Prize; Canada Council Act	New Canadian Library begins publication under the editorship of Malcolm Ross; Northrop Frye, *Anatomy of Criticism*; John Marlyn, *Under the Ribs of Death*; Mordecai Richler, *A Choice of Enemies*; Jacques Languirand, *Les Grands Départs*
1958		Yves Thériault, *Agaguk*; Norman Levine, *Canada Made Me*; Marcel Dubé, *Un simple soldat*; Jacques Ferron, *Les Grands Soleils*; Michel van Schendel, *Poèmes de l'Amérique étrangère*; Prix France-Canada founded (1982: Prix Québec-Paris)
1959	Maurice Duplessis, Premier of Quebec, dies, ending "La grande noirceur"; St. Lawrence Seaway completed	*Canadian Literature* begins publication under the editorship of George Woodcock; *Liberté* established; Mordecai Richler, *The Apprenticeship of Duddy Kravitz*; Sheila Watson, *The Double Hook*; Irving Layton, *A Red Carpet for the Sun*; Hugh MacLennan, *The Watch That Ends the Night*; Gratien Gélinas, *Bousille et les justes*; Marie-Claire Blais, *La Belle Bête*; Gilbert Langevin, *À la gueule du jour*

Chronology

Year	Historical	Literary and Cultural
1960	Quiet Revolution 1960–6; Rassemblement pour l'indépendance nationale (RIN) founded; Status Indians acquire the right to vote; regular jet-service Toronto–Vancouver	Margaret Avison, *Winter Sun*; Phyllis Brett Young, *The Torontonians*; Margaret Laurence, *This Side Jordan*; Brian Moore, *The Luck of Ginger Coffey*; Jean-Paul Desbiens, *Les Insolences d'un frère untel*; Gérard Bessette, *Le Libraire*; *Châtelaine* begins publication
1961	Parent Commission begins work	Margaret Atwood, *Double Persephone*; *TISH* begins publication (1961–9); Jean Le Moyne, *Convergences*
1962	Trans-Canada highway completed	Marshall McLuhan, *The Gutenberg Galaxy*; Earle Birney, *Ice Cod Bell or Stone*; Rudy Wiebe, *Peace Shall Destroy Many*; Gilles Marcotte, *Une Littérature qui se fait*; Jacques Ferron, *Contes du pays incertain*
1963	Lester Pearson Prime Minister (1963–8); Jacques Ferron founds the Rhinoceros Party; the Front de libération du Québec (FLQ) plants its first bomb (at the English-speaking CKGM radio station)	Solange Chaput-Rolland and Gwethalyn Graham, *Chers ennemis / Dear Enemies*; Farley Mowat, *Never Cry Wolf*; Leonard Cohen, *The Favourite Game*; Margaret Laurence, *The Tomorrow-Tamer*; *The Prophet's Camel Bell*; Mordecai Richler, *The Incomparable Atuk*; *Parti pris* begins publication (1963–8); Pierre Vadeboncœur, *La Ligne du risque*; Gatien Lapointe, *Ode au Saint-Laurent*
1964		Marshall McLuhan, *Understanding Media*; Margaret Laurence, *The Stone Angel*; Jane Rule, *Desert of the Heart*; Earle Birney, *Near False Creek Mouth*; Paul

Chronology

Year	Historical	Literary and Cultural
		Chamberland, *L'Afficheur hurle*; *Terre Québec*; Claude Jasmin, *Ethel et le terroriste*; Jacques Renaud, *Le Cassé*; Jean Basile, *La Jument des Mongoles*; film: Gilles Groulx, *Le Chat dans le sac*; Michel Brault, Pierre Perreault, *Pour la suite du monde*
1965	Canada adopts the Maple Leaf flag	George Grant, *Lament for a Nation*; Carl F. Klinck et al., *Literary History of Canada in English*; Hubert Aquin, *Prochain épisode*; Marie-Claire Blais, *Une saison dans la vie d'Emmanuel* (Prix Médicis); Claire Martin, *Dans un gant de fer*; Jacques Godbout, *Le Couteau sur la table*; Roland Giguère, *L'Âge de la parole: poèmes inédits 1949–1960*; Jacques Ferron, *La Nuit*; Jacques Brault, *Mémoire*; first performance of "Mon pays" by Gilles Vigneault; Prix France-Québec founded (now France-Québec Jean-Hamelin); Edmund Wilson, *O Canada: An American's Notes on Canadian Culture*; film: Gilles Carle, *La Vie heureuse de Léopold Z*; Arthur Lamothe, *Poussière sur la ville*
1966	Medical Care Act	Leonard Cohen, *Beautiful Losers*; Réjean Ducharme, *L'Avalée des avalés*
1967	Centennial of Confederation; Expo 67 in Montreal; René Levesque founds the Mouvement souveraineté-association	House of Anansi founded by Dave Godfrey and Dennis Lee; Marshall McLuhan, *The Medium Is the Massage*; George Ryga, *The Ecstasy of*

Chronology

Year	Historical	Literary and Cultural
		Rita Joe; John Herbert, *Fortune and Men's Eyes*; P. K. Page, *Cry Ararat!*; Scott Symons, *Place d'Armes*; Jacques Godbout, *Salut Galarneau!*; Glenn Gould, *The Idea of North*; Yves Préfontaine, *Pays sans parole*; André Prévost, Michèle Lalonde, *Terre des hommes* (oratorio); Michel Brault, *Entre la mer et l'eau douce*; Gérald Godin, *Les Cantouques*; Pierre de Grandpré, ed., *Histoire de la littérature française du Québec*, 4 vols., begins publication (1967–9)
1968	Pierre Trudeau Prime Minister (1968–79; 1980–4); Parti Québécois founded	Dennis Lee, *Civil Elegies*; Margaret Atwood, *The Animals in That Country*; bill bissett, *awake in the red desert*; Alice Munro, *Dance of the Happy Shades*; Mordecai Richler, *Cocksure*; Margaret Atwood, *The Animals in That Country*; Hubert Aquin, *Trou de mémoire* (refuses Governor General's Award); Pierre Vallières, *Nègres blancs d'Amérique*; Michel Tremblay, *Les Belles-Sœurs*; Denis Héroux, *Valérie*; Roch Carrier, *La Guerre yes sir!*; Fernand Dumont, *Le Lieu de l'homme*; Victor-Lévy Beaulieu begins *La Vraie Saga des Beauchemin*
1969	Official Languages Act passed; White Paper	Harold Cardinal, *The Unjust Society: The Tragedy of Canada's Indians*; George Grant, *Technology and Empire*; Jacques Ferron, *Le Ciel de*

Chronology

Year	Historical	Literary and Cultural
		Québec; Robert Kroetsch, The Studhorse Man; Milton Acorn, I've Tasted My Blood; Margaret Atwood, The Edible Woman; Victor-Lévy Beaulieu, Race de monde!; film: Arthur Lamothe, Le Mépris n'aura qu'un temps; Pierre Perreault, Les Voitures d'eau
1970	October Crisis; Royal Commission on Status of Women reports; "Citizens Plus" (also known as the "Red Paper") published as Aboriginal response to the Canadian government's White Paper proposing removal of special status for Native people; the Drybones Case	Margaret Atwood, The Journals of Susanna Moodie; Michael Ondaatje, The Collected Works of Billy the Kid; Susan Musgrave, Songs of the Sea Witch; Robertson Davies, Fifth Business; John Glassco, Memoirs of Montparnasse; Margaret Laurence, A Bird in the House; Dave Godfrey, The New Ancestors; Audrey Thomas, Mrs. Blood; Anne Hébert, Kamouraska; Rudy Wiebe, The Blue Mountains of China; Margaret Atwood, The Circle Game; Procedures for Underground; First Nuit de la poésie: Michèle Lalonde recites "Speak White"; Gaston Miron, L'Homme rapaillé; Jacques Ferron, L'Amélanchier; Nicole Brossard, Suite logique; le Grand Cirque ordinaire, T'es pas tannée, Jeanne d'Arc?; film: Claude Jutra, Mon Oncle Antoine
1971	Introduction of Canada's Multiculturalism Policy	Alice Munro, Lives of Girls and Women; George Ryga, Captives of a Faceless Drummer; Paul-Marie Lapointe, Le Réel absolu: poèmes 1948–1965; Antonine Maillet, La Sagouine; Michel Tremblay, A toi, pour toujours, ta Marie-Lou;

xxxi

Chronology

Year	Historical	Literary and Cultural
1972		Paul-Marie Lapointe, *Le Réel absolu: Poèmes 1948–1965*; Juan García, *Corps de gloire*; Margaret Atwood, *Survival: A Thematic Guide to Canadian Literature*; *Surfacing*; bp nichol, *The Martyrology*; Carol Bolt; *Buffalo Jump*; Ann Henry, *Lulu Street*; Fernand Ouellette, *Poésies: poèmes 1953–1971*; Gilles Hénault, *Signaux pour les voyants*; First Rencontre québécoise internationale des écrivains, organized by *Liberté*; film: Gilles Carle, *La Vraie Nature de Bernadette*
1973	Calder Case decided by the Supreme Court, leading to Nisga'a Treaty in 1996	Maria Campbell, *Halfbreed*; Dennis Lee, "Cadence, Country, Silence: Writing in Colonial Space" (*Liberté*); Rudy Wiebe, *The Temptations of Big Bear*; Rick Salutin / Théâtre Passe Muraille, *1837: The Farmers' Revolt*; James Reaney, *Sticks and Stones* (first play of the Donnelly trilogy); Herschel Hardin, *Esker Mike and His Wife, Agiluk*; David Freeman, *Of the Fields, Lately*; Michel Tremblay, *Hosanna*; André Brassard, *Il était une fois dans l'Est*; Réjean Ducharme, *L'Hiver de force*; film: Jean-Pierre Lefebvre, *Les Dernières Fiançailles*
1974		Margaret Laurence, *The Diviners*; Hubert Aquin, *Neige noire*; Chief Dan George, *My Heart Soars*; Michael Cook, *Jacob's Wake*; Madeleine Ferron, Robert Cliche, *Les Beaucerons, ces insoumis, 1735–1867*; Madeleine Gagnon, *Pour*

Chronology

Year	Historical	Literary and Cultural
		les Femmes et tous les autres; film: Michel Brault, Les Ordres; Anne-Claire Poirier, Les Filles du Roy
1975	Cultural Property Export and Import Act; James Bay and Northern Quebec Agreement	Lee Maracle, Bobbi Lee: Indian Rebel; Jacques Brault, Chemin faisant; L'en dessous l'admirable; Poèmes des quatre côtés
1976	Quebec referendum on sovereignty defeated	Sharon Pollock, The Komagatu Maru Incident; Marian Engel, Bear; Margaret Atwood, Lady Oracle; Jack Hodgins, Spit Delaney's Island; Louky Bersianik, L'Euguélionne; Théâtre du Nouveau Monde, La Nef des sorcières; Gilles Marcotte, Le Roman à l'imparfait
1977	Report, Berger Commission: Northern Frontier, Northern Homeland; Charter of the French language (Loi 101) adopted in Quebec; Passage of the Canadian Human Rights Act	F. R. Scott, Essays on the Constitution; Timothy Findley, The Wars; Jack Hodgins, The Invention of the World; Dennis Lee, Savage Fields: An Essay on Literature and Cosmology; Bharati Mukherjee, Clark Blaise, Days and Nights in Calcutta; Josef Škvorecký, The Engineer of Human Souls; George Walker, Zastrozzi; Rudy Wiebe, The Scorched-Wood People; Claude Gauvreau, Œuvres créatrices complètes; Gabrielle Roy, Ces Enfants de ma vie; France Théoret, Bloody Mary; film: Allan King, Who Has Seen the Wind
1978	Immigration Act	Margaret Atwood, Two-Headed Poems; Alice Munro, Who Do You Think You Are? Aritha van Herk, Judith; Michel Tremblay, La Grosse Femme d'à côté est enceinte (first volume of the Chroniques du Plateau-Mont-

Chronology

Year	Historical	Literary and Cultural
		Royal); 25th Street Theatre, Paper Wheat; Pierre Vadeboncœur, Les Deux Royaumes; Gilles Cyr, Sol inapparent; François Charron, Blessures; Jacques Poulin, Les Grandes Marées; Denise Boucher, Les Fées ont soif; Réjean, Ducharme, HA ha! ...
1979		Antonine Maillet, Pélagie-la-Charrette (Prix Goncourt); Mavis Gallant, From the Fifteenth District
1980	"O Canada" officially adopted as national anthem	George Bowering, Burning Water; Robert Kroetsch, The Crow Journals; Judith Thompson, The Crackwalker; David Fennario, Balconville; Nicole Brossard, Amantes; Jovette Marchessault, Tryptique lesbien; Yolande Villemaire, La Vie en prose; film: Francis Mankiewicz, Les Bons Débarras
1981		Joy Kogawa, Obasan; Timothy Findley, Famous Last Words; Mavis Gallant, Home Truths; Margaret Atwood, Bodily Harm; F. R. Scott, Collected Poems; John Gray, Billy Bishop Goes to War; Louis Caron, Le Canard de bois; Alice Poznanska-Parizeau, Les Lilas fleurissent à Varsovie; Jean-Pierre Ronfard, Vie et Mort du Roi boiteux; Yves Beauchemin, Le Matou; Patrice Desbiens, L'Homme invisible/The Invisible Man
1982	Patriation of Constitution, Charter of Rights and Freedoms	Michael Ondaatje, Running in the Family; Anne Hébert, Les Fous de Bassan (Prix Fémina); Alice Munro, The Moons of Jupiter; Marie Uguay,

Chronology

Year	Historical	Literary and Cultural
		Autoportraits; Marco Micone, *Gens du silence*
1983	Ice storm in Quebec, Ontario and New Brunswick	Beatrice Culleton Mosionier, *In Search of April Raintree*; Penny Petrone, ed., *First People, First Voices*; Sam Selvon, *Moses Migrating*; Makeda Silvera, *Silenced*; Susan Swan, *The Biggest Modern Woman of the World*; Margaret Atwood, *Bluebeard's Egg*; Régine Robin, *La Québécoite*; Gérald Godin, *Sarzène*; Francine Noël, *Maryse*
1984	Jeanne Sauvé becomes the first woman to be appointed Governor-General; body of John Torrington, member of the Franklin Expedition, discovered	Timothy Findley, *Not Wanted on the Voyage*; Jacques Brault, *Agonie*; *Moments fragiles*; Jacques Poulin, *Volkswagen Blues*; Gabrielle Roy, *La Détresse et l'enchantement*; Michel Beaulieu, *Kaléidoscope ou les Aléas du corps grave*
1985	Air India disaster	Jeannette Armstrong, *Slash*; Fred Wah, *Waiting for Saskatchewan*; Margaret Atwood, *The Handmaid's Tale*; Bharati Mukherjee, Clark Blaise, *The Sorrow and the Terror*; Arlette Cousture, *Les Filles de Caleb*; Dany Laferrière, *Comment faire l'amour avec un nègre sans se fatiguer*; Robert Lepage, *La Trilogie des dragons*; René-Daniel Dubois, *Being at Home with Claude*
1986		Robert Lepage, *Vinci*; Alice Munro, *The Progress of Love*; Jane Urquhart, *The Whirlpool*; Gérald Godin, *Soirs sans atouts*; André Belleau, *Surprendre les voix*; Sylvain Trudel, *Le Souffle de l'harmattan*; Normand de

Chronology

Year	Historical	Literary and Cultural
1987		Bellefeuille, *Catégoriques un deux et trois*; film: Denys Arcand, *Le Déclin de l'empire américain*; Michael Ondaatje, *In the Skin of a Lion*; Rohinton Mistry, *Tales from Firozsha Baag*; Michael Ignatieff, *The Russian Album*; Carol Shields, *Swann*; Fernand Séguin, *La Bombe et l'orchidée*; Fernand Ouellette, *Les Heures*; Nicole Brossard, *Le Désert mauve*; Jean Larose, *La Petite Noirceur*; film: Patricia Rozema, *I've Heard the Mermaids Singing*; Jean-Claude Lauzon, *Un Zoo la nuit*
1988	Canadian Multiculturalism Act; Free Trade Agreement; the federal government officially apologizes to Japanese Canadians for Second World War internment	Tomson Highway, *The Rez Sisters*; Daphne Marlatt, *Ana Historic*; Lee Maracle, *I am Woman: A Native Perspective on Sociology and Feminism*; Paul Yee, *Saltwater City: The Chinese in Vancouver*; Pierre Nepveu, *L'Écologie du réel*; Christian Mistral, *Vamp*; Gilles Maheu, *Le Dortoir*
1989	Fall of the Berlin Wall; end of the Cold War	Tomson Highway, *Dry Lips Oughta Move to Kapuskasing*; Maria Campbell and Linda Griffiths, *Jessica*; Harry Robinson, *Write It on Your Heart*; Mordecai Richler, *Solomon Gursky Was Here*; Jacques Poulin, *Le Vieux Chagrin*; Louis Hamelin, *La Rage*; Monique Larue, *Copies conformes*; Pierre Morency, *L'Oeil américain*; film: Denys Arcand, *Jésus de Montréal*
1990	Meech Lake Accord fails; Oka Crisis	Lee Maracle, *Oratory: Coming to Theory*; Thomas King, ed., *All

Chronology

Year	Historical	Literary and Cultural
1991		*My Relations: An Anthology of Contemporary Canadian Native Fiction*; Nino Ricci, *Lives of the Saints*; Alice Munro, *Friend of My Youth*; George Elliott Clarke, *Whylah Falls*; SKY Lee, *Disappearing Moon Cafe*; Dionne Brand, *No Language Is Neutral*; Aritha van Herk, *Places Far from Ellesmere*; Réjean Ducharme, *Dévadé*; Hélène Dorion, *Un visage appuyé contre le monde*; Lise Tremblay, *L'Hiver de pluie*; Michel Tremblay, André Gagnon, *Nelligan* (opera); film: Cynthia Scott, *The Company of Strangers*
		M. NourbeSe Philip, *Looking for Livingstone*; Monique Mojica, *Princess Pocahontas and the Blue Spots*; Bennett Lee, Jim Wong-Chu eds., *Many-Mouthed Birds: Contemporary Writing by Chinese-Canadians*; Rohinton Mistry, *Such a Long Journey*; Douglas Coupland, *Generation X: Tales for an Accelerated Culture*; Élise Turcotte, *Le Bruit des choses vivantes*; Suzanne Jacob, *L'Obéissance*; Normand Chaurette, *Les Reines*
1992	Conviction of Louis Riel revoked; Louis Riel Day introduced (16 November)	Michael Ondaatje, *The English Patient* (Booker Prize); Daniel David Moses and Terry Goldie, eds., *An Anthology of Canadian Native Literature in English*; Harry Robinson, *Nature Power*; François Ricard, *Les Littératures de l'exiguïté*; film: Jean-Claude Lauzon, *Léolo*

Chronology

Year	Historical	Literary and Cultural
1993		Thomas King, *Green Grass, Running Water*; *One Good Story, That One*; Jeannette Armstrong, *Looking at the Words of Our People: An Anthology of First Nations Literary Criticism*; Pierre Trudeau, *Mémoires politiques*; Jane Urquhart, *Away*; Carol Shields, *The Stone Diaries* (1995 Pulitzer Prize); Guillermo Verdecchia, *Fronteras Americanas / American Borders*; Timothy Findley, *Headhunter*; Jacques Poulin, *La Tournée d'automne*; Fernand Dumont, *Genèse de la société québécoise*; Paul Chanel Malenfant, *Le Verbe être*; film: François Girard, *Trente-deux films brefs sur Glenn Gould*
1994	Charlottetown Accord fails	M. G. Vassanji, *The Book of Secrets* (first Giller Prize); Shyam Selvadurai, *Funny Boy*; Hiromi Goto, *Chorus of Mushrooms*; Louise Halfe, *Bear Bones and Feathers*; Neil Bissoondath, *Selling Illusions: The Cult of Multiculturalism in Canada*; Alice Munro, *Open Secrets*; Anne-Marie Alonzo, *Lettres à Cassandre*; Gaëtan Soucy, *L'Immaculée Conception*; film: Atom Egoyan, *Exotica*
1995	Quebec referendum on sovereignty narrowly defeated	Wayson Choy, *The Jade Peony*; Rohinton Mistry, *A Fine Balance*; Ying Chen, *L'Ingratitude*; Marie-Claire Blais, *Soifs*; film: Robert Lepage, *Le Confessionnal*; Charles Binnamé, *Eldorado*;

Chronology

Year	Historical	Literary and Cultural
1996	Nisga'a treaty	Mort Ransen, *Margaret's Museum*; Margaret Atwood, *Alias Grace*; Anne Michaels, *Fugitive Pieces*; Anita Rau Badami, *Tamarind Mem*; Gail Anderson-Dargatz, *The Cure for Death by Lightning*; Guy Vanderhaeghe, *The Englishman's Boy*; Ann-Marie MacDonald, *Fall on Your Knees*; Larissa Lai, *When Fox Is a Thousand*; Shani Mootoo, *Cereus Blooms at Night*; Robert Lepage, *Le Polygraphe*
1997		Mordecai Richler, *Barney's Version*; Dionne Brand, *Land to Light On*; P. K. Page, *The Hidden Room*; Jane Urquhart, *The Underpainter*; David Adams Richards, *Lines on the Water: A Fisherman's Life on the Miramichi*; Daphne Marlatt, *Mothertalk: Life Stories of Mary Kiyoshi Kiyooka*; Louis Saïa, *Les Boys*; Wajdi Mouawad, *Littoral*
1998		Alice Munro, *The Love of a Good Woman*; Anne Carson, *Autobiography of Red: A Novel in Verse*; Jack Hodgins, *Broken Ground*; Wayne Johnston, *The Colony of Unrequited Dreams*; Barbara Gowdy, *The White Bone*; Carol Shields, *Larry's Party* (Orange Prize); Gaétan Soucy, *La Petite Fille qui aimait trop les allumettes*; Pierre Nepveu, *Intérieurs du Nouveau Monde*; France Daigle, *Pas pire*; film: Manon Briand, *2 secondes*; Denis Villeneuve,

Chronology

Year	Historical	Literary and Cultural
1999	Nunavut established; Adrienne Clarkson becomes Governor-General	*Un 32 août sur terre*; François Girard, *Le Violon rouge* Gregory Scofield, *Thunder through My Veins*; Alistair MacLeod, *No Great Mischief* (2001 IMPAC Dublin Literary Award); Caroline Adderson, *A History of Forgetting*; Bonnie Burnard, *A Good House*; Wayne Johnston, *Baltimore's Mansion* (2000, first Charles Taylor Prize for Literary Non-Fiction); Robert Bringhurst, *A Story as Sharp as a Knife: The Classical Haida Mythtellers and Their World*; Claude Beausoleil, *Exilé*; Émile Ollivier, *Mille eaux*
2000		Michael Ondaatje, *Anil's Ghost*; Margaret Atwood, *The Blind Assassin* (Booker Prize); Poul Ruders's opera of *The Handmaid's Tale* premieres in Copenhagen; David Adams Richards, *Mercy Among the Children*; Elizabeth Hay, *A Student of Weather*; Nega Mezlekia, *Notes from the Hyena's Belly*; Timothy Findley, *Elizabeth Rex*; Michael Redhill, *Building Jerusalem*; Marie Laberge, *Le Goût du bonheur: Adelaïde / Annabelle / Florent* (trilogy); Luc Plamondon, *Notre-Dame de Paris*; Denis Villeneuve, *Maëlstrom*; Nancy Huston, *Pérégrinations Goldberg*
2001	World Trade Center attacked, Canada shelters thousands of stranded passengers	*Canada: A People's History* (CBC-SRC); Jane Urquhart, *The Stone Carvers*; Richard Wright, *Clara Callan*; Yann Martel, *Life of Pi* (2002 Booker

Chronology

Year	Historical	Literary and Cultural
		Prize); Alice Munro, *Hateship, Friendship, Courtship, Loveship, Marriage*; Timothy Taylor, *Stanley Park*; Nelly Arcan, *Putain*; Nancy Huston, *Dolce Agonia*; film: Zacharias Kunuk, *Atanarjuat*
2002		George Bowering becomes Canada's first poet laureate; Austin Clarke, *The Polished Hoe*; Wayne Johnston, *The Navigator of New York*; Carol Shields, *Unless*; Rohinton Mistry, *Family Matters*; Guy Vanderhaeghe, *Last Crossing*; Michael Redhill, *Martin Sloane*; Timothy Taylor, *Silent Cruise*; Michel Tremblay, *Bonbons assortis*
2003	SARS virus outbreak in Toronto	Margaret Atwood, *Oryx and Crake*; Barbara Gowdy, *The Romantic*; David Adams Richards, *River of the Brokenhearted*; Michel Basilières, *Black Bird*; David Odhiambo, *Kipligat's Chance*; Frances Itani, *Deafening*; Ann-Marie MacDonald, *The Way the Crow Flies*; Jack Hodgins, *Distance*; M. G. Vassanji, *The In-Between World of Vikram Lall*; Elizabeth Hay, *Garbo Laughs*; Chester Brown, *Louis Riel: A Comic-Strip Biography*; Michel Tremblay, *Le Cahier noir*; Gil Courtemanche, *Un dimanche à la piscine à Kigali*; Nancy Huston, *Une Adoration*; film: Denys Arcand, *Les Invasions barbares*
2004	Maher Arar Inquiry (Report 2006)	Alice Munro, *Runaway*; Carol Shields, *The Collected Stories*; Miriam Toews, *A Complicated*

Chronology

Year	Historical	Literary and Cultural
		Kindness; Thomas Wharton, *The Logograph*; Robert Alexie, *Porcupines and China Dolls*; Wayson Choy, *All That Matters*; Nadine Bismuth, *Scrapbook*; Alain Gagnon, *Jakob, fils de Jakob*; Sergio Kokis, *Les Amants d'Alfana*; Michel Tremblay, *Le Cahier rouge*; Lise Tremblay, *La Héronnière*
2005	Michaëlle Jean becomes Governor-General	Noah Richler, "This Is My Country, What's Yours?" (CBC Radio); Margaret Atwood, *The Penelopiad*; Tomson Highway, *Kiss of the Fur Queen*; Joseph Boyden, *Three Day Road*; George Elliott Clarke, *George & Rue*; Dionne Brand, *What We All Long For*; Wayson Choy, *Searching for Confucius*; Anne Compton, *Processional*; Anosh Irani, *The Cripple and His Talismans*; Camilla Gibb, *Sweetness in the Belly*; David Gilmour, *A Perfect Night to Go to China*; Joan Clark, *An Audience of Chairs*; David Bergen, *The Time In Between*; Lisa Moore, *Alligator*; Nelofer Pazira, *A Bed of Red Flowers*; Edeet Ravel, *A Wall of Light*; Aki Shimazaki, *Hotaru*; Michael Redhill, *Goodness*; Marie-Claire Blais, *Augustino et le chœur de la destruction*; Michel Tremblay, *Le Cahier bleu*
2006	Stephen Harper (Conservative) becomes Prime Minister after twelve years of Liberal Government; Quebec's "nation" motion approved by	Mavis Gallant becomes first English-language writer to win Prix Athanase-David; Rawi Hage, *De Niro's Game* (2008 IMPAC); Margaret

Chronology

Year	Historical	Literary and Cultural
	House of Commons; Valiants' Memorial inaugurated in Ottawa; in Quebec City, archeologists discover the foundations of forts occupied by Cartier and de Roberval between 1541 and 1543; Eva Ottawa elected Grand Chief of the Atikamekw tribe, the first Amerindian woman in Quebec to obtain this position; federal government issues official apology to Chinese-Canadians for Head Tax and Exclusion Act	Atwood, *The Tent*; *Moral Disorder*; Alice Munro, *The View from Castle Rock*; P. K. Page, *Hand Luggage*; Jane Urquhart, *A Map of Glass*; Rudy Wiebe, *Of This Earth: A Mennonite Boyhood in the Boreal Forest*; Wayne Johnston, *The Custodian of Paradise*; Drew Hayden Taylor, *In a World Created by a Drunken God*; Vincent Lam, *Bloodletting and Miraculous Cures*; Anita Rau Badami, *Can You Hear the Nightbird Call?*; Peter Behrens, *The Law of Dreams*; Dionne Brand, *Inventory*; Anosh Irani, *The Song of Kahnusha*; Janice Kulyk Keefer, *Midnight Stroll*; Don McKay, *Strike / Slip*; Heather O'Neill, *Lullabies for Little Criminals*; Morris Panych, *What Lies Before Us*; Michael Redhill, *Consolation*; Steve Keewatin Sanderson, *Darkness Calls*; Timothy Taylor, *Story House*; Sylvain Trudel, *La Mer de la tranquillité*; Andrée Laberge, *La Rivière du loup*; Myriam Beaudoin, *Hadassa*; Nancy Huston, *Lignes de faille*; Jacques Poulin, *La Traduction est une histoire d'amour*; film: Sarah Polley, *Away from Her*
2007	Ninetieth anniversary of the Battle of Vimy Ridge; memorial to victims of Air India disaster (1985) unveiled in Vancouver	First performance of *The Penelopiad* at Stratford-upon-Avon, UK; Margaret Atwood, *The Door*; Michael Ondaatje, *Divisadero*; Douglas Coupland, *The Gum Thief*; Barbara Gowdy, *Helpless*; Elizabeth Hay, *Late Nights on*

Chronology

Year	Historical	Literary and Cultural
		Air; Sharon Pollock, Man Out of Joint; Anosh Irani, The Bombay Plays; Carolyn Smardz Frost, I've Got a Home in Glory Land: A Lost Tale of the Underground Railroad; Lorna Goodison, From Harvey River: A Memoir of My Mother and Her Island; Lawrence Hill, The Book of Negroes (Someone Knows My Name in US edition; 2008 Best Book Commonwealth Writers' Prize); Kulyk Keefer, The Ladies' Lending Library; James Bartleman, Raisin Wine: A Boyhood in a Different Muskoka; David Chariandy, Soucouyant; Marie Clements, Thunderbird; Neil Smith, Bang Crunch; Michel Tremblay, La Traversée du continent; Lise Tremblay, La Sœur de Judith; Nancy Huston, Passions d'Annie Leclerc; Michel Biron, François Dumont, Élisabeth Nardout-Lafarge, Histoire de la littérature québécoise; film: Guy Maddin, My Winnipeg
2008	The federal government issues an official apology to former Indian Residential School students; Truth and Reconciliation Commission established; BC offers official apology to Sikhs for Komagata Maru Incident; Bouchard-Taylor Commission on Accommodation Practices Related to Cultural Differences (Province of Quebec) reports; Canada launches new search for	Margaret Atwood Payback: Debt and the Shadow Side of Wealth (nominated for the 2009 National Business Book Award); Atwood wins Prince of Asturias Prize for Literature; Joseph Boyden, Through Black Spruce; Nino Ricci, The Origin of the Species; Caroline Adderson, Pleased to Meet You; Drew Hayden Taylor, The Berlin Blues; Fred Wah, Sentenced to Light; André Alexis, Asylum; Stan Dragland, The Drowned

Year	Historical	Literary and Cultural
	Franklin expedition; Barack Obama elected 44th President of the United States	*Lands*; Rawi Hage, *Cockroach*; Maggie Helwig, *Girls Fall Down*; D. Y. Béchard, *Vandal Love*; Tom Lilburn, *Orphic Politics*; Daphne Marlatt, *The Given*; Morris Panych, *Benevolence*; Paul Quarrington, *The Ravine*; Diane Schoemperlen, *At a Loss for Words*; Jaspreet Singh, *Chef*; Mary Swan, *The Boys in the Trees*; Mariko and Jilian Tamaki, *Skim*; M. G. Vassanji, *A Place Within: Rediscovering India*; Shani Mootoo, *Valmiki's Daughter*; Jacob Scheier, *More to Keep us Warm*; Rebecca Rosenblum, *Once*; Marie-Claire Blais, *Naissance de Rébecca à l'ère des tourments*; Victor-Lévy Beaulieu, *La Grande Tribu*; Dany Laferrière, *Je suis un écrivain japonais*; Michel Pleau, *La Lenteur du monde*; Hervé Bouchard, *Parents et amis sont priés d'assister*; Laurence Prud'homme, *La Danse de la Méduse*; Maurice Henrie, *Esprit de sel*; Michel Vézina, *La Machine à l'orgueil*; Hélène Rioux, *Mercredi soir au bout du monde*; film: Sturla Gunnarsson, *Air India 182*

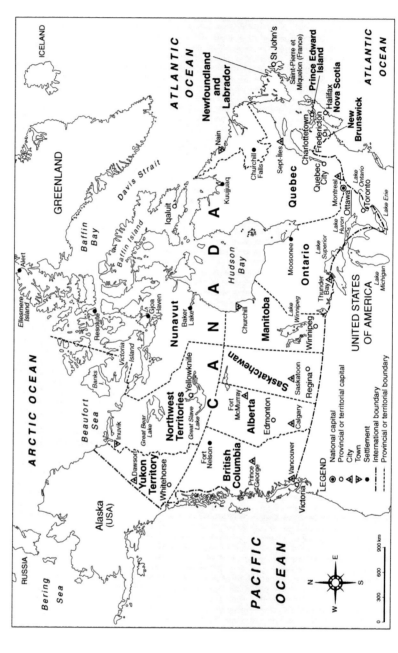

Map 1: Canada

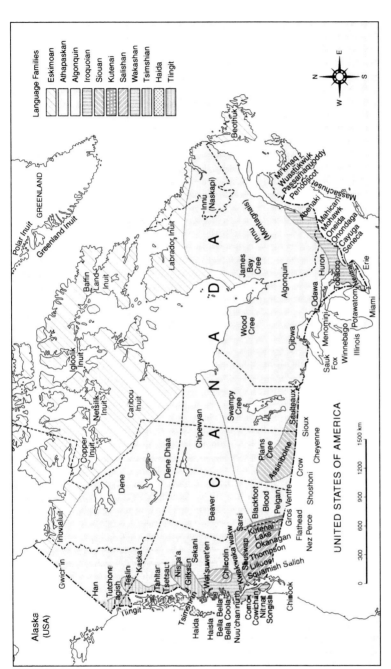

Map 2: Tribal distributions in and near Canada at time of contact* (based on O. P. Dickason, *Canada's First Nations: A History of Founding Peoples from Earliest Times*, 3rd edn. [Oxford: Oxford University Press, 2002] p. 47)

* Various different spellings of Native tribal groups and place-names are currently in use.

Introduction

CORAL ANN HOWELLS AND EVA-MARIE KRÖLLER

In 1917 Canadian literature made its first appearance in *The Cambridge History of English Literature* as a modest twenty-page chapter entitled "English-Canadian Literature" by Toronto academic Pelham Edgar, along with a series of other chapters on literatures of the Empire like "Anglo-Irish Literature," "Anglo-Indian Literature," "The Literature of Australia and New Zealand," and "South African Poetry." Almost exactly ninety years later, this substantial *Cambridge History of Canadian Literature*, co-edited by two women scholars, with its thirty-one chapters written by a distinguished company of Canadian and international contributors, offers convincing evidence for the establishment of Canadian literature as an important scholarly field and for its current standing. Between then and now there have been numerous literary histories, encyclopedias, and anthologies in English and French, produced in a continual process of inventory-taking on the state of the nation and its literature.[1]

Interestingly, these have been concentrated in particular periods of national crisis or celebration, notably in the post-war 1920s, in the decade of cultural nationalism centered on the Centennial of the Canadian Confederation in 1967, and most recently since the mid-1990s with its radical reassessments of the nation and its literary heritage. This *Cambridge History of Canadian Literature* is situated in the context of newly defined discourses of nationhood, national culture, and literary production which are both specific to Canada and related to larger theoretical questions which have widened the parameters of nation, history, and literature.[2]

---

1 For a chronological list of literary histories of Canada up to 1996, see E. D. Blodgett, *Five-Part Invention: A History of Literary History in Canada* (Toronto: University of Toronto Press, 2002), pp. 20–2.
2 It is symptomatic of this development that a number of other literary histories have appeared almost concurrently with this volume, including Michel Biron, François Dumont, Élisabeth Nardout-Lafarge, *Histoire de la littérature québécoise* (Montreal: Boréal, 2007), and Reingard M. Nischik, ed., *History of Literature in Canada: English-Canadian and*

Indeed, to write the history of any national literature in the era of globalization is problematical, where tensions persist between "national" and "global, diasporic, transnational," where national identities have become pluralized, and where the contemporary emphasis on diversity stimulates – and indeed necessitates – the revisionist reading of that literature from its beginnings so that we may understand the relation between the present and the past in different and more inclusive ways.[3] One striking feature of Canada's literary history is that it has always been a fractured discourse, notoriously difficult to define along chronological or national lines. Even the concept of literary history needs to be re-examined in a New World context where the first encounters between Europeans and Indigenous peoples highlight the differences between written records and other semiotic systems not covered by writing. The problem of multiple beginnings and conflicting allegiances continues with Canada's fraught bilingual and bicultural traditions which are written into the history of its European colonization and which continue to feature in its postcolonial politics. Since the 1970s the country's official multiculturalism has in many ways bypassed traditional English and French dichotomies, and most recently developments in response to globalization have raised social and cultural issues which are crucially different from both biculturalism and multiculturalism.

This *History* acknowledges the conceptual challenges posed by changing meanings of "Canadian" as an identity category and by periodic reformulations of Canada as an imagined community: such instabilities and shifts are represented within our narrative. What this volume offers is a nuanced reassessment of contemporary literary production in English and French, together with a reconfiguring of the literature and national myths of earlier periods, drawing attention to ethnic, cultural and regional diversities that were sometimes submerged in previous paradigms. The visual images in this volume are an important component of the narrative. Strategically placed in specific chapters, they function to underline arguments about different

---

French-Canadian (Rochester: Camden House, 2008), a revised translation of Konrad Gross, Wolfgang Klooss, Reingard M. Nischik, eds., *Kanadische Literaturgeschichte* (Stuttgart: Metzler, 2005).

[3] The *Cambridge History of Canadian Literature* is one of several volumes already published or in preparation by Cambridge University Press that re-examine the literatures of the former Commonwealth and other previously colonial cultures. Some of these volumes focus on national literatures (the volumes in preparation on Australian and Indian literature, for example), while others transcend national boundaries (the two-volume *Cambridge History of African and Caribbean Literature* published in 2004 and the forthcoming *Cambridge History of Postcolonial Literature*).

Introduction

forms of graphic representation, from an early eighteenth-century drawing annotated in French of a tattooed Indigenous warrior to contemporary cartoons and comic books.

Of course, this *History* measures its differences against earlier literary histories, among which our major predecessor is Carl F. Klinck's monumental *A Literary History of Canada: Canadian Literature in English*, first published as a single volume in 1965. A three-volume version appeared in 1976, followed by a fourth volume, edited by W. H. New in 1990. This pioneering work was the first multi-authored comprehensive history of Canadian literature in English, and in that Centennial period a parallel volume on Canadian literature in French was also planned. That did not eventuate, though Pierre de Grandpré's *Histoire de la littérature française du Québec* appeared 1967–9, and Klinck's volume was published in French translation in 1970. The publication of Grandpré's four-volume history of writing in French well before Klinck's multi-volume version is a reminder that Quebec has collected the evidence of its "patrimoine" much more systematically than the English Canadians, a phenomenon which persists into the present with the now seven-volume *Dictionnaire des œuvres littéraires du Québec*, which has no exact equivalent in English.

Klinck and Northrop Frye in his famous "Conclusion" to Klinck's *History* were very aware of the double nature of Canada's literary traditions: "Every statement made [about English-Canadian literature] ... implies a parallel or contrast with French-Canadian literature."[4] They envisaged a consistently comparative study of both literatures, whereas our approach is designed to highlight major connections and differences between the two linguistic traditions. Anglophone and francophone materials are treated comparatively in appropriate locations throughout (for instance, in the chapter on nineteenth-century histories and historical novels), while on the other hand the distinctive history of francophone writing is recognized with a final section devoted exclusively to writing in French from across Canada. Two of these chapters, written by scholars from Quebec and Franco-Ontario, were translated into English for this volume.

Klinck saw the production of literary history as a cultural project of national significance designed to give Canadians "a studied knowledge of ourselves" (p.xi). His emphases were – inevitably for that period – Eurocentric and territorial, though his definition of literature was a very catholic one. He includes essays on folk tales and folk songs, travel books, autobiography and

---

4 Northrop Frye, "Conclusion," in *A Literary History of Canada*, ed. Carl F. Klinck (Toronto: University of Toronto Press, 1965), pp. 823–4.

3

children's books (incidentally these four are among only six essays written or co-authored, by women out of a total of forty) as well as essays on historical writings, philosophy, religion, and the natural sciences. Indeed his approach was remarkably pragmatic for its time, and his authors make passing reference to oral storytelling traditions of "[t]he Indians and Eskimos" (p. 163) and to the new post-1940s phenomenon of novels where "the backgrounds ... are Continental" (p. 709), the first recognition of the multiethnic dimension in Canadian literature. Such coverage implies an incipient recognition of the cultural pluralism which has become Canada's signature in following decades.

In 1971 Canada was the first country in the world to introduce an official multiculturalism policy, and subsequent changes in the social and ideological contexts within which images of Canadianness were reconstructed may be charted through creative writing, the media, new literary histories and revisions of those histories which were published in quick succession. The academic industry surrounding Canadian literature grew rapidly during the 1980s at home and abroad, encouraged by government sponsorship of Canadian Studies internationally as a branch of foreign policy, and for the first time ever, two Canadian literary histories were published in London: W. J. Keith's *Canadian Literature in English* (1985) and W. H. New's *A History of Canadian Literature* (1989). Both have been republished in Canada since 2000, with supplementary chapters.

The 1990s bore witness to symptoms of crisis as literary and cultural critics struggled to reconceptualize narratives of the nation. That revisionist emphasis has merely gained impetus in the twenty-first century. The traditional Anglo-French paradigm of Canadian literary heritage might now be considered as one of Canada's national myths, given the light thrown on the nation's origins by new critical perspectives and recent archival research. Far from being a double-stranded narrative of two "founding nations," Canadian literary history now begins to look more like a multi-plot novel with different beginnings and different narrative imperatives, as formerly marginalized voices and suppressed histories are assuming their proper place within a restructured and increasingly diversified literary tradition.[5]

This volume seeks to maintain a balance between the conventional chronological design and canonical genre treatment characteristic of traditional

---

5 We have looked more closely at these questions in a joint address, "Switching the Plot: From *Survival* to the *Cambridge History of Canadian Literature*," to the 2008 meeting of the International Council of Canadian Studies. A revised version of the lecture appears in the conference proceedings, *Canada Exposed / Le Canada à découvert*, ed. Pierre Anctil, André Loiselle, Christopher Rolfe (Brussels: Peter Lang, 2009), pp. 45–60.

literary histories, and a revisionist approach which interrogates and blurs those category divisions. Our aim is to demonstrate continuities and interconnections across decades and even centuries, with chapters on history and myth, nineteenth-century nature-writing and contemporary environmental writing and publishing history in Canada, while figures like Margaret Atwood and Michael Ondaatje cannot easily be accommodated under historical or generic headings, and chapters like "Canada and the Great War" illustrate the ways in which certain traumatic events resonate way beyond their particular historical moment.

We also include non-canonical genres, like comic books, as evidence of the continuing presence of popular culture and its resonance. In particular we recognize the significant new directions which Canadian literature has taken over the past twenty-five years or so. Over half the volume is devoted to literary production since the 1960s, paying detailed attention not only to major international literary figures but also signaling the emergence of new cultural and literary paradigms with the advent of Aboriginal and multicultural writing in the two major languages. Braided together, all these narratives bear witness to a multiplicity of traditions which contribute to the ever-increasing complexities within Canadian literature.

Writing as diverse as this also comes with typographical challenges. In general, we use the English version of names that have accents in French but none in English (for instance Québec / Quebec, Montréal / Montreal), except, of course, when they are part of a quotation in French or part of a publisher's name or a book title. This means that in our coverage of writing in French, it has sometimes been necessary to use the two versions side by side. "Native" and "Indigenous" are spelled with capital letters when they refer to "Aboriginal." On the advice of the authors contributing the chapters in this area and of other scholars, this volume uses these terms interchangeably, although arguments exist that favor one over the other. Because their printed versions are approximations of oral languages, the names of Aboriginal tribes can be spelled in a variety of ways. We have opted for consistent spelling, but we are aware of the compromise involved in this decision.

Most chapters have been provided with subheadings to assist the reader, but in a few cases they have been left out because they would have interrupted the argument.

PART ONE

*

OLD AND NEW WORLD, LA NOUVELLE-FRANCE, THE CANADAS, DOMINION OF CANADA

1
Native societies and French colonization

BARBARA BELYEA

To explain why the Aztec empire crumbled before a small force of conquistadors, Tzvetan Todorov opined that the most important cause of its defeat was the absence of writing in Mexican culture. The Mexicans' drawings and pictographs recorded experience, not language, and so they lacked the mental structures fostered by phonetic, grammatically organized writing. Aztec leaders lacked the ability to perceive and respond to new situations which writing presumably creates.[1]

It is tempting to smile and dismiss such an evolutionist, Eurocentric, politically incorrect view of a non-European culture. But Todorov's bias, whether writing is understood as a transcription of language or a pervasive system of difference, is close to the heart (so to speak) of other literary scholarship.[2] The business of literary criticism has always been the analysis of written texts. Since the mid-twentieth century the structuralist and post-structuralist leveling of all representative forms to language, understood in terms of grammar and writing, has determined the focus and premises of other disciplines such as history and anthropology. The classic distinction between savagery and civilization is presented as a technical difference between orality and writing, and some leading anthropologists such as Clifford Geertz claim to "read" culture like a document. Nothing has really changed, however: the wolf is now the wolf in sheep's clothing; concepts of primitivism and savagery are still at the core of anthropological and ethnohistorical practice. Todorov's study of the Aztecs is an example of the risk that an oral / literate opposition entails: by its logic, he is led to assert that Aztec leaders were culturally, even mentally inferior to the Spanish invaders who

---

[1] Tzvetan Todorov, *La Conquête de l'Amérique: La question de l'autre* (Paris: Seuil, 1982), pp. 104–10.
[2] See, for example, Jacques Derrida, *De la grammatologie* (Paris: Minuit, 1967) and Roland Barthes, *Le Grain de la voix* (Paris: Seuil, 1981), pp. 9–13.

destroyed their world. "Know what [the writer] thinks a savage is," Geertz remarks, "and you have the key to his work."³

We can weigh Todorov's claims by examining journals and memoirs produced during roughly two centuries of French colonization in North America. The French, both secular and religious, who documented early contact with Native societies from Acadia to the Great Plains include Cartier, Champlain, Lescarbot, Sagard, Lejeune, Radisson, La Salle, Lahonton, La Vérendrye, La Potherie and Charlevoix. All of these authors routinely used the term "Sauvages" to describe the people who welcomed and traded with them, who became their allies in war, but who resisted, at least in the short term, their efforts to change beliefs and subvert traditional ways of life. As their knowledge of Native societies extended to tribes living beyond the St Lawrence valley, the French in America modified their views of the "Sauvages"; they retained the term but used it ambivalently.

The first recorded contact between Europeans and Natives in what is now Canada took place on July 6, 1534. After touring the Gulf of St Lawrence, Cartier dropped anchor in the Baie des Chaleurs and sent out an exploratory longboat. The crew found more than they bargained for: up to fifty canoes and "ung grant nombre de gens quelx fessoint ung grant bruict et nous fessoint *plusieurs* signes," inviting them to trade for furs. The boat crew were outnumbered; they feared for their lives and quickly turned back to the ships. Seven canoes followed the boat, the paddlers "dansant et fasiant *plusieurs* signes de voulloir nostre amytié nous disant en leur langaige *napou tou daman asurtat*." The crew signed their refusal. When their signs were ignored, they opened fire.⁴

This encounter is interesting for the limited communication that was possible between the two parties. Notwithstanding the journalist's good ear for the language, or possibly a crew member's previous familiarity with it (the transcribed words are recognizably a Mi'kmaq invitation to friendship), interaction was limited to gestures before lapsing into open hostility.⁵ The boat crew's refusal to trade is explained not only by unequal numbers but also by reference to an earlier description by European explorers to "gens effarables et sauvaiges." Seeing Montagnais or Beothuks west of Belle Isle had already

---

3 Clifford Geertz, *The Interpretation of Cultures* (New York: Basic Books, 1973), p. 346.
4 Jacques Cartier, *Relations*, ed. Michel Bideaux (Montreal: Presses de l'Université de Montréal, 1986), pp. 110–11, 333: "a crowd of people who shouted and gesticulated to us ... dancing and indicating that they wanted our friendship ... calling to us in their language, 'Friends, each of your counterparts in this nation asks for your good will.'" The translations in the following are my own.
5 Ibid., p. 331.

given the French an impression of Native marginality and impenetrability: "Ilz se voistent de peaulx de bestes ... Ilz se paingnent de certaines couleurs tannees."[6] To the French these wild, daubed figures seemed scarcely human.

The text of Cartier's Mi'kmaq encounter is more accessible, most of us would say more reliable, than Native stories of "des hommes prodigieux & espouventables" crowded onto an "Isle mouvante."[7] To judge from the Mi'kmaq readiness to sell furs, there must have been earlier occasions for trade with European ships. While we can only guess at previous encounters, in Cartier's *Relations* the meeting between French and Natives snaps into focus. A specific date is given; the place has been identified; the details give an impression of exactness – *one* boat was launched from Cartier's ships and *seven* canoes pursued it, the paddlers shouting *napou tou daman asurtat*. Its detail and the day-by-day progress of the ships may even lull the reader into thinking that the account is a transcript of Cartier's own journal. But this confidence would be misplaced: Cartier's authorship is established only by inference, and there is no original text. Although a manuscript exists, it resembles a later version translated and published by an Italian compiler of voyages in 1556. Hakluyt in turn translated the Italian text for his *Principall Navigations* published in 1600. For 240 years, until the French manuscript was discovered, these translations were the only record of Cartier's first voyage. The textual uncertainty of Cartier's *Relations* is not exceptional: Champlain may not have written the earliest text attributed to him, and the *Voyages* of 1632 may have been compiled by a Jesuit ghostwriter.[8] A number of works claiming to be eyewitness accounts owe a great deal to earlier texts: Sagard's *Grand voyage du pays des Hurons* borrowed heavily from Champlain and Lescarbot, just as Charlevoix's *Journal d'un voyage ... dans l'Amérique septentrionale* relied heavily on Lafitau's *Mœurs des sauvages amériquains*. Most of these writers claimed to report what they themselves had seen, at least what they had heard while in America. In fact earlier texts contributed as much to their accounts as their own experience.

An exchange of signs during Cartier's meeting with Stadaconé villagers on the Gaspé coast plainly revealed French intentions in the New World. The

---

6 Ibid., p. 101: "frightful, savage people who are dressed in animal skins ... They paint themselves with colors which make their skin look like tanned hide."
7 Paul Lejeune, *The Jesuit Relations and Allied Documents*, ed. Reuben Gold Thwaites, 23 vols. (New York: Pageant, 1954), vol. V, pp. 118–20: "amazing, fearsome men" "[on] a moving island."
8 François-Marc Gagnon, "Le *Brief discours* est-il de Champlain?", in *Champlain: la naissance de l'Amérique française*, ed. Raymonde Litalien and Denis Vaugeois (Sillery: Septentrion, 2004), pp. 83–92.

ships traded with 200 men, women and children considered to be savages "car c'est la plus pouvre gence qu'il puisse estre au monde ... Ilz sont tous nudz ... Ils n'ont aultre logis que soubz leurs *dites* barques ... Ilz mangent leur chair quasi crue ... "[9] Seeing that their poor appearance posed no threat, Cartier chose this place to erect a thirty-foot cross on which he hung a shield painted with lilies and a plaque inscribed with the words "Vive le Roy de France." The French gathered around the cross and fell to their knees in adoration. Then they explained to the Stadaconé villagers what the cross represented: "leur fismes signe regardant et leur monstrant le ciel que par icelle estoit nostre redemption dequoy ilz firent *plusieurs* admyradtions" – remarkably succinct theology, all things considered, and the first of many lessons taught to the Native peoples of Canada.[10] The conjunction of religious, national, and royal emblems gave the French authority, in their view, to take possession of territory in the Americas. The Stadaconé chief Donnacona was not persuaded, however: "nous fit une grande harangue nous monstrant *ladite* croix et *faisant* le signe de la croix avec deux doydz et puis nous monstroit la terre tout alentour de nous."[11] Although the French could not understand a word of the chief's "harangue," his gestures communicated disapproval of the cross and appeared to insist that all the land belonged to him. As with the Mi'kmaq, the French response to Donnacona's signs was violent. Two young men, Taignoagny and Domagaya, were forced on board one of the ships, "dequoy furent bient estonnez,"[12] a phrase, indicating the Natives' reaction when Cartier abducts them, that allows us to see them just for a moment not as marginal objects of French observation and power, but as human beings who feel surprise and dismay.

Probably to ensure a passage home, the two captives told Cartier about a rich kingdom of the Saguenay as well as a great river flowing into the gulf where he had found them. French interest in the New World was limited to three objectives: to find a water route to Asia, to discover gold and copper mines, and to claim possession of the territory they traveled through. Given these aims, news of wealth farther west was a powerful attraction that the

---

9 Cartier, *Relations*, pp. 114–15: "These are the poorest people in the world ... They are entirely naked ... Their only shelter is under their canoes ... They eat their meat almost raw ... "
10 Ibid., p. 116: "To explain the cross we made signs, pointing to the sky as the source of our redemption, at which they expressed their awe and wonder."
11 Ibid., p. 116: "He made a long speech, pointing to the cross and making a sign of the cross with two fingers, and then he indicated the land all around us, as if he wished to say that all this land belonged to him."
12 "At which they were greatly surprised."

narrows of Stadaconé (Quebec) and rapids above Hochelaga (Montreal) could not discourage. For the next two centuries, French explorers and cartographers were driven by wishful thinking to produce, by discovery and invention, seductive maps that kept the royal government interested and impatient for more. The search for a navigable passage accounts for Champlain's early interest in Lake Ontario; later he would draw the Great Lakes as a single wide channel, with a northern sea not far away.[13] Two centuries later, La Vérendrye beguiled the Minister of Marine with rumors of a western sea and of mountains shining with bright stones.[14] Lahontan produced a suggestive map of a "Rivière Longue"; Charlevoix compared the plains Sioux to Tartars, remarking that their country west of Lake Michigan would yield "des découvertes utiles, surtout par rapport à la Mer du Sud."[15] In response the great French cartographers – Sanson, Delisle, Coronelli, Bellin and Buache – filled in the western half of their maps with rivers, mountains and lakes stretching to the Californian coast, or brought this coast within reach by inventing an immense "Mer de l'Ouest."[16] Searching for a passage and precious minerals, pausing now and then to admire the fertility of regions they explored, the French were ambivalent about the continent's Native inhabitants. These people could be useful as guides and hunters; their canoes and snowshoes were indispensable tools; but their languages, beliefs, and customs, their complex alliances and enmities frustrated the French, who tried to impose their own agendas of discovery, exploitation and conversion. However useful or difficult, Native societies had to be reckoned with: the legendary Royaume du Saguenay, rich in mines and the door to Asia, insensibly became the *pays d'en haut*, a vast territory in which the French were partners rather than rulers.

The two sides were not impenetrable. The security and prosperity of New France depended on alliances with Native leaders and a brisk trade in furs; in turn, trade and alliances depended on good communication. As early as 1610, Champlain authorized an exchange by which Brûlé, his own "garçon,"

---

13 Champlain, *Carte géographique de la Nouvelle France* (1612), "[Le Canada] faict par le Sr de Champlain" (1616) and *Carte de la Nouvelle France* (1632). The maps are reproduced in Litalien and Vaugeois, eds, *Champlain*, pp. 314–15, 320, 322–3.
14 Pierre Gaultier de Varennes de la Vérendrye and His Sons, *Journals and Letters*, ed. Lawrence J. Burpee (Toronto: Champlain Society, 1927), pp. 43–9, 52–60.
15 Louis Armand de Lom d'Arce, Baron de Lahontan, *Œuvres complètes*, ed. Réal Ouellet, 2 vols. (Montreal: Presses de l'Université de Montréal, 1990), vol. I, pp. 416–17; François-Xavier de Charlevoix, *Histoire de la Nouvelle France*, 3 vols. (Paris: Didot, 1744), vol. I, p. 347: "useful discoveries, especially with respect to the Pacific Ocean."
16 This "Mer de l'Ouest" appears in numerous maps. See, for example, Library and Archives Canada, National Map Collection 7110, Nicolas Sanson, *L'Amérique septentrionale* (1650); LAC NMC 6333, Pierre du Val, *Le Canada faict par le Sr de Champlain* (1653).

and Savignon, a young Huron man, could learn each other's language.[17] Brûlé and his successors were key figures in the cultural evolution of the *pays d'en haut*; by the late seventeenth century hundreds of colonists in the Laurentian valley had deserted their fields to live with Native bands. These *coureurs de bois* formed the French personnel of the fur trade. Radisson and Chouart dit Groseilliers, notable *coureurs*, were among the first traders to venture beyond Michilimackinac, but when the colony's strict regulations robbed them of profits, they presented their next business plan to the English.[18] Like Brûlé, who defected to the Kirke brothers during their siege of Quebec, Chouart, Radisson and other *coureurs de bois* felt next to no loyalty to the colonial administration. They were at home in the half-way culture of the Great Lakes, a vast territory characterized by tribal displacement, shifting alliances and shared ways of life. Slowly the French who ventured beyond the colonies became more or less acculturated: traders married into the groups who furnished their pelts; missionaries lived with those they hoped to convert. Journals relating to Cavelier de la Salle's exploration of the Mississippi are evidence of the cultural métissage that characterized this region during the seventeenth century. Although they accepted torture, most French commentators stopped short of openly approving cannibalism, both of which were rites of victory in Native wars.[19] Far down the river, Cavelier de la Salle and his men found meat – alligator and a side of ribs – in an abandoned canoe. They ate it all before realizing that the ribs were human, but they were not shocked at the discovery. "Cette chair étoit meilleure que celle de Caymant" was the journalist's only remark.[20]

Knowledge of Native languages and ways of life qualified the *coureurs de bois* to facilitate the conduct of daily business and the negotiation of formal

---

17 Samuel Champlain, *Œuvres de Samuel Champlain*, ed. C.-H. Laverdière, 2nd edn., 5 vols. (Quebec: Séminaire de Quebec, 1870), vol. IV, p. 53.

18 Pierre Esprit Radisson, *Voyages of Peter Esprit Radisson: Being an Account of His Travels and Experiences Among the North American Indians, from 1652–1684*, ed. Gideon D. Scull (Boston: Prince Society, 1885); Marcel Trudel, *La Population du Canada en 1666* (Sillery: Septentrion, 1995), pp. 243, 267: the census for Trois Rivières notes that Chouart and Radisson were out of the country.

19 Gilles Havard, *Empire et métissages: Indiens et Français dans le Pays d'en haut, 1660–1715* (Sillery: Septentrion, 2003), pp. 744–6; Gabriel Sagard, *Le Grand Voyage du pays des Hurons*, ed. Jack Warwick (Montreal: Les Presses de l'Université de Montréal, 1998), pp. 242–3; Lejeune, *Jesuit Relations*, vol. V, p. 28; Christophe Regnaut, *The Jesuit Relations and Allied Documents*, ed. Reuben Gold Thwaites, vol. XXXIV, pp. 24–37.

20 "The ribs were better than the alligator." Texas State Archives, Nicolas de la Salle, "La Salle M. S. 1682," p. 28; see Nicolas de la Salle, *Découvertes et établissements des Français*, ed. Pierre Margry, 6 vols. (Paris: D. Jouaust, 1876–86), vol. I, pp. 547–70: this entry does not appear in Margry's edition. Nicolas de la Salle was a member of the 1682 expedition led by René-Robert Cavelier de la Salle; apparently the two men were not related.

alliances. By the 1640s priests who lived with Native bands or served at frontier missions could also act as interpreters. But while the *coureurs'* acculturation was considerable, the missionaries' acceptance of Native cultures was minimal. Lejeune, for example, continued to see Native inhabitants in terms of lack: the Montagnais lived deprived of comfortable lodgings, adequate food, refinement of manners and knowledge of the world. Above all they lacked the Word of God, for which they needed the skills of reading and writing. Lejeune's conviction of technical superiority shaped his report of an incident similar to the writing lesson in *Tristes tropiques*.

> [Quantité] d'Alguonquains nous estans venus voir, l'un d'eux me voya[n]t escrire, print une plume & voulu faire le mesme: mais voyant qu'il ne faisoit rien qui vaille, & que je sousriois, il se mit a souffler sur ce qu'il avoit escrit, pensant le faire en aller comme de la poudre. Je leur fis dire à tous que nous estio[n]s venus pour les instruire.[21]

Writing aroused interest equal to wonder at the noise and efficacy of guns, the size of European ships, the use of navigational instruments and the mechanism of clocks. The missionaries' job was to enlighten the "Sauvages" as well as to convert them.

Theater animated the written word; it provided another mode of French instruction by combining several forms of representation. In 1616, for example, Lescarbot mounted a masque called *Le Théâtre de Neptune* in the harbor of Port-Royal. The Governor of the colony, playing himself, recited lines from Lescarbot's text, received tributes from four "Sauvages" (probably Frenchmen in Native dress, since their speeches were in French), and generally signified the pompous might of the French state. "La musique achevée, la trompette sonne derechef & ... les Canons bourdonnent de toutes parts ... "[22] Lescarbot's pageant was impressive because it was dramatic: it made the figurative actual, thus narrowing the gap between ideal and real. The French were at home with such theatricality. Church liturgy and court protocol produced the same idealizing effect; schools, especially Jesuit schools, produced plays designed to prepare their pupils for public life by honing their rhetorical skills. Writing

---

21 Lejeune, *Jesuit Relations*, vol. V, p. 134: "Among many Algonquins who came to see us was one who, seeing me write, took a pen and wished to do the same: but seeing that he could not produce anything significant, and that I was smiling, he began to blow on what he had written, in an effort to disperse the marks like powder. I told them by an interpreter that we had come to instruct them."
22 Marc Lescarbot, *The History of New France*, ed. W. L. Grant, 3 vols. (Toronto: Champlain Society, 1914), vol. III, pp. 473–9: "As soon as the music ends, the trumpet sounds again and ... the cannons boom on all sides."

was valued primarily as an aid to public speaking, which involved other forms of representation, especially dress and gestures, to reinforce the sense of the words.[23] To promote their imperial themes, the officials of Port-Royal lost no opportunity to impress the locals with French magnificence and to indicate the ideal relationship between French and Native. Even if Mi'kmaq actors did not play the four "Sauvages" in Lescarbot's production, the role of humble petitioners amid this display of French ceremony and power would have demonstrated what the French expected of Natives in real life.

The French believed they were superior to Indigenous societies because for almost two centuries they defined savagery in negative terms. Natives did not possess the skills and inventions that had allowed Europeans to discover the New World. They were naked ("Ilz sont tous nudz"), without the arts of civilization. Gradually certain commentators reconsidered this judgment, laying the groundwork of the Philosophes' social criticism in the mid-eighteenth century.[24] The most obvious Native skill was oratory, recognized long before the fictional "bon sauvage" was transported to France in the figure of Lahontan's Adario. In 1603 Champlain remarked that Montagnais leaders at Tadoussac "parlent fort pozément, comme se voullant bien faire entendre ... Ils usent bien souvent de ceste façon de faire parmi leurs harangues au conseil."[25] Champlain began a long tradition of imitating the allegories and rhetorical figures that he and others in his time considered characteristic of Native oratory, even to the extent of dramatizing these figures, as in a pageant, with actions and objects. Sagard was present when the General of the French fleet threw a sword into the St Lawrence to assure the killers of two French men that their fault was entirely forgiven and forgotten. Forgiveness of enemies was not in their moral lexicon, but the Natives who had contact with the French were no less adept at theatrical performance. Hurons who witnessed this scene seemed to approve Champlain's speech; then, according to Sagard's report, they laughed all the way back to their villages.[26] While colonial administrators were often misled by a grave demeanor, missionaries were observers behind the scenes. "Je ne crois pas

---

23 See Lahontan, Œuvres complètes, vol. I, p. 432: Lahontan regards even torture in theatrical terms : "ces tragédies réelles ... ce spectacle" / "these real-life tragedies ... this spectacle."
24 François-Xavier Charlevoix, Histoire de la Nouvelle France, 3 vols. (Paris: Didot, 1744). Charlevoix was indebted for many of his observations and attitudes, including increased respect for North American Natives, to Joseph-François Lafitau, Mœurs des sauvages amériquains, comparées aux mœurs des premiers temps (Paris: Saugrain and Hochereau, 1724).
25 Champlain, Œuvres, vol. I, p. 13: "They speak very deliberately, so as to be clearly understood ... They often employ this style while making speeches in council."
26 Sagard, Le Grand Voyage, p. 175.

qu'il y aye de nation sous le ciel plus mocqueuse & plus gausseuse que la nation des Montagnais," wrote Lejeune. "[L]eur vie se passe à manger, à rire, & à railler les uns des autres."[27]

Often content to play the role of the Governor's children, Native orators saved their best rhetoric for their own councils. Charlevoix, who had observed nations of the Mississippi and Great Lakes closely enough to perceive their multiple forms of representation, reserved his admiration for their debates. "Le premier coup d'œil de ces Assemblées, n'en donne pas une idée bien avantageuse," he conceded. "Nulle marque de distinction, nulle préseance; mais on change bien de sentiment, lorsqu'on voit le résultat de leurs Délibérations."[28] The councils consisted of speeches with long intervals of smoking. There was no jockeying for position, no visual display of wealth or power. What is more, the council members delivered their orations without emphatic gestures. "[L]'Orateur ... alla droit au Fait. Il parla lontems, et posément ... Son air, le son de sa voix, & son action, quoiqu'il ne fît aucun geste, me parurent avoir quelque chose de noble & d'imposant."[29] Nothing in Charlevoix's French experience – the liturgy's processions and prescribed gestures, its secular counterpart in courtly etiquette, the stylized movements of baroque theater – could explain the persuasive power of Native eloquence, which seemed untutored and purely *oral*.[30]

However, Native rhetorical skill was not quite so "naked" as Charlevoix claimed in his *Journal*: he and other French writers had many occasions to remark objects in council meetings that were used to regulate discussions and lend authority to decisions. The calumet, adorned with feathers, sometimes etched with animal figures, was smoked at intervals. Its use kept the tone of negotiations calm and reasonable by inserting periods of reflective silence between speeches. To ensure that decisions were remembered and honored, wampum belts were exchanged. The white and purple shell patterns of

---

27 Lejeune, *Jesuit Relations*, vol. VI, p. 242: "I do not think there is a nation under heaven more sardonic and facetious than the Montagnais. Their life is spent eating, laughing, and mocking each other."
28 Charlevoix, *Journal d'un voyage fait par ordre du roi dans l'Amérique septentrionale*, ed. Pierre Berthiaume, 2 vols. (Montreal: Presses de l'Université de Montréal, 1994), vol. I, pp. 539–40: "At first sight these assemblies do not show to advantage ... No badges of distinction, no hierarchy of rank and honour – but this impression soon gives way when one learns the result of their deliberations."
29 Ibid., vol. I, p. 541: "The orator ... went straight to the point. He spoke deliberately and for a long time. ... His manner, the timbre of his voice, the stance of his body though he made no gesture, struck me as rather noble and imposing."
30 Normand Doiron, "Rhétorique jésuite de l'éloqence sauvage au XVIIe siècle: les *Relations* de Paul Lejeune," *Dix-Septième Siècle* 173.4 (1991), pp. 375–402.

wampum belts were sometimes decorative abstract designs, sometimes figures representative of the agreement under discussion.³¹ La Potherie told of a council that wished to verify an earlier decision; to do so, "on leur fit la lecture de ce Collier pour éviter la confusion."³²

The range of semiotic modes practiced by Indigenous cultures in contact with the French colonial régime included not only oratory with its pipe and wampum (the mode proper to "oral" societies) but also three important graphic forms of representation: body decoration, figurative signs and maps.

Body decoration impressed the French from the first recorded moment of contact. Cartier's sight of Natives in the Gulf of St Lawrence was of men clad in skins and fearsomely painted. A century later, when Lejeune met Montagnais at Tadoussac, he compared them to Mardi-gras revellers: "je voyais ces masques qui courent en France à Caresme-prenant."³³ Lejeune "read" the paint as disguise: the Montagnais were inscrutable; Lejeune's first contact with them repeated Cartier's experience. In contrast, Sagard observed young men applying body paint before he viewed the effect. He also noted that some of the men were tattooed; their bodies and faces were scored into compartments "avec des figures de serpens, lezards, escureux & autres animaux ... ce qui les rend effroyables & hydeux à ceux qui n'y sont pas accoustumez." Hurons and their neighbours were proud of their tattoos not only for their aesthetic value but because the pricks "leur causent de grandes douleurs, & en tombent souvent malades."³⁴ Tattooing was an act of bravado, a kind of torture, self-inflicted, which mirrored the painful deaths meted out to one's enemies. And torture, in turn, was a kind of justice: the law of vengeance was inscribed on the bodies of those abandoned by their manitous and defeated in war.³⁵ The proper attitude to torture was a willingness to suffer it, to be proud and careless of life.

---

31 For photographs and detailed descriptions, see William N. Fenton, "Return of Eleven Wampum Belts to the Six Nations Iroquois Confederacy on Grand River, Canada," *Ethnohistory* 36.4 (Fall 1989), pp. 392–410, and Elisabeth Tooker, "A Note on the Return of Eleven Wampum Belts to the Six Nations Iroquois Confederacy on Grand River, Canada," *Ethnohistory* 45.2 (Spring 1998), pp. 219–36.
32 Baqueville de la Potherie, *Histoire de l'Amérique septentrionale*, 4 vols. (Paris: Nion and Didot, 1721), vol. IV, p. 220: "This wampum belt was read in order to avoid confusion."
33 Lejeune, *Jesuit Relations*, vol. V, p. 22: "I saw those masked revellers who run loose in France just before Lent."
34 Sagard, *Le Grand Voyage*, pp. 228–9: "with designs of snakes, lizards, squirrels and other animals ... which makes them seem frightening and hideous to those who are not used to it ... these pricks cause them great pain and they often fall ill as a result."
35 Pierre Clastres, *La Société contre l'état* (Paris: Minuit, 1974), pp. 152–60.

Figurative signs, what Charlevoix called "des espèces d'Hieroglyphes,"[36] were intimately associated with rituals and tradition. At a curing ceremony conducted by the "Sorcier" who so irritated Lejeune, a woman "marquoit sur un baston triangulaire ... toutes les chansons qu'ils disoient."[37] Similar song records on boards and bark scrolls were part of the Midéwiwin legacy preserved for generations by Ojibwa shamans and now in various museums. Other Midé scrolls depicted the westward migration of the Ojibwa's healing knowledge and the ritual re-enactment of this journey in the initiation rites of its members. The signs were stylized pictures of animals, places, actions, and medicine power. Although each drawing consisted of only a few strokes, the images were far from crude or simple. Instead they were *simplified*, reduced to essential traits.[38] By extension, the figures of ritual were associated with tribal leadership and came to be used as signatures on European treaties. As Charlevoix observed, "Le Chef de chaque Famille en porte le nom, & dans les actions publiques on ne lui en donne point d'autre. Il en est de même du Chef de la Nation, & de celui de chaque Village." The chiefs had personal names "outre ce nom, qui n'est, pour ainsi dire, que de représentation."[39] For example, the name sign of Kondiaronk, a Huron chief and Lahontan's model for Adario, was the figure of a muskrat; hence he was known to the French as "le Rat." La Potherie noted in 1701 that "Tous les Députez ratifierent la Paix en mettant chacun leurs armes, qui étoient un Orignac, un Castor, un Chevreuil, un Cerf, un Rat musqué, & une infinité d'autres animaux."[40]

Indigenous maps, no less than European maps, were spatial constructs operating outside the oral limits all too often assigned to Indigenous societies. The graphic nature of Native maps is often overlooked because of the dialogue that prompted their creation: the explorer asked for directions;

---

36 Charlevoix, *Journal d'un voyage*, vol. I, pp. 451, 512: "a kind of hieroglyphics." See Derrida, *De la grammatologie*, pp. 119–42, 397–427, on the eighteenth-century interest in hieroglyphics and other non-phonetic writing.

37 Lejeune, *Jesuit Relations*, vol. VI, p. 204: "a woman marked all the songs they chanted on a triangular stick."

38 See, for example, Garrick Mallery, *Picture-Writing of the American Indians*, 2 vols. (New York: Dover, 1972), vol. I, pp. 31–130, 227–57.

39 Charlevoix, *Journal d'un voyage*, vol. I, p. 554: "The head of each family bears the name of that family, and in public affairs he always goes by that name, which is strictly representative. Otherwise he has a name which designates him more specifically."

40 La Potherie, *Histoire* vol. IV, p. 254: "All the representatives ratified the peace treaty by each appending their 'arms' – a moose, a beaver, a deer, a stag, a muskrat and many more animals."

the informant responded with a map.[41] Like the figurative signs, Native maps were simplified, conventional designs that were used and understood over most of North America. Their characteristic pattern is often perceptible in the maps of the best French cartographers. Features of La Vérendrye's "Carte Tracée Par les Cris," for example, were incorporated into maps drawn by two royal geographers, Bellin and Buache. Inclusion of Native maps was a stopgap in anticipation of scientific data.[42] Ideally, according to Lahontan, the French explorer should be equipped with an astrolabe, a plane table, several compasses, a lodestone, two large watches, and paper for writing up his journals and drawing his maps.[43] In contrast to the explorer laden with instruments and paper records, Natives could find their way without even a compass and produce their geographical knowledge from memory. French commentators regarded Native cartography with the same ambivalence as they did Native oratory and tattooing: all three forms of representation relied on memory and / or were focused on the body.[44] The French saw these forms as more proof of the lack which defined savagery; at the same time, the skill of Native mapmakers and orators as well as the startling effect of body paint and tattoos never failed to impress them.

French understanding of these various forms of representation increased with time and familiarity. But even Frenchmen who moved away from the Laurentian colonies and into the *pays d'en haut* often failed to connect attitudes and practices, and thus fell short of understanding a world view at odds with their own. If Indigenous practices were strange and complex, their governing attitudes should still have been evident. From the Gulf of St Lawrence to the Great Plains, two virtues dictated honorable behaviour in Native societies: courage before enemies and generosity to friends. Although the French could be courageous enough, missionaries failed to be generous even with signs of their faith. When a Montagnais chief asked Sagard to give him a rosary, Sagard refused, for fear he would not get another one. The young Franciscan later noted the appropriate response without seeing how it related to his own ungenerous behavior: when a sick woman dreamed that her cure depended on the chief's cat, "ce Capitaine en fut adverty, qui aussi tost luy envoye son

---

41 Mark Warhus, *Another America: Native American Maps and the History of Our Land* (New York: St. Martin's Press, 1997) assumes that traditionally Indigenous societies were oral cultures and that Native maps must somehow be "oral" as well.
42 Barbara Belyea, "Amerindian Maps: The Explorer as Translator," *Journal of Historical Geography* 18.3 (1992), pp. 267–77; Barbara Belyea, *Dark Storm Moving West* (Calgary: University of Calgary Press, 2007), pp. 51–73.
43 Lahontan, *Œuvres complètes*, vol. I, p. 436.
44 Charlevoix, *Journal d'un voyage*, vol. II, pp. 622–7.

Plate 1. Louis Nicholas, "Chief of the Illinois nation. He is armed with his pipe and his spear," c. 1700.

chat bien qu'il l'aymast grandement."[45] Lejeune was just as uncomprehending. "Nostre Sauvage," he wrote, "voudroit bien vivre avec nous comme frere, en un mot il voudroit entrer en communauté de tout. Je te donneray, dit-il, de

---

45 Sagard, *Le Grand Voyage*, p. 205: "when this chief learned of the woman's dream, he immediately sent her his cat although he loved it dearly."

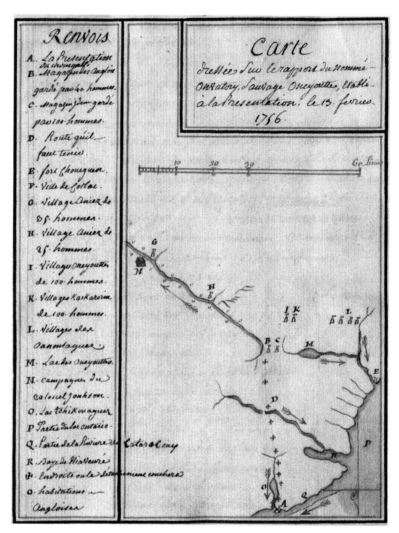

Plate 2. "Map drawn up from the account of the aforesaid Onouatary, an Oneida Savage, recorded, at the presentation of February 13, 1756, in Gaspard–Joseph Chaussegros de Léry's journal of the winter campaign, 1756."

tout ce que j'ay, & tu me donneras de tout ce que tu as."[46] Lejeune's answer was firm: if the French lived as equals with the Montagnais and treated them as brothers, "ce seroit nous perdre en trois jours."[47] So when Champlain invited Native traders to be brothers with the French, they could not believe he was serious. "Ils se mire[n]t à rire; repartans: Tu nous dis toujours quelque chose de gaillard pour nous resjouyr."[48] Despite their own use of kinship terms to describe their relationship with various Native groups, the French were slow to understand these terms as other than empty or approximate metaphors. Natives who used them were prepared to take them literally, that is, to treat their new allies as family members. Traditionally the only alternative to kinship was enmity. The nations of the *pays d'en haut* overcame their enemies by incorporating them, either by cannibalism or by adoption into their own communities. In contrast, most of the French, *coureurs de bois* excepted, offered a strange blend of apparent generosity, interest and distance: they could be prodigal with presents and seem friendly enough, but there was a line most of them would not cross. That line defined them as civilized and separated them from the "Sauvages."

During the late seventeenth century the Indigenous nations of the Great Lakes, accustomed for decades to French traders and missionaries, were slowly drawn into closer ties with the colonial government. They relied on "Onontio," the French governor, to mediate their differences and to supply them with goods in times of want. Colonial officials' willingness to play the roles of protector and provider was driven by their own need for a safe and prosperous fur trade in the *pays d'en haut*, as well as by the faint hope of exacting real obedience to the French crown. In 1671 the colonial administration arranged the first of a series of grand alliances: a meeting of fourteen nations confirmed agreements made by the *coureurs de bois* Radisson, Perrot, and Chouart dit Groseilliers. Four Jesuits acted as interpreters, and the negotiations concluded with a ceremony of possession: the cross, the king's arms, the gunfire and the *Te Deum* were the same signs by which Cartier had claimed the Gulf of St Lawrence.[49]

---

46 Lejeune, *Jesuit Relations*, vol. V, pp. 170–72: "Our Savage would like to live with us like a brother, in short, he would like to share everything with us. I will give you all that I have, he says, and you will give me all that you have."
47 Ibid., vol. VI, p. 258: "in three days we would have nothing left" – this in spite of knowing how important generosity was to the Montagnais.
48 Ibid., vol. V, p. 210: "They laughed and answered, You always tell us a joke in order to make us feel good."
49 Havard, *Empire et métissages* pp. 209–10.

Indigenous leaders were well aware of French strengths and weaknesses. When, for example, Governor La Barre hid the poor condition of his forces behind a flowery negotiation for peace in 1684, the Iroquois leader Grangula cut through the French rhetoric with some of his own: "Ecoute, *Onnontio*, je ne dors point, j'ai les yeux ouverts, & le Soleil qui m'éclaire, me fait découvrir un grand Capitaine à la tête d'une troupe de Guerriers qui parle en someillant."[50] But the Native nations also had weaknesses. The following year, when Hurons traded their furs at Montreal, one of their leaders (possibly Kondiaronk) assured the French "qu'ils savent bien le plaisir qu'ils font aux habitans du *Monreal*, par raport au profit que ces mêmes habitans en retirent; que ces peaux étant estimées en France, & au contraire les Marchandises qu'on leur troque étant de petite valeur."[51] The Huron orator knew of the French traders' high markup and said so. He also knew that his speech would do nothing to change the situation: the Huron–French alliance ruled out trade with the English; Huron traders were obliged to accept the French rate of exchange if they wanted European goods. Meanwhile colonial officials played on the vanity of chiefs by giving them presents, inviting them to dine at the Governor's house, bestowing titles and medals, and in certain cases befriending them. The Huron chief Michipichi was nicknamed "Quarante-Sols" because he angled for the title and pay of a captain in the French army.[52] According to Charlevoix, Kondiaronk was actually granted this status.[53]

With the help of such chiefs, the colonial government's relationship with inland tribes was reconstructed during the 1690s. War, disease, and wavering English support forced the five Iroquois nations to negotiate for alliances with the French and with the nations of the Great Lakes. Frontenac and his successor, Callières, saw their chance to organize a general alliance of all nations in territory claimed by the French crown, from Acadia to the Great Lakes. After several years of negotiation, ratification of the agreement was set for midsummer 1701.

---

50 Lahontan, *Œuvres complètes* vol. I, p. 307: "Listen, Onontio, *I'm* not asleep, *my* eyes are wide open, and the sun which lights my way has shown me a great chief at the head of a troop of warriors who is sleeping as he speaks."
51 Ibid., vol. I, pp. 316–17: "... that they well knew the pleasure they gave to the inhabitants of Montreal by virtue of the profitable trade of these same inhabitants – that these pelts were prized in France, and that by contrast the goods that they traded were of little value."
52 Antoine Laumet de la Mothe, Sieur de Cadillac, *Découvertes et établissements des Français*, ed. Pierre Margry, vol. V, pp. 309–10.
53 Charlevoix, *Histoire de la Nouvelle France*, vol. II, p. 278.

The Great Peace of Montreal saw 1,300 representatives of forty nations camped outside the town. As well as the usual rivalries and injuries, an infectious fever threatened to sabotage the proceedings. Callières moved forward to the treaty-signing as quickly as he could, given the inevitable speeches and ceremonies. The treaty format was not the usual series of articles specifying points agreed to; instead it was the text of the Governor's "parolle" on the day of signing, together with the summarized responses of eighteen chiefs. The document has been described as the intersection of writing and orality, a transcription of "harangues" by the chiefs and the Governor himself. The Governor welcomed the delegates as his children, reminded them of their promises to maintain the general alliance, and offered to settle any disputes. The delegates addressed the Governor as "mon pere" and promised to obey him. The only surviving copy of this treaty is now in the Archives nationales de France.[54]

Although it is the official document marking the Peace of 1701, the treaty text is poor evidence of the extraordinary occasion it claims to represent. It is too short, too sketchy, and its exclusive emphasis on obedience to Onontio can be misread. Fortunately there are supporting documents, notably La Potherie's account published twenty years later. La Potherie followed the twelve-day event from the arrival of inland canoes to the farewell speeches. On the first day the Iroquois met their former enemies at the Sault St Louis, addressing them as "mes freres"; then all the important men met at the lodge of Arioteka, chief of the calumet. La Potherie gave a hint of the delegates' expectations and the adjustments they were obliged to make on the level of diplomatic protocol, by observing various forms of representation that marked the entente. The old enemies smoked the calumet, although "les Iroquois furent un peu surpris de ce que ils ne leurs en presenterent point un nouveau. Ils s'attendoient à y répondre par un present de fusils, de chaudieres, de chemises & de couvertures."[55] The Iroquois politely ignored the oversight while the assembled crowd listened to music and waited for the first banquet. The next day the delegates arrived at Montreal: cannon volleys saluted them and they camped along the town's wooden palisade.

---

54 Archives nationales de France, fonds de Colonies CIIA, vol. XIX, ff. 41–4. Gilles Havard, *The Great Peace of Montreal of 1701*, tr. Phyllis Aronoff and Howard Scott (Montreal and Kingston: McGill-Queen's University Press, 2001), pp. 112–18, reproduces the treaty and its signatures.
55 La Potherie, *Histoire* vol. IV, pp. 194–200, quotation at p. 197: "the Iroquois were a bit surprised that they were not presented with a new calumet. They expected to respond to this gift with a present of guns, kettles, shirts and blankets."

And so on: La Potherie described every day of the event in comparable detail. By reporting the speeches at length, he furnished plentiful evidence of serious negotiations right up to the treaty-signing. Callières and his officials met with the chiefs in succession; these meetings were not audiences to hear petitions but discussions to reach a mutually acceptable arrangement. The Native leaders had been asked to bring their captives to Montreal so that they could be returned to their own people. The exchange of captives was a usual procedure in European peace negotiations; in America, French officials hoped that it might break the traditional vendettas and impose colonial law on the *pays d'en haut*. Many chiefs acceded to this request, although a couple of them regretted that they had already eaten their prisoners. The Iroquois decision to attend without captives threatened the peace; eventually a plan for their release was approved, but not before the Governor "se trouva fort déconcerté ... à cause de nos Alliez qui avoient lieu de se plaindre extrêmement de nous."[56] The ritual of the calumet was instrumental in keeping tempers in check, while gifts of wampum guaranteed the spoken promises.

As well as offering thirty-one wampum belts, colonial officials confirmed the negotiations with their own brand of pomp and display. An unforeseen occasion offered itself when Kondiaronk, one of the principal advocates of the alliance, died shortly before the treaty was signed. The funeral became an occasion of rapprochement: Iroquois chiefs mourned the Huron as they would one of their own, while the colonial administration spared no effort or expense to provide grave clothes, a decorated coffin, a solemn procession and high mass in the cathedral. On the day of the treaty signing, all the gentlemen and ladies gathered at a large field outside the town; all the delegates sat, nation by nation, facing a "sale" made of leafy branches that mimicked as much as possible an interior venue of royal magnificence at home, beside which the government's wampum belts were displayed. More long speeches were delivered, a number of them reported in La Potherie's account. This day might have passed like the others except for the French determination to mark it with their own kind of solemnity, believing it was necessary to confirm this great alliance with a splendid entertainment; to this end the French contributed more presents, invited the delegates to a feast, sang the *Te Deum*, saluted with muskets and cannon, and committed their understanding of the event to paper.[57] Some elements of this ceremony recalled previous claims of

---

56 Ibid., vol. IV, pp. 218, 223–5: "We were very worried and frustrated ... our allies had cause to be very disappointed in us."
57 Ibid., vol. IV, pp. 240–57, quotation at p. 252.

possession, and the terms of the document seemed to demand tighter colonial control. In fact, the French were slowly withdrawing from the region and had recently abandoned all but three of their military posts inland.[58] The Peace of Montreal was a sort of masque dramatizing what the French wished to happen and what they tried, by ceremonial means, to bring about. The success of the Montreal treaty was mixed. Although Iroquois no longer attacked the Laurentian colonies, the French were never more than allies with nations of the *pays d'en haut*.

We are left with the treaty document, which reveals French aims in its text but includes more than this text. The chiefs were asked to ratify the new general alliance; they did so by drawing their name-signs on the last pages of the document.[59] Strictly speaking, these figurative signs subscribed not to the treaty text but to the negotiations that the text was supposed to record. Yet, as signatures, the identity marks are no more mnemonic ("oral") than Callières's own signature. They are a graphic form of representation – an *Indigenous* graphic form, in no way derivative of, or related to, European writing. They remind us not (as Todorov would conclude) that the Indigenous nations were inferior to French culture and therefore vulnerable to French power, but that French–Native relationships were built on a range of semiotic modes: French literacy and Native oratory were only two forms of representation, neither of which was practiced in isolation from other forms.

Since both sides used the full range of their own forms as well as borrowing from the other, often the effect was unpredictable. For example, Miskouensa, the Fox chief from west of Lake Michigan, painted his face and donned a wig for the treaty-signing. When he rose to speak, he bowed to the Governor, bending his knee and sweeping the wig like a hat from his head. The French *beau monde* tittered at the sight; La Potherie reported, "[m]algré le sang froid que l'on est obligé d'avoir devant des gens qui sont d'un si grand flegme."[60] But when Miskouensa bowed to Callières, who was laughing at whom, and for whose benefit? The chief's odd combination of dress and gesture was saturated with significance. At the most solemn and important moment of the Peace of Montreal, when the French paper was on the table ready for final

---

58 Havard, *Empire et métissages*, pp. 71, 452–7; Richard White, *The Middle Ground: Indians, Empires, and Republics in the Great Lake Region, 1650–1815* (Cambridge: Cambridge University Press, 1991), pp. 143, 148.
59 Yann Guillaud, Denys Delâge, and Mathieu d'Avignon, "Les Signatures amérindiennes: Essai d'interpretation des traités de paix de Montréal de 1700 et de 1701," *Recherches amérindiennes de Québec* 31.2 (2001), pp. 21–41.
60 La Potherie, *Histoire* vol. IV, p. 247: "in spite of the poker face that one is supposed to maintain in the presence of such stolid people."

assent, Miskouensa's standup comic performance added his own theatrical version of the alliance to the mix of declarations and interpretations. Both sides had spent days in negotiation to achieve a new kind of mutual understanding; now they took refuge in laughter which confirmed their own forms of representation and momentarily distanced those of the other.[61]

What are we to make of Miskouensa's wordless parody, of the great peace of Montreal, of French–Native contact since Cartier? Three remarks seem appropriate. First: the main evidence of this period is in the form of French written records, a fact of survival requiring careful analysis of the recorded situations to assess the various semiotic codes in play. Second: the range of representative forms elicited from the evidence cannot be reduced to, or adequately conveyed by, a single signifying process. All societies organize and communicate experience by using multiple forms of representation; to classify a culture as "oral" or "literate" is to distort its communicative and expressive capacity by privileging one form over the others. This second remark is valid whether writing is defined as phonetic transcription or used as the metaphor of all signification. And last, in answer to Todorov's claim of mental superiority: the "Sauvages," from Donnacona to Kondiaronk and Miskouensa, were remarkably intelligent and kept the French guessing for 200 years.

61 Havard, *Empire et métissages*, pp. 758–9.

2

Reports from la Nouvelle-France: the Jesuit *Relations*, Marie de l'Incarnation, and Élisabeth Bégon

E. D. BLODGETT

The problem

The early globalization of New France, its evangelization and exploration, after a few years in Acadia, began in earnest in the 1630s, the same decade in which the Jesuit-trained René Descartes's *Discours de la méthode* appeared, a text that formed the foundation of modern, rationalist philosophy. Just as our world is post-Cartesian, the formation of Canada was earnestly its opposite, and their ideological differences form the basis of a debate begun in Quebec in the nineteenth century between the liberal, secular historian François-Xavier Garneau and the more conservative, ecclesiastical historian Jean-Baptiste-Antoine Ferland. Inasmuch as the liberal side has prevailed, the missionary work of the Jesuits and its written legacy, not to speak of their influence on Marie de l'Incarnation, tends to be put aside, as, for example, a recent history in English has done.[1] To neglect these texts, especially the Jesuit *Relations*,[2] simply because they inscribe an ideology that does not fit the contemporary doxa would be to distort the sense of Canada's arrival into history. It is to forget that, before the "empire writes back," it writes; and by merely writing, it claims an ideological and discursive territory that extends well beyond its initial frontiers. That they have not been entirely neglected is apparent from novels, poems and plays such as Leonard Cohen's *Beautiful*

---

1 For example H(enry). V(ivian). Nelles, *A Little History of Canada* (Don Mills: Oxford University Press, 2004).
2 Note on translations: The translations of the Jesuit *Relations* are taken from Reuben Gold Thwaites, ed., *The Jesuit Relations and Allied Documents: Travels and Explorations of the Jesuit Missionaries in New France*, 73 vols. (Cleveland: Burrows, 1896–1901). My referencing system follows that of Conrad Heidenreich's *Huronia* (Toronto: McClelland and Stewart, 1971). 8:179, for example, stands for volume 8, p. 179. The translations from Marie de l'Incarnation and Élisabeth Bégon are mine.

Losers, Laure Conan's *À l'œuvre et à l'épreuve*, Brian Moore's *Black Robe*, Archibald Lampman's "At the Long Sault," Delaware playwright Daniel David Moses's *Brébeuf's Ghost*, and E. J. Pratt's *Brébeuf and his Brethren*.

The Jesuit *Relations* are annual reports that began in 1611 in Acadia and lasted for a few years until 1616. They resume as letters, at least, in Quebec in 1626. Because of their heterogeneous character, written by many authors and reflecting a variety of preoccupations, they are, taken as a whole, closer to chronicles than instances of plotted historiography. For literary history they are especially valuable because of the imaginary world they evince. As a result, they provoke a number of questions: to what end is character constructed, how is the narrative order controlled, what kind of ethical structures are implied, where do they draw their text models from? In other words, how can they be read in respect of character, plot, and intention?

The intention is deceptively simple: to "convertir les Sauvages" (8:178).[3] Conversion, as the Jesuits predict with ironic prescience, is required so that God "dominabitur a mari usque ad mare."[4] But in order for the Church to triumph, a knowledge of Aboriginal languages was of the first necessity, because no real exchange is possible otherwise.[5] The use of language in general, however, was even more important, and it takes one to the heart of matter for the Jesuits and their desire to "convertir le trafic de la terre en celui du ciel, vouloir mourir dans la Barbarie" (8:222).[6] So it is that the activity of the Jesuits is directly connected to their *Relations*. To act is perforce to write, and taken together they constitute a discursive practice, which is at least as old as the Middle Ages, and which is founded on the accuracy of the written, rather than the spoken, word (see 39:148). Without an acquaintance with Descartes, the Jesuits are, nevertheless, implying the assertion: I write, therefore, I am. This may appear to be an existential gesture, but it is primarily a theological and social one, and all the words the Natives are prompted to say turn (convert) them into other theological and social agents, beginning with their assimilation.[7]

---

3 "To convert the savages."
4 "He will have dominion from sea to sea," Psalms 72:8, cited 18:238; this verse forms the motto of Canada, adopted in the nineteenth century.
5 Similarly, Marie de l'Incarnation, after learning Algonquin and Innu, took up the study of Huron at fifty, which resulted in a subsequently lost dictionary. Marie de l'Incarnation, *Correspondance*, ed. Guy Oury (Solesmes: Abbaye Saint-Pierre, 1971), p. 390.
6 "To convert the business of earth into that of heaven, to be willing to die in the midst of Barbarism."
7 See Yvon Le Bras, *L'Amérindien dans les Relations du père Paul Lejeune* (Sainte-Foy: Les Editions de la huit, 1994), p. 142.

As a consequence, the *Relations* are most fruitfully understood as more than simply language. It is a language designed to assert, to confirm, and to establish, all of which taken together constitute an act of possession. It is performative in a theological sense; their language is composed of discursive practices that, as Foucault puts it, "forment systémiquement les objets dont ils parlent."[8] Furthermore, because of the textual models that are drawn upon, notably, the saint's life, the Bible, ecclesiastical history, and the manner in which they narrate the world, they inevitably construct characters (priests and Natives) as they were in existence before the *Relations* began to articulate them. Thus, the process by which New France was made was not a discovery, but a testimony to the way things were since late antiquity.

The texts and theology

This means that a recovery, no matter how brief, of the significant events that the *Relations* provide (that is, a second-order history based upon them as primary documents) is not adequate to determine how they function as either literary or social history. The general title used by their last editor, Reuben Gold Thwaites, is deceptively simple: *The Jesuit Relations and Allied Documents*. They consist of relations, a practice begun by Ignatius Loyola, which are annual reports on the state of the missions, written for the most part in French, but also in Latin and Italian. Other genres include the journal, which are frequently travel diaries, but often simply notations of daily events, and the letter, which normally treats of desiderata, such as Father Paul Le Jeune's appeal to the King to save the colony. That they reached more than one reader is evident in Claude Chauchetière's expression of unhappiness that one of his letters was not kept confidential (63:144). The *Relations* were published, for the most part, annually.

While letters may be relatively personal, the relations and journals construct different but complementary worlds the motivations of which govern how their material is to be construed. The Jesuit Fathers assumed, first of all, that their readers would know that the world is constructed on the two planes of the temporal and the spiritual along which secular and divine events are enacted. A not uncommon pair of entries in a journal reads as follows for the month of January 1659: "22 Marie boutet [sic] receut 1 habit aux Ursulines.

---

8 "Systematically shape the objects they talk about." Michel Foucault, *L'Archéologie du savoir* (Paris: Gallimard, 1969), p. 67.

27 retournerent aux 3 Rivieres les 3 francois" (45:78).⁹ The quotidian character of these events and their lack of both connection and consequence mark them as purely temporal. Because the *Relations* generally have the sub-theme of conversion, they order the world with the consequence provided by the extra-temporal frame. For example, the journal just cited notes in an entry for 12 September: "Un françois nommé L'Epine tüé aux 3 riv. par les Iroquois" (45:114).¹⁰ By contrast, Father Antoine Daniel's final moments before his martyrdom (1648) continued to inspire so many of his congregation that he baptised them as a group. Here, consequence, coded as it is, is highly charged (and well rhymed). The passage introduces the reader to the double *agon* of the *Relations*, in which a priest faces possible death from ubiquitous enemies ("Infidels") and rebellion from those who refuse conversion. The moments of climax that the *Relations* contain overcome this *agon* through baptism and martyrdom, the two moments when the temporal world is ordered in clear contrast with that of the journals into a vertical, as opposed to a horizontal, perspective.

It is hardly accidental that the two modes of narration bear a cruciform relation to each other, inasmuch as the Christ of the Jesuit Fathers was Christ crucified, despite the fact that their most frequently quoted Gospel is that of Matthew, which is perhaps most famous for its chapter known as the Beatitudes (Matt 5:1–10). Matthew may be said, however, to have been privileged because of his emphasis on the authority of Christ established by his place in the temporal world conceived as the history of salvation, achieved through his crucifixion and resurrection. Matthew's Christ also legitimizes missionary activity as coterminous with apocalypse: "And this gospel of the kingdom will be preached to the whole inhabited earth for a testimony (martyrion) to all the nations, and then the end will come" (Matt 24:14). As Father Le Jeune asserts in an early *Relation*, they found themselves in life and in death, where death always signifies another world akin to Dante's.

The effects of Jesuit ideology

Such a vision has consequences. A primary consequence was the effect that the missions had on First Nations over a vast area that ranged from Acadia to what is now Labrador, Quebec, Ontario, Michigan, Wisconsin, and the lands bordering the Mississippi as far as New Orleans, as well as the Saguenay as far

---

9 "Marie boutet took the veil at the Ursulines. The 3 frenchmen returned to 3 rivers."
10 "A frenchman named L'Epine was killed at 3 Rivers by the Iroquois."

as Hudson's Bay. While conversion was the object, knowledge of Aboriginal peoples was the means. Many Jesuits learned the several languages of the Iroquois, Hurons, Algonquins, Innu (Montagnais), and others, and all seem to have been assiduous ethnographers. Furthermore, they brought to their task a clear, medieval sensibility, a resolute adherence to the principles of the Counter-Reformation, and rigorous grounding in the education of the early modern period. Although their judgments reflect their ideological formation, their observations on Aboriginal life in these regions are invaluable.

The purpose of their observations was, of course, not entirely scientific. As Father Jérôme Lalemant remarks, his report is designed to move the faithful with compassion (17:212), and knowledge of them is also useful as a means of acquiring trust. To the disciplined eye of a Jesuit, life in a Native village appeared disorderly. It is frequently mentioned how the children are treated with great indulgence, and that there is no legal system that corresponds to the Roman tradition, although a method of dealing with murder that corresponds to the Germanic Wergeld is noted. The three major vices of the missions, it is often observed, are drunkenness, superstition, and lewdness, to which a host of others can be added, especially gluttony and the love of pleasure. Superstition, naturally, exercises Natives continually, and both conversations and descriptions of it are provided. All Aboriginal theology is classified as fable, which includes the divination of animals and the belief in Manitou. Along with regular castigations of jugglers or magicians (shamans), the empowerment of dreams is regularly remarked upon, especially as the instigator of vice and a constant threat to the life of the missionary. Father de Carheil, discussing the Iroquois, is cited in a letter remarking that dreams are the means by which Native people are directly reached by the divine. Hence they are the soul of their religion and the spirit that speaks to them is the master of their lives. At the same time, the soul, contrary to Roman Catholic belief, leaves the body in dream and embarks upon personal quests.

Great effort is expended in trying to refute such claims with the help of medieval dream psychology in order to replace the Native notion of dreams with a Christian one. Sometimes replacement is spontaneous. For example, when a sick old man dreams of heaven, his dream consists of the torture of captives that was related to him by a man one cubit in height. This dream is countered by an elder who also dreamed of heaven as a place where all wishes were fulfilled. The second dream is considered by the Jesuit reporting as sufficient proof against the first dream, and an indication that most dreams are inventions. Nevertheless, even as inventions they are useful. When a sick man dreams of Father Julien Garnier giving him medicine, he is told that this is a message from God, "Le grand Maistre de nostre vie."[11] The man receives baptism and dies.

Of greater use for the cause of conversion was the figure of the Manitou. The Manitou, who appears first among the Acadian *Relations* and is discussed often into the final volumes, is the divine figure recognized by most First Nations whom the Jesuits encountered. According to Father Joseph Jouvency, the Aboriginals worship a Deity lacking definite character or regulated worship. He is the active principle of dreams, and he makes the animal world sacred. He is the cause of sickness and death. What endows him with a certain complexity is that he is construed in a dualistic fashion. For the Montagnais, for example, he is "toute Nature superieure à l'homme, bonne ou mauvaise" (12:6).[12] Not only is he omnipotent, he is also omniscient; and thus the Jesuits, because of their superior knowledge of earth and sky are also considered Manitous.[13]

His dominant characteristic, however, is his maliciousness, and often he is likened to the devil, but for real evil, his wife is to blame. Because the Manitou was a nature spirit, his presence is implicit in various etiological legends, which are readily dismissed as ridiculous fables. But because of the Aboriginal tendency to perceive the sacred as a ubiquitous presence, they were not immune to the possibility of superior divine powers, which becomes evident in their conversion. As Le Jeune reports of their success with the Iroquois, God turns all their religious tendencies, false as they may be from a Roman Catholic point of view, to his advantage. Thus, in a certain measure, the Aboriginal people were already prepared for what the Jesuits assumed to be their religious fulfillment.

The Jesuits from the first were fascinated by differences in customs, and their interest generated a long list of oppositions between Europeans and First Nations. Marriage, of course, was of interest, and polygamy, for example, was proscribed, but the practice among the Hurons of remaining chaste as if they were siblings during the first four months of marriage is looked upon with approval. An obvious leitmotif of the *Relations* is the interest taken in the cruel and whimsical treatment of captives, whether Native or foreign, which begins soon after Le Jeune's arrival at Tadoussac. As soon as the prisoners arrive, the torture begins, and his witness of it prompts him to remark that, if the Jesuits

---

11 "The Great Master of our lives."
12 "All Nature superior to man, good or bad."
13 Or they were thought to be *Okhi*, which were extraordinary beings (12:244). According to Marie de l'Incarnation, their signal power lay in their ability to write (*Correspondance*, p. 918).

had been captured by the Iroquois, they would likely have been tortured as well, since they lived with the Montagnards, enemies of the Iroquois. This a spontaneous and understandable conjecture, but it takes us, at the threshold of Le Jeune's many years of reporting, to the heart of the *Relations* as theological, historical, and literary narratives. On the one hand, the comment announces the theme of martyrdom, at once a hope and a fear, and, on the other, it raises the several issues of style which give these narrations their peculiar stamp.

Narrating martyrdom

Whether coterminous with conversion or not, death by martyrdom was the deep desire of the Jesuits in Canada. In Father Claude Dablon's *Relation* of 1676–7, it is remarked that their chief occupation is to suffer. As Marie de l'Incarnation writes, in this way they become true imitators of Christ (p. 106). The missionary life as an *imitatio Christi* was inscribed in their characters, and Brébeuf was known to receive visions of Christ crucified. His desire was to follow this example, and the Jesuits' fear is less of death than of losing the opportunity of living the sacrifice in which their occupation constantly places them.

Perhaps for this reason the narratives of the martyrs are among the most memorable. They are, indeed, designed to be memorable.[14] Of them all, Brébeuf is most known, at least in English Canada, because of E. J. Pratt's poem "Brébeuf and his Brethren" (1940), and before that his presence is most palpable in Francis Parkman's *The Jesuits in North America in the Seventeenth Century*, where he is remembered as "that masculine apostle of the Faith – the Ajax of the mission."[15] Although the account that Parkman provides follows that of Father Paul Ragueneau's *Relation* and imitates its succinctness, he does not notice the singular manner in which it becomes, at least, a twice-told tale. The narrator, although not an eyewitness, begins by relating the martyrdom, asserting its credibility by indicating that he has seen captives treated like Brébeuf. He notes that some of the details are unusual, such as the use of scalding water in mockery of the holy baptism, and the removal of his speech organs to prevent his efforts at conversion. The narrator continues the story at his point of entry after finding the body, and his presence is clearly asserted by

---

14 See Pierre Dostie, *Le Lecteur suborné dans cinq textes missionnaires de la Nouvelle-France* (Sainte-Foy: Les Editions de la huit, 1994), p. 225.
15 Francis Parkman, *The Jesuits in North America in the Seventeenth Century*, 2 vols. (Boston: Little, Brown, and Company, 1910), vol. I, p. 188.

Plate 3. Eric Gill, *The Martyrdom of Jean de Brébeuf*.

the clause, "Je ne doute pointe" (34:32).¹⁶ The second account follows death with acts of veneration and virtual resurrection. To make his point, he repeats the clause, "Jay veu et touché" (34:34),¹⁷ eight times to underscore the gestures of recognition that turn simple piety into Baroque corporeal emphasis, and no effort is spared to prepare Brebeuf and Lalemant's remains as relics. All that remained was sanctification (resurrection, in effect), which came in 1930.

The story, however, does not end with this report. Without being aware of it, the narrator was participating in the distinguishing design of the *Relations*, for no narrative is sufficient in itself, and the central stories fold into the *Relations* as a whole in multi-layered textualization. Brébeuf appeared to Father Charles Simon and Mother Catherine de St. Augustin as an apparition, and Brébeuf's efficacy as a relic is reported as leading to the conversion of a heretic (50:86–8). The only other martyr who found such an echo in fiction is Charles Garnier, who is given a more sentimental role in Laure Conan's novel

---

16 "I do not doubt."
17 "I saw and touched."

À l'œuvre et à l'épreuve (1891). There remains, however, the story of Isaac Jogues, whose only thorough narrative memorialization, outside the correspondence of Marie de l'Incarnation, is in the *Relations* themselves, and there he plays an extraordinary role, despite the fact that in Parkman's catalogue of heroes he merits no more than a sentence as an afterthought.[18]

No one appears better fitted for martyrdom than Jogues, and in a sketch of his virtues it is remarked that he possessed a rare sense of humility and that he wanted to be treated as if he were nothing. Jogues was the paradigm of the Jesuits as martyrs, and the relationship between Jesuit and Aboriginal was complementary: each is construed to enhance the continuous *agon* of early French settlement in Canada. His torture is particularly valuable because, since he survived it, he could serve as his own eyewitness. Although one might assume his personal report sufficient, in the *Relations* he is frequently scrutinized, and the first mention of his torture is brief, limited to the damaged fingers and amputated thumb. Jogues's own account is remarkable to the degree that he makes its object not his, but his companion's, torture. His account of the initial attack of the Iroquois is placed fully on René Goupil: "Les ennemis ... se ietterent sur nous comme des chiens enragez a belles dents, nous arrachant les ongles nous escrasans les doigts, ce qu'il enduroit avec beaucoup de patience et de courage" (28:118).[19]

As the narrative unfolds, Goupil is constructed as its hero. Jogues signals his presence of mind and the fact that he was always preoccupied with God: "Il le donnoit a lui en holocauste pour estre reduit en cendres p(ar) les feus des Iroquois que la main de ce bon Pere allumeroit" (28:120).[20] Goupil's humility and obedience to those who had captured him confound Jogues. Running the gauntlet and suffering mutilation are endured by Goupil with an uncommon gentleness. Suffering the ordeals of fire, which seemed to be a nightly activity for some six days after daily torture on the scaffolds, Jogues again puts Goupil forward, claiming that he, Jogues, had received greater power of endurance from nature. The reverence with which he treats Goupil's remains is one that one would bestow on the relics of one who had died as a martyr for Christ. After a few more summary comments, the document ends, an extraordinary testimony of self-abnegation and true to the character of its author.

---

18 Parkman, *The Jesuits*, vol. I, p. 195.
19 "The enemies ... fell upon us like mad dogs, with sharp teeth, tearing out our nails, and crushing our fingers, which he endured with much patience and courage."
20 "He gave himself to him as a sacrifice, to be reduced to ashes by the fires of the Iroquois, which that good Father's hand would kindle."

Self-abnegation, charity, and piety – traits generally perceived in saintly behavior – may be noted not only in countless, anonymous converts, but also in those like (St.) Kateri Tekakwitha, whose trials and death (1680) are celebrated in Chauchetière's history of the Mission of the Sault and who received another epiphany in Leonard Cohen's *Beautiful Losers* (1966). Characteristically, references to Takakwitha continue to recur in subsequent volumes, following the practice of layering noted already. In Chauchetière's letters of 1694, we find her treated as local legend and relic. In 1696, she continues to attract processions and people seeking cures, and further mention is made of her in 1735.

Intertextuality in the *Relations*

Repetition, of course, is a mode of veneration, and it is grounded in the medieval view of the world that the Jesuit Fathers perpetuated. It derives in many ways, perhaps primarily, from the practice of *lectio divina*.[21] The world was oriented in Scripture and to a lesser extent in the classical writers included in the curriculum, as well as a limited number of Church Fathers. Pliny is cited by the historian Marc Lescarbot, an Aboriginal is praised for speaking with rhetoric worthy of Aristotle and Cicero, Virgil's famous curse on the thirst for money (*Aeneid* III, 57) is cited, and the riddles of Oedipus. Lescarbot also cites Tacitus on the Germans, who are a model of the classical primitive ideal. Thus, he is implied, at least, in the frequent evocations of such an ideal as apparent among First Nations, among whom the Jesuits inhabit a golden age. Of the Fathers, St. John Chrysostom is mentioned, St. Ambrose, Tertullian, and St. Augustine, as well as such Church Doctors as St. Isidore, Bede, and St. Bernard. The largest share of citations is drawn, of course, from the Bible, but all the texts suggest the extent to which the world is perceived in terms of canonized narrative. It is also the program by which the temporal world is conjoined with the spirit and, indeed, made spiritual.[22]

There are two major uses of citation: either to point a moral or, more significantly, to demonstrate how the world is seen as palimpsest. The former is significant in respect of the narrative form that the *moralitas* bestowed upon the exemplary life. Thus, the obituary of Mme de la Peltrie is graced with two

---

21 See Jean Leclercq, *The Love of Learning and the Desire for God: A Study of Monastic Culture* (New York: Fordham University Press, 1960), ch. 5.
22 See Rémi Ferland, *Les Relations des Jésuites: Un art de la persuasion* (Sainte-Foy: Les Editions de la huit, 1992), p. 120.

citations, each in two parts, drawn from Ecclesiastes 1:13 and Wisdom 3:1, which are designed to show that her death was a day of blessing and her soul was in God's hand. Of far greater significance is the manner in which the Bible, among other texts, not only explains human life, but also implies that life, because of the analogies that are always possible, repeats or imitates Scripture. For this reason, all the missionaries can cite St. Paul's "Quotidie morimur" (1 Cor 15:31), and David's "Anima mea in manibus meis semper" (Psalms 119:109), "qu'il porte son ame entre ses mains; ou plustost qu'elle est à chaque moment dans les mains; [sic] des plus infideles de tous les peuples" (47:184).[23] The first citation is varied, as often in the *Relations*, to fit the situation (the verb as adapted from *morior* [I die]), but both adaptation and usage testify to the sense of human life as always in some way prefigured in biblical writing.

St. Augustine is used in the same way when Brébeuf is cited as praying to God for help, and a voice replies: "Tolle, Lege," which echoes St. Augustine's *Confessions*. Moreover, he then *takes* and *reads* a copy of Thomas à Kempis's *The Imitation of Christ* and by chance falls on the chapter concerning the cross as the royal way. His death is thus prescribed, so to speak, and his life, as those of other missionaries, is a fulfillment, and where the Psalmist chants "venientes venient cum exaltatione portantes manipulos suos" (11:18),[24] the Jesuits believed that they themselves held the sheaves. For the missionaries, the sentence refers to the metaphor of the harvest of souls (baptism), and particularly, as it is drawn from Luke, it implies a request for more harvesters.

Hence, while the Jesuits travelled through vast regions of North America, they were in fact moving through the Bible and all the auxiliary texts which belong to its interpretation. They represent figures possessed of a divine register. The *Relations* are striking in that they prompt the reader to take them as narratives that *read* life as allegorical and real, that is, spiritual and temporal. Reading, which is always *lectio divina*, conjoins the two, making them mutually empowering. As if a character in fiction, Brébeuf is constituted in the *Relations* as, at least, a re-enactment of St. Augustine and Christ.[25]

---

23 "That he carries his life in his hands, or, rather, that it is every instant in the hands of the most faithless of all peoples."
24 "They shall came exalting, bearing their sheaves."
25 The process is discussed at length in Erich Auerbach's essay "Figura" in *Scenes from the Drama of European Literature*, tr. Ralph Manheim (New York: Meridian Books, 1959), pp. 11–76.

Conversions and style

Not surprisingly, the landscape in which these events occur has a dual function. Careful observation is made of the water routes across the land; the lush country of the Iroquois is noted. Le Jeune implies, however, in a series of questions that the real sense of sufficiency lies in the opportunity it affords for union with God. The landscape may have attractions and the wherewithal to live, but its true value lies in its capability of bearing the medieval, monastic values from which this thinking emerges. Such a perspective also affected the more imaginative Aboriginals, and one had a dream (obviously a "good" dream) on three occasions in which he saw Christ against the sky, his cross all red with blood, and elsewhere it is described how erecting a cross on Good Friday transformed a forest into a sacred wood. The same landscape is readily perceived as the Kingdom of God, which was the purpose of its creation, and later many heretics are caused to find the road to Paradise by way of Canada. It is where, as opposed to France and the corruption of all the Louvres and the Palaces, sainthood is possible (25:32). In sum, to live in New France means to live in the bosom of God and to breathe the air of His guidance. Consequently, it is the home of Apostolic man.

In short, everything – nature and people – is converted, and what appears to be a system of parallels and analogies is overcome by the structure of Jesuit, that is medieval Roman Catholic, theology, which is articulated in the peculiar style of the *Relations*. The dominant genres of the Jesuit documents are the *Relations* and the *Journals*, and they bear approximately the same relationship to each other as the distinction Hayden White draws between chronicle and annal. The latter lacks a "narrative component," especially those journals constructed as diaries, while the chronicle "aspires to narrativity, but typically fails to achieve it" by failing to reach "narrative closure."[26] As he goes on to argue, some chronicles violate this rule and are more artistically fashioned. Although the *Relations* have closure in the pathetic appeal of the last of four Jesuits remaining after the eviction of the order from Canada who requested a small pension, they are all governed by one consideration: "Nous ne sçavons pas ce que Dieu nous reserve" (34:206).[27] This inability to know the future is what distinguishes the *Relations* from fiction and historiography, both of which are plotted with an end in mind. As a consequence, a reader is constructed

---

26 Hayden White, *The Content of the Form: Narrative Discourse and Historical Representation* (Baltimore and London: The Johns Hopkins University Press, 1987), p. 5.
27 "We know not what God reserves for us."

who ineluctably inhabits a present the significance of which is supplied largely by the Bible and related texts. A sense of the past is constructed by the manner in which events are repeated, but their meaning is contingent on existence as a present or remembered past. When the past is remembered, it is often transmuted into epiphany.

Marie de l'Incarnation

Canada was thus written into history in the first century of its existence by the hand of God, and what the Jesuits asserted was quietly affirmed in the letters of Marie de l'Incarnation. Ideologically akin, she differs from them in one primary respect: her passion is private; theirs, public. None of the correspondence of the Jesuits compares on a personal level with Marie's efforts, for example, to respond to her son's reproaches that she abandoned him before he was fully weaned.[28] But a biological mother is not a Mother Superior, which Marie was from her arrival in Quebec (1639) until her death (1672). Despite her yielding to the force of divine love, she still considers herself the cruellest of all mothers. Limited as it is, the reply suggests the degree to which Marie's personal life was imbricated into her official life. With all the finesse of her contemporary, Mme de la Fayette,[29] Marie explores the nuances of the spiritual life in a later letter to her son, in which it becomes apparent that the heart of her life is a continuous exercise of growing closer to the Holy Spirit, and those who do this the best are the Jesuit martyrs, whose hearts were filled with the spirit of the Word and the love of the cross.

Given the fact that she felt a vocation for the religious life long before her marriage, her meditations on the life of the spirit are not surprising. Without her other talents for business affairs and administration, however, developed for a few years after her husband's death, the success of the Ursulines in Canada may not have been so brilliant as it was.[30] She was fully aware that without commerce the country was worthless in the temporal world, and the relation between the temporal and the spiritual in her thinking was almost seamless.

---

28 She abandoned him fully when she entered a convent in Tours, which affected him so deeply that, at the instigation of his young friends, they stormed the convent in an effort to retrieve her. See Claude Martin, *La Vie de la Vénérable Mère Marie de l'Incarnation* (Paris: Chez Louis Billaine, 1677), p. 181.
29 Her novel, *La Princesse de Clèves* (1678), is generally considered the first psychological novel.
30 See Marie-Emmanuel Chabot's article in the *Canadian Dictionary of Biography Online*, ed. Ramsay Cook and Réal Bélanger.

In another letter to her son, she discusses the recent deaths of several missionaries as union with the divine. She concludes this section of her letter by reminding him of his unworthiness, and then without transition continues to observe that she agrees with his sense that, if money is lacking, there is a possibility that their Bull will be prevented from going to Rome and, even more important, without military support, the problem of the Iroquois makes all plans fruitless. Indeed, she shares the opinion of the Jesuits that only a Crusade against the infidel, a name frequently applied by Marie and the missionaries to the Iroquois, can solve the problem. As an administrator, she fiercely defended the constitution of the Quebec Ursulines against the plans of the newly arrived Bishop Laval, and generally was successful. As the director of a convent, her opportunities for ethnographical observation were limited, but she complains that after some thirty years they had not been able to "civiliser que sept ou huit, qui aient été francisées" (p. 828).[31] Nevertheless, toward the end of her life she answered a number of questions from her son, most of whose answers he might have gotten from the *Relations*, with the possible exception of the story of a virgin who gave birth to a great Man.

In most respects Marie's construction of the world complements that of the Jesuits. In one, however, she lets one see more deeply into the motivations they shared. She articulates the quotidian and temporal with more personal presence, but what she admires in the Jesuits she reveals in herself from her earliest letters. The supreme commitment of the Roman Catholic Church in New France was to sacrifice, and Marie was not alone in craving a death as blessed as that of Father Jogues. If suffering was not to occur, then abandonment to the spiritual and flight from the temporal was the one solution, and Marie's giving up of her son was an initial step. The other was union with Christ or the bridegroom mysticism that is the most common form in the Catholic contemplative life, which she refers to as her ordinary inner life (p. 19). From her earliest letter (1626), we read: "... Après ces sacrifices de la pénitence, mon esprit étoit rempli de tant de nouvelles lumières qu'il étoit offusqué et éblouy ... de la grandeur de la Majesté de Dieu" (1, see 36, 318 and passim).[32] She discovers that God was like a vast ocean which, breaking beyond its shores, "me couvroit, m'inondoit, et m'enveloppoit de toutes

---

31 "Civilize seven or eight, who had been made French." It should be remembered that the missionaries gave all the baptized Natives Christian names as part of the assimilation process.

32 "... After these penitential sacrifices, my spirit was filled with such new light that it was offended and dazzled ... by the grandeur of God's Majesty."

parts" (1).³³ The same metaphor of God as an ocean recurs in one of her final visions (929), and it is in the ocean or abyss where her nothingness is lost. Divine wisdom has purified her soul, which is the nearest she comes to death by fire. Martyrdom is spoken of as part of the erotic character of her relationship with Christ as the bridegroom; and not being sent to New France, a calling kindled through reading the first *Relations*, was another martydom.

Although more personal, mystical, and ecstatic in her self-representation than the missionaries, Marie is one with them in spirit. And if the *Relations* were not enough to persuade her director immediately of her desire to go to New France, surely her dream of the future Ursuline convent must have had an effect. In another letter to him she remarks that she sees nothing that is nearer her heart than a life "qui transforme en Jésus."³⁴ One might infer that the narrative of the Jesuits works through a continuous coincidence between the realities of their daily lives and that of Scripture; Marie's narrative is enlivened through contemplative experience in which the difference between Marie and the divinity is hard to distinguish.³⁵ In turn, her writing draws upon a long discourse of mystical devotion at least as old as St. Augustine. In these two dominant narratives the discursive articulation of Canada takes its rise.

Élisabeth Bégon

Contemporaneous with Marie de de l'Incarnation and the later *Relations* of the Jesuits, the letters of Élisabeth Bégon to her son appear to be somewhat of an anomaly. Worldly, and without commitment to the life of religion, they address her personal life, her family, the upper class, and the largely administrative concerns of her immediate society. Never intended for a public audience, they remained undisturbed for almost two centuries in the Archives Nationales du Québec until published in 1932 under the anodyne title *Rapport de l'Archiviste de la Province de Québec (1934–35)*. Although Bégon conducted a continual correspondence with a variety of respondents, these, addressed to Michel de Villebois de La Rouvillière, her son-in-law, appear the only preserved letters and have now been given the more arresting title of

---

33 "That infinite Majesty was in my view like a huge and vast sea which, reaching the point of breaking beyond its bounds, covered me, inundated me and enveloped me on all sides."
34 "Which transforms into Jesus."
35 See Martin, *La Vie de la Vénérable Mère Marie de l'Incarnation*, in which she speaks of her soul as "consubstanciel & égal à son père" ("of the same substance and equal to her father"), p. 111.

Lettres au cher fils, qualified on the title page as *Correspondance d'Élisabeth Bégon avec son gendre (1748–1753)*. The correspondence began after the deaths of Bégon's husband and daughter, and after her son-in-law had moved to Louisiana to take a position in the colonial finance department. His daughter was put into the guardianship of Mme Bégon.

What gives the letters their particular charm is their artless character. They appear as the conversation of a woman who has lived close to power (her father-in-law was an Intendant, the chief royal representative, while her close friend is the interim Governor), has heard all the scandals, and is acquainted with the many pitfalls that surround the ambitious and powerful. In a word, unlike the reports of the Jesuits and the religious self-awareness of Marie, these letters are not "official." Part of this character may be attributed to their brevity. They are intimate communications in the style of a personal diary shared with her son-in-law. As a consequence, the letters shed a light on daily life in New France and France in the eighteenth century, which is of inestimable value for the understanding of "la petite histoire" as it affects the domestic lives of the colonists, as well as those whose political shadow, such as that of the Intendant Bigot, continues to endure. Thus, in an early letter, for example, the evocation of Quebec's harsh winter climate is combined with a reference to the colonial official whose presence makes this forbidding environment tolerable: "Il nous est tombé cette nuit, cher fils, un pied de neige, ce qui m'a fait grogner dès le matin. Que tu es heureux d'être dans un pays exempt de ces froids! Je tremble d'avance lorsque je pense que nous voilà pour neuf mois dans la neige. Mais il ne tiendra pas à moi si je n'en sors pas l'automne prochain. Que ferai-je en [sic] Canada seule, si M. de Galissonnière [the interim Governor] s'en vas?"[36]

The collection may be divided into two parts: the first consists of letters from Canada, the second, and by far the largest part, of letters from France. Neither the climate of Quebec nor the interests of her family prompt her desire to go to France. Primarily she wishes to be reunited with her son-in-law in the hope that eventually he will take up a position in the home government. He died, however, in Louisiana in 1753, and because of the dependence on sea voyages for the transmission of letters and, one supposes, her son-in-law's

---

36 "A foot of snow fell for us last night, dear son, which has made me grumble since morning. How lucky you are to be in a country exempt from this cold! I am trembling in advance when I think that here we are for nine months in snow. But it won't be my fault if I don't leave next autumn. What will I do alone in Canada, if M. de la Galissonnière leaves?" *Lettres au cher fils: Correspondance d'Élisabeth Bégon avec son gendre (1748–1753)*, ed. Nicole Deschamps (Montreal: Boréal, 1994), p. 47.

discretion with his friends concerning Élisabeth, she was still, ironically, writing to him letters full of motherly advice until her death two years later.

While artless, the letters are in no sense naive. In an early letter her true feelings burst eloquently forth: "Que te dirai-je, cher fils? Je ne sais rien, que je t'aime? – Cela ne t'est pas nouveau. – Que je m'ennuie de ton absence? – Tu dois le savoir. – Que je suis presque toujours malade? – Mon âge y contribue. Que te dire?" (p. 54).[37] Such is the plaintive note that, in various degrees of intensity, animates the letters. It is a voice that both reveals a profound and intimate knowledge of a social world that angered the religious authorities of the era, particularly in New France, and betrays a deeper psychological life that can be considered Oedipal, at least to a certain extent. How reciprocal his love for her might have been is almost impossible to determine. His letters, few as they were, do not seem to have been preserved, and her responses address mainly his illness and his difficult relationship with the governor of Louisiana. Referring to his last letter in her own last letter, she responds to her son-in-law's request to stay out of his affairs, her letters suggesting that he may have considered her a meddling mother-in-law, and nothing more.

If one considers, however, the voices of all these major figures of New France, notably, Jogues, Marie de l'Incarnation, and Élisabeth Bégon, one is tempted to wonder at the psychological states they were in, no matter how ideologically acceptable they may then have appeared to be. The states of exaltation common to the Jesuits and Marie may possibly, though shared with mystics elsewhere, have been the only way to manage the difficulties of such lives in such a place at such a time. They lived heroically by finding suitable biblical paradigms and acting on them. In contrast, Bégon was not tempted to follow such a path and, while not entirely typical of her class and society (her in-laws referred to her as "l'Iroquoise"), she understood and used them both to perfection. She was in love in socially unacceptable circumstances, however, and the world changed in her eyes, and the snows of Canada, the expense of living in France, the absence of love return as tragic leitmotifs. What passions will societies accept? Hers, if fully known, would have made of her a complete outcast, and she found no narrative that gave her life a kind of sense other than that of mother, which her "dear son" refuses. Yet she writes on, signing herself as "ta mère qui t'aime plus que tu ne l'aimeras jamais"

---

37 "What shall I say to you, dear son? I know nothing [but] that I love you? – That's not new to you. – That your absence is always hard on me? – You must be aware of it. – That I'm almost always sick? – My age is a factor. What to say to you?"

(p. 345), ironically echoing Marie.[38] And how is one to imagine her, alone in her room, writing: "Je suis piquée au vif, cher fils. Comment, tu as une mère qui ne respire que pour toi et tu ne lui écris point!" (p. 336).[39]

Jean LeMoyne remarks that through the letters of Mme Bégon one sees Canada as it entered the temporal world, but in a repressed state.[40] The temporal world, however, bears a complementary relationship to the sacred world, and one cannot fail to see in both the continuous practice of learning to live with solitudes – those of both inner and outer spaces. And, while born in Canada, Bégon considered that escape from solitude was possible, by settling in the mother country. Her son-in-law, however, never followed, and her solution was to concentrate all her passion on his absence. In her way, she entered into the same family drama of her religious contemporaries, discovering that there were only two roles that seemed to draw out the best qualities in a person. The Jesuits, while Fathers, all sought to imitate the life of the eternal Son, while Marie and Élisabeth became transcendent Mothers. No other stories appeared appropriate as founding narratives.

---

38 "Your mother who loves you more than you will ever love her."
39 "I am cut to the quick, dear son. Really! You have a mother who does not breathe except for you and you do not write to her at all!"
40 Jean LeMoyne, *Convergences* (Montreal: Hurtubise-HMH, 1977), p. 86.

3

Migrations, multiple allegiances, and satirical traditions: from Frances Brooke to Thomas Chandler Haliburton

MARTA DVOŘÁK

At the close of the Seven Years' War in 1763, which gave England almost total control of the continent of North America until the American Revolution, only a handful of English administered a newly conquered population of 60,000 French Canadians. It has been asserted that this period witnessed "a literature of information rather than a literature of imagination."[1] It is indeed for its documentary qualities that certain critics appreciate *The History of Emily Montague* (1769), published in England but nonetheless the earliest novel to emanate from the North American continent. The quality of its descriptions of the Kamouraska region has effectively incited critics to treat it as travel literature.[2] Yet the writer Frances Brooke (1724–89) undeniably reconfigured the topography, institutions, and social interactions of the French and English elites in the newly acquired colony of what is today Quebec, struggling notably, as Susanna Moodie would, with the gap between Old World diction and decorum, and New World landscape – the embodiment of Burkean sublimity.

The History of Emily Montague

Moving in the literary circles of Samuel Richardson, Samuel Johnson, and Fanny Burney, Mrs. Brooke was an established editor, translator, playwright, and novelist (*The History of Lady Julia Mandeville*, 1763) before leaving England to reside in Quebec City in 1763. As well as a travel book intended for an

---

[1] Alfred G. Bailey, "Overture to Nationhood," in Carl F. Klinck, ed., *Literary History of Canada: Canadian Literature in English*, 3 vols. (Toronto: University of Toronto Press, 1976 [1965]), vol. I, p. 78.
[2] James J. and Ruth Talman, "III. The Canadas 1763–1812," in Klinck, ed., *Literary History*, p. 99.

English readership in search of exotic settings and mores, *Emily Montague* has been labelled a romance (although almost totally devoid of the conventional melodramatic trappings the genre had adopted), a novel of sentiment, or a novel of manners, and the book has often been reduced to an uneventful love story. The 228 epistolary exchanges, essentially among three sets of lovers,[3] have been dismissed as a merely amusing account "of social occasions, including the flirtations of the military and seigneurial classes."[4] In the Introduction to the New Canadian Library edition, Carl F. Klinck, too, insisted on Frances Brooke's "special interest in the niceties of courtship and love."[5] This is to ignore the series of letters written by the officer William Fermor to an unidentified earl back in England, giving information on "the political and religious state of Canada."[6]

Among his analyses of the unrest in the older Thirteen Colonies, Fermor affirms that the Americans would not have refused submission to the stamp act or disputed the power of the legislature if it had not been for the restraints laid on their trade with the French and Spanish settlements. Rhetorically skillful, the judgment is shrewd and progressive-minded, but it is interestingly at war with the conservative bias of birth and position which calls up the parent / offspring analogy Susanna Moodie would later develop: "A good mother will consult the interest and happiness of her children, but will never suffer her authority to be disputed" (242). William H. New was among the first critics to acknowledge the indirect political strategy of the novel, namely the political ends underlying the literary artifice, remarking how the author re-examined conventional attitudes toward the social order in general and the colonies in particular.[7]

For several reasons, then, this remarkably crafted epistolary novel, published when the genre was but burgeoning even in the metropolis, deserves to be investigated on its own merits. It serves moreover as an exemplar through which to demonstrate the issues this chapter addresses. Both following and preceding huge political and territorial upheavals, it stages the initial

---

3 Alongside the central pair of lovers based in Quebec for most of the novel, the Colonel Ed. Rivers and Emily Montague, we find Emily's friend Arabella Fermor and her suitor, the Captain Fitzgerald, as well as – back in England – Colonel Rivers's sister, Lucy, and his friend, John Temple, also paired off.
4 Bailey, "Overture," p. 78.
5 Carl F. Klinck, "Introduction," in Frances Brooke, *The History of Emily Montague* (Toronto: McClelland and Stewart, 1991 [1769]), p. viii.
6 Frances Brooke, *The History of Emily Montague*, ed. Mary Jane Edwards (Ottawa: Carleton University Press, 1985), p. 162. All further quotations will be from this edition.
7 William H. New, *A History of Canadian Literature*, 2nd edn. (Montreal: McGill-Queen's University Press, 2003 [1989]), pp. 58–9.

adjustments in the triangular configurations and shifting allegiances between England, the rebellious Thirteen Colonies, and (formerly French) Canada, and the slow process of identity construction and cultural differentiation which unfold in the later works under scrutiny. This discussion will show the tension and ambivalence which accompany acculturation on the march, and the modes and strategies which make Canadian writing distinctive, yet position it within a cultural continuum and a transnational perspective. Brooke oscillates between transgression and conservatism, within the dynamics of satire and sentimentalism, two major traits of nineteenth-century Canadian literature. Underpinning the novel is a strong didactic streak also identifiable in the other authors to be investigated, who all subscribe to the double function of literature – to teach and to entertain.

To the reader alert to the play of intertextuality in *Emily Montague*, the aesthetic conventions of epistolary fiction not only tell stories with a feeling of immediacy and conveniently credible shifts in point of view, but also convey fascinating discussions of a well-read, even learned, author, on the political, social, religious, philosophical, and aesthetic issues that preoccupied her age. As both the daughter and the wife of Anglican clergymen, Brooke's Protestant mindset and bias are evident in her criticism of the regular clergy, "an institution equally incompatible with public good, and private happiness" (p. 16). Her choice of metaphor and playfully satirical manner of giving a concrete shape to abstract principles are fresh and striking in Letter 8, penned by one of her several correspondents, Ed. Rivers, newly arrived in the colony:

> [T]he parochial clergy are useful every where, but I have a great aversion to monks, those drones in the political hive, whose whole study seems to be to make themselves as useless to the world as possible. Think too of the shocking indelicacy of many of them, who make it a point of religion to abjure linen, and wear their habits till they drop off. (p. 26)

William Fermor posits that the British settlements in America are superior to the French for both climatic and religious reasons. French indolence is allegedly due to the excesses of summer heat and winter chill, but also to Catholicism, "a religion which encourages idleness" (p. 209), notably by the excessive number of religious holidays. All the while advocating that the French Canadian population be allowed to worship "in the manner in which they have been early taught to believe the best, and to which they are consequently attached" (p. 210), Major Fermor surmises that English colonization will better the lot of the people, and that a more liberal education will notably lead them by degrees to the Church of England.

The discourse anticipates Max Weber's premise associating Protestantism with capitalism, through a certain work ethic, individualism, and equation of prosperity and virtue. It is also redolent of Montesquieu's theory that mores are regulated by climate, virtue and morality being an affair of the weather. That civilization and the arts are inseparable from climatic conditions is equally suggested by Arabella Fermor, a strong, witty, Austen-like protagonist (ironically named after the vacuous coquette in Pope's *The Rape of the Lock*). In a letter to Lucy describing the severities of a winter in which the strongest wine freezes in a room which has a stove in it, Arabella declares: "I no longer wonder the elegant arts are unknown here; the rigour of the climate suspends the very powers of the understanding; what then must become of those of the imagination? ... Genius will never mount high, where the faculties of the mind are benumbed half the year" (p. 103). As the letters progress, however, the reader witnesses a process of acculturation; Ed. Rivers plans to take up lands with his future wife, Emily Montague, and Arabella writes to Lucy, now become Mrs. Temple, that she "had rather live at Quebec, take it for all in all, than in any town in England, except London" (p. 281).

In what amounts to a novel of education, the cultivated Arabella, alongside Ed. Rivers, is often the author's mouthpiece. Arabella has been encouraged to read widely by a progressive-minded father, and her voice is that of a woman of the Enlightenment, her letters often pleading for tolerance and acknowledgment of cultural relativity, and suffused with Deism. In an age marked by Rousseau's treatises *Du Contrat social* and *Émile* (both 1762), most of the protagonists accept the philosopher's basic premise that the human being is naturally good. Arabella Fermor declares that "the business of education is ... less to give us good impressions, which we have from nature, than to guard us against bad ones, which are generally acquired" (p. 239). Arabella's progressive stances on education and the equality of the sexes anticipate Mary Wollstonecraft's *A Vindication of the Rights of Woman* (1792), which contested Rousseau's theories concerning women. Tackling the debate on nature and nurture, like her father, who deplores "the limited and trifling educations" women are generally allowed (p. 243–4), Arabella argues that gender differences are culturally transmitted and inculcated. An equally radical stance is adopted by Ed. Rivers, quite subversive in its comparison of European and Huron civilizations. The progressive-minded colonel's praise of the Indians' social institutions serves in the manner of a foil to criticize certain English practices, much as Sir Thomas More in *Utopia* satirized his contemporary society by describing an exotic one. Rivers castigates the European system which deprives women of political rights, pointing out that "The sex we have so unjustly excluded from power in Europe have a great share in the Huron government" (p. 34), and affirming that "*we* [men] are the savages, who so impolitely deprive you of the common rights of citizenship" (pp. 34–5). Colonel Rivers condones civil disobedience in women, and his position is all the more radical as Rivers makes an analogy with the Thirteen Colonies' demands to participate in the decisions of government.

The egalitarian opinions that the protagonist voices are subversive, all the more so as they are placed in the mouth of a member of the ruling gentry. Praising the Hurons' classless society amounts to criticizing an English society organized around the privileges of birth and class, and even to putting into question the institution of monarchy. Colonel Rivers admires the egalitarianism of the Hurons, who know no lords: one Huron declared proudly, "'we are subjects to no prince; a savage is free all over the world'" (p. 33). The officer's praise of a people "unawed by rank or riches" who respect their equals "without regarding the gaudy trappings, the *accidental* advantages, to which polished nations pay homage" (p. 33, emphasis added) strangely resembles the subversive ultra-republican sentiments which were growing south of the border.

It is Mrs. Brooke's often advanced positions on questions continuing to preoccupy our planet today which account for the interest in love and marriage which many critics have dismissed as superficial. Among the numerous literary and philosophical texts quoted by the protagonists, we find Pope's *Essay on Man*: "True self-love and social are the same" (p. 370). Ed. Rivers glosses the quotation, explaining that "those passions which make the happiness of individuals tend directly to the general good of the species." By equating public and private happiness, his stance anticipates Adam Smith's *Inquiry into the Nature and Causes of the Wealth of Nations* (1776), which laid the foundations of capitalism and democracy, arguing that by promoting one's individual interests, one promotes the general good. Adam Smith significantly also authored the treatise *The Theory of Moral Sentiments* (1759), the seminal text of sentimentalism, which argued that virtue stems from natural moral sentiments. Mrs. Brooke's focus on love and marriage is consequently philosophical and political, driven by a didactic purpose. Domestic felicity is thus the foundation of social stability and harmony, and Rivers castigates the conventional arranged marriage, centered on economic considerations. A radical analogy with prostitution anticipates better-known iconoclastic texts such as Wollstonecraft's *A Vindication of the Rights of Woman* (1792), William Godwin's *Enquiry Concerning Political Justice* (1793), and Friedrich Engels's *The Origin of the Family, Private Property and the State* (German original, 1884).

Brooke's position championing the marriage of affection is both backward- and forward-looking. It participates in the pre-Romantic current, but is also rooted in eighteenth-century optimism and sentimentalism. Ed. Rivers and Emily Montague's courtship and marriage are paths to virtue, and it is precisely Rivers's sensitivity and empathy which make him good. Rivers's goodness is, of course, rewarded, in a conservative dénouement studded with melodramatic disclosures, mistaken identities, and a *deus ex machina*. The young man who would have been content making his modest means go further in the colony with a penniless wife ends up back in England with a large fortune bequeathed to himself, to his mother, and to his wife, by a father-in-law, once ruined, now rich, who had been given up for dead. Brooke thus chooses to plot the resolution in a conventional, even conservative, stance with respect to wealth and social position. The doubleness of the discourse concerning issues such as power, property, and propriety is rooted in both an ideological ambivalence or aporia, and the dual stance of satire. Brooke's use of the popular sub-genre of the romance to treat serious social and political issues can be positioned in a cultural continuum: it anticipates not only the nineteenth-century ironic voices of McCulloch, Haliburton, and Howe, but also Sara Jeannette Duncan's early twentieth-century romantic novel, *The Imperialist* (1904), satirizing the provincialism of the Canadian middle class.

The United Empire Loyalists

The American Revolution that Brooke dimly foresaw sent roughly 50,000 refugees into the Canadas (over two-thirds to the Maritime provinces), and harbored the satirical production in the Maritimes of United Empire Loyalist poets such as Jonathan Odell (1737–1818), who fled from New Jersey in 1776, the Harvard-educated Anglican minister Jacob Bailey (1731–1808), charged with sedition and driven from Maine to Nova Scotia in 1779, and, for a brief period, Joseph Stansbury (1742–1809), a former British agent who returned to the new republic of the United States in 1785 after a mere two-year exile in Nova Scotia. Having spent the Revolution in New York behind British lines, then moving to England in 1783, Odell was appointed a year later to the political post of provincial secretary of New Brunswick. Bailey served as parish priest at Cornwallis and then Annapolis Royal. The Reverend was well known for his sermons and his prose descriptions of Nova Scotia through the travel motif and the celebration of the local that Joseph Howe was later to take up. Bailey, like Odell, is best known for his Hudibrastic verse. Among his verse satires investigating social and political concerns is the long poem "The Adventures of Jack Ramble, the Methodist Preacher" targeting evangelical itinerant preachers as McCulloch would later do, and denouncing the increase of religious dissent as a factor of social instability. Odell published four major Loyalist satires in heroic couplets while in New York. The best known, *The American Times* (1780) issued as a pamphlet, sketched satirical portraits of the leaders of the rebel cause. During his New Brunswick period, Odell satirized the absenteeism of governor Thomas Carleton, and tackled the American bungling of the War of 1812 in parodic poems such as "The Agonizing Dilemma."

Most interesting perhaps is Bailey's "Journal of a Voyage from Pownalboro' to Halifax," an incomplete autograph record of his forced emigration, which can be found in W. S. Bartlet's biography, *The Frontier Missionary: A Memoir of the Life of the Rev. Jacob Bailey* (1853). The manuscript provides an illuminating depiction of the American Revolution from the ex-centric angle of a Loyalist mindset. While the Preface to the biography regrets but excuses Bailey's "mistaken conscience" in maintaining his allegiance to the British crown,[8] Bailey does not mince his words when relating his escape from "tyranny, oppression, and poverty" (p. 159), but accuses the rebels of implementing "faction, sedition, and turbulence," and pities the common people finding themselves under the dominion of the Congress, "cruelly harrassed [sic] and persecuted by a number of inexorable tyrants, who had got all the power into their hands" (p. 162). Adopting the lofty diction meant to suit elevated subjects, Bailey amplifies his sentences through recurrent alliteration, personification, and periphrasis. The sun rising is "the splendid orb of day peeping over the eastern hills," the birds singing in the trees are "the tuneful tribe, amidst the trembling grove" (p. 129). He does have an eye for the telltale detail qualified to generate readerly sympathy, evident when he describes his confinement under the hold in the boat taking him to the Bay of Fundy, where the passengers may choose between closing the hatchway and suffocating or opening them and drowning (p. 146).

Bailey excels with the apologue or fable, deployed for didactic purposes. The author relates how one of the confined hens escaped onto the deck, and, refusing to be captured, flew overboard to its doom, "struggling and cackling upon the waves" (p. 148). The witless fowl, that "foolish flutterer," stands of course for human folly in general, for those periphrastic "animals who fondly boast of reason" hurrying "into ruin." More precisely, it stands for rebellious colonials, and more especially rebel Americans, on a course of

---

8 George Burgess, "Preface," in William S. Bartlet, *The Frontier Missionary: A Memoir of the Life of the Rev. Jacob Bailey* (Boston: Ide and Dutton, 1853), p. vii.

self-destruction. The lesson driven home is that the freedom of independence is illusory, and that the colonial condition termed slavery and bondage bestows security and stability. If the literary output of Bailey and his fellow U. E. Loyalists was modest, it did stage, as we have seen, certain adjustments in the triangular political and cultural configurations of the age, and played an undeniable role in defining and confirming Canada's identity and values as anchored in order, stability, and tradition. Descendants of this group – such as William Kirby and Archibald Lampman – were to go on contributing to the Canadian literary scene.

Moreover, the United Empire Loyalists were a complex group of people whose definitions of "loyalty" varied according to their backgrounds. In joining the British, Black Loyalists, for example, were motivated by their desire for freedom, while Aboriginal Loyalists like Joseph (Thayendanegea) and Molly Brant (Koñwatsiátsiaiéñni) asserted the interests of their own people within the confrontation between the American revolutionaries and the British. We know of three memoirs, by Boston King, David George and John Marrant, that describe Black Loyalists' experience of the American Revolution, their escape to Nova Scotia and departure for Sierra Leone. First published in 1798 in the *Methodist Magazine* and told from hindsight when he received schooling at Kingswood Methodist School near Bristol to assist him in his work as missionary in Africa, King's story follows the genre of the conversion narrative and much of it emulates the model of pietist language and plot.

But the circumstances he evokes are so extreme and his imagery so physical that the memoir poignantly alternates between parable and realism. At the age of twelve, for instance, he had a dream "that the world was on fire" (p. 15). His vision is of the Last Judgement, but it also reads like a premonition of "the horrors and devastation of war" (p. 21) that nevertheless allow him an adventurous escape from being routinely "beat and tortured most cruelly" by his master for offenses he did not commit such as losing nails that were "very dear at that time, it being in the American war" (p. 16). The narratives of King, George and Marrant reach into the present as the "*ur*-texts" of "classical Africadian concerns," though these men's departure from Nova Scotia brought such literary expression for many years to a virtual stop.[9]

---

9 George Elliott Clarke, "The Birth and Rebirth of Africadian Literature," in *Odysseys Home: Mapping African-Canadian Literature* (Toronto: University of Toronto Press, 2002), pp. 122, 110. "Africadian" is Clarke's word creation, combining "African" and "Acadian." The story of the Black United Empire Loyalists has been retold in Lawrence Hill's *The Book of Negroes* (2007), which is discussed in the chapter on multiculturalism and globalization.

Boston King's mother learned "some knowledge of the virtue of herbs" (p. 15) from the Indian slaves on the plantation, and the motivation for Blacks and Aboriginals from these backgrounds to join the Loyalists may have been similar. For distinguished Mohawk leaders like Joseph Brant and his sister Molly Brant, an additional important question was how to protect the territorial interests of their people during and after the conflict. Brant traveled twice to England to represent Aboriginal claims, and his visits were highly publicized because his imposing presence – captured in a portrait by George Romney – served the British cause.[10] Molly Brant's literary presence is conveyed in her letters though it is not certain that these are from her own hand. Joseph Brant translated the Gospel of Mark into Mohawk, thus contributing to a lively print culture generated by the migration of some 2,000 Aboriginal Loyalists, including Mohawk, into Upper Canada. Many of them were "literate Anglicans"[11] and required prayer books and Bibles in sufficient copies.

Thomas McCulloch, Joseph Howe, and Thomas Chandler Haliburton

The first half of the nineteenth century was marked by three prominent colonial figures from Nova Scotia whose often topical writings (which, as we have seen with Brooke, strain towards didactic, political ends) converge and interweave: Thomas McCulloch (1776–1843), who immigrated from Scotland, and Canadian-born Joseph Howe (1804–73) and Thomas Chandler Haliburton (1796–1865). Joseph Howe is best remembered as a politician and a statesman. He was also a writer and owner, publisher, and editor of one of the best newspapers in British North America, the liberal *Novascotian*, in which he published essays, poems, and two series of sketches, the *Western Rambles* (1828) and the *Eastern Rambles* (1829–31),[12] written during his journeys throughout the province. Howe explicitly aligned himself within a tradition shared by the likes of Laurence Sterne and Chateaubriand, but advocated the pleasures of "travelling at home" rather than abroad (all the while keeping up learned allusions to Milton, Shakespeare, Byron, Spenser, Sterne, and Smollett). In the

---

10 Stephanie Pratt, "Joseph Brant (Thayendanegea)," in Jocelyn Hackforth-Jones, ed., *Between Worlds: Voyagers to Britain 1700–1850* (London: National Portrait Gallery, 2007), pp. 56–67.
11 Joyce M. Banks, "Print for Communities," in Patricia Lockhart Fleming, Gilles Gallichan, Yvan Lamonde, eds., *History of the Book in Canada*, 3 vols. (Toronto: University of Toronto Press, 2004), vol. II, p. 282.
12 Later collected under the title *Western and Eastern Rambles: Travel Sketches of Nova Scotia*, ed. M. G. Parks (Toronto and Buffalo: University of Toronto Press, 1973).

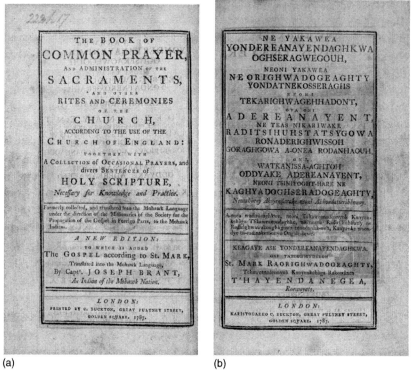

Plate 4. a) and b) *Gospel of St. Mark* in English and Mohawk, translated by Joseph Brant, 1787.

wake of McCulloch's *The Mephibosheth Stepsure Letters*, which appeared serially to huge acclaim in the Halifax weekly *The Acadian Recorder* in 1821–3, Howe's travel sketches both celebrated and exposed the province's respective virtues and shortcomings – deploring, like McCulloch before him, "the idleness of many, and the baneful extravagance of a great many more" (88). Howe posits that idleness is due to man's "natural antipathy to labor" (81), stemming from a nostalgia for the Garden of Eden, "where *there was nothing to do*" (81–2). With benevolent Horatian satire, Howe suggests that bipeds follow a consoling syllogism: "'Adam,' say they, 'did not work in Eden – Adam was very happy while he staid there – ergo, if we do not work we shall be very happy too'" (p. 81). Yet the gentle irony shifts towards a more severe, even Hobbesian, vision of humanity: "The brutes labour while the rein is in their mouths, and the whip on their withers – and let but necessity slacken the ribbons, and lay aside the scourge of poverty and want, and what becomes of man's superiority over the beast he drives?" (p. 82–3).

Howe took into account the relatively substantial Black population in Nova Scotia that existed from the eighteenth century on.[13] Many of the Black slaves who fled northward during the American Revolution arrived in Nova Scotia, forming the basis for Africville, though approximately a thousand of them accepted the offer of free passage to Sierra Leone in 1791–2. These were joined in 1796 by a second group of "maroons" from Jamaica, who left for Sierra Leone by 1800. A third group was transplanted from the Chesapeake Bay area to Nova Scotia by the British fleet in 1814–15, during the British attacks on Washington and Baltimore. In a sketch dated 31 July 1828, Howe periphrastically describes his encounter with "a goodly bevy of sable beauties, with their unsophisticated feet, and their woolly heads, adorned, not with 'the likeness of a kingly crown',[14] but with tubs and baskets of fair dimensions" (p. 55). The author observes that it has been the fashion to revile these people for laziness, and "for the heinous sin of not immediately accustoming themselves to a climate half a dozen degrees colder than it was where they were born" (p. 55). Howe incites the reader to modify such a mindset through empathy: "suppose good folks, that you were suddenly caught up and cast into Maryland – stripped to your trowsers, and a hoe put into your hand, do you think that hoeing Tobacco and Corn would come a bit more easy to you, under the burning rays of the sun, than cutting down trees and clearing land is to the negro, in a country where everything is opposed to his accustomed habits?" (pp. 56–7).

Thomas McCulloch's *Letters of Mephibosheth Stepsure* (generally known as *The Stepsure Letters*) were originally published in serial form and anonymously. They were not collected into a manuscript (entitled *The Chronicles of Our Town, or, A Peep at America*) and published in book form till 1862, well after the author's death, when sixteen letters out of a total of twenty-five were published to begin with. The letters caused great controversy when they first appeared, and various critics attacked them not only for their ideas on social reform, but also for their earthiness. Through the epistolary mode which generates a strong narratorial presence and an illusion of veracity, McCulloch

---

13 Owning Black slaves in Quebec and Upper Canada was not uncommon until the Parliament of Upper Canada began to phase out slavery by abolishing the purchase or importation of new slaves in 1793, before the British Crown abolished slavery throughout all of its colonies in 1834 (see Parks, *Western and Eastern Rambles*, p. 56 for this and most other historical background information in this paragraph).
14 Howe indicates that the quotation is from Milton, *Paradise Lost* II, 1. 673.

chose the digressive, episodic structure of oral storytelling favored by eighteenth-century writers such as Fielding and Sterne. Perfectly suited to that double function of literature – to teach and to entertain – the digressive style is a staple technique of both moralists and humorists.

One could easily attribute the profoundly didactic dimension of *The Stepsure Letters* to the fact that McCulloch was a learned Presbyterian clergyman with strong ideas on social and educational reform, having left Scotland to settle in Nova Scotia, where he taught philosophy, logic, and science as well as theology at the Pictou Academy he founded. Yet that would be to ignore the witty character of his writing, which has influenced humorists and satirists for almost two centuries. An extended parable on idleness and industriousness, *The Stepsure Letters* is rooted in an ancient tradition, sharing affinities with works ranging from Bunyan's *The Pilgrim's Progress* and Pope's *Moral Essays* to Richardson's *Pamela*, Defoe's *Moll Flanders*, Hogarth's *The Rake's Progress*, and Thoreau's *Walden*. The narrator Mephibosheth, aptly named like the lame grandson of the biblical King Saul, but ironically also going by the surname Stepsure, is a living example of self-reliance and success through hard work. In addition to his deformity, he was left orphaned and destitute, and so, in keeping with current Nova Scotian legislation, he was auctioned off to the lowest bidder to earn his keep as a bound servant. Thanks to rational management, industriousness, regularity, and simple tastes, Stepsure makes his small farm prosper, while he observes with the benevolent detachment of an ironist the follies, vanity, extravagance and sloth of his neighbors, who generally get their just deserts. The social evils which they illustrate range from smuggling and drinking and gaming to poor housekeeping and child rearing, all susceptible of tearing apart the social fabric of home and community. The point is often hammered home in admirably compact structures, through parallelism, echo, and antithesis:

> Were any of my neighbours to be called a rogue he would be mightily offended; and among us, were one person to take a penny from the pocket of another, the whole town would cry out against such a sinful and shameful transaction. But cheating the whole community at once, was so far from being considered as either sin or shame, that Deacon Scruple, who allowed nothing to be sung in his vessel but hymns, was the greatest smuggler of the whole. (p. 31)[15]

---

15 Thomas McCulloch, *The Mephibosheth Stepsure Letters*, ed. Gwendolyn Davies (Ottawa: Carleton University Press, 1990 [1862]), p. 31.

One of McCulloch's characters, Saunders, declares that "[n]othing ... has prevented our town from being one of the wealthiest places in the world, but want of industry and want of economy" (p. 189). The huge *but*, structurally ironic, conveys the values the author espouses. These, along with industriousness and economy,[16] are the land, the home, and stability – essentially the values of an agrarian society (shared by Howe, and, to a certain extent, Haliburton), not unremarkable in a period of post-war economic depression restricted further by colonial trade policies, and exacerbated by a suspicion of the republican urbanization to the south. Commerce is suspect: "Merchants are very useful; and we cannot do without them: but they live by the labour of other people; and they usually live well" (p. 98). For McCulloch, buying rather than producing is frowned on, and buying on credit even more so: "though our soil is excellent, and farms very easily got; the most of our townsfolk would rather ride two days round the country to make a bargain, than give the ground one day's labour" (p. 29). Drinking and gambling threaten social order and stability, as shown by the neat paradox of the neighbour's son who likes his glass of grog over a game of cards: "though Hob is not a quarrelsome young man, his name was frequently called over in court, in assault and battery cases" (pp. 12–13).

The didacticism which at times may seem overly explicit to a contemporary reader corresponded to a taste of the times; even in popular literature readers expected to find a moral, which satisfied them much as a happy ending satisfies us today. Alongside Parson Drone's overtly didactic sermons, however, McCulloch displays an arsenal of modes of indirection, unfurling a wide range of rhetorical devices which have served great satirists throughout the ages. These range from metonymy, personification, circumlocution, and irony to understatement and its corollary, exaggeration, which culminate in the burlesque and the carnivalesque. The overall narrative dynamics, as we shall see, are dialogic, not only systematically engaging with the response of the reader, as does Howe, but also transmitting another's speech in a double-voiced fashion which for ironic and ultimately corrective purposes Haliburton would hone to perfection (and which is one of the trademarks of contemporary Canadian writing, notably in Margaret Atwood's writing).[17]

---

16 St. Jean de Crèvecœur had already deplored in 1782 in *Letters of an American Farmer* that Nova Scotians preferred to depend on government subsidies rather than on their own industry.
17 See Marta Dvořák, "Margaret Atwood's Humor," in Coral Ann Howells, ed., *The Cambridge Companion to Margaret Atwood* (Cambridge: Cambridge University Press, 2006), pp. 114–29.

Rather than a plot anchored in causality and chronology, the reader finds at the heart of the narrative pattern of *The Stepsure Letters* an apparently random series of flat characters or "humors" exemplifying every type of virtue or vice, as signaled by their names. There are Mr. Soakem and Mr. Tipple, the tavern-keepers, Mr. Holdfast and Mr. Catchem, the old and new sheriffs, Justice Choakem, and Widow Scant. Many of these are mere metonymies, figuring and giving shape to an abstract idea. Other characters are sketched out into fuller portraits. There is Squire Worthy, the peacemaker of the town, who took the lame orphan Mephibosheth, whom no one wanted, as a bound servant. There is Bill Scamp, a case study as it were of unguided youth gone astray, and a warning to overindulgent parents who expect to be taken care of in their old age. McCulloch's rhetorical mastery is visible in the adroit chiasmus: "I have frequently heard Mr. Drone tell [Bill's father], that, when he was striving to leave a farm worthy of his son, he should take care to leave a son worthy of the farm" (p. 76). For McCulloch is a satirist, directing ridicule, as would Haliburton, at certain institutions (the magistrature, the military, the Church), mindsets (colonial and frontier), social practices (the frolic, bundling, borrowing), and deviations from cultural traditions (wearing store-bought finery instead of homespun). That practices such as dressing above one's station had been targeted centuries before by satirists from Chaucer to Sir Thomas More indicates to what extent McCulloch's stance is a conservative one in a community infected by the ultra-republicanism of its southern neighbor, which has constructed its identity on the leveling of hierarchies. However, McCulloch's writing is distinctive, not so much the matter of the telling as the manner.

Personification is rife, shifting from earnestness to playfulness. The description of old Whinge places *The Stepsure Letters* in line with didactic works such as Bunyan's *The Pilgrim's Progress*: "As Whinge had no industry, want lived in his house; and where want does not scrape acquaintance with industry, it becomes the companion of discontent" (p. 127). But the playful description of Mrs Whinge and her expansionist lice – who "became dissatisfied with the country, and began to emigrate" – not only castigates a lack of domestic cleanliness, but also generates hilarity with its extended personification, analogy, and circumlocution (p. 136). The oblique mode of circumlocution informs us humorously of certain social practices of the time, such as that of locking up those who could not pay their creditors and auctioning off their property: "Our sheriff is a very hospitable gentleman; and, when any of his neighbours are in hardships, he will call upon them, and even insist upon their making his house their home" (p. 12). McCulloch's humorous manner anticipates that of Haliburton, and subsequently Mark Twain and Stephen Leacock, notably the techniques Twain would go on to recommend: apparent gravity, deferral, and underemphasis, associated with a sense of pace.

Understatement is a trademark feature in McCulloch's writing, engendering the incongruity that produces laughter. To produce even greater counter-expectation, the author at times combines understatement with its rhetorical opposite: exaggeration – source of caricature and the burlesque. With such an outrageous combination, McCulloch moves into the mode of oral storytelling known as the yarn or tall tale. McCulloch's high burlesque episodes involve making unheroic cultural references collide with an elevated register. The reader also finds occasions of low burlesque, combining an elevated subject with a low style. The author was criticized for using images "unworthy of a grave moralist" (p. 434).

The essential principle of grotesque realism is degradation, a practice which generates carnivalesque laughter by undermining elevated subjects through the low or trivial, notably the life of the belly. Insisting on the functions of the lower body can challenge institutions and social practices, as Swift was notorious for doing, and, conservative though he was, McCulloch's gleeful allusions to Judge Grub hiding his bare nether end in bed when his trousers were being mended is a reminder of the vanity of public honors and dignities of office. Since cleanliness is praised elsewhere as the heart of domestic comfort and harmony, a scatological circumlocution describing the bleached trail left on the side of the house by the pails of urine tossed out the bedroom window serves to underline the uncivilized nature of its inhabitants. Emphasizing the undignified processes of ingestion, digestion, and elimination calls attention to our animal functions and relativizes human pretensions.

McCulloch's writing is often heteroglossic, containing two or three simultaneous levels of discourse for ironic purposes. The irony is structural rather than verbal, resting on narratorial or authorial duplicity. When Stepsure relates how Jack, in need of funds, camps out with friends in the woods to cut down lumber, the utterance which justifies the men's drinking and gambling is no longer the narrator's voice, but the collective voice, the speech of current opinion, which intrudes through free direct speech: "Without a little spirits, as every youngster knows, the fatigue of lumbering would be intolerable. Besides, persons who must quit their labour at dusk, cannot sleep all the long nights of winter; and when they are sitting in the camp, they need something along with a game at cards, to make them cheery and keep out the cold" (22). The double-styled utterance invites readers to keep their distance, and to deduce that Jack is pushing his family deeper into debt. In such intersections of two utterances and two belief systems, we can remark that the diffused authorial voice often blames while seeming to praise. Over a decade before Susanna Moodie deplores the fact that New World young women all consider themselves young ladies and scorn learning domestic skills, McCulloch gives a voice to current opinion, ostensibly praising his young neighbors for accomplishments which the reader is brought to infer are not the essential ones:

> As for the girls, they are intrusted to Mrs. McCackle, who, I assure you, does ample justice to their education ... When they return home to get husbands and manage families, they can paint flowers and make filigree work to admiration. They can also sing and dance delightfully. (p. 169)

That such arts are of not much help in managing a household in an agrarian economy requiring a high degree of self-sufficiency is suggested in the device of enumeration, and particularly in the binary periodic sentence in which the protasis or rising first segment (... manage families) and the apodosis (paint flowers ...) are at odds. McCulloch's ironic passage on women's education is part of a broader satirical passage targeting those who, believing themselves better than the station for which they are qualified, eschew the diligence required for economic improvement, let alone stability. Through the indirect mode of social irony, McCulloch suggests that the economic depression of the times is attributable to the mindset of the inhabitants of the province. McCulloch is an ironist whose satiric pose sets up complex relationships of connivance and distance between reader, narrator, and characters. His satiric pose conveys the implicit affirmative values that the authorial voice defends as well as the negative values that it attacks. Since irony resides not only in the writer's ability to represent textually, but also in the receiver's process of perception, successful reception requires certain shared frames with respect to values, cultural and aesthetic context, or at the very least a readerly sensibility to authorial intent. As a result, McCulloch can be unfairly misconstrued by those who read his writings through the filter of their modern sensibility and taste.

In the wake of *The Stepsure Letters* and his own *Western and Eastern Rambles* Joseph Howe also published Haliburton's "Recollections of Nova Scotia," twenty-one sketches equally inspired by McCulloch's manner of exposing and ridiculing the follies of the natives of Nova Scotia, or Bluenoses. These satirical sketches, published in three series beginning in 1835, were written in the aftermath of the arrival in Nova Scotia of thousands of United Empire Loyalists,[18]

---

18 The population of Upper Canada more than tripled in less than two decades between the 1820s and 1840s. Late Loyalists, who were rarely literate, were often motivated more by the offer of land grants than by issues of allegiance.

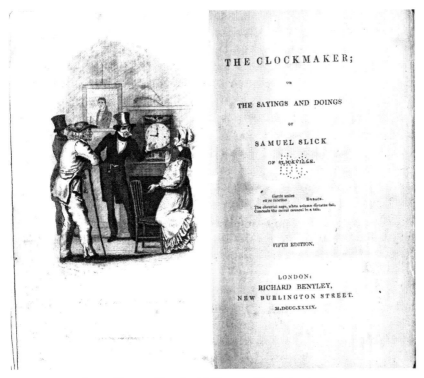

Plate 5. Thomas Chandler Haliburton, *The Clockmaker*, 1839.

and the economic crash which finally occurred in the mid-1830s. Revolving round the dramatic monologues of a brash Yankee pedlar named Sam Slick (at the origin of the term "Uncle Sam"), they were subsequently brought together to become the first Canadian bestseller as *The Clockmaker; or the Sayings and Doings of Samuel Slick of Slickville* (1836). The exuberant dialogues and polyphonic monologues in vernacular idiom of the trickster figure Sam, a visiting English squire, and a plethora of other characters also steeped in the social biases of their time and place allow Haliburton to examine the triangular relations of the Canadian colony with the neighboring United States as well as Great Britain, and satirize all three arenas through the polyphonic confrontation of cultures. His irony operates within the paradigms of distance and normativity. With amused detachment, the shifting points of view highlight flaws ranging from colonial provinciality and laziness to American arrogance and ruthlessness and British pretentions and shortsightedness.

Haliburton resorts essentially to the devices of caricature, parody, and burlesque, all features of Menippean satire, as is his recourse to dialogue and dialogic monologue. The derision often rests on the use of social types of the period, such as the Black servant, for comedic purposes. Alongside the Horatian satire are more militant instances of satire, often targeting a simplistic form of abolitionism equating freedom and welfare. In "Training a Carriboo," the old, sick, freed slave Pompey makes a rueful parallel between his bought freedom and his present starvation, serving as an exemplum to one of Haliburton's central ideas: the equivalence of Black slavery and abusive white wage labor practices.[19] His oxymoronic term "white nigger" underlines his metaphorical use of racial terms, Black signifying positions of powerlessness ranging from the colonist who has no voice in government to factory laborers discarded when old and sick. In "The White Nigger," Haliburton unsettles easy certainties through the device of the biter being bit. The squire points out to Sam that when Jefferson penned the Declaration of Independence, he really meant that all *white* men are created equal, for the self-evident truth the preamble declared was in fact an "'untruth, in a country which tolerates domestic slavery.'"[20] Sam counterattacks and points out that "'the blue noses sell their own species – they trade in white slaves'" (p. 161). To the indignant squire, incredulous that the "human cattle sales" (p. 162) Sam refers to could occur in the British Empire where slavery was at present abolished, the Yankee pedlar relates an auction he witnessed at which an old couple were separated and sold off. The custom of auctioning off paupers to the lowest bidder, for whom they work for their keep, is defamiliarized for the local readership, and revealed as an inhumane practice. A Bluenose companion of Sam's, a witness to his indignation, functions as the reader's representative: "'I never seed it in that are light afore, for its our custom, and custom you know will reconcile one to most any thing" (p. 164).

Born into a Loyalist family which migrated from New England to Nova Scotia at the time of the American Revolution, Haliburton was a member of the provincial legislature, then a judge. In life as in his dialogic texts which value American resourcefulness all the while that they castigate American brashness, Haliburton – like Brooke – was both progressive and conservative: he supported the perpetuation of colonial ties with the metropolis, and, all the

---

[19] See George Elliot Clarke, "White Niggers, Black Slaves: Slavery, Race and Class in T. C. Haliburton's *The Clockmaker*," *Nova Scotia Historical Review* 14.1 (1994), pp. 13–40.

[20] Thomas Chandler Haliburton, *The Clockmaker: Series One, Two, and Three*, ed. George L. Parker (Ottawa: Carleton University Press, 1995 [1836]), p. 161.

while criticizing what had become an abusively powerful oligarchy[21] and promoting certain institutional reforms, opposed those who held that the ministers of provincial government should be responsible to the people of Nova Scotia, and not to the British crown,[22] a change which he feared would logically lead to unwanted independence, and to the province being annexed by the United States.[23] Haliburton authored historical and political treatises, but was particularly well known in Great Britain and the United States for his fiction, rivalling Dickens in popularity. His *Clockmaker* series subjects the local community to the cross gaze, language, and mind set of strangers: both a Yankee and a visiting Englishman, representatives of political and economic ascendancy over the colony, before confronting American and then English mores from an external vantage point. His satirical writing includes further Sam Slick adventures in *Sam Slick's Wise Saws and Modern Instances* (1853) and *Nature and Human Nature* (1855), but also the many-voiced, Slick-less *The Old Judge, or Life in a Colony* (1849), depicting Nova Scotian life at an earlier period. In a mirror reversal of *The Attaché* series (1843–4) which defamiliarized and satirized the imperial center through the peripheral perspective of North Americans, *The Old Judge* resorts to the subversive outsider's point of view (in this case a visiting Englishman's) to depict the flaws of the Nova Scotian vantage point. Insinuating that the colonials have been infected by the ultra-republican spirit of their newly emancipated neighbour, the English traveler skewers the man in the street's pretensions to political savvy by ironically juxtaposing occupational incompetence with the complexities of statesmanship allegedly mastered.

Inspired by the stances and textual practices of Thomas McCulloch, Haliburton is nonetheless the one who strongly influenced North American anecdotal humor. Haliburton combines the genres (anecdote, sketch, parable, and exemplum) best adapted to imparting a lesson. Anticipating Twain's *Puddn'head Wilson*, he strews his pieces with inventive, imagistic aphorisms. "Brag ... is a good dog, but hold fast is better" says Sam (p. 129). "[W]hat's got over the devil's back is commonly lost under his belly," says a trader who refuses to resort to smuggling (p. 369). The exuberant tales are highly dialogic:

---

21 If supported by the Governor, the Executive Council, the members of which were appointed by the British Crown, could, and systematically did, block any legislation passed by the House of Assembly.
22 The Rebellions of 1837 resulted from the denial of responsible government, which was eventually achieved in the Maritimes in 1848.
23 We should keep in mind that this was in the wake of the War of 1812, which saw the invasion of the Canadian colony by an expansionist United States.

even Sam Slick's monologues are full of rapid framed dialogues which iterate "Yes, says he / Well, says I." They generate the headiness of speed, but also the theatrical effect of the scene, which is conducive to transmitting the didactic message inherent in satire. Concrete analogies abound: we learn that "it is about as easy to find a good inn in Halifax,as it is to find wool on a goat's back" (p. 17) or that Slick "never see'd an Englishman, that did'nt cut his words as short as he does his horse's tail, close up to the stump" (p. 45). Circumlocution and paradox generate hilarity: "I don't know as I ever cheated a man myself in my life ... but if a chap seems bent on cheatin' himself, I like to be neighbourly and help him to do it" (p. 372).

McCulloch was adept at transcribing vernacular speech, but kept it for direct discourse. Howe experimented timidly with incorporating idiolect into the narration for satirical social antithesis, inciting the reader to smile, for instance, at English cockney travelers returning home and amazing their neighbours with "the istory of their adwentures."[24] But with his polyphonic dramatic monologues, Haliburton moved North American regional dialects close to the narration itself, blazing the trail for vernacular idiom as the form for storytelling in Canadian and American writing, from Twain to Salinger. Haliburton was also the first writer to develop the tall tale, as in the story of how he made Jim Munroe marry his sister Sally by swinging him upside down like a rabbit till one leg was half a yard longer than the other. Haliburton's audaciously inventive play with language lives on. Many of the phrases that the author coined or that deviated from standard usage have passed into mainstream language as expressions and proverbial sayings, such as "stick-in-the mud," "upper crust," "as large as life and twice as natural," "[a]n ounce of prevention is worth a pound of cure," or "[a] nod is as good as a wink to a blind horse."[25]

Canadian writers were among the first to engage in questions of identity construction and cultural differentiation. Nourished by the complex perspective stemming from the multiple allegiances of migration, a strong satirical tradition thrived in their culture-making, and set the foundations for what was to become a distinctive feature of Canadian cultural production.

---

24 Howe, *Western and Eastern Rambles*, p. 49, original emphasis.
25 See R. E. Watters, "Sam Slick," in *On Thomas Chandler Haliburton*, ed. R. A. Davies, (Ottawa: Tecumseh, 1979), p. 246.

4

Writing in the Northwest: narratives, journals, letters, 1700–1870

BRUCE GREENFIELD

Up to the middle of the nineteenth century, all travel reportage about the lands north and west of the Great Lakes was beholden either to the British Admiralty or to the large fur companies, in particular the North West Company and the Hudson's Bay Company. Vast distances, severe climate, and sparse population ruled out anything like independent travel or travel for its own sake. The naval expeditions of James Cook and George Vancouver charted the Pacific coast of North America during the later eighteenth century. Then, in the early nineteenth century, the British navy undertook to survey the Arctic coastline, beginning with the land expeditions of Captain John Franklin. The design and reporting of these expeditions reflected what Mary Louise Pratt has referred to as the post-Enlightenment "knowledge-building project of natural history." Informed by a "planetary" sense of the knowledge-gathering errand, the ship-based scientific expedition "became one of Europe's proudest and most conspicuous instruments of expansion."[1] Expeditions such as those of Cook and Vancouver included scientific specialists, and their elegant and prestigious published accounts were imitated by aspiring travelers-turned-writers, as the genre became one of the most popular and profitable of British publishing.[2] Lacking anything like the support of a group of naval vessels, the fur traders who were almost solely responsible for communicating knowledge of the interior of the continent nonetheless aspired to publish "voyages" that shared some of this prestige and glamor. For most of the fur trade travelers, however, writing was initially a response to the record-keeping requirements of the large commercial organizations in which they labored. The transcontinental and oceanic span of these

---

[1] Mary Louise Pratt, *Imperial Eyes: Travel Writing and Transculturation*, 2nd edn (London and New York: Routledge, 2008 [1992]), pp. 23–4.
[2] G. R. Crone and R. A. Skelton, "English Collections of Voyages and Travels, 1625–1846," in *Richard Hakluyt and his Successors*, ed. Edward Lynam (London: Hakluyt Society, 1946), p. 78.

enterprises was itself an artifact of written documents, with letters and reports of many kinds flowing up and down the hierarchy, and back and forth through space.

Over 3,000 linear meters of Hudson's Bay Company documents now housed in the Archives of Manitoba are an astonishing monument to such an organization, within which lie many examples of individual creativity. European men were the authors of most of these documents, and most of their letters, reports, and formal narratives address audiences of their peers. Exceptional texts by women exist, however, and readings of the male-authored letters and narratives by Sylvia van Kirk, Jennifer S. H. Brown, and Susan Sleeper-Smith, among others, have teased out the lives of women who, in the case of the fur trade especially, were of vital importance. The lives of Native inhabitants are vividly present in many narratives, and these sources, along with oral tradition, have enabled an historiography centered on Aboriginal experience.[3] Many of the published works discussed in this chapter can now be read online in their entirety.

Early Hudson's Bay Company travelers

In the Hudson's Bay Company (HBC) factories, or trading establishments, on the margins of Hudson's Bay, remote from European as well as Native North American life, most employees were indentured servants and apprentices, more or less unskilled laborers, with literate clerks and managers guiding affairs. Native traders brought their products to the factories to exchange, and for the first decades of its activity few HBC servants ventured beyond the neighborhood of the factory. Competition from French traders was always a factor, however, and the HBC made periodic inland ventures, notably those of Henry Kelsey in 1690, Anthony Henday in 1754, and Matthew Cocking in 1772. The three young clerks made similar journeys southwestward into the plains for the purpose of attracting trade, in each case living and traveling with a Native group whose annual round included a visit to the HBC factory.

Extant journals by these three men consist of daily logs noting directions, distances, and conditions of travel, typically not revised into

---

3 See R. David Edmunds, "Native Americans, New Voices: American Indian History, 1895–1995," *American Historical Review* 100.3 (June 1995), pp. 717–40; Richard White, *The Middle Ground: Indians, Empires, and Republics in the Great Lakes Region, 1650–1815* (Cambridge: Cambridge University Press, 1991); Jennifer S. Brown and Elizabeth Vibert, eds., *Reading Beyond Worlds: Contexts for Native History* (Peterborough: Broadview Press, 1996).

narrative form.[4] To such basic notations as Henday's "Travelled none. Indians killed a few beaver" the journalists added details about what they had to eat, the activities of their companions, and prospects for trade. Especially in the journals of Henday and Cocking, the accumulation of these brief notes, along with passages of more complex observation, produce a concrete and lively sense of the day-to-day lives of the journalist and his Native companions. An exception to mainly terse journal notations is Kelsey's narrative account of the first year of his two-year journey, which he renders in the form of rhymed decasyllabic couplets. Kelsey writes that he set forth "Through Gods assistance for to understand / The natives language & to see their land."[5]

If the primary qualification for undertaking such journeys was the wit and stamina to adapt to life as lived in local conditions, the ability to produce a written account was also essential. James Isham's instructions to Henday, typical of what each traveler received, emphasize journal keeping, taking "all the observations and Remarks that occur to your View, be it Ever so trifling."[6] Journals were forwarded, along with the Factor's commentary, to the company's directors, but they also furnished information for the factors' own compositions. Three of the four surviving copies of Henday's journal are found in the manuscripts of "Observations on Hudson's Bay," a memoir by Andrew Graham, second in command at York Fort during the period of Henday's travels,[7] and James Isham completed his own "Observations" in 1743. Such accounts are not narrative histories, but they are also not journals. Isham's includes vocabularies, descriptions of plants and animals and of the people he knows. He refers to books and other documents, and his account is clearly a product of many earnestly spent hours. Though he lacked the authority of a traveler's direct observation, the factor could still address his audience in London from an exotic location.[8]

---

4 Matthew Cocking, "An Adventurer from Hudson Bay: Journal of Matthew Cocking, from York Factory to the Blackfeet Country, 1772–73," in *Transactions of the Royal Society of Canada*, ed., intro. and notes by Lawrence J. Burpee, 3rd Series, vol. II (1908), pp. 89–121; Anthony Henday, "York Factory to the Blackfeet Country: The Journal of Anthony Hendry [sic], 1754–55," in *Transactions of the Royal Society of Canada*, ed. Lawrence J. Burpee, 3rd Series, vol. I (1907), section II, pp. 307–64; Henry Kelsey, *The Kelsey Papers*, intro. John Warkentin (Regina: Canadian Plains Research Center, University of Regina, 1994).
5 Ibid., pp. 1–2.
6 Barbara Belyea, ed., *A Year Inland: The Journal of a Hudson's Bay Company Winterer* (Waterloo: Wilfred Laurier University Press, 2000), p. 41.
7 Ibid., p. 17.
8 Andrew Graham, *Andrew Graham's Observations on Hudson's Bay, 1767–91*, ed. Glyndwr Williams, intro. Richard Glover (London: Hudson's Bay Record Society, 1969); James

Given the long history of British interest in travel narratives and the culture of record keeping within the HBC organization, it is remarkable that so little of what was written about the Northwest achieved publication, a fact that reflects the HBC's policy of active discouragement.[9] Samuel Hearne's *A Journey from Prince of Wales's Fort, in Hudson's Bay, to the Northern Ocean* (1795) is a literary landmark, the first fully realized travel narrative to be published about northern Canada.[10] Hearne's account of the three journeys that eventually brought him to the mouth of the Coppermine River on the Arctic coast unites the experiential authority of the traveler's journal with the access to documents and the time for reflection afforded by Hearne's subsequent position as Factor at Prince of Wales Fort, near modern Churchill, Manitoba. Like other travel accounts, Hearne's published text may reflect some attention from an editor or ghost writer.[11] Like Kelsey, Henday, and Cocking, Hearne traveled by attaching himself to a Native band, in this case Chipewyans, who modified their peregrination to include the mouth of the Coppermine River. Hearne succeeded thanks to the leadership of Matonabbee, a respected Chipewyan chief, whose skills, experience, and authority guided and protected Hearne during the eighteen months and twenty-two days of the journey. Hearne's narrative is in many respects an account of the decisions of Matonabbee and of the daily life of the group he leads, Hearne's own goals being registered in astronomical notations, descriptions of key sites, and his copious and astute accounts of the wildlife of the boreal forests and barren grounds. The most interesting story, however, is that of his deeply fraught relationship with his traveling companions, who elicit his admiration, respect, fear, and antipathy.

The North West Company

Alexander Mackenzie's *Voyages* (1801) was part of a campaign to advance the standing of the North West Company (NWC), the main competitor of

---

Isham, *Observations on Hudson's Bay, 1743, and Notes and Observations on a Book Entitled A Voyage to Hudson's Bay in the Dobbs Galley, 1749*, ed. and intro. E. E. Rich and A. M. Johnson (Toronto: Champlain Society, 1949).

9 I. S. MacLaren, "English Writings about the New World," in *History of the Book in Canada*, ed. Patricia Lockhart Fleming, Gilles Gallican, and Yvan Lamonde, 3 vols. (Toronto: University of Toronto Press, 2004), vol. I, p. 39.

10 Samuel Hearne, *A Journey from Prince of Wales's Fort in Hudson's Bay to the Northern Ocean in the Years 1769, 1770, 1771 and 1772*, ed. J. B. Tyrrell (Toronto: Champlain Society, 1911 [1795]).

11 See I. S. MacLaren, "English Writings about the New World," p. 39.

the HBC until the two concerns merged in 1821. Mackenzie positions the narratives of his voyages within his vision of a continent-spanning trading system founded on his extensions of geographic knowledge. His purposefulness engenders a strong narrative line and considerable suspense. Mackenzie's Pacific narrative is the first account to render the experience of ascending and descending the canyon-confined torrents of the western cordillera, what would become a topos of western North American travel narratives. The human environment within the narrow valleys of the Coastal Ranges also emerges as a series of challenges, and as a second novel pattern in his narrative. Whereas Hearne and his fellow HBC travelers encountered unfamiliar peoples from within the company of a large Native group who knew the terrain and its inhabitants, Mackenzie, though he depended heavily on local guides and information, traveled with his own small group of employees, and was typically passed from village to village, and then from language group to language group, usually with a guide who knew little beyond the next village. Local guides had to be wooed, rewarded, and sometimes compelled to go the distance to the next community. The fears and hostility of each new group had to be assuaged, and their assistance secured. This human geography is perhaps the richest register of Mackenzie's movement through time and space. Mackenzie's thoughts and feelings are also part of the story, as he plans, threatens, and charms his way from village to village, the worst moments inducing "a state of mind which I scarce wish to recollect, and shall not attempt to describe." Mackenzie's own journal for the Pacific voyage having disappeared, it is impossible to know whether such expressions reflect the interventions of William Combe, known to have "edited freely" Mackenzie's work.[12]

Mackenzie's *Voyages* was widely reviewed, translated, and reprinted, and within months of its publication Mackenzie was knighted, all of which made an impression on Mackenzie's colleagues. Simon Fraser's editor suggests that Fraser was "jealous" of Mackenzie, and that Fraser had publication in mind when he undertook his 1808 descent of the river that came to bear his name.[13] Like Mackenzie, Fraser renders the cataract and canyon landscape in vivid terms, describing how "The water ... rolls down this extraordinary passage in

---

12 Alexander Mackenzie, *Voyages from Montreal on the River St. Laurence, through the Continent of North America, to the Frozen and Pacific Oceans, in the Years 1789 and 1793* (London: T. Cadell and W. Davies, 1801), p. 273; W. Kaye Lamb, ed. *The Journals and Letters of Sir Alexander Mackenzie* (Toronto: Macmillan of Canada, 1970), p. 47.
13 Simon Fraser, *Letters and Journals, 1806–1808*, ed. and intro. W. Kaye Lamb (Toronto: Macmillan Co. of Canada, 1960), p. 37.

tumultuous waves and with great velocity. ... [T]he great difficulty consisted in keeping the canoes ... clear of the precipice on one side, and of the gulphs [sic] formed by the waves on the other. However, thus skimming along like lightning, the crews cool and determined, followed each other in awful silence." When rapids become impassible altogether, Fraser describes scaling tremendous walls of rock by means of steps and ladders that local people had constructed for their own use. "The country through which we passed this day was the most savage that can be imagined," says Fraser, "yet we were always in a beaten path."[14] As he was also handed on from village to village, relying always on locals to provide for the next stage of the journey, Fraser's encounters with friendly, inscrutable, or hostile people reflect and magnify his own desires and anxieties. Though unpublished during his lifetime, Fraser's journals are ambitious, with cultivated allusions and skillful turns of phrase.

Presumably Fraser and Mackenzie are included among those to whom Alexander Henry (the elder) referred as "a parcel of Boys and upstarts."[15] Among the first Anglo-Americans to launch himself in the fur trade after the fall of New France, during his first expeditions Henry was regarded as an enemy by Ojibwas still allied with the French. Henry describes the 1763 massacre of the British garrison at Michilimackinac, his own escape from which depended on Wawatam, an Ojibwa who earlier had adopted Henry and who, after the attack, ransomed and sheltered him during an entire winter. The first half of Henry's *Travels and Adventures in Canada and the Indian Territories* (1809) has some elements of a captivity narrative, and of sensational fiction. The second part recounts Henry's later journey to the prairies, and is more purely a travel narrative.[16] Writing many years after the events, Henry claims to base his often very detailed memoir on notebooks, though none is known to survive.

Peter Pond's important maps, as well as his geographical theories, stimulated and guided the explorations of Mackenzie, his junior colleague. An exact contemporary of Henry, Pond, too, seized opportunities in Canada after the fall of New France, eventually extending the NWC network as far as Lake Athabasca. There is strong evidence that Pond aspired to publish the pungent,

---

14 Ibid., pp. 75–6, 79.
15 David A. Armour, "Alexander Henry," in *Dictionary of Canadian Biography Online*, www.biographi.ca.
16 *Travels and Adventures in Canada and the Indian Territories between the Years 1760 and 1776* (New York: I. Riley, 1809).

lively, and indecorous memoir of his life and travels that he wrote late in his life, but the manuscript languished for a century.[17]

The writings of David Thompson are a unique monument in Canadian exploration and travel. Known during his life as an exceptional geographer, nothing other than his maps and some newspaper articles saw publication until long after his death. Yet more than 100 extant notebooks document his work, travel, correspondence, personal thoughts, virtually without a lapse from 1785, when he was fifteen, to 1851, six years before his death. Moreover, in 1845, at the age of seventy-five, Thompson began to write the narrative of his life and work, bringing the perspective of his old age to bear on the detailed records of his active years. The resulting travel narrative and memoir, what Thompson called his "Travels," remained unpublished until 1916.[18]

From the outset of his travel narrative Thompson portrays himself as a writer in training. At the Grey Coat Hospital in Westminster, a charity school, Thompson received a practical education, in preparation for an apprenticeship as a clerk with the HBC. Speaking of his first winter with the HBC, at Fort Churchill (1784–5), he complains that "for all I had seen in their service neither reading nor writing was required." A year later, an encounter with a graduate of the same school, who after thirteen years in the country "had lost all his education," is a disturbing possibility for a young man eager to improve himself. Thus Thompson's subsequent encounter with Philip Turnor, the HBC's chief surveyor, seems providential, "the best thing that ever happened" to him. In 1794, Thompson himself was appointed surveyor, but only two years later he left the HBC to join the rival NWC, justifying his abrupt defection by explaining that the NWC had commissioned him to survey the country from Lake of the Woods to the Rocky Mountains, with "every necessary I required to be at my order."[19]

The manuscripts that Thompson referred to as his "Travels," were first edited by J. B. Tyrell, and published as *David Thompson's Narrative of his Explorations in Western American 1784–1812*.[20] Arranged by Tyrell in roughly

---

17 Bruce Greenfield, "Creating the Distance of Print: The Memoir of Peter Pond, Fur Trader," *Early American Literature* 37.3 (2002), pp. 415–38. Pond's narrative is available in *Five Fur Traders of the Northwest*, ed. Charles M. Gates (St. Paul: Minnesota Historical Society, 1965).
18 William E. Moreau, "'To Be Fit for Publication': The Editorial History of David Thompson's Travels, 1840–1916," *Papers of the Bibliographical Society of Canada*, 39 (Fall 2001), pp. 17–18.
19 *David Thompson's Narrative, 1784–1812*, ed. Richard Glover (Toronto: Champlain Society, 1962), pp. 19, 43, 132.
20 David Thompson, *David Thompson's Narrative of his Explorations in Western American 1784–1812*, ed. J. B. Tyrell (Toronto: Champlain Society, 1916).

chronological order, Thompson's career and travels can be seen as falling into three periods. The first includes his life in the HBC factories along the Bay, as well as inland, where Thompson lived in close association with Cree and Chipewyan peoples. The second period begins with Thompson's move to the North West Company, where he first undertook a survey of the country westward from Lake of the Woods as far as the foothills of the Rocky Mountains. The journeys of this period include a visit to the Mandan villages on the upper Missouri, his survey of the headwaters of the Mississippi, and a winter spent with the Peeagan or Blackfeet, in the tent of Saukamappee, an old man whose life story Thompson records at length. During the third period Thompson ventures across the mountains in a series of famous journeys culminating in his descent of the Columbia River to the Pacific Ocean.

Into the framework of his narrative of travel Thompson inserts biographies, ethnographies, local histories and stories, descriptions of wildlife, and essays on such broad topics as the geography of the Great Plains and their rivers. Thompson's accounts of Native people spring from close personal acquaintance, and generalizations spring from particular instances. Cree dances, he explains,

> have a religious tendency, they are not, as with us, dances of mere pleasure, of the joyous countenance: they are grave, each dancer considers it is a religious rite for some purpose; their motions are slow and graceful; yet I have sometimes seen occasional dances of a gay character. [One such occurred on] a fine, calm, moonlight night, the young men came with the Rattle and Tambour, about nine women formed the dance, to which they sung with their fine voices, and lively they danced hand in hand in a half circle for a long hour; it is now many years ago, yet I remember this gay hour.[21]

Thompson's wildlife descriptions also convey a sense of being specifically sited, with the presence of the observer communicated indirectly.

> In autumn, the last three days of the geese appear to be wholly given in cleaning and adjusting every feather of every part ...; the Manito of the geese, ducks and other fowls had given his orders, they collect, and form flocks of, from 40 to 60, or more. ... The order is given, and flock after flock, in innumerable numbers, rise ... Thus in two, or three days, these extensive marshes, swarming with noisy life, become silent, and wholly deserted.[22]

At his best, Thompson achieves a remarkable integration of information, the lived experience of the young traveler, and the synthetic vision and reflective

---

21 *David Thompson's Narrative*, ed. Glover, p. 81.
22 Ibid., p. 26.

comments of the elderly author. These and other strengths make Thompson's narrative the richest and most important of its kind in Canada.

Early nineteenth-century journals

Thompson's journal keeping was a widely shared practice that produced other excellent writing among his peers. Alexander Henry (the younger), Daniel Harmon, and Peter Skene Ogden left copious journals dealing with the first decades of the nineteenth century, when the fur trade was pushed westward to the Pacific coast. Harmon's journal is exceptional in its focus on the routine affairs of a trader's life. He is aware of the great journeys of Thompson and Fraser, and of the North West Company's "deep-laid plans" to open up water communication with the Pacific. Harmon, meanwhile, will "attend to the little affairs of New Caledonia! and pass the summer in this place."[23] Scion of a pious Vermont family, Harmon presents his years in the Northwest as a period of trial and exile, his disapproval throwing into strong relief the mores of life upstream from Montreal – the drinking, the non-observance of the Sabbath, the practice of taking a "country wife." According to his own reckoning, Harmon often needed less than a fifth of his day to fulfill his duties. Reading and writing helped pass the time, Harmon's journal affording unique testimony to the importance of books, letters, and literate exchange in this environment. The high points of his year are when he meets his friends to discuss books and read each other the letters and journals that they themselves have penned.[24]

Although Alexander Henry (the younger) drowned on the Columbia before he had any occasion to revise his journals, their almost 800 published pages include some of the best writing in the field. His entries for 1800–1, for example, a period spent in the Red River valley in Minnesota, vividly convey the activities of the trader's garrison. He describes the labors of his employees, as well as their celebration of Catholic feast days with special allowances of flour, sugar, and "strong wine." Henry characterizes his relationships with his Chippewa trading partners as being openly based upon the self-interest of both parties. Alcohol seems to have been central to this relationship; Natives value it highly, and Henry restricts and grants access to suit his own interests, noting its destructive effects upon the drinkers themselves, in the form of

---

23 Daniel Williams Harmon, *Sixteen Years in the Indian Country: The Journal of Daniel Williams Harmon 1800–1816*, ed. W. Kaye Lamb (Toronto: Macmillan, 1957), p. 159.
24 Laura J. Murray, "Fur Traders in Conversation," *Ethnohistory* 50.2 (Spring 2003), pp. 289–91.

fights and neglect of the necessaries of existence. Without isolating "natural history" in lists and descriptive essays, Henry conveys a detailed account of the rich wildlife of the Red River valley and the surrounding plains. "[A] most delightful country," according to Henry, adding that "was it not for the perpetual wars, the natives might be the happiest people upon earth." Henry's ironic lucidity is a notable literary achievement among fur-trade writers, as is his gift for comic effects, seen here as he describes a false alarm in the garrison:

> My men who had just placed their kettle of meat in the middle of the Fort ... had got up from around their kettle, and were now standing, and gaping and stareing [sic]. ... Some had pieces of meat sticking out of their mouths, others with their mouth full, others again with large bits in their hands, whilst some had let them drop to the ground.[25]

Peter Skene Ogden's reputation as a writer derives from his "Snake Country Journals," which recount a series of expeditions during the years 1824 through 1830, in present-day Oregon, Idaho, California, Nevada, Utah, and Wyoming.[26] In addition to his journals, he is thought to be the author of *Traits of American-Indian Life and Character* (1853). Perhaps the strongest impression conveyed by Ogden's account of his explorations is of their unremitting drudgery. His party's labors and privations seem prodigious. "[T]he life of a trapper," he says, "in four years makes a young man look almost as if he had reached the advanced age of sixty." Ogden himself, managing dozens of men, their wives, children, and horses in unfamiliar country, where local people are often hostile, suffers "anxiety greater than few can form any Idea off [sic]."[27] Ogden's comments express sympathy for his companions and for the peoples he encounters, as well as biting criticism, and his frequent laments are infused with wit. Ogden, like Henry, seems to have enjoyed writing, and he often describes himself alone in his tent, working on his journal.

John Jacob Astor's 1811 trading venture to the Columbia River became the subject of numerous accounts, including three by members of the seaborne branch of the expedition. Gabriel Franchère's original journal in French is a modest and meticulous young clerk's diary, intended, he says, for family and

---

25 Alexander Henry, *The Journal of Alexander Henry the Younger, 1799–1814*, ed. Barry M. Gough, 2 vols. (Toronto: Champlain Society, 1988–92), vol. I, pp. 55, 64.
26 Peter Skene Ogden, *Peter Skene Ogden's Snake Country Journals, 1824–25 and 1825–26*, ed. E. E. Rich and A. M. Johnson (London: Hudson's Bay Record Society, 1950); *Peter Skene Ogden's Snake Country Journal, 1826–27*, ed. K. G. Davies and A. M. Johnson (London: Hudson's Bay Record Society, 1961); *Peter Skene Ogden's Snake Country Journals, 1827–28 and 1828–29*, ed. Glyndwr Williams (London: Hudson's Bay Record Society, 1971).
27 Ogden, *Snake Country Journal, 1826–27*, pp. 94, 27.

friends. Franchère describes the voyage around Cape Horn, daily life in the trading establishment they called Astoria, as well as life in the villages of the lower Columbia Valley. A disciplined observer of people and events, his own person remains somewhat effaced. Much later in his life, he would publish an English version of his experiences.[28] Ross Cox's *Adventures on the Columbia River* (1831) addresses a popular audience, promising "extraordinary escapes" and gratification to all those whose tastes favor "'battle murder and sudden death.'"[29] His Natives are foils for adventurous whites, and occasionally objects of his disdain. Often closely paralleling Franchère's account, Cox fills the vacuum of Franchère's reserve, readily supplying adjectives, adverbs, and action scenes, even some that he did not himself witness. Alexander Ross wrote two books about the Pacific Northwest and a third about the Red River colony, where he lived after retiring from the trade. *Adventures of the First Settlers on the Oregon or Columbia River* (1849) includes many vivid personalities, along with Ross's insights into how character traits figure in conflicts and decisions. Ross's tone is often satiric, and although he views particular Native figures through the same satiric lens that he focuses on the whites, his accounts of the two peoples he knows best, the Chinooks and the Okanagans, are respectful, dispassionate, and specific. There are many signs throughout the first two books that Ross's attitudes toward the enterprise of the fur trade were ambivalent.[30] Fred Stenson's novel *The Trade* (2000) skillfully peoples a fictional narrative with characters and events of the early nineteenth-century fur trade in the prairies and foothills.[31]

Epistolary perspectives

Both as personal and semi-public communications letters include more of the domestic, the affective, and the tentative, as compared to exploration journals and narratives. People not mentioned at all in exploration narratives find a place in letters, and some of the same events appear in a very different light.

---

28 Gabriel Franchère, *The Journal of Gabriel Franchère, 1811–1814* (Toronto: Champlain Society, 1969); *Narrative of a Voyage to the Northwest Coast of America, in the Years 1811, 1812, 1813, and 1814*, trans. and ed. J. V. Huntington (New York: Redfield, 1854).
29 Ross Cox, *Adventures on the Columbia River*, 2 vols. (London: H. Colburn, 1831), vol. I, pp. vii–viii.
30 Alexander Ross, *Adventures of the First Settlers on the Oregon or Columbia River* (London: Smith, Elder and Co., 1849); *The Fur Hunters of the Far West: a Narrative of Adventures in the Oregon and Rocky Mountains* (London: Smith, Elder and Co., 1855); *The Red River Settlement: Its Rise, Progress, and Present State* (London: Smith, Elder and Co., 1856).
31 Fred Stenson, *The Trade* (Vancouver: Douglas and McIntyre, 2000).

Most significantly, women achieve a representation that more closely accords with reality, especially when they themselves write the letters.

A collection of letters received by James Hargrave at York Factory includes routine exchanges among managers of the HBC, as well as personal news, with most authors capturing succinctly and often with some wit the matters at hand.[32] Much more personal, sometimes ribald and naughty, are the letters of Francis Ermatinger to his brother Edward. Mainly posted in the Columbia district, Francis wrote to his brother throughout his career, speaking casually of mutual acquaintances, critically and satirically of his superiors, and somewhat facetiously of his own affairs, particularly of his reputation for being "fond of [Ladies]."[33] His chatty letters afford a young man's perspective on the sexual mores of fur trade society. Archibald McDonald, a colleague of Francis Ermatinger in the Columbia District from 1821 to 1844, also wrote to Edward Ermatinger, often discussing brother Francis's complicated personal affairs.[34] McDonald's own life was simpler, however, his first "country marriage" ending with his wife's death in childbirth, and his second, to Jane Klyne, the daughter of a French-Canadian man and a Métis woman, lasting until his own death. McDonald's annual letters to friends include accounts of Jane, their growing family, and the pleasures he found there. We learn about the system of partnerships and promotions within the HBC, who is due, who is overlooked, which elderly, ineffectual factors are squatting on their lucrative Chief Factorships. McDonald's letters provide a running commentary on events and personalities, from the early days of European presence in the Columbia Valley to the beginning of the overland wave of American settlers. The view from the apex of the HBC organization is conveyed in letters and reports by its famous Governor-in-Chief, George Simpson. His rendering of persons and places is resolutely instrumental, but the world as it appeared to this deft manager assumes a vivid and particular form, and the voice that would exert influence for forty years is suave and concise.[35]

---

32 *The Hargrave Correspondence, 1821–1843*, ed. G. P. de T. Glazebrook (Toronto: Champlain Society, 1938).
33 Francis Ermatinger, *Fur Trade Letters of Francis Ermatinger: Written to his Brother Edward during his Service with the Hudson's Bay Company, 1818–1853*, ed. Lois Halliday McDonald (Glendale, CA: Arthur H. Clark, 1980), p. 63.
34 Archibald McDonald, *This Blessed Wilderness: Archibald McDonald's Letters from the Columbia, 1822–44*, ed. Jean Murray Cole (Vancouver: University of British Columbia Press, 2001).
35 George Simpson, *Journal of Occurrences in the Athabasca Department, 1820 and 1821*, ed. E. E. Rich (Toronto: Champlain Society, 1938); *Fur Trade and Empire; George Simpson's Journal; Remarks Connected with the Fur Trade in the Course of a Voyage from York Factory to Fort George and back to York Factory 1824–1825*, ed. Frederick Merk (Cambridge, MA: Harvard University Press, 1931).

The letters of Letitia MacTavish Hargrave provide a unique account of fur-trade life, based on her decade at York Factory, from 1840 to 1851, where her husband James Hargrave was Chief Trader, and subsequently Chief Factor. Along with Governor Simpson's wife, Frances Ramsay Simpson, and Catherine Turner MacTavish, the British wife of Letitia's uncle, John George MacTavish, Hargrave was among the first British-born women to marry an HBC officer and live in remote postings. Written to her parents and sisters about three times each year, her letters describe her own domestic environment, but they also convey her considerable knowledge of the HBC's personnel and affairs. Hargrave's letters are typically vivid and observant, and often astute about the world in which she found herself.

At York Hargrave managed the household of a gentlewoman, with a lady's maid and nurse, a butler, and a cook. Winter carriole rides were almost the only occasions for her to leave the immediate confines of the Fort, since the surrounding ground was swampy when not frozen. Her accounts of herself mingle complaint with appreciation: "I am as well pleased with York as at first, but I only am so from never thinking. You may believe that the eternal barreness [sic] of white water & black pines are not very enlivening to the spirits. The sky is always beautiful night or day, the Aurora being magnificent & the stars very bright."[36]

Secure as she seems to have been in her own circumscribed middle-class household, everything around her spoke of radically different arrangements, to which she was alert. As Margaret MacLeod, the editor of Hargrave's *Letters* explains, and as Sylvia van Kirk subsequently explored so memorably, most long-time factors, clerks, and servants of the fur trade effected "country marriages," in the early years of the trade with Native women, and then subsequently with the daughters of such relationships.[37] Some of these lasted a lifetime, but many ended when the man decided to retire to Britain or Canada, leaving behind the woman and their children. Provision for wife and children varied, and many women contracted subsequent relationships with other men in the trade.

According to Letitia, her uncle, John MacTavish, "has certainly 6 daughters" by at least two women, prior to his marriage to Catherine Turner. Frances Simpson, meanwhile, is thought not to know "that she has more encumbrances than Mrs Mactavish," though Mrs. Simpson herself confesses

---

36 Letitia Hargrave, *The Letters of Letitia Hargrave*, ed. Margaret Arnett MacLeod (Toronto: The Champlain Society, 1947), p. 146.
37 Ibid., pp. xxiv–xxv, xliii–xliv, lv–lvi.

that she "was always terrified to look about her in case of seeing something disagreeable." Hargrave confronts these matters fairly directly. She may consider "the state of society ... shocking," but she is forthright in her accounts of people and their relationships.[38] She is also alive to the grief and jealousy that were part and parcel of inequitable social arrangements. She seems to have got on well with several formidable wives she encountered in the factory environment over the years, and she relates their stories with a certain sympathy for the complexity and difficulty of their lives. Her contact with Native people who are not part of the circle of company society at the Fort seems to have been limited, but there are nice moments when she describes how her young son is kissed and admired by women and men visiting the fort. The story of Métis people and their roots in the fur trade is extended in Christine Welsh's documentary film, *Women in the Shadows*, where she journeys in search of her own Métis foremothers.[39]

One learns much from the Hargraves' letters about the importance and logistics of fur-trade letter writing. In addition to the official letters that were the main means by which individuals reported on their activities, many private and personal letters circulated as well, cementing alliances, sustaining friendships, and providing news and entertainment. In the Hargraves' York posting, letter writing was tied to the arrival of the summer ships in the Bay and to the dispatches sent overland via Red River, the Great Lakes, and Canada. Marathon composition sessions preceded each departure, Letitia coordinating letters to family members, which remained open until the last possible moment, in one instance in the hope that Letitia would give birth before the ship sailed. In such circumstances, good letters were highly valued. Letters received by James Hargrave frequently laud his epistolary skill, and the careful preservation of Letitia's suggests the esteem in which they were held.[40] Letters typically reached audiences well beyond the addressee, being read aloud, copied, circulated among friends and family, and occasionally printed in newspapers. Collected and published letters constitute the actual or pretended basis of books like Catherine Parr Trail's *The Backwoods of Canada*.

The collection *Undelivered Letters to Hudson's Bay Company Men on the Northwest Coast of America, 1830–57* turns the tables by publishing letters written

---

38 Ibid., pp. 35, 36, 84.
39 Christine Welsh, *Women in the Shadows* (National Film Board of Canada, 1991).
40 Hargrave, *The Letters of Letitia Hargrave*, pp. xv–xvi.

from home to men in HBC service.[41] As the editors explain, these letters give voice to mothers, wives, girlfriends and other family and friends of men working on the faraway west coast of America. Some are the products of only modest writing skill, yet they bear telling witness to the concerns of the authors, and the volume recovers voices mostly absent from public discourses of the time.

Settlement and adventure

Interest in western settlements was growing during the 1850s, when two expeditions were commissioned to report on the possibilities, the British Colonial Office's, led by John Palliser, and that of the Upper Canada government, reported on by Henry Youle Hind. The Palliser Report is based on the journals kept during the three summers that Palliser and his party explored the plains and mountains of southern Canada.[42] Palliser's big-game hunting enthusiasms surface occasionally in gallops after buffalo, but for the most part, the persona avoids enthusiasm, and the journals' unpretentious particularity yields vivid impressions of places and people. Covering much the same territory, and published in the same year as Palliser's report, Hind's account is much longer, with a meandering organization.[43] Palliser and Hind depended on the HBC for logistical support, but in their reports, the personnel and practices of the trade have an air of quaint antiquity. It is a nice coincidence that in 1857, on his way to the prairies for the first time, Palliser meets Sir George Simpson, HBC Governor, returning from one of his last trips to inspect his domain. The same year, Simpson testified before a British House of Commons committee that the western countries were unsuitable for settlement; Palliser's report argued the opposite.

Robert Michael Ballantyne's *Hudson Bay* (1848) anticipates this shift in point of view away from the fur trader. Though his book sprang from his apprentice years with the HBC, Ballantyne exhibited little aptitude or enthusiasm for

---

41 Judith Hudson Beattie and Helen M. Buss, eds., *Undelivered Letters to Hudson's Bay Company Men on the Northwest Coast of America, 1830–57* (Vancouver: University of British Columbia Press, 2003).
42 John Palliser, *Papers Relative to the Exploration by Captain Palliser of that Portion of British North America which Lies between the Northern Branch of the River Saskatchewan and the Frontier of the United States; and between the Red River and Rocky Mountains* (London: G. E. Eyre and W. Spottiswoode, 1859).
43 Henry Youle Hind, *Narrative of the Canadian Red River Exploring Expedition of 1857, and of the Assinniboine and Saskatchewan Exploring Expedition of 1858* (London: Longman, Green, Longman, and Roberts, 1860).

his clerkship, and he may have had his literary ambitions even as he embarked for Hudson's Bay at the age of sixteen. He kept a journal from the outset, wrote letters home, and used his later postings on the lower St Lawrence to begin writing the book that was published within a year of his return to Scotland. He renders the northern landscape with vivid enthusiasm, along with hunting, traveling by canoe and sled, and other activities that a young man would appreciate. He seems less interested in the Native inhabitants and the laboring men in the trade. His point of view is suggested on the first page, where he expresses the hope that he may have the "satisfaction" of giving readers information on "those wild, uncivilized regions in the northern continent of America."[44]

Also beholden to the HBC for transportation and support, but not actually in their employ, Paul Kane traveled three summers and two winters between 1845 and 1848, from Toronto, across the prairies, up the Athabasca River, down the Columbia, spending about six months in the Columbia district, including a visit to Victoria. Appearing a decade later, *Wanderings of an Artist among the Indians of North America* (1859) aspired to document Native people and their lives, following the example of the American artist, George Caitlin. Kane's approach is, of course, visual, but he reports stories he hears and the histories of the different individuals and peoples he meets, his book being a lively and concise account of the origins of his sketches.[45]

Stimulated by accounts of transcontinental journeys in American territories during the 1840s and 1850s, Canadian "adventure tourism" begins in earnest with Viscount Milton and Walter Butler Cheadle's *The North-West Passage by Land* (1865), which recounts their two-year journey across the continent in British territory.[46] A look at Cheadle's own journal makes it clear that he was the main author of the book.[47] The pair traveled from the settlements in present-day Minnesota and Manitoba to the HBC factories at Carlton, Edmonton, Rocky Mountain House, Kamloops, the settlements of the lower mainland in BC, and finally Victoria. Between these outposts, however,

---

44 Robert Michael Ballantyne, *Hudson's Bay; or, Every-day life in the Wilds of North America, during Six Years' Residence in the Territories of the Honourable Hudson's Bay Company* (Edinburgh: W. Blackwood, 1848), p. 1.

45 Paul Kane, *Wanderings of an Artist among the Indians of North America, from Canada to Vancouver's Island and Oregon, through the Hudson's Bay Company's Territory and Back Again* (London: Longman, Brown, Green, Longmans and Roberts, 1859).

46 Walter Butler Cheadle and Viscount Milton (William Wentworth-Fitzwilliam), *North-West Passage by Land* (London: Cassell, Petter, and Galpin, 1865).

47 Walter Butler Cheadle, *Cheadle's Journal of Trip across Canada, 1862–1863*, intro. and notes by A. G. Doughty and Gustave Lanctot (Ottawa: Graphic Publishers, 1931; rprt. Edmonton: M. G. Hurtig, 1971.)

particularly in the mountains, the routes were barely discernible, the traveling hard and dangerous, and their party suffered many privations. Cheadle renders the pleasures and trials of wilderness travel very vividly. He is open-spirited and open-minded, but sometimes his vocabulary reflects the trends of the time, marginalizing Aboriginal and mixed-blood people with terms like "squaws" and "half-breeds." Initially interested in "sport," and drawn to the thrills of buffalo hunting on horseback, with its "spice of danger," the young men later depend on hunting for survival, an experience that grounds their understanding in a new reality – their own hunger and that of their Native companions.[48]

The prospect of advancement in the British army spurred the Anglo-Irish William Francis Butler to come to the Red River colony in present-day Manitoba, during the period of the first uprising of Métis people led by Louis Riel. Butler saw events there as a "speck" in the context of British overseas interests, and in *The Great Lone Land* (1872) Butler speaks from within the organization that manages an empire.[49] That said, he sympathizes with the struggles of Métis and Indian inhabitants, and he is an enthusiast for the scale, grandeur, and wildness of the western landscape. Purple prose and a certain lofty confidence in British institutions date this work, but the author's muscular engagements with water, wind, and snow on a vast scale remain vital and interesting.

The far north

"Long, fatiguing, and disastrous" are the adjectives with which John Franklin concludes his *Narrative of a Journey to the Shores of the Polar Sea* (1824).[50] Intended to explore the Arctic coast of Canada eastward from the mouth of the Coppermine River, Franklin's first expedition picked up northern exploration where Hearne and Mackenzie left off, reflecting the British admiralty's renewed interest following the Napoleonic wars. Despite its slight contribution to geographical knowledge, the expedition's sponsors in the navy actively encouraged publication of the narrative, and the resulting fine volume attracted a lot of interest.[51] Franklin was promoted and then trusted with a

---

48 Cheadle, *North-West Passage*, p. 62.
49 William Francis Butler, *The Great Lone Land: A Tale of Travel and Adventure in the North-West of America* (Toronto: Macmillan, 1910 [1872]), p. 7.
50 John Franklin, *Narrative of a Journey to the Shores of the Polar Sea, in the Years 1819–20–21–22*, 2 vols. (London: J. Murray, 1824), vol. II, p. 399.
51 I. S. MacLaren, "English Writings about the New World," p. 37.

second expedition to explore the coast in both directions from the mouth of the Mackenzie River (1825–7). Some of Franklin's initial notoriety surely stemmed from his account of the suffering undergone during the first expedition's return journey from the Arctic coast, when all were reduced to near starvation, with nine men succumbing, and two others meeting violent deaths. These human costs would seem to be what Franklin has in mind when he apologizes at the end of his narrative for "the melancholy detail into which I felt it proper to enter."[52] Admired for his courage as well as his actual achievements, Franklin's fame was amplified to the level of myth after 1845, when his naval expedition disappeared without a trace. Determining his fate became the focus of more than thirty expeditions in the following decades, as well as of research and speculation continuing to the present time.

Inevitably, Franklin's first narrative tends to be read ironically, with his ultimate fate in mind, but it is at least as interesting viewed in terms of its original novelty. Prior to Franklin, Hearne and Mackenzie were the only Europeans to have traveled overland to the northern coast, Mackenzie having somewhat clandestinely cobbled together the personnel for a rapid descent of the river that came to bear his name, and Hearne by putting himself into the hands of a band of Chipewyans, whose itinerary was adapted to accommodate his mission. Although Franklin's journey into "unexplored territory" northeast of Great Slave Lake was only possible because of Native guides and Canadian *voyageurs* recruited by the fur companies, Franklin, an officer in the navy, his expedition conceived and financed by the Admiralty, thought of his expedition as an autonomous entity with goals that transcended the interests of all concerned. Franklin presents his expedition as having come not "for the purpose of traffic, but solely to make discoveries," and these abstract ideals, which hark back to the naval expeditions of Cook and Vancouver, may be seen as a source both of the expedition's suffering and of the published narrative's considerable interest.[53] The persons of four educated officers, and the financial support of the British navy, brought a new level of observation to bear on the Canadian north, though Franklin evidently overestimated the ability and/or the willingness of local people to support him.

In earlier parts of the narrative, reporting conditions that were relatively benign, all are eager to capture as much as possible of what is seen and heard. Franklin and his fellow officers bring the eyes of tenderfoot travelers to country and people that have become unremarkable to fur trade personnel.

52 Franklin, *Narrative*, vol. II, p. 395.
53 Franklin, *Narrative*, vol. I, p. 316.

Their awkwardness in canoes and their raw wounds from snow shoes make the conditions of travel readily imaginable. They were made uneasy by the stillness of the vast landscapes, but cold clear nights, with howling wolves, also aroused their sense of pleasure. Franklin records a number of remarkable stories of Native life, and seems to have spent considerable time during the first winter collecting information about the inhabitants of the country. Despite a certain latinate loftiness, Franklin's prose is mostly concise, and often vivid.

Franklin's sense of his party as disinterested observers also kept them recording data, collecting specimens, writing and safeguarding their journals even as starvation loomed. In the later stages of the narrative, recounting their overland return from the coast, the accumulating details of their daily ordeal yield an intensity and suspense that is probably unique in Canadian travel literature. Here observation occurs from the level of men for whom each step is a painful, deliberate effort, for whom an additional few centimeters of snow may render walking impossible, for whom the rancid marrow of an otherwise clean-picked deer carcass means energy for another day's survival. Yet they write in the direst circumstances, carrying their journals strapped to their bodies. When George Back, separated from the main party, sends a messenger to find out if Franklin is still alive, his only instruction, should Franklin be dead, is to collect as many of his papers as possible.

John Richardson, Robert Hood, and George Back, Franklin's team of officers, all kept journals. The most notable is that of George Back, now published along with most of his fifty-seven watercolor sketches.[54] Back's comments are more candid and personal than Franklin's public narrative, and his subsequent *Narrative of the Arctic Land Expedition to the Mouth of the Great Fish River* (1836) retains in a public account some of the strengths of his journals, an ability to convey the impact of Arctic landscapes, and a lively engagement with people encountered en route.[55]

Having provided logistical support for Franklin's first two expeditions, the HBC later dispatched several of its personnel to pick up where his land

---

54 *Arctic Artist: The Journal and Paintings of George Back, Midshipman with Franklin, 1819–1822*, ed. C. Stuart Houston, commentary by I. S. MacLaren (Montreal and Kingston: McGill-Queen's University Press, 1994); Robert Hood, *To the Arctic by Canoe, 1819–1821: The Journal and Paintings of Robert Hood, Midshipman with Franklin*, ed. C. Stuart Houston (Montreal: McGill-Queen's University Press, 1994 [1974]); John Richardson, *Arctic Ordeal: The Journal of John Richardson, Surgeon-Naturalist with Franklin, 1820–1822*, ed. C. Stuart Houston (Kingston: McGill-Queen's University Press, 1984).

55 George Back, *Narrative of the Arctic Land Expedition to the Mouth of the Great Fish River, and along the Shores of the Arctic Ocean, in the Years 1833, 1834, and 1835* (London: J. Murray, 1836).

explorations had left off. In 1836, Thomas Simpson, the ambitious younger cousin of HBC Governor George Simpson, was appointed second in command under the experienced trader Peter Warren Dease, with orders to continue the survey of the Arctic coastline. Their explorations over the next three summers are recounted in Simpson's *Narrative of the Discoveries on the North Coast of America* (1843). Edited by his brother Alexander, after Simpson's untimely death in 1840, the style is concise, conveying a lively sense of landscapes, local people, and the activity of traveling. As well, Simpson's tone suggests his ambition, and his interest in cultivating a metropolitan audience.[56]

An exceptionally adept trader and surveyor, John Rae was from the outset of his service in the HBC a noted student of Indigenous ways and a pioneer in the deployment of northern customs and technologies in the service of Arctic exploration. Moreover, in writing about his travels he speaks from a vantage point attuned to northern life, from within, as it were, the snow huts that his party constructed many nights. Rae's accounts of his four expeditions between 1846 and 1854, organized around systematic charting of the country, describe his small party's daily activities, leaving the impression of a much friendlier environment than Franklin's narratives.[57] Following Rae, more expeditions organized their traveling in the far north in cooperation with Indigenous peoples, adapting their technologies to the purpose of exploratory travel. The many works of Canadian Vilhjalmur Stefansson convey the fruits of a life-long engagement with the peoples of the Arctic. The film *The Journals of Knud Rasmussen* (2006) is based upon the Danish anthropologist's 1922 visit to Igloolik in Canada's eastern Arctic.[58]

Many in the Northwest began writing in fulfillment of a clerk's duties. The genre of the exploration narrative, with its popularity and prestige, offered a further avenue for the ambitious. Good writing could win advancement within the company, even as publication promised recognition in wider society. The act of composition itself, moreover, came to engage the best of these writers, so that discoveries occurred on the page, as well as in the field. Letters, reports, and full-fledged narratives document the lives of generations of Europeans and Native peoples in the Northwest, and they also testify to the craft and creativity of their authors.

---

56 *Narrative of the Discoveries of the North Coast of America: Effected by the Officers of the Hudson's Bay Company during the Years 1836–39* (London: R. Bentley, 1843).
57 John Rae, *Narrative of an Expedition to the Shores of the Arctic Sea in 1846 and 1847* (London: T. and W. Boone, 1850).
58 Norman Cohn and Zacharias Kunuk, *The Journals of Knud Rasmussen* (Kunuk Cohn Productions, Igloolik Isuma Productions, Barok Film, 2006).

5

Literature of settlement

CAROLE GERSON

Introduction

In the terrain that would eventually become the Dominion of Canada, it is not surprising that the literature of exploration was written almost entirely by men. By contrast, canonical narratives of settlement were largely penned by women. From an historical perspective, Central Canada's settlement literature began with the texts that were written in the first half of the nineteenth century to entice emigrants from the British Isles to the New World. According to Carl F. Klinck, between 1815 and 1840 approximately 100 "travel and emigrant books about Upper Canada" appeared in Britain, of which he distinguishes William Dunlop's *Statistical Sketches of Upper Canada for the use of Emigrants* (two editions in 1832 and a third in 1833) as "the most engaging of the lot."[1] Also popular was John Howison's much-reprinted *Sketches of Upper Canada* (1821, 1822, 1825), which integrates advice for prospective emigrants with an account of his own travels and observations. Eyewitness testimonials were considered especially credible, such as T. W. Magrath's *Authentic Letters from Upper Canada* (1833), a copy of which was owned by the Moodie family.[2]

The early 1830s saw the appearance of several important works of this nature, including the novels *Lawrie Todd; or, The Settlers in the Woods* (1830) and *Bogle Corbet* (1831) by Scottish writer John Galt, which reflect his experience in planning communities under the aegis of the Canada Company in the 1820s, and a tract by William Cattermole, whose recruiting lectures would soon entice John and Susanna Moodie to immigrate to Upper Canada. The generic nature of Cattermole's *Emigration. The Advantages of Emigration to Canada ...* (1831) is borne out by the degree to which its structure was followed in subsequent texts, such as *A Plea for Emigration: or, Notes of Canada West in*

---

1 Carl F. Klinck, Introduction, William Dunlop, *Tiger Dunlop's Upper Canada* (Toronto: McClelland and Stewart, 1967), p. xi.
2 In the Patrick Hamilton Ewing Collection at Library and Archives Canada.

its *Moral, Social, and Political Aspect: with Suggestions Respecting Mexico, West Indies, and Vancouver's Island for the Information of Colored Emigrants* (1852) by Mary Ann Shadd, the region's first Black woman author, who argued that Upper Canada was the best refuge for Black Americans seeking to escape the ramifications of the Fugitive Slave Law of 1850. Like Cattermole, Shadd opens with a discussion of the physical geography and climate of the colony; both claim that Canada's cold weather is less extreme and healthier than commonly believed. Both then describe the soil and its fruits, the price of land, and the monetary value of crops and animals. Such details of agriculture are followed by attention to social issues and descriptions of existing communities. Cattermole presents towns in descending order of significance (from York to Queenston), outlining their layout, population, churches, institutional development, and professional and business opportunities. Shadd, in contrast, turns directly to the community that concerns her most: the "colored" people of southern Ontario, and the ways that fugitive slaves can prosper in Canada's "colored settlements"[3] in and around Chatham as well as in Toronto.

Other than Shadd, authors of immigrant handbooks were invariably male, as, with the exception of Ann Cuthbert Knight and Isabella Valancy Crawford, were authors of long narrative poems, another genre that characterizes early settlement writing. Less numerous than works in prose, narrative poems first appeared in Lower Canada, composed in familiar formats such as heroic couplets or Spenserian stanzas. Well-known examples from Nova Scotia – Oliver Goldsmith's *The Rising Village, with Other Poems* (London, 1825; St. John, NB, 1834) and Joseph Howe's *Acadia* (Montreal, 1874) – were matched by several efforts from Upper Canada, including Knight's *A Year in Canada, and Other Poems* (Edinburgh, 1816) and Adam Hood Burwell's *Talbot Road: A Poem* (in the *Niagara Spectator*, 1818). Following Standish O'Grady's production of *The Emigrant* in Montreal in 1841, there appeared two additional poems bearing the same title, one an obscure narrative by John Newton, published in Hamilton in 1846, and the other a well-known work by Alexander McLachlan, published in Toronto in 1861.

While publication is a useful criterion for discerning Canada's early literature, much was penned for more limited dissemination. Shared manuscript documentation was a long-standing practice of female diarists and correspondents; for example, during her five years' residence in Upper Canada, where her husband served as Lieutenant Governor from 1791 to 1796, Elizabeth Simcoe maintained a diary, frequently sending sections to her children and friends

---

3 Mary A. Shadd, *A Plea for Emigration: or, Notes of Canada West* (Detroit: s.n., 1852), p. 22.

back in England. In a similar fashion, settlers like Anne Langton often wrote privately for family and friends, intending to circulate their words in manuscript rather than in print. An unmarried woman who joined the family of her brother, John Langton, in the Peterborough area in 1837, Anne Langton wrote copious letters that were saved by relatives and also maintained a journal that was meant to be read by others. "Did you ever write a journal with the intention of sending it to any one? I think it would be difficult to do it with simplicity," she recorded in 1838.[4] In 1881 she composed *The Story of Our Family*, printed in Manchester for private circulation. Such writers become known after publication of their private correspondence and journals; in Langton's case, this process began with *Langton Records: Journals and Letters from Canada, 1837–1846* (Edinburgh, 1904) and continued with *A Gentlewoman in Upper Canada: The Journals of Anne Langton* (Toronto, 1950). Characterized by optimism and good humor, these texts provide fulsome details of domestic life in the bush. In a similar fashion, Irish-born Frances Stewart, who settled in Douro Township in 1822 and became an intimate friend of the Traills following their arrival in the mid-1830s, entered Canada's national print culture when selections from her letters were issued posthumously as *Our Forest Home: Being Extracts from the Correspondence of the late Frances Stewart* (1889; rpt 1902).

The major authors

Within this context, the major works that constitute Central Canada's canonical settlement narratives were shaped by a singular common feature of their authors' biographies: the arrival of several women who had previously established literary careers in Britain and quickly incorporated their Canadian experience into their oeuvre. Whether visitors (Anna Brownell Jameson, 1794–1860) or immigrants (sisters Susanna Strickland Moodie [1803–85] and Catharine Parr Strickland Traill [1802–99]), their perspectives were shaped by their original environment and their books about Canada were published in England for British readers. After the unexpected death of their father in 1818, the young Strickland women followed their elder sister, Agnes, into London's genteel literary circles, where, during the 1820s, they eked out a living by writing children's books and contributing poetry and prose to literary periodicals and annuals. Both married Scottish army officers of declining fortune who sought to improve their material situation by emigrating to British North

---

4 Barbara Williams, ed., *A Gentlewoman in Upper Canada: The Journals, Letters and Art of Anne Langton* (Toronto: University of Toronto Press, 2008), p. 175.

America in 1832. Also self-supporting, Anna Brownell Jameson was a well-known author of eight books – principally non-fiction – when she followed her estranged husband to Canada in 1836 in order to arrange for a formal separation.

Susanna Moodie was the first of this trio to appear in print in Canada: some of her poems even preceded her, appearing in the Cobourg *Star* in the fall of 1831, well before the Moodie family sailed from Edinburgh on 1 July 1832.[5] During the 1830s, Mrs. Moodie developed a prominent profile in Upper Canada's newspapers and magazines and in the New York *Albion* before becoming a major contributor to the *Literary Garland* (Montreal, 1838–51) and similar refined periodicals. However, Catharine Parr Traill was the first to issue a book about the New World when the Society for the Diffusion of Useful Knowledge published *The Backwoods of Canada: Being Letters from the Wife of an Emigrant Officer, Illustrative of the Domestic Economy of British America* (London, 1836). Its anonymous author was not yet identified when the volume was read by Anna Jameson in preparation for her own voyage to Canada later that year. "The book interested me," Jameson wrote to her friend, Ottilie von Goethe, "and pleased me very much, and it is thought to give so favourable a view of things, that they say it has made many persons emigrate." However, its contents also caused her to fear the coming winter: "The account in the book I sent you is enough to give one cold, only to read it. – It was the part I liked least, and I must say I shiver at the idea of my dressing-gown freezing to my skin and cracking when I take it off."[6] The extent to which Traill's optimistic description of her first years as a settler may have informed Jameson's account of her eight-month visit, published shortly after her return as *Winter Studies and Summer Rambles in Canada* (1838), is a topic that remains to be explored.

Anna Jameson

While the Strickland sisters authored many books about Canada from the perspective of settlers with a long-term commitment to their new home, Jameson's Canadian material is confined to a single title in which she

---

5 Carl Ballstadt, Elizabeth Hopkins, and Michael Peterman, eds., *Susanna Moodie: Letters of a Lifetime* (Toronto: University of Toronto Press, 1985), pp. 73–4. The poems were likely brought to Canada by the father-in-law of her brother, Samuel Strickland, who had emigrated in 1825.
6 G. H. Needler, ed., *Letters of Anna Jameson to Ottilie von Goethe* (London: Oxford University Press, 1939), pp. 59–60.

entertains European readers with her exotic experiences and personal opinions. She arrived as a recognized author of both travel-writing and cultural criticism, having published two books about her tours of the Continent as well as studies of historical and fictional women ranging from queens of England to Shakespeare's heroines. Accustomed to a cosmopolitan literary sphere, Jameson cast a critical eye on the colony's relatively crude social and cultural life. Toronto she likened to "a fourth or fifth rate provincial town, with the pretensions of a capital city"[7] and she initially judged Niagara Falls' reputation for sublimity to be "false or exaggerated" (p. 57). Much of her book's "winter studies" section records her study of German literature; it is in the second part, "summer rambles," that she claims the novelty requisite of the travel genre: "While in Canada, I was thrown into scenes and regions hitherto undescribed by any traveller ... and into relations with the Indian tribes, such as few European women of refined and civilised habits have ever risked, and none have recorded" (p. 9). Her casual idiom – "thrown into" – belies her careful plan to travel as extensively possible in order to satisfy her curiosity and also produce a saleable book. Similarly, the trope of modesty, which characterizes the preface in which the phrase appears, ironically highlights the substantial size of what she called her "little book" (which filled three volumes), while the powerful intellect displayed in her discussion of German literature and analysis of the conditions of women renders her text far more weighty than her self-deprecating description of it as "'fragments' of a journal addressed to a friend" (p. 9). As with Traill's first Canadian work, which purported to be a series of letters written to her mother, Jameson adopted the apparently private mode of writing to a close female confidante in order to offer the general reader a sense of intimacy within a very public medium, a strategy that in both instances yielded commercial success.

Jameson's visit to Canada, although undertaken reluctantly, brought both mental and physical liberation. When trapped indoors by winter she exercised her intellect, and when freed by the coming of spring, she undertook a "wild expedition" (p. 542) that began with a return to Niagara in June. She traveled overland to Hamilton and thence to Chatham, where she took a steamboat to Detroit. In mid-July she caught another steamer to Mackinaw, where she met the American ethnologist, Henry Schoolcraft, and Jane, his half-Native wife. Together the party travelled 94 miles to Sault Ste. Marie in a *bateau*, a small open boat rowed by five *voyageurs*, reaching Manitoulin Island in time for the

---

7 Anna Brownell Jameson, *Winter Studies and Summer Rambles in Canada* (Toronto: McClelland and Stewart, 1990 [1838]), p. 65.

annual Indian conclave. Jameson continued eastward on Lake Huron by canoe, returning to Toronto on August 17. Despite her claim to have traveled alone, she was never entirely by herself and was protected by her identity as "the 'chancellor's lady'" (p. 262). However, the unescorted nature of her journey attracted the attention of reviewers, who commended her for being the intrepid yet feminine figure she had deliberately constructed. Throughout her journey, in addition to taking notes Jameson filled her sketchbook. Omitted from her published volume, these drawings have survived, enabling us to see how her various self-depictions, in the words of Wendy Roy, "[represent] in concrete terms her solitude in terms of gender, and her femininity, gentility, and cultural origins."[8] Roy finds that Jameson's images tend to complement her written text, although at times they counter specific statements.

Ever the urbane cosmopolitan, on the lookout for both adequate bookshops and noble savages, Jameson discovered that first-hand experience of frontier North America, in its various stages of settlement, produced "inconsistent and apparently contradictory emotions and impressions" (p. 303). She achieved some resolution by identifying both the sublime and the picturesque in the terrain and its inhabitants. In addition to frequently commenting on the painterly aspects of specific scenes, she used painterly language to describe the landscape and she arranged the content of her pictorial sketches according to prevailing Romantic conventions.[9]

Jameson's travels brought her into direct contact with Aboriginal North America. In typical touristic mode, her written account links her preparatory reading to her visits to historic sites, such as the scene of Pontiac's siege of Detroit in 1763. "[I]t is *one* thing," she declared, "to read of these events by an English fireside, where the features of the scene – the forest wilds echoing to the war-whoop – the painted warriors – the very words scalping, tomahawking, bring no definite meaning to the mind, only a vague horror; – and quite *another* thing to recall them here on the spot, arrayed in all their dread yet picturesque reality." She validated Pontiac as "a man of genius" by likening him to "Caractacus or Arminius in the Roman history" (p. 334). When she reached Mackinaw, where she became good friends with the American Indian agent, ethnologist Henry Schoolcraft, and especially with his wife, Jane, daughter of an Irish fur trader and a Chippewa woman, Jameson's

---

8 Wendy Roy, "'Here is the picture as well as I can paint it': Anna Jameson's Illustrations for *Winter Studies and Summer Rambles in Canada,*" *Canadian Literature* 177 (Summer 2003), pp. 103–4.
9 Roy, "Here is the picture," pp. 105, 107.

engagement with the local culture was less directly mediated by European paradigms. The tinge of novelty prevails instead when *Winter Studies* presents the first print publication of three Indigenous stories "from Mrs. Schoolcraft's translation" which "have at least the merit of being genuine. Their very wildness and childishness, and dissimilarity to all other fictions, will recommend them to you" (p. 403).[10] Many of Jameson's visual sketches of anonymous Indigenous figures display a similar ethnographic quality, albeit several name their subjects and depict them as individualized human beings.

Jameson does not hesitate to point out the white man's failure – "Wherever the Christian comes, he brings the Bible in one hand, disease, corruption, and the accursed fire-water, in the other" (p. 310) – and approvingly quotes Sir Francis Bond Head's remark that "The fault of our executive is, that we acknowledge the Indians our *allies* yet treat them, as well as call them, our *children*" (p. 351). Yet she is also uncertain about the nature and future of Aboriginal people, who strike her as being "an *untameable* race" (p. 322) with little that she can recognize as being of cultural or intellectual value. "The taciturnity of the Indians," she opines, "does not arise from any ideas of gravity, decorum, or personal dignity, but rather from the dearth of ideas and of subjects of interest" (p. 402). She is eager to record their appearance and customs from the perspective of a relatively sympathetic imperialist, even though to do so may require discomfort: "The truth is, that a woman of very delicate and fastidious habits must learn to endure some very disagreeable things, or she had best stay at home" (p. 434). Her feminist interest in Native women led to her concern about their status and her delight in making the acquaintance of the cultivated mixed-race McMurray and Schoolcraft sisters, whose full-blooded mother, Mrs. Johnston, honored Jameson with "adoption" and a Chippewa name for being the first European woman to shoot the local rapids, albeit while a passenger in a Native-steered canoe.

The Strickland sisters: Susanna Moodie and Catharine Parr Traill

For Anna Jameson, as for Frances Brooke nearly a century earlier, travel to British North America represented a dramatic episode that contributed fresh material and a significant book to a London literary career. For the Strickland

---

10 See Robert Dale Parker, ed., *The Sound the Stars Make Rushing through the Sky: The Writings of Jane Johnston Schoolcraft* (Philadelphia: University of Pennsylvania Press, 2007).

sisters, however, emigration revealed the many difficulties involved in transferring an established literary life from the imperial center to the colonial periphery. Of the two, Susanna Moodie has achieved greater posthumous reknown, due in part to her appearance as an archetypal pioneer figure in Margaret Atwood's book of poems *The Journals of Susanna Moodie* (1970). Equally prolific, Catharine enjoyed a literary association with the New World that spanned seven decades, beginning with *The Young Emigrants; or, Pictures of Canada* (London, 1826). This unrealistically optimistic children's story, written long before Traill had any idea that she herself was destined to emigrate, was based on "scenes and events ... communicated to the writer by the members of a very amiable family, who emigrated to America in 1821."[11] Traill's last book was *Cot and Cradle Stories* (Toronto, 1895), issued after she had achieved distinction as the eldest living writer in the British Empire.

In the early 1830s, following rather late marriages to fellow half-pay army officers Thomas Traill and John Wedderburn Dunbar Moodie, the Strickland women emigrated to Douro township, near present-day Peterborough, in eastern Ontario. On the shores of Lake Katchewanooka, the Moodies and Traills took up adjoining grants of uncleared land beside the lot already occupied by their young brother, Samuel Strickland, sent to Upper Canada in 1825 to learn farming. For many years, critics constructed a dichotomy between the sisters, based on the different personas they constructed for their major books about their first years in the colony. The sunny temperament of the narrator of Traill's *The Backwoods of Canada* (1836) contrasts sharply with the often regretful and emotional narrator of Moodie's *Roughing It in The Bush; Or, Life in Canada* (1852). Subsequent publication of several volumes of the sisters' letters as well as a full-length dual biography has added considerable nuance to our understanding of their personal and professional lives as they descended into unprecedented poverty due to their husbands' incompetence as settlers. The public nature of the sisters' books tells little about their supportive companionship during many years of child-bearing which yielded five surviving children for Susanna and seven for Catharine. As they struggled to maintain their families in the bush and towns of Upper Canada, they found that writing became even more necessary for survival than it had been during their maiden days in England.

The manuscript of *The Backwoods of Canada*, which drew primarily on Catharine's first two years in the colony, was submitted for publication

---

11 Catharine Parr Traill, *The Young Emigrants; or, Pictures of Canada* (London: Harvey and Darton, 1826), p. iii.

early in 1835, before her greatest trials. With just one child to care for and the family's financial resources still intact, Catharine took a cheerful view of pioneer life, affirming that proper information would inevitably lead to agricultural and material success. Published in London in January 1836 as parts 57 and 58 of the Library of Entertaining Knowledge, *Backwoods* opens with an introduction by its editor, Charles Knight, extolling the book's unique value as "a faithful guide to the person on whose responsibility the whole comfort of a family depends – the mistress." "Indeed," he continues, "a woman's pen alone can describe half that is requisite to be told of the internal management of a domicile in the backwoods," and "well-educated females," who are "the pioneers of civilization in the wilderness," will especially benefit from Traill's honest representation of "facts in their real and true light."[12] These facts were selected, as Michael Peterman notes, to create "a narrative carefully crafted both to reassure British families with members already in the Canadas and to encourage wives and daughters of the families who were facing immigration to the colonies."[13] Some details regarding conflict, illness and delays were omitted, while others, such as the name of Traill's ship and the identities of people she met, were modified.[14] Structured as a series of eighteen letters to her mother dated from July 1832 to May 1835, Traill's narrative follows the usual traveler's mode of describing the natural and human scenery through the lens of European taste, noting, "To me nothing that bears the stamp of novelty is devoid of interest" (*Backwoods*, p. 40). On the difficult journey to their uncleared land, Traill met misadventure with determined cheerfulness, admitting that "sometimes I laughed because I would not cry" (p. 82). As the Traills painstakingly cleared their lot and built their farm, Catharine coped with privation by adopting the watchwords "Hope! Resolution! and Perseverance!" (p. 93). Her book provides advice about various practical matters such as how to make maple sugar and construct a root-cellar, and closes with images of future self-sufficiency that were to prove illusory. The Traills' "trust soon to enjoy the comforts of a cleared farm" (p. 226) would be broken by illness, crop failure, economic depression, and the Rebellion of 1837.

As with many of the works that Traill published in England, the production of this manuscript was overseen by Agnes Strickland, whose career as a London author of royal biographies blossomed after the departure of her youngest sisters. Yet despite Agnes's best efforts, Traill received a total of only

12 Catharine Parr Traill, *The Backwoods of Canada*, ed. Michael A. Peterman (Ottawa: Carleton University Press, 1997 [1836]), pp. 1–3.
13 Ibid., Introduction, p. xxvii.
14 Ibid., Introduction, p. xxvii.

125 pounds for this volume, which "was reissued at least eight times in London over the next twenty years," translated into German and French, and widely read by immigrants, including those sponsored by the Canada Company.[15] Its status as a Canadian classic was confirmed with the appearance of the first Canadian edition in 1929 and a scholarly edition in 1997 that incorporates later changes Traill wished to make.

Traill attempted to capitalize on the success of *Backwoods* with a sequel titled "Forest Gleanings." Unable to place the manuscript with a London or Edinburgh publisher, Agnes sold sections to various magazines, particularly *Chambers's Edinburgh Journal*. This periodical, along with *Sharpe's London Journal* and *The Home Journal*, would continue to publish pieces by Traill through the 1850s. Versions of these sketches also appeared in Toronto's *Anglo-American Magazine* in 1852–3, in a series likewise titled "Forest Gleanings."[16] During the 1850s, Traill also published in the *Snow Drop; or, Juvenile Magazine* (Montreal), and the *Maple Leaf* (Montreal).

The Backwoods of Canada entwines two major strands of Traill's subsequent Canadian writing: domestic advice for women, amplified with recipes and other forms of instruction, and delight in natural history – especially botany – which she regarded as a route to the Divine: "The simplest weed that grows in my path, or the fly that flutters about me, are subjects for reflection, admiration, and delight" (*Backwoods*, p. 14). The first strand culminated in *The Female Emigrant's Guide, and Hints on Canadian Housekeeping*, issued by subscription in Toronto in 1854–5, a venture that probably brought her no income at all.[17] The second strand yielded a series of titles about nature for both children and adults that included *Lady Mary and Her Nurse; or, A Peep into the Canadian Forest* (London, 1856), *Canadian Wild Flowers* (Montreal, 1868), and *Studies of Plant Life in Canada* (Ottawa, 1885). The two themes converge in Traill's major book for children, *Canadian Crusoes: A Tale of the Rice Lake Plains* (London, 1852), a narrative that also involves another of her ongoing interests, Canada's Indigenous inhabitants.

Like Anna Jameson, Moodie and Traill were intrigued by, and friendly with, Aboriginal women. *The Backwoods of Canada* and *Roughing It in the Bush* both sympathetically describe frequent interactions with the Chippewa

---

15 Ibid., Introduction, pp. xxxvi–vii, xl, xlii.
16 Michael A. Peterman and Carl Ballstadt, eds., *Forest and Other Gleanings: The Fugitive Writings of Catharine Parr Traill* (Ottawa: University of Ottawa Press, 1994), p. 8.
17 Carl Ballstadt, Elizabeth Hopkins, and Michael A. Peterman, eds., *I Bless You in My Heart: Selected Correspondence of Catharine Parr Traill* (Toronto: University of Toronto Press, 1996), pp. 24–5.

inhabitants of Upper Canada, who were being displaced by European settlers, a process presented by the Stricklands as the inevitable fate of a people they believed to be destined for extinction. Initially espousing the idealization of the Noble Savage inherited from British Romanticism, the sisters each progressed from curiosity to esteem, admiring the skills, crafts, and family practices of their "Indian friends." They felt a particular bond with Native women, on whom they projected their own maternal anxieties about the welfare of their children and their ability to survive in a difficult environment.[18]

Not a proponent of imaginative literature per se, Traill wrote *Canadian Crusoes* as a juvenile fictionalized survival guide. Set in the 1770s, this Robinsonade recounts the adventures of three Canadian adolescents – two Scots siblings and their half-French cousin – who survive quite handily while lost in the woods for several years. The "Friday" role is given to a Mohawk girl whom the European children name "Indiana" after saving her life, and who in turn saves them with her woodlore and hunting skills. The overt didacticism expressed in Traill's unsubtle imparting of facts, and her advocacy of a highly gendered social code for the settler children, are subverted by her presentation of Native characters. While the young white heroine learns to be a model housewife, Aboriginal women present strong countervailing images of knowledge and power. The story concludes when the rescued children are conveniently old enough to pair up in marriage. Herself a future grandmother of part-Native children, Traill sanctioned miscegenation in a Canadian society that drew strength from a blend of French, First Nations and Scottish heritages so long as the English language and British values prevailed.

Despite this book's considerable success in both Britain and the United States, its author's earnings were paltry. Traill received 50 pounds for the first British edition of 2,000 copies and a "present" of 50 dollars from the American firm that produced many impressions of its pirated edition. The second British edition brought her just 25 pounds more.[19] In 1867, she received another 40 from Nelson of Edinburgh for two corrected and retitled children's books: a new edition of *Lady Mary and Her Nurse* reissued in 1869 as *Afar in the Forest; or, Pictures of Life and Scenery in the Wilds of Canada* and the 1882 edition of *Canadian Crusoes* reissued as *Lost in the Backwoods. A Tale of the Canadian Forest*, under which title it remained in print for many decades.

18 See Carole Gerson, "Nobler Savages: Representations of Native Women in the Writings of Susanna Moodie and Catharine Parr Traill," *Journal of Canadian Studies* 32.2 (Summer 1997), pp. 5–21.
19 Catharine Parr Traill, *Canadian Crusoes: A Tale of the Rice Lake Plains*, ed. Rupert Schieder (Ottawa: Carleton University Press, 1986 [1852]), pp. xxxi–v.

Economic woes continually pursued Traill, along with the personal stress of coping with the increasing emotional depression of her husband, who died in 1859. The family moved frequently, and lost their home to fire in 1857. Yet even on the brink of starvation and despair, Catharine maintained her equilibrium, her letters recording the strong religious faith and social and family connections that sustained her until the age of ninety-seven. Now published, these letters document not only her extraordinary resilience, but also her centrality to the expanding generations of her offspring, relatives, and friends, who consoled and sheltered one another, fostered each other's children to enable them to obtain schooling and employment, and maintained a network of correspondence by copying and resending their letters.

Whereas Catharine wrote mostly prose, Susanna was best known as a poet during her first decade in the New World. Some of the verse she published in North America was recycled from *Enthusiasm; And Other Poems* (London, 1831). In Canada, more attention was paid to her poems on local topics: "The Sleigh-Bells. A Canadian Song" was reprinted many times following its first appearance in the *Albion* (New York) in 1833, as were "The Canadian Woodsman" (1834) and "Canadians Will You Join the Band. A Loyal Song" (1837).[20] John Lovell's founding of the *Literary Garland* in Montreal in December 1838 gave Moodie fresh inspiration and much-needed cash. Most of the colonies' early literary periodicals were short-lived ventures that commenced with enthusiasm and petered out in frustration. Run by the country's most savvy publisher, the *Garland* was distinctive for both its relative longevity and its regular payment to contributors. In *Roughing It in the Bush*, Moodie claimed that she "actually shed tears of joy over the first twenty-dollar bill" she received from Montreal,[21] although she allowed the dramatic exigencies of her narrative to advance the date of this event by a year. In the summer of 1839 she established her presence as one of the journal's major authors; by the time it folded in 1851, she had contributed some seventy poems, nine serialized novels, and twenty-one shorter pieces of prose. Traill, in contrast, published only a dozen pieces in the *Garland*.

In 1840 the Moodies moved to Belleville, on the north shore of Lake Ontario. Here they became more directly involved in the colony's literary life with the founding of the *Victoria Magazine*, which they edited from September 1847 until August 1848. Styled "A CHEAP PERIODICAL for the CANADIAN PEOPLE,"

---

20 John Thurston, *The Work of Words: The Writing of Susanna Strickland Moodie* (Montreal and Kingston: McGill-Queen's University Press, 1996), pp. 234–6.
21 Susanna Moodie, *Roughing It in the Bush; or Life in Canada*, ed. Carl Ballstadt (Ottawa: Carleton University Press, 1988 [1852]), p. 441.

the magazine aimed to induce "a taste for polite literature among the working classes" in order to stimulate "the mental improvement of the masses,"[22] expressing a meliorist philosophy that pervades the Moodies' other writings. The *Victoria Magazine*'s published list of 781 subscribers shows that it was supported primarily by residents of Belleville, with most other readers scattered in towns and settlements between present-day Toronto and Montreal. Other than a few pieces that Agnes sent from England and several by such local authors as Rhoda Anne Page, the majority of the contents, whether identified or not, were penned by the Moodies themselves, on topics ranging from classical Rome to current humor. Catharine's sole contribution was a two-part European story she had written at the age of sixteen. Unable to sustain the role of "literary philanthropists,"[23] the Moodies seemed destined to learn many things the hard way, from the unreliability of land speculators to the capriciousness of colonial cultural economics.

Susanna Moodie's Canadian career, characterized by acute awareness of the need to cater to different markets at home and abroad, was shaped by confidence and control. These features sometimes escape readers inclined to merge the naive, emotional and vulnerable character of "Mrs. Moodie," created to serve as protagonist in *Roughing It in the Bush*, with the real-life Susanna Moodie, the seasoned writer who carefully constructed an appealing narrative of culture shock and adaptation through which to dramatize her retrospective story of emigration and issue stern cautions to future settlers. Sometimes the boundaries between author and character blur, as when Moodie's pioneer persona claims that in the Canadian backwoods, in order to obtain social approval she "tried to conceal [her] blue stockings beneath the long conventional robes of the tamest common-place" (*Roughing It*, p. 215). Moreover, Moodie advised fellow author Louisa Annie Murray that "[t]he low esteem in which all literary labor is held in this country renders it every thing but a profitable employment";[24] this kind of statement has been taken to represent the failure of Canadians to appreciate and support a national literary culture. Yet, when we examine Moodie's publishing history, we see how fully she participated in a flourishing transatlantic print culture: the latter remark was written just as she embarked on her most productive decade, which saw six books published by Richard Bentley in London between 1852 and 1856. Two of these were Moodie's major Canadian titles, *Roughing It in the Bush*

---

22 "Editor's Table," *Victoria Magazine* 1.12 (August 1848), p. 287.
23 Ibid., p. 288.
24 Ballstadt, Hopkins and Peterman, *Letters of a Lifetime*, p. 99.

and its sequel, *Life in the Clearings versus the Bush*; the remainder were novels bearing little relation to Canada, despite their original serialization in the *Literary Garland*.

From the 1830s through the 1850s, Richard Bentley provides an important lens through which to examine the transatlantic literary relations of two major Canadian authors: immigrant Susanna Moodie and emigrant Thomas Chandler Haliburton. Quick to exploit British interest in American writers, Bentley added many significant names to his list, totaling more than fifty by 1857.[25] He issued titles on North America in various genres, with a predilection for travel and exploration, settlers' narratives, and fiction. Hence Bentley's crucial involvement with two of Canada's major authors of the early Victorian era is scarcely a coincidence.

Richard Bentley's acquaintance with the Moodies began with his publication of John Moodie's *Ten Years in South Africa* (1835) and resumed in 1851 when he received Susanna's manuscript that would appear as *Roughing It in the Bush*. Although Susanna never met her English publisher in person, they developed a warm epistolary friendship over the years he issued her books, the last in 1867. Tension arose when Bentley also published the only book to appear under the name of Susanna's brother, Samuel Strickland's *Twenty-seven Years in Canada West* (1853). Instigated and edited by big sister Agnes in order to restore her family's dignity which she felt had been denigrated by the coarseness of *Roughing It*, Sam's book was worse written and better paid. However, the success of *Roughing It*, followed by *Life in the Clearings*, restored the Moodie–Bentley relationship. Moodie hosted the visit of Bentley's son, Horace, to Upper Canada in 1858 and he assisted her in obtaining a grant from the Royal Literary Fund in 1865.

The Bentley connection enabled Moodie to cultivate a double audience. At home, she wrote for Canadians in her extensive contributions to the periodical press, while her books were all published in England and addressed a British audience. Without an English publisher, Moodie's book production would have been vastly diminished. Throughout the nineteenth century, Canadian book publication was, in George L. Parker's words, "almost an act of faith,"[26] and Americans preferred to pirate Canadian-authored work than to pay for it. Subscription publishing was the norm, but rarely likely to yield the envisioned income, as John Moodie learned with his *Scenes and Adventures, As a Soldier*

---

25 Royal A. Gettmann, *A Victorian Publisher: A Study of the Bentley Papers* (Cambridge: Cambridge University Press, 1960), p. 25.
26 George Parker, *The Beginnings of the Book Trade in Canada* (Toronto: University of Toronto Press, 1985), p. 67.

and Settler, During Half a Century (1866).[27] Today, one cannot help speculating whether Susanna Moodie's relationship with Bentley might have been less sanguine if she had known of his financial arrangements with Thomas Chandler Haliburton, which rendered Haliburton "undoubtedly the best-paid author in nineteenth-century Canada" according to Parker.[28] Whereas Moodie's earnings for her seven Bentley books seem to have totalled somewhat above 350 pounds, Haliburton received 300 pounds for the single volume of the second series of *The Clockmaker* (1838) and he requested 500 for the third (1840).[29]

In addition to seeing Moodie's professional career in relation to multiple audiences, appreciation of the full story contained in her major book requires attention to its double narrative: its simultaneous and at times contradictory stories of pioneer acculturation and literary accomplishment. *Roughing It in the Bush* is a composite volume that assembles sketches, essays and poems to create a somewhat autobiographical narrative that follows the Moodies from their arrival in 1832 through their first unhappy year on their cleared farm near Cobourg and their subsequent years on their uncleared land in Douro. It concludes with their 1840 escape from the woods to the town of Belleville, where they would enjoy a period of prosperity after John obtained the post of Sheriff of Victoria District. The book's self-contained chapters demonstrate Moodie's talent for entertaining and lively sketches of characters and events, even while expressing displeasure with the impertinences of disrespectful Yankees or disgust at the drunkenness that occurred at logging-bees. Last minute withdrawals and substitutions resulted in differing contents in the first few editions, with two chapters appearing later in *Life in the Clearings*. Three chapters and several poems by John Moodie and another chapter and poem by Samuel Strickland give *Roughing It* some aura of a family scrapbook.

A reading of this book that seeks an affirmative story of authorship finds its traces between the sections that celebrate such domestic successes as learning to bake bread and milk cows. In the preliminary pages, the sisterly dedication to Agnes Strickland, "Author of the 'Lives of the Queens of England,'" asserts a literary lineage, as does the publisher's advertisement that identifies Moodie as "a member of a family which has enriched English literature with works of very high popularity" and as the Susanna Strickland known for "a volume

---

27 Carole Gerson, "Mrs. Moodie's Beloved Partner," *Canadian Literature* 107 (Winter 1985), pp. 34–45.
28 Parker, *Beginnings of the Book Trade in Canada*, p. 65.
29 Carole Gerson, *Canada's Early Women Writers: Texts in English to 1859* (Ottawa: CRIAW, 1994), p. 23; Richard A. Davies, ed., *The Letters of Thomas Chandler Haliburton* (Toronto: University of Toronto Press, 1988), pp. 86, 109.

of Poems published in 1831."³⁰ At the same time, the epigraph on the original title page establishes a claim to tell the truth: "I sketch from Nature, and the picture's true; / Whate'er the subject, whether grave or gay, / Painful experience in a distant land / Made it mine own." This assertion of veracity contrasts sharply with Moodie's critique of the fraudulent misrepresentations of the New World in "public newspapers and private letters," described a few pages later in her Introduction (p. 4).

Moodie's authorial skill is directly evident in her adaptation of sketches originally published in Canadian periodicals for a local readership, to suit a two-volume work issued in England and addressing a middle-class British female audience. Unlike Catharine, whose *Backwoods* related recent events, Susanna drew on reflection and hindsight. Nearly half her chapters in the first edition of *Roughing It* were based on the eight sketches that originally appeared in the *Literary Garland* and the *Victoria Magazine* in 1847 and 1848. In these first versions, Moodie wrote to members of her own community who didn't need practical advice or to be reminded that a standard men's meal consisted of "potatoes and pork, washed down with a glass of whiskey," details later added to her book (p. 487). Nor did she depict her neighbors as speaking substandard English or as being squeamish about frontier medicine or relatively crude humor. Whether the modifications for British readers were made by Moodie herself or by an English editor, they dramatize her text by adding exclamation marks to the narrator's style and using dialect to reinforce class distinctions. Thus a simple opening question to readers of the *Literary Garland*, premised on familiarity – "READER, have you ever heard of a place called Dummer?"³¹ – acquired gothic overtones when revamped to stress strangeness: "Reader! have you ever heard of a place situated in the forest-depths of this far western wilderness, called Dummer?" (*Roughing It*, p. 463). Refinement of both content and language resulted in "damn" being changed to "hang," reductions in sexual innuendo concerning the marital adventures of old Woodruff, and the replacement of explicit bodily details by genteel circumlocution in the account of Brian the Still Hunter's suicide attempt. Changes in details range from inserting a plug for her sister as "the author of 'the Backwoods of Canada'" (p. 475) to discarding the presence of her husband in her account of landing at Grosse Isle upon their arrival in Canada. In this instance, Canadian readers were originally told that "My

---

30 Moodie, *Roughing It in the Bush*, pp. ix–x.
31 Mrs. Moodie, "Canadian Sketches. No. II. The Walk to Dummer," *Literary Garland* 5.3 (March 1847), p. 101.

husband alone remained"³² on board with Susanna and her daughter, whereas for British readers this episode of companionship was transformed to pathos: "My husband went off with the boats ... and I was left alone with my baby" (p. 16). In a similar fashion, *Roughing It*'s account of her years near Peterborough blurs the proximity of her sister and her brother in order to stress her sense of isolation. Whereas the purpose of the first sketches was to share stories and experiences with local readers, the thesis of the later book is that the strenuous work of clearing the land is best undertaken by those who are accustomed to manual labor. As a warning to middle-aged, middle-class immigrants not to replicate the Moodies' errors, *Roughing It* represents a sequel to Traill's *Backwoods*, recounting experiences of settlement through the sagacity of hindsight.

The only one of her books to be published in Canada during her lifetime, *Roughing It in the Bush* attained canonical status with the Toronto edition of 1871, for which Moodie wrote a new preface titled "Canada. A Contrast." Now reconciled to her life in a country that was quickly maturing into nationhood, Susanna Moodie concluded her personal and literary life on a celebratory note, marveling at the progress that had occurred during less than forty years, and anticipating "the fulfilment of a great and glorious destiny" (p. 674).

---

32 S. M., "Scenes in Canada. A Visit to Grosse Isle," *Victoria Magazine* 1.1 (September 1847), p. 15.

6

History in English and French, 1832–1898

E. D. BLODGETT

"But we *ought* to know about it," said Hélène. "It's history."
"That makes it all the worse. If it were fiction I wouldn't care."[1]

Fiction and history before Confederation

Although the events of history are always at the mercy of the historian, some moments seem to be worthy of greater investment than others. In the cultural history of Canada, the decades of 1760 and 1830 are clearly seminal. The first marks the end of the French zone of influence in North America as an extension of French rule. This is also the period when, in the course of early settlement, various visions of what came to be called British North America were put forth. While the country was to acquire such a name, the name masked a continual competition between the changing perspectives toward First Nations, on the one hand, and anglophone and francophone Canada, on the other. It was also the decade in which the printing press arrived in the former French colony. 1830 stood for the decade in which the argument, particularly between anglophone and francophone Canada, took on a more violent character and led to a series of decisions and compromises that issued in the Act of Confederation. It marks, then, the second major *prise de conscience* of the changed colony when, among other things, the efforts toward creating national literatures began to bear serious fruit.

1830 was a decade that came to an end in a failed attempt by both French and English Canada to persuade the Crown of the virtues of responsible government. The new decade concluded with the *Report* by Lord Durham (1839), which contained the remarkable observation that the French in

---

[1] Mercer Adam and A. Ethelwyn Wetherald, *An Algonquin Maiden: A Romance of the Early Days of Upper Canada* (Montreal and Toronto: Lovell and Williamson, 1887), p. 199.

Lower Canada were "a people with no history, and no literature."[2] Given such cultural deficiencies, assimilation could be their only fate. It was a decade that plunged the Canadas into an identity crisis, which the *Report* proposed to resolve simply through union and responsible government. It articulated what had become the task of the 1830s and what would remain the task for at least a century, which was to articulate the narratives that would provide consensual identities for several cultures. The dominant discursive modes for tracing the arguments, at least in the nineteenth century, were fiction and history. As modes of perceiving the past, they both pose problems specific to their methods of recovery. Since most of the world either believes or accepts that historical time is linear, rather than cyclical, it is not only implicit that there is a *plan événementiel* that implies sequence, but also that there are accidents that cannot be foreseen. Why at the Battle of the Plains of Abraham, one might ask, did Montcalm choose to attack Wolfe without waiting for Bougainville to attack from the rear? The answer to such questions requires that the historian take what evidence is provided and develop a persuasive argument that will put order in the events so that the resulting sequence appears reasonable. Inasmuch as history is not historiography, fiction is less so, but it bears, nevertheless, a double relation with history both as it happens and as it is written.

The period we are addressing took much of its ideology from European Romanticism, for which history was charged with providing primary knowledge of human activity in the gradual diminution of transcendent explanations. Thus both genres were in many ways given the not insignificant task of developing identities and national aspirations, and often representing moral positions that competed in many ways with the sense of morality provided by religion. Rather than a scene of the unforeseen, history was asked to become an informing spirit. To this end, its use in fiction was to place characters in extreme situations, so that the moral vigor of their actions could be seen with greatest clarity. Hence, certain moments are privileged in which large issues are at stake, notably, *le grand dérangement* or deportation of the Acadians in 1755, the Battle of the Plains of Abraham, the American War (1812–14), the revolts of 1837–8, and, for French Canadian writers, the renewed wars of the late seventeenth century with the Iroquois and American settlers. The history that imaginative writing drew upon, and vice versa, was constructed as ideological and moral drama. It did so by satisfying the appetite of both

---

2 Gerald M. Craig, ed., *Lord Durham's Report* (Toronto: McClelland and Stewart, 1963), p. 150.

anglophone and francophone Canada for historical narrative that, in the process of articulating national identity models, provided heroic deeds, legitimated the dominant ideological perspective, and authenticated the moral compass of the novel.

Inasmuch as we are considering a long period in the history of Canada, I have divided it into two periods, the first one ending in 1866, just before Confederation. Political and cultural activities in the Canadas before 1867 were characterized by constant struggle, apparent in the major historians of the period, that is François-Xavier Garneau and John MacMullen. While the struggles did not cease after that date, they assumed a changed character, particularly because appeals could be made to what appeared a more settled political situation.

Searching for identities: 1832–1844

The fiction that draws its inspiration from historical writing is historical romance, and the relation of romance to history is more complementary than oxymoronic. The beginning of such fiction in Canada is John Richardson's *Wacousta; or, The Prophecy: a Tale of the Canadas* (1832). It poses the fundamental problem of all historical romance: too much history can overwhelm the romance. Richardson's solution to this dilemma was stated candidly in the Introduction to the 1851 edition: "The story is founded solely on the artifice of Ponteac [sic] to possess himself of these last two British forts. All else is imaginary."[3] The complexity of the solution reflects, nevertheless, the social and political situation in the Canadas in the early years of the nineteenth century. The novel seizes upon antinomies of "new" and "old" worlds, already developed in the detached gaze of Frances Brooke's *The History of Emily Montague* (1766) and skillfully toyed with in Julia Catherine Beckwith Hart's *St. Ursula's Convent, or, the Nun of Canada* (1824) and energizes them to a degree that comes close to destroying their previous difference. Wacousta, a former Cornishman adopted by the Ottawa, seems in the course of the narrative to change his being, while continually moving between his European and Native character. By so doing, he at once dramatizes and problematizes the theme of identity which motivates the genres of both romance and national historiography. Wacousta is driven by one

---

3 John Richardson, *Wacousta or, The Prophecy; A Tale of the Canadas*, ed. Douglas Cronk (Ottawa: Carleton University Press, 1987 [1832]), p. 585.

desire: to avenge the treachery of his former comrade, Colonel de Haldimar, who persuaded Wacousta's fiancée to marry him in a brief absence of Wacousta.

The full story of deceit and treachery, however, is not revealed until near the end. As a consequence, the hero of conventional romance – youthful and innocent – is perceived as the opposite: old, embittered, and implacable, but capable of exposing both sides of his character, and going so far as to murder two of the children of the colonel who most resemble his former beloved. Delaying revelation enhances the sense of mystery and allows for the characteristic blurring of identities common to romance, but in a manner that emphasizes the grotesque and the brutal, as if romance, when thrust upon the raw conditions of life in the new colony (the time period directly follows the Cession of Canada to England in 1763) could only unravel.

The first francophone novel,[4] François-Réal Angers's *Les Révélations du crime ou Combray et ses accomplices: Chroniques canadiennes de 1834* (1837), as its subtitle implies, prefers history to imagination. While closer to what might now be called "docu-drama," it owes a great deal to the romantic valorization of subjectivity, making use of the device of confession, which allows the perpetrator of the crime to speak apparently *in propria persona*, to give personal perspectives, employ flashbacks, provide conversations, and lift the chronicle above the level of being merely a police report. Like romance, furthermore, it responds to a taste for violence and, especially, characters placed in extreme situations.

The wake of Lord Durham: 1839–1858

The decade of the 1830s concluded in rebellion and Lord Durham's *Report* (1839). While neither fiction nor historiography, it influenced both profoundly. Its recommendations of constitutional reform along British lines reverberate both in francophone history and in anglophone ideology. It prompted a dual identity that separated the Canadas at the same time as it united them. French Canada was driven to identify with its past, and English Canada began to dramatize the virtues of loyalty to the Crown, for, as the *Report*, asserts: "The attachment constantly exhibited by the people of these Provinces

---

4 Because of its more enduring reception, *Le Chercheur de trésors ou L'Influence d'un livre* by Philippe Aubert de Gaspé *fils* is often credited with being first, but it appeared a few months later (John Hare, ed., *Les Révélations du crime ou Combray et ses accomplices* [Montreal: Réédition-Québec, 1969], p. iv, note 3).

towards the British Crown and Empire, has all the characteristics of a strong national feeling."⁵

While not a direct response to the *Report*, Richardson's *The Canadian Brothers; Or, The Prophecy Fulfilled. A Tale of the Late American War* (1840), plays down the author's preoccupation with disguise so prevalent in his first novel in order to lay a greater emphasis on Durham's theme of loyalty. It begins with a challenge to one of the brothers' loyalty and subsequently relates loyalty to the nation to *affaires d'honneur*. The central spring of the action is the curse laid on the de Haldimar family at the beginning of *Wacousta* which is fulfilled at the end of *The Canadian Brothers*, first in an act of fratricide that occurs at the end during the battle of Queenston Heights (1813) and finally in the murder of the last of the de Haldimar family. In this instance, the two brothers are innocent victims, which places the moral onus on Wacousta and his influence. It implicitly condemns the rebel leader. An initial francophone response is Régis de Trobriand's *Le Rebelle: histoire canadienne* (1842) set during the Rebellion of 1837. Against the battle of St. Charles, it poses three figures: the rebel hero (Laurent de Hautegarde), his beloved, and his rival (Barterèze) who is in league with the British. Both names appear allegorical, implying a political struggle. Curiously, the woman is the daughter of a loyal Irish immigrant, whose son is killed by the rebel, destroying the hope of Alice's father for a match that would have joined the two peoples. The conclusion is unclear: either Alice, in her allegorical role as a future Quebec, died broken-hearted or entered a convent. The ideological implication is, however, clear: no union is possible.

Joseph Doutre's *Les Fiancés de 1812* (1844) is one of the many novels that poses a problem of genre. Although it comes close to history in the hero's saving Châteauguay, thus evoking a famous battle won by French Canadian forces under the command of De Salaberry, most of the novel avails itself of the techniques of comic romance. The hero's beloved is almost immediately seized by pirates (whose chief later turns out to be her brother whom she has never known); nearly at the same time the hero himself saves her father's life without the father's recognizing him. In true romance fashion, an object the hero loses in saving the father turns up later so that his identity is revealed, causing the repressive father to overlook the hero's impoverished upbringing and to give his permission for the marriage. An interesting subplot is provided by the hero's friend. He marries a Native woman, who

---

5 Gerald M. Craig, ed., *Lord Durham's Report* (Toronto: McClelland and Stewart, 1963), p. 143.

satisfies contemporary standards by becoming civilized and fluent in French in less than two years. Like most romance plots, the hero's success in war and love depends on subterfuge. The endurance of the book depends less on its plot than its preface, which resolutely declares its moral difference with the more frivolous French novel of the period. Although unpersuasive, the argument set a pattern for future novel writers as a means of developing personal autonomy.

Although moral difference became a necessary motif in the rhetoric of autonomy in the course of the century, it was not believed in the instance of Doutre, who was a member of the liberal Institut canadien, which was often sternly attacked by Church authorities. Equally liberal, but more consistent in his practice, François-Xavier Garneau's epoch-making *Histoire du Canada depuis sa découverte jusqu'à nos jours* in 1845 (second edition 1852) earned him the title of French Canada's national historian. The title signals immediately the theme of "discovery," and thus rivals somewhat the role of Columbus, implying the large role played by French explorers in North America. Although not French Canada's first historian (that was Pierre-François-Xavier de Charlevoix), Garneau was the first to make history modern in the sense of such French Romantics as Jules Michelet. In so doing, he provided the first and most durable riposte to the deprecatory remarks of Lord Durham and a number of other English Canadian historians, such as William Smith and Robert Christie. He gave French Canada a usable past along with a *"projet de société"* and so gestured toward countless twentieth-century postcolonial histories.

Historiography, of course, is a work always in process, and those historians who last do so on the strength of the voice employed and the ideology distilled. Garneau is striking to the extent that, while continually memorializing a glorious past and celebrating heroes who survive against great odds, the romantic rhetoric one might expect is reduced to the barest essentials. His frequently cited description of the Iroquois destruction of the village of Lachine in 1689 is a fine example of horror that is notable precisely for its lack of enhancement: "Ils ouvrent le sein des femmes enceintes pour en arracher le fruit qu'elles portent, et contraignent des mères à rôtir vifs leurs enfants."[6] Speaking of the defence of Quebec and the failed effort to recapture it in 1760, he remarks: "Quant à l'armée, le simple récit de ses combats et ses travaux

---

6 "They open the womb of pregnant women and tear out the fruit they bear, and force mothers to roast their children alive." François-Xavier Garneau, *Histoire du Canada depuis sa découverte jusqu'à nos jours*, 6 vols. (Montreal: François Beauval, 1976 [1845]), vol. I, p. 388. Translations are my own.

suffit pour faire son éloge."⁷ The consequence of the unadorned account bestows upon the narrative its allure of authority, providing order, solidity, and the sense of inevitability that carries tragedy with it. Garneau's favorite words are verbs designed to shape history as action and forward movement. His portraits are rare, but incisive. In preparing Montcalm for service in New France, his life, career, and faults are given in a few sentences: he is timid in strategy but so bold in combat as to go beyond prudence.⁸ The style, then, combined with his contempt of the French monarchy and the colonial government, foregrounds his mid-century liberal ideology of social and individual autonomy.⁹

The second historiographical response to Durham is contained in the four volumes of James Huston's *Le Répertoire national: ou, le recueil de littérature canadienne* (1848–50), which consists of a miscellany of material gathered from a number of sources that form a kind of historical pulse of French Canadian culture. It reprinted, for example, Patrice Lacombe's *La Terre paternelle* (1846), and contained a number of texts that are designed to shape national identity, particularly from the perspective of the Church. Compared, however, with Octave Crémazie, who created for French Canada the durable historical poem, the poets gathered in the *Répertoire* are not much better than gifted amateurs. Much of Crémazie's durability may be attributed to the efforts of Father Henri-Raymond Casgrain, who lauds him as "notre premier poète national" and links him conspicuously in the same essay with Garneau, "notre historien national."¹⁰ This was no small praise, as Casgrain assumed a central role in the institutionalization of French Canadian literature in the second half of the nineteenth century. The link with Garneau is not entirely gratuitous, however, and the sharing of themes, particularly in Crémazie's "Le Drapeau de Carillon (1858)," a poem frequently set to music because of its nationalistic fervor and memorializing of Montcalm's defeat of the British at Fort Ticonderoga (1758), is clearly evident. Set at the end of France's reign in Canada, it celebrates Canadian intrepid heroism despite Bourbon weakness. Unlike that of Garneau, Crémazie's style is highly rhetorical and unstintingly elegiac. But the intent is at once shared and indicative of a

---

7 "As for the army, the simple account of its battles and efforts suffices as elegy." Ibid., vol. III, p. 274.
8 Ibid., vol. III, p. 108.
9 See Serge Gagnon, *Le Québec et ses historiens de 1840 à 1920* (Quebec: Les Presses de l'Université Laval, 1978), p. 292.
10 Henri Raymond Casgrain, "Le Mouvement littéraire au Canada" (1866), in *Œuvres complètes*, 4 vols. (Montreal: Beauchemin et fils, 1896), vol. I, pp. 365, 355.

constant nineteenth-century preoccupation: Carillon's flag emerges as a sign for the symbolic capital the French Canadians invested in "leur langue et leur foi."[11]

Constructing French Canada as tragedy: 1862–1865

The role of symbols is of course paramount in national identity formation, and sometimes, in their absence, they require creation *ex nihilo* in order to enter time. Evangeline was one such figure, invented by Henry Wadsworth Longfellow (1847), reinvented in free translation by Pamphile Le May[12] (1865), and subject of several operas, of which two were produced in the nineteenth century. She was also the model for a statue by sculptor Philippe Hébert, commissioned by the Dominion Atlantic Railway and erected outside the memorial church in Grand-Pré. Fiction brought her into history, and necessarily, inasmuch as every effort was made to suppress the documentation of what is known as *"le grand dérangement"* ("great upheaval"). Thomas Haliburton, for example, was unable to discover any records in his history of 1829, suggesting that the parties involved in the forced removal may have "carefully concealed" all the incriminating documents.[13] Furthermore, while Longfellow heard the story of the Acadians from the American historian George Bancroft, the historic level of the story is not explored in the poem.[14] Longfellow prefers to think of it as a story set in "the forest primeval" (a prehistoric moment), and to allow it to unfold in a kind of Edenic America, where Evangeline spends her life chasing the elusive Gabriel. The elements of pastoral romance are privileged: the invading army can serve as pirates, and the separation of the lovers before marriage is a convention, as well as the reunion, bittersweet as it is at the end of their lives. Because, however, the lovers represent the family, the central socially ordering principle of

---

11 Octave Crémazie, *Œuvres complètes* (Montreal: Beauchemin et fils, 1896), p. 137. For a sober account of the battle, see Garneau, *Histoire*, vol. III, pp. 159–68. The French army was outnumbered in the order of five to one.
12 The name has also been spelled LeMay and Lemay.
13 Thomas Chandler Haliburton, *An Historical and Statistical Account of Nova Scotia*, 2 vols. (Halifax: Joseph Howe, 1829), vol. I, p. 196, note.
14 John Mack Faragher, *A Great and Noble Scheme* (New York: Norton, 2005), p. 455. Garneau, whom Faragher does not mention, had, however, commented at some length on the removal of the Acadians, citing the initial French source, Guillaume-Thomas-François de Raynal, *Histoire philosophique et politique des établissements et du commerce des Européens dans les deux Indes* (Amsterdam: La Haye, 1770), extensively (*Histoire*, vol. III, pp. 81–8).

Acadia, and their adventures are construed as a collective symbol of a violently repressed history, they thus transcend romance and fiction.[15]

The problems posed by *Evangeline* are somewhat inverted in Philippe Aubert de Gaspé's *Les Anciens Canadiens* (1863), a novel of which 15 per cent consists of notes and explanations. The author's intent is to situate his novel in history in such a way as to blur the fictional by the truth-claims inherent in historiography, thus prompting Casgrain's comment in his biography of the author: "il n'y a presque pas une ligne de cet ouvrage qui n'ait sa réalité dans la vie de notre peuple."[16] Such a reality is more than "effects of the real," as Roland Barthes would remark.[17] It is, rather, an effect of the true, which distinguishes the historical novel from realism. His use of Garneau also sets a pattern for subsequent novels. Rather than cite him, he praises him for his efforts to give French Canada a remembered past, thus not drawing on him for support, but treating him implicitly as a fellow historian.[18] He shares his themes of the abandonment of New France by the monarchy and the loyalty of French Canadians, but without explicitly citing him as a source, suggesting the real possibility of an independent, mutual perspective.[19] The historicity of the novel is of two kinds: major tableaux, such as the battle of the Plains of Abraham, and scenes that belong to "la petite histoire," that is, the story of private lives, making it typical of a novel of manners.[20] In this respect, it responds to an interest in selected aspects of history forming a national past that writers like James MacPherson Le Moine provided in *Maple Leaves*, collected at intervals from 1863 to 1906.

As for the plot, the protagonist is Archibald Cameron of Locheill, whose Jacobite father sided with Bonnie Prince Charlie and lost at Culloden. Consequently, he is treated as an outsider in the British army, supporting his ambiguous but sympathetic relationship with the d'Haberville family. Because of his efforts to assist the French Canadians during the siege of Quebec, which included saving his friend Jules d'Haberville's life, he is

---

15 According to Christoph Irmscher, Le May's changes tended to "mythicize" Longfellow's text. See *Longfellow Redux* (Urbana and Chicago: University of Illinois Press, 2006), p. 249.
16 "There is scarcely a line in this work that does not have its reality in the life of our people." Casgrain, *Œuvres*, vol. III, p. 273.
17 Roland Barthes, S/Z (Paris: Seuil, 1970), p. 88: "le rire, le gant sont des effets du réel" ("the laugh, the glove are effects of the real"), my translation.
18 Philippe Aubert de Gaspé, *Les Anciens Canadiens* (Montreal: Boréal, 2002 [1863]), p. 237.
19 Ibid., pp. 236, 288, 349.
20 Gaspé's use of the domestic, local past is often that of an eye witness, which suggests that the line between fiction and non-fiction is deliberately blurred. Casgrain's institutionalizing of Aubert de Gaspé through biography has a similar effect.

subsequently forgiven by the d'Haberville family for his part in destroying their house, and for being on the wrong side, except by Blanche who, faced with a dilemma worthy of Corneille, prefers duty to sentiment and refuses to marry him. In this respect she follows a pattern set by Alice in Trobriand's *Le Rebelle*, ideologically incarnating, despite the intimate friendship they enjoy for the rest of their lives, the honor that Louis XV so easily abandoned.

Georges Boucher de Boucherville's *Une de perdue, deux de trouvées* (1849–51, 1864–5) in its publication history alone suggests its divided character. The first thirty-three chapters were published separately, and it was later completed with material that allowed it to move from being an adventure novel to historical fiction. In this respect, it seems to have been primarily a means of making money for its author, but its dual character did not prevent it from becoming quickly canonized. Besides being frequently republished, it was given pride of place in the first significant history of the literatures of Canada.[21] While the first part, set mostly in New Orleans, is romance, in which the hero endeavors to recover his inheritance and saves the heroine from pirates, the sequel is set in Quebec during the Rebellion. Much of the second part is based on personal experience, and the author mentions himself in passing as one of the *patriotes*. Striking, however, is the use of the hero in the sequel who easily consorts with both sides, despite his sympathies for the *patriotes* because of an infatuation with a sister of one their leaders. The theme of liberty, raised in the slave revolt in the first part, is strangely elided in the sequel, and the hero marries the English Governor General's cousin. Of note is his freed slave, Trim, reminiscent of Native companions in James Fenimore Cooper, who is looked upon as his closest friend and treated like a bodyguard. Like many other Canadian heroes, Pierre de St-Luc represents upper-class interests that remove him from what may be called a people's history, and allows him to project an identity model of someone capable of duty but easily drawn into the plot of romance.

Searching for autonomies: 1664–1866

The first appearance of a major historical novel in English following Richardson's *The Canadian Brothers* was Rosanna Leprohan's *Antoinette De Mirecourt; or, Secret Marrying and Secret Sorrowing* (1864),[22] which was, like a

---

21 See Edmond Lareau, *Histoire de la littérature canadienne* (Montreal: John Lovell, 1874), p. 289.
22 An earlier novel, *Le Manoir de Villerai: Roman canadien* (1861), has not earned the same reputation.

number of her other novels, immediately translated into French and as well received in translation as in English. It is more romance than historical fiction,[23] but its setting just after the Conquest and its dramatization of interaction between the upper-class English and French give it a historical allure. The plot is simple, consisting of the trials of Antoinette, who secretly marries an English fortune hunter, but refuses consummation after realizing her error and is not released from her vows until another suitor kills her husband in a duel, allowing her to marry the man she loves. The book was praised in both cultures for its moral fortitude. Of ideological interest is the fact that, although her father wants her to marry a French Canadian, she prefers a British officer, as paternal as her father, who is willing to save her honor. The very fact that she marries an Englishman is already somewhat scandalous, but despite Leprohon's fine cultural sense, her sensibilities are English enough to permit it.

The period before Confederation ends with Edward Hartley Dewart's *Selections from Canadian Poets* (1864), which contains some biographical notes and critical commentary. It is the first anglophone effort to gather some of its poetry.[24] As such, it is a significant early record of national identity formation,[25] despite the usual Victorian position on the moral ideals of poetry with which the Introduction is imbued. Significantly, in respect of national identity, he raises the matter of Canada's "colonial position," which has had a negative effect on the development of "an indigenous literature,"[26] and so the anthology plays a significant, if limited, role when compared to French Canadian collections of the period, in moving toward an autonomous history of one's own.

Such a history is implicitly the purpose of most historical fiction, and Napoléon Bourassa's *Jacques et Marie: Souvenir d'un people dispersé* (1865-6) is the major text of the nineteenth century designed to recover the Acadian losses of the years 1755-62. Relying frequently on Haliburton and other sources, he carefully interweaves the historical and the psychological levels of the novel, centering the issues on Marie, who is torn between saving her parents and marrying a British officer or following her father's advice and

---

23 Rosanna Leprohan, *Antoinette De Mirecourt; or, Secret Marrying and Secret Sorrowing* (Ottawa: Carleton University Press, 1989 [1864]), p. 236.
24 Brief biographies of notable Canadians had already been compiled by Henry J. Morgan in his *Sketches of Celebrated Canadians, and Persons Connected with Canada, from the Earliest Period in the History of the Province Down to the Present Time* (Quebec: Hunter, Rose, 1862).
25 Edward Hartley Dewart, "Introductory Essay," in *Selections from Canadian Poets* (Toronto: University of Toronto Press, 1973 [1864]), p. ix.
26 Ibid., p. xiv.

remaining Acadian for Jacques. Not only does she choose the latter, but her moral fortitude so touches her rather cynical British suitor that he makes noble gestures for the French cause and dies a Catholic convert. The close rapport between the Acadians and the Mi'kmaqs is illustrated in the figure of Wagontaga, who only supports the Acadians as a free spirit, suggesting the same kind of figure as representations of Tecumseh. It is evident that Marie is used as a kind of allegory for Acadia and designed, like many other female characters, to carry the moral conflict of such a role. Unlike her father, who knows the past conveys its meaning, she must learn it and manifest its suffering in her torn emotions. She becomes a kind of figure of sanctity in the process, anticipating the heroines of Laure Conan who gradually accommodate a male world.

Canada besieged: 1868–1880

Other than the passage of the British North America Act, which brought three decades of unrest and debate to a kind of conclusion, the year 1867 produced no historical fiction but it found a historiographic response in the second edition of John MacMullen's *The History of Canada: From its First Discovery to the Present Time* (1855, 1868). Although the title echoes Garneau's, it is unacknowledged; and its *retentissement*, at least among general readers and subsequent anglophone historians, seems almost as broad, even if he is rarely referred to now. The second edition has been selected because of the close coincidence of Confederation with which it concludes. Confederation legally symbolizes MacMullen's theme, namely, the emergence of responsible government, encompassing two cultures in a single nation and fulfilling the proposals of the Durham *Report*.[27] In contrast to Garneau's emphasis on *la survivance*, it became the master-narrative of anglophone history in the nineteenth century, and only someone of "British descent" could have written it.[28]

Joseph Marmette's *François de Bienville, scènes de la vie canadienne au XVIIe siècle* (1870) at once confirms the promise of his *Charles et Éva* (1866) and establishes his presence as author of historical fiction. Frequently appealing to the female reader, Marmette follows the pattern of placing the heroine

---

27 M. Brook Taylor, *Promoters, Patriots and Partisans: Historiography in Nineteenth-Century English Canada* (Toronto: University of Toronto Press, 1989), p. 154.

28 John MacMullen, *The History of Canada from Its First Discovery to the Present Time* (Brockville: McMullen and Co., 1868 [1855]), p. 478. See also Carl Berger, *The Writing of Canadian History: Aspects of English-Canadian Historical Writing 1900 to 1970* (Toronto: Oxford University Press, 1976), p. 2.

between two males, one a Bostonian, the other French. Although the choice is clear, the representation of the Bostonian becomes increasingly monstrous as the siege of Quebec continues (1690). Every effort is made to follow historical evidence for the life and death of Bienville in order to assure the reader, through the appeal to documented evidence drawn from Garneau, Jean-Baptiste-Antoine Ferland,[29] Pierre-François Xavier Charlevoix, and others, that the story is more than fiction. If the heroine is to be construed allegorically as French survival in North America, then she is, like many others, a sign of sacrifice for enduring against overwhelming odds. Despite MacMullen's belief in a united country, sacrifice is the shared theme between the two cultures. Loyalty to the respective mother countries is also tested, which is why in the case of anglophone novels the War of 1812 is exemplary and why francophones prefer the Rebellion of 1837–8. Thus, Agnes Maule Machar's *For King and Country: A Story of 1812* (1874) addresses a border war (1812) along both geographical and ideological lines, allowing Ernest Heathcote understanding of both the American and the Canadian positions. Remaining consistently in favour of the Loyalist cause, he wins the mind of the woman he loves, her Tory father, and his British rival. In a text that includes Scottish, English and American immigrants, as well as Tecumseh, it is evident that history is used to present a number of identity possibilities, held firmly in control through the filter of an Anglo-Canadian ideological narrative perspective.

If Richardson errs too far in the direction of imagination, John Talon Lespérance's *The Bastonnais: Tale of the American Invasion of Canada 1775–76* (1877) may be accused of depending too much on historiography. The sentimental level of the plot, however, engages two couples, and the conclusion sharply modifies the reader's expectation. Their marriages are designed, as they frequently are, to mark significant ideological compromises between enemies, in this instance between French Canadians, an American, and the son of a Scottish immigrant who is perfectly assimilated into the culture of Quebec. The historical foundation of the novel is the American siege of Quebec of 1775–6 and the possibilities it poses for liberation from British

---

29 Next to Garneau, Ferland is the other major francophone historian of the nineteenth century. His history covers the period of la Nouvelle-France from a decidedly ecclesiastical perspective as a gift "à la religion et à la patrie." See his *Cours d'histoire du Canada*, 2 vols. (Quebec: Augustin Côté, 1861), vol. I, p. xi. Although novelists continued to cite Garneau as well as Ferland, see Réjean Beaudoin, *Naissance d'une littérature: Essai sur le messianisme et les débuts de la littérature canadienne-française (1850–1890)* (Montreal: Boréal, 1989).

"tyranny." Historiographical references are frequent, especially to Simon Sanguinuet's journal *L'Invasion du Canada par les Bastonnois* (1870), and, combined with the narrator's self-representation in the last paragraph, are designed to lift the novel above the constraints of fiction into a zone of truth.

More fluid is the approach of William Kirby in *The Golden Dog* (1877), written, nevertheless, within the shade of Le Moine, Benjamin Sulte, and Francis Parkman. Next to *Wacousta*, it is the one anglophone novel of the nineteenth century that has best stood the test of time and, indeed, in both cultures. Like most of the historical fiction of the period, its ideology is Tory, and it delights in the decadence of the French regime at the end of its reign in North America. It draws on most of the conventions of Gothic romance, aligning good against evil, allowing the latter the greater scope, and revelling in terror and horror. When the heroine's brother is sufficiently corrupted and tricked into murdering her future father-in-law, the merchant who runs Le Chien d'or, she refuses marriage and withers away from tuberculosis. The interplay of history and legend is also romantic to the point where historical characters such as l'Intendant Bigot expressly lose their historical veracity, allowing the novel, which Parkman urged to see in print,[30] to challenge implicitly the convention of truth. Not unnoticed in Quebec, it received a grateful reception through Le May's felicitous translation (1884), which was prefaced by an editor's note, generally thought to be Le May's, praising its representation of the distinctive character of life in New France.[31]

W. H. Withrow's *Neville Trueman, The Pioneer Preacher: A Tale of the War of 1812* (1880) like Machar's novel also chooses the American War as a test of loyalty. In this instance, the figure tested is an American Methodist preacher who, in Canada when the Americans attacked, is constructed as a border-figure who chooses Canada, thus articulating the ideological perspective of the novel. As a preacher, he represents the moral point of view of the novel, which eventually overcomes the Tory desires of the heroine's father to have his daughter marry a British captain. The relationship to historiography is especially striking, inasmuch as the historian most frequently cited is the author himself, a popular historian dismissed by his contemporary John G. Bourinot

---

30 See Carole Gerson, *A Purer Taste: The Writing and Reading of Fiction in English in Nineteenth-Century Canada* (Toronto: The University of Toronto Press, 1989), p. 114.

31 In a subsequent Preface, the historian Benjamin Sulte, whose own history privileges the *habitant* of New France, praised Kirby at Parkman's expense, because Parkman failed to see the people of New France and make it known. See *Le Chien d'or*, trans. Pamphile Le May (Quebec: Librairie Garneau, 1926 [1916]), p. 11.

as a historian lacking in originality.³² Since he was also a Methodist preacher, the use of history is primarily a moral and ideological reinforcement of the argument designed, as the concluding pages repeat, to illustrate the theme of Canadian patriotism.

Canadianizing First Nations: 1851–1887

It is now evident that the historian Francis Parkman was not above challenges of the novel, and he was accused in 1985 by by the American historian Francis Jennings of being mendacious and in fact writing fiction. Nevertheless, *The Oregon Trail* (1847–9) established him as a brilliant historian, and his *Montcalm and Wolfe* (1884) was considered a masterpiece. In Victorian English Canada his work was held in the same regard as that of Garneau in French Canada, and while we might consider it fiction today, it was then considered "truth" and fit easily within the dominant ideological order of things. This would be true of both his denigrating representation of First Nations, which may be found everywhere in the *History of the Conspiracy of Pontiac, and the War of the North American Tribes against the English Colonies after the Conquest of Canada* (1851), and his negative understanding of the French regime in North America. Both fit with his dominant theme of the superiority of Anglo-American culture, as the last paragraph of the first chapter of *Montcalm and Wolfe* asserts, consisting of a series of oppositions that invariably establish Anglo-America as the natural future. His denigration of the French included Acadia, and he easily underplayed their expulsion, exciting the wrath of Father Casgrain, one of his promoters in French Canada.³³

The Natives of North America are normally given ideological functions in both the historiography and fiction of the nineteenth century. The "noble savage" is the inverse of Parkman's representation; and when the Native appears, especially in narratives of the War of 1812, it is primarily as part of the ideological dynamics of the story. As we have seen, that war in fiction was a test of loyalty to the Crown, and every nationality was tested. The Native, such as Tecumseh, who passed the test, was "noble." Thus, Charles Mair in his serious five-act play, *Tecumseh: A Drama* (1886), contrasts Tecumseh with his brother, and the latter is found wanting. But Tecumseh's loyalty to General Brock is sufficient to make him appear as reliable as any United Empire

---

32 See Taylor, *Promoters*, p. 255.
33 Casgrain, *Œuvres*, vol. II, pp. 294–335.

Loyalist, which in light of Tecumseh's own politics appears forced.[34] Laura Secord in Sarah Anne Curzon's play (1887) by the same title is on the point of death at the end of Act II, when she is rescued by friendly Native Americans and safely brought to the British at Beaver Dam. The larger frame within which they are placed is that of the heroic woman, which is clearly downplayed in MacMullen's *History*.[35]

In Mair and Curzon it is evident that the historical moment informs and defines the psychological level of the plays. In *An Algonquin Maiden: A Romance of the Early Days of Upper Canada* (1887) by G. Mercer Adam and A. Ethelwyn Wetherald, the drive toward parliamentary reform of the 1820s is merely ideological background. The purpose of the novel is to set the opposition between radical reform and unswerving Toryism, represented to a degree by Allan Dunlop and Commodore MacLeod, whose daughter he eventually marries, forming a compromise between the two extremes. They have nothing ostensibly to do with the Algonquin maiden with whom MacLeod's son is infatuated. This level of the novel addresses the manner in which she is excluded from upper-class Upper-Canadian society in time-honored fashion. Edward "discovers" she is nature, and thus ever at odds with "culture."[36] As she is the last, in a sense, of her people, her subsequent suicide is an exorbitant sacrifice for the orderly emergence of responsible government. Finally, if we assume the title underlines the primary plot, the secondary plot concerning reform appears only as a means of establishing ideological identities, suggesting that the novel comes closer to pseudo-historical fiction.

The Canadas become Victorian: 1887–1898

Louis Fréchette's *La Légende d'un peuple* (1887) was perhaps inevitable: Garneau's sobriety simply needed lyric effusion to be fulfilled. Less an epic than a series of episodes published separately from 1882 to 1886, it not only calls to mind Victor Hugo's *La Légende des siècles* but also inscribes France as its implied reader in the dedication and at moments in the text. Its meta-narrative is that of France's abandonment of her colony, interwoven with the quest for liberty. The poem is structured to foreground heroes whose role is to find recognition. Its three parts celebrate a history of discovery and settlement, the struggle against the English, and efforts to keep the flame of freedom alive

---

34 See James Wilson, *The Earth Shall Weep: A History of Native America* (New York: Grove Press, 1998), pp. 154–5.
35 MacMullen, *History*, p. 281.
36 Adam and Wetherald, *An Algonquin Maiden*, p. 192.

after the Conquest. The struggle for the most part is dramatized as an affair of masculinity, and when, for example, the Ursuline Convent is celebrated, it is because of the ash tree that "vit tous nos héros."[37]

John Hunter-Duvar's five-act tragedy *De Roberval: A Drama* (1888) is distinguished, for one reason, because it is one of the few texts devoted to a colonizer. His colony failed after a year. When he returned seven years later, he perished at sea, and it is implied that this was because of his refusal to assist his niece in her affair with a man beneath De Roberval's respect. The other reason it is distinguished is for the question it raises about Canada: "... is't a country in the world at all?"[38] Edmond Rousseau's preface to his novel *Les Exploits d'Iberville* (1888) raises a concern found among most novelists in Victorian Canada, particularly after Zola, regarding the moral utility of novels.[39] Like Marmette, he does not hesitate to note historians, usually Ferland, and it is evident the sentimental plot is subordinate to the main plot of d'Iberville's heroic action in order to "faire aimer et connaître une de nos gloires nationales."[40] Like anglophone novelists, he selects incidents which exalt the hero who overcomes impossible odds. As he also notes in his preface, the text is a "compilation,"[41] but it is compiled in order to carry the "frivolous" reader through three explicit steps to reach the moral vision of the novel: 1) Yvonne's escape from American captor to reunite with future husband, 2) d'Iberville's brilliant seamanship accompanied by the valor of Yvonne's suitor, which demonstrate glory, and 3) use of text as ideological polemic through references to Ferland. It is maladroit, but exemplary.

The same moral imperative governs W. D. Lighthall's Introduction to his *Songs of the Great Dominion: Voices from the Forests and Waters, the Settlements and Cities of Canada* (1889). The history he provides is simple enough: it begins with Jacques Cartier. The land is settled by Samuel de Champlain and filled with the romance of New France, which disappears in the panorama of the Conquest, and which is followed by the arrival of the Loyalists and "a steady unfolding of culture and power," an arrival which is grandly related to the *Aeneid*'s exiles' founding of Rome.[42] The book is designed to represent

---

37 Louis Fréchette, *La Légende d'un peuple* (Montreal: Éditions Beauchemin, 1941 [1877]), p. 85. ("Sees all our heroes.")
38 John Hunter-Duvar, *De Roberval: A Drama* (Saint John: J. and A. McMullen, 1888), p. 48.
39 For anglophone Canada, see Gerson, *Taste*, p. 29. Edmond Rousseau, *Les Exploits d'Iberville* (Quebec: C. Darveau, 1888), pp. viii–ix.
40 "In order to bring about loving and knowing our national glories." Rousseau, *d'Iberville*, p. 61.
41 Rousseau, *d'Iberville*, p. 10.
42 William Douw Lighthall, *Songs of the Great Dominion* (London: W. Scott, 1889), pp. xxii and xxiii.

the major male Confederation poets, a few women, and, in a revealing appendix, a few francophone poems chosen for their medieval charm. The identity model provided by history springs from the discourse of British Imperialism. A more balanced perception of the French character of Canada is provided by Machar and Thomas G. Marquis in their *Stories of New France* (1890), dedicated to George Monro Grant and Charles G. D. Roberts, two stolid central Canadians. Shaped, as the Authors' Preface remarks, in the spirit of Parkman and Fréchette, its aim is to confederate the peoples of Canada through "gradual and peaceful fusion."[43]

Robert Sellar's *Hemlock: A Tale of the War of 1812* (1890) takes its place among other novels of the War of 1812 that celebrate loyalty, especially on the part of First Nations. The eponymous hero is a Native chief who is a modelled on both the "noble savage" figure of Tecumseh and Emily Brontë's Heathcliff. Loyalty goes beyond the Crown and includes the relationship between Hemlock and the British officer Morton, as well some German immigrants. Hemlock dies over half-way through the novel, opening the rest of the plot to the heroic deeds of Morton and his eventual marriage to a settler's daughter, Maggie Forsyth, thus linking Old and New Worlds to the advantage of Canada as Morton finds more to admire in North America.

Laure Conan's *À l'œuvre et à l'épreuve* (1891), written under the influence of Casgrain, is one of the few novels devoted to the missionary work of the Jesuits. Already having shown a talent for psychological analysis in her *Angéline de Montbrun* (1881–2), Conan conjoins both history and psychology in her second novel to a degree not found among earlier novelists. Her theme, as in her other novels, is sacrifice, and, in this instance, the heroine is more or less abandoned by Father Garnier, who becomes a martyr. Textually, the novel operates on several levels, making use of self-representation in the heroine's diaries and imagined letters from Father Garnier, and also drawing verbatim upon the *Relations* of the Jesuits. The narrator further supports the historicity of the text with references to Garneau, Parkman, Chateaubriand, Ferland, and Casgrain. The great test is both Garnier's and hers as she learns to sublimate her love. Ideologically, the novel is a perfect product of the late nineteenth-century French Canadian Messianic narrative.

Designed to inspire the reader, historical fiction in the nineteenth century in Canada is rarely deliberately humorous. Robert Barr's *In the Midst of Alarms* (1894) has a tenuous claim on history through both its humor and its brief

---

43 Agnes Maule Machar and Thomas G. Marquis, *Stories of New France: Being Tales of Adventure and Heroism From the Early History of Canada* (Boston: D. Lothrop, 1890), n.p.

dramatization of the Fenian Raid of 1866. Most of it consists of a sentimental love story that is only coincidentally related to the abortive raid. Gilbert Parker's *The Seats of the Mighty: Being the Memoirs of Captain Robert Moray, Sometime an Officer in the Virginia Regiment and Afterwards in General Amherst's Regiment* (1896) constitutes the other extreme in its lack of humor and inflated rhetoric, and, in spite of the author's emphasis on destiny in the Introduction, privileges chance as much as the other romances of the period, as has been done since Greek Antiquity.

His work, esteemed, but not quite on par with that of either Sir Walter Scott or William Kirby, depended on bold deeds and, emphatically in this instance, on the bravery of a young woman against a shrewd and powerful antagonist. The luck of the hero, Captain Moray, brings down Quebec in 1759 and earns the love of the woman who braves French power, inaugurating a Canada that appealed to late Victorian Imperialism. Moray is based on the *Memoirs of Major Robert Stobo of the Virginia Regiment* (1800), but the woman and her enemy were invented for the sake of the novel. The strength of the novel rests upon the characters as the sources of its motivation and moral tenor, so that the Conquest is closely woven into Moray's desire to save his beloved, who suffers temptation unscathed and reaches the point where her father overlooks the Protestant religion of Moray.

The final history of the period, *A History of Canada* (1897), was narrated by Charles G. D. Roberts, and its structure and style are both characteristic of its author's narrative skill. It carries MacMullen's theme – the triumph of responsible government – but within a form of clearly marked triumphalism. Its three parts are stated early: French Dominion, English Dominion, and Confederation, and the latter, according to the argument's conclusion, held out the possibility of Imperial Federation. The center, from 1812 to 1848, is dominated by the pressure for responsible government, a theme kept alive in John Charles Dent's *The Last Forty Years: Canada Since the Union of 1841* (1881).[44] Roberts was also a translator of Aubert de Gaspé's *Les Anciens Canadiens* (*Canadians of Old* [1890]), and in his Introduction he notes the author's central preoccupation, namely, "a loving memory for his people's romantic and heroic past," and then remarks that "it would be well for the distant observer to view the French Canadians through the faithful medium which de Gaspé's work affords him."[45] Beyond language and certain institutions, French Canada appears to have no other place in the Dominion seeking a place in the Empire.

---

44 See Taylor, *Promoters*, p. 250.
45 Charles G. D. Roberts, *Canadians of Old* (Toronto: Hart, 1891 [1890]), p. 4.

Appropriately, the last francophone historical novel of the century, Ernest Choquette's *Les Ribaud: Une idylle de 37* (1898), echoes *Les Anciens Canadiens*, especially because of the morally difficult position in which Dr. Ribaud's daughter is placed when she falls in love with a British officer during the Rebellion of 1837. Dr. Ribaud has lost his son, who duelled with a British officer in defence of Quebec, and he himself represents all the values that the father does in Aubert de Gaspé's novel. The other echo is that the daughter's lover finds a way to avoid fighting the *patriotes* by allowing another officer, Archie Lovell, to impersonate him. The echo of Archie (Cameron) of Locheill seems rather deliberate. The central issue, however, is the theme of sacrifice and redemption that the daughter must act out as she learns that her father, like the father of the d'Haberville family, represents tradition and the French presence in North America. Since the daughter is the maternal future of the people, her choice of an appropriate husband must conform with the ideology of the father. Fortunately, the village priest sanctions the union that the father finally sees is morally acceptable, permitting the union that never quite occurs in Aubert de Gaspé's novel.

How fitting such a conclusion of this conflicted century seems to be in its earnest search for an identity in a country that so often seemed at odds with itself. Lord Durham's hopes and recommendations that French Canada might eventually disappear were met with various responses from both sides of the cultural divide, coming to temporary closure in a symbolic marriage that, characteristic of the high moral tone of the century's literature and history, transfigures both sides of the conflict through supreme acts of sacrifice. The century of progress it may have been, but progress only made possible through an understanding that nations emerge in catastrophe.

PART TWO

*

THE POST-CONFEDERATION PERIOD

7
Post-Confederation poetry

D. M. R. BENTLEY

Prelude and the precursors of the Confederation group

"Whereas the Provinces of Canada, Nova Scotia, and New Brunswick have expressed their Desire to be federally united into One Dominion under the Crown of the United Kingdom of Great Britain and Ireland. ..." When the British North America Act, of which these are the opening words, came into effect on July 1, 1867, the ground was prepared for the growth of what many expected would be a robustly northern national culture. Some seeds had already been sown and more were expected quickly to follow. While Confederation was barely a gleam in its fathers' eyes, one of its most eloquent proponents, Thomas D'Arcy McGee, published a collection of *Canadian Ballads* (1858). During the Dominion's infancy even one of its most vehement opponents, Joseph Howe, was persuaded to assemble for publication a selection of the verses that would appear posthumously in 1874 in his *Poems and Essays*. In that year, "the Canadian Burns," Alexander McLachlan, followed *The Emigrant, and Other Poems* (1861) with *Poems and Songs* (1874), and in 1877 the arch-Tory William Kirby followed *The U. E.: A Tale of Upper Canada in XII Cantos* (1859) with *The Golden Dog (Le Chien d'or: A Legend) of Quebec* (1877). An English translation of Philippe-Joseph Aubert de Gaspé's racially conciliatory historical romance *Les Anciens Canadiens* (1863) had preceded Confederation and another would follow, albeit not until 1890, by which time Edward Hartley Dewart's anticipatory *Selections from Canadian Poets* (1864) had given way to William Douw Lighthall's stridently Canadian *Songs of the Great Dominion* (1889). In the interim, Louis Honoré Fréchette's *Les Fleurs boréales* (1879) had won the prestigious Prix Montyon of the Académie Française. Here is "our first national poet," enthused Nicholas Flood Davin; "his imagination ... is steeped in local tints ... The heroes of Canadian history call forth the deepest and most touching notes of his lyre ... The national poet is a singer, in whose song we find his time and country.''[1]

In English Canada, Fréchette's signal success provided food for disconcertment as well as celebration. With publishing houses enough, newspapers in every city and town of any size hungry for poems to grace their pages, and magazines on both sides of the Canada–US border eager to publish poems on Canadian subjects, the condition of Canadian poetry seemed robust enough. But were verses about Canada's "[l]akes ... mighty rivers ... snowy landscapes ... bright skies ... vast solitudes ... [and] sonorous pines" (p. 272) necessarily the ingredients of a literature of distinction in both senses of the word? Were such volumes as Charles Mair's *Dreamland and Other Poems* (1868) and John Reade's *The Prophecy of Merlin and Other Poems* (1870) in any way comparable to *Les Fleurs boréales*, let alone to volumes published during the same decade by Tennyson, Swinburne, Whitman, Whittier, and other English and American poets? Was English Canada's failure to produce a poet of Fréchette's stature evidence of cultural or even racial inadequacy? By the late 1870s and early 1880s, the misgivings that such questions reflect were becoming increasingly apparent in Ontario and the Maritimes, but in 1880 they began to be allayed by the publication of a collection of poems the cosmopolitan themes and technical virtuosity of which could sustain the proposition that, at last, English-Canadian poetry had transcended mediocrity and provincialism. That volume was *Orion, and Other Poems* by Charles G. D. Roberts, and within a year it had prompted the best-known Eureka moment in Canadian poetry – a moment of the kind described by Margaret Avison in "Voluptuaries and Others" as a "lighting up of the terrain / That leaves aside the whole terrain ... / But signalizes, and compels, an advance in it."[2]

Romantic nationalism and the formation of the group

The setting for that moment was the grounds of Trinity College, Toronto in May 1881. Its Archimedean figure was Canada's finest nineteenth-century poet, Archibald Lampman, who was then in the second year of a degree in Classics. Ten years later, in "Two Canadian Poets," a lecture delivered before the Literary and Scientific Society of Ottawa, where he was by then working

---

[1] Nicholas Flood Davin, "Great Speeches," *Rose-Belford's Canadian Monthly and National Review* new series 7 (March 1881), p. 272.
[2] Margaret Avison, *Always Now: The Collected Poems*, 3 vols. (Erin: The Porcupine's Quill, 2003), vol. I, p. 117.

in the Post Office Department, Lampman recalled what happened with the vividness of a flashbulb memory:

> One ... evening somebody lent me *Orion and Other Poems* ... Like most of the young fellows about me I had been under the depressing conviction that we were situated hopelessly on the outskirts of civilization, where no art and no literature could be, and that it was useless to expect that anything great could be done ... I sat up all night reading and re-reading "Orion" in a state of the wildest excitement and when I went to bed I could not sleep. It seemed to me a wonderful thing that such work could be done by a Canadian, by a young man, one of ourselves. ... A little after sunrise I got up and went out into the College grounds ... [E]verything was transfigured for me beyond description, bathed in an old world radiance of beauty, the magic of the lines that were sounding in my ears, those divine verses, as they seemed to me, with their Tennyson-like richness and strange earth-loving Greekish flavour. I have never forgotten that morning, and its influence has always remained with me.[3]

How soon after that momentous morning the two poets were in contact is not known, but within eighteen months Roberts was writing to Lampman at length about various literary "schemes" and about his desire to move from his native New Brunswick to Ontario in order "to get together literary and independent Young Canada, and to spread ... [the] doctrine ... [of Canadian Republicanism] with untiring hands."[4]

Almost certainly the driving force behind Roberts's plan was Joseph Edmund Collins, the transplanted Newfoundlander and professional journalist whom he had come to know while teaching in Chatham, New Brunswick in 1879–82. Collins was staying with Lampman when Roberts wrote to him about his plans and hopes, and he was already working covertly to enhance Roberts's literary reputation and place him in a professorship at the University of Toronto. (The attempt failed, though Roberts did get to Toronto in 1883–4 as editor of *The Week*, a "Journal of Literature, Politics, and Criticism," and in 1885 he took up a professorship at King's College in Windsor, Nova Scotia, where he remained until 1897.) Whatever the immediate sources of Roberts's plan, however, the ancestry of his conception of Young Canada lay in the Young Ireland and (to a lesser extent) Young England movements and, beyond these, in German Romantic nationalism and the German

---

3 Archibald Lampman, *Essays and Reviews*, ed. D. M. R. Bentley (London, ON: Canadian Poetry Press, 1996), pp. 94–5.
4 Charles G. D. Roberts, *Collected Letters*, ed. Laurel Boone (Fredericton: Goose Lane Editions, 1989), p. 29.

Counter-Enlightenment. A belief in the interdependence of literature, especially poetry, and national identity was central to these precursors, as was an environmental determinism that posited an affective relationship between a nation's physical environment (landscape, climate), the mentality of its inhabitants, and hence, its artistic productions. Neither Roberts nor Lampman was entirely convinced that the characteristics of Canadian literature were or would be environmentally determined but both gave voice to the doctrine. "Our climate with its swift extremes is eager and waking," wrote Roberts in "The Outlook for Literature: Acadia's Field for Poetry, History and Romance" (1886), "and we should expect a sort of dry sparkle in our page, with a transparent and tonic quality in our thought."[5] In "Two Canadian Poets" Lampman identified different environmental influences and literary outcomes to make a similar point:

> In the climate of this country we have the pitiless severity of the climate of Sweden with the sunshine and sky of the north of Italy ... A Canadian race ... might combine the energy, the seriousness, the perseverance of the Scandinavians with something of the gayety, the elasticity, the quickness of spirit of the south. If these qualities could be united in a literature, the result would indeed be something novel and wonderful.[6]

Inspired by a zealous form of patriotism known at the time as "Canadianism," Roberts figured the new Dominion as a "Child of Nations, giant-limbed" that was heir to a great heritage of "Saxon force ... Celtic fire," and heroic resistance to American incursion, but still immaturely dependent on Mother Britain,[7] and he set about identifying poets – men – of sufficient youth, skill, accomplishment, and potential to give Canada the poetry of distinction that it deserved – indeed, required – if it was to achieve national manhood. After Lampman came Bliss Carman, Roberts's cousin and fellow New Brunswicker, then William Wilfred Campbell, an Ontarian whose first two collections were published in New Brunswick while he was living there from 1888 to 1890, then Lampman's Ottawa friend and fellow civil servant Duncan Campbell Scott,

---

5 Charles G. D. Roberts, *Selected Poetry and Critical Prose*, ed. W. J. Keith (Toronto: University of Toronto Press, 1974), p. 261.
6 Lampman, *Essays and Reviews*, p. 93.
7 Charles G. D. Roberts, *Collected Poems*, ed. Desmond Pacey and Graham Adams (Wolfville, NS: Wombat Press, 1985), p. 85. By 1888 Roberts had ceased to support Canadian independence and come to regard imperial federation with Britain and her other dependencies as the best way to protect Canada from economic and political union with the United States. It was apparently the annexationist beliefs of the proprietor of *The Week*, Goldwin Smith, that caused Roberts to resign his editorship of the journal after only a few months.

and finally the most peripheral and least gifted of the group and its only Quebecker, Frederick George Scott. With the exception of D. C. Scott, whose father was a Methodist minister, all six poets had personal or family connections with the Church of England (in fact, F. G. Scott was an Anglican priest, as was Campbell until 1891). Without exception, all were born in the early 1860s and thus came to maturity after Confederation.

In retrospect, Roberts was inclined to add such writers as E. Pauline Johnson, Helena Coleman, and Albert E. Smythe to his "little band."[8] In their heydey in the early 1890s, however, "the 1860s group" or, as they would come to be known, "the poets of Confederation" or simply "the Confederation poets," were six young men bound in a "loose Confederation"[9] under Roberts's leadership who to a greater or lesser extent shared his belief that "workmanship"[10] was a more indispensable ingredient of a literature worthy of Canada than were blatantly Canadian themes and subjects. At their peak in the *annus mirabilis* of 1893, members of the group enjoyed a level of international and national recognition unprecedented in English-Canadian literature and never since surpassed in Canadian poetry. Their poems were appearing regularly in newspapers and magazines in England and the United States as well as Canada, and each had at least one substantial and well-received collection to his name: Lampman, *Among the Millet, and Other Poems* (1888), F. G. Scott, *The Soul's Quest and Other Poems* (1888), D. C. Scott, *The Magic House and Other Poems* (1893), Carman, *Low Tide on Grand Pré: A Book of Lyrics* (1893), Campbell, *Snowflakes and Sunbeams* (1888), *Lake Lyrics and Other Poems* (1889), and *The Dread Voyage: Poems* (1893), and Roberts himself *In Divers Tones* (1886) and *Songs of the Common Day, and Ave: An Ode for the Shelley Centenary* (1893) as well as *Orion, and Other Poems*.

Literary influences and therapeutic nature

The Hellenic title of Roberts's first collection and the allusions to Tennyson's *In Memoriam* and Wordsworth's "Intimations" Ode in the titles of the second and third reflect in small the classical background and Romantic-Victorian roots of the Confederation group as a whole. Heavily exposed to the Classics at school, all turned to Greek and Roman literature, mythology, and history for themes and forms, all but F. G. Scott wrote of Pan as either the embodiment of

---

8 Roberts, *Collected Letters*, p. 173.
9 W. J. Keith, *Canadian Literature in English* (New York: Longman, 1985), p. 33.
10 "Workmanship," "craftsmanship," and their cognates are terms that appear frequently in Roberts's essays and letters; see, for example, *Selected Poetry and Critical Prose*, p. 258 and "Edgar Fawcett," *The Week* 1.30 (26 June 1884), p. 472.

Nature or a type of the poet, and in "The Pipes of Pan" (1886) and "Favorites of Pan" (1895) Roberts and Lampman contrived to render Pan's spirit present in the New World. Carlylean to the core and keen to distance themselves from other and earlier Canadian writers such as Charles Sangster, whom they regarded as technically and intellectually inferior,[11] they found their heroic *beaux-idéaux* in the Romantic Poet and the Victorian Sage and Man of Letters. To Roberts, Keats was the "glorious ... Titan of poets,"[12] Wordsworth was a poet whose "influence" was to be welcomed because his work is "so high, so ennobling, so renovating to the spirit,"[13] and Arnold was "second to no living English writer in prose or verse ... so tolerant, so lucid and unprejudiced, so broad in his grasp, and so exquisite in his expression."[14] "Keats has always had such a fascination for me and has so penetrated my whole mental outfit that I have an idea that he has found a sort of faint reincarnation in me," wrote Lampman in 1894; "I am only just now getting quite clear of the spell of that marvellous person; and it has taken me ten years to do it."[15] In "Shelley" (1887) and "Ave: An Ode for the Shelley Centenary" (1893), first Carman and then Roberts associated beloved portions of the New Brunswick landscape with the spirit and character of the English poet, and in "Ode for the Keats Centenary" (1921) D. C. Scott envisages the Canadian Arctic as an appropriate refuge for the anti-modern "Spirit of Keats" and implores that Spirit to "unfurl [its] deathless wings" in Canada and to "Teach us ... Beauty in Loneliness."[16] Scholars may have underestimated the extent to which the Confederation group's perceptions of the Romantics were mediated by Arnold, Pater, and other Victorians, but the use of such terms as "Northern Romanticism"[17] to describe their work has the merit of identifying one of its primary matrices.

It is but one indication of the extent to which the poets of the Confederation group sought to emulate the English Romantics that debts to Wordsworth's

---

11 "[T]his writer's verse ... [is] not worth a brass farthing," remarks J. E. Collins of Sangster in his chapter on Canadian "Thought and Literature" in *The Life and Times of the Right Honourable Sir John A. Macdonald: Premier of the Dominion of Canada* (Toronto: Rose, 1883), p. 496; "[h]is name only appears here that he may not be confounded with Canadian poets."
12 Roberts, *Collected Letters*, p. 40.
13 Roberts, *Selected Poetry and Critical Prose*, p. 274.
14 Roberts, *Collected Letters*, p. 30.
15 *An Annotated Edition of the Correspondence between Archibald Lampman and Edward William Thompson (1890–1898)*, ed. Helen Lynn (Ottawa: Tecumseh Press, 1980), p. 119.
16 D. C. Scott, *Poems* (Toronto: McClelland and Stewart, 1926), pp. 153–4.
17 Tracy Ware, ed., *A Northern Romanticism: Poets of the Confederation* (Ottawa: Tecumseh Press, 2000).

"Tintern Abbey," Keats's "Ode to Autumn," and other poems with a substantial landscape component can be discerned in the imagery, diction, syntax, stanza forms, and overall attitudes of many of their most characteristic and important works. To be sure, the seaside setting and dactylic rhythm of Robert's first masterpiece, "Tantramar Revisited" (1886), are Swinburnian, but the tone and mood of its opening lines and much that follows are those of Wordsworth's great return poem: "Summers and summers have come, and gone with the flight of the swallow; / Sunshine and thunder have been, storm, and winter, and frost ... Only in these green hills, aslant to the sea, no change!"[18] In "April" (1888) Lampman appropriately uses the season of burgeoning to establish the theme of psychological and spiritual regeneration through immersion in the natural world as a major theme of *Among the Millet, and Other Poems*, but the manner in which he does so is redolent of "Ode to Autumn": "Pale season, watcher in unvexed suspense, / Still priestess of the patient middle day, ... / Maid month of sunny peace and sober gray, / Weaver of flowers in sunward glades that ring ..."[19] The lake of Campbell's *Lake Lyrics* is Lake Huron and the cadences of many of the lyrics are again Swinburnian, but the "ghost-like shores," the "looming" "Crags," the "Wastes of desolate woods," and the "great forms" "Towering stern"[20] of poems such as "The Winter Lakes" (1889) which Campbell himself regarded as the strongest in the collection, come trailing clouds of gloom from the boat-stealing episode and elsewhere in *The Prelude*.

The Carman of "Low Tide on Grand Pré" (1893), the lyric that records his seminal mystical experience, had been spiritually inclined since boyhood. The F. G. Scott who recalls "imbibing the ... mysterious life message" of some "glorious old trees" in "In the Winter Woods" (1906)[21] was an orthodox Christian. The D. C. Scott who meditates on the spiritual progress of humanity in "The Height of Land" (1916) was something of a neo-Platonist. Yet all three poets came to Canadian Nature, as did their three *confrères*, with a Wordsworthian "sense sublime / Of something ... deeply interfused" in all things,[22] and with the correspondingly vague terminology of Romantic-Victorian natural supernaturalism: "Spirit of life or subtler thing ... / The secret of some wonder-thing" (Carman),[23] "a subtle bond ... linking / Nature's

---

18 Roberts, *Collected Poems*, p. 78.
19 *The Poems of Archibald Lampman*, ed. Duncan Campbell Scott (Toronto: Morang, 1900), p. 4.
20 William Wilfred Campbell, *Poems* (Toronto: William Briggs, 1905), pp. 346–7, 352.
21 F. G. Scott, *Collected Poems* (Vancouver: Clarke and Stuart, 1934), p. 177.
22 *Poetical Works of William Wordsworth*, ed. E. de Sélincourt, 2nd edn., 5 vols. (Oxford: Clarendon Press, 1952 [1940–9]), vol. II, p. 262.
23 *Bliss Carman's Poems* (Toronto: McClelland and Stewart, 1931), p. 4.

offspring through and through" (F. G. Scott),[24] "Something [that] comes by flashes / Deeper than peace, – a spell / Golden and inappellable" (D. C. Scott).[25]

This is not to say that the work of the Confederation group was shaped only by the English Romantic-Victorian tradition. While at college, Lampman was impressed by German patriotic poetry and his most important long poem, *The Story of an Affinity*, although composed in 1892–4 and not published until 1900, originated in an 1884 plan to write "a strictly Canadian poem, local in its incident and spirit, but cosmopolitan in form and manner ... sober and realistic ... in the metre of [Longfellow's] Evangeline but more like [Goethe's] Hermann and Dorothea or ... [Edmund Gosse's] translations from ... [the] Swedish poet [Johan Ludvig] Runeberg."[26] Campbell was heavily influenced by Poe as well as Longfellow, and in 1892 he praised the "tales" of the Norwegian writer Bjørnstjerne Bjørnson as mirrors of his country and its people, "who are so much akin to us" in their northernness.[27] In the same year, D. C. Scott expressed his admiration for Ibsen's *Hedda Gabler* and *The Lady from the Sea* as well as for the *Journal intime* of the Swiss writer Henri Frédéric Amiel. A major influence on his thinking on spiritual matters are the essays of the Belgian *symboliste* Maurice Maeterlinck, whose plays were translated in the mid-1890s by Carman's friend and collaborator Richard Hovey and lie centrally in the background of Scott's and Roberts's first collections of short fiction, *In the Village of Viger* (1896) and *Earth's Enigmas: A Book of Animal and Nature Life* (1896). Mallarmé and other French *symbolistes* are presences in the *Vagabondia* volumes (1894–1901) of Carman and Hovey. Perhaps surprisingly, French Canadian writing had little impact on the group, with the honorable exception of Roberts, who translated the 1890 version of *Les Anciens Canadiens* and, before that, a clutch of poems by Fréchette.

Quite the reverse is true of American writing. With the possible exception of F. G. Scott, all members of the Confederation group were deeply influenced by Emersonian Transcendentalism and Thoreauvian primitivism. With the escalating dissent of Campbell, all wrote poems of refined sentiment and delicate form in the manner of Thomas Bailey Aldrich and looked to Boston and *The Atlantic Monthly* (which he edited from 1881 to 1890) as literary centers. Without exception, all recognized the distinctiveness and power

---

24 F. G. Scott, *Collected Poems*, p. 6.
25 D. C. Scott, *Poems* (Toronto: McClelland and Stewart, 1926), p. 47.
26 Quoted in Carl Y. Connor, *Archibald Lampman: Canadian Poet of Nature* (New York and Montreal: Louis Carrier, 1929), p. 78.
27 Barrie Davies, ed., *At the Mermaid Inn: Wilfred Campbell, Archibald Lampman, Duncan Campbell Scott in* The Globe *1892–93* (Toronto: University of Toronto Press, 1979), p. 112.

of Whitman as well as Poe and Longfellow but resisted the un-Canadian exuberance of Whitman's long line and democratic spirit, a momentary deviant in this respect being Lampman, whose "To Chicago," a celebration of the "White City" at the 1893 Columbian Exhibition in Chicago, is fittingly Whitmanesque.

At least to some extent all came to the natural world with eyes alerted to its sights and sounds by the essays of the New England naturalist John Burroughs and his followers. Indeed, the descriptions of the natural world in several of the most accomplished and anthologized of the group's poems, including Lampman's "Heat" (1888), "The Frogs" (1888), and "In November" (1895) and several of Roberts's *Songs of the Common Day* derive in considerable part from Burroughs' observations about the creatures and feelings associated with various seasons of the year in *Birds and Poets, With Other Papers*. Nor is the reason for this hard to find. "April seems to come a little sooner, and to be a little more luxuriant in southern New England than it used to be in New Brunswick ... [b]ut her traits are very little changed," wrote Carman twenty years after moving permanently to New York in 1890: "The frogs pipe, the maples and wild cherries break in bloom, the golden-wing calls from the hardwood ridges, the blood-root is white along the roadsides ... [t]rilliums, too ..."[28] The political system changed at the border, but the natural world remained much the same.

So too did its function as a therapeutic agent in contemporary thinking and writing about modernity. Drawing on sources as diverse as Wordsworth, Arnold, Emerson, S. Weir Mitchell (the inventor of the rest-cure), George Miller Beard (the author of *American Nervousness, Its Causes and Consequences*), and Hovey's wife Henrietta Russell (a proponent of Delsartean mind-body-spirit harmonization), the poets of the Confederation group regarded time spent in the natural world as an antidote to the psychological and physical wear and tear inflicted by modern urban life. "[My] design for instance in 'Among the Timothy,'" explained Lampman in 1889, "was not in the first place to describe a landscape, but ... the effect of a few hours spent among the summer fields on a mind in a troubled or despondent condition."[29] Campbell regarded a book "that will charm and soothe, rather than worry or excite," as a valuable aid to the "draughts" and "voices" of Nature in "blow[ing] out ... sickly

---

28 *Letters of Bliss Carman*, ed. H. Pearson Gundy (Montreal: McGill's-Queen's University Press, 1981), p. 174.
29 Quoted in James Doyle, "Archibald Lampman and Hamlin Garland," *Canadian Poetry: Studies, Documents, Reviews* 16 (Spring–Summer 1985), p. 40.

fancies from heart and brain ... quiet[ing] tired nerves and reviv[ing] jaded energies"[30] and Roberts ascribed to the animal stories that he began to write in the late 1880s the capacity not only to "free ... us for a little from the world of shop-worn utilities and from the mean tenement of self," but also to provide the "gift of refreshment and renewal."[31] Both of the Scotts produced works in the therapeutic mode, and for Carman from the 1890s onwards mind-cure and personal harmonization were prime *raisons d'être* of his work. The *Vagabondia* volumes, the books and chapbooks that became *The Pipes of Pan* series (1902–5), and the collection of essays that he published during the same period are works aimed at ministering to the psychosomatic illnesses of their primarily American readers.

International and national recognition

In view of the cosmopolitan and southerly orientation of the Confederation group, it is scarcely surprising that their individual and collective rise to prominence in Canada was preceded by recognition in Britain and the United States. Roberts received plaudits on both sides of the border for *Orion, and Other Poems*, but nothing on the scale achieved by Lampman near the end of the decade when a slightly belated and highly laudatory (though not entirely unmixed) review of *Among the Millet, and Other Poems* appeared in the January 1889 issue of *The Spectator* (London) and was quickly reprinted in *The Globe* (Toronto) and echoed in *The Week* (Toronto). The best was yet to come, however: in the "Editor's Study" in the April 1889 number of *Harper's New Monthly Magazine* (New York) none other than the "Dean" of American Letters, William Dean Howells, heaped lavish praise on Lampman's book. By the end of the year, William Sharp had followed suit in the November 23 issue of *The Academy* (London), and in the March 1890 number of *Harper's* Howells went further, proclaiming Lampman one of the ten North American poets who had "finally g[iven] us a splendid and unsurpassed literature" and "achieved a place in the British classics."[32]

D. C. Scott's turn in the limelight came in December 1890 when "The Reed-Player" (1893), a Pandean lyric that anticipates his masterpiece in the *symboliste*

---

30 Davies, ed., *At the Mermaid Inn*, p. 111.
31 Charles G. D. Roberts, *The Kindred of the Wild; A Book of Animal Life* (Boston: L. C. Page, 1935 [1902]), p. 29.
32 William Dean Howells, "Editor's Study," *Harper's New Monthly Magazine* 79 (March 1890), p. 646.

mode, "The Piper of Arll" (1898), was judged by *The Independent* to be the best poem to have appeared in an American periodical during the entire year. In 1891 Campbell's turn came when the editor of *The Inter-Ocean* (Chicago) pronounced his Poe-esque rendition of a macabre German folk legend, "The Mother" (1893), "the nearest approach to a great poem ... in current literature for many a long day" and placed it "in ... [the] same category" as such poems as Milton's "Ode on the Morning of Christ's Nativity" and Shelley's "To a Skylark."[33] British, American, and Canadian reviews of Carman's *Low Tide on Grand Pré* were "ruinous in [their] praise."[34] Roberts's *Songs of the Common Day and Ave* was less profusely extolled, but nevertheless garnered strong reviews in *The Independent* (which compared "Ave" to Keats's "Ode to a Nightingale")[35] and *The Academy* (where Sharp judged the same poem a "noble ode [in which] Roberts measures himself with the chiefs in lyrical mastery").[36] F. G. Scott's plaudits were longer in coming and less lavish, but come they did in the March 2, 1895 issue of *The Speaker* (London), where "Samson," a brief narrative in his second collection, *My Lattice and Other Poems* (1894), which casts its biblical and Miltonic hero as a defiant Romantic Prometheus, is declared "splendid," beyond criticism, and "probably the best American poem for many years."[37]

The greatest beneficiaries of these accolades were Lampman, Campbell, and D. C. Scott: Howells's praise of Lampman prompted calls for his promotion to a sinecure in the civil service; the enthusiastic reception of "The Mother" procured Campbell a position as librarian in the Department of the Secretary of State in Ottawa; and Scott's more modest success, combined with the location of all three poets in Ontario, resulted in *At the Mermaid Inn*, a weekly column in *The Globe* that ran from 6 February 1892 to 1 July, 1893. For Carman, Roberts, and F. G. Scott the early 1890s were also a period of kudos and high visibility in Canada not only because they were showered with praise in Canadian newspapers and magazines, but also because laudatory articles about them and their fellow poets in American magazines were

33 [T. H. Sudduth], review of "The Mother" by William Wilfred Campbell, *The Inter-Ocean* (Chicago) 20 (5 April 1891), p. 4.
34 *Letters of Carman*, p. 74.
35 Review of *Songs of the Common Day, and Ave* by Charles G. D. Roberts, *The Independent* 45 (9 March, 1893), p. 17.
36 William Sharp, Review of *Songs of the Common Day, and Ave: An Ode for the Shelley Centenary* by Charles G. D. Roberts, *The Academy: A Weekly Review of Literature, Science, and Art* 44 (21 October, 1893), p. 335.
37 Anon., Review of *My Lattice and Other Poems* by Frederick George Scott, *The Speaker* (March 2, 1985), p. 249.

readily available and eagerly excerpted in Canada. F. G. Scott was spared Edward William Bok's fulsome praise of the "growing school of young Canadian writers" working primarily in poetry in the April 1, 1893 of the Toronto *Globe*,[38] but in "The Singers of Canada" by Joseph Dana Miller in the May 1895 number of *Munsey's Magazine* (New York) he is included in the rapturous celebration of "the achievements and the prospects of the northern school to which Carman, Roberts, Lampman, and Campbell belong."[39] With patriotic pride mitigated only by the regret that "the American public are better acquainted with the work of our poets than are Canadians," *The Globe* observed on October 7, 1893 that "the splendid work ... of the bright coterie whose verse appears in the current magazines and in their printed volumes, has given gratifying prominence to the poetic literature of their country."[40]

For the Confederation group as a whole, the most significant publication of the early 1890s was without doubt *Later Canadian Poems* (1893), an anthology edited by J. E. Wetherell, ostensibly for use in Ontario schools. At Lampman's urging and because of its alphabetical organization, the volume begins with a selection of the work of George Frederick Cameron, whose *Lyrics of Freedom, Love and Death* had appeared posthumously in 1887. At its heart, however, are "selections from the productions" of all six members of the group: "the best known of our younger ... poets."[41] Very well received on both sides of the border, it garnered its most substantial and telling Canadian review in the July 7, 1893 number of *The Week*, where the historian and Tennyson scholar Samuel Edward Dawson makes no mention of Cameron and gives separate and considered attention to each member of the group. Although crediting Lampman with, "perhaps, the greatest power of expression," Dawson observes that the anthology as a whole is remarkable for being, "not an aggregation of poems selected solely because they were written by Canadians," but a collection characterized by "an evenness of literary workmanship ... which shows that we have writers who are justly claiming recognition in English literature, solely because of their literary skill and inherent poetic power."[42] The review's genteel nod to Lampman may have

---

38 Edward William Bok, "Young Canadian Writers from an American Standpoint," *The Globe* (April 1, 1893), p. 17.
39 Quoted in Alexandra J. Hurst, ed., *The War among the Poets: Issues of Plagiarism and Patronage among the Confederation Poets* (London, ON: Canadian Poetry Press, 1994), p. 10.
40 Anon., "Canadian Poets," *The Globe* (October 7, 1893), p. 20.
41 J. E. Wetherell, ed., *Later Canadian Poems* (Toronto: Copp, Clark, 1893), p. iii.
42 Edward Dawson, Review of J. E. Wetherell, ed., *Later Canadian Poems*, *The Week* (July 7, 1893), pp. 756–7.

dismayed Roberts, but he must have been gratified by Dawson's emphasis on "workmanship" and by his comment that "we can tender this little volume to our brothers and sisters of the English tongue in distant lands, with more satisfaction than any other of the collections that have fallen into our hands."[43]

Cameron is the only poet in *Later Canadian Poems* who is ignored in Dawson's review, but short shrift is given to the six women writers – Johnson, Agnes Ethelwyn Wetherald, Susie Frances Harrison, Agnes Maule Machar, Isabella Valancy Crawford, and Sara Jeannette Duncan – whose poems languish in a twenty-five page "Supplement" at the end of the anthology that Wetherell describes as "an addition to the original plan of the book."[44] Two of the writers thus marginalized had published substantial collections of poems by 1893 and three others would publish substantial collections by the end of the decade: Crawford's *Old Spookses' Pass, Malcolm's Katie, and Other Poems* had appeared in 1884 and Harrison's *Pine, Rose and Fleur de Lis* in 1891. Johnson's *The White Wampum* and Wetherald's *The House of the Trees and Other Poems* would appear in 1895, and Machar's *Lays of the "True North" and Other Canadian Poems* in 1899. (Duncan did not publish a collection of poems, but her novel *The Imperialist* [1904] is one of the most important works of the post-Confederation period.) Like the Montreal poet Rosanna Leprohon before them and like several female poets who came to prominence in the ensuing decades, Wetherald, Harrison, and Machar have until recently received scant scholarly attention, part of the reason being the masculinist bias within and surrounding the Confederation group and its modernist successors. In great measure because of the mythic patterns and Amerindian figures deployed in *Malcolm's Katie*, Crawford eventually found sympathetic critics among followers of Northrop Frye and among critics seeking connections between Canadian literature and Native materials. More recently, a combination of feminism and Aboriginal Studies has returned Johnson to the spotlight – *returned* because that is where she most definitely was after February 1892 when she began to exploit her Native ancestry and striking looks by reciting her poems in Indian costume. No other poet of the period came closer than Johnson to becoming part of the Confederation group, but that possibility was precluded by her sex and, perhaps even more important, by the cloud of opprobrium that was about to descend on the "bright coterie."

---

43 Ibid., p. 757.
44 Wetherell, ed., *Later Canadian Poems*, p. iii.

"War among the Poets"

Since early 1893, Campbell had been publishing pieces in *At the Mermaid Inn*, *The Week*, and elsewhere that contained initially veiled but increasingly bellicose remarks about the excessive "polish," the absence of "great subject matter," and the preponderance of "word-painting" in contemporary poetry, as well as dark hints about the prevalence of a "fraternal system of back-scratching ... and back-biting" in the North American literary arena.[45] In the summer of 1895, his *casus belli* came in the prominence accorded to other members of the Confederation group by Miller in "The Singers of Canada" and he launched first an anonymous attack on the article and then a pseudo-nymous attack on Carman, accusing him of being "the most flagrant imitator" – in a word, plagiarist – "on this continent."[46] Towards the end of the summer, the "War among the Poets," as it was quickly dubbed, was further fueled by Campbell's accusation that Roberts and Carman had engaged in "log-rolling"[47] – the mutual praise of one another's work – a charge not without foundation both in the practices of the two men and in Roberts's careful orchestration of critical responses to the work of the Confederation group. It is no more coincidental that Carman was editor of *The Independent* than it is that Sharp was a friend of Roberts or, indeed, that Roberts dragooned at least one writer from outside the group, the Windsor, Nova Scotia poet George M. Acklom, into defending Carman against the charge of plagiarism.[48] The covert tactics learned from Collins and used so effectively for over a decade had rebounded with a vengeance.

By the end of 1895, the "War among the Poets" was nearly over, but it had spawned a myriad of responses in newspapers throughout Ontario and the Maritimes, a Byronic satire on Carman and his supporters by the Ottawa poet Charles Gordon Rogers, and a mock-epitaph for Campbell by Carman in *The Chap-Book* (Boston), which he edited from 1894 to 1896.[49] In 1896 came *The Poetical Review*, a Popean satire of "Scribblers in the Service of Folly" by the Fort William, Ontario poet Alexander Charles Stewart that lambasts each member of the group in turn – Robert as the perpetrator of "tantramarian

---

45 Davies, ed., *At the Mermaid Inn*, pp. 313–16, 331, and see Hurst, ed., *War Among the Poets*, pp. 1–9.
46 Quoted in ibid., p. 30.
47 See ibid., pp. 116–22.
48 See Roberts, *Collected Letters*, p. 205, and Hurst, ed., *War among the Poets*, pp. 93–9.
49 See ibid., pp. 47–99 (letters and articles in newspapers), pp. 99–111 (Rogers's "Bards of the Boiler-Plate"), and pp. 113–15 (Carman's article).

nonsense," Carman as a participant in log-rolling, Campbell as a pedlar of "mimicked Tennysonian rant," Lampman as a soporific observer of "midsummer," D. C. Scott as purveyor of "specious phrase," and F. G. Scott as a concocter of "mutilated verse" that "he alone sh[ould] read."⁵⁰ The reputation and the morale of the group had been irreparably damaged, and, to make matters worse, readers were showing a growing preference for fiction over poetry.⁵¹ In June 1895, Roberts left his post at King's College and in February 1897 he moved to New York. On 10 July of that year readers of *Saturday Night* (Toronto) were treated to "The Plaint of Poets Unemployed," a sympathetic treatment of the Confederation group's predicament in which one of their staunchest supporters, the Toronto writer Thomas O'Hagan, envisaged them appealing for "ruth and pity" to the "gods and goddesses, that ha[d] been well disposed to us, / (To us poor proud Parnassians) in the good old days that were ..."⁵²

Dénouement and aftermath

In the wake of the "War among the Poets" and the departure of Roberts, the Confederation group more obviously became what it had been in the process of becoming for some time: six highly individualistic writers whose affinities, where they existed, were more related to proximity and friendship than aesthetics and patriotism. In New York, Roberts and Carman joined Hovey and other apostles of the avant-garde in flouting convention and celebrating the pleasures and mysteries of erotic love and the open road, Roberts in *New York Nocturnes and Other Poems* (1898) and *The Book of the Rose* (1903) and Carman in the *Vagabondia* volumes, the *Pipes of Pan* series, and *Sappho: One Hundred Lyrics* (1903), a collection that is remarkable both as a fusion of lyrical power and Unitrinian philosophy and as a precursor of Imagism. In Ottawa, Lampman and Scott remained on cordial terms with Campbell and in sporadic contact with F. G. Scott, but their principal interactions were with one another. Lampman's "The City of the End of Things" (1900) and "The Land of Pallas" (1900) both of which date from the early-to-mid-1890s, reflect an interest in urban problems and socialist theories, as does the title poem

---

50 *The Poetical Review: A Brief Notice of Canadian Poets and Poetry*, ed. D. M. R. Bentley, *Canadian Poetry: Studies, Documents, Reviews* 1 (Fall/Winter 1977), pp. 69, 74–83.
51 See Frank Luther Mott, *A History of American Magazines*, vol. IV: *1741–1850* (Cambridge, Mass.: Harvard University Press, 1957 [1930]), pp. 111, 120.
52 Thomas O'Hagan, "The Plaint of Poets Unemployed," *Saturday Night* 10 (10 July 1897), p. 7.

of D. C. Scott's *Labor and the Angel* (1898). Such poems as "Temagami" and "The Lake in the Forest" that were to have been published in *Alcyone*, the collection that was in press at the time of Lampman's premature death in 1899, participate in the turn towards the landscapes, spirituality, and peoples of the Canadian north that finds expression in the so-called "Indian" poems and short stories of Scott's *New World Lyrics and Ballads* (1905), *The Green Cloister: Later Poems* (1935), and *The Circle of Affection, and Other Pieces in Prose and Verse* (1947), pieces whose apparent sympathy for Native people has seemed to many to be at odds with the policies that their author pursued as Secretary and then Deputy Superintendent General of Indian Affairs.

Not until they were all in their fifties were the surviving members of the Confederation group again provided with a common cause in the form of the First World War. Since the mid-1890s, Campbell had been trumpeting about Canada's place in the "Greater Britain" of the Empire, so he eagerly threw himself into the war effort with *Sagas of Vaster Britain – Poems of the Race, the Empire and the Divinity of Man* (1914). Always the most physically active of the group, Roberts enlisted in the British army. For his part, F. G. Scott enlisted in the Canadian army and served as senior chaplain to the First Canadian Division. On the home front, Carman worked to bring the United States into the war and D. C. Scott ensured the smooth running of the Department of Indian Affairs and the Royal Society of Canada. All five wrote war poems, none with the popular success of John McCrae's "In Flanders Fields" (1915), let alone the stark realism of a Wilfred Owen or a Siegfried Sassoon.

There is a curious, even uncanny, appropriateness to the fact that Campbell died of pneumonia on New Year's Day 1918, for the war was both the end of one era and the beginning of another. "The Victorian days belong to history [and] I believe the new days will be better," Carman had written in April 1917, "but I doubt if any of the men who came to maturity before the great war will be able to find the new key, the new mode, the new tune."[53] The wave of national confidence that swept Canada in the 1920s resulted in the lionization, first of Carman and then of Roberts: between 1921 and his death in 1929, Carman undertook several reading and lecture tours in central, western, and eastern Canada, and in 1925 Roberts returned from Europe to undertake similar tours of Ontario and the West, the success of which persuaded him to embark on a further tour of the Maritimes and to settle permanently in Toronto, where he died in 1943, the year before F. G. Scott. In 1931, the Canadian Authors Association unveiled a memorial cairn near Lampman's

---

53 *Letters of Carman*, p. 244.

birthplace in Morpeth, Ontario, and in 1954 Carman was at last granted his wish to have "a scarlet maple / For the grave-tree at [his] head"[54] in the cemetery in Fredericton where he was buried. Roberts and D. C. Scott were among the honored guests at the unveiling of the Lampman memorial, but no member of the group was left to attend the dedication of Carman's scarlet maple. With Scott's death in 1947, a generation had passed and, with it, a way of thinking and writing about Canada and the world that modernism, the New Criticism, and other forces would continue to render unappealing within the academy for many years to come. In the 1960s the tide began to turn, however, and the ensuing decades have witnessed a growing appreciation of the Confederation poets both individually and as a group.

54 *Carman's Poems*, p. 209.

8
Writing by Victorian naturalists

CHRISTOPH IRMSCHER

What is here?

"Science does not always appear, as on the present occasion, in holiday attire," Mr. William Dawson, the Principal of McGill College, warned the members of the Montreal Society of Natural History and assorted guests on a May evening in 1856. More than 150 ladies and gentlemen, the *"elite* of the city and neighborhood," had shown up for the soirée the society had organized in honor of Sir William Logan, the Director of the Geological Survey of Canada. The guests were having fun. After the requisite speeches, they inspected the museum, peered through three powerful microscopes that had been set up for their amusement, and partook of the refreshments in the library. But now it was Mr. Dawson's turn. Science, he declared, means sacrifice. "It scales every mountain, gropes in every mine, toils through every wilderness, boils its camp kettle by all streams, pores over the minutest objects, anatomises the least agreeable creatures, stifles itself in laboratory fumes, breaks stones like a road maker, and carries loads like a porter." A true scientist, Mr. Dawson added, is someone people look at and say: "[He] has seen better days." As if he realized that he wasn't about to convert anyone in the audience who wasn't already a scientist, he quickly shifted gears: really, what he meant was that science was, above all, a way of getting people to talk to each other – which was precisely the purpose of a fine natural history society like the present one. Just in time.[1]

The Montreal Society of Natural History, founded in 1827, had begun inauspiciously, with only a handful members and a shoestring budget. In its early years, it would collect whatever came its way or was given to it, a live porcupine, for example, lichens and sea-weeds sent by a lady from Boston,

---

1 "Proceedings at the Soiree," *Twenty-Eighth Annual Report of the Natural History Society of Montreal* (Montreal: Rose, 1856), pp. 12–23.

some insects from China, the plant specimens a member had pressed between the pages of his books while studying medicine in Berlin, even a few plaster casts of classical statues they got from London (and which some dedicated member had to glue together after they arrived in Montreal smashed into smithereens). But, almost casually, the members also began to compile more specific collections, of certain types of Canadian minerals, for example, or of local birds ("almost all the birds found in this part of the world," the society's Council boasted in 1833). *Pace* Mr. Dawson (who would go on to develop quite a reputation, and not a good one, for opposing Darwin), natural history was everybody's business, and one didn't need to look terrible to be considered a naturalist: "The animal and vegetable kingdoms, the rocks and the mountains, are open to the investigation of all," the Council noted in 1859. In fact, natural history was a natural cure for dejection; good health to us all, as Walt Whitman would have said.[2]

The annual reports of the Montreal Society of Natural History are more than a quaint reminder of the way things were. In fact, a continuous line reaches from the fraying paper on which they were printed to the full-page illustrations of richly colored, lusty apples bursting with sap published, towards the end of the century, in the volumes of *The Canadian Horticulturalist* to the delicate drawings that accompany Christopher Dewdney's recent natural history poems, his attempt to imagine a Canadian "geography / for every phase of our lives."[3] It is my contention here that Canadian nature writing came into its own during the Victorian period, which is often falsely regarded as a time when benign and somewhat benighted amateurs ventured out (though never too far) into the field and found nothing beyond what their colonialist myopia allowed them to see.[4] The patient stocktaking of Canadian nature, begun by the early explorers but taken to new heights by the Victorians, suggests that – rather than Frye's agonized "Where is here?" – a different question became central to the minds of Canadians, "*What* is here?"[5] It is a truly open-ended question, one that points us to the inherent ecological

---

2 *Fifth, Sixth, Seventh Annual Reports of the Council of the Natural History Society for 1831–32, 1832–33, and 1833–34* (Montreal: Gazette Office, 1834), p. 13; *Report of the Council of the Natural History Society of Montreal, for the Year 1859* (Montreal: Lovell, 1859), pp. 5–6; Walt Whitman, *Leaves of Grass: The First (1855) Edition* (New York: Penguin, 2005), p. 96.
3 Christopher Dewdney, *Signal Fires: Poems* (Toronto: McClelland and Stewart, 2000), p. 18.
4 For the established reading of Victorian science in Canada, see Carl Berger, *Science, God, and Nature in Victorian Canada* (Toronto: University of Toronto Press, 1983).
5 See Northrop Frye, "Conclusion," in Carl F. Klinck, ed., *Literary History of Canada: Canadian Literature in English* (Toronto: University of Toronto Press, 1965), p. 826. See also my chapter on "Nature-Writing" in Eva-Marie Kröller, ed., *The Cambridge Companion to Canadian Literature* (Cambridge: Cambridge University Press, 2004), pp. 94–114.

ramifications of Victorian nature writing in Canada, informed as it is by the realization that, while nature is very important to us, we are perhaps not all that important to nature.

All the loveliness for Canada

The Tiger Swallowtail, the Violet Tip, the Pearl-border Fritillary, the Archippus, the Camberwell Beauty, the Spring Azure, the Tawny-edged Skipper, the Angleshades, the Green Emperor, the Streaked Hooktip, the Twin Goldspot, the Spangled Orange, and the Crimson Underwing – Philip Henry Gosse knows his butterflies and moths from the inside out.[6] In *The Canadian Naturalist* (1840), insect names roll off the writer's tongue like the lines of so many yet-to-be-written poems. Born in Worcester, England, Gosse (1810–88) had followed his brother William to Carbonear, Newfoundland, where he indentured himself for six years as a clerk in the counting-house of Messrs. Slade, Elson, and Co., the owners of seventy schooners that went cod-fishing or sealing off the coast of Labrador. In Newfoundland, Gosse became entranced with creatures so light and soft they seemed intended to make him forget the dreariness of a life dominated by double-entry book-keeping.[7] From 1832 to 1835, Gosse produced drawings of more than 250 of such insects, which he included in his *Entomologia Terrae Novae*, the first scientific entomological study ever undertaken in Newfoundland. However, *The Canadian Naturalist*, his first published book, was based loosely on the author's own experiences in a different region – Compton, Lower Canada, where he had moved in 1835 in an attempt to make a living as a farmer.[8]

Gosse structured his book as a series of conversations between a Canadian farmer (the "Father") and his son Charles, newly arrived from England. With his parent acting as an enthusiastic guide on their joint rambles through the neighborhood, Charles's initial reservations about Canadian nature don't last long. Come June he is hooked: "It seems almost a contradiction in terms, for a naturalist to be in low spirits," he cries out, "everything he sees tends to

---

6 Throughout this chapter I will insert modern species names – if needed and if they are significantly different from nineteenth-century nomenclature – in lower case. Names by which animal or plant species were known to the authors themselves are left capitalized.
7 Edmund Gosse, *The Life of Philip Henry Gosse, F. R. S.* (London: Kegan Paul, Trench, Trübner & Co., 1890), pp. 77–81. William had left Worcester for Newfoundland five years earlier, when he was only fourteen; see Ann Thwaite, *Glimpses of the Wonderful: The Life of Philip Henry Gosse, 1810–1888* (London: Faber and Faber, 2002), pp. 27–37.
8 Philip Henry Gosse, *The Canadian Naturalist: A Series of Conversations on the Natural History of Lower Canada* (London: Van Voorst, 1840).

enrapture and delight him." Charles is particularly entranced with the "various transformations to which insects are subject: the same individual, Proteus-like, taking new forms and presenting new objects of examination to our admiring eye" (p. 226). The caterpillars of the Forked Butterfly (known as the tortoiseshell today) and Orange Comma Butterflies which he had collected a few weeks ago are now in their pupal stage, and the chrysalis of the Banded Purple Butterfly (the white admiral) has finally yielded its prize, "an insect of remarkable beauty." In Gosse's eyes, Canadian nature is distinguished by its capacity to surprise and confound the human observer.[9] The father's and son's rambles thus often turn into ramblings, but for Gosse this lack of linearity isn't a problem. The very unpredictability of his method becomes one of the strongest assets of a book that revels in the power of detail – the intoxicating plenitude of "what is here" – and pits the slowness of the metamorphosis of insects against the hurried glances uncomprehending humans give their environment.

Gosse soon permanently exchanged his plough for the pen and the rocky soil of Lower Canada for the gentler pastures of southern England. Unhampered by his hardening evangelicalism, he became one of Britain's most prolific and popular natural history writers, using his considerable influence to argue, against Darwin, that species were created and not born. Adam, he claimed, had come into life with a full-sized belly button, no mother involved. As Gosse contended, the moment in which we first look at an animal or plant – any such moment, really – is "the very first moment of its life."[10] Behind the obvious craziness of this theory stands a serious desire to celebrate nature in all its fullness. Intense, brilliant, and enigmatic, Gosse, inspired by his years in Quebec, developed a view of nature that demands – but paradoxically doesn't really *need* – the human observer's full engagement.

The commitment to precise observation Gosse shared with a fellow immigrant from England, Catharine Parr Traill (1802–99). From the moment of her arrival, Traill seems to have embraced her new home. Watching the sun set over Lake Ontario in August, "with a radiance such as my English eyes had never yet looked upon," she asked her husband if he had ever seen anything "so glorious." "Yes, many a time, in Italy and in Switzerland," responded Thomas Traill uncooperatively. His passionate wife, however,

---

9 Christoph Irmscher, "Nature Laughs at Our Systems: Philip Henry Gosse's *The Canadian Naturalist*," *Canadian Literature* 170/171 (Autumn–Winter 2001), pp. 58–86.
10 Philip Henry Gosse, *Omphalos: An Attempt to Untie the Geological Knot* (London: Van Voorst, 1857), p. 252.

became determined, "to claim all the loveliness for Canada, the country of our adoption and henceforth our home."[11]

Traill was, as Margaret Atwood said later, a "practical coper."[12] And resilient she definitely was. As if to anticipate the way her story would be told by future generations, Traill once likened herself to the Carpetweed, a pesky, persevering little nuisance that "flourishes under all circumstances, however adverse."[13] The comparison was not a careless one: native Canadian plants had become Traill's abiding passion. In 1868, the year after the establishment of the Dominion of Canada, she published *Canadian Wild Flowers*, in collaboration with her niece, Agnes Fitzgibbon (1833–1913). Five hundred copies were printed by John Lovell of Montreal, each of them adorned with ten lithographed botanical sketches drawn on stone by Fitzgibbon. In her preface, Traill worried that the more scientifically inclined among her readers would be disappointed by her book's accessibility, while others would deplore the excess of scientific terminology. But this was really only a tongue-in-cheek way of saying that here she had attempted to please both audiences and to offer something that, in a modest way, could claim to be *both* science and art.[14]

To that end, Traill plays the botanist whenever she can, flaunting her knowledge of technical language and casually inserting adjectives like "turbinate" or "campanulate" into her prose. At the same time, her text is also laced with quotations from her favorite poets – Robert Herrick, Lord Byron, Felicia Hemans, William Cullen Bryant, and Henry Wadsworth Longfellow among them – and she does not shy away from poetic conceits herself, as when she compares the buds of the Showy Lady's Slipper to "the appearance of slightly flattened globes of delicately-tinted primrose coloured rice-paper" and its fully opened blossoms to "the curious face and peering black eyes of the ape" (pp. 60–1).[15]

In her drawings, Fitzgibbon similarly tries to combine solid science with aesthetic effect. Typically, her beautiful designs place a plant with large flowers at the center of the composition and surround it with smaller-flowering

---

11 Catharine Parr Traill, *Pearls and Pebbles; or, Notes of an Old Naturalist* (London: Sampson Low, Marston, and Company, 1894), pp. 45–6.
12 Margaret Atwood, *Strange Things: The Malevolent North in Canadian Literature* (Oxford: Clarendon, 1995), p. 99.
13 Catharine Parr Traill, *Studies of Plant Life in Canada: Gleanings from Forest, Lake and Plain* (Ottawa: Woodburn, 1885), p. ii.
14 *Canadian Wild Flowers, Painted and Lithographed by Agnes Fitzgibbon, with Botanical Descriptions by C. P. Traill* (Montreal: Lovell, 1868), p. 8.
15 Unsurprisingly, Traill is often regarded as an anachronistic *littérateur*; see Charlotte Gray, *Sisters in the Wilderness: The Lives of Susanna Moodie and Catharine Parr Traill* (Toronto: Penguin, 2000 [1999]), p. 301.

Plate 6. Plate III from Catharine Parr Traill and Agnes Fitzgibbon, *Canadian Wildflowers* (1868): "Yellow Adder's Tongue (*Erythronium Americanum*), Large White Trillium (*Trillium Grandiflorum*), Wild Columbine (*Aquilegia Canadensis*)."

plants which thus create a kind of decorative frame – here (Plate 6) a group including the large-flowered White Trillium, a plant Traill preferred to call "Adder's Tongue" (another common name, "Dog-toothed Violet," she deemed inappropriate), and the Rock Columbine (wild columbine). Fitzgibbon relishes the contrast between the single showy flower of the Trillium in the middle and the smaller flowers that surround it: while the slightly averted yellow flower of the lily on the left mirrors, in reduced form, the Trillium's more expansive petals, the drooping blossoms of the Columbine on the right and at the top provide a subtle visual counterpoint. Fitzgibbon thus essentially *stages* her flowers. At the same time, she also fulfills the basic requirements of botanical illustration, bending and turning her specimens in such a way that the viewer can see both sides of the leaf and look right into the flower, even to the point of being able to count (in the case of the Trillium) the six stamens surrounding the ovary with its three stigmas.

There is no doubt that Fitzgibbon's compositional tricks, like Traill's pretty personifications, serve to civilize the wild flowers, fitting them into frames and patterns that are no longer those of nature itself. As Traill sees it, the movement from the wild woods to the settler's backyard will in fact be good for flowers like the Wood Anemone, which will " become larger and handsomer" as a result (p. 83). But she also knows that what works for some flowers isn't good for others. "Some indeed of the forest plants," sighs Traill, "have disappeared and we see them no more. Types are they of the native race, the Indian children of the land, fast passing away" (*Pearls and Pebbles*, p. 131).

For Traill, who was proud of her Ojibwa name (*Peta-wan-noo-ka*, "red cloud of the dawn," given to her because of her "rosy English complexion"),[16] the connection between the endangered wildflowers and the First Nations is not a merely figurative one. In fact, attempting to preserve the vanishing wisdom of the "herb-seeking medicine men of the native tribes," she adds yet another dimension to the mix of art and science in *Wild Flowers* and turns her book into a modern-day "domestic Herbal of the Wild Plants of Canada" (p. 8). The heated juices of the Indian Turnip are an excellent "remedy in violent colic" (p. 10); the root of the Pitcher Plant has been said to lessen the symptoms of smallpox; the Wood Geranium may yield "a gargle for sore throats and ulcerated mouth" (p. 42); and the Hepatica can be used to produce a "mild tonic" good for people with liver disease (p. 78).

But as much as Traill wants to think of her wildflowers as made for the sake of humans, she also realizes that in many cases the shrinking Canadian wilderness might be the only place where they can still be found intact. Notwithstanding the writer's temptation to personify them, Canadian wildflowers are so attractive precisely because they are *not* human. The name of the anemone, for example, derives from the Greek word for "wind," because the flower's "cheerful" blossoms were said to open "only when the wind was blowing" (pp. 81–2). But, jokes Traill, Canadian anemones don't seem to have heard this explanation: "Whatever the habits of the Anemone of the Grecian Isles may be, assuredly in their native haunts in this country, the blossoms open alike in windy weather or in calm; in shade or in sunshine" (p. 81).

---

16 Traill, *Pearls and Pebbles*, p. 181.

From the outside looking in

Gosse's and Traill's literary stocktaking of Canadian nature marks only one strand in Victorian Canadian natural history writing. Many books published during this period were indeed written from precisely the perspective of the casual, hurried, and often self-important observer that both of them had hoped to eliminate from Canadian writing: immigrants or travelers from England with a vaguely military background and some basic understanding of natural history who regarded Canada as a kind of gigantic self-serve store where they could hunt, shoot, and fish to their heart's content. The books they produced – with titles such as *Three Months Among the Moose*, *Forest Life in Acadie*, *Field and Forest Rambles*, or *At Home in the Wilderness* (the latter came with the promising subtitle, *Being Full Instructions How to Get Along, and to Surmount All Difficulties by the Way*) – were intended as bedside reading for the folks back home who were toying with the idea of roughing it out, fishing rod and breechloader in hand, in the wilds of a new country.[17]

John Keast Lord (1818–72), for example, the author of *At Home in the Wilderness*, who served on the English Boundary Commission in British Columbia, never wavered in regarding "the old country" as his home. His account, titled *The Naturalist in Vancouver Island and British Columbia* (1866), is replete with references to the specimens he collected in the Canadian West that could now be inspected, appropriately classified and mounted, in the British Museum, as if this were where they really belonged. Lord's charge – to help mark the border along the forty-ninth parallel between British Columbia and the United States – left him plenty of time to explore a country where one could pick up pond turtles as easily as one would gather hedge-snails in Devonshire.[18] His folksy style steers clear of scientific jargon (except in the taxonomic lists he appended to his second volume) in favor of creating the impression of easy familiarity with the living, breathing world of western Canadian animals. Frequently addressing his readers directly ("Picture to

---

17 [Rev. Joshua Frazer], *Three Months Among the Moose: "A Winter's Tale" of the Wilds of Canada, by a Military Chaplain* (Montreal: Lovell, 1881); Captain Campbell Hardy, *Forest Life in Acadie: Sketches of Sport and Natural History in the Lower Provinces of the Canadian Dominion* (New York: Appleton, 1869); Andrew Leith Adams, Staff-Surgeon Major, *Field and Forest Rambles, with Observations on the Natural History of Eastern Canada* (London: King, 1873); "The Wanderer" [i.e. John Keast Lord], *At Home in the Wilderness, Being Full Instructions How to Get Along, and to Surmount All Difficulties by the Way* (London: Hardwicke, 1867).

18 John Keast Lord, *The Naturalist in Vancouver Island and British Columbia*, 2 vols. (London: Bentley, 1866), vol. II, p. 101.

yourself"; "Imagine, if you can"; vol. I, pp. 142–3), Lord prides himself on his ability to cut to the chase and admit prejudice where prejudice is due. The skunk smells so bad, he states, that this can't be so only for defensive purposes, and, as far as he is concerned, the crows of British Columbia, the hoarse screams of which drown out the sweet songs of other birds, can go straight to hell (vol. II, pp. 9, 67).

Lord's science was natural history done with an axe, not the dissecting knife. After all, he had been sent to British Columbia with the assignment to help cut an arbitrary line through the wilderness. It seems richly ironical that the most memorable of the animals Lord meets are precisely the ones that jeopardize neat categories – the viviparous fish, for example, in whose placental sacs the offspring are arranged like the wedge-shaped pieces inside an orange; the Urotrichus, a blind, pig-snouted, furry animal, half shrew, half mole, found on the Chilliwack prairie, whose powerful forefeet look like garden-tools; and the Sewellel, which got its name from the Chinook word for the robes made from the animal's pelts, a strange cross between a beaver and a squirrel and far too "rat-like" in appearance to tempt Lord's palate. Especially in the case of the latter creature, which passes its life in dark burrows, shambles uneasily when it walks, and eats slimy vegetable matter only, Lord feels compelled to ask: "Why was this ... made?" (vol. I, p. 358).[19]

Oddly, Lord, who spends his nights in mosquito-infested canvas tents, finds himself irresistibly drawn to the hidden habitations of Canadian animals, as if there were a cure for his own loneliness in the dank, grass-lined holes of the Urotrichus, dug by a creature that thinks, sees, and feels with its nose and therefore needs no sun to brighten its days, or in the conical bulrush mansions built, "how I am at a loss to imagine," by the muskrat (vol. II, pp. 77–8). The animals of British Columbia inhabit a world in which he will always be an intruder, someone who is less rebuffed than simply ignored. In his appendix, Lord recounts, with comical earnestness, his repeated attempts to make a rattlesnake, "[v]ery sluggish in all its movements, and remarkably fond of creeping in the dust," take an interest in him: "I have again and again teased a large rattlesnake with a twig, but never succeeded in provoking [it] to attack me" (vol. II, p. 304).

---

19 Lord's "Urotrichus" is *Neurotrichus gibsii*, the American shrew mole; the Sewellel is more commonly referred to as the "mountain beaver," even though the animal "is not a beaver and only occasionally a mountaineer." See *The Imperial Collection of Audubon Animals*, ed. Victor H. Cahalane (New York: Bonanza, 1967), p. 51.

Lord's lingering reservations about parts of the Canadian fauna are shared by a Scots army officer, William Ross King (1822–90), whose remarkably successful book, *The Sportsman and Naturalist in Canada* (1866), did much to shape contemporary European perceptions of Canadian wildlife.[20] For King, the skunk is simply a "horrid little animal" (no argument here, Mr. Lord!); often did he have to run, "with suspended breath," past a spot where a skunk had just crossed (pp. 17–18). Where Mr. Lord likes to picture his animals in their homes, Major King, of the 74th Highlanders, prefers to visualize them in a pot, "stewed or made into a curry" (p. 32). Many remarks are about the tasty flesh of animals he has caught. King takes particular pride in having served squirrel to a fellow officer ("who had often expressed his disgust at the idea," p. 32) and preparing it so well that his colleague didn't notice. And thus he merrily eats his way through the Canadian fauna, frequently complaining that the resources are constantly diminishing, but blissfully unaware of the inherent irony of his position.

But though he might sometimes come across as a trigger-happy carnivore with a conscience the size of a breeze-fly's brain, King is in fact an accomplished writer whose prose, given time and the right occasion, will take wing. Poignantly, he is at his best when describing animals he is about to shoot, a moose, for example, attracted by a fake call of a female, which stands before the hunter concealed behind a tree, "bellowing in tones that ring startlingly through the forest depths, stamping impatiently, and turning his shaggy head, now in one direction now in another, the large ears moving continually backwards and forwards, the mane erect, his enormous antlers glancing in the moonlight, and his breath wreathing in the night air" (p. 53). The prize is worth the effort, as King reminds himself: the flesh of the moose is tender, like beef.

King, who has stalked wildebeest and springbok in South Africa and alligators in Malabar (p. 56), is a woodcraftsman, one who is able to follow tracks "invisible to unaccustomed eyes" (p. 57), stepping lightly over dead leaves, moss, and rocks, breathing in the air scented with the moose's warm musky odor, straining every nerve, constantly worried that a small bird darting through the thicket or a tiny chipmunk scampering away over dry leaves might betray his presence to the sensitive ears of the enormous animal he is

---

20 Major W. Ross King, *The Sportsman and Naturalist in Canada, Or Notes on the Natural History of the Game, Game Birds, and Fish of That Country* (London: Hurst and Blackett, 1866). Darwin uses King's Canadian book as a resource in his *Descent of Man* (1871); see notes 41 and 52 in chapter XIII, note 8 in XVII, and note 3 in XVIII. For King's biography, see his obituary in *Scottish Notes and Queries* 4.5 (October 1890), pp. 83–4.

pursuing. Like his American model, the expert bird-hunter and ornithologist John James Audubon, frequently cited in King's pages, the Major has no patience for the "closet-naturalists."[21] He will remind his readers that he has in fact touched, laid his hands on the creatures he writes about. He knows, for example, that the long, straight hair of the caribou breaks off when handled roughly or that the feathers of the snowy owl are "a mass of the softest down" (p. 109). King's willingness to open his senses to the experience of Canada is exemplary, and his prose drips with a sense of giddy excitement and personal involvement that we do not find in more staid writers like Gosse and Traill. Along with him we stand on the frozen ground in winter, covered with snow as "pure and bright as on the day it fell," and look up at the azure sky, so clear and brilliant that we feel, as King certainly does, impelled to "almost boisterous mirth" (p. 97). In the spring, when the woods are blue with hyacinths, we listen, as he does, to the snakes and centipedes rustling under the dry leaves (p. 113).

Major King, mind you, is not an indiscriminate hunter. He strongly disapproves of those who go after wild turkeys in any other season than in the late fall, "when, after a summer diet of strawberries and wild fruit," they are "so wild and difficult of approach as to require no inconsiderable amount of skill in stalking" (p. 136). And King unequivocally admires the pugnacity of the prairie hen, demonstrated in the illustration he supplies in which the cock, upright, alert, and unafraid, framed by a clump of flowers on one side and a tuft of rough grass on the other, stares down the viewer, not allowing the prairie to dwarf him into insignificance (see Plate 7). King realizes that ultimately there is something a bit pathetic about humans "worming," *ventre à terre* (p. 199), their way through the grass in pursuit of birds – a far cry from the upright position that usually serves as the mark of human distinctiveness and distinction.

Like King, Major John J. Rowan was a military man, and, like King's book, Rowan's wry account, *The Emigrant and Sportsman in Canada* (1876), published ten years later, seems to suggest that Canada is a country mostly for guys with guns.[22] But Rowan's reminiscences are already shaped by a distinctly

---

21 See, for example, John Audubon, *Writings and Drawings*, ed. Christoph Irmscher (New York: Library of America, 1999), pp. 210, 271, 745, and 847 ("crazed Naturalists of the closet").
22 John J. Rowan, *The Emigrant and Sportsman in Canada: Some Experiences of an Old Country Settler, With Sketches of Canadian Life, Sporting Adventures, and Observations on the Forests and Fauna* (London: Stanford, 1876). While Rowan spent his life in complete obscurity, his only book became famous enough to attract the attention of Thomas Hardy, who refers to it in chapter 44 of *The Mayor of Casterbridge* (1886), where he compares his protagonist Henchard's wanderings around Casterbridge to "that of the Canadian woodsman."

Plate 7. "Prairie Hen (*Cupidonia Cupio*)," chromolithograph from
W. Ross King, *The Sportsman and Naturalist in Canada* (1866).

post-Confederacy perspective: his aim is to give prospective immigrants an honest picture of what life over here is really like. In Rowan's confident assessment, Canada is becoming safely independent. It will never be annexed by the United States, because, as Rowan amusingly explains, the physical differences between Americans and Canadians have become too pronounced to allow for cohabitation. Reliance on the "hewers of wood and drawers of water from Africa, from China, and from Ireland," along with the dreadful liquor they drink, has impoverished the muscles of the average Americans, while the "native born Canadian ... is sprung from a well-grown and muscular parentage" (pp. 43, 51).

Like King, Rowan seems ready to lay "a yellow eye" (in Emily Dickinson's phrase)[23] on everything that has feathers or fur or swims in Canada's rivers. *Almost* everything, that is. The mere image of a deer being chased to exhaustion and then having its throat cut, its "wild and beautiful eye" breaking, sickens him: "Of all butchery this is the worst" (p. 66). At heart, he is a trapper, not a hunter. Rowan identifies with those Canadian animals that are as hardy and gritty as he would like to think he is, too: the gutsy otter with an old steel trap embedded in his tail who will nevertheless scare the salmon into jumping onto the ice, where he devours them, or the crippled Canada Jay (he prefers to call him "meat bird"), who has roped other birds into delivering food to him (p. 317). One particularly feisty otter, "a savage fighter" like all of his species (p. 332), escapes with Rowan on his skates in hot pursuit ("My skating at the best is not swanlike," Rowan admits). The chase doesn't go well – Rowan falls and lands on top of the otter ("I actually felt his breath on my face, and for one dreadful second there seemed a probability that I should come to the ignominious end of being eaten by an otter," p. 334). With fireworks dancing before his eyes, prostrate on the ice, his gun broken, Rowan helplessly watches as one of his Native associates brutally "polishes off" the animal.

The rough, sinewy world of furry woodland creatures, with snarling fangs, extended claws and all, as it was pictured in Audubon's *Viviparous Quadrupeds of North America*, comes alive again in Rowan's book. It is precisely their wildness that makes these animals so appealing. Domesticate the mink and its fur will soon be useless. Rowan confesses to having a soft spot for skunks ("[a]nyone who has watched an old skunk, with two or three young ones playing about her" couldn't help liking them, he claims [p. 341]), and he is half inclined to believe the Natives when they say that porcupines, clumsy and slow by the day, will run as fast as dogs at night (he knows already that they're "capital climber[s]"; p. 343). Despite his fondness for such scrappy, savvy creatures, Rowan's interest in them is always determined by what they're good for: woodchucks, for example, make "excellent pouches for tobacco" (p. 344). But then his favorite animals, too, are driven by purely pragmatic considerations in their interactions with others: the fisher, for example, "eats any animal food it can get" and will not shy away from devouring a whole porcupine, quills and all, or a caribou carcass (p. 340). The little ground squirrels of Ontario may seem cute to you, but you don't truly know what they're like until you've seen one of them dragging off the bleeding corpse of

---

23 Dickinson, "My Life had stood – a Loaded Gun –" (c. 1863), *The Complete Poems of Emily Dickinson*, ed. Thomas H. Johnson (Boston: Little, Brown and Company, 1960), p. 369.

a chicken it has just killed. In this world, Rowan, the expert shooter and discriminating consumer of animal meat, is just one more link in a cycle by which nature constantly renews itself. Settler, beware. There is little room for sentimentality here, and humans as well as animals cannot expect that their efforts to leave a mark will last. When Rowan shoots a little beaver he roasts him over a fire built of the wood the beaver himself has just cut, for very different purposes, of course. "[Y]oung beaver, roasted whole, is rather like sucking pig," notes Rowan, smacking his lips (p. 358).

Apples, full of sap and color

"The consumption of the coarsest products only, will tend to make coarse men," said the horticulturalist Delos White Beadle in 1872, a remark that seems intended for someone like John Rowan.[24] With a more staid and perhaps less hungry audience in mind, Beadle (1823–1905), the owner of a nursery in St. Catharines, Ontario, had written his *Canadian Fruit, Flower, and Kitchen Gardener*, a handbook for "all who love good fruit, pretty flowers, and choice vegetables" (p. xvii). Beadle's gardening book was an achievement not only because of its subject matter ("[h]itherto there has been no work devoted to these subjects ... by a Canadian, embodying his own actual experience" [p. xvii]) but also as an aesthetic object in its own right. Ornamental borders graced its dark green cloth covers; the title itself appeared, in gold leaf, in a small central circle on the front cover, surrounded by vines. Three splendid chromolithographs featuring fruits, vegetables, and flowers lent emphasis to the author's argument that Canadians were failing en masse to render their lives beautiful. "Too little is done to make home attractive," Beadle complained (p. 190). Long before the heyday of the City Beautiful movement, Beadle argued that usefulness and beauty were intimately connected. Grow a kitchen garden but never forget to "twine some flowers in the strands of daily toil" (p. 270).

Even in the extensive sections offering concrete advice Beadle doesn't put the brakes on his exuberance, calling the celery "delightful," beets "pleasing to the eye," and a rose-colored variety of radish "tender and excellent." (The kohlrabi, on the other hand, a "sort of above-ground turnip," doesn't pass muster. It possesses, writes Beadle acidly, "no special qualities that we

---

24 D. W. Beadle, *Canadian Fruit, Flower, and Kitchen Gardener* (Toronto: Campbell, 1872), p. 190. On Beadle's achievements, see Pleasance Crawford's entry in *Dictionary of Canadian Biography*, general ed. Ramsay Cook, 14 vols. to date (Toronto: University of Toronto Press, 1994), vol. XIII, pp. 46–8.

can discover.")[25] He does realize that the volatile climate places limits on his dream in which he envisions all of eastern Canada transformed into a flourishing garden full of ripening fruit, ruddy vegetables, and fragrant flowers. But if the treasures of the tropics do not grow naturally in this northern land, there is an abundance of hardy shrubs (from the Barberry to the White Fringe), easy-to-cultivate herbaceous flowers (from the Achillea to the Yucca) as well as tough annuals (from the Aster to the Salpiglossis) that will amply repay the gardener's efforts. Canada *does* require work, but the results are spectacular. With a little care on the part of the cultivator, even the pansy could be "grown here in great beauty, unfolding its lovely flowers in abundant profusion through the spring and autumn months" (p. 307).

However, such profusion is fragile, easily threatened. Unconcerned about the consequences, Canadians continue to hew down their trees by the wagonload. As the forests dwindle, the winters will become harsher, too. What underlies Beadle's worries for the aesthetic well-being of his fellow citizens, then, are strong environmental concerns, the hope that Canadians will, before it is too late, learn to appreciate "the influence of frequent belts of timber ... upon the life and health of ourselves, of our stock, of our crops and our orchards" (p. 94). But the realistic Beadle also knows – and these words seem eerily prophetic today – that "thoughts of immediate advantage" will always displace efforts to plan "with reference to the needs and comforts of years yet in the distance" (p. 33).

Canadian Fruit, Flower, and Kitchen Gardener, written by a Canadian-born horticulturist who rejects the yardstick of the "old country" as a way of measuring the success of the new, marks a turning point in Canadian botanical writing. Yet it is sobering to see how the gain of a new perspective – one that looks from the inside out rather than from the outside in – is already connected with a powerful vision of future irreversible losses, the fear that the Canadian project might be doomed before it has even begun.

The hidden subject of Beadle's book, the intimate connection between horticulture and Canadian identity, was also the underlying theme of *The Canadian Horticulturist*, the monthly magazine Beadle edited from 1878 to 1886 on behalf of the Fruit Growers' Association of Ontario. His successor was Linus Woolverton (1846–1914), a nurseryman from Grimsby, Ontario. What united the contributors to *The Canadian Horticulturist* was a special interest in apples. The September 1888 issue, for example, included a sparkling chromolithograph of the "Princess Louise" or "Woolverton Apple," first

---

25 Beadle, *Canadian Fruit*, pp. 215, 201, 249, 227.

shown in 1879, a product of editor Woolverton's Maplehurst Fruit Farm (Plate 8). Naming a new Canadian apple was not a trifling matter: a committee of the Fruit Grower's Association had, after much deliberation, chosen "Princess Louise," the name of the Viceregal Consort. From the article accompanying the illustration it is not entirely clear whether the intention was to honor the beautiful princess or the apple or both;[26] interestingly, some committee members had favored the homelier "Woolverton." And yet this was no ordinary apple – its skin is free from blemishes, we're told, and it has a waxy luster, "as though it had been highly polished" (Woolverton is quoting his fellow apple enthusiast Beadle here). In fact, no description will give the reader even an inkling of the extreme beauty of the fruit, its luminous carmine color and its fragrance. Bite into it, and you'll be overwhelmed even more: "The flesh is pure white, like that of the Snow apple, tender, juicy and nearly as melting, with a richer flavor and higher aroma." And then editor Woolverton, bursting with parental pride (after all, this is *his* apple), takes the unusual step of criticizing his own publication. According to him, the chromolithograph of the Woolverton apple, made after a painting by Evvy Smith, the daughter of the Vice-President of the Fruit Growers' Association, falls far short of the savory fruit's splendid reality.[27]

With apples such as these, who needs friends? Zealously, Woolverton and his friends kept track of bad harvests in Europe, because they meant a greater market share for their apples, the harbingers of Canadian pride abroad. In the *Canadian Horticulturist*, the whole business of fruit-improving and apple-growing turns into a metaphor for the nurturing of Canadian independence from Europe.[28] No wonder that some committee members had preferred "Woolverton," the plainer designation, to "Princess Louise," a reminder of their dependence on the old country. Knowing *what* precisely is here, the goal of previous naturalists, is one thing – *adding to it* is yet another matter entirely.

And pride in Canadian fruit-growing did not remain limited to the East. In 1909, J. T. (John Thomas) Bealby (1858–1943) reported on his successes as a

---

26 At Rideau Hall, Princess Louise painted her bedroom door with a *trompe l'œil* pattern of blossoming apple boughs; see Sandra Gwyn, *The Private Capital: Ambition and Love in the Age of Macdonald and Laurier* (Toronto: McClelland and Stewart, 1984), p. 187.

27 "The Princess Louise," *The Canadian Horticulturist* 11.9 (1888), pp. 193–5. For more on Linus Woolverton, see Pleasance Crawford's article in *Dictionary of Canadian Biography* (Toronto: University of Toronto Press, 1998), vol. XIV, pp. 1082–4.

28 On the connections between improving Canadian fruits so that "they no longer resembled the [European] original" and Canadian identity, see Suzanne Zeller, *Inventing Canada: Early Victorian Science and the Idea of a Transcontinental Nation* (Toronto: University of Toronto Press, 1987), pp. 198–9.

Plate 8. E. E. S. (i.e. Evvy Smith), "Princess Louise or Woolverton. For the Canadian Horticulturalist," from *The Canadian Horticulturalist* 11.9 (1888).

professional fruit-grower on land he had acquired on the Kootenay River, eighteen kilometers below Nelson, British Columbia. His self-congratulatory memoir, *Fruit Ranching in British Columbia,* was preceded by an advertisement in which Bealby identified himself as the "winner of hundreds of prizes for fruit." Pages and pages are devoted to figures and statistics, documenting the heavier yield, the greater certainty of a crop, and lower cost of land in British Columbia when compared to England.[29] More autobiographically tinged asides – about moronic cows eating dynamite ("nothing happened"), horses that refuse to be led, skunks lusting after the settlers' chickens – offer some comic relief, but the image that Bealby wants to plant in the reader's mind is an unambiguously positive one. It is a vision of "plum trees with the fruit hanging on them as thick as ropes of onions, the pear trees trailing their branches on the

---

29 J. T. Bealby, *Fruit Ranching in British Columbia,* 2nd ed. (London: Adam and Charles Black, 1911 [1909]). The Cambridge-educated Bealby was the English translator of E. T. A. Hoffmann's *Weird Tales* (1885) and Sven Hedin's memoir *Through Asia* (1898). See Edwinna von Baeyer and Pleasance Crawford, eds., *Garden Voices: Two Centuries of Canadian Garden Writing* (Toronto: Random, 1995), p. 43.

PEAR TREE,
Showing Pendulous Habit Caused by Weight of Fruit.

Plate 9. "Pear Tree, Showing Pendulous Habit Caused by Weight of Fruit," Photograph in J. T. Bealby, *Fruit Ranching in British Columbia*, 2nd edn. (1911).

ground through sheer inability to hold up their load of fruit ... the apples colouring day after day under the bright autumn sunshine" (p. 192; Plate 9).

The cookbooks published towards the end of the century similarly took pride in what they regarded as a typically Canadian – and export-worthy – conjunction of natural abundance and human ingenuity. In the revised edition of *The Galt Cook Book*, a compilation, first published in 1877, of "thoroughly tried and tested" recipes specifically for "[i]nexperienced housekeepers," editors Margaret Taylor and Frances McNaught bragged that copies of their book had been sent "to China, Egypt, India, South Africa, Australia, and other remote countries."[30] Apples are important here, too – in the form of pies,

---

30 Margaret Taylor and Frances McNaught, eds. and comps., *The New Galt Cook Book: Revised Edition. A Comprehensive Treatment of the Subject of Cookery with Abundant Instructions in Every Branch of the Art – Soups, Fish, Poultry, Meats, Vegetables, Salads, Bread, Cakes, Jellies, Fruits, Pickles, Sauces, Beverages, Candies, Sick Room Diet, Canning &c. &c. Including Valuable Tested Recipes in All Departments, Prepared for the Housewife – Not For the Chef* (Toronto: McLeod and Allen, 1898), pp. [iii]–iv.

dumplings, pudding, and jelly (one particularly enticing recipe, submitted by Miss Nettie Crane, is for "iced apples" [p. 200]) – but they represent only a fraction of the material that is ground, pureed, pounded, and kneaded in the course of the book's 450 recipe-filled pages.

Cookery means, as the book's epigraph by Ruskin makes clear, "the knowledge of all fruits and herbs and balms and spices, and of all that is healing and sweet in fields and groves, and savory in meats."[31] However, the advice housekeepers get here is often less than healing and sweet. "[S]plit the skin on the back of the neck" of the chicken, the reader is encouraged; then use your fingers to "[l]oosen the pipes" around it (p. 41). If you want your frogs nicely fried, says Mrs. Taylor, you need to skin them well and cook their hind legs in saltwater for five minutes (p. 51). This is a book preoccupied above all with liquids: the juices that drip out of slabs of delicious meat, the stews flavored with wine, the asparagus soup poured over slices of toast, the oysters smothered in white-pepper sauce, the calf brains soaked in cold salt water, the thick, oozy stream of scalding vinegar added to the small pieces of salmon and cabbage in a recipe for "Salmon Salad." Most of the recipes are restrained in tone, focused on the essentials – what to get, how to cut, chop, or slice it, how long to boil it, and what to pour over it. On a few occasions, however, the writer's excitement will break through: "There is scarcely any pickle more delicious than mushrooms," writes someone only identified as "S. B. C.," though even in this case pragmatism takes over: "provided they are properly done" (p. 147). The collaborative product of scores of nature-savvy, confident women authors, *The Galt Cook Book* refuses to play into stereotypes of Victorian femininity. A few dishes (the haggis, tripe, and trifle, for example) are traditional "old country" fare, to be sure, but consider especially the remedies offered in the section called "Cookery for the Sick," which indicate an irrepressible desire to engage directly with what Canadian nature has to offer: the witch-hazel, good for bruises and swelling and cheaper than arnica; Canadian balsam, which helps with rheumatism; the slippery elm bark, which, once boiled and sweetened, will cure the reader of her hiccups. Catharine Parr Traill would have approved.

Indefinitely pure

The ornithological equivalent of the recipes prepared by the women of Galt came in 1885, when the coal merchant Thomas McIlwraith (1824–1903), of

---

31 A slightly inaccurate quotation from John Ruskin, *The Ethics of the Dust: Ten Lectures to Little Housewives on the Elements of Crystallisation* (London: Smith, Elder, & Co., 1866), p. 138.

Hamilton, Ontario, published his *Birds of Ontario*, a handbook for nature enthusiasts and specimen collectors, the true guardians of natural history.[32] Local in emphasis, McIlwraith's book was as practical in intent as the recipes collected by Margaret Taylor and Frances McNaught. Yet many of McIlwraith's entries have an urgency that is no longer justified by the purpose of documentation.

Canadian ornithology was still in its infancy then. In the 1870s, when the young Ernest Seton Thompson, growing up in Toronto, wanted to read up on the birds in his immediate environment, his best resource was a slim volume by Alexander Milton Ross, *The Birds of Canada*, which he bought at Piddington's Book Store on Yonge Street after months of cutting firewood.[33] Dr. Ross (1832–97), a physician from Belleville, Ontario, had been an active member of the Underground Railroad, a "red-hot abolitionist," in the words of President Lincoln. He personally conducted scores of slaves from Alabama, Georgia, and Kentucky to their freedom in Canada.[34] Throughout his *Birds of Canada*, Ross is evidently impressed with the ability of birds to go wherever they please, something he knows only too well humans aren't able to do. His prose is serviceable, condensed to the point of fragmentation ("Feeds upon insects"; "Nest, upon the ground") or, in a few cases, even silence: "This very common bird," he writes about the phoebe, "is too well known to need a description" (p. 29). Equivocation is not his game: "The Canada Goose," Ross states with confidence, "is thirty-five inches long" (p. 99). When it comes to praising his birds, Ross's prose rarely soars higher than the adjective "pretty." Therefore, those moments in which he permits himself to become involved in his own text are more powerful than they would normally be, such as when he is talking about the "indescribably sweet and musical" song of the White-throated Sparrow: "I have frequently heard it at night, when passing through the woods" (p. 59).

Compared to the restrained Ross, McIlwraith is the Homer of Canadian bird life. Organized like a field guide, beginning with the Diving Birds and

---

32 The following quotations are from the second edition, *The Birds of Ontario: Being A Concise Account of Every Species of Bird Known to Have Been Found in Ontario, with a Description of Their Nests and Eggs and Instructions for Collecting Birds and Preparing and Preserving Skins, Also Directions How to Form a Collection of Eggs* (Toronto: Briggs, 1894).

33 John G. Samson, ed., *The Worlds of Ernest Thompson Seton* (New York: Knopf, 1976), p. 25; Alexander Milton Ross, *The Birds of Canada: With Descriptions of their Plumage, Habits, Food, Song, Nests, Eggs, Times of Arrival and Departure*, 2nd ed. (Toronto: Rowsell and Hutchison, 1872 [1871]).

34 See Ross's *Recollections and Experiences of an Abolitionist; from 1855 to 1865* (Toronto: Rowsell and Hutchison, 1875).

ending (as did Ross's book) with the Perchers, *Birds of Ontario* is in reality a poetic homage to Canadian birds as well as a lament for the lost connection between them and their human fans. Birds, you see, may share the world of humans, but they don't *have* to. In a country where humans settle down – like McIlwraith himself, who had left his native Scotland for Hamilton in 1853 and stayed – birds remain migrants, some defiantly so, and their temporary residences in Ontario are often annoyingly inaccessible to the humans who pursue them: all the nests of the Long-billed Marsh Wren that McIlwraith has seen "have been so placed that they could only be reached by wading or in a boat, and sometimes they were among the reeds on a quaking bog where approach was impossible" (p. 397).

One obvious remedy for the grief faithless migratory birds cause a collector like McIlwraith is to double one's appreciation for those who elect to stay, such as the White-breasted Nuthatch or the Snowbird, and for those who go the extra mile and do "good work" for Canadian farmers, like the Rose-breasted Grosbeak, who will visit the farmer's fields and snap up the potato bugs. However, the most poignant aspect of the story McIlwraith tells in *Birds of Ontario* concerns not the behavior of birds but the role humans have played in their gradual disappearance. The more thickly the province becomes settled, the fewer Bald Eagles are to be found here; the birds now "seek for greater retirement elsewhere" (p. 210). In winter, "strings of drowned, draggled cowheens" (the local name for the Long-tailed Ducks) may be seen dangling from the clotheslines outside the shacks on the beach. Many of these birds, after getting caught in the fishermen's gill-nets, will end up as swine food, a sad end "for the beautiful, lively *Clangula hyemalis*" (p. 86). Some birds, like the American Herring Gulls, adjust and feed on the city's trash drifting in the bay; others, like the White-winged Scoters, wash up dead on the shore soon after their arrival, a fact that the coal merchant McIlwraith, with his many personal and financial ties to local industry, knows could be related to "the emptying of the city sewage and refuse from the oil refineries into the bay" (p. 92).

In the face of such present and future losses, McIlwraith's prose becomes the place, the only one, where he can hold on to his beloved birds, where the "what is here," steadily diminishing as it is, can be made to appear to last. A small bird like the White-throated Sparrow thus becomes a complex work of art, to be caressed slowly by the writer's pen, even when we are given a taxonomic description: "With the crown black, divided by a median white stripe, bounded by a white superciliary line and yellow spot from the nostril to the eye; below this a black stripe through the eye; below this a maxillary black stripe bounding the indefinitely pure white throat, sharply contrasted with the dark ash of the breast and sides of the neck and head" (p. 319). McIlwraith recalls having come across one of these little sparrows, thirty miles west of Hamilton, near a gloomy little pond, on a warm July evening. It had appeared out of nowhere, mounting the top of a tree and, "his whole attitude indicating languor and weariness," drawled out its plaintive, familiar song "Old Tom Peabody, Peabody" (p. 320). At the time, the bird seemed perfectly at home where it was. By the end of October, however, it was gone; as far as McIlwraith was concerned, it might as well have been gone for good.

9
Short fiction

GERALD LYNCH

Two of the most eminent post-Confederation Canadian poets, Charles G. D. Roberts (1860–1943) and Duncan Campbell Scott (1862–1947), were also innovative short story writers. Of course, innovation should not be taken as the sole measure of a new country's literary achievement, especially when its literature already exists within a larger, established tradition. But artistic invention can signal a cultural coming-of-age as well as abundant vitality, as it does for the Canadian short story in this period. Roberts's *Earth's Enigmas: A Volume of Stories* (1896) was the first of his many collections of realistic animal stories, instituting a body of work the importance of which continues to grow. And Scott's *In the Village of Viger*, published the same year, was paradigmatic for the Canadian short story cycle, a genre that has continued attractive to Canadian writers. Such late nineteenth-century short stories by these and many other writers – adventurously realistic with respect to nature and adopting the practices of local color fiction – were widely praised for their convincing representations of wilderness and animals, and for their attention to linguistic and other particularities of place as small town and region. The other major short story writer of the post-Confederation period, Stephen Leacock (1869–1944), is perhaps the most internationally popular writer Canada has produced, if for a conventional kind of short story: humorous-satiric fiction. What is true, though, of any greatwriters view of literary history is true also of these writers and this survey: Roberts, Scott, and Leacock were the products of a whole post-Confederation culture that, like the Anglo-American nineteenth century itself, was prolific in its production of short story writers and the newspapers, magazines, miscellanies, and books in which they published. The present chapter will take some account of these enabling developments in the milieu of post-Confederation Canadian short fiction, then focus on the achievements of the three major writers.

It is not fortuitous that Roberts and Scott wrote the kinds of short fiction that were seen best to represent Canada, and perceived so not only from the perspective of the United States and Britain but also from within Canada's rapidly growing urban centers. Since Confederation in 1867, Canadians, galvanized by the nationalist urgings of such political-cultural forces as the Canada First Movement, were encouraged to look to their literature for a definitive reflection of themselves as Canadians. Beginning already to experience a modern alienation from nature, the increasing number of Canada's urbanites longed to reconnect with the natural world and to reaffiliate through fiction with their small-town origins (impulses that Leacock both satisfied and satirized). In service to this search for national identity and roots, poetry was accorded its traditional pride of place, but the popular interest was vested in wilderness adventure stories (Roberts), local color stories (Scott, Leacock), and humorous stories in a distinctively Canadian ironic voice expressive of the diversity that collectively was settling into a middle way philosophically, politically, and culturally.

Although the English-Canadian short story from Confederation to the First World War was often romantic, it was by no means exclusively so. All the kinds of stories that flourished elsewhere in the Anglo-American world flourished in Canada and were regularly published as well in a wide array of American magazines. In the best short stories of this period, there is a sophisticated mix of the romantic and the realistic, just as Leacock's parodic stories often poke fun at the excesses of romantic and realistic formulas. Roberts's achievement in the realistic animal story could seem alone to contradict the received critical opinion that nineteenth-century Canadian fiction was preponderantly romantic or, at the other extreme, that Canadian literature is at its best when realistic and documentary, but those animal stories are also about the secret lives of the periphrastic "furry kindred," those equally real other Victorians after Darwin. And Scott's seminal short story cycle, *In the Village of Viger*, is a tour de force of nineteenth-century story types, including such romantic forms as the Gothic tale, the folk tale, and the ghost story, while it is also, by definition as local color fiction, keenly observed realism.

Canadian markets and minor writers

Although the opportunity offered by the American market was instrumental in the success of the Canadian short story (more below), numerous homegrown magazines also contributed. These often ephemeral publications were many, and a number were longer-lived, with all having a voracious appetite for material. They included, for example, *Rose-Belford's Canadian Monthly and*

National Review (1872–82), the *New Dominion Monthly* (1867–79), and the *Canadian Illustrated News* (1869–83). The prolific writers who contributed to them included such stalwarts as May Agnes Fleming (1840–80), Rosanna Mullins Leprohon (1829–79), Ethelwyn Wetherald (1857–1940), Susie Frances Harrison (1859–1935), Agnes Maule Machar (1837–1927), Louisa Murray (1818–94), and Joanna Wood (1867–1927). Most of these writers had been forgotten until the recuperative work of the closing decades of the twentieth century (such as that of Lorraine McMullen and Sandra Campbell).[1] As a result some, such as Wetherald, Harrison and Machar, have become better recognized as significant contributors to the development of the literary short story in Canada.

To these lesser known writers can be added a number of the better known in what must nonetheless remain a necessarily selective survey. The social-political writer Nellie McClung (1873–1951) successfully employed the short story to didactic purposes in such collections as *The Black Creek Stopping-House* (1912), in which the stories, if salted with some wit, rely on pathos to fictionalize lessons and examples of Christian reform. As such, McClung's fictional practice is exemplary of a broad reformist movement in turn-of-the-century Canada. Lucy Maud Montgomery (1874–1942), still among the most popular and prolific writers from the period (some 500 short stories alone), steadily supplied the Canadian and American magazine markets with local color short stories in the style of her series of novels featuring Anne Shirley (of Green Gables fame) and other Prince Edward Island characters. The equally popular E. Pauline Johnson (1861–1913), best known for her performance poetry of Native Canadian life, was another steady contributor of short stories. In her collections *Legends of Vancouver* (1911) and *The Shagganappi* (1913), Johnson retells Native Canadian legends and tales, making them her own in the writing, as well as adventure stories of Native and pioneer life in Canada. Such stories as those mentioned above are not, as Canadian literary historians had first dismissed them, merely romantic or amateurish. They are fully realized short fictions as accomplished and important in their historical-cultural contexts as any that came afterwards.

Apart from Roberts, Scott, and Leacock, the more accomplished short story writers of the period were Isabella Valancy Crawford (1850–87), the

---

[1] See for example, Lorraine McMullen and Sandra Campbell, eds., *Pioneering Women: Short Stories by Canadian Women, Beginnings to 1880* (Ottawa: University of Ottawa Press, 1993); *Aspiring Women: Short Stories by Canadian Women, 1880–1900* (Ottawa: Tecumseh, 1993); and *New Women: Short Stories by Canadian Women, 1900–1920* (Ottawa: University of Ottawa Press, 1991).

aforementioned Susie Frances Harrison, and Sara Jeannette Duncan (1861–1922). The Irish-born Crawford, best known for her long poem "Malcolm's Katie: A Love Story" (1884), depended for a living (as main supporter of her fatherless family) on the income from her writing for various newspapers and magazines, if mainly in the publications of the period's leading entrepreneur, New York's Frank Leslie, and most often in his *Frank Leslie's Chimney Corner* through the 1870s and 1880s.[2] Consequently Crawford specialized in such popular fictional forms as romantic stories, comic stories of high-and-low society, and fairy tales, all of which were full of local color, sharply realized dialogue, and an impressively rendered Irish dialect. Occasionally, in such stories as "In the Breast of the Maple" and "Extradited" (the latter first published, not insignificantly, in Toronto's *The Globe*), she displays a talent for compelling realistic depictions of the larger problems facing the new nation and an interest in what might be termed a more authentic local color, albeit still in melodramatic backwoods tales.

Harrison's collection *Crowded Out! and Other Sketches* (1886), and especially the excellent title story and "The Idyl of the Island," are now read as exploring themes of distinctly Canadian national interest. Furthermore, in its stories' recurrent representation of Quebec provincial life, *Crowded Out!* anticipates one of the era's signal achievements in Scott's *In the Village of Viger*. In this regard, Harrison can also be seen to have practiced a local color fiction of Quebec life that is superior to the work of at least two of her better-known male contemporaries. E. W. Thomson (1849–1924) was writing a similar kind of local color story – dialect fiction of French-Canadian life – in numerous works such as those first collected in *Old Man Savarin* (1895), fictions which can be seen as pandering somewhat to American and British tastes for the exotic *à la Canadienne*. And the exceedingly popular Gilbert Parker (1862–1932), who lived in England while giving wide currency to the Northwest adventures of his recurring French-Canadian hero, Pierre, in such collections as *Pierre and his People: Tales of the Far North* (1892), was also retailing clichés to a non-Canadian readership, and doing so with short fictions set in areas of Canada that, remarkably, he had never visited.

Excepting the three focal authors of the present chapter, Sara Jeannette Duncan was the most gifted short story writer of the time, as she was unarguably its preeminent Canadian novelist. Her work as a journalist and

---

2 See Michael Peterman, "Writing for the Illustrated Story Papers in the 1870s: Individuality and Conformity in Isabella Valancy Crawford's Stories and Serialized Fiction," *Short Story* 13 (Spring 2005), pp. 73–87.

role as bestselling author are discussed in chapters by Janice Fiamengo and Michael Peterman respectively. Best known for her novel set in Canada, *The Imperialist* (1904), Duncan published only one collection of short stories, but it is a fairly flawless example of the genre: *The Pool in the Desert* (1903). In this short fiction (some of the stories approach novella length), which is proficient in its display of a Jamesean realism informed by William Dean Howells's theories of local color writing, the lives of girls and women in colonial Anglo-India may attract the most interest, but the stories also depict the frustrations of the displaced female artist and knowledgeably probe looming social-political problems, especially in its title story and "A Mother in India." In "The Heir Apparent," a short story published in the American *Harper's Bazaar* in 1905 and not collected till late in the twentieth century, Duncan shows that her skill at portraying perceptive female characters in Canadian society is not limited to her best-known Canadian novel.

Cross-border publishing: American markets

As stated, "The Heir Apparent" was published first in an American magazine, as was "A Mother in India" (*Scribner's*). This was not only Duncan's usual practice (along with those magazines already mentioned, she published stories in *Century* and *Atheneum*) but also that of her ambitious Canadian compatriots. Typical of the times' cross-border publishing opportunists, in 1887 Duncan pointed out to her fellow Canadians that "[t]he market for Canadian literary wares is New York, where the intellectual life of the continent is rapidly centralising."[3] And Roberts in "The Poet is Bidden to Manhattan Island" had some serious poetic fun with this early literary brain drain, advising the poet to "recognize / The side on which your bread is buttered!" and concluding:

> You've piped at home, where none could pay,
> Till now, I trust, your wits are riper.
> Make no delay, but come this way,
> And pipe for them that pay the piper![4]

As literary historians James Doyle and Nick Mount have shown, most important to professional writers such as Roberts, Scott, Leacock, and Duncan were the many widely circulated, so better paying, American magazines and

---

3 Quoted in James Doyle, "Canadian Women Writers and the American Literary Milieu of the 1890s," in Lorraine McMullen, ed., *Re(Dis)covering Our Foremothers* (Ottawa: University of Ottawa Press, 1990), p. 30.
4 Charles G. D. Roberts, *In Divers Tones* (Boston: E. Lothrop, 1886), pp. 130–2.

newspapers published mainly in New York (supplemented by those in Philadelphia, Boston, Detroit, and Chicago). This wider market for their writing was a great encouragement to Canada's short story writers, poets, journalists, and editors. Such a market made possible for the first time the professionalization of Canadian writing, from ephemeral newspaper sketches to short stories, to serialized novels in weekly and monthly magazines, to eventual book publication. Along with those already mentioned (*Harper's*, *Scribner's*, and so on), Canadian short story writers regularly found a venue for their work in such American magazines of the period as *The Atlantic Monthly*, *The Illustrated American*, *Literary Digest*, *Youth's Companion*, *Littel's Living Age*, *Truth*, and the *New England Magazine*. Important Canadian writers and editors such as Roberts and Bliss Carman were influential in shaping the policies of these American magazines, and in selecting their contributors. Many, such as E. W. Thompson and Peter McArthur (1866–1924), followed the practice of Carman, who at various times edited the New York magazines *The Chap-Book*, *The Independent*, and *Current Literature* and regularly solicited the writings of both his fellow Canadians struggling to make a living in the United States and those who remained back home. McArthur, as editor at *Truth* in New York, was instrumental in the early development and encouragement of Leacock: between 1895 and 1897, *Truth* published some two dozen of Leacock's first comic stories.

So the burgeoning American market had an obviously favorable impact on the success of the post-Confederation Canadian short story. Robert Barr (1850–1912), for instance, who was remarkably prolific and successful as a writer of many kinds of short stories, capitalized by publishing some fifteen collections, with many featuring his "fastidious French detective who is often seen as a precursor to Agatha Christie's Hercule Poirot."[5] But looked at another way, American magazine editors, insistently marketing Canada as either a stereotypically picturesque substitute Europe or a wilderness of adventurous possibility untouched by urban sophistication, also had a deleterious, or at least a constricting, effect. Voracious US market forces must answer for the very high production of forgettable local color stories and vicarious wilderness adventure tales, while remaining those same forces that also created the conditions for Roberts's realistic animal stories and Scott's *Viger*. A similar ambiguous influence obtains even in Leacock's most celebrated work, *Sunshine Sketches of a Little Town* (1912), if in this case the culprit is North American urbanism more than the American publishing market. Although commissioned by the

---

5 Misao Dean, Headnote to Robert Barr, in *Early Canadian Short Stories: Short Stories in English Before World War I*, Canadian Critical Editions (Ottawa: Tecumseh, 2000), p. 185.

Montreal Star as a series of stories for his Canadian readership (the stories of its companion volume, *Arcadian Adventures with the Idle Rich* [1914], were first published via an American syndicate), *Sunshine Sketches* is nonetheless, like *Viger*, a short story cycle in which the charming idyll of small-town Canadian life conflicts with, as it ironically satisfies, the homesick nostalgia of modern North American urbanites.

More unambiguously, it is highly likely that Leacock abused his best talent in churning out "funny pieces" for an idolizing British and American readership. As a staple of American magazine fiction, undoubtedly selected over material that would have conveyed a more sophisticated image of Canada, such local color stories and wilderness adventure tales helped to entrench internationally a cliché about Canada that would prove difficult to alter. As a result, early Canadian short stories were most often read for their sentimental didacticism or exotic local color features rather than for the literary innovations that they also exhibited. For example, Norman Duncan (1871–1916) published *The Soul of the Street: Correlated Stories of the New York Syrian Quarter* (1900), an undervalued linked series of stories set in New York's "Arab Quarter," but he remains best known for formulaic adventure and local color stories set in Newfoundland and Labrador (though at least one of these books, *The Way of the Sea* [1903], is original and accomplished in depicting the life of Newfoundland fishing communities).

Along with the Canadian magazines mentioned earlier and the publishing opportunities in the United States, there were more general-interest magazines in Canada also requiring a constant supply of short stories for that überliterary Victorian readership: *Dominion Illustrated News* (1862–4), *Grip* (1873–94), *The Week* (1883–96), and *The Canadian Magazine* (1893–1939). In retrospect, the most important was the highly influential *The Week*. Although primarily an organ of social and political culture, it regularly published short fiction by numerous authors as well as the sketches and journalism of Sara Jeannette Duncan in her "Saunterings" column. The last quarter of the nineteenth century also saw the rise and demise of many short-lived publications devoted to topical comic writings, with the most important being the exceptionally long-running *Grip*. It published a large number of prose parodies and sketches in each issue, short comic stories of the kind that would later win Leacock international acclaim. (In fact, Leacock published his first professional piece in *Grip* in 1894, the still hilarious "A, B, and C: The Human Element in Mathematics.") It is only in recent years that some of the lesser-known writers of comic fictions are being recovered and valued for their contributions to the development of the Canadian short story. As Michael Peterman has shown, the Irish-Canadian James McCarroll (pseud. Terry Finnegan, 1814–92) is one such;[6] interestingly, McCarroll was also an influential editor in New York who helped in the success there of such fellow Canadians as Isabella Valancy Crawford.

Charles G. D. Roberts

To turn to the first of the three major writers who will be the focus of the remainder of this chapter, there is little bombast in claiming that Charles G. D. Roberts created a sub-genre of the English short story with the publication of "Strayed" in the July 1889 issue of *Harper's Young People*: the realistic animal story, which may prove to be Canada's unique contribution to literature in English. Roberts's first collection of animal stories, *Earth's Enigmas* (1896), sold poorly, and the professional writer abandoned the form. But in one of those mysteries of creative synchronicity, the realistic animal story was also being pioneered by Ernest Thompson Seton in the stories first collected in *Wild Animals I Have Known* (1898). Seton's book achieved instant popularity, which was immediately capitalized on by Roberts in his return to animal stories in numerous collections and even whole novels over the next three decades. In retrospect it seems perfectly natural that a late nineteenth-century Canadian, Roberts, at home in semi-wilderness surroundings and educated in the classical tradition, would write about animals in an original manner – realistically and sympathetically. Seton may well have been the better naturalist, and it may be truer to literary history to credit both Seton and Roberts with the invention of the realistic animal story, but any lover of fiction will agree that Roberts was by far the better writer.[7]

Roberts would eventually publish some 250 realistic animal stories in what amounts to a catalogue of the era's most important publications and, simultaneously, some of its most ephemeral: *Harper's Monthly, Lippincott's Monthly Magazine, Current Literature, Harper's Young People, Outing, Frank Leslie's Popular Monthly, The Independent, Century Illustrated Magazine, The Windsor Magazine, Chamber's Journal, Hampton's Magazine, Canadian Magazine, Sunday Magazine, Sunset,* and *Saturday Evening Post.* The universe of these animal

---

6 Michael Peterman, *James McCarroll, Alias Terry Finnegan: Newspapers, Controversy and Literature in Victorian Canada* (Peterborough: Peterborough Historical Society, 1996).
7 Roberts was a great admirer of Seton; see "The Animal Story," in Terry Whalen, ed., *Charles G. D. Roberts: Selected Animal Stories* (Ottawa: Tecumseh, 2005), pp. 221–2. Further references to Roberts's stories will be from this edition and given parenthetically within the text.

stories is roughly governed by the Darwinian law of survival of the physically and mentally fittest. Big animals are beaten and eaten by bigger animals, and smart predators by smarter. Death most often descends from higher up the chain, often literally swooping down on the unsuspecting or careless. Darwin rules, but he does so with some consideration for chance and luck, and, equally relevant, in a natural world of much beauty and enduring mystery. (The brief "In the Deep of the Grass" from 1904's *The Watchers of the Trails: A Book of Animal Life* neatly illustrates all of these generalizations.) Never before in fiction had the furtive lives of wilderness animals been so closely observed, and never before had readers been led to empathize with the Other as real animal.

Roberts himself provides an excellent entrée to the realistic animal story. His introduction to *The Kindred of the Wild: A Book of Animal Life* (1902), his second collection, amounts to an essay on the new genre. First surveying the history of animals in literature, he recognizes his post-Darwinian moment: "men were forced at last to accept the proposition that, within their varying limitations, animals can and do reason" (p. 220). Acknowledging further the extent to which evolutionary theory has broken down the barriers between human and animal (and using his characteristic periphrasis), he observes that "[l]ooking deep into the eyes of certain of the four-footed kindred, we have been startled to see therein a something, before unrecognised, that answered to our inner and intellectual, if not our spiritual selves" (p. 220). Although Roberts often warned against anthropocentrism, the concluding exclusion in the preceding – "if not our spiritual selves" – is key to understanding his own persistent humanism (more below).

He proceeds to define the new kind of animal story as, "at its highest point of development ... a psychological romance constructed on a framework of natural science" (p. 221). And in concluding his introductory essay, Roberts clarifies his view of the real purpose of the realistic animal story: "[t]he clear and candid life to which [it] reinitiates us, far behind though it lies in the long upward march of being, holds for us this quality. It has ever the more significance, it has ever the richer gift of refreshment and renewal, the more humane the heart and spiritual the understanding which we bring to the intimacy of it" (p. 222). In other words, the realistic animal story ultimately serves a humanistic purpose in making its responsive readers more fully human, because the "intimate" reading of such stories tests the limit of our ability to sympathize imaginatively with the animal other.

There are as many kinds of Roberts's animal stories as there are of other equally prolific authors' human stories. He devotes exacting attention to all forms of animal life from the ephemeral existence of insects to the life-span of a bull moose, often including humans as just another animal of distinct superiority and failings. But his multifarious animal stories can helpfully be grouped into categories, somewhat arbitrarily labeled, with most of the following examples taken from *The Kindred of the Wild* (1902). There are slice-of-animal-life stories, such as "The Lord of the Air," wherein a male eagle and his mate are rearing their chicks until the male is trapped by a wily Native for sale to an American trophy hunter. By dint of a regal disdain, patience and speedy action, and luck, the eagle escapes back to his mountain aerie, where he resumes his rule over a feudally disposed natural world that is also sublime and mysterious (its animal inhabitants are in communication by means that seem telepathic). There are stories of predatory combat, such as "When Twilight Falls on the Stump Lots." In it, agrarian incursion into its habitat forces a she bear, for the sake of her cubs, to stalk a farmer's calf. In the climactic confrontation with the calf's mother, the naturally superior bear slips into an "unnatural" depression (an effect most likely of the clearing of land) and is mortally gored by the cow. The calf and injured cow are rescued by a farmer, the bear's unprotected cubs are eaten by foxes, and in a conclusion that is deeply ironic only if read in isolation from Roberts's view of man as the uppermost omnivore in nature's food chain, the calf is "tended and fattened, and within a few weeks [finds] its way to the cool marble slabs of a city market" (p. 99). There are full animal biographies, such as "The King of the Mamozekel," which recounts the life of a New Brunswick bull moose from birth to maturity, analyzing his psychology in terms of youthful trauma and presenting the adult bull as primarily governed by the need to mate. Like the eagles, the moose are seen to be thinly populating a world of much beauty and mystery, if a space that is at one point also invaded by ruthless, technology-assisted trophy hunters who are nonetheless bested by the big moose.

And there are numerous examples of what may broadly be termed animal adventure stories. "Strayed," for example, from Roberts' first collection, *Earth's Enigmas*, tells the compressed tale of a domesticated ox's escape into the wild, where it has threatening encounters with predators till killed by a panther (pp. 37–40). Typically more than a simple wilderness adventure story, "Strayed" can also be read as cautionary with regards to one's place in the world, and instructive also about the extent to which the domestic sphere has become alienated from wilderness. There are even animal stories indebted in whole or part to such genres as the detective story, the romantic tale, the comic anecdote, and, in at least one instance, the marooned-on-a-desert-island yarn ("King of Beasts," first published in *The Windsor Magazine* in 1912, and most revealing, as its title indicates, of Roberts's view of the animal man's place atop the order).

The most engaging of Roberts's animal stories are those that involve interaction between animals and humans. His second published story, "Do Seek Their Meat From God" (*Harper's Monthly*, December 1892), is remarkable for the degree to which it exhibits the themes of animal life that would continue to interest Roberts. As in "When Twilight Falls on the Stump Lots," the action is generated by civilization's incursion into wilderness habitat, this time the territory of two panthers. The panthers, hunting (like the she bear) to satisfy their ravenous cubs, chance upon a child abandoned in an isolated cabin in the woods. The owner of the cabin is a derelict settler whose neighbor is an industrious pioneer. The good settler chances to be returning home with store-bought provisions when he hears the abandoned child crying in the cabin. Hungry himself and imagining his waiting supper, he thinks he will let the bad settler look after his own child. But as the child sets up a greater wail, the man is overpowered by his sympathetic imagining of his own child in similar circumstances. He sets down his provisions and investigates the crying. In this story of parallel lives moving towards confrontation, he comes into the cabin's clearing just as the panthers enter it from the other side, and he shoots both, just managing to save his own life. In the cabin he discovers that the child is his own son who had come to the cabin seeking the playmate who, with his own father, had departed the sparse settlement. The story ends with the father out hunting one day and coming upon the skeletal remains of the panthers' cubs.

Obviously, human and animal have much in common: both seek to ensure the lives of their offspring and, since reproductive success *is* success in nature, will do what is necessary. Where man and animal differ essentially in Roberts is in the human capacity for imagined, sympathetic identification with the other, that most human quality Roberts wished his innovative realistic animal stories to encourage. That faculty, call it the empathetic imagination, would appear to be the saving grace of humans (indeed, much reader sympathy is elicited even for the preying panthers, who would never turn aside from their meal for the sake of another's cubs and who clearly exhibit no sentimental response to the prospect of eating the boy; nor can they, Roberts states explicitly [p. 31]). As was suggested earlier, it is no surprise that a highly educated imaginative writer of late nineteenth-century Canada entangled with the real post-Darwinian animal world would come to such a conclusion about what is distinctively best in human beings. Roberts's "man" is both a part of the animal world and apart from it – atop it in the highest reach of what

Roberts calls our "spiritual selves." Ecological theorists may view such a reading as anthropocentric, but it seems the only realistic conclusion to be drawn from Charles G. D. Roberts's animal stories.

Duncan Campbell Scott

In 1896, at the beginning of the Anglo-American modern short story, Duncan Campbell Scott published his seminal short story cycle, *In the Village of Viger*.[8] Throughout the post-Confederation period, Scott also published many other stories, mostly in the American *Scribner's Magazine* beginning in 1887, where most of the *Viger* stories were first published, but also in Toronto's *Massey's Magazine* in the 1890s.[9] Scott, often recognized as Canada's first writer of realistic short fiction (in 1928 Raymond Knister dedicated the first modern anthology of Canadian short stories to him),[10] also published wilderness adventure stories, historical romances, ghost stories, detective stories, and even a comic tale in the manner of Leacock, "How Uncle David Rouse Made His Will" (in Toronto's *The Globe* in 1907).[11] With "Charcoal" (which was first published as "Star Blanket" in the *Canadian Magazine* in 1904) he wrote a short story on the same subject as his best-known poems, the so-called Indian poems. Based on an actual court case and very much realistic in execution, "Charcoal" tells the pathetically tragic story of one confused Native's struggle to accommodate himself to a world no longer essentially Native or yet wholly European-Christian. Thus "Charcoal" illustrates Scott's abiding interest in times of transition, in the violent disturbance of what was once a thing at "rest" (an important word in Scott's writings signifying a pure state) before it transforms into whatever it will become, whether for Natives or for the residents of the small Quebec town of Viger experiencing the first incursions of metropolitan modernity.

The coherent whole of *In the Village of Viger* will most likely remain Scott's greatest achievement in the short story. Although there may be claims for the antecedence of other linked-story collections, it is doubtful that as fully formed a short story cycle can be found earlier anywhere. Certainly there are earlier

---

8 Duncan Campbell Scott, *In the Village of Viger* (Toronto: McClelland and Stewart, 1996 [1896]). All further references are to this edition and are given parenthetically in the text.
9 See Carole Gerson, "The Piper's Forgotten Tune: Notes on the Stories of D. C. Scott and a Bibliography," *Journal of Canadian Fiction* 16 (1976), p. 138.
10 Raymond Knister, ed., *Canadian Short Stories* (Freeport, New York: Books for Libraries Press, 1971 [1928]).
11 Tracy Ware, ed., *The Uncollected Short Stories of Duncan Campbell Scott* (London: Canadian Poetry Press, 2001), p. 159.

coherent collections, by such as Charles Dickens, Ivan Turgenev, Nikolai Gogol, and Washington Irving, including such earlier Canadian works as Thomas McCulloch's *The Letters of Mephibosheth Stepsure* (ser. 1821–3) and, most importantly, Thomas Chandler Haliburton's *The Clockmaker: or, the Sayings and Doings of Sam Slick of Slickville* (1836). But with *Viger* there comes into the literary world a new genre best called the short story cycle, and even the Canadian short story cycle.[12]

Forrest L. Ingram provided the first definition of the short story cycle: "*a book of short stories so linked to each other by their author that the reader's successive experience on various levels of the pattern of the whole significantly modifies his experience of each of its component parts.*"[13] Story cycles develop by means of what Ingram called "the dynamic patterns of RECURRENCE and DEVELOPMENT" (Ingram, p. 20). Occupying the gap between the miscellaneous collection of stories and the novel, the short story cycle can be seen thus as an ideal form for the writers of such a middle-way country as Canada. Where modern and contemporary story cycles most often focus on character and questions of identity, such as Alice Munro's *Who Do You Think You Are?* (1978), the story cycles of the post-Confederation period, such as *Viger* and Leacock's *Sunshine Sketches of a Little Town*, achieve coherence by dwelling on place, the small town. Further, the concluding stories of cycles bring to fulfillment the recurrent patterns of the preceding fiction, reintroducing the stories' major characters and central images, and restating in a refrain-like manner the main concerns of the whole. Typically, the final stories of such cycles of place return, or attempt to return, readers and characters alike to small-town origins, a distinctively Canadian feature that has been termed "the return story."[14]

As stated earlier, *Viger* comprises a virtuoso's gallery of nineteenth-century story forms: sketch ("The Bobolink"), folk tale ("The Pedler"), Gothic/Ghost Story ("The Tragedy of the Seigniory"), local color ("Josephine Labrosse"), realistic ("No. 68 Rue Alfred de Musset"), psychological ("The Desjardins," "Sedan"), and comic ("The Wooing of Monsieur Cuerrier") – all in a seamless blend of romantic and realistic styles, with the two modes sometimes commingling. Knister not only dedicated 1928's *Canadian Short Stories* to Scott but

---

12 It should be noted that American Sara Orne Jewett's story sequence *The Country of the Pointed Firs* was also published in 1896, but it does not compare favorably with *Viger*.
13 Forrest L. Ingram, *Representative Short Story Cycles of the Twentieth Century: Studies in a Literary Genre* (Paris: Mouton, 1971), p. 19. Italics in original.
14 See Gerald Lynch, *The One and the Many: English-Canadian Short Story Cycles* (Toronto: University of Toronto Press, 2001), pp. 28–32.

concluded his stock-taking introduction by praising the signal achievement of *Viger* specifically: "a perfect flowering of art is embodied in one volume, *In the Village of Viger*, by Duncan Campbell Scott. It is work which has had an unobtrusive influence; but it stands out after thirty years as the most satisfyingly individual contribution to the Canadian short story."[15]

The cycle form of *In the Village of Viger* is especially appropriate to its subject. The realistic nineteenth-century novel, the only plausible alternative, would not have been as suited to figuring the subsumption of the small community of Viger by the expanding metropolis and the consequent fragmentation of many of those humanistic values that Scott held: interdependent community, tradition (history), duty and responsibility, work, tolerance, and family. The discontinuous narrative of the story cycle provided Scott with a form ideally suited to the depiction of the dissolution and tentative reconstitution of familial and, by extension, communal life. *Viger*'s primary manifestation of the effects of the confrontation between past and future is the destabilization of the traditional family. Fractured families are the most telling symptom of the dark themes of *Viger*'s stories – urban sprawl, New World versus Old World, exploitation of labor, and such – as well as being the further cause of problems: crime, madness, dislocation, failed romance, betrayal, and so forth.

The opening paragraph of *Viger*'s first story, "The Little Milliner," with its bold announcement of the book's subject of transitional times, constitutes a projection of the whole story cycle. Quoted in its entirety, it serves here as illustration both of the genre's proleptic and recurrent technique and of Scott's concise symbolic style:

> It was too true that the city was growing rapidly. As yet its arms were not long enough to embrace the little village of Viger, but before long they would be, and it was not a time that the inhabitants looked forward to with any pleasure. It was not to be wondered at, for few places were more pleasant to live in. The houses, half-hidden amid the trees, clustered around the slim steeple of St. Joseph's, which flashed like a naked poniard in the sun. They were old, and the village was sleepy, almost dozing, since the mill, behind the rise of land, on the Blanche had shut down. The miller had died, and who would trouble to grind what little grist came to the mill, when flour was so cheap? But while the beech-groves lasted, and the Blanche continued to run, it seemed impossible that any change could come. The change was coming, however, rapidly enough. Even now, on still nights, above the noise of the

---

15 Knister, *Canadian Short Stories*, p. xix.

frogs in the pools, you could hear the rumble of the street-cars and the faint tinkle of their bells, and when the air was moist the whole southern sky was luminous with the reflection of thousands of gas-lamps. But when the time came for Viger to be mentioned in the city papers as one of the outlying wards, what a change there would be! There would be no unfenced fields, full of little inequalities and covered with short grass; there would be no deep pools, where the quarries had been, and where the boys pelted the frogs; there would be no more beech-groves, where the children could gather nuts; and the dread pool, which had filled the shaft where old Daigneau, years ago, mined for gold, would cease to exist. But in the meantime, the boys of Viger roamed over the unclosed fields and pelted the frogs, and the boldest ventured to roll huge stones into Daigneau's pit, and only waited to see the green slime come working up to the surface before scampering away, their flesh creeping with the idea that it was old Daigneau himself who was stirring up the water in a rage. (pp. 3–4)

The ten following short stories are illustrations of, and variations on, the theme of destabilizing transitional times announced in this opening paragraph: what Viger was, what it is "in the meantime," and what it will become. Scott shows here that Viger, rather than being the "pleasant Viger by the Blanche" that he describes in the book's prefatory poem or the Arcadia he will describe in the opening of the actually vicious "Sedan" (p. 30), is a small town in the path of a booming metropolis about to "embrace" it – "not a time that the inhabitants looked forward to with any pleasure."

The details of the opening paragraph also reveal that Viger's flour mill – one of a rural community's foundational institutions – will remain shut down because flour is produced more cheaply in the industrialized city. Thus Scott introduces the theme of dislocation resulting from technological progress – modern production methods – a theme that is recurrently developed in subsequent stories (for example, "Josephene LaBrosse" and "Paul Farlotte"). The ominous advance of such metropolitan/modern changes is signaled further by the foreboding "rumble of the street-cars" and in the portrayal of the city as a colonizing Pandemonium on the horizon, advancing northwards and lighting up the "southern sky ... with the reflection of thousands of gas-lamps." Then there is the catalogue of emphatic negations that places Viger under threatened erasure: "no unfenced fields," "no deep pools," "no more beech groves," and "the dread pool ... would cease to exist." The ugliest image in this opening paragraph, the "green slime" that comes "working up to the surface" of old Daigneau's pit (a disused mine), might be seen as adumbrating the evil effects of the pursuit of material wealth, another theme that, recurrently developed, is central in such dark stories as "No. 68 Rue Alfred de Musset,"

"The Tragedy of the Seigniory," and "The Pedler." St. Joseph was the protector of the Holy Family and remains the patron saint of the family and of Canada itself; thus he can be viewed with his "naked poniard" as protecting those threatened Viger families living in the houses that cluster about the church.

Viger's return story, "Paul Farlotte," plays a final variation on the cycle's theme of fractured family, but does so in concert with a number of motifs from the cycle's preceding stories: madness, duty, industrialization and progress, Old World vs. New, and the need for self-sacrifice. Like the return stories of the best Canadian short story cycles, "Paul Farlotte" functions as peroration to *Viger*, returning to the cycle's dominant theme, fractured family, and refiguring it in a powerful, because cumulative, manner, reiterating key images and even repeating phrases from earlier stories. Read in this way, "Paul Farlotte" can be seen to offer a possible answer to the question that Scott implicitly asks throughout his innovative *fin-de-siècle* short story cycle: What is family to mean in the alienating, dislocating, industrializing, urbanizing, maddening modern world that is coming? *Viger*'s return story shows an answer in self-sacrifice, a painful shifting of national loyalty from Old World to New, and, in effect, a redefinition of "family" itself.

Stephen Leacock

Like Scott with *Viger*, Stephen Leacock wrote his two masterpieces, *Sunshine Sketches of a Little Town* and *Arcadian Adventures with the Idle Rich* (1914) as short story cycles. But Leacock was wholly a humorist and satirist. His first short stories were published in the 1890s in such magazines as *Grip* and New York's *Truth*, when the latter was edited by Canadian Peter McArthur. "My Financial Career" was first published in New York's *Life* in 1895 (also when McArthur worked there), and that classic working of the humor of discomfort provided the opening story of Leacock's first miscellaneous collection, the self-published *Literary Lapses* (1910). This book still exhibits some of Leacock's best work in the short comic story: "Boarding-House Geometry," "The Awful Fate of Melpomenus Jones," "Hoodoo McFiggin's Christmas," and the aforementioned "A, B, and C: The Human Element in Mathematics." He would continue to produce such gems throughout a long career, but Leacock's primary contribution to the Canadian short story will remain those companion volumes, *Sunshine Sketches* and *Arcadian Adventures*, with the *Sketches* being the most important not only in the continuum of Canada's short fiction but of its fiction period. As Mordecai Richler, Canada's great comic novelist of the second half of the twentieth century, observed, the Sketches was "the first work to establish a Canadian voice."[16]

The stories of Sunshine Sketches were first serialized in the Montreal Star from 17 February 1912 to 22 June 1912. Between then and its publication in book form later that year, Leacock added an autobiographical preface and revised the stories, dividing one into two and combining two others into one. In structurally reorganizing the opening and middle parts of the book, he gave prominence to the character of Josh Smith, who dominates the opening and closing stories on business and politics. And these revisions created in the book's middle – stories four through nine – two three-story sections, with the first group satirizing Mariposan religion and the second ultimately valorizing its romance. This symmetrical center of the Sketches opposes three stories on the failure of Mariposa's institutionalized religion to meet simply the spiritual needs of its Anglican parishioners with three on the redemptive value of love, marriage, and family.

The stories proper of Sunshine Sketches are grouped, then, into five thematic sections: 1) stories one and two, concerning Josh Smith and Jefferson Thorpe respectively, oppose real and illusory business in Mariposa; 2) story three, the much anthologized "The Marine Excursion of the Knights of Pythias," uses the ship trope to portray in microcosm the social life of Mariposa aboard the Mariposa Belle; 3) stories four through six deal with religion; 4) stories seven through nine center on romance; and 5) stories ten and eleven humorously satirize political life. Schematized so, the two-story business and political sections of the Sketches (dominated by Smith) can be seen structurally to frame the social, religious, and romantic concerns of the town. This is what might be expected in the fiction of a professor of political economy (which Leacock was): the practical realities of business and politics come first and last, while at the center of the book are found the spiritual realities of religion and love.

This whole is further framed, opening with the preface and closing with the short return story, "L'Envoi: The Train to Mariposa." In "L'Envoi" an anonymous auditor – a "you" now resident in the City – boards a train bound for Mariposa, confronts his face mirrored in a darkened window, and realizes that he will be unrecognizable to those among whom he once lived. But if "L'Envoi" depicts an abortive return to the small town for the urban auditor, it remains instructive for that other "you" aboard the imaginary train, the reader

---

16 Mordecai Richler, Introduction to Stephen Leacock, Sunshine Sketches of a Little Town (London: Prion, 2000 [1912]), p. xiii.

of "such a book as the present one."[17] As return story, *"L'Envoi"* recapitulates the importance of recovering the conservative, humanist values that Leacock associated with Mariposa – interdependent community, a cherishing of ancestors and history, anti-materialism, romance and family – reminding the reader of what "home" means and how "Mariposa" with all its faults must be remembered in the modern urban present if there is to be any hope for a worthwhile future.

Regrettably, *Sunshine Sketches* nonetheless ends in a city's "Mausoleum Club." *Arcadian Adventures with the Idle Rich* begins and ends there. Thus the two can be read as an extended work of fiction, as companion volumes, as an ideologically continuous work that turns on the hinge of the *Sketches'* return story. Both books anatomize their subjects – the small Canadian town and the big American city – portraying in roughly the same order such fundamental institutions as business, religion, marriage, and politics. But where the *Sketches* looks fondly and ironically to a past time, in the hope of recovering the communal values that characterized small-town Canada, the *Adventures* peers at the present (c. 1914), with the intention of exposing the individualism and crass materialism that rampant capitalism has thrown up in the form of a metropolitan American plutocracy. Thus the stories of *Arcadian Adventures* satirize such early twentieth-century phenomena as stock-market scams, the hunger for religious experience, the back-to-nature vogue, doctrinal-ditching efforts toward a pecuniary ecumenism, and the hypocritical movement for municipal reform.

Arcadian Adventures depicts the pursuit of wealth and power as initially the competitive but eventually the monopolistic enterprise of a central clique of plutocrats. The first story of the cycle, "A Little Dinner with Mr. Lucullus Fyshe," concerns the cutthroat practices of two financial predators, Fyshe and Asmodeus Boulder, and ends in determined vengefulness. The next two stories – "The Wizard of Finance" and "The Arrested Philanthropy of Mr. Tomlinson" – contrast the present decadent metropolis with an earlier American pastoral ideal figured in the Tomlinsons and their farm. "The Yahi-Bahi Oriental Society of Mrs. Rasselyer-Brown" continues to chip away at the urban mock-Arcadia, with Leacock lampooning the empty lives and spurious culture supported by crass materialism. In "The Love Story of Mr. Peter Spillikins," the plutocracy asserts control over romantic love itself: the myopic Spillikins mistakes the gold-digging Mrs. Everleigh for the mother lode of

---

17 Stephen Leacock, *Sunshine Sketches of a Little Town*, Canadian Critical Editions, ed. Gerald Lynch (Ottawa: Tecumseh, 1996 [1912]), p. 141.

love, while the potential for true love and natural family (of the redemptive kind portrayed in *Sunshine Sketches*) promised in the "Little Girl in Green" is thwarted. In the *Adventures'* stories on religion – "The Rival Churches of St. Asaph and St. Osoph" and "The Ministrations of the Rev. Uttermust Dumfarthing" – Leacock's ostensible subjects are the idolatry of wealth and power, expedient ecumenism (the "United Church Limited"), and, more subtly, monopoly capitalism. The reader of *Arcadian Adventures* might well wonder at this point in the story cycle: if business, society and culture, love, and religion have fallen to the increasingly concerted machinations of the so-called plutorians, can plutocratic political rule be far behind? The *Adventures'* return story, "The Great Fight for Clean Government," answers this question with a negative more deadening than *"L'Envoi's"* frustrated return to Mariposa.

All those in *Arcadian Adventures* who are close to the center of Leacock's conservative-humanist satiric norm – the Tomlinson family, the Little Girl in Green, the Rev. McTeague – are defeated by the ascendant plutocracy in what emerges in the return story as a satiric triumph of dullness and darkness. The only real opposition to the benighted plutocracy is suggested not by the return story of *Arcadian Adventures* but by the closing words of *Sunshine Sketches*: "the little Town in the Sunshine that once we knew." By recovering the values that Leacock associated with the small-town Canadian community, by knowing again what "once we knew," the we of the *Sketches'* Mausoleum Club might avoid the spiritual dead end that is so insistently depicted in *Arcadian Adventures with the Idle Rich* – Leacock's short story cycle set in an American city and published in the first year of the First World War.

Many of the short story writers discussed in this chapter – and certainly Roberts, Scott, and Leacock – continued to publish well into the twentieth century, but their most important fiction was published in the post-Confederation period, roughly 1867 to 1914.

10

Bestselling authors, magazines, and the international market

MICHAEL PETERMAN

In the late 1860s and 1870s publishers and writers in the new Dominion were paying close attention to the dramatic changes affecting the conditions of print culture. Many were industrial and had international implications; collectively, they created a new range of opportunities to be tested and exploited. This chapter considers various ways in which, quite apart from the vexing matter of copyright protection,[1] these new conditions affected Canadian writers and publishers. By the 1880s, in fact, the era of the bestseller had dawned and the scramble to profit from new publishing opportunities was evident both in the United States and Canada.[2]

In the wake of the American Civil War, it was clear that, in New York and Boston, newspapers, magazines, and books were being printed faster and in much greater volume than ever before. Technical improvements abounded. Paper was cheaper, automated typesetting was increasingly efficient, woodcuts were being integrated more effectively (the application of photographs was imminent), and large steam presses meant printing firms could operate day and night. Distribution was faster and advertising aggressive both within the printed text and by agents seeking to develop national markets. Newspaper production and book publishing could now occur on an unprecedented scale and at much reduced costs per unit. As well, in the northeastern United States large niche markets were opening up and expanding, although the conservative media of the time deemed much of this new production

---

1 See George L. Parker's detailed study of copyright restrictions affecting Canadian publishers in the nineteenth century and the ways in which several publishers sought to challenge them in *The Beginnings of the Book Trade in Canada* (Toronto: University of Toronto Press, 1985).
2 Clarence Karr reports that the term "bestseller" emerged in the 1880s and was in common use by the 1890s. See *Authors and Audiences: Popular Canadian Fiction in the Early Twentieth Century* (Montreal and Kingston: McGill-Queen's University Press, 2000), p. 28.

cheap and merely popular – that is, non-literary and of lesser consequence than traditional publications.

In Canada, by contrast, markets remained much smaller and highly regional, despite the optimism and cultural excitement generated by Confederation. In fact, what had been true during colonial days remained in effect for many publishers well after 1867; there were few attempts to capitalize operations on a large scale or to encourage local talent and a readership for Canadian writing. In fact, most of the writers and publishers in Canada prior to 1870 had been born elsewhere; they thought of publishing opportunities and literary production in terms of their homelands. It remained a cultural given to them that Britain and America were the sites of serious authorship and consequential publishing. Canada remained a fledgling country in which localized newspapers, conceived and justified on political and economic grounds, were the main medium of communication.

Though a small number of entrepreneurs sought to test wider publishing markets after Confederation, their opportunities were no match for the action generated in centers like New York, Boston, and Chicago. Ambitious publishers like John Lovell in Montreal and Hunter, Rose in Toronto were well aware of the liabilities involved in publishing local authors. They specialized in meeting the needs of local businesses and competing for government contracts. In seeking to wrest a portion of the demand for international literary material, they tapped into the dominant American and British markets by publishing inexpensive reprints. Their approach was both conservative and entrepreneurial. Native-born writers were not blind to the realities governing the Canadian marketplace; accordingly, while they sought out local publication, they vigorously looked elsewhere to sell their literary wares.

South of the border many magazines and newspapers were noisily contending for diverse audiences. Mass-market publishers like Frank Leslie, Beadle & Adams, Street & Smith, and George and Norman Munro flooded the burgeoning marketplace with inexpensive newspapers, story magazines and dime novels, geared to serve a range of tastes and appetites. Promising their readers exciting narratives, engaging characters, and family entertainment, they aimed their products at specific audiences – women, men, adolescents, and children. They paid their authors attractive fees and guaranteed them wide distribution and name recognition. In this sense American business culture was far more attuned than Canada to the nurturing of literary aspirations, so long as the writers geared their texts to the marketplace they served.

Thus, a writer in Concord, Massachusetts or Peterborough, Ontario could identify an opportunity, seek out a connection, and produce what he or she could, recognizing that in the publishing world the fittest efforts were likely to find a home, regardless of nationality. At least, there was the opportunity for an aspiring writer to make a living. In Canada, with far fewer paying opportunities and a culture deeply mired in fierce religious denominationalism and the application of Victorian niceties, only a handful of writers could make their living at home. Many were not slow to make their way south in search of publishing positions and literary connections. As Nick Mount has demonstrated, there was a flood of expatriate talent to American centers after 1880.[3] Not all, however, went south, at least in the wake of Confederation. One such stay-at-home was Isabella Valancy Crawford (1850–87).

Isabella Valancy Crawford

Crawford's story provides a striking example of those conditions. Talented and ambitious, she set out in the early 1870s to find outlets for her fiction in both the Canadian and American story markets. Dublin-born but Ontario-raised, she was only twenty-two in 1872, when, with the help of a fellow Irish-Canadian named James McCarroll, her novel *Wrecked! or, The Rosclerras of Mistree* was serialized in *Frank Leslie's Illustrated Newspaper* (October 26, 1872–March 29, 1873). McCarroll (1814–92) had left Toronto under a cloud in 1866 and was then working as an editor for the Frank Leslie Company in New York City.[4] It was just five years after Confederation and the breezes of Canada-First[5] enthusiasm were brisk. In that same year, Crawford won a Canadian story contest initiated by a Montreal magazine called *The Hearthstone*, owned by George-Édouard Desbarats, the highly regarded publisher of *The Canadian Illustrated News*. Her prize-winning novel, *Winona; or, The Foster Sisters*, began serialization in the first issue of *The Favorite*, *The Hearthstone's* successor. It ran

---

3 Nick Mount, *When Canadian Literature Moved to New York* (Toronto: University of Toronto Press, 2005). Mount uses census figures to conclude "that between 1880 and 1900 upwards of two hundred Canadian writers either quit their profession or quit their country" (p. 7). Most of them moved south to take up available opportunities.

4 McCarroll had been one of Toronto's most prominent poets and humorists in the early 1860s before becoming disenchanted with Canadian politics and aligning himself with the Fenian movement in Buffalo. By 1872 he was working as an editor for Leslie in New York City.

5 See Isabella Valancy Crawford, *Winona; or, The Foster Sisters*, ed. Len Early and Michael Peterman (Peterborough: Broadview Press, 2007), pp. 15–30, 65 and the *Dictionary of Canadian Biography* entry on Desbarats, by Claude Galarneau (Toronto: University of Toronto Press, 1990), vol. XII, pp. 246–50. The *DCB* entry makes no reference to *The Favorite* or to the Desbarats–Crawford legal case.

in twelve instalments from January 11 to March 29, 1873. Thus, not only was Crawford able to compare two components of the emerging North American market for serialized fiction, but she was soon to learn some hard lessons about their differences.

Frank Leslie's large and self-promoting publishing empire in New York City helped to open up a writing career for her; the prominence of the serialization of "Wrecked" brought her name before a large sector of the North American reading public. In any given week, Leslie's *Illustrated Newspaper* sold between 150,000 and 300,000 copies depending on the newsworthiness of the stories covered by his reporters and illustrators. With a wide distribution keyed partly to the burgeoning rail networks, Leslie likely paid her according to going rates although she was a virtual unknown.[6] For a young writer whose family was struggling to maintain genteel appearances in the wake of her father's ill health and financial struggles, immediate remuneration for literary services was most welcome.

By contrast, Crawford's Canadian experience was neither pleasant nor profitable. After the editor of *The Hearthstone* informed her by letter of her success, Desbarats decided to downplay the results of the contest and thus avoid paying Crawford the $500 that she had won. The list of winners promised by *The Hearthstone* was never formally announced. More disappointing still, after "Winona" and several other Crawford poems and stories had appeared in *The Favorite*, the magazine still refused to pay her.

Despite his solid reputation, Desbarats was, by early 1873, experiencing serious financial constraints. Even as he was revamping *The Favorite*, he was involved in an attempt to enter the New York City market for illustrated newspapers with a daily called the *New York Graphic*. Facing cash shortages on several fronts, he withheld payments to Crawford, thus leaving her no recourse but a lawsuit. In the fall of 1873 she took her claim to the Peterborough Assizes, where she won her suit for $605.48. The judge ruled that there was no legitimate defence for Desbarats's actions. Despite the court's finding, however, Crawford faced a major second disappointment, for, in 1875, Desbarats was forced to declare bankruptcy. Anecdotal evidence suggests that finally she received a mere $100 of the money that he owed to her.[7]

---

6 See Joshua Brown, *Beyond the Lines: Pictorial Reporting, Everyday Life, and the Crisis of Gilded-Age America* (Berkeley: University of California Press, 2002) for the best available information on Frank Leslie's illustrated newspaper. Circulation of the newspaper is dealt with throughout the study.
7 See the Introduction to *Winona; or, The Foster Sisters*, pp. 21–30.

The lesson was clear. The solid and successful Frank Leslie paid promptly and distributed widely while Desbarats failed to pay; neither had he managed to develop a sustaining readership for his story magazine. Little wonder that Crawford wrote most of her subsequent prose for Leslie and the American story market.

Her experiences in 1872–3 determined the direction of Crawford's brief literary career. While she did not hesitate to send her poetry to Toronto newspapers and Canadian magazines in the 1870s and 80s, she felt betrayed by "the High Priests of Canadian periodical literature."[8] However, she accepted such conditions as a given. Thus, she prepared her material the better to meet the needs of the transnational and popular market represented by Frank Leslie. While she later observed that she had "not [been] very seriously injured by the process,"[9] she likely meant was that she was able to find paying work in *Frank Leslie's Chimney Corner* and his *Popular Magazine*, and with other American publishers, thus earning money to support herself and her widowed mother. A later generation of writers would not hesitate to move south in search of paying work and greater opportunities.

Publishing in Canada

The period from 1867 to 1915 provides a fascinating glimpse of the myriad ways in which Canadian writers and publishers conducted their careers and businesses. After a brief period of post-Confederation optimism, the 1870s and 1880s were decades of economic depression and stagnation, so much so that "original book publishing almost disappeared in Canada" in the 1880s.[10] The bulk of the readership in English-speaking Canada demanded the popular books of prominent British and American authors; moreover, they wanted them at attractive prices. In such a restricted market Canadian writers had little traction or cachet. As George Parker has aptly observed, "The Canadian market was at best a small and uncertain one, where occasionally a popular book sold well enough to warrant a local printing."[11] Thus, there was little call to promote home-based literary output. From Thomas D'Arcy McGee in the

---

8 The quotation is from a letter Crawford wrote to the editor of a new Toronto magazine *Arcturus*. See "Editorial Notes," *Arcturus: A Canadian Journal of Literature and Life* (February 19, 1887), pp. 83–4.
9 Ibid.
10 See George L. Parker's "The Evolution of Publishing in Canada," in *The History of the Book in Canada*, 3 vols. (Toronto: University of Toronto Press, 2005), vol. II, p. 21.
11 Parker, *The Beginnings of the Book Trade*, p. 170.

1860s to Graeme Mercer Adam in the 1870s to Archibald Lampman in the 1890s, those who sought to encourage Canadian literary talent spoke for a small and dispersed number of like-minded literary nationalists, not the general readership.

The three decades between 1870 and 1900 produced " a cycle of advances and traumatic setbacks" that kept book publishing in Canada in a subsidiary state.[12] The 1870s saw the emergence of a number of publishing firms eager to supply Canadians with inexpensive reading material. Largely based in Toronto and Montreal, firms like Hunter, Rose and Company, the Belford Brothers, George Munro, the Dawson Brothers, and John Lovell were cautious operations. Their main fortes were inexpensive reprints of writers like Mark Twain and Wilkie Collins, textbooks for Canadian schools, and books published by subscription. Certain firms, notably the Belfords and John Lovell, boldly violated copyright laws by "pirating" bestselling international authors for the Canadian market, thus challenging conditions that favored the rights of British and American publishers and allowed them to treat the Canadian market as an extended fiefdom. The result was indignation and legal action.

When, by contrast, George Maclean Rose published the first Canadian edition of Susanna Moodie's *Roughing It in the Bush* in 1871, it may well have been as much the result of his friendship with Moodie's son-in-law, John Vickers, a successful Toronto businessman, as the still-simmering notoriety of the book. Connections mattered. Assessing the general state of Canadian publishing in *The Canadian Bookseller* a year later, Graeme Mercer Adam astutely observed, "We have not been *producers*, to any extent" though "as re-producers, in the publication of American reprints, etc., our book firms have been active to an unusual degree."[13]

Magazines in Canada during these decades suffered a parallel fate. Venturesome undertakings were typically short-lived and usually undersubscribed. Nothing quite like *The Literary Garland* (1839–51) arose to fill the void created by its demise. Rollo and Adams published the short-lived *British-American Magazine* in Toronto (1863–4), while *Belford's Monthly Magazine* merged with *The Canadian Monthly and National Review* to become *Rose-Belford's Canadian Monthly and National Review* (1878–82). Story-magazines such as Desbarats attempted in the early 1870s failed to take hold.

---

12 Ibid., p. 166.
13 Quoted in ibid., p. 175. Italics in original.

As conditions improved, general and public interest magazines had the best runs into the new century; in them, literary material usually took a back seat to politics and economics. *The Canadian Illustrated News* (1869–83) and its successor *The Dominion Illustrated* (1888–95) did promote a few Canadian writers, but they favored prominent international authors. Magazines associated with the outspoken Goldwin Smith, known to many as Canada's most famous man of letters, included *The Canadian Monthly and National Review* and *The Week* (1883–96). The latter did foster the early journalistic work of emerging writers like Sara Jeannette Duncan and Lily Lewis and was, for a time, edited by Charles G. D. Roberts. Smith, who became a leading advocate of annexation by the United States, was himself not confident that one could talk seriously about such a thing as Canadian Literature. John Wilson Bengough's *Grip* (1873–94) specialized in lively caricature and satire, successfully carrying on the tradition established in the 1860s by *The Grumbler* (Toronto). Various religious (*The Christian Guardian*) and agricultural magazines of longish tenure included some poetry and fiction in their pages, but no durable literary magazine emerged to foster Canadian writers. A climate of conservatism and indifference to literary talent persisted in turn-of-the-century Canada. Duncan was particularly forthright about the state of cultural malnutrition in Ontario in several of her columns for *The Week*.[14]

Publishing in the United States

South of the border opportunities abounded. There were many chances to work in the publishing trade or to find paying outlets in established or new newspapers and magazines. What Clarence Karr has called "the golden age of hardcover fiction"[15] was opening up on many fronts. Personal initiative or useful connections were the key if writers wished to find work that paid. Writers like Charles G. D. Roberts, Bliss Carman, May Agnes Fleming, Palmer Cox, James De Mille, Marshall Saunders, Charles Gordon, Nellie McClung, Arthur Stringer, Lucy Maud Montgomery, Sara Jeannette Duncan, and Gilbert Parker found their own ways – or ways were found for them – to make their marks as writers, in large part through American opportunities and connections. New York City and other centers offered professional work and

---

14 See, for example, "Saunterings," *The Week* (September 30, 1886), p. 707.
15 Karr, *Authors and Audiences*, p. 40.

publishing opportunities, cosmopolitan experience, bohemian adventure, the experience of cultural difference, and access to literary and cultural communities such as were impossible to find in most Canadian towns or cities.

The phenomenon of the bestseller emerged in the 1880s as a result of changes in the publishing industry and the rapid increase in population and readership. New York quickly made itself the center of such activity, undermining Boston's former eminence, even as Chicago and, more modestly, Montreal and Toronto sought to become centers of publishing activity. In New York mass-market publishers like Frank Leslie, Beadle & Adams, Street & Smith, and George and Norman Munro flooded the burgeoning market with inexpensive newspapers, magazines and dime novels, geared to a range of readerships and tastes. Writers everywhere could test their mettle simply by submitting manuscripts. It is a curious anomaly that among the few Canadian writers of the 1860s and 70s to test these new markets, the two most successful – May Agnes Fleming (1840–80) and James De Mille (1833–80) – were born in the same New Brunswick town. By comparison, Isabella Valancy Crawford's contributions from Ontario were on a smaller scale. Together they pioneered differing processes whereby talented and ambitious Canadians found outlets in the American market.

May Agnes Fleming

The case of May Agnes Fleming is indicative of committed personal initiative.[16] A quiet teenager at a convent school in her native St. John, May Agnes Earlie (Early) was an omnivorous reader and a devotee of writers like Charles Dickens. Schooled in reading, writing and music by the nuns, she began to write stories at a young age, the first of which she sent off to a popular story paper, the *New York Mercury* (1838–60). Using the cozy penname Cousin May Carleton, she was surprised and delighted when the magazine bought the story and sent her three gold American dollars.

Thus encouraged, she sent off short stories to the *Sunday Mercury* and other papers like *The Western Recorder* and the Irish-Catholic *Boston Pilot* between 1857 and 1863, occasionally including Canadian scenes and characters in her narratives. Having established a reputation as a storywriter, she was invited in 1868 at a better rate of pay to contribute serialized novels to *Saturday Night*, a

---

16 For more detail, see Lorraine McMullen, "May Agnes Fleming: 'I Did Nothing but Write,'" in *Silenced Sextet: Six Nineteenth-Century Canadian Women Novelists*, ed. Carrie MacMillan, Lorraine McMullen, and Elizabeth Waterston (Montreal and Kingston: McGill-Queen's University Press, 1992), pp. 52–81.

Philadelphia magazine; the novels would then be produced in book form in the Beadle & Adams's "cheap" novel series. In the early 1870s Fleming received a still better offer from Street & Smith; she signed an exclusive contract to publish her serials in their magazine, the *New York Weekly*, after which they were issued in book form in the "New Eagle" series. G. W., Carleton also published her books in the 1870s, offering her a 15 percent royalty.

In the meantime May Agnes had married a boilermaker named John Fleming and was raising four children in St. John. Deeply committed to her writing, she persuaded her husband in 1875 to move to New York to pursue her opportunities better. However, as her fame grew, John's drinking and disgruntlement increased. When the marriage ended in divorce, the children remained with the mother. Writing was her true husband. Leading a quiet and genteel life in Brooklyn, she carefully monitored her precarious health and produced a new novel every spring, attentive to the popular formulae of serial fiction and the need to include attractive elements of the exotic and sensational, the mysterious and adventurous.

Writing made her a wealthy woman. By the late 1870s she was earning in excess of $10,000 a year. At the time of her premature death she was among North America's most popular fiction writers. Certainly, she was "Canada's first best-selling novelist."[17] Such titles as *Sybil Campbell; or, The Queen of the Isle* (1861), *Eulalie; or, A Wife's Tragedy* (c. 1864), and *The Baronet's Bride; or, A Woman's Vengeance* (1868) suggest her firm grasp of sensational and Gothic plotting. The cover of each Smith & Street novel featured a fetching female face and Fleming's name in bold print; each sold for ten or twenty cents. Often, they carried no date but were reprinted for years. It is testimony to her fame that, after her premature death in 1880, "new" Fleming novels continued to appear. David Skene-Melvin has calculated that, of the forty-two novels attributed to her, twenty-seven were published after her death (p. 9). Given her deliberate writing schedule later in her brief life (a novel a year), it is clear that several of her novels were later repackaged and retitled for fresh consumption.

James De Mille

James De Mille's career proceeded along more affluent, middle-class lines. His influential Loyalist and Baptist father had helped to found the Horton Academy (Wolfville) and was a Governor of Acadia College; James attended

---

17 David Skene-Melvin, *Investigating Women: Female Detectives by Canadian Writers – An Eclectic Sampler* (Toronto: Simon and Pierre, 1995), p. 9. *Sybil Campbell* was republished under several different titles (see MacMillan et al., *Silenced Sextet*, p. 60).

both schools before embarking on a European tour with his brother. On his return he pursued a Masters degree at Brown University in Rhode Island and while there wrote several pieces that were accepted for publication by *Putnam's Monthly* (New York). However, an ambitious attempt to establish a bookstore in St. John left De Mille seriously in debt. Seeking an income by which to meet both his losses and daily needs, he accepted an appointment in 1860 to teach the Classics at Acadia even as he wrote stories for his brother's Baptist magazine, *The Christian Watchman*. Five years later he was made the chair of History and Rhetoric at what was then Dalhousie College in Halifax.

Writing provided a very profitable secondary income for De Mille. His first book, *The Martyr of the Catacombs: A Tale of Ancient Rome* (1865), was a historical romance set in Italy, a country he had come to love in his travels. In Halifax he dovetailed his two careers with great success. A popular professor and scholar at Dalhousie, he wrote *The Elements of Rhetoric* (1878) and honed his extraordinary linguistic skills and classical knowledge.[18] Meanwhile he set out to experiment with popular narrative, testing the markets for boys' books, mystery and adventure, and humor and satire. With remarkable facility, he often produced two books a year while keeping up his university demands. *The B. O. W. C.* [The Brethren of the White Cross]: *A Book for Boys* (1869) dramatized boyish adventures in the Minas Basin area in a spirit of fun that was relatively free of Victorian moral uplift while *The Dodge Club: or, Italy in 1859* (1869) gently satirized the aggressive and chauvinistic attitudes of American men travelling abroad. Mark Twain may well have learned some important lessons from both books.

Over the final fifteen years of his life De Mille produced some twenty-five novels for the popular press in New York and London, becoming in the process one of Canada's bestselling authors. Like Fleming, he commanded a substantial income. Working with a higher level of publisher, most notably Harper Brothers in New York, Lee & Shepherd in Boston, and Chatto & Windus in London, he set his scenes in Europe, America, Italy and the Bay of Fundy region, and seasoned his stories with parody, satire, and verbal dexterity. Ironically, his most famous book, *A Strange Manuscript Found in a Copper Cylinder* (1888), was published posthumously, though it was likely written much earlier in his career. Its popularity at the turn of the century was comparable to that of other well-known, utopian novels of the time by H. G. Wells and Jules Verne, and

---

18 Patricia Monk, *The Gilded Beaver: An Introduction to the Life and Work of James De Mille* (Toronto: ECW Press, 1991), pp. 188, 135.

was reinvigorated by its inclusion in the New Canadian Library (1969) and the Centre for Editing Early Canadian Texts project in 1986.

The Appeal of American Markets

The heyday of turn-of-the-century Canadian success stories in the burgeoning American marketplace began in the 1890s. By then, New York was "the most exciting and modern city," as well as the busiest literary market, "in the world."[19] With story magazines and hardcover novels clearly established as the major types of literary exchange, "New York dominated the continent."[20] Well-known American and Canadian writers alike – from William Dean Howells to Bliss Carman – came to North America's new literary capital to assume editing positions, and to experience its rich cultural exchange, energy, and social extremes. Among the Canadians to take up residence or formal positions in New York in these years were Charles G. D. Roberts, Ernest Thompson Seton, Peter McArthur, Arthur Stringer, Palmer Cox, Norman Duncan, Agnes Laut, and even long-time Canadian nationalist Graeme Mercer Adam.

Nick Mount documents the careers of some thirty prominent writers who came from Ontario, English-speaking Quebec and the Maritimes in the 1890s to find work and make careers for themselves as writers. In all, 200 or more individuals came and went across the unprotected border in search of work and fame. Many made a good living and found better opportunities to work at their profession than were available in Canadian centers. Some had striking successes.

In terms of authoring bestselling books only a handful of Canadians writing between 1890 and 1915 struck gold. Five of those careers are the subject of Karr's detailed study, subtitled "Popular Canadian Fiction in the Early Twentieth Century." Interestingly, several who wrote "American" bestsellers – Marshall Saunders, Ralph Connor, Lucy Maud Montgomery, and Nellie McClung – stayed in Canada and developed their careers at home. It was a matter of marrying a particular kind of narrative with a supportive publisher and a capacious target audience. By contrast, Gilbert Parker, Robert Barr, and Sara Jeannette Duncan moved abroad and did much of their popular writing in England or, in Duncan's case, in both England and India. Only Arthur Stringer made a career for himself in the United States, relying on his versatility and acute eye for challenging subject matter.

---

19 Karr, *Authors and Audiences*, p. 139.
20 Mount, *When Canadian Literature Moved*, p. 10.

Certain characteristics define these writers and their most successful undertakings. All came from rural or small-town backgrounds where they had enjoyed relatively affluent upbringings and educations. Most had a strong connection, either familial or communal, to organized religion, and several of them became well known because of publication by a religious press. Stringer alone broke that mould. All were attentive to the need to celebrate and preserve core human values in an increasingly modern world in which urbanization, industrialization, and technological improvements were occurring at a rapid pace. In addition to Church values, they celebrated "the importance of order, civility, family, and community"[21] and they dramatized the need for a culture of social improvement to meet new challenges.

As Karr has argued, they took careful note of the aspects of the modern unfolding before them but sought strategies in their fiction to preserve values that were threatened by modernistic change. Generally, they arranged their plots and characters to avoid issues pertaining to sexuality and sexual appetite, psychological complexity, and the deeper roots of social problems. For her part, Duncan sought a greater complexity in her representation of the difficulties of social interaction and political realities; she sought and reached a more literary and fastidious audience, resistant to popular conventions, melodramatic plotting, and one-dimensional characters. Arthur Stringer brought issues of sexuality and urban crime before his readers in challenging ways.

Bestselling women writers

As the careers of several successful women writers will be treated in other chapters, only brief mention will be made here of their particular bestsellers and the circumstances associated with them. Marshall Saunders (1861–1947) caught the wave of large-scale public attention in North America with *Beautiful Joe: The Autobiography of a Dog* (1894), a novel about the trials of an abused dog that she wrote for a contest sponsored by the American Humane Society. A Nova Scotian and a Baptist minister's daughter, she won the $200 prize. She then had to search for a publisher, the American Baptist Publication Society of Philadelphia. With revisions included to protect copyright, Jarrold and Sons, the publisher of Anna Sewell's path-breaking *Black Beauty* (1877), published the book in London.

Saunders was no beginner when her warm-hearted novel awakened a spirit of middle-class outrage at the mistreatment of animals. Its solid early

---

21 Karr, *Authors and Audiences*, p. 25.

sales – over 200,000 in the first year – proved the basis of a steady consumer interest. Issues of education and social justice preoccupied her thinking and played well to early twentieth-century readers, who welcomed sweetened moral uplift in their reading. Temperance and the iniquities of child labor were among subjects she featured in other works but throughout her career she remained known for her animal stories. Because of the popularity of *Beautiful Joe*, especially with young readers, she became the first Canadian writer to sell over a million copies of a novel. By the 1930s the novel had reportedly sold over seven million copies and been translated into numerous languages.[22]

An aspiring writer from Prince Edward Island, Lucy Maud Montgomery (1874–1942) very deliberately began building an audience for her fiction at an early age. Growing up in an affluent Scots Presbyterian family, she sent out stories and poems to numerous periodicals, tasting publication at age sixteen. Aiming first at Sunday School papers and rural audiences, she soon advanced to magazines of greater literary prominence. Her apprenticeship was "long and hard."[23] Indeed, it was nearly twenty years later, in 1908, that she published her first novel, *Anne of Green Gables*, the book by which later generations of Canadians and young women worldwide have identified her.

Accounts of Montgomery's career necessarily emphasize that her Boston publisher, Louis Coues Page, took advantage of her by means of a long-term contract and unfair terms. Delighted as she was to become a published novelist (the novel had been turned down four times), she was not prepared to be so grievously disadvantaged. "It would be difficult," writes Clarence Karr, "to find another publisher who treated a star author as wretchedly as Page did [her]" (Karr, p. 71).

Still, with the public success of *Anne* and its sequels, readers saw Montgomery's free-spirited and plucky protagonist, Anne Shirley, through girlhood to motherhood and a career as a teacher. For many of them Montgomery captured the complexity of girlhood and adolescence even as she celebrated a rural world of picket fences and painted cottages. Ably, she made rural Prince Edward Island attractive for modern, urban readers and, while she memorialized young heroines like Anne and Emily of New Moon, she held firmly to the traditional values of motherhood and a woman's place in the home. A spirit of independence and a conservative outlook were never

---

22 See Elizabeth Waterston, "Margaret Marshall Saunders: A Voice for the Silent," in MacMillan et al., *Silenced Sextet*, pp. 137–68.
23 Karr, *Authors and Audiences*, p. 41.

at odds in her heroines. Of all the Canadian writers who made a success in the American bestseller market of the day, Montgomery alone has seen her star continue to shine both nationally and internationally. Seldom have a Canadian character and her setting persisted so strongly in readers' minds and seldom has a Canadian book had such sustained success.

Like Saunders but in a more politically activist mode, Nelly McClung (1873–1951) succeeded in marrying her social views to pleasing narrative. Her *Sowing Seeds in Danny* (1908) launched a trilogy of Pearlie Watson novels and a successful writing career that provided one of the first sustained looks at community life in western Canada. Her career, like Saunders's, had its start through a Canadian religious press, for it was the work of Edward Caswell, on behalf of the Toronto-based Methodist Book and Publishing House, that opened the door for that book and McClung's career. The MBPH was becoming less denominational and more nationalistic in the 1890s and was taking an increasing interest in books by Canadian writers. The firm would not only provide a publisher in Canada for several writers like McClung but would train many of the individuals – Thomas Allen, John McClelland, and George Stewart among them – who would push forward the book-publishing business in Canada in the next generation.

Sara Jeannette Duncan (1861–1922) was a much more accomplished writer than either Saunders or McClung. Well trained as a journalist, she knew how to entertain and challenge her readers. As a novelist she could write both light-hearted social comedy (*Those Delightful Americans*) and politically charged, satiric novels (*Set in Authority*) for both the American and British markets. The former, she knew, sold better than the latter, but she ably maintained her popularity over three decades, despite the disappointing sales of her Canadian novel, *The Imperialist* (1904). Duncan did not hesitate to employ an agent (A. P. Watt & Son) in her pursuit of profitable publishing arrangements.

Ralph Connor

No literary star shone brighter in the Canadian sky than the Rev. Charles Gordon (1860–1937). He became a publishing phenomenon when he began to write about the challenges faced by a Presbyterian minister assigned to bring religion to the rough-edged miners and ranchers in the Rocky and Selkirk Mountains. Adopting the penname Ralph Connor, Gordon found a large readership hungry for his blend of fast-paced, often violent adventure and the glorification of Christianity and the hearth. His sketches about his ministerial work in the west were first serialized in the *Westminster Magazine*

(Toronto) at the urging of his university friend, James Macdonald, another keen Presbyterian minister. A year later he adapted them to book form under the title *Black Rock* (1898). Editions, legitimate or pirated, quickly appeared in Canada, the United States and England. *The Sky Pilot: A Tale of the Foothills* (1899) also built its narrative around the challenges facing a manly, sensitive minister assigned to a corrupt and violent frontier community. By deliberate and dramatic means the pistol-packing minister and his small band of supporters bring a new awareness of personal and social responsibility to the once-corrupt inhabitants.

These two novels brought Connor immediate fame. Each sold close to a million copies in less than a decade and spoke powerfully to a wide readership, many of whom wrote grateful letters to the author describing their personal reactions. As Karr summarizes, "there was a general consensus in the reviews and in readers' letters that no one could read Connor without becoming a better person" (Karr, p. 87). He thought positively about human nature and wrote with a Christian passion that made his readers feel better about themselves and the future that lay before them. A strong underlying faith, based on the promises Connor found in the "sky pilot" Himself, bathed these narratives in a warmth that came from the author's confidence in the inevitable victory of right thinking over the sins of the flesh.

Connor hit a sympathetic note for readers hungry not only for adventure but for assurances of social order in the fast-changing, complex world in which they lived. His books offered hope. He leavened a series of bloody encounters, accidental deaths, and murders by dramatizing an effective confrontation with alcoholism, gambling, violence, and self-indulgence. Though his sales would be strong from novel to novel, often approaching 60,000 copies per book in Canada alone (where a sale of 5,000 was regarded as a triumph for a Canadian writer), he would never duplicate the great success of his first two books. Publishing records indicate that sales for his first five novels topped two million dollars. In a career covering nearly forty years, he wrote twenty-three works of fiction and thirty-two volumes overall.

The Man from Glengarry: A Tale of the Ottawa (1901) and its sequel *Glengarry School Days: A Story of Early Days in Glengarry* (1902) were among his first five books but, unlike the first two, they have enjoyed a much longer shelf life and are still valued by Canadian readers. Their vivid renderings of time and place and their affection for Canada's Scottish past appeal more to contemporary audiences than the adventures of a frontier minister. Indeed, *The Man from Glengarry* provides a warm localized narrative that Connor sought to expand into a hymn to Canada's incipient nationalism. In *Corporal Cameron of the North*

West Mounted Police: A Tale of the Macleod Trail (serialization 1908; book publication 1912), he allowed the Mounties to stand in for religious leadership, but generally, though he tried to meet the demands of his publishers and readers, he had little skill in plotting, in rendering romantic relationships, or in dealing with sex. Still, even after the First World War his books meant large print runs in Canada, the United States and Britain.

Caring friends facilitated Connor's writing career. Regularly, they pushed him to deliver manuscripts though he was on occasion so slow that the opportunity for serialization prior to book publication was missed. Nevertheless, Connor would admit in 1915 that he had been "extremely fortunate in my publishers" (Karr, p. 66). William E. Robertson replaced the Rev. James Macdonald at the Westminster Company, which went into book publishing largely on the strength of Connor's solid sales. Volume by volume, Westminster could count on Connor to sell between 10,000 and 60,000 copies in Canada. In arranging his contracts with other publishers, collecting royalties, and negotiating film deals, Robertson functioned much like an agent on Connor's behalf. Highly prominent book publishers like Fleming Revell in Chicago (and then Revell's protégé, George H. Doran) and Percy Hodder-Williams of Hodder and Stoughton in London became, like Robertson, close personal friends. Doran, a Canadian who became a major publisher in New York, owed his initial success to the sales of Connor's *The Foreigner: A Tale of Saskatchewan* (1909).

Gilbert Parker

Gilbert Parker (1860–1932) became a world traveler before he began tapping the potential of a writing career. His life is an exhilarating example of the Canadian with a capacity to challenge and reinvent himself internationally. Born near Kingston, he was educated in Ottawa and at Trinity College, Toronto, where he studied for the Anglican ministry even as he excelled in elocution. After deciding against a career in religion, he spent several years teaching in Canada before sailing for the South Seas. He settled in Australia in 1886, where he took up journalism with the Sydney *Morning Herald*. Beyond his journalism and sketch writing, he wrote his first play, an adaptation of Goethe's *Faust*, which was performed in Sydney.

Four years later he moved to London. Committed to making his living by the pen he wrote sketches and stories for popular magazines while trying his hand at romantic novels. His first book, *Round the Compass*, appeared in Australia in 1892. Canadian friends were helpful. Poet Bliss Carman, then living in New York and editing *The Independent*, published one of his adventure stories set in the Canadian Northwest. Not long thereafter, Parker made an éclat with the publication of his first book, *Pierre and His People: Tales of the Far North* (1892) in New York and London. Though some critics bemoaned his unrealistic portrayal of the romantic Métis gambler, Pretty Pierre, many readers welcomed the bracing narrative, strong characters, and exotic setting in the book. As with Connor, the Canadian West provided an attractive locale for turn-of-the-century readers.

Once launched, he was steadily productive, producing novel after novel that increased media attention to his work. Shifting from the Northwest (which he had never visited) to the romance of early French-Canadian history, the realm popularized by the American historian Francis Parkman, he wrote *The Trail of the Sword* (1894), *When Valmond Came to Pontiac* (1895) and his best-remembered book, *The Seats of the Mighty* (1896). The latter, his first to be published separately in Canada (by Copp, Clark), dramatized the British conquest of French-Canada by General James Wolfe in 1859. It drew on historical documents and the cogent advice of well-informed Canadian friends. So popular was *Seats* that Parker adapted it for Herbert Beerbohm Tree, who chose the play to open his plush new theatre, Her Majesty's, on the occasion of Queen Victoria's sixtieth anniversary. Though Parker worked hard on the adaptation, the production lasted only five months before shifting to America. Its failure did not, however, diminish his literary reputation or his writing income, rumored to be several thousand pounds a year. He had established himself as a very marketable writer and London literary figure before he married Amy Vantine, an American heiress, in 1895. Thereafter, while keeping up his writing at the rate of a book a year (always preceded by magazine serialization), he turned increasingly to politics. In 1900 he was elected a British MP and served with distinction for three terms, offering his strong support for the idea of Imperialism along with his literary countrymen, Sara Jeannette Duncan and Stephen Leacock. Parker was knighted in 1902 for his contributions to Canadian literature and made a baronet in 1915. So solid was his popularity that in 1913 Scribner's celebrated his achievements by publishing the "Imperial Edition" of his works.

Like Ralph Connor, Parker proved that, insofar as historical romances and adventure fiction required, Canadian settings would indeed attract readers. He knew that Canada had provided his best material and he took pride in the eminence he had achieved. In a letter to Charles G. D. Roberts in 1928 he wishfully declared himself one of Canada's truly important writers of fiction.[24]

---

24 John C. Adams, *Seated with the Mighty: A Biography of Sir Gilbert Parker* (Ottawa: Borealis Press, 1979), p. 191.

Literary historians have since done much to diminish his status both because he wrote "bad" history (though some readers still enjoy his books today) and because he promoted suspect values while catering to the formulae of popular fiction.

Arthur Stringer

Finally, Arthur Stringer (1874–1950) had a startlingly productive career both in writing and film, though he never succeeded on the bestseller list as strongly as did Connor or Parker. He was proud of the breadth of his subject matter and was steadily productive over a long career, often generating strong sales. Like Duncan, his posthumous reputation has suffered in part because, despite his multi-faceted prominence in New York during his lifetime, his Canadian roots have not served him well in sustaining his importance with later American critics. Indeed, even after he became an American citizen in 1937, an editor turned down a submission by him on the grounds that he would only publish "American."[25] Today he is remembered mostly in Canada and, then, largely on the basis of a small part of his output; a trilogy of prairie novels beginning with *The Prairie Wife* (1915), which has earned him a place among early western regionalists. However, when he died, he was regarded in Canada as one of the country's most accomplished writers.

Stringer's protean and resilient writing career was watched over and abetted by his capable agent Paul Reynolds. He began as a journalist and produced over sixty books, though he remained most serious about his poetry, producing a dozen collections. But it was as a fast-paced, racy novelist that he made his largest waves and sustained his popular reputation over nearly four decades. Producing a novel a year, he tapped into various markets, often in path-breaking ways. Crime novels such as *The Wire Tappers* (1906) tested genteel standards with regard to motivation and womanly behavior in the dark recesses of the criminal underworld. In *The Wine of Life* (1921) he studied the behavior of a film star who, in marriage, retreated from the limelight to a rural farm and then, after several years, divorced her husband to return to the excitement of New York. Drawing on his own first marriage to the original Gibson Girl, actress Jobyna Howland, and his life with her on his farm north of Lake Erie, he explored both masculine and feminine attitudes to marriage and divorce in ways that challenged the conservative standards of many reviewers and readers, just as in the prairie trilogy he followed the

---

25 Karr, *Authors and Audiences*, pp. 198–9.

struggles of a New England socialite who became a rancher's wife in Alberta. Other areas he explored included the Canadian wilderness, American city life, and life in New York's slums. His work has been dismissed as too hastily written and maudlin, but such assessments overlook Stringer's extraordinary range and his courageous inquiry into subjects that most of his contemporaries avoided. A full retroactive study of his personal life and writing career is called for.

Indeed, Stringer's writing took him beyond novels and poems. When opportunities in silent films beckoned, he proved adept at screen writing on his own and as a "script doctor" for the studios. He spent a winter in Hollywood writing scripts in 1917–18 and scored his biggest success with *Man-Handled*, a film starring Gloria Swanson. Though he wrote numerous scripts before the advent of the talkies, he was steadily resistant to the lures of film writing, largely because the process, involving so many hands, compromised his autonomy as a writer.[26]

Bestselling novels had their visual and dramatic appeal to filmmakers; hence, it ought not to be surprising that opportunities presented themselves to other Canadian writers included here, notably Montgomery and Connor. But it is their compelling and bestselling narratives for which they remain known and which in retrospect help us to define the tastes and values of the rapidly expanding reading public in North America and Britain before the First World War. They mark vivid spots on a spectrum of change from the Victorian to the modern and show, in early guise, the ability of talented Canadians to make their way within the realm of American cultural opportunity.

26 Karr, pp. 174–8.

11

Textual and social experiment in women's genres

JANICE FIAMENGO

In the decades following Confederation, Canada was a nation struggling to define itself at a time of economic upheaval, ethnic division, and political and religious uncertainty; it was both a forbidding and fruitful time to be a writer, and particularly to be a woman writer, ostensibly barred by her sex from political debate and self-display. Yet when Lily Lewis wrote for *The Week* in 1888 that "The time has come for this Canada of ours to be revealed by other tongues, other pens, and in other languages than that of the railway magnate or emigration agent,"[1] she obviously counted herself and fellow women among those who would reveal the new nation; and her confidence was not misplaced. Women played an increasingly public role in post-Confederation Canada, contributing with confidence and authority to an emerging print culture centered in the newspaper and magazine industries and the fledgling domestic book trade. Amidst heated debates about the health of the race, the decline of Christianity, women's rights, class warfare, and the Indian problem, the voices of women were not only tolerated but increasingly sought after for their social awareness, moral influence, and personal touch. Working creatively in genres ranging from the newspaper sketch, campaign speech, and advice column to the personal memoir, patriotic poem, and social problem novel, Canadian women crafted compelling personae who spoke powerfully and persuasively to a large audience, both at home and internationally.

In a country as regionally diverse as Canada, only a few generalizations can be advanced to explain the significant entry of women into print at this time. Marjory Lang has pointed to a steady increase in the number of professional female writers, mostly journalists, from 1891 (the first year for which census figures are available) until 1921, with a marked spike during the decade of the

---

[1] Louis Lloyd (Lily Lewis), "Montreal Letter," *The Week* (February 9, 1888), p. 169.

First World War.[2] The formation of the Canadian Women's Press Club in 1904 demonstrated women's sense of collective identity and enabled them to lobby for better pay and professional recognition. Paul Rutherford has emphasized the dramatic rise in literacy – with figures in the range of 94 percent for Ontario by the last two decades of the nineteenth century[3] – an increase that created a much larger, more sophisticated reading audience than had existed previously. In addition, changes in print technology and in communications generally (the telegraph, for example) helped create an efficient system of information exchange and a public ever more eager for news, stories, and entertainment. Newspapers in the 1880s were moving away from political patronage toward "soft" journalism to attract advertisers – human interest stories, fashion news, personal advice, all subjects deemed appropriate to women – at the same time as new developments in household technology were beginning to free women from domestic work. Greater ease of travel, increased educational opportunities, and widespread interest in social reform all contributed to women's willingness and ability to enter the public sphere; historians of women have noted that a majority of social activists in this period were also writers. Although lucrative markets drew some to the United States and abroad, many women spent at least a part of their careers in Canada. Particularly congenial to them were fiction with a moral purpose, investigative and personal journalism, and platform performance and speech-making, genres they shaped and adapted with rhetorical ingenuity. The following pages offer a glimpse into the literary endeavors they pursued and the extraordinary success they achieved.

Agnes Maule Machar and Letitia Youmans

Some sense of the differing literary aims, rhetorical modes, and career paths of post-Confederation women is suggested through the contrast between two near-contemporaries, Agnes Maule Machar (1837–1927) and Letitia Youmans (1827–96), both of whom came to public prominence in the 1870s and embodied the values of Victorian Canada in their piety, hopefulness, and belief in social action. While Machar published prolifically, yet pseudonymously, believing literature an essential work of nation-building, Youmans published only one volume near the end of her life, subordinating writing

---

2 Marjory Lang, *Women Who Made the News: Female Journalists in Canada, 1880–1945* (Montreal: McGill-Queen's University Press, 1999), p. 5. See also pp. 11–20.

3 Paul Rutherford, *A Victorian Authority: The Daily Press in Late Nineteenth-Century Canada* (Toronto: University of Toronto Press, 1982), p. 28. See also pp. 24–35.

to activism. Both, though, made persuasive words their medium and were compelled by a sense of national mission. Machar, whose penname, Fidelis, signified faithfulness, was a novelist, poet, biographer, and essayist, and daughter of a Presbyterian clergyman, John Machar, who co-founded Queen's College, Kingston, which became one of Canada's most prestigious universities. She never married and spent her life in Kingston and at her summer cottage near the Thousand Islands, writing her morally uplifting and socially earnest works.

Her early books – a biography entitled *Faithful Unto Death: A Memorial of John Anderson, Late Janitor of Queen's College* (1859) and a novel *Katie Johnstone's Cross: A Canadian Tale* (1870), which won a Toronto publishing firm's contest for the best Sunday School novel – belong to the genre of the spiritual biography, a narrative in which the individual's life is read against the Christian outline of faith, trial, and spiritual triumph. In employing this pattern, Machar placed herself in the company of many popular women writers of the mid-nineteenth century, notably Harriet Beecher Stowe (1811–96) in antebellum America and, in Canada, Margaret Murray Robertson (1821–97), in whose popular evangelizing novels, such as *Christie Redfern's Troubles: An American Story* (1866) and *Shenac's Work at Home: A Story of Canadian Life* (1868), the spiritual purification of the young heroine is the focus. Such novelists were united by the belief that fiction should present clear lessons for living, emphasizing personal and community regeneration through God's grace. Robertson's nephew, Charles Gordon (1860–1937), who wrote under the penname Ralph Connor, masculinized the pattern at the end of the century, applying it to rollicking tales of frontier adventure and muscular Christianity such as *The Sky Pilot: A Tale of the Foothills* (1899) and *The Man From Glengarry: A Tale of the Ottawa* (1901), in which faith, exuberant fighting, and the building of the country are closely interconnected.

Machar's emphasis on social regeneration was more intellectually and theologically daring than Robertson's in its willingness to tackle the relationship of modern science to belief, and it was at least as ambitious as Connor's in reaching to embrace all the poor and neglected in her midst: the factory workers, street urchins, disabled, elderly, and outcast whose suffering touched her social conscience. As part of a circle of progressive intellectuals clustered around Queen's and active in a variety of good causes, Machar wrote to promote prohibition, free compulsory schooling for poor children, shelters for the destitute, soup kitchens and employment bureaus, and the protection of wilderness parks and endangered songbirds. These social and ecological concerns sprang from her belief that suffering was an affront to God. At a time when the problems of industrial capitalism, with its slums, work stoppages, and brutal competition, led many Canadians to approve Marxist or loosely socialist systems, and when scholarship on the Bible and the discoveries of Darwin caused the disillusioned to question the veracity of Scripture, Machar insisted that only Christianity could provide the spiritual and moral foundation for a just society. Her passionate defense of her faith, however, did not prevent her also from lamenting and criticizing the Church's failure to put its teachings into practice, as she did perhaps most trenchantly for *The Week* in "Voices Crying in the Wilderness" (1891). All of her writings, for which she earned many literary prizes, articulated an applied faith.

In defending religion, she entered into debate with the rationalist W. D. LeSueur (1840–1917) in the pages of the élite *Canadian Monthly and National Review* on the continuing relevance of Christian doctrine to modern life. In such articles as "Prayer and Modern Doubt" (1875) and "The Divine Law of Prayer" (1876), her ability to counter LeSueur on points of theology, logic, science, and philosophy – and the commitment to truth and fairness she maintained throughout – ultimately led her adversary to confess that, of all the opponents with whom he had argued, Fidelis's answers were the most satisfying. Her rhetorical and logical ability, in combination with the impression she gave that winning the argument *per se* was a less important goal than winning readers away from error into life-giving faith, established Machar as one of Canada's premier intellectuals and moralists.

Her credentials as a social reformer – one of the group of socially oriented Christians whose concern for justice identified them with the Social Gospel – were also confirmed in articles such as "Our Lady of the Slums" (1891), a tribute to the Salvation Army and a call for thoroughgoing outreach to the poor, and "Unhealthy Conditions of Women's Work in Factories" (1896), a detailed denunciation of the factory system, both articles published in *The Week*. Her industrial novel *Roland Graeme: Knight: A Novel of Our Time* (1892) was the culmination of her efforts to apply Christianity to the social order. Set in a small American factory town, it tells of an idealistic young intellectual who, having lost his faith, still holds to principles of co-operation and brotherhood as the basis of social life; he attempts to heal the economic and social rifts between the owning and the laboring classes before the festering discontent of the workers can erupt in the violence of despair. While the novel may strike modern readers as timid in its proposed solutions to capitalist exploitation, Machar's commitment to improving workers' conditions, through union organizing and strike activity if necessary, placed her in the vanguard of progressive movements of her day. In novels such as *For King and*

Country: A Story of 1812 (1874) and *Marjorie's Canadian Winter: A Story of the Northern Lights* (1893), Machar sought to increase readers' sympathetic understanding of the American republic and French Canada respectively. Her radical sympathy is everywhere evident, perhaps most markedly in "Quebec to Ontario, A Plea for the Life of Riel, September, 1885," a poem calling for clemency for Louis Riel, arrested leader of the Northwest Rebellion.

Letitia Youmans shared many of Machar's convictions, but her early experiences and upbringing in rural and small-town Ontario had formed her for a different life. Lacking Machar's élite education and social connections, Youmans did not aspire to a writing or speaking career until it was, she claimed, thrust upon her. After working as a schoolteacher and then marrying a widower and raising his eight children, she was inspired in 1874 to found a Canadian chapter of the Woman's Christian Temperance Union in order to combat the drunkenness and violence she witnessed in her community; in 1877 she became the first president of the Ontario WCTU and eventually, in 1885, of the Dominion WCTU. At first timidly and with trepidation, but soon with greater confidence, she found herself occupying a central role in the mass political campaigns to legislate prohibition that swept North America in the 1870s and 80s; traveling across Canada, the United States, and the British Isles, she addressed crowds of up to 10,000 people. Towards the end of her life, she wrote her political autobiography, *Campaign Echoes: The Autobiography of Mrs. Letitia Youmans, the Pioneer of the White Ribbon Movement in Canada* (1893), in which she reveals herself an astute tactician sensitive to rhetorical effect and galvanized by the opportunity to participate in a mass movement. The memoir also provides a fascinating record of women's public speech in Victorian Canada.

Describing her political education as an arduous but exhilarating coming to voice, Youmans explains how she gained the courage to speak only because she believed her children to be "under the sentence of death"[4] from the liquor trade. Addressing an audience was terrifying until she realized that words were being given to her by "another and a higher source"[5] (p. 108). By attributing her untrained eloquence to God, she could boast of her words' power to inspire listeners – a fact attested by the tremendous increase in WCTU membership in Ontario. Over the course of various campaigns, she began to master the gestures and language of emotional appeal: quoting from her speeches, she demonstrates how stirring calls to community solidarity and thundering denunciations of complicity became effective weapons in the

---

4 Letitia Youmans, *Campaign Echoes* (Toronto: Briggs, 1893), p. 106.
5 Canada First was a nationalist movement of the Post-Confederation period.

rhetorical arsenal of temperance. Particularly important to that rhetoric was her transformation of domestic imagery – mothering, child-protection, housekeeping – into a narrative of heroic resistance, a technique that Nellie McClung and many other temperance and suffrage activists would adopt in the early twentieth century. In repeatedly emphasizing her role as a vehicle for God's will, an obedient soldier in the temperance war – which, she left no doubt, was a war for the lives of children and the soul of Canada – Youmans figured herself as one who had accepted a divine commission and could therefore, without shame, place the autobiographical I at the center of her narrative.

Christian heroism

Such pious, alternately self-effacing and self-glorifying narratives were popular in mid- to late-nineteenth-century North America. The writings of Frances Willard (1839–98), the American president of the Worldwide WCTU (and friend of Youmans) provide one well-known model of subversive but divinely sanctioned heroism. A notable Canadian version can be found in *Lights and Shades of Mission Work; or Leaves From a Worker's Notebook* (1892) by Bertha Carr-Harris (née Wright) (1863–1949), which tells of devoted self-sacrifice in the cause of evangelism. Speaking of herself in the third person throughout the narrative, preferring the passive voice and collective nouns (usually "the workers") to avoid self-reference, this leader of the youth wing of the WCTU in Ottawa tells how she helped to establish the Home for Friendless Women in her hometown and carried the Hull mission, organized to evangelize French Catholics in the city of Hull, Quebec, through a rocky beginning. A good part of her text, as she emphasizes, is a document of failures and adversity: of indifferent listeners, fumbled speeches, even the Lord's Prayer mis-recited. But beneath the self-effacing prose and admissions of inarticulacy, the reader recognizes the excitement of a hard-fought battle.

The thrill of conflict is particularly evident when Wright describes the bitter opposition she and fellow workers experienced in Hull, where they were pelted with stones and pieces of wood as they tried to address a gathering crowd in February, 1890. At the height of the violence, they were "surrounded and dragged out into the street and kicked about the face and head,"[6] being saved from more serious injury only by the intervention of the police; the

---

6 Bertha (Wright) Carr-Harris, *Lights and Shades of Mission Work* (Ottawa: Free Press, 1892), p. 89.

incident touched off debate in the Ottawa *Citizen* and even the House of Commons.⁷ That the workers chose to return to Hull, refusing an offer of an armed escort, demonstrated their righteous conviction. Amidst continued violence and threats, the prayer meetings continued: "fire arms were freely discharged, the building bombarded with stones, windows and doors smashed and it seemed for a time as though hell were let loose. The meeting was held notwithstanding, and if ever there was earnest pleading with God for the lost in the City of Hull, there was then."⁸ The contrast between the prayers of the women and the vociferations and missiles of their audience demonstrates Wright's relishing of dramatic effect.

Christian reforming energies could be put to more overtly self-aggrandizing purposes, as in the case of Anna Leonowens (1831–1915), who traveled through Asia with her husband and then, after his death in Malaysia, supported herself and her young son by teaching English to the many children and wives of King Mongkut of Siam (now Thailand). She wrote of the experience in her popular *An English Governess at the Siamese Court: Being Recollections of Six Years in the Royal Palace at Bangkok* (1870), a fictionalized autobiography that combines a narrative of female independence and missionary zeal with the orientalizing exoticism so popular in travel accounts of the period. (The story was eventually adapted into a stage musical and film, *The King and I*.) Depicting her experience as a dramatic contest between the forces of paganism, superstition, and injustice and "the Great Hearts of a lonely woman and a loving child,"⁹ Leonowens filled her account of the Siamese court with the barbaric splendor readers expected, emphasizing both the depravity and the humanity of the King with whom she vigorously debated, and lavishing pathetic eloquence on "those ill-fated sisters of mine, imprisoned without a crime" (p. 103), whom she longed to liberate into Christian freedom. Leonowens' association with Canada occurred only after the publication of this volume when she moved to Halifax in 1876, where she spent the next two decades working for woman suffrage and founding a number of key cultural institutions, including the Shakespeare Society and the Victoria School of Art and Design.

---

7 Sharon Anne Cook, *"Through Sunshine and Shadow": The Woman's Christian Temperance Union, Evangelicalism, and Reform in Ontario, 1874–1930* (Montreal and Kingston: McGill-Queen's University Press, 1995), pp. 4–6.
8 Carr-Harris, *Lights and Shades*, p. 92.
9 Anna Harriette Leonowens, *The English Governess at the Siamese Court* (Oxford: Oxford University Press, 1988 [1870]), p. 67.

Sara Jeannette Duncan

Not all women were so devout as the reformers whose conviction of godly mission urged them into print. Some, in fact, such as the witty and ironical Sara Jeannette Duncan (1861–1922), cultivated an arch, mocking stance precisely to avoid association with earnestness or orthodoxy. Now best known as a novelist, Duncan launched her career as a journalist in the mid-1880s, making her name at the *Washington Post* (1885–6) before returning to Canada to write for the Toronto *Globe*, the *Montreal Star*, and *The Week*, earning a wide readership for her lively, often provocative columns. As the first Canadian woman to work full-time in a newspaper office, she was conscious of her status as a pioneer and determined not to be type-cast as a dour feminist with eye-glasses, pinched lips, and ugly clothes. Thus, when she wrote her report on the Washington suffrage convention of 1886, she was careful to note not only the force of suffragists' arguments (she had already declared her support for the cause), but also their style of dress and mannerisms, approving one who looked like she would have "flirted strategically" on behalf of the franchise.[10] Toward the sincere do-gooder or strident platform speaker, she was often cool and sometimes contemptuous – as when she interviewed a WCTU local organizer whose earnest, rather humorless conviction forms a striking contrast to her own ironical intelligence;[11] Duncan always preferred sharp analysis to missionary zeal.

The typical women's column was either practically feminine – advice on household products and stain removal – or frivolously feminine – society reporting, as exemplified by Amaryllis (Agnes Scott, 1863–1927) in the Ottawa *Free Press* in the 1890s. Duncan's columns were a bit of both, but mainly she took the whole field of human activity as her domain, discussing matters such as copyright law, long a sore point for Canadian authors; Canadian culture (once declaring Ontario "one great camp of the Philistines");[12] and imperial trade policy. Her forthright statements of opinion ranged from measured support for woman suffrage to acid-tongued ridicule of feminist excess; from endorsement of British imperial ideals to criticism of colonial injustice; and from praise of American social energy to irritated analyses of Canada's colonial cringe. Rarely in full sympathy with any movement or ideology, she adopted a variety of dissenting and approving postures,

---

10 Sara Jeannette Duncan, "Woman Suffragists in Council," *The Week* (March 25, 1886), p. 261.
11 Sara Jeannette Duncan, "Woman's World," *The Globe* (November 2, 1886), p. 6.
12 Sara Jeannette Duncan, "Saunterings," *The Week* (September 30, 1886), p. 707.

speaking by turns as a skeptic, an idealist, or a coquette, and crafting a complex, opinionated persona whose rhetorical dexterity protected her from charges of dogmatism or shrillness. In the process, she transformed a conventional women's column into a widely read forum for challenging ideas.

After three years of newspaper work, Duncan and a journalist friend convinced their editors to finance a trip around the world in search of original material for their papers. Upon ending the tour in London, Duncan published *A Social Departure: How Orthodocia and I Went Round the World By Ourselves* (1890), her most successful book-length narrative, in which she established herself a master of self-mockery and sparkling social observation. In India, Duncan had met and become engaged to Everard Cotes, a museum official with the colonial government, and in 1890, she left Canada for good to make a new life in Calcutta and Simla. There she turned her literary energies mainly to novels, publishing works that explore national types and describe the experiences of women and dreamers in conservative societies. Social critique was always a mainstay of her fiction, whether she was criticizing the gap between ideal justice and its flawed practice in Anglo-India (as she did in *Set in Authority* [1906] and *The Burnt Offering* [1910]), examining the perils facing a New Woman in *A Daughter of To-day* (1894), or narrating the comic trials of a young wife adapting to Anglo-Indian society in *The Simple Adventures of a Memsahib* (1893). Her most polished and rewarding novel is perhaps *The Imperialist* (1904), a portrait of small-town Ontario (based on Brantford, Duncan's hometown) at once nostalgic and critical, which examines the fragility of political and personal idealism. Duncan's virtuoso stylistic skills, controlled irony, and acute powers of observation give her best writing a lasting charm.

Although never as well known as Duncan, the young "Orthodocia" of the travels, Lily Lewis (1866–1929), a Montreal native, was a writer of note in her day. Having already published a series of sketches entitled "Montreal Letter" under the pseudonym Louis Lloyd in *The Week* from 1887 to 1888 (and probably also "Our Paris Letter" and "Letter from Italy" in 1886–7 as L. L.) in which she developed her skills in wit and word painting, she used her trip with Duncan to train her satirist's eye on the typical foibles of fellow travelers and native inhabitants. In her travels across Canada by train and through Japan and India, she recorded amusing and telling incidents that frequently made her and "Garth" (Duncan's pseudonym) the center of the comedy: uncomfortable lodgings in Moosomin, communication failures with a Japanese reporter, and misguided attempts to improve relations between natives and rulers in India. Her frequent condescension is offset by exuberant self-mockery and skillful recreation of exotic scenes as she perfected the jaundiced perspective of the train traveler and the embarrassed uncertainty of the *ingénue* abroad. That Lewis never built on her early promise as a writer seems to have been due more to unfortunate personal circumstances than to any lack of ability.[13] The pattern she and Duncan established, in which European and exotic travel became the occasion for literary journalism, was further developed by Nova Scotian Alice Jones (1853–1933), who published sophisticated articles on Italian art and North African culture for *The Dominion Illustrated* and *The Week* in the early 1890s.

Journalists

Following in the eclectic journalistic footsteps of Duncan, if arguably bolder in her exploits, Alice Fenton Freeman (1857–1936), a Toronto schoolteacher, wrote under the penname Faith Fenton. Her column for *The Empire*, "Woman's Empire" (1888–95), combined fashion advice with social satire, and book reviews with discussions of Theosophy and women's rights; the column regularly ended with answers to readers' letters about courtship and careers. Creating an outspoken persona by turns sentimental and tough-minded, she reported on high society events, murder trials, institutes for the unfortunate, and visits from dignitaries and performers, including Susan B. Anthony, acclaimed American suffragist, and Lady Ishbel Aberdeen, wife of the Governor General.

Over time, Fenton's social views, particularly regarding the position of women, became more daring as her role as a journalist took on a greater bravura: she began to travel, sometimes using her growing fame to gain access to important personages – visiting John A. Macdonald at his summer residence – and at other times making incognito visits to the Toronto underworld, disguising herself as a vagabond to spend a bedbug-plagued night at the House of Industry. She camped in the wilds of Quebec, scolding her English-Canadian readers for their failure to embrace *la belle province*, and took in the sights at the Chicago World's Fair in 1893, with particular attention to the meetings of the International Council of Women, an organization she would showcase when she became editor of the *Canadian Home Journal* after losing her position at *The Empire*. She capped an intrepid reporting career by traveling to the Klondike in the employ of the *Globe*, laboring by foot up the marshy Teslin Trail to Dawson City, in 1898, to report on the vigor and squalor of the

---

13 See Peggy Martin, *Lily Lewis: Sketches of a Canadian Journalist* (Calgary: University of Calgary Press, 2006).

Gold Rush West, confirming her reputation as a pioneer journalist and dauntless traveler.

Kathleen Blake Coleman (1856–1915), an Irish immigrant and single parent who supported her two children by her pen, had lamented the demise of "Woman's Empire" even though, as author of the rival "Woman's Kingdom" at the *Mail*, she may have picked up some of Fenton's bereft readers when *The Empire* merged with *The Mail* in 1895. Coleman's five-year-old Saturday column was already the most successful in the country and would continue so until her resignation in 1911. The syndicated feature of one or more pages, containing an editorial, a "Pot-pourri" section of sketches and reviews, and one or more columns of "Correspondence," in which Kit answered questions from readers, attracted fan letters and requests from across Canada and the United States. Readers wrote to confess their unrequited or illicit loves, lament their personal dissatisfactions, and ask for advice about such matters as breaking into journalism, growing a thick moustache, or dealing with a son who dressed in girls' clothing. This was women's territory – Kit had been hired by the paper precisely to attract female readers, to fill the role of the maternal advisor often missing or irrelevant in the lives of a newly mobile, urban generation – but her persona and style were so engaging that many men wrote to her too. Wilfrid Laurier declared himself a devoted reader.

Like other popular female journalists, she traveled and indulged occasionally in stunt journalism, once disguising herself as a man to walk the slums of London, England; ultimately, she established her fame as the first woman war correspondent when sent to Cuba to cover the Spanish-American war in 1898. Mainly, though, she was known for her advice. Opinionated, feisty, sympathetic, and droll, she charmed many, enraged a few, and emerged as the champion of the lonely-hearted, erring, and socially outcast. She was unafraid to tackle deeply controversial issues – advising women to leave abusive husbands, Christians to be less judgmental, and men to rethink the sexual double-standard – without compromising her respectability or womanliness, and her many-sided personality, which could be playful, somber, sentimental, and satirical in a single column, kept readers interested in what she had to say. Many must have chuckled when she responded to "A Sinner" tartly: "You write me that you are in the 'same case as when last I heard from you, and you want my advice.' No you don't. If you did you would have taken it when you got it, and have married the mother of your child."[14] As a lapsed Catholic still respectful of the Roman faith in Protestant Toronto, and as an

---

14 Kit (Kathleen Blake Coleman), "Woman's Kingdom," *The Mail* (December 27, 1890), p. 5.

educated and well-traveled cosmopolitan who sometimes expressed scorn for Toronto the Good, she brought Canadians into contact with a wider world. Most importantly, perhaps, she made them feel they knew her and were intimately known by her – yet remained protective of her dignity and mystery. To make correspondents feel individually loved while insisting that she did not care ever to meet them was in itself an achievement.

E. Pauline Johnson (Tekahionwake)

While writers such as Duncan, Fenton, and Coleman made travel part of the human-interest dimension of their writing, Canada's most famous writer-performer made her living by it, crisscrossing the continent (and crossing the Atlantic to London) to recite her verse and prose sketches in an exotic Native outfit, performing in grand theaters, ramshackle saloons, and many venues in between. Daughter of a British-born Quaker mother and a Mohawk father of the Six Nations Reserve near Brantford, Ontario, Pauline Johnson, or Tekahionwake (1861–1913), presented herself as an ambassador for the Iroquois, promoting the Native point of view to enraptured audiences, who thrilled to her war whoops, authentic-seeming costuming, dramatic verse, and dark beauty. Often greeted with titillated curiosity as much as respectful interest, Johnson negotiated a variety of conflicting expectations and became skilled at balancing the anger of a dramatic ballad such as "The Cattle Thief" (1894), which demands "Give back our land and our country,"[15] with erotic lyrics about the Canadian landscape and the romance of the canoe. Her denunciations of injustice were also softened by comic monologues, teasing exchanges with audience members, and rousing patriotic poems such as "Canadian Born" (1900), all guaranteed to please a crowd. Although explicitly Native content never formed the majority of her verse or prose fiction, it was nearly always the material that audiences found most remarkable. As the traveling life became wearying, she increasingly published prose fiction and essays in popular American magazines, using the materials of her life ("My Mother," 1909) and stories of her people ("Mothers of a Great Red Race," 1908) to educate audiences about the contributions of Native people to white societies past and present. Not everyone in her audiences heard the challenge launched by her writings, but her work spoke deeply to many fans and readers.

---

15 Pauline Johnson, "The Cattle Thief," in *The White Wampum* (London: John Lane, 1895), p. 15.

Social problem novels

Johnson's social critique set her apart from her contemporaries, many of whom thought little about the situation of Native peoples, or thought in clichés. But it also linked her to a small group of Canadian novelists who, influenced by international literary currents, wrote didactically about social problems. Anger at injustice is the keynote of Joanna E. Wood's *The Untempered Wind* (1894), an indictment of the cruelty inflicted by rural villagers on a young woman, Myron, who has the misfortune to be "a mother, but not a wife."[16] Wood's insistence on the sanctity of her heroine's unlawful sexual union – "under no more sacred canopy than the topaz of a summer sky" (p. 6) – and on her further purification through motherhood makes clear the feminist-maternalist politic grounding this anti-idyll, in which a woman's faith and self-sacrificing love outweigh social convention. A *fin-de-siècle* fascination with degeneration is suggested in the narrative emphasis on the pure beauty and healthy maternity of the outcast heroine, whose physical vitality contrasts with the bodily weakness, deformity, and sexual sadism of the villagers. Myron's ultimate death, after tending the sick during a cholera epidemic, denies the villagers their one potential source of spiritual and physical regeneration. Wood (1867–1927) was a native of Queenston, Ontario, who traveled widely and was influenced by the avant-garde poetics of Algernon Charles Swinburne (1837–1909); her later novels continue to focus on passionate womanhood.

Also evoking the specter of degenerative disease but linking it to an urban environment, Maria Amelia Fytche's *Kerchiefs to Hunt Souls* (1895) articulates the conflict between the New Woman's desire for independence through fulfilling work and her age-old longing for an all-consuming love. The novel follows Dorothy Pembroke, a Canadian schoolteacher, who leaves her position, her country, and her sensible suitor to travel to Paris, where she is pursued and won by a dissolute aristocratic artist soon revealed to be a scoundrel. This man first claims her as his muse and then abandons her, informing her that the Protestant rites through which their marriage was solemnized in England are meaningless to him, a Catholic, and not legally binding in France. Upon learning that he is about to marry another, wealthier, woman, Dorothy contemplates killing him before falling ill. The novel explores how an intelligent woman is led to participate in her own degradation, which she mistakes for passionate devotion. The social factors that make

---

16 Joanna E. Wood, *The Untempered Wind* (Ottawa: Tecumseh Press, 1994 [1894]), p. 6.

women psychologically vulnerable to exploitation are suggested in scenes in which the friendless Dorothy, upon her arrival in Paris, is made to feel ashamed for seeking lodgings or enquiring about employment. At the end, Dorothy is reunited with her Canadian lover and rescued from the near-deadly illness and potential insanity that are, the narrative suggests, the consequences of sexual passion for women. Whether the link between passion and degradation is a truth for all times or the consequence of a misogynist order is not clarified in this interesting, if strained, novel. Fytche (1844–1927) lived without marrying in Halifax and St. John.

A host of social issues informs the fiction of Nova Scotian Margaret Marshall Saunders (1861–1947), whose *The House of Armour* (1897) has child poverty and the injustices of the factory system among its subjects. But Saunders is best remembered today for novels and short stories about the mistreatment of animals. A devoted animal lover herself (and in old age an increasingly eccentric one), Saunders based the story of *Beautiful Joe: An Autobiography* (1893), which won a competition sponsored by the American Humane Society, on a real dog she had known – a mongrel rescued from an abusive owner – and on her sister Laura, who had died at age seventeen. Told in the first person by Joe, it surveys a range of animal abuses, from the docking of horses' tails to the neglect of farm animals to the slaughter of birds for women's hats, stories of innocent suffering designed to teach young readers their duty to the lower order.

The novel does not ultimately question human beings' right to use animals for pleasure and profit – nor to kill them for food – but its focus on their moral responsibility to prevent animal suffering, even when such prevention entails lowered profits – gives ethical substance to the sentimental narrative. Saunders went on to publish numerous novels in which animals tell their stories of suffering and survival, including *Nita, the Story of an Irish Setter* (1904) and *Princess Sukey: The Story of a Pigeon and Her Human Friends* (1905). Typical of much humane literature (the period saw the establishment of humane societies across North America), these animal autobiographies reflect a Christian vision of social order as a hierarchy of interlocking relationships of mutual responsibility, dependency, and compassion.

Moral and Christian themes dominate the novels of Lily Dougall (1858–1923), whose *The Madonna of a Day* (1895) identified the two possible types of New Woman: at the novel's beginning, the heroine, an unconventional freethinker, meets a clergyman on a train platform and delights in shocking him with her cigarette smoking and emancipated manner. But after a train wreck throws her into the clutches of a gang of ruffians in the British Columbia

Rockies, she emerges as the "Madonna" of the title, a pure-hearted woman whose mission is the moral reform of wayward men. Many of the period's novels about the modern woman imagine her the regenerator of society and mankind. Flora MacDonald Denison's *Mary Melville; The Psychic* (1900), though adamantly non-Christian, presents a variation on this theme of social salvation. The heroine (a thinly disguised version of Denison's deceased sister, Mary Merrill, a mathematical prodigy thought to possess supernatural and telekinetic abilities) is a model of the spiritual and psychic powers of the human soul that await unlocking. Denouncing the cruelty and superstition of orthodox Christianity, the novel calls for a worldwide spiritual and social revolution to usher in universal brotherhood and equality.

Suffragists and social reformers

A few years after the novel's publication, Denison (1867–1921) became a leading activist in the suffrage movement and was hired as the women's columnist for the Toronto *Sunday World* (1909–13), a radical people's daily. The vote for women was not Denison's only passion: her wide-ranging and unorthodox interests included parapsychology, free thought, Theosophy (a syncretic Eastern-influenced religion), vegetarianism, and the poetic philosophy of Walt Whitman. In the final years of her life, she ran a nature retreat at Bon Echo, north of Toronto, where Canadian and American artists and free spirits gathered to discuss socialism and to commune with Whitman in séances. For the four years that she wrote her weekly column at the *World*, however, suffrage was Denison's main public focus and she its tireless champion. Attempting to rouse the slumbering sisterhood of Toronto, she developed a revolutionary language that envisioned the women's movement as a spiritual solution to the world's ills.

Rejecting the Christian framework and middle-class outlook of Canadian moderates, Denison articulated an alternative perspective in which suffrage was not only a basic right and a means to social improvement, but also a cosmic assault on injustice: it was "the greater part of the Great Spirit of the age fighting for a real democracy, a real brotherhood."[17] Suffrage workers, within this conception, were not simply political activists but glorious martyrs whose example and self-sacrifice would usher in a new world order. Her

---

17 Flora MacDonald Denison, "Under the Pines," Toronto *Sunday World* (December 4, 1910), p. 7.

spiritual emphasis and transformative vision made Denison a compelling voice for the feminist revolution in the years just prior to the First World War. That hers was a voice on the radical fringe is suggested by Denison's resignation, likely forced, from the presidency of the Canadian Suffrage Association in 1914.

A more moderate and even more compelling voice for suffrage belonged to Nellie Letitia McClung (1873–1951), an activist associated with the western provinces of Manitoba and Alberta. McClung first came to public attention with her novel *Sowing Seeds in Danny* (1908). Like L. M. Montgomery's *Anne of Green Gables*, published in the same year and equally popular at the time, it told the story of an imaginative and energetic little girl whose optimism transforms her community. Unlike Montgomery's novel, *Danny* has a reforming focus: Pearlie intervenes to solve the ills of her community, and in the sequel, *Purple Springs* (1921), she becomes a suffrage activist. Here McClung fictionalized her own adventures during the suffrage struggle of 1914 and 1915, years that made her famous across Canada and led to the publication of her landmark collection of essays, *In Times Like These* (1915).

In Times Like These had its germination during the Manitoba election campaign of 1914 when McClung fought against the corruption-ridden Conservative government in support of the Liberals, who had made woman suffrage their platform and expressed willingness to hold a plebiscite on prohibition. Her strategy was to shadow Premier Rodmond Roblin on the campaign trail: when he spoke in a particular town, McClung spoke there a few days later, ridiculing his arguments and advancing her own. A brilliant mimic from childhood, she delighted audiences by mocking his verbal mannerisms and characteristic rhetorical tactics. Moreover, she won audience respect and sympathy with her keen wit, forthright style, and compelling logic. Although she was never officially part of the Liberal campaign team and insisted on paying her own travel expenses (defraying costs by charging admission to her talks), she became the most feared opponent of the Conservative machine, hated enough to be burned in effigy in Brandon and bitterly caricatured by party loyalists. The Liberals did not defeat the Conservatives at that time, but McClung was decisive in preparing the way for Conservative collapse one year later, and her formulation of the aims of woman suffrage and of maternal feminist ideology shaped the women's movement for decades to come.

Both on the campaign trail and in the witty, poignant essays she based on her speeches, McClung had a remarkable ability to revitalize well-known figures of speech and expressions, appealing to what was familiar in social discourse while creating fresh humor or relevance through a shift in emphasis or a redefinition. Responding to the time-worn adage that the corrupt world of politics was no place for a woman, for example, she declared that "Any man who is actively engaged in politics, and declares that politics are too corrupt for women, admits one of two things, either that he is a party to this corruption, or that he is unable to prevent it – and in either case something should be done."[18] When Premier Roblin told of his chivalrous regard for women, his preference that they be protected from the world, she declared that "chivalry is a poor substitute for justice" (p. 42). Her particular ability to puncture clichés – she was fond of saying that "If women are angels we should try to get them into public life as soon as possible, for there is a great shortage of angels there just at present" (p. 51) – enabled her to transform the standard images and aphorisms of her opponents, particularly their sentimental references to domesticity, into pro-feminist assertions, as when she proclaimed memorably that "Women have cleaned up things since time began; and if women ever get into politics there will be a cleaning-out of pigeon-holes and forgotten corners, on which the dust of years has fallen, and the sound of the political carpet-beater will be heard in the land" (p. 48).

Such reform-minded optimism and determination were the keynotes of many western writers and activists in McClung's wide circle, including her close friend, Edmonton-based Emily Murphy (1868–1933), best known for her work as police magistrate in the Edmonton women's court and her campaign, as part of the Famous Five, to have women legally declared persons in 1929. But she first established her authority as a social reformer and prairie expert through her contributions to Canadian magazines and newspapers, and through the publication of four collections of personal sketches, the most widely known in her day being *Janey Canuck in the West* (1910). This was an intimate story of pioneer life, full of humorous personal anecdotes and self-consciously broad-minded accounts of prairie peoples, especially the Doukhobor settlers. Her commendation of the Doukhobors as future citizens of promise – tough, frugal, simple, and devout – and the lively vigor and friendly curiosity conveyed by her narrative established Murphy's persona as the archetypal western woman, full of common sense and moral wisdom, with a saving touch of buoyant irreverence.

While Murphy was a reformer exhilarated by the opportunity to build a community from the bottom up (she wrote of Edmonton in *Janey Canuck* that "It is good to live in these first days when the foundations of things are being

---

18 Nellie L. McClung, *In Times Like These* (Toronto: University of Toronto Press, 1972), p. 48.

laid, to be able, now and then, to place a stone or carry the mortar, to set it good and true"),[19] Winnipeg journalist Francis Marion Beynon (1884–1951) was a radical whose questioning spirit and vehement pacifism ultimately placed her at odds with most of her feminist colleagues. The younger sister of Lillian Beynon Thomas, herself a columnist for women at the *Manitoba Free Press*, Beynon took charge of the *Grain Growers' Guide* women's page, "The Country Homemakers," where she advocated for women's equality and the easing of the burdens of farm life. Answering readers' questions about home decorating, household chores, babies' hiccoughs, "foreign bodies in the ear,"[20] and many other subjects, she also sought to educate women about their political rights and responsibilities. What was needed, she advocated, was nothing less than "A new spirit of national motherhood."[21] Her language here was very close to McClung's, a friend whose activism she frequently recorded and commended. She was also not afraid to disagree, as she did when McClung accepted Prime Minister Borden's Wartime Elections Act, which gave the vote to female relatives of soldiers while withdrawing it from foreigners naturalized after 1902. Her argument against McClung's hasty compromise was so persuasive that she was able, a few weeks later, to publish McClung's frank retraction.

Beynon was appalled by the outbreak of the First World War, which shattered her faith in social improvement, and which she deplored for provoking uncritical patriotism and conformism. As she lamented the war-profiteering and political self-interest that led nations to send their sons to die on the battlefields, her views were increasingly in conflict with mainstream Canadian opinion. In 1917, after resigning or being fired from her position, she left Winnipeg for New York, seemingly because Canada had become unbearable. In New York with her sister, she wrote and published *Aleta Dey* (1919), a personal summation of the promise and failure of the prairie progressive movement. As a fictional autobiography about the narrator's years growing up on a Manitoba farm, it tells of a difficult rebellion: "I think I was born to be free," the narrator reports on the first page, "but my parents, with God as one of their chief instruments of terror, frightened me into servility."[22] Following her conscience, the heroine becomes a suffragist and war-resister, whose

---

19 Emily Ferguson (Murphy), *Janey Canuck in the West*, 3rd ed. (Toronto: Cassell, 1910), p. 305.
20 Francis Marion Beynon, "The Country Homemakers," *Grain Growers' Guide* (February 9, 1916), p. 10.
21 Beynon, "The Country Homemakers" (October 1, 1913), p. 9.
22 Beynon, *Aleta Dey* (Peterborough: Broadview Press, 2000), p. 11.

death at the end, from injuries received in a scuffle with a crowd while she is making a pacifist speech, indicts the violence of a supposed democracy. In her earlier disquisitions on social justice, the narrator rejects both capitalism and socialism in favor of a radical Christian ethic of love, peace, and self-giving, telling her socialist friend Ned that "Your socialist commonwealth will be a new kind of hell for anyone who happens to have an original mind" (p. 146). Having given up hope in current socio-economic systems, she can offer only a summons to "a new idealism of faith and service" (p. 146).

Beynon's fellow suffragist, reformer, and journalist in Winnipeg was E. Cora Hind (1861–1942), whose writing took her in a direction unlike that of any of her sister activists: to become a world expert on the agricultural market. After working as a stenographer, Hind put her knowledge of farming to use for Maclean's Publications and later the *Manitoba Free Press*, where she began work as commercial and agricultural editor in 1901. In this position, she visited wheat-producing areas across the country to predict a yield based on the condition of the wheat and the number and plumpness of kernels. Her fame was decisively established in 1904 when, contrary to experts from Chicago predicting a disastrously low yield of 35 million bushels due to rust disease, Hind predicted a crop of 55 million bushels. When the official count came in at 54 million, Hind's position as the pre-eminent crop forecaster in North America was set.[23] From then on, she surveyed the crop every summer until she was seventy-two, publishing forecasts in the *Free Press* September issue the accuracy of which seemed to many almost supernatural. She was trusted so completely that grain dealers came to set their prices according to her predictions, and her importance to the national economy was widely acknowledged. Highly respected by men not known for progressive ideas about women, she was willing to brave public disapproval when, as in 1913, her forecast was low. As a suffragist, she advocated for women perhaps most successfully by showing the extraordinary ease with which a woman could do a man's work; her writing was forthright, unpretentious, and seemingly without ego.

Like many other women writers in Post-Confederation Canada, Hind attained unprecedented prominence and legitimacy. As traditional sources of authority weakened during this time of rapid urbanization and secularization, and as the temperance and suffrage campaigns highlighted women's potential as compelling and compassionate social leaders, readers increasingly

---

23 Carlotta Hacker, *E. Cora Hind* (Don Mills: Fitzhenry and Whiteside, 1979), pp. 37–40.

turned to them for practical advice, information, moral guidance, a social vision – and provocative entertainment as well. Whether by intriguing audiences with their unorthodox views and bold self-portraits or by reassuring them through their moral conviction and stirring rhetoric, women writers made a significant contribution to the public culture of Victorian and Edwardian Canada.

12

Canada and the Great War

SUSAN FISHER

We have come to view the First World War as a pointless bloodbath, a "monstrous and futile Valley of Death."[1] Yet during the war years and indeed for decades after, many Canadians thought otherwise. In September 1914, two Methodist clergymen, Samuel Chown and A. Carman, described the good that had already come from the "crushing evil" of the war: "There has been such a manifestation of the patriotism of our people as to enkindle our souls to ardor and admiration. We are aroused to emulate heroic sacrifices and valiant deeds. We come all of us to feel we have a country, a land we call our own, and to unite in its protection and service. In these seven-fold hotter fires, our varied elements are fused to beauty and to strength."[2] After just a month of war, the hottest fires were yet to come – the Second Battle of Ypres, Vimy Ridge, Passchendaele – but already, in Chown and Carman's prescient address, Canada's war was taking on a mythic dimension as a nation-forging crucible. The victory at Vimy Ridge in 1917 – when the four Canadian divisions, composed of men from across the country, advanced over a height of land that neither British nor French troops had been able to take – is still identified as "the key to making Canada a nation."[3]

On April 9, 2007, ninety years after the battle, the monument at Vimy Ridge (which is Canada's largest war memorial) was rededicated after several years of restoration. Speaking at the rededication ceremonies, the Queen declared that "those who seek the foundations of Canada's distinction will do well to begin here, at Vimy." In his speech Prime Minister Stephen Harper said that "every nation has a creation story to tell; the First World War and the Battle

---

[1] Sandra Gwyn, *Tapestry of War: A Private View of Canadians in the Great War* (Toronto: HarperCollins, 1992), p. xxii.
[2] Samuel Chown and A. Carman, "Address of the General Superintendents to the General Conference of 1914," *Christian Guardian* Supplement (September 23, 1914), p. 3.
[3] J. L. Granatstein and Norman Hillmer, "Canada's Century," *Maclean's* (July 1, 1999), p. 23.

of Vimy Ridge are central to the story of our country."[4] It has been argued that this view of the war began as a way to justify its terrible cost.[5] Out of a population of 8 million, Canada sent 600,000 to the war, of whom more than 60,000 died. The war also exacted a price at home, not only in the grief that struck so many families but also in the lasting bitterness of the Conscription Crisis of 1917–18. Quebeckers who opposed conscription were vilified as traitors; they in turn viewed English Canada as racist. The four civilians shot during unrest in Quebec City in April 1918 were also casualties of war, long remembered by Quebeckers.

Patriotic verse

Canada did not officially enlist writers in the war effort (as Britain did with the War Propaganda Bureau), but they nonetheless produced patriotic literature.[6] Poems, stories, letters, and eyewitness accounts abounded in newspapers and magazines; numerous small volumes of war verse appeared. Amateurs or minor figures were responsible for most of this work, but virtually every significant writer of the period wrote about the war. Bliss Carman, for example, produced a panegyric to Maréchal Foch, "The Man of the Marne." Robert Stead's eulogy "Kitchener of Khartoum" (considered by Lorne Pierce to be one of the outstanding poems of the war years) praised Kitchener as "a nation's master mind." Even Canon Frederick George Scott, who served as Senior Chaplain to the First Division and knew the realities of the fighting, did not deviate from prevailing pieties. In "The Crown of Empire," Scott described the war as an imperial duty: "A Mother's voice was calling us, / We heard it over-sea, / The blood which thou didst give us / Is the blood we spill for thee." His "On the Rue du Bois" apotheosized the fallen soldier by identifying him with Christ.[7] Marjorie Pickthall made the same comparison in "Marching Men": "Under the level winter sky / I saw a thousand Christs go by. / They sang an idle song and free / As they went up to calvary."[8]

---

4 Quoted in Doug Saunders, "From Symbol of Despair to Source of Inspiration," *The Globe and Mail* (April 10, 2007), p. A5.
5 See Jonathan F. Vance, *Death So Noble: Memory, Meaning, and The First World War* (Vancouver: University of British Columbia Press, 1997), p. 9.
6 See Peter Buitenhuis, *The Great War of Words: British, American and Canadian Propaganda and Fiction 1914–1933* (Vancouver: University of British Columbia Press, 1987).
7 J. E. Wetherell, ed., *The Great War in Verse and Prose* (Toronto: Ministry of Education for Ontario, 1919), pp. 18, 80, 83, 75. Pierce's assessment of Stead's poem is cited in Vance, *Death So Noble*, p. 174.
8 Marjorie Pickthall, *The Selected Poems of Marjorie Pickthall*, ed. Lorne Pierce (Toronto: McClelland and Stewart, 1957), p. 78.

Associated with the motif of Christ-like sacrifice was the idea of resurrection (a connection reinforced by the fact that Vimy took place on Easter Monday). Many poems, including the most famous poem of the war, "In Flanders Fields," employed voices from the grave, as if dead soldiers acquired immortality. Robert Service (who had been a stretcher bearer) adopted the device in "Pilgrims": *"But never, oh! never come sighing, / For ours was the Splendid Release; / And oh! but 'twas joy in the dying / To know we were winning you Peace"* (italics in original).[9] Duncan Campbell Scott's "To a Canadian Aviator Who Died for His Country in France" also denies death: the aviator is a "swift soul immortal / [m]ounting in circles, faithful beyond death." In his sonnet "To a Canadian Lad Killed in the War," Scott offers the nation-building value of the war as consolation: "Thou in thy vivid pride hast reaped a nation."[10]

In contrast to such poetry, with its conventional sentiments and diction, are the war poems that constitute nearly a quarter of E. J. Pratt's *Newfoundland Verse*. Pratt's poems of the war display intense grief mingled with religious doubt, not a combination that could be perceived as patriotic; they have been described as "some of the best Canadian poetry to come out of the First World War."[11] "Before a Bulletin Board" memorably describes Pratt's horror at seeing the names of the killed and missing of the Newfoundland Regiment after the battle at Beaumont-Hamel: "God! How should letters change their color so? / A little *k* or *m* stab like a sword."[12] Equally poignant and unsentimental is Charles G. D. Roberts's villanelle, "Going Over (the Somme 1919)." The poem contrasts the trenches with a soldier's dream of home, each battlefield sensation paired with a dream counterpart – a flare over the trenches with dusk in a garden, the sergeant's order with a girl's voice, the din of war with the twilight "hush."[13] "Going Over" is a superb Canadian example of what Paul Fussell, in describing British poetry of the First World War, called ironic pastoral.[14]

---

9 Wetherell, ed., *The Great War*, p. 152.
10 Duncan Campbell Scott, *The Complete Poems of Duncan Campbell Scott* (Toronto: McClelland and Stewart, 1926), pp. 307, 124.
11 David G. Pitt, *E. J. Pratt: The Truant Years 1882–1927* (Toronto: University of Toronto Press, 1984), p. 166.
12 E. J. Pratt, *Newfoundland Verse* (Toronto: Ryerson, 1923), p. 104.
13 Carole Gerson and Gwendolyn Davies, eds., *Canadian Poetry from the Beginnings through the First World War* (Toronto: McClelland and Stewart, 1994), pp. 217–18.
14 Paul Fussell, *The Great War and Modern Memory* (New York: Oxford University Press, 1975), pp. 231–69.

Fictions of war

In *Dubious Glory: The Two World Wars and the Canadian Novel*, Dagmar Novak classifies novels of the war period as romances: "While not totally ignoring the brutality of the war, they choose to promote the positive themes of patriotism and honour, religious idealism and sacrifice."[15] *The Sky Pilot in No Man's Land* by Ralph Connor [Charles Gordon] is one of the better books of this kind – better in the sense that Connor, a preacher and a skilled author of bestsellers, knew how to deliver cathartic sentiment and moral uplift. As chief Protestant chaplain to the Canadian forces, he had been at the Ypres Salient and at the Somme. The convincing battle scenes in *Sky Pilot in No Man's Land* show his first-hand knowledge of trench warfare, yet no horror diminishes the faith of his protagonist Barry Dunbar, outdoorsman, musician, and chaplain. Even when his father (who has been serving as a Sergeant Major) is killed, Barry is "chiefly conscious of a solemn, tender pride that he was permitted to share that glorious offering which his Empire was making for the saving of the world."[16] This is a novel in which Muscular Christianity goes to war. Barry's qualifications as a peerless physical specimen are guaranteed right from the outset of the novel, when he is spied skinny dipping in a lake in the Foothills country: "What an Apollo!" (p. 9) gasps the American who happens to come across him. At first priggish, given to chiding the men about swearing and drinking, Barry matures into a compassionate and heroic leader. He is also a distinctly Canadian hero: he marries his VAD sweetheart in Scotland while on leave and, finding a convenient canoe nearby, paddles away with his Phyllis for a few days of camping.[17] Yet, despite such silliness, when Barry dies (having offered his body to shield a wounded man from shrapnel), one is touched. His bride takes the news bravely: "His body was beautiful, his soul was beautiful, his life was beautiful, and the ending, oh, was beautiful" (p. 349).

Harold R. Peat's *Private Peat* (a Canadian bestseller in 1918) is jocular, not sentimental, but it too was clearly meant to comfort those at home. In his summary of victories from Ypres to the Somme and Courcelette, Peat writes, "We plugged right on and soon we put the 'Vim' into Vimy."[18] Peat

---

15 Dagmar Novak, *Dubious Glory: The Two World Wars and the Canadian Novel* (New York: Peter Lang, 2000) p. 7.
16 Ralph Connor, *The Sky Pilot in No Man's Land* (Toronto: McClelland and Stewart, 1919), p. 188.
17 The VADs were members of the Voluntary Aid Detachments established by the British Red Cross to assist the military in time of war. The VADs worked primarily in hospitals and convalescent homes.
18 Harold R. Peat, *Private Peat* (Toronto: McLeod, 1917), p. 175.

asserts that "Boys come through without a scratch ... There is every reason to believe that you will get your boy back" (p. 216). He reassures women that the boys "gather together in the trench and we talk of mother – mother – mother" (p. 218).

An even more lighthearted treatment is John Murray Gibbon's *The Conquering Hero*. Gibbon's novel pictures Canada as a rugged Eden in contrast to the hell of the battlefields: "when it was hailing shrapnel ... I kept myself together thinking of that valley out in B. C., where father and I cleared thirty acres or so beside the creek ..."[19] (So does Connor's *Sky Pilot in No Man's Land*, which begins with two backcountry trips in Alberta.) Gibbon blithely asserts that "[i]t was the smart uniforms that reconciled our women to the Canadian army ... when they paraded as the best dressed men in the country, every girl agreed that this was a righteous war" (p. 140). Jo, a young woman in Robert Stead's *Grain*, has much the same thought: "Nothing was further from her hopes than that anything should happen to [her sweetheart] Gander, but in those early stages the risk of casualty was considered small [and] to wear a uniform and march away with bands playing was an heroic gesture." Jo, to her credit, ultimately recognizes that Gander, who keeps on growing wheat throughout the war, is indeed a hero, even in overalls.[20]

The women's war

Much of what was written during the war was aimed at female readers on the home front. In Jean Blewett's "The Little Refugee," a mother who has lost her son is bitter about the war. But when he miraculously reappears on Christmas Eve bearing a mutilated Belgian orphan, she changes her mind: "God bless Great Britain! I – I didn't know she fought for this ... I would give a dozen sons if I had them to give!"[21] L. M. Montgomery's poem "Our Women" portrays three archetypal females: a bereaved "bride of a day" who smiles because her husband "died with a smile on a field of France"; a proud "[m]other of one" whose son now "sleeps in a chilly bed"; and a weeping woman whose sorrow is that "I have none of love or kin to go." Katherine Hale's very popular poem "Grey Knitting" depicts the woman at home as

---

19 John Murray Gibbon, *The Conquering Hero* (Toronto: Gundy, 1920), pp. 86–7.
20 Robert Stead, *Grain* (Toronto: McClelland and Stewart, 1926), p. 137.
21 Jean Blewett, *Heart Stories* (Toronto: Warwick Bros. and Rutter, 1919), p. 29. The charge that Germans had cut off the arms of Belgian children was the "key Allied myth of 1914." See John Horne and Alan Kramer, *German Atrocities, 1914: A History of Denial* (New Haven: Yale University Press, 2001), p. 204.

a latter-day Penelope who, with her "little wooden needles," weaves "the web of love": "I like to think that soldiers, gaily dying / For the white Christ on fields with shame sown deep, / May hear the tender song of women's needles, / As they fall fast asleep."[22]

Nellie McClung's *The Next of Kin* is much more realistic about the cost of war. In this collection of vignettes and poems, McClung set out to show "how this war is hitting"[23] Canadian women, ranging from her own experience when her son joins up, to the plight of a Ukrainian farm girl whose education is ended when the teacher joins up. (The farm girl goes to the city alone and manages to recruit a replacement – an art-school graduate who finds knitting dull but gladly takes on the "real, full-sized woman's job" [p. 168] of running a rural school.) McClung had been a pacifist, but, like many liberal reformers, she ended up supporting the war as a necessary and even morally uplifting crusade. Though sentimental, *The Next of Kin* is enlivened by McClung's gift for satire: she drily depicts, for example, the society woman who saves for the Patriotic Fund by reducing her cook's wages (p. 42).

Some women writers explored the ironic circumstance that the war, despite its terrible cost, had brought benefits to women.[24] In J. J. Sime's short story "Munitions!" a domestic servant finds new friends and freedoms when she takes a job in a munitions factory.[25] The protagonist of Francis Beynon's *Aleta Dey* overcomes her timidity and becomes a defiant pacifist, even though her lover is a soldier.[26] Montgomery's *Rilla of Ingleside* presents, as Jonathan Vance has noted, the "stock characters that peopled Canada's memory of the war": a sensitive soldier who gives his life as a sacrifice; a rugged outdoorsman who regards the war as a great adventure; brave mothers and stalwart sisters who are proud when their menfolk enlist.[27] Yet it also "contains subversive

---

22 The poems by Lucy Maud Montgomery and Katherine Hale appear in John W. Garvin, ed., *Canadian Poems of the Great War* (Toronto: McClelland and Stewart, 1918), pp. 158, 73.
23 Nellie McClung, *The Next of Kin: Those Who Wait and Wander* (Toronto: Thomas Allen, 1917), p. 17.
24 See Donna Coates, "The Best Soldiers of All: Unsung Heroines in Canadian Women's Great War Fictions," *Canadian Literature* 151 (Winter 1996), p. 67. In 1917, some women – military nurses and the close relatives of men serving overseas – were enfranchised federally.
25 J. G. Sime, "Munitions!" *New Women: Short Stories by Canadian Women 1900–1920*, ed. Sandra Campbell and Lorraine McMullen (Ottawa: University of Ottawa Press, 1991), pp. 326–33.
26 Francis Beynon, *Aleta Dey* (Peterborough, ON: Broadview, 2000 [1919]).
27 L. M. Montgomery, *Rilla of Ingleside*, 1920 (Toronto: Seal-Random House, 1996); Vance, *Death So Noble*, p. 175.

elements that challenged contemporary attitudes to the war."[28] Among the residents of Glen St. Mary is a pacifist; although he is a malicious fool, his speech against the war is both sensible and Christian. A similarly ambivalent scene is Bruce Meredith's "sacrifice" of his cat to God: was the slaughter of young soldiers as senseless as the drowning of beloved Stripey? These subtle challenges, combined with Montgomery's strong female characters and her humorous depiction of small-town Canada, help explain why *Rilla*, alone of all the war books of its time, is still in print as a trade title.

Quebec voices

In contrast to the "plethora of verse and prose" about the war in English Canada was the virtual silence of Quebec writers.[29] A few plays were presented, such as Aimé Plamondon's *Âmes françaises*, the main theme of which was devotion to Mother France. Journalist Olivar Asselin's fervent manifesto, "Pourquoi je m'enrôle," explained that his motives were the defense of British institutions, the atrocities in Belgium, and the preservation of French intellectual traditions.[30] Eyewitness reports appeared in the newspapers: the front page of the April 1, 1915 edition of *La Presse* was devoted to the account by Major Émile Ranger of his company's journey from Salisbury Plain to the trenches – "écrit au jour le jour, du plus vif, du plus palpitant intérêt, de l'odyssée de nos vaillants soldats."[31] But such materials had little effect on enlistment. As Ringuet would assert in his 1938 novel *Trente Arpents*, "the peace-loving people of Quebec were not in the least interested in the Great European Madness."[32] There is no francophone equivalent of Garvin's *Canadian Poems of the Great War*. The only francophone war novel of this period is Ulric Barthe's *Similia Similibus*, which depicts a German take-over of Quebec City. Although the German invasion is ultimately revealed to be only the dream of an overwrought journalist, it is "une sorte

---

28 Amy Tector, "A Righteous War? L. M. Montgomery's Depiction of the First World War in *Rilla of Ingleside*," *Canadian Literature* 179 (Winter 2003), p. 73.

29 J. D. Logan and Donald G. French, *Highways of Canadian Literature: A Synoptic Introduction to the Literary History of Canada (English) from 1760 to 1924* (Toronto: McClelland and Stewart, 1924), p. 18.

30 Olivar Asselin, "Pourquoi je m'enrôle," *Liberté de pensée: Choix de textes politiques et littéraires* (Montreal: Editions TYPO, 1997).

31 "Written day by day, of the most vivid, stirring interest, about the odyssey of our valiant soldiers." Quoted in Pierre Vennat, *Les "Poilus" québécois de 1914–1918: Histoire des militaires canadiens-français de la Première Guerre mondiale*, 2 vols. (Montreal: Méridien, 1999), vol. I, p. 56. Unless otherwise indicated, translations are my own.

32 Ringuet [Philippe Panneton], *Trente Arpents* [*Thirty Acres*], tr. Felix and Dorothea Walter (Toronto: McClelland, 1960 [1940]), p. 144.

d'avertissement qui devrait stimuler l'enrôlement."[33] As one character darkly observes, "Une chose certaine, c'est que ce qui est arrivé à la Belgique pourrait bien nous arriver."[34]

From one war to the next

In 1918, William Douw Lighthall predicted that the War School of poets would be more important than the poets of Confederation: "as the war is a greater, wider, nobler event for us than Confederation, its influence will be so much the stronger."[35] J. D. Logan and Donald G. French in *Highways of Canadian Literature* devoted an entire chapter to "Hymns of War," claiming that the war had "caused a genuine Renascence of the Poetic Spirit."[36] A 1922 editorial in the *Canadian Bookman* hailed the new "golden era" for Canadian literature.[37] The founding of such journals as the *Canadian Forum, Canadian Historical Review*, and *Dalhousie Review* reflected this post-war confidence. Canada had embarked on a new "hour of self-supporting, self-conscious, independent nationhood."[38]

But as modernism began to take hold, Canadian poets turned their back on what Lighthall had optimistically called "our Homeric Age."[39] *New Provinces*, the 1936 anthology that championed the cosmopolitan poetry of the Montreal Group, included only one poem of the war, E. J. Pratt's "Text of the Oath," which describes war enthusiasm as "a virus in the air ... / [b]reathing romance on sleet and mud."[40] This break between war writers and modernists is strikingly different from what has been observed in Canadian painting: several of the most important twentieth-century painters – David Milne, Fred Varley, A. Y. Jackson, James Morrice, and Arthur Lismer – worked as official

---

33 "A sort of warning that should stimulate enlistment." Ulric Barthe, *Similia Similibus ou La guerre au Canada: Essai romantique sur un sujet d'actualité* (Quebec: Imprimerie Cie du "Telegraph," 1916), pp. 243.
34 "One thing is certain, which is that what happened in Belgium could well happen to us," ibid., p. 242.
35 William Douw Lighthall, "Presidential Address: Canadian Poets of the Great War," *Transactions of the Royal Society of Canada*, vol. XII, 3rd series, 1918, p. 61.
36 Logan and French, *Highways*, p. 344.
37 Quoted in James Mulvihill, "The Canadian Bookman and Literary Nationalism," *Canadian Literature* 107 (Winter 1985), p. 49.
38 Lorne Pierce, quoted in ibid., p. 50.
39 Lighthall, "Presidential Address," pp. LXI–LXII.
40 F. R. Scott and A. J. M. Smith, eds., *New Provinces: Poems of Several Authors*, introd. Michael Gnarowski (Toronto: University of Toronto Press, 1976 [1936]), p. 42.

war artists, and that experience had a direct influence on their subsequent work in Canada.[41]

In the 1920s, returned soldiers appeared frequently in Canadian fiction. They feature in several of Bertrand Sinclair's novels, even though Sinclair himself was not a veteran. In *Burned Bridges*, Wesley Thompson comes home from war with only minor injuries, but a "hidden sickness of racked nerves in an unmaimed body" has made him unfit for duty. He heads up the coast in pursuit of his sweetheart, where, as in all of Sinclair's returned-soldier novels, love in the wilderness heals the wounds of war. In *The Inverted Pyramid*, a working-class radical named Andy Hall has come home with two fewer fingers and three medals. When a society dowager makes a pious remark about sacrifice, Andy is quick to correct her: "Go to some slaughterhouse and watch pigs and sheep die with squeals and bleats and blood spurting out of their throats. Substitute men for pigs and sheep, and you have war."[42]

Like Sinclair, Hubert Evans paints British Columbia as a benign wilderness where men broken by war can heal themselves. Evans's returned soldier in *The New Front Line* decides to homestead in the Coast Range in the "new front line of pioneering."[43] When he and his wife finish their cabin, they look with pride at the rock fireplace they have built, a cenotaph in the wilderness: "that homely column of stone stood for yet another victory ... a fresh success in winning for themselves the kind of life they wanted" (p. 271).

At the end of the 1920s, a new kind of war writing began to appear. It was bitter, naturalistic, explicit. In an article in the *Canadian Defence Quarterly*, Lieutenant-Colonel F. C. Curry decried this "sudden flood of 'exposure literature'" as obscene. In an otherwise muddled critique, Curry made the insightful point that gruesomeness was no guarantee of accuracy.[44] Canadian war books of this period such as Charles Yale Harrison's *Generals Die in Bed*, Peregrine Acland's *All Else Is Folly*, and Philip Child's *God's Sparrows*, are certainly gruesome. Harrison's novel, laconically written in the present tense, depicts hideous injuries, visits to prostitutes, looting, and the killing

---

41 See Dean F. Oliver and Laura Brandon, *Canvas of War: Painting the Canadian Experience 1914–1945* (Vancouver: Douglas and McIntyre, 2000); Maria Tippett, *Art at the Service of War: Canada, Art, and the Great War* (Toronto: University of Toronto Press, 1984).
42 Bertrand W. Sinclair, *Burned Bridges* (New York: Grosset and Dunlap, 1919), p. 274; *The Inverted Pyramid* (Toronto: Goodchild, 1924), p. 266.
43 Hubert Evans, *The New Front Line* (Toronto: Macmillan, 1927), pp. 291.
44 F. C. Curry, "The Trend of the War Novel," *Canadian Defence Quarterly* 7:4 (July 1930), p. 519.

of prisoners.[45] W. J. Keith has described *Generals Die in Bed* as a "minor masterpiece," but it was reviled by veterans as "a gross and shameful slander."[46]

All Else Is Folly and *God's Sparrows* were not received so negatively, perhaps because they are ambivalent about the war. To Acland's protagonist Alec Falcon, "the whole thing was nothing but a gigantic futility, a world-embracing insanity ... He would like to live till the War was over, 'if only,' he said with sudden passion, 'to damn it.'"[47] But in the epilogue, set in 1924, Falcon goes to see his old regiment muster at the armories, and when he hears "the shrill summons of the pipes" (p. 342), he realizes that "he would have signed away his liberty, his life, for another war" (p. 343). In *God's Sparrows*, when the war breaks out, Pen Thatcher tries to quash his son's excitement: "This isn't romance, Dan! It is not a page out of the Iliad. It's the Devil let loose in the world."[48] Yet Child describes Ypres as "less a name than the symbol of a generation's Calvary" (p. 108), and he defends the soldiers against the presumption that they were dupes in a pointless war: "the thousands went into battle not ignobly, not as driven sheep or hired murderers ... but as free men with a corporate if vague feeling of brotherhood because of a tradition they shared and an honest belief that they were doing their duty in a necessary task. He who says otherwise lies, or has forgotten" (p. 146).

Perhaps the best book of the inter-war years was Will Bird's *And We Go On*. Bird served with the 42nd Battalion, the Black Watch of Canada, from 1916 to 1919. Like Curry, he was offended by the new war books, which he described as "putrid with so-called realism."[49] He complained that they "portray[ed] the soldier as a coarse-minded, profane creature ... Vulgar language and indelicacy of incident are often their substitute for lack of knowledge, and their distorted pictures of battle action are particularly repugnant. On the whole, such literature, offered to our avid youth, is an irrevocable insult to those gallant men who lie in French or Belgian graves." *And We Go On* aims to correct these misrepresentations. It is an odd book, colored by Bird's belief in psychic phenomena: he felt his brother, who had died on the battlefields in

---

45 Charles Yale Harrison, *Generals Die in Bed: A Story from the Trenches* (Toronto: Annick, 2002 [1928]).
46 W. J. Keith, *Canadian Literature in English*, rev. edn. 2 vols. (Erin: Porcupine's Quill, 2006 [1985]), vol. II, p. 28. Veterans' attacks on *Generals* quoted in Vance, *Death So Noble*, p. 194. See also Jonathan F. Vance, "The Soldier as Novelist: Literature, History, and the Great War," *Canadian Literature* 179 (Winter 2003), pp. 22–37.
47 Peregrine Acland, *All Else Is Folly: A Tale of War and Passion* (Toronto: McClelland and Stewart, 1929), p. 180.
48 Philip Child, *God's Sparrows* (Toronto: McClelland and Stewart, 1978 [1937]), p. 82.
49 Will Bird, *And We Go On* (Toronto: Hunter-Rose, 1930), p. 5.

1916, watched over him and saved his life on numerous occasions. It is also somewhat ragged. (The version published in 1968 as *Ghosts Have Warm Hands* is a more orderly narrative.)[50] But the very shapelessness of Bird's story reflects the chaos of war. Bird and his fellow soldiers spend hours waiting or being sent hither and thither. They march for miles in rain and darkness. They sleep in the mud; on one occasion, Bird nearly drowns in his bed. And always, there is death, not just in battle but at random, from snipers' bullets or stray shells. Perhaps the most agonizing passage is Bird's description of Passchendaele, where the mud, studded with corpses of men and animals, became the real enemy. One reviewer declared it a book that "everybody should read fully to appreciate the valor of the private soldier … It is true … yet no war fiction I have read can compare with it for intensity of interest."[51]

Two Quebec war novels from the inter-war period, Laetitia Filion's *Yolande, la fiancée* and Claudius Corneloup's *La Coccinelle du 22e*, exhibit none of the new battlefield realism, and they are silent about the Conscription Crisis at home. The young heroine of Filion's novel asks, "Qu'est-ce que cela pourrait bien nous faire à nous, ici au Canada, s'il y avait la guerre en Europe?"[52] Yolande's fiancé Henri and her brother Jean go off to war in the autumn of 1915. Henri loses his legs in a shell blast and releases Yolande from their engagement because no woman could marry a *mutilé de guerre*. Jean returns unharmed; the greatest injury he sustains is learning that his fiancée, the flighty Lucienne, has not been devoted to him.[53] Although Corneloup's *La Coccinelle du 22e* takes place on the battlefields, it too is more concerned with romance than with war. In the mode of *The Three Musketeers*, one central hero, Messidor, does daring deeds with the aid of three brothers-in-arms: Brumaire, Ventôse, and Germinal (all named after months of the Republican calendar, an odd choice for men raised in Quebec). A private detective before the war, Messidor spends most of his time tailing a suspected spy. Corneloup's fanciful treatment of the war seems at odds with his own experience. An emigrant from France, he joined the 22nd Regiment (the Van Doos) when war broke out. In 1917, he wrote a letter to Henri Bourassa (then editor of *Le Devoir*) in which he opposed conscription. Highly critical of British officers, the letter resulted in a court-martial for Corneloup. He later returned to active

---

50 Will Bird, *Ghosts Have Warm Hands* (Toronto: Clarke, Irwin, 1968).
51 *Canadian Magazine* 75.17 (January 1931), p. 17.
52 "What could that have to do with us here in Canada, if there is a war in Europe?"
53 Laetitia Filion, *Yolande, la fiancée* (Lévis: Le Quotidien 1934), p. 33.

service and after the war produced a memoir of his regiment, *L'Épopée du 22ᵉ* (1919).⁵⁴

Even with the outbreak of the second war, Canadians continued to write about the first. Hugh MacLennan was too young to have served in the Great War, but *Barometer Rising*, his 1941 novel about the Halifax Explosion (which MacLennan had witnessed as a child), gives a vivid picture of the nation at war. Like authors of the returned soldier generation, MacLennan applied the wartime vocabulary of sacrifice and heroism to the task of building a stronger Canada. As the reviewer for *Queen's Quarterly* put it, the protagonist Neil Macrae "finally wins through to the vision of a Canada strong and indispensable in a new order uniting England and America."⁵⁵

MacLennan's second novel, *Two Solitudes*, deals more directly with the war. In the rural parish of Saint-Marc-des-Érables, villagers accept the view of their priest that French Canadians ("the only real Canadians")⁵⁶ should feel no obligation to the English "who had conquered and humiliated them, and were Protestant anyway." Nor should they go to war for the sake of France: "she had deserted her Canadians a century and a half ago ... then turned atheist" (pp. 154–5). While the novel is set chiefly in Quebec, it also describes the war's national impact: "from one end to the other the war ate into everyone's mind ... Names like Ypres, Courcelette, Lens, Vimy, Cambrai, Arras, the Somme, had become as familiar and as much part of Canada as Fredericton, Moose Jaw, Sudbury or Prince Rupert" (pp. 202–3). When at last the troops return home, MacLennan sums up their bitter experience:

> Some of them had lived through half a week of the first gas attack, breathing through rags saturated with their own urine while they fought the Germans before Ypres. Some had existed in the cellars of Lens for weeks, gnawing their way underground through the town like rats, wall by wall ... Some had won medals. Some had acquired trench feet, scars, clap, gas-burns, syphilis and hallucinations that came in the night.

In this remarkable passage, which carries on for twelve sentences of sustained anaphora, MacLennan's prose attains a near-biblical dignity.

Little Man by G. Herbert Sallans, which in 1942 won both the Ryerson Fiction Prize and the Governor-General's award, begins with George Battle's

---

54 Claudius Corneloup, *La Coccinelle du 22ᵉ* (Montreal: Beauchemin, 1934). Corneloup's story appears at the website of Library and Archives Canada, www.collectionscanada.gc.ca.
55 Hugh MacLennan, *Barometer Rising* (Toronto: McClelland and Stewart, 1958 [1941]); E. H. W. "Fiction," *Queen's Quarterly* 48 (Winter 1941), p. 428.
56 Hugh MacLennan, *Two Solitudes* (Toronto: General, 1991 [1945]), p. 6.

first day in the trenches. It ends twenty-six years later, when George's son is killed in action over Britain. Sallans's novel is unusual in that it portrays the inter-war years as a hectic, disillusioning interlude between installments of war. Not surprisingly for a novel published in 1942, it ends with George and his wife, despite the loss of their son, displaying Churchillian resolve: "[t]hey had reeled, as from an onslaught for which they had fashioned no weapons. Yet somehow they had stood ... There could be no swerving any more, no hesitancy and no fear."[57]

One Quebec novel of the 1950s treats the first war. In Jean Simard's *Mon fils pourtant heureux*, the narrator offers a vivid portrait of his maternal grandmother, whose eldest son died in France in 1915. She wears his military cross on her chest and rereads the telegram announcing his death. In contrast to her patriotic grief, the narrator notes that his own father married in 1914, as did many others, in order to avoid having to enlist.[58]

Rediscovering the Great War

In the 1960s and 1970s, the Great War continued to appear in Canadian fiction for the simple reason that no account of the early twentieth century could ignore it. In Robertson Davies's *Fifth Business*, Dunstable Ramsay considers himself "born again" at Passchendaele. Davies uses the war chiefly as an instrument in Ramsay's spiritual and intellectual transformation, but the riotous celebration in Deptford when the VC-winning hero returns home suggests the war's importance in communities across the country.[59] The title story of Margaret Laurence's *A Bird in the House* describes how the death of a young man in the First World War darkens the lives of three generations: his mother, his brother, and his niece. Laurence's *The Diviners* also shows the long shadow of the war: Christie Logan, the adoptive father of narrator Morag Gunn, is a victim of shellshock. Reduced by his illness to being Manawaka's garbage man, tending the "Nuisance Grounds," Christie sees all the town's dark secrets. The story he tells about the war – "Christie's Tale of the Battle of Bourlon Wood" – seems to belong both to the world of the repressed that the Nuisance Grounds represent and to the proud warrior history of Christie's (and Morag's) Scottish ancestors.[60]

57 G. Herbert Sallans, *Little Man* (Toronto: Ryerson, 1942), p. 419.
58 Jean Simard, *Mon fils pourtant heureux* (Ottawa: Cercle du Livre de France, 1956), pp. 21, 42.
59 Robertson Davies, *Fifth Business* (Toronto: Macmillan, 1970), p. 72.
60 Margaret Laurence, *A Bird in the House* (Toronto: McClelland and Stewart, 1989 [1963]); *The Diviners* (Toronto: McClelland and Stewart, 1974), p. 73.

But these are only passing elements in novels focused more squarely on other themes. When Timothy Findley's *The Wars* appeared in 1977, it was the first novel in thirty years to focus chiefly on the war, and it self-consciously emphasized its status as a reconstruction, not a memoir. Presented as the notes of a researcher (identified only as "you"), *The Wars* attempts to explain why Robert Ross, son of an affluent Toronto family, went mad in France, shooting two men and embarking on a quixotic attempt to save some horses. Horribly burned in the fire that ended his mutiny, Ross was court-martialed and died soon after the war. In recounting Ross's story, Findley depicts the awfulness of trench warfare and the suffering that drove men mad, but much in this novel seems not to belong to the war. The cruellest incident occurs when Robert is raped in a wash-house by unseen assailants. It seems a startling departure from the war as it was represented by veterans. Perhaps reticence prevented them from recording such events, or perhaps Findley was projecting a nightmarish fantasy from his own time onto the backdrop of the war. The plural noun of his title suggests that it is not solely a historical novel.[61]

Louis Caron's *L'Emmitouflé*, published in the same year as *The Wars*, reflects a very different memory of the war. In Caron's novel, the return to Massachusetts of a Franco-American draft-dodger in the Vietnam era becomes a frame for the story of Uncle Nazaire, who fled to the woods to avoid conscription in the First World War. Timid but not cowardly, Nazaire does not want to die in a war that means nothing to him. He hides out in the woods until the war is over, and the suffering he endures makes him a kind of hero among his people. The narrator recognizes that his own resistance to the Vietnam War is a legacy of his uncle's actions during the First World War.[62]

Since *The Wars*, an astonishing number of Canadian writers have returned to the Great War. Its resurgence is partly a demographic phenomenon: the writers who came of age in the 1960s and 1970s are the last generation to have known the soldiers of the Great War. It is also political: as Canada's military commitments and losses have increased, so has our interest in our military past. But the new work about the war is very different from that of earlier decades. Herb Wyile has observed that historical novelists of our day "are much less inclined to construct patriotic narratives ... than to dramatize the exploitation, appropriation, and exclusion that such narratives ... have often

---

61 Timothy Findley, *The Wars* (Toronto: Clarke, Irwin, 1977).
62 Louis Caron, *L'Emmitouflé* (Paris: Laffont, 1977); *The Draft Dodger*, tr. David Homel (Toronto: Anansi, 1980).

served to efface."[63] In Great War novels, this tendency has meant, among other things, a shift away from protagonists of Scottish or English descent, and a greater emphasis on women. But it has also led to anachronism. In Jane Urquhart's *The Stone Carvers*, the protagonist Klara and her lover (both carvers on the Vimy Memorial) choose as their trysting spot a rusting bunk in the Grange tunnels; these were dug into the ridge in 1917 in order to bring Canadian troops to the front. Klara perceives their "secret lovemaking" as "a life source pulsing deep in the earth." Klara is German-Canadian, her lover Italian-Canadian, and their union under Vimy Ridge symbolizes renewal and reconciliation. But surely in 1936, when the monument was unveiled, veterans and the bereaved would have found such a scene both preposterous and offensive.[64]

Urquhart's earlier novel *The Underpainter* also deals with the aftermath of war. Two Canadians – a soldier who lived through Passchendaele, and a nurse who survived the bombing of the military hospital at Étaples – return home irretrievably damaged in heart and mind. In this novel, the war matters not for its own sake but for the noble luster it lends to Urquhart's characters.[65] A similar impression is created by Mary Swan's novella *The Deep*, which focuses on twin sisters who become volunteer aides in France. Just as Findley used "interviews" to reconstruct Ross's story, Swan uses various speakers to explain why the sisters commit suicide after the armistice.[66]

The book jacket of Joseph Boyden's *Three Day Road* describes it as "inspired in part by real-life World War I Ojibwa hero Francis Pegahmagabow," and in his acknowledgments, Boyden declares that "I wish to honour the Native soldiers who fought in the Great War ... especially ... Francis Pegahmagabow." The most decorated Native soldier of the Great War, Pegahmagabow fought in the Second Battle of Ypres and at Passchendaele, where his work as a scout was invaluable. Canada's Native soldiers numbered at least 4,000, about one in three of the able-bodied Native men of military age.[67] But it is not clear that Boyden's novel honors them. Xavier and Elijah, the Cree soldiers of *Three Day Road*, do not, as Pegahmagabow did, come home to serve their communities

---

63 Herb Wyile, *Speculative Fictions: Contemporary Canadian Novelists and the Writing of History* (Montreal: McGill-Queen's University Press, 2002), p. 4.
64 Jane Urquhart, *The Stone Carvers* (Toronto: McClelland and Stewart, 2001), p. 356.
65 Jane Urquhart, *The Underpainter* (Toronto: McClelland and Stewart, 1997).
66 Mary Swan, *The Deep* (Erin: Porcupine's Quill, 2002).
67 Joseph Boyden, *Three Day Road* (Toronto: Viking-Penguin, 2005). For background on Pegahmagabow and other Native soldiers, see Janice Summerby, *Native Soldiers, Foreign Battlefields* (Ottawa: Veterans Affairs Canada, 2005).

in peacetime. Xavier, wounded in the war, becomes a morphine addict. (There is no evidence that morphine addiction occurred among Canadian soldiers, for whom alcohol and nicotine were the drugs of choice.) Elijah, a sharpshooter, goes "windigo" on the Western Front, killing the enemy not out of duty but from bloodlust.[68]

In 1920, the Plains Cree writer and Anglican priest Edward Ahenakew declared that the war had elevated the Native man: "For the first time since the Treaty of 1876 the Indian has stood side by side with the white man upon the same plane and with equal chances ... he will never again be content to stand aside, giving no voice to matters that affect him."[69] Perhaps Ahenakew was naive – Native veterans did not share in land grants under the Soldier Settlement Act, nor did they receive equal pensions until 1936 – but there is no reason to presume that Native soldiers were degraded by the war, as Boyden's characters are. Boyden's 2008 novel, *Through Black Spruce*, carries on the story of Xavier's family; one of the narrators is his grandson, whose name – Will Bird – presumably alludes to the Great War memoirist.[70]

Other recent novels about the Great War seem less conspicuously engaged in projecting the attitudes of the present onto the war. *No Man's Land*, by Kevin Major, an award-winning writer of novels for adolescents, provides a sober and restrained account of "the single greatest disaster" in Newfoundland history: the battle at Beaumont-Hamel on the first day of the Somme. Left on their own by the failure of earlier advances, Newfoundlanders were mowed down as they tried to climb over bodies and cut through the German wire. About 780 men went over the top; only sixty-eight mustered the following day. Most of *No Man's Land* takes place on the day before the battle, moving inexorably toward the twenty minutes in which so many died. Photographs of the Regiment on the cover and at the back of the book remind us that, as Major puts it in his acknowledgments, "*No Man's Land* is a fiction, but the battle ... is not."[71]

In *Broken Ground* Jack Hodgins recreates life in one of the Soldier Settlements established when land grants were awarded to veterans. His

---

68 Windigo (sometimes wendigo or witiko) is an Algonquian and Northern Athapaskan term referring to a cannibalistic giant who haunts the woods; a person forced to eat human flesh in order to survive is believed to be possessed by the windigo.
69 Reverend E. Ahenakew, *Address* (Battleford: Battleford Press, 1920), n.p.
70 See Vance, *Death So Noble*, pp. 345–50, 250f., for a discussion of Native veterans. Joseph Boyden, *Through Black Spruce* (Toronto: Penguin, 2008).
71 Kevin Major, *No Man's Land* (Toronto: Doubleday, 1995). See book jacket, acknowledgments unpaginated. Major has adapted this novel for the stage: *No Man's Land: A Play* (St. John's, NL: Pennywell-Flanker, 2005).

fictional community of Portuguese Creek is based on Merville on Vancouver Island, where Hodgins's own parents lived. Scenes of war figure relatively little in *Broken Ground*; a fire that rips through the settlement in 1922 is more dramatically described, and the community's collective memory of the fire seems to stand for the war's lasting impact on this group of returned soldiers. In the acknowledgments, Hodgins cites scholars such as Modris Eksteins, Jay Winter, and Paul Fussell, whose ideas about memory and the Great War are reflected in the novel's self-conscious examination of "remembering, and remembering of earlier rememberings."[72]

In *Deafening* (2003), Frances Itani set out to write a novel about her deaf grandmother, but it turned into a novel about war: "I felt ... that I could not possibly set a book during this period and pretend that the war did not exist." While much of *Deafening* does deal with Grania, a young deaf woman, it also depicts the battlefields where her husband Jim serves as a stretcher bearer. Chapter epigraphs drawn from documentary materials anchor the novel in the period: the reader never loses sight of what men and women of the time believed. The wide range of sources for these epigraphs – letters from the front, articles in the *Canadian* (the newspaper of the Ontario School for the Deaf), newspaper advertisements, and official documents – attest to the research underlying this novel, as do the extensive acknowledgments. Although Jim is the focalizer for the war scenes, Grania is the central character. Thus *Deafening* is particularly good in depicting how families at home dealt with bereavement, invalid soldiers, and then the influenza epidemic.[73]

The protagonist of Alan Cumyn's war novel *The Sojourn* and its sequel *The Famished Lover* is named Ramsay Crome – possibly after Chrome yellow, the vivid color of a figure in Colin Gill's *Canadian Observation Post*, the painting on the dust jacket of *The Sojourn*. Cumyn is faced with a problem that Evelyn Cobley sees as characteristic of First World War narratives: "a fairly predictable sequence of events and a repertoire of conventional themes and images."[74] Moving up the lines, being at the front, going on patrol, having leave in London – the same episodes inevitably recur. Others have tried to break away from this inherent monotony by emphasizing the home front

---

72 Jack Hodgins, *Broken Ground* (Toronto: McClelland and Stewart, 1998), p. 330.
73 Frances Itani, *Deafening* (Toronto: HarperCollins, 2003). Interview material from Sasan Fisher, "Hear, Overhear, Observe, Remember: A Dialogue with Frances Itani," *Canadian Literature* 183 (Winter 2004), p. 50.
74 Evelyn Cobley, *Representing War: Form and Ideology in First World War Narratives* (Toronto: University of Toronto Press, 1993), p. 132.

(as in *Deafening* and *Broken Ground*) or by focusing on unusual participants (as in *Three Day Road*) or on a specific engagement (*No Man's Land*). But Cumyn is stuck with familiar, almost generic material. In *The Sojourn*, he attempts to transcend it by making Crome an artist and by using a sustained metaphor of the soldiers as helpless animals. But, in a sense, Cumyn is defeated by his own research, which serves only to supply details that declare "this is authentic" without ever quite making Ramsay Crome and his war real.[75]

The return to the First World War has been most evident among novelists, but others – anthologists, playwrights, children's authors, and poets – have also rediscovered the war. *We Wasn't Pals: Canadian Poetry and Prose of the First World War* makes work by writers like Acland, Peat, W. W. E. Ross, and Frank Prewett accessible to modern readers; so too does Muriel Whitaker's *Great Canadian War Stories*.[76] The most successful play about the First World War has been *Billy Bishop Goes to War*, John Gray's musical about the legend of Canada's VC-winning air ace, but Anne Chislett, Wendy Lill, R. H. Thomson, David French, Kevin Kerr, and Stephen Massicotte have also written plays about the war's impact on Canada.[77] More than two dozen children's books about the war, ranging from picture books to young adult novels, have appeared since 1990.[78] David Macfarlane's memoir, *The Danger Tree*, describes how the war affected his Newfoundland relatives; when it appeared in the United States in 2001, *The Atlantic Monthly* named it one of the best

---

75 Alan Cumyn, *The Sojourn* (Toronto: McClelland and Stewart, 2003); *The Famished Lover* (Fredericton: Goose Lane, 2006).
76 Barry Callaghan and Bruce Meyer, eds., *We Wasn't Pals: Canadian Poetry and Prose of the First World War* (Toronto: Exile, 2001); Muriel Whitaker, ed., *Great Canadian War Stories* (Edmonton: University of Alberta Press, 2001).
77 John Gray with Eric Peterson, *Billy Bishop Goes to War* (Vancouver: Talonbooks, 1981); Anne Chislett, *Quiet in the Land* (Toronto: Coach House, 1983); Wendy Lill, *The Fighting Days* (Vancouver: Talonbooks, 1985); Guy Vanderhaeghe, *Dancock's Dance* (Vancouver: Talonbooks, 1996); R. H. Thomson, *The Lost Boys: Letters from the Sons in Two Acts, 1914–1923* (Toronto: Playwrights Canada, 2001); David French, *Soldier's Heart* (Vancouver: Talonbooks, 2002); Kevin Kerr, *Unity (1918)* (Vancouver: Talonbooks, 2002); Stephen Massicotte, *Mary's Wedding* (Toronto: Playwrights Canada, 2002); Vern Thiessen, *Vimy* (Toronto: Playwrights Canada, 2008). See also Donna Coates and Sherrill Grace, eds., *Canada and the Theatre of War* (Toronto: Playwrights Canada, 2008), vol. I.
78 See, for example, Stephanie Innes and Harry Endrulat, *A Bear in War* (Toronto: KPk-Key Porter, 2008); Hugh Brewster, *At Vimy Ridge: Canada's Greatest World War I Victory* (Toronto: Scholastic, 2006); Arthur Slade, *Megiddo's Shadow* (Toronto: Harper Trophy Canada-HarperCollins, 2006); Jean Little, *Brothers Far From Home: The World War I Diary of Eliza Bates* (Markham: Scholastic, 2003); Sharon E. McKay, *Charlie Wilcox's Great War* (Toronto: Penguin, 2004); Linda Granfield, *Where Poppies Grow: A World War I Companion* (Toronto: Stoddart, 2001).

books of the year.⁷⁹ In late 2008, Paul Gross's *Passchendaele*, the most expensive Canadian film ever made, was released, and the novel based on his screenplay spent several weeks on the national best-seller list. Gross also wrote the foreword for *Passchendaele: An Illustrated History*, the tie-in children's book by Norman Leach.⁸⁰

In recent poetry, the war is observed from a distance. (An exception is Ted Plantos's collection, *Passchendaele*, in which the speaker is a soldier.)⁸¹ Raymond Souster (who has written several poems about both world wars) recounts in "Vimy Ridge" his father's experience of what "[a]ll the history books call ... / a great Canadian victory": "... for my father / it was only digging / a gun-pit behind the Ridge, / and finding the skeletons / of two French *poilu* [sic]."⁸² Marilyn Bowering's collection *Grandfather Was a Soldier* describes her pilgrimage to the Western Front, a journey motivated by "A few brown photographs. / A silence two generations old." The poems are framed with documents, beginning with her grandfather's attestation papers and ending with his discharge certificate.⁸³

Perhaps the most powerful Canadian poem of the Great War is Alden Nowlan's "Ypres: 1915." The speaker is no patriot – "[s]ometimes I'm not even sure that I have a country" – yet the image of the Canadians at the Second Battle of Ypres, who famously held their ground in the gas attack, remains stirring. A second scene, describing a television interview with a veteran of Vimy Ridge, adds to this impression of Canadian toughness. A final picture of war features a soldier who thinks, as he faces the enemy, "you want this God damn trench / you're going to have to take it away / from Billy MacNally / of the South End of Saint John, New Brunswick." The speaker admits that these images are " nothing / on which to found a country," yet he takes pride in thinking "that in some obscure, conclusive way" soldiers like Private MacNally "were connected with me / And me with them."⁸⁴

---

79 David Macfarlane, *The Danger Tree: Memory, War, and the Search for a Family's Past* (Toronto: Macfarlane Walter and Ross, 1991); Benjamin Schwarz, "(Some of) the Best Books of 2001," *The Atlantic Monthly* (December 2001), p. 150.
80 Paul Gross, dir., *Passchendaele*, Rhombus Media / Whizbang Films, 2008; *Passchendaele* (Toronto: HarperCollins, 2008); Norman Leach, *Passchendaele: An Illustrated History* (Regina: Coteau, 2008).
81 Ted Plantos, *Passchendaele* (Windsor: Black Moss, 1983).
82 Raymond Souster, *Collected Poems of Raymond Souster*, 10 vols. (Ottawa: Oberon, 1984), vol. V: 1977–83, p. 43.
83 Marilyn Bowering, *Grandfather Was a Soldier* (Victoria: Porcépic, 1987), p. 2.
84 Alden Nowlan, *Selected Poems* (Concord: Anansi, 1996), pp. 63–5.

In 1933, Will Bird predicted that "[w]ithin twenty years the veterans will have gone to their last roll-call – then they can bury ... everything regarding the Great War. It will then be of no interest."[85] But Bird was wrong. Although the hundreds of thousands who fought on the Western Front are gone now, they still haunt the Canadian imagination.

---

85 Will Bird, "Preface," *The Communication Trench: Anecdotes and Statistics from the Great War* (Ottawa: CEF Books, 2000 [1933]), n.p.

PART THREE

*

MODELS OF MODERNITY, POST-FIRST WORLD WAR

13
Staging personalities in modernism and realism

IRENE GAMMEL

Canadian modernism, realism, and romance made for comfortable, and at times, not so comfortable bedfellows during the first decades of the twentieth century. "A salutary move has been to circumscribe or define Canadian modernism in a non-canonical way – usually in order to accommodate it, at least partly but paradoxically, to its old enemies, realism and romanticism," writes Glenn Willmott.[1] Dean Irvine echoes this approach while also emphasizing that Canadian modernism has remained somewhat under-examined in the scholarly literature because of its hybrid attributes.[2]

A review of early twentieth-century prose reveals a rich array of modernist forms, more specifically the exuberant play with self-portraiture and multiple selves found in the life-writing and fiction of numerous Canadian authors who lived during the modernist era. Their works may well constitute the most central and experimental articulation of Canadian modernism in prose, allowing authors to stage cross-cultural, controversial, and even conflicted identities – personal and public, sexual and political, regional and national. In New York, the influx of a group of European artists created an important ferment that stimulated radically modern expressions of art and literature during the First World War era; so too in Canada, the influx of European voices stimulated literary production and energized cross-Canadian literary and cultural dialogue. These authors play with hybrid genres, as well as exploring modernity at the interface of the textual and visual, thereby submitting distinctly Canadian contributions to the global movement of international literary modernism. A well-kept secret, this Canadian modernism deserves more critical attention.

---

1 Glenn Willmott, *Unreal Country: Modernity in the Canadian Novel in English* (Montreal and Kingston: McGill-Queen's University Press, 2002), p. 42.
2 Dean Irvine. "Introduction," in *The Canadian Modernists Meet* (Ottawa: University of Ottawa Press, 2005), pp. 1–13.

Many of these writers have been categorized as realists, naturalists, journalists, or romance writers. However, a re-examination of their contributions to life-writing reveals a shared preoccupation with modernist concerns in content, narrative, and form, even as there is a great diversity among them. Canadian prose texts involve a staging of the modern personality, and authors as diverse as Frederick Philip Grove, Georgina Binnie-Clark, Kathleen Strange, Robert Stead, Martha Ostenso, L. M. Montgomery, Mazo de la Roche, Elizabeth Smart, Morley Callaghan, and John Glassco articulate and challenge the aesthetic and literary values typically associated with modernism. An important focus will be F. P. Grove and L. M. Montgomery, representing western and eastern Canada respectively. Both of these national icons posthumously startled their readerships when it was revealed they had led secret lives. Grove and Montgomery are prominent examples of the creative labor entailed in the construction of a public and private persona during the modern era. The performative and narrative manipulations characteristic of modernist life writing draw attention to pan-Canadian literary dialogues that have remained hitherto unacknowledged or uninvestigated.[3] They also undermine the conventional oppositions that pit eastern sentimentalism against western realism, traditionalism against experimentalism, rural against urban, conservative against progressive. These dialogues reveal distinctly Canadian preoccupations with modernist concerns and narrative forms.

Modernist masquerades: F. P. Grove

In 1946, Frederick Philip Grove (1879–1948), author of innovative and commercially successful nature sketches and novels (*Over Prairie Trails*, 1922; *The Turn of the Year*, 1923; *Settlers of the Marsh*, 1925; *A Search for America*, 1927, among others), received the Governor General's Award for non-fiction, for what was assumed to be his autobiography, *In Search of Myself* (1946). In 1973, his biographer Douglas O. Spettigue, however, revealed the autobiography as an elaborate lie that had allowed Grove to reinvent himself after he settled in Manitoba in 1912 and resumed his writing career during the 1920s.[4] Spettigue also revealed a remarkable and omitted history: Grove's prison incarceration for fraud in

---

3 The list of authors and works discussed here is by no means complete. For instance, Sinclair Ross's *As for Me and My House* (1941), according to Irvine (*The Canadian Modernists Meet*, p. 8) "the most critically studied modernist novel in Canada," is discussed elsewhere in this volume.

4 For biographical and textual studies, see D. O. Spettigue's *FPG: The European Years* (Ottawa: Oberon, 1973); Margaret Stobie, *Frederick Philip Grove* (New York: Twayne,

Germany, and his hidden identity as the German writer Felix Paul Greve, a well-known author and translator among *fin-de-siècle* European writers such as Stefan George, H. G. Wells, and André Gide. Grove's biographers often collapse the two identities under the acronym "FPG" to designate the complex Greve/Grove dyad. The play afforded by this double name has opened up a way of rereading his works with an eye alert to artificial identities. His case is similar to that of other famous Canadian literary con-men such as the Scotsman Archibald Belaney (Grey Owl) and African-American Sylvester C. Long (Chief Buffalo Child Long Lance), who both assumed Native personae and became Canadian and international celebrities. Grove's German biographer Klaus Martens argues that all three artists crossed national and racial boundaries not to defraud, but rather to escape persecution or social prejudice, or to seek new identities that were in harmony with nature.[5] And yet this staging of identities has an ethical ambiguity, like Jay Gatz's shady rebirth and renaming in Fitzgerald's 1925 modernist classic *The Great Gatsby*. As Paul John Eakin writes, "When life writers fail to tell the truth, then, they do more than violate a literary convention governing nonfiction as a genre; they disobey a moral imperative."[6]

More recent discoveries regarding FPG's nine-year intense and rocky relationship with Else Plötz point to the depth of Grove's deception. His biographers tacitly assumed that FPG had never married, but had lived in a common-law relationship with the German artist who called herself his wife and was also the inspiration for his two German novels, *Fanny Essler* (1905) and *Maurermeister Ihles Haus* (1906). Ironically, Grove's lie was protected by the *Datenschutzgesetz*, the stringent German data protection law. In my book on Greve's wife, I was able to disclose that, on August 22, 1907, Felix Paul Greve had indeed married Else Plötz in Berlin-Wilmersdorf.[7] Else Plötz is better known today as the Baroness Elsa von Freytag-Loringhoven, an original and controversial member of the New York Dada circle after her separation from FPG. In 1910, she had followed him to the United States and by September the couple had drawn the attention of *The New York Times*, which reported that "Mrs. Elsie Greve" was arrested on the crowded Fifth Avenue in Pittsburgh because she was "dressed in men's clothes and puffing a cigarette." She was

---

1973); Irene Gammel, *Sexualizing Power in Naturalism: Theodore Dreiser and Frederick Philip Grove* (Calgary: University of Calgary Press, 1994), and Klaus Martens, *F. P. Grove in Europe and Canada: Translated Lives* (Edmonton: University of Alberta Press, 2001).

5 Klaus Martens, ed., *Over Canadian Trails: F. P. Grove in New Letters and Documents* (Würzburg: Königshausen and Neumann, 2007), p. 152.

6 Paul John Eakin, *The Ethics of Life Writing* (Ithaca, NY: Cornell University Press, 2004), pp. 2–3.

7 Irene Gammel, *Baroness Elsa: Gender, Dada, and Everyday Modernity – A Cultural Biography* (Cambridge, MA: MIT Press, 2002), pp. 144–5.

Plate 10. Baroness Elsa von Freytag-Loringhoven in Costume, c. 1920.

"walking by the side of her husband, F. P. Greve of New York."[8] A modern figure par excellence, Elsa staged her androgyny and sexual assertiveness in photography by Man Ray and others.[9] But her flamboyant modernity was also a dangerous liability for her husband and may have contributed to his desertion of her; Greve left his wife in Sparta, Kentucky, in the fall of 1911.

8 Anonymous. "She Wore Men's Clothes: On Walking Tour with Husband, Mrs. Greve Explains – Police Let Couple Go," *The New York Times* (September 17, 1910), p. 6.
9 Elsa von Freytag-Loringhoven was photographed and filmed by Man Ray and Marcel Duchamp (Gammel, *Baroness Elsa*, pp. 286–313).

After first traveling west and then north, he arrived in Manitoba in 1912. Here he assumed the name Frederick Philip Grove and became a teacher, husband, father, and writer who supported family values and had a vision for building Canada's national literature. This new life, however, was based on a dangerous lie. With the onset of war, in 1914, the thirty-five-year-old Greve married twenty-two-year-old school teacher Catherine (Tena) Wiens. On the marriage certificate, he indicated his new identity as the forty-one-year-old Moscow-born widower Frederick Philip Grove. Having never obtained a divorce, he remained legally married to Elsa – a secret that must have weighed heavily on him and may have taken its psychological toll, considering the crippling migraines and hypochondria that had also marked stressful times in Germany. As a writer, he was condemned to remain obscure; had the Baroness Elsa ever discovered his new identity, he might have faced blackmail and exposure. In an unpublished document, the Baroness described him with an oxymoron, calling him a mixture of "honesty – dishonesty," a blend of "echt – unecht," someone who was self-deceived.[10]

Grove's autobiographical fiction is a palimpsest of masquerading characters pointing toward the implied author of the text. In *A Search for America*, the polyglot idealist immigrant Phil Branden turns his back on the United States to become a resident in Canada. "I have been a teacher since; and not only a teacher, but the doctor, lawyer, and business-agent of all the immigrants in my various districts." The ending invites the reader to blur the line between the fictional man and the author: "And twenty-seven years after the end of my rambles I published the first of my few books."[11] Grove gave a voice to the land-hungry pioneers of the West, but also cloaked his past in the ostensible honesty of the prairie pioneer novel. The genre was a screen that protected his new self, for a prairie western novel would not have piqued the reading interests of the cosmopolitan Baroness.

Published *after* Elsa had returned to Berlin, *Settlers of the Marsh* achieved notoriety in Canada with its frank and graphic depiction of sexuality on a prairie pioneer farm; rape, abortion, promiscuity, adultery, and sexual aversion expose the breakdown of domestic and heterosexual relationships. Embedded within the naturalist genre was a work of confessional fiction. As Grove wrote in a December 13, 1924 letter to his friend Arthur Phelps, his goal had been, "to put the corrupt, sexually hypertrophied woman of French

---

10 Elsa von Freytag-Loringhoven, "Seelisch-Chemische Betrachtung," Elsa von Freytag-Loringhoven Papers. University of Maryland Archives. My translation.
11 F. P. Grove, *A Search for America* (Ottawa: The Graphic Publishers, 1927), p. 448.

upper-class novels on the *soil*."¹² Clara Vogel, who can be read as Elsa's alter ego, dyes her hair with henna leaves, applies make-up and refuses to do the housework – just like Elsa. When the infamous widow seduces the puritanical Swedish immigrant farmer Niels Lindstedt, he feels compelled to marry her, as perhaps Greve had felt compelled to marry Elsa after their notorious affair in 1902 which resulted in the very public and acrimonious break-up of her previous marriage.

Not only was *Settlers* a working through of his relationship and separation from his first wife, but it resonated with modern-day anxieties regarding the New Woman. As a sexual initiator, Clara Vogel threatens to unman and engulf Niels Lindstedt, whose aversion to sex is palpable: "Distasteful though they were, he satisfied her strange, ardent, erratic desires."¹³ Expressions of male emasculation are a hallmark of much modernist writing; impotency and anxiety figure prominently in major literary works such as Hemingway's *The Sun Also Rises*, D. H. Lawrence's *Lady Chatterley's Lover*, and T. S. Eliot's *The Love Song of J. Alfred Prufrock* and *The Waste Land*; as well as in visual art such as *The Bride Stripped Bare by her Bachelors, Even* (*The Large Glass*) by Marcel Duchamp, in which sex is deferred. In *Settlers of the Marsh*, Grove was articulating the modernist era's sexual anxieties in trying to contain the specter of the erotically assertive New Woman. Meanwhile, in New York, the Baroness's poetry and art excoriated the males in the New York Dada circle as in her 1918 "Love-Chemical Relationship," which poetically engaged Duchamp's *Large Glass* as an articulation of a heterosexual stalemate.¹⁴

Grove's new role as spokesperson for the young Canadian nation was promoted in advertisements, lecture tours, essays, and fiction. *Over Prairie Trails* was endorsed by L. M. Montgomery as a book which "should be in the library of every educational institution in Canada."¹⁵ Similarly, *Settlers of the Marsh* was propagated with the question: "Is It the Great Canadian Novel?" According to a 1925 promotion brochure, the immigrant's perspective was Grove's most valuable contribution: "As an adopted son he is able to see a developing Canada and Canadian conditions from some standpoints as a native could not do nor understand, and his outline of pioneer Canadian life

---

12 F. P. Grove to Arthur Phelps, December 23, 1924, in Martens, ed., *Over Canadian Trails*, p. 218.
13 F. P. Grove, *Settlers of the Marsh* (Toronto: Ryerson Press, 1925), p. 192.
14 Elsa von Freytag-Loringhoven, "Love-Chemical Relationship," *The Little Review* 5.2 (June 1918), pp. 58–9.
15 The endorsement for *Over Prairie Trails* is by L. M. Montgomery and appeared in *The Montreal Gazette* (April 11, 1923), n.p.

is therefore all the more interesting."¹⁶ In the accompanying photo, Grove sits at the table writing, the eyes turned downward, hair combed flat like a priest's, and dressed in a homely knitted sweater. In "Felix Paul Greve, the Eulenburg Scandal, and Frederick Philip Grove," Richard Cavell has argued that homosexual panic may also have contributed to FPG's decision to leave Germany and may have prompted Grove to refashion himself as a heterosexual icon for the Canadian nation.¹⁷

Indeed, FPG staged himself as a new and upright Canadian citizen. In carefully constructed self-portrait photography he posed on a self-made raft on Lake Winnipeg; or with his wife and daughter camping in the outdoors, the tent in the background; or sitting by the beach wearing old-fashioned clothing, his wife knitting, a collapsed umbrella pitched like a flag pole in the photo's center. Each photo represents the self-conscious pose of the Canadian pioneer writer and travel narrator, the author in touch with the natural world. A stunning transformation from the manicured and dressed-to-the-hilt dandy pose that so impressed André Gide, these apparently natural poses are nonetheless no less constructed, as the careful choice of props reveals. Grove was an excellent photographer, arranging a vision of himself, his family, his writing, and the landscape.¹⁸

Speaking with a "guttural" German accent, while claiming to be Swedish, FPG never fit neatly into national categories, just as his aesthetic did not fit any particular style or genre. He was more at home in the hybrid realm, and one of his favorite fictional poses was that of the traveler, crossing countries, continents, professions, and languages. In his fiction and non-fiction, Grove similarly crossed borders. Although his eco-consciousness harks back to the American nature writer Henry David Thoreau, whose work he had read and annotated, his nature prose calls up the destructive effects of human progress in surrealist images. In *Over Prairie Trails*, for example, the new drainage ditches built by the province look "like naked scars on Nature's body: ugly, raw, as if the bowels were torn out of a beautiful bird and left to dry and rot on

---

16 A copy of an unpaginated, multi-page advertisement for *Settlers* of *c*. 1925 (source unknown) is held in L. M. Montgomery's Red Scrapbook, No. 2, *c*. 1913–1926, [p. 116], Lucy Maud Montgomery Collection, University of Guelph Archives.
17 Richard Cavell, "Felix Paul Greve, the Eulenburg Scandal, and Frederick Philip Grove," *Essays on Canadian Writing* 62 (Fall 1997), pp. 12–45.
18 Some of these photos appear in Klaus Martens's 2007 *Over Canadian Trails*: the original photographs are held in a private collection (Leonard and Mary Grove), as well as in the University of Manitoba Archives, where some of Grove's work has also been made available electronically.

Plate 11. F. P. Grove and family, Lake Winnipeg, 1923. The text on the back of the photograph reads: "A summer afternoon of the family on one of the as yet unchartered beaches of Lake Winnipeg. The hats as well as the rest of the clothes are those discarded for outer wear 375 years ago."

its plumage."[19] Similarly, in *The Turn of the Year*, he sought out the hard and concrete image that would become a hallmark of modernism: "First the male willows only hold up their yellow phalli ... Then the poplars hang out their red tassels pregnant with yellow dust."[20] The western prairie was the canvas on which Grove painted the frantic dance of the hailstones, which rained down on once proud canes of sweet corn, now pitiable stumps in a melodramatic setting. But in the same texts he could also rhapsodize about the beauty and texture of snow and fog.

Marked by flashbacks, time shifts, and unreliable narration, *The Master of the Mill* (1944) is Grove's most experimental and self-consciously modernist work. Set in fictional Langholm, Ontario, the novel also reflects Grove's move to Ontario in 1929, after the shocking death of his young daughter May two years earlier. Narrated through the lens of the aging and not always reliable Samuel Clark, the novel traces the development of the Clark flour empire from his father Rudyard's small family-run business in 1888 to an internationally renowned corporation – a huge and fully automated industrial

---

19 F. P. Grove, *Over Prairie Trails* (Toronto: McClelland and Stewart, 1922), pp. 36–7.
20 F. P. Grove, *The Turn of the Year* (Toronto: McClelland and Stewart, 1923), p. 75.

machine – constructed under the management of Sam's son Edmund in 1923. An allegory of Canada's development into an industrial nation, *The Master of the Mill* is also a satire of the Freudian *Wiederholungszwang*, which is played out by three generations of Clark males at the head of the mill. Fraudulent insurance schemes reveal the ethical ambiguity of the modern corporate machine, reflected in the ostensible shifts of narrative perspectives. Using another modernist theme, the text reveals that the male icons of power who command the mill are impotent, exposing their control to be a chimera.

Realism and beyond: Martha Ostenso and Robert Stead

The ways in which Grove both exploits and surpasses the naturalist and realist tropes in masquerades also alerts us to the complexity of the realist prairie novel in general. Consider, for example, Martha Ostenso's *Wild Geese* (1925, reprinted in 1926, movie adaptation *After the Harvest* in 2001) and Robert Stead's *Grain* (1926); the former is a commercially successful collaboration with her husband Douglas Durkin, and the latter is influenced by Stead's work as a publicist for the Department of Immigration and Colonization, which colors the novel with war publicity. Obscuring the name of Ostenso's male collaborator seemed to influence responses to her novel during an era when women writers and activists were making headway in claiming female sexual and creative agency. When Norwegian-born Ostenso (1900–63) was awarded the prestigious Dodd, Mead, and Company Prize for the best North American novel in 1925, F. P. Grove felt deeply threatened by the success of the twenty-five-year-old female writer. "It is the old story: only trash wins a prize," he quipped. "In fact, how could a young girl know anything of the fierce antagonisms that discharge themselves in sex?"[21] His reasoning was disingenuous considering the role that sexually liberated Elsa had played in Grove's life. That Ostenso's work was subsequently revealed to be the result of collaboration ironically mirrors Grove's own situation: his writing had benefited greatly from Elsa's input. The "young girl" evoked by Grove was a nostalgic fiction: Ostenso was a woman writer who defied bourgeois mores by living with a married novelist (who became her husband many years later). The stereotype of the "young girl" was clearly being dismantled

---

21 Desmond Pacey, ed., *The Letters of Frederick Philip Grove* (Toronto: University of Toronto Press, 1976), p. 26.

by woman writers, who transformed the image of the western woman farmer and writer.

Indeed, Canadian modernity is perhaps most provocatively articulated through tales that figure prominently the New Woman's public presence, agency and rights. The women in fiction – such as Ostenso's Judith Gare in *Wild Geese*, Jo Burge in Stead's *Grain*, and Ellen Amundsen in *Settlers* – are androgynous and rebellious. They are unconventional in their dress and sexual demeanor: Judith becomes pregnant out of wedlock, for example, while Ellen chooses to stay single. Often performing male tasks, they love the land and handle the machinery and livestock with as much skill as the men.

In the same novels, mirroring the modernist crisis of masculinity in the prairie setting, male pioneering is depicted as stagnant and rigid. A case in point: Stead's anti-hero William Stake, nicknamed Gander, is a slave to the land and his home. His intense attachment hampers his psychological development and his ability to form meaningful relationships. Similarly, Grove's male prairie pioneers – Abe Spalding in *Fruits of the Earth* (1933), Niels Lindstedt in *Settlers*, John Elliot in *Our Daily Bread* (1928) – are all larger-than-life empire builders who fail because they lack the nimble linguistic flexibility of their female counterparts.[22] They stammer, stutter, and bumble, caught in a linguistic crisis. Where Ostenso's female immigrants talk eloquently and with distinctly ethnic accents, the male immigrants are often caught in what Canadian writer-critic Robert Kroetsch has aptly described as "the grammar of silence."[23]

In his examination of the evolving world, Grove treats the monomaniacal patriarch with sympathy and nostalgia, depicting his bafflement when confronted with a modern world of flux. In contrast, Martha Ostenso's *Wild Geese* exorcizes the patriarch Caleb Gare as a demonic figure who tries to hold on to old power structures by bullying, blackmailing, and whipping his family into submission. '[A] spiritual counterpart of the land, as harsh, as demanding, as tyrannical as the very soil from which he drew his existence," he recruits the unpaid workers from within his immediate family, yoking them to the land. His daughter – "Judith, vivid and terrible, who seemed the embryonic ecstasy of all life" – tries to kill her father.

---

22 E. D. Blodgett, "*Alias* Grove: Variations in Disguise," *Configuration: Essays in the Canadian Literatures* (Toronto: ECW, 1982), pp. 112–53.
23 Robert Kroetsch, "The Grammar of Silence: Narrative Pattern in Ethnic Writing," *Canadian Literature* 106 (Autumn 1985), p. 65.

The novel ends with a melodramatic *deus ex machina*, a prairie fire during which Caleb ventures into the muskeg and is sucked into the "irresistible" and "insidious" land. After his death, peace returns. Quiet and serene, the women triumph as survivors and are integrated once again into the larger social community from which they were alienated under Caleb's rule. "I wonder just what the mystery was with the Gares," the teacher Lind Archer muses: "It seemed to vanish with Caleb."[24] The locale evokes the Interlake district in Manitoba, where Ostenso taught school, but the setting is unidentified; the novel is left suspended in a timeless and anonymous setting that opens the novel to both Canadian and American readers. "For a novel in which 'place' plays such a central role, Ostenso seems not to have wanted to 'place' it," Deborah Keahey writes in *Making It Home: Place in Canadian Prairie Literature*.[25]

How does farming technology, perhaps, make the rural prairie relevant to modernism? Albert Einstein's relativity theory and the advent of new technologies including phonography, radiography, chronophotography, and cinematography in the early twentieth century shaped international literary modernism. The modernist novel is concerned with an accelerated world and new experiences of visual and aural perception.[26] The privileged symbol for the modern world, the car is the vehicle of liberated sexual traditions and accelerated speed. "A car?" Mr. Stake scoffed in Stead's *Grain*, "One o' them rantin' automobilly-goats? No, sir!" Although the car first gets little respect on the prairie farm, half-way through the novel in the third year of the war, Gander's father purchases a Ford – the symbol of a small-town prairie world in transition. In *Grain*, the male protagonist's identity is entangled in his love of machinery, in particular the steam thresher: "And although Gander was a boy not touched by the romance of books here was something that stirred him deeply – the romance of machinery, of steam, which, at the pull of a lever, turned loose the power of giants!"[27] His erotic fixation on the machine displaces his sexual desire, causing him to defer the consummation of a sexual relationship with "his girl" Jo Burge.

Grain pictures female erotic desire as intensely frustrated. When Jo Burge, tired of waiting, leaves Gander to marry Dick Claus, her problem is further

---

24 Martha Ostenso, *Wild Geese* (New York: Grosset and Dunlap, 1926), pp. 35–6, 35, 351, 355.
25 Deborah Keahey, *Making It Home: Place in Canadian Prairie Literature* (Winnipeg: The University of Manitoba Press, 1998), p. 15.
26 Sara Danius, *The Senses of Modernism: Technology, Perception, and Aesthetics* (Ithaca: Cornell University Press, 2002).
27 Robert Stead, *Grain* (New York: Doran, 1926), pp. 180, 61.

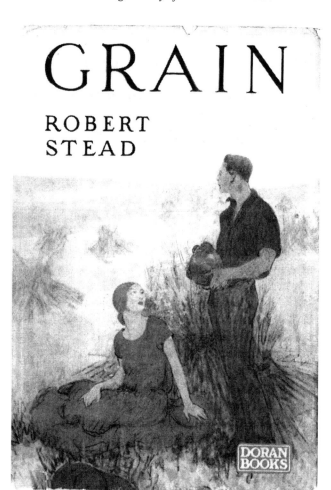

Plate 12. Cover Image, Robert J. Stead's *Grain*, 1926.

exacerbated when her husband returns from the war an invalid; their marriage, like Lady Chatterley's, appears to be devoid of sex. With *Settlers* and *Grain*, the modernist heterosexual stalemate enters the realm of prairie fiction. Ironically, however, the first-edition cover of *Grain* pictures a woman with flaming hair and red dress lounging on the hayfield and gazing up at a strapping male standing tall and proud and scanning the horizon. The novel was marketed as *A Romance of the True Northwest*, as the subtitle on the spine underscores, but the novel's sardonic modernist allusions seem to complicate and even contradict the conventional romance.

Modern homesteaders: Georgina Binnie-Clark and Kathleen Strange

Wheat and Woman (1914) and *A Summer on a Canadian Prairie* (1910) are personal and humorous accounts of farming as seen through the lens of a confident and vivacious writer. Born in Dorset, England, the British travel writer Georgina Binnie-Clark (1871–1955) made her home in the Qu'Appelle Valley, Saskatchewan, in 1905. As a single woman homesteader, she soon found herself stumbling into the sexist loop-holes of the Canadian homestead law. According to the Dominion Lands Act of 1872, men were entitled to receive 160 acres of land by paying the government just $10, but the same agreement did not apply to women. Binnie-Clark was forced to pay $5,000 for her farm. It was a clear case of sexual discrimination that prompted her to spearhead the women's homesteader movement. Her narrative contributed to a literature that was increasingly interested in the single woman, in egalitarian relationships, and in post-Victorian ideals and rhetoric: "Lost my temper and blasphemed badly and loudly and bitterly," Georgina Binnie-Clark notes in her account of the harvest troubles in September 1906.[28]

Still, Binnie-Clark was privileged compared to others. The cover picture of the 2007 edition emphasizes her gentility, portraying the homesteader-writer as a Victorian lady with hair piled high, glancing winsomely over her left shoulder. Binnie-Clark was less financially vulnerable than some of the other homesteaders in her area, who did not receive life-saving stipends from home. She was never really in danger of starvation or of ending up homeless. According to her writings, her battles against frost, fire, and unequal laws, her frustration and melancholy, her seemingly endless stream of misfortunes never left her too dejected. After a trip to New York in 1908, Binnie-Clark received many offers to translate her homesteading experience into lucrative literature: "All the world was interested in Canada; I was possessed of practical and first-hand information. Offers of work from various magazines approached my pen."[29] There was a market for this type of literature as seen in the success of American author Willa Cather (*O Pioneers!*, 1913 and *My Ántonia*, 1918), as well as the female homesteader stories so popular in some of

---

28 Georgina Binnie-Clark, *Wheat and Woman* (Toronto: University of Toronto Press, 2007), p. 167.
29 Ibid., p. 275.

the American mass-market magazines including the *Atlantic, Collier's* and *Outlook*.[30]

A journalist and writer, Binnie-Clark was attuned to the nuances of self-representation. Her style is marked by evocative descriptions and a dry, self-deprecating humor. Although there is a progression from naivety to experience, the tone is also that of a travel narrative in which an outsider observes the landscape as both quaint and exotic: "And the gophers! Crouched on their haunches with their dainty little forepaws dropped in a most convincing attitude of supplication." When the chore boy leaves, she tries her hand at milking. At the end of two hours of pulling and pressing and squeezing, Binnie-Clark claims: "I had about a quart of Molly's milk in the pail, and I hadn't even looked at the hard cow." Trying to ease her cramped limbs, Georgina gets up. Molly, "fed up from the prolonged ceremony, walked off gaily, kicking over the pail in her exit!"[31] The reader imagines more swearing on a Sabbath! Although Binnie-Clark's activism did not garner as much attention as the suffrage movement, which involved Manitoban writer Nellie McClung, it was nonetheless prompted by the same feminist desire for social transformation – to make women independent agents in the farming community. Suffrage was granted in 1916 in Alberta, Manitoba, and Saskatchewan two years before the federal law was passed, but it took until the 1930s for Western women homesteaders to win equal rights.[32]

"To Farm Women – Pioneers All" was also the motto of Manitoba writer and farmer Kathleen Strange (1896–1968), who was born in London and immigrated with her husband to Canada. "On a stiflingly hot day of July, in the year 1920," Kathleen and Harry arrived at Fenn, in Central Alberta. The town consisted of a grain elevator, a train depot, and a general store. *With the West in her Eyes: The Story of a Modern Pioneer* (1937) is a personal account of Strange's struggle on the western farm.[33] The memoir also established Strange as a significant literary figure in Canada; she would eventually become the President of the Winnipeg Writers' Club, and Vice-President of the Winnipeg Branch of the Canadian Authors Association. The inside cover of the first edition I was able to find shows a harvested wheat field with the farm in the

---

30 Dee Garceau, "Single Women Homesteaders and the Meanings of Independence: Places on the Map, Places in the Mind," *Frontiers: A Journal of Women Studies* 15.3 (1995), p. 9.
31 Binnie-Clark, *Wheat and Woman*, pp. 135, 133.
32 Shawne McKeown, "How Women Won the West," *The National Post* (March 2, 2004), p. A10.
33 Kathleen Strange, *With the West in Her Eyes: The Story of a Modern Pioneer* (Toronto: George J. McLeod, 1937), pp. v, 3.

background, a decidedly rural scene; but the book nevertheless also included a promotional page (perhaps part of the dust jacket?) with a photo of Strange in which she looks like a racy city flapper, with a bob and a mischievous sideways glance at the camera. Strange asserts her determination to break traditional roles by wearing male breeches on the farm: "Defiantly I went on wearing the offending garments, and in time apparently wore the resistance down" (p. 41). Her social pioneering extends to dancing, which seems to split the Fenn social scene in two opposing factions: "Fists were shaken in angry faces. Many unflattering remarks were passed … The room began to resemble a sort of verbal battle-field" (p. 122). Yet she emerges triumphant.

Where Grove sees nature as a force indifferent or hostile to humans, to be tamed by the settler, Strange's tone is more pragmatic and offers yet another perspective on the idea of "spring," so pervasive in modernist writings by Eliot, W. C. Williams, e.e. cummings, and Edna St. Vincent Millay: "Spring comes to the prairies clothed in beauty, but the prairie farmer seldom has time to appreciate or enjoy it" (p. 150). Strange's narrative looks at marriage and motherhood, miscarriages and childbirth. She also locates the technological symbols of modernism on the prairie farm, enjoying "a 'wireless set' – a home-made radio, constructed by a radio engineer in London who was a friend of ours" (p. 137). Technology connects the rural and the urban, the regional with the wider international world: "Not only were we successful in tuning in on stations all over Canada and the United States, but we actually managed to connect up with London itself" (pp. 137–8). Indeed, it is the family's connectedness with the global world that allows the Strange family business to flourish; Kathleen and Harry launch a seed business after finding out that northern-grown seed is desirable in other parts of the world and win the World's Grand Prize at the Chicago Exhibition in 1923 for their seeds.

The woman farmer experimenting with new identities is the true heroine in Strange's memoir. In the spring, a neighbor, Mrs. de Graff helped her husband to cut logs and build their house, in which all but three of her sixteen children would be born: "Of such stuff were the pioneer women of Western Canada made!" (p. 242). The inclusion of these narratives in a discussion of Grove, Stead, and Ostenso compels us to consider the extent to which the figure of the female pioneer operates as a metonymy for Canadian modernism. For Kathleen, pioneering had a gendered political meaning: it meant to be an equal partner and to work side by side with her husband on the farm. In 1930, the Stranges moved to the city (presumably Winnipeg), where Harry became the new director of an agricultural research department. For Kathleen, the urban space brought an ironic setback of sorts that relegated her to the traditional home: "On the farm I was a *real* partner with my husband, sharing with him in almost every detail of his daily work" (p. 292). Far from being a space of backwards conservatism, the western prairie farm had been a space for the city woman to claim sexual equality. The western homesteader woman's memoir had become the canvas for writing multiple and complex modern female selves.

In what ways do these writers shape the new nation in their literature? The 1920s were marked by a fervent nationalism in Canada, as witnessed by the formation of the Group of Seven, the Canadian Authors Association (founded in Montreal in 1921), and the United Church of Canada (in 1925). Enveloped in an imperialist perspective, Binnie-Clark often speaks of Canadians as if they were a thoroughly foreign group, even though most of them were first- or second-generation immigrants from England and Ireland (hardly far removed from her own cultural context). In contrast, Kathleen Strange focuses on the diversity of different nations. A few people in the district have Scotch, English or American heritage, but more were from Central Europe: "Among them were French, Germans, Dutch, Swedes, Norwegians, Russians, Finlanders, Poles and even one Chinese – a conglomerate of races that merged and mingled surprisingly well when one considered their widely divergent racial characteristics and traits" (p. 110). Martha Ostenso's work is also populated by multicultural communities of Icelanders, Swedes, Hungarians, "Half-breeds," and "Indians." In *In Search of Myself*, Grove gives himself a mixed identity; his father is English-Swedish, his mother Scotch; his nurse a mixture of French and Scotch. Concerned with the identity of the new writer, *In Search of Myself* – originally titled "My Life as a Writer in Canada"[34] – contains long catalogues of European, Canadian, and American cities, writers, poets, literati, publishers, and periodicals, creating a Whitmanesque archive for his new nation, filling up the vast space with cross-cultural references, albeit Eurocentric ones. In a letter written to Desmond Pacey on January 30, 1945, he complained about his status as an "incomer Canadian."[35]

Romantic moderns: L. M. Montgomery, Mazo de la Roche, and Elizabeth Smart

In March of 1923, in Rapid City, Manitoba, F. P. Grove received a letter from Prince Edward Island-born author L. M. Montgomery (1874–1942). Effusively

---

34 F. P. Grove, *In Search of Myself* (Toronto: Macmillan, 1946), p. 11.
35 Pacey, ed., *The Letters of Frederick Philip Grove*, p. 462.

praising *Over Prairie Trails* – "Rarely have I read a book which gave me so much pleasure" – she invited him to write more about the mysterious and lonely "White Range Line House" he described in his book.[36] (As if heeding Montgomery's advice, he made the house central in *Settlers*.) She promptly also included the lonely house with its windows nailed shut in the autobiographical *Emily* trilogy she was writing, calling it the "Disappointed House." Coincidentally, in each text, the house figured as a symbol for failed heterosexual romance. More positively, it also figured in a pan-Canadian intertextual dialogue. L. M. Montgomery garnered fame as the beloved author of bestselling fiction, most notably the *Anne* series. Published and selling well in the United States, as well as in Canada, her nostalgia-driven romance and satire of rural Canada appears, on the surface, to be a kind of anti-modernist response to the technological, political, and social changes that were sweeping Canada. Still, Montgomery was a woman of her era, and modernist and nostalgic expressions were not so much the antithesis as a condition of modernity, permitting readers to fantasize about the security of the past even as they traveled the road of the modern.

After settling in Ontario in 1911, Montgomery described her own struggle to become a writer in Canada within the context of a *Künstlerroman*, her autobiographical *Emily* series (1923, 1925, 1927). Emily, like Montgomery, decides to undertake her apprenticeship in Canada and not in New York, where so many earlier Canadian poets and writers (for example, Bliss Carman, Charles G. D. Roberts) had settled and built distinguished careers. The tone of *Emily* is darker than the *Anne* series, but it is her journals that were the proverbial bombshell when they were published posthumously (1985, 1987, 1992, 1998, 2004). Their tenor departed radically from the romance of her fiction, revealing the cracks in her public façade. Dated March 23, 1942, the last entry sounds the depths of modernist suicidal despair: "Since then my life has been hell, hell, hell. My mind is gone – everything in the world I lived for has gone – the world has gone mad. I shall be driven to end my life."[37] Beginning in 1889, Montgomery's journals are a self-consciously crafted literary record intended for publication. Her developing self is embedded in the metaphors of modernity – the telephone, the car, silent movies, "talkies" and fashion.

---

36 L. M. Montgomery to F. P. Grove, letter 10 March 1923, University of Manitoba Archives MSS 2, Box 3, Fd. 10, p. 1.
37 M. Rubio and E. Waterston, eds., *The Selected Journals of L. M. Montgomery*, 5 vols. (Toronto: Oxford University Press, 1985–2004), vol. V: *1935–1942*, p. 350. For a full exploration of these issues, see I. Gammel, ed., *The Intimate Life of L. M. Montgomery* (Toronto: University of Toronto Press, 2005).

During her honeymoon to London, England, on September 18, 1911, Montgomery records her impressions of glimpsing an airplane in nearly sublime terms: "we beheld a flying machine soaring across the sunset sky like some huge bird."[38] Moreover, when touring Prince Edward Island, the Ontario resident dazzled her fellow Islanders with her new automobile. The iconic author of the serene east coast idyllic turns out to have been deeply affected by technologies of mobility and flight.

Darker and more complex metaphors of self – illness, depression, sexual desire, and frustration – assert themselves to contradict and dismantle the public self Montgomery had created in her formal memoir *The Alpine Path: The Story of My Career* (1917). The author's intense romantic female friendships and the fifty-five-year-old's expressions of lesbian panic have prompted readers to reconsider her sexual and domestic conservatism. Sitting beside her husband just after their wedding ceremony, Montgomery recollects: "I felt a sudden horrible inrush of *rebellion* and *despair*. I *wanted to be free*! I felt like a prisoner – a hopeless prisoner." The very self-consciousness of repressing such feelings over decades of marriage – "Either I must conquer it or die" – is a modernist expression par excellence.[39] A political conservative with little interest in women's suffrage, Montgomery asserted herself rhetorically throughout her journal as a modern woman who emotionally rebelled against the constraints of conventional marriage, even as she outwardly conformed, staying married to her husband until her death. Conservative and subversive Montgomery claimed multiple modern roles for herself – businesswoman, public speaker, and celebrity author.

Unreliable first-person narration is a paradigmatic theme in modernist fiction, reaching its apotheosis with novels such as Ford Madox Ford's *The Good Soldier* (1915). The retrospective disclosure that Montgomery's habit was to record events not as they occurred but weeks, months, years, and even decades later, draws attention to her narrative manipulations and revisions of the past, situating her as an unreliable first-person narrator of her own biography. "Are we to regard the diarist as functioning like the 'untrustworthy narrator' in a modern novel?" the editors of her journals, Mary Rubio and Elizabeth Waterston, ask, questioning the author's portrait of her husband.[40] Montgomery rewrote her journals at various times during her life, often

---

38 M. Rubio and E. Waterston, eds., *The Selected Journals of L. M. Montgomery*, vol. II: *1910–1921* (Toronto: Oxford University Press, 1987), p. 77.
39 Ibid., p. 68.
40 M. Rubio and E. Waterston, eds., *The Selected Journals of L. M. Montgomery*, vol. III: *1921–1929* (Toronto: Oxford University Press, 1992), p. xii.

omitting important events. The author's play with multiple selves is perhaps best exemplified in a 1902 self-portrait photograph of her in her Cavendish bedroom. She poses fully dressed with a parasol, gloves, and a hat with a polka dot veil obscuring her face. She is revealing herself but simultaneously hiding behind the veil, a staging of the self in a visual palimpsest.

Like L. M. Montgomery, Mazo de la Roche (1879–1961) found her fountain of creativity in an imaginary dream world and first made a splash when her novel *Jalna* (1927) won the prestigious *Atlantic Monthly* prize. Set in southern Ontario, the fictional Whiteoak family home Jalna would give birth to fifteen sequels, and sell millions of copies internationally, but the books did not enjoy the enduring popularity of Montgomery's Avonlea. Mazo de la Roche's 1957 *Ringing the Changes: An Autobiography* sets up a number of compelling identities: a woman writer and international celebrity; friend and life partner of another woman, Caroline Clement; mental patient undergoing electro-shock treatment; single mother who adopts two children; and international traveler living in a succession of memorable houses. The labor involved in the staging of these public and private selves is collaborative. Decisions are made in partnership with Caroline Clement, who, like Alice B. Toklas for Gertrude Stein, helped with editing and typing, as well as with housekeeping and decorating. When *Jalna* became an international success, together they prepared "for the ordeal of publicity to come. Always have I hated publicity."[41]

And yet, as Joan Givner has revealed in her 1989 biography *Mazo de la Roche: The Hidden Life*, the author of these lines carefully controlled her image through selective truth telling, evasions, and embellishments.[42] Like Montgomery in her journals, de la Roche staged her personae in *Ringing the Changes* in photos: as an eleven-year-old, with a sideways look away from the camera, serious and dramatic in a genteel Joan-of-Arc pose with a studded blouse and long flowing hair. In the frontispiece, "Myself – London 1936," the professional woman's steady gaze confronts the camera directly. Posing in her gorgeous home Vale House, de la Roche is enveloped by leaded-glass windows, exquisite furniture, and stylistic arrangements – revealing the artistic hand of Caroline Clement. Caroline also destroyed de la Roche's personal diaries when she died. The two blond haired adopted children in the photos are the epitome of the cute and beautiful angel child; her adopted daughter

---

41 Mazo de la Roche, *Ringing the Changes: An Autobiography* (Toronto: Macmillan, 1957), p. 188.
42 Joan Givner, *Mazo de la Roche: The Hidden Life* (Toronto: Oxford University Press, 1989). See also Heather Kirk, *Mazo de la Roche: Rich and Famous Writer* (Montreal: XYZ Publishing, 2006).

Plate 13. L. M. Montgomery, "Myself in 1902,"
self-portrait photograph taken in her bedroom in Cavendish.

Esmée said that her mother lost interest in her when she outgrew this stage of beauty. Control and embellishment were essential to the author's self-representation.

If Grove, Montgomery, and de la Roche were experts at staging the modern *Künstler* through socially acceptable masks, Ottawa-born poet and writer Elizabeth Smart (1913–86) presents the opposite end of the writing spectrum by reveling in notoriety. When Smart's first book, *By Grand Central Station I Sat Down and Wept* (1945), was published, her mother was so offended that she bought the copies and burned them in order to prevent their circulation.

A fascinating piece of Canadian modernist life writing, with echoes of James Joyce's *Ulysses*, the semi-autobiographical prose poem was based on Smart's affair with a married man and the father of her four children, the British modernist poet George Barker (who had affairs with many other modernist writers including American Emily Coleman). The rhapsodic and insubordinate narrator declares sublimated love to be repulsive, claiming a new speech for female erotic pleasure. Her staged self is frenzied and hyperbolic, but also daring and original as a transgressive experiment: "I am over-run, jungled in my bed, I am infested with a menagerie of desires: my heart is eaten by a dove, a cat scrambles in the cave of my sex, hounds in my head obey a whipmaster who cries nothing but havoc as the hours test my endurance with an accumulation of tortures."[43] This story of adultery is strung together by a journey from Ottawa to California and New York. It is also a modernist retelling of the tale of Dido, the woman mourning the desertion of her lover in Virgil's *Aeneid*. Smart's journals, posthumously published as *Necessary Secrets* (1986) and *On the Side of Angels* (1994), also enact the more destructive aspects of the modernist artist, a personality consumed by addictive love and alcohol abuse. Yet her break from a bourgeois home and frankness in writing about sexuality, with an articulation of both the pleasure and frustration of sexual love, make the text a classic of Canadian modernism.

Cosmopolitan modernism: Morley Callaghan and John Glassco

Given that urbanism and cosmopolitanism are highly topical aspects of canonical modernism, one must ask: how are these issues being investigated and challenged by Canadian writers? As in the case of other books inspired by the First World War, some of the texts discussed here too have acquired additional resonance from publications that appeared long after the fact, most notably Morley Callaghan's *That Summer in Paris* (1963), and John Glassco's autobiographical *Memoirs of Montparnasse* (1970), which talk of their lives in Paris during the 1920s, where they encountered James Joyce, Gertrude Stein, Ernest Hemingway, Djuna Barnes, Robert McAlmon, and Kay Boyle. The modernist memoir of the 1920s jazz age is a popular genre in the American literary tradition; examples include Margaret Anderson's *My Thirty Years' War* (1930), W. C. Williams's *Autobiography* (1951), Matthew Josephson's *Life Among*

---

43 Elizabeth Smart, *By Grand Central Station I Sat Down And Wept* (London: Paladin, 1991), p. 23.

the Surrealists (1962), and Hemingway's *A Moveable Feast* (1964). Morley Callaghan had first encountered Hemingway when they both worked for the Toronto *Daily Star*. Ostensibly prompted by Hemingway's suicide, Callaghan's memoir is also a companion to Hemingway's own memoir of the expatriate circle in Paris, *A Moveable Feast*, which would be published a year after Callaghan's memoir in 1964. In the center of his memoir, Callaghan stages his infamous 1929 fight with Hemingway (with Fitzgerald as the incompetent timekeeper). Just as Hemingway's memoir is vindictive in its portraits of Stein, Ford, and F. Scott Fitzgerald, so Callaghan's memoir is designed to challenge the Hemingway legend; the larger-than-life American celebrity writer was literally knocked out by the shorter Toronto man (and lesser known author).

Lawyer, writer, journalist, and boxer Morley Callaghan (1903–90) is also the author of two experimental plays. His dramatic interests have shaped his memoir, which appears to portray the modernist writer's self in theatrical terms: "Callaghan creates a narrative persona for his voice that performs the same tasks as a casting director, a lighting designer, and a costume designer."[44] Such performance and staging of selves, once again, raises the usual questions of reliability. The "tangled friendships" of the memoir title mask the fact that the streets, salons, and cafés of Paris during the 1920s were the stage for a "pissing contest" of sorts for male literary egos, creating what Richard Dellamora has called a "masculinist modernism."[45]

The memoir genre typically included a visual narrative in photographs. Callaghan's portrait, eyes penetrating above a smirky smile and debonair moustache, performs the same kind of theatrics that Hemingway projected into his brooding poses. Callaghan's narrative tone similarly mirrors Hemingway's bellicose assertiveness, condescension and showmanship as the two men sniff out each other's weaknesses: Hemingway stutters; Callaghan is a novice. Hemingway is clumsy; Callaghan needs help pitching his stories. It is a memoir of rivalries rather than of friendships, of confrontations more than bonding. "Who does impress you, Morley?" F. Scott Fitzgerald asks the young Callaghan, offended by Callaghan's superior attitude toward other writers. "Would this impress you, Morley?"[46] The drunken Fitzgerald gets on his

---

[44] Marianne Perz, "Staging *That Summer in Paris*: Narrative Strategies and Theatrical Techniques in the Life Writing of Morley Callaghan," *Studies in Canadian Literature / Études en littérature canadienne* 22.1 (1997), pp. 96–7.

[45] Richard Dellamora, "Queering Modernism: A Canadian in Paris," *Essays on Canadian Writing* 60 (Winter 1996), p. 258.

[46] Morley Callaghan, *That Summer in Paris: Memories of Tangled Friendships with Hemingway, Fitzgerald, and Some Others* (Toronto: Macmillan, 1963), pp. 153, 154.

knees, trying to complete a ludicrous headstand. The shocking gesture disrupts a social visit. Fitzgerald's headstand is more than an expression of inebriation: Fitzgerald is ridiculing Callaghan's pretension with something equivalent to the shock of Dada shenanigans.

"A whisper had gone the rounds that Greenwich Village was washed up: Paris was the new frontier," Callaghan writes;[47] the narrator's posing as a vanguard player in Paris, however, is not entirely persuasive. In 1929, rather than paving the way, he was following the trend of the Paris literary pilgrimage that had begun in the early twenties. Callaghan's retrospective account of his life among the modernists presents a view of Parisian life from the perspective of an appreciative yet alien outsider: "In Toronto, Paris indeed became my city of light." He is accompanied by his wife Loretto – who "had the advantage of not being steeped in bad writing" and instead is steeped in washing and folding his handkerchiefs.[48] The Irish-Catholic writer-lawyer from Toronto is a bit of a tourist in Paris, like the New Jersey poet-doctor William Carlos Williams, who spent a sabbatical year in Paris in 1924 but never felt truly comfortable among the rowdy expatriate crowd. It is Loretto who finds her way around the city, while the narrator occasionally indulges in cliché, as when he calls Paris "the lovely Babylonian capital."[49]

In contrast, Montreal-born writer John Glassco (1909–81) presents an intimate mingling with the modernists in Paris. Glassco offers colorful portraits of famous literati he encountered in salons and cafés, at parties and in dance halls, and invokes many examples of sexual transgression, gender-boundary crossing, and inebriation. An accomplished translator of Québécois poetry and the organizer of the 1963 "English Poetry in Quebec" conference, Glassco is also a significant figure in Canadian queer culture, and the author of several works of pornography. He wrote his memoir in response to Morley Callaghan's staunchly heterosexual ethos; Callaghan not only slighted Sylvia Beach, the American publisher of James Joyce's *Ulysses*, as "a bit severe and mannish," but also depicted the boy-couple John Glassco and Graeme Taylor with condescension. A drunken Robert McAlmon, publisher of the Contact Press, proclaims in Callaghan's memoir: "I'm bisexual myself, like Michelangelo, and I don't give a damn who knows it."[50] As critic Richard Dellamora writes, Callaghan was outing Glassco's (and, we might add, McAlmon's)

---

47 Ibid., p. 113.
48 Ibid., pp. 36, 35, 180.
49 Ibid., pp. 157, 116.
50 Ibid., pp. 89, 134.

Plate 14. Graeme Taylor, John Glassco, and Robert McAlmon on the beach at Nice, c. 1928.

homosexuality during a time when male homosexuality was criminalized in Canada.[51]

Although Glassco did not explicitly refer to his homosexuality in *Memoirs of Montparnasse*, he left behind his notebooks and drafts that clearly reveal his homosexual life in Paris. Also, the visual self-portraiture inserted in the 1995 edition of the book depicts Robert McAlmon, John Glassco and Graeme Taylor in a homoerotic group photo in which all three men lounge in bathing suits on the beach at Nice: McAlmon slim and muscular like a model; Glassco in the centre, slender, with Taylor on his right; naked skin touches in what looks like a snapshot of physical freedom. At the same time, the memoir is ambivalent about same-sex love. It derides the lesbianism of Willa Torrance (the writer Djuna Barnes) and her lover Emily Pine (the sculptor Thelma Wood): "I felt more than ever out of place among these women, whose faded asexuality was marked by the kind of fiercely possessive passion that is generally and more properly expended on cats and dogs."[52]

---

51 Dellamora, "Queering Modernism," pp. 258–9.
52 John Glassco, *Memoirs of Montparnasse* (Toronto: Oxford University Press, 1995), p. 33.

Like other authors discussed in this chapter, who created intricate works that made readers ask questions about their reliability and truthfulness, so Glassco made full use of fiction, fabricating a story about how his *Memoirs* came about. He asserts that the first three chapters were written in Paris in 1928 at age eighteen; and the rest of the book throughout 1932 and 1933, when he was convalescing in the Royal Victoria Hospital. Yet Philip Kokotailo's research on the manuscripts at the Library and Archives of Canada have revealed that the entire memoir was written and revised much later, during the 1960s. "[O]ne quarter of the book *was* lies," Glassco admitted in a June 2, 1965, journal entry: "Man Ray never discussed Jane Austen with me; Joyce held no conversation with me about Ulysses."[53] Glassco too was driven by the beautiful lie that is at the heart of a number of Canadian authors of the modernist era.

In his essay "Tradition and the Individual Talent" (1919), T. S. Eliot claimed that modern writers should free themselves from old Romantic practices: "The progress of an artist is a continual self-sacrifice, a continual extinction of personality."[54] But the writers discussed in this chapter often departed from Eliot's doctrine, making the text a theater for staging their personalities and artistic lives, while also drawing attention to the artifice and the masquerades behind the selves. Drawing attention to the *Künstler*, they reveal the labor inherent in crafting a plethora of selves, as writers and immigrants at home or as travelers meeting an international group of modernists abroad. The opportunities afforded by the Canadian landscape, the rewriting of old roles and identities within new contexts, the claiming of rights on the homestead and in urban spaces, have created a distinct – albeit obscured – modernism that pulsates through the realist novel, the settler narrative, and even the romance. Although critics such as Robert Kroetsch have quipped that Canadian literature went straight from Victorianism to postmodernism, the Canadian modern lives at times in places where we least expect it, including the prairie homestead or the old Maritime farm house.[55]

---

53 Glassco quoted in P. Kokotailo, *John Glassco's Richer World: Memoirs of Montparnasse* (Toronto: ECW Press, 1988), p. 73.
54 T. S. Eliot, "Tradition and the Individual Talent" (1919), in *Selected Essays 1932 and 1950* (New York: Harcourt, Brace and World, 1964), p. 7.
55 Thanks to Nicola Spunt for her probing questions about modernism, which have found their way into this essay; and to Gaby Divay, Joan Givner, Mary Grove, Gina Vaccaro, and Kate Zieman for help in locating rare manuscripts, books, and photography.

14

E. J. Pratt and the McGill poets

ADRIAN FOWLER

Modernism took its time crossing the Atlantic, and when it arrived in downtown Toronto, it was as if it had eaten too much roast beef and drunk too much claret during its first-class passage. It was introduced to the Canadian nationalism of the 1920s. It was taken to see the Group of Seven. It fell asleep during a debate at the Arts and Letters Club about whether Bliss Carman was a better poet than Wilson MacDonald, and it didn't wake up for twenty years.[1]

This view of modernism's arrival in Canada by a talented contemporary writer can be corroborated by a glance at the introductions of two major anthologies of Canadian poetry at the time of the First World War. In *The Oxford Book of Canadian Verse* (1913), after anxiously taking up most of his Preface considering at least five different sets of criteria to define Canadian poetry, Wilfred Campbell gives up and concedes that "the true British-Canadian verse, if it has any real root and lasting influence, must necessarily be but an offshoot of the great tree of British literature, as the American school also is, though less obviously."[2] Campbell then goes on to justify the inclusion of poems by the Duke of Argyll, Governor General of Canada from 1878 to 1883. In a similar vein, John W. Garvin, in his "Editor's Foreword" to *Canadian Poets* (1916), gives a soaring characterization of poetry which, "at its height, implies beauty and the driving force of passion." He then contemplates the past and future glories of Canadian poets in the following terms: "Love of Nature has been their chief source of inspiration; but themes based on love of humanity and man's kinship with the Infinite Life, have steadily gained of late in number and potency, and the Great War must necessarily arouse a more intense

---

1 David Macfarlane, *The Danger Tree* (Toronto: Macfarlane, Walter and Ross, 1991), p. 43.
2 Wilfred Campbell, "Preface," in *The Oxford Book of Canadian Verse* (Toronto: Oxford University Press, 1913), p. viii.

interest in human and divine relationships."³ Campbell and Garvin show no awareness that the world has changed. The wholesale rejection of nineteenth-century forms of artistic expression, the crushing disillusionment and overwhelming sense of cultural fragmentation emanating out of the Great War, are apparently not on the radar screen. Was this Canada at the advent of the modern age?

To a large extent it was, but there are also early signs that the winds of change were being felt by some poets and critics. Arthur Stringer, in the Preface to his collection, *Open Water* (1914), points out the obsolescence of traditional forms of meter and rhyme to express contemporary themes. The poet's "apparel has remained mediaeval. He must still don mail to face Mausers, and wear chain-armour against machine-guns ... pathetically resplendent in that rigid steel which is an anachronism and no longer an armour."⁴ In a witty essay in *Canadian Bookman* (1919), J. M. Gibbon adopts a light-hearted, ironic tone to make a similar case for *vers libre*. Gibbon shows himself to be well aware of Harriet Monroe, her ground-breaking literary magazine *Poetry* (Chicago), founded in 1912, and *The New Poetry*, the anthology Monroe co-edited with Alice Corbin Henderson in 1917. He approvingly mentions Carl Sandburg, Edgar Lee Masters, Ezra Pound, Richard Aldington, T. S. Eliot, Conrad Aiken, and he quotes Pound's dictums for the new poetry. He laments the omission of Bliss Carman from *The New Poetry*, albeit acknowledging that Carman's recent verse has lost its original fire, and, in general, conceding that most Canadian poetry is minor. Gibbon concludes on a "man-the-barricades" note: "The times are moving. Dynasties are falling, are being swept away. The whole world is aflame with a war against the over-bearing tyranny of military caste. The voice today is the voice of the people ...."⁵

Yet another case for modern forms and modern subject matter comes from Frank Oliver Call, in the Foreword to his collection *Acanthus and Wild Grape* (1920). Both an iron foundry and a Venetian palace, Call says, have the capacity to inspire poetry, but "perhaps the foundry has the greater power." And while the acanthus leaves carved on a Corinthian column are beautiful, the wild grape embracing a ruin may be "more beautiful still in its natural freedom."⁶

---

3 John W. Garvin, "Editor's Foreword," in *Canadian Poets* (Toronto: McClelland, Goodchild and Stewart, 1916), pp. 5–6.
4 See Louis Dudek and Michael Gnarowski, eds., *The Making of Modern Poetry in Canada: Essential Articles on Contemporary Canadian Poetry in English* (Toronto: Ryerson Press, 1970 [1967]), p. 5.
5 Ibid., p. 20.
6 Ibid., pp. 21 and 23.

These graceful analogies reflect a Canadian politeness in advancing the cause, but in his Foreword Call shows himself to be aware that modernism is more than a matter of style and form; it also includes a new kind of material on which to work.

Stringer, Gibbon and Call indicate that the major innovations in modernism were being favorably received by some writers in Canada almost as soon as they were emerging in the United States and Europe. The impact of these innovations upon poetic practice is another matter. The effect of imagism upon Canadian poets of the 1920s has been observed in the work of W. W. E. Ross, R. G. Everson, Raymond Knister, Dorothy Livesay, and E. J. Pratt.[7] But despite the efforts of A. J. M. Smith, F. R. Scott and others during the 1920s to repudiate the achievement of Sir Charles G. D. Roberts, Duncan Campbell Scott, Archibald Lampman and Bliss Carman, and import the practice of Eliot and Pound, Canadian poetry moved beyond the legacy of the Confederation poets without a revolution.

E. J. Pratt

Although not revolutionary, a significant break with the prevailing style of Canadian poetry became evident with the publication of E. J. Pratt's first collection, *Newfoundland Verse*, in 1923. E. K. Brown, from the perspective of 1943, saw much in it that seemed at one with the established tradition, but Northrop Frye, from the perspective of 1958, was surely closer to the mark in saying that "[t]he noises that exploded in *Newfoundland Verse*, the pounding of surf, the screaming of wind, the crash of ships on rocks, rudely shattered" the mood of the Romantic lyric as practiced by Carman, Scott and Marjorie Pickthall.[8] Pratt's attitude towards nature, as exemplified in "Newfoundland," "The Toll of the Bells," "The Shark," and the short narrative "The Ice-Floes," is unsentimental and unromantic. As he later wryly observed, "[w]e lost the habit of interrogating nature as a kind mother whose task it was to lead us from joy to joy, who never did betray the heart that loved her."[9] Although he ascribed this view generally to the influence of Thomas Hardy, it was

---

7 See Ken Norris, "The Beginnings of Canadian Modernism," *Canadian Poetry* 11 (Fall–Winter 1982), p. 57; and Sandra Djwa and R. G. Moyles, eds., *E. J. Pratt: Complete Poems*, 2 vols. (Toronto: University of Toronto Press, 1989), vol. I, p. xxi.
8 E. K. Brown, *On Canadian Poetry* (Ottawa: Tecumseh, 1973 [1943]), pp. 147–8; and Northrop Frye, "Editor's Introduction," in *The Collected Poems of E. J. Pratt* (Toronto: Macmillan, 1962 [1958]), p. xxvi.
9 The E. J. Pratt Collection, Victoria University in the University of Toronto. Quoted in Sandra Djwa, *E. J. Pratt: The Evolutionary Vision* (Vancouver: Copp Clark, 1974), p. 18.

probably Pratt's scientific training in evolutionary theory and, even more so, his background growing up on the coast of Newfoundland that made it difficult for him to maintain a Wordsworthian view of nature.

In any event, if *Newfoundland Verse* did not clearly indicate that things had changed in Canadian poetry, Pratt's next publications, *The Witches' Brew* (1925) and *Titans* (1926), left no one in doubt. In the first of these, Pratt is plausibly said to have created an innovative amalgam out of models as diverse as Milton's *Paradise Lost*, Byron's *The Vision of Judgement*, Burns's "Tam O'Shanter," and the Newfoundland balladeer Johnny Burke's "The Kelligrew's Soiree."[10] More to the point, given the times, may be its wicked put-down of the puritanism that characterized the prohibition era in Canada. The passage of many decades has obscured the stifling repressiveness of the period, but it is easily recovered by reading pieces such as Douglas Bush's "A Plea for Original Sin," which only half-jokingly foresaw no future for Canadian letters until Canadians learned to obey the injunction to "sin gladly."[11] To cast a whale as a warrior-king and a *tyrannosaurus rex* as a tragic hero now seems breathtakingly anthropomorphic, despite Sandra Djwa's justification that the works are beast fables, yet the energy and virtuosity of Pratt's verse in *Titans* are undeniable.[12] Barker Fairley, in a review of *Titans* in *The Canadian Forum*, was taken aback by the bold originality of Pratt's subject and style. At the same time, he precisely defined the colonial mentality of Canadian letters during the 1920s when he declared enthusiastically that *Titans* could not have been written by an Englishman – as though this were the true measure of achievement. He credited Pratt not only for "seeing with primal freshness" but also for "avoiding the weary vision of older cultures."[13]

The McGill Fortnightly Review and *The Canadian Mercury*

Modernism in Canadian poetry, however, is usually traced back not to Pratt but to the McGill (or Montreal) poets, especially A. J. M. Smith and F. R. Scott, who established a literary magazine in November 1925 while students at McGill University. The story has seemed less and less straightforward as it has come under critical and scholarly scrutiny in recent years, but it is fair to say that a programmatic attempt to advance modernism as an aesthetic emerged for the first time in Canada in the pages of the *McGill Fortnightly*

---

10 Djwa, pp. 40–9.
11 *The Canadian Forum* 2.19 (April 1922), pp. 589–90.
12 Djwa, *E. J. Pratt: The Evolutionary Vision*, p. 68.
13 *The Canadian Forum* 7.77 (February 1927), p. 149.

Review.[14] Smith, a graduate student in English at the time, had already edited the *McGill Daily Literary Supplement*, an insert in the university's student newspaper. Scott, a law student who had just returned to Canada after having studied history at Oxford on a Rhodes Scholarship, was invited to join the editorial board, but then the *Literary Supplement* was cancelled after a dispute over advertising revenues, prompting Smith and Scott to establish the *McGill Fortnightly Review* as a stand-alone publication financed by subscription.

To read the *Fortnightly Review* now is to see just how much a student production it was. The first editorial outlined in diplomatic terms the nature of the dispute that led to its creation (with one or two gibes at the advertising manager who was cast as the villain in the piece); declared its editorial policy of promoting independent thought and providing a forum for dissenting opinions; lamented the change in the constitution of the *McGill Daily* requiring it to assume neutrality on all controversial issues and avoid opposition to decisions of the Student Council; announced in glowing terms the appointment of Bliss Carman to give lectures on Canadian literature and provide direction to student writers subject to the "furor poeticus"; complained about the use of the Harold Lloyd Rugby Trophy and the McGill Band for commercial advertising; censured undergraduates who booed the decisions of the referee in a recent McGill Varsity game; and acknowledged a grant of fifty dollars from the Arts Undergraduate Society.

The well-established humorist Stephen Leacock, celebrating twenty-five years as a professor of political economy at McGill, contributed a whimsical meditation on "The Flight of College Time," and a young Eugene Forsey, on the verge of being nominated for a Rhodes Scholarship, offered a witty analysis of the predicament of the minority government of Mackenzie King. Initiating the practice of pseudonymous writing, Scott, under the guise of "Nordic," objected in a mock-Socratic dialogue to the establishment of a Scarlet Key Society at McGill on the grounds that it aped an American tradition. Finally, there were three reviews and two poems – a translation of epigrams "from the Italian of DeRossi" by F. R. Scott and "What Strange Enchantment" by Vincent Starr, a pseudonym for Smith. The editorial board listed the names of A. P. R. Coulborn, A. B. Latham, F. R. Scott, A. J. M. Smith and, as managing editor, L. Edel. The magazine sold for 10 cents.

There is little in the first eight-page edition of the *Fortnightly Review* to indicate that a catalyst of momentous cultural change had emerged. What is pronounced is the impatience that the young authors had with the stifling

14 Norris, "Beginnings," pp. 56–66.

authoritarianism that seemed to pervade the McGill campus from the top down. In the second issue of the journal, the editors confront this climate of oppression and claim the right to voice dissenting opinions. This declaration of freedom of speech caused Scott and Smith to be called before the Principal of McGill, Sir Arthur Currie, who unsuccessfully attempted to intimidate them into accepting an advisory board to ensure that McGill's "esprit de corps" should not be damaged through "dangerous doctrines," perhaps even "Bolsheveki" ones.[15] Later, Scott was actually present when Currie explained his practice of vetting visiting speakers with the Intelligence Bureau in Ottawa.[16]

The *Fortnightly Review* was courageous but not foolhardy in the way it combated this repressiveness. Satiric poetry published under a pseudonym was used as frequently as carefully worded, unsigned editorials. Political conservatism was associated with literary philistinism. Over the eighteen months of its life, the *Fortnightly Review* conveyed the view that Canada was mired in mediocrity, and that great attainments in intellectual life and the arts were to be found elsewhere. Thus Canadian Book Week is mercilessly lampooned because it boosts second-rate Canadian books, doing "considerable harm to good literature."[17] The McGill debating team is lambasted for its "ponderous arguments" and "clumsy fumblings" while their opponents from Cambridge display an ability to "sweep ... aside" all positions "with a single thrust, a brilliant epigram."[18] An exhibition of the Royal Canadian Academy of Art is damned with faint praise, despite positive comments on the work of J. E. H. Macdonald, A. Y. Jackson and R. W. Pilot, and the review ends with a wry comment upon the dearth of nude studies – "what a contrast to a Parisian Salon!"[19]

Smith later observed with apparent delight and satisfaction that "when we were on the *Fortnightly* there was not a single Canadian poet we paid much attention to, certainly not an old poet like Bliss Carman, Charles G. D. Roberts, Archibald Lampman or Duncan Campbell Scott."[20] He and Scott had actually read little Canadian poetry, but they were predisposed to believe that it was not of a very high quality.[21] The internationalism of the *McGill*

---

15 Quoted in Sandra Djwa, *The Politics of the Imagination: A Life of F. R. Scott* (Toronto: McClelland and Stewart, 1987), p. 84.
16 Ibid., p. 86.
17 *McGill Fortnightly Review*, 1.2 (5 December 1925), p. 9.
18 *Fortnightly*, 2.3 (1 December 1926), p. 23.
19 *Fortnightly*, 1.2 (5 Dec 1925): 14.
20 Quoted in Norris, "Beginnings," p. 60.
21 See Djwa, *Politics of the Imagination*, pp. 90–1; and Patricia Morley, "The Young Turks: A Biographer's Comment," *Canadian Poetry* 11 (Fall–Winter 1982), p. 67.

Fortnightly Review was fueled by a sense of colonial inferiority on the part of its young editors. As they saw it, the nation's literary scene, embodied in the Canadian Authors Association, displayed a smug insularity that was absurd and embarrassing. The *Fortnightly* demonstrated their determination to upset the complacency of Canadian literary life by introducing the latest experiments in modernism as practiced in the great cities of Europe and America.

In addition to clever commentaries on student issues, the *Fortnightly* published a number of ambitious poems, some timely reviews of contemporary writers, and three probing essays by Smith on modernism in literature. The first of these essays, "Symbolism in Poetry," is a didactic and derivative rendering of the work of Arthur Symons with reference to Blake, Verlaine, and Yeats that justifies a "certain amount of obscurity, evocation, and suggestion" as natural to symbolist poetry.[22] The second, "Hamlet in Modern Dress," a more insightful and articulate essay on the poetry of T. S. Eliot, especially "The Waste Land," highlights modernist preoccupations with disintegration and sterility and explains Eliot's interest in the decadence of Jacobean drama.[23] The third essay, "Contemporary Poetry," attempts to account for the techniques of "The New Poetry" through reference to James Stephens, who argued that the enormously accelerated tempo of modern living had outstripped the literary conventions bequeathed by a "leisured society."[24] Smith is somewhat at a loss to describe with confidence the characteristics of the new verse, recognizing that it is not simply a matter of form or diction. Noting that all the "ultra moderns" are "poets of disillusion," he comments that some critics have detected in their work "the symptoms of deep decadence."

This point contradicts the later view that modernism involved the overthrow of aestheticism and its outgrowth decadence. In his examination of the early poetry of Scott and Smith, including poems published under pseudonyms in the *McGill Fortnightly Review*, Brian Trehearne has shown how the young Canadian modernists were simultaneously under the influence of aestheticism and decadence, and, in Smith's case, at least, this influence continued into his mature years as a poet.[25] Trehearne cites the work of Morse Peckham, J. E. Chamberlin and Jacques Barzun, who, in different ways, make a persuasive case, in general, for an essential continuity in the transition from these forms of late Romanticism into modernism (pp. 19–21). As Trehearne points out, one

---

22 *Fortnightly*, 1.2 (5 December 1925), pp. 11–12, 16.
23 *Fortnightly*, 2.1 (3 November 1926), pp. 2–4.
24 *Fortnightly*, 2.4 (15 December 1926), pp. 31–2.
25 Brian Trehearne, *Aestheticism and the Canadian Modernists: Aspects of a Poetic Influence* (Kingston and Montreal: McGill-Queen's University Press, 1989), chapters 4 and 6.

need only recall the outrageous dandy Anthony Blanche in Evelyn Waugh's *Brideshead Revisited*, declaiming "The Waste Land" out the windows of Lord Sebastian Flyte's rooms at Christ Church, Oxford, to grasp the plausibility of this view (p. 157).

Since Scott had just returned from Oxford, the allusion to the world of *Brideshead Revisited* is not far-fetched. It is true that the *Fortnightly* contains poems that show the hard edge in language, imagery, and sentiment that came to characterize Scott's mature work. These range from "Sweeney Comes to McGill," a clever parody of Eliot's Sweeney poems, to "Below Quebec," an uncompromising and ironic observation on love in a cold climate, to "Proud Cellist," an ambiguous comparison of wood and flesh as instruments, and, of course, "The Canadian Authors Meet," a poem that has become his signature comment on the tiresome old fogies who represented the Canadian literary establishment, as he and Smith saw it. On the other hand, there are also several poems, most of them written under the pseudonym of Brian Tuke, in which Scott displays intense aspirations after absolute beauty, rarefied expressions of the ecstasy of failure and despair, and morbid attractions to death and the tragic style of death-in-life. But Scott would not be the first young person to entertain contradictory tendencies as he sought his way in the world. Indeed, Trehearne convincingly argues that this internal conflict is revealed in one of Scott's most acclaimed poems, "Overture," and is the source of its powerful tension (pp. 160–3). Here the absolute aesthetic values evoked by the playing of a Mozart sonata in the first two stanzas give way at last to a rhetorical question that suggests a call to action – "But how shall I hear old Music?" ... [which] "seems a trinket on a shelf, / A pretty octave played before a window / Beyond whose curtain grows a world crescendo."

Similarly, Trehearne contends that an analysis of Smith's early poetry demonstrates the strong influence of English aestheticism and decadence, and that his adoption of modernist principles was gradual and by no means complete at the time he was editing the *Fortnightly*. Poems published there that survived to be associated with the modernist Smith, such as "The Lonely Land" and "The Sorcerer" (originally "Not of the Dust") appeared at first in a significantly less modernist style. Furthermore, many poems published in the *Fortnightly* were not ultimately included in the Smith canon and these are either "tentatively modern" or "loosely Romantic" (p. 243). Finally, it is noteworthy that the first of Smith's *Fortnightly* essays, "Symbolism in Poetry," articulates the values of aestheticism rather than modernism. Even when Smith's status as a modern is no longer in question, Trehearne defines a core set of "artistic principles" – intensity, craft and detachment – essential to his identity as a writer – that are fundamental tenets of aestheticism. Yet Trehearne believes that Smith consciously rejected aestheticism, reading his poem "Nightfall" as a representation of this shift in sensibility.

The *McGill Fortnightly Review* published its final issue in April 1927, when Smith left to do a Ph.D. at Edinburgh University, but in December 1928 *The Canadian Mercury* appeared, designated "A monthly Journal of literature and opinion published in Montreal," with an editorial board consisting of F. R. Scott, Leo Kennedy, Jean Burton and Felix Walter. A. J. M. Smith was listed as a contributor in the first issue for his poem, "Proud Parable." Although *The Canadian Mercury* was aimed at a broader readership than the *Fortnightly*, it still announced itself with a generous modicum of youthful swagger as "striving to contribute ... to the consummation of that graceful ideal, the emancipation of Canadian literature from the state of amiable mediocrity and insipidity in which it now languishes."[26] The supercilious style evokes 1920s Oxford, once again giving credence to Trehearne's thesis about the influence of aestheticism. Perhaps it is recalled through Scott's personal experience or vicariously through those much-praised Oxbridge debaters. In any event, the scorn for the puritanical and philistine values of mainstream Canadian life, however justified, now seems pretentious. The superiority of the tone is only marginally alleviated by the self-mockery of the statement "The editors are all well under thirty and intend to remain so."

The Canadian Mercury survived for only seven months, and a survey of the seven issues reveals many of the themes that dominated the *Fortnightly*. Stephen Leacock is once again wheeled in, this time for the more serious purpose of delineating "The National Literature Problem in Canada," the main problem being that "there is no such thing as a Canadian way of writing."[27] Leacock points out that other national literatures in English have a strong identity – the Scottish, the English and the American – but that Canada shares the literary heritage of these countries rather than displaying one of its own. Some months later, Leo Kennedy offers this brutal assessment: "with rare exceptions the best prose and poetry hitherto produced in Canada compares unfavourably even with the eyewash poured annually from third rate British and United States presses."[28] Lacking a worthwhile literary tradition of their own, Kennedy remarks, "the young men are inclined, and wisely, to look abroad for that which will influence them."

---

26 *The Canadian Mercury*, 1.1 (December 1928), p. 3.
27 Ibid., p. 8.
28 "The Future of Canadian Literature," *The Canadian Mercury*, 1.5–6 (April–May 1929), pp. 99–100.

It is characteristic of the McGill Group to assume, despite evidence to the contrary, that prospective poets would be young men. In the meantime, *The Canadian Mercury* addresses the backwardness of Canadian literary and intellectual life by publishing the work of a new generation. Kennedy contributes fiction and poetry, as well as criticism; A. M. Klein makes his debut with a couple of poems; Dorothy Livesay appears as the author of a short story entitled "Heat"; and Leon Edel provides a regular "Montparnasse Letter" full of arch commentary about the literary scene in Paris. David Lewis and S. I. Hayakawa author reviews. Eugene Forsey, now at Oxford, writes about "The Future of Canadian Politics"; and Douglas Bush, from the University of Minnesota, warns against American-bashing. A. J. M. Smith and F. R. Scott continue to publish their poetry; and Smith shows that he is still under the influence of T. S. Eliot (not to mention Herbert Grierson, the acclaimed editor of John Donne, under whose supervision he was doing his doctorate at Edinburgh) by contributing "A Note on Metaphysical Poetry."

Pratt continued

In the meantime, E. J. Pratt had moved on. The poet whom Barker Fairley had admired for being "more at home with whales, octopuses, and dinosaurs than with his fellowmen," published in 1930 his epic tale of human heroism at sea, *The Roosevelt and the Antinoe*.[29] The poem launched Pratt's practice of documentary realism and this, with the exploration of human heroism, must have seemed like a 180-degree turn from the comic fantasy of "The Witches' Brew" and the naturalistic allegories of *Titans*. In any event, the reader of *The Roosevelt and the Antinoe* can hardly doubt the originality of Pratt's vision or the power of his narrative style. Pratt's interest in science and technology, specifically his knowledge of geology, biology, and physics, and his fascination with the philosophical and moral implications of evolutionary theory, all make him seem modern in the broad sense of the word, and certainly in comparison with the Canadian poets who preceded him. But Pratt was little influenced by literary modernism as exemplified by Eliot, Pound and Joyce. Some years older than Eliot and Pound, and the same age as Joyce, Pratt had developed his style in Canada independent of such influences. By the 1920s he had found his own unique voice and stood alone – a poet who, having broken with traditional poetry in Canada, owed almost nothing to contemporary poetry in Europe.

29 *The Canadian Forum* 7.77 (February 1927), p. 148.

The Roosevelt and the Antinoe was Pratt's fifth book of poetry. Although it appeared to mixed reviews in the United States, it was enthusiastically received in Canada, and favorably in England. In David Pitt's words, "Pratt (whether validly laurelled or not) was left without a visible rival on the national horizon."[30] The self-proclaimed heralds of modernism – Smith, Scott, Kennedy, and Klein – had thus far published only in literary magazines, mostly edited by themselves. The work of the Toronto poet Robert Finch had similarly not yet been collected in book form. Of the "new" generation, only Dorothy Livesay, at the precocious age of nineteen, had published a volume of verse – Green Pitcher (1928), brought out by Macmillan after a favorable endorsement by Pratt, who was employed by the publisher as reader.[31] During the next few years, while he worked on Many Moods (1932) and The Titanic (1935), Pratt was to cross paths again and again with these emerging writers. Macmillan brought out Livesay's second collection, Signpost, in 1932, and published Leo Kennedy's The Shrouding one year later, again apparently with strong support from Pratt.[32] Given his national profile, and his influence at Macmillan, it is not surprising that in late 1933 Pratt was approached by F. R. Scott, who asked him to be part of a McGill Group project to publish an anthology of "new poetry."[33] Appearing in 1936, after two years of wrangling, New Provinces: Poems of Several Authors eventually included the work of Robert Finch as well as Pratt and the McGill Group.

Modernist controversies, New Provinces, and poetry magazines of the 1940s

In the attacks launched on the Canadian Authors Association (CAA) by the McGill Group and others throughout the 1920s, Pratt had been exempted from criticism and even occasionally singled out for qualified approbation. Although such new lights as Raymond Knister, Douglas Bush, A. J. M. Smith and F. R. Scott may have been puzzled by Pratt's fantasies about krakens and whales and sea cats – which did not, after all, follow very closely the dictates of Eliot and Pound – they regarded him at least as a fresh voice. Furthermore, he was popular, and so they decided that he was someone they should work with.

---

30 David G. Pitt, E. J. Pratt: The Master Years, 1927–1964 (Toronto: University of Toronto Press, 1987), p. 69.
31 Ibid., p. 70.
32 Leon Edel, "Memories of the Montreal Group," The E. J. Pratt Lecture, 1984 (St. John's: Memorial University of Newfoundland, 1986), p. 22.
33 Pitt, E. J. Pratt, p. 142.

Pratt, for his part, was flattered by their attention. Although earlier wary of the "Montreal gang," he evinced such a desire to be accepted by the new generation of writers that he began to distance himself from the CAA.[34] When approached by Scott, Pratt was enthusiastic about the chance to participate in what he imagined might be a giant leap forward in Canadian poetry. He made comparisons to the effect of the Group of Seven upon Canadian art, tried (without much success) to organize some of his famous "stag" parties to bring the group together, and in the course of the project indicated that his critical standards and his poetic practice were being reformed as a result of the association with his new colleagues.

Not that the discussions and negotiations over the next two years were to be without tension or rancor. On the contrary, they constitute a classic case study of the stereotypical clash of literary egos. Smith's criticisms of the work of Pratt and Finch were characteristically blunt. Taken aback, Pratt asked Scott, "Who is this man Smith?"[35] Several months later it was Pratt's turn. Claiming to be speaking for Finch as well, he declared that Smith's "'Hyacinth for Edith' ... exhibits no trace of originality" and suggested that "the middle part of 'Shadows There Are' is pretty flat."[36] Smith argued that some good left-wing verse should be included and he suggested they consider inviting Dorothy Livesay to be part of the project. Livesay's credentials as a radical socialist were certainly impeccable and, given that by this time she was better published than any of the group with the exception of Pratt, it is surprising that the invitation did not materialize. Ironically, Peggy Kelly has concluded, after a thorough sifting of the records, that it may have been the socialist Scott who stymied Livesay's involvement because he was under pressure at McGill to tone down his activities and was uneasy being associated with someone whose politics were to the left of his.[37]

The most divisive moments of the collaboration, however, had to do with finding a publisher for the anthology and with the manifesto that Arthur Smith felt should herald the new poetry. Although he was a great supporter of Pratt, Hugh Eayrs, President of Macmillan Canada, was skeptical about the financial prospects for a poetry anthology in the midst of the Great Depression. In November 1934, Eayrs set the condition that the poets themselves subsidize

---

34 Ibid., pp. 54, 58–9.
35 Michael Gnarowski, "Introduction," *New Provinces: Poems of Several Authors* (Toronto: University of Toronto Press, 1976), p.xiii.
36 Quoted in Pitt, *E.J. Pratt*, p. 155.
37 Peggy Kelly, "Politics, Gender, and *New Provinces*: Dorothy Livesay and F. R. Scott," *Canadian Poetry* 53 (Fall–Winter 2003), pp. 59–61.

the publication to the amount of 250 dollars to be raised through subscriptions. The Montreal poets rejected this condition, deciding to seek another publisher, but when after a year had passed they were unsuccessful, they finally came to terms with Eayrs's demands.

Smith's Preface proved, if anything, to be more of an obstacle to publication. A full-frontal attack on the sorry state of Canadian letters reminiscent of the *Fortnightly Review* and *The Canadian Mercury*, the Preface outlines the conventional expectations of Canadian poetry lovers with delicious irony: "The most popular experience is to be pained, hurt, stabbed or seared by beauty – preferably by the yellow flame of a crocus in the spring or the red flame of a maple leaf in autumn."[38] By the end of the third paragraph, Smith reaches this unambiguous verdict: "The fundamental criticism that must be brought against Canadian poetry as a whole is that it ignores the intelligence. And as a result it is dead" (p. xxviii). The Preface then goes on to outline the values that animate the poetry promoted in the collection. Poetry should be "pure" (meaning that "a poem exists as a thing in itself"), and after that it might be imagist, metaphysical or satirical. Finally Smith goes on to predict the collapse of capitalism and to recommend that the poet should learn to "play his part in developing mental and emotional attitudes that will facilitate the creation of a more practical social system" (p. xxxi).

Not surprisingly, this did not go down well with Pratt. But Pratt was not the only dissenter. In a letter to Scott, he claimed that Finch did not approve of the impression that was being given that "Canadian literature had to wait for us to get its first obstetrical success" and that Eayrs did not like what he called the "nose-tweaking."[39] When it was clear the Preface would have to go, Scott informed Smith, who fumed, "Who the hell are Finch and Pratt to object to the preface. If I am willing to let my poems come out in the same book with Pratt's insipid stuff, he can take the preface."[40] Exasperated by the internecine warfare, Scott put his foot down, substituted a much-watered-down, half-page preface of his own, and *New Provinces* finally appeared in the spring of 1936.

The anthology would certainly have represented a challenge for those nourished on the tradition of the Confederation poets. The verse is uniformly well crafted, muscular in structure, diction and rhythm, but it is also difficult and frequently obscure. Much of it has an uncompromising bluntness and austerity that probably reflected the influence of Smith. On the other hand, it

---

38 "A Rejected Preface," in Gnarowski, *New Provinces*, p. xxvii.
39 Quoted in Pitt, *E. J. Pratt*, p. 189.
40 Quoted in Kelly, "Politics," p. 58.

is conventional in its versification. Most of the poems are written in meter and rhyme, with some experimentation with the rhythms of speech and recourse to occasional or half-rhyme for greater flexibility. The modernist bias (via Eliot) in favor of sixteenth- and seventeenth-century literature, especially the Jacobean dramatists and the metaphysical poets, is evident in some of the diction such as "[m]augre" (Finch, "The Excursionists"), "leman" (Kennedy, "Epithalamium"), "horrid air" and "limn" (Smith, "Shadows There Are"), "mandrake" (Smith, "The Offices of the First and Second Hour") and in direct allusions to Malfi and Denmark (Smith, "Prothalamium").

Echoes of Eliot are everywhere – in such phrases as "maculate streets of Amsterdam," "He and His God are under interdict" and "My life lies on a tray of cigarette-butts" from Klein's "Out of the Pulver and the Polished Lens" and his "Soirée of Velvel Kleinburger," and in the verse form and supercilious tone of Scott's "The Canadian Authors Meet." The hypnotic rhythms of e.e. cummings's "all in green went my love riding" are expertly recalled in Finch's "The Five Kine." Even Pratt's selections are dark and hard-edged ("The Prize Winner" and "From Java to Geneva") or bitterly satiric ("Text of the Oath" and "The Convict Holocaust"). Despite the obviously derivative nature of much of the work, several poems published in *New Provinces* have since entered the canon of modernist poetry in Canada – Klein's "Out of the Pulver and the Polished Lens," Scott's "The Canadian Authors Meet," and Smith's "The Lonely Land."

Almost as striking as the exclusion of Livesay is the isolation of Pratt. Although he was the only one of the group who had established a national reputation at this point, he was accorded eight pages, the smallest number of any contributor. Klein was given ten; Foster, Kennedy, and Scott eleven; and Smith thirteen. And Pratt was the only one of the contributors who is not lauded, or even mentioned, in Smith's "Rejected Preface." Given Pratt's profile, his influence with the only publisher the group could find, and his welcoming attitude towards the younger poets, it is hard to avoid seeing a certain arrogance, mean-spiritedness and even exploitation in their treatment of him. *New Provinces* barely concealed the rifts and jealousies that characterized the uneasy partnership.

As it turned out, Eayrs's caution about the marketability of the anthology proved to be right. *New Provinces* sank like a stone in the water. So did its companion critical volume, W. E. Collins's *The White Savannahs*, published one month afterwards, which provided an independent critical justification for the "new poetry," with essays on Pratt, Livesay, Scott, Klein, Smith, and Kennedy, as well as Archibald Lampman, Marjorie Pickthall and Marie Le

Franc by way of introduction. *New Provinces* was favorably reviewed by E. K. Brown in *New Frontier*, Edgar McInnis in *The Canadian Forum*, and Burns Martin in *The Dalhousie Review*, and that was about it.[41] Ten months later, Scott reported to Pratt that eighty-two copies had been sold, and he had purchased ten of them.[42] Although both volumes seem ground-breaking in retrospect, their impact at the time was negligible.

By the time *New Provinces* appeared, Pratt's flirtation with modernism was over. In taking on the editorship of the *Canadian Poetry Magazine* in 1935 at the behest of Pelham Edgar, he was working, in effect, for the dreaded Canadian Authors Association, of which Edgar was now President. He had won the Governor General's Award for *The Fable of the Goats and Other Poems* (1937), and had just published his second great "epic" of the 1930s, *The Titanic* (1935). Pratt was at the height of his powers and the end of the decade was to see the publication of another substantial work, *Brébeuf and His Brethren* (1940). Although conceptually flawed in its assumption that the Aboriginals needed saving by the White man's God, for which Scott took him to task in his own poem entitled "Brébeuf and His Brethren," Pratt's work won him a second Governor General's Award. He was now successful beyond the measure of any other Canadian poet.

A. M. Klein published his first collection of poetry, *Hath Not a Jew*, in 1940, and followed it with three further publications of poetry during the 1940s. Smith's first collection, *News of the Phoenix*, appeared in 1943, and Scott's *Overture* followed in 1945. Robert Finch began an impressive series of publications with *Poems* in 1946. Pratt's work continued to appear throughout the 1940s – the war narratives, *Dunkirk* (1941) and *Behind the Log* (1947), and the collection of lyrics *Still Life and Other Verse* (1943). In 1952, he published his saga of the building of the Canadian Pacific Railway, *Towards the Last Spike*, winning his third Governor General's Award. Almost as productive as Pratt and Klein, Dorothy Livesay brought out three collections during the 1940s. Smith, Finch, Klein, and Livesay were all honored with Governor General's Awards for their work during that decade. Leo Kennedy, on the other hand, gave up the practice of poetry for the writing of advertising copy. "Look, I have taken down the sign from above the door," he wrote forlornly to Leon Edel.[43]

Pratt stepped down as editor of the *Canadian Poetry Magazine* in 1943, succeeded by his protégé Earle Birney. But by then, as editor of *CPM* and as

---

41 Pitt, *E. J. Pratt*, pp. 190–1.
42 Gnarowski, "Introduction," p. xxi.
43 Leon Edel, "Introduction," Leo Kennedy, *The Shrouding: Poems* (Ottawa: Golden Dog Press, 1975 [1933]), n.p.

chief poetry reader for Macmillan, his influence on the development of Canadian poetry was probably unprecedented. In the meantime, during the 1940s, Livesay and Scott were associated with the establishment of two important poetry magazines – *Contemporary Verse* (Vancouver, 1941) and *Preview* (Montreal, 1942). *Contemporary Verse*, edited by Alan Crawley with significant support from Livesay, Doris Ferne, Anne Marriott and Floris Clarke McLaren, continued until 1952. *Preview*, edited by Patrick Anderson and others, including Scott, Klein, and P. K. Page, merged in 1945 with its Montreal rival, *First Statement*, edited by John Sutherland, to form *Northern Review*. Although the production values of these magazines were primitive by today's standards, and the circulations in the range of 100 or less, they were responsible for the publication of many poets who have since entered the Canadian canon.

As for A. J. M. Smith, through his editing of *The Book of Canadian Poetry: A Critical and Historical Anthology* (1943), and his critical articles, in particular his Introduction to the anthology and his earlier essay, "Canadian Poetry: A Minority Report" (1939), he continued to provoke debate around the direction Canadian poetry should take. His distinction between the "cosmopolitan" and the "native" in the Introduction to *The Book of Canadian Poetry* led Sutherland to respond with an anthology of his own, *Other Canadians: An Anthology of the New Poetry in Canada 1940–46* (1947). By the 1940s, the internationalism of the McGill poets was being tempered by the nationalism of Sutherland and the *First Statement* group, including Irving Layton.

From the perspective of the twenty-first century, Pratt and the McGill poets not surprisingly seem to be creatures very much of their times, all of them limited and blinkered in their ways – Pratt with his stag parties and golf games, his anthropomorphism and ethnocentricity, Smith and Scott with the essentially derivative and colonial nature of their internationalism, all of them with their "masculinist" assumptions about literature and life. Legacies are difficult to trace. Birney was close to Pratt and somewhat influenced by him in his poetics, but Pratt famously founded no school. A line can be drawn from the McGill Group through Layton and Louis Dudek to Leonard Cohen, but then what? The smug self-satisfaction and impenetrable philistinism of bourgeois Canadian society in the years between the wars definitely needed a lesson in humility, and Smith and Scott, and their compatriots, were up to the job. In the long run, they did literature a great service in opening Canada up to the world, even if in doing so they betrayed a quintessentially colonial sense of their country's inferiority. Pratt's response to Canada's stifling cultural atmosphere was less theoretical and more personal but perhaps just as effective.

Ernest Sirluck, a regular member of Pratt's circle later to become President of the University of Manitoba, recalled that, whereas Pelham Edgar, Pratt's mentor, had made his protégés feel that they lived in "a remote corner of the culture of the world," Pratt made them feel that they "were at the centre of the culture of Canada."[44] If Declan Kiberd is right in pointing out that "[a]t the heart of modernist culture is a distrust of the very idea of culture itself," modernism would not by itself prove the salvation of Canadian literature.[45] Canada needed to accept itself as a culture before the advances of the 1970s and 1980s could take place, before its literature could enable it to invent itself as a country offering a haven for different cultures. Pratt's respect for Canada's past and his optimism in its future, embodied in his literary leadership as well as in his poetic achievement as Canada's great myth-maker (despite his well-documented limitations), were critical in this evolution from a colonial to a postcolonial society.

44 Quoted in Pitt, *E.J. Pratt*, p. 119.
45 Declan Kiberd, "Introduction," James Joyce, *Ulysses* (Toronto: Penguin, 1992 [1922]), p. xlix.

15
The 1940s and 1950s: signs of cultural change

CORAL ANN HOWELLS

Looking back to the late 1930s, the novelist Hugh MacLennan described Canada as "an uncharacterized country," unrealized and unappreciated by Canadians themselves, while the rest of the world "had never thought about Canada at all, and knew nothing whatever about us."[1] By contrast, in the late 1950s he was speaking confidently about a national transformation: "There are many evidences that the Canadian scene at the moment can provide themes as significant to old countries in Europe, and to the United States, as can be found anywhere. If this is true, there is no need any longer to ask whether there can be a Canadian literature. There is one now."[2] This magisterial overview by the major literary spokesman for Canadian nationalism in the 1940s and 50s provides a framework for this chapter. These twenty years form a border zone between old and new, when the patterns of colonial Canada were radically disrupted by the Second World War, followed by the optimistic years of post-war reconstruction and attempts to forge a new national consciousness for an independent North American nation. Canadian Confederation seemed complete when Newfoundland joined in 1949, but the province's discontent lingers into present-day politics and literature. Inevitably this was a period of conflicting political and cultural interests: nationalism versus regionalism, biculturalism and bilingualism; literary modernism versus traditionalism; voices of British-centered cultural authority versus the "other" voices of regional writers, ethnic writers, women, and French Canadians. Altogether these unresolved tensions produced a far more contentious and livelier literary culture than many historians have been willing to acknowledge.

---

1 Hugh MacLennan, "Where Is My Potted Palm" (1952), reprinted in *The Other Side of Hugh MacLennan*, ed. Elspeth Cameron (Toronto: Macmillan, 1978), p. 46.
2 Hugh MacLennan, "Literature in a New Country," in *Scotchman's Return and Other Essays* (Toronto: Macmillan, 1960), p. 138.

During these two decades Canadian cultural politics and questions around Canadian identity assumed new importance and a measure of diversity. Wartime issues like the Quebec Conscription Crises of 1942 and 1944 (echoing the troubles of 1917) and the internment and dispersal of Japanese Canadians under the War Measures Act were followed by the Canadian Citizenship Act in 1947, the Revocation of the Chinese Exclusion Act that year, and the granting of federal voting rights to Japanese Canadians in 1948. These immediate post-war changes were signs of the shift in attitudes as codified in the 1948 United Nations Universal Declaration of Human Rights. Canada's own Bill of Rights would be passed in 1960, though Canadians' tolerance for racial others was still very limited and innovative multiculturalism policies were only developed in the 1970s.[3] The most important post-war cultural initiative was the setting up of the Royal Commission on National Development in the Arts, Letters and Sciences in 1949 under the chairmanship of Vincent Massey – the first step towards "a coherent, state-supported, federal policy for culture and the arts."[4] The resultant Massey Report (1951) instigated the creation of new national institutions, and signaled developments that would underpin Anglo-Canadian and to a lesser extent Quebec cultural nationalism in the 1960s and 70s.

In literature, the main debates centered on the struggles between modernism and traditionalism, though these contestations were played out differently in fiction and poetry. Whereas in fiction the dominance of realism and issues around regional and national identity tended to occlude modernist modes of writing, in anglophone poetry at least the emphasis was rather the opposite, with the traditionalists on the defensive. As John Sutherland, founder of the Montreal modernist journal *First Statement*, declared in his submission to the Massey Commission (1949), Canadian poetry had "caught something of the experimental temper of twentieth-century literature everywhere, and, in form and expression, it has reacted against the more conservative techniques of the romantic nature poets."[5] Indeed, so had the novel, but the conflictual discourses around modernism in poetry were not paralleled in fiction. Given their different priorities, fiction and poetry will be analyzed separately in this chapter.

---

[3] Ross Lambertson, *Repression and Resistance: Canadian Human Rights Activists, 1930–1960* (Toronto: University of Toronto Press, 2005), p. 371.
[4] Maria Tippett, *Making Culture: English-Canadian Institutions and the Arts Before the Massey Commission* (Toronto: University of Toronto Press, 1990), p. 184.
[5] Reprinted in *The Making of Modern Poetry in Canada: Essential Articles on Contemporary Canadian Poetry in English*, ed. Louis Dudek and Michael Gnarowski (Toronto: Ryerson, 1967), p. 67.

Fiction

Trying to chart a course through cross-currents, I have chosen to begin from the Governor General's Literary Awards – possibly a crude critical tool, but one that highlights the gap between the anglophone establishment's view of what Canadian literature should be and the real diversity of fiction being published in this period.[6] If the list of Award winners tells one story, then those who never featured on that list tell another. Not surprisingly, what is left off the list is modernist experimental fiction (what Ondaatje calls "outriders – books that burn or splash on the periphery ... the beginnings of the contemporary novel in Canada"),[7] ethnic minority writing, much francophone fiction, and new writers who would come to prominence later, like Robertson Davies and Mordecai Richler. Award winners included some of Canada's best-known authors, while there are others whose work has sunk into virtual oblivion.

There are some writers who were not GG Award winners but whose texts have become classics, such as Sinclair Ross, whose novel *As for Me and My House* (1941) is one of the most frequently analyzed works in Canadian literature. The entire period has recently been receiving renewed scholarly attention, with the reissue of novels by Gwethalyn Graham, Phyllis Brett Young, and Irene Baird, and the publication of numerous biographies.[8] Then there were the bestsellers, notably the historical romances of Thomas B. Costain – *The Black Rose* and *The Silver Chalice* were made into Hollywood

---

6 This chapter deals only with writing in English or English translation, following the pattern of the prestigious Governor General's Awards up to 1959, when prizes for writing in French were introduced. These awards, Canada's first national literary prizes, were started in 1937 under GG Lord Tweedsmuir at the instigation of the Canadian Authors Association, with prizes awarded for two books published in 1936. Designed to publicize Canadian writing, these annual awards for best works of fiction, poetry, drama and non-fiction were administered and adjudicated by the CAA until 1959, when the Canada Council assumed responsibility and the awards system was revised. Sponsored since 1988 by the BMO Financial Group, the GG Awards retain their status as official national literary accolade with currently fourteen categories and substantial monetary prizes.
7 Michael Ondaatje, Afterword to Howard O'Hagan's *Tay John* (Toronto: McClelland and Stewart, 1989), pp. 271–2.
8 See Gwethalyn Graham, *Swiss Sonata* (London: Cape, 1938) and *Earth and High Heaven* (Philadelphia: Lippincott, 1944), both reissued by Cormorant Books, 2003; Phyllis Brett Young, *Psyche* (1959) and *The Torontonians* (1960), both published in Toronto by Longmans, Green and Co., and reissued by McGill-Queen's University Press in 2007 and 2008 respectively; Irene Baird, *Waste Heritage* (Toronto: Macmillan, and New York: Random House, 1939), reprinted 1973, and reissued by University of Ottawa Press, 2007. For biographical studies of Sinclair Ross, Gabrielle Roy, Elizabeth Smart, Sheila Watson, Ethel Wilson, and Adele Wiseman consult the Bibliography in this volume.

films in the 1950s – and Thomas H. Raddall's tales of Nova Scotia's past (*His Majesty's Yankees*, 1942).

The dominant figure in fiction writing from the start of the Second World War to the end of the 1950s was Hugh MacLennan. He won five GG awards in this period. A Maritimer who had studied Classics at Oxford and Princeton before returning to Montreal, MacLennan wrote novels which addressed questions of contemporary national significance such as Canadian identity, Anglo-French divisions in Quebec, Canadian–American relations. MacLennan also believed in the importance of history to establish a sense of national awareness. His first novel, *Barometer Rising* (1941), allegorizes Canada's dawning sense of national independence during the Second World War through the Halifax Explosion of 1917, which blew apart the city and the old Nova Scotian colonial hierarchy, and his most famous novel, *Two Solitudes* (1945), is an attempt to move beyond historic enmities between English and French in Quebec to embrace an ideal of national unity.

That historicizing consciousness is evident through *The Watch That Ends the Night* (1958) right up to his last dystopian novel, *Voices in Time* (1980). The frequent allusions to Homeric epic and the Bible function as amplification, binding present events in Canada into a universalized context: "But time is more than now, more than twelve o'clock, or any particular century. It is also ourselves. It is millions of people and many nations."[9] MacLennan's double role as visionary and chronicler puts some strain on the realist mode of his fictions for, though he is obsessed with chronology and documentary details (a Canadian novelist must "be something of a geographer, an historian, and a sociologist"),[10] there are strange fissures in these realistic novels where MacLennan incorporates elements from epic and romance and even modernist features. Though critics have recognized modernist strategies in *Watch*, they are there in *Two Solitudes* as well, a realist fiction which views the present through a historical lens but which also features the young male protagonist's unfinished novel about Canada, a self-reflexive parallel with MacLennan's own deferred vision of national unity at the end of his novel.

MacLennan's principal model for his representation of French Canadians was *Thirty Acres* by Ringuet (pseudonym for Philippe Panneton). The book was originally published as *Trente Arpents* in Paris in 1938 and translated into English in 1940, when it won a GG Award. This realist novel is a twentieth-century revision of the nineteenth-century *roman du terroir*, where rural

---

9 Hush MacLennan, *The Precipice* (Toronto: Collins, 1948), p. vii.
10 MacLennan, "Where Is My Potted Palm," p. 46.

stability is being destroyed by the forces of modernization. It is a tragic story of loss and inevitable change which ends without hope, for the Quebec idyll exists nowhere except in the memory of a dispossessed old farmer now living in exile in the Franco-American community of a shabby American factory town. A curious connection might be made between *Thirty Acres* and Germaine Guèvremont's *The Outlander* (1950). (The two-part original, *Le Survenant* [1945] had won prizes in Quebec and France. A sequel, *Marie-Didace*, was published in 1947. All three parts were included in the translation, *The Outlander*.) Guèvremont's novel, generally regarded as the ultimate *roman du terroir*, celebrates Quebec's rural myth, which Ringuet had already shown in its early stages of disintegration. However, the very title generates unease, for "Outlander" is close to "outlandish," and "survenant" carries connotations of the unexpected and the uncanny. The unknown young man who appears at the farmhouse door is a reminder that there is a wider world waiting outside the parish and, like the Outlander's Poe-esque word "neveurmagne," this reads more like the death knell to a way of life than a celebration.

Urbanization, industrialization, mass migration to the city – all the phenomena of modernity – assume center focus in Gabrielle Roy's *The Tin Flute*, the first urban realist novel produced in Quebec. Published in French as *Bonheur d'occasion* the same year as *Two Solitudes* and translated into English in 1947, the novel won many awards and became a bestseller in Canada, the United States, and France. Roy, a Franco-Manitoban, had worked as a journalist in Montreal on her return from Europe in 1939, and her novel had its genesis in her 1941 research for a series of newspaper articles. It focuses on the shabby French working-class district of Saint-Henri, an urban slum close to the railway lines, and on the poverty-stricken lives of one family of rural immigrants, the Lacasses, in the last year of the Depression up to the Second World War. Roy measures the impact of mass unemployment and the perpetual struggle against poverty principally through the lives of women, and her liberal social sympathies shape a compassionate psychological analysis which reveals the failed dreams and moral compromises by which survival is achieved.

The ironic ending brings together masculine and feminine escape strategies, where dreams of prosperity are fulfilled for the unemployed French Canadians only by joining the army. Roy presents a much less exalted view of the war than MacLennan's: "So this was how salvation came to the suburb! Salvation through war!"[11] The ending opens onto an uncertain future,

---

11 Gabrielle Roy, *The Tin Flute*, tr. Alan Brown (Toronto: McClelland and Stewart, 1980), p. 375. This superseded the first English edition, tr. Hannah Josephson (New York:

for women at home and for men going abroad to war. In her later fiction Roy turned away from urban poverty back to the rural Manitoba of her youth, in *La petite poule d'eau* (1950) and in her second GG Award-winning *Street of Riches* (1957; first published 1955 in Montreal as *Rue Deschambault*). These are no rural idylls, however, for misery, poverty, and women's desire for escape are as pervasive in the country as in the city.

Two Solitudes and *The Tin Flute* both end with the outbreak of the Second World War, a reminder that the war haunts the Canadian imagination throughout this period. Novels set in pre-war Europe include Gwethalyn Graham's *Swiss Sonata* (1938), Philip Child's *The Day of Wrath* (1945), Winifred Bambrick's *Continental Revue* (1946) and the Austrian Jewish immigrant Henry Kreisel's *The Rich Man* (1948), all of them filled with a sense of impending catastrophe and the threat from Nazi Germany. War novels set in Canada tend to emphasize domestic disruption and troop departures; there is a determinedly patriotic tone in English Canadian novels of the 1940s, though French Canadian dissidence is registered not only in *The Tin Flute* but also in Roger Lemelin's satirical comments in *Les Plouffe* (1948) / *The Plouffe Family* (1950). One of the earliest war novels, G. Herbert Sallans's *Little Man* (1942) links the First and Second World Wars and contains a remarkably modernist urge to chronicle these events through a new kind of Canadian novel celebrating the "Little Man, transfigured, supreme, and sublime, who will win the war."[12]

Gwethalyn Graham's *Earth and High Heaven* (1944) is a woman's wartime romance set in Montreal, which not only won the GG Award but also topped the *New York Times* Best Seller list. Its distinctive feature was its passionate condemnation of anti-Semitism at home: "After all, we Canadians don't really disagree fundamentally with the Nazis about the Jews – we just think they go a bit too far."[13] The Gentile–Jewish love story is rather overburdened by earnest debates which were restaged during the 1950s by Jewish Canadian writers. None of the other war novels has stood the test of time any better than Graham's – neither Earle Birney's *Turvey: A Military Picaresque* (1949) nor the GG Award winners of the 1950s, David Walker's *The Pillar* (1952), Lionel Shapiro's *The Sixth of June* (1955), and Colin McDougall's *Execution* (1958).[14] With the advent of the Korean War and the Cold War, the Second World War was overshadowed by new international and domestic anxieties.

> Reynal and Hitchcock, 1947). The French original reads as follows: "Ainsi donc le salut leur était venu dans le faubourg! Le salut par la guerre!" (*Bonheur d'occasion*, 2 vols. [Montreal: Société des Éditions Pascal, 1945], vol. II, p. 521).
> 12 G. Herbert Sallans, *Little Man* (Toronto: Ryerson, 1942), p. 419.
> 13 Gwethalyn Graham, *Earth and High Heaven* (Philadelphia: Lippincott, 1944), p. 51.
> 14 These are GG Award dates.

The slightly maverick Morley Callaghan from Toronto, friend and admirer of Hemingway and Scott Fitzgerald, who had made his name as a novelist and short story writer in the 1920s and 30s, returned to fiction in the early 1950s with his GG award winning novel *The Loved and the Lost* (1951). Set in a wintry, snow-covered Montreal, this is a story about a doomed love affair and the murder of a white girl who flouts social convention and racial taboos by living alone in the dominantly Black area of St Antoine. However, this is not a novel about race relations, and the social context functions as symbolic backdrop to the moral drama, for Callaghan has taken a melodramatic plot and turned it into an allegory of post-war urban Canada with its glaring social inequalities, its racial intolerance, and the split identities of many of its citizens. The enigmatic heroine, an early hippie with a taste for Negro jazz, is suspected by both Whites and Blacks (and by the hero, who is in love with her) of being a loose woman. She cannot survive and after her murder he is left derelict, standing lonely and lost in the dead, white Montreal winter landscape. The novel is a strange mixture of realism and symbolic resonance, contrasting with the social realism of Hugh Garner's *Cabbagetown* (1950; unexpurgated text 1968) set in Toronto during the Depression.

A very different figure, Robertson Davies, born in small-town Ontario, should be included here, for, though his international fame came with the Deptford trilogy in the 1970s, he was already a member of the literary establishment from the early 1940s, editor of the *Peterborough Examiner*, one of Canada's best-known playwrights, author of *The Diary of Samuel Marchbanks* (1947), and of the Salterton trilogy (*Tempest-Tost*, 1951; *Leaven of Malice*, 1954; and *A Mixture of Frailties*, 1958). These early works are social comedies satirizing Canadian provincialism in the tradition of Duncan and Leacock, but already Davies's interest in theatricality and his fascination with Jungian psychoanalysis and myths, the hallmarks of his later fiction, are apparent.

Turning now to the outriders who offered sub-versions of Canada's story in the 1940s and 50s, we notice the prominence of westerners and Maritimers, diasporic writers (for the first time), and expatriates who wrote about Canada from the outside. Of the major prairie novelists, Sinclair Ross and W. O. Mitchell, Ross is the emblematic outrider figure, a writer from Saskatchewan whose first novel was about a failed prairie artist and who regarded his own career as a failure. A modernist before his time, Ross's short stories were practically ignored, and he always had difficulty in placing his novels. Contemporary reviewers praised or criticized *As For Me and My House* for all the wrong reasons, reading it within the Western realist tradition epitomized by Robert Stead's *Grain* (1926) but failing to appreciate Ross's modernist techniques – his alienated artist figures, his attention to language, and debates about significant form. His use of the diary model comes close to a woman's interior monologue, for it is Mrs Bentley and not her husband, the frustrated painter turned clergyman, who tells the story, a mode which Ross described as "something like cross-writing."[15] Surely "cross-dressing" is lurking close behind this comment, given Ross's own secret homosexual identity. Ironically, when the novel was first published, the *New York Herald Tribune* reviewer (February 23, 1941) thought that the author was a woman (see Stouck, p. 106). Recent gender and queer theory have opened new perspectives on this novel, while it has also been read as prairie Gothic.

By contrast, W. O. Mitchell was a well-known figure, a television script writer and later playwright, and his first novel, *Who Has Seen the Wind* (1947), won immediate popularity. (It was made into a major film in 1977.) A crucial difference between these novels is one of tone, for Ross's harsh narrative of survival changes to comic survival with Mitchell, though he treats the same serious social issues as Ross – drought and the Depression, satire on the social hypocrisy of prairie small-town life – defusing his criticism by focalizing the narrative through a young boy's consciousness. Mitchell also uses modernist fictional techniques, but disguises these appropriations through his down-home realism and folksy humor. Thirty years later in *How I Spent My Summer Holidays* (1981) Mitchell returned to the *bildungsroman* form, though innocence is here shockingly damaged by darker intimations of violence.

Moving further west into British Columbia, we enter the territory of modernist mythmaking, with Howard O'Hagan's *Tay John* (1939), Emily Carr's *Klee Wyck* (1941), Sheila Watson's *The Double Hook* (1959) and Malcolm Lowry's *October Ferry to Gabriola* (posthumously published 1970). O'Hagan presents the colonial heritage of the Canadian West as myth, not in the American heroic mode but as a story of the disastrous consequences of progress for the Indigenous population, sometimes reminiscent of Conrad's *Heart of Darkness*, though closer in feeling to Farley Mowat's *The People of the Deer* (1952). Set in the remote Rocky Mountains at the time of land surveying and railway building, the novel emphasizes the violence of these colonization processes, while Tay John is a tragic hero out of Native myth who emerges as a miraculous child from his mother's grave only to vanish back into the earth at the end. But O'Hagan is a white mythographer, his hero is of mixed race, and the storytellers are all Europeans, so that Native myths are recast within a hybridized narrative mode, just as Tay John represents the clash of Native and

---

15 David Stouck, *As For Sinclair Ross* (Toronto: University of Toronto Press, 2005), p. 98.

White cultures in his own body and his life story. Likened by an American entrepreneur to a totem pole, he remains as unfathomable as the wilderness.

O'Hagan was virtually unknown in Canada till *Tay John* was resurrected in 1974, though Emily Carr's autobiographical sketches in *Klee Wyck* were immediately popular in Canada and Britain and won a GG Award for non-fiction. Her success is attributable to several factors, not least because she was already a famous painter (Carr was seventy when *Klee Wyck* was published), and because as a writer she had the devoted support of Ira Dilworth, the provincial director for CBC Radio, who became her editor, confidant, and literary agent. *Klee Wyck* presents an intensely visual celebration of landscape, exploring the mysterious poetry of the coastal forests of British Columbia and Vancouver Island. Carr saw Native culture and myth as the distinctive signature of British Columbia, though she always regarded herself as a late-comer from the European world, engaged in retrieving the vestiges of a myth-centered culture which was already lost. The Haida totem poles in her art stand as signposts to a holistic spiritual vision of Nature which she had to reconstruct in her subjective relation to myth as a modernist artist.

One enthusiastic reader of *Klee Wyck* was Sheila Watson, whose novel *The Double Hook* also celebrates the spirit of British Columbia, though Watson's territory is the dry upland interior and her stylistic affinities are with High European modernism. Acknowledged since the 1970s as Canada's first major modernist prose writer, in the 1940s and 50s Watson had great difficulty in getting her fiction published, and when her husband Wilfred Watson's myth-opoeic poems *Friday's Child* (1955) won the GG Award, she was still an obscure name with only two stories in print, a measure of the different status of modernism between the genres. Watson had been a schoolteacher up in the Cariboo region during the Depression, and that landscape became the setting for *The Double Hook*, begun in 1946 in Toronto, though Watson insisted that her imagery was not realistic but symbolic of the modern condition of spiritual alienation.[16] This extraordinary novel fuses influences from *The Waste Land*, the Bible, and Native legends about Coyote the trickster, for Watson finds the modernist aesthetic solution to confusion in the role of the artist as mythographer. *The Double Hook* was published in 1959, only to be greeted by most reviewers with bewilderment if not hostility. Oddly, it was nominated for a GG Award, though predictably MacLennan's *The Watch That Ends the Night*

---

16 F. T. Flahiff, *"Always Someone to Kill the Doves": A Life of Sheila Watson* (Edmonton: NeWest Press, 2005), p. 62.

won. When *Deep Hollow Creek* (written sixty years earlier and published 1992) was nominated for a GG Award, Ondaatje's *The English Patient* took the prize.

There is something subversive about the women prose writers of British Columbia, the third of whom is that ladylike figure Ethel Wilson, whose praise of *The Double Hook* stood out against the current of critical opinion in 1959. Wilson was in love with the landscape of British Columbia and saw herself not as a nationalist writer but a regional one. Her career as a published novelist began late; she was nearly sixty when *Hetty Dorval* appeared in 1947, and she adopted the post-war feminine persona of the well-off doctor's wife who took up writing as a hobby, though her correspondence reveals a long apprenticeship going back to the early 1930s, and after *Hetty Dorval* she published five more novels and short story collections, including her best-known novel, *Swamp Angel* (1954). This mild duplicity characterizes her fiction, for, like Jane Austen, whom she "read and re-read," the apparent decorum of her elegant narrative style and her domestic concern with women's lives conceal a disturbing awareness of contingency and the irrationality of human behavior. Her stories are filled with women who take risks, (Hetty Dorval, Topaz, Lilly, Nell Severance and Maggie Lloyd) in feminine versions of heroic quest narratives: "'We have no immunity and we may as well realize it. You won't be immune ever, at that lake Maggie' (nor anywhere else, thought Maggie. No one is.)"[17] That parenthesis is symptomatic of Wilson's style, where much that is seemingly peripheral slips inside the boundaries of conventional realism, as her novels shift almost imperceptibly into modernist territory of epiphany, symbolism, and mythic patterning. Wilson deftly positions her writing in a middle ground (a no man's land, but a woman's land) between realism and modernism.

The claim of that nomadic English modernist Malcolm Lowry to being considered a Canadian writer rests principally not on his residence (1940–54) in a squatter's shack at Dollarton, North Vancouver, where he finished his most famous novel *Under the Volcano* (1947), but on his writing about the coastal wilderness of British Columbia. His novel *October Ferry to Gabriola*, begun at Dollarton and unfinished at his death in Sussex in 1957, encodes Lowry's double vision, combining imaginative delight in the grandeur of the natural world with a tormented metaphysic in his homeless protagonist's quest through a modernist waste land. Lowry's legacy can be seen in Timothy Taylor's Vancouver novel *Stanley Park* (2001), a postmodern deconstruction of the wilderness aesthetic which paradoxically opens a space in the wilderness

---

17 Ethel Wilson, *Swamp Angel* (New York: Harper and Brothers, 1954), p. 206.

for the city's homeless, with the Park seen as "a living theatre of rootedness ... reborn from distant tragedy."[18]

By the 1950s modernism had become an unacknowledged presence in Canadian fiction, still largely ignored by the literary establishment but practised by authors themselves, from western Canadian writers to Ernest Buckler in the Maritimes (and beyond it, if we consider Elizabeth Smart's modernist hymn to erotic love *By Grand Central Station I Sat Down and Wept*, published 1945 in London but banned at her mother's request by Prime Minister Mackenzie King and not published in Canada till 1981). Like the westerners, Buckler had no time for self-conscious literary nationalism and his writing is unmistakably regional, set in the Annapolis Valley of his native Nova Scotia. Some of his stories belong to the oral tradition of the Tall Tale and their ironic humor and idiomatic dialogue may be compared with his fellow Nova Scotian Thomas H. Raddall's *The Pied Piper of Dipper Creek* (1939) which won a GG Award in 1943.

While Raddall remained committed to realism with overtones of romance and myth in *The Nymph and the Lamp* (1950), Buckler's best-known novel, *The Mountain and the Valley* (1952), is closer to Joyce's *Portrait of the Artist as a Young Man*, for his focus was on interiority and his superb descriptions of landscape and farming activities are filtered through the consciousness of his artist protagonist David Canaan (a name as allegorically resonant as Stephen Dedalus). The novel displays the aesthetic patterning of modernist art, highlighted through narrative structure, poetic language, and symbolic imagery. In a typically self-reflexive gesture Buckler shows his protagonist scribbling a story called "Thanks for Listening" in his notebook, though the novel he dreams of writing remains inside his head. That unwritten novel is written by Buckler, who is inside and outside his protagonist's consciousness, and who completes the narrative pattern by braiding together the novelist's art and domestic craft. In the 1960s Buckler continued to write stories, a second novel, and a memoir, and in the 1970s two collections of his work were published; these are supplemented by Marta Dvořák's edited volume in 2004.[19]

Up until 1950 Canada was one of the "white" countries of the British Commonwealth. Its image was that of an English-speaking nation with a francophone minority, and under the Canadian Citizenship Act of 1947 all Canadians were British subjects. Notwithstanding the fact that Canada's

---

18 Timothy Taylor, *Stanley Park* (Toronto: Vintage Canada, 2001), p. 194.
19 Marta Dvořák, ed., *Thanks for Listening: Stories and Short Fictions by Ernest Buckler* (Waterloo: Wilfrid Laurier Press, 2004).

population had included small ethnic minority groups since the late eighteenth century and larger urban Jewish communities, only with the influx of post-war immigrants did that traditional image begin to change. It was Jewish Canadian writers who first registered as a presence on the Canadian literary scene, with A. M. Klein, born in the Ukraine but brought up in Montreal, regarded as the founder of a Jewish Canadian tradition. Known primarily as a poet, Klein wrote one novel, *The Second Scroll* (1951), a modernist epic like *Ulysses*, representing a synthesis of Jewish and Christian cultural traditions. Mordecai Richler is the mythographer of Jewish Canadian working-class identity through his novels set in the neighborhood of St Urbain Street in Montreal, though Winnipeg's North End features in Jewish and other ethnic minority fiction.

Adele Wiseman, a second-generation Jewish Canadian born and brought up in Winnipeg, was the first woman novelist to write about the Holocaust and Jewish diasporic experience in Canada, and *The Sacrifice* (1956) was the first Jewish Canadian novel to win a GG Award. It follows realistic conventions in depicting the lives of poor working-class immigrants in Winnipeg's Jewish ghetto during the Depression, though its most striking feature is the way that social realism is shaped into the contours of myth as the Old Testament story of Abraham and Isaac is revised in a modern North American context. Wiseman's success was not repeated in her later work in the 1970s and she remains a somewhat marginal literary figure. It is worth mentioning that Winnipeg features in the first Ukrainian and Hungarian Canadian novels written in English: Vera Lysenko's *Yellow Boots* (1954) and John Marlyn's *Under the Ribs of Death* (1957).

Richler began publishing in the 1950s and went on to become one of Canada's best-known writers, chronicling Jewish diasporic experience through comedy and satire. He left Montreal for Europe in 1950, where he lived for most of the next twenty years. His first novel to attract popular notice was *The Apprenticeship of Duddy Kravitz* (1959) though it was actually his fourth. These early novels deserve more attention, for they sketch out the social and moral parameters of his later fiction. Beginning as an analyst of post-war European culture with *The Acrobats* (1954) and *A Choice of Enemies* (1957), Richler, like James Joyce, soon "returned" to the city from which he had escaped, with *Son of a Smaller Hero* (1955) and then more confidently with *Duddy Kravitz*. This reflects Richler's shift from the existential angst of wartorn Europe to the new prosperity of post-war North America, though the features of cultural breakdown are evident in both locations. Richler's versions of Eliot's waste land develop from the rather febrile modernist pastiche of *The Acrobats* to the carnivalesque satire of *Duddy Kravitz* with its trickster hero. Duddy personifies the ruthlessness of the new capitalist era, though the multiple dimensions of Richler's satire are most evident in his representations of St Urbain Street, where through a dazzling display of modernist fictional techniques he creates a textual space for this ethnic community on the margins of the powerful WASP majority culture. Richler wrote the screenplay for the 1974 film version and returned to St Urbain Street in his novels of the 1970s and 80s. Recursive patterns are evident up till the end, when, four decades after *The Acrobats*, he revisited 1950s Paris in *Barney's Version* (1997), his last novel.

As a supplement to the cultural nationalism so vigorously promoted by MacLennan, two expatriate writers, Mavis Gallant and Norman Levine, offer a more nuanced perspective on Canadianness at the end of the 1950s. Gallant, who left Montreal for Europe in 1950, settled in Paris. Levine, a Jewish Canadian from Ottawa, sailed from Montreal for England in 1949, following the opposite trajectory to Belfast-born Brian Moore, who emigrated to Montreal in 1948 and published his Irish immigrant novel *The Luck of Ginger Coffey* in 1960. In her two short story collections and her first novel published in the 1950s Gallant's own experience of being a Canadian in Europe is depersonalized in the manner of the high modernists, transformed into her ironic analyses of unhappy Anglo-American expatriates in scenarios recognizable from Richler's *The Acrobats*. *Green Water, Green Sky* (1959) reflects the post-war malaise in a peculiarly claustrophobic domestic form with its anatomy of a young North American woman's descent into madness in Venice and her incarceration in a private mental asylum in Paris. Gallant's fragmented modernist narrative perfectly mirrors the process of mental disintegration, where the borders between reality and fantasy become hopelessly blurred as if under water.

In apparent contrast, Levine gives a very personal account of his ambivalent responses to his native country in the mid-1950s in *Canada Made Me* (1958). Written in laconic Hemingwayesque style, Levine's record of his cross-country visit offers a kind of moral mapping which has striking parallels with Gallant's European analyses (and with Richler's as well), highlighting alienation and failure in a country enjoying a new era of prosperity. Focusing on the underside of city life, Levine pays attention to Canada's own underprivileged population in the immigrant communities of Ottawa, Montreal, and Winnipeg, the Displaced Persons from Europe (or DPs, as they were known) working in the Algoma mines, and the Native people whom he meets at the North Vancouver Mission. Like MacLennan he is "something of a geographer, an historian, and a sociologist," though he views Canada from a very different perspective. Levine's counter-narrative to the swelling tide of cultural nationalism was published in London, but not in Canada till 1979.

Poetry

To address the volatile situation of poetry in the 1940s and 50s, the best evidence is provided by the numerous anthologies, prefaces, essays, and poets' memoirs of the period, the annual poetry reviews in the *University of Toronto Quarterly* by E. K. Brown and Northrop Frye, together with editorial statements and creative writing in the little magazines produced by different groups in different places across Canada, which are arguably "the most important single factor behind the rise and continued progress of modernism in Canadian poetry."[20] Pratt, Smith, and Klein remain the most significant presences in the 1940s, all of them winning GG awards in this decade and Pratt again in 1952 for his epic *Towards the Last Spike*. As Earle Birney commented in 1949: "[T]he only living poet among us who sells half as well as a dozen second-rate Canadian novelists is Ned Pratt."[21]

However, this period also saw an unprecedented revival of poetic energies across the country, with young writers from Montreal to Vancouver committed to the modernist doctrines of making it new for Canadian poetry "in the revolutionary world of today."[22] Out of the swirl of divergent trends towards innovation and revolt against outmoded literary conventions, leading poets of the 1940s include the Montrealers Patrick Anderson, Ralph Gustafson, Louis Dudek, P. K. Page, and Miriam Waddington, westerners Earle Birney and Dorothy Livesay, also Raymond Souster from Toronto, while new names in the 1950s include Jay Macpherson, Anne Wilkinson and Margaret Avison from Toronto, James Reaney from small-town Ontario, and from Montreal Irving Layton (heralded by Frye in 1956 as "the most considerable Canadian poet of his generation")[23] and the young Leonard Cohen.

The significance of Montreal in the development of modernist English poetry inevitably prompts questions about the relationship between English

---

20 Dudek and Gnarowski, eds., *The Making of Modern Poetry*, p. 203.
21 Earle Birney, *Spreading Time: Remarks on Canadian Writing and Writers 1904–1949* (Montreal: Véhicule, 1989), p. 145.
22 Preface to *The Book of Canadian Poetry: A Critical and Historical Anthology*, ed. A. J. M. Smith (Chicago: University of Chicago Press, 1943), p. 3.
23 Northrop Frye, *The Bush Garden: Essays on the Canadian Imagination* (Toronto: Anansi, 1971), p. 70.

and francophone literature in this period, to which the answer is that they remained virtually distinct literatures in Canada throughout the 1940s and 50s. Only four Quebec novels translated into English appeared on the GG Awards list, two of them by Gabrielle Roy, whose sympathies were on the side of Canadian unity. Lemelin's humorous satire *Les Plouffe / The Plouffe Family* (1948/1950) deserves mention again as from it developed the popular 1950s Radio-Canada / CBC weekly television series, *La Famille Plouffe* (1953–7) / *The Plouffe Family* (1954–7), one of the rare cases of Anglo-French crossover in this period. (The cast performed episodes in French and in English on consecutive evenings.) It was only in the 1960s that translations of Quebec literature increased, thanks to the efforts of individuals like John Glassco and encouraged by the Official Languages Act (1969), followed by Canada Council funding for translations in the early 1970s.

Looking back to the debates about poetry and poetics in the 1940s, one striking feature is the extent to which they all shared the characteristics of an Emergent Nation syndrome, lamenting Canada's colonial mindset and, like MacLennan, wishing to see the country affirming its own national and cultural identity so as to take its place in an international context. Controversies arose as to how Canadian poetic traditions should be reshaped in breaking away from Victorian poetics and how best to articulate a distinctively Canadian representation of modernity, when modernism itself was a highly contested term.

A. J. M. Smith's influential anthology *The Book of Canadian Poetry: A Critical and Historical Anthology* (1943) might be taken as the flagship of the new poetics, for his Introduction laid out the main lines of debate for the decade. Smith, himself a poet and promoter of modernism since his McGill days in the 1920s, a co-editor of *New Provinces* anthology (1936) and a member of the *Preview* group, used his selection of English-Canadian poems from the end of the eighteenth century to the contemporary period to construct a pattern of development from "narrow parochialism"[24] toward a new international awareness, where Canadian poets are "importing something very much needed in their homeland" (p. 31). However, it was his division of modern poetry into a "native" and a "cosmopolitan" tradition which became notorious. He was attacked in print and on radio from East and West for his snobbery and literary colonialism, and later his "cosmopolitan" coinage was ridiculed by Miriam Waddington on the basis of first-hand experience: "My

---

24 Smith, ed., *Book of Canadian Poetry*, p. 31.

own word for it is not cosmopolitan but colonial – the very thing the *Preview* group professed to abhor."[25]

These arguments around terminology need to be seen in their social context, which is best reflected in E. K. Brown's GG Award-winning essay *On Canadian Poetry* (1943), written, like Smith's controversial Preface, while he was teaching in the United States, and echoed with variations in Birney's numerous essays and broadcasts. There was a general complaint about public indifference to literature, about publishers' negative attitudes and lack of government support for the arts (a frequent complaint made to the Massey Commission), while Brown emphasized the fissures in Canadian cultural life between centralist and regional agendas and between English and French Canada, ending his rather pessimistic account with a choice of Canada's master poets: Lampman, D. C. Scott, and Pratt. (No wonder that, when Birney characterized the "representative Canadian poet" in 1947, he described this composite figure as "three-quarters male").[26] Birney's analysis of the cultural climate immediately post-war was similar, though in his vigorous refutation of Smith's cosmopolitanism he spelled out a more positive future for Canadian writing: "Meantime the most cosmopolitan service a Canadian poet can do is to make himself such a clear and memorable and passionate interpreter of Canadians themselves, in the language of Canada, that the world will accept him as a mature voice, and be the readier for that to accept Canada as a mature nation."[27]

The role of the little magazines was crucial in providing a public space for new writings as well as theoretical debate and polemical argument about the relationship between writers and society in the 1940s and 50s.[28] Many were small-scale productions dominated by the agendas of particular editors or coteries, though two had their own presses (First Statement Press and Contact Press), and several survived for over a decade, profiling the multiple perspectives on modern poetry. In this brief summary I shall mention only the most influential or contentious, beginning with the *Canadian Poetry Magazine* (1936–68) published by the Canadian Authors Association, first edited by Pratt and then briefly (1946–8) by Birney. His ambition was to transform it into a

---

25 Miriam Waddington, *Apartment Seven: Essays Selected and New* (Toronto: Oxford University Press, 1989), p. 31.
26 Birney, *Spreading Time*, p. 104. See also Carole Gerson, "Field-notes of a Feminist Literary Archaeologist," in *Canadian Canons: Essays in Literary Value*, ed. Robert Lecker (Toronto: University of Toronto Press, 1991), pp. 46–56.
27 Birney, *Spreading Time*, p. 76.
28 See Ken Norris, *The Little Magazine in Canada 1925–80* (Toronto: ECW Press, 1984).

national outlet for contemporary work, and though he resigned in frustration with the CAA, he did succeed in publishing most of the leading poets of the 1940s: Pratt, Klein, Smith, Anderson, Dudek, Robert Finch, Ralph Gustafson, Livesay, Anne Marriott, Raymond Souster, Waddington, as well as early work by Fred Cogswell, Roy Daniells, P. K. Page, Al Purdy, James Reaney and Anne Wilkinson, plus four poems by Lowry, two translations "from the Eskimo,"[29] and some French Canadian poetry (the first English-Canadian editor to do so).

The second wave of modernism was represented by the two Montreal journals *Preview* (1942–5), edited by Anderson, whose preference was for "cosmopolitan" poetry, and *First Statement* (1942–5), edited by Sutherland, who argued for poetry with popular appeal and a measure of realism which he thought lacking in Canadian writing. Curiously given their different manifestos, many poets published in both, with even Anderson appearing in *First Statement*. In 1945 the two journals merged to become *Northern Review* (1945–56), which Birney the westerner argued should be called "Eastern Review,"[30] though by 1948 after bitter quarrels and resignations Sutherland was left in sole charge and remained so till his death in 1956. The west coast magazine *Contemporary Verse* (1941–52), edited by Alan Crawley though founded by four women poets (Livesay, Floris McLaren, Anne Marriott, and Doris Ferne),[31] reversed much of the gender bias of the eastern magazines, while publishing many of the male poets and the young Ontarian myth poets Reaney and Jay Macpherson.

New magazines in the 1950s, notably Souster's *Contact* (1952–4) and Dudek's *CIV/n* (1953–4) and *Delta* (1957–66), signaled a shift in the post-war sociocultural scene away from Britain towards the United States. Once again their literary manifestos declared that poetry in Canada needed a new start, this time energized by American influences, and in these journals the names of Black Mountain poets Charles Olson and Robert Creeley appeared beside more familiar Canadian names, as well as one significant new name – Leonard Cohen – in 1954, plus an eclectic selection of European and Latin American poets in translation. The shifts, controversies, and confusion of these two decades when Canadian poetry was reinventing itself as modernist and international, provide a context for the work of individual poets, many of whom started writing during or just after the war and continued as significant

---

29 Birney, *Spreading Time*, p. 128.
30 Ibid., p. 142.
31 Gerson, "Field-notes," p. 208.

voices into the 1970s and 80s, while a few, like Cohen, Page, Webb, and Avison, have continued into the twenty-first century.

Dorothy Livesay's poetic career stretches back to the 1920s, when her first collection, *The Green Pitcher*, was published in 1928, though as a woman poet with socialist and Communist political sympathies she was marginalized by the male modernist establishment and quite scandalously omitted from *New Provinces* (1936). However, she continued to work for left-wing causes and to write politically engaged poetry, served on the editorial board of *New Frontier*, and co-founded *Contemporary Verse*; in the mid-1940s her *Day and Night* (1945) and *Poems for People* (1947) won GG Awards. The much-anthologized title poem "Day and Night" is an excellent illustration of her social poetry of this period both in its themes and its technical skill. A passionate indictment of the dehumanizing effects of modern industrial society combined with a fiercely optimistic belief in the survival capacity of human emotions, this is a long poem in the modernist style. Its sequence of six sketches varies in form from blank verse to echoes of Negro spirituals to short rhymed stanzas with mechanical rhythms, while the various fragments are linked by the "night and day" refrain.

Her "Fantasia, for Helena Coleman" in the same volume is in contrast a very private poem of descent into the creative underworld, not unlike Adrienne Rich's "Diving into the Wreck." In the late 1940s Livesay turned to radio verse drama, the best known being *Call My People Home* (1950), a multi-voiced narrative chronicling the dispersal of Vancouver's Japanese Canadians after Pearl Harbor from the victims' points of view. These were followed by two new collections in the 1950s. Livesay's combination of a public political voice and a private lyric voice which she saw as the mark of women's poetry continued to characterize her later woman-centered poems, where she explored female sexuality and desire (from *The Unquiet Bed*, 1967, to her collected poems in *The Self-Completing Tree*, 1986).

Earle Birney, like Livesay, whom he had met when they were graduate students with Northrop Frye at the University of Toronto in the early 1930s, also started from a marginalized position, not because of gender but because of region, for he was a westerner. After serving in the war he settled in Vancouver, where he was a professor of Old and Middle English at the University of British Columbia till his retirement in 1965. He started the first department of creative writing in Canada and soon assumed a public voice defending literature on CBC radio. With his first collection, *David and Other Poems* (which won a GG Award in 1942), Birney announced himself as a landscape poet but of a very different kind from the Ontario Maple Leafers, for his long title poem in blank verse presents what Atwood in *Survival* called a narrative of "Death by Nature." In his vast Rocky Mountain landscape, where a young climber falls to his death, it is the fearsome aspect of the sublime which is emphasized through uncanny imagery of pointing fingers, claws, and talons, an apprehension of the otherness of Canadian wilderness which is also expressed in his later poems "Bushed" and "North of Superior."

"Vancouver Lights" invokes the Prometheus myth in a poem about the city's wartime blackouts, using landscape to script a political protest about Canada's involvement in a European war, while "The Road to Nijmegen," written while on active service in the Netherlands, again deploys landscape – this time one of manmade devastation – to articulate the terrible crisis of human values caused by war. Birney's endless inventiveness finds expression in his satiric war novel *Turvey* (1949) and his 1952 radio verse drama *Trial of a City: A Public Hearing into the Proposed Damnation of Vancouver*, which combined environmental concerns with Birney's democratic view of Canadian history, where the voices of an explorer, a pioneer, and a Native headman along with government ministers and a local housewife all give evidence at the trial. Birney's most celebrated poems belong to the 1960s and 70s (the concrete poem "ALASKA PASSAGE," "The Bear on the Delhi Road," and "A Walk in Kyoto"). His lively memoir, *Spreading Time* (1980), was reissued in 1989 as one of the most valuable accounts of the Canadian poetry scene in the 1940s.

Many of the writers in the Montreal little magazines published their first volumes of poetry in the mid-1940s: in 1945 Anderson's *A Tent for April*, Layton's *Here and Now*, Waddington's *Green World*, and in 1946 Dudek's *East of the City*, Page's *As Ten, as Twenty*, and Souster's *When We Are Young*. Anne Marriott, already well known for her long narrative poem "The Wind Our Enemy" about the 1930s Saskatchewan drought, won the GG Award for *Calling Adventurers* (1941), while Gustafson (who lived in London and New York till the early 1960s) had published *The Golden Chalice* in 1935, which was followed by his first modernist collection *Flight into Darkness* (1944).

Most of these poets worked in a variety of genres, writing novels and essays about politics and culture; several of them were actively involved in founding journals and editing anthologies, all symptomatic of a lively, slightly incoherent, emergent modernist literary culture. Waddington's description of "small enclaves of like minded people"[32] is perhaps a misnomer when one considers the differences in ideology and in concepts of poetry between, for example, Gustafson's "Mythos" and Waddington's lyrics, or between the urban realism

---

32 Waddington, *Apartment Seven*, p. 27.

of Dudek's "From a Library Window" or "A Street in April" and the streaks of surrealism embedded in Souster's colloquial verses like "Flight of the Roller Coaster." Of all the young Montreal poets of the 1940s Page and Layton have emerged as the most innovative and distinguished.

P. K. Page was already a familiar name in Canadian and American little magazines and the author of a prose romance, *The Sun and the Moon*, published under the pseudonym Judith Cape (1944) before her first volume of poems was published in 1946. Both the "cosmopolitan" influence of British and American modernists and the unique quality of Page's double vision are evident in "Stories of Snow" and "The Bands and the Beautiful Children," which figure the imaginative transformations of reality, while her concern for women's unspoken anguish shapes "The Stenographers," "Typists," and "Portrait of Marina," who "walked forever antlered with migraines" in Page's second collection *The Metal and the Flower* (1954).[33]

In both these volumes Page's characteristic imagery of vision is evident, for eyes are everywhere: eyebeams, glass eyes, empty eyes, mad eyes, eyes looking at works of art. For Page the border blur between the visible and the visionary is at the center of her art, facilitating the crossovers in her work between poetry and painting. She married Arthur Irwin in 1950 while working in Ottawa for the National Film Board, and when he became a diplomat she accompanied him to Australia in 1953 and then to Brazil, Mexico, and Guatemala (1957–64). In Brazil she discovered her vocation as a visual artist, and while she was in Mexico she made the acquaintance of the women surrealist painters Remedios Varo and Leonora Carrington. Some later collections like *Cry Ararat!* (1967), *The Glass Air: Poems Selected and New* (1985) and *Brazilian Journal: A Memoir* (1987) include her original paintings and drawings (under her painter's name P. K. Irwin).

Whereas Page's poetry fuses the visionary and the material worlds, Layton's is characterized by its celebration of the life of instinct and imagination and preoccupied with the questions of sex, religion, and death. Layton began publishing in *First Statement*, and his first volume, *Here and Now*, was produced by First Statement Press. Between 1945 and 1960 he published thirteen volumes of poems, the best of which were collected in *A Red Carpet for the Sun* (1959), which won a GG Award. Always a flamboyant and iconoclastic figure who set out to *épater la bourgeoisie* in his poems, polemical essays, and public readings, Layton believed in the poet's role as prophet, addressing contemporary moral and political dilemmas in verses which range widely

---

33 P. K. Page, *The Metal and the Flower* (Toronto: McClelland and Stewart, 1954), p. 48.

through satire and urban realism to erotic love lyrics, extraordinary animal poems, and poems about poetry. With his Montreal Jewish background (his mentor was A. M. Klein, just as in turn he would be Leonard Cohen's), Layton saw himself as a poet with a European sensibility, influenced by Nietzsche, Yeats, and D. H. Lawrence and then in the 1950s by the Black Mountain poets, but always at odds with Canadian puritanism and parochialism ("From Colony to Nation," "Paging Mr. Superman"), a stance he once described as a lover's quarrel with his country.

Among his best poems of this period are those celebrating the poet's craft and the powers of the imagination ("The Poetic Process," "The Birth of Tragedy," and "The Cold Green Element") and those illustrating his empathy with non-human life ("The Bull Calf" and "Sheep"). "For Mao Tse-Tung: A Meditation on Flies and Kings," which holds life and death, social satire and poetic ecstasy together in a structure of paradox, is emblematic of Layton's late 1950s poetry, and a line from it provided the title for his only GG Award-winning volume, *A Red Carpet for the Sun*. Layton continued to write prolifically, passionately, and controversially until the 1980s; he produced his autobiography, *Waiting for the Messiah* (1985), and was nominated for the Nobel Prize.

Northrop Frye's mapping of the 1950s poetry scene in his annual reviews for the *University of Toronto Quarterly* provides a pan-Canadian overview, though my selection of new voices is limited to five, four of them women and four of them writing from outside Montreal, a significant shift of gender emphasis and location from the 1940s. Only Phyllis Webb lived in Montreal, having moved there after graduating from the University of British Columbia and Birney's creative writing group; her first collection, *Even Your Right Eye* (1956), suggests a modernist poet's critical self-consciousness in relation to literary tradition ("Marvell's Garden") and her rather despairing focus on the contemporary world, "[k]nowing that everything is wrong" ("Lament"). Anne Wilkinson's voice is unmistakably feminine in her poem "Lens" from her second volume, *The Hangman Ties the Holly* (1955):

> My woman's eye is weak
> And veiled with milk;
> My working eye is muscled
> with a curious tension.[34]

---

34 *The Collected Poems of Anne Wilkinson*, ed. A. J. M. Smith (Toronto: Macmillan, 1968), p. 48.

Margaret Avison, also a Toronto poet, was already widely published in Canadian and American little magazines before her first book, *Winter Sun*, appeared in 1960, containing poems written over twenty-five years. Distinguished by their formal elegance, many of them enact the moment of active commitment to the creative process or the sad consequences of its refusal, with her sonnet "Snow" describing the positive choice as "a jail-break [a]nd re-creation."[35]

To end with two poets whose work is embedded in the mythic 1950s, Jay Macpherson and James Reaney, we note that both of them acknowledge the shaping influence of Northrop Frye's graduate classes on literary symbolism and myth. (It is also worth noting that Leonard Cohen's first book [1956] was entitled *Let Us Compare Mythologies*.) Macpherson, who had privately published *O Earth Return* (1954), won the GG Award in 1957 for *The Boatman*. Structured as a modernist poetic sequence in a dazzling variety of short verse forms and modeled on the biblical myth of the Flood, it ranges widely and wittily in its intertextual references across classical myths and the English literary tradition from Anglo-Saxon riddles through nursery rhymes and the psalms to *Finnegan's Wake*. Feminist critics have remarked on Macpherson's revisioning of patriarchal myths in a manner that prefigures Atwood's in poems such as "Sibylla," "Sheba," "Isis," and "Helen." Macpherson produced one later privately printed collection, *Welcoming Disaster* (1974), and the two sequences were reprinted by Oxford University Press in *Poems Twice Told* accompanied by the author's illustrations in 1981.

Reaney's poetry is, unlike Macpherson's, based firmly in its regional location of southwestern Ontario, where he was born and brought up, and Reaney writes out of that rural landscape with its folkloric traditions, transforming it into fantastic literary forms. He won GG Awards for *The Red Heart* (1949) and *A Suit of Nettles* (1958), and it is the latter which best displays his comic wit and erudition. Modeled on Edmund Spenser's *Shepheardes Calendar*, though full of playful allusions to his literary predecessors both Canadian and British, it consists of twelve eclogues (like Spenser's poem) cast in the mode of satire and caricature reminiscent of Chaucer's *The Parliament of Fowls* and *The Nun's Priest's Tale*, fusing pastoral conventions with references to contemporary life in metropolitan and small-town Ontario. Though primarily a poet, Reaney branched out as a playwright in the 1960s, winning a GG Award for poetry and drama in 1962 with *Twelve Letters to a Small Town* and *The Killdeer and Other Plays*, and in the 1970s produced his Ontario Gothic trilogy *The Donnellys* (1973,

---

35 Margaret Avison, *Winter Sun* (Toronto: University of Toronto Press, 1960), p. 17.

1974, 1975) and *Wacousta!* (1978).³⁶ He also founded *Alphabet* (1960–71), a journal devoted to iconography, the first issue of which featured an essay on myth by Jay Macpherson.

Frye's concluding remarks in his final poetry review for *University of Toronto Quarterly* (1959) may seem like an echo of MacLennan's statements with which this chapter opened, though Frye is a little more realistic in his assessment of a Canadian literature which is still in the making: "Poetry is of major importance in the culture, and therefore in the history, of a country, especially of a country that is still struggling for articulateness."³⁷

---

36 These are performance dates.
37 Frye, *The Bush Garden*, p. 126.

16

The Centennial

EVA-MARIE KRÖLLER

In 1967, Canada celebrated the 100th anniversary of Confederation and to mark the occasion, Montreal staged an international exhibition on two islands in the St. Lawrence, the Île St.-Hélène and the Île Notre-Dame. Expo 67 was to become the most successful of its kind in the twentieth century, praised for a "sophisticated standard of excellence [that] almost defies description."[1] Described as "a multi-sensory total-environment poem,"[2] Expo brought millions of Canadians and international visitors to a city said to possess such "verve and panache"[3] that citizens from the more remote regions were carefully coached in the media on how to measure up to the place. A microcosm of global competition, most notably between the United States and the Soviet Union and their satellites, an encyclopedia of the latest technological developments, and a compendium of 1960s popular culture, ranging from the campy exhibits of the United States to a "color-splashed display of Carnaby Street's mad-mod styles" in the British pavilion,[4] Expo 67 was also a unique opportunity to see important collections of art both traditional and modern, for which participating nations had all but ransacked their museums. The effect on Canadian visitors and artists was profound.

Expo 67 and the Centennial cannot explain everything about Canadian literature in the 1960s, but they are a useful springboard for this discussion, which, in its emphasis on aspects of the cultural institution, serves as a companion piece to the previous chapter with its focus on the Governor General's Awards. These chapters also share an interest in the development, through the 1940s, 1950s, and 1960s, of urban writing and the cosmopolitanism imported during the post-war

---

1 Ada Louise Huxtable, "A Fair with Flair," *The New York Times* (April 28, 1967), p. 18.
2 Donald F. Theall, "Expo 67: Unique Art Form," *arts/canada* 24 (April 1967), p. 3.
3 Mark Satin, ed., *Manual for Draft-Age Immigrants to Canada* (Toronto: House of Anansi, 1968), p. 62.
4 "Miniskirts Mix with Tradition at Britain's Bold Entry for Expo," *The Globe and Mail* (April 22, 1967), p. 11.

years into Canadian culture by refugees from European fascism. Authors writing in English and French who supported national unity, such as Gabrielle Roy and Hugh MacLennan, continued to play a central role even as counter-culture and Quebec separatism made their influence felt.

Expo's media too combined the traditional with the new. Interactive film was the most celebrated medium of Expo 67, but contributing nations devised educational schemes that drew especially school children into the displays of books, as a reporter for the Canadian women's magazine *Châtelaine* observed approvingly on a visit to the French Pavilion's *Musée des écrivains*, where buttons could be pushed to hear famous authors' voices.[5] By separating the amusement park La Ronde from the exhibition site proper, organizers further underlined the pedagogic seriousness of the event and their desire that the Exposition should be dignified and respectable (Pilotte, p. 58). This distinction had not always been successfully made in the sleazy "midway" ambiance of previous expositions, but now citizens were instructed not to expect an "ordinary fair with honky-tonk atmosphere," and they were told to dress formally for the occasion.[6]

The Pavilion of Canada proclaimed its own educational priorities by including "[a] reference library containing over 3000 volumes in English and French and in 26 other languages spoken and written in Canada."[7] As in other areas of Expo, the presence of both film and books underscored the confluence of the traditional and the new, rather than the wholesale replacement of one by the other. Canada's most celebrated scholars crossed the borderline between the written word and the cinematic medium with aplomb. Northrop Frye advised the makers of the National Film Board's experimental *Labyrinth* on the intricacies of the Theseus myth and then, after exploring the Expo site, planned to write his next book "in the fullest quest or labyrinth form."[8] The influence of Marshall McLuhan, whose book *The Gutenberg Galaxy* was published in 1962, was so pervasive in virtually all media that Expo has been called "McLuhan's Fair."[9]

---

5   Hélène Pilotte, Michel Monticelli, and Chet Rhoden, "Fête dans les îles," *Châtelaine* 8.8 (August 1967), p. 60. This magazine exists in both English and French editions, the contents of which are not always identical.

6   Vivian Wilcox, "What to Wear to Expo," *Chatelaine* 40.3 (March 1967), p. 55. Also see Eva-Marie Kröller, "'Une Terre humaine': Expo 67, Canadian Women, and *Chatelaine/Châtelaine*," in *Expo 67: Not Just a Souvenir*, ed. Rhona Richman Kenneally and Johanne Sloan (Toronto: University of Toronto Press, 2010 [forthcoming]).

7   *Information Manual Expo '67* (Montreal: no publ., 1967), Section 26, p. 6.

8   Northrop Frye, *The "Third Book" Notebooks of Northrop Frye, 1964–1972: The Critical Comedy*, in *Collected Works of Northrop Frye*, 31 vols. (16 vols. to 2005), (ed. Michael Dolzani (Toronto: University of Toronto Press, 2002), vol. IX, p. 87.

9   Donald F. Theall, *The Virtual Marshall McLuhan* (Montreal and Kingston: McGill-Queen's University Press, 2001), p. 126.

In her study of the Pavilion of Quebec, Pauline Curien includes a list of the books on display, the vast majority of them published in the 1960s.[10] Besides reprints of classics like Germaine Guèvremont's *Le Survenant*, Félix-Antoine Savard's *Menaud, maître draveur*, and Emile Nelligan's *Poésies complètes*, there are key separatist works that had appeared by 1967 such as Claude Jasmin's *Ethel et le terroriste* (1964, tr. 1965) and Hubert Aquin's *Prochain épisode* (1965, tr. 1967), along with Solange Chaput-Rolland's proclamation of disillusionment with federalism, *Mon pays, le Québec ou le Canada?* (1966, tr. 1966). The impact of this potentially seditious *salon du livre* may have been limited because its unfortunate location in the Pavilion made it difficult to find, but the presence of these books is symptomatic nevertheless, as is the way in which English-Canadians responded to their publication. Translation of Jasmin's, Aquin's and Chaput-Rolland's books was almost instant, and the 1960s publication list of any of the large anglophone publishing houses demonstrates that citizens trusted in books to help them understand the threat that separatism posed to the nation. McClelland and Stewart issued a steady stream of such works, ranging from 1965 reprints of Lord Durham's infamous *Report* (1839) and of Mason Wade's *French-Canadian Outlook: A Brief Account of the Unknown North Americans* (1946) to Peter Desbarats, *The State of Quebec* (1965), Marcel Faribault, *Some Thoughts on the Mounting Crisis in Quebec* (1967), and Richard Jones, *Community in Crisis* (1967).[11] Given the message of brotherhood devised for the Fair, the books displayed in the Pavilion of Quebec reflected the strains within the Canadian body politic with surprising candor.

Expo became an important stepping stone for writers who soon established themselves as some of Canada's most influential public figures. Métis poet Duke Redbird wrote a poem entitled "Indian Pavilion"; Michèle Lalonde composed the script for André Prévost's oratorio *Terre des hommes*, that was staged at the opening gala at Montreal's Place des Arts; Leonard Cohen – who released his first album in 1967 – performed at the Katimavik;[12] Hubert Aquin contributed a film to the cinema programme at the Quebec Pavilion; Nicole Brossard organized jazz and poetry events at the Youth Pavilion; and Margaret Atwood was the winner of the 1967 Centennial Commission Poetry Competition, one of the first in a long list of honors headed her way.

---

10 See Pauline Curien, "L'Identité nationale exposée: Représentations du Québec à l'Éxposition universelle de Montréal 1967 (Éxpo 67)," Ph.D. thesis, Université Laval, 2003, pp. 387–91.
11 See Carl Spadoni and Judy Donnelly, *A Bibliography of McClelland and Stewart Imprints, 1909–1985: A Publisher's Legacy* (Toronto: ECW Press, 1994).
12 Inuktitut for "meeting place," the Katimavik was an inverted pyramid dominating the Canadian Pavilion.

Several of these authors, however, sharply changed direction shortly afterwards. In 1968, Aquin refused to accept his Governor General's Award for political reasons, along with Leonard Cohen, whose explanation was a mixture of the personal and the political.[13] Poet Michèle Lalonde is now much better known for her poem "Speak White" (1968), originally composed for one of the *Poèmes et chansons de la résistance* performances but especially acclaimed for Lalonde's recital at the *Nuit de la poésie* in support of Quebec citizens, many writers and artists among them, who were arrested under the War Measures Act of 1970.[14] The poem draws disconcerting parallels between French Canadians' colonization by the English, the race riots in Watts, and the escalating war in Vietnam, and its topical urgency bears little resemblance to the idealism of Lalonde's verse for the oratorio. For his part, Duke Redbird became an important activist in Canadian Native movements, assuming the position of Vice-President of the Native Council of Canada in 1975, and obtaining a Master's degree in political science in 1978. Because of the significance of their careers as a whole, several of these authors are further discussed elsewhere in this volume, in chapters on forms of non-fiction, on poetry, drama and fiction in French, Indigenous poetry and prose, and multiculturalism and globalization.

The ambition of Centennial organizers to project a unified, globally connected image of Canada is reflected in the writing of the decade, but perhaps more importantly it is challenged in it. Thus, in their different and often contradictory ways, Expo and Canadian literature became laboratories of national identity.[15] Even under the spell of the festivities, Hugh Hood's enthusiastic "It's too much, baby; it's something else, total environment, Romantic synaesthesia, the way things are"[16] exists in contrast with more critical voices. F. R. Scott's poem "The Indians Speak At Expo '67," published in *Trouvailles* (1967), alludes to the candor of the Pavilion of Canada's Indians by combining the captions from exhibits in a "found" text. The result illustrates the exploitation of Native people by the white man, who "could not have lived / Or moved / Without Indian friends."[17]

---

13 See Mordecai Richler, "Êtes-vous canadien?," *The Great Comic Book Heroes and Other Essays* (Toronto: McClelland and Stewart, 1978), p. 23.
14 The War Measures Act was invoked in response to the kidnapping of British trade commissioner James Cross and Liberal politician Pierre Laporte by the independentist FLQ (Front de libération du Québec), and to the murder of Laporte.
15 This is Curien's expression in "L'Identité nationale," p. 27: "[Les expositions] sont véritablement un laboratoire de négociation des identités nationales."
16 Hugh Hood, "It's a Small World," *Tamarack Review* 44 (Summer 1967), p. 71.
17 F. R. Scott, "The Indians Speak At Expo '67," in *Collected Poems* (Toronto: McClelland and Stewart, 1981), p. 277.

Quebec *indépendantistes* too were inspired in ways that federal organizers had been eager to avoid. In the middle of the festivities, General de Gaulle of France, "ce géant arrogant, les bras levés en croix,"[18] famously proclaimed "Vive le Québec libre!" from the balcony of Montreal's City Hall. The Canadian government was quick to express its displeasure, but in *Le Cahier rouge* (2004), one of several books that describe the impact of Expo even well after the event, Michel Tremblay's Céline Poulin echoes the response of many Québécois when she declares herself both incensed and exhilarated by the General's nerve. Tremblay's intention, in describing a fictive transvestite brothel operating behind the scenes at Expo and its occupants' response to daily events, was to move behind the façade of an event that he now feels was "trop astiqué, trop poli" and therefore badly in need of some retrospective subversion.[19] One of his characters' favorite targets is Montreal's ambitious mayor, Jean Drapeau, who was instrumental in bringing Expo to his city and wanted its seedier quarters cleaned up in preparation. The result, according to Pierre Vallières's hostile view, was not the vibrant city celebrated in Expo commercials, but "une ville ... d'une moralité de vieille fille sèche et laide."[20]

In Oskar Matzerath fashion, Tremblay's story is told by a dwarf, who moves from waiting tables in a hamburger joint to playing hostess in the bordello, where she hands out "menus" describing the sexual specialties on offer. The daily variety show is entitled "Expo Follies," spelled with two *l*s to make "folies" look more English. A similar desire to puncture the smooth surface motivates Robert Majzels's novel *Hellman's Scrapbook* (1992), in which the central character finds a job at the amusement park after crossing "from the austerity of the pavilions to the crazy colours, streamers and balloons of La Ronde."[21] In yet another narrative apparently inspired by Günter Grass's *The Tin Drum* (1959, tr. 1962) and in parallel to 1960s Canadian fictions such as Aquin's *Prochain épisode* and Kroetsch's *The Studhorse Man*

---

18 "This arrogant giant, with his arms flung out," Michel Tremblay, *Le Cahier rouge* (Montreal: Leméac, 2004), pp. 23–4. The two other volumes in the trilogy are *Le Cahier noir* (2003) and *Le Cahier bleu* (2005). By fall 2008, only the first two volumes had been translated, both by Sheila Fischman, as *The Black Notebook* (Vancouver: Talonbooks, 2006) and *The Red Notebook* (Vancouver: Talonbooks, 2008) respectively. Unless otherwise identified, translations in the following are my own.

19 "Too slick, too polished," Caroline Montpetit, "Michel Tremblay: Les Dessous d'une ville propre," *Le Devoir* (November 20–1, 2004), http://www.ledevoir.com/2004/11/20/68971.html. Accessed 15 March 2009.

20 Pierre Vallières, *Nègres blancs d'Amérique*, 1968 (Montreal: Typo, 1994), p. 249. "A city [clothed in] the purity and morality of a dried-up, ugly old maid." Translation from Vallières, *White Niggers of America*, tr. Joan Pinkham (Toronto: McClelland and Stewart, 1971), p. 146.

21 Robert Majzels, *Hellman's Scrapbook* (Dunvegan: Cormorant Books, 1992), pp. 128–9.

(1969), David Hellman writes his account from a mental institution, where he has been placed following an attempt to burn his hands.²² Gifted with the ability to read the thoughts of others as soon as he touches their hands – including those of his father, a survivor of the Holocaust – he performs this act perhaps as a token of responsibility for the sufferings of the world: the self-immolation of a Buddhist monk in the Christian Pavilion's harrowing film *Le Huitième Jour* might have been his inspiration.

In elaboration of the "scrapbook" theme, Majzels's novel includes clippings from Montreal's newspapers, both in English and French, some of which are placed to conceal substantial parts of the text so that the reader must guess what is underneath. This insistence on probing below the surface of its media image is found in other comments on Expo as well. Several authors thought the theme of *Terre des hommes* and its symbols were wanting because they were not inclusive enough or even completely inappropriate for the times. Fernande Saint-Martin, art critic and editor of *Châtelaine*, suggested that "une terre humaine" would have been a better acknowledgment of those less privileged, including women,²³ and Hugh Anderson, the central character in Scott Symons's novel *Place d'Armes*, finds the Renaissance philosophy behind the exhibition so preposterous that he recommends "no one need attend it. One might call it World Without Man" because "it will show better, be seen to advantage even, on TV!"²⁴ The sharpest criticism came from an editorial in the magazine *arts/canada*, which focused on Alexander Calder's giant sculpture "Man" and asked: "What after all, in this 1967 world of mass communications, mass control and mass revolution, is Man, that we should be mindful of him?"²⁵

The buffed image that these authors deplore did, however, sometimes contain the potential of such energetic reinvention that not only fresh concepts but also new stereotypes were created in the process. Canada's identification with an inhospitable north, entrenched at previous international exhibitions, was one of the images that was modified. Although there were line-ups for the popular pavilions, even critical visitors remembered the site as a place where they "spent ... exhilarating hours simply strolling about,"²⁶

---

22 See Patricia Merivale, "Portraits of the Artist, *Canadian Literature* 140 (Spring 1994), pp. 100–2.
23 Fernande Saint-Martin, "Le Peuple de Montréal doit-il être sacrifié aux touristes? (éditorial)," *Châtelaine* 9.5 (May 1968), p. 1.
24 Scott Symons, *Place d'Armes* (Toronto: McClelland and Stewart, 1978 [1967]), p. 238.
25 "The editor's page," *arts/canada* 24.4 (April 1967), n.p.
26 Richler, "Expo 67," in *The Great Comic Book Heroes*, p. 116.

where many enjoyed their first "Baked Pineapple Canoe," along with live music, dance, and theater performances previously inaccessible to them, and where they were surrounded by all the amenities of a city but few of its problems. Futurist buildings like Buckminster Fuller's geodesic dome and Moshe Safdie's Habitat joined with the serenity of quiet canals and Venetian gondolas to create "a separate world where the troubles of life were left behind and where the mind could be set free to dream."[27] Expo paid due attention to Canada's northern dimensions, especially in the theme pavilion "Man and the Polar Regions," where visitors viewed displays on geology, meteorology, and transport and enjoyed refreshing blasts of simulated polar air,[28] but overall coordinators managed to create an almost Mediterranean atmosphere on the Expo islands.

The result was so effective that it permanently changed the appearance of Montreal: in imitation of the *terrasses* on the Expo islands, new outdoor cafés sprang up all over the city during the summer months, vividly described as a particularly appealing characteristic in American mystery-writer Kathy Reichs's *Déjà Dead* (1997): "When summer arrives in Montreal it flounces in like a rumba dancer" and "Life moves into the open."[29] For a bestselling popular novel like Reichs's book to select Montreal (or any Canadian city) as a setting – even if a map is included to be on the safe side – great changes had to have taken place since Gwethalyn Graham gambled with (and, surprisingly, won) the US sales of *Earth and High Heaven* by doing the same in the 1940s. Even as late as the beginning of the 1960s, the title of Phyllis Brett Young's *The Torontonians* (1960) about life in the suburbs was changed by its British and American publishers to eliminate the reference to Toronto, and in the previous year, Hugh MacLennan, describing the difficulties of "writing books about Canadians living in their own country," entitled one of his essays "Boy Meets Girl in Winnipeg and Who Cares?"[30] Along with the extensive changes to Montreal's cityscape during the 1960s in anticipation of a dramatic increase in population that then failed to materialize, Expo was a

---

27 Gary R. Miedema, *For Canada's Sake: Public Religion, Centennial Celebrations, and the Re-making of Canada in the 1960s* (Montreal and Kingston: McGill-Queen's University Press, 2005), p. 116.
28 *Expo 67: Guide Officiel/Official* (Toronto: MacLean-Hunter, 1967), p. 51.
29 Kathy Reichs, *Déjà Dead* (New York: Scribner, 1997), p. 15. Kathy Reichs is a forensic anthropologist, whose work is divided between the University of North Carolina and the Province of Quebec. See also the comments of Curien's informants on the ways in which Expo permanently changed the city, "L' Identité nationale," p. 323.
30 Hugh MacLennan, "Boy Meets Girl in Winnipeg And Who Cares?," in *Scotchman's Return and Other Essays* (Toronto: Macmillan, 1960 [1959]), p. 118–19.

major factor in creating an urban and urbane dimension to Canadian culture.[31]

Because the northern displays were not only a place of information but also one to cool off from the sunshine outside, they became incorporated into a southern ambiance that had little to do with the city's harsh and long winters. Elizabeth Hay does not write about Expo, but she formulates the paradox well through one of the characters in her novel *Late Nights on Air* (2007), for whom the north is a place of personal escape and refuge: "The North was the tropics made simple and cool."[32] Such individualized readings of the north ignore its identity as a distinctive ecological environment and home to Indigenous people, and Hay redresses the balance by focusing on the Berger inquiry into the effects of the Mackenzie Valley gas pipeline on the Native environment. At Expo, these blunt questions were raised in the Pavilion of Canada's Indians, for which artists Norval Morrisseau and George Clutesi had been commissioned to paint large murals and to which Duke Redbird and Chief Dan George contributed poems.

The Pavilion provided a thorough re-education on Native issues for some visitors, and in imitation of the Confederation Train and Caravans that took exhibitions of Canadian historical artifacts across the country, Native artists and activists created the "Indian Traveling College" to spread the message of the Pavilion further abroad. Several of the activities organized by Aboriginal people parodied or reversed official versions that left them out or involved them insufficiently. Fourteen Nova Scotia Mi'kmaqs, for example, paddled "from Cape Breton to Montreal to relive an 1894 treaty signing between their people and the Quebec Iroquois," that is, not with the purpose of commemorating the Centennial of Confederation, and they proceeded in the opposite direction to the celebrated Centennial Canoe Pageant retracing the traditional *voyageur* routes.[33] In addition to possibly offering a variation on the title of George Grant's *Lament for a Nation* published two years earlier, Chief Dan George's "A Lament for Confederation" (1967) is one of many parodies, by Native people and others, of the Canadian national anthem, concluding

---

31 See the exhibition catalogue: André Lortie, *The 60s: Montreal Thinks Big* (Montreal and Vancouver: Canadian Centre for Architecture/Douglas and McIntyre, 2004).
32 Elizabeth Hay, *Late Nights on Air* (Toronto: McClelland and Stewart, 2007), p. 162.
33 Pierre Berton, *1967: The Last Good Year* (Toronto: Doubleday, 1997), p. 48. See Misao Dean, "The Centennial Voyageur Canoe Pageant as Historical Re-enactment." *Journal of Canadian Studies* 40.3 (2006), pp. 43–67. The Pageant was the idea of Gene Rhéaume, first Métis Member of Parliament (1963–5) since Louis Riel, but the involvement of Native people in this event was minimal.

on the imperious prophecy "So shall the *next* hundred years be the greatest in the proud history of our tribes and nations."³⁴

Established authors co-operated in creating Expo's vision of harmony, at least to an extent. Some of these efforts were abortive, despite the distinction of the people involved. Robertson Davies, then the first Master of Massey College, was invited by the Performing Arts Division of the Centennial Commission to collaborate with regional playwrights on "a play that could be performed by amateurs across the country."³⁵ *The Centennial Play*, first (and apparently last) performed at the Ottawa Little Theatre in early 1967, was not a success, but at least it was staged. By contrast, *The Centennial Spectacle*, a *plein-air* historical pageant to be created on Parliament Hill by Tyrone Guthrie with the assistance of Davies, the composer Louis Applebaum, the poet Robert Finch and the playwright Gratien Gélinas among others, was cancelled before it ever saw the light of day. The official reason was that the event would have conflicted with the presence of the Queen, but one wonders if the prospect of "Britannia and La Belle France [being] hustled into the hold of a liner and deported" had something to do with the decision (Grant, p. 444).

In 1963, Gabrielle Roy and Hugh MacLennan, along with F. R. Scott, André Laurendeau and Davidson Dunton (co-chairmen of the Royal Commission on Bilingualism and Biculturalism), museum curators, scientists, and city planners, gathered in Montebello, Quebec, in 1963 to work out the details of the theme. *Terre des hommes* was borrowed from another writer, Antoine de Saint-Exupéry. MacLennan wrote promotional texts for the new Place des Arts in Montreal, scripts for CBC television specials on Expo, and the narrative for McClelland and Stewart's coffee-table book *The Colour of Canada*, as well as looking forward – mistakenly as it turned out once the reviews were in – to the publication of his novel *Return of the Sphinx* in the Centennial year.³⁶

In his Preface to the commemorative album, Expo's Commissioner General Pierre Dupuy views the discussions at Montebello as the communal composition of an ambitious "hymne à la grandeur de l' Homme."³⁷ Echoing Dupuis's

---

34 Chief Dan George, "A Lament for Confederation" (1967), in Jeannette C. Armstrong and Lally Grauer, eds., *Native Poetry in Canada: A Contemporary Anthology* (Peterborough: Broadview Press, 2001), pp. 2–3.
35 Judith Skelton Grant, *Robertson Davies: Man of Myth* (Toronto: Viking, 1994), p. 443.
36 Elspeth Cameron, *Hugh MacLennan: A Writer's Life* (Toronto: University of Toronto Press, 1981), pp. 337–8.
37 "A hymn to the greatness of Man," Pierre Dupuy, Preface, *Terre des hommes/Man and his World* (Ottawa: Canadian Corporation for the 1967 World Exhibition, 1967), p. 16. Joyce Marshall's parallel English version, steering away from a direct translation, renders this as "Here, with unparalleled grandeur, Man's noblest endeavours speak for themselves."

elevated tone, Gabrielle Roy cites Matthew Arnold, Saint-Exupéry, Georges Bernanos, Teilhard de Chardin, Shakespeare, and Shri Aurobindo, but her observations are interspersed with gritty descriptions of the manual labor involved in creating the "[a]cier, béton et verdure"[38] of the Expo site, and in translating into reality an engineering feat to rival the building of the Eiffel Tower for the 1889 Paris exhibition. Truckload after truckload of fill from the excavations for Montreal's new Metro system were transported across town to help create one of the islands for the Fair, as Roy recalls. These scenes were later given a burlesque turn in Tremblay's memoir *Un Ange cornu des ailes de tôle* (1994),[39] where the writer's family grimly decides they need not go to Expo because with never-ending hellish noise Expo has already come rumbling by their house, one pile of dirt at a time.

Roy, by contrast, is delighted with the result of these labors, and the undulating canvas covering one of the pavilions evokes for her, "par quelle mystérieuse association d'idées!," the "rencontre du Camp du Drap d'Or."[40] She does not further explain this allusion. Average anglophone readers of Joyce Marshall's translation that runs parallel with Roy's text apparently cannot be expected to understand that the "Camp" refers to an encounter of François I and Henry VIII in 1520 to confirm the friendship between their nations and to provide an opportunity for English and French to impress each other with their magnificence. In the English version, the scene reminds Roy "of all things, of that moment in history when the awestricken armies of England encountered François the First's troops on the battlefield, resplendent with the 'Cloth of Gold'" (p. 42).

Is it possible that Roy's emphasis on the splendor of the French, without due attention to that of the English, gives away sympathies not completely in keeping with this diplomatic context? Certainly, the rather free translation illustrates that – as in the *salon du livre* of the Pavilion of Quebec – Expo's conciliatory theme was sometimes tripped up by its educational mandate: despite the added historical information, there is little to indicate that *both* parties went out of their way at the "Camp du drap d'or" to display their prowess. Over Roy's protests, the original version of her Introduction was extensively revised by the publisher, removing many of the specific references and transforming her essay into a stilted humanist manifesto almost completely devoid

---

38 "Steel, concrete, parkland," "Le Thème raconté par Gabrielle Roy / The Theme Unfolded by Gabrielle Roy," *Terre des hommes*, p. 42.
39 Michel Tremblay, *Birth of a Bookworm*, tr. Sheila Fischman (Vancouver: Talonbooks, 2003).
40 "By what mysterious association of ideas!"; "Field of the Cloth of Gold."

of specific reference.[41] The accusatory self-irony of "Nous avons aussi dans notre composition nationale un peu du sang des peuplades indiennes que l'on n'a pas réussi autrefois à exterminer tout à fait" was clearly not welcome, nor were several other sharp comments about the "cent pièces du monde déchiré"[42] that organizers preferred to see submerged in Expo's happy mosaic.

The discrepancy between the French and English versions in Roy's text highlights a more general phenomenon. Organizers created bilingual signage that would reflect the recommendations of the Royal Commission on Bilingualism and Biculturalism (1963–9), but here too the difficulty was to locate an idiom that was completely parallel in the two languages. Expo was derided by separatists for its bastardization of the French language by coining such linguistically dubious creations as "Centre bilingual centre," "Centre validation centre," "Visit-visitez Expo" and "Support Supportons Expo 67," all evidence – according to the magazine *Parti pris* – of the determination of the "fédérastes" to play at speaking French and thereby entrench anglophone domination.[43] *Parti pris* editors were particularly bemused by instructions on rolls of paper-towels or on cereal boxes that provided unwitting separatist encouragement by asking users to "séparer" this or that.[44] With their strategic placements of pavilions to articulate the sometimes complicated relationships of nations, or parts of nations, to each other, the Expo islands offered a compact environment in which to study the connections between cultural identity and space. Like the product instructions, some of these connections were planned one way by organizers and read another by visitors. Thus, Hélène Pilotte, co-founder of l'Hexagone publishers and reporter for *Châtelaine*, perceives the proximity of the French and Quebec pavilions as a family reunion, and she considers it appropriate that the Pavilion of France should insert itself between Quebec and Great Britain, even if Expo strategists probably meant to underscore the proximity between all three.[45]

In the background of these political readings of the Expo site linger influential publications of the decade, *Les Insolences du Frère Untel* and *Nègres*

---

41 See François Ricard, *Gabrielle Roy: Une vie* (Montreal, 1996), pp. 426–7, for an account of this disagreement.
42 "And in our national make-up we also have some Indian blood from those peoples whom we never quite succeeded in exterminating"; "a hundred fragments of a torn world." Quoted from Gabrielle Roy, *The Fragile Lights of Earth: Articles and Memories 1942–1970*, tr. Alan Brown (Toronto: McClelland and Stewart, 1982), both quotations p. 204.
43 "Colonialisme quotidien: centre bilingual centre," *numéro du centrenaire: aliénation et dépossession*, Parti pris 4.9–12 (May–August 1967), pp. 19–20.
44 Pierre Maheu, "signe des temps?" *Parti pris* 4.9–12 (May–August 1967), p. 222.
45 Pilotte et al., "Fête," p. 60.

blancs d'Amérique foremost among them, both made quickly available in English translation. One of several Québécois texts illustrating that members of the Catholic Church were crucially involved in moving the Quiet Revolution along, *Les Insolences* (1960) was first published anonymously in the daily *Le Devoir* as Letters to the Editor. They were translated as *Impertinences of Brother Anonymous* in 1962, sold in thousands of copies in both versions, and were revealed to have been written by Jean-Paul Desbiens, a Marist brother and teacher. Desbiens became an educational advisor in Premier Jean Lesage's Liberal government based on the impact made by *Les Insolences*. Here, as in Chief Dan George's "A Lament for Confederation," the text originates in a parody of "O Canada," albeit an involuntary one. Proceeding from a compilation of the anthem as school children understood (or rather, misunderstood) the verse and bristling with epigraphs from theologians, philosophers, and literary authors, the book amounts to an ambitious social manifesto.

The target is a provincial educational system that, propped up by archaic religious principles and regulations, fails to provide students with the intellectually challenging academic preparation that would equip them for the modern world and ensure a firm sense of cultural identity. In particular, Desbiens attacks as a sign of decay the spread of *joual*,[46] a working-class French characterized, among other features, by its liberal adaptation of anglophone vocabulary. To encourage such language is to give in to "décomposition," he avers, and he cites Edgar Allen Poe's Gothic stories to underline the type of rotting he means. Although they use populist elements of the sermon, political oratory, and newspaper editorial and are famous for their polished wit, the individual letters making up *Les Insolences* consistently draw on the form of a rigorously developed *exemplum* to make their point. His pervasive irony notwithstanding, Desbiens never questions the standards he seeks to implement.

Although he dismisses Desbiens as a "fonctionnaire" (p. 56),[47] Pierre Vallières shares his rejection of *joual* in his book *Nègres blancs d' Amérique: autobiographie précoce d'un "terroriste" québécois*, published in 1968 by *Parti pris*, and available in translation as *White Niggers of America* three years later. Written in New York and Montreal jails, *Nègres blancs* interleafs Marxist analysis of Quebec's social condition with a narrative of the episodes in the author's life that have led to his current political convictions and incarceration

---

46 Jean-Paul Desbiens, *Les Insolences du frère Untel* (Ottawa: Éditions de l'homme, 1960), p. 24. The word reflects a mispronunciation of *cheval*. The term was popularized in the 1950s and 1960s by the journalist André Laurendeau, but was in circulation well before then.

47 Pierre Vallières, *Nègres blancs d'Amérique* (Montreal: Typo, 1994 [1968]), p. 56. Translated as "functionary" in *White Niggers*, p. 18.

for participating in a demonstration in front of the United Nations Building. Vallières explains that the provisional nature of his text is due to the haste with which the manuscript was rushed into print and the conditions under which he had to write it. In its unfinished presentation if not in the reasons he gives for it, Vallières's memoir resembles the meta-texts of international postmodernism that are associated with the 1960s, but its *bildungsroman* elements (family, education, sexual initiation) also draw strongly on the traditional Quebec imaginary.

Like *Les Insolences*, *Nègres blancs* abounds with literary allusions, but unlike Desbiens's, Vallières's reading is steeped in the classics of Quebec literature as well as its most recent publications: Gabrielle Roy, Louis Hémon, Ringuet, Claude-Henri Grignon, Marcel Dubé, André Major, Roland Giguère, Jacques Ferron, Gaston Miron are only some of the names that populate his book. He attacks the myths that have helped to entrench Quebec's enslavement and that are endorsed by invented traditions such as the cult of St. John the Baptist, patron saint of Quebec (p. 54). (His attack is prescient because rioting crowds decapitated the figure of the saint during a Saint-Jean Baptiste parade in 1969, resulting in the suspension of the event for the following twelve years.) Vallières is blisteringly misogynist both in the description of his own amorous adventures and in his dissection of female myths that he believes to have kept French-Canadian men in servitude to the Church and to capitalism. In an allusion to the *filles du roi* he claims that "plusieurs colons préféraient se faire coureurs de bois plutôt que d'être contraints d'épouser une femme qu'ils ne connaissaient pas et dont souvent ils ne voulaient pas, parce qu'elle avait mauvais caractère, était laide ou stupide" (p. 64).[48]

Claire Martin's chilling memoir about domestic abuse and the restrictions of female education, *Dans un gant de fer* (1965–6), provides an antidote to this aspect of Vallières's views. For both, however, coercive parents and educators are representative of an intolerably repressive society. Divided into "La Joue gauche" and "La Joue droite,"[49] in ironical allusion to the Sermon on the Mount, Martin's memoir has been called "le premier ouvrage explicitement féministe en littérature québécoise,"[50] and the author's rage at the brutality

---

48 "[M]any colonists preferred to become *coureurs de bois* rather than be forced to marry a woman whom they did not know and often did not want because she was ill-tempered, homely, or stupid," Vallières, *White Niggers*, p. 22.
49 "The left cheek," "the right cheek."
50 "The first explicitly feminist work in Quebec literature." Patricia Smart, "Introduction," in Claire Martin, *Dans un gant de fer* (Montreal: Les Presses de l'Université de Montréal, 2005 [1965]), p. 7. Translation in Claire Martin, *In an Iron Glove*, tr. Philip Stratford (Toronto: Ryerson Press, 1968), p. 81.

and bigotry inflicted on her in her youth leaps off the page even thirty years later when she writes about them. Unlike Vallières's ragged narrative and proletarian ideology, Martin's writing is polished and her social background shaped by "tout ce que la ville de Québec comptait de 'mondain,'"[51] but both authors perform personal and collective therapy through their writing. Without Martin's skillful irony, the descriptions of abuse she and her siblings suffer at the hands of their violent father would be unbearable, but the studied impartiality also makes them even worse because it reflects the lasting pyschological damage. To recollect one particularly horrendous beating that drives her to the brink of suicide, the author likens the escalating assault to a boxing match, and she hones texture and rhythm of her language to appalling finesse: "Deuxième manche: re-ballon, re-mouchoir et relavage des mains paternelles."[52]

Influenced by Colette, André Gide and Marcel Proust, Martin does not mention a single author from Quebec. She does deride Catholic arbiters of literary taste such as Henri-Raymond, Casgrain and Camille Roy for helping to make literature into another oppressive tool through which to control French Canadians in general and women in particular. The lack of appropriate books is the source of many of her grievances, and she considers it a crime not to provide an intelligent child with a well-sorted library. In Quebec and in English-speaking Canada, the reception of her work tested the established boundaries of literature in more ways than one. Accused of vengeful sensationalism by some of her critics, Martin's narrative nevertheless created an unprecedented echo among readers, who contacted her by the dozens because they identified with her account or even sought her advice for similar situations. As a result, this sophisticated memoir doubles as both a Gothic tale and advice column.

It also vividly illustrates, along with Desbiens's and Vallières's books, that traditional historiography and biography no longer adequately demarcated the field of non-fiction. In the absence of an appropriate category, Philip Stratford's translation of *La Joue droite* won the Governor General's Award for fiction. Unlike Aquin and Cohen, Martin accepted her award, but she did challenge another institution. Elected a Fellow of the Royal Society of Canada

---

51 "The very cream of ... society in the city of Quebec," Martin, *Gant de fer*, p. 162; *Iron Glove*, p. 81.
52 "Second round: punching bag, handkerchief and paternal washing of hands all over again," Martin, *Gant de fer*, p. 336; *Iron Glove*, p. 236.

in 1968, she resigned two years later because, despite her protests, RSC correspondence insisted on addressing her as "cher monsieur" or "cher confrère." It was not the symptom she objected to, she explained in her letter of resignation, but the patriarchal disease revealed by it, and so: "J'abandonne."[53]

The malaise of Québécois society and the threat of separatism were so pervasive during the 1960s that it is possible to forget that polarization along English and French lines was not the only form of diversity in Canadian society, and that there were members of the population and writers from different backgrounds and with different concerns. Mordecai Richler, on a visit from London during "our very golden Expo summer," barely recognized the city where he was born: "I rode into the city on multi-decked highways, which swooped here, soared there, unwinding into a pot of prosperity, a downtown of high rise apartments and hotels, the latter seemingly so new that they could have been uncrated the night before."[54] From the air or on the underground Metro, the class and linguistic barriers that have traditionally divided Montreal may have seemed obliterated, but to the careful observer they were still vividly present and had even been strengthened. In Roch Carrier's *Le Deux-millième étage* (1973),[55] the demolitions that preceded the building frenzy and the people displaced by them certainly provide an alternative view to the "cornucopia"[56] that spread out below Richler as he flew into Dorval Airport. Richler himself, however, is one of the foremost authors to have depicted Montreal's ethnic richness. In *The Street* (1969) he writes about the Jewish community of his childhood on Montreal's St. Urbain Street, a milieu from which he also draws in his novel *St. Urbain's Horseman* (1966). He evokes a richly diverse immigrant community previously described by A. M. Klein and, in Yiddish, by Chava Rosenfarb. "This is a third identity in the divided city," Sherry Simon has explained, "a buffer zone that defines itself in opposition to the polarized identities around it."[57]

Apart from defining itself in relation to the anglophone and francophone communities, this group is remarkable for its internationalism, and if Expo opened Canadian culture to global influences, there were citizens whose migrant backgrounds already gave them worldwide connections. Many of

---

53 Martin, "Lettre de démission de la Société royale du Canada," in *Dans un gant de fer*, "Appendices," pp. 638–9.
54 Mordecai Richler, *The Street* (Toronto: McClelland and Stewart, 1969), p. 11.
55 Roch Carrier, *They Won't Demolish Me!*, tr. Sheila Fischman (Toronto: House of Anansi, 1973).
56 Richler, *The Street*, p. 11.
57 Sherry Simon, *Translating Montreal: Episodes in the Life of a Divided City* (Montreal and Kingston: McGill-Queen's University Press, 2006), p. 60.

these links were formed out of bitter necessity and had little to do with the glib mottos of the Fair. Rosenfarb, an Auschwitz survivor, was born in Łódź, Poland, lived in Belgium after the war, and arrived in Quebec in 1950: she has described her reception in Montreal[58] "by ... the city's most respected Yiddish writers" and detailed the vibrant literary community she found in the city that was also known as the "Jerusalem of the North."[59] Following volumes of poetry and drama published in London and Montreal between 1947 and 1958, her book *Aroys fun gan Eiden* (*Outside of Eden*) appeared in Tel-Aviv in 1965. Other works, including translations, appeared in Syracuse and Melbourne. A similarly complex case is that of the essayist, short story writer, and journalist Jacob Beller, who arrived in Quebec in 1960, via Austria and South America, before leaving for Israel in the late 1960s. He too published several works in Yiddish in New York and Buenos Aires, as well as *Jews in Latin America* (in English) in 1969.

In Rosenfarb's story "The Greenhorn," the same words have entirely different meanings for Barukh, a concentration-camp survivor newly arrived in Montreal, and for his French-Canadian co-workers. His knowledge of French from having "lived in Paris for a while"[60] raises the young man in their esteem, but they do not understand, nor does the extent of his trauma allow him to explain, that his travels through Poland, Czechoslovakia, Austria, and Germany to "the God-blessed country of Canada" have been those of a DP, not a privileged tourist (p. 15). A mirror image of their wanderings, the survivors' language is a complex and confusing mixture of accents. In "Edgia's Revenge," Edgia's accent "contribute[s] to the continental ambience" of the boutique the narrator has opened in Montreal, but she resents the linguistic distinctiveness of her speech for "prevent[ing her] from becoming a new person" and so protecting her from others who might remember her collaborationist past.[61] Rosenfarb deliberately chose to write in Yiddish in order to preserve its role as "a vehicle of memory."[62] Along with other authors who have chosen not to write in one of Canada's official languages, her oeuvre belongs to an

---

58 See Chava Rosenfarb, "Canadian Yiddish Writers," Pierre Anctil, Norman Ravvin, Sherry Simon, eds., *New Readings of Yiddish Montreal / Traduire le Montréal yiddish / Taytshn un ibertaytshn Yiddish in Montreol* (Ottawa: Ottawa University Press, 2007), p. 11.
59 Simon, *Translating Montreal*, p. 90.
60 Chava Rosenfarb, "The Greenhorn," *The Survivors: Seven Short Stories*, tr. Goldie Morgentaler (Toronto: Cormorant Books, 2004), p. 4. With the exception of "A Friday in the Life of Sarah Zonabend," all stories were previously published in Yiddish between 1974 and 1994.
61 Rosenfarb, "Edgia's Revenge," in *The Survivors*, p. 104.
62 Simon, *Translating Montreal*, p. 93.

alternative, underground canon until it becomes translated. The transnational status of such writing could not be better illustrated than by the fact that the Yiddish original of "The Greenhorn" first appeared in an anthology entitled *Kanadish antologie* published by Yosef Lifshits-fond fun der literatur-gezelshaft baym Yivo in 1974, in Buenos Aires.

While the distinctive quarters of Montreal's Jewish population gave such travelers an instant, if not always unproblematic, community, other visitors to the city came to it precisely because it liberated them from previous connections. Their reasons could be sexual, as in Scott Symons's *Place d'Armes* (1967), in its full title *Combat Journal for Place d'Armes: A Personal Narrative*, in which the narrator describes his escape from conservative Toronto into the homosexual milieu and "the seethe of sound that was a seethe of people"[63] in Montreal, even if Ontario will follow him in the "blanched, blandiloquent, indelibly cubicle" shape of its Pavilion at Expo (p. 237). In imitation of the "old-fashioned journal and notebook" that the narrator finds "lying in the bargain pile on a gate-leg table" (p. 22), the book includes picture postcards, tourist brochures, maps, and newspaper clippings tucked into a pocket in the inside cover. Taking the technique of *mise-en-abyme* to extremes, Symons juggles several different narratives, telling the same story from different perspectives (and in different fonts). The resulting vision of Montreal is oddly paradoxical. As an expert in antique furniture and a connoisseur of architecture, Hugh Anderson scrutinizes Old Montreal with painstaking care, and the narrative contains one of the most consummately urban topographies in Canadian literature. At the same time the city seems mostly a pretext for his ego, one that, despite the graphic descriptions of sex with male prostitutes, looks like a museum display of furniture and architecture, and so contrasts with the intimate knowledge of the same milieu displayed in Tremblay's novels.

Much of the dialogue during these scenes is conducted in French, but here it is used to provide the privacy of a secret code. The book includes a map of Old Montreal with a personalized itinerary superimposed on it in red ink. This map outlines the gay district, and alternative names have been sketched in for various buildings to go with this new context. The narrative itself traces additional routes for the narrator's professional, name-dropping self, such as his lunches with "Lisette – executive secretary to the Head of Expo 67 for Quebec" (p. 233). The uproar with which *Place d'Armes* was received illustrates the conservative strains that continued to determine Canadian sexual mores. Three years before Symons's novel,

63 Symons, *Place d'Armes*, p. 17.

Jane Rule published *Desert of the Heart*, also controversial because its subject matter was lesbian romance. Here, the casinos of Reno, Nevada, assume the role of a safe zone where sexuality forbidden elsewhere becomes possible. In her later novel, *The Young in One Another's Arms* (1977), Rule, who had moved to Vancouver in the 1950s, located the setting in Kitsilano, a part of town then famous for its population of hippies and American draft evaders.

As refugees from the draft to serve in Vietnam, young American men poured into Canada "in the largest politically motivated exodus since the American Revolution."[64] One of them, the activist Mark Satin, edited the *Manual for Draft-Age Immigrants to Canada*, a publication that was so successful that it became a profit engine for the House of Anansi, with a total of 25,000 copies printed in 1968, the year it first appeared.[65] The *Manual* surveys the formalities of applying for an immigrant visa to Canada, underlining that "[v]isitors with long hair, untidy dress or peace buttons are detained more often than others."[66] Included is a commentary on Canadian schools, in which the University of Alberta fares badly because the "weather [is] too cold to make hippiness possible," the University of Manitoba is dismissed as "bland and square," and Brock University collects minus points for being "small-townish" (pp. 72, 73). Because of their cosmopolitanism, McGill University and Université de Montréal are given high rankings, as is the city itself, which "is a very exciting place to be" (p. 62) even if, in the year after Expo, immigrants are advised that they must expect an economic slump.

The book provides a brief list of literary works by Callaghan, Richler, Laurence, Cohen, Saint Denys-Garneau, and Dennis Lee compiled by Dave Godfrey as an introduction to Canadian literature, but the *Manual* itself has acquired cult status as a document of Canadian-American relations, in which the characteristics of the "ideal" American immigrant are outlined along with those of the culture ready to receive him. As Rachel Adams has illustrated, the draft evader becomes a literary figure and less-than-admirable character in such Canadian novels as Atwood's *The Robber Bride* and Richler's *Barney's Version*, and American ones that include Joyce Carol Oates's *Crossing the Border* (1976) and Valerie Miner's *Movement* (1982). In these books, Canada as a whole often functions as a blank space in which draft evaders live in exile, reviled by their own nation for their alleged failure to live up to its patriotic ideals, and

---

64 Rachel Adams, "'Going to Canada': The Politics and Poetics of Northern Exodus," *The Yale Journal of Criticism* 18.2 (2005), p. 409.
65 Atwood's *Survival* was another such source of revenue, as she relates in the Introduction to the 2004 edition of the book.
66 Satin, *Manual*, pp. 8–9.

eyed with resentment and suspicion by their Canadian hosts even as the latter "claim draft dodgers as evidence of national tolerance and resistance to US imperialism."[67] Billy, in *The Robber Bride*, exploits his Canadian girlfriend Charis's naivety, leaving her pregnant with their daughter when he returns to the United States. He turns informer to save his own skin, but later lives down and out in Washington. Some of this story may be one of Zenia's typical fabrications, but it helps to release Charis from his spell. No matter what the details of his biography, Billy is presented as a sponger on Canadian innocence and a moral poltroon.

Adams criticizes such depictions as declaring the draft evader's "political commitments ... irrelevant" and "undermin[ing] the seriousness of his protest" (p. 416). By contrast, the Canadian authors who write about him consider the threat he poses to their country the most important issue. In *The Struggle for Canadian Universities: A Dossier* (1969), editors Robin Mathews and James Steele identified one aspect of the threat by investigating the influx of Americans into Canadian universities. This, they argued, merely continued the previous colonizing domination by British scholars.

Other Canadians, thought that their country was too preoccupied with its own problems. Reading the newspaper the morning after General de Gaulle's speech, Tremblay's Céline is shocked to find that the headlines describing his performance have almost completely displaced the story of Black riots in Detroit, and she wonders about her compatriots' sense of perspective. Visitors to Expo, who saw in it primarily an opportunity to educate themselves, complained that there was not enough to tell them about political upheaval around the world. This was not a concern raised by visitors to the Christian Pavilion who were shown Charles Gagnon's haunting film *Le Huitième Jour / The Eighth Day*, mentioned earlier in connection with *Hellman's Scrapbook*. On the contrary, many found the merciless and wordless collage of images showing battlefields, concentration camps, nuclear explosions, and self-immolations too brutal to bear. The entire Pavilion "explicitly questioned Expo '67's declaration of hope that with more cooperation and more technology, the progress of humanity was assured" (Miedema, p. 174). Against the background of the sometimes horrendous world events and social revolutions during the 1960s, Canadian literature too acknowledged its international responsibilities and their implications for the nation's multi-ethnic population.

---

67 Adams, p. 431.

The books that did address these concerns tended to be marketed as sensations. In *Canadian Literature*, McClelland & Stewart and Macmillan promoted Jessie L. Beattie's *Strength for the Bridge* (1966), a novel about "[t]he shocking treatment of Japanese Canadians during the last war ... described in vivid detail," and Charles E. Israel's *Shadows on a Wall* (1965), a book about "[t]he Brandons, an intelligent, sophisticated couple [who] suffer bitter conflict provoked by their adoption of a teenaged Negro girl."[68] Publishers' advertisements are rarely a reliable way to judge a book, but, in their clichéd language and plots, the novels themselves prove only too clearly how radical (and delayed) a book Joy Kogawa's *Obasan* (1981) really was. A more cogent discussion of racial issues occurs in a response, also in *Canadian Literature*, by the Jamaican poet and scholar Lloyd W. Brown to a review of Austin Clarke's *The Meeting Point* (1967). Challenging Miriam Waddington's criticism that the tone was too strident and the problems depicted artificial, Brown alleges that her judgments are informed by racial cliché and an escapist desire for universalism. His views are not free of sexual and ethnic stereotypes either, but the rebuttal is nevertheless significant, especially as it complicates the parallels that might, or might not, be drawn between the situation of two marginalized groups, Blacks and Jews.[69] "Negro visitors" to Expo were assured that they would not have to suffer discrimination, but it is revealing that such clarifications had to be issued in the first place.[70]

Postcolonialism and Canadians' involvement in organizations like CUSO (Canadian University Services Organization) resulted in a number of books about Africa. Among these, Dave Godfrey's *The New Ancestors* (1970), a novel set in "Lost Coast," a fictional country modeled on Nkrumah's Ghana, was the most acclaimed.[71] Told in a variety of competing narratives, the book tells the story of Michael Burdener, who has redefined Rudyard Kipling's notion of "the white man's burden" to mean the obligation to spread rebellion among the citizens of Lost Coast. Notebook entries, newspaper articles, letters, and the transcript of a lecture all combine to make Burdener's persona increasingly elusive even as they make his ideology more precise. The author further undermines conventional character development when he delays the "genealogy" of

---

68 *Canadian Literature* 28 (Spring 1966), 24 (Spring 1965), inside covers.
69 Lloyd W. Brown, "Austin Clarke in Canadian Reviews," *Canadian Literature* 38 (Autumn 1968), pp. 101–4.
70 "Negroes assured on Expo housing," *The New York Times* (March 22, 1967), p. 2.
71 Given Expo's theme, it is worth pointing out that Godfrey was also co-editor, with Bill McWhinney, of a collection of volunteers' memoirs, ominously entitled *Man Deserves Man: CUSO in Developing Countries* (Toronto: Ryerson Press, 1968).

the characters and Burdener's place among them almost a hundred pages into the book, in the medical file documenting his mother-in-law's mental illness. Burdener ("white, personal acquaintance")[72] is married to an African woman, whose own mother is the daughter of a woman "of good [African] lineage" and a "Canadian sailor ... possible deserter" (p. 90).

Throughout, sexual exploitation mirrors colonialism and neo-colonialism, and the British and Americans are equally censored for the imperialist arrogance they direct at Africans, and at "those cautious little Canadians" who look after "all essential affairs" (p. 17). Burdener rouses his students to "steal [the colonizer's] tricks for [their] society" (p. 161). In incorporating non-English vocabulary and refusing to explain it, *The New Ancestors* employs a classic postcolonial strategy. Godfrey's "A Note on the Missing Glossary" elaborates that he "wanted to point out to scholars the clear gaps ... in the libraries they have helped form." In a reminder of the letter-writing campaigns that were both art form and activist tool of counter-culture, the author does offer to mail "a set of the author's notes" if required, in return for postage (p. 444).

Margaret Laurence's books about Africa are not associated with CUSO, but her translation of Somali tales and poems, *A Tree for Poverty* (1954), was reprinted in 1970 for the use of Peace Corps volunteers. Her novel *This Side Jordan* (1960), the memoir-travelogue *The Prophet's Camel Bell* (1963), the stories collected in *The Tomorrow-Tamer* (1963), and a study of Nigerian writers, *Long Drums and Cannons* (1968), must be mentioned here as well. The liberal humanism that informs Laurence's experience, even as she cites postcolonial critics like O. Mannoni, has led some critics to fault her for seeking to establish universal understanding where none is to be had. At the same time, Laurence's faith in human communication, no matter what the cultural barriers, is tempered by her persistent self-scrutiny and by the layered irony with which she recounts her "Very Best Intentions," as one of her essays in *Heart of a Stranger* (1976)[73] has it, in dealing with cultures that she is not adquately equipped to comprehend, linguistically or otherwise.

Writing about Africa was also writing about Canada and its experience of colonialism, Laurence explains in an essay written in honor of George Woodcock.[74] The question of what analogies are appropriate between

---

72 Dave Godfrey, *The New Ancestors* (Toronto: New Press, 1972), p. 93.
73 Margaret Laurence, "The Very Best Intentions," in *Heart of a Stranger* (Toronto: McClelland and Stewart, 1976), pp. 33–43.
74 "Ivory Tower or Grassroots?: The Novelist as Sociopolitical Being," in *A Political Art: Essays and Images in Honour of George Woodcock*, ed. W. H. New (Vancouver: University of British Columbia Press, 1978), p. 17.

disenfranchized groups has been raised by critics who have taken a new look at some of the key texts of the Centennial decade. Thus, George Elliott Clarke surveys instances where Quebec intellectuals have equated their colonization with the lot of Black people, especially Vallières and Lalonde in *Nègres blancs d'Amérique* and "Speak White" respectively, but also Hubert Aquin in *Trou de mémoire* (1969). Clarke is restrained in his criticism, but his characterization of Vallières's book as a "splenetic *cri-du-cœur*" suggests that his observations are not entirely complimentary.[75] For its exclusive emphasis on the Québécois population despite a society rich in diverse ethnic groups, "Speak White" has furthermore been the target of Italian Canadian poet Marco Micone, who renamed the poem "Speak What,"[76] rewriting the original to reflect his own immigrant experience and the new literatures and languages that have shaped his imagination. The tone is as bitter and accusatory as that of "Speak White," but now it is the former victims who have slipped into the skin of the oppressors and "sound like them more and more" (p. 14). Neil ten Kortenaar's chapter in this volume looks at such "revisions" in the context of multiculturalism and globalization.

The dual task of defining Canadian culture for the Centennial and opening it up to the world created a multitude of problems and questions that resonated well after the 1960s. Woodcock, editor of the first scholarly magazine devoted to Canadian literature in 1959, endeavored to establish standards of excellence that would guarantee respect. Alongside full-page displays of poems by Ralph Gustafson or A. J. M. Smith sponsored by the Hudson's Bay Company, early issues of the magazine characterized Northrop Frye as "The Kant of Criticism," printed reviews of authors who had nothing to do with Canadian literature (G. B. Shaw, the Pre-Raphaelites), advertised books by Robert Graves and Arnold Bennett, featured letters by Naïm Kattan from Montreal ("une ville internationale"), by Robert McCormack from Toronto, and by D. A. Cameron from London, and dealt firmly with Phyllis Brett Young's *The Torontonians* as belonging to "women's magazine fiction," therefore as negligible despite its success.[77]

The earnest tone of culture-defining in *Canadian Literature* has its comic but no less forceful counterpart in Mordecai Richler's frequent sallies against "Maple Leaf Culture Time." This is the heading under which he collected

---

75 George Elliott Clarke, *Odysseys Home: Mapping African-Canadian Literature* (Toronto: University of Toronto Press, 2002), p. 165f.
76 Marco Micone, *Speak What*, with an analysis by Lise Gauvin (Montreal: vlb éditeur, 2001 [1989]).
77 Robert McCormack, "Letter from Toronto," *Canadian Literature* 7 (Winter 1961), pp. 54–8.

his responses to the various initiatives – by the Canada Council, the Canadian Authors Association, and the editors of monumental reference works like the *Oxford Companion to Canadian History and Literature* (1967) – toward fostering a well-documented and funded Canadian literature. Such activities would have the reverse effect, he suggested, and lead to parochialism instead of promoting a culture worth its salt.[78] By the early 1970s at the latest, such views had become intolerable to nationalist critics, who accused Richler of viewing Canada from an expatriate's perspective, of not pulling his weight in creating a homegrown, independent culture, and of not even paying the targets of his criticism the compliment of getting his facts right.[79] With Atwood's *Survival* (1972), no matter how strong the irony infusing that volume, the pendulum swung toward a preoccupation with Canadian themes, a tendency that was challenged soon enough in Frank Davey's influential essay "Surviving the Paraphrase," first delivered as a lecture in 1974.[80]

Among the more spectacular exhibits at Expo's Dutch Pavilion was an enormous book, measuring ten by twelve feet. The pages were turned automatically, showing licenses for Dutch-Canadian marriages, poems by children whose parents had explained the role of Canadians in the liberation of the Netherlands to them, and letters exchanged between citizens of the two countries.[81] Like many books of the Centennial decade, this one too incorporates a multitude of genres and media to formulate its theme. It is a technical novelty, as well as a traditional medium. It is a book of reckoning, a collective memoir, a dialogue, a manifesto, a partnership agreement, and a romance. To a nation sometimes shaken to its roots by civic and global conflict, books were still a place to look up the questions, if not always find the answers.[82]

---

78 See Richler, "Maple Leaf Culture Time," "Êtes-vous canadien?", "Expo 67," *The Great Comic Book Heroes*, pp. 15–20, 21–6, 104–18.
79 Donald Cameron, "Don Mordecai and the Hardhats," *Canadian Forum* (March 1972), pp. 29–33.
80 See Frank Davey, *Surviving the Paraphrase: Eleven Essays on Canadian Literature* (Winnipeg: Turnstone Press, 1983).
81 Pilotte *et al.*, "Fête," p. 60.
82 With thanks to Réjean Beaudoin, André Lamontagne, Janice Fiamengo, Monika Kin Gagnon, and Goldie Morgentaler for scholarly advice.

17

Forms of non-fiction: Innis, McLuhan, Frye, and Grant

DAVID STAINES

In one of his final interviews, Herbert Marshall McLuhan (1911–80) reflected on the people who had strongly influenced him. Harold Adams Innis (1894–1952), McLuhan claimed, "is the only man since the beginning of literacy 2,400 years ago who ever studied the effects of technology, and I think that is an amazing thing in view of the numbers of great minds that had this opportunity. He's the only human being that ever studied the effects of literacy on the people who were literate."[1]

Harold Innis

A rural southwestern Ontarian by birth and upbringing, Innis graduated from McMaster University in History and Political Economy (BA, 1916), then enlisted and was sent overseas; the war in Europe was, for him, a deeply moral cause. "If I had no faith in Christianity I don't think I would go, but it is as He said, you must desert everything take up the cross and follow me," he wrote to his sister.[2] The experience of the horrors of war, however, left him an avowed agnostic, robbing him of his Baptist faith and his plan to become a preacher.

Innis returned to McMaster for his master's degree in Political Economy (1918), then went to the University of Chicago for his doctorate (1920). Under his supervisor, the economic historian Chester Whitney Wright, he wrote as his thesis, "A History of the Canadian Pacific Railway." Although employment offers came his way, he declined these "on a chance that a Canadian university will send in an application."[3] He accepted a position in the Department of

---

[1] Marshall McLuhan, "Violence as a Quest for Identity," *Understanding Me*, ed. Stephanie McLuhan and David Staines (Toronto: McClelland and Stewart, 2003), p. 273.
[2] From the Innis Family Papers, University of Toronto Archives, letter to his sister and all, April 4, 1916.
[3] Ibid., letter to his mother and all, February 6, 1920.

Political Economy at the University of Toronto in 1920, where he became the first Canadian Head of the Department in 1937 and the first Dean of the School of Graduate Studies in 1947, two positions he held until his death from cancer just after his fifty-eighth birthday.

In his first book, *A History of the Canadian Pacific Railway* (1923), an expanded version of his thesis, Innis employed charts, statistics, and a linear narrative to map the growth of a Canadian transcontinental railway, showing in the course of its development that the patterns of transportation must have existed in the country before the arrival of the railroad. A strong railway system reveals the country's underlying unity: "Canada was a geographic and economic unit. He saw, what now seems so obvious, that the geographic lines of the country were as much east-west as they were north-south."[4] And it is this unity that remains central in the author's mind.

The book's concluding chapter begins:

> The history of the Canadian Pacific Railway is primarily the history of the spread of western civilization over the northern half of the North American continent. The addition of technical equipment described as physical property of the Canadian Pacific Railway Company was a cause and an effect of the strength of that civilization. The construction of the road was the result of the direction of energy to the conquest of geographic barriers. The effects of the road were measured to some extent by the changes in the strength and character of that civilization in the period following its construction.[5]

In these words, Innis was already laying out plans for his subsequent studies of the fur trade and fisheries that reveal how Canada's lines of communication have been first constructed by the people who used the country's natural river systems prior to the coming of the railroad.

In *The Fur Trade in Canada* (1930), subtitled "An Introduction to Canadian Economic History," Innis explains in his Preface that "[a]n interest in this subject has followed from a study on the Canadian Pacific Railway. A sense of the incompleteness of that volume and of all volumes which have centered on the subject and on the subject of Canadian confederation is the occasion for this work."[6] Arising, then, from his railway study and adopting the same exhaustive patterns of charts, statistics, and a linear narrative, the new book

---

4 Ramsay Cook, *The Maple Leaf Forever: Essays on Nationalism and Politics on Canada* (Toronto: Macmillan, 1971), p. 145.
5 Harold A. Innis, *A History of the Canadian Pacific Railway* (Toronto: McClelland and Stewart, 1923), p. 287.
6 Harold A. Innis, *The Fur Trade in Canada: An Introduction to Canadian Economic History* (New Haven: Yale University Press, 1930).

shows dramatically that the routes established by the fur trappers mark the general routes of subsequent travel. And he demonstrates that a British economic model, which highlights the price and quantity of trade goods, was unsuitable for a new country like Canada, whose economic problems, like those of any young country, cannot be wholly defined by a study of the economics of older countries.

Consequently, Innis developed his theory of staples or raw materials: "Staples illuminated the ties between government, business, and society, and consequently linked economics to geography, political science, and sociology. And it tied all of them to the study of Canadian history."[7] Canada grew up, Innis shows, providing a series of staples, for example fur and fish, for the imperial centre. And as the trading centres became centralized, the staples led to monopolies, for example, the Hudson's Bay Company, the imprint of the staple leaving its own lasting impact on the economic development of the young country.

In his conclusion to *The Fur Trade in Canada*, Innis asserts:

> The most promising source of early trade was found in the abundance of fish, especially cod, to be caught off the Grand Banks of Newfoundland and in the territory adjacent to the Gulf of St. Lawrence. The abundance of cod led the peoples concerned to direct all their available energy to the prosecution of the fishing industry which developed extensively.[8]

For the next ten years, Innis plotted the development of an international trade in codfish from 1497 until 1936. The result of his research was *The Cod Fisheries* (1940), appropriately subtitled "The History of an International Economy." From his seminal work on the fur trade within Canada, he now mapped, once again with charts, statistics, and a linear narrative, how cod created a society that was diverse and decentralized; indeed, the story of the fisheries offered evidence that Canada was a country of distinct economics, distinct interests, and distinct needs. The book proves that "Ottawa's needs were not greater than those of Canada's constituent parts."[9]

With its linear story moving from the French, Spanish, and English centers to the rise of the economies of the Atlantic provinces and finally to the Post-Confederation tariffs that penalized these once-prosperous provinces, *The Cod Fisheries* is the "international" account of economic rivalries that expands

---

7 William Westfall, "The Ambivalent Verdict: Harold Innis and Canadian History," *Culture, Communication, and Dependency: The Tradition of H. A. Innis*, ed. William H. Melody, Liora Salter, and Paul Heyer (Norwood, NJ: Ablex Publishing, 1981), p. 39.
8 Innis, *The Fur Trade in Canada*, p. 387.
9 Barry M. Gough, "Innis Update," *The London Journal of Canadian Studies* 2 (1985), p. 8.

Innis's fur trade boundaries to encompass the United States and Europe. *A History of the Canadian Pacific Railway*, *The Fur Trade in Canada*, and *The Cod Fisheries* form a trilogy that maps the growth of a young country through its transportation systems and its staples of fur and fish. Canada was no longer an artificial construct that came into being by accident; it was a natural community based on geographic and economic lines. The country, Innis often stated, "emerged not in spite of geography but because of it."[10]

In his final three books, *Empire and Communications* (1950), *The Bias of Communication* (1951), and *Changing Concepts of Time* (1952), now regarded as the forerunners of communication studies,[11] Innis turned "from the trade-routes of the external world to the trade-routes of the mind,"[12] concentrating on the packaging of information in societies from ancient Egypt to the present day and exploring the interconnections between the durability of empires and the forms of communication that sustained them. By focusing on the impact of communications on the stability of empires, his final researches further explained the patterns of economic growth in Canada and other civilizations.

In his later work Innis grew increasingly aphoristic. "[T]heir opacity, their maddening obscurity, their elliptical quality," James W. Carey proclaims,[13] and Ronald B. Hatch observes, "With its piling up of details, Innis's prose often presents readers with difficulties, and the later books are especially cryptic. In his aphoristic style, he appears to be struggling to evade the constraints of his own medium, the printed word."[14] For Marshall McLuhan, however, the style reflected Innis's thinking:

> the later Innis inevitably adopted a discontinuous style, an aphoristic, mental-camera sort of procedure which was indispensable to his needs. For in his later prose the linear development of paragraph perspectives is abandoned

---

10 Innis, *The Fur Trade in Canada*, p. 397. For an overview of Innis's work as an historian, see Carl Berger, *The Writing of Canadian History: Aspects of English-Canadian Historical Writing 1900–1970* (Toronto: Oxford University Press, 1976), pp. 85–111. For Innis's philosophy, see Harold A. Innis, *Staples, Markets, and Cultural Change*, ed. Daniel Drache (Montreal and Kingston: McGill-Queen's University Press, 1995), pp. xiii–lv, and James Bickerton, Stephen Brooks, and Alain-G. Gagnon, *Freedom, Equality, Community: The Political Philosophy of Six Influential Canadians* (Montreal and Kingston: McGill-Queen's University Press, 2006), pp. 14–34.
11 For a full account of Innis as a communications theorist, see Paul Heyer, *Harold Innis* (Lanham: Rowman and Littlefield, 2003).
12 Marshall McLuhan, "The Later Innis," *Queen's Quarterly* 60 (1953), p. 385.
13 James W. Carey, "Culture, Geography, and Communications: The Work of Harold Innis in an American Context," in Melody et al., eds., *Culture, Communication, and Dependency*, p. 73.
14 "Harold Adams Innis," *Encyclopedia of Literature in Canada*, ed. W. H. New (Toronto: University of Toronto Press, 2002), pp. 527–8.

almost entirely in favour of the rapid montage of single shots ... This prose calls for steady contemplation of what is happening on the page. It is not intended to deliver an idea or a concept in a formula or in a package.[15]

And in 1980 Herman Northrop Frye (1912–91) confessed his own ignorance at the time of Innis's achievement: "It is no great credit to me that I entirely missed the significance, at the time, of the later work of Harold Innis, which appeared around 1950–2. I found the prose style impenetrable and the subject-matter uncongenial." And he goes on to point out Innis's lasting glory:

> he had something of what I call the garrison mentality in him, the university being still his garrison for all the obscurantism in it that he comments on so dryly. Perhaps it is not possible to hold a vision of that scope and range steadily in one's mind without a more passionate commitment to society as well as to scholarship.[16]

In 1920 there were few Canadian economists,[17] fewer still with Innis's fine historical sensitivity, for he was "a born historian, with a tremendous irrepressible interest in the facts of experience."[18] The historian stands behind all his writings from a study of the Canadian railway to the history of communications throughout the world's history.

In his life and in his many books, beginning with his doctoral thesis, Innis was passionately devoted to, and proud of, his own country. Yet Canada was still largely unknown both to its citizens and to the world. As a consequence, Innis considered his writings an ongoing attempt to explain Canada to Canadians so that they would understand and appreciate themselves and their place in the world.

Marshall McLuhan

Born in Edmonton, Alberta, and raised in Winnipeg, Manitoba, McLuhan grew up in a nominally Baptist family, attending the University of Manitoba, where he had planned to become an engineer. He read his way out of engineering, however, and into English literature, receiving his BA (1933) in

---

15 McLuhan, "The Later Innis," p. 389.
16 Northrop Frye, "Across the River and Out of the Trees," *University of Toronto Quarterly* 50 (Fall 1980), pp. 10–11.
17 See Innis's article, "The Teaching of Economic History in Canada," *Contributions to Canadian Economics* 2 (1929), pp. 52–68.
18 Donald Creighton, *Harold Adams Innis: Portrait of a Scholar* (Toronto: University of Toronto Press, 1957), p. 59. See also S. D. Clark, "The Contribution of H. A. Innis to Canadian Scholarship," in Melody et al., eds., *Culture, Communication, and Dependency*, pp. 27–35.

English and Philosophy and his MA (1934) in English with a thesis on George Meredith. He then attended Cambridge University where he obtained his second BA (1936) and MA (1940) and his Ph.D. (1943) in English with a dissertation on "The Place of Thomas Nashe in the Learning of His Time."

From his reading of G. K. Chesterton and Hilaire Belloc in the early 1930s, McLuhan converted to Catholicism in 1937 with the Hopkins scholar John Pick serving as his godfather. Devoutly disciplined in the practice of his faith and a daily communicant at mass, he kept his religion well in the background of his writings, although it played a major role in his thinking.[19]

After his years in Cambridge, McLuhan taught as a sessional lecturer for one year at the University of Wisconsin. There he quickly realized that he could not reach his students directly through literature; they were more conversant with comic books than with the novels of Charles Dickens:

> I confronted classes of freshmen and I suddenly realized that I was incapable of understanding them. I felt an urgent need to study their popular culture: advertising, games, movies. It was pedagogy, part of my teaching program. To meet them on their grounds was my strategy in pedagogy: the world of pop culture. Advertising was a very convenient form of approach.[20]

In addition to his many early articles on Coleridge and Keats, Shakespeare and Tennyson, not to mention such contemporary figures as T. S. Eliot, James Joyce, and Ezra Pound, McLuhan developed his method of explorations or "probes" of popular culture, thus bridging his interest in literature with his students' interest in popular culture. After teaching at Saint Louis University (1937–44) and Assumption University (1944–6) in Windsor, Ontario, he joined the Department of English at Saint Michael's, the Roman Catholic College in the University of Toronto, where he and his wife Corinne were invited to dinner first by Northrop Frye, then a young professor of English at Victoria, the United Church College at the University of Toronto, and his wife. McLuhan remained in Toronto until he suffered a major stroke in September 1979, spending the last months of his life incapable of reading or speaking more than a few phrases. In his sleep he died on December 31, 1980.

As the dustjacket of *The Mechanical Bride: Folklore of Industrial Man* (1951) states, McLuhan "has never limited his interests to 'literature' as such but has applied his vigorous intellectual curiosity to all facets of the contemporary

---

[19] For an early view on the role of Catholicism in McLuhan's thinking, see Walter J. Ong, "The Mechanical Bride: Christen the Folklore of Industrial Man," *Social Order* 2.2 (February 1952), pp. 79–85.

[20] "a dialogue: Q. & A.," in *McLuhan: Hot & Cool*, ed. Gerald Emanuel Stearn (New York: Dial Press, 1967), p. 268.

scene."²¹ This, his first book, studies a mass of advertisements, comic strips, and newspaper front pages to show the connections among them, attempting

> to set the reader at the center of the revolving picture created by these affairs where he may observe the action that is in progress and in which everybody is involved. From the analysis of that action, it is hoped, many individual strategies may suggest themselves. But it is seldom the business of this book to take account of such strategies.²²

This final remark is the center of McLuhan's later theories, for he never proposes strategies; he seeks only to look, to watch, and to observe.²³ The answers are beyond the book's pages; there informed readers can draw their conclusions. As McLuhan later observes, "I have no *theories* whatever about anything. I make observations by way of discovering contours, lines of force, and pressures."²⁴

As the book's title, *The Mechanical Bride*, indicates, technology and sex are the general patterns of thought in the public consciousness, and McLuhan points out the places where these items operate, "the widely occurring cluster image of sex, technology, and death which constitutes the mystery of the mechanical bride."²⁵ The book is "really a new form of science fiction, with ads and comics cast as characters. Since my object is to show the community in action rather than *prove* anything, it can indeed be regarded as a new kind of novel."²⁶ A study of "[p]opular icons as ideograms of complex implication,"²⁷ the volume aims to free the public from advertising's sinister manipulations.

Although a fascinating protest against capitalism, industrialism, and mechanistic automatism, *The Mechanical Bride* soon dated itself as a new tribalism occurred with the advent of television: "*Mechanical Bride* is a good example of a book that was completely negated by TV. All the mechanical assumptions of

---

21 Herbert Marshall McLuhan, *The Mechanical Bride: Folklore of Industrial Man* (New York: The Vanguard Press, 1951).
22 Ibid., p. v.
23 Frye observed that *The Mechanical Bride*, "his first and I think his best book ... has no specific reference to Canada, but it was, I think, written in Canada, and reflects the perspective of a country committed to observing rather than participating actively in the international scene" (Northrop Frye, "Criticism and Environment," in *Adjoining Cultures as Reflected in Literature and Language*, ed. John X. Evans and Peter Horwath [Tempe: Arizona State University, 1983], p. 19.)
24 "To William Kuhns, December 6, 1971," *Letters of Marshall McLuhan*, ed. Matie Molinaro, Corinne McLuhan, William Toye (Toronto: Oxford University Press, 1987), p. 448.
25 McLuhan, *The Mechanical Bride*, p. 101.
26 From an undated letter to his mother, probably written in the fall of 1952, *Letters of Marshall McLuhan*, p. 217.
27 "To Ezra Pound. June 30/48," ibid., p. 194.

American life have been shifted since TV; it's become an organic culture."²⁸ The book, however, brought McLuhan into Innis's orbit:

> It was through *The Mechanical Bride* that I met him. When I heard that he had put it on his reading list, I was fascinated to find out what sort of an academic would put a book like *The Mechanical Bride* on a reading list. So I went around and met him and we became acquainted for the few years of his life that remained.²⁹

Based in part on Innis's *Empire and Communications* and *The Bias of Communication*, *The Gutenberg Galaxy: The Making of Typographic Man* (1962), McLuhan's second book, argues persuasively that every new medium of communication alters entirely the outlook of the people who use it. Thus Innis maintained that print, ushered into the pattern of human communication by Gutenberg, brought about the spread of nationalism, and McLuhan's book demonstrates that the basic Western experience has been shaped by the invention of print. Gutenberg, therefore, created a new emphasis on privacy and separateness as well as an extraordinary change in the human senses. With the advancement of print, "there is more complete separation of the visual sense from the audile-tactile. This involves the modern reader in total translation of sight into sound as he *looks* at the page."³⁰

Arguing in a radial rather than a linear style and with the close reading of a New Critic, McLuhan shows that every technology creates a new human environment, and technological environments, which are not merely passive containers of human beings, but are active processes that reshape people and other technologies, too. In speaking of his own age, he further points out that "the human family now exists under conditions of a 'global village' ... The new interdependence recreates the world in the image of a global village."³¹ This image foresaw the pervasive use of e-mail as a form of community language and the World Wide Web as an electronic village.

In this book McLuhan credited Innis with so much of his thinking, for Innis "explained why print causes nationalism and not tribalism; and why print causes price systems and markets such as cannot exist without print. In short, Harold Innis was the first person to hit upon the *process* of change as implicit in

---

28 McLuhan, "a dialogue: Q. & A.," p. 267.
29 McLuhan, "Violence as a Quest for Identity," p. 273.
30 Marshall McLuhan, *The Gutenberg Galaxy: The Making of Typographic Man* (Toronto: University of Toronto Press, 1962), p. 93.
31 Ibid., p. 31. In a letter to Jacqueline Tyrwhitt of December 23, 1960, he had written: "Today with electronics we have discovered that we live in a global village, and the job is to create a global *city*, as center for the village margins" (*Letters of Marshall McLuhan*, p. 278).

the *forms* of media technology. The present book is a footnote of explanation to his work."³² *The Gutenberg Galaxy* won the Governor General's Award for non-fiction, a form of acclaim that increased McLuhan's reputation. And the chair of the selection committee for the award was McLuhan's colleague, Northrop Frye.

Whereas *The Gutenberg Galaxy* concentrates mainly on the effects of print in society, *Understanding Media: The Extensions of Man* (1964), McLuhan's third book, studies the effects of the communication networks on twentieth-century people. The new technologies are now influencing and shaping everyday life and culture; people are becoming victims of the electric age all about them. McLuhan probes its complexity, watching the globe turn itself into a village and throwing people back again into the life of the tribe.

Certain fundamental concepts stand out in McLuhan's argument. The book opens, for example, with his famous phrase, "The medium is the message," implying that in the electric age structure and configuration yield to simultaneity of apprehension. There are also hot and cool media: "Hot media are, therefore, low in participation, and cool media are high in participation or completion by the audience. Naturally, therefore, a hot medium like radio has very different effects on the user from a cool medium like the telephone."³³ Furthermore, "A cool medium, whether the spoken word or the manuscript or TV, leaves much more for the listener or the user to do than a hot medium."³⁴

Above all else McLuhan realizes that it is the artist who has the singular ability to observe the true nature of this contemporary world: "The artist is the man in any field, scientific or humanistic, who grasps the implications of his actions and of new knowledge in his own time. He is the man of integral awareness."³⁵ Furthermore,

> The power of the arts to anticipate future social and technological developments, by a generation or more, has long been recognized. In this century Ezra Pound called the artist "the antennae of the race." Art as radar acts as "an early alarm system," as it were, enabling us to discover social and psychic targets in lots of time to prepare to cope with them.³⁶

---

32 Ibid., p. 50.
33 Marshall McLuhan, *Understanding Media: The Extensions of Man* (New York: McGraw-Hill Book Company, 1964), p. 36.
34 Ibid., p. 278.
35 Ibid., p. 71.
36 Ibid., p. xi.

And it is as an artist that McLuhan saw his own proper role: "the greatest artists of the 20th Century – Yeats, Pound, Joyce, Eliot – had discovered a totally different approach, based on the identity of the processes of cognition and creation. I realized that artistic creation is the playback of ordinary experience – from trash to treasures."[37] The position of the artist is the highest level of participation in the probing of contemporary reality: "The only person who can actually see and sample and savour the time he is actually living is the artist. And this is why he is such a disagreeable character. The other people are nostalgically oriented towards the past."[38] The principal function of art is "to anticipate change and to invent new models of experience that will enable us to come to terms with change before its full impact can erase earlier achievement."[39] McLuhan sees himself, therefore, as an artist, using his books as probes into the complexities of the contemporary world. And in 1980 Frye suggests that "it is perhaps time for a sympathetic rereading of *The Gutenberg Galaxy* and *Understanding Media* and a reabsorption of McLuhan's influence."[40]

After these three books, McLuhan began to work with friends and associates. In 1968, for example, Harley Parker joined with him in writing *Through the Vanishing Point: Space in Poetry and Painting*, and in 1970 Wilfred Watson co-authored with him *From Cliché to Archetype*. In 1969 Eugene McNamara collected McLuhan's essays on literature in *The Interior Landscape: The Literary Criticism of Marshall McLuhan, 1943–1962*.

While McLuhan's object of study was the modern universe in its various states of being, he did comment briefly on Canada in some of his essays. In his 1952 "Defrosting Canadian Culture," he focused briefly on Canada's artistic outlook. The Canadian, "located between two great communities, the English and the American, is provincial to both. He would, therefore be in a superb position to develop habits of critical insight if the development of such habits were not paralyzed by colonial timidity or Scottish caution."[41] At the University of Toronto in 1967, McLuhan delivered the Marfleet Lectures. In the first of two, "Canada, the Borderline Case," he studies the effect of having so many borderlines in one country.

37 Marshall McLuhan, "Playboy Interview: Marshall McLuhan," *Playboy* 16.3 (March 1969), p. 74.
38 Marshall McLuhan, "The World and Marshall McLuhan," *Journal of Canadian Studies* 1.2 (August 1966), p. 44.
39 Marshall McLuhan, "Romanticism Reviewed," *Renascence* 12.4 (Summer 1960), p. 209.
40 Frye, "Across the River and Out of the Trees," pp. 11–12.
41 Marshall McLuhan, "Defrosting Canadian Culture," *The American Mercury* 74 (March 1952), p. 95.

> As the U.S.A. becomes a world environment through its resources, technology, and enterprises, Canada takes on the function of making that world environment perceptible to those who occupy it. Any environment tends to be imperceptible to its users and occupants except to the degree that counter-environments are created by the artist.[42]

In this view, Canada is a counter-environment to the United States.

In one of his final essays, "Canada: The Borderline Case," an expansion and refinement of his earlier lecture, McLuhan develops carefully his idea of the unique nature of his own country. Having lived so long in a colonial world where a sense of identity is minimal, yet situated beside the powerful presence of the United States, the Canadian is now the person best prepared to respond to the growing complexities of the modern world. "Canada has no goals or directions, yet shares so much of the American character and experience that the role of dialogue and liaison has become entirely natural to Canadians wherever they are."[43] To the people who have often complained about the absence of any Canadian identity, McLuhan concludes: "The low-profile Canadian, having learned to live without such strongly marked characteristics, begins to experience a security and self-confidence that are absent from the big-power situation."[44]

Always stationed resolutely north of the forty-ninth parallel, McLuhan observes without being a participant in the action of the main world. From his carefully constructed position in a colonial environment, he becomes the perfect observer of the United States from his detached perspective. In his criticism, be it literary, social, or communications, he remains true to his statement:

> I do not have a point of view on anything. I am interested only in modalities and processes ... My main theme is the extension of the nervous system in the electric age and thus the complete break with 5000 years of mechanical technology. This I state over and over again. I do not say whether it is a good or bad thing. To do so would be meaningless and arrogant.[45]

Northrop Frye

Born in Sherbrooke, Quebec, and raised in Moncton, New Brunswick, Frye moved in 1929 to Toronto and to Victoria College, which became his home for

---

42 Marshall McLuhan, "Canada, The Borderline Case," in McLuhan and Staines, eds., *Understanding Me*, p. 106.
43 Marshall McLuhan, "Canada: The Borderline Case," in *The Canadian Imagination: Dimensions of a Literary Culture*, ed. David Staines (Cambridge, MA: Harvard University Press, 1977), p. 227.
44 Ibid., p. 247.
45 "To Robert Fulford, June 1st, 1964," *Letters of Marshall McLuhan*, p. 300.

the rest of his life. He obtained his BA (1933) in Honors English and Philosophy, then went to Emmanuel College, the United Church's theology college, where he was ordained in 1936. "I enrolled at Victoria College in Toronto with the ministry in mind," he later acknowledged. "But as soon as I got to university I knew that was where I wanted to stay. I found myself in a community where I felt I had something to contribute."[46] Although he remained a United Church minister, conducting services until the end of his life, his interest lay in poetry, especially the prophetic poetry of William Blake. Consequently, he accepted a Royal Society of Canada fellowship in 1936 to pursue English studies at Merton College Oxford (MA 1941). In 1939 he returned to Victoria College, where he taught until his death in 1991.

Frye's achievement rests with his many books devoted to studies of Blake, the nature of literary criticism, romance, and ultimately the Bible. These books make him one of the twentieth-century's preeminent English-speaking critics and literary theorists.

Frye's first book, *Fearful Symmetry* (1947), a study of Blake's poetry and criticism, proposes that the poet's prophecies reshape the biblical myth of the creation, fall, redemption, and apocalypse. The book moves beyond Blake himself to focus on the role of myth and symbol in various literary genres, a concern of all his subsequent explorations. And his next book, *Anatomy of Criticism* (1957), presents a theory of literature as shaped by mythology. Setting out to refute the aestheticism of New Criticism and open up literary criticism by substituting for so-called value judgments a disciplined and teachable schematic access to literature, *Anatomy of Criticism* outlines a verbal universe of archetypes, symbols, and rhetoric that binds all literature together. This universe includes desired and detested worlds, the former expressed by comedy and romance, the latter by tragedy and irony.

In the 1960s and 1970s Frye turned to the romance tradition, publishing *A Natural Perspective: The Development of Shakespearean Comedy and Romance* (1965) and *The Secular Scripture: A Study of the Structure of Romance* (1976), as well as books on *T. S. Eliot* (1963), *The Return of Eden: Five Essays on Milton's Epics* (1965), and *Fools of Time: Studies in Shakespearean Tragedy* (1967). All this time he was writing articles on cultural history, bringing these together in his final great studies, *The Great Code: The Bible and Literature* (1982), his detailed account of biblical language and typology, and its companion volume, *Words with Power: Being a Second Study of "The Bible and Literature"* (1990), which

---

46 Northrop Frye, "Beginnings," *Today Magazine* 3 (January 1981), p. 3.

reveals the degree to which "the canonical unity of the Bible indicates or symbolizes a much wider imaginative unity in secular European literature."[47]

Throughout his career Frye was a devoted student of his country's culture. He began his critical work as a reviewer for *Acta Victoriana*, the Victoria College undergraduate literary magazine, and later for the *Canadian Forum*. As a reviewer he saw himself "as a nurse, that is, as somebody bringing along a culture that was not yet wholly mature but showed so many signs of it."[48] In these early articles he sees Canada as a bleak country, overcome by "a feeling of the melancholy of a thinly-settled country under a bleak northern sky, of the terrible isolation of the creative mind in such a country, of resigning oneself to hardship and loneliness as the only means of attaining, if not serenity, as least a kind of rigid calm."[49]

In 1950 the editor of the *University of Toronto Quarterly* invited Frye to take over the annual survey of the country's poetry in its "Letters in Canada" issue. Frye accepted, knowing that these reviews demanded a more constant and more detailed attention to Canadian poetry than did his earlier reviews. They also provided Frye with an opportunity to read closely the increasing body of poetry being written in Canada. The reviews themselves reveal Frye the practical critic, sharing his insights while working out his larger theories.

Frye approached his new duty as an occasion to work out his growing understanding of mythic patterns within the specific parameters of one art form in one country. These reviews were, he later reflected, "an essential piece of 'field work' to be carried on while I was working out a comprehensive critical theory. I was fascinated to see how the echoes and ripples of the great mythopoeic age kept moving through Canada, and taking a form there that they could not have taken elsewhere."[50] In writing his detailed analyses of each year's poetry, he contributed more than any other critic to establishing the standards by which Canadian poetry might be judged. His achievement as a reviewer was to give "our writers some strong and honest assurance that they were at last out of the parish and standing with their peers on high, new ground."[51]

---

47 Northrop Frye, *Words with Power: Being a Second Study of "The Bible and Literature"* (Toronto: Viking, 1990), p. xx.
48 David Cayley, *Northrop Frye in Conversation* (Concord: House of Anansi Press, 1992), p. 135.
49 Northrop Frye, "The Narrative Tradition in English-Canadian Poetry," in *The Bush Garden: Essays on the Canadian Imagination* (Toronto: House of Anansi Press, 1971), p. 146.
50 "Preface," in ibid., pp. viii–ix.
51 Malcolm Ross, "Northrop Frye," *University of Toronto Quarterly* 41 (Winter 1972), p. 173.

When Frye announced his retirement from publicly studying Canadian poetry, he admitted: "During this period I acquired my own sense of the context, in time and space, that Canadian culture inhabits ... the Canadian scene became a kind of cultural laboratory in which to study the relation of criticism to its environment."[52] The long reviews serve the same function in Frye's Canadian writings as does his study of Blake in his non-Canadian criticism. "I think it advisable for every critic proposing to devote his life to literary scholarship," he wrote,

> to pick a major writer of literature as a kind of spiritual preceptor for himself, whatever the subject of his thesis. I am not speaking, of course, of any moral model, but it seems to me that growing up inside a mind so large that one has no sense of claustrophobia within it is an irreplaceable experience in humane studies. Some kind of transmission by seed goes on here too.[53]

For Frye's non-Canadian studies, that major writer was Blake, but Frye had no major writer as a kind of spiritual preceptor in his own country. In lieu of the absent master-worker, he collectively made the books he reviewed his preceptors, and these books serve as his literary training, which in turn prepared him for his later commentaries that embody his vision of his country, its history, its culture, and its future. From 1960 on Frye wrote no more reviews of Canadian literature; he devoted himself, instead, to commentaries on the cultural life of his country, his role now that of a cultural theorist who articulated the myths he saw shaping the books he read and the country he was inhabiting.

1965 saw the publication of the *Literary History of Canada*, and Frye prepared an elaborate Conclusion to this immense project. He used this opportunity to bring together many of the themes that have characterized his understanding of the Canadian imagination. "Canada has, for all practical purposes, no Atlantic seaboard. The traveller from Europe edges into it like a tiny Jonah entering an inconceivably large whale, slipping past the Straits of Belle Isle into the Gulf of St. Lawrence, where five Canadian provinces surround him, for the most part invisible," he begins. And once the settler has made his home, "he then becomes aware of the longitudinal dimension, the southward pull toward the richer and more glamorous American cities."[54]

---

52 Frye, "Criticism and Environment," p. 9.
53 Northrop Frye, "The Search for Acceptable Words," *Daedalus* 102 (Spring 1973), p. 19.
54 Northrop Frye, "Conclusion," in *Literary History of Canada: Canadian Literature in English*, ed. Carl F. Klinck et al. (Toronto: University of Toronto Press, 1965), p. 824.

The garrison emerges as a central feature of Frye's understanding of the struggling literary voice in his country.

> Small and isolated communities surrounded with a physical or psychological "frontier," separated from one another and from their American and British cultural sources: communities that provide all that their members have in the way of distinctively human values, and that are compelled to feel a great respect for the law and order that holds them together, yet confronted with a huge, unthinking, menacing, and formidable physical setting – such communities are bound to develop what we may provisionally call a garrison mentality.

And this mentality changes as the center of Canadian life moves to the metropolis, the garrison mentality beginning "as an expression of the moral values generally accepted in the group as a whole, and then, as society gets more complicated and more in control of its environment, it becomes more of a revolutionary garrison within a metropolitan society."[55] In adding his detailed Conclusion, the most often reprinted and consulted essay on Canadian literature, Frye offered a paradigm of the literary patterns that stand behind English-Canadian literature.

In his later essays, Frye's perspective on Canada within its North American terrain underlies many of his observations. Not a continentalist himself, he argues that "[a]n independent Canada would be much more useful to the United States itself than a dependent or annexed one would be, and it is of great importance to the United States to have a critical view of it centred in Canada, a view which is not hostile but is simply another view."[56] This vision complements McLuhan's similar assertion: "Since the United States has become a world environment, Canada has become the anti-environment that renders the United States more acceptable and intelligible to many small countries of the world; anti-environments are indispensable for making an environment understandable."[57]

Many of Frye's later essays are explorations of Canadian culture. All the time he was writing his books on the Bible, he was drawn back to his own country, now as the spokesperson for a vibrant Canadian culture, "the indestructible core of a human society, so far as it is a human society and

---

55 Ibid., pp. 830, 834.
56 Northrop Frye, "Conclusion," in *Literary History of Canada: Canadian Literature in English*, ed. Carl F. Klinck *et al.*, 2nd edn., 3 vols. (Toronto: University of Toronto Press, 1976), vol. III, pp. 320–1.
57 McLuhan, "Canada: The Borderline Case," in Staines, ed., *Canadian Imagination*, p. 227.

not a mere aggregate of atoms in a human mass."[58] Frye is a careful critic of the country that has occupied his attention all his life. He could not write the definitive book on Canadian culture because, as he noted in his conclusion to the second edition of the *Literary History of Canada*, "It would be an affectation for me to pretend not to notice that I am extensively featured in this book myself."[59]

In addition to his many books on a variety of literary subjects, Frye was also the most respected critic of his country's literature; as he himself sensed, he was a vital participant in Canada's cultural evolution.

George Grant

Born and raised in Toronto, George Parkin Grant (1918–88), one of Canada's foremost philosophers, obtained his BA (1940) from Queen's University, where his paternal grandfather, George Monro Grant, had been principal. His maternal grandfather, George Parkin, was equally instrumental in the field of education as principal of Upper Canada College and author of many books. Awarded a Rhodes Scholarship, George Grant went to Balliol College, Oxford, where he obtained his D.Phil. (1945) in Theology.

During the war years Grant, a pacifist, underwent a religious conversion which determined much of his philosophic bent. "I just remember going off to work one morning and I remember walking through a gate; I got off my bicycle and walked through a gate, and I believed in God. I can't tell you more, I just knew that was it for me. And that came to me very suddenly," he recalled. The moment was "a kind of affirmation that beyond time and space there is order ... an affirmation about what is, an affirmation that ultimately there is order. And that is what one means by God, isn't it? That ultimately the world is not a maniacal chaos – I think that's what the affirmation was."[60]

Grant returned to Canada, teaching in the Department of Philosophy at Dalhousie University (1947–60), in the Department of Religion at McMaster University (1961–80), and as Killam Professor of Political Science at Dalhousie University (1980–4). He died of pancreatic cancer in 1988.

---

58 Northrop Frye, "The Cultural Development of Canada," *Australian-Canadian Studies* 10.1 (1991), p. 15.
59 Frye, "Conclusion," in *Literary History of Canada*, ed. Klinck et al., 2nd edn., vol. III, p. 319.
60 David Cayley, *George Grant in Conversation* (Concord: House of Anansi Press, 1995), pp. 48–9.

Grant was a conservative philosopher who held to his strong Christian beliefs. Studying modern technology, he saw it as the evil driving force behind modern culture. As a consequence, he turned to the great philosophers of the past, particularly Plato, to show that people can recognize the true and the good through their use of reason; thus they can direct technological change rather than be subject to it. In all his discussions Grant identified himself with traditional Canadian conservatism, which defended community values against the individualism he saw embedded in contemporary liberal thinking.

In his first book, *Philosophy in the Mass Age* (1959), his most optimistic work, Grant seeks to locate the Judeo-Christian tradition as an important element in the nature of human freedom while still seeking to maintain the equally central concept of the classical notion of a natural order. Essentially a wide-ranging attempt to bridge ancient and modern cultures, especially the wide chasm that separates the moral wisdom of the classical world and contemporary society, which is rooted in technological progress, the book reveals, first of all, the wealth of Grant's readings. Believing that Hegel had written a synthesis of the Greek and the Christian worlds, further combining them with modern empiricism, Grant produces a significant work which he hopes will make modern society aware of its own urgent need for a moral structure.

Seven years later, Grant wrote an introduction to a new edition of *Philosophy in the Mass Age*. His views on technology had undergone a dramatic change. Now he could lament: "I no longer believe that technology is simply a matter of means which men can use well or badly. As an end in itself, it inhibits the pursuit of other ends in the society it controls. Thus, its effect is debasing our conceptions of human excellence."[61]

In *Lament for a Nation: The Defeat of Canadian Nationalism* (1965), his second book and a phenomenal bestseller, Grant laid out his conservative philosophy in a dramatic manner. Affirming that Canada's traditional ties to England connected the country to a tradition of strong communal values that took precedence over ideas of unlimited individual liberty, he now lamented the inevitable passing of such a communally based nation: "To lament is to cry out at the death or at the dying of something loved. This lament mourns the end of Canada as a sovereign state."[62]

While the book arises out of Prime Minister John Diefenbaker's defeat in the 1963 election – Grant saw Diefenbaker as the symbol of the old Canadian conservatism – the book's true concern was with the encroaching nature of

---

61 George Grant, *Philosophy in the Mass Age* (Toronto: Copp Clark, 1966), p. vii.
62 George Grant, *Lament for a Nation* (Toronto: McClelland and Stewart, 1965), p. 2.

the United States. He demonstrates that all Liberal governments in Canada since 1940 have made the American control of Canada inevitable at the same time that this control meant the complete obliteration of traditional Canadian values, including the traditions of British justice and British common law. Although Grant's thesis that Canada had become little more than an American branch-plant made the task of preserving Canadian nationalism a hopeless enterprise, *Lament for a Nation* had an exceptionally wide influence on proponents of Canadian nationalism, including Margaret Atwood and Dennis Lee.

The theme of American imperialism resurfaced in Grant's next book, *Technology and Empire: Perspectives on North America* (1969), a small collection of previously published articles, where American culture homogenizes the cultures of the world, especially Canada's. Britain's influence against this impulse has dwindled since 1945, when Britain decided to follow politically the American way. And Grant argues further that North American universities have also been adversely affected by American technology, leaving faculty and students unable to accommodate themselves to a genuinely humane understanding of the meaning of human existence.

Grant's subsequent books were again collections of lectures or previously published articles. In *Time as History* (1969), he examines Nietzsche, insisting that there are indeed eternal values. Basic Christian ideas and ideals soundly limit what can be done to and with human beings. Without some possible external framework, technological mastery leads to catastrophes. And in *English-Speaking Justice* (1978), Grant returns to a stinging critique of liberal ideology through a conservatively coherent attack on the philosophy of John Rawls.

Always a maverick outsider to the philosophic mainstream of his own society, Grant was a faithful, indeed devout, adherent to his Anglican religion and its British principles of order, becoming, therefore, an outsider because of his conservatism. Long an admirer of Harold Innis,[63] he slowly became less and less enamored of his master. Although he admired Northrop Frye's public stand as an educator and as a critic, he lost his admiration in the disparaging comments he made about Frye's less than conservative approach to biblical studies.[64] And while he disliked Marshall McLuhan's seemingly uncritical

---

63 For Grant's indebtedness to Innis, see Robert E. Babe, "The Communication Thought of George Grant (1918–1988)," in *Canadian Communication Thought: Ten Foundational Writers* (Toronto: University of Toronto Press, 2000), pp. 182–206, and "Lament: The Anguished Conservatism of George Grant," Bickerton et al., *Freedom, Equality, Community*, pp. 35–54.

64 For Grant on Frye, see "The Great Code," *The Globe and Mail* (February 27, 1982), p. E17.

study of modern technology, he came to admire his public positions on issues that appealed to his conservatism.[65]

Grant "managed to stir the imagination and steel the determination of nationalists, socialists, communitarians, ecologists, student activists, and all manner of Canadians who shared his premonitions about the long-term implications of the dominant ideology of technological liberalism and the kind of society it was fostering." In this way, therefore, he "seems the natural inheritor and extension of an important part of Harold Innis's intellectual legacy, though a much more public and dramatic expositor of that legacy than ever was Innis."[66] Throughout Grant's writings exists his profound and compelling Platonism with its insistence on stability rather than change and on community rather than individuality.

These four – Harold Innis, Marshall McLuhan, Northrop Frye, and George Grant – are the pillars of prose non-fiction. The pioneer of this quartet, Innis came to the University of Toronto and made it the important home for all his economic, historical, and communications studies. McLuhan also made the university home for his literary criticism and communication studies. And Frye made it home for his literary theories. Grant, the only one to be born in Toronto, resided for twenty years at McMaster University in nearby Hamilton, bringing his philosophical musings to a wider audience through his writings and his radio broadcasts. All four were devoted academics whose teaching supported and enhanced their original writings.

---

65 Although Grant thought that McLuhan accepted and therefore endorsed the technological advances in contemporary society, he wrote to him on April 19, 1978: "Let me say how much I admire what you have said recently about abortion and about child pornography. So many people who become well-known cease to speak on what may be an unpopular side. I very greatly admire the fact that you have not ceased to speak" (in *George Grant: Selected Letters*, ed. William Christian [Toronto: University of Toronto Press, 1996], pp. 301–2).
66 Babe, "Lament," pp. 53–4.

PART FOUR

*

AESTHETIC EXPERIMENTS,
1960 AND AFTER

18
Quartet: Atwood, Gallant, Munro, Shields

ROBERT THACKER

In 1955, when she was about sixteen, Margaret Atwood announced to the other girls she lunched with at Leaside High School in Toronto that she intended to be a writer.[1] Five years before that, Mavis Gallant had quit her job at the Montreal *Standard* and moved to Paris resolved to do the same thing. "I believed that if I was going to call myself a writer, I should live on writing." The first story she had submitted to *The New Yorker* came back, she has also recalled in the Preface to her *Selected Stories* (1996), "with a friendly letter that said, 'Do you have anything else you could show us?'"[2] She did, and the second story she sent, "Madeline's Birthday," was accepted and appeared in that magazine on September 1, 1951 – it proved to be the first of over a hundred stories she would first publish there. By 1955 too, Alice Munro had appeared with half a dozen stories in such Canadian outlets as the *Canadian Forum*, *Mayfair*, and *Queen's Quarterly* and had four broadcast on CBC radio, but her second daughter was born that year so mostly her time was spent being a mother and wife in West Vancouver. Her initial appearance in *The New Yorker*, the first of over fifty stories ultimately, would not happen until 1977. In 1955, Carol Warner was still an undergraduate at Hanover College in Indiana; she would not become Carol Shields until 1957, when she married. She began publishing poetry and criticism in the early 1970s, subsequently establishing herself as a writer.

Together, this quartet constitutes the leading English-Canadian writers of the latter half of the twentieth century, and neither Atwood nor Munro gives any indication of easing up at the beginning of the twenty-first. Others might be asserted as equally significant, perhaps Michael Ondaatje or Margaret Laurence, yet very few critics doubt the importance of the massed oeuvres

---

[1] Atwood includes this episode in *Negotiating with the Dead: A Writer on Writing* (Cambridge: Cambridge University Press, 2002), p. 14.
[2] Mavis Gallant, "Preface," in *Selected Stories* (Toronto: McClelland and Stewart, 1996), p. xiii.

produced by these four writers since the 1950s. Each found her subject in that decade when the myriad social changes wrought to post-war European and North American societies were everywhere evident. This time was inauspicious for women generally, and for women writers particularly, yet each of these figures has demonstrated an exceptionally precise understanding of the era, its social and cultural mores, and in particular its attitudes towards gender as they were transformed during the 1960s and 70s. They did so by drawing upon traditional forms and by consistently pressing at boundaries, innovating when few models were available. Through this work, though to varying degrees, they became spokespersons for their profession and nation while achieving international reputations.

Margaret Atwood

Of the four, Atwood stands apart and ahead of the others by the breadth of her appeal. Her work, according to critic John Moss, "bridges the gap between popularity and highbrow literariness. She offers illusory proof that art is relevant to everyday life."[3] Atwood captures the trajectory of what each writer was doing by harkening back to her high-school self in the 1950s in a recent story, "The Art of Cooking and Serving." After an epiphanic confrontation with her mother, the narrator writes that she "felt set free, as if released from an enchantment" and later concludes, "[A]lready in spirit I was off and running – to the movies, to the skating rinks, to the swooning blue-lit dances, and to all sorts of other seductive and tawdry and frightening pleasures I could not yet begin to imagine."[4] Any one of these four might have formulated this realization. Each was akin to Isabel in Munro's story "White Dump" (1986). At a critical moment in her life, considering what she has abandoned and what she is about abandon for something else, Isabel "felt herself newly, and boundlessly, resourceful."[5]

Atwood has dissected the writer's role with characteristic élan in *Negotiating with the Dead: A Writer on Writing* (2002), the published version of a series of six Empson lectures she gave at Cambridge University in 2000. There, in the first lecture, she poses two key questions – "What is 'a writer,' and how did I become one?" – then she sets about answering them by telling her own

---

3 John Moss, "Scuba Diving with Margaret Atwood," *Books in Canada* 36.3 (2007), p. 10.
4 Margaret Atwood, "The Art of Cooking and Serving," in *Moral Disorder* (New York: Nan A. Talese/Doubleday, 2006), p. 23.
5 Alice Munro, "White Dump," in *The Progress of Love* (Toronto: McClelland and Stewart, 1986), p. 307.

story. To set oneself out as a writer at all was overreaching enough for any woman, but to do so in 1950s Canada was an act of even greater hubris. In Canada, real writing came from elsewhere, from Great Britain, the United States, or France. Significantly, the first epigraph Atwood offers to this chapter is from E. K. Brown's *On Canadian Poetry* (1943), where he characterized Canada as a colony, a place which "lacks the spiritual energy to rise above the routine, and that it lacks this energy because it does not adequately believe in itself."[6] As Atwood details in her account, this was the place where she grew up and where she became aware of herself as a writer. What she calls her "first real collection of poetry," *The Circle Game*, appeared the year before Canada's Centennial celebrations in 1967, which sparked the widespread cultural nationalism that characterized English-Canada during the 1960s.[7] Atwood and her work were at the forefront of this transformation, as were Gallant – writing in *The New Yorker* about the uprisings in Paris during May 1968 – and Munro, whose work explicitly details the changing cultural mores in southwestern Ontario from the 1940s on. Publishing later and so under the potential influence of the others, the American-born Shields draws upon her own experiences in her stories and novels, tracing the fragmentations of ordinary contemporary life for men and women with humor and pathos.

Since the publication of *Surfacing* and *Survival* in 1972, Atwood has been what might be called a "phe-nom," that is, a phenomenal cultural presence, a public intellectual par excellence. She has been omnipresent as a cultural commentator. Drawn to the dystopic – *Surfacing*, *The Handmaid's Tale* (1985), *Oryx and Crake* (2003) – Atwood continues to link her writing to the present cultural moment. As a result of this commitment, her works include two large volumes of topical essays – *Second Words* (1982) and *Moving Targets* (2004; republished for the British market as *Curious Pursuits* in 2005). When she introduced Atwood as the 1987 Humanist of the Year, human rights activist Vera Freud called her "a dangerous person" and continued, saying that she "has become a most powerful and far-reaching voice for the defense of Mother Earth, human dignity, and freedom."[8] In a review of *Moral Disorder*, Alice Truax asserted that "Apocalypse is never very far away in Atwood's writing.

---

6 E. K. Brown, *On Canadian Poetry* (Ottawa: Tecumseh, 1977 [1943]), p. 14.
7 Atwood, *Negotiating*, p. 16.
8 Vera Freud, "Margaret Atwood," *The Humanist* (September–October 1987), p. 5. Particularly in her environmental work, Atwood often joins forces with Graeme Gibson. Gibson's *The Bedside Book of Birds: An Avian Miscellany* (Toronto: Nan A. Talese, 2005) is an eclectic anthology which illustrates the respectful and imaginative cataloguing that must go with such activism.

True, it isn't always on a grand scale ... but it always feels big; even personal tragedies tend to carry the weight of malevolent disaster."⁹ While it is possible to see Gallant, Munro, and Shields as technically better writers than Atwood, the broad audience she has reached in her articulation of what threats confront us all at the outset of the twenty-first century is unsurpassed.

Atwood has cultivated and influenced her broadest audience through prose, though she began as a poet and indeed remains one. In 2004 the University of Ottawa held a symposium on Atwood and called it, fittingly, "Margaret Atwood: The Open Eye." Its title was taken from one of Atwood's best-known poems, "You Fit Into Me," which embodies the jarring effects of shocking juxtapositions so characteristic of her writing. Also fittingly, Atwood herself spoke. Throughout her career and in clear contrast to the other writers considered here Margaret Atwood has been a perennial presence as her work has been published: commenting, challenging, cajoling, and reminding. As *Negotiating with the Dead* demonstrates, Atwood is a writer who, from the beginning, has understood the public role of the writer. She first assumed that role in a Canada teeming with nationalist ambitions. More recently, since her international reputation has made her Canada's leading writer abroad, Atwood has moved her activism to a wider stage, writing and speaking out unequivocally on questions of human dignity the world over, while she has served as President of PEN, Canada 1984–86, and is currently (in 2013) Vice President of PEN International. Analyzing the concept of literary celebrity, Lorraine M. York underlines Atwood's conflicted responses to her own iconic status in her interviews, essays, comics, and novels, showing how Atwood "reproduces her own star image as performed satire."¹⁰

Emerging in the 1960s as a poet offering stark poems replete with antilyrical imagery like that of "You Fit Into Me" from the aptly titled *Power Politics* (1971), Atwood's nationalism put her at the very center of what was called "CanLit," the literary manifestation of cultural nationalism, which was intent on creating Canadian literature for Canadians to read, intent on rediscovering lost authors, intent on shaping another view of life in North America apart from the American way. Atwood became involved in the work of the House of Anansi Press, publishing her thematic guide to Canadian Literature, *Survival* (1972), as an avowed bestseller to help support Anansi's other books. A partial explanation for Atwood's early prominence were some of the subjects in her early work. In *The Animals in That Country* (1968) she first

---

9 Alice Truax, "A Private Apocalypse," *The New York Times Book Review* (October 15, 2006), p. 20.
10 Lorraine M. York, *Literary Celebrity in Canada* (Toronto: University of Toronto Press, 2007), p. 107.

published "Progressive Insanities of a Pioneer," a powerful poem which, by focusing a pioneer's vain attempts to impose his cultural assumptions on nature, defined the traditional but increasingly outmoded view of nature as something to be controlled and managed. It also shaped Canada as a still-new place, where the pioneer spirit was not far distant: "Things / refused to name themselves; refused / to let him name them."[11] Derived in part from her own experiences growing up when every summer her family moved north into the bush, Atwood's early poems focused on concerns central to the study of Canadian literature.

This is most apparent in *The Journals of Susanna Moodie* (1970), where Atwood personifies and adopts the voice of the genteel nineteenth-century English immigrant author of *Roughing It in the Bush* (1852) as a means of articulating the same relations found in "Progressive Insanities." She was engaged as well in a recovery project for, while known to scholars, Moodie had little of the iconic status that *The Journals* accorded her subsequently. It is possible to see Atwood's version of Moodie as something separate from the historical Moodie herself. As scholars have asserted the biographical Moodie in compelling detail, Atwood's Moodie has remained a vivid counter-presence.[12] Just after Moodie's ghost is last seen on a bus on St Clair Avenue in Toronto in the final poem, Atwood offers an Afterword which addresses her attraction to Moodie, asserting that this pioneering woman offers a historical mirror to contemporary Canadian obsessions: "If the national mental illness of the United States is megalomania, that of Canada is paranoid schizophrenia."[13] Embodying this condition, Susanna Moodie speaks out in an exemplary poem, "The Double Voice."

While Atwood has continued to publish poetry, the early 1970s saw a shift to prose; here *Survival*, with its emphasis on the tropes of wilderness and victimhood as the distinctive marks of Canadian literature, must be noted, but the shift was primarily to fiction. Her first two novels, and especially the dystopic *Surfacing*, which became something of a cult feminist text, transformed her reputation, first in Canada and then internationally. In her third novel, *Lady Oracle* (1976), creating a protagonist who is also a writer, Atwood

---

11 Margaret Atwood, "Progressive Insanities of a Pioneer," *Selected Poems* (Toronto: Oxford University Press, 1976), p. 63.
12 Among the foremost scholars on Moodie is Michael A. Peterman; see Susanna Moodie, *Roughing It in the Bush*, ed. Michael A. Peterman, Norton Critical Edition (New York: Norton, 2007 [1852]).
13 Margaret Atwood, "Afterword," in *The Journals of Susanna Moodie* (Toronto: Oxford, 1970), p. 62.

explored this topic of fame directly. The next novel, *Life Before Man* (1979), is a multi-voiced representation of Toronto in the mid-1970s and is partially set in its Royal Ontario Museum. Just about the same time, Sandra Djwa observed that the "circumference of Margaret Atwood's imagination ... is often contained by Canada's national and literary boundaries. It is almost as if she consciously sets herself down, right in the middle of the Canadian literary landscape, and tries to orient herself by filtering Canadian experience through archetypes of her poetic sensibility."[14] Much has been made of Atwood's Canadian ambivalence towards the United States, since the opening of *Surfacing*, where, in the first sentence, the narrator notices that "the disease is spreading up from the south,"[15] but a more nuanced formulation of this relationship is found in her essay "Canadian–American Relations: Surviving the Eighties." Explaining the need for a distinctive "home-grown" Canadian culture to an American audience, Atwood asserts that English-Canadians had "become addicted to the one-way mirror of the Canadian–American border – we can see you, you can't see us – and had neglected that other mirror, their own culture."[16]

Atwood's first novel, *The Edible Woman* (1969), is replete with social satire and wry humor. *Surfacing* proved to be both more striking and a very different thing altogether – a stream-of-consciousness narrative which allowed a wide range of possible interpretation, as it looked back to modernism and also offered the fragmentation of postmodernism.[17] Both these novels speak to their respective cultural moments, but *Surfacing* captures the movement of a whole culture while *The Edible Woman* takes the more conventional novelistic approach by telling an individual's story. Stepping back from Atwood's work, the reader may see this alternation recurring throughout her career. What is more, her experiments with narrative modes, for example, dystopia as opposed to a more realistic social critique, are complemented by Atwood's generic range: along with poetry, novels, and non-fiction, she has published collections of short stories and children's books.

After *Surfacing*, Atwood's prime dystopic work is *The Handmaid's Tale*. Like its predecessor, it captured the cultural moment of the 1980s, but because by

---

14 Sandra Djwa, "The Where of Here: Margaret Atwood and a Canadian Tradition," *The Art of Margaret Atwood*, ed. Arnold E. Davidson and Cathy N. Davidson (Toronto: Anansi, 1981), p. 22.
15 Margaret Atwood, *Surfacing* (New York: Bantam, 1996 [1972]), p. 3.
16 Margaret Atwood, *Second Words* (Toronto: Anansi, 1982), p. 385.
17 Philip Kokotailo, "Form in Atwood's *Surfacing*: Toward a Synthesis of Critical Opinion," *Studies in Canadian Literature* 8.2 (1983), pp. 155–65.

then Atwood's reputation was well established beyond Canada's borders, its effect was far broader. Imagining Gilead, a futuristic United States controlled by men who had their beginnings in the Religious Right then ascendant in Reagan's America, Atwood creates a story told by Offred, a "handmaid," a woman held in virtual slavery and valued only for her ability to reproduce. Like the others of her class, she is required each month to copulate ritualistically with the commander, a man who controls her and whose wife is barren owing to past environmental devastation. Atwood presents Offred's own tale, and follows it in Orwellian mode with "Historical Notes on *The Handmaid's Tale*," an account of "the Twelfth Symposium of Gileadean Studies" held in Arctic Canada in June 2195, long after Gilead has disappeared.[18] Here a male professor describes the provenance and veracity of Offred's narrative and also speculates as to whether or not she may have escaped Gilead to live a life of her own choosing.

Atwood's cautionary purpose is clear, and she reached a wide audience with it. The novel was made into a major motion picture in 1990, directed by Volker Schlöndorff, based on Harold Pinter's screenplay adaptation, and starring Faye Dunaway and Robert Duvall, and then in 1997–8 into an opera by the Danish composer Poul Ruders (first performed 2003/4). *Oryx and Crake* presents a much grimmer vision of global rather than national catastrophe, where the entire human race and civilization are on the brink of extinction. In a post-apocalyptic world devastated by climate change and genetic engineering, Snowman, the only survivor (as he thinks) of his friend Crake's bioterrorist plot, drags out his existence in the company of a group of genetically modified humans called Crakers, so unlike himself that he feels like an alien. Atwood's satire has become ferociously Swiftian and her challenge more radical as she asks, What does it mean to be human? In the end, she leaves open a glimmer of hope, though her warnings of catastrophe have become increasingly urgent.

But if Atwood's prolific art is singular for her visions of the future, she has neglected neither the past nor the present, as *Alias Grace* (1996) and *The Blind Assassin* (2000) readily demonstrate. In the former, Atwood returns to a historical recovery project similar to her early use of Moodie to reconstruct the true story of an Irish maid named Grace Marks, who served time in the Kingston penitentiary for her part in an infamous 1843 double murder at a farm on the edge of Toronto. Taking a succession of quilting motifs as her central metaphor, Atwood presents numerous historical texts to complement her

---

18 Margaret Atwood, *The Handmaid's Tale* (New York: Fawcett Crest, 1986 [1985]), pp. 379–95.

narrative, itself made up of different narratives by different narrators, including Grace Marks herself. In so doing, Atwood presents a novel that gives a reader the sense that she is gaining a deeper understanding of what occurred. On the contrary, no certain illumination is achieved. By offering what Earl G. Ingersoll calls "a patchwork of texts, some 'true' and others 'fictional,'" Atwood presents in *Alias Grace* – just as its title implies – an illusion of understanding. The book is an avowed metafiction, one that the reader enjoys with a sense of impending understanding but, upon scrutiny, she realizes that no understanding is possible. As Ingersoll argues, "the reader is likely to be perplexed by what may well seem a collection of quilting blocks, ready perhaps to be assembled according to the reader's sense of 'pattern.'"[19] *Alias Grace* appeals to a textualizing intelligence as does *The Blind Assassin*, where Atwood combines her understanding of Ontario high society with its social history and the position of women within it. The novel offers one old woman's lifelong reminiscence which is woven into the larger frame of a science fiction, also called *The Blind Assassin*. In effect, there are three stories here. For this book, and doubtless also in recognition of her entire oeuvre, Atwood won the Booker Prize in 2000.

She is far from done yet, continuing to produce books at an astonishing rate: *The Penelopiad* appeared in 2005, *The Tent* and *Moral Disorder* in 2006, and another book of poems, *The Door*, in 2007. In *The Penelopiad* she returns to her feminist revisions of ancient myths, retelling Homer's *Odyssey* through the voices of Penelope, Helen of Troy, and Penelope's twelve hanged maids as she shifts the emphasis from male heroics to mock epic and domestic drama. In Atwood's version, Penelope emerges as a trickster figure as duplicitous and seductive as Odysseus himself, while the maids' counter-narratives highlight the dark underside of classical epic. *The Penelopiad* was rewritten as a play script by Atwood herself and first performed at Stratford-upon-Avon in 2007. Legendary women reappear in various contemporary guises in both recent poetry collections: Salome, Helen of Troy ("It's Not Easy Being Half Divine"), and the Cumaean Sibyl, now a voice inside a bottle in *The Tent* and then again in *The Door* as a crusty old fortuneteller, one of Atwood's own personas. As well as topical concerns related to environment and human rights, these collections contain elegies, tender love poems, and a remarkable series in *The Door* about poets and poetry ("Heart" and "Poetry Reading").

---

19 Earl G. Ingersoll, "Engendering Metafiction: Textuality and Closure in Margaret Atwood's *Alias Grace*," *American Review of Canadian Studies* 31–3 (2001), pp. 387–8.

Atwood's dazzling variety of poetic forms is matched by her experiments with the short story in *Moral Disorder*, a collection which almost becomes a story sequence though the last two personal stories disrupt that formal pattern. At the same time, all these stories are linked as they figure symptoms of disorder in the lives of individuals, in relationships, or in the body politic. "The Bad News" comes first in a collection that might be described as Gothic domesticated, as the uncanny surfaces in stories like "The Entities," while a network of dark tunnels winds under the seemingly everyday, till with a final swirl of narrative artifice in "The Boys at the Lab," all the characters vanish into the forest. Margaret Atwood and her works exceed any attempt to contain them. Atwood confirmed her status as public, and sometimes prophetic, intellectual with her 2008 Massey Lectures, published as *Payback: Debt and the Shadow Side of Wealth* in the midst of a worldwide economic recession. The essay combines a personal memoir of learning about the significance of money with wide-ranging reflections about its place in literature and myth, and sharply worded conclusions about public responsibility. A new novel, *The Year of the Flood*, was announced for 2009.

Mavis Gallant

Mavis Gallant, by contrast, offers a career that in many ways is the mirror-opposite of Atwood's. If Atwood set herself in the center of Canadian literary sensibilities since the mid-1960s before growing to international writing celebrity, then Gallant has been singular by her invisibility in Canada during much of the same time. Having left Montreal for Paris in 1950, Gallant became, and for a long time remained, a vague presence in Canadian writing, focusing in her fiction on situations in war-torn Europe rather than on specifically Canadian subject matter. Her invisibility has been punctured from time to time – when a selection of her stories, *The End of the World and Other Stories* (1974) appeared from the New Canadian Library or when *Home Truths: Selected Canadian Stories* (1981) won a Governor General's Literary Award for fiction – but unlike Atwood and Munro in the 1970s, she was much better known to readers outside Canada than inside the country. This has appeared to change in recent years; in 1996 her *Selected Stories* was published, her *Paris Stories*, selected and introduced by Michael Ondaatje, appeared in 2002, and the companion volume, *Montreal Stories*, selected and introduced by Russell Banks, in 2004. Then in late 2006 Gallant received the Prix Athanase David, the leading literary prize given by the province of Quebec, one never before given to a writer whose literary language is English. This award is all the more singular in that it represents recognition across her country's two cultural solitudes. There is a certain retrospective quality about the recognition of Gallant in her home place which is not without its ironies: in 2008, Gallant was projected into the popular consciousness when her 1979 collection *From the Fifteenth District* was one of the five books selected for the CBC Radio competition "Canada Reads." In 2009, a collection of "missing stories" entitled *Going Ashore* was published.

Gallant's long absence as a Canadian writer calls for comment in view of her considerable productivity. By the time she was gaining real critical attention in Canada at the beginning of the 1980s, she had published several collections, two novels (*Green Water, Green Sky*, 1959, and *A Fairly Good Time*, 1970) and over ninety stories. But she continued to live in Paris, most of her stories were published in *The New Yorker*, and she worked closely with American, not Canadian, publishers until the 1970s, when her association with Macmillan and then McClelland and Stewart began. Neil K. Besner summarized these effects: "How, Canadian readers have asked, are we to understand Gallant's leaving Canada at twenty-seven in 1950? In what senses is Gallant an expatriate writer? Or an exile? And how are we to look at Gallant's thirty-five year association with *The New Yorker*?"[20] It is perhaps worth noting that Gallant's dissociation from Canada and Canadianness is nothing like as absolute as these questions might suggest, though she has always resisted attempts to label her writing. As she has so memorably commented: "[I]t surely signifies more than lightheadedness about English that 'expatriate' is regularly spelled in Canadian newspapers 'expatriot.' Whether they know it or not, Canadian artists are supposed to 'Paint Canadian.'"[21] More than these biographic matters, there is also the "other difficulty" that "Gallant's stories seem to resist interpretation": "[C]lose readings of Gallant's stories run the risk of bogging down in a mass of details, all significant, none representative."[22]

In "Madeline's Birthday," her first *New Yorker* story, for instance, such details abound but are not readily summarized. The story concerns Madeline, her mother Mrs. Tracy, and a German Jewish refugee boy, Paul, also staying in the Tracys' Connecticut house one summer, on the morning of Madeline's birthday. The characters are sharply drawn, in indicative detail, and the thin plot has to do with Paul's relation to Madeline, and the latter's birthday. It is mostly recalled. Once the characters and their relations are established, an

---

20 Neil K. Besner, *The Light of Imagination: Mavis Gallant's Fiction* (Vancouver: University of British Columbia Press, 1988), p. ix.
21 Mavis Gallant, "An Introduction," in *Home Truths: Selected Canadian Stories* (Toronto: Macmillan, 1981), p.xii.
22 Besner, *Light*, pp. ix, x.

incident occurs which leaves Madeline crying, but this passes. Mrs. Tracy has a telephone conversation with her husband, who is in New York. Then the story stops, leaving the characters still in a day's morning, heading for breakfast.[23]

As with this birthday, Gallant conceives and structures her stories around a crucial image or situation so that in reading, one feels a center from which a character's inner life may be glimpsed in a single flash. In her 1982 essay "What is Style?" Gallant made the point of such moments precisely: "[T]his is what fiction is about ... that something is taking place and that nothing lasts. Against the sustained tick of a watch, fiction takes the measure of a life, a season, a look exchanged, the turning point, desire as brief as a dream, the grief and terror that after childhood we cease to express. The lie, the look, the grief are without permanence. The watch continues to tick where the story stops."[24] Gallant's stories register both that moment in time and also the jarring of incompatible frames of reference, so that the reader is led through the complex interplay of differences to a recognition of states of mind and feeling the final meaning of which remains elusive.

With characteristic irony Gallant has observed: "I still do not know what impels anyone of sound mind to leave dry land and spend a lifetime describing people who do not exist."[25] Yet this is just what Gallant has done, and her stories – including her few novels – stand testament to her accomplishment and to the ringing compulsion of what she says of the workings of fiction in "What is Style?" That she has done so on her own terms from her particular vantage point as a Canadian woman writer living alone in Paris is everywhere evident in her work. While it is possible to select further from her stories to make this point in greater detail, an extended non-fiction piece published in two subsequent issues of *The New Yorker* in 1968 better illustrates her own point of view. Based on the uprisings in Paris in May of that year, "The Events in May: A Paris Notebook" is Gallant's own vision of what was happening around her – and, as such, it details her authorial perspective. Attending a meeting at the National School of Oriental Languages, Gallant comments in passing that "Louis Hémon went to the Langues Orientales. He is still my favorite Frenchman, because of his life, but scarcely anyone has ever heard of him here. Always have to identify him by a book I do not much like – 'Maria Chapdelaine.'" Such a remark captures Gallant's ongoing reference to "home

---

23 Mavis Gallant, "Madeline's Birthday," *The New Yorker* (September 1, 1951), pp. 20–4.
24 Mavis Gallant, "What is Style?" *Canadian Forum* (September 1982), p. 6.
25 Mavis Gallant, "Preface," in *Selected Stories*, p. x. Gallant has frequently discussed the beginning of her stories in images. See, for example, the interview with Pleuke Boyce entitled "Image and Memory," in *Books in Canada* (January–February 1990), p. 30.

truths," the phrase she later used as a title. Whatever she thinks of Hémon's *Maria Chapdelaine* (1916), Gallant mentions this text because it reminds her of her homeland.

Her sense of separateness from the French whom she lives among is even more evident when she asks:

> Why is it when [President] de G[aulle] speaks I always feel like a foreigner? If I had ordinarily felt like a foreigner in France, I would not have stayed here more than a weekend. But whenever he manifests himself, something about the way he thinks, the things he says, and the reactions he arouses in people – even in friends – always leave me thinking: Thank God I am not a refugee; I can pick up and leave whenever I like.[26]

Gallant's position, that of an outsider realizing culture as a web of historical resonances, a person (in a phrasing borrowed from Munro) "trying to understand the danger, to read the signs of invasion" in Paris in May 1968, and mediating what is happening in the city she knows and loves, characterizes her contingent point of view.[27] That position of disengagement is coded into the title of *Overhead in a Balloon: Stories of Paris* (1985) and may be seen as her distinctive signature throughout her fiction.

Gallant has maintained that "like every other form of art, literature is no more and nothing less than a matter of life and death. The only question worth asking about a story ... is, 'Is it dead or alive?'"[28] Gallant's stories live by the ways she assembles the details about her characters' lives, many of whom are exiles and refugees, some of whom are Canadian or American expatriates in Europe, and all of whom are outsiders, detached from the people among whom they happen to be living. Her stories are never about belonging but about isolation or random encounters in places that are both real and unreal, with people who are seen but not really seen, speaking across gaps of language and understanding. Her intense interest in the politics and history of post-war Europe and the psychological consequences of the Second World War is most poignantly represented in *The Pegnitz Junction* (1973), where, as Besner has argued, "recent history has swamped individual experience, distorting characters' sense of the present, because the past has been suppressed, misinterpreted, or 'buried.'"[29]

---

26 Mavis Gallant, "The Events in May: A Paris Notebook by Mavis Gallant II," *The New Yorker* (September 21, 1968), pp. 66, 128. Collected in *Paris Notebooks: Essays and Reviews* (Toronto: Macmillan, 1986).
27 Alice Munro, "Images," in *Dance of the Happy Shades* (Toronto: Ryerson, 1968), p. 35.
28 Gallant, "What is Style?" p. 6.
29 Besner, *Light*, p. 93.

These stories, which highlight the widespread geographical and psychological displacement suffered as the result of war, might be seen as the prototypical fictions of globalism, which has become such a significant phenomenon in twenty-first-century literature. However, Gallant offers a reversal of view, writing as a Canadian in Europe about the shifting populations of refugees, many of whom would constitute the post-war wave of immigrants to Canada. As Besner also notes, Gallant's stories live through the welter of personal and historical details that are either asserted or (more usually) implied, their interconnections creating a resonant understanding of the image central to the story's meaning, as with the Pegnitz Junction as a place emblematic of a nation's recent social trauma.

Gallant's fascination with urban social history encompasses not only European cities but also her native Montreal, which she revisits in several collections, notably *Home Truths* and *Across the Bridge* (1993), a Canadian dimension of her writing which has been neglected by critics until recently.[30] The six linked Linnet-Muir stories, written in the 1970s and published together in *Home Truths*, are of special interest for their reconstruction of multiethnic Montreal society between the 1920s and 1940s with its social, religious, and linguistic divisions between English and French Canadians: "Montreal was a city where the greater part of the population were wrapped in myths and sustained by belief in magic."[31] It is also an example of semi-fictional life writing, for Gallant gives us a series of portraits of the artist as a young woman and also as a child and her realization of unbelonging in her home town. Returning to the theme of displacement on a global scale and to its intimate refigurings, Linnet even traces correspondences between her own condition and that of newly arrived European war refugees ("Varieties of Exile"). For Gallant the most disturbing home truth is that the condition of being lost or even "dislocated, perhaps forever"[32] is not specific to nomads and exiles in post-war Europe but experienced most painfully at home in Canada ("Orphans' Progress," "Up North"). As she wrote in her introduction to *Home Truths*, "I have sometimes felt more at odds in Canada than anywhere else, but I never supposed I was any the less Canadian."[33]

---

30 See Kristjana Gunnars, ed., *Transient Questions: New Essays on Mavis Gallant* (Amsterdam: Rodopi, 2004).
31 Mavis Gallant, "Between Zero and One," in *Home Truths*, p. 245.
32 Mavis Gallant, "Virus X," in *Home Truths*, p. 204.
33 Mavis Gallant, "Introduction," in *Home Truths*, p. xiv.

Alice Munro

Like Gallant, Alice Munro has made the short story her primary form, and like her has found an outlet for her stories in *The New Yorker*, publishing them at roughly the same rate over about half the time. Yet if Gallant is known especially for fictions of unhomeliness, then Munro offers quite another thing, a succession of characters rooted in their particular place – also Munro's own home place – Huron County, southwestern Ontario. This distinction between Gallant and Munro is important because, while Gallant was not seen in Canada, when Munro's work began appearing in *The New Yorker* in March 1977 the reaction in Canada was quite different, celebratory and focused. By then, nationalism had come to the fore in English-speaking Canada, and Munro's stories were most emphatically drawn from Canadian conditions. Indeed, recalling the reactions occasioned by the first stories Munro submitted to *The New Yorker*, Charles McGrath, her first editor there, commented that William Shawn, the magazine's longtime chief editor, was bothered by "'the violence, the intensity of emotion, the rawness of the setting and what people [did]'" in Munro's stories.[34] However, partly because of these qualities, the magazine quickly bought two of them and Munro's long relationship with *The New Yorker* began.

Munro's career breaks neatly into two sections. She began writing while she was still a teenager; during the 1950s and 60s she worked in obscurity, known only to the few people who followed Canadian writing closely. Beyond her husband, who encouraged her writing throughout their marriage, and Robert Weaver, a literary and cultural programming producer at the CBC, Munro knew very few people who were even aware that she wrote. This began to change when she came to the attention of Earle Toppings, an editor at the Ryerson Press, during the early 1960s. He suggested the idea of a first book. *Dance of the Happy Shades*, which included stories written over a dozen years, was published in 1968; it won the Governor General's Award and so brought Munro a new level of reputation. Following it with *Lives of Girls and Women* (1971) and *Something I've Been Meaning to Tell You* (1974), Munro was well established among leading Canadian writers when her marriage broke up in 1973 and she returned to Ontario. On her own for the first time and so in need of greater support from her writing, Munro hired Virginia Barber, a New York agent, in 1976. Barber established Munro's work as a presence in the United

---

34 See Robert Thacker, *Alice Munro: Writing Her Lives* (Toronto: McClelland and Stewart, 2005), p. 321 and *passim*.

States through *The New Yorker* and other commercial magazines and also through book publication by Alfred A. Knopf, who published the Governor General's Award-winning *Who Do You Think You Are?* (1978) under the title used in the United States and Britain, *The Beggar Maid: Stories of Flo and Rose* (1979). Once Barber became involved, the second phase of Munro's career began; her stories would appear in *The New Yorker* and, every few years since 1979, a new collection would be published by Knopf.[35]

Just as this process was beginning, after Munro had published two stories in *The New Yorker*, McGrath wrote Munro to tell her that they had decided against "Chaddeleys and Flemings" – a long, two-part story that ultimately became the opening of *The Moons of Jupiter* (1982). Shawn had overruled McGrath and the other fiction editors there, believing that Munro's story was too close to autobiography. Distancing himself from the decision, McGrath wrote, "I don't know whether it's autobiographical or not, but it's my feeling that you've taken the material of reminiscence and turned it into something much stronger – a moving, complicated work of fiction."[36] Though certainly not overly concerned about her fiction's autobiographical underpinnings, Munro is herself well aware of this issue. In *The View from Castle Rock* (2006), where she decided to include three patently autobiographical pieces that she had published before but had held from her books, Munro offers a foreword that addresses the question of reminiscence versus fiction directly. Writing of the three – "Home" (1974), "Working for a Living" (1981), and "Hired Girl" (1994) – Munro explains her hesitation about them:

> In other first-person stories I had drawn on personal material, but then I did anything I wanted to do with this material. Because the chief thing I was doing was making a story. In the stories I hadn't collected I was not doing exactly that. I was doing something closer to what a memoir does – exploring a life, my own life, but not in an austere or rigorously factual way.

Concluding this paragraph, Munro asserts that autobiography and memoir are shaped by narrative artifice: "These are *stories*."[37]

---

35 Munro began attracting the attention of critics in the late 1970s and 80s. An important early book is *Probable Fictions: Alice Munro's Narrative Acts*, ed. Louis K. MacKendrick (Downsview: ECW, 1983). Two omnibus review essays by Robert Thacker allow readers to gauge the critical progress of Munro's work until the late 1990s. "Go Ask Alice: The Progress of Munro Criticism," *Journal of Canadian Studies* 26.2 (1991), pp. 156–69, and "What's 'Material'?: The Progress of Munro Criticism, Part 2," *Journal of Canadian Studies* 33.2 (1998), pp. 196–210.
36 Charles McGrath to Alice Munro, November 1, 1977, Alice Munro fonds, University of Calgary, 37.2.30.5.
37 Alice Munro, "Foreword," *The View From Castle Rock* (Toronto: McClelland and Stewart, 2006), p. x. See also Alice Munro, "What is Real?" *Canadian Forum* (September 1982), pp. 5, 36.

When she started sending him new stories in 1984, McGrath was impressed: "You're sending in these stories faster than I can edit them, and each one is more dazzling than the last. I feel the way Rilke's editor must have felt – if he had one."[38] The stories he was dealing with became *The Progress of Love* (1986), Munro's strongest collection. Of the eleven it contains, *The New Yorker* first published five; the others were placed elsewhere after McGrath and his colleagues had declined them. The last two they took, "The Progress of Love" (1985) and "White Dump," became the opening and closing stories of *Progress*, anchoring the volume. Each of these stories takes up a trio of women – daughter, mother, and grandmother – as a way of examining "the progress of love" through the generations. Paired together, these two stories look back at what Munro had done in her previous work and forward toward the complex narrative structuring so distinctive of her art.

"The Progress of Love," a story the title of which, as Magdalene Redekop has noted, both echoes that of a satiric poem by Swift ("Phillis, Or, The Progress of Love") and offers the image of life as a parade, is among Munro's most profound examinations of familial inheritance and the duplicitous powers of storytelling.[39] Here the female narrator comes to realize after her mother's death that a story about her parents which she had believed to be true is one that she has invented for herself. As she tracks through memories of her mother and the mother's stories about *her* mother, strange crises are revealed in these women's lives – the grandmother's threatened suicide in the barn, the mother's burning of her family inheritance in the kitchen stove – but strangest of all is her daughter's reconstruction of that act of wastage as evidence of her parents' married love, when it is a false memory. In this multi-stranded meditation on three women's interconnected lives, many possible meanings are generated, but no single interpretation could accommodate them all. Is it a story about familial love or about family hatreds, or does it collapse the distinction between these emotions, leaving just the sediment in the present narrator's memory, "the stories, and griefs, the old puzzles you can't resist or solve"?[40]

---

38 Charles McGrath to Alice Munro, October 15, 1984, Alice Munro fonds, University of Calgary, 396/87:2.13.
39 Magdalene Redekop, *Mothers and Other Clowns: The Stories of Alice Munro* (London: Routledge, 1992), p. 175.
40 Alice Munro, "The Progress of Love," in *The Progress of Love* (Toronto: McClelland and Stewart, 1986), p. 14.

"The Progress of Love" is a tour de force story through its retrospective cast and its explicit use of an autobiographical context. There are suggestive parallels with Munro's maternal grandmother and great-grandmother in the Ottawa valley, since the womanizing great-grandfather of the story and his religious daughter were among Munro's ancestors. Arguably, such probings of family-based relations have been constant concerns in Munro's work from the beginning, and indeed all her previous books contain stories in which autobiographical and ancestral materials are used and shaped. Yet with "The Progress of Love" – both the story and the entire collection – clear distinctions can no longer be made between fact, personal and collective memory, and invention, so fulfilling McGrath's prediction that Munro was heading toward "a moving, complicated work of fiction" when he rejected "Chaddeleys and Flemings" at Shawn's behest.

Less frequently noted than the title story, "White Dump" offers an ironic comment on love's progress, for over a fifteen-year span it chronicles the breakup of a marriage and its aftermath. It is a story told in three parts from the perspectives of a daughter, a grandmother, and a mother who leaves her husband and children for a man she has just met. As these women's stories circulate around the husband's fortieth birthday in 1969, the year of the first moon shot, they offer three different versions of that day's events in an intricately woven narrative which meshes together domesticity, random violence, and a woman's transgressive sexual desire. With its shifts in chronology and point of view, the story looks like an assemblage of anecdotes – the family's birthday treat with a plane ride down the Rideau lakes, the birthday dinner, and the beginning of the wife's love affair with the pilot, sometimes viewed up close and sometimes retrospectively.

Yet patterns are made, not through a unifying plot but through a succession of startling otherworldly images, each of which captures the human wonder that ultimately is Munro's actual subject here. The first moon shot and the family's first plane ride resonate against the key image of the "White Dump" evoked by the wife at the birthday dinner. That image binds together childish anticipation of the sweetness of a shining pile of white candy swept up from the local biscuit factory floor and a woman's romantic fantasy of erotic desire and fulfillment. As the story shifts between different frames of emotional reference it resonates against all the other partial histories of love in this volume, where "love" with its promises, its disillusions, and refigurings seems to signal the mystery surrounding relationships between men and women. The reader's response to the volume is rather like that of the narrator of the first story, who describes her responses to her mother's stories: "I always had a feeling, with my mother's talk and stories, of something swelling out behind. Like a cloud you couldn't see through, or get to the end of."[41]

Since the 1980s Munro's stories have become increasingly complex and elusive with their shifting narrative perspectives, their apparent digressions, their spatial and temporal gaps, and their multiple layers of meaning. Certainly there are thematic continuities in the stories between collections as Munro revisits familiar fictional territory, but there are also shifts of emphasis which reveal new dimensions of experience or something previously overlooked. For example, her continuing fascination with women's romantic fantasies and the secrets of female desire may be traced through all the later collections, from "Five Points" (*Friend of My Youth*, 1990) and one of her rare Australian stories, "The Jack Randa Hotel" (*Open Secrets*, 1994), through the title story in *The Love of a Good Woman* (1998) and "What Is Remembered" (*Hateship, Friendship, Courtship, Loveship, Marriage*, 2001), to "Passion" (*Runaway*, 2004) and "The Ticket" (*The View from Castle Rock*, 2006). With their shimmering variations, these stories are all related to Munro's attempts to articulate emotional and imaginative experience traditionally devalued as feminine. In a similar way she writes against the neglect of the feminine in Canada's colonial history with the stories of two women, one a Victorian poetess in "Meneseteung" (*Friend of My Youth*) and the other a working-class woman who tells stories to save her life in "A Wilderness Station" (*Open Secrets*). Both these women resist conventional feminine roles, and both are dismissed by society as eccentrics. In the course of her narrative investigations Munro expands the short story form to accommodate features from such disparate genres and sub-genres as psychobiography, dream narratives, epistolary and travel writing, jokes, Gothic fiction and murder mysteries, though wryly remarking that they do not "satisfy in the same way as a traditional mystery or romance would."[42] In this context, Richard B. Wright's *Clara Callan* (2001) deserves mention as a male writer's investigation into the secret emotional lives of two sisters from the 1930s, as does Joan Barfoot's psychological analysis of a murderous housewife in *Dancing in the Dark* (1982), all of whom might have come out of a Munro story.

There has been an increasing emphasis on ageing and the shadows of approaching death in Munro's work, on retrospection, and the unraveling of life's plots. A brilliant example would be the last story in *Hateship, Friendship*,

---

41 Ibid., p. 13.
42 Pleuke Boyce and Ron Smith, "A National Treasure: An Interview with Alice Munro," *Meanjin* 54.2 (1995), p. 227.

Courtship, Loveship, Marriage about a woman in the early stages of Alzheimer's disease, made into the film *Away from Her* in 2007, directed by the young Canadian actor-turned-director Sarah Polley and starring Julie Christie and Gordon Pinsent. Yet, as if in compensation, many of these stories see individual lives through a wider angle of vision, introducing overarching patterns intimated through allusions to Greek myths, Shakespeare, and other literary texts, which seem to overlap present circumstances, shifting the frame of reference into further dimensions of imaginative apprehension, though with no ultimate revelation. Munro does not deal in the supernatural but she does deal in mysteries and secrets, and stories like "Carried Away," "Open Secrets," and "Powers" challenge the limits of conventional realism with their glimpses of alternative realities and indecipherable signs which hint at hidden, possibly inaccessible meanings. Such shifts of emphasis have prompted new directions in Munro criticism, paying attention to her revisions of ancient myths or to the postmodern features of her narratives with their metafictional commentary and their unsettling supplements and deferrals.[43]

Munro has never had the popular success of Atwood or Shields, possibly because of her devotion to the short story form, which she has redefined. For this she is widely admired as a writer's writer, and there is at least one published essay on "How to Write like Alice Munro."[44] But perhaps Munro's narrative aesthetic is most suggestively articulated by one of her protagonists in a story which is both lucid and resistant to any final interpretation: "She seems to be looking into an open secret, something not startling until you think of trying to tell it."[45] In an odd and perverse way, Munro seems to have been approached as an ongoing discovery and source, especially for other writers who long to achieve similar effects themselves, of wonderment. Reviewing *Runaway* (2004) in *The New York Times Book Review*, Jonathan Franzen dissects the probable reasons for her putative neglect – mostly owing to Munro's devotion to the form of the short story – and makes one crucial, though over-the-top, point: "Read Munro! Read Munro!" He calls it a "simple instruction."[46] Munro's standing in both the United States and in Canada was highlighted further with *Alice Munro's Best: Selected Stories*

---

43 See Héliane Ventura and Mary Condé, eds., *Alice Munro: Writing Secrets*, Special issue of *Open Letter* 11.9/12.1 (2003–4).
44 Kim Aubrey, "How to Write like Alice Munro," *The Writer's Chronicle*, 38 (2005), pp. 12–18.
45 Alice Munro, "Open Secrets," in *Open Secrets* (Toronto: McClelland and Stewart, 1994), p. 160.
46 Jonathan Franzen, "Alice's Wonderland," *The New York Times Book Review* (November 14, 2004), p. 16.

published for the American market in 2006 by Knopf, in Canada in 2008 by McClelland and Stewart, and in the United Kingdom, also in 2008, as *Carried Away: A Selection of Stories* by Everyman's Library. Atwood provided a celebratory Introduction for all three editions. Munro's publishers announced a new volume, *Too Much Happiness*, for 2009, the year her stature was confirmed by the award of the Man Booker International Prize.

Carol Shields

Carol Shields's first novel, *Small Ceremonies*, was published in 1976, and, recalling her response to it, Munro said, "You just get that shiver when you come across a real writer, and I had that with her."[47] That novel is about white Canadian middle-class family life, told by a woman who is married to an English professor and is the mother of two teenaged children; she is also a writer who is finishing a biography of Susanna Moodie. It offers a shadowy parallel with Shields's own life at the time: married to a Canadian academic (who was not an English professor), the mother of five children, author of *Susanna Moodie: Voice and Vision* (her University of Ottawa Master's thesis, published 1976) and of two volumes of poetry (*Others*, 1972 and *Intersect*, 1974). Such biographical speculation on connections between fiction and real life is encouraged by Shields's domestic realism and by her own fascination with the genre of biography throughout her writing career.

That career pattern is an interesting variant on the other three considered in this chapter, for though Shields published three more novels and a short story collection in Canada in the 1970s and early 80s, it was only with *Swann: A Mystery* (1987)[48] and *The Republic of Love* (1992) that she began to attract much critical attention. Her breakthrough into real literary celebrity came with *The Stone Diaries* (1993), which won the Governor General's Award in Canada and was nominated for the Booker Prize in Britain that year, and then received the Pulitzer Prize in the United States in 1995. By the time she died in 2003, Shields had become an internationally popular writer. Her output during those last eight years was remarkably prolific: she published two more novels (*Larry's Party* and *Unless*), another collection of stories, her biography of Jane Austen (2001), three plays, and a co-edited anthology of women's reminiscences, *Dropped Threads: What We Aren't Told* (2001). *Dropped Threads 2* appeared in

---

47 Maria Russo, "Final Chapter," *The New York Times Magazine* (April 14, 2002), p. 35.
48 This was the first novel by Shields to appear in Britain, published as *Mary Swann* (London: Fourth Estate, 1990).

2003, and her *Collected Stories*, published on the first anniversary of her death, contains the previously unpublished story "Segue," part of the unfinished novel she was working on before her death.

Through her immensely varied output there are continuities of subject matter and interest which are signaled in *Small Ceremonies*, the most important coded into the concept of "narrative hunger," that fascination with storytelling as an attempt to glimpse the mystery of other people's lives and to enlarge one's own life, which is first expressed by the protagonist in that novel, again in interviews, and in her essay "Narrative Hunger and the Overflowing Cupboard," delivered as an address at her *alma mater*, Hanover College, Indiana, in 1996.[49] That hunger has led her in the dual directions of biography and fictive biography/autobiography, though her stated preference is for the fictional modes of life writing: "[B]iography and history have a narrative structure, but they don't tell us much about the interior lives of people. This seems to me to be fiction's magic, that it attempts to be an account of all that cannot be documented but is, nevertheless, true."[50]

In her two most popular novels, *The Stone Diaries* and *Larry's Party*, Shields negotiates with generic conventions in different ways, first in the autobiography of a woman who believes that, if her life story were ever to be written, it would be "an assemblage of dark voids and unbridgeable gaps"[51] and then in the biography of a male subject who feels an outsider in his own life: "This was his history, but none of it, it seemed, reflecting *him*."[52] Shields treats biography in a very postmodern way, appropriating it in order to question the very foundation on which the biographical project is based. *The Stone Diaries* takes the form of a traditional biography with a family tree at the beginning, chapter titles running from "Birth, 1905" to "Death," and a selection of family photographs, though from the beginning its aberrations foreground the difficulties attendant on both biography and autobiography. Opening with Daisy Goodwill's telling the story of her own birth in the first person, Shields moves the reader through Daisy's life by various narrative shifts, highlighting the contingency of attempting to textualize or indeed to capture any life. Filled with humor and often painful irony, this novel ends just after Daisy is "laid to rest" with a wry little joke. Her "final (unspoken) words" are "I am not at peace," and, looking at the beautiful spring pansies on her coffin, one of the

---

49 Published in Edward Eden and Dee Goertz, eds., *Carol Shields, Narrative Hunger, and the Possibilities of Fiction* (Toronto: University of Toronto Press, 2003), pp. 19–36.
50 Marjorie Anderson, "Interview with Carol Shields," *Prairie Fire* 16.1 (1995), p. 150.
51 Carol Shields, *The Stone Diaries* (London: Fourth Estate, 1993), p. 76.
52 Carol Shields, *Larry's Party* (London: Fourth Estate, 1997), p. 171.

mourners says, "Someone should have thought of daisies."[53] Attempting a comprehensive assessment of the novel, David Williams focuses on "the primary question about the narrative act: "Is Daisy the subject of her own story? Or is she the object of someone else's story? Is her life told by many narrators ... or is her telling subject to the judgement of an omniscient narrator"?[54] *Larry's Party* destabilizes the biographical genre by offering a "spatial figuring of Larry's life story rather than staying within the constraints of a [conventional] temporal pattern,"[55] structuring his life story like a garden maze, full of digressions and doublings back where "the path to a maze's goal is always shortened by turning away from the goal."[56] Once again Shields is refashioning biography to try to account for the unrecorded moments in her subject's life.

Shields's interest in revisions of genre is symptomatic of her unassumingly feminist commitment as a writer. "Women's writing has already begun to dismantle the rigidities of genre," as she remarked in her Hanover College lecture,[57] and in *The Republic of Love* she revises women's popular romance, critiquing the courtship plot with its clichés of language and feeling in a manner which the critic Faye Hammill argues is comparable with Jane Austen's complex and often parodic revisions of eighteenth-century sentimental fiction. Hammill also notes that *Swann* "revises the narrative form of the detective mystery,"[58] though Shields's most spectacular narrative experiments are to be found in her short stories. Here again there is a strong gender inflection, as her comments on women's storytelling in her essay "Arriving Late: Starting Over" clearly show.[59] That essay locates the moment of her breakaway from realism in 1983 with her first short story collection, *Various Miracles*. Shields confesses her disaffection for the linear short story design, which she describes with a surprisingly ribald hint at its gender affiliations "modeled perhaps on the orgasmic pattern of tumescence followed by

---

53 Shields, *The Stone Diaries*, p. 361.
54 David Williams, "Making Stories, Making Selves: 'Alternate Versions' in *The Stone Diaries*," *Canadian Literature* 186 (2005), pp. 10–11.
55 Coral Ann Howells, "Larry's A/Mazing Spaces," in *Carol Shields and the Extra-Ordinary*, ed. Marta Dvořák and Manina Jones (Montreal and Kingston: McGill-Queen's University Press, 2007), pp. 115–35.
56 Shields, *Larry's Party*, p. 152.
57 Carol Shields, "Narrative Hunger and the Overflowing Cupboard," in Eden and Goertz, eds., *Carol Shields, Narrative Hunger*, p. 35.
58 Faye Hammill, "*The Republic of Love* and Popular Romance," in Eden and Goertz, eds., *Carol Shields, Narrative Hunger*, pp. 61.
59 Carol Shields, "Arriving Late: Starting Over," *How Stories Mean*, ed. John Metcalf and J. R. (Tim) Struthers (Erin: Porcupine's Quill), pp. 244–51.

detumescence, an endless predictable circle of desire, fulfilment, and quiescence" (p. 248), together with her preference for an episodic structure of apparently random moments and coincidences where ordinariness splits open to reveal the extra-ordinary.[60]

These stories represent Shields's first postmodern metafictional experiments – she claimed that postmodernism gave her "a breath of that precious oxygen of permission"[61] – which led to her reformulation of genre conventions in *Swann* and her subsequent novels. In her other two collections, *The Orange Fish* and *Dressing Up for the Carnival*, Shields continues to push against the limits of realism with her emphasis on women writing and reading, using fiction to reshape reality ("Hazel," "Collision"), revealing contours of myth under the everyday,[62] and her delight in word play and intertextuality.[63] This narrative and stylistic experimentation is at its most exuberant in her third carnivalesque collection, which begins with a parade in the title story, moves into the surreal with a story like "Reportage" (where a Roman arena is unearthed on the Canadian prairie), to end ironically and humorously with "Dressing Down" in its delicate slippages of voice and tone between a staid Victorian marriage and a summer nudist camp, the Club Soleil.

These stories may seem a far cry from the more conventional narrative forms of her biography of Jane Austen and *Unless*, though in both there are new departures with the emphasis on female narrative self-consciousness and also on feminine anger and possible ways of articulating it decorously in fiction. In her biography Shields identifies with Austen's strategies of deception and irony, while *Unless* reads like a savage reprise of *Small Ceremonies*, where the Happy Families plot is shattered by the trauma of a teenage daughter's inexplicable desertion, an interesting case of delayed exposition where the reasons for such behavior are only revealed at the end. Here Shields's characteristic concerns with family relations and female friendships, focused through a women writer's consciousness are filtered through the lens of feminist protest: *"But we've come so far,* that's the thinking. So far compared with fifty or a hundred years ago. Well, no, we've 'arrived' at the new millennium and we haven't arrived at all. We've been sent over to the

---

60 See Simone Vauthier, "Closure in Carol Shields's *Various Miracles*," in *Reverberations: Explorations in the Canadian Short Story* (Concord. Anansi, 1993), pp. 114–31.
61 Shields, "Narrative Hunger," p. 34.
62 See Héliane Ventura, "Eros in the Eye of the Mirror: The Rewriting of Myths in Carol Shields's 'Mirrors,'" in Dvořák and Jones, eds., *Carol Shields and the Extra-Ordinary*, pp. 205–20.
63 See Marta Dvořák, "Disappearance and 'the Vision Multiplied': Writing as Performance," in ibid., pp. 223–37.

side pocket of the snooker table and made to disappear."[64] Though the novel is wrenched into a comic resolution, its conveniently fabricated quality is obvious both to the narrator and to the reader: "The uncertainty principle; did anyone ever believe otherwise?"[65] The fragility of that ending is a reminder that beneath Shields's fictions of domesticity and order, or of wilder narrative invention, there is a sense of women's dissatisfaction and restlessness which persists, from the first sentences of *Small Ceremonies*: "Sunday night. And the thought strikes me that I ought to be happier than I am,"[66] to the final sentences of "Segue": "What is my position in the universe, in the fen and bog of my arrangements? The reply comes promptly, mocking my tone of high seriousness: if it weren't for my particular circumstances I would be happy."[67]

In Atwood's second Empson lecture at Cambridge, she addressed the relation between the writer, the reader, and the text: "A book may outlive its author, and it moves too, and it too can be said to change – but not in the manner of the telling. It changes in the manner of the reading ... works of literature are recreated by each generation of readers, who make them new by finding fresh meanings in them."[68] Atwood continues to contextualize her observations in both learned and personalized ways, and it should be no surprise that Atwood mentions Gallant, Munro, and Shields in the course of those lectures. With them, she shares the last several decades of the twentieth century and the first years of the twenty-first; with them, she shares literary reputation at home and abroad; with them, finally, she shares the position of being among Canada's and the world's preeminent writers. That privileged status may change as time passes and other writers and readers emerge, Atwood knows, but there can be no doubt about it in the first decade of the twenty-first century. It is there in the texts these women writers have made and are continuing to make, "newly, and boundlessly, resourceful" as they are.

---

64 Carol Shields, *Unless* (Toronto: Random House Canada, 2002), p. 99.
65 Ibid., p. 318.
66 Carol Shields, *Small Ceremonies* (London: Fourth Estate, 1995), p. 1.
67 Carol Shields, "Segue," in *The Collected Stories* (Toronto: Random House Canada, 2004), p. 20.
68 Atwood, *Negotiating*, p. 50.

19

The short story

W. H. NEW

In 1965, recognizing that publishers had released relatively few short story collections during the previous decade, the *Literary History of Canada* predicted that the genre was dying.¹ Instead, short fiction thrived, copious and flexible. By the first decade of the twenty-first century approximately fifty collections were appearing every year, the increase in numbers coinciding with social growth, changes in the means of production, and extended critical attention. While markets for the genre remained fragile, short fiction nevertheless became more visible and more varied, with publishers seeking further ways to attract commercial attention and new writers keen to address readers in a different manner and voice. New stories ranged widely in subject and form: from Alice Munro's Altmanesque collections, where western Ontario radiates into story-making, to Rohinton Mistry's layered sequence set in Toronto and Bombay; from Alistair MacLeod's memorializing Cape Breton cadences to the serious comedy of Austin Clarke and Thomas King; from Mavis Gallant's and Guy Vanderhaeghe's dances with temporality to the rhetorical adventures of Audrey Thomas, Tamas Dobozy, Mark Anthony Jarman, Douglas Glover, Thomas Wharton, and Lisa Moore. Numerous writers, such as Nancy Lee, Rachel Wyatt, Jack Hodgins, and Bill Gaston, dramatized the particularity of gender, place, and social politics. Some, such as Olive Senior, Adam Lewis Schroeder, and Joseph Boyden, focused on issues relating to ethnic and colonial history. Still others – among them Elizabeth Brewster, Kristjana Gunnars,

---

1 See Hugo McPherson, "Fiction 1940–60," in Carl F. Klinck et al., eds., *Literary History of Canada: Canadian Literature in English* (Toronto: University of Toronto Press, 1965), pp. 704–6. In volume 4 of the second edition of *Literary History of Canada*, David Jackel strives to correct this perception, focusing on short fiction written between 1972 and 1984 but surveying the emergence of the genre in Canada in the decades prior to that time as well; see his "Short Fiction" in W. H. New et al., eds., *Literary History of Canada* (Toronto: University of Toronto Press, 1990), pp. 46–72. Allan Weiss's bibliography of stories published between 1950 and 1983, *A Comprehensive Bibliography of English-Canadian Short Stories, 1950–1983* (Toronto: ECW, 1989), is an invaluable reference resource.

Timothy Findley, Barry Dempster, Ken Mitchell, Mark Frutkin, and David Watmough – established their primary reputation with their poems, plays, or novels, but also published noteworthy collections of stories. The history of the genre during these decades thus demonstrates a series of differing designs, due in part to radical changes in technology, strategic developments in the publishing industry, and the emergence of succeeding generations of writers, all coping with the demands of the medium and the institutions of communication, and eager to express their understanding of their own time in the world.

Several established writers continued to write, some not publishing even their first collections until after 1960: Henry Kreisel (*The Almost Meeting*, 1981), Howard O'Hagan (*The Woman Who Got on at Jasper Station*, 1963), A. M. Klein (*Short Stories*, 1983), Joyce Marshall (*Any Time at All*, 1993). Ethel Wilson displayed her range of styles – satiric, Gothic, didactic – in *Mrs. Golightly and other stories* (1961). James Reaney's stories were not assembled till *The Box Social* (1996). Barry Callaghan's collection of his father's *Esquire* and *Scribner's* stories, *The Lost and Found Stories of Morley Callaghan* (1985), confirmed the elder writer's reputation as an urban moralist. Sinclair Ross's stories of sexuality, depression, and savage uncertainty (familiar to magazine readers in the 1930s and 1940s) appeared to critical acclaim in *The Lamp at Noon and other stories* (1968); fourteen years passed before a second collection appeared. W. O. Mitchell's *Jake and the Kid* (1961) assembled anecdotal sketches that had become familiar to CBC radio listeners in the 1950s; they pose dilemmas in the life of a crusty farmhand and a boy from "Crocus, Saskatchewan," then amiably resolve them. Unlike Mitchell's secure world, Malcolm Lowry's was always precarious, as is evident in the fractured identities of the character Sigbjørn Wilderness in Lowry's posthumously published *Hear us O Lord from Heaven Thy Dwelling Place* (1961). Syntactically complex, this collection reads "knowledge" as a terrifying comfort and "translation" as a dislocating comedy; it closes powerfully with "The Forest Path to the Spring," a paean to the healing grace of nature.

Although Margaret Laurence and Norman Levine also started to publish in the 1950s, their careers flourished in subsequent decades, when they also strongly influenced the writers who followed, such as Jack Hodgins and John Metcalf. Hodgins read Laurence and recognized the legitimacy of writing about a particular locale. Metcalf praised Levine for his style and his freedom from nationalist bias. Others praised Levine's insight into social status and Laurence's concern for cultural diversity and women's independence. But the early 1960s was also a time when established critics were celebrating *Hugh Garner's Best Stories* (1963) for its ostensible "realism," leading Ryerson Press to invite Garner to introduce, and so "validate," Alice Munro's first book, *Dance of the Happy Shades* (1968). One sign of ensuing change was the effective disappearance of Garner from critical commentary, and the increasing international celebration of Levine, Hodgins, Laurence, and Munro.

Collectively, these interconnected careers also show writers turning to alternative forms. The conventional short story followed a textbook pattern: rising action, climax, denouement. Stressing character development, it might hinge on a moment of recognition or "epiphany," or, if plot-driven, arrange events so as to permit closure, generally to reaffirm order in the world. Raymond Knister had already broken away from this rough design, experimenting with free indirect discourse and "open endings," techniques that Mavis Gallant and others honed, and that quickly became mainstream. Several separate volumes on the literary practice of individual writers (for example, Munro, Gallant, Blaise) did appear in the late twentieth century, but those that deal with writers who have published both short fiction and novels (for example, Atwood, Bowering, Hodgins, Mistry, Hood) tend to emphasize the longer form (and, in connection with Atwood and Bowering, their poetry). Moreover, while the essays in Drew Hayden Taylor's *Me Funny* (Vancouver: Douglas and McIntyre, 2005) illuminate the role of humor in Native communities, humor in the work of such writers as Gallant, Atwood, Wyatt, Gartner, and Arnason remains unexamined in detail. As of 2008, extended studies of writers both established (Birdsell, Burnard, Matt Cohen, Levine, Richards, Ray Smith, Ron Smith, Thomas, Vanderhaeghe) and more recently published (for example, Dobozy, Fleming, Gaston, Henderson, Lee, Lyon, Moore, Redhill, Svendsen, Taylor, and Wharton) also wait to be written. Mitchell's vernacular speech, Klein's and Kreisel's acuity about ethnic culture, Ross's imagery, Marshall's appreciation of social and gender differences, the political parables of francophone writers (Jacques Ferron's *Contes du pays incertain*, 1962; Gilles Vigneault's *Tales sur la pointe des pieds*, 1972): these, too, showed how storytelling techniques shaped the substance of the story being told. Successful writers from 1960 onwards took this maxim to heart, and refined their craft. In the process, lines blurred between story, essay, long poem, lyric sequence, travel anecdote, radio drama, autobiography, novella. The short story both contracted (to "flash-fiction" of fewer than 100 words) and expanded (to *c.* 30,000 words). No longer did Edgar Allan Poe's definition of the form,[2] as a prose narrative that could be read at a single sitting, easily apply.

---

2 Poe's influential review of Nathaniel Hawthorne's *Twice-Told Tales* appeared in *Graham's Magazine* in May 1842; it has been much reprinted, as in Charles E. May, ed., *The New Short Story Theories* (Athens: Ohio University Press, 1994), pp. 60–4.

Although several writers, including Mavis Gallant and Timothy Taylor, included novellas within their story collections, this long form seldom separately found a publisher – Warren Cariou's *The Exalted Company of Roadside Martyrs* (1999) and John Metcalf's *Girl in Gingham* (1978) are exceptions. Scarcely represented in anthologies, novellas tended to be overlooked by critics and readers alike. A dearth of anthologies was not the issue; scores appeared, from those designed for use in junior schools to those that affirmed the aesthetic priorities of a particular literary coterie.[3] Most focused on a single subject, region, gender, ethnicity, or sexual identity, or conversely surveyed a range of styles, topics, and forms. Whereas Robert Weaver's multi-volume series *Canadian Short Stories* tended to privilege realist storytelling conventions, collections edited by George Bowering (*And other stories*, 2001, for example) leaned towards minimalism and *bricolage*. Metcalf's *Sixteen by Twelve* (1970), Wayne Grady's *The Penguin Book of Canadian Short Stories* (1980), Michael Ondaatje's *From Ink Lake* (1990), and W. H. New's *Canadian Short Fiction* (1986; 2nd ed. 1997) variously collect Native tales, early sketches and romances, realist psychodramas, and contemporary metatexts. That the work of Alice Munro should appear in a wide range of anthologies testifies not only to its craft and status in critical circles but also to two contrasting ways of reading Munro's work – as realist and representational, and as rhetorical and psychological, glimpsing human behavior partially, through image and embedded narrative.

Three annual series – *Best Canadian Stories*, *Coming Attractions* (both from Oberon Press), and *The Journey Prize Anthology* (from McClelland and Stewart) – showcased new writers or the best of a given year's work. "Best" stories had been collected by numerous earlier editors as well, though in practice their versions of "best" had loosely privileged modernist realism. Geoff Hancock, whose efforts to highlight the strength of the contemporary short story involved him editorially in the influential *Canadian Fiction Magazine* (1971–97), resisted this tendency by championing *Magic Realism* (1980): that is, the uncontradictory presence of the surreal within the real, as in works by Stephen Guppy and W. P. Kinsella. Eric McCormack's *Inspecting the Vaults* (1987) combines magic realism with the macabre. Other challenges to realist conventions came from writers who devised speculative and alternative worlds. Examples include Robert Sawyer, Candas Jane Dorsey, and

---

3 It should be emphasized that much valuable commentary appears in anthologies, in editorial introductions, commentaries, and notes – some of which has been subsequently assembled in critical anthologies, for instance, John Metcalf and J. R. (Tim) Struthers, eds., *How Stories Mean* (Erin: Porcupine's Quill, 1993).

Nalo Hopkinson, who published sf[4] stories in the various *Tesseracts* anthologies that began, with Judith Merril's urging, in 1985.

These changes in style, strategy, and critical taste had ramifications within academia and industry. With some exceptions, larger publishers tended to be conservative, making decisions based on perceived value, established reputation, and likelihood of sale. For example, Laurence, Munro, Gallant, Mistry, MacLeod, and Atwood all published with McClelland and Stewart, while Thomas, Blaise, Hodgins, Basil Johnston, Thomas King, Janice Kulyk Keefer, Bonnie Burnard (*Casino*, 1994), Dennis Bock (*Olympia*, 1998), and Tamas Dobozy appeared variously with HarperCollins, Doubleday, Viking Penguin, and for a time Macmillan, although these writers did publish with more than one publisher over the course of their careers. Previously unknown writers were more likely to be first published by Porcupine's Quill, Oolichan, Talonbooks, Cormorant, Anansi, Raincoast, Turnstone, Arsenal, or Polestar.

In the 1970s, developments in technology – coupled with government support for publication, partly to fend off American control over book distribution in Canada – led to numerous smaller publishers developing attractive lists, often locally oriented or avant-garde. As they moved from hand-cranked mimeograph machine to photo-offset printing to computer graphics, small publishers could produce high-quality print runs outside centers that had largely controlled the industry. With still further developments in computer technology in the 1990s, all publishers found that radical notions of what constituted "the page" were possible to render visually. With changes in print design came new ways of imagining how stories should look, new strategies for reading them, and consequently new challenges for reviewers in both little magazines and commercial journals.

Journals became agents of change. In place of the romances that filled the pages of *Collier's* and other large-distribution magazines, small journals such as *Geist*, *Descant*, *Rampike*, *dANDelion*, *Brick*, and *TickleAce* – and internet sites – found room for non-linear and self-reflexive narratives, and for exchanges about practice and style. Academic curricula opened to courses in short fiction and theory; critical journals such as *Short Story*[5] emerged. Writers' collectives

---

4 In contemparary usage, especially among aficionados, who make the distinction, "sf" refers to both "science fiction" and "speculative fiction" (that is, those works that emphasize the scientific principles behind a fiction and those that hypothesize a fantasy).

5 The history of short fiction in Canada has been influenced by events and organizations outside the country as well as within. The journal *Short Story* is one of several enterprises sponsored by the international Society for the Study of the Short Story (chartered in 1994); among the organizers of this Society are such distinguished American short story critics as Mary Rohrberger, Susan Lohafer, and Maurice Lee.

such as Newfoundland's Burning Rock provided discussion, training, and support, as did writers' retreats (Banff, Sage Hill) and academic workshops. Writers' Workshop at the University of Iowa attracted many Canadian students, including Jarman, Kinsella, and Clark Blaise, who later became its director. In the 1960s a few Canadian universities established creative writing programs; several more followed over the next thirty years. Among accomplished short story writers who served as faculty are Alistair MacLeod at Windsor, Jack Hodgins at Victoria, and Linda Svendsen and George McWhirter at the University of British Columbia. By 2000, publishers had discovered a number of creative writing school graduates at the start of their careers, especially those – K. D. Miller (*A Litany in Time of Plague*, 1994, in part about AIDS), Genni Gunn (*Hungers*, 2002), Charlotte Gill (*Ladykiller*, 2005), and others – who took illness, anger, and urban trauma for their subject. These publishers were seeking a younger generation of writers in order to reach the new century's readers, and, by this time, literary voices that bristled with attitude had become *de rigueur*.

Books and journals were not the only media through which narrative was told. Just as radio readings and dramatic adaptations of short stories altered how short fictions could be received – through voices and sound effects – so did film versions of stories affect both the manner of storytelling and the impact on observers. Film versions of short fiction sometimes fixed for spectators how they visualized characters and scenes; by transforming verbal imagery into visual sign, they could render setting symbolically; they could also use fade-out or flashback to dramatize transitions and time changes, add a musical score, alter relationships, or simplify a plot-line. The National Film Board produced cinematic adaptations of several short stories in the 1960s – Hugh Hood's "The Red Kite" in 1965, Joan Finnigan's folktale-form "The Best Damn Fiddler from Calabogie to Kaladar" in 1968. Mordecai Richler's "The Street" appeared in 1986. The greater number of adaptations were released in the 1980s: Munro's "Thanks for the Ride" (1983), Guy Vanderhaeghe's powerful "Cages" (1984), the same year that two of Sinclair Ross's most anthologized stories appeared as films: "One's a Heifer" (dir. Anne Wheeler) and "The Painted Door" (dir. Bruce Pittman). Hodgins's nostalgic "The Concert Stages of Europe" (1985) was followed by versions of stories by Callaghan, Findley, Ernest Buckler, Brian Moore. From 1996 through 2004 (in cooperation with Atlantis Films), the NFB produced "Short Story Video Collections," packaging new videos with re-releases of earlier films. Each narrative in video form lasted thirty minutes – the NFB's intention being to reach school audiences and home viewers through television. Sheldon Currie adapted his Gothic story about a Nova Scotia mine disaster, "The Glace Bay Miners' Museum," into the prize-winning 114-minute film, "Margaret's Museum" (dir. Mort Ransen), which, with additional private funding, was released internationally to theatre screening.

Social and technological developments, which questioned paradigms of uniform nationhood, challenged assumptions about fixed or consistent identity, and disrupted existing patterns of communication, had a rough counterpart in several forms of "experimental" prose, such as that of Matt Cohen, D. M. Fraser, J. Michael Yates, Dave Godfrey, Brian Fawcett, George Bowering, Douglas Glover, and the writers associated with the Montreal Story Tellers. Yates's *The Abstract Beast* (1971) asked what relation exists between the conventions of storytelling and public assumptions about reality. Godfrey's political fables in *Death Goes Better with Coca-Cola* (1967; rev. 1973) used literary fantasy and the *I Ching* to attack corporate globalism, and cautionary tales in *Dark Must Yield* (1978) to encourage global social responsibility. Cohen – the range of his work sampled in *Night Flights* (1978) – probed ethnic rivalries in Ontario and Europe in his later writings, but in his earlier tales let loose a surreal imagination: Columbus reappears in a circus sideshow, Galahad teaches school, a mechanic's brain fills up with dust. Fraser's *Class Warfare* (1974) probed strategies of organization – the demands of songs and examination questions, the plight of someone who lives on "Masterpiece Avenue." Fawcett's *My Career with the Leafs* (1982) adapts sports metaphors to an analysis of other games that people play, and *Capital Tales* (1984) culminates in a conversation with Thomas Carlyle on the idea of progress and unbridled capitalism.

Bowering's numerous collections of essays and stories (for example, *Standing on Richards*, 2004), adopt a jaunty, even prankish, manner towards events and institutions – which does not disguise a seriousness about living intently, about finding value by scraping beyond the clutches of cliché. Glover, too, challenges conventional story form, openly espousing the postmodern philosophy of language-as-game-playing, whereby narrative does not lead *to* the ratification of some moral premise but carries the reader *through* a linguistic field. "Story" happens when reader and writer *participate* in what Glover calls "modules" – units of composition – as in *Notes Home from a Prodigal Son* (1999). For instance, the eighteen separate units in the title story of *Dog Attempts to Drown Man in Saskatoon* (1985) tell of a man and woman separating, a blind man's dog drowning, Wittgenstein's fragmentations of holistic structure, an art gallery and what one sees there, and the contradictoriness, the inconsistency, of the self-aware style. By following the fragmentation, the reader does not reassemble details into a closed plot but rather enters the mindset of the narrator, with all its insights, ironies, defense mechanisms, explanations, and seemingly free associations, until the cumulative weight of clarification drowns him as he comes to believe that no understanding can ever be final.

Clark Blaise's short fictions (for example, *A North American Education*, 1973) might well be read in relation to his life, an interpretation reinforced by the multi-volume reprint of his work (2000–) according to setting: "Pittsburgh," "Southern," "Montreal," "World." Yet the individual stories derive their force less from setting than from style: Blaise takes the reader into character through language, by crafting a rhetorical form that illuminates the set of mind that preoccupies him. "Eyes" adopts a fiercely threatening second-person point of view; "A Class of New Canadians" dances between a claim on fluency and a lust for power; "Salad Days" deals with lost language and Alzheimer's disease, playing metatextually with its own composition. As with Blaise, so with Ray Smith, in *Cape Breton Is the Thought Control Centre of Canada* (1969); Leon Rooke, in more than a dozen collections, including *Cry Evil* (1980) and *Who Do You Love?* (1992), where absurdity crops up as an ordinary dimension of daily life; Raymond Fraser (*Rum River*, 1997); and John Metcalf, mentor of numerous writers who published with Tim Inkster's Porcupine's Quill Press, among whom are Vivette J. Kady (*Most Wanted*, 2005), Ramona Dearing (*So Beautiful*, 2004), Keath Fraser (*Telling My Love Lies*, 1996), Sharon English (*Zero Gravity*, 2006), and Steven Heighton. Heighton's stories include both comic and emotionally wrenching narratives ("Five Paintings of the New Japan," *Flight Paths of the Emperor*, 1992; "To Everything a Season," *On Earth as It Is*, 1995).

All of them learned something of their craft from Norman Levine (*Thin Ice*, 1979) and Hugh Hood. Levine's pared-back tales give the illusion of translucency, of character and landscape viewed directly, without the interference of an observer; far from simple, they testify to the power of choosing the exact word. Hood's effective sketch sequence *Around the Mountain: Scenes from Montreal Life* (1967) reappeared as one of the several volumes of his *Collected Stories*, a series that began in 1990 with *Flying a Red Kite*. Carefully composed, by rhythm as well as image, the sketches and stories stress the importance of arranged detail, balanced sentences, phrases working incrementally (often in threes) to reveal the shape or shades of recognition. Informed by Roman Catholic conscience and iconography, Hood's writing turns on moral questions. Blaise's work grows out of the shifting dialects of his cross-border life, Smith's through Cape Breton vernacular. Metcalf's is influenced by the aesthetics of modern British stylists, and by a passion for the musicality of prose, using punctuation to score cadence.

Though differing significantly in age, Blaise, Metcalf, Fraser, Smith, and Hood came together in the 1970s to form a group called The Montreal Story Tellers;[6] the aim, Metcalf avers, was less to express a common aesthetic than to sell books – though the camaraderie of performing together soon led to an appreciation of each other's styles of storytelling. Publishers of the day had proved reluctant to accept short story collections, and bookstores equally reluctant to stock them when they did appear, on grounds that stories did not sell. The Story Tellers' plan was to read stories aloud, to school and other groups, stressing cadence through performance and thus enticing readers into listening well. Various writing festivals (starting with the Harbourfront reading series in Toronto in 1974 and the Vancouver International Writers Festival in 1988) also actively drew attention to the aural effectiveness of short fiction. Metcalf and Blaise went on not only to read and write with power, but also to inform and explain. Metcalf edited a careful selection of Hood's work, *Light Shining Out of Darkness and Other Stories* (2001);[7] Blaise edited what his subtitle calls the "best" stories of Metcalf, *Standing Stones* (2004). Over time, they came to be among the most influential editors and teachers of their generation.

A contrast between Margaret Laurence and Audrey Thomas demonstrates further how changes in short story form interconnected with contemporary social issues. While both writers addressed Africa, memory, and women's experience – thus articulating both private and civil tension – they differed in strategy. Thomas's stories, from the beginning, live *in language*, whereas Laurence departed slowly from conventional patterning. Thomas's first story, "If One Green Bottle ..." (collected in *Ten Green Bottles*, 1967), won an *Atlantic Monthly* prize in 1965 while the author was still studying Old English; several collections appeared by 2001. *The Tomorrow-Tamer and Other Stories* (1963), which Laurence wrote mainly in Vancouver after having lived in East and West Africa from 1950 to 1957, depicts an external world where character is central and closure desirable. A disfigured man takes a job as a performer; a

---

6 For studies of the group's aims and accomplishments, and for the writers' memoirs, see Robert Lecker, *On the Line* (Downsview: ECW, 1982) and J. R. (Tim) Struthers, *The Montreal Story Tellers* (Montreal: Véhicule, 1985).

7 *Light Shining Out of Darkness* (2001) was one of several volumes of "selected short stories" edited by invitation for McClelland and Stewart's New Canadian Library; other volumes include Joyce Marshall's *Any Time at All and Other Stories* (1993, selected by Timothy Findley), Mavis Gallant's *The Moslem Wife and Other Stories* (1994, selected by Mordecai Richler), and Stephen Leacock's *My Financial Career and Other Follies* (1993, selected by David Staines).

post-Independence hairdresser learns how to adapt her skills to her new clientele; a woman stands as a figure of shelter for a world now full of strangers. *The Tomorrow-Tamer* expresses responsible concern about distress in modern Africa, and hope (despite the misapprehensions of missionaries and educators) for cross-cultural understanding in a better future. Critics have asked what "better" means in these stories: does it equate with a reclaimed African past, Euro-American notions of progress, or a personal vision of tolerance and understanding?

Learning from African writers – for instance, her friend Chinua Achebe – that she could look at her own past and society creatively, Laurence turned in the eight connected stories of her more adventurous book, *A Bird in the House* (1970), to write about Manitoba. Sequentially this series recounts Vanessa MacLeod's troubling encounters, as she grows up, with family, death, poverty, war and madness, ethnicity, and education. As narrator, Vanessa must come to terms with both grief and influence; she must revisit her home (that is, revisit the past) to reconcile herself with the autocratic grandfather whom she resists and resembles, and to recognize that her most powerful connection has been with her mother, whom she only in retrospect begins to appreciate. Individual stories can be read for their insights into Depression society and their claim on artistry as one form of affirmation and escape. "Horses of the Night" (the title alluding to a phrase in Ovid's *Amores* – *O lente lente currite noctis equi!* – reiterated in Christopher Marlowe's *The Tragical History of Dr. Faustus*) is a technically sustained dramatization of slow decay, continuing love, and a fierce, necessary assertion of independence. Balancing the voice of the child Vanessa with that of the literarily more sophisticated adult narrator, the book also reveals how gender and social politics can alternatively codify, control, or enable choice.

Thomas's stories also dramatize gender and social politics, as do her novels *Mrs. Blood*, *Latakia*, and *Intertidal Life*, all of which began as short fiction. But from *Ten Green Bottles* on, Thomas asks readers to understand her characters' dilemmas through broken syntax, the fragmentation of conventional vocabulary, patterns of sound, and paths of association. In her essays, Thomas writes of the fascination of language, whether visual (the "other" in *mother*, the "over" in *lover*), aural and bilingual (the *pain* that bread makers sell fresh each day), or allusive (textual references to archetype and fairytale). Linguistic twists often comically uncover covert narratives. Consulting phrase books with oblique success, characters travel away from anglophone North America, discovering who they are only when they find out that the language they have taken for granted will no longer serve them.

The "other country" that the stories visit is psychological as well as geographical – Thomas's characters being repeatedly concerned with loss, especially the loss of a child. "If One Green Bottle ..." follows the stream-of-consciousness thoughts of a woman in labor, her waves of language all the more painful when they cease in stillbirth. "The More Little Mummy in the World" (*Ladies & Escorts*, 1977) logs the fractured observations of a woman in Mexico as she visits a cemetery on the Day of the Dead and struggles to come to terms with an abortion her (ex)-lover has insisted on. "Breaking the Ice," in *The Path of Totality* (2001), moves towards reconciliation: not in closure, but in celebration, when desire proves less painful and love within the characters' reach.

The overlapping motifs in such stories – dislocation, marginality, travel, diaspora, the reality of language, competing realities of entitlement and community – presented formal challenges of a sort that several writers met by combining related stories into unified collections, variously called *cycles, sequences, composites*.[8] Titles such as Hodgins's *The Barclay Family Theatre* (1981) and Munro's *The Beggar Maid: Stories of Flo and Rose*, 1979 (the American title of *Who Do You Think You Are?*, 1978) emphasize this loose connectedness. As early as George Elliott's eloquent first collection, *The Kissing Man* (1962), it was clear that a powerfully elliptical series could incrementally reveal how the known but unstated secrets of a small town could destroy trust, but also how touch and love could sometimes heal. By 1980 some publishers had found that book-length sequences also sold because of how they contained an embedded continuous narrative. Commercial motives aside, the story-sequence/cycle appealed to writers for a different reason: it allowed them to suggest unity and disparity at the same time. The deliberate fragmentation that was part of the form's intent and appeal called attention to interruption (in time, in point-of-view), to progress that happens only by revisiting the past or by taking into account the compelling validity of alternatives, and to the possibility that

---

8 The terms are widely (but sometimes contradictorily) used in short story criticism; for further definitions see Rolf Lundén, *The United Stories of America: Studies in the Short Story Composite* (Amsterdam: Rodopi, 1999); Forrest L. Ingram, *Representative Short Story Cycles of the Twentieth Century* (The Hague and Paris: Mouton, 1971); Gerald Lynch, *The One and the Many: English-Canadian Short Story Cycles* (Toronto: University of Toronto Press, 2001); Robert M. Luscher, "The Short Story Sequence: An Open Book," in Susan Lohafer and Jo Ellen Clarey, eds., *Short Story Theory at a Crossroads* (Baton Rouge and London: Louisiana State University Press, 1989), pp. 148–67; Gerald Kennedy, ed., *Modern American Short Story Sequences* (Cambridge: Cambridge University Press, 1995); W. H. New, "Edges, Spaces, Borderblur: Reflections on the Short Story Composite in Canada," in Ignacio M. Palácio Martínez et al., eds., *Fifty Years of English Studies in Spain (1952–2002)* (Santiago de Compostela: Universidade de Santiago de Compostela, 2003), pp. 83–100.

inconclusiveness (the "open ending" of so many post-realist fictions) stages life more faithfully than does closure.

Hodgins's first collection, *Spit Delaney's Island* (1976), was arranged into book form after separate stories had already appeared. Using the device of the "frame" to unify the tales – the opening and closing stories depict Delaney's fear of, then accommodation to, life – Hodgins works within a consistent sense of place and tone: his rural Vancouver Island comes alive through comedy that hovers at the edge of despair. Hodgins also adapted two of these stories, "Every Day of His Life" and "Three Women of the Country," along with a later story, "Mr. Pernouski's Dream," into the libretto of *Eyes on the Mountain*, an opera by Christopher Donison, performed in 2001. Rohinton Mistry's cycle *Tales from Firozsha Baag* (1987) also works with recurrent characters and a consistent sense of place; it, too, was shaped into book form after many separate stories had been published in early versions. With the self-reflexive final story "Swimming Lessons" in hand, Mistry revised all eleven stories so that the connections among them might resonate, emphasizing choice and balance.

At once funny and achingly aware of loss, Mistry's book reconstructs the diversity of a largely Parsi "baag" or apartment complex in Bombay, then traces the growth of the main character Kersi as he leaves childhood games behind and emigrates to a slowly familiar Toronto. Along the way, drawing on Zoroastrian ritual and Gujerati words, the book deals with issues as wide-ranging as petty competition, confused sexuality, social injustice, class, category, and human decency. Structurally, the stories interconnect through images of food, game-playing, water ("swimming"), and the Parsi holy element of fire. Several examples of successful and failed emigration also bring coherence to the tales, as does a series of portraits of boys who grow into different kinds of men: Kersi himself, his social worker brother Percy, as well as a servant, a thief, and various friends who are killed, who turn their back arrogantly on the past, or who flail about in uncertainty, unable to admit openly who they have become. Each story – "Auspicious Occasion," "Squatter," "Exercisers" – resonates with precise detail; with "Swimming Lessons," these details take on a further dimension. Writing to his mother and father (*mai* and *bap*), Kersi reveals himself to be the internal narrator of all the stories. Writing to and about *"mai-bap"* – that is, *India* – Mistry implicitly argues for his home country and his adopted country to enter into a productive dialogue.

Many story sequences portray moments in a single character's growth, often in the context of a small town or against the mores of a non-"mainstream" cultural community. The appeal of such works can derive from revelations of behavior, details of locale, or clashes between traditions and assumptions. Examples include David Bezmozgis's stories of a Russian Jewish émigré in *Natasha and Other Stories* (2004); Wayson Choy's novel of Vancouver's Chinatown *The Jade Peony* (1995), which began life as a 1977 short story; Michael Winter's tales of Gabriel English, growing up in Newfoundland in *One Last Good Look* (1999); and the six Linnet Muir stories in Mavis Gallant's *Home Truths* (1981). Characteristically, growing-up narratives tell of childhood idyll or trauma, youthful romance, sibling rivalry, death, and some form of commitment to the future. The writing life often constitutes one paradigm of escape, a way of prevailing over voicelessness. Realism is the dominant mode. With several collections, a range of characters might be taken as variations on a single personality: Andy Quan's *Calendar Boy* (2001), about gay young men discovering adulthood and sexuality; Madeleine Thien's *Simple Recipes* (2001), about Canadian-Asian women in dysfunctional families; Russell Smith's *Young Men* (1999), where four urban men tell of relationships gone sour; Kevin Patterson's *Country of Cold* (2003), where the subsequent lives of a highschool class trace narratives of loneliness and disillusion. Even the multiple characters in Kevin Armstrong's *Night Watch* (2002), at sea in the South Pacific, can be read as the contrary faces of a voyager away from, but seeking, home.

Collections of related stories do not necessarily combine into "cycles." Their unity can rely on formal strategy, as in Ron Smith's deft variations on intimacy in families, *What Men Know About Women* (1999), where couples age together, a father reconnects with his son, and friends rally to help heal a marriage – but where the sequence of stories (anecdote, parable, first-person, third-person, extended narrative) records at the same time a mini-history of the short story genre. Unity can also derive from sensibility more than form, as in Michael Redhill's riffs on honesty, *Fidelity* (2003); Russell Wangersky's *The Hour of Bad Decisions* (2006), where characters cannot find creative ways to expressive their inner lives, and are led to violence, work, or thwarted relationships instead; Michael Trussler's *Encounters* (2006), where radiance and ruin intertwine because implicitly irrational desire interrupts the banalities of urban domesticity; or Leo McKay's *Like This* (1995), where a sense of the surreal disarranges "plain tales" of molestation and survival. Here, unity derives more from emotional tension than from recurrent characters.

Relatedly, Guy Vanderhaeghe's stories – *Man Descending* (1982), *The Trouble with Heroes* (1983), *Things as They Are?* (1992) – interrogate family dynamics (love, shame, dependence, masculinity) to ask what stories people tell each other and themselves. What is truth, in the words of expatriates, teachers, con-artists, monks? What is history, with its sharp shocks and lingering power? Dialogues read as though recorded directly from life, but authenticity is always in question. Family life in Vanderhaeghe's stories reveals layers of emotional upheaval. Constrained behind decorum, suppressed by convention, ironized against fear of exposure, emotions come to the surface, but tensions mount anyway, because the stories insist that surfaces lie.

The unique voices of Alistair MacLeod and Mavis Gallant probe family and society against the dynamic workings of memory and time. Gallant's meticulous, concretely realized writing – much of it printed first in *The New Yorker* – is sampled in *The Selected Stories* (1996). Included are such powerful stories as "The Fenton Child," "The End of the World," the several stories and fables about people whose uprooted lives are shaped by European war and the hiatus between war and peace ("The Moslem Wife," "The Latehomecomer"), and the comic satires of life in modern France as experienced by a character named Henri Grippes. All respond to careful listening: "listening," because the idiom is sure – the dialogues convey the unsaid as well as the said, the nuances of implied knowledge and intuited power that underscore the history of actions and affairs. Serious and fiercely intelligent, but also deviously funny, these stories dramatically re-enact modern history by probing the limits of perception and, when perceptions collide, the foibles of desire.

Island (2000) combines MacLeod's two earlier collections, *The Lost Salt Gift of Blood* (1976) and *As Birds Bring Forth the Sun* (1986), a total of sixteen stories that date from as early as 1968 and that were read first on CBC radio or printed first in *Massachusetts Review, Fiddlehead, Atlantic Advocate, Tamarack*, and other little magazines. Though few, these remain some of the most powerful stories of the time, the scenes and images precisely visualized, emotionally wrenching. They focus on Cape Breton fishermen, farmers, coal-haulers – characters who, the stories say, respond strongly only to things that are real. The narrators belong to a succeeding generation, for whom other occupations are an option but memory inescapable, making tensions between parents and children a recurrent motif. Yet rebellion, however extreme, never separates. Memory is a rhythm of persistence in MacLeod's world, stilled in the heritage of Nova Scotia and sounded in its storytelling traditions, cadences of speech and patterns of repetition, folklore allusions, Gaelic phrases, and names.[9]

---

9 See Gwendolyn Davies, "Alistair Macleod and the Gaelic Diaspora," in *Tropes and Territories: Short Fiction, Postcolonial Readings, Canadian Writing in Context*, ed. Marta Dvořák, William H. New (Montreal: McGill-Queen's University Press, 2007), pp. 121–33.

Within this set of mind, modern history only means anything because a cultural memory persists to animate and disarrange it. In "The Road to Rankin's Point," a man copes with the death of his grandmother, hearing again in the darkness the old songs she once sang. In "Winter Dog," a collie that saves a man from a winter death is later shot because he is deemed too violent; told as a memory, against the backdrop of children's play in the snow, this story develops through images of containment: fences, chains, snares, ice – and of the dead, who return to shore when the winter sea releases them. In "The Boat," a young man turns away from the sea, where his lobster-fisherman father has died, but not from memories of the family trawler, which comes to embody for him his childhood – the past, its secrets, and all that has changed. Releasing these narratives into speech, MacLeod takes on the role of the *sennachie*, the Gaelic teller of legends and tales, who, by keeping alive the people's history, keeps alive the people themselves.

Some writers thus used the story sequence/cycle to imagine a whole community, whether in the Miramichi, as in David Adams Richards's *Dancers at Night* (1978), where the closed-mouthed characters communicate as much by gesture as through speech, or in the equally dour world of W. D. Valgardson's Icelandic Manitoba (*Bloodflowers*, 1973). Other writers focused on sensibilities shaped by ethnic diversity, such as the colonial Zanzibar tales of M. G. Vassanji, or the colonial South Pacific as seen by Adam Lewis Schroeder (*Kingdom of Monkeys*, 2001), or various tales of racism and resistance by Philip Kreiner, Bharati Mukherjee, J. J. Steinfeld (*Dancing at the Club Holocaust*, 1993), Neil Bissoondath (*Digging Up the Mountains*, 1985), Shirley Faessler, and Vincent Lam. Frequently such subjects took comic form, sometimes to exaggerate the foibles of small towns, as in the Alberta of Gail Anderson-Dargatz's *The Miss Hereford Stories* (1994); or of individuals, as when David Donnell's *The Blue Ontario Hemingway Boat Race* (1985) chases the young journalist Ernest Hemingway around a fictional Toronto; or of social rituals, as in Roch Carrier's memoir of boyhood desire and chagrin, *The Hockey Sweater* (tr. Sheila Fischman, 1979; made into a popular NFB animated short film, *The Sweater/Le Chandail*, 1980), which amusedly evokes institutional rivalries between Montreal and Toronto. At other times, an often brittle comedy shapes a way of surviving displacement, as when Austin Clarke's stories (sampled in *The Austin Clarke Reader*, 1996) portray Caribbean characters and voices nostalgically, but distinguish sharply between perception and desire, or when André Alexis's *Despair and Other Stories of Ottawa* (1994) follow dream logic past surface differences into a community governed by the surreal bureaucracy of the unconscious. In *A Planet of Eccentrics* (1990) and *Laterna*

Magika (1997), Ven Begamudré highlights the borderless appeal of storytelling, affirming South Asian and East European narratives to be equally part of a contemporary writer's inheritance in North America.

For First Nations and Métis writers, "inheritance" is complicated by those aspects of colonization that imposed trauma – making unexamined attempts to read their works according to "postcolonial" or "diasporic" models consequently suspect. Only in the twenty-first century are the numbers of people with First Nations heritage returning to pre-colonial numbers; those among them who are writers (Joseph Boyden, Drew Hayden Taylor, Eden Robinson, Thomas King) and storytellers (Basil Johnston, Harry Robinson) asserted their place in contemporary Canada both by retelling traditional stories for a new audience and by devising tales of present-day life. The thirteen stories in Boyden's *Born with a Tooth* (2001) tell of dissatisfactions in a Cree community, then of individuals who resist the hierarchies of dismissal: the Church, with its fearsome and punitive attacks on tradition; the residential school, with its burden of sexual abuse and denial of Native languages; the state police, with a history of violence to overcome. The aim of resistance here is to reclaim health. Johnston's work follows other patterns, from tale-telling (*The Star-Man*, 1997) to instructional anecdotes about a contemporary Anishnabe reserve (*Moose Meat & Wild Rice*, 1978) to narrative accounts of traditional rituals, legends, songs, and prayers (*Ojibway Heritage*, 1976). In his hands, the Moose Meat Reserve regains self-respect. The Hobbema Reserve tales of W. P. Kinsella (*The Moccasin Telegraph*, 1983; *The Miss Hobbema Pageant*, 1989) provide a contrast, for – comic in intent, widely enjoyed, but told from outside the culture – their stance came under attack when the political climate questioned their "authenticity." In general, any parody that was not somehow self-aware became hard to sustain.

Hayden Taylor's work – his stories (*Fearless Warriors*, 1998) and essay anthology (*Me Funny*, 2005) – nevertheless shows how Native storytelling recurrently uses a teasing humor to reintegrate individuals into the cohesiveness of the group, and relies on laughter to diffuse tensions between groups. Comedy can thus reconfigure the power relations that divide Native and Métis from White. Stories by Thomas King – reinforced by his lecture series *The Truth About Stories* (2003), which insists on the importance of *listening* – further embody the principles Taylor elucidates. In *One Good Story, That One* (1993) and *A Short History of Indians in Canada* (2005), King writes deceptively simple fables of cultural encounter and Native survival: deceptive, because the playful vocabulary, with its allusions to both European and Native history, does more than entertain. It skewers overzealous preachers, comfortable politicians, folktale collectors, naive husbands, and uninformed anthropologists alike. In "Borders," a Blackfoot woman embarrasses government officials when she refuses to identify her citizenship according to current national models and consequently gets stranded at a border crossing. "A Seat in the Garden" overturns social stereotypes. "A Coyote Columbus Story" hints that explorer-tricksters might even yet be tricked. Comedy is political. Short fiction by Native writers is further discussed in the chapter on Indigenous poetry and prose.

Like ethnicity, region, family, and livelihood, gender also came to function as a motif of identity and community, particularly in the wake of feminist political movements during the 1960s and the "new feminism" that followed. The writings of Janice Kulyk Keefer (*The Paris-Napoli Express*, 1986) and Carol Shields (*Various Miracles*, 1985) use exact detail to elucidate their female characters' actions and political context. Political themes also inform both Atwood's *Moral Disorder* (2006), where a story sequence dramatizes the chaos of fear, the unknown that the characters equate with the future, and Munro's adamantly affirmative stories in *The Love of a Good Woman* (1998), where women in later life recall making possibly unwise choices (for love) but refuse to regret having done so. All four writers resist simplistic social allegory and easy thematic enclosure. In Munro's carefully crafted stories, where each storyline gives rise to another that is equally precise and elusive – even in *The View from Castle Rock* (2006), the most autobiographical of her collections – art and life remain apart. Robert Thacker's chapter on Atwood, Munro, Shields and Gallant comments further on these writers.

Perhaps because of the wide appeal of these stories – to students, reviewers, prize-givers, members of book clubs – as well as because of the intrinsic interest of the subjects they addressed, publishers began in the 1970s to release numerous collections of subject-centered stories, sometimes highlighting the subjects as though they were "exotic" as well as "topical." Scores of books appeared depicting the traumatic experience of individual women and some men, especially in "regional" surrounds. Also foregrounded were issues relating to alternative sexual choices, the ostensible distinctiveness of various social enclaves, and the intrinsic character of many immigrant families. Such collections tended to be marketed for their validity, authenticity, and social significance as much as for their textual sophistication – and therefore for the cultural "relevance" of the dilemmas they portrayed. Some sustained more than sociological interest. Singling out a few names, however, among the fifty or so writers whose texts warrant more extended commentary, simply suggests the range of their topics: choice, time, community, survival. Ann

Copeland portrays a woman who leaves convent life in middle age (*At Peace*, 1978), Margaret Gibson discloses the dimensions of madness (*The Butterfly Ward*, 1976), Gertrude Story tracks the progress of a Saskatchewan woman (in a trilogy beginning with *The Way to Always Dance*, 1983), Sandra Birdsell narrates tales of sisterhood (*Night Travellers*, 1982), Anne Fleming tells of adolescent high-jinks and lesbian love (*Pool-Hopping*, 1998), Mary Borsky looks at Ukrainian Alberta (*Influence of the Moon*, 1995), Linda Svendsen at the West Coast (*Marine Life*, 1992). Repeatedly, family shapes place, which in turn shapes family. Out of each writer's particular observations of the world – whether social, sexual, spatial, or sectarian – emerged a fiction of validation, a fiction that could observe ignorance, loneliness, pain, and lies, neutrally or passionately, but try still to affirm the power to live.

These works generally adapted documentary models, whether testing out conventional gender roles or affirming a difference in perspective. For those women who sought alternatives to male models of rise, fall, exploration, and return, however, another stylistic strategy promised differences in effect. For many – writers and theorists alike – Nicole Brossard's stories illustrated francophone feminist practice and the possibility of adapting language theories to fiction – which led some writers to express the self through body rhythms, to dramatize how pregnancy and menstrual cycles informed characters' behavior. Cassandra replaced Odysseus as a gendered prototype. Dialogue progressed obliquely – critically, but often with laughter as well. A few writers' tales – those of Rachel Wyatt, Zsuzsi Gartner, and Elizabeth Hay, for instance – used wit as a way of exposing urban and suburban behavior without altogether condemning it. In others – those, for example, of Edna Alford in *The Garden of Eloise Loon* (1986) – spirituality provided a kind of sustenance in the face of life's complications. But especially for younger writers and their readers, destructive relationships proved a more compelling interest. Eden Robinson's *Traplines* (1996) records the psychopathology of the reserve system; Nancy Lee's *Dead Girls* (2002), drawing inferentially on real-life legal cases, renders the sociopathic conditions that drive men to violence against women; and in the wide range of forms represented in Annabel Lyon's *Oxygen* (2000), fragments coalesce in revelation or slide by like strangers, touching without touching: ostensibly neutral utterance masks extraordinary depths of hope and its counterpart, despair.

Still other stories tested a range of structural innovations, as in Margaret Atwood's clipped fairytales, or those of David Arnason – for example, "Girl and Wolf," *The Circus Performers' Bar* (1984). Anne Cameron, in *Daughters of Copper Woman* (1981), sought to retell Native women's tales, while Sheila

Watson (her stories collected in *A Father's Kingdom*, 2004) followed classical models. Diane Schoemperlen, whose storytelling antecedents are Franz Kafka and Gertrude Stein, turns dreams and grammatical experiments into narrative in *Red Plaid Shirt* (2002). And in his most reprinted story, the title work in *Where Is the Voice Coming From?* (1974), the novelist and cultural commentator Rudy Wiebe composed a metatextual inquiry that asks how anyone can "know" history, especially the history of the Cree Chief Big Bear, when "knowledge" comes to them in translation.

While Atwood's longer stories about language and fraught love (*Bluebeard's Egg*, 1983; *Wilderness Tips*, 1991) follow patterns familiar from her novels, the *mélange* of strategies collected as early as *Good Bones* (1992) or as late as *The Tent* (2006) reveals a writer fascinated by the narrative potential of everything from parable, parody, and diary note to recipe and sf proposition. In stories characteristically sustained over several pages, Carol Windley (*Visible Light*, 1993) and Caroline Adderson (*Bad Imaginings*, 1993) demonstrate a gift for crafting point-of-view. By reducing perception to a few carefully arranged (hence intensified) scenes and phrases, Lisa Moore eloquently favors metaphor and minimalism in *Open* (2002), as does John Gould in the fifty-five "short-short-stories" ("Cotton," "The End of the Day") in *Kilter* (2003). In Bill Gaston's *Mount Appetite* (2002), diary form and meditation jostle with comedy, as in a first-person "exorcism" of Malcolm Lowry called "A Forest Path"; in this volume, formal variation is part of what a reader must learn to read. Extending this principle, Thomas Wharton, in *The Logogryph* (2004), composes an extended set of prose forms, the book as a whole drafting the possibility that language has its own reality, that it dreams its way beyond the words that readers imagine they are reading. In the stories of Tamas Dobozy – especially *Last Notes* (2005) – the barriers between fiction and essay start to blur: narrative pretends to be confessional confessing to be narrative, landscape absents itself from the eye of an artist, the mindset of "dislocation" is revealed through conflicting cadences of insight and uncertainty. "Story" here begins not in topic but in text, when the rhythms of speaking and listening coincide.

The work of American writers influenced these dances with form: not *The New Yorker* (which gave space to Munro and Gallant) but Raymond Carver and Amy Hempel for their stylistic economy, David Foster Wallace and the pages of *Rolling Stone* for explosive encounters with politics and popular culture. In the cross-border writings of Mark Anthony Jarman – *New Orleans Is Sinking* (1998), *19 Knives* (2000) – language bursts in play, voice taking over from print as sentences rush forward as obsessively as characters do. Dobozy finds *bricolage* here: a strategy – using fad and fashion (the products that power sells) – to take on and take apart the forces that exercise North American power.[10] Jarman's is a world of methodone and fast cars, Guinness and pop theology, cancer, bikers, stern blondes, and (in "Eskimo Blue Day") officials who override – who cannot hear – the inarticulate syllables of love and pain.

Among other books seeking ways to interrupt conventional realist techniques, Paul Glennon's *How Did You Sleep?* (2000) favors a cross between science fiction and satire; Barry Webster's *The Sound of All Flesh* (2005) combines musical idiom with mordant verbal photojournalism; Robert Rawdon Wilson's *Boundaries* (1999) invents alternative worlds, where game theory arranges behavior in ways that mirror the conventionally "real." Timothy Taylor, in *Silent Cruise* (2002), builds number theory and technological terms into his studies of personality. Greg Hollingshead, in *The Roaring Girl* (1995), relies on the surprise appearance of the erratic in ordinary life to set narrative in motion. Lee Henderson's non-linear tales in *The Broken Record Technique* (2002) achieve something comparable: technology expresses connection better than families do, crudity stands in for expression when real feeling is suppressed, time repeats or collapses inside the prose form. While Seán Virgo's *White Lies and Other Fictions* (1980) represents reality lyrically, Clint Burnham's anti-narrative *Airborne Photo* (1999) favors the gritty blunt language of drugs and the social underclass; Derek McCormack's *Dark Rides* (1996) explores the back alleys of cities and sexuality; Nathan Sellyn's *Indigenous Beasts* (2006) portrays men's obsession with rage and escape, their fear of exposure, their drift into loneliness; Craig Davidson's visceral *Rust and Bone* (2005) explodes in episodes of violent sex and sport: fetishes, compulsions, organ ruptures, intrusions into others' space – the whole book resonates with father–son rivalries, and though the characters seem to want to reclaim belief, the narratives suggest that only magic will permit them to do so. Ellipsis is stronger here than affirmation.

Whether formal disruption or some long-familiar strategy of continuity comes to characterize the next decades of the short story – or more likely, as talented new writers appear, a reconfiguration that takes these and other possibilities all into account – the genre in the early twenty-first century clearly is not dying. Nor is it merely an "apprentice form" for would-be novelists, as some commentators once averred. More like the lyric poem than the novel in some ways, the short story form calls upon its readers to perceive the breadth

---

10 See Tamas Dobozy, "Fables of a Bricoleur: Mark Anthony Jarman's Many Improvisations," *Tropes and Territories*, pp. 323–30. See also Douglas Glover, "How to Read a Mark Jarman Story," *New Quarterly* 21.2–3 (Winter 2002), pp. 115–21.

of vision that is condensed into a small compass. As the writers of the later twentieth century sought ways to express this sensibility, they faced both technical challenges and commercial barriers. Modes of communication were altering; the economics and politics of publishing required them to deal with changing patterns and demands, not only of fashion but also of editorial practice, cost, distribution, and readership. Artfully stretching the dimensions of language, they continued to listen for the music of their time and place and the abrupt rhythms of discord. Probing values, pondering behavior, their narratives do not shy away from hunger, anger, raw language, and irrational action. Often critical of unexamined habits and institutional lethargy, they acknowledge imperfection. But they celebrate human dignity as well.

20

Canadian drama: performing communities

ANNE NOTHOF

Canadian theater historiography

Theater, like historiography, is a process of analyzing and evaluating a society's past and present. It articulates particular places and times to address private and public issues that may transcend these particularities, and helps to shape the society it reflects. Theater history can be read as voicing a national narrative or as countering a national narrative, as culturally validating or iconoclastic. In Canada, where a vast and diverse geographical and social landscape challenges imaginative configuration, theater has developed in diverse communities which resist the imposition of a cultural center. A persistent loyalty to local and regional place troubles the imperative to articulate a coherent national identity. Nor should Canadian theater be read in evolutionary terms, as a chronological development through clearly discernible phases. Its origins and forms speak to its collaborative, dynamic, amorphous, and performative nature.

Theatrical ritual and performance have existed in Canada long before colonization in the form of First Nations ceremony and dance. However, these Indigenous performances have been occluded by a long-standing historical assumption that the first performance was a Masque entitled *Le Théâtre de Neptune en la Nouvelle France* at Port Royal, Acadia (now Nova Scotia), written in 1606 by Parisian lawyer Marc Lescarbot, and enacted in barges and canoes by *voyageurs* dressed in Native regalia to celebrate the return of a French official from an exploratory sea voyage. By contrast, this historical moment has also been interpreted from a postcolonial perspective as enacting "the incorporation of this vast and (to the European eye) savage wilderness into the template of the French cultural imaginary."[1]

---

[1] Alan Filewod, *Performing Canada: The Nation Enacted in the Imagined Theatre* (Kamloops: University College of the Cariboo, 2002), p. xii.

With the arrival of more settler-invaders from Britain and France, British officers assisted by local amateurs performed popular farces and melodramas from England and plays by Shakespeare and Molière in garrison theaters across the country. Opulent theater venues constructed in the late eighteenth and early nineteenth centuries in urban centers housed resident companies and touring productions from the United States and Britain. In response to the preponderance of British and American culture, semi-professional regional "Little Theaters" were established early in the twentieth century, including the Hart House Theatre (1919) at the University of Toronto, which introduced experimental European works and produced new Canadian plays such as *Marsh Hay* (1923; 1974)[2] by Merrill Denison and the expressionist plays of the Canadian north by Herman Voaden, including *Rocks* (1932; 1993), *Hill-Land* (1934; 1984), and *Ascend as the Sun* (1942; 1993).

The Dominion Drama Festival was founded in 1932 by a group of community theater enthusiasts from across the country assembled by the Governor General of Canada, the Earl of Bessborough. The DDF provided a stimulus for playwriting and production, with competitions held in thirteen regions of Canada, but with regional and national adjudication by British judges. Although the DDF fostered the largest number of amateur acting groups per capita of any country in the world, very few made the transition to professional status, and very few Canadian plays were performed. During the 1940s and 50s playwrights such as Gwen Pharis Ringwood (*Still Stands the House*, 1938), Robertson Davies (*At My Heart's Core*, 1950), and John Coulter (*Riel*, 1950; 1962), who wrote critically about Canadian history and society, were an anomaly on the stage. However, during the same period, as in Australia and New Zealand, national radio broadcasts of new Canadian plays, such as the historical epics of Ringwood and Elsie Park Gowan, and the social satires of Len Peterson and W. O. Mitchell, helped to foster a sense of a national community. Indeed the CBC was created as an instrument of Canadian culture to unite a widely dispersed population; and contemporary playwrights such as Rachel Wyatt and Judith Thompson have continued to reach a wide audience through the medium of radio drama.

The Stratford Festival was ceremoniously launched in 1953 as Canada's answer to a national theater, although its mandate is to produce Shakespeare and other foreign classics, generously supplemented by American musicals. In an attempt to address the dearth of new Canadian plays on its stages, Stratford launched a series featuring Canadian "works in progress" in its Studio Theatre

---

2 First production date and first publication date are provided, where possible. One date only is given when performance and publication occurred in the same year.

in 2002, including the first of a trilogy of plays loosely based on an imaginative and provocative nineteenth-century history of British royalty entitled *The Swanne* by Peter Hinton. Since 1975, popular Canadian drama has been showcased just down the highway from Stratford at the more modest Blyth Festival, held every summer in a small farm community.

With federal funding from the Canada Council, regional theaters were established in major cities across Canada in the late 1950s and early 1960s, with mandates typically directed toward the development of a community theater culture through the production of British and American plays, although many of these theaters also produced new Canadian works in small second spaces, and established educational outreach programs to schools through touring and youth workshops. Ottawa's National Arts Centre was built in 1969 to act as a showcase of the best of the country's live arts, to develop the performing arts in the Ottawa region, and to assist the Canada Council in the development of performing arts across Canada. In the 1970s the NAC hosted productions from theaters across the country, including ambitious remounts of John Coulter's epic play, *Riel*, and of John Murrell's *Waiting for the Parade*. In 2002 it provided a platform for the first Magnetic North Theatre Festival, which recruits new works from across Canada in order to promote an awareness of the diversity of Canadian theater, and is produced in alternate years in different cities. Although the NAC facilitates a collaborative network, it does not function as a touchstone for the style or content of Canadian drama.

Alternative theaters

Postcolonial narratives of Canadian theater history identify the beginnings of a distinctive Canadian drama and an awareness of a theatrical tradition with the founding of small theater companies as "alternatives" to the established professional regional theaters which accessed most of the Arts Council funding. Their productions were typically anti-establishment, challenging liberal assumptions of a safe homogeneity in Canadian society, and performed in a variety of unconventional spaces. Although they explored a wide range of theatrical styles and structures – from improvisation to dance, from epic to absurd – these alternative theaters did not initiate identifiably Canadian themes or forms; rather, they embraced the techniques of British and European collectivist and modernist theater. In Toronto, George Luscombe's Workshop Productions (1959)[3] employed the expressionist theatrical techniques of British director

---

3 "Toronto" was added as a prefix in 1963.

Joan Littlewood to create plays that disrupted traditional theater practice, using ensemble acting and minimal scenography. Their documentary style has characterized much of Canadian theater, film, and television production since then; for example, the theater company's most popular production, *Ten Lost Years* (1974; 1983), collectively enacted Barry Broadfoot's history of the Depression in the Canadian West through song and anecdote.

The 1967 Centennial celebrations provided an impetus to the proliferation of alternative theaters across Canada, as did the Canada Council's Local Initiatives Grant and "Opportunities for Youth" federal program, which enabled graduates from university theater departments to build their own companies. Between 1970 and 1973 more than fifty original Canadian plays were produced in Toronto's alternative theaters, and by 1975 twenty-five alternative theaters were located in Toronto alone.

Under the guidance of Paul Thompson, who had absorbed the innovative ideas of Roger Planchon while in France, Toronto's Theatre Passe Muraille (1968) explored the constituency of local communities and issues through a process of collective creation: a group of actors researched a subject, pooled their ideas, and improvised episodic scenes and dialogue. *The Farm Show* (1972; 1976) dramatized the stories and customs of the farming town of Clinton, Ontario, through mime, song, and poetry. Theatre Passe Muraille's populist epics, such as Rick Salutin's *1837: The Farmers' Revolt* (1973; 1975), tried "to demonstrate the political significance of past events in relation to the present and, above all, to discover a national mythology within the material provided by Canadian history."[4] Its style of docudrama, which interrogated traditional nationalist narratives, influenced the work of playwrights across the country, including Carol Bolt's *Buffalo Jump* (1972), an account of the "On-to-Ottawa" protest march during the Depression; Linda Griffith's *Maggie and Pierre* (1979; 1980), an irreverent portrait of Prime Minister Trudeau's marriage; and John Gray's *Billy Bishop Goes to War* (1978; 1981), a satiric deconstruction of the Canadian First World War flying ace.

The tendency of some theater critics to imagine Theatre Passe Muraille's *The Farm Show* as a seminal "founding" Canadian play has been reinforced by Michael Healey's comic revisiting of the circumstances under which it was created in his play, *The Drawer Boy* (1999), which also interrogates the social values of an Ontario farming community and the cultural values of theater. *The Drawer Boy* replays the adventures of a young actor from

---

4 Renate Usmiani, *Second Stage: The Alternative Theatre Movement in Canada* (Vancouver: University of British Columbia Press, 1983), p. 47.

a Toronto theater group which visits the rural Ontario home of two elderly bachelor farmers to research farm life for a new play. In doing so, he demonstrates the way in which a collective creation appropriates and changes the lives of its subjects. As Miles tells Morgan, "We're here to get your history and give it back to you."[5] *The Drawer Boy* enacts the power of storytelling in creating and interpreting reality; it also provides a self-reflexive, ironic consideration of the making of Canadian drama. Its many productions across the country and abroad have included a revival at Theatre Passe Muraille in 2007 to celebrate its fortieth season, thus reinforcing a misconceived view of Canada as a pervasively rural and culturally naive society. Healey's subsequent plays, however, paint a more complex political and social portrait of the country: *Plan B* (2002), which speculates on a federal government strategy should the separatists win a Quebec referendum, is an urban, political allegory in which personal intimacy is paralleled to the relationship between English and French Canada; *Generous* (2006; 2007) returns to the inanities of Canadian politics with a satiric look at selfish people inspired by self-preservation to be selfless.

Since its inception in 1971 the Tarragon Theatre, housed in a renovated warehouse in Toronto, has been instrumental in developing a substantive body of Canadian works, first under the direction of Bill Glassco (1971–82), then under Urjo Kareda (1982–2002), and Richard Rose. Again, ironically, an iconic Canadian theater found its inspiration in a British model – the Royal Court Theatre in London. Glassco established playwrights' workshops and a playwright-in-residence program, which supported writers such as David French, Judith Thompson, Joan MacLeod, Guillermo Verdecchia, Michael Healey, and Jason Sherman. He also encouraged the production of Quebec plays in English, initiating the premieres of translations of most of Michel Tremblay's plays. Tarragon plays have been performed in regional and alternative theaters across the country and beyond, although they are often regionally focused in setting and subject. This is particularly true of David French's autobiographical cycle of "Mercer" plays, *Leaving Home* (1972), *Of the Fields, Lately* (1973; 1975), *Salt-Water Moon* (1984; 1985), *1949* (1988; 1989), and *Soldier's Heart* (2002), which explore the conflicts within three generations of a Newfoundland family, uprooted and relocated to Toronto. French's plays enact passionate confrontations in which the characters are fighting for their integrity, their beliefs, their hopes and desires. Their status in the Canadian canon was confirmed by the positive critical reception of Toronto's

---

5 Michael Healey, *The Drawer Boy* (Toronto: Playwrights Canada Press, 1999), p. 34.

Soulpepper Theatre production of *Leaving Home* in 2007; Soulpepper, founded in 1997, is a repertory company with a mandate to present Canadian interpretations of international theater classics.

Toronto's Factory Theatre, established in 1970 by Ken Gass to develop and perform exclusively Canadian works, has produced more than 220 new Canadian plays on its main stage, and 600 more in workshops,[6] including David Freeman's portraits of the institutionalized lives of men with cerebral palsy in *Creeps* (1971; 1972) and *Battering Ram* (1972). Factory Theatre has also produced most of George F. Walker's plays, from the absurdist comedy *The Prince of Naples* (1971; 1972) to the Black social satires in the *Suburban Motel* cycle (1997–8).

Toronto Free Theatre was founded in 1971 by playwrights John Palmer, Martin Kinch, and Tom Hendry to provide a milieu in which talented newcomers could learn and work. It initially specialized in controversial and transgressive theater, with free admission. When it merged with the mainstream theater CentreStage in 1987 to form the Canadian Stage Company under co-directors Bill Glassco and Guy Sprung, the intention was that it function as a national theater company, although its purview and impact are more regional than national.

During the 1970s alternative theaters with similar objectives established themselves across the country: the Mummers in St. John's, the Great Canadian Theatre Company in Ottawa, the 25th Street Theatre in Saskatoon, Workshop West and Theatre Network in Edmonton, Alberta Theatre Projects in Calgary, Tamahnous Theatre in Vancouver. Socially engaged collective works such as Theatre Network's *Two Miles Off* (1975), 25th Street Theatre's *Paper Wheat* (1977; 1978), and the Mummers' *They Club Seals, Don't They?* (1978) toured across the country, generating a wide range of response – from anger to enthusiastic empathy. This touring practice linked communities which were geographically disparate but socially similar, enabling audiences to see themselves from a broader perspective as participating in a larger history. The mandate of Edmonton's Theatre Network typifies the idealistic community focus of these alternative theaters: to develop plays about Alberta for Albertans, to form a network of understanding between different communities in Alberta and in the nation. Since its inception in 1975 Theatre Network has premiered more than 100 new Canadian works, including Raymond Storey's coming-of-age play, *The Last Bus* (1987); Frank Moher's poignant

---

6 These numbers are provided on the Factory Theatre website: http://www.factory-theatre.ca/history.htm

consideration of old age and unemployment, *Odd Jobs* (1985; 1986); Lyle Victor Albert's autobiographical monologue on the challenges of cerebral palsy, *Scraping the Surface* (1996; 2000). Theatre Network has collaborated with many other theaters across the country, including the 25th Street Theatre, Prairie Theatre Exchange in Winnipeg, Playwrights' Workshop in Montreal and the Blyth Festival in Ontario. In effect, a distinctive Canadian drama has developed from the networking of small community theaters that foster local playwrights. Some of the plays developed by anti-canonical theaters of the 1970s and 80s now constitute the Canadian canon,[7] ironically reinforcing the idea of a traditional Canadian play as realistic, rural, domestic.

Interrogating communities

Since the 1960s many Canadian plays have attempted to expose the dislocations and discords endemic in a postcolonial society: racial conflict, social disparities, alienation, isolation, adjustment, and resistance. George Ryga dramatized the tragic struggle for survival of a Native woman in a white society in *The Ecstasy of Rita Joe* (1967; 1971); James Reaney portrayed the violence amongst Irish immigrant families in southwestern Ontario during the nineteenth century in his trilogy *The Donnellys* (1973–5; 1975). Both playwrights disrupted traditional play structure through the use of fluid action and montage, and an expressionistic, minimal set. Montreal playwright David Fennario probed the cultural conflicts of francophone and anglophone communities in two of his bilingual plays: *Balconville* (1979; 1980), set on a tenement balcony in Montreal, depicts the linguistic, social, and cultural clashes among three families; *Condoville* (2005) revisits the same characters twenty-five years later. The residents of the tenement are now threatened by up-market forces, and must co-operate to resist the encroachment of gentrification. Racial and homophobic tensions have replaced the language tensions of *Balconville* with the arrival of two new tenants – a gay, mixed-race couple.

Other playwrights have revisited Canadian history to assert or debunk national myths: Michael Cook delineated the grim realities of the Newfoundland fishery in *The Head, Guts and Soundbone Dance* (1973; 1974) and *Jacob's Wake* (1974; 1975); John Murrell portrayed Canadian wartime society in the 1940s from the various perspectives of five women in Calgary who keep the home fires burning or extinguished in *Waiting for the Parade*

---

7 Chris Johnson, "'Wisdome Under a Ragged Coate': Canonicity and Canadian Drama," in *Contemporary Issues in Canadian Drama*, ed. Per Brask (Winnipeg: Blizzard, 1995), p. 27.

(1977; 1980). Murrell's *Farther West* (1984; 1985) dramatizes a prairie prostitute's catastrophic search for absolute freedom, and his opera libretto for *Filumena* (2003), set in a mining town in the Crowsnest Pass in 1921, sketches a sociological portrait of a young Italian woman hanged for murder – an historical event interpreted very differently by Sharon Pollock in her play *Whiskey Six Cadenza* (1983; 1987).

Sharon Pollock has tackled contentious moral and social issues in her plays for over forty years, continually experimenting with style and structure. She has revisited events in Canadian history that have been forgotten or misrepresented: *Walsh* (1973) reveals how the federal government's decision to starve Sitting Bull out of Canada resulted in the decimation of the Sioux Nation; *The Komagata Maru Incident* (1976; 1978) shows the consequences of the British Columbia government's refusal to allow the debarkation of Sikhs from the Punjab in Vancouver; *One Tiger to a Hill* (1980; 1981) shows how a repressive and intransigent prison system inevitably leads to violence. One of her many radio plays, *The Making of Warriors* (1991), juxtaposes the stories of Anna Mae Pictou Acquash, a Mi'kmaq woman murdered for her involvement in the American Indian Movement, and Sarah Grimke, an American abolitionist and suffragette. The overlapping of these women's lives points to systemic injustices against Blacks, Natives, and women. In *Fair Liberty's Call* (1993; 1995), set in New Brunswick after the American Revolution, Pollock dramatizes the fragmentation of a family torn apart by conflicting loyalties to Britain and the United States; the play deconstructs what she considers the Canadian identity – "upholding compromise over compassion, legality over justice."[8] *Man Out of Joint* (2007; 2008) is an excoriating interrogation of a post-9/11 world in which freedoms are abrogated, and justice is denied.

In each play, she presents the scenario from different perspectives, inviting (or provoking) the audience to make up its own mind as to who is guilty and who is innocent. Pollock is preoccupied by the moral choices that individuals make, and the consequences of those choices. She tries to make sense of the world around her – to "get it straight," like the "madwoman" in her self-reflexive monologue *Getting It Straight* (1988; 1992). In her later plays she focuses on the struggles of creative women to express themselves in a patriarchal society: *Moving Pictures* (1999; 2003) examines the life and career of filmmaker and actor Nell Shipman; *Angel's Trumpet* (2001; 2003) dramatizes the endgame played by Zelda and F. Scott Fitzgerald.

---

8 Brian Hutchinson, "Restored 'Theatre of Risks,'" *The Financial Post* (20 March 1993), p. S5

Canadian women playwrights are actively engaged in deconstructing the myth of equity and freedom in Canadian society. Wendy Lill sympathetically delineates failed or compromised good intentions in her plays about women – how they are often defeated by social patterns and political structures. In *The Fighting Days* (1983; 1985) she portrays the women's suffrage movement in Manitoba, focusing on the journalist and political activist Francis Beynon and her differences with Nellie McClung. The monologue *The Occupation of Heather Rose* (1986; 1987) is the confession of a nurse who has left her post in northern Ontario, defeated by the systemic poverty and problems of a Native reserve and her own prescriptive attitudes. *Sisters* (1989; 1991) provides a critical look at a Native residential school run by nuns, and *All Fall Down* (1993; 1994) delineates the response of a community to an accusation of child molestation in a daycare facility. *The Glace Bay Miners' Museum* (1995; 1996) provides a young woman's perspective on the disasters inflicted on family and community by the local mine in which most of the men work. *Chimera* (2007) explores the contentious issue of stem-cell research.

Judith Thompson's surrealistic psychological portraits of the socially and mentally crippled are attempts to provoke change by showing the horror and violence, both latent and overt, in modern society. She probes the dark side of human nature, the reality of evil, the fear, the loss of moral direction which results in predatory behavior. Her characters struggle with their sins, their self-hatred, their guilt. They grapple with the "animal" within and without – in *The Crackwalker* (1980; 1981), *White Biting Dog* (1983), *I Am Yours* (1987; 1989), *Lion in the Streets* (1990; 1992), *Sled* (1997), *Perfect Pie* (2000), *Capture Me* (2004; 2006). Thompson's early plays were nurtured at the Tarragon Theatre, where they premiered at regular intervals, but they are rarely produced on the main stages of Canada's regional theaters. When *The Crackwalker* and *Lion in the Streets* were produced in London, England, critics were confounded by the physical energy and verbal onslaughts of these plays from a former colony they had assumed to be safe and boring.

Modern Canadian drama is often characterized by ironic self-reflection, staging life as tragi-comedy. The black comedies of Morris Panych and George F. Walker investigate fraught communities and relationships where hope is continually deferred; they may even question whether community is possible. They place their existential interrogations in generalized locations, not specific to a Canadian environment – the ledge of an apartment building, a restaurant scullery, a suburban motel room – and they raise broad philosophical questions on human interaction and isolation, on the nature of good and evil, and on the relationship between fantasy and reality. The apparently pointless and repetitive acts portrayed on the stage reflect the futility of human endeavor. The protagonists sustain themselves with verbal sparring or aimless actions. Life is a waiting game, a vigil at a deathbed.

Morris Panych's absurdist theater shares the *angst* and black humor of Samuel Beckett's *Waiting for Godot* and *Endgame*. Like Beckett's, his characters are balanced between hope and despair: their only salvation appears to be through a sympathetic engagement with another isolated human being. In his metatheatrical *7 Stories* (1989; 1990) seven characters engage in role-playing to create a sense of purpose in their lives, but all are guilty of *mauvaise foi*, denying the possibility of freedom, and thereby choosing to remain objects in the world, at the mercy of circumstances. In assuming social roles that invalidate conscious choice, they validate their denial that choice is possible. The suicidal witness to these fabricated lives stands on the ledge of their seven-story apartment building, which also functions as a stage on which he thinks he is playing out his last scene unobserved, but where he is in fact very visible. Although the play is rife with miscommunication and misunderstanding, the act of storytelling is shown to provide a way of coming to terms with incomprehension. Having flown off the ledge from which he has intended to jump, the Man concludes, that "[he] forgot [his] own story ... and [he] flew ... flew on the wings of someone else's."[9] Art provides a necessary perspective from which to see the world, although it may be only a momentary delusion.

In *Vigil* (1996) a solitary young bank clerk impatiently awaits the death of a silent, bedridden woman he believes is his aunt, filling the time with memories and self-reflections, while slowly developing a relationship with her, only to discover it is too late. *Lawrence & Holloman* (1998) explores the relationship between two antithetical personalities – one an optimist, the other a pessimist. Holloman's name alludes to the title of T. S. Eliot's poem "The Hollow Men," which delineates the modern world as being without values, without conviction, ending "Not with a bang, but a whimper."[10] In Panych's play, however, Holloman's life does end with a "bang": he is accidentally shot by Lawrence after he has failed at an attempt at suicide. His nihilistic interpretation of life as a joke is in one sense validated, but Lawrence's final words – that there is some meaning, "[a] brilliant and complex kind of logic"[11] – are also ironically validated, in that all of Holloman's efforts to destroy Lawrence have

---

9 Morris Panych, "7 Stories," in *Modern Canadian Plays*, vol. II, 4th ed., ed. Jerry Wasserman (Vancouver: Talonbooks, 2001), p. 182.
10 T. S. Eliot, "The Hollow Men" [1925], in *Selected Poems* (London: Faber, 1961), p. 80.
11 Morris Panych, *Lawrence & Holloman* (Vancouver: Talonbooks, 1998), p. 127.

resulted in his own destruction. Holloman's testing of Lawrence with a series of disasters also recalls the trials of Job; in this light, then, the disasters can be read as tests of the human spirit. *Girl in the Goldfish Bowl* (2002; 2003) is set in the home of a dysfunctional family which the mother continually threatens to leave. The point-of-view is that of the ingenuous, ebullient young daughter who imagines that her dead goldfish has metamorphosed into a young man who emerges from the sea to save them all. He doesn't.

Like Morris Panych, George F. Walker establishes a dialectic between nihilism and humanism in his plays. A recurrent theme is the attempted indoctrination of a recalcitrant humanist into an anarchic, anti-humanist position. In his *East End* trilogy, Walker explores the possibility of operative humanist values, usually through the character of a woman who defies social anarchy and irrationality. According to critic Jerry Wasserman, in these earlier plays, "Walker's women ... act from a sense of personal imperative based on a vested familial or communal interest in the social world in which they intervene. And in place of the men's rhetorically inflated ideological gigantism, they adopt attainable goals and pragmatic strategies."[12] Nora in *Better Living* (1986; 1988) is what Walker terms a "possibility character" who practices the doctrine of "betterism." His dysfunctional characters fight against impossible odds, believing they can win despite their suffering and the power of the enemy – whether social or ontological; they are both comic and heroic. In the six plays which comprise the *Suburban Motel* series, the scenario is darker and the prospects for betterment are considerably reduced; the "heroines" may still embody some degree of hope and desperate courage, but their futures are tenuous.

Each play is enacted in a shabby motel room on the edge of society, in which the lives of the inhabitants have been reduced to psychic survival. In *Problem Child* (1997) a desperate mother who works as a prostitute struggles to retrieve her baby daughter from social services, battling with an intransigent social worker while her husband becomes emotionally embroiled in television talk shows. His concern for the plight of the television host's victims and his crusade to change the format to a more compassionate one provide a satiric comment on the confusion of reality and illusion that characterizes contemporary Western society. The alcoholic motel manager is a choric wise fool, obsessed with the lack of justice in the world. He can keep himself on an even keel only by attempting to "suck up what little dirt [he] can."[13] But there are

---

12 Jerry Wasserman, "'It's the Do-Gooders Burn My Ass': Modern Canadian Drama and the Crisis of Liberalism," *Modern Drama* 43:1 (Spring 2000), p. 41.
13 George F. Walker, "Problem Child," in Wasserman, ed., *Modern Canadian Plays*, vol. II, p. 380.

certain stains on the carpet that he cannot remove. Walker provides no easy resolution to the problems, nor any redemption for the characters, although each one expresses humanist values that seem to escape the notice of the social worker – compassion, justice, love. Their inability to live these values provides sufficient comment on the human tragedy they embody.

Family portraits

Modern Canadian drama is also singularly preoccupied with family dynamics – the conflicted relationship of parents, the desperate desire of their offspring to leave home, and their reluctant realization that leaving the past behind is an impossibility. This pattern may be construed as a paradigm for the Canadian psyche – the urge to free oneself from a perceived oppressive colonial past and to realize an illusive autonomous identity. In Pollock's *Blood Relations* (1980; 1981) this is effected through the murder of the parents, when "Lizzie Borden [takes] an axe."[14] In Pollock's autobiographical portrait, *Doc* (1984; 1986), the daughter exorcises the ghosts of mother and grandmother through a confrontation with a father who has prioritized his patients over his family. The plays of Joanna McClelland Glass are also emotionally violent – deeply entrenched in her childhood years in Saskatchewan, surviving a dysfunctional family. *Canadian Gothic* (1972; 1977) portrays the psychologically debilitating consequences of living in isolation on the prairies, and the conflict between a repressive father and his free-spirited wife and daughter. *If We Are Women* (1993; 1994) depicts the fraught relationships of a young woman writer, her illiterate mother from Saskatchewan, her intellectually sophisticated mother-in-law, and her rebellious teenage daughter. *Trying* (2004), set in 1967, is based on Glass's working relationship as a young Canadian from the prairies with octogenarian Francis Biddle, Attorney General under President Franklin D. Roosevelt and a judge during the Nuremberg trials. The intersections of American and Canadian perspectives and of youth and age inform many of Glass's plays.

A "prairie Gothic" sensibility characterizes the rural plays of other Saskatchewan and Alberta playwrights: in *Still Stands the House* (1938) by Gwen Pharis Ringwood, *Sky* (1989) by Connie Gault, *Gravel Run* (1988; 1991) by Conni Massing, and *MacGregor's Hard Ice Cream and Gas* (2005) by Daniel Macdonald, women imprisoned by social restrictions, isolated in their homes

---

14 Sharon Pollock, "Blood Relations," in *Blood Relations and Other Plays*, ed. Anne Nothof (Edmonton: NeWest Press, 2002), p. 8.

by the vast expanse of the prairies, try to escape by roundabout and tortuous routes, defying patriarchal authority, and disturbing conventional and social models. The atmosphere of these plays is charged with irrational violence, mystery, even horror, as the unspeakable is played out, although the pervasive mood may be either tragic or comic.

Joan MacLeod's plays explore the often unacknowledged tensions and conflicts in an apparently peaceful Canadian society, considering the complexities of personal and political relationships in a lyrical, allusive style characterized by evocative imagery and layered themes. However, she also believes in the power of the imagination to transform reality and to enable hope: despite natural and political cataclysms, individuals can recreate their lives. Her monologue *Jewel* (1987; 1989) is spoken by a young woman to her dead husband, who drowned during the sinking of an oil rig off the coast of Newfoundland, as she attempts to get her own life back into gear. *Toronto Mississippi* (1987; 1989) explores the complex dynamics between a mother and her mildly autistic daughter, and their responses to an absentee husband/ father who lives out his fantasies as an Elvis impersonator, and who enables his daughter to imagine a world beyond her mental limitations.

The motivation behind *Amigo's Blue Guitar* (1990) was the "appalling" refugee policies in Canada, which MacLeod personally encountered while involved with refugee sponsorship programs in Toronto. It is set on a Gulf island off the west coast of British Columbia, a place of refuge and retreat, but where the wreckage of other places and events washes up on the beaches. The family of an American draft dodger has sponsored a Salvadoran refugee, but their response to his painful history is compromised by selfish personal motives, which finally the refugee, Elias, violently resists. *The Hope Slide* (1992; 1994) is a complex monologue which tracks the inner journey of an actress, recollecting her turbulent girlhood in terms of her preoccupation with the Doukhobors, who settled in the Canadian west. The Doukhobors' struggle for the freedom to live as they choose becomes a metaphor for her own aspirations and social defiance. MacLeod's "millennium play," *2000* (1996; 1997), is set on the "margins" of Vancouver, where the city meets the mountains – a precarious space between the "civilized" and the "savage," and portrays a technologized consumer culture that cannot entirely displace the elemental forces of nature. As in most of her plays, domestic space is both fraught and comforting: despite its conflicts, it shapes the values which guide individual actions. In her monologue *The Shape of a Girl* (2001; 2002) an adolescent girl discovers a frightening correspondence between the senseless murder of a teenager by her schoolmates and her own social behavior.

Similarly, Margaret Hollingsworth focuses on the dangerous spaces inhabited by women in their relationships in her collection of plays entitled *Endangered Species* (1988). Home can be claustrophobic, restrictive, even violent; the walls that define domestic space may exclude or confine, restrict or protect. Sally Clark also explores the ways in which women respond to male control and power. In *Moo* (1988; 1989) the protagonist aggressively pursues a relationship over a fifty-year period, defying the conventional roles prescribed for women by society; in *Life without Instruction* (1991; 1994) the seventeenth-century Italian painter Artemisia Gentilleschi avenges her rape by a perspectives instructor.

Gay and lesbian communities

Life without Instruction was commissioned by Nightwood Theatre, a collective company founded in Toronto in 1979 by a group of women interested in developing plays by, about, and for women. Nightwood's most popular play is a satiric comedy by Ann-Marie MacDonald, entitled *Goodnight Desdemona (Good Morning Juliet)* (1988; 1990), in which MacDonald revisions Shakespeare's tragedies in terms of comedy, creating from the female victims of the tragic heroes a nymphomaniac (Juliet) and a warrior (Desdemona). The point of entry into their stories is effected by a female academic who is writing a thesis proposing that there is a missing Wise Fool in *Romeo and Juliet* and *Othello*. If he were reinstated, the tragedies would be comedies. By the end of the play, Constance discovers that she is the Wise Fool, and that she has been transformed into an independent, confident woman, a paradigm for a feminized postcolonialism. She has learned from Desdemona "To live by questions, not by their solution";[15] and from Juliet to trade certainties for confusion. Ironically, recent productions which foreground the comedy in the clever pastiche of Shakespeare have sublimated the radical feminist and gay issues raised by the play.

In Canada gay and lesbian theater initially asserted itself as alternative, although it has been rapidly absorbed into the mainstream. John Herbert's seminal play *Fortune and Men's Eyes* (1967), which graphically portrays the consequences of prison brutality in terms of gay dynamics, was first produced in New York because there were no Canadian theaters willing to take the risk, but has since been inscribed in the Canadian academic canon. The Toronto theater company Buddies in Bad Times was founded in 1979 as an

---

15 Ann-Marie MacDonald, *Goodnight Desdemona (Good Morning Juliet)*. (Toronto: Coach House Press, 1990), p. 85.

experimental theater to explore the relationship of the printed word to theatrical image, and came out as gay and lesbian in 1985 under the direction of playwright Sky Gilbert, who asserted in the theater's manifesto that "[j]ust as Canada is multi-cultural, it is multi-sexual, and the encouragement of queer culture (as opposed to its oppression) encourages a lively exchange of ideas and images about our sometimes very different experiences of life."[16] For Gilbert queer culture means sexual, radical, non-linear, redefining form as well as content. His play *Drag Queens on Trial* (1985) features the transvestites from Herbert's *Fortune and Men's Eyes* and from Tremblay's *Hosanna* (1972; 1973) as his heroines' defeated older sisters who have failed to enact an aggressively transgressive behavior and language.

Canadian gay and lesbian drama no longer relies exclusively on theaters with a gay mandate: the works of Tremblay and Michel Marc Bouchard, for example, are produced in regional theaters across the country, and by tourist-oriented companies such the Shaw Festival in Niagara-on-the-Lake. Brad Fraser's violent, sexually explicit *Unidentified Human Remains and the True Nature of Love* (1989; 1990) has been performed in Canada, Britain, Australia, and the United States. All of Fraser's subsequent plays graphically demonstrate the terrifying isolation of urban existence, the brutality of exploitative relationships, a sub-culture of drugs and prostitution, including *Poor Super Man* (1994; 1995), *Martin Yesterday* (1997; 1998) – originally commissioned by the BBC as a radio play – and *Snake in Fridge* (2000; 2001), commissioned by the Royal Exchange Theatre in Manchester, England. Fraser's plays are written in the style of film segues – brief scenes are juxtaposed and intercut; dialogue is abrupt and truncated, conjuring images of popular culture, television violence, and pornography. Occasional extended monologues interrupt the stichomythic exchanges, amplifying the portrait of an increasingly diverse and dysfunctional society in which an official multicultural civility only thinly conceals virulent racism, frustration, and rage. In *Snake in Fridge*, the Black youth, Travis, encounters an escalating verbal race riot in the civilized halls of the Bank of Nova Scotia while making a payment on his student loan, which prompts even the teller to respond, "You goddamn third world gooks can't talk this way in a bank."[17]

The highly individualistic and metatheatrical plays of Daniel MacIvor, created for his own company, da da kamera (founded in 1986), are set in a

---

16 Quoted in Robert Wallace, "Theorizing a Queer Theatre: Buddies in Bad Times," in Brask, ed., *Contemporary Issues*, p. 146.
17 Brad Fraser, *Snake in Fridge* (Edmonton: NeWest Press, 2001), p. 82.

dysfunctional, hyperactive, and competitive consumerist environment which precludes interpersonal relationships. *Never Swim Alone* (1991; 1993) enacts a series of competitive male rituals on a beach, with a female referee in the lifeguard's seat, who finally becomes the victim of their pointless, narcissistic behavior. MacIvor's monologue *Monster* (1998; 1999) engages the audience in oedipal revenge fantasies, and his two-hander *In on It* (2001) interrogates the relationship between memory and reality. His final play for da da kamera was *A Beautiful View*, produced by Buddies in Bad Times in 2006; it portrays the fluctuating relationship of two women through three split-ups and reunions until they both come to appreciate their final view of life.

Ethnic theater communities

Ethnic drama – interpreted as other than Anglo / French and Native – has a long history in Canada, although it still exists primarily on the margins of mainstream theater in the small arts or community theaters of cities with a large immigrant population, such as Vancouver, Montreal, and Toronto. Since 1981 Montreal's Teesri Duniya Theatre (meaning "Third World"), under the direction of Rahul Varma, has supported the development and production of South-Asian plays, and works by other minority cultures. Varma's own plays, including *Counter Offence* (1996; 1999), interrogate racism and social inequities in Canadian society. *Bhopal* (2001; 2005) marked the twentieth anniversary of the explosion at the Union Carbide chemical plant in Bhopal, India, causing the death of 8,000 people within the following days, and poisoning 500,000 with cyanide.

According to critic and playwright Uma Parameswaran, South-Asian theaters are "in the process of forging a new national cultural identity in Canada, an identity that will be a composite of many heritage cultures."[18] In Toronto, Cahoots Theatre Projects (founded in 1986) has a mandate to develop, produce, and promote new Canadian theater reflective of Canada's diverse cultural mosaic. Its productions have included works by Métis playwright Daniel David Moses (*The Moon and Dead Indians* 1993; published in *The Indian Medicine Shows: Two One-Act Plays* 1995); and by Chinese-Canadian playwright Marty Chan (*Mom, Dad, I'm Living with a White Girl*, 1995; 1996). In Chan's satiric examination of political correctness, the psychological defense of a son against his parents' opposition to his relationship with a *gwai mui* is to

---

18 Uma Parameswaran, "Protest for a Better Future: South Asian Canadian Theatre's March to the Centre," in Brask, ed., *Contemporary Issues*, p. 117.

demonize his parents as villains from B-movies – a sinister dragon lady and her henchman who seek world domination. However, he finally realizes that in erasing his heritage, he destroys something of himself, and that "[t]he young tree has deep roots."[19]

The lecture/monologue *Fronteras Americanas* (Tarragon Theatre, 1993) by the former artistic director of Cahoots, Guillermo Verdecchia, demonstrates the difficulty of crossing "border zones," and shows how Canada constructs otherness and marginalizes difference as exotic. *A Line in the Sand* (1995; 1997), written with Marcus Youssef for the New Play Centre in Vancouver, enacts the disastrous consequences of the torture and murder of a sixteen-year-old Palestinian on the relationship between a Canadian soldier and another young Palestinian during Operation Desert Shield in 1990. In 2004 Verdecchia collaborated with Marcus Youssef and Camyar Chai on the political satire, *The Adventures of Ali & Ali and the Axes of Evil* (2005). Billed as "a divertimento for warlords," it takes a wild and wide swipe at American aggressive imperial practices: two guys from the Middle East find themselves in North America post-9/11 during the "War on Terror," and attempt to survive by selling anything they can to the audience.

African-Canadian playwright Djanet Sears dramatizes the ethnic diversity of Canadian society by creating new theatrical forms for her own work and through her involvement with the Obsidian Theatre and the AfriCanadian Playwrights Festival in Toronto. In *Afrika Solo* (1987; 1990) she explores possible identities for a Black woman – "British by birth, Jamaican on her Mother's side, Guyanese on her fathers [sic], presently living in Canada, claiming Canadian citizenship."[20] The play reconstructs her history in terms of a trip to Africa. As does Verdecchia in *Fronteras Americanas*, she discovers a rich, varied history that dispels negative and limiting stereotypes, and confronts the hegemonic whiteness of Western audiences. Sears' *The Adventures of a Black Girl in Search of God* (2002; 2003) explores the disastrous interpersonal consequences of a woman doctor's feelings of guilt over her daughter's death, her dying father, and her divorce from her preacher-husband. Rainey rants against the powerlessness of God, while seeking some form of salvation. The focus is less on race and difference than on a personal quest for meaning.

Montreal's Black Theatre Workshop, established in 1972 to develop and perform plays by and for African Canadians, has produced Andrew Moodie's

---

19 Marty Chan, "Mom, Dad, I'm Living with a White Girl," in *Ethnicities: Plays from the New West*, ed. Anne Nothof (Edmonton: NeWest Press, 1999), p. 167.
20 Djanet Sears, *Afrika Solo* (Toronto: Sister Vision, 1990), p. 11.

satiric comedy, *Riot* (1995; 1997), about the impossibility of being politically correct in Canada; George Elroy Boyd's tragic history of slavery, *Wade in the Water* (2003), and Vadney S. Haynes' hilarious comedy about Black identity, *Blacks Don't Bowl* (2006; 2007). Boyd's other plays have been produced in his native Nova Scotia, tracing the fraught history of Black immigration and alienation in that province: *Gideon's Blues* (1990; 1996) dramatizes the downward spiral of an educated Black man whose ambitions for himself and his family are thwarted by racism; *Consecrated Ground* (1999) depicts the consequences to a Black family of the razing of Africville on the outskirts of Halifax in the 1960s, and the relocation of its 400 residents to more "progressive" public housing, despite the efforts of the advocates of Black heritage to save it.

Poet, novelist, librettist, and playwright George Elliot Clarke scrutinizes the history of the Black community in Nova Scotia in *Whylah Falls: The Play* (1997; 1999) and in the libretto for the opera, *Beatrice Chancy* (1999). Lorena Gale explores the unacknowledged history of slavery in Canada in *Angélique* (1998; 2000), which reenacts the story of a slave imported from Madeira and bought by a Montreal businessman for his wife, but exploited as his mistress. Although accused of arson, and hanged in 1734, in the play she proclaims her innocence, and foresees the city "swarming with ebony"[21] – her brothers and her sisters of the future. Canadian drama is increasingly preoccupied with diversity and complexity, and eroding a white majority Eurocentrism. The amorphous identity of Canada remains provisional, continually reconstituted and debated.

Community festivals

The form and content of Canadian theater is also stretched and challenged in annual summer Fringe Festivals, hosting unvetted productions on a "first come first served" basis. Since 1982 the inaugural Edmonton International Fringe Festival has grown into the largest theater festival in North America, hosting over 200 shows over ten days to audiences of 300,000. Subsequently, similar festivals, staged in cities from Halifax to Victoria, have provided a network for traveling local and international productions. Some playwrights whose work has premiered at Fringe Festivals have continued to write for theater companies in regular seasons of plays; for example, Stewart Lemoine has created witty, philosophical comedies of manners for his company, Teatro La

---

21 Lorena Gale, "Angélique," in *Testifyin': Contemporary African Canadian Drama*, 2 vols. ed. Djanet Sears (Toronto: Playwrights Canada Press, 2003), vol. II, p. 70.

Quindicina, including *At the Zenith of the Empire* (2005; 2007), which features Sarah Bernhardt in her 1913 performance of *La Dame aux camélias* in Edmonton's second Empire Theatre. The play provides a metatheatrical and metahistorical exposition of the importance of community theater practice. In her concluding speech, Bernhardt points to the ephemerality of theater, and importance of continuity:

> That the Empire is beautiful is not to be denied, but I think it could come down tomorrow and the loss would be less profound than you'd expect. All that was most valuable here is gone by the end of every night. It's taken away by the people who came and watched and listened. These buildings that we call theatres ... some last, some don't, and this is surely how it's always going to be, but the thing is to see that whenever you may lose one ... you find another. A smaller one, a bigger one, it doesn't matter ... but they must always be replaced.[22]

Vern Thiessen launched his playwriting career at the Edmonton Fringe with *The Courier* in 1988 (2006), a monologue which investigates the ethics of conflicted loyalties and national identities during wartime. Since then he has created complex moral investigations of other crucial historical moments: Fritz Haber's invention of Zyklon B and Einstein's work on nuclear chain reactions in *Einstein's Gift* (2003); and Canada's involvement in the First World War in *Vimy* (2007; 2008).

Enacting possible worlds

Canadian playwrights have addressed and defined local communities and histories, but they have also undertaken metaphysical inquiries into the ways in which reality may be constructed and perceived, and the fluid, shifting nature of character. In John Mighton's *Possible Worlds* (1990; 1992) the protagonist believes that he lives in many times and places at the same time, and falls in love with different incarnations of the same woman, while detectives attempt to discover who is responsible for removing the brains of intelligent victims. "Possible worlds" connotes the multifaceted nature of reality and of perception; it is also a metaphor for the many possible incarnations of lives and events through theater.

In 2000 John Mighton's play was made into a film directed by Robert Lepage, whose plays are similarly preoccupied with shapeshifting and the amorphous nature of reality and truth. In *Polygraph* (1989, English-language

---

22 Stewart Lemoine, *At the Zenith of the Empire* (Edmonton: NeWest Press, 2007), p. 133.

premiere; 1990) the lie-detector operates on many different levels: truth is multivalent, and all the characters are actors, living out fantasies or concealing trauma: their personal crises become indicators of cultural and political collisions. Lepage's plays are linguistically polyphonic, suggesting the intercultural nature of Canadian society, but also the confusion and misunderstanding that can result, for example in *The Dragon's Trilogy* (1985) and *Tectonic Plates* (1988). Cultures are always borrowed or stolen; they can never be wholly authentic or inauthentic. Perhaps because of their transcultural themes and images and their imaginative theatricality, Lepage's complex creations have traveled around the world.

Canada's most extravagant theatrical export, however, is Cirque du Soleil, an internationally acclaimed circus/theater company based in Montreal, founded in 1984 by a group of Quebec street performers to celebrate a colonizing moment: the 450th anniversary of Jacques Cartier's landing. Its performances, staged in giant tents or site-specific theaters, are loosely structured around a narrative which links a series of spectacular acrobatics by artists from around the world – all set to a dynamic and evocative urban tribal musical score, and featuring opulent or minimalist exotic costumes. By 1988 the Cirque was touring extensively in the United States, and by 1992 it had visited Europe and Japan. In 1992 it established a permanent circus in Las Vegas, and in 1998 it opened another mega-production in a specially conceived house at the Bellagio Hotel, entitled *O* – a pun on the French word for "water" – which was performed in, around, and above a gigantic pool. Other productions include *Alegria*, *Quidam*, and *Dralion*, most of which have been directed by Franco Dragone, with soundtracks composed by René Dupéré. In 2002 the company launched *Varekai*, directed by Quebec playwright Dominic Champagne.

The making of theater in Canada ranges from monologue to mega-musical, from community-based to globally marketed. It connects individuals, communities, and countries, crossing aesthetic and national borders. Its diversity reflects the limitations, challenges, and successes of a multicultural country.

21
Poetry

KEVIN McNEILLY

Between 2001 and 2004, the Bank of Canada issued its updated series of bills, each denomination depicting on its verso a collage of thematically linked cultural images, microscopically captioned with a brief excerpt from a literary text.[1] The series, under the title "Canadian Journey," aims both to reflect the diversity of Canadian cultural experience and to produce a sense of common tradition and shared values from within that diversity, so the texts chosen for the bills consist of poems – John McRae's "In Flanders Fields" for the ten-dollar bill – or stories – Roch Carrier's "The Hockey Sweater" for the five – that Canadians of any ethnic or linguistic background will likely have encountered either in school or in the media.

The two lines (like other texts, presented in both official languages) on the back of the 100 dollar bill are not so widely known, perhaps because they question how we can be said to share any such history: "Do we ever remember that somewhere above the sky in some child's dream perhaps / Jacques Cartier is still sailing, always on his way always about to discover a new Canada?" This couplet is reshaped from the last six lines of Miriam Waddington's poem "Jacques Cartier in Toronto," from her 1992 collection *The Last Landscape*. Its inclusion on Canadian currency is significant not only because it honors Waddington's significant contributions to Canadian literary culture, but also because it poses directly the question of how poetry and national history entwine. "Wanting to write the stories of ordinary Canadians," Waddington opens "The Writer," a prose poem from the same volume, "I discover there are no ordinary Canadians." What Canadians share, as cultural history, is for her exactly this want, the open-ended question of our present-day self-fashioning.

Writing any history of recent and contemporary poetry involves confronting the ways in which that poetry attempts to frame its own historical sense:

---

1 Bank of Canada. http://www.bankofcanada.ca/en/banknotes/general/character/2001-04.html.

how and why poetry might matter to national cultural history, or how aesthetic work historicizes itself. English-Canadian poetry after 1960 is informed by a set of interwoven pluralities – of voice, of perspective, of form, of culture – that present themselves in a braid of four principal tendencies: modernist formalism, reflexive postmodern experimentation, confessional free-verse lyric and ethno-poetic pluralism. This welter of cross-currents is best modeled historically and poetically as polyrhythm, a multiplying set of resonances and interconnections; as P. K. Page, probably English Canada's most important poet of the last fifty years, puts it in a 2007 interview for CBC radio, self-aware poets are drawn to the confluences of "rhythm and rhythm and rhythm."[2]

Locating poetic voice

As a barometer of cultural sanction, the Governor General's Literary Award (for poetry or drama) went in 1960 to Margaret Avison, for her first book, *Winter Sun*, a masterful collection mixing modernist free verse, influenced by Dylan Thomas and A. J. M. Smith, with crafted formal pieces, including sonnets – some of her most frequently anthologized poems, such as "Butterfly Bones" – and stanzaic lyrics outwardly informed by her reading of metaphysical poetry. Avison's early writing – her next collection, *The Dumbfounding*, is published in 1966 – appears in retrospect more reactive than innovative, a tendency that reflects her immediate historical context as an emergent Canadian poet. She had lived and studied in the United States, where she encountered writers such as Robert Creeley and Denise Levertov who were evolving a poetry that combined American idioms with universalizing mythopoeia. Notably, Irving Layton's collection *A Red Carpet for the Sun* (1959, his first publication with McClelland and Stewart) also registers the impact of Black Mountain verse, and was praised by William Carlos Williams as well as Northrop Frye. But both Avison and Layton – respectively representing the new and established voices of 1960 – refuse a direct colloquial mode or confessional matter, preferring the stylized language of symbol and image. Avison's conversion to Christianity in 1963 will reinvigorate her work, and her monumental three-volume collected poems *Always Now* (2003–5) testifies to a plural and evolving poetic imagination.

The sway of Northrop Frye's biblically informed criticism can be felt in the poetry of the early 1960s, though not so much in Avison's poems as in the

---

2 CBC Radio, "Words at Large." http://www.cbc.ca/wordsatlarge/.

work of James Reaney, whose regionalist formalism draws unapologetically on his mentor's analysis of Canadian poetry, published as Frye's "Annual Surveys" in the *University of Toronto Quarterly* from 1950 to 1960, articles that argued for a Canadian canon based on a formative, determinist conception of landscape and religion within the Canadian "imagination." Frye's University of Toronto colleague Jay Macpherson wrote poetry that versified Frye's biblical thematics. While her two collections appeared in print outside the 1960s – the archly formal *The Boatman*, 1957, and the more subtly domesticated *Welcoming Disaster*, 1974 – she did publish the libretto for a cantata by composer John Beckwith, *Jonah*, in James Reaney's hand-made journal ALPHABET in June 1964. Although essentially a "little magazine," ALPHABET (produced from 1960 to 1971) epitomizes Reaney's regionalist aesthetic, in its combined attention to the local – much of his work concentrates on content linked to Reaney's "Souwesto" (that is, southwestern Ontario) small-town cultural background – and to the archetypal, both literary and religious (that is, Protestant Christian).

ALPHABET saw to print early work by poets as diverse as Margaret Atwood, Colleen Thibaudeau, bill bissett, George Bowering and bp Nichol. Reaney's work insisted on locating the subject and voice of a text in its immediate Canadian setting – whether Ontario or elsewhere – but also deferred to a broader canon for any yardstick of literary value; poetry comes from here, and is about here ("Where is Here?" Northrop Frye famously asks), but it uses forms and language from a European colonial heritage. For example, Bowering's *Kerrisdale Elegies* (1984), which represent for many readers a high-point in his poetic oeuvre, are – however much a product of urban Vancouver life and however inherently suspicious of central Canadian formal literary pieties – a transplanting of Rainer Maria Rilke's famous *Duino Elegies* (1923) into a Canadian context; the poems confront the issue of cosmopolitan measure for local work, and ironically ask how we, as citizens of this place, can articulate any vital "need" for our own poetry.

Reaney's preoccupation with local voice remained an influence on Bowering and others, even if the younger poets sought to critique the Eurocentric premises of his Frygian thought. Reaney, Bowering writes in 1972, remains important not because of Frye but because he can "feel / the tug" of his earth.[3] Poets such as Don McKay would acknowledge Reaney as motivational, and McKay's own poetry from the 1970s emerges from close interest in local physiography, in the forms and textures of region. *Butterfly on*

---

3 See "James Reaney" in *George Bowering Selected: Poems 1961–1992*, ed. Roy Miki (Toronto: McClelland and Stewart, 1993), pp. 64–5.

Rock: A Study of Themes and Images in Canadian Literature (1970), a critical overview by the poet and critic D. G. Jones (and titled after an Irving Layton poem), synthesizes and reworks Frye's formal influence on Canadian poetry in the 1960s, arguing that poets aim to resolve in their work the deep-seated colonial conflict between Eurocentric cultural heritage and an unruly autochthony. The conceptual tensions in Reaney's poetic are for Jones mitigated by an imaginative, grounded solidarity of voice and concern.

But little such resolution occurs in the 1960s. The poetry of the remainder of the decade bears witness to a waning of this and other formalisms. Poet-diplomat R. A. D. Ford continued to publish his formally rigorous poems, eventually gathered in his selected, *Coming From Afar* (1990). *New Provinces* modernist Robert Finch – in *Dover Beach Revisited* (1961) and *Silverthorn Bush* (1966) – reaffirmed his Arnoldian cultural conservatism and exacting style. P. K. Page, ever a resilient and unrepentant formalist, published no collection of poems (after 1954) until 1967, when *Cry Ararat!* appeared, consisting as much of retrospective as new work. Daryl Hine left Canada for Europe in the early 1960s, before settling in Chicago and going on to become editor (from 1968 to 1978) of the internationally prestigious journal *Poetry*. His cosmopolitan style – linked by its formalism and homoeroticism to the work of Americans James Merrill and, especially, Richard Howard – finds no amenable home in this country, despite his continued interest in writing about Canadian subjects, and Hine becomes something of a poetic "resident alien" (also the title of a 1975 poetry volume).

Instead, many poets articulate a preference for engaged and expressive writing, with an increasing emphasis on vernacular free verse. The death of E. J. Pratt in 1964 marks a break between the modernism of an earlier generation – their work canonized by Frye – and a more troubled and various coterie of new voices. The positive critical reception in 1965 of Al Purdy's *The Cariboo Horses* denotes a turning point in Canadian poetry. Purdy had published *Poems for All the Annettes* in 1962, and would follow with *North of Summer: Poems from Baffin Island* in 1967, both of which interrogate the poet's uneasy and fluid relationships to landscape and history, whether Ameliasburg Ontario or the Northwest Territories. As Dennis Lee makes clear in his Afterword to Purdy's 1986 *Collected Poems*, the key shift in Purdy's work is a move away from the strictures of Anglocentric form toward expressive freedom and directness,[4] as well as an increased emphasis on process, the poet's modulating engagement with a sense of time and place.

---

4 See Dennis Lee, *Body Music: Essays* (Toronto: Anansi, 1998), pp. 73–102.

The poems of New Brunswicker Alden Nowlan, notably his collection *Bread, Wine and Salt* (1967), continued to investigate a kind of luminous intimacy, coupling confessional free verse with diffident restraint. Milton Acorn, who moved to central Canada from Prince Edward Island (where he would return in 1981), saw his poetry undergo a shift similar to Purdy's, as his writing veered away from closed metrical patterns to freely flowing lines. Acorn's early achievements were recognized by a special issue of *The Fiddlehead* (number 56, Spring 1963).[5] When Acorn's *I've Tasted My Blood: Poems 1956–1968* (edited by Purdy, as was an earlier book, *The Brain's the Target*, 1960) did not win the 1969 Governor General's Award, a number of writers including Irving Layton, Margaret Atwood, Eli Mandel and Joe Rosenblatt named him "The People's Poet" the following year, a label that bespoke Acorn's populism as well as the admiration of his peers.[6] The Milton Acorn People's Poetry Award was established in 1987 in Acorn's memory.

Layton's *Collected Poems* appeared in 1965, closing off a chapter in his career. Layton would continue to be praised as a major voice in Canadian poetry, but his own increasingly cranky relationship to Canadian literature was tied to a blunter, polemical style that bore little trace of his elaborate lyricism. At virtually the same cultural moment, Dorothy Livesay's committed work underwent a renaissance. Livesay's poetry had been associated with modernism and with leftist politics. On her return to Western Canada (from Zambia) in 1963, Livesay found her work re-energized by the Vancouver writing scene (including the establishment of a separate Department of Creative Writing at the University of British Columbia by Earle Birney). Livesay's *The Unquiet Bed* (1967) and *Plainsongs* (1969) bracket the republication in 1968 of her long poems from the 1930s and 1940s as *The Documentaries*. The titles of these books suggest much about Livesay's poetic preoccupations: empirical engagement with societal and cultural realities, a directness of voice and an aspiration to political disquiet. Moreover, she sought – in a paper republished in Eli Mandel's 1971 anthology *Contexts of Canadian Criticism* – to instantiate what she called "the documentary poem" as a Canadian genre, coupling her address to the factual present with a historically minded nationalism symptomatic of the poetry produced around the Centennial.

---

5 Founded at Fredericton, New Brunswick, in 1945 as an outgrowth of the Bliss Carman Society, *The Fiddlehead* has claimed to be Canada's oldest surviving poetry journal. See the online catalogue of the Fred Cogswell / *Fiddlehead* papers at the University of New Brunswick http://www.lib.unb.ca/archives/finding/Fiddlehead/fiddle.html.
6 See Chris Gudgeon, "Taste of Victory: The Night the 'People's Poet' Tasted Triumph." *Canadian Forum* 75.854 (1996), pp. 10–13.

Earle Birney would retire from teaching in 1965, but his writing – which extended the landscape-focused modernism of E. J. Pratt – continued to explore the formal and conceptual limits of the poetic. His fulminating influence on establishing a distinctively west coast poetry scene was substantial. Birney coupled a sense of political engagement with restless experimentalism, and his writing would come to include concrete and typographically innovative poetry, complex associative free verse and collaborative performances with musicians. The engaged intelligence of both Birney and Livesay would have a significant impact on poets emerging in the 1970s and 1980s, such as Tom Wayman, whose poetry addresses the sensuousness in human work and common experience – seeking out shared values and concerns in everyday life.

Alternatives

Phyllis Webb had worked as a journalist in Montreal in the late 1950s, interacting with a number of prominent poets there including F. R. Scott, Louis Dudek, Irving Layton, and Eli Mandel; she lived in Vancouver from 1960 to 1964 (returning again to the west coast from Toronto in 1969, where she worked for CBC Radio), and felt the influence of Birney as well as a group of literati at the University of British Columbia including George Woodcock (then editor of *Canadian Literature*) and Warren Tallman. *The Sea Is Also a Garden*, her third collection, which appeared in 1962, marks a shift away from social to spiritual politics, but a spirituality tied more to an exploration of female essence than to organized religion; her feminism intersects with Livesay's efforts to revalue women's empowerment through a recovery of suppressed voices.

In the summer of 1963, Webb interviewed visiting American poets at the university, including Robert Creeley, Robert Duncan, Charles Olson, and Denise Levertov,[7] and their influence – particularly of Creeley's verbal minimalism – can be felt in her subsequent collection, *Naked Poems* (1965): "a new alphabet," she writes, "gasps for air" in her compact, honed lines.[8] This vertical influence suggests a closer poetic kinship for west coast Canadian writers with established American postmodernists than with central Canadians. Webb's "new alphabet" wasn't Reaney's ALPHABET. The American-style cosmopolitan modernism from which Webb and others in British Columbia derive

---

7 See Pauline Butling, *Seeing in the Dark: The Poetry of Phyllis Webb* (Waterloo: Wilfrid Laurier University Press, 1997), p. 146.
8 See Phyllis Webb, *Naked Poems* (Vancouver: Periwinkle Press, 1965).

their poetics differs from the Frygian modernity of either A. J. M. Smith or E. J. Pratt.

This alternative poetics might best be framed as a product of work published in the little magazine *TISH*, which appeared, as homemade mimeographs, around the University of British Columbia from 1961 to 1969. The "TISH Group" of poets who contributed to the magazine included George Bowering, Fred Wah, Frank Davey, Lionel Kearns, Jamie Reid, and Daphne Marlatt. Their poetry was reshaped by techniques of "composition by field" and improvisational "projective verse" – practices developed by Robert Duncan and Charles Olson – that emphasized the spatial rhythms of the page and the corporeal rhythms of breath and pulse as structural bases for composition, as well as the specific use of the typewriter as a writing "instrument." Wah and Reid would increasingly emphasize the relationships between their poetry and jazz performances, while Marlatt (in her best-known long poem *Steveston*, 1974) would develop a distinctive poetic linked to geographical and historical space. Marlatt's influence on avant-garde women's poetry in Canada was significant through the 1980s and 1990s, and her poems and essays – such as *Touch to my Tongue* (1984) and "Musing with Mothertongue" – contribute to establishing a significant counter-canon of feminist and queer poetry within the Canadian scene.

By contrast, George Bowering would come to emphasize (in serial poems such as *George, Vancouver*, 1970) regional geography and history, interrogating popular ideologies of heroic masculinity while rejecting what he perceived as the anthropocentrism of Ontario-style regionalism. While Bowering's perspective tends characteristically to be ironic rather than pious, his provocative poetic investigations of place contribute a body of foundational cultural work. Fred Wah's poetry and prose would increasingly center on his "hyphenated" status as a Chinese-Canadian, as he sought to produce a language responsive to the fraught and complex dynamics of multiculturalism. Later poets – especially from in and around Vancouver – such as Roy Miki would also follow Wah and take up the challenges presented by the language-politics of a multicultural idiom. (Miki's acclaimed *Surrender* [2001] also incorporates many of bp Nichol's experiments with language to address the nature of the culturally mixed voice.)

Frank Davey goes on after *TISH* to found the critical journal *Open Letter* (1965–); his writing since then documents his shift away from Black Mountain poetics toward an interest in L=A=N=G=U=A=G=E poetry and related experimentation with the limits of poetic meaning. Even as his work becomes more abstract and, arguably, academic, Davey maintains a strong interest in popular culture (as do a number of the former *TISH* poets – Reid, for instance, would write a biography of Canadian pop-jazz pianist and singer Diana Krall).[9] A special issue in 1991 of the poetry journal *West Coast Line* entitled "Beyond TISH" – guest-edited by Douglas Barbour – examines the lasting influence of the group's grass-roots upheaval of Canadian poetics.

Milton Acorn also lived in Vancouver in 1967, and was a member of the founding collective of the *Georgia Straight* alternative newspaper. A resurgent populism – at times blatantly nationalistic, at others doggedly resistant – inflects the poetry of the late 1960s and early 1970s. Itinerant Montrealer Leonard Cohen, who is further discussed in the chapter on poetry, drama, and the postmodern novel, had become a leading young voice with the publication of *The Spice-Box of Earth* in 1961, a Canadian bestseller at the time, establishing Cohen's characteristic mix of lyric sensuality and ironic detachment. His *Selected Poems* appeared from McClelland and Stewart in 1968, the same year as his first recording, *Songs of Leonard Cohen*. While poetry, along with his novels (including *The Favourite Game*, 1963, and *Beautiful Losers*, 1966), had given Cohen a substantial cultural profile, he appears still to have sought the more popular and less rarefied role of folk troubadour, as a Canadian Bob Dylan.

Torontonian Margaret Atwood seeks out what she takes to be submerged or repressed archetypes of the popular Canadian imagination; while she has attained international stature as a writer of fiction, her work as a poet – beginning in 1964 with *The Circle Game*, followed in 1968 by *The Animals in That Country* and in 1970 by *The Journals of Susanna Moodie* – focuses more acutely than her prose, with a dry detached lyricism, on addressing the underside of a deeply rooted Canadian psyche, a mentality that for Atwood remains shared, if unacknowledged, among Anglo-Saxon-descended Central Canadians. Her work in all genres is discussed in a separate chapter, along with the writing of Munro, Shields, and Gallant.

The poetry of bp Nichol anticipates by a decade the innovations and experiments of the L=A=N=G=U=A=G=E movement south of the border; much of Nichol's work concerns itself with transgressing aesthetic categories, incorporating pop-culture conventions of comic books, for example, into complex and whimsical graphic scores and concrete poems. Nichol attended the University of British Columbia between 1960 and 1963, where he encountered the work of *TISH*; he moved to Toronto in the mid-1960s, and began to publish hand-drawn, genre-bending writing with new small presses such as

---

9 Janie Reid, *Diana Krall: The Language of Love* (Markham: Quarry Music Books, 2002).

Coach House. A mix of abstraction and playfulness characterizes his best work, embodied in his long (six-volume) serial poem *The Martyrology* (1972–88, with posthumous volumes appearing in 1990 and 1992).[10]

Nichol's poetry preoccupies itself with what he calls in one poem the additional "l" that converts the word "word" into "world": how both to describe and to enact an articulation between graphic representation and lived experience, between form and action.[11] His performances with the sound-poetry group The Four Horsemen, which included Steve McCaffery, Paul Dutton, and Rafael Barreto-Rivera, pushed the limits of sense in pursuit of that articulation; Nichol participated through the 1980s in experimental forays into recording and printing, and the avant-garde work of artists and composers such as Michael Snow and R. Murray Schafer emerges in parallel with his innovations. Nichol's aesthetic allegiances tended to be international, as he forged nascent artistic relationships with the work of American and European avant-gardists such as Bob Cobbing or Henri Chopin. His deconstructive approach to language and culture impacted as well on West Coast writers such as Colin Browne and Jeff Derksen, who participated in founding the Kootenay School of Writing in Vancouver (moving from Nelson, British Columbia) in 1984, an artists' collective that aims to foster experimental, marginalized, and off-the-wall creative work.

The polystylism that informs the poetries of Nichol, McCaffery, and other Toronto writers would pave the way for the surreal poetry of Christopher Dewdney, whose work is (he writes) "warped out of science" and natural history.[12] The son of archeologist and novelist Selwyn Dewdney, Christopher Dewdney grew up in London, Ontario, and his writing registers the immediate impact of James Reaney's Souwesto regionalism – but instead of local geography, Dewdney looks (like a postmodern E. J. Pratt) to geology as a node at which texture and archetype coalesce, and jar. His *A Palaeozoic Geology of London, Ontario: Poems and Collages* appeared from the Coach House Press in 1973; subsequent work, including *Predators of the Adoration: Selected Poems*,

---

10 An online version of *The Martyrology* can be found at the Coach House Books website http://archives.chbooks.com/online_books/martyrology/?q=archives/online_books/martyrology. The electronic format of the poem would have appealed to Nichol, who also experimented with crafting a series of "action poems" on his Apple IIe computer, collectively entitled *First Screening*, emulated versions of which can be found online at Jim Andrews's website, http://www.vispo.com/bp/introduction.htm.
11 See *The Martyrology*, book 3, section 8, lines 2, 101–2.
12 See the Christopher Dewdney page at the "Canadian Poetry" website from the University of Toronto Library: http://www.library.utoronto.ca/canpoetry/dewdney/. See also Christopher Dewdney and Karl E. Jirgens, ed., *Children of the Outer Dark: The Poetry of Christopher Dewdney* (Waterloo: Wilfrid Laurier University Press, 2007), pp. 41–6.

1972–82 (1983) and *Signal Fires* (2000) develop his admixture of skewed lyric and pataphysical play. The factual language of science is treated by Dewdney as a literal discourse, as raw linguistic material for making poems.

New publics

Michael Ondaatje achieved international fame as the author of *The English Patient* (1992), but his career before his success as a novelist focused primarily on poetry (of which he has published at least fourteen books, including *Handwriting*, 1998). Ondaatje's writing evinces a latter-day aestheticism, focusing on sensuous imagery and enacting meditations on the fleshly hues and textures of cultural difference. His earlier extended poems and mixed-genre collages focus on American cultural icons such as Billy the Kid or jazz trumpeter Buddy Bolden. Ondaatje's Sri Lankan background begins to appear more pervasively as a subject in collections such as *Secular Love* (1984) and *The Cinnamon Peeler* (1992), but his perspective remains attentive to its Canadian context. southwestern Ontario becomes a locale from which to address the dynamics of cultural displacement and diaspora that also inform, historically, the uneasy reflexive voices of post-1960 poetry.

Ondaatje taught at the University of Western Ontario from 1967 to 1971, where he established strong artistic and personal ties to the founding editors of Brick Books, which would grow to be one of the most significant small presses publishing poetry in Canada. Brick Books emerged in 1977 – from the small presses Applegarth Follies and the Nairn Publishing House, which had been provisionally edited since 1975 by writer and critic Stan Dragland – under the collaborative editorship of Dragland and poet Don McKay.[13] (The journal *Brick* diverged from the publisher in 1985.) In its thirty-odd years, Brick Books has seen to print many of the most prominent of Canadian poets, including major titles from P. K. Page (*Hologram: A Book of Glosas*, 1994), Margaret Avison (*Concrete and Wild Carrot*, 2002), John Reibetanz (*Mining for Sun*, 2000), Don McKay (*Lependu*, 1978), A. F. Moritz (*Rest on the Flight into Egypt*, 1999), Jan Zwicky (*Songs for Relinquishing the Earth*, 1998),[14] as well as important collections from emergent and established voices including John Donlan, Colleen Thibaudeau, Robyn Sarah, Phil Hall, Patrick Friesen, Méira Cook, Adam Dickinson, Robert Kroetsch, Michael Crummey, Russ Leckie, and

---

13 http://www.brickbooks.ca/?page_id-2.
14 The 1998 edition replicates a hand-made version of the book self-published by Zwicky in 1996.

Dennis Lee (among many others). The other editors of the press, including poet Barry Dempster, continue its legacy. While the press can claim in its roster a mix of poets with varying aesthetics, certain tendencies do emerge in its titles: an emphasis on the lyric as a viable expressive form, particularly in the context of an increasingly depersonalized postmodernism, a renewed insistence on confessional free verse, and an attention to landscape and ecology.

McKay would act understatedly as a key presence in Anglo-Canadian poetry throughout the 1980s and 1990s, editing work by major and emergent poets for McClelland and Stewart's poetry series. McClelland and Stewart is probably the most prestigious publisher in the country, and its roster of poets shapes Canadian readers' sense of the contemporary poetic canon. Its key authors have included McKay, Robert Bringhurst, Lorna Crozier, George Bowering, Dennis Lee, Margaret Avison, Dionne Brand, Leonard Cohen, Margaret Atwood, Michael Ondaatje, Steven Heighton, Patrick Lane, Tim Lilburn, John Steffler, John Reibetanz, and Miriam Waddington, as well as new voices after 2000 including Michael Crummey, Sonnet l'Abbé, and Anne Simpson. While no single poetic philosophy unites these poets, there are notable leanings in the choices made by the publisher, often centering on a perception (if not the actuality) of cultural nationalism, on ethnic and social plurality, and on an address to place and history in the poetry.

In 2000, publisher Avie Bennett gave control of McClelland and Stewart to the University of Toronto, to ensure its continuation as what the federal Ministry of Heritage dubbed "a Canadian entity."[15] But as early as 1958, McClelland and Stewart had issued titles in its "New Canadian Library" series in a concerted effort to form the Canadian canon. The series would include anthologies of historical and recent poetry, such as *Poets of Contemporary Canada 1960–1970*, edited by Eli Mandel; works on poetics such as *Masks of Poetry: Canadian Critics on Canadian Verse*, edited by A. J. M. Smith in 1962; selections from poetry by Al Purdy and Irving Layton; and biographical studies of the poetry of Leonard Cohen, E. J. Pratt, Earle Birney, and James Reaney. The series was reactivated in 1988 by David Staines of the University of Ottawa, and continues its reissue program to the present.[16]

---

15 Bennet donated a 75 percent share of the company to the University, while the remaining 25 percent was purchased by the American publisher Random House, an indication – perhaps ironically, given the press's nationalistic mandate – of increasing American ownership of Canadian cultural properties. McClelland and Stewart. http://www.mcclelland.com/about/index.html.

16 The work of canon recovery and promotion continues in other contexts as well. The Summer 2007 issue of *ARC*, a poetry journal, consists of an anthology of "lost" Canadian

Through the 1970s and 1980s, McClelland and Stewart also published retrospective selections and collected poems by Irving Layton (*The Darkening Fire* and *The Unwavering Eye* [1975], later re-edited and combined as *A Wild Peculiar Joy* [1982, revised 2004]), F. R. Scott (*Collected Poems*, 1981), Al Purdy (*Collected Poems*, 1986), Ralph Gustafson (*Selected Poems*, 1972, followed by *Fire on Stone*, 1974), A. J. M. Smith (*The Classic Shade: Selected Poems*, 1978), and Earle Birney (*Ghost in the Wheels: Selected Poems*, 1977). In *Configurations at Midnight*, a 1992 verse memoir, Gustafson claims to have striven in his work for "Exact measure / In spontaneous grace," melding a careful and acute formalism to spontaneity of expression.[17] This tension between order and immediacy informs both Gustafson's work and that of his contemporaries.

Dennis Lee's *Civil Elegies* (1968, revised 1972) probably gives the fullest range of any contemporary poet to this involved problematic of self, citizenship, and civic voice. Under the influence of the philosopher George Grant, Lee's poem – consisting of a series of nine meditative "elegies" loosely modeled on Rilke, set in Toronto's Nathan Phillips Square in front of City Hall – strive to enact ("Better however to try," the poem suggests) a sense of homecoming, of contemporary belonging to a national polity, a society that is at once, as the poem puts it, "strangest" and "nearest."[18] Lee has probably had more influence as a theorist about poetics and as a poetry editor; his essays "Cadence, Country, Silence: Writing in Colonial Space" (1973) and "Polyphony: Enacting a Meditation" (1979) have had an immeasurable impact on discussion about the nature of subjectivity and voice in the aftermath of colonial influence in Canada.[19]

"Cadence," for Lee, names the material immediacy of existential rhythm, the local "here and now" in which time and space unfold; catching at its unresolved textures, for Lee, offers a means of grappling poetically with the work of participation in one's own culture and place, however unstable or uncertain that context may be. Lee argues that poets can embrace contradictions, rather than attempt to resolve them artificially in their work. Lee's poetry also has a populist aspect, mitigating the philosophical abstraction of his mature work (an abstraction he insists on avoiding, despite himself). He wrote song lyrics and script material for the children's program *Fraggle Rock* in the 1980s (along with bp Nichol), and is best known for his collection of

---

poets – including George Faludy, Philip Child, Douglas LePan, Cheng Sait Chia, Audrey Alexandra Brown, Dorothy Roberts and Avi Boxer, among others – who the editorial claims need to be brought back to a national readership.
17 Ralph Gustafson, *Configurations at Midnight* (Toronto: ECW, 1992), p. 44.
18 Dennis Lee, *Civil Elegies and Other Poems* (Toronto: Anansi, 1972), p. 57.
19 Both essays are collected in Dennis Lee, *Body Music: Essays* (Toronto: Anansi, 1998).

children's poetry, *Alligator Pie* (1974). Despite their young audience, these poems address – with playful irony – the establishment of iconic and canonical figures in Canadiana.

Alongside Lee's commitment to civic poetics, an amount of social satire and politically engaged poetry appeared in the 1970s. F. R. Scott – associated with A. J. M. Smith and the McGill Group of modernists published in the seminal anthology *New Provinces* in 1936 – still composed scathing satiric poems, although his best-known work had appeared in the 1940s and 1950s. His son Peter Dale Scott has produced a trilogy of long poems – *Coming to Jakarta: A Poem about Terror* (1988), *Listening to the Candle: A Poem on Impulse* (1992), and *Minding the Darkness: A Poem for the Year 2000* (2000) – that employ a mixed mode of fractal structure and academic analysis to address the fraught politics of globalization. Dorothy Livesay's selected poems *The Self-Completing Tree* appeared in 1986, and demonstrated her continuing importance as a socially and culturally engaged artist, focusing in particular on her intense commitment to feminist causes.

Lee's influence has been more decisive on aesthetics than on politics. A 1996 symposium at Trent University in Peterborough, Ontario, entitled "Polyphony," saw a group of poets and critics gather to explore and extend Lee's multivalent poetics. This informal coterie, including Don McKay, Robert Bringhurst, Stan Dragland, Tim Lilburn, Roo Borson, Kim Maltman and Jan Zwicky, had been debating poetics and building affiliations since the mid-1980s, and their essays appear in two collections, edited by Lilburn: *Poetry and Knowing* (1995) and *Thinking and Singing* (2002). Their work concentrates from multiple angles on encountering through lyric poetry a sense of the open, unresolvable multiplicity of human (and non-human) existence, emphasizing crucial thematics of ecology and otherness.

These poets have been nominated for and won major literary prizes, and their loose cohesion as a group has created a critical mass in Canadian poetry. Borson's work revisits Eastern spirituality to investigate its essential foreignness, as well as to the fine dynamics of consciousness and of image. Bringhurst's poems (gathered in two selections, *The Beauty of the Weapons*, 1982, and *The Calling*, 1995) combine philosophical interest (informed by both Zen and Pre-Socratic thought) in the non-human world with honed attention to the "music" of human existence. His sculptural, spare translations and adaptations of poet-thinkers, whether ancient or modern, aspire to look and to listen beyond the surface dynamics of nation and culture to recover a "polyphonic" form that might enact lost human kinship with earth and with being itself.

Lilburn's poetry reflects his background in Jesuit theology, seeking to recuperate a radical mysticism through encounters with landscape and history, as in the title poem from *Kill-site* (2003), in which the poet locates himself in a turf bunker in rural Saskatchewan, inviting earth to speak through him, a practice for Lilburn of thoughtful disavowal and humility. Don McKay's poetry emerges from Souwesto regionalism to cultivate an ecology of difference, while remaining attentive to his immediate natural contexts; his poems often demonstrate an ornithological focus not to reproduce some sort of latter-day Keats–nightingale relation, but to listen – a key concept in McKay's work, notable throughout his selected poems, *Camber* (2004) and his Griffin Poetry Prize-winning *Strike / Slip* (2006) – at the limits of human comprehension. Jan Zwicky's poems emerge from an interest in place (often, her originary geography of Alberta) and in philosophical history to take up a lyric ecology: a reimagining of human dwelling and of "home" that undoes one's personal relationship to what Northrop Frye named "here," moving away from archetypes and categories toward a radical openness Zwicky calls (following the philosopher Simone Weil, perhaps) "grace."[20] She outlines her poetics in two philosophical books – *Lyric Philosophy* (1992) and *Wisdom and Metaphor* (2003) – that incorporate multi-voiced collages of texts, poems and even musical scores into their fabric.

History and form

The mid-1970s saw a variety of poetic work that offered, as Lee did, revisionist versions of cultural history. Gwendolyn MacEwen's poetry (represented in *Afterworlds*, 1987) concentrates on revivifying forms and figures derived from Jungian psychology and from alchemical mysticism. She reworks Greek and Egyptian myths, emphasizing female or goddess archetypes: while her poems usually acknowledge the present tense of their making – that they are artifacts of a Canadian mind – they also aim to comprehend a cosmopolitanism of the sacred, and MacEwen appears to have understood her texts as human rituals. By contrast, the recalcitrant skepticism of John Newlove's poems (as in *Lies*, 1972, or his selected *The Fat Man*, 1977) refuses nationalist pieties or belief of any sort in favor of ironic contrariety, which he traces as an anti-nationalist lineage in reimagining the anti-heroic fates of such historical figures as Métis rebel Louis Riel or explorer Samuel Hearne.

---

20 See Jan Zwicky, "Lyric, Narrative, Memory," in *A Ragged Pen: Essays on Poetry and Memory*, ed. Robert Finley (Kentville, NS: Gaspereau Press, 2006), pp. 93–100.

Manitoban poet and novelist Robert Kroetsch incorporates found texts into his work to re-examine and to critique nationalist historicisms as well as regionalist fantasies of the plenitudes of place. In books such as *Seed Catalogue* (1977) and *The Ledger* (1975, revised 1979), Kroetsch creates arbitrary historical palimpsests, while juxtaposing ("with no effort / or pretension / to literary merit," he ironically notes)[21] his own failing efforts to wrest sense or meaning from artifacts of a lost, marginal past. As his long poem *Field Notes* (two volumes, completed in 1989) affirms, Kroetsch commits to a brand of postmodernism – he co-founded (with William Spanos) *Boundary 2*, a journal for postmodern writing, in 1972 – that emphasizes contingency and dehiscence to deconstruct the myths of self and place.

A new generation of poets – in the wake of Kroetsch, although not his followers – takes up various inflections of postmodernism. Erin Mouré's deconstructive texts deploy fragmentation and disruption to interrogate societal and cultural norms, and to undermine gender-based and social hierarchies of power: her poems (in her selected *The Green Word*, 1994) present what amount to crafted discursive interventions in a mediatized world. Lisa Robertson's *Debbie: An Epic* (1997) and *The Weather* (2001) incorporate techniques derived from American L=A=N=G=U=A=G=E poetry and from Gertrude Stein to critique the dynamics of patriarchal power and to reinstantiate a knowing and motile woman's perspective. Christian Bök's *Eunoia* (2001) develops language techniques from Dada-influenced performances and texts (including, for example, the French writer Georges Perec's alphabetic experiments). The small press work of Ottawa-based poet rob mclennan pursues an uneasy and shifting relationship with extemporaneity, informed by a creative mistrust of the status quo: "the present is a small thing & moves very fast," he writes in *harvest: a book of signifiers* (2001).[22] Recent poetry tends instead to inhabit those gaps, differences and alterities.

The House of Anansi Press was founded in Toronto in 1967 by Dennis Lee and David Godfrey, and throughout its forty-year history has published poetry in both the postmodern and lyric lineages, often concentrating on work that bridges these two tendencies. Anansi was purchased in 2002 by Scott Griffin, founder of the Griffin Poetry Prize, and its poetry program was reinvigorated by the arrival of Newfoundland-born Ken Babstock as poetry editor. Babstock's three collections – *Mean* (1999), *Days into Flatspin* (2001) and *Airstream Land Yacht* (2006) – have had a substantial impact on recent writing, and Babstock's

---

21 See Robert Kroetsch, *The Ledger* (Coldstream: Brick / Nairn, 1975), [p. 24].
22 rob mclennan, *harvest: a book of signifiers* (Vancouver: Talonbooks, 2001), p. 125.

work is admired for its rhythmic vitality, its artfully skewed syntax, and its arresting idiomatic spin. Babstock has forged artistic connections with American and British poets of note – Charles Simic, Don Paterson, and Simon Armitage – while encouraging new work by young and established Canadian poets such as Kevin Connolly (*drift*, 2005), Barbara Nickel (*Domain*, 2007) and Erin Mouré (*O Cadoiro*, 2007). Recent poetry by David O'Meara (*Storm still*, 1999) and Karen Solie (*Short Haul Engine*, 2001) offers in divergent idioms the assured results of a vital new direction in Canadian poetry.

In the late 1980s around Montreal, a strain of Anglo-Québécois writing strengthened its voice, centering on the reactionary poetics of David Solway. Solway's technically masterful poetry re-examines literary history and claims to cultural authority. He also calls for a revaluation of artistic standards, promoting the work of Robyn Sarah, Eric Ormsby, Peter van Toorn, and others as accomplished poetry unjustly overlooked because of the predominance of confessional, postmodern, or multicultural writing, which he disdains as second-rate. Solway's strident writing has given impetus to a resurgence of formalism in English-Canadian poetry, and the work of Carmine Starnino, Elise Partridge, Todd Swift, and Stephanie Bolster owes its positive reception if not to his influence then to a resurgence of interest in traditional form, for which he serves as bellwether.

Preeminent among Canadian poets, P. K. Page produces work that is nonetheless *sui generis*. Her poetry – encyclopedic in its formal range, global in its subject matter – is like no other, her style instantly recognizable. Her cosmopolitan sensibility, a result of decades spent as a diplomat's wife posted to Australia, Brazil, and Mexico (among a few other countries), gestures toward a preoccupation with cultural and existential otherness, a pervasive sense of being (as Canadian) a perennially displaced person. This homelessness – what she calls in one famous text being a "permanent tourist" – becomes a creative advantage for Page, as she finds herself renewing her means of seeing and understanding. The intersection of the visual and the visionary forms the crux of her poetic efforts, and while her work tends either to assume or rework traditional meter and structure, Page insists on conceptual openness and clear-eyed attentiveness to a multiplicitous and often contrary world. She is hardly a cultural nationalist, preferring to question the basis of the human need to locate or to define: in her work, "here" becomes another elsewhere. Her two-volume collected poems (*The Hidden Room*, 1997) testify to a restless and vital poetic intelligence.

Page's poetic pluralism offers not so much influence as companionship to a number of poets. Ottawa's Diana Brebner, whose posthumous selected poems *The Ishtar Gate* (2005) was edited by Stephanie Bolster, meshes a preoccupation about the enabling limits of form and distance with an often confessional subject matter, particularly in her last poems addressing her illness from cancer. Her work is remarkable for its originality and its metaphorical urgency. Vancouver-based W. H. New taught Canadian and Commonwealth literatures at the University of British Columbia, and has been influential as an academic in the creation of a Canadian literary history. Late in his scholarly career, New began to publish books of poetry, by 2009 numbering nine; his work combines a pluralist sensibility, preoccupied with the construction and transgression of cultural boundaries, and an acutely formal ear. His first book, *Science Lessons* (1996), offers a sequence of reimagined sonnets to address the tensions and slippages between linguistic play and empirical claims to surety in our sense of place and land. Edmontonian E. D. Blodgett taught Comparative Literature since 1966 at the University of Alberta, but has also published numerous volumes of poems, including *Apostrophes: Woman at a Piano* (1996). Blodgett's writing is highly allusive – both in form and in content – and he has collaborated with francophone Canadian poets to investigate the cross-cultural dynamics of literary translation.

Cultural pluralities

While such poets have focused on creative displacements, there have also been a number of resurgences of regional and culturally specific sensibilities through the last decades of the twentieth century. In Nova Scotia through the early 1980s small presses such as Pottersfield (founded in 1979 by poet and novelist Lesley Choyce) promulgated work that found its history and community on the east coast: looking back to the Confederation poets, Maritime writers attempted to secure their own lineage, and the work of Alden Nowlan and others early in these decades promised the emergence of a distinctive set of east coast voices. Fred Cogswell's poetry (as represented by his 1983 *Selected Poems*) melds an interest in the local – particularly the natural world around Fredericton, New Brunswick – with traditional forms. Cogswell was also a notable translator of Québécois poetry.

Anne Compton, an academic at the University of New Brunswick in Fredericton and Saint John, writes poetry of imagistic verve, examining domestic experience and the landscapes of the Atlantic, especially around the Bay of Fundy, as her award-winning *Processional* (2005) demonstrates. Anne Simpson, living in Antigonish, Nova Scotia, addresses the limits of language in her remarkable poems. Mixing traditional form and free verse, her texts assess the enmeshment of wonder and delusion in a post-September 11 context. Her collection *Loop* was awarded the Griffin Poetry Prize for 2004, honoring a poetry that inhabits its subjective present while addressing the fraught incursions of mass media and globalization within poetic language. Michael Crummey draws on the landscapes of Newfoundland. The poems in *Hard Light* (1998) seek a direct language addressing common experience and the physical facts of work and place.

The most visible of east coast poets is George Elliott Clarke, who extends this regional aesthetic to an encounter with the politics of race. Clarke is a vernacular formalist, mixing African-Canadian orality with Eurocentric traditions. His *Execution Poems: The Black Acadian Tragedy of "George and Rue"* (2001), published by the Annapolis Valley's Gaspereau Press, fuses Black history with a depiction of racial violence: from absolute difficulty Clarke recovers lyricism, as he suggests in his best-known collection *Whylah Falls* (1990). Clarke's writing draws attention to work by African-Canadian poets, among them M. NourbeSe Philip – who melds Caribbean cultural heritage with postmodernism – and Wayde Compton – whose hiphop-influenced work addresses the complex dynamics of cultural boundaries. Dionne Brand faces the complexities of tracing racial and cultural origins. Her collection *No Language Is Neutral* (1990) initiates a project to examine the politics of language, how heritage both limits and enables. Brand's title – a line borrowed from Antillean poet Derek Walcott's *Midsummer* (1984)[23] – is frequently cited by her readers as a crucial framing of the irresolvable plurality of languages. Her long poem *Inventory* (2006) confronts the possibilities of producing lyric in a world devastated by militarism.

Recent years have seen the emergence of poets of Native backgrounds, as discussed at greater length in the chapter on Indigenous poetry and prose. Daniel David Moses mixes a studied formalism with close attention to Native story (in his collection *Delicate Bodies*, 1992). Novelist Thomas King published poems in a 1990 issue of *Canadian Literature* (then edited by W. H. New), work influenced by the hybrid texts of Okanagan storyteller Harry Robinson, whose idiosyncratic combination of traditional orature and playful colloquy impacted powerfully on the appearance of aesthetically complex, recognizably Native literary styles. Collections from Cree poet Louise Bernice Halfe and Métis Gregory Scofield, though stylistically

---

23 See section LII of Derek Walcott's *Midsummer* (New York: Farrar, Straus, and Giroux, 1984), [p. 64].

divergent, focus on recounting personal history and dealing with social challenges faced by Native people.

The most notable publication of Native Canadian literary work in recent years was the poetic translation by Robert Bringhurst of Haida oral narratives, first gathered in 1900–1 by ethnographer John Swanton. Bringhurst makes a convincing case, in his introduction to this material, for treating the extended works of Haida mythtellers Skaay and Ghandl as powerful works of world literature. As non-Native, however, Bringhurst has run into considerable political resistance from the Haida people – a conflict which does not take away from the merits of his translations, but which nonetheless troubles the possibility of their unselfconscious reception by a non-Native audience. The three-volume edition of this work, published by Douglas and McIntyre in 2002 as *Masterworks of the Classical Haida Mythtellers*, not only established Bringhurst as a preeminent poet-translator, but also gives Native Canadian oral poetry a non-specialist visibility it had previously lacked.

Bringhurst's translation of Ghandl (*Nine Visits to the Mythworld*, 2000) was nominated in 2001 for the inaugural Griffin Poetry Prize. Established by businessman Scott Griffin, it consists of two annual prizes: one for work by a Canadian, and one for international authors. The rationale is to counteract a general perception of poetry's diminishing contemporary audience, and to promote Canadian poetry on a world stage. The first Canadian prize went to Anne Carson, whose work has received international accolades, including a MacArthur Foundation "Genius" grant and the T. S. Eliot Prize. Her oeuvre is discussed in the chapter on poetry, drama, and the postmodern novel.

Epitomised by Carson's writing, what remains notable about the current conflicted state of Canadian writing is not a need to resolve its difficulties, but rather to remark that poetry depends on such unresolved pluralities for its material impetus. The Canadian "voice" consists not in refusing nationalist poetics, but in their multiplicity, their polyrhythms. Carson's emergence among others on the world stage marks a new development in Canadian work.

22
Poetry, drama, and the postmodern novel

IAN RAE

"Generic instability is undeniably a fundamental characteristic of postmodern writing," as Marta Dvořák argues.[1] Given this instability, one might assume that genre theory no longer functions as a useful tool for interpreting the novel. However, Fredric Jameson argues that traditional genres do not disappear from postmodern fiction, so much as resurface in dissonant states of juxtaposition.[2] Genre analysis takes on a heightened importance in this context because it illuminates the complex ways in which authors break down literary codes and force readers to negotiate overlapping frames of generic and cultural reference. This intersection of formal and cultural concerns can be illustrated by surveying two prominent traditions of cross-genre experimentation in Canada. The first combines lyric with novelistic techniques, while the second, which evolves from a different set of circumstances, yet enters into dialogue with the poet-novelist tradition, adapts dramatic devices to the novel. By compelling these dissimilar genres to intermingle, the authors illustrate how cultures interact in Canada through form as well as declarative statements.

Leonard Cohen

The work of Leonard Cohen exemplifies the poet-novelist phenomenon. A student of the novelist Hugh MacLennan at McGill University, and a Jewish writer in English who revered the poet-novelist A. M. Klein as a surrogate father-figure, Cohen produced two landmark novels about crossing cultural solitudes in the 1960s. *The Favourite Game* (1963) depicts the attempts of Lawrence Breavman to break out of his Jewish Westmount enclave. Breavman courts

---

[1] Marta Dvořák, "Fiction," *The Cambridge Companion to Canadian Literature*, ed. Eva-Marie Kröller (Cambridge: Cambridge University Press, 2004), p. 165.
[2] Fredric Jameson, *Postmodernism, or, The Cultural Logic of Late Capitalism* (Durham: Duke University Press, 1991), p. 371.

WASP and Québécois women, immigrates briefly to the United States, and celebrates and satirizes his Jewish heritage. However, Breavman fails to establish successful relationships because his intimates do not conform to the romantic ideals of his poetry. Cohen therefore concludes the novel by imagining a mode of interpersonal contact based on a children's game that involves producing and comparing idiosyncratic shapes in the snow. The function of this game in valorizing difference anticipates the importance of games in postmodern theory. As Jean-François Lyotard argues in *The Postmodern Condition*, "[t]he social bond is linguistic, but is not woven with a single thread. It is a fabric formed by the intersection of at least two (and in reality an indeterminate number) of language games, obeying different sets of rules."[3] Lyotard replaces the grand narratives of modernism with a multiplicity of micro-narratives generated by language games in which ludic elements break down generic codes and emphasize the ways in which distinct systems interact. Likewise, Cohen rewrote a monolithic draft of *The Favourite Game* to give it the whorling dynamic of the spinning game. He achieved this effect by framing the novel with selections of poetry from *The Spice-Box of Earth* (1961) and modeling his prose on the imagistic and recursive narratives of his poetic practice.

Genre and character are linked in *The Favourite Game* because Cohen exposes the emotional limitations of his protagonist through a simultaneous critique of Breavman's lyric poetry. Cohen's second novel, *Beautiful Losers* (1966), counteracts this solipsism by diversifying the range of genres deployed within the narrative, employing multiple narrators, and elaborating on the social and erotic functions of games. *Beautiful Losers* depicts a love triangle between an anglophone historian, a Québécois separatist, and a Mohawk woman as they collaborate on the hagiography of the Mohawk "saint" Catherine Tekakwitha. The historical breadth of the novel and its depiction of Montreal as the locus of a dynamic new nation invoke the epic genre, but Cohen places all the triumphal conventions of the epic – the celebration of a unified race, religion, and nation – *en abyme*. Cohen associates the epic with European fascism and the violent colonization of the Iroquois in North America. He counteracts the imperative of mastery in the genre's conventions by embracing tropes of translation, in which one relinquishes (not always successfully) a solipsistic sense of control in favor of plural identities and ongoing inventions of self and community.

---

3 Jean-François Lyotard, *The Postmodern Condition: A Report on Knowledge*, tr. Geoff Bennington and Brian Massumi (Minneapolis: University of Minnesota Press, 1984 [1979]), p. 40.

Michael Ondaatje

Michael Ondaatje's only book of literary criticism is *Leonard Cohen* (1970), and Ondaatje's early novels testify to Cohen's influence. Cohen's fame as a poet, novelist, and musician suggested an interdisciplinary model to the young immigrant to Canada from England and Ceylon (now Sri Lanka). Ondaatje's first novel, *Coming Through Slaughter* (1976), about an imaginary friendship between the New Orleans jazz pioneer Buddy Bolden and the white photographer E. J. Bellocq, can, like *The Favourite Game*, be read as a long poem about crossing racial and artistic barriers.[4] The guiding premise in these novels is that artistic breakthroughs can only be achieved by translating elements of one medium and culture into another. Thus Ondaatje's subsequent memoir of his youth in Ceylon, *Running in the Family* (1982), "playfully runs from one genre to another, it deliberately postpones the naming of its genre," even as it attempts to reconcile Ondaatje's Canadian present to his Ceylonese past.[5] However, there is also a haunted aspect to Ondaatje's humorous portrait of life on colonial estates: the instability of the book's generic framework highlights the fact that the burgher ruling class into which Ondaatje was born (his lineage combines Dutch, Sinhalese, and Tamil) has been overthrown.[6] In the predominantly Sinhalese country that achieved its independence in 1948 and redefined itself as the socialist republic of Sri Lanka in 1972, the legacy and heirs of this class are disappearing and dispersed.

Ondaatje addresses his Torontonian identity more directly in *In the Skin of a Lion* (1987), which rewrites the *Epic of Gilgamesh* (c. 1700 BC). In the Sumerian poem, the gods must invent a new kind of hero, the wild man Enkidu, to counteract the tyranny of Gilgamesh, the ruler of a city famed for its monumental architecture. Ondaatje initially seems to follow this epic model as he stages a power struggle between the son of a logger (Patrick Lewis) and an urban financier (Ambrose Small). However, Ondaatje multiplies the heroic characters to include women, immigrants, and urban laborers in a manner that ultimately dismantles the epic model. In its place, Ondaatje fashions a

---

4 Michael Greenstein, *Third Solitudes: Tradition and Discontinuity in Jewish-Canadian Literature* (Montreal: McGill-Queen's University Press, 1989), p. 124.
5 Smaro Kamboureli, "The Alphabet of the Self: Generic and Other Slippages in Michael Ondaatje's *Running in the Family*," in *Reflections: Autobiography and Canadian Literature*, ed. K. P. Stich (Ottawa: University of Ottawa Press, 1988), p. 79.
6 Note that the Ondaatje family is English-speaking and has strong affinities with British values and culture. See Cynthia Wong, "Michael Ondaatje," *Asian American Novelists: A Bio-Bibliographical Critical Sourcebook*, ed. Emmanuel S. Nelson (Westport: Greenwood Press, 2000), pp. 288–95.

more decentered narrative based on a variety of games and a play: a square dance, a fire-lit game of tag on ice, and a piece of theater in which women exchange an animal pelt to signify their right to partake in a communal story. Patrick's adopted daughter Hana eventually takes control of the story she collects in the frame tale of *In the Skin of a Lion* and gathers a similar community around herself in the sequel, *The English Patient* (1992), set in Italy at the end of the Second World War.

Much as Klein and Cohen turned to the poet's novel to address the state of cultural devastation and fragmentation following the Shoah, Ondaatje combines lyricism with historical fragments to address questions of race, memory, and cultural geography in the period between the defeat of fascism in Italy and the nuclear Holocausts at Hiroshima and Nagasaki. In *The English Patient* and *Anil's Ghost* (2000), which examines the effects of the Sri Lankan civil war on nationals and prodigals in the 1990s, Ondaatje uses the lyric voice to address apocalyptic events obliquely, without making the mistake of trying to encapsulate the entire experience. Instead, Ondaatje configures mosaics of fragments that serve as formal analogues for his preferred theme of multicultural community formation, in which the "filial search for father and fatherland is replaced ... by a project of affiliation" that also accounts for spaces of contestation.[7]

In *Divisadero* (2007), the author works against his own conventions. The story begins with a typical (for Ondaatje) hybrid family unit in California: a father, his daughter Anna, and two adopted children, Coop and Claire. The family, which initially forms in response to the death of Anna's mother and Coop's parents, is shattered by the father's violent reaction to his discovery that Coop and Anna have become lovers. Ondaatje's fascination with the theme of adultery in *Coming Through Slaughter* and *The English Patient* is here replaced by various forms of incest. The siblings are divided and the narrative follows their separate journeys across the United States and France. Whereas most of Ondaatje's novels compensate for the proliferation of cultural histories by cultivating a strong sense of place, this novel is named after a street in San Francisco that is only mentioned twice in the novel. The characters in *Divisadero* are always moving on to the next place. They evolve away from, instead of toward, each other. No epiphany or artistic text serves to unite the disparate sections of the novel, as with Bolden's parade performance or the English patient's copy of Herodotus.

---

7 Susan Spearey, "Cultural Crossings: The Shifting Subjectivities and Stylistics of Michael Ondaatje's *Running in the Family* and *In the Skin of a Lion*," *British Journal of Canadian Studies*, 11.1 (1996), p. 134.

Although one character is modeled on the American poet Edward Dorn and another on the imaginary French poet and novelist Lucien Segura, *Divisadero* heightens the lack of security (*segura* is Spanish for secure) in artistic and scholarly enterprises. The characters in *Divisadero* are stock Ondaatje figures in that they make a performance of their respective crafts and use them to reconstruct a lost past, but they do not use their skills to document suppressed histories (*Slaughter*, *Skin*) nor to uphold a political principle (*Anil*), but rather to generate some temporary and personal consolation. They do not seek the elusive truth of a complicated situation, but rather, following a quotation from Nietzsche in the prefatory passage that opens the novel, they use art to protect themselves from a truth about their lives.[8]

George Bowering

The clash between East and West is usually a domestic one in the poetry and prose of George Bowering. Although issues of race are central to Bowering's novel *Shoot!* (1994), about the Métis McLean gang, his roots in the British Columbian interior compel him to configure cultural solitudes in regional terms and align his work with western poet-novelists such as Sheila Watson and Robert Kroetsch.[9] Bowering's novel *A Short Sad Book* (1977) is an encyclopedic parody of eastern Canadian myths that uses poetic word plays to dismantle regional biases without rejecting the national project. As Linda Hutcheon argues in *A Poetics of Postmodernism*, parody is a device that subverts generic codes from within by turning their conventions against themselves.[10] One of Hutcheon's principal examples in *The Canadian Postmodern* is Bowering's *Burning Water* (1980), which juxtaposes a narrative about the voyage of George Vancouver to British Columbia in 1792 with meditations on the writing process (depicted as a voyage of discovery) by the metafictional author.

Burning Water draws on canonical tales of sea voyages by the likes of Coleridge and Melville, but Bowering takes parody one step further in this novel to include self-parody. Bowering explains in his prologue that the novel rewrites *George, Vancouver: A Discovery Poem* (1970): "In the late sixties I was a

---

8 The original quotation from Nietzsche reads: "Wir haben die *Kunst*, damit wir *nicht an der Wahrheit zu Grunde gehn*." See Friedrich Nietzsche, *Der Wille zur Macht*, in *Gesammelte Werke*, 23 vols. (Munich: Musarion Verlag, 1926), vol. XIX, section 822.
9 George Bowering, "Sheila Watson," in *Encyclopedia of Literature in Canada*, ed. W. H. New (Toronto: University of Toronto Press, 2002), p. I, 199.
10 Linda Hutcheon, *A Poetics of Postmodernism: History, Theory, Fiction* (New York: Routledge, 1988), p. 5.

poet, so I wrote a poetry book about Vancouver and me. Then a radio play about us, and on the air we all became third persons. But I was not satisfied. The story of the greatest navigational voyage of all time was not lyrical, and it was certainly not dramatic. It was narrative. So I began to plan a novel."[11] The fragmented syntax of this passage underscores the evolution of the narrative as a series of generic stages culminating in the novel.

Furthermore, by emphasizing the manner in which he overhauled a serial poem and converted it into a historical novel, Bowering recuperates an etymological dimension of "parody" that relates to narrative poetry. Martin Kuester demonstrates that early Greek forms of parody involved "an innovation in the technique of recitation of epic poetry: the poem is no longer recited in a singing fashion but in the normal tone of an actor speaking dialogue."[12] In rewriting a long poem as a radio play and doubling his "George" narratives, Bowering recovers the Greek sense of parody as a shift in the register of performance. In rewriting of *George, Vancouver* as *Burning Water*, he aligns his novel with Renaissance interpretations of this notion of parody:

> In the same way that satire developed out of tragedy, and mime out of comedy, parody stems from rhapsody. Whenever the rhapsodists interrupted their recitation, those entered the stage who jokingly, for the mind's relaxation, inverted everything that had previously been performed. For this reason they were called parodists, as they undermined the serious message by means of another, ridiculous one. Parody is thus an inverted rhapsody that is drawn towards a ridiculous meaning through a change in voices.[13]

Kuester does not apply these insights to *Burning Water* in his chapter on Bowering, but Bowering does perform a variation on the shift from rhapsody to dramatic parody to revisionist history in his various attempts to highlight and undermine Vancouver's colonial project. "Serious ridiculousness" is an apt description of Bowering's tactical use of humor in his parodic works.

Daphne Marlatt

Before Bowering was designated Canada's inaugural poet laureate in 2002, he constructed himself as marginal to central Canada's literary establishment. However, marginality depends on where one constructs the margin and situates the self. In the same period, Daphne Marlatt was combatting the

---

11 George Bowering, *Burning Water* (Toronto: Penguin, 1994 [1980]), n.p.
12 Martin Kuester, *Framing Truths: Parodic Structures in Contemporary English-Canadian Historical Novels* (Toronto: University of Toronto Press, 1992), p. 6.
13 Ibid., Kuester's translation from the Latin of Julius Caesar Scaliger, pp. 8–9.

marginalization of her lesbian sexuality by patriarchal values, including those of Bowering and her elder male peers in the *TISH* group of poets.[14] As Marlatt shifted from the long poem to novel in the 1970s, she became increasingly critical of the role narrative conventions play in shaping female desire and behavior. Her novella *Zócalo* (1977) and her first novel *Ana Historic* (1988) interrogate the constraints imposed on women by myth, history, and photography with the aim of opening a discursive space for a burgeoning lesbian identity. As Caroline Rosenthal observes of *Ana Historic*, "Marlatt takes apart the very frames that 'freeze' her protagonist into a specific 'feminine act' ... Through her textual devices Marlatt shows that heterosexuality is a *regulatory fiction*, which 'frames' men and women into one story by ruling out more complex constructions of gender and sexual identity."[15] Marlatt uses puns, anagrams, parodies, and self-reflexive criticism to position her writing between generic frames because the conventions of the major genres have been tailored to heterosexual and patriarchal standards. The Heraclitan aesthetics of the *TISH* group (which did not necessarily accord with the male poets' desire for dominance in a literary milieu), as well as Marlatt's work in French–English translation, compel her to think of form as a negotiation and a kinetic process.

Marlatt also points out in the preface to *Ghost Works* (1993) that her fascination with crossing borders, genres, and genders is an "immigrant's preoccupation."[16] Even as Marlatt fought to recover her "mothertongue" from the influence of her literary father-figures in the 1980s, she was forced to confront the impact on this tongue of her British colonial upbringing in Penang. Her second novel, *Taken* (1996), explores the complicity of women in the colonial process by juxtaposing the Japanese invasion of Malaya in her mother's generation with the first Gulf War in her own. This military context dampens the emancipatory euphoria of the climax of *Ana Historic* by suggesting that the power dynamics of patriarchal families can resurface in lesbian relationships: "Breaking the marriage script, we broke the familial ties we each were meant to perpetuate. And yet, so many strands of the old scripts that compose us wove the narrative, then unreadable, unread, that made me recognize you when you walked into that crowded café."[17] On the other hand, women's

---

14 See Daphne Marlatt, "Given This Body. An Interview with Daphne Marlatt," interview by George Bowering, *Open Letter* 4.3 (Spring 1973), p. 35; Daphne Marlatt, *Readings from the Labyrinth* (Edmonton: NeWest, 1998), p. 145.
15 Caroline Rosenthal, *Narrative Deconstructions of Gender in Works by Audrey Thomas, Daphne Marlatt, and Louise Erdrich* (Rochester: Camden House, 2003), p. 67.
16 Daphne Marlatt, *Ghost Works* (Edmonton: NeWest, 1993), p. viii.
17 Daphne Marlatt, *Taken* (Toronto: Anansi, 1996), pp. 77–8.

complicity in war and colonization furthers Marlatt's argument for feminist revisionism, because she believes that women require means of challenging patriarchy in order to participate in postcolonial transformations.

Joy Kogawa

Joy Kogawa's *Obasan* (1981) links domestic to public space by focusing on the historical mistreatment of Japanese Canadians. In *Obasan*, a thirty-six-year-old Alberta schoolteacher named Naomi Nakane meditates on her experience as a five-year-old girl caught up in the evacuation, internment, and deportation of Japanese Canadians during and after the Second World War. Along with its sequel *Itsuka* (1992), the novel chronicles Naomi's growing involvement with the Japanese Canadian redress movement and the achievement in 1988 of a settlement with the federal government for violations of Japanese Canadian rights. Although Roy Miki has rightly criticized the conclusions of *Obasan* and *Itsuka*, which suggest that racial conflict for Japanese Canadians has been overcome, these novels have played an enormous role in raising public awareness of Japanese Canadian history.[18] In 2006, this legacy was recognized by the public purchase of Kogawa's childhood home (the model for the family home seized in *Obasan*), which will be converted into a residence for writers-in-exile and an educational center for human rights issues.

Although Kogawa is known primarily as a novelist, she adapted the lunar symbolism, apocalyptic imagery, and concentric structure of her long poem "Dear Euclid" in *A Choice of Dreams* (1974) to shape *Obasan*, as well as incorporating elements of short lyrics from the same collection, such as "What Do I Remember of the Evacuation," into her prose. Kogawa makes this cross-genre aesthetic explicit in a 1998 interview: "The first draft of *Obasan* was written in the same way that I wrote poetry, that is just following the dreams, not knowing where I was going, one thing after another. I had not taken any courses in novel writing and didn't even read a lot of novels. I didn't know what writing a novel meant at all. I just did it. When I was finished that first draft, I was told to forget it. I didn't."[19]

This process of dreaming, drafting, and learning the power of narrative is clearly inscribed in the novel, as the metafictional author Naomi struggles to convert her lyrical meditations into a narrative that will mitigate the

---

18 Roy Miki, *Broken Entries: Race, Subjectivity, Writing* (Toronto: Mercury, 1998), p. 139.
19 Joy Kogawa, "Journey in Search of Some Evidence of Love: An Interview with Joy Kogawa," by Linda Ghan, Chieko Mulhern, and Ayako Sato, *The Rising Generation* 114.2 (May 1, 1998), p. 14.

alienation of individuals in her family by situating their personal crises within a historical context and an interpersonal matrix. Kogawa's interview statement also underscores a fact that she develops into a key theme in the novel: for every political act of remembering there are institutional powers that encourage forgetting. The structures of expectation produced and perpetuated by genre conventions serve these powers by determining what and how one remembers. Kogawa therefore links generic transformation to her larger project of historical revision by recasting poetry as prose, lineating prose as poetry (the biblical epigram), and revising the documentary techniques of the historical novel through incursions of lyricism.

The lyrical epigram and short piece of poetic prose at the outset of *Obasan*, which together establish the key symbols of Naomi's quest, also partake of the tradition of "haibun," a form of poetic travelogue made famous by writers such as Matsuo Bashō in *Narrow Road to the Interior* (1694). Haibun pairs haikus with short, elliptical prose poems in a narrative linked by key images; it thereby furthers the juxtapositional aesthetic of the haiku, which balances two distinct images. Much as Bashō converted haiku from a witty drinking game into a serious poetic genre, he developed haibun into a respected form of poetic meditation that explores existential questions through poignant images, yet avoids philosophical jargon.

Haibun emerged at the intersection of classical Chinese poetry and the Japanese Zen tradition and thus Fred Wah makes use of the form in his long poem "This Dendrite Map: Father / Mother Haibun" (1986), which reflects on his Chinese-Scots-Swedish ancestry. "This Dendrite Map" also facilitated the poet's transition to prose in *Diamond Grill* (1996), which furthers his musings on racism and hybridity by developing a portrait of his father's Chinese-Canadian diner in Nelson, British Columbia. Most of the short chapters in *Diamond Grill* are a page in length and feature an opening sentence lineated as two lines of poetry that runs into the prose paragraph below, thereby confusing the distinction between poetry and prose while maintaining the visual appearance of haibun. Wah and Kogawa look beyond European models of generic crossover to narrate journeys into the western interior that differ significantly from the official myths of peace, order, and good government.

Anne Michaels

Kogawa's protagonist is haunted by the disappearance of her mother following the nuclear bombing of Nagasaki, but Anne Michaels aims to raise awareness of genocide from a Jewish perspective in *Fugitive Pieces* (1996), which explores the impact of the Shoah on two generations of Canadians. Michaels follows the precedents of her poet-novelist predecessors by investigating the historical record and probing its absences through poetry. Although critics such as Theodor Adorno forbade the writing of poetry in the immediate aftermath of the Shoah,[20] Susan Gubar argues that poetry in the late twentieth and early twenty-first centuries serves as an effective complement to the documentary record: "As the testimonies of those individuals who personally survived the Holocaust draw to a close, poetry's opacity and figural density write what cannot be written so as to excavate, preserve, or, at least, evoke the transmitted and untransmitted memories of those obliterated in or incapacitated by the Shoah."[21] Michaels thus follows Klein and Cohen in moving away from realist modes of narrative and towards poetic forms of discourse inspired by Jewish ritual.

Yet Michaels uses the verbal resources of rituals such as the kaddish to connect Jews to other faiths in a multicultural community. Annick Hillger argues that Michaels writes in the tense of a "messianic time" rooted in the kabbalistic tradition, wherein the tragic trajectory of linear time is overcome by correspondences that link the present to a utopic moment.[22] This emphasis on temporal interconnection in *Fugitive Pieces* has profound implications for the unorthodox family and marital units in the novel. Like *Beautiful Losers*, *Fugitive Pieces* is a novel about orphans and the way that they create family units through complex forms of adoption and nurturing.[23] Michaels's family units cut across blood lines in a fashion analogous to her vertical reading of history as a cross-section or core sample of time.

Anne Carson

Fugitive Pieces builds on the themes and devices of Michaels's acclaimed poetry collections *The Weight of Oranges* (1985) and *Miner's Pond* (1991). The lyrical style and recursive structure of her novel support her claim that the long poem can serve as a means of transforming the short lyric form into a

---

20 Theodor Adorno, "Cultural Criticism and Society," *Prisms*, tr. Samuel and Sherry Weber (Cambridge: MIT Press, 1981 [1955]), pp. 17–34.
21 Susan Gubar, "Empathic Identification in Anne Michaels's *Fugitive Pieces*: Masculinity and Poetry after Auschwitz," *Signs* 28.1 (Autumn 2002), p. 273.
22 Annick Hillger, "'Afterbirth of Earth': Messianic Materialism in Anne Michaels' *Fugitive Pieces*," *Canadian Literature* 160 (Spring 1999), pp. 29, 41.
23 Barbara L. Estrin, "Ending in the Middle: Revisioning Adoption in Binjamin Wilkomirski's *Fragments* and Anne Michaels's *Fugitive Pieces*," *Tulsa Studies in Women's Literature* 21.2 (Fall 2002), p. 280.

"narrative of relation."[24] However, Anne Carson's *Autobiography of Red: A Novel in Verse* (1998) subverts the priority booksellers give to prose fiction by recasting the novel as an amalgam of genres involved in the reading of verse. Carson's novel consists of an essay on the ancient Greek poet Stesichoros, translations of his fragments, appendices on the legendary blinding of Stesichoros by Helen of Troy, a rewriting of his long lyric poem *Geryoneis* as a gay romance, and a concluding interview. The "Romance" at the center of the novel recalls the origins of the *roman* in medieval romance, but Carson's career as a classicist gives her a broader perspective on the evolution of the genre. In her treatise on ancient Greek lyric, *Eros the Bittersweet* (1986), Carson states that the "terms 'novel' and 'romance' do not reflect an ancient name for the genre. Chariton refers to his work as *erōtika pathēmata*, or 'erotic sufferings': these are love stories in which it is generically required that love be painful. The stories are told in prose and their apparent aim is to entertain readers."[25]

Carson made her name as a poet through accounts of erotic suffering such as "The Glass Essay" in *Glass, Irony and God* (1995) and "The Anthropology of Water" in *Plainwater* (1995). These long poems are widely admired, but the model for Carson's novel in verse is "Mimnermos: The Brainsex Paintings," an experiment in combining translations of the fragmentary corpus of the Greek poet Mimnermos with an essay and three mock interviews with the ancient poet. *Autobiography of Red* furthers the ludic dimension of "Mimnermos" by shifting the narrative context rapidly between Greek antiquity (Homer, Stesichoros), modernist high culture (Dickinson, Stein, Picasso), and postmodernist pop culture (graffiti, airplane novels).

Carson challenges the mimetic basis of the realist novel by building phenomenological connections between moods, thoughts, and sensations, instead of tracking realist continuities in time and space. The setting of *Autobiography of Red* shifts suddenly from the Mediterranean to North and South America, while absorbing a vast array of cultural referents. Carson is interested in diasporic populations, including Stesichoros's Himera, because "[a] refugee population is hungry for language and aware that anything can happen."[26] Thus Sherry Simon compares Carson's poetry to that of Klein by reading it through the polyglot sensibility of their Mile End neighborhood in Montreal, in which "there is a widening of the frame of reference. No one vocabulary

---

24 Anne Michaels, "Narrative Moves: An Interview with Anne Michaels," by anonymous, *Canadian Notes & Queries* 50.1 (1996), p. 18.
25 Anne Carson, *Eros the Bittersweet* (Normal: Dalkey Archive Press, 1998 [1986]), p. 78.
26 Anne Carson, *Autobiography of Red* (New York: Knopf, 1999 [1998]), p. 3.

will suffice, no one channel can access the multiple planes of expression. Just as visual and plastic arts today abandon the single frame, the written word expands its reach."[27] The experience of translation in this neighborhood serves as a guide for the migration of lyric into the novel, where the lyric voice unframes an established generic code and invents a new, multiplanar one.

Autobiography of Red concludes with a dialogue between two speakers who seem to be a part of "concealment drama," wherein Gertrude Stein supplants Stesichoros as leader of the chorus.[28] Critics tend to ignore this section, and indeed the impact of drama on the Canadian novel is under-examined, in contrast to the abundance of critical comparisons of fiction to photography and film. The second section of this chapter will attempt to redress this oversight by examining a prominent pair of writers (Davies and Findley) closely tied to the establishment of Canada's most influential theater, the Stratford Shakespeare Festival, as well as two novelists who critique the Eurocentrism of that theater tradition (MacDonald and Clarke).

Robertson Davies

The plays and novels of Robertson Davies exemplify many of the contradictions of twentieth-century Ontario, as it transformed itself from the heartland of a British colony into the most ethnically diverse province in a modern North American state. All at once, Davies is an anglophile and a cultural nationalist, a supporter of "Stratford's old-country, highbrow mission of artistic 'pilgrimage'" and a consultant to the Massey-Lévesque Commission in the 1950s, which sought to fund distinctively Canadian art forms.[29] Ellen MacKay therefore argues in "Fantasies of Origin: Staging the Birth of the Canadian Stage" that Davies's writing is the product of "a theatre history in which loyalty divided between old worlds and new is understood to be constitutive of the Canadian theatre, and not its impediment."[30] Davies's plays and novels build on the ambivalences of a colonial state in transition.

In his dramatic work, "Davies carefully develops the metaphors of life as play and the world as stage," and these Shakespearean metaphors carry over into his first novel, *Tempest-Tost* (1951), which dramatizes the difficulties

---

27 Sherry Simon, "Hybrid Montreal: The Shadows of Language," *Sites: The Journal of the 20th-Century / Contemporary French Studies* 5.2 (Fall 2001), p. 321.
28 Carson, *Autobiography of Red*, p. 147.
29 Ellen MacKay, "Fantasies of Origin: Staging the Birth of the Canadian Stage," *Canadian Theatre Review* 114 (Spring 2003), p. 11.
30 Ibid., p. 14.

of staging an amateur production of *The Tempest*.³¹ Although Davies's fascination with the English Renaissance is often dismissed as "old-fashioned," the term is misleading because Davies uses the passions, appetites, and verbal virtuosity of Shakespearean theater to critique a colonial culture attached to puritan notions of English identity. Several of Davies's novels (including *Tempest-Tost*) have been converted into plays that satirize puritan fears of the body, the cosmopolitan, and the non-conformist. However, productions such as the Broadway adaptation of *Leaven of Malice* (1954) by Tyrone Guthrie in 1960 have struggled with the importance of intellectual banter to Davies's prose; indeed, despite their extensive use of dialogue, novels such as *What's Bred in the Bone* (1985) are talkative in a way that theater cannot allow.³² Following Davies's own analysis, Michael Peterman notes that Davies's dramatic plots are more streamlined:

> he favours [a] "single, dominating character," identifies largely with him (whatever his venial sins), and conspicuously arranges the secondary characters so as to throw a positive light upon him and his predicament. Insisting upon "a fairly simple and direct line of action," he establishes a conflict of values that, however it is amplified intellectually, is essentially melodramatic. The "good guys" either side instinctively with or learn to see the value of the protagonist's view of life. The "bad guys" either can't see that value or by choice refuse to support it.³³

Davies's novels exhibit this melodramatic structure in their use of psychological archetypes and Jungian ideas of naming as fate.

However, the novel gives Davies more space to develop his talent for characterization, more opportunity to include opposing views, more context for his Shavian wit. Although his novels uphold an aristocratic world view, they exhibit greater sympathy for conventionally unheroic characters. Davies's most critically acclaimed novel, *Fifth Business* (1970), is based on the premise that the lead character, Dunstan Ramsay, plays a minor role of vital importance: "Those roles which, being neither those of Hero nor Heroine, Confidante nor Villain, but which were none-the-less essential to bring about the Recognition or the denouement were called the Fifth Business in drama and opera companies."³⁴ This passage derives from an epigraph to *Fifth*

---

31 Michael Peterman, "Bewitchments of Simplification," *Canadian Drama / L'Art dramatique canadien* 7.2 (1981), p. 106.
32 Susan Stone-Blackburn, "The Novelist as Dramatist: Davies' Adaptation of *Leaven of Malice*," *Canadian Literature* 86 (Autumn 1980), pp. 71–86.
33 Peterman, "Bewitchments of Simplification," p. 96.
34 Robertson Davies, *Fifth Business* (Toronto: Macmillan, 1970), n.p.

Business that Davies attributes to a Danish theater critic, but which Davies fabricated for the novel.[35] Such ruses highlight Davies's postmodern sense of playfulness, which is complemented by his carnivalesque confusions of social, sexual, and religious mores in circuses and magic shows. However, Davies still cherishes modernist aspirations of the absolute. The Deptford Trilogy and the Cornish Trilogy employ intricate framing devices that contrast different perceptions of key events, moving back and forth between narrative levels and time periods, testing the bias of one perceiver against that of another, while ultimately affirming transcendental values.

Timothy Findley

As a successful novelist, Timothy Findley shares with Davies a fundamental paradox: the novel enables him to elaborate on ideas, characterizations, and historical details in a way drama does not permit, yet he owes the formal complexity of his novels to his dramatic training. Among the landmarks of Findley's dramatic career, Carol Roberts notes that "Findley acted in the inaugural season at the Stratford Festival, was the National Arts Centre's first playwright-in-residence, and wrote the script for CBC Television's first feature-length colour film."[36] Findley shares Davies's love of intermingling realist description with sections of dialogue that lift the story out of narration and into the theatrical moment, which Findley insists is "always *now*."[37] Findley uses transcripts, monologues, and dramatizations of various kinds to transform his narratives into verbal events. Unlike Ondaatje, who employs these devices to highlight a poignant anecdote from his archival research, or simply to establish a mood and idiom, Findley uses the spoken word as a storytelling medium. Findley's novels are populated with gossips, speechmakers, *raconteurs*, debaters, and characters haunted by voices, such as Lucy in the parody of the biblical flood narrative, *Not Wanted on the Voyage* (1984). The author encourages his audience to get caught up in these verbal performances by periodically restricting the presence of the narrator or freeing characters to tell (and edit) their own story. Yet one should heed Findley's cautionary assessment of Davies's novels, which applies to his own fiction – "Davies' books are not just plays in disguise. What they are are *theatres*" – because they

---

35 Judith Skelton Grant, *Robertson Davies: Man of Myth* (Toronto: Viking, 1994), p. 483.
36 Carol Roberts, "The Perfection of Gesture: Timothy Findley and Canadian Theatre," *Theatre History in Canada / Histoire du théâtre au Canada* 12.1 (Spring 1991), p. 22.
37 Timothy Findley, *Spadework* (Toronto: HarperCollins, 2001), p. 17.

conspicuously frame their verbal performances and periodically test the stability of the mimetic fourth wall.[38]

While one can trace connections between the careers, characters, and formal techniques of Davies and Findley, Findley brings a much more critical eye to the magic of theater than Davies does. Barbara Gabriel argues that Findley's *Famous Last Words* (1981) interprets "the Fascist moment on the world stage as a problematic of *power* and *consent* ... National Socialism and Italian Fascism made conscious use of theatre and the new technologies of photography and film to mobilize mass support, reworking an existing semiotic field to produce new gendered meanings and power relations centred on a charismatic figure."[39] The interplay between power, charisma, and consent is central to most of Findley's works, and its critique ranges from his early appraisal of the Hollywood star system in the novel *The Butterfly Plague* (1969) to his portrait of a gay director's seduction of a married actor in his Stratford novel, *Spadework* (2001), as well as his final plays, *The Trials of Ezra Pound* (1994) and *Elizabeth Rex* (2000). Whereas Davies mocks the Canadian reputation for humility in favor of a new definition of heroic masculinity, Findley's most acclaimed novel, *The Wars* (1977), begins with an epigraph from Euripides and then works through a variety of ancient and modern definitions of heroism to make, finally, a virtue of the gentleness that Davies shunned. Yet, in Findley, this gentleness emerges out of a history of violence and complicity.

Findley's appraisal of desire's connection to power reflects his status as a pioneering gay writer in a predominantly heterosexual literary milieu. He foregrounds the presence and subversive power of gay men throughout history, but he does not always endorse the uses to which this power is put, as Marlatt does for her lesbian characters. Findley's novels often pair sexual with moral ambivalence, and the crises in his narratives demand that characters (and readers) interpret ambivalent actions.

Ann-Marie MacDonald

Ann-Marie MacDonald better resembles Marlatt in the affirmative stance and lesbian perspective she brings to her plays, such as the feminist parody

---

38 Timothy Findley, "Robertson Davies," in *Robertson Davies: An Appreciation*, ed. Elspeth Cameron (Peterborough: Broadview, 1991), p. 35.
39 Barbara Gabriel, "'The Repose of an Icon' in Timothy Findley's Theatre of Fascism: From 'Alligator Shoes' to *Famous Last Words*," *Essays on Canadian Writing* 64 (Summer 1998), p. 151. See also Anne Geddes Bailey, *Timothy Findley and the Aesthetics of Fascism* (Vancouver: Talonbooks, 1998).

of Shakespearean conventions, *Goodnight Desdemona (Good Morning Juliet)* (published in 1990). Born in Germany to Canadian parents of Scotch and Lebanese descent, the author of *The Arab's Mouth* (published in 1995) achieved widespread fame after her first novel, *Fall on Your Knees* (1996), won a Commonwealth Writer's Prize for best first fiction and appeared on Oprah's Book Club. At once accessible and stylistically complex, *Fall on Your Knees* employs many standard devices of the multi-generational family saga. The novel begins with a meditation on family photos that is reminiscent of Findley's *The Piano Man's Daughter* (the head of the household, James Piper, is a piano tuner with a sick daughter named Lily). The branches of the Piper family tree are continually elaborated in narrative and pictorial form. Death certificates mark several chapter endings. Diary entries appear to explain plot twists. However, by the time the final book of the novel circles back to the first, MacDonald has revised the tourist's image of Cape Breton as a Celtic idyll and incorporated the industrial, multicultural heritage of the region by highlighting the place of Arab, Eastern European, and African Nova Scotians in the community.

The plot of *Fall on Your Knees* revolves around repressed secrets of incest and death in the Piper household, which aligns the fiction with the Gothic novel and ghost story. However, the performative dimension of MacDonald's novel ultimately exceeds the conventions of these genres. One of the main characters, Kathleen, is a lesbian opera singer whose sexual abuse at the hands of her father sets in motion a variety of operatic themes: incest, war, domestic violence, original sin, death-by-guilt, a quest for redemption. MacDonald mimics Kathleen's vocal virtuosity by moving through every available register and constantly expanding her range of generic and cultural expression. Whereas MacLennan proposed the musical principle of counterpoint as a means of balancing cultural differences in *Two Solitudes* (1945), MacDonald's novel shatters this classical poise with Irish and Arabic folk songs, French Catholic hymns, Harlem jazz, and Cape Breton fiddle music. As the settings shift from Nova Scotia to New York City, the characters cross racial, national, and linguistic boundaries in an effort to realize their aspirations in new places and media.

The novel is told retrospectively to an ethnomusicologist, but the novel does not simply counterpose two time periods. The recollections of the characters are distorted because "memory plays tricks. Memory is another word for story, and nothing is more unreliable."[40] Crucial scenes in the novel

---

40 Ann-Marie MacDonald, *Fall on Your Knees* (Toronto: Vintage, 1997 [1996]), p. 270.

are replayed differently in the characters' memories, as they struggle with denial and the rationalization of trauma. Telling these stories helps the women narrators piece together their complex family history, but only through music do they experience transitory moments of clarified identity and sexual emancipation. In *Fall on Your Knees*, race and desire are issues of the repression, resurgence, and recombination of sound, as well as skin.

George Elliott Clarke

MacDonald's novel draws attention to the labor of African-Canadians in a predominantly white province, but the career-long project of George Elliott Clarke has been to raise the profile of African Nova Scotians as a cultural community distinct from white Nova Scotians, African Americans, and the metropolitan communities of African Canadians outside the Maritimes. African Nova Scotians, for whom Clarke coined the term "Africadian" by combining "African" and "Acadian," descend primarily from the Loyalists who migrated from the United States following the American Revolution and the War of 1812–14, as well as the northward flights of escaped slaves.

Clarke refers to Africadians as an "epic people" and *Whylah Falls* (1990) is his most explicit attempt to write the epic of Africadia.[41] Whereas most poet-novelists dismiss the ethnic aspirations of epic, Clarke points to "the destruction of Africville" in Halifax in the 1960s as "a symbol of what happens to a culture which does not vigorously assert its right to exist."[42] Yet the essay that introduces the tenth anniversary edition of *Whylah Falls* makes clear that Clarke's epic model is built on the lyric. Clarke maintains that the lyric, by "evolving various symbolist, imagist, social realist, and projectivist mutations, was the only poetic form to survive the piggery of capital and the slaughterhouse of war" in the twentieth century.[43] He claims that "[t]he poem survives now by gathering unto itself all of the powers of the novel" (p. xiii), and proceeds to link his treatment of the novel to a wide variety of literary currents, including the mythic narratives of Michael Ondaatje and the African American tradition of lyrical prose by Jean Toomer and Toni Morrison. Thus, for Clarke, the "lyric sequence is [at once] the epitaph of the epic" (p. xxiv) and "a memory

---

41 George Elliott Clarke, quoted in "Innovations in Arts and Culture," by anonymous, *University of Toronto National Report* (2002), p. 12.
42 George Elliott Clarke, *Fire on the Water: An Anthology of Black Nova Scotian Writing*, 2 vols. (Porters Lake: Pottersfield, 1991), vol. II, p. 11.
43 George Elliott Clarke, *Whylah Falls* (Victoria: Polestar, 2000 [1990]), p. xiii.

of its grandeur" (p. xvi) because this reconfigured lyricism invents mythic underpinnings for a distinct society.

Like *Coming Through Slaughter*, *Whylah Falls* uses the song cycle as a model for recuperating Black oral history and modes of performance. *Whylah Falls* takes its cue from the famous contralto "Portia White (1913–1968), [Clarke's] great aunt, who sang a way through the wilderness," and builds a song cycle out of bits of gospel, blues, jazz, opera, letters, archival photographs, newspaper clippings, and quotations from western poetry in order to celebrate Africadian hybridity.[44] Clarke reclaims the African elements within western culture through characters such as Othello, Pushkin (who was proud of his Moorish grandfather), and Pablo (an allusion to Picasso's obsession with African masks), all of whom are listed in his *Dramatis Personae*.

More importantly, *Whylah Falls* pays tribute to the poetic speech rhythms, oral storytelling traditions, and fight against racial persecution of the Africadian community of Weymouth Falls in southwest Nova Scotia, where Clarke served as a social worker in 1985. Clarke's emphasis on orality makes the performance of later works, such as the libretto *Beatrice Chancy* (1999) and *Québécité: A Jazz Fantasia in Three Cantos* (2003), both logical and vital. Moving away from the stage, his novel *George and Rue* (2005) furthers his interest in the storytelling idiom of rural Acadia, as it combines sections of Africadian and standard English to recount the story of a murder in New Brunswick that exposes the economic disparities between the Black and White communities. Clarke explored this same story in the lyric voice in his collection *Execution Poems* (2000), which was originally part of the novel but evolved into a separate collection, and he reprises it in the poem "George & Rue: Coda" in *Black* (2006).[45]

Postmodern literature thus embraces the pairing of formal and cultural hybridity, but it is less concerned with achieving the stasis of a definitive form or cultural identity than the modern novels that doubled generic and cultural concerns, such as MacLennan's *Two Solitudes*, Klein's *The Second Scroll* (1951), and Sheila Watson's *The Double Hook* (1959). Instead of attempting a fusion of cultures through a process of thesis, antithesis, and synthesis, postmodern novels accentuate the disjunctures and deferrals already present in the modernist classics. Postmodern novels push the discourse of hybridity away from synthetic unity towards syncretic multiplicity. However, to say that

---

44 Clarke, *Fire on the Water*, vol. I, n.p.
45 Clarke explains the development of *Execution Poems* and *George & Rue* in the "P. S. Ideas, interviews and features" supplement appended to the end of *George & Rue* (Toronto: HarperCollins, 2006 [2005]), p. 18.

postmodern novels depict a new multicultural Canada is to obscure a key point. The novels in this chapter tell stories about cultural communities that largely predate the official multiculturalism legislation of 1971. The novels may cater to a market that craves pluralist interpretations of Canadian history, but their literary reputations rest on the innovative formal strategies they devise for placing Canada's diverse cultural heritages in a state of interaction.

One consequence of this emphasis on revising historical narrative is that, with the exception of *Beautiful Losers*, there is a tendency to ignore contemporaneous aspects of what Davies would call "low culture" in Canadian postmodernism, when compared to other literatures. On the other hand, in an age when novels began to read increasingly like treatments for a Hollywood screenplay, Canadian authors have found ways to renew the engagement of the novel with small-market art forms, such as poetry and theater, without foregoing cinematic techniques. Against the backdrop of world wars and racially motivated violence, these novelists imagine alternatives to apocalyptic conflict. To do so, they create heterogeneous literary forms that underscore the process of forging communities from diverse histories and cultural sources.

23

Comic art and *bande dessinée*: from the funnies to graphic novels

JEAN-PAUL GABILLIET

The Super Heroes Stamp Pack issued by Canada Post on October 2, 1995 sported the likeness of Superman, the quintessential American superhero. It may have seemed a prank to many Canadians but it was actually a quirk of fate: Superman's co-creator Joseph Shuster (1914–92) was born in Toronto and moved with his family to Cleveland at age ten. Much later, in the 1960s, Mordecai Richler interpreted the "Man from Krypton" as a metaphor of the "Canadian psyche," that is, a convenient self-image for individuals with great abilities yet content to live under the disguise of a self-effacing alter ego.[1]

However debatable Richler's tongue-in-cheek contention may be, it at least implies that comics are no different from any other narrative species: they simultaneously tell stories and impart collective representations. Today's Canadians are often unaware of their country's comic art heritage – they know at best that Lynn Johnston, the author of the long-running soap-opera-cum-sitcom newspaper comic-strip "For Better or For Worse" (since 1979) is one of them. And yet, from the political commentaries of editorial cartoons to the escapism of twentieth-century comic strips to the mature creativity of present-day graphic novels, English-language comics and French-language *bande dessinée* have been vivid elements in the landscape of Canadian news and entertainment media since the mid-nineteenth century.

From cartoons to comics

Before comics there was political and satirical cartooning. The short-lived *Punch in Canada*, which appeared in Montreal in 1849, opened the way to many other humorous weeklies, but the first significant illustrated journals were

---

1 Mordecai Richler, *The Great Comic Book Heroes and Other Essays* (Toronto: McClelland and Stewart, 1978), pp. 122–4.

born in the wake of Confederation: following the staid *Canadian Illustrated News*, which made its debut in Montreal in 1869, the more biting Toronto-based cartoon weekly *Grip* relied as of 1873 on the satirical political drawings of John Wilson Bengough throughout its twenty-two-year run. One of the first recurrent characters in Canadian editorial cartoons at the time was Johnny (sometimes Jack) Canuck. He was traditionally depicted as a wholesome young man wearing the simple clothes of an *habitant* (in the earliest versions), farmer, or logger, as opposed to the frock coat and top hat of his famous counterparts and often contentious interlocutors, John Bull and Uncle Sam.[2]

One prominent early figure of Canadian cartooning in the late nineteenth century was Henri Julien: a frequent contributor to American and French periodicals, he became the country's first full-time newspaper cartoonist when the Montreal *Star* hired him in 1888. Among his contemporaries was Palmer Cox, a Quebec-born expatriate to the USA who gained fame thanks to his pixie-like characters "the Brownies," which featured in several bestselling collections from the late 1880s.[3] The next generation of talented cartoonists at the beginning of the new century included Arthur G. Racey, who succeeded Julien at the Montreal *Star*, J. B. Fitzmaurice in *The Vancouver Daily Province*, and Bob Edwards, founder of the satirical *Calgary Eye-Opener* in 1902 and its publisher for twenty years. In Quebec, more than seventy French-language humor periodicals appeared and disappeared in the second half of the nineteenth century. One remarkable actor in this field was caricaturist Hector Berthelot, the publisher of several satirical titles; as "Père Ladébauche,"[4] a penname he adopted in 1878, he posed as an obnoxious critic of contemporary society who eventually became a major character in Quebec popular culture until the mid-twentieth century.

For many North American cartoonists the shift from political drawing to comic strips *per se* happened after the turn of the century, following the emergence of comic supplements in Sunday newspapers in the mid-1890s and the multiplication of comic strip pages on weekdays in the 1910s. From the start of the twentieth century, American syndicates regarded Canadian newspapers as part of their domestic market and accordingly provided them with

---

2 Nineteenth-century cartooning has been documented by John Bell in his groundbreaking *Canuck Comics* (Montreal: Matrix Books, 1986), pp. 19–21 and his more recent *Invaders from the North: How Canada Conquered the Comic Book Universe* (Toronto: Dundurn Group, 2006), pp. 21–3.
3 Roger W. Cummins, *Humorous but Wholesome: A History of Palmer Cox and the Brownies* (Watkins Glen, NY: Century House, 1973). See also Nick Mount, *When Canadian Literature Moved to New York* (Toronto: University of Toronto Press, 2005), pp. 60–6.
4 "Father Excess." My translation.

cheap comic strips for both weekday and Sunday editions. In this admittedly unfavorable context, the first Canadian-made newspaper comics were published in the Québécois liberal daily *La Patrie*: early in 1904 Albéric Bourgeois (1876–1962) launched "Les Aventures de Timothée" featuring an opinionated dandy bumbling along in modern urban Quebec. The strip's popularity ushered in a string of other comics appearing in the same newspaper and its main competitor, *La Presse*. After defecting to *La Presse* early in 1905, Bourgeois took up in comic-strip form H. Berthelot's "Père Ladébauche" – by then a classic of Quebec's satirical press. For more than forty years, Bourgeois provided illustrations and chronicles featuring the loud-mouthed stereotypical Quebecker and remained the leading graphic satirist of the province until the early 1950s.

By the 1910s the competition of cheaper American and French comics had practically killed off French-Canadian strips, and they remained quite uncommon until the 1970s. The national origins of the 301 strips running in Quebec newspapers from 1930 to 1950 broke down as follows: more than 85 percent from the USA, 9 percent from France, 5 percent from Quebec, 0.6 percent from English Canada – where newspapers hardly ever considered purchasing material that did not come from the United States.[5] Two exceptions were the now largely forgotten Brownies-like "Doo Dads" by Winnipeg artist Arch Dale, a strip that enjoyed short-lived North American syndication in the early 1920s, and the more memorable "Birdseye Centre," drawn by Jimmy Frise for the *Toronto Star* from 1921 to 1947. The 1930s were the golden age of American adventure strips in which one Canadian stood out: Halifax native Harold Foster created two masterpieces of the medium, "Tarzan" in 1929 and "Prince Valiant" in 1937. By contrast, Toronto writer Ted McCall's and artist Charles R. Snelgrove's "Robin Hood and Company" was the period's only Canadian syndicated strip (1935–40).

Between the world wars most of the comics produced in Quebec outside newspapers were *Images d'Épinal*-like broadsheets,[6] a format considered by Catholic authorities more respectable than the American speech balloon comic-strip. The Société Saint-Jean-Baptiste de Montréal's three *Contes*

---

5 Yves Lacroix, "La Bande dessinée dans les journaux québécois (1930–1950)," *La Nouvelle barre du jour* 110–111 (February 1982), pp. 101–9, as cited in Bell, ed., *Canuck Comics*, p. 104.

6 *Images d'Épinal* refers to the comic-strip broadsheets published in the nineteenth century by the Pellerin company based in Épinal, a small town in northeastern France. The stencil-colored prints featured humorous or edifying comic-strip woodcuts essentially devoted to folk themes, military subjects, storybook characters. Hawked by peddlers across the country, the Épinal prints were mainstays of popular culture in pre-First World War France.

historiques series (1919–21), presenting captioned strips – some of which were scripted by the traditionalist historian Lionel Groulx – were bestsellers that led to the publication of the edifying monthly children's magazine *L'Oiseau bleu* (1920–40). In 1935 the Trois-Rivières-based Association Catholique des Voyageurs de Commerce commissioned broadsheet adaptations of Catholic-content novels subsequently inserted in leading newspapers and magazines. Catholic publishers converted to the American comic-book format only during the Second World War and after: Fides (*Hérauts*) and the Compagnie de Publications Agricoles (*Exploits héroïques et d'aventures illustrés, Illustrés classiques*) issued translations of American comics whereas the Centrale de la Jeunesse Étudiante Catholique (JEC) mixed Québécois material with French and American comics in *François* (launched in 1943). The sister title for girls, *Claire*, came out in 1957, during a two-year period when Quebec-made material once again found its way into children's magazines: *Claire*'s flagship strip was Nicole Lapointe's "Jani," featuring a modern, self-assured flight attendant, while Fides published dozens of stories by the prolific French-born Maurice Petitdidier, whose strips were reprinted in numerous collections. Franco-Belgian and American competition eventually brought about the demise of JEC and Fides titles by the mid-1960s.

Wartime boom and post-war slump

Comics publishing in Canada has suffered from the same problems that have chronically plagued the country's culture as a whole: the daunting competition of inexpensive – because previously amortized – French, British, and American material, the limited domestic interest in, and appeal of, home-made cultural products, the difficulty for national producers of having to distance themselves from foreign models and formats, and finally, the insufficient size of the domestic market to support a national comics industry. By the late 1930s the newborn comic-book industry emerging in New York City likewise developed by extending distribution networks into Canada and dumping thousands of American-made funnybooks retailing for a dime a copy – regardless of the exchange rate on either side of the border.

Yet a totally unexpected "Golden Age" of English-Canadian comic-book publishing occurred after the December 1940 "War Exchange Conservation Act" restricted the importation of non-essential goods from countries outside the sterling bloc, thereby cutting off the flow of American pulps and comic books and creating an overnight demand that had to be met by domestic publishers. Despite their brief careers, the Canadian "Whites" (thus nicknamed because, unlike American four-color comic magazines, their interior pages were printed in black and white) left a lasting imprint on the minds of 1940s children and teenagers. They remain to this day emblematic of Canada's Second World War-era ultra-patriotic popular culture, which earned them the honor of a major National Gallery exhibition in 1972, "Comic Art Traditions in Canada, 1941–45," soon after M. Hirsh and P. Loubert's 1971 study *The Great Canadian Comic Books* introduced post-war generations to this previously neglected part of their national heritage.

The first Whites publishers, Vancouver's Maple Leaf and Toronto's Anglo-American, released their inaugural titles in March 1941. Maple Leaf's *Better Comics* offered original material with a clear Canadian slant (it introduced former Disney artist Vernon Miller's "Iron Man," the first Canadian superhero), while Anglo-American's tabloid-sized *Robin Hood and Company* reprinted generic adventure fare; the Toronto publisher subsequently specialized in reprints, with the notable exception of Ted McCall's and artist Ted Furness's "Freelance," chronologically the second Canadian superhero and the only one whose popularity warranted stardom in his own comic book throughout the war.

The next important Whites manufacturer was Toronto's Bell Features, a company born in 1942 from the acquisition by brothers Cy and Gene Bell of Hillborough Studios, a short-lived venture founded in the summer of 1941 whose single title *Triumph-Adventure Comics* had spawned the first Canadian superheroine, "Nelvana of the Northern Lights." Based on Inuit legends, Nelvana was jointly created by writer-artist Adrian Dingle, who illustrated all her stories, and the Group of Seven's Frank Johnston. The daughter of a human mother and Koliak, King of the Northern Lights, she could travel at the speed of light on a giant aurora borealis ray to fulfill her mission as protector of the people of the north (that is, Canadians) from her home base in Nortonville, Ontario.

The success of the Bells' first comic, *Wow* (cover-dated September 1941), packaged by French-Canadian artist Edmund Legault, prompted them to hire Nelvana creator Adrian Dingle as art director of a five-title line of Canadian-content humor and adventure magazines: *Funny, Joke, Active, Commando,* and *Dime. Dime*'s first issue featured another fondly remembered wartime superhero: the brainchild of sixteen-year-old cartoonist Leo Bachle, "Johnny Canuck" was a contemporary adventurer bearing the name of the cartoon character impersonating Canada in the nineteenth century.

A relative latecomer, Montreal's Educational Projects, filled the niche of educational periodicals from late 1942; its flagship title, *Canadian Heroes*, sold

Comic art and *bande dessinée*: from the funnies to graphic novels

Plate 15. "Nelvana of the Northern Lights," drawn by Adrian Dingle, *c.* 1945.

slowly until the introduction of a "realistic" national superhero, George M. Rae's "Canada Jack." Four other publishers hoping to cash in on the comic-book bonanza emerged in 1944 (Feature) and 1945 (F. E. Howard, Rucker, Superior) but the momentum that had gathered since 1941 was cut short by the lifting of the ban on imports in the summer of 1945. Superior, Anglo-American, and Bell weathered the crisis by marketing reprints of US comics but all their competitors had folded by late 1946. Superior, which survived into the next decade by publishing exceptionally gruesome horror titles, was eventually brought down by the mid-1950s North American moral panic over comic books.

Plate 16. Steven Keewatin Sanderson, *Darkness Calls*, 2006.

Until the end of the next decade the few comic books produced in Canada were mostly educational and promotional giveaways mainly cranked out by Toronto's Ganes Productions and Halifax's Comic Book World. Public-service comics have been a long-lasting, albeit often overlooked, segment of this industry; their social relevance as a means to reach out to disenfranchised communities has increased over the years. A recent example was the nation-wide launch, in 2006, by the Vancouver-based "Healthy Aboriginal Network" of a comic-book series dealing with public health issues for Aboriginal teenagers.[7] In *Darkness Calls*, artist Steve Keewatin Sanderson stages a battle between two Cree spirits, Wesakechak and Weetigo, over a suicidal young boy, who finally proclaims to them his will to live.

Counter-culture, nationalism, avant-garde: cartooning in colonial space

The 1960s was a time of change for comics: the medium in which output had from the early twentieth century traditionally been geared to children then became an important means of expression for the counter-culture, both because it was affordable and because it appealed to baby-boomers. Unlike its American and European counterparts the Canadian literary avant-garde used comics to produce innovative expressive forms. The earliest such endeavor was *Scraptures*, a special issue of the Toronto experimental magazine *grOnk* entirely conceived by concrete poet bp nichol, and the first of a series of *Scraptures* "sequences" that he produced into the 1980s. His life-long fascination with the medium's form and content found its first outlet in "Bob the Cat," a comic-strip begun in 1960 whose character was reincarnated as the protagonist of the 1965–8 "Captain Poetry" poems finally published in 1971. He was later dissatisfied with these because he felt he had failed to control the parodic voice of a masked cartoon superhero.[8] He created numerous other pieces of comics-form poetry, many of which are found in his *Allegory* series, *Zygal*, *The Martyrology Book 6* and *Gifts: The Martyrology Book[s] 7&*.

---

7 Eva Salinas, "Comics Shed Light on the Darker Side of Native Life; Format Helps Get Message Out, Artist Says," *The Globe and Mail* (14 August 2006), p. S1.
8 Carl Peters, ed., *bp nichol Comics* (Vancouver: Talonbooks, 2002), p. 25; Susan E. Billingham, *Language and the Sacred in Canadian Poet BP Nichol's The Martyrology* (Queenston, ON: Edwin Mellen Press, 2000), p. 274. Born Barrie Phillip Nichol, the poet chose the penname of "bp nichol" but this spelling is not always reproduced correctly in texts about him. Carl Peters's book collects all his comics-inspired pieces.

While bp nichol was the only avant-garde writer, either inside or outside Canada, to engage in comics-based visual poetry, a few other similar projects did come into existence at the beginning of the 1970s. Also a small press, Toronto's Coach House produced in 1969 *Snore Comix* (labelled "the first Canadian underground comix"[9] by John Bell in his seminal 1986 study *Canuck Comics*), with contributions by Victor Coleman, Greg Curnoe, and Michael Tims – the first of a three-issue run that featured bp nichol himself and several actors of the local pop art and Dada scene. Other remarkable contributions to comics avant-gardism by Coach House were the all but impenetrable "visual novels" by the British-born artist Martin Vaughn-James: *The Projector* (1971), *The Park* (1972), and *The Cage* (1975) came in the wake of *Elephant*, his first opus published by New Press in 1970. In Quebec the avant-garde's interest in comics came in the form of innovative visuals by Chiendent, a group of artists (Marc-Antoine Nadeau, André Montpetit, Michel Fortier) gathered around the surrealist poet Claude Haeffely; their work appeared briefly in the mainstream magazines *Maclean's* and *Perspectives* in 1970.

Still the broad thrust of counter-culture was more political than aesthetic and whatever traits were shared by English-Canadian and Québécois comix boiled down to their emphasis on satire and the political critique of contemporary Canadian realities. The "springtime of Quebec comics," celebrated in 1971 by journalist Georges Raby,[10] mainly consisted in sporadic publications designed by and for college students to assist the agenda of the Quiet Revolution: among many others, *MA(R)DE IN KEBEC* (Sherbrooke, 1970–2), *BD* (1971–3), *L'Hydrocéphale illustré* (University of Montreal, 1971–2), *La Pulpe* (Ottawa, 1973–5), *L'Ecran* (1974), *Prisme* (1974–7), and *Baloune* (1977–78) exemplified the diversity of contemporary French-Canadian comics publishing.

Comics occasionally proved popular vehicles for nationalist discourse as in Robert Lavaill's comic-strip adaptation of Léandre Bergeron's Marxist interpretation of Quebec history, *Petit manuel d'histoire du Québec* (1971), Pierre Fournier's 1973 one-shot *Les Aventures du Capitaine Kébec*, featuring a hippie Québécois superhero, and J. Guilemay's Astérix-inspired "Bojoual le Huron Kébékois" album series (1973–6), featuring a villain bearing an uncanny resemblance to Prime Minister Trudeau. Classic Québécois cartoonists like Albéric Bourgeois and Albert Chartier (1912–2004) were also co-opted by cultural nationalists during this period. By the mid-1970s Chartier's

---

9 Bell, *Canuck Comics*, p. 75. "Comix" refers to underground comic books as opposed to their mainstream counterparts.
10 Georges Raby, "Le Printemps de la bande dessinée'," *Culture vivante* 22 (September 1971), pp. 12–23.

"Onésime" had been the longest-running comic-strip in Quebec history, published uninterruptedly in the *Bulletin des agriculteurs* since late 1943. The thin, pipe-smoking, no-nonsense Laurentides farmer with a knack for bringing on disaster was featured for six decades in monthly one-page gags that testify to the societal changes experienced by the rural and small-town Quebec middle class after the Second World War.

The first major Canadian underground newspapers that prominently featured comics were Montreal's *Logos* and Vancouver's *Georgia Straight*, both founded in 1967. By 1970 the *Straight* began to publish the work of Nova-Scotia-born Rand Holmes (1942–2002), who was to become the country's most remarkable comix artist, equally recognized and sought after on both sides of the forty-ninth parallel throughout a thirty-year career. Besides providing exquisitely rendered covers and spot illustrations for the *Straight*, Holmes created "Harold Hedd," an easy-going Vancouver freak obsessed with drugs and sex. His stories were so many vehicles for biting satire, often directed against Prime Minister Trudeau, particularly at the time of the October Crisis, when he invoked the War Measures Act, and his government's half-hearted criticism of the American military involvement in Vietnam. The Prime Minister was also the main target of *Fuddle Duddle*, published in Ottawa in 1971–2.[11]

As was the case in the United States, the heyday of Canadian comix was from 1970 to 1973; afterwards, the American withdrawal from Vietnam and the incipient global depression helped to deflate the counter-cultural movement. The era ended with the release of two flamboyant one-shots from Vancouver, the *Georgia Straight*'s pornographic *All Canadian Beaver Comix* and Leo Burdak's *Gearfoot Wrecks*, a scathing satire of the Watergate scandal. Besides Rand Holmes, Canadian comix produced a handful of excellent creators, in particular Saskatoon's Dave Geary (*Nature Comix*, the Dadaist *Bridge City Beer Comix*) and Vancouver's Brent Boates and George Metzger.

English-Canadian radicalism rarely took the comics route, with the notable exception of *She Named It Canada Because That's What It Was Called*. Issued by the Corrective Collective, this eighty-page feminist history of Canada originally printed as a handout for a women's conference held in Vancouver in 1971 warranted two successive reprintings with revisions. The one significant instance of political satire in the late 1970s was not a comic book but the

---

11 "Fuddle Duddle" was the phrase Trudeau claimed to have actually uttered after opposition MPs accused him of having mouthed the F word at them in the House of Commons in February 1971.

page of satirical cartoon strips introduced in the progressive Toronto publication *This Magazine* by one of its editors, Rick Salutin. After he convinced Margaret Atwood to become a regular collaborator, she created "Kanadian Kultchur Komics," a tongue-in-cheek cartoon-strip she wrote and drew (with admittedly limited graphic skills) under the pseudonym Bart Gerrard. Appearing next to more overtly parodic comics, like Mike Cherkas's "Mary Worth in Westmount" and "Canazan: Lord of the Academic Jungle" (with John Sech) or Mike Smith's "Correct Line Comix," Atwood's nineteen irreverent strips featured a gallery of memorable caricatures – a chain-smoking American

Plate 17. Margaret Atwood, "Survivalwoman," 1975.

superhero with a paunch and five-o'clock shadow named Superham, the naive pro-independence Québécois seductress Amphibianwoman, and the self-deprecatory Survivalwoman, a Canadian superheroine whose only exceptional attributes were snowshoes and a defeatist mentality. Atwood used the cartoon form to debunk the English Canadian intellectuals' left-wing dogmatism and she expressed skepticism toward Quebec's sovereignist government as well as disillusionment with the Liberals' ostensible commitment to cultural nationalism.

Laying the foundations of a Canadian comic-book industry

From the mid-1970s to the mid-1990s North American comic books (outside Quebec) experienced a twofold transition. First, the non-mainstream production evolved from "undergrounds" characterized by their largely counter-cultural content to "alternatives" that proposed stories fitting into mainstream genres (superheroes, fantasy, science fiction) with added elements of sex and/or satire to appeal to adolescent and young adult readers. Second, the transition took place as comic-book reading was changing into a cultural niche the primary material for which was supplied by a growing network of specialty bookstores catering to fans on average older than the previous decades' pre-adolescent dime-store customers. An equivalent phenomenon happened in Quebec as alternative comics publishing evolved in response to the maturing of France's comics market in the wake of the May 1968 student revolt.

Despite these domestic developments foreign competition remained as difficult to challenge as ever. Within a few years, the scattered small-press production of comic books riding the wave of Western counter-culture and local cultural nationalism in the late 1960s evolved into a small-scale industry of one-shots and titles enjoying runs rarely exceeding a couple of issues. Although a number of Canadian cartoonists have become on-and-off fan favorites working for mainstream American publishers (for example, John Byrne, Todd McFarlane, Stuart Immonen, Darwyn Cooke), occasionally introducing Canadian concepts (for instance John Byrne's superhero team "Alpha Flight" for Marvel Comics in the early 1980s), there is no Canadian periodical comic book that has decisively succeeded in American mainstream production.

In the ten years after 1974 numerous alternative English-Canadian publishers appeared: Toronto's Orb, Andromeda, Peter Dako (*Casual Casual Graphix Magazine*); Calgary's CKR (*Captain Canuck*); Montreal's Matrix

Graphic Series (*Mackenzie Queen*); Vancouver's Jim McPherson (*Phantacea*) and Stampart (*Fog City Comics*, a post-underground title comprising many superb Rand Holmes graphics). The period's most interesting publishing ventures were Toronto publisher Bill Marks' Vortex – with *Mister X*, a title of paranoid and counter-utopian science fiction beautifully illustrated by Seth, and Ty Templeton's comedic *Stig's Inferno* – and, above all, Aardvark-Vanaheim (A-V) in Kitchener, Ontario. Founded in 1977 by Deni Loubert to publish her partner Dave Sim's comics, A-V was the home of one the most remarkable achievements in Canadian comics, Sim's series *Cerebus the Aardvark*. Besides its flagship title, A-V also promoted several alternative artists, including Vancouver creator Arn Saba's charming *Neil the Horse Comics and Stories*, whose cartoony artwork illustrated short funny-animal stories revolving around the author's fascination with the golden age of American musical comedy.

The mid-1980s comic-book market bubble, fueled by fan speculation, generated many other short-lived titles. Some among these were xeroxed pamphlets (John MacLeod's *Dishman* and Chester Brown's *Yummy Fur* in Toronto, Colin Upton's *Big Thing* in Vancouver) following the pioneering example of Vancouver's David Boswell's self-published *Reid Fleming, The World's Toughest Milkman* (1980), the small-press *Jam-Pac*, Winnipeg, a collection of five mini-comix published by the Free-Kluck collective in 1981, and K. G. Cruickshank's *No Name Comix* (1984), whose experimental agenda was reminiscent of the late 1960s bp nichol-type material. Conversely some authors contributed to foreign publications (for example Vancouver's Carol Moiseiwitsch's strips for American underground magazines). By the late 1980s, several future important creators had managed to emerge in the comics field. Among them was Douglas Coupland: before turning to the novel, he began exploring the culture of the post-baby-boomer rat race in the Toronto magazine *Vista*. His "Generation X" comic-strip (1988–9), written in collaboration with cartoonist Paul Rivoche, featured Brad, an aspiring yuppie desperately craving the success of his older and tiresome role-model bosses John Boomer and Mr. Ward.

Modern Québécois comics came into their own with the 1979 launch by Ludcom-Croc of *Croc* ("fang," but also the first syllable of the verb *croquer*, meaning both "to bite" and "to sketch"), a magazine inspired by two contemporary mainstays of the satirical press, the American *National Lampoon* and the French *Pilote*. Edited by the triumvirate of 1970s comics agitators Jacques Hurtubise, his partner Hélène Fleury, and Pierre Huet, the monthly magazine experienced a slow start but turned out to be a 189-issue success story that came to an end fifteen years later after having boosted the careers of a number of high-profile cartoonists (Claude Cloutier, Lucie Faniel, Pierre Fournier, Serge Gaboury, Réal Godbout, Caroline Merola, and others). Despite the failure of the aptly named comics-only magazine *Titanic* in 1983–4 (featuring Garnotte, Henriette Valium – pseudonym of Patrick Henley – Jules Prud'homme, Sylvie Pilon, Rémy Simard) Lucdom-Croc became highly visible throughout the 1980s through licensing, incursions into radio and television, and comics albums (Hurtubise's *Le Sombre vilain*, Réal Godbout and Pierre Fournier's "Michel Risque" and "Red Ketchup" series). In the 1980s most Québécois cartoonists worked for, or were discovered by, Hurtubise, even when they contributed to other publications like *Cocktail* (six issues in 1981) or the neo-underground title *Iceberg* (1983–5, 1990–4). *Croc*'s decline began in 1987 when it had to deal with competition from a Quebec City-based newcomer, Sylvain Bolduc's *Safarir*. Largely inspired by *Mad Magazine*, the new title emphasized burlesque humor rather than socio-political satire, appealing to many faithful readers of Hurtubise's magazine, which eventually folded in 1994. *Safarir* has since become an essential outlet for many cartoonists, both established and new.

Since the mid-1980s, the Québécois comics industry has greatly benefited from two other major sources of creativity. A large number of neo-underground fanzines of variable quality (*Baloney Comix, EXIL, Gratte-Cellules, Guillotine, Spoutnik, Tabasko*) have been training grounds for beginners, many of whom have graduated to professional status (Grégoire Bouchard, Fidèle Castrée, Jean-Pierre Chansigaud, Leanne Franson, Alexandre Lafleur, Marc Tessier). Moreover, the influence of French comics publishing has brought about the emergence of a number of publishers of hardcover and softcover albums, who anticipated by a few years the American conversion to the graphic novel format: fairly large houses like Yves Millet's Éditions du Phylactère, cartoonist Rémy Simard's Kami-Case (now a branch of Éditions du Boréal), Mille-Iles, Soulières (formerly Falardeau) and smaller presses like D'Amours, Romanichels, and Raz-de-Marée.

Despite the dynamism of various local comics scenes (for instance *Drippytown*, the sporadic anthology title featuring the production of young Vancouver cartoonists), English-Canadian comics and Québécois *bandes dessinées* typically continue to receive very little exposure until they are picked up by publishers in the United States or France. However, the adjustment of the North American comics industry to the graphic novel format in the last decade of the twentieth century has shifted the market into a positive direction for high-profile Canadian comics creators.

The age of the graphic novel

Graphic novels, that is, hard- or soft-cover comics designed to be marketed in bookstores rather than periodicals outlets, have existed for decades in North America although both the comic-book industry and the book trade did not acknowledge the commercial viability of this format before the late 1980s. The term "graphic novel" was first coined in 1964 by American fan and critic Richard Kyle to refer to a possible long-term evolution of comic narratives toward formats transcending the then standard saddle-stitched four-color pamphlet that included stories no more than twenty pages long. Few North Americans were familiar with the comic albums that Europeans had been reading since the 1930s and they were generally unaware of the thick *manga* that the Japanese had been reading avidly since the 1950s. The *albums de bande dessinée* issued by French and Belgian publishers connected with the Catholic Church were available in Quebec as far back as the 1930s but their relatively expensive retail prices limited their visibility. They were read by urban middle-class children and never became staples of local francophone popular culture. In Quebec (as in France during the same period) comic albums enjoyed a modicum of cultural legitimacy that comic books had yet to obtain in English Canada.

This explains why the *album* was the format chosen by Éditions du Cri in 1970 to publish two avant-garde comic books, *Oror 70 (Celle qui en a marre tire)* by André Philibert and *L'Œil voyeur* by Tibo (pseudonym of Gilles Thibault). Dealing with the drug culture, free love, the rejection of the establishment, and Quebec independence against a psychedelic backdrop, these two books may be considered the first Canadian graphic novels. Another remarkable precursor, released in 1978, was *Now You're Logging*, a detailed documentary account of coastal logging in Depression-era British Columbia along with some romance, written and drawn by Bus Griffiths (1913–2006), a former wartime-era contributor to Vancouver's Maple Leaf Publishing. The book had no connection with the French *album* tradition nor with the then barely nascent graphic novel, and was indeed much closer to the tradition of educational comics. The graphic novel as a medium likely to compete with saddle-stitched pamphlets came of age in the 1990s with the unexpected success of Art Spiegelman's *Maus*, the growing global popularity of Japanese *manga*, and the increasing interest of bookstores in the new format thanks to both its literary potential, touted by mainstream media, and the profitability that came with its newly respectable reputation. Since the 1990s Canadians have fared very well in high-end graphic novels, as testified by two successful alternative publishing ventures, Aardvark-Vanaheim's *Cerebus* and Montreal's Drawn & Quarterly (D&Q).

If there is such a thing as a "great Canadian graphic novel," Dave Sim's sixteen-volume, 6,000-page *Cerebus* is its closest contender. Describing it as the life story of a short-tempered, sword-wielding talking aardvark in the fictitious world of Estarcion is about as informative as summarizing Joyce's *Ulysses* as a day in the life of Leopold Bloom in 1904 Dublin. Completed between 1977 and 2004, *Cerebus* is one of the medium's most remarkable and troubling achievements, partly because of its length – although quite a few *manga* series are several thousand pages long – but mainly because of its unprecedented creative scope. A comic-book fan who by his early twenties had turned into a self-taught professional cartoonist, Sim decided in 1979 that his self-published black-and-white title – originally a parody of the Marvel Comics heroic fantasy titles – would become a unique creative entreprise spanning 300 monthly installments – no more, no less. In terms of sheer popularity, *Cerebus* towered above the rest of English-Canadian comics throughout the 1980s. Moving, sometimes in alternation, between slapstick, melodrama, fantasy, magic realism, autobiographical writing, pamphleteering, and even religious exegesis (in the penultimate volume), it is a tentacular narrative tapping into popular culture (including the Marx Brothers, the Rolling Stones, Warner Bros. cartoon characters) and all the significant English-language comic-book concepts of the late twentieth century as well as the writings of Oscar Wilde, F. Scott Fitzgerald, and Ernest Hemingway. To appraise Sim's work proves challenging because of the chasm between form and substance. On the one hand he is one of the most accomplished graphic storytellers in the world; he has assimilated all the possibilities of visual narration inaugurated by his most prestigious American predecessors and transcended them by stretching the potential of text-image relationships to the limits of visual characterization, page design, and lettering. At his best, he is also an exceptionally gifted dialogist. On the other hand, the comic became a vehicle of controversial ideas in volumes 5 through 16. These chronicle Cerebus's personal downfall under the matriarchal theocracy led by Cirin, a giant female aardvark cast as the protagonist's evil double. Although it requires a reader willing to ignore the narrative's problematic elements, *Cerebus* remains an unparalleled creative experiment.

Sim was, until the early 1990s, a vocal mouthpiece of North American alternative comics publishing, but Aardvark-Vanaheim ceased publishing other artists after the late 1980s. The Canadian publisher who became the most active promoter of Canadian cartoonists is Chris Oliveros, founder of

D&Q. This Montreal publishing house debuted in 1990 with an eponymous quarterly anthology title featuring artwork of varying interest by North American and European alternative creators. Out of this informal creative crew emerged several outstanding authors whose work has earned them international recognition. The first one was Julie Doucet (b. 1965): after noticing her French-language fanzine *Dirty Plotte*[12] self-published in the late 1980s, Oliveros went on to publish her material in English under the same title (1990–8). Doucet's stream-of-consciousness pieces revolve around the trials of the female life (particularly menstruation and other bodily excretions), rendered in a neo-underground "grungy" visual and narrative vein influenced by Robert Crumb's no-holds-barred autobiographical cartooning. This work made her extremely popular in American and European alternative comics circles by the mid-1990s. After spending time abroad she published less surreal, often autobiographical stories (*My New York Diary*, 1999; *The Madame Paul Affair*, 2000; *Journal*, 2004) before announcing in 2006 her decision to give up comics.

Oliveros's next major discoveries, Seth and Chester Brown, came from the Toronto scene. After a short stint with Vortex Comics in the mid-1980s, Seth (born Gregory Gallant in 1962) in *Palooka Ville* put his deceptively simple style influenced by *New Yorker* cartoonists at the service of wistfully intimist narratives steeped in his nostalgia for pre-1960s artifacts and popular culture: *It's A Good Life, If You Don't Weaken* (1996), a would-be autobiographical *bildungsroman* in which the author conducts a lengthy investigation about an obscure (actually fictitious) *New Yorker* cartoonist; the yet unfinished *Clyde Fans* (2004) about the family history behind an electric fan business in 1957 Ontario; in collaboration with his father John Gallant, *Bannock, Beans and Black Tea* (2004), a moving illustrated memoir of the latter's childhood in Depression-era Prince Edward Island; and the ironic multiple-viewpoint fable on comic-book collecting *Wimbledon Green: The Greatest Comic Book Collector in the World* (2005).

Chester Brown (b. 1960) is a very idiosyncratic creator; though neither as controversial nor as stylistically brilliant as Dave Sim, he is even more mystical. His early 1980s mini-comic *Yummy Fur* contained disconcerting one-pagers (whose panels were arranged at random with altered dialogues) and the bizarre, esoteric story *Ed the Happy Clown*, which transposed surrealist automatic writing to comic-strip narration. After *Yummy Fur* was picked up by

---

12 *Dirty Plotte* contains a double-entendre on "plot" and "plotte." The latter is *joual* for the female genitalia.

Vortex in 1986, Brown moved progressively toward painfully intimate autobiographical teenage-guilt narratives (*The Playboy, I Never Liked You*) while working on colloquially rendered adaptations of the Gospels that he continued after joining the D&Q stable in 1991. After the relative failure of *Underwater*, an unfinished series chronicling an infant's perception of the world from his birth, Brown started working on *Louis Riel: A Comic-Strip Biography*, which earned him international acclaim in 2003.

Among the other significant comics authors revealed by D&Q since the late 1990s are the gay Toronto artist Maurice Vellekoop (b. 1964), whose eclectic illustration work has been showcased in *Vellevision: A Cocktail of Comics and Pictures* (1997), David Collier, who emerged as a major creator of short stories in *Just the Facts* (1998), *Surviving Saskatoon* (2000), and *Portraits from Life* (2001), and two Québécois cartoonists – Michel Rabagliati (b. 1961), whose "Paul" series has been published by Montreal's Éditions de la Pastèque since 1998, and Guy Delisle (b. 1966), whose travelogues about his experience as a supervisor of animation work in Asia, *Shenzhen: A Travelogue from China* and *Pyongyang: A Journey in North Korea*, were published in France in the early 2000s. While D&Q has been the leading Canadian alternative comics publisher, its American counterpart Fantagraphics has also opened its catalogue to Canadian creators Ho Che Anderson (b. 1969) and Dave Cooper (b. 1967). Anderson, a Black artist, first came up with a brilliant biography of Martin Luther King (*King*), but his subsequent *Pop Life* series set in Toronto showcased noirish artwork decidedly superior to his narrative skills. In a totally different vein, Cooper has written and drawn, in deliberately cartoony style, increasingly disturbing graphic novels revolving around male sexual paranoia: *Suckle* (1997), *Crumple* (2000), *Ripple* (2003).

Having overcome the stigma of comics as art for children, the graphic novel typifies the medium's ability to engage fiction and autobiography. It has proved a narrative genre where some Canadians have excelled and gained worldwide recognition. In this case, the gradual legitimization of comic art in Western countries since the 1980s has benefited Canadian publishers of highbrow material. Their books have enjoyed greater visibility and prestige both on the international market and among critics of mainstream literary production.[13]

---

13 I am grateful to Dr. Virginia Ricard for her attentive reading of this chapter.

24
"Ghost stories": fictions of history and myth

TERESA GIBERT

The organizers of the 1967 Centennial of Canadian Confederation promoted greater cohesion across social, political, and ethnic tensions in an intrinsically pluralist country. Even after the Centennial Commission had ceased to provide generous funds, many Canadian artists were committed to this project, but it became increasingly difficult to avoid the question whether such cohesion did not come at great cost to too many of the country's constituents. This was a period when Canada's collective memory was questioned, cultural icons were dismantled and unified visions of history and the mythology contested. More than ever before, Canadian artists began to view the beginnings of their country critically rather than nostalgically. The "ghost history"[1] that haunts Canadian literature in the post-1960s is the symbolic representation of those elements of the country's society that were previously barred from consciousness, and it is appropriate that revivals of the ghost story have been a preoccupation in contemporary Canadian criticism.

The *revenants* include Aboriginal people and immigrants who did not fit the two "founding nations," as well as parts of the country – such as Newfoundland, the last province to join Confederation – whose unfulfilled aspirations illustrate the strains within the Canadian body politic. While as late as 1960 the historian W. L. Morton stipulated that "[t]here is but one narrative line in Canadian history,"[2] literary revisions of history and myth have increasingly served not

---

[1] This is Wayne Johnston's term, though numerous other writers – Joseph Boyden, Margaret Sweatman, and Michael Crummey among them – use similar concepts. See Johnston's interview with Herb Wyile, "An Afterlife Endlessly Revised: Wayne Johnston," in *Speaking in the Past Tense: Canadian Novelists on Writing Historical Fiction* (Waterloo: Wilfrid Laurier Press, 2007), p. 111. For a discussion of the "ghost story" in contemporary Canadian literature and postcolonial writing generally, see, for example, Pamela McCallum, ed., *Postcolonial Hauntings*, special issue of *Ariel* 37.1 (2006).

[2] W. L. Morton, "The Relevance of Canadian History," lecture to the Canadian Historical Association (1960), included in Morton, *The Canadian Identity*, 2nd edn. (Toronto: University of Toronto Press, 1972 [1961]), p. 89.

"Ghost stories": fictions of history and myth

only to bridge the many divisions, but also to make them even more obvious. Writers from Aboriginal and from multicultural backgrounds that have shaped the Canadian demographic from the 1980s onwards have tackled these questions on their own terms, sometimes writing back against mainstream narratives and at other times bringing completely new geographies and histories into Canadian literature. Daniel David Moses's aptly named play *Brébeuf's Ghost*, subtitled "A Tale of Horror," draws on *Macbeth* for inspiration. Here, the story of the famous Jesuit priest is reinterpreted against the seventeenth-century story of an Ojibwa migration across the Canadian Shield, while in her poetry Marilyn Dumont talks back to Prime Minister John MacDonald, and Armand Ruffo in his verse addresses Duncan Campbell Scott, Post-Confederation poet and civil servant in the Department of Indian Affairs. Rohinton Mistry's novels do not concern themselves with the classic dilemmas of Canadian history at all. Instead, they require extensive knowledge of the history of the Mughal Empire, the Indian Partition, and the regime of Indira Gandhi.

Because their writing raises special research questions, these authors are discussed in separate chapters on contemporary Aboriginal and multicultural writing. By contrast, the following discussion will focus on authors who may write about, but do not write from, the Aboriginal position. When authors covered here write from a multicultural perspective, it is generally rooted in the older migrations from European countries. Like all classifications, however, these too can be difficult to maintain, as is apparent in the case of Ann-Marie MacDonald, whose ancestry is Scottish and Lebanese.

In drawing out "the mysterious, the buried, the forgotten, the discarded, the taboo,"[3] post-1960s Canadian authors often rely on postmodernist techniques, specifically those associated with "historiographic metafiction," defined by its most influential theorist, Linda Hutcheon, as "fiction that is intensely, self-reflexively art, but is also grounded in historical, social and political realities."[4] Although it introduced innovative narrative methods into Canadian literature, historiographic metafiction represents at least in part a logical sequel to earlier literary preoccupations with history, such as the nineteenth-century historical novels in English and French analyzed by E. D. Blodgett in this volume. The connection to other modes, realism among them, may at times therefore be as strong as that to postmodernism.

---

3 Margaret Atwood, *In Search of Alias Grace: On Writing Canadian Historical Fiction*, Charles R. Bronfman Lecture in Canadian Studies (1996) (Ottawa: Ottawa University Press, 1997), p. 19.
4 Linda Hutcheon, *The Canadian Postmodern: A Study of Contemporary English-Canadian Fiction* (Toronto: Oxford University Press, 1988), p. 13.

In keeping with the narrative model provided by Walter Scott, historical fiction like *Les Anciens Canadiens* is not intellectually or formally naive. Its understanding of "the buried" and "the forgotten" does differ crucially from the hidden narratives exposed in its contemporary equivalent, but these earlier novels – often encrusted with prefaces, notes, and epilogues that both question and support the main narrative – are in their own way as fractured as the complicated reality they represent.[5] In other words, technique alone does not necessarily make a historical novel conservative, nor does it guarantee innovation.

Like their predecessors, the novels under discussion in this chapter draw on the scholarly apparatus of positivism only to undermine its scientific premises, of which historiography provides one. Barbara Gowdy's *The White Bone* is more readily classified as an ecological fable than metafictional history, but the glossaries, footnotes, maps, and genealogical tree that populate the book and the uses to which they are put nevertheless point in that direction, as well as borrowing the conventions of the scientific treatise. Here, human history has receded and the rationalist perspective has been swiveled so radically that it is replaced by the history and outlook of those who are traditionally the specimens. In this case, these are a herd of elephants on a quest for "the white bone" that will guide them to a place of safety from ivory poachers, "slaughterers – a new and stunningly voracious generation," or even from the more harmless safari tourists, "a different breed entirely. Peaceful. Entranced."[6] In Gowdy's book, Romantic and Gothic elements parody the encyclopedism that props up the truth claim of the historical novel, and they do so using the self-reflexive approach that is typical of the new historical novel.

Echoing Bram Stoker and E. T. A. Hoffmann, along with Jorge Luis Borges and Italo Calvino, Thomas Wharton's *Salamander* (2001) begins and ends in a shelled-out bookshop in Quebec City just before the 1759 Battle of the Plains of Abraham. In between, the narrative returns to a time fifty years earlier to tell the story of the printer Nicholas Flood, who sets out to create "an infinite book."[7] In the employ of an eastern European aristocrat, who has created a robotic castle featuring a "ceaseless migration of bookcases," Flood is loath to

---

5 See, for example, Katie Trumpener, *Bardic Nationalism: The Romantic Novel and the British Empire* (Princeton: Princeton University Press, 1997). See also Gordon Bölling, *History in the Making: Metafiktion im neueren anglokanadischen historischen Roman* (Heidelberg: Universitätsverlag Winter, 2006), pp. 38–48. Thanks to Eva-Marie Kröller for her assistance.
6 Barbara Gowdy, *The White Bone* (Toronto: HarperCollins, 1998), pp. 56, 73.
7 Thomas Wharton, *Salamander* (Toronto: McClelland and Stewart, 2001), p. 40.

become no more than a cog in the Count's ingenious machine, defying him – at least temporarily – by loving his daughter Irene, whose bed he must board, "like a pirate," as it travels by on its rails by night (pp. 21, 97). Insistent on his own creativity, Flood derives some of his inspiration from an individual volume, not the ensemble, of an old encyclopedia, the *Libraria technicum*. In this eccentricity he resembles the priest and the schoolteacher in Urquhart's *Away*, who shuffle knowledge as if it were a deck of cards, by reading outdated volumes of the *Encyclopaedia Britannica* passed on by their landlords, and then making random articles the subject of impassioned debate.

These allusions to nineteenth-century works that combine historical fiction, Romanticism and Gothicism are all the more worth pointing out as the novels under discussion have consistently embraced forms of narrative that pose questions similar to experimental metafiction, but use self-reflexive techniques the latter shares with traditional fiction. These techniques include *mise en abyme*, unreliable narrators, multiple narrators, stories within stories, and pastiche, along with a host of textual genres that call into question by their sheer variety the information contained in each, such as letters, diaries, travelogues, testimonials, newspaper reports, tracts, poems, and songs (in Susan Swan's story of Anna Swan the giantess from Nova Scotia in *The Biggest Modern Woman of the World*, 1983) or theatre bills, signs, telegrams, comics, tabloids, academic writing, and radio programs (in Mordecai Richler's *roman-à-clef* of the Bronfman family, *Solomon Gursky Was Here*, 1989). At times, words and the paper they are written on are so foregrounded that passions seem "aroused less by [a lover's] charms than his stationery" (Wharton, p. 88).

Indeed, few Canadian novels adopt the "extreme revisionist and deconstructionist"[8] tendencies that are found in international postmodernism, while many channel their questions through well-established character types such as the maniacal collector or archivist whose overflowing library, stuffed filing cabinets, and boxes of specimens still do not guarantee the capture of reality or even a reliable record. For example, Urquhart's *Away* – a novel set against the background of the Irish potato famine and the resulting mass emigrations to North America – probes the insufficiency of classificatory systems through the practices of a pair of amateur naturalists, the Sedgewick brothers. Osbert and Granville signal their family resemblance to Walter Scott's obsessive antiquary and their distance from the natural environment by keeping "the strange, delicate life-forms that exist ... in the coastal tidepools" in an

---

8 Herb Wyile, *Speculative Fictions: Contemporary Canadian Novelists and the Writing of History* (Montreal and Kingston: McGill-Queen's University Press, 2002), p. 253.

aquarium until "these enigmatic creatures" turn into "putrid soup."[9] Marian Engel's *Bear* (1976) follows an opposite trajectory when Lou, an archivist from Toronto sent to catalogue the library of a nineteenth-century English settler on an island in Lake Huron, becomes obsessed with a wilderness creature. Here, in a feminized version of the Canadian wilderness myth, female sexual fantasy mingles with stories about bears scribbled on old scraps of paper and a vision of the Great Bear constellation.

Stereotypical Englishmen who conscientiously catalogue the world around them, but have difficulty understanding it, inhabit several of these novels: the painter Charles Gaunt in Vanderhaeghe's *The Last Crossing* (2002), a novel set in the nineteenth-century frontier country of the North American West, is one; the botanist Edward Byrne in Thomas Wharton's *Icefields* (1995), a story told against the backdrop of the Columbia Icefields in the Canadian Rockies, is another. Often these men are complemented by companions (some perhaps equally stereotypical) who teach them, or attempt to teach them, about the significance of the imagination. The Sedgewicks, for example, are contrasted with Moira (Mary O'Malley), for whom cabbages and teapots – washed ashore by the hundreds in "bands of colour" and "ribbons of glitter" – become magical objects, serving as passports to an "otherworld" (pp. 6, 8). After her emigration to Canada, she herself acquires a potent guide in Exodus Crow. In *The Last Crossing*, the mentors for these magic realms include Charles Gaunt's lover Lucy Stoveall, Métis guide Jerry Potts, and the *bote* or *berdache*, a "creature both male and female, yet more than either,"[10] who becomes Addington Gaunt's Native companion. The success of these encounters often hinges on the willingness of the "disciple" to be taught a new language. Lucy Stonewall despairs that she and Charles Gaunt will ever learn to communicate, because her idiom is "all knots to him that he can hardly pick apart" (p. 319).

The closeness of history and myth informs many of these novels, but the result is generally not to endorse either of them unconditionally. Commenting on Findley's *The Wars*, Ondaatje's *In the Skin of the Lion* and Hodgins's *The Invention of the World*, as well as *Away*, Herb Wyile sees them all as "resist[ing] the allure of myth as a retreat from history ... but without returning to history as a retreat from myth."[11] This mutually corrective function is significant because the postmodern aesthetic of these narratives, their "focus on play, on dissolving grand narratives and foundations, on deconstructing binary

---

9 Jane Urquhart, *Away* (Toronto: McClelland and Stewart, 1993), pp. 85.
10 Guy Vanderhaeghe, *The Last Crossing* (Toronto: McClelland and Stewart, 2002), p. 355.
11 Wylie, *Speculative Fictions*, p. 210.

oppositions, on transgression," can militate against the ethical requirement to "mak[e] moral judgements."[12] Although the ideological underpinnings of critics' objections can differ, Ondaatje's work in particular has been the focus of such criticism, because his typically ornate style and mythical plots draw so much attention to themselves that they can distract the reader from the seriousness of the questions implied in his material. Writing about "Marxism as an Ersatz Religion" in selected Canadian texts (1987), Christian Bök suggests that Ondaatje's *In the Skin of a Lion* (1987) "deploys ... serious, religious motifs in a way that reflects his own distance from the Marxist milieu, a distance that offers greater room in which to romanticize the mystical grandeur of proletarians who agitate for social reform."[13] He asserted throughout his career that his main project as a writer was to expose the seductions of fascism, but Timothy Findley's narratives play so knowledgeably with its aesthetic that, even as they proclaim to abhor it, they sometimes appear complicit in its goals.[14] Conversely, other critics have suggested that Findley's oeuvre is divided between an aesthetic that is postmodern and an ethic that is not.[15]

The question of what is "right" and "wrong" in these novels is an area where readers can be as vocal as the critics, and where critics may be so personally involved in the subject that they side with the readers. Is it ethical for writers to manipulate a history with which their audience is familiar and the details of which concern them personally? Of the authors under discussion it is perhaps Wayne Johnston who stirred up the most impassioned debate when he took liberties with the biography of Joe Smallwood, Premier of Newfoundland, but Susan Swan too had to defend her reinvention of Anna Swan against protest from her character's real-life descendants.[16] In the typical fashion of historical novelists, Johnston and Swan have responded to such criticism by providing disclaimers, some of them fanciful.[17] The controversy – involving other prominent natives of Newfoundland in Canadian public life

---

12 Jennifer L. Geddes, ed., "Introduction," in *Evil After Postmodernism: Histories, Narratives, and Ethics* (London and New York: Routledge, 2001), p. 2.
13 Christian Bök, "The Secular Opiate: Marxism as an Ersatz Religion in Three Canadian Texts," *Canadian Literature* 147 (Winter 1995), pp. 21f.
14 See Diana Brydon, *Writing on Trial: Timothy Findley's Famous Last Words* (Toronto: ECW, 1995), p. 77.
15 See Dagmar Krause, *Timothy Findley's Novels Between Ethics and Postmodernism* (Würzburg: Königshausen and Neumann, 2005).
16 See Susan Swan, "Preface," in *The Biggest Modern Woman of the World* (Toronto: Key Porter, 2001 [1983]), n. p.
17 At the end of his novel about American Arctic explorers Robert Peary and Frederick Cook, *The Navigator of New York* (Toronto: Knopf Canada, 2002), p. 484, Johnston inserts the following disclaimer: "This is a work of fiction. At times, it places real people in

such as Sandra Gwyn and Rex Murphy[18] – over Johnston's departure from established fact in Smallwood's life prompted the author to assert that his goal was "not factual accuracy but narrative and fictional plausibility," and that his intention was to write a "work of art that would express a felt, emotional truth that adherence to an often untrustworthy and inevitably incomplete historical record would have made impossible."[19] Some authors' dismissive view of "a culture that reveres realistic fiction" and their criticism of "readers [who are] constantly confusing the short stories of fiction with the nonfiction features" (Swan, n. p.) suggests, however, that these writers may not always have thought through the complex public expectations that come with the genre they have chosen.

Much of this fiction concentrates on uncovering the local histories that are often submerged in sweeping national narratives, such as the Winnipeg of the 1916 General Strike in Margaret Sweatman's *Fox* (1991) or the rural Nova Scotia of Swan's *The Biggest Modern Woman of the World*. In fact, a reader might acquire a detailed, historical understanding of Canadian communities and customs by reading these novels. The vivid evocation of the "horrific groaning reft with hysterical shrieks" produced by an ungreased Red River Cart, along with the picture of "York boats, ugly, cumbersome vessels propelled by sweeps and a square sail," are reason enough on their own to read painstakingly researched books like *The Last Crossing* (pp. 275, 281) or Michael Crummey's *River Thieves* (2001). Using the conventions of the adventure story enriched with precise details about the harsh life of seafaring and trapping in Newfoundland, Crummey's novel talks about the extinction of the Beothuk and develops an ingeniously plotted love story involving both actual and fictional characters from Newfoundland's history. Nearly extinct vocabularies, "a kind of taxidermy, words that were once muscle and sinew preserved in these single wooden postures," are revived in a narrative preoccupied with reading words and human beings or, more often, misreading them.[20]

Major cities like Toronto, too, have local stories buried below the official ones. Michael Redhill's *Consolation* (2006) interweaves the apothecary Jem Hallam's nineteenth-century narrative with the contemporary story of David Hollis, a "forensic geologist" with a particular interest in the untold histories of

> imaginary space and time. At others, imaginary people in real space and time. While it draws from the historical record, its purpose is not to answer historical questions or settle historical controversies."
>
> 18 See, for example, Sandra Gwyn, "Conjuring Smallwood: A New Novel Brilliantly Evokes an Era, If Not Its Main Protagonist," *Maclean's* 111.45 (November 9, 1998), p. 85.
> 19 Wayne Johnston, "Truth vs. Fiction," *The Globe and Mail* (November 23, 1998), p. D1.
> 20 Michael Crummey, *River Thieves* (Toronto: Doubleday Canada, 2001), n. p.

Toronto: "Squinting academics had stroked the John Graves Simcoe papers with cotton gloves (the city's founder! the holy grail!) and taken down every last *bon mot* muttered by him or any of his bucktoothed relations ... And yet, David had somehow ferretted out an unknown eyewitness with a story of early Toronto."[21] Hallam, an immigrant to Toronto, abandons his original profession to become a photographer, and Hollis's obsession (inherited by his widow Marianne) is to locate the photographic panorama of the city created by Hallam and his associates and lost in shipwreck.

In exploring the local, however, these novels also address its connections to the world at large and they often do so by updating traditional genres such as the picaresque novel, the travelogue, and the epistolary novel along with the fable and parable. An ambitious compendium of literary styles, *Solomon Gursky Was Here* (1989) is set against the vividly realized Montreal of a specific time and social class, especially Westmount (built on the grounds of what was once "an Indian burial ground"),[22] but periodically, the reader is reminded of world events framing this local milieu. Among these the Watergate scandal stands out because the tapes at its center – some erased, others not – suggest to the narrator the "[f]ragments. Tantalizing leads. Tapes, journals, trial transcripts" (p. 411) that both aid and obstruct his own investigation into the Gurskys' family history. In addition, the novel contains sweeping parodies of the Franklin Expedition (a historical episode obsessively revisited in Canadian writing), suggesting that one Ephraim Gursky avoided the lead poisoning that killed the crew of the *Erebus* and *Terror* by eating a diet of schmaltz herring and other "Jewish soul food" (p. 432). The parody incorporates the legend of the Wandering Jew and Aboriginal trickster narratives, braiding both into an ominous subplot of impending environmental disaster: fearing "another ice age" (p. 347), one of the Gurskys has a modern replica of Noah's Ark on standby.

Equally ambitious is Margaret Sweatman's *When Alice Lay Down With Peter* (2001), a family saga in which some characters "[don't] really believe in death"[23] and not in gender roles either. "You look like a girl," Alice McCormack says to her granddaughter Helen: "I never thought I'd see the day when a McCormack woman would go off wearing women's clothing" (p. 228). The story is told by Blondie McCormack, daughter of immigrants from the Orkneys, whose recollections embrace the Riel Rebellion, the Boer

21 Michael Redhill, *Consolation* (Toronto: Random House, 2006), p. 12.
22 Mordecai Richler, *Solomon Gursky Was Here* (Toronto: Penguin, 1989), p. 165.
23 Margaret Sweatman, *When Alice Lay Down With Peter* (Toronto: Alfred A. Knopf, 2001), p. 287.

War, the Sinking of the *Titanic*, the Great War, the Wall Street Crash, the Depression, the rise of fascism, the Second World War, and the Cold War. Based on the history of St. Norbert in Manitoba, the novel tries out various literary genres as it proceeds, including classical myth, the Old Testament ("that radical rag," p. 188), the picaresque novel, the ghost story, and agitprop theatre. There are also pastorals of the Red River landscape where "[t]he ash leaves sounded like water. They stood lopsided in a row. Under them, creamy blossoms of saskatoons and tiny buds of rose" (p. 165). Again and again, Sweatman's characters find themselves at the tragic junction of the local and the world. This connection comes into especially sharp focus in writing about Canadians and the First World War, a subject we examine in a separate chapter, which in its attention to a multitude of genres also illustrates that the subject is not restricted to fiction.

Although revisions of history became a particularly prominent subject from the 1980s onwards when feminism, multiculturalism and Aboriginal awareness made an indelible impression on Canadian literature, there are earlier works to be considered as well, on their own and in relation to the more recent ones. Prominent writers of the 1960s and 1970s, such as Margaret Laurence and Robert Kroetsch (born in 1926 and 1927 respectively), deplored that they had been brought up largely ignorant about their local history. In "Books That Mattered to Me," Laurence recalls her emotional response when she first read W. L. Morton's *Manitoba: A History* (1957), a book that finally taught her about her native province – a fine irony considering Morton's interpretation of Canadian history quoted earlier in this chapter.[24] Likewise, in "The Moment of the Discovery of America Continues," Kroetsch explains how the children of his generation were deprived of whole chapters of Canadian history. His questions about buffalo wallows and tipi rings, for example, remained unanswered and, though he was a Canadian of German descent, he was expected to recite the names of British kings and prime ministers. His response was to become a writer: "I responded to those discoveries of absence, to that invisibility, to that silence, by knowing I had to make up a story. Our story."[25] The writers who shared Kroetsch's desire to fill in such absences rewrote their past and that of their readers.

A substantial body of Canadian historical fiction published since the 1970s addresses the complexities of the country's colonial status. Margaret

---

24 Margaret Laurence, "Books That Mattered To Me," in *Margaret Laurence: An Appreciation*, ed. Christl Verduyn (Peterborough, ON: Broadview Press, 1988), p. 245.
25 Robert Kroetsch, *The Lovely Treachery of Words: Essays Selected and New* (Toronto: Oxford University Press, 1989), p. 2.

Laurence, Robert Kroetsch and Rudy Wiebe all perceive their own region, the Canadian prairies, as a social palimpsest composed by the different people who occupied it. While she lived in Africa during the 1950s, geographical distance gave Margaret Laurence the perspective to compare the effects of two forms of colonialism in two continents. Back in Canada, she applied her insights to the exploration of the Canadian past, especially in *The Diviners* (1974), the last of her five works set in Manawaka, an imaginary small town in Manitoba modeled after Laurence's hometown of Neepawa. Three retrospective devices assist the author in intertwining past and presence: old photographs, childhood scenes recalled or invented by the adult protagonist, and stories from Scottish and Métis backgrounds.

The Diviners bridges the gap between public and private history when Morag, who has a daughter with a Métis, looks for her family origins in Scotland but realizes that her country is Canada, where she was born, not the Scottish Highlands of her ancestors. Nevertheless, the theme of colonization connects the plight of the impoverished Scots Highlanders with that of the prairie Métis. The former were the victims of the Highland Clearances, which forced them to abandon their clans and emigrate. The Métis in turn became the victims of the Scottish settlement of the prairies, implemented at the expense of the Indigenous population. Those who were "once the prairie horse-lords" ended up compelled to live "in ramshackledom, belonging nowhere."[26]

Rudy Wiebe too has written fiction about the heritage of communities to which he belonged either by ancestry or by shared local geography. Reflecting on displacements in Europe and Canada, he recalls that in the eighteenth century his Mennonite ancestors had dispossessed the Ukrainians and the Cossacks when they settled on the steppes of the Ukraine. They had done the same again in the following century, when they "became the unwitting beneficiaries of violence that had been applied to suppress and dominate the aboriginal peoples" in southern Manitoba and the plains of Saskatchewan.[27] Objecting strongly to the derogatory portrayal of "Indians" in Canadian Depression novels, Wiebe describes Aboriginal peoples with empathy and respect, from *First and Vital Candle* (1966), a novel set in an Ojibwa community in northern Ontario, to *A Discovery of Strangers* (1994), where he creates the voice of a strong-willed Yellowknife woman, and *Stolen Life: The Journey of a*

---

26 Margaret Laurence, *The Fire-Dwellers* (London: Macmillan, 1969), p. 225.
27 Linda Hutcheon, "Interview with Rudy Wiebe," *Other Solitudes: Canadian Multicultural Fictions*, ed. Linda Hutcheon and Marion Richmond (Toronto: Oxford University Press, 1990), p. 84.

Cree Woman (1998), a memoir written in collaboration with Yvonne Johnson, Big Bear's great-great-granddaughter.

Wiebe adopts Native and Métis perspectives in *The Temptations of Big Bear* (1973) and *The Scorched-Wood People* (1977), set in the prairies between 1876 and 1888 and 1869 and 1885 respectively. The protagonist of *Temptations* is the Cree Chief Big Bear, whose suppressed story and silenced voice Wiebe is determined to recover. *The Scorched-Wood People* focuses on the Northwest Rebellion and its political and spiritual leader, Louis Riel, who is depicted not as a fanatical rebel, but as a wise prophet sacrificing himself for the cause of his people. Riel is contrasted with Sir John A. Macdonald, traditionally honored as founding father of the Confederation and one of Canada's longest serving Prime Ministers in Canadian history. In the novel, however, he is characterized as an utterly amoral politician.

A number of Wiebe's novels deal with the themes and settings of his Mennonite background. *Peace Shall Destroy Many* (1962) describes the challenge that the Second World War posed for pacifists. *The Blue Mountains of China* (1970) traces, over the course of a hundred years, the migrations of four Russian-born families that suffered religious persecution and were scattered all across the world. *My Lovely Enemy* (1983) is told from the perspective of a Mennonite historian who investigates the story of a defeated nineteenth-century Cree chieftain. The protagonist of *Sweeter Than All the World* (2001), another Mennonite searching for the meaning of life through the study of history, looks at his own ancestral history. His narrative covers five centuries, from the story of sixteenth-century Weynken Wybe (who was burned at the stake for her faith) to Elizabeth Katarina Wiebe's traumatic experiences in the Second World War. Sandra Birdsell's *The Russländer* (2001) also tells the traumatic story of Russian Mennonites and their mass migration in the 1920s, this time through the voice of an old immigrant woman. Katharine Vogt Heinrichs's story, recorded in a taped interview at an old people's home in Winnipeg, forms part of the Mennonite-heritage narrative.

Wiebe constantly blends past and present, often using circular constellations because he is convinced that history is cyclical as well as fragmentary and provisional. His narratives are full of gaps and abrupt changes, and they conceal information as much as they reveal it. Furthermore, he creates a tension between the written and the spoken word, illustrating how the former is given more credence than the oral. Despite his meticulous research, Wiebe insists that an accurate account is in fact impossible, since the act of recording necessarily implies a biased perspective. Like other writers of his generation, Wiebe rejects the notion that there is absolute truth in any single version of history. His religious faith, however, does lead him to believe in the possibility of Truth beyond human logic.

Like Wiebe, Robert Kroetsch turned to the prairies for material about the Canadian past, but he addressed the question of history differently. He explained the reasons for his "considerable disdain or distrust for history" by pointing out that its narrative "begins from meaning instead of discovering meanings along the way," whereas "myth dares to discover its way toward meanings."²⁸ Rejecting the vision of historians as limited and commending the Canadian fiction writers who undertake "the radical process of demythologizing the systems that threaten to define them," Kroetsch adopted the role of transgressive mythmaker.²⁹ Postmodernist and postcolonial theories underpin his burlesque rewriting of Old World myths both biblical and classical. For example, *The Studhorse Man* (1969), a novel set in Alberta at the end of the Second World War, is a parody of the Homeric and Virgilian quests.

Kroetsch parodies Ulysses's wanderings, because in spite of his admiration for *The Odyssey*, he wanted "to get free of it," "get loose," "re-tell the story," and "re-enact it in [his] own way."³⁰ In *Gone Indian* (1973), a self-conscious narrative about a mock hero who wants to emulate Grey Owl and be transformed into "the truest Indian of them all,"³¹ the author combines various myths (of origin, the Fall, western freedom) and then proceeds to strip them of their aura. *Badlands* (1975), about an expedition down the Red Deer River and into the Alberta Badlands in search of dinosaur skeletons, is a novel about paleontology and about two different views of the past, one seeing it as permanent and the other as vanishing. Kroetsch describes the mythic story of a prairie town called Big Indian in *What the Crow Said* (1978), and documents the writing of this novel in *The Crow Journals* (1980), where he also acknowledges the influence of Gabriel García Márquez's magic realism.

A similar relocation of Old World myths, this time with a feminist emphasis, is to be found in the novels of Aritha van Herk. Taking her models from the heroines of biblical and classical myth in *Judith* (1978), *The Tent Peg* (1981), and *No Fixed Address* (1986), she recontextualizes these figures in the lives of her contemporary protagonists: a prairie woman pig farmer (*Judith*), a cook on a mining expedition to the Far North (JL in *The Tent Peg*) and a traveling

---

28 Shirley Neuman and Robert Wilson, eds., *Labyrinths of Voice: Conversations with Robert Kroetsch* (Edmonton: NeWest Press, 1982), p. 133.
29 Robert Kroetsch, "Unhiding the Hidden: Recent Canadian Fiction" (1974), in *The Lovely Treachery of Words*, p. 58.
30 Donald Cameron, *Conversations with Canadian Novelists*, vol. I (Toronto: Macmillan, 1973), p. 91.
31 Robert Kroetsch, *Gone Indian* (Toronto: NeWest Press, 1973), p. 94.

saleswoman for ladies' underwear (Arachne in *No Fixed Address*). Combining a celebration of transgressive female energy with an exploration of prairie and northern space, she charts locations which are not only geographical but also cultural, historical, and imaginary, establishing a fictional cartography which blurs the boundaries between prairie realism and the dimensions of fantasy and myth.

Preoccupied with the ethics of recording history, Timothy Findley's self-reflexive play with history and myth covers a wide range of postmodern modes. All his works, from *The Last of the Crazy People* (1967) onwards, seek to rescue stories from oblivion in order to confront rather than efface the past. The narrator of *The Wars* (1977), a very skeptical historian, undertakes this difficult task by examining accounts and sifting through evidence, but he is forced to conclude at a crucial point that "[h]ere is where the mythology is muddled."[32] Looking at fascism and its sympathizers, *Famous Last Words* (1981) mixes real and fictional characters, including Hugh Selwyn Mauberley (from Ezra Pound's poem), Edward VIII, Wallis Simpson, and Adolf Hitler, and – in a fictional equivalent of Susan Sontag's essay "Fascinating Fascism" – raises disturbing questions about the seductiveness of totalitarianism.[33]

Truths and lies play an important role in the detective novel *The Telling of Lies* (1986), where the protagonist's incarceration in a Japanese prisoner of war camp in Java during the Second World War is recalled. The bombing of Hiroshima and Nagasaki haunts Findley's fiction, and images of nuclear warfare and ecological disaster pervade it. *Not Wanted on the Voyage* (1984), a parody of the Flood that anticipates Julian Barnes's sly variation of the myth in *History of the World in 10½ Chapters* (1989), is an expression of this apocalyptic vision. Noyes, wife of the patriarch Dr. Noyes (a man for whom the world is strictly divided into "No" and "Yes"), smuggles her blind cat Mottyl onto the ark and unsuccessfully attempts to do the same with a disabled child. The subordinates populating the lower decks find ways to rebel against Dr. Noyes's despotism, but the ending of the novel is ambiguous. Will this world be saved? Is this world worth saving?

A similar desire to challenge history centered on wealth and political power "from the lower decks" motivates Michael Ondaatje's fiction. In *The English Patient* (1992), the Second World War and its aftermath are viewed from the perspective of a random group of people in an abandoned Italian villa – a

---

32 Timothy Findley, *The Wars* (Toronto: Penguin, 1996 [1977]), p. 209.
33 Susan Sontag, "Fascinating Fascism," in *Under the Sign of Saturn* (New York: Farrar, Straus, and Giroux, 1980), pp. 73–105.

severely burned man, a nurse, a morphine addict, and a sapper – all of them psychologically or physically scarred. *In the Skin of a Lion* (1987) tells the story of immigrant workers in 1917 Toronto and draws inspiration from oral history, especially the interviews that Lillian Petroff conducted with the Macedonian bridge-builder Nicholas Temelcoff. Ondaatje deliberately avoided dwelling on the Asian community that had settled in the city because he wanted "to step away from a private story into a public one, a social one," thus avoiding "a personal saga."[34] This does not mean that he has failed to tell the story of Asians elsewhere in his works. The sapper in *The English Patient* is Sikh, *Anil's Ghost* (2000) talks about war-torn Sri Lanka, and Ondaatje's memoir *Running in the Family* (1982) is the "personal saga" of his family. But his preoccupation with neglected voices notwithstanding, Ondaatje has always resisted being slotted as the writer of a specific ethnic group. In its diversity, his oeuvre has resisted categorization and so perhaps inclusion into a new "master narrative," that of multiculturalism.

Mordecai Richler, by contrast, readily focused on the people of his own background, the European Jews who immigrated to urban Canada and their descendants. The inhabitants of the working-class St. Urbain Street neighborhood where he grew up provided the realistic elements for his satiric portraits of mid-twentieth-century Montreal Jewish life, which existed alongside the Roman Catholic francophones and the WASP (White Anglo Saxon Protestant) establishment. Both *Joshua Then and Now* (1980) and *Barney's Version* (1997) show a character's life against a vividly rendered contemporary panorama, starting from an underprivileged childhood in St. Urbain Street, young adulthood in Europe, marriage to a WASP woman, and the achievement of fame and fortune in Montreal. Prompted by middle-age crises, both characters uncover their past. Joshua Shapiro, the son of a gangster and a stripper, is only a boy when he learns about the Spanish Civil War, but he becomes so fascinated with it that Spain is the destination of the two most important journeys of his life. Reality and fantasy are humorously juxtaposed in many of Richler's works. He uses and abuses the Golem myth in *St. Urbain's Horseman* (1971), which casts the scoundrel Joey Hersh as the legendary avenger. Because of its caustic wit and intellectual boldness, Richler's writing has often been controversial. The Jewish community has objected to his irreverent depiction of Jewish life, particularly in *The Apprenticeship of Duddy Kravitz* (1959), and to his assertion that media attention has turned the Holocaust into

---

34 Linda Hutcheon, "Interview with Michael Ondaatje," in *Other Solitudes*, p. 199.

kitsch.³⁵ Likewise, his satiric and widely published attacks on Quebec nationalism, collected in *Oh Canada! Oh Quebec!: Requiem for a Divided Country* (1992), have bitterly provoked francophone Canadians.

The ravages of war have prompted many writers of Canadian historical fiction to fix their attention on individual ethnic groups affected by strife, but ethnicity is not their only focus. Daphne Marlatt looks at Japanese internment camps in Sumatra during the Second World War in *Taken* (1996), a novel which also talks about the Gulf War. Her main concern, however, are the women who have been excluded from history. "[W]omen's experiences of war – rape, famine, destruction of their families and homes – are often callously viewed as just 'collateral damage' in the grand heroic narrative of war," she has said,³⁶ and she has gone so far as to claim that "[t]he patriarchal oppression of women and colonialism are two different faces of the same coin."³⁷ Marlatt's lesbian feminism aims to revise the "great diorama of history" with a concept that respects women.³⁸ Marlatt conceived *Ana Historic* (1988) as "a woman's version of history"³⁹ that plays on the meaning of the Greek preposition "ana-," meaning "on, back, toward, throughout." Her book recounts the lives of three women: the autobiographical story of a contemporary narrator called Annie, that of her dead mother Ina, and that of an archival Mrs. Richards, who is identified as a "young and pretty widow" in Alan Morley's book *Vancouver: From Milltown to Metropolis* (1961).⁴⁰ While conducting research for her husband in the municipal archives of Vancouver, Annie discovers a number of gaps in the record and decides to use her imagination to fill them. For example, she invents the first name Ana for Mrs. Richards, gives her a life story as Vancouver's first school teacher and composes a fictitious diary on her behalf.

Marlatt's method of intertwining contemporary and historical narratives resembles Guy Vanderhaeghe's approach in *The Englishman's Boy* (1996). In 1952, the narrator of this novel, which is more strongly indebted to the realist

---

35 See Robert Fulford, "Seventy Years of Glorious Trouble" (obituary), *The National Post* (July 4, 2001), p. A1; Richler, "The Holocaust and After" (1966), reprinted in *Shovelling Trouble* (Toronto: McClelland and Stewart, 1972), pp. 84–96.
36 Sue Kossew, "History and Place: An Interview with Daphne Marlatt," *Canadian Literature* 178 (Autumn 2003), p. 54.
37 Janice Williamson, *Sounding Differences: Conversations with Seventeen Canadian Women Writers* (Toronto: University of Toronto Press, 1993), p. 191.
38 Daphne Marlatt, "Subverting the Heroic: Recent Feminist Writing on the West Coast," *British Columbia Reconsidered: Essays on Women* ed. Gillian Creese and Veronice Strong-Boag (Vancouver: Press Gang, 1992), p. 304.
39 George Bowering, "On Ana Historic: An Interview with Daphne Marlatt," *Line* 13 (1989), p. 98.
40 Alan Morley, *Vancouver: From Milltown to Metropolis* (Vancouver: Mitchell Press, 1961), p. 48.

tradition than the previous works discussed, connects two different settings: that of the 1873 massacre of the Assiniboine at Saskatchewan's Cypress Hills and that of the 1920s film industry of Hollywood. In the sequel, *The Last Crossing* (2002), Vanderhaeghe also examines popular myths of the Canadian Wild West, but here he sets them against Victorian England, concluding that the west was not as wild and anarchic as reported, and nineteenth-century Britain not as genteel and ordered. The apparently lawless frontiersmen turn out to be morally superior to their civilized counterparts, but both find themselves pre-judged by stereotypical convention. An English gentleman rapes and strangles a young girl, while an American horse-trader is falsely accused. Painstaking historical research goes into Vanderhaeghe's fiction, and his Master's degree in history has given him formal preparation for the task.

Like Vanderhaeghe, David Adams Richards has been reluctant to accept the label "regionalism" for his writing, though both authors have focused on specific Canadian regions, the Saskatchewan prairies and the Miramichi Valley respectively. Richards finds the designation condescending,[41] but "social realist regionalist" is nevertheless the description most frequently applied to his gritty depictions of social reality in New Brunswick.[42] The Miramichi Trilogy – *Nights Below Station Street* (1988), *Evening Snow Will Bring Such Peace* (1990), and *For Those Who Hunt the Wounded Down* (1993) – and works like *Mercy Among the Children* (2000) and *River of the Brokenhearted* (2003) give voice to inarticulate, uneducated, financially deprived and alienated characters whom the author always treats with love and respect. The details of human interaction in nameless rural communities of New Brunswick and a mill town (probably inspired by Richards's native Newcastle, formerly a prosperous shipping hub on the Miramichi River) are recorded with realistic precision. At the same time, these narratives transcend the small geographic space in which they are located. In a manner reminiscent of William Faulkner's Yoknapatawpha County, Richards evokes universal human struggles through the microcosm of the Miramichi world, and the region's harsh climate and barren landscape mirror the lives of working-class people and social outcasts whose existence is dominated by poverty, violence and despair.

The oppressive sense of failure that characterizes Richards's writing is softened into an elegiac tone in the work of one of his greatest admirers, Alistair MacLeod. Although MacLeod was born in Saskatchewan and spent

---

41 Andrew Garrod, "[Interview with] David Adams Richards," in *Speaking for Myself: Canadian Writers in Interview* (St. John's: Breakwater Press, 1986), p. 221.

42 Kathleen Scherf, "[Interview with] David Adams Richards: He Must Be a Social Realist Regionalist," *Studies in Canadian Literature* 15.1 (1990), pp. 154–70.

his childhood in Alberta, he later moved with his family to Nova Scotia, where their Gaelic-speaking forebears had settled in the eighteenth century. MacLeod has explored the human condition through a compelling portrait of the alienation and exile endured by the Canadian descendants of the Scottish immigrants who settled in Cape Breton and whose families have remained deeply attached to their Celtic origins. Communities of coal miners and fishermen disintegrate as the young migrate to distant cities in search of employment. The indifference of authorities both present and past is illustrated in his first novel, *No Great Mischief* (1999). The title comes from General James Wolfe's insistence that Highland soldiers be sent into the front lines of the Battle of the Plains of Abraham because there would be "no great mischief if they fell."[43]

Another Maritime author, Newfoundlander Wayne Johnston, looks at the determinist influence of landscape in his fiction, but his technique is more experimental than that of Richards and MacLeod. In his first three novels – *The Story of Bobby O'Malley* (1985), *The Time of Their Lives* (1987), and *The Divine Ryans* (1990) – he examines Newfoundland's history through the past of individual families, and he also chronicles three generations of his own family – fiercely opposed to Confederation with Canada – in the memoir *Baltimore's Mansion* (1999). But his acknowledged "first foray into historical fiction" was *Human Amusements* (1994), where he exchanged Newfoundland's isolated villages for 1960s Toronto, and investigated how a television program could turn a real man into a myth.[44] Out of that novel grew *The Colony of Unrequited Dreams* (1998), a fictional biography of the rise of Joseph R. "Joey" Smallwood (1900–91) from working-class underdog to first Premier of Newfoundland.

Johnston's interest in what he calls "ghost history" (the theme of Frost's poem "The Road Not Taken") pervades most of his work, which is haunted by glimpses of what might have been if, in the 1948 referendum, more Newfoundlanders had voted for independence rather than Confederation. His novels invoke Newfoundland's potential for nationhood as they emphasize its political, economic, and psychological colonization by Britain, the United States, and the rest of Canada. Drawing on the postmodern and postcolonial modes, Johnston intersperses Smallwood's first-person account, in *The Colony of Unrequited Dreams*, with excerpts from Fielding's *Condensed History of Newfoundland*, a satire that parodies D. W. Prowse's monumental *A History of Newfoundland* (1895). The journalist Shelagh Fielding becomes the

---

43 Laurie Kruk, "Alistair MacLeod: 'The World is Full of Exiles,'" in *The Voice is the Story: Conversations with Canadian Writers of Short Fiction* (Oakville: Mosaic, 2003), p. 160.
44 Wyile, "An Afterlife Endlessly Revised," p. 106.

protagonist of *The Custodian of Paradise* (2006), a novel relating the mysteries of Fielding's damaged past.

Fielding's obsession with the spectral figure of the Provider has its equivalent in the ghosts that haunt Ann-Marie MacDonald's Gothic *Fall on Your Knees* (1996) and its Cape Breton setting. This novel – replete with daughters abused by their fathers, unmarried mothers prevented from keeping their children, and other generational secrets – upsets conventional wisdom about families and nation building. Ann-Marie MacDonald has explained that she finds the inspiration for her stories in the collision between national myths of peaceful homogeneity on the one hand and multiracial conflict and linguistic tension on the other. At least seven different languages come into play in *Fall on Your Knees* where they serve as "[r]epositories of history."[45]

Ann-Marie MacDonald's use of Maritime Gothic parallels Barbara Gowdy's exploration of the weird world of southern Ontario Gothic, but Gowdy goes to greater extremes. Her gallery of bizarre characters includes a dysfunctional family in *Falling Angels* (1989), Siamese twins, a two-headed man who survives after committing a brutal self-decapitation, a female exhibitionist and a necrophiliac woman in the short-story collection *We So Seldom Look on Love* (1992), a nymphomaniac and a reincarnated brain-damaged baby confined to a closet in *Mister Sandman* (1995), and a self-deceiving child abductor who sees himself as a rescuer rather than as a predator in *Helpless* (2007). The latter, set in Toronto's Cabbagetown, is a bold exploration of pedophilia in a morally inconsistent society which condemns people for giving in to the temptations planted by the media. Gowdy examines a different type of infatuation in *The Romantic* (2003), where self-destructive Abel and passionate Louise enact a 1960s suburban version of the medieval love story of Abélard and Héloïse.

The mythology of Niagara Falls dominates Jane Urquhart's novel *The Whirlpool* (1986). The title refers to the swirling waters about a mile downstream from the falls, "the only part of the river which is entirely Canadian."[46] The whirlpool becomes a symbol of "a geography of fierce opposites. Order on one side and, nearer the water, sublime geological chaos" (p. 31). The book traces the personal histories of four daydreamers bound together by a magnetism that attracts them to this haunted space in the summer of 1889: a poet, a military historian, a lapsed housewife who admires Robert Browning's poetry, and finally the owner of a funeral home, who keeps a record of the nameless

---

45 Melanie Lee Lockhart, "'Taking Them to the Moon in a Station Wagon': An Interview with Ann-Marie MacDonald," *Canadian Review of American Studies* 35.2 (2005), p. 141. The interview was held in 1998.
46 Jane Urquhart, *The Whirlpool* (Toronto: McClelland and Stewart, 1986), p. 86.

"floaters" pulled from the river below the falls. She keeps their personal effects in numbered canvas sacks in the futile effort to make "some sense out of the chaos of the deaths around her" (p. 165).[47] The circular movement of the whirlpool conveys a visual image of how history works, staying "in one spot, moving nowhere and endlessly repeating itself" (p. 49).

Likewise, the title of *Away* (1993) points to its central trope, which evokes both the displacement of exiles and the experience of humans drawn into the realm of the supernatural. Mary O'Malley leaves Ireland during the potato famine and settles on an Ontario homestead. However, long before she left Rathlin Island, she was already "away" because her spirit was carried "off with the fairies" when a dead shipwrecked sailor cast a spell on her and became her "daemon lover" (p. 45). History, geography and myth are interwoven in the narrative. The historical account, which spans several generations of the O'Malley family, depicts the oppression that the Irish Catholics suffered in the Old and New Worlds, but the author avoids a chronicle of prejudice and exploitation and presents a multi-dimensional portrait of her ancestral past instead. Urquhart does not idealize her ethnic background. She points out, for example, that the Irish "brought the hate with them across all that ocean ... across all that water," so that the rivalries between Catholics and Protestants traveled from one continent to another (p. 198).

Urquhart pays "attention to marks made by previous human activity on the landscape" using her characteristic mythopoeic mode.[48] Her vivid depictions of Ontario contain frequent references to Ojibwa legends, such as the story of The Sleeping Giant, "the human-shaped peninsula of rock" on the north shore of Lake Superior, which is described at the beginning of *The Underpainter* (1997).[49] In *A Map of Glass* (2005), the erosion of historical memory is symbolized by a hotel that is buried beneath layers of sand.

Gowdy's and Urquhart's explorations of the past often have a sinister quality, but Jack Hodgins, who thinks that "[e]very story is an experiment in magic,"[50] entertains readers with the interplay of the material and the spiritual. The grotesque extravagance of his characters may be serious or comic, but they are never menacing. Judging from his fiction, British Columbia's beauty and mild climate have tinged the literature of this province with optimism.

---

47 Urquhart draws on the "little floaters book" kept by the grandmother of her husband, artist Tony Urquhart.
48 Herb Wyile, "Confessions of a Historical Geographer: Jane Urquhart," in *Speaking in the Past Tense*, p. 100.
49 Jane Urquhart, *The Underpainter* (Toronto: McClelland and Stewart, 1997), p. 2.
50 Jack Hodgins, "An Experiment in Magic," in *Transitions II: Short Fiction, a Source Book of Canadian Literature*, ed. Edward Peck (Vancouver: CommCept, 1978), p. 238.

"Ghost stories": fictions of history and myth

Hodgins's works, inspired by anecdotes and tall tales from his farming and logging community in the Comox Valley and by the oral traditions of his Irish ancestry, assume that people (authors, readers, and characters alike) can shape history, but are themselves shaped by geography that is both real and imagined.

The title of his first novel, *The Invention of the World* (1977), suggests that the world has been invented rather than created. In this parodic narrative, the oral historian and geographer Strabo Becker tries (but fails) to compile the "true" history of Vancouver Island by combining factual knowledge with legend, in telling the story of the community of "The Revelations Colony of Truth." Its mythic founder is Donal Keneally, an Irish messiah said to have been conceived in the union of a peasant girl with "a monstrous black bull."[51] Keneally's origins are a mix of biblical, classical, and Celtic myths, but as a mock hero and false savior he casts doubt on all of them. This skepticism also informs Hodgins's later books, *The Resurrection of Joseph Bourne* (1979) and *Broken Ground* (1998).

In 1996, Margaret Atwood delivered the annual Charles R. Bronfman Lecture in Canadian Studies at the University of Ottawa. Drawing on her experience of writing *Alias Grace*, she talked about the writing of historical fiction from the perspective of someone who had experienced personally how Canadian history had once been taught in the nation's schools. "The main idea behind the way we were taught Canadian history seemed to be reassurance," she asserted, "as a country, we'd had our little differences, and a few embarrassing moments – the Rebellion of 1837, the hanging of Louis Riel, and so forth – but these had just been unseemly burps in one long gentle after-dinner nap. We were always being told that Canada had come of age."[52] Atwood's formulation is polemic and therefore selective, but her novel along with others discussed in this chapter has gone a long way towards confronting the inequities and stirring readers out of their reassurance.

---

51 Jack Hodgins, *The Invention of the World* (Toronto: Macmillan, 1977), p. 71.
52 Atwood, *In Search of Alias Grace*, p. 19.

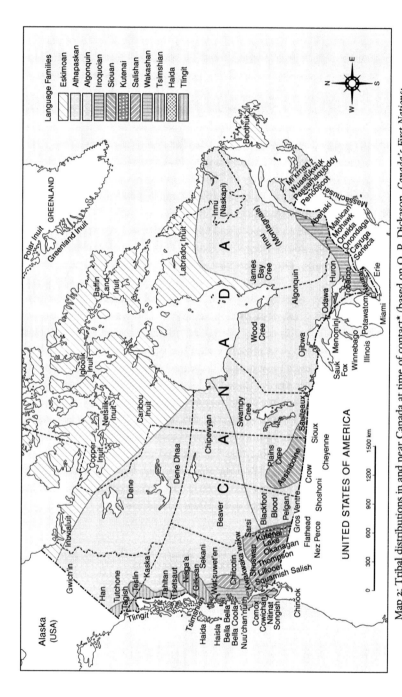

Map 2: Tribal distributions in and near Canada at time of contact* (based on O. P. Dickason, *Canada's First Nations: A History of Founding Peoples from Earliest Times*, 3rd edn. [Oxford: Oxford University Press, 2002] p. 47)

* Various different spellings of Native tribal groups and place-names are currently in use.

25

Indigenous writing: poetry and prose

LALLY GRAUER AND ARMAND GARNET RUFFO

Describing her first encounters with contemporary Indigenous literature in the late 1960s and early 1970s, Okanagan writer and educator Jeannette Armstrong remembers listening to Duke Redbird read his poems on CBC radio, or hunting through Indian newspapers to search out poems "scattered like gems" in their pages. To her, these works reflected "[n]ot unrequited love and romance, not longing for motherland, not taming the wilderness nor pastoral beauty ... nor placing the immigrant self," standard themes of Canadian literary criticism at the time, but rather "our own collective colonized heritage of loss, pain, anger and resistance, and of our pride and identity as Native."[1] Armstrong defines the early stages of a literature in Canada which is not synonymous with Canadian literature, although it has developed side by side with other contemporary Canadian writing.

In saying what Indigenous literature in the 1970s was not, she implies particular relationships to self and community, history and political power, land and story. Her comments also evoke a heady time of protest, of Black and Chicano pride imported from south of the border, and of an intense search for cultural alternatives – taken on by both Indigenous and non-Indigenous Canadians – towards a white, Anglo-Saxon, middle-class society that often saw its own assumptions as universal, or, if it acknowledged difference, as superior. Since then, Canadian literature has branched into many literatures, forms and perspectives. Contributing its own richness, Indigenous literature has also flourished, yet it remains inextricably involved with survival. It addresses Canadian readers of all backgrounds, exposing profound and subtle effects of colonialism and offering alternative points of view.

---

[1] Jeannette C. Armstrong, "Four Decades: An Anthology of Canadian Native Poetry from 1960 to 2000," in *Native Poetry in Canada: A Contemporary Anthology*, ed. Jeannette C. Armstrong and Lally Grauer (Peterborough: Broadview, 2001), pp. xviii, xvi–xvii.

Some writers assert Indigenous identities to protect and insure the continuity of cultures – cultures often regarded as obstacles in the way of perceived national and global economic interests – or they write to disturb the complacency and comfortable entitlement of individuals who ignore the continuing oppression of Indigenous peoples in Canada. At the same time, this writing is engaged in the process of redefining literature, undoing the reductive representations that obstruct any understanding of Indigenous ways of being and knowing, and inventing forms to accommodate perspectives which are complex, varied, traditional, and changing. Plains Cree Métis writer and scholar Emma LaRocque challenges readers to respond when she asks, "Here are our voices – who will hear?"[2]

Renewal

The 1970s became a period of extraordinary growth and renewal for Indigenous literature in Canada partly because changing conditions made it easier for authors to get into print. In 1969, Pierre Trudeau's White Paper proposing an end to Indian status, purportedly in the interests of a "just society," sparked a protest movement of pan-Indian nationalism fueled by Cree organizer Harold Cardinal's dissection of "extermination through assimilation" in *The Unjust Society* (1969).[3] The controversy reached a changing population. Second World War veterans who had experienced a sense of equality in the military were once again subjected to paternalism and discrimination on the home front and began to organize and assert Indigenous rights. Residential schooling, which contributed a legacy of abuse and alienation, also produced educated individuals who became leaders in the development of regional and national politics. Enfranchisement but also poverty brought growing numbers of people from reserves and isolated communities to cities. While they continued to be marginalized in urban centers, some graduated from colleges and universities, and English was becoming a common language.

A consequence of the immediate and widespread rejection of the White Paper was the development of journalism. Following the fiasco of their proposed new Indian policy, the Canadian government made some attempts to accommodate Indigenous peoples. Stable government funding was acquired by national organizations such as the National Indian Brotherhood,

---

[2] Emma LaRocque, "Preface," in *Writing the Circle: Native Women of Western Canada*, ed. Jeanne Perreault and Sylvia Vance (Edmonton: NeWest, 1990), p. xv.
[3] Harold Cardinal, *The Unjust Society: The Tragedy of Canada's Indians* (Edmonton: Hurtig, 1969), p. 1.

the Native Council of Canada, the Native Women's Association of Canada, and Friendship Centres newly established across the country. They began to finance regular publications which became vehicles and catalysts not only for political writers, but also for authors of poetry, fiction, and memoirs.

Most contributors to these newspapers reached an Indigenous audience that had not seen itself in Canadian literature. By the end of the 1970s, poets such as Chief Dan George, Rita Joe, Duke Redbird, and Wayne Keon had their own books published by small presses and the loss, pain, resistance, and pride Armstrong describes is evident in their work, manifesting itself in diverse forms and literary expressions. Chief Dan George envisioned Canada's Centenary in 1967 as a day of mourning for Indigenous people in his famous piece of oratory, "A Lament for Confederation," delivered at the Empire Stadium in Vancouver and reprinted in many Indian newspapers. In his poem "Words to a Grandchild," included in his collection *My Heart Soars* (1974), George quietly affirms Indigenous identity, asking that his hearer value "the silent ways," understand the meaning of a non-materialist culture, and be attentive to the land and the forces of nature around him.[4]

Taken together, these works demonstrate an ambivalence about the potential to come to terms with Canadian society. In his oration on Confederation, George turned his lament into a hopeful vision for the future, in which his people grasp and turn the tools of the "white man's success," such as education, to the betterment of Indigenous people in a land shared with Canadian society, "*our* great land."[5] "Words to a Grandchild," however, articulates an alienation between different cultures and ways of life: "Our ways are good / but only in our world." The "white man" occupies another world, where the grandchild "will walk like a stranger." Dan George was a logger and longshoreman, and Chief of the Sleil Waututh First Nation of Burrard Inlet. He became a successful actor after an injury at work and in 1972 received honorary degrees from Simon Fraser University and the University of Brandon. Nevertheless, his writing implies a continuing experience of colonialism.

If "Words to a Grandchild" counsels a thoughtful distance from Canadian society, Wayne Keon's poetry playfully engages in cultural mix as a way of enabling Indigenous writing. Keon, an Ojibwa who grew up in Elliott Lake near Sudbury, Ontario, published one of the first anthologies of Indigenous poetry, *Sweetgrass* (1972), as well as three works of poetry in the 1990s. In his

---

4 Chief Dan George, *My Heart Soars* (Saanichton: Hancock House, 1974), pp. 13–22.
5 Chief Dan George, "A Lament for Confederation," *TAWOW* 2.1 (Spring 1971), pp. 10–11. Emphasis added. Reprinted in Armstrong and Grauer, eds., *Native Poetry in Canada*, pp. 2–3. TAWOW is a salutation in Plains Cree language which literally means "there's room."

early poem "an opun letr tu bill bissett," Keon refers, in both form and content, to a debt to poet bill bissett: "deer bill / i don't think / i evr met yu ... i used sum of / yr lines."[6] Keon adapts to his own style bissett's strategy of idiosyncratic spelling which, among other things, works to contest boundaries between the spoken and written word as well as between language and visual image.[7] Introducing elements of oral storytelling, chanting and ritual, and contemporary pictograph into his own writing, Keon communicates an exuberant counter-cultural creativity that thumbs its nose at the hierarchy of purity and correctness implied by standard English.

Post *Halfbreed*

Poetry was the vehicle many early Indigenous writers used to approach literary writing, with its connection to the spoken voice and its flexibility of language and form. It provided a popular form for protest and expression for many influenced by the songs of artists such as Buffy Sainte Marie. Writers whose lives were transient or who struggled to survive could write poetry without taking the extended blocks of time needed for a novel or a play. Rita Joe, a Mi'kmaq from Nova Scotia, recalls beginning to write poetry "two lines, now and then" in 1969, publishing her first work, *Poems of Rita Joe*, in 1978[8] and two more collections of poetry in 1988 and 1991. However, it was an autobiography, Maria Campbell's *Halfbreed* (1973), which profoundly influenced writers in the following decades. Published alongside other memoirs which brought a range of experience to the page, from a traditional life on the land as in John Tetso's *Trapping Is My Life* (1970) to the dislocation caused by residential school recorded by Jane Willis in *Geniesh: An Indian Girlhood* (1973), *Halfbreed*'s strong protest against the dispersal and persecution of the Red River Métis struck a chord with readers in an era of political activism and protest against the war in Vietnam. Her story reframed Canada as a site of rebellion, not just reform. It spoke out about a history of racism that challenged a complacent belief in a tolerant society, and associated the word "halfbreed" with pride rather than shame. Campbell's account of her own personal history and Scottish-Cree-Métis family network both affirmed the identity of the Red River Métis

---

6 Originally printed in *Sweetgrass*, ed. Wayne, Orville and Ronald Keon (Elliot Lake, ON: W. O. K. Books, 1972); reprinted in Armstrong and Grauer, eds., *Native Poetry in Canada*, p. 86.
7 This includes the lower case spelling of his own name.
8 Armstrong and Grauer, eds., *Native Poetry in Canada*, p. 13.

and at the same time exposed how government regulations colluded in fixing identities using categories of "Indian," "halfbreed," and "white."

Telling the story of her people forced to the margins of Canadian society, onto the edges of road lines and crown lands in Saskatchewan which gave them the name of "Road Allowance People,"[9] Campbell was now speaking out through a mainstream press, McClelland and Stewart. Her work represented a powerful breakthrough that encouraged other writers. Delaware poet and playwright Daniel David Moses has called her "The Mother of Us All,"[10] and Métis poet Gregory Scofield refers to her as his "Mom Maria" in his autobiography, *Thunder Through My Veins* (1999). Métis/Saulteaux scholar Janice Acoose points to the importance of Campbell's portrayal of Métis and Indian women, especially the grandmother figure of Cheechum, as "resourceful and dynamic," undoing stereotypes encountered in Canadian literature of "squaw drudge, Indian princess and suffering victim."[11]

Writing itself was a political act for many authors in the 1970s and 1980s who began to break down a wall of silence constructed by racism, poverty, shame, and fear. Writers were often themselves activists. Campbell's *Halfbreed* told of her own development as an organizer. Lee Maracle, of Cree and Salish ancestry, spoke in her early autobiography *Bobbi Lee: Indian Rebel* (1975) about coming to political consciousness through working with migrant laborers in the orchards of British Columbia and on the inner-city streets of Vancouver and Toronto. Others employed autobiography, fictional autobiography, polemic, satire, and humor to challenge, persuade, and entertain their readers, as in Odawa author Wilfred Pelletier's *No Foreign Land* (1973), Métis author Howard Adams's *Prison of Grass: Canada from the Native Point of View* (1975), Ojibwa author Basil Johnston's *Moose Meat and Wild Rice* (1978) and Cree author Joseph F. Dion's *My Tribe, The Crees* (1979). Like Campbell and Maracle, who fostered Indigenous writing through teaching and workshops, these writers were also activists and teachers who used their writing as political tools.

Alongside the growth of writing, issues of control and autonomy emerged. Writers of the 1980s looked for alternative methods of collaboration and publishing as misrepresentation by non-Indigenous authors and publishers

---

9 Maria Campbell, *Halfbreed* (Toronto: McClelland and Stewart, 1973), p. 13.
10 As reported by Lenore Keeshig-Tobias, Interview, in *Contemporary Challenges: Conversations with Canadian Native Authors*, ed. Hartmut Lutz (Saskatoon: Fifth House, 1991), p. 83.
11 Janice Acoose, "Campbell: An Indigenous Perspective," in *Looking at the Words of Our People: First Nations Analysis of Literature*, ed. Jeannette Armstrong (Penticton: Theytus Books, 1993), p. 141.

came under scrutiny. For example, the anthology *Many Voices: An Anthology of Contemporary Canadian Indian Poetry* (1977), edited by Marilyn Bowering and David Day, included non-Indigenous poets writing "Indian poetry." An important section of *Halfbreed* was left out of the final printed form by McClelland and Stewart, according to Campbell.[12] Lee Maracle's *Bobbi Lee: Indian Rebel* was initially published under the name of her collaborator Don Barnett, who taped and edited it.[13] Partly in response to such problems, Indigenous presses were established in the early 1980s which then published the majority of contemporary writers throughout the 1990s and into 2000. Pemmican Publications was founded in Winnipeg in 1980 (with a mandate to give Métis writers an outlet). That same year Randy Fred established Theytus Books in Nanaimo, BC, and two years later moved it to Penticton, where it was bought by the Okanagan Indian Educational Resources Society. Both presses were important to the publishing of the first modern novels by Indigenous writers in Canada.

First novels

In Search of April Raintree, published by Pemmican in 1983, was written by Beatrice Culleton, a Métis who had grown up in foster homes in or near Winnipeg.[14] Her work, first drafted in 1981 in response to the suicide of her sister, becomes a device for reimagining her own experience and identity. Culleton has described the process as a way to "rethink the way I've been living. Kind of blind … But while I was writing that's what I realized about myself: that I had to accept my identity …"[15] Culleton's story about two sisters sent to different foster homes, one who attempts to assimilate as white (April) and the other who embraces her Native roots (Cheryl), was at first celebrated for its raw authenticity.[16] It has remained a much-read, contemporary classic; a critical edition was reissued by Peguis Publishers in 1999. More recent literary critics examine the ways in which the novel complicates identity, reading Culleton's two sister protagonists not simply as opposites, but as "permeable

---

12 Maria Campbell, Interview, in Lutz, ed., *Contemporary Challenges*, p. 42.
13 An expanded, revised edition was published by Women's Press (Toronto) in 1990.
14 Culleton later resumed her family name Mosionier and published later works, including the revised critical edition of *In Search of April Raintree*, under the name Beatrice Culleton Mosionier.
15 Beatrice Culleton, Interview, in Lutz, ed., *Contemporary Challenges*, p. 98.
16 See for example, Armin Wiebe's review in *Prairie Fire* 4.5 (July–August 1983), pp. 49–51.

and melded selves,"[17] and acknowledging the author's recognition of the role of racism in the construction of Indigeneity.[18]

In the novel *Slash*, published by Theytus Press in 1985, Jeannette Armstrong focuses on the identity of a people rather than of an individual, responding to a need felt by the Okanagan people in Penticton to convey the history of the militant movement of the 1960s and 1970s to the youth in her community. The novel communicates not only a contemporary history of the effects of colonialism in the Okanagan, but also an Indigenous perspective on the resistance to it, both local and cross-border. The work also suggests that resistance through activism is not sufficient to ensure the continuation of Indigenous peoples and cultures in Canada. Through a narrative that dramatizes learning, the young male protagonist, Slash, realizes the importance of Aboriginal rights as different from democratic rights and begins to understand his people's long history of connection to the land as a source of power and ethics.

Inspired and encouraged by Beatrice Culleton, Ojibwa writer Ruby Slipperjack published *Honour the Sun* with Pemmican in 1987,[19] taking fiction in a new direction through her development of narration and point-of-view. Slipperjack takes the reader inside the mind of a young girl named Owl, who lives in a small Ojibwa community established alongside CN railway lines in northern Ontario. She describes Owl's moment-to-moment observations and emotions, whether admiring the shape of a tree branch in the water or interpreting the look on her mother's face. However, the book remains reticent about other parts of Owl's life, such as her time in residential school or her mother's struggle with alcoholism. Slipperjack's use of indirection, gaps and silences have been variously interpreted as a way of writing mainly for an informed Indigenous reader rather than a non-Native reader,[20] or as a way of inscribing a cultural form of communication in which silence can both speak and leave things unsaid. Slipperjack has talked about how in her own Ojibwa community, "[w]ords are very, very rare." Similarly, in Owl's family and community "[t]here are some things ... like [facial] expressions, like a shrug of a shoulder, that can mean so much. How do you put that into

---

17 Helen Hoy, *How Should I Read These? Native Women Writers in Canada* (Toronto: University of Toronto Press, 2001), p 93
18 Margery Fee, "Deploying Identity in the Face of Racism," *In Search of April Raintree* by Beatrice Culleton Mosionier, critical edition (Winnipeg: Peguis, 1999), pp. 211–26.
19 Jennifer David, ed., *Story Keepers: Conversations with Aboriginal Writers* (Owen Sound: Ningwakwe Learning Press, 2004), p. 27.
20 See Thomas King, "Godzilla vs. Post-Colonial," *World Literature Written in English* 30.2 (1990), pp. 10–16.

writing, and in another language too?"²¹ Slipperjack's second novel, *Silent Words* (1992), continues to work with these narrative issues

Recovering cultures

In both *Halfbreed* and *Slash*, the recovery of cultures and traditions is shown to be important to individual characters and to communities. A similar perspective in eastern Canada connected the recovery of culture to the vitality of Indigenous literature. In 1986 in Ontario, Cree playwright (and later novelist) Tomson Highway, Ojibwa poet and storyteller Lenore Keeshig-Tobias, and Delaware poet and playwright Daniel David Moses formed "The Committee to Re-Establish the Trickster," dedicated, as Moses later put it, "to the idea that the Trickster is emblematic of our different world view and the different literature connected to it." Their discussions reverberated in mythic and comic theater and writing, what Moses calls a recognition of "the funny" and "the strange," noting that both cultural differences and resemblances were important to the group.[22] For Highway, the paradoxical Cree trickster is hero and god, animal and human, "a bolt of electricity – like a poke in the bum – that is basically ... hysterically funny."[23] Not restricted to either male or female gender, the trickster circulates in Highway's plays to subvert the patriarchal grip of government and Church on Indigenous communities. Highway's novel and fictional autobiography *Kiss of the Fur Queen* (1998) revolves around the magical figures of the fox and the fur queen in their many disguises as it tells the story of the brothers Jeremiah and Gabriel Okimasis, born to a nomadic Cree family in northern Manitoba, and their transformations into dancer and writer.

When Daniel David Moses reminisces about the trickster, he underlines that he had to relearn Indigenous cultural traditions. Growing up on the Six Nations reserve in southern Ontario in the 1950s and 1960s, Moses experienced a range of cultural influences, including Christian, Longhouse, or Iroquoian traditional spiritual and political systems, and his Delaware heritage. He recalls his education as providing him with "a western mind," and he sees his writing as "'growing up'" when it developed from the lyric poetry of *Delicate Bodies* (1980) to his ghost-haunted, multi-dimensional plays such as *Coyote City* (1990,

---

21 Ruby Slipperjack, Interview, in Lutz, ed., *Contemporary Challenges*, pp. 212, 206.
22 Daniel David Moses, "The Trickster's Laugh: My Meeting with Tomson and Lenore," *American Indian Quarterly* 28.1/2 (2004), pp. 109, 110.
23 Noah Richler, *This Is My Country, What's Yours? A Literary Atlas of Canada* (Toronto: McClelland and Stewart, 2006), p. 132.

produced in 1988) and *The Indian Medicine Shows* (1995, produced in 1996).[24] His second poetry collection, *The White Line* (1990), combines ironic, postmodern, and trickster-inspired play with the surreal, using symbol and dream.

The word "rediscovery" can also suggest reinvention through new creative forms and contexts. One of these contexts was the university. Educated writers with strong roots in their communities such as Jeannette Armstrong, Tomson Highway, and Daniel David Moses were joined by a number of others in the 1990s, such as Armand Garnet Ruffo, Thomas King, Louise Halfe, Marilyn Dumont, and Marie Annharte Baker. Circulating writing and ideas within North American literature, international literature, and the postcolonial and postmodern movements, these writers and others embraced new approaches and strategies. An Indigenous post-secondary institution was also established. In 1989, Jeannette Armstrong, Lee Maracle, and others founded the En'owkin International School of Writing, Canada's only creative writing program led by and designed for Indigenous people. It has since expanded, under the directorship of Armstrong, to include Indigenous studies, fine arts, and language teaching, while establishing joint programs with the Universities of Victoria and British Columbia. During the 1990s many Native authors from across the country passed through the doors of the En'owkin Centre as teachers or students, contributing to a national network.

Educating audiences

Published by small presses, the work of many writers of the 1970s and 1980s had been limited in distribution and readership. In her preface to the anthology *Writing the Circle: Native Women of Western Canada* (1990), Emma LaRoque suggests some of the reasons for this state of affairs, pointing out that "[l]inguistic, cultural, geographic and social distances fostered by colonial forces prevented the development of a broadly based Native intellectual community," while, at the same time, many academics in mainstream universities still turned to non-Indigenous writing about Native subjects, putting Indigenous scholars in the position of "having to educate" audiences "before we could even begin dialoguing with them!"[25] Compiling anthologies in the 1980s and early 1990s was part of that education. Penny Petrone, a scholar at Lakehead University, published the groundbreaking, *First People, First Voices* in

---

24 "Daniel David Moses," *An Anthology of Canadian Native Literature in English*, 3rd edn., ed. Daniel David Moses and Terry Goldie (Toronto: Oxford University Press, 2005), p. 355.
25 LaRocque, *Writing the Circle*, p. xxii.

1983 (followed by *Northern Voices* on Inuit writing in 1988 and *Native Literature in Canada: From the Oral Tradition to the Present* in 1990), while other anthologies providing inside perspectives also appeared. Maria Campbell published *Achimoona* (1985), from her writing workshops, and Theytus in collaboration with the En'owkin Centre published *Seventh Generation* edited by Heather Hodgson (1989), focusing primarily on a new generation of poets.

In the 1990s, two important kinds of anthologies brought Indigenous writing to broader audiences and helped stimulate new writing. *All My Relations* (1990), edited by Thomas King, a writer and scholar of Cherokee and Greek heritage, collected stories published in the late 1980s presenting a range of styles and perspectives by such writers as Basil Johnston (Ojibwa), Beth Brant (Mohawk), Harry Robinson (Okanagan), and Ruby Slipperjack which reached an enthusiastic mainstream and academic audience.[26] In August of 1990, Theytus Books published *Gatherings: The En'owkin Journal of First North American Peoples* under the guidance of Opsakwayak Cree publisher Greg Young-Ing. *Gatherings* employed a policy of inclusiveness to promote writing in Native communities, featuring the work of children and Elders, as well as published authors and scholars. An issue of *Gatherings* edited by Jeannette Armstrong entitled *Looking At the Words of Our People: A First Nations Analysis of Literature* (1993) became the first collection of literary criticism devoted to writing by and about Indigenous peoples. Among others, it was followed by *(Ad)dressing Our Words: Aboriginal Perspectives on Aboriginal Literatures* (2001), edited by Armand Garnet Ruffo.

Voice on the page

Indigenous literature is intimately linked to knowing and rediscovering oral traditions, which include a vast body of poetry, narrative, and drama. These traditions communicate an inherently sacred worldview in which humankind and the natural world are integrated into a holistic relationship based on kinship, beginning in pre-settlement times and including many post-settlement narratives: stories written down by recorders, as in the Cree stories collected by James Stevens and Haida stories reinterpreted by Robert Bringhurst; stories put into writing by Indigenous authors with collaborators; those written down by Native writers like Basil Johnston, George Blondin (Dene), Louis Bird (Cree); or transformed into film, as in the Inuit feature

---

26 King had already published many of the works in the anthology in a special issue of the literary journal *Canadian Fiction Magazine* 60 (1987).

film *Atanarjuat: The Fast Runner* (2000). These stories participate in ongoing traditions not by reproducing word-for-word accuracy but by transmitting ethics through the recurrence of certain key elements that reflect a philosophy while passing on practical knowledge of customs, habitat changes, mapping, and land uses. The multiple functions of Indigenous storytelling have been recognized in the Mackenzie Valley Pipeline Inquiry (the Berger Inquiry) in the mid-1970s, the Royal Commission on Aboriginal Peoples in the early 1990s, and the Delgamuukw decision of 1997 when the Supreme Court of Canada ruled for the first time that the concept of Aboriginal title existed. The use of oral storytelling in this and other land claims underscores the significance of ongoing oral traditions.

Oral traditions are not only defined by characteristic genres but by appropriate contexts and protocols. For the Ojibwa, sacred stories are reserved for telling at night in winter (but not for the Okanagan, for example). Certain stories have power and are seen as owned by particular persons or families. Sometimes individuals are chosen to inherit stories but storytellers may choose to whom they will pass on their stories. To retell or use a story requires permission which may be easily given or be earned through respectful service or the payment of gifts. Writers who do not understand the existence of a set of rules different from their own have sometimes complained that not being able to use a story implies censorship. In 1990, when Ojibwa storyteller Lenore Keeshig-Tobias spoke out at national academic conferences and wrote in *The Globe and Mail* against "stealing native stories," she used the example of the film *Where the Spirit Lives* (1989), about a young girl taken to residential school and her struggle to maintain her culture. Keeshig-Tobias's main concern is the assumption by non-Indigenous filmmakers that it was their story to tell. She points out the colonial context of inequality in which appropriation takes place, and condemns the way Native stories are misinterpreted, marketed, and consumed by mainstream writers and media with little or no commitment to Indigenous communities.[27] Maria Campbell has written about the appropriation of her own life stories in *The Book of Jessica* (1990), which she co-authored with Linda Griffiths.[28] A respectful approach to storytelling is one of the themes Thomas King takes up in his Massey lectures published in *The Truth About Stories: A Native Narrative* (2003).

---

27 Lenore Keeshig-Tobias, "Stop Stealing Native Stories," *The Globe and Mail* (January 26, 1990), p. A7; Interview, in Lutz, ed., *Contemporary Challenges*, p. 82.
28 See also Maria Campbell, "Introduction," in *Stories of the Road Allowance People* (Penticton: Theytus, 1995).

Indigenous stories have also been misunderstood or misinterpreted by popularizers and scholars. Following a history of oral stories collected and translated into English by missionaries, anthropologists, and writers, James Stevens's *Sacred Legends of the Sandy Lake Cree* (with illustrations by Cree artist Carl Ray) first appeared in 1971, but was revised as *Sacred Legends* in a 1995 edition that gave equal credit to Ray. Harry Robinson's stories, *Write It On Your Heart: The Epic World of an Okanagan Storyteller* (1989) brought something new to the process. In transcribing the stories, culled from over a decade of visits and recording sessions with Robinson, musicologist Wendy Wickwire attempts to reproduce on paper the *sound* of Robinson's stories. Fidelity to Robinson's characteristic diction and syntax and laying out words on the page using shortened lines and blank space to signal pauses for breath or emphasis were some of Wickwire's methods of conveying Robinson's style and tone. Thomas King has acknowledged Robinson's important influence on his construction of voice in the short story collection *One Good Story, That One* (1993) and in *Green Grass, Running Water* (1993).[29]

For Maria Campbell, writing in the 1980s, English sounded spiritless, like "lecturing."[30] In *Stories of the Road Allowance People* (1995) she moves out of the standard English of *Halfbreed*, telling stories in Cree-influenced and French-inflected English, "the dialect and rhythm of my village and my father's generation." She spent hours listening to "old men's stories," which she paid for not only in offerings of blankets and tobacco, but "by re-learning and re-thinking my language."[31] Campbell sees herself not as an author, but as a translator, mediating between cultures. Beautifully illustrated by Sherry Farrell Racette, the stories also convey their own powerful images. In "Rou-Garous" (a motif that appears in French-Canadian folklore as "loup-garou"), a woman takes the form of a wolf:

> George he look up
> an dis big animal he jump in front of dah
> car an all he can member when he hit it
> was dat it was a woman dat look at him. (p. 40)

Typical of these stories, the narrator incorporates many perspectives which invite interpretative possibilities – is the "rou-garou" a devil, a powerful shape-shifter, or "a woman dat look at him" and is being defamed for her independence? – leaving it to readers to make their own meaning.

---

29 "On Thomas King," ed. Margery Fee, special issue of *Canadian Literature* 161 / 162 (1999), p. 72.
30 Campbell, interview, in Lutz, ed., *Contemporary Challenges*, p. 49.
31 Campbell, *Stories of the Road Allowance People*, p. 2.

Likewise, Louise Halfe, a Cree from Saddle Lake, Alberta, who received a bachelor's degree in social work from the University of Regina in 1991 and published her first book of poetry, *Bear Bones and Feathers*, in 1994, reclaims voices that have often been dismissed as illiterate and illegitimate, making them powerful and healing. In poems such as "Der Poop," addressed to the Pope, she uses a voice that is reminiscent of her mother's Cree-accented English,[32] playfully but seriously challenging the authorities by putting the power of punning and eloquence in the mouth of an uneducated speaker writing on "dis newspaper / I found it in da outhouse" (p. 102). The poem plays with outhouse humor in the word "poop" and lines like "stay/out of my pissness," but at the same time it grounds the sacred in the body. In her book-length "epic" poem *Blue Marrow* (1998), nominated for the Governor General's Award for poetry, Halfe gives voice to Indigenous women involved in the fur trade who have been written out of history. Petticoat grandmother, Wandering Stone grandmother, *nôhkom* Michif and others interweave Cree, formal English, and French-inflected English, creating a dynamic sense of presence.

Story and history

The intersecting of past and present is important in the work of Armand Garnet Ruffo. In "Poem for Duncan Campbell Scott," from his first collection of poems, *Opening in the Sky* (1994), he reframes through Ojibwa perspectives the post-Confederation poet and civil servant in the Department of Indian Affairs who came to make treaty with his ancestors in northern Ontario. His book-length poem *Grey Owl: The Mystery of Archie Belaney* (1997) returns to this territory, but its subject is an imposter, a once-respected spokesperson who came to be exposed as a fake Indian. Ruffo, whose great-grandparents adopted Archie Belaney into their family, explores issues of identity, authenticity, and imposture. *At Geronimo's Grave* (2001), a collection of poems clustered around the figure of Geronimo, a renowned Apache warrior of the nineteenth century, undermines the nostalgia with which popular culture often views such figures. Similarly, Joan Crate calls up the past as a way of looking at present identity in *Pale as Real Ladies: Poems for Pauline Johnson* (1989), a collection that locates her own life as a poet and woman "of mixed nations (Cree and five million other things)" in the historical figure of Mohawk Pauline Johnson, also of mixed heritage.[33]

---

32 "Louise Halfe," in Armstrong and Grauer, eds., *Native Poetry in Canada*, p. 240.
33 "Joan Crate," in Armstrong and Grauer, eds., *Native Poetry in Canada*, p. 227.

Some writers have focused on more recent history. Lorne Simon's posthumously published *Stones and Switches* (1994), the first novel by a Mi'kmaq writer in Canada, sets his protagonist Megwadesk in the Depression era and approaches the spiritual world of the Mi'kmaq through the young fisherman who must enter the dream-world to battle witchery on the reserve. Lee Maracle uses fiction to record the complex effects of colonialism on individual lives, mediating colonial and Indigenous ways of knowing through the perspectives of her contemporary female protagonists. Her novel *Sundogs* (1992) probes the significance of 1990, the year of the Mohawk stand for sovereign territory at Oka, Quebec, against 2,500 Canadian soldiers sent to Kanesatake and Kahnawake by Prime Minister Brian Mulroney, while *Ravensong* (1993) explores the devastating effects of a 1950s flu epidemic on a Salish village near North Vancouver, its plight ignored by an inwardly turned colonial society. Joseph Boyden, a southern Ontario writer with Irish, Scottish, and Ojibwa roots, writes about the participation of Cree soldiers in the First World War in *Three Day Road* (2005). A second novel of a planned trilogy, *Through Black Spruce* (2008), follows descendants of Boyden's protagonist, Xavier Bird, into a fraught contemporary world spanning the unpopulated terrain of the James-Bay Cree and the glamorous haunts of New York's young fashionable people. Through intertwining monologues, both novels set up an exchange between generations which establishes connection rather than conflict.

The insidious effects of residential school on Indigenous communities across Canada are revealed and dissected in several works. In *Indian School Days* (1988) Basil Johnston chronicles residential school life in Spanish, Ontario, with a comic flair and ironic eye, rewriting the English "school days" account in a Canadian setting. Although catalogued as fiction, Salish writer Shirley Sterling's *My Name is Seepeetza* (1992) is based on the experiences of the author, her sisters and friends who attended the Kamloops Residential School in the 1950s. Teetl'it Gwich'in writer Robert Arthur Alexie, born in Fort McPherson, Northwest Territories, and living in Inuvik, employs a driving pace and vivid language in his novel *Porcupines and China Dolls* (2002), communicating James Nathan's and Jake Noland's repressed anger and alienation before their disclosure that they were sexually abused in residential school liberates them from their trauma. The title refers to the institutional haircut which serves as a metonymical figure in so many accounts for the violence inflicted on Indigenous lives through government regulation such as residential schools. Alexie's novel not only recounts personal history, covering a few days in the lives of his middle-aged protagonists, but uses memory and dream to situate their story within the struggle for survival of two generations in the fictional community of the people of the Blue Mountains. The often tragic events of the story are countered by the irreverence of Alexie's narration.

Authenticity and subversion

Both Basil Johnston and Robert Arthur Alexie use humor to undermine and combat the toxic effects of residential schools. While these schools operated on the policy that the Indian – sometimes viewed as savage or subhuman in particular institutions – had to be removed from the child, other limiting concepts of Indigenous peoples were also destructive. Reductive notions of authenticity, stemming from bigotry or political correctness, are targets for satire taken on by Drew Hayden Taylor in *Funny, You Don't Look Like One: Observations from a Blue-Eyed Ojibway* (1996), the first of several volumes of humorous writing. Because the blue-eyed, blonde Taylor did not "look like" an Indian, it was often hard for others, not only whites but sometimes Indigenous people, to assimilate his "pinkness" into their images of Indigeneity.[34]

Green Grass, Running Water also addresses the cultural construction of "authenticity" in a racist and colonial society. One of King's characters is the Cree actor Portland Looking Bear, who has to wear make-up and a false nose in order to look "authentically" Indian. The situation is simultaneously humorous and tragic, fictional and a reality known by everyone who knows Iron Eyes Cody, one of the many historical figures King imports into his novel. An Italian-American actor claiming Cree and Cherokee heritage, Cody was famous in the 1970s for his portrayal on posters and in public service announcements of an "Indian" shedding a tear when confronted with litter. The novel's mixing of Christian and Indigenous creation stories has many implications, but one of them addresses the stereotypical notion that being a "real Indian" means following fixed and unchanging traditions uncontaminated by contact with other cultures. In a story told by First Woman in the novel, a character called Ahdamn is naming animals and plants, getting it wrong so many times that the Bear suggests "[w]e got to get you some glasses." But getting it wrong is sometimes getting it right, such as when he calls the Cedar Tree a "telephone book."[35] King's humorous subversion of the Christian creation story's assertion of male dominion over the world also comments on Indigenous storytelling, underscoring the idea that creation is an ongoing

---

34 Drew Hayden Taylor, *Funny, You Don't Look Like One: Observations from a Blue-Eyed Ojibway* (Penticton: Theytus, 1996), p. 10.
35 Thomas King, *Green Grass, Running Water* (Toronto: HarperCollins, 1993), p. 41.

process, often enabled by a trickster figure, with no exact beginning and no cut-off date. It includes both Cedar Trees and telephone books, Elks and microwave ovens (some creations being tricksterish errors). In Harry Robinson's creation stories, echoes of Bible stories also appear, and his coyote tales expand to include the creation of the Panama Canal and Neil Armstrong's trip to the moon. Similarly, King's novel creates a structure in which Indigenous stories incorporate into their cosmology Christian stories, colonial history, and the modern world in an ongoing, ever-adjusting story cycle.

In his novel *Keeper'n Me* (1994) Ojibwa writer Richard Wagamese recounts the story of his protagonist's return, after trying on a series of makeshift identities, to the White Dog Reserve and to a sense of place and belonging, learning that "land is a feeling"[36] which can be located "as much inside his people as it is under their feet."[37] In her first collection of poetry, *A Really Good Brown Girl* (1996), Métis poet Marilyn Dumont considers how the inside is affected by the outside, and how identity can become destabilized when subject to different social and cultural contexts. In her prose poem "Leather and Naughahyde" the narrator tells a "treaty guy" that she's Métis "like it's an apology and he says, 'mmh,' like he forgives me, like he's got a big heart and mine's pumping diluted blood ..." (p. 58). "It Crosses My Mind" from the same work articulates the intersecting perspectives and histories that undermine the poet's ability to identify herself as "Canadian" on an application form for a job: "there are no lines for the stories between *yes and no*" (p. 59).

All Indigenous literature can be thought of as counteracting the erasure of identities and stories. At the same time, there have been institutional efforts such as removal of land, outlawing rituals and Indigenous knowledge, defining and limiting Indian "status," and residential schooling, which attempt to end Indigeneity, and writers have tried to analyze the effects of these policies, seeking ways to reconnect with their cultural heritage. For Gregory Scofield, finding a "half-breed" identity has been necessary to accept himself as a "whole individual" of both Cree and European ancestry,[38] and his four works of poetry reflect different stages of alienation and belonging. An interest in the connections between poetry and song runs through his more recent work as he experiments with diverse forms such as country music in *I Knew Two Métis Women: The Lives of Dorothy Scofield and Georgiana Houle Young* (1999) and Cree

---

36 Richard Wagamese, *Keeper 'n Me* (Toronto: Doubleday, 1994), p. 155.
37 Armand Garnet Ruffo, "Why Native Literature?" in *Native North America: Critical and Cultural Perspectives*, ed. Renée Hulan (Toronto: ECW Press, 1999), p. 116–17.
38 David, ed., *Story Keepers*, p. 35.

language and traditional song in *Sakihtowin-maskihkiy ekwa peyak-nikamowin / Love Medicine and One Song* (1997). The latter work contests the stereotype of the masculine, stoic Indian by representing homosexual love, at the same time grounding this eroticism in images of prairie land and sky. His poetry, along with the work of other Indigenous poets from Canada, the United States, Australia, and Aotearoa (New Zealand), has been anthologized in the innovative collection *Without Reservation: Indigenous Erotica* (2003), edited by Anishnaabe poet Kateri Akiwenzie-Damm and published by Kegedonce Press, established on the Cape Croker Reserve in Ontario by Akiwenzie-Damm in 1993.

Recovering Indigenous identity and accepting herself as a "'mixed race person,'" through a workshop with Mohawk poet Beth Brant was an important breakthrough for Métis poet Joanne Arnott. Her prose poem "Like an Indian: Struggling with Ogres" from *My Grass Cradle* (1992) evokes the "anxiety ... and flat out denial" concerning Indigenous heritage that was present in her family.[39] A quality of vulnerability and toughness that can be found in Arnott's poems characterizes the teenagers caught in dysfunctional families in Haisla writer Eden Robinson's collection of short stories *Traplines* (1996). In most of these stories, Robinson refrains from defining the identities of her characters as Indigenous (or not), potentially "trapping" readers into confronting their own preconceptions. In her novel *Monkey Beach* (2000), nominated for the Governor General's Award for fiction, Robinson conveys a brooding sense of immanent evil which some critics have described as Gothic. This evil makes appearances in monstrous forms throughout, but Robinson also suggests that nurturing powers co-exist with destructive ones. In this work, the setting of Haisla territory near the town of Kitimat in northern British Columbia is clearly mapped for the reader. This description, however, is only one of many ways the novel represents the mixed territory of land and sea and its meanings in Haisla culture. Robinson's use of surface detail combined with indirection and silences is reminiscent of Ruby Slipperjack's aesthetic.

Robinson's young Haisla protagonist Lisamarie Hill is named after Elvis Presley's daughter and inhabits a world of contemporary popular culture, as do the characters in Dogrib author Richard Van Camp's *The Lesser Blessed* (1996), a novel set in the Northwest Territories. Van Camp's vibrant language, bilingual slang, and neologisms convey a society of teenagers in which trauma and humor, heavy metal music and Dogrib creation stories co-exist. Both works suggest the potential for consumer culture to provide alluring but

---

39 "Joanne Arnott," in Armstrong and Grauer, eds., *Native Poetry in Canada*, p. 282.

destructive alternatives to Indigenous traditions but also show characters who creatively adapt aspects of contemporary culture to their own needs, and illustrate the potential for subtle critique of a market-driven cultural environment.

Both Saulteaux poet Annharte and Marvin Francis, a Cree from Heart Lake First Nation in northern Alberta, adapt urban street smarts, tricksterish humor, and performance to their poetry. Annharte, raised in Winnipeg, has written about "borrowing" language: English is a "borrowed language" that has been forced upon Indigenous peoples, but she also deliberately borrows street talk and "underclass English vocabulary."[40] Annharte recycles language, as in the poet's definition of herself in "Raced Out to Write This Up" from her first collection, *Being on the Moon* (1990): "I'm a half a half breed / a mixed bag breed of bread and butter bred."[41] In "Tongue in Cheek, if not Tongue in Check" from her chapbook *Coyote Columbus Cafe* (1994), the "coyotrix" takes a "simple" definition from the "Coyote dictionary." She evokes coyote's subversive potential when she compares his discourse to "dew on a cactus" as well as the trickster's scatological humor when she advises not to "do it on a cactus unless desperate," and mixes in references to manufactured kitsch and marketing tactics: "do it in mucho grande southwest deco portraits / or see entry, urine sample. Scratch and sniff."[42]

Marvin Francis takes on advertising, branding and selling in *city treaty: a long poem* (2002), which plays with the boundaries of Indigenous and consumer culture, land and city, past and present, "high" literature and getting high on the street. Francis, who described himself as a "bush poet" with an "urban / rural lens," remembers the second-hand books that sustained him while working on a railroad gang, especially the first book of poetry he ever read, Michael Ondaatje's *The Collected Works of Billy the Kid*.[43] He died in 2005, while in the process of getting a PhD at the University of Manitoba in Winnipeg.

Author and scholar Warren Cariou, who supervised Francis's doctorate, has described *city treaty* as "a streetwise anti-globalization manifesto for the indigenous world" and links Francis's perspective to Jeannette Armstrong's novel *Whispering in Shadows* (2000). Both works use artist figures to

---

40 Marie Annharte Baker, "Borrowing Enemy Language: A First Nation Woman Use of English," *West Coast Line* 27.1 (1993), p. 60.
41 Annharte, "Being on the Moon" (Winlaw: Polestar, 1990), p. 61.
42 Annharte, *Coyote Columbus Cafe* (Winnipeg: Moonprint Press, 1994), p. 19.
43 *Reading Writers Reading: Canadian Authors' Reflections*, ed. Danielle Schaub (Edmonton: University of Alberta Press, 2006) p. 120.

interrogate and critique the effects of globalization on Indigenous cultures.[44] One of the solutions the novel suggests is to re-establish a connection and balance between human and land. As Armstrong says in her essay "Land Speaking," "All my elders say that it is land that holds all knowledge of life and death and is a constant teacher ... Not to learn its language is to die."[45] Armstrong has recently advocated writing in Native languages as a way of not only recovering this interaction with the land, but also exploring and developing Indigenous aesthetics.[46] Creating space for diverse directions and connections, urban, land-centered, local, and global, Indigenous writers continue to redefine literature in Canada.

44 Warren Cariou, "'How Come These Guns Are so Tall': Anti-Corporate Resistance in Marvin Francis's *City Treaty*," *Studies in Canadian Literature / Études en littérature canadienne* 31.1 (2006), pp. 149, 156.
45 Jeannette Armstrong, "Land Speaking," in *Speaking for the Generations*, ed. Simon J. Ortiz (Tucson: University of Arizona Press, 1998), p. 176.
46 Jeannette Armstrong, "The Aesthetic Qualities of Aboriginal Writing," in *Studies in Canadian Literature / Études en littérature canadienne* 31.1 (2006), pp. 20–30.

26
Contemporary Aboriginal theater

HELEN GILBERT

Indigenous theater in Canada, like its artistic counterparts in Australia and Aotearoa/New Zealand, has become a significant force in the nation's cultural repertoire over the past twenty-five years, capturing the attention of both local audiences and the international performing arts market, notably at major festivals. Not only has there been a rapid expansion in the number and variety of performance works created by Canada's First Peoples since the mid-1980s but also a concerted attempt to develop industry structures – publicity networks, production companies, training schools, and research laboratories – that will ensure the continued visibility of Indigenous artists *in* theater across the nation. This cultural project has been an important part of the broader campaign by Aboriginal Canadians to address the multiple effects of European colonization and thereby reclaim forms of agency. The power of performance to expose and reconfigure social relations has been evident on several fronts, not least of which is the contested terrain of representation itself. As practitioners and scholars have observed, Aboriginal theater-makers necessarily contend – in a very visceral and visual way – with the particular burden of stereotyped Indigeneity that has accumulated over centuries through images of "Indianness" circulated in a wide range of pedagogical and imaginative texts. In this context, one of the key achievements of this theater has been to stage the mechanisms by which Indigeneity is constructed, envisaging, in the process, more flexible and varied representations of Aboriginal cultures and practices.

Canada's adoption of multiculturalism in 1971 as an official model of social organization helped to lay the foundations for Aboriginal theater's development, both in terms of opening up avenues for Aboriginal artists and projecting a more inclusive vision of the nation. In the earlier years of the twentieth century, Aboriginals had been effectively excluded from the public stage, both by laws (in place from 1916 to 1951) prohibiting costumed performance[1] and by widespread social and political marginalization. While Aboriginal themes animated a small number of non-Indigenous dramas, such as Gwen Pharis Ringwood's *Maya*, or *Lament for Harmonica* (1959),[2] Aboriginal characters in this period were generally played by white actors and tended to be fashioned in liberal humanist modes that intimated, however unintentionally, the tragic demise of a doomed race.

George Ryga's widely acclaimed dramatization of urban Native life in *The Ecstasy of Rita Joe* (1967; 1970) follows this pattern, although its expressionistic treatment of the protagonist's rape and murder arguably moves beyond a simply mimetic reproduction of Aboriginal trauma. The premiere production featured film actor Chief Dan George as Rita Joe's father but Aboriginal performers were otherwise conspicuously absent. Despite its limitations, the play is credited with helping to inspire later efforts by Aboriginal theater-makers because it staged issues of concern to them in a highly politicized way at a time when the merits of assimilation were only just beginning to be questioned. Such visibility proved a mixed blessing as the text's rapid incorporation into the canon of Canadian literature and its wide dissemination through college syllabi initially made it a kind of ur-text against which fledgling Aboriginal works might be measured. Yet, the play's national circulation *as a performance piece* also provided a vehicle for Aboriginals to enter main-stage representation. Actor Margo Kane (Cree/Salteaux/Blackfoot), for example, came to prominence in the lead role of Rita Joe for Prairie Theatre Exchange's 1982 production, before developing her current praxis as a storyteller and director. Various other non-Indigenous playwrights followed in Ryga's wake, expanding the range of plays centrally concerned with Aboriginal–white encounters. Herschel Hardin's northern tragedy *Esker Mike and His Wife, Agiluk* (1971; 1973), Sharon Pollock's historical drama *Walsh* (1973), and Henry Beissel's biting satire *Inook and the Sun* (1973; 1974) are cases in point. By the late 1970s, Canadian theater audiences were thus familiarized with

---

1 The 1914 amendment to the Indian Act forbad Indians in several provinces from participating in exhibitions, performances, stampedes, or pageants in Aboriginal costume without the consent of government representatives. This prohibition added to the ban on west coast potlaches in force from the 1880s. Wendy Moss and Elaine Gardner-O'Toole, Law and Government Division, "Aboriginal People: History of Discriminatory Laws," Government of Canada Depository Services Programme, 1991, http://dsp-psd.pwgsc.gc.ca/Collection-R/LoPBdP/BP/bp175-e.htm, accessed February 4, 2008.
2 Single dates in parentheses after plays refer to the first production unless otherwise noted and may also indicate publication date where the year is the same. Where two dates are given, they specify the premiere production and first publication respectively. Where texts have been workshopped before public audiences as part of an on-going development process, production dates may be somewhat arbitrary.

certain (limited) portraits of Indigenous cultures that would influence – and haunt – subsequent representations. Plays penned by Aboriginals themselves include Nona Benedict's *The Dress* (published 1970) and George Kenny's *October Stranger* (1977), adapted from his book *Indians Don't Cry* (1977) with the help of actor Denis Lacroix. Though not much remarked upon at the time, these works are now cited as pioneering literary efforts in Aboriginal terms.

Aboriginal theater practitioners of this era had already begun to hone their skills through organizations such as the Association for Native Development in the Performing and Visual Arts, established in Toronto in 1972, which negotiated opportunities to stage Aboriginal works while providing a forum for information and skills exchange. Its founder, James Buller, also created the Native Theatre School, a summer workshop that has now expanded into a three-year post-secondary training programme run by the Centre for Indigenous Theatre. Elsewhere, ad hoc collectives sprang up to nurture local performance activities. Nanaimo's Tillicum Theatre (1973–5) on Vancouver Island and the Atchemowin (storytelling) group in Edmonton (*c.* 1976–8) are among the documented examples. The following years saw an expansion and consolidation with the formation of a number of influential theater companies, among them Spirit Song in Vancouver in 1981 (now defunct), Native Earth Performing Arts in Toronto in 1982, and De-ba-jeh-mu-jig in West Bay on Wikwemikong Unceded Indian reserve, Manitoulin Island, in 1984. Various cultural events, notably the World Indigenous Theatre Festival staged in outer Toronto (1980) and then Peterborough (1982), and the Festival de Théâtre des Amériques (1985–2006; now Festival TransAmériques), which particularly encouraged emerging artists, afforded additional avenues for Aboriginal Canadians to showcase their work while forging links with First Nations communities in other countries. Around this time, professional and amateur initiatives began to diverge, the latter often being community-based and concerned with youth groups and/or "at risk" constituencies, although there have been numerous crossovers between the two. Dramatists associated with such community work include Tsimshian activist-educator Valerie Dudoward, whose play *Teach Me the Ways of the Sacred Circle* (1985; 1986) explores Indigenous values and philosophies in an urban setting, and Mi'kmaq actor-director Ida Labillois-Williams, who produced, among other works, *I Hear the Same Drums/Le son du même tambour* (1987), a bilingual performance addressing challenges faced by the French-speaking Montagnais/Naskapi.

In the professional realm, two key events in 1986 combined to draw mainstream attention to Aboriginal theater. The first was the performance at Toronto's Theatre Passe Muraille of *Jessica*, starring Kuna/Rappahannock performer Monique Mojica, which won the Dora Mavor Moore award for Outstanding New Play and was shortlisted for a Chalmers Award. A loose adaptation of Métis writer Maria Campbell's highly acclaimed autobiography, *Halfbreed* (1973), the play was initially co-written by Campbell, non-Aboriginal actor/playwright Linda Griffiths, and director Paul Thompson. It had enjoyed a successful season in Saskatoon in 1982 despite considerable tensions between Campbell and Griffiths, who "browned up" to play the lead role. Subsequently, Griffiths revised the script, initially without consultation, in what is now well documented as a painful collaboration dogged by disagreements over authenticity and agency.[3] The play charts a spiritual journey, Jessica's movement towards self-discovery and healing after a difficult childhood, a broken marriage, drug addiction and prostitution. This journey is presented as a dream-vision via a series of flashbacks and dramatic transformations contained within a ceremony invoking animal spirits, vividly realized as masked figures, to guide the protagonist in confronting her past. Insistently theatrical and structured to convey a sense of cultural origins, *Jessica* modelled a way of dramatizing Aboriginal lives that avoided the aesthetic of injury permeating texts such as *The Ecstasy of Rita Joe*.

Aboriginal women were similarly the focus of the second notable 1986 event, the staging of Cree playwright Tomson Highway's exuberant, if poignant, portrait of reservation life in *The Rez Sisters* (published 1988), which also won a Dora Mavor Moore Award. Initially workshopped at De-ba-jeh-mu-jig but produced by Native Earth Performing Arts and Act IV Theatre Company in Toronto, the play premiered at the Native Canadian Centre before moving into largely mainstream venues for a sell-out national tour, followed in 1988 by a season at the Edinburgh Festival. *The Rez Sisters* was remarkable not only for its creation of seven meaty roles for Indigenous women but also for its earthy comedy as shaped by the trickster, Nanabush, who galvanizes and directs the action. Partly modeled after Michel Tremblay's *Les Belles-Soeurs* (1968; 1972), which probes the spiritual malaise of seven working-class Québécois women in Montreal, Highway's play pivots around the protagonists' determination to win "the biggest Bingo in the world," thereby securing the means to improve their impoverished lives. Social realism is the predominant mode of both plays, but Highway charges his narrative with mythopoeic force, elevating the women's quest from its mundane context

---

3 The revised playscript, together with a dialogue between Campbell and Griffiths charting their collaborative process, was published as *The Book of Jessica* (Toronto: Coach House, 1989).

to a fantastical world where transformation (in Aboriginal terms) is possible. With the trickster's intervention, the Rez sisters learn to value what they have and to use their own energy and ingenuity to solve their problems.

With the 1989 premiere of *Dry Lips Oughta Move to Kapuskasing*, his second installment in a projected cycle of seven "Rez" plays, Highway consolidated his position as a playwright of note. *Dry Lips* garnered a Chalmers Award for best new Canadian drama, among other accolades, and had a season at Toronto's prestigious Royal Alexandra Theatre after its initial run at Theatre Passe Muraille. The play, a companion piece and refractive mirror to *The Rez Sisters*, concentrates on the lives of seven Aboriginal men living on the now-familiar Wasaychigan Hill Reserve. Again it features Nanabush as a dynamic structural force but unfolds as a darker and more confronting work, particularly in its critique of the Church and its related institutions as key sites of colonial violence. The plot revolves around Zachary's and Big Joey's efforts to develop separate businesses on the reservation, a mean-spirited contest played out against an off-stage hockey competition mounted by the community's women in an unsettling gender reversal. Where the male trickster in *The Rez Sisters* oversees a regenerative movement in the women's lives, his female counterpart in *Dry Lips* functions primarily to illuminate the deep-seated divisions that plague the reservation. The play's graphic representation of misogyny, rape and alcoholism has troubled some viewers, though Highway defends his material as exposing the poisoned legacies of the past as a prelude to cultural healing. Critics such as Kimberley Solga support this view, arguing that Nanabush's exaggerated sexuality conforms to the trickster logics of teaching by negative example, while the multi-layered staging provides a space for radical gender critique.[4]

Highway's subsequent Rez drama, *Rose*, written in the early 1990s, adopts a similarly controversial mode but is even bolder in its vision. After failing to secure a professional production, the play was mounted in 2000 by students at the University of Toronto in a short season that sold out before opening night. Structured as a spectacular cabaret, *Rose* (published 2003) brings together the key characters from the earlier plays in a pitted "battle of the sexes" for the metaphorical soul of Wasaychigan Hill. Once again Nanabush is both *provocateur* and symbolic center in a dream-like narrative that casts violent conflicts between the community's men and women in mythic terms. This

---

[4] Kimberly Solga. "Violent Imaginings: Feminist Performance Spaces in Tomson Highway's *Dry Lips Oughta Move to Kapuskasing*," in *Space and the Postmodern Stage*, ed. Irène Eynat-Confino and Eva Soromová (Prague: Divadelni Ústav, 2000), pp. 71–81.

shape-shifting trickster figure encompasses three Roses, each connected to the central female character, Emily Dictionary. One Rose is her former lover, the legendary activist Rosabella Baez who committed suicide some years earlier; another is her unborn child, Rosetta, aborted after Emily was savagely beaten while pregnant; the third is her half-sister, Chief Big Rose, the community's new leader, whose ascension into the spirit world after an untimely assassination marks the play's shattering climax.

While *The Rez Sisters* and *Dry Lips* brought Highway international fame and have been widely taught within Canada and abroad, his contribution to Aboriginal theater extends well beyond these plays. From 1986 to 1992 as artistic director of Native Earth, he developed the company's profile while producing several works. These include *Aria* (1987; 2003), an integrated set of monologues for a solo actress; *New Song ... New Dance* (1988), a multimedia performance created with his brother René, an acclaimed dancer; and *The Sage, The Dancer and the Fool* (1989), a "mini-*Ulysses*" co-devised with Billy Merasty and René Highway, which dramatizes one day in the life of an Aboriginal youth. Highway was commissioned by Western Canada Theatre and the Secwepemc Cultural Education Society to write *Ernestine Shuswap Gets Her Trout* (2004; 2005), a tragi-comic account of how Indigenous tribes in British Columbia's Thompson River basin were dispossessed of their land, along with their hunting and fishing rights. Again, Highway creates memorable female characters, stressing their underlying spirit of co-operation in the face of adversity. This apparently unflinching faith in Aboriginal women's integrity, although open to charges of romanticism, is perhaps what marks the thematic coherence of his stage works. Theatrically, his mastery of illusion, spectacle, and transformation enlarges conceptions of what performance might encompass while reviving the expressive Aboriginal energies subdued by colonialism.

The late 1980s and early 1990s saw the emergence of several other significant Aboriginal playwrights. Prominent among these is Daniel David Moses (Delaware), whose expansive oeuvre presents – and interrogates – historical, mythical, and contemporary versions of Indigenous culture, sometimes in the one composite text. In theatrical terms, Moses's work is distinguished by its deftness in "making the relations between performer, story and audience visible"[5] so as to unsettle dominant constructions of Aboriginal cultures and

---

5 Robert Appleford, "Making Relations Visible in Native Canadian Performance," in *Siting the Other: Revisions of Marginality in Australian and English-Canadian Drama*, ed. Marc Maufort and Franca Bellarsi (Brussels: P. I. E.-Peter Lang, 2001), p. 234.

open up a dynamic, interactive space in which more enabling subjectivities may be forged. Moses also enlists the subversive figure of the trickster in this project, variously manifest as a ghost or numinous presence. He explains that such ghosts exist to probe the power of whiteness, "spook its metaphors," and dismantle its racialized hierarchies.[6] At the beginning of his first play, *Coyote City*, which premiered in 1988 (published 1990) at the Native Canadian Centre and was shortlisted for a Governor General's Award, an apparently drunken Indian[7] confronts the audience in an uncomfortable moment designed to mimic the stereotyping that so often characterizes white representations of Indigeneity. This figure is one of Moses's spooks; having died in a knife fight six months earlier, he returns to lure his grieving lover, Lena, to Toronto's Silver Dollar tavern, here metaphorized as a contemporary underworld of prostitution, alcoholism, and cultural amnesia. The play, inspired by a Nez Percé story titled "Coyote and the Shadow People," charts Lena's physical and psychological journey toward this abyss. Her tragic failure to resist its seductions accounts for the circularity of the narrative, which ends with another ghost's drunken tirade spoken directly to the audience.

Following *Coyote City*, Moses reintroduces some of its characters in three other loosely related dramas to form a tetralogy of "city plays" exploring the construction of contemporary Aboriginal identities. *Big Buck City* (1991; 1998), shaped as a farcical rendition of the Christian nativity myth, focuses on the miraculous birth of Lena's child, Babe Fisher, fathered by Johnny (as spirit-lover) with the help of a trickster/ghost/street-kid, Ricky Raccoon, who orchestrates much of the action. Babe Fisher then becomes the astronaut heroine of the next play, *Kyotopolis* (1993; 2008), an outrageously imaginative sci-fi tale that spoofs – and spooks – media representations of Aboriginality and the genre of science fiction itself. In *City of Shadows* (1995), the last offering in this series, Moses stages a "theatrical séance" during which the ghosts of characters in the previous dramas review their earthly experiences. *Kyotopolis* has attracted the most scholarly attention among these later works, not least because of its dense narrative texturing and its extended engagement with the "optics"/politics of multimedia representation. Although styled as a futuristic fantasy, the play is haunted by history's ghosts, manifest in the nightmarish visions experienced by some of the characters. In this respect,

---

6 Daniel David Moses, "How My Ghosts Got Pale Faces," in *Speaking for the Generations: Native Writers on Writing*, ed. Simon J. Ortiz (Tucson: University of Arizona Press, 1998), p. 147.
7 I use "Indian" where the plays themselves have deployed the term and to denote stereotypical or contested representations of Native peoples.

Babe's mythic flight into the cosmos connects the spaces of past, present, and future in a metaphysical vision that projects "wholeness" as the desired teleology for Aboriginal nations. Such wholeness is not to be confused with notions of authenticity, Moses suggests, through his pointed satire of the reality effects produced by media technologies and his insistent foregrounding of the colonizing spectatorial gaze directed at Aboriginal peoples.

Moses has also written a number of "historical" dramas that take a different tack in probing colonialism's wounds but are equally concerned with the intricacies of representation. *Almighty Voice and His Wife*, a complex metatheatrical work first produced at the Great Canadian Theatre Company in Ottawa in 1991 (published 1992), revisits the story of a Cree warrior whose presentation in Anglo-Canadian histories seemed unsatisfactory to Moses. Using just two actors, his multi-layered response to the 1897 manhunt leading to Almighty Voice's death by cannon fire unfolds in starkly contrasting sequences: firstly as a quasi-realist lyrical drama, then as a variety performance using whiteface (a ghostly inversion of blackface) and conventions of the nineteenth-century minstrel show to re-examine the events just staged. The minstrel routines, overlaid with images drawn from other popular entertainments such as Wild West shows, are essentially acts of subversive ventriloquism. They not only clarify ways in which power is exercised in creating racist stereotypes but also reveal the internalized racism that compromises Aboriginal efforts at self-determination.

Moses maintains this focus on the hybrid genealogies of Indigenous performance in *The Indian Medicine Shows* (published 1995), comprised of two short companion pieces staged together at Theatre Passe Muraille in 1996. The first of these, *The Moon and Dead Indians*, focuses on the genocide of Indigenous tribes on the American frontier, manifest through the haunted landscape that encompasses a young settler. The second, *Angel of the Medicine Show*, brings one of the "disappeared" back into visibility, albeit as a theatrical trope: the Wild Indian of the Medicine Shows. In *Brébeuf's Ghost* (1996; 2000), subtitled "A Tale of Horror in Three Acts," Moses draws loosely on Shakespeare's *Macbeth* to structure his epic account of tensions between Iroquois and Ojibwa tribes in the seventeenth century, here reimagined as a conflict shaped and energized by a martyred Jesuit missionary's cannibal-ghost. Taken together, these historical dramas make an important contribution to a nationwide campaign by Aboriginal artists to expose and revise the limiting portraits of Indians proffered by a range of authoritative texts. As oral histories, the plays also speak indirectly to sovereignty issues by probing the debatable circumstances of colonial conquest and the ways in which it has been recorded. Moses's recent plays *The Ballad of Burnt Ella* and *Songs of the Tall Grass* were developed in tandem and staged together as *Songs of Love and Medicine* in 2005. Described in publicity materials as "a dark farce" and a "bright tragedy,"[8] these works continue a long-term interest in reinterpreting mythic (children's) stories and also extend his productive experimentation with genre.

The early 1990s marked the recognition, at the national level, of a number of cutting-edge, small-scale works by Aboriginal women, notably Monique Mojica and Margo Kane, each of whom has made substantial contributions to the wider field of Aboriginal theater practice. Mojica had by this time developed a considerable profile as an actor following her celebrated performance in *Jessica* and her powerfully evocative rendition of a trickster-like Ariel in Lewis Baumander's adaptation of Shakespeare's *The Tempest* in Toronto (1987 and 1989), which was set on the Queen Charlotte Islands and presented as a parable of colonialism. Mojica's iconoclastic, self-devised performance piece, *Princess Pocahontas and the Blue Spots* (1990; 1991), introduced Canadian audiences to the woman-centered mode of Indigenous "story-weaving" pioneered by New York's Spiderwoman Theater, the members of which include her mother, Gloria Miguel. Co-produced in 1990 by Theatre Passe Muraille and Nightwood Theatre, this version of the Pocahontas legend confronts a maelstrom of images comprising the semiotic field of female Indianness constructed by popular cinema and storybook accounts of European settlement across the Americas. The play encompasses present and mythic realms as well as the colonial time/space of the 1607 Jamestown colony (in what is now Virginia) and the Spanish conquests of Indigenous cultures in Peru and Mexico. Mojica (as actor) focuses on the multiple roles played by Aboriginal women in such enterprises, bodily inhabiting, so as to rework, the stereotypes of traitor, whore, Indian princess, mistress, and Cigar Store Squaw that circumscribe contemporary Indigenous women's efforts to carve a meaningful place in their societies. A similar deconstructive project drives *Birdwoman and the Suffragettes*, Mojica's 1991 radio-drama about the Shoshone translator, Sacajawea, who aided American explorers Lewis and Clark in their attempt to find an overland route to the Pacific coast.

Mojica's mode of historiographic inquiry is premised on a model of pan-Aboriginality that connects Canadian Indigenous rights campaigns and land disputes – expressed most famously by the 1990 Mohawk blockade during the

---

8 See *Songs of Love and Medicine* by Daniel David Moses, http://www.queensu.ca/drama/library/songs/songs.htm, accessed December 12, 2007.

Oka Crisis in Quebec – to the political resurgence of Indigenous groups in other parts of North and South America. As Ric Knowles argues, such transnationalism was and is important "at a time when Native political struggles were increasingly against the governments, legislative bodies and armies of Nation States."[9] Implicit in Mojica's presentation of pan-Aboriginality lies a demand that we recognize current cross-border territories and affiliations based on Indigenous demographies existing before colonization. This reconfiguration of (first) nationhood also informs her more recent, co-devised text, *The Scrubbing Project*, written and performed with fellow Turtle Gals Ensemble members Jani Lauzon and Michelle St John in 2002 at Toronto's Factory Studio Café, then redeveloped for a national tour in 2005–6.[10] Using the paradoxical but enabling concept of *"living* with genocide," the play investigates the attempted "scrubbing out" of Aboriginal women's identities and material cultures across the generations, through rape, child removal policies, residential school education, and internalized racism. Despite its dark subjects, the performance is leavened by vaudeville and popular comedy routines as part of the story-weaving process that aims to celebrate the fluidity and adaptability of Aboriginal women's lives. Mojica has continued to develop this kind of syncretic dramaturgy in various contexts, notably in collaboration with Cree playwright and director Floyd Favel.[11]

Margo Kane's dramas are less epic in their canvas, though her work, based mostly in western Canada, has been equally influential. She was a founding member of Spirit Song in the 1980s and in 1992 established Full Circle First Nations Performance, also based in Vancouver, which consists of a diverse ensemble of actors, singers, clowns, writers, and musicians focused on exploring modern Aboriginal theater. Her loosely autobiographical solo piece, *Moonlodge* (1990; 1994), drew wider attention to her skills when it was staged at Vancouver's Women in View Festival in 1990 and has since enjoyed a number of productions in various cities in Canada and the USA, as well as being adapted for CBC radio. Kane showcased the play in the very popular "Wimmin's Business" programme at the pre-Olympic Festival of the Dreaming in 1997 in Australia and has also performed it in Ireland. While part of its appeal has no doubt been the author's extraordinary talents as a storyteller, the play's short length belies its complexity. Concentrating on the experiences of a

---

9 Ric Knowles, "Translators, Traitors, Mistresses, and Whores: Monique Mojica and the Mothers of the Métis Nations," in Maufort and Bellarsi, eds., *Siting the Other*, p. 255.
10 *The Scrubbing Project* is published in *Staging Coyote's Dream*, vol. II, ed. Monique Mojica and Ric Knowles (Toronto: Playwrights Canada Press, 2009).
11 Floyd Favel has also published under the name of Floyd Favel Starr.

woman "scooped" from her Aboriginal family as a child, Kane, like Mojica and Moses, targets commoditized versions of Indigeneity as both ludicrous and pernicious. In performative terms, as the solo actor embodies the many characters and forces affecting the woman's efforts to shape her own identity, the text strives towards a reintegration of the fragmented Native subject even while demonstrating its ontological impossibility. Kane's subsequent solo piece, *Confessions of an Indian Cowboy* (published 2001), which has been staged in various versions since 1998, mostly in western Canada, enacts a similar project in its historical exploration of relations between Aboriginals and Whites, and the contradictions of Métis subjectivity – in this case, of being both "Cowboy" and "Indian." Kane has devised a number of other solo pieces, while her noted collaborative work is *The River Home* (1994), a multi-media installation combining mask dance and storytelling traditions to present an ecological vision of First Nations' relationships with their physical environments.

Cree writer/performer Shirley Cheechoo has also worked as a solo artist, though she founded De-ba-jeh-mu-jig as a collaborative venture and has co-written plays for the company as well as developing its profile during a period as artistic director before turning to film as her primary interest. Her *Path With No Moccasins* (1991; 1993), a wry, intimate, and sometimes harrowing memory piece, was initially self-produced in 1991 before touring across North America to general acclaim. In a different mode, Beatrice Mosionier's *Night of the Trickster* (1993) addresses the failure of the justice system to respond adequately to crimes that have particularly affected Indigenous women. Like Mojica's and Kane's self-devised pieces, these plays enact a form of gendered "re-membering" that locates violence toward Aboriginal women as central to the "material technologies of colonisation."[12] Such depictions are particularly important in countering the tendency to present rape, sexual abuse, and other bodily harm as emblematic of wider forms of oppression endured by Indigenous peoples, as Ryga's and, arguably, Highway's plays do. The work of women theater-makers has also been pioneering in its adaptation of multi-voiced solo performance as a distinctive strand of the larger repertoire of Aboriginal arts.

Aboriginal comedy forms another identifiable genre, particularly as fashioned by Ojibwa playwright Drew Hayden Taylor, whose prolific output has

---

12 Ric Knowles, "The Hearts of Its Women: Rape, Residential Schools, and Re-membering," in *Performing National Identities: International Perspectives on Contemporary Canadian Theatre*, ed. Sherrill Grace and Albert Reiner-Glaap (Vancouver: Talonbooks, 2003), p. 245.

helped to popularize Canadian Indigenous works across North America and in Europe. Sometimes positioned as part of a second wave of Aboriginal theater that has continued to diversify the field, Taylor's oeuvre features a quartet of "blues" plays unified by their uproarious tone and situational comedy, and a number of tragicomedies that focus on the complexities of postcolonial identity. The blues quartet satirizes the excesses of "yuppie" Aboriginals, white "wannabes," pow-wow spiritualism, and all manner of claims to cultural authenticity. The first of these plays, *The Bootlegger Blues*, produced by De-ba-jeh-mu-jig in 1990 (published 1991), revolves around the farcical efforts of a teetotalling woman to bootleg 143 cases of beer for a church fundraiser, much to the horror of her daughter's upwardly mobile de facto husband. In *The Baby Blues* (1995; 1997), Taylor pokes fun at an aging fancy dancer with a penchant for young women, but reserves his more pointed quips for white political correctness, as caricatured in the "wannabe" Summer, whose proud claim to be "one sixty-fourth Native" marks a romantic quest for Indianness. *Buz'Gem Blues* (2001; 2002) parodies stereotypes of the wise elder, the brave warrior, and the noble savage. In the final installment of the quartet, *Berlin Blues* (2007; 2008), a German conglomerate offers to finance an Ojibwa theme park with all the kitsch imaginable, a proposition that promises temporary financial gains but also a permanent loss of dignity. Across all these plays is a trickster sensibility that delights in mimicry and deflating pretensions, while demonstrating that "real" Aboriginal culture is hybrid, adaptive, and, above all, redolent with comedy.

This insistence on hybridity likewise underpins Taylor's critically acclaimed satire *alterNatives* (1999; 2000), which provoked outrage among some viewers and an anonymous bomb threat to one theater company in Vancouver in 1999. Part dinner-party farce, part serious dissection of cross-cultural relations, the play stages a volatile conversation about Aboriginality, attacking not only outsiders' ignorance but also insiders' smugness. The action centers on a Jewish Professor of Native Literature and her Aboriginal partner, an aspiring science-fiction writer, whose ill-matched guests are a politically correct Anglo-Canadian couple (vegetarians) and a pair of self-styled "Über-Indians" (meat-eaters) ardent in their campaign to overturn white cultural norms. Any pretence at politeness soon unravels, along with the various relationships, as the characters deliberately set out to provoke one another, laying bare deep-seated prejudices and insecurities. The showy destructiveness of this farce, targeted specifically at "selective traditionalism" and the myths of authenticity, is another manifestation of Taylor's trickster aesthetics.

His tragicomedies attempt a more nuanced exploration of Aboriginal societies. Three of these plays deal with the repercussions of forced adoption in a serial story of a middle-class lawyer, Janice, removed from her family as a toddler and now struggling to reconcile her newly discovered Indigenous family/heritage with the non-Aboriginal world to which she has been so thoroughly assimilated. The trilogy begins with *Someday* (1991; 1993), which concentrates on a fraught mother–daughter reunion after their thirty-five-year separation. This play's award-winning sequel, *Only Drunks and Children Tell the Truth* (1996; 1998), develops the Janice character by revealing aspects of her "White" world and, more particularly, her anger and guilt over her mother's death. In *400 Kilometres* (1999; 2005), the saga ends with a symbolic promise of cultural renewal as Janice, now pregnant to an Aboriginal man who invites her to return to her natal community, determines to find ways to integrate her separate families and histories. Taylor's mastery of the "one-liner," together with his pastiche of popular culture genres, lightens the tone of the narrative while working to undermine facile cultural assumptions. His interest in broken families continues in the 2004 drama *In a World Created by a Drunken God* (published 2006), when an Aboriginal man is approached unexpectedly as a potential kidney donor for his estranged white father, who abandoned him as a child. This play adds an ethical dilemma to the more general exploration of identity politics in a socially complex situation.

Taylor has also written "youth-oriented" dramas, including *Toronto at Dreamer's Rock* (1989; 1990), about a teenager's questioning of what it means to be Indian, and *Education Is Our Right* (1990), which responds to a 1989 Indian Affairs cap on the budget for post-secondary education; and two plays about growing up, *Girl Who Loved Her Horses* (1995; 2000) and *The Boy in the Treehouse* (2000). While his humorous perspective is not unique among Aboriginal dramatists, his pioneering work has shaped that perspective into generic forms of comedy that enable a critique as well as a celebration of Aboriginal societies. Ian Ross (Ojibwa) follows in this mode with *fareWel* (1996; 1997), which premiered at the Prairie Theatre Exchange and became the first Aboriginal play to win a Governor General's Award. This gritty satire takes up the 1990s debate about Indigenous self-determination through the story of a reservation community that refuses welfare and decides to govern itself when its corrupt chief disappears to Las Vegas. Ross's subsequent play, *The Gap* (2001), explores a developing relationship between an Aboriginal man and a French woman, engaging with the conventions of romantic comedy to deliver its political observations on the breaches between Canada's constituent cultures.

Whereas Taylor and Ross have made their mark by Aboriginalizing popular stage genres, west coast writer, performer, and director Marie Clements (Métis) is at the vanguard of a distinctive experimental theater that combines mythopoeic elements with historicized social and political commentary. Her work typically employs a rich collocation of visual and aural images while integrating ritualistic and realistic gestures, action, and dialogue. *Age of Iron* (1993; 2001), her powerful debut play, draws on classical Greek mythology to examine colonization and its aftermath, blending the story of the fall of Troy with the history of First Nations peoples in North America. Here, various legendary Trojans are reimagined as Aboriginal street warriors in an urban battle for survival against discrimination, poverty, and violence. Cassandra is both seer and prostitute, an emblematic figure who carries the wounds of Native residential school, while Hecuba appears as a tragic bag-lady fussing over her plastic dolls, surrogates for the daughter she unwittingly exiled. Mythical Aboriginal figures also inhabit this social landscape in the form of a menacing half-boy, half-bird street kid cum trickster, Raven, and his antithesis, Earth Woman, the land's nurturing spirit. Clements adds another layer to her rich dramaturgy with contrasting choruses – representing the solidarity of Aboriginal sisterhood and the pervasive system of imposed (white) governance – that punctuate the street warriors' efforts to survive their multiple oppressions. Despite their difficulties, the play ends on a triumphant note, positioning colonization (past and present) not only as a time of loss but also as an age of "transition, bravery and courage."[13]

Many of Clements's subsequent plays have followed in this epic, imagistic mode, now seen as one of the defining characteristics of her work. *The Unnatural and Accidental Women* (2000) blends news reportage, slapstick comedy, storytelling, *film noir*, and Aboriginal ritual, loosely structured in the shape of a revenge drama, to probe the serial murder of a number of women in Vancouver's downtown eastside, home to the Firehall Arts Centre, where the play premiered. The victims' parallel stories, each culminating in a confrontation with the murderer, are presented as a collage of realist and surreal scenes that recuperates the subjectivity and sense of community they have been denied. The central narrative is framed with a complex intertext of sounds and projected images that positions systematic violence against Aboriginal women in the context of the wider destruction of resources – natural and human – visited upon Canada by European settlement and subsequent urban

---

13 Marie Clements, "Notes to *Age of Iron*," in *DraMétis: Three Métis Plays* (Penticton: Theytus, 2001), p. 194.

development. This environmentalism, a recurring sub-theme in Clements's oeuvre, is explicitly developed in *Burning Vision* (2002; 2003), which tackles the subject of atomic warfare by tracing the passage of uranium mined on Dene territory as it is transported across land and water to the apocalyptic fires of Hiroshima and Nagasaki. Structured in four movements, the narrative presents a fragmentary, mythic version of history that incorporates the prophetic vision of a Dene medicine man in the late 1800s to offer a trenchant critique of the racism and xenophobia that fuel cycles of rationalized genocide. This haunting play enjoyed a national tour after its Vancouver premiere and featured at the 2003 Festival de Théâtre des Amériques; it also won a Canada–Japan literary award in 2004.

In her recent offering, *Copper Thunderbird* (2007), Clements presents a multi-layered portrait of Anishinaabe painter, shaman, and womanizer Norval Morrisseau, widely revered as the "father" of modern Aboriginal art in Canada. Her other plays include *The Girl Who Swam Forever* (1995), which dramatizes a young girl's attempt to disengage from the experience of residential school; *Look What You Made Me Do* (1995), about cycles of domestic violence in Native communities; and *Urban Tattoo* (1998), a solo piece on the themes of identity, survival, and the inscription (tattoo) of culture as embodied memory. These innovative works contribute to Clements's reputation as an artist engaged in "creating a postcolonial, postmodern iconography" for our times.[14] An accomplished actor, Clements founded Urban Ink in 2001 to develop Aboriginal and multicultural works and was artistic director of the company until 2007. Her overriding concern with women's lives is part of a broadly feminist project that has similarly preoccupied theater-makers such as Yvette Nolan (Algonquin/Irish), who has produced a number of short experimental dramas including *Blade* (1990; 1995), *Video* (1992; 1995), and *Job's Wife* (1992; 1995). Nolan, currently at the helm of Native Earth Performing Arts, has made substantial contributions to Indigenous theater's recent development through her work as a director and dramaturge. She is also author of *Annie Mae's Movement* (1998; 1999), which combines documentary with myth to honor/re-member the murdered Mi'kmaq activist Anna Mae Aquash, a key figure in the American Indian Movement in the 1970s.

Floyd Favel, founder of Takwakin Performance Workshop in Saskatchewan, is another important theatrical innovator, who, like Clements, strives to find new vocabularies to convey the complexities of contemporary Aboriginal

---

14 Reid Gilbert, "'Shine on us Grandmother Moon': Coding in First Nations Drama," *Theatre Research International* 21.1 (1996), p. 31.

culture. His training includes work with Tukak Teatret in Denmark and such luminaries of experimental theater as Jerzy Grotowski and Suzuki Tadashi, whose influences he meshes with Aboriginal gestural languages, oratory, symbol, and ceremony to develop a modern Indigenous performance style rooted in ancestral tradition. Favel is distinguished by his penetrating engagement with Western texts and genres, which he boldly refashions. His best-known play, *Lady of Silences* (1992; 2005), draws on Jean Genet's *The Blacks* to explore the self-loathing that plagues an Aboriginal community whose internalized "white" value system creates a deep schism between the aspirations and lived realities of its members. First staged at Catalyst Theatre in Edmonton in 1992 and then reworked in 1998, the text revolves around issues of territoriality linked to the murder of a white woman, consciously adopting the generic conventions of detective drama but evading its tidy resolutions. *House of Sonya* (1997) revisits the European canon in a radical adaptation of *Uncle Vanya* that transposes Chekhov's vision of a dissipated pre-revolutionary society to an Aboriginal reservation in Saskatchewan. Favel has also written *All My Relatives* (1990; 2002), about Indigenous transitions from a rural to an urban lifestyle, and *Governor of the Dew* (1999; 2002), a fable of first contact and the genesis of the Métis Nation. His current work-in-progress is *Artaud and the Tarahumaras*, a reflection on art and exile based on the legendary French director's visit to Mexico in 1935.

In the realm of movement/image-based performance, Huron-Wendat theater-maker Yves Sioui Durand has pioneered a unique practice, based on pan-American Indigenous mythologies, which foregrounds dance, music, and visual imagery as its expressive medium. His early piece, *Le Porteur des peines du monde* (1983; 1992), won the Prix Américanité at the 1985 Festival de Théâtre des Amériques, appeared at various venues in Europe and was produced at the Banff Centre in 1995 in an English version. This ritual drama presents a mythic tale about the sun, which carries the sufferings of Aboriginal peoples in its daily passage across the sky before reappearing, cleansed, with the new dawn. In 1985 Sioui Durand co-founded (with Catherine Joncas and John Blondin Déné) Montreal-based company Ondinnok, the only French-language Aboriginal theater in Canada. Along with various community projects, the company's subsequent dramas include *La Conquête de Mexico* (1991; 2001); *Atiskenandahate, voyage au pays des morts* (1988), an Aboriginal version of the Orpheus story; *Ukuamaq* (1993), based on an Inuit legend; and *Kmùkamch Vasierindien* (2002), which explores ancient ties between Asia and America. As well as collaborating with artists such as Robert Lepage, Sioui Durand has been remarkable in his efforts to reach out to Indigenous groups across the

Americas. In a similar vein, Toronto company Red Sky Performance, founded in 2000 by Sandra Laronde, has enjoyed commercial success with its spectacular dance-dramas and mythic presentations of pan-Aboriginality. Jane Moss discusses francophone Native theater further in the chapter on drama in French.

If the task of professional and experimental theater by Aboriginal artists over the recent decades has been to innovate and extend in terms of themes, styles, genres, and performance vocabularies, community theater has aimed to connect individuals and groups, build bridges between cultures, and agitate about particular causes. Tunooniq Theatre, established in Pond Inlet on Baffin Island in 1986, has achieved national recognition, serving not only its local constituency but also distant Inuit settlements across northern Canada and Alaska. The company's widely toured interactive dramas *Changes* (1986; 1999) and *In Search of a Friend* (1988; 1999) draw on Inuit dance, drumming, song and games, with the text performed mostly in Inuktitut, to suggest solutions to problems such as the loss of cultural traditions and the harmful effects of alcohol. Sen'klip Theatre in Vernon, British Columbia, established in 1987, is another notable grass-roots company, having expanded its initial youth education mandate to encompass a popular ecotourism venture that uses theater to develop environmental awareness. More recently created community groups include Kehewin Native Dance Theatre, set up by Melvin and Rosa John in 1991 at the Kehewin Cree Nation in Alberta, and the Saskatchewan Native Theatre in Saskatoon (incorporated 1999), which has developed into a vibrant arts and cultural organization under the direction of its founder, veteran Cree actor Kennetch Charlette.

Some important community theater projects have involved work with non-Aboriginal practitioners. A prominent early example is *No' Xya'* (1987; 1991), devised by David Diamond and Headlines Theatre in Vancouver in close collaboration with the Gitksan and Wet'suwet'en Hereditary Chiefs. Influenced by forum theater techniques, this docudrama presents opposing perspectives on a disputed Aboriginal land claim against the provincial government in 1984, incorporating dance and traditional regalia to convey the tribal structures and migratory patterns of the land's original inhabitants. In a related mode, Rachel Van Fossen and Daryl Wildcat created the massive pageant *Ka'ma'mo'pi cik/The Gathering* (1992; 1997), which recasts colonial history as a process of dialogue and mutual accommodation, to bring together Aboriginal and non-Aboriginal communities in Saskatchewan's legendary Qu'Appelle valley. This kind of community-building has been evident in numerous other projects, with most professional Aboriginal companies also engaged in outreach work of some kind.

The consolidation of structures and organizations necessary to nurture Aboriginal theater and the inspirational work of its many pioneers have provided a robust environment for emerging artists in the twenty-first century. Among these, Shuswap writer-performer Darrell Dennis has drawn attention with *Trickster of Third Avenue East* (2000; 2005), and *Tales of an Urban Indian* (2003; 2005), a semi-autobiographical monodrama that charts a young man's difficult journey from a reservation in northern British Columbia to adult life in the city. Vancouver-based Métis playwright Penny Gummerson won a Jessie Richardson Award for outstanding new play for *Wawatay* (2002; 2005), a family-focused drama that uses the metaphor of the northern lights to suggest the gathering of newly departed souls to commence their journey to the spirit world. Among other highly promising writers is Tara Beagan, whose work attempts to bring together aspects of her Thompson River Salish and Irish Canadian heritages. Her probing exploration of the after-effects of foetal alcohol syndrome in *Dreary and Izzy* (2005; 2007) has been followed by innovative historical dramas including *The Fort at York* (2007).

The diversification of both professional and community work over the last three decades has produced an Aboriginal theater that is vibrant, polyvocal, syncretic and frequently resistant to categorization. Like other Indigenous art forms in Canada, this work has necessarily served at least two different constituencies: its own distinct communities and the broader postcolonizing society from which many audience members are drawn. As this brief survey suggests, Aboriginal theater has wrestled with the legacies of colonialism in original and provocative ways; it has also looked forward to imagine different futures for Indigenous peoples and to forge new cultural and artistic allegiances, facilitating a pronounced if uneven shift in the nation's performing arts culture.[15]

---

15 I would like to thank Daniel David Moses for his contribution to this essay. His generously shared information and comment on early drafts has enabled a fuller account of contemporary Aboriginal theater than I would have otherwise been able to produce.

27

Transcultural life-writing

ALFRED HORNUNG

Since the 1980s, life-writing has become a recognized and productive genre, incorporating the traditional forms of autobiography, memoir, journal, and biography as well as adding sub-genres such as advice columns, letters to the editor, obituaries, video tapes, performance, and online lives. As such, life-writing has simultaneously developed into a privileged form of self-expression and into a major field of scholarship. More than representations of self, such texts represent their subjects in relation to their cultures, tracing their interactions over periods of time. In the course of the twentieth century, these subjects and cultures were primarily defined with reference to a nation and its official language. A seemingly homogeneous allegiance to a national code could, however, not be fully realized in classic immigration countries like Australia, Canada, and the United States. Waves of immigration since the end of the nineteenth century have challenged uniform national credos and transformed mainstream societies. The end to colonial rule in Third World countries and the appeal of free economic markets in the First World have created new patterns of global migration in the second half of the twentieth century.

With the transition from a modern to a postmodern age, the processes of acculturation changed from the demands of assimilation to the recognition of cultural differences. The long-held belief in a monocultural model of society gave way to the reality of multicultural nations. Canada is one of the few countries which has officially recognized her cultural heritage of immigrants by adding the Multiculturalism Act to her Constitution in 1988. Forms of life-writing which have appeared since then affirm the spirit of this legislation, though they often relate stories of discrimination of past and present in different cultures. Thus the practice of life-writing has become a form of intercultural negotiation with the goal of realizing a transcultural form of existence.¹ Canadian autobiographers use their often experimental life-writing to situate themselves in their new country of residence, but also to maintain connections to their countries of origin. The self which governs these texts is primarily oriented along ethnicity and gender and differs radically from the belief in a unified self once formulated by European Enlightenment thinkers. Rather, this self derives its flexibility from the transitory and multicultural experiences that also affect the political status of nation states. Transcultural life-writers challenge beliefs in national allegiance and geographical boundaries. In this sense, contemporary Canadian autobiographers provide viable models for the interaction of displaced individuals in a multi-ethnic democratic society and project a new relationship with their environment.

One of the important features of the global age is an increase in migration. Such migrations have long been part of world history and have influenced the formation of nations and modern societies. Causes for such migrations have been climate changes, wars, expulsion, ethnic cleansing, ensuing poverty and economic need. They also include forms of forced migration, such as slavery, or the movement of migrant workers who follow the demands of the labor market in industrialized societies. Australia, Canada and the United States have traditionally been the goal of these migrations, but since the second half of the twentieth century, European countries have also had to confront the societal and cultural changes caused by the presence of migrants. Canadian forms of life-writing, which look back to a longer history of migration, may, therefore, serve as models of acculturation elsewhere. The life-stories of a great number of writers who immigrated to Canada in the course of the twentieth century begin with the disastrous effects of the collapse of empires and the struggle for power. Most writers with a European background refer to the pogroms at the turn of the last century and to the two World Wars as their reasons for migration to Canada, a safe place of refuge from persecution.

The multicultural frame of Europe rests on the Austro-Hungarian Empire and its transformation after the First World War. Anna Porter's *The Storyteller: Memory, Secrets, Magic and Lies* (2000), Modris Eksteins's *Walking Since Daybreak: A Story of Eastern Europe, World War II, and the Heart of Our Century* (1999), Janice Kulyk Keefer's *Honey and Ashes: A Story of a Family* (1998), and Hanna Spencer's *Hanna's Diary, 1938–1941* (2001) interweave their personal stories with a vast historical panorama. Porter's family history, which

---

1 See, for example, the special issue on "Cross-Cultural Autobiography," *a/b: Auto/Biography Studies* 12.2 (Fall 1997), ed. Joseph and Rebecca Hogan.

begins with her grandfather Vili in 1899 and traces the lives of three generations from Hungary via New Zealand to the author's new home in Toronto, connects the succession of fourteen generations with the history of Hungary from 1456 to the 1990s. This historical and generational panorama is dominated by opposites in cultural and political ideology, ranging from the Huns and the Romans to the Turks and finally the Nazis and Soviets. After the Revolution of 1956, the family manages to leave the country and settle in New Zealand, before Anna Porter begins her publishing career in England. She moves to Canada in 1969, where she marries and sees her two daughters develop into "true Canadians."[2]

A similar kind of political and historical background informs Modris Eksteins's writing. The University of Toronto historian uses the craft of his profession for an analysis of his own family history. For him, "[t]he year 1945 stands at the center of our century and our meaning."[3] Born in 1943 in Latvia, Eksteins begins with the birth of his grandfather Jānis in 1874, child of a Latvian chambermaid and a Baltic-German baron. This union connects his family with the history of the Baltic States, beginning with their colonization by the German Hansa and the dominant influence of the Austro-Hungarian Empire until the Baltic gained independence in 1991, following Nazi and Soviet occupation. His childhood memories recollect the dismal days as a Displaced Person in refugee camps in northern Germany until the family ships out to Canada, courtesy of the International Refugee Organization.

Janice Kulyk Keefer begins with the stories of her grandmother's native village, Staromischyna, Ukraine, which at the grandmother's birth in 1902 belonged to the Austro-Hungarian Empire, but at her mother's birth twenty years later to the newly created Polish Republic. In her narrative, the Canadian-born author tries to follow poetically the remapping of the European landscape and the shuffling of national and cultural allegiances by focusing on the women in the family. Once the women arrive in Canada in 1935, they face a difficult period. Feeling excluded from the company of WASPs, Kulyk Keefer associates with Jewish women in Toronto in whose meetings she hears about the anti-Semitism in the Ukraine and Poland as well as the Greek-Catholic origin of her family, problematically aligning her own life with that of the Jews and identifying with Anne Frank.

---

2 Anna Porter, *The Storyteller: Memory, Secrets, Magic and Lies*, 2000 (Toronto: Anchor Canada, 2001), p. 343.
3 Modris Eksteins, *Walking Since Daybreak: A Story of Eastern Europe, World War II, and the Heart of Our Century* (Boston: Houghton Mifflin, 1999), p. x.

The Russian Orthodox world of 1920s Orenburg and the subsequent displacement to Poland in the course of the Second World War re-emerges in the memory of Irena F. Karafilly's mother, who suffers from Alzheimer's disease. The narrative of *The Stranger in the Plumed Hat: A Memoir* (2000), which starts out as a way for the daughter to cope with this stressful situation, turns out to be "a factual account of my mother's story – the story she kept trying to tell."[4] The relapse into the soothing Russian and Polish languages of her early life in Europe at the same time hastens her mother's dementia. When the disease sets in she challenges her doctor's medical diagnosis with her own: "'My *memory* make [sic] me crazy!'" (p. 15) In memory she relives her marriage to a Polish Jew, life in Łódź after the war, their nine-year stay in Israel and their initial difficulties of settling in Montreal. Karafilly's mother relives her experience as a migrant in Israel and immigrant in Canada as a patient in St. Mary's hospital in the 1990s, isolated, sanitized, and strapped to a bed.

The escape from the turmoil of war is especially crucial for the survivors of the Holocaust who seek refuge in North America. The Jewish experience alluded to in Keefer's and Karafilly's stories is augmented and authenticated by the survivor stories of Jack Kuper, Hanna Spencer, and Lisa Appignanesi.[5] In the memories of forced migration triggered by disease, it is her parents' declining health which reconnects Lisa Appignanesi with her European Jewish heritage in *Losing the Dead* (1999; 2000). The opening chapter, "Legacies," captures the moment of her father's death from diabetes in a London hospital, where he lapses into the Yiddish language of his Polish past. Similarly, the ravages of Alzheimer's disease send her mother back to her Polish life, so that the daughter feels compelled to write all of this experience down "to anchor myself against the rudderless ship of her mind."[6] It is only at the end of her parents' lives that the daughter makes an effort to reconstruct her Polish roots by recovering her mother's Jewish past in Poland and by relating the history of the Jews in Poland who had become – by the twentieth century – assimilated modern Jews as a result of a multicultural world in which they had lived since the eighteenth century. Their escape from the Warsaw Ghetto and from the concentration camps by fleeing to France and

---

4 Irena F. Karafilly, "Author's Note," *The Stranger in the Plumed Hat: A Memoir* (Toronto: Viking, 2000), n.p.
5 See Susanna Egan and Gabriele Helms, "Generations of the Holocaust in Canadian Auto/biography," in *Auto/biography in Canada: Critical Directions*, ed. Julie Rak (Waterloo: Wilfried Laurier University Press, 2005), pp. 32–51.
6 Lisa Appignanesi, *Losing the Dead: A Family Memoir* (London: Vintage, 2000 [1999]), p. 7.

then to Canada enforced their ethnic origins before they were able to blend into a new environment.

While Karafilly and Appignanesi work through the memory of their parents, other writers try to recall the effects of the war and persecution on their childhood and adolescence in their narratives. Kuper's *Child of the Holocaust* (1967) is the survival story of nine-year-old Jakob Kuperblum in Poland. As one of many Jewish orphans he is rescued by the Canadian Jewish Congress, brought to Canada and adopted in Toronto. Hanna Spencer uses the form of the diary to record the story of her survival in Czechoslovakia, a nation created after the First World War in 1918 after the collapse of the Austro-Hungarian Empire. Living with the Sudeten Germans she writes six volumes of her diary in German, recording the political changes after the *Anschluss* of the Sudetenland in 1938 which force her to flee to England and from there to Canada. Frank Oberle's migration from Germany to Canada becomes the topic of the first of his two volumes of autobiography written after his political career in British Columbia and with the government of Canada. *Finding Home: A War Child's Journey to Peace* (2004) takes him back to his childhood in Forchheim, near the Black Forest, where he was born in 1932.[7] The experience of Hitler's war begins with his family's relocation to Poland in 1940 and attendance of a Hitler Youth school, ending with his escape from the advancing Red Army in 1945. Dissatisfied with his life in post-war Germany, he seeks his fortune in the New World and emigrates to Canada in 1951, joined by his wife Joan (Hanna) and their daughter fifteen months later.

In most of these writings, the reconstruction of a past, often including that of parents and grandparents, is in the foreground. The stories are either told from direct personal experience of the Old Country and the hardship of migration, or retold from stories passed on by earlier generations. The direct telling of their own life-story by Modris Eksteins and Frank Oberle or of parts of their lives in Jack Kuper and Hanna Spencer is motivated by gratitude to Canada, which, in Oberle's words, represents "finding home." Although Canada is not part of Jack Kuper's Holocaust story, the epigraph in which "[t]he author wishes to express his gratitude to the people of Canada" governs the narrative. Hanna Spencer spends the second part of her diary praising the welcome reception by Canadian organizations and their rescue missions and speaking fondly of "our very own farm" in New Haven, Ontario.[8] Modris

---

7 The second volume is *A Chosen Path: From Moccasin Flats to Parliament Hill* (Surrey: Heritage House Publishing, 2005).
8 Hanna Spencer, *Hanna's Diary, 1938–1941: Czechoslovakia to Canada* (Montreal: McGill-Queen's University Press, 2001), p. 122.

Eksteins parallels the historical juxtaposition between Eastern Europe and North America with the fateful year of 1945, which for him is the turning point in the progress from old regimes to new democratic societies. Hence, he analyzes the demise of the Hapsburg and German empires and the collapse of the fascist and communist ideologies in Europe from the perspective of his life in Canada and feels that he has become part of "the postmodern, multicultural, posthistorical mainstream."[9] Along with an assessment of the struggle of the Baltic States for freedom, he has lavish praise for his new home.

> Despite superficial setbacks and difficulties, this land, this "peaceful kingdom," proved to be, for our family and for most immigrants, a haven of perfectly poetical nature, a shelter from a world of deprivation and horror, a land of plenty, a country never occupied, never bombed from the air, a veritable Eden. (p. 83)

These alternations between narratives devoted to the new country of Canada on the one hand and the Old Country on the other are frequently substantiated by visits back home in search of family roots. These travels become the basis for a linkage between the two worlds. While writers like Oberle or Eksteins, who personally remember their countries of origin, proudly endorse their new and successful Canadian lives or research their biographically based historical work, the return trip becomes more essential for writers who come by their knowledge mostly through their parents' stories. Appignanesi, Keefer, Porter, and Karafilly rely on their own impressions from visits, often accompanied by friends or children. Some writers receive additional information about their European lives by reconnecting with relatives in Canada.

Lisa Appignanesi's two trips back to Poland in 1988 and 1997 are motivated by questions left open about her Jewish past after her father's death and the failure of her mother's memory, badly affected by Alzheimer's disease. While the impressions of her first trip are rather superficial because of the uncooperative demeanor of officials and her inadequate knowledge of Polish, she profits from the political changes of post-communism and the company of her Polish-speaking New York friend during her second trip.[10] Through research in archives and visits to concentration camps and her family's homes she reconstructs wartime Jewish history, filling in gaps with scraps of memory

---

9 Eksteins, *Walking Since Daybreak*, p. xi.
10 See Mary Besemeres, "The Family in Exile, Between Languages: Eva Hoffman's *Lost in Translation*, Lisa Appignanesi's *Losing the Dead*, Anca Vlasopolos's *No Return Address*," *a/b: Auto/Biography Studies* 19.1/2 (Summer 2004), pp. 239–48.

from her mother's stories and her own imagination. Aptly, Part Two describing this visit is called "Excavations," as the information is culled from the missing dead. By the time the two friends leave Poland, they feel that they have come closer to the recovery of their past, thus making amends for not having previously paid attention to their "childhood stories of war and emigration."[11]

The collapse of communism at the end of the twentieth century facilitates the return of naturalized Canadians to their East European homes, from which they were forced to migrate in the first half of the century. Keefer's two return trips to the Ukraine in 1993 and 1997 turn out to be important exercises in living memory, an answer to the author's rhetorical question: "Are we, in the end, only what we can remember?"[12] Porter's visits in 1996 and 1998 to Hungary, where she spent her childhood and school years, are less an attempt at reconstruction – as in Appignanesi's case – than a wish to see again the places of her youth and show them to her daughter. These visits do not really add to the narrative, but create a thread of continuity for the next generation to connect with the mother's past.

All of these life-stories about interactions of the Old World in Eastern Europe with the new country of Canada are written from the perspective of migrants successfully settled in North America. Writers, artists, publishers, academics, or politicians praise Canada's system of political freedom over the persecution of difference in war-torn Europe. Yet most of these writers also mention the multicultural syncretism in Eastern Europe before the two world wars, with Yiddish functioning as a means of communication that transcended state lines and national boundaries. Pre-war and post-war maps included in these books mark the destruction of the Austro-Hungarian and Prussian Empires and the creation of new states. This knowledge of political and cultural transformation informs the process of acculturation in Canada. Despite the initial feeling of discrimination against immigrants from Eastern Europe, and despite the newcomers' perception of Canada as a *"terra incognita"*[13] or "a nation-less state,"[14] Canada is gradually seen as the basis for establishing new connections. These writings create maps out of words[15]

---

11 Appignanesi, *Losing the Dead*, p. 87.
12 Janice Kulyk Keefer, *Honey and Ashes: A Story of Family* (Toronto: HarperFlamingoCanada, 1998), p. 320.
13 Appignanesi, *Losing the Dead*, p. 13.
14 Eksteins, *Walking Since Daybreak*, p. 18.
15 See Karafilly's quotation from Adrienne Rich's poem "Diving into the Wreck" in the epigraph of her memoir.

and tell stories "that will speak across any number of borders ... trying to build a bridge out of words."[16]

The temporal succession of generations which governs most life stories has its spatial equivalent in a border-crossing network of co-operation. It is also worth noting Isabel Huggan's account in *Belonging: Home Away from Home* (2003) of transcultural experience in reverse. Using a hybridized memoir-short story form, Huggan refashions the tropes of nomadism and exile from the perspective of a white middle-class Canadian woman who finds herself for reasons having to do with her husband's profession (like Margaret Laurence and Audrey Thomas before her) making her home in a foreign country – France. However, she is too wise to conflate very different experiences of homesickness, recognizing her own privileged position compared with those who will never be able to return home, "and you feel ashamed, and you stop."[17]

The collapse of empires in Europe and the resultant reconfiguration of the political landscape, responsible for migration to, and life-writing in, a new country, had its repercussions and equivalents in Asia. The imperialist goals of European and American colonial powers and their engagement in Japan and China in the course of the nineteenth century led to political and cultural confrontations which resulted in two Sino-Japanese Wars in 1894–5 and 1937–45. Encouraged by German imperial and fascist forces, Japan opened the Asian frontline of the world wars. The resulting radical transformations and economic need caused the migration of a first generation of Chinese and Japanese workers to North America toward the end of the nineteenth century. Unlike most European immigrants, male bread-winners in Asian families generally first arrived on their own. Against their original intention, they stayed on and had their families join them. With few exceptions, their children were born in Canada, grew up in ethnic communities, often not learning their parents' language and receiving their education in an English-language environment. Knowledge about their ancestors' home country came from family stories and mythic tales or occasional journeys "back home."

In these life-stories, many writers stress the importance of childhood recollected in middle age, with reference to the difficulties created by immigration policies and discriminatory practices against the acceptance of Asians, including the relocation of Japanese Canadians after Pearl Harbor.

---

16 Keefer, *Honey and Ashes*, pp. 7–8.
17 Isabel Huggan, *Belonging: Home Away from Home* (Toronto: Alfred A. Knopf Canada, 2003), p. 21.

While all writers situate the origin of their family's migration in the turmoil and hardship at the end of the nineteenth century and recover their forebears' path to Canada from stories and cultural customs, Michael David Kwan relives in *Things That Must Not Be Forgotten: A Childhood in Wartime China* (2000) his actual experiences in China from the mid-1930s to the late 1940s. Thanks to his father's international connections, education in Cambridge, and position as "administrator of one of China's major railways,"[18] Michael lives a privileged life without any material want. Even in the early days of the Japanese invasion and the initial ideological battles between Chiang Kai-shek's Kuomintang and Mao Zedong's communists the family resides comfortably in the foreign community separated from the Chinese in the Legation Quarter of Beijing. Kwan's real problem is a lack of emotional and cultural ties. As the child of a Chinese father and a young Swiss mother, who abandons the family and is divorced, he grows up in the care of a Chinese nanny and increasingly becomes aware of his status as a mixed-blood Chinese and a half-caste Eurasian (ch. 3).

This mixed cultural identity is also reflected in his linguistic oscillation between English and Chinese. Early on he learns to counteract the xenophobic attitude of Hester, the British wife of the Findlay-Wu family, in whose care he lives temporarily, and the Chinese teachers and fellow students in school. When his father marries Hester's sister Ellen and dismisses Michael's Chinese nanny to make him accept his new mother, the young boy is devastated. The reversal of his father's social and political status as part of a system of betrayal in war times creates the basis for a meaningful relation among them, which allows them to survive false allegations and hardship. Kwan's escape from China in the final days of the war to Hong Kong is the stepping stone for his migration to Canada in 1963, while his parents find refuge in Australia. Although Canada never appears in Kwan's narrative, his life in Vancouver is the backdrop against which the story is set. In an interview he pointed out that he did not experience any discrimination in Canada and faced more problems with the diverse groups of Chinese in Vancouver than with Caucasian Canadians.[19]

In *Paper Shadows: A Chinatown Childhood* (1999), Wayson Choy narrates a different kind of Chinese childhood. Born in 1939 in Vancouver as a third-generation Chinese immigrant, he was raised in Chinatown. In the

---

18 Michael David Kwan, *Things That Must Not Be Forgotten: A Childhood in Wartime China* (Toronto: Macfarlane Walter and Ross, 2000), p. 4.
19 Jeannine Cuevas, "An Interview with Michael David Kwan" (2000), www.Kiriyamaprize.org.

story of his childhood experiences, he interweaves his life-story with the history of Chinese immigration to Canada, restrictive Canadian immigration politics, and the militant aggression of Japan in China and in Pearl Harbor. His narrative culminates in the celebration of Japan's surrender in 1945. Although Choy is surrounded by Chinese culture in Chinatown, he grows up within competing cultural systems, juxtaposing the tradition of the Chinese opera with American cowboy films. Thus he prefers to be a cowboy or a Robin Hood character to identifying with Chinese mythic characters on stage and rejects the idea of going back to Old China. Resisting his mother's efforts to educate her son in the Chinese language and culture, he affirms his intercultural situation by speaking *"Chinglish."*[20] In the Chinatown school, he notes the ignorance of his teachers who "saw our peasant Chinese faces, but not our in-between souls" (p. 234). Rather than wanting to be Chinese, he drops out of Chinese school and affirms that he is a Canadian (p. 238).

As an adult with a teaching career in Toronto, Choy comes upon two family secrets. One concerns his grandfather's first wife, who was left behind with her son, Choy's father, when he embarked for Canada in 1903. During his absence, his wife committed adultery and brought shame on the family. With hindsight, Choy begins to understand why his father was dismissed by his grandfather's second wife. The second secret concerns Choy's biological parents. Coincidentally he finds out that he is an adopted child, possibly fathered by an actor of the Chinese opera in Vancouver. Although he rejected Chinese culture as a child, these intercultural relations between China and Canada have motivated him to explore the lives of 1930s and 1940s Chinese-Canadians in two novels, *The Jade Peony* (1995) and the sequel *All That Matters* (2004). Along with the video biography *Wayson Choy: Unfolding the Butterfly* (2003) and the documentary *Searching for Confucius* (2005) describing his trip to China, these texts convey Choy's belief that being Chinese-Canadian and a member of an ethnic minority is only a stage in acquiring Canadian identity.[21]

Canadians of Japanese descent, like the scientist David Suzuki, tell a different kind of story, albeit with the same message of allegiance to Canada. In two partially overlapping autobiographical works, *Metamorphosis: Stages in a Life* (1987) and *David Suzuki: The Autobiography* (2006), Suzuki strongly affirms from the beginning his identity as a monolingual Canadian citizen, born in 1936 in Vancouver of second-generation Japanese parents. Japan's attack on Pearl Harbor sets off a series of discriminatory measures, including relocation

---

20 Wayson Choy, *Paper Shadows: A Chinatown Childhood* (Toronto: Viking, 1999), p. 83.
21 Don Montgomery, "An Interview with Wayson Choy" (2002), www.asiancanadian.net.

from the west coast to the interior, segregation in internment camps and the Canadian government's efforts to repatriate Japanese Canadian citizens after the war. While Suzuki represents this process of disruptive acculturation from a scientist's perspective in *Metamorphosis*, he looks at the same history from a political one in *The Autobiography* nineteen years later, as is evident in the title of that book's first chapter: "My Happy Childhood in Racist British Columbia."[22] In the course of his education and professional life he learns, however, to deal with prejudice and he gains the respect of Canadians as a scientist and environmentalist with his own popular TV series whose work transcends national borders.

War in Southeast Asia and its political consequences result in new patterns of migration and travel as well as different kinds of life-stories. Suzuki reports on the "repatriation" of his maternal grandparents to a defeated Japan, where they died from "culture shock and disillusionment" shortly thereafter.[23] In the more liberal and increasingly multicultural climate of Canada from the 1970s on, the changed political order in the country of their ancestors motivates Asian-Canadians to reconnect with their cultural origins. The lifestories describing these short-term trips or longer stays are generally related to their professional activities as journalists (Jan Wong, Yi Sun-Kyung), writers (Clark Blaise, Bharati Mukherjee, M. G. Vassanji, Michael Ondaatje) or academics (Arun Mukherjee).

Yi Sun-Kyung and Jan Wong belong to the second and third generation of immigrants from, respectively, Korea and China, whose life-writing is part of their careers as journalists. While Jan Wong was born in 1953 in Montreal of Canadian-born Chinese parents, Yi Sun-Kyung spent the first nine years of her life in South Korea before her family moved to Regina, Saskatchewan. For different reasons and on assignment for different Canadian media, they each make two visits to the country of their ancestors and come back with changed political ideologies. As described in her memoir *Red China Blues: My Long March from Mao to Now* (1996), Jan Wong's rebellious 1960s spirit leads her to criticize her family's difficult adjustment to Canada and to adopt Maoism under the influence of anti-Vietnam activities in North America and Europe. Dedicated to her political conviction as "a Montreal Maoist"[24] the McGill student is one of two North American students chosen to study at Peking University for the academic year of 1972–3.

22 David Suzuki, *The Autobiography* (Vancouver: Greystone Books, 2006).
23 David Suzuki, *Metamorphosis: Stages in a Life* (Toronto: Stoddart, 1987), p. 25.
24 Jan Wong, *Red China Blues: My Long March from Mao to Now* (New York: Anchor Books, 1997 [1996]), p. 16.

Part of her political intention during this stay is "to do manual labor to reform my thinking" (p. 25). Classified as an "Overseas Chinese," she is acquainted by her "minders" with her ancestral home in Taishan, South China. As a result, she also learns about her grandparents' immigration stories at the turn of the past century. Between 1972 and 1994 Wong spends a total of fourteen years in China, first as a student, then as a journalist after an eight-year intermission to study at Columbia University in New York. The title and subtitle of her book express her transformation, the "red china blues" caused by her "long march from Mao to now." The structural arrangement of her experiences in four parts, reminiscent of John Milton's *Paradise Lost*, stands for her gradual disillusionment with Mao's paradise and her renewed allegiance with Canada after the collapse of the Communist world.

A similar ideological basis underlies Yi Sun-Kyung's Korean-Canadian life story, *Inside the Hermit Kingdom: A Memoir* (1997). The prologue in 1975 Seoul depicts through the eight-year-old child's eyes the political opposition between the free South Korea protected by the Americans, for whom her father works, and the "evil" communist North Korea separated by the Demilitarized Zone (DMZ). This black and white worldview, which seems to be supported by the image of North America she has gained from Hollywood pictures, later colors the impression of Korea she derives from watching the American television series *MASH*. Being sworn in as a Canadian citizen in 1979 is not "a day of celebration and pride" for her; instead she feels "a sense of loss," remembering her adolescent "dream of going back to Korea."[25] She feels increasingly divided in her cultural affiliation when she visits Korea, first North Korea in 1994, then South Korea in 1995 on assignment for the CBC.

Her visit of North Korea shortly after Kim Il-Sung's death is shaped by the guides and translators, the "senior" and the "junior minder" (p. 98) who escort the "'reporter-teacher'" (p. 100) on her official program. In Seoul one year later, she registers the changes since her childhood, the westernization of South Korea and the corruption in the political system. The author deplores the lack of freedom of speech and – back in Canada – fights off attempts by agents of the Korean Embassy in Toronto to edit her report (p. 234). Viewing the DMZ from the southern side, she feels that the divide is unbridgeable: "Like the nation itself, I was divided, caught in an emotional paralysis" (p. 219). She is torn between an emotional attachment based on illusions and a rational acceptance of Canada. Finally she consoles herself with

---

25 Yi Sun-Kyung, *Inside the Hermit Kingdom: A Memoir* (Toronto: Key Porter, 1997), p. 24.

her parents' motivation for leaving Korea: "We came to Canada for your future" (p. 219).

The division between different cultures informs *Days and Nights in Calcutta* (1977; 1995), co-authored by Clark Blaise and Bharati Mukherjee following their one-year stay in India in 1973–4. The book combines the perspectives of the American-raised Canadian husband and of the Indian-born Canadian wife. For Blaise this project involves the encounter with his wife's Indian world, her ancestors and family history, while for Mukherjee it represents a reconnection with her childhood in India. Blaise's journal precedes that of his wife, and his perceptions are those of an outsider recording features of non-Western life new to him as well as aspects of post-Independence Indian politics. Her journal conveys the perceptions of someone who has returned reluctantly after fourteen years of absence. Noting differences between America's and India's public life, she is puzzled by the ease with which citizenship can be acquired, but cultural roots cannot: "... changing citizenships is easy, swapping cultures is not."[26] When she revisits her former homes and attends social events, she experiences nostalgia without establishing any real connection.

In the Epilogue, she comments on her in-between position and feels more "as an immigrant than an exile" (p. 296), who has exchanged the old image of India for an imaginary one. Thus she opts for a cultural syncretism which conjoins "Hindu imagination with an Americanized sense of the craft of fiction" (p. 298). The book, originally published in 1977, is given an additional level of meaning in the 1995 paperback edition. The couple's perspective has changed. The common thread is "the distant rumble of Canadian racism" and the disintegration of the Canadian identity that one of them was born into and that the other acquired (p. xiii). Also influenced by their analysis of the Air India disaster of 1985, Mukherjee questions the rhetoric of multiculturalism in Canada, which marginalizes "its non-white citizens exclusively on the basis of race," and she justifies her decision to abandon her Canadian citizenship for a career at the University of California at Berkeley. In the final analysis, this "accidental autobiography" provides the aesthetic space for her "risky journey from exile to settler and claimant" (p. 302).

Unlike *Days and Nights in Calcutta*, novelist M. G. Vassanji's *A Place Within: Rediscovering India* (2008) is told from a single perspective, but the author speaks "on behalf of [his] family after seventy, eighty, a hundred years" of living outside of India. Born in Nairobi, Tanzania, Vassanji relates his

---

26 Clark Blaise, Bharati Mukherjee, *Days and Nights in Calcutta* (Saint Paul: Hungry Mind Press, 1995 [1977]), p. 169.

numerous travels to India in a narrative that combines personal memoir with scholarly investigation. Recurrent visits to tombs alternate with travels by train, creating a dynamic of myth and modernity, stasis and movement, but "the journey is endless."[27]

M. G. Vassanji's and Bharati Mukherjee's writing fits the label of postcolonial literature which literary critic Arun Mukherjee, not a relation of Bharati Mukherjee, sees as the focus of her professional life. *Postcolonialism: My Living* (1998) describes her evolution from an Indian woman born in 1946 as a British subject to an Indian citizen on August 15, 1947 and finally a South Asian-Canadian in Toronto. In a series of articles and talks, Arun Mukherjee rightly claims her life to be exemplary of the postcolonial condition and the political freedom that follows colonial power. As a Commonwealth scholar at the University of Toronto, she begins to acquire from 1971 on the critical vocabulary used by Western critics in dealing with postcolonial literature. Stressing the interrelation of lived experience and theoretical concepts, of teaching and theorizing, Arun Mukherjee criticizes the assumptions of Western critics who base their analyses on homogenized constructions of the Third World.

These scholarly preoccupations, she feels, have outlived their usefulness, and, moving away from them, Mukherjee now feels equipped to talk only about her native India and South Asia. A result of these stereotypes, Mukherjee claims, was the neglect of ethnicity, race, and women in postcolonial criticism. The inclusion of ethnicity and race in discussions of Canadian literature and the acceptance of colored people as part of Canadian society are first steps in a new understanding of South Asian writers and critics like herself who live between two worlds, rejecting a nostalgic view of India and deploring the inability to become fully Canadian.[28] Arun Mukherjee's own life and profession become a transnational project of reading, writing, and teaching, which incorporates the responses of her students in the classroom and the modification of curricula in the "metropolitan centres of Euro-America" (p. 179). This critique is also directed against colleagues from Third World countries teaching at First World universities who have forgotten their own origin.

Michael Ondaatje's postmodern and postcolonial autobiography *Running in the Family* (1982) is the author's attempt to reconnect with his past in Sri Lanka during two visits in 1978 and 1980, after leaving in 1954 at the age of eleven. His intention was to travel back to restore in writing the ties with his family

---

27 M. G. Vassanji, *A Place Within: Rediscovering India* (Toronto: Doubleday Canada, 2008), p. 3.
28 Arun Mukherjee, *Postcolonialism: My Living* (Toronto: TSAR, 1998), pp. 35–6.

and relatives. "In my mid-thirties I realized I had slipped past a childhood I had ignored and not understood."[29] Guided by maps and documents, he reconstructs the colonial times of the Dutch and the English in Ceylon from 1600, with an emphasis on the 1920s and 1930s. He writes: "The maps reveal rumours of topography, the routes for invasion and trade, and the dark mad mind of travellers' tales appears throughout Arab and Chinese and medieval records. The island seduced all of Europe. The Portuguese. The Dutch. The English" (p. 64). Ondaatje's own life and writing reflects these diverse origins.

The intercultural experiences made by Canadian citizens on their travels (Sun-Kyung, Ondaatje), during extended stays (Wong, Blaise/Mukherjee) or at international conferences (A. Mukherjee) in the country of ancestors take on a different dimension for visible minorities in the country of residence. While David Kwan's and Wayson Choy's memories of their childhood in, respectively, China and Vancouver focus on the interpersonal negotiation of a cultural identity within the Chinese community, writers in mixed-race relations growing up and living in Canada stress the difficulties of interracial unions between people of color and white Canadians. Novelist Lawrence Hill, whose African-American father and white American mother emigrated to Toronto after their marriage in the 1950s, investigates in his autobiographical narrative *Black Berry, Sweet Juice: On Being Black and White in Canada* (2001) what it means to be Black and white in Canada.

The book is based on his own experience and on interviews conducted with thirty-four mixed-race Canadians, who – like him – recall their first encounter, at the moment when their racial awareness, was awakened, with whites who insult them for their ethnic difference. The only way they can refute the racist equation of whiteness and Canadianness is to embrace their Black identity in Canada.[30] Disappointed in his hopes of finding the answer to his question in Africa, Hill discovers after his return from a summer project in French-speaking Niger that he has more in common with his friends from Quebec. When he studies at Université Laval in 1978, his difference shifts from color to language, "from being black to being an *anglais*" (p. 203). Encounters of racism, Hill feels, are part of socialization in societies in which race is accepted as social construct. Raising his own biracial children, he instills in them the pride of being a Black Canadian and calls on other African-Canadian parents to follow suit. This is also the eloquent message of Barack Obama, elected forty-fourth

---

29 Michael Ondaatje, *Running in the Family* (Toronto: McClelland and Stewart, 1982), p. 22.
30 Lawrence Hill, *Black Berry, Sweet Juice: On Being Black and White in Canada* (Toronto: HarperFlamingoCanada, 2001), p. 29.

President of the United States in 2008. In his memoir *Dreams From My Father: A Story of Race and Inheritance* (1995; rev. 2004), he talks about his exposure to different ethnicities and cultures in Hawai'i, Indonesia, Africa and North America, and how these have determined his identity and political beliefs.

The loss of civil rights as a result of mixed-race relationships is the topic of Velma Demerson's *Incorrigible* (2004). Her relationship with a Chinese man in Toronto leads to her arrest in 1939. When she marries him after her release from ten months in Toronto's Mercer Reformatory for Females, she loses her Canadian citizenship, as she does not realize until later. Throughout her memoir she tries to reconstruct the difficult situation of her family, the troubled marriage of her English immigrant mother to a dark-skinned Mediterranean, and their divorce. Demerson's portrayal of hidden and open forms of discrimination against non-white members of Canadian society, which include her father's objection to her relationship with an "oriental" and turning her over to the police, has an additional sexist aspect. Demerson is sentenced for her improper and morally "incorrigible" behavior under the *Female Refuges Act* of the 1930s. The austere conditions in the Reformatory are compounded by medical experiments carried out without the patients' consent. Treatment for alleged venereal disease endangers her unborn son. Researching these experiments on women and non-white immigrants in the 1980s is for Demerson a process of healing.

The special role of the Indigenous people and their interactions with Canadian society form an important part of transcultural life-writing. It ranges from Chester Brown's comic-strip biography of the nineteenth-century Métis fighter *Louis Riel* (2003) to the identification of Black and Asian immigrants with the Aboriginals, their rise to political office and their struggle for the preservation of the environment. A sense of loss and alienation seems to jeopardize their successful integration into mainstream Canadian society, as Maggie de Vries's biography of her sister shows. In *Missing Sarah: A Vancouver Woman Remembers Her Vanished Sister* (2003) she tries to understand why Sarah, who was adopted into her family as an eleven-month-old baby, did not become part of the family like her adopted brother Mark. The decisive difference between them is color and ethnic origin. As a child with a mixed-race background of Black, Aboriginal, Mexican Indian and white parents, Sarah feels like "the literal black sheep of the family," as she writes in her journal.[31] Her foster parents' divorce and the frequent

---

31 Maggie de Vries, *Missing Sarah: A Vancouver Woman Remembers Her Vanished Sister* (Toronto: Penguin Canada, 2004 [2003]), p. 6.

dislocations contribute to her feelings of insecurity and emotional distance. At the age of fourteen she runs away and becomes a drug addict and a prostitute. After giving birth to two children, she disappears in 1998 and is presumed murdered. Maggie de Vries's book, which started out as a private effort to know her dead sister better, has become an autobiography of her family, a memorial for Vancouver's so-called "missing women" as well as a sociological investigation.[32]

While de Vries's emphasis gradually shifts to criminal investigation, ethnic writers find points of connection between the different races and they move beyond the national borders to a transnational dimension. Thus, Dionne Brand in *A Map to the Door of No Return: Notes to Belonging* (2001) identifies with her Black diaspora, but also establishes cross-cultural links with the Natives of Canada, like the Salish Indians in Vancouver, with her ancestral Africans, or with Chinese migrants. David Suzuki, whose childhood and youth are overshadowed by the discrimination against the Japanese during and after the war, sides with African-Americans during a research assignment in Oak Ridge, Tennessee, and joins the National Association for the Advancement of Colored People (NAACP). The analogy which he draws in *Metamorphosis* between the American treatment of Blacks and the Canadian treatment of Natives changes to an analogy between Aboriginal and Asian immigrants based on "our shared genetic heritage" in his *Autobiography* (p. 11). This affinity between Canada's cultural history and the global situation can be deployed to address political and environmental emergencies.

In *The Sorrow and the Terror: The Haunting Legacy of the Air India Tragedy* (1987), Clark Blaise and Bharati Mukherjee analyze the Air India tragedy of June 1985 as a plot masterminded by a Sikh terrorist cell in Vancouver. The death of 329 people, whose plane crashed into the Atlantic Ocean off the coast of Ireland en route from Canada to India, turns into a nightmare for relatives and officials of several nations. Although most of the passengers were Canadians, the political authorities refer to them as people of Indian descent without acknowledging their national identity. Because India owns the carrier, it controls the investigations and legal proceedings, while Ireland organizes the rescue operations and the identification of the victims. Canada, however, fails to mourn the dead in an official ceremony as Canadian citizens. It was not until July 2007 that a memorial was dedicated in Vancouver. In their analysis, Blaise and Mukherjee see Canada's immigration policies of the 1970s and the

---

32 See Valerie Raoul, "You May Think This, but: An Interview with Maggie de Vries," *Canadian Literature* 183 (Winter 2004), pp. 59–70.

adoption of a multicultural society as the cause for the terrorist act. Rather than insisting on assimilation, the Canadian concept of a cultural mosaic – they argue – nurtured a form of religious fundamentalism among the "undereducated and underemployed Sikh youth."[33] For the authors the Air India disaster is a Canadian tragedy.

Investigations and trials did not yield any conclusive results. Yet, there is evidence that this tragedy might have been prevented by Canadian authorities. On May 3, 2007, Ontario Lieutenant Governor James Bartleman, in charge of the intelligence analysis and security branch of the Department of External Affairs in 1985, stated on CBC News that he had received a document warning of an imminent terrorist attack. Presenting this document at a committee meeting on Sikh extremism, he was rebuffed by a senior RCMP officer who had received the same information, but apparently did not consider it significant. This response could, in Blaise's and Mukherjee's opinion, be cited as proof that a question of national security was treated as an issue affecting a visible minority and therefore one that did not receive first priority. Their broadside attack on Canada's Multiculturalism Act which – in their mind – rewards visible minorities' "resistant diversity, not their ability to assimilate" (p. 199) does not, however, reflect the modified multicultural reality of contemporary Canadian society at the beginning of the twenty-first century. In addition to the successful naturalization of European immigrants, there are prominent examples of the acceptance and integration of ethnic minorities. James Bartleman, Rudy Wiebe, and David Suzuki, among many others, represent three representative lives whose identification with Canada forms the basis of their life-writing.

Bartleman, Wiebe, and Suzuki look back at their early lives from the vantage points of accomplished careers as a politician, a writer, and a scientist. Their difficult ethnic beginnings in the 1930s and 1940s as children of mixed race and immigrants from Russia and Japan respectively are overcome by adopting a post-ethnic position and appealing to transnational co-operation for the preservation of the planet earth.[34] In *Raisin Wine: A Boyhood in a Different Muskoka* (2007), James Bartleman relates the first thirteen years of his life from 1940 to 1953 in the Muskoka region. It is the life-story of his parents, a Chippewa woman and a white man who made their home with four children in Port Carling, Ontario, on the Indian reserve. Bartleman, who speaks of

---

33 Clark Blaise, Bharati Mukherjee, *The Sorrow and the Terror: The Haunting Legacy of the Air India Tragedy* (Markham: Viking, 1987), p. 177.
34 David Hollinger, *Postethnic America: Beyond Multiculturalism* (New York: Basic Books, 1995).

himself as "the boy," describes life in a natural environment, without the trappings of modern technology. In retrospect his childhood appears to him secure and charming. He remembers his mother caring for the family while his father adopts a happy-go-lucky attitude and is more interested in preparing his home-brew raisin wine. In his recollection, Bartleman emphasizes the Native side, the birthright of the nations who lived on the land before the arrival of the white man. The ideological divide between Native rights and mainstream Canadian politics is most conspicuous when his Native grandfather dies: "Like all native Canadians of the period, he lived and died as a nonperson, not recognized as a full citizen under Canadian law."[35] Speaking from the perspective of his distinguished career in the diplomatic service and the Canadian government, Bartleman takes pride in the emancipation of Native people and the recognition of all ethnic groups.

Rudy Wiebe's *Of This Earth: A Mennonite Boyhood in the Boreal Forest* (2006) retells the first fifteen years of his life as the child of Mennonite immigrants in Saskatchewan. Like Bartleman, Wiebe fondly remembers the openness of the Canadian landscape which has inspired his imagination from the start. His love for the Canadian land begins with his birth "at the Canadian geographical co-ordinates of 'S. W. 31–52–17 West 3rd' on Thursday, October 4, 1934" in a log hut before the family homestead was finished.[36] This vast space is his source of energy and creation: "Standing barefoot in the turned soil behind our house, I know: Of this earth my cells are made" (p. 367). Wiebe's identification with the land also includes the preservation of his Mennonite ancestors' religion and culture. The history of his family and by implication the history of the Mennonites contribute to his Canadian identity. Tracing this history back to the Anabaptists in Friesland and Holland and their persecution, he sees the root of his Canadian existence in Adam Wiebe, "the Frisian ancestor of all Russian Mennonite Wiebes, who in 1616 sailed from Harlingen on invitation by the Free City of Danzig to become its water engineer" (p. 229). Against all opposition, the community is kept intact by their faith and their language, Russian Mennonite Low German.

These possessions represent the fundamentals of their lives and sustain Wiebe's family when it arrives in 1930. Religion and language are the ramparts for their lives in the Boreal forest "on the edge of white settlement" in difficult economic times and during the Second World War (p. 11). Among Wiebe's

---

35 James Bartleman, *Raisin Wine: A Boyhood in a Different Muskoka* (Toronto: McClelland and Stewart, 2007), pp. 44–5.
36 Rudy Wiebe, *Of This Earth: A Mennonite Boyhood in the Boreal Forest* (Toronto: Alfred A. Knopf Canada, 2006), p. 23.

many sources for his narrative are the diary of his sister Helen, who died prematurely in 1945, the hymn books of the Mennonite congregation, and a number of family photographs. Visits back to his parents' home in Russia in 1997 and conversations with his remaining relatives in Canada complete the picture. At the end of the memoir the family moves to Coaldale in Alberta, where he witnesses "a daily Canadian multicultural manifestation more than twenty years before Ottawa named that an official policy" (p. 384). Rudy Wiebe's and James Bartleman's respect for the land complements their commitment to a modified multicultural Canadian society. David Suzuki develops these concerns and commitments into an ecological program.

Suzuki's two autobiographies document how the once predominantly negative implications of racial difference have given way to a fruitful co-operation of all humans for the sake of the preservation of the environment. He adopts this post-ethnic position during his second marriage to Tara Cullis, who emigrated from England with her parents at the age of five. Ethnic difference is no longer an issue, neither for his father nor his in-laws. The Japanese racial legacy, which dominates most of *Metamorphosis*, moves into the background. This new perception makes it easy to transfer his teaching and research from the classroom and lab to his popular CBC series *The Nature of Things with David Suzuki*, which expands to a global network of research for his television audience.

Thirteen out of eighteen chapters of *The Autobiography* are dedicated to a description of these ecological projects. They are based on his first encounter as a young professor in genetics with Aboriginal people when he learns from them a basic respect for human beings and nature. Immigrants to Canada as well as environmentalists – he argues – have ignored the "broader cultural and spiritual needs" of Indigenous people and their right "to remain who they are" (p. 133). In continuation of his father's "Japanese tradition of nature-worship" (p. 395), he is involved in environmental projects worldwide and has made his influence felt in political decisions at the Earth Summit in Rio de Janeiro and the Kyoto Convention on Climate Change. Suzuki's belief in the interdependence of all human beings on earth, regardless of their ethnicity or race, appears to be one of the essential requirements for the well-being of multi-ethnic societies. All writers discussed here aspire to such a goal in their transcultural life-writing, which can serve as models for existing in a post-national world.

28

Multiculturalism and globalization

NEIL TEN KORTENAAR

In the last decades of the twentieth century, English Canadian and Québécois literature became increasingly defined by their relations to a world much larger than Britain, France, and the United States. How those other languages, races, and cultural traditions manifest themselves in Canada is commonly called "multiculturalism." How English Canada and Quebec locate themselves in relation to other places and cultural traditions is called "globalization." There is, however, another definition of "globalization," equally common but with the opposite meaning, which refers to increasing cultural homogenization and subordination to the English language and international capital. Both definitions must be remembered for both express a truth.

Different kinds of difference

This chapter will discuss the authors from Asia, Africa, and the Caribbean most responsible for making literature in Canada multicultural, but, in order to establish a context, we must first make some important distinctions. The presence of other languages and races in Canada is nothing new: Canada has always imported cheap labour to do the work English Canadians did not want to do, and immigration is central to the nation's self-definition as a place that people choose to come to. English Canadian literature has long included writers from ethnic minorities, such as Mordecai Richler and Rudy Wiebe, but their presence did not make that canon multicultural in the way it has so resoundingly become. As long as decolonization and the forging of a national identity were the great projects of literature in both French and English, as they were until the 1970s, the experience of people who spoke other languages, looked different, or did not identify with the national history could be ignored. No sooner had the two national literatures established themselves, however, than they faced a demand for the recognition of difference and of the plurality of identities. The demand came from the margins, but it answered a need built into the project of both national literatures to be recognized as cosmopolitan.

Even as literary multiculturalism affirms minority communities and what they have inherited from the past, it assures that the national literatures appear directed toward the future. The result: the success of foreign-born writers at finding readers both inside and outside Canada has altered all notions of what is central in the national literatures. In 1992 Michael Ondaatje, born in Sri Lanka, became the first Canadian to win the Booker Prize, for his novel *The English Patient*, the film version of which won the Academy Award for best picture in 1997. In 2007, with *Divisadero*, he became the first Canadian novelist since MacLennan to win five Governor General's Awards. Rohinton Mistry, born in Bombay, is probably the most read Canadian writer, especially since his novel *A Fine Balance* (1995) became a Book Club selection of Oprah Winfrey, the American television host, in 2001. And M. G. Vassanji, born in Kenya, who won the inaugural Giller Prize in 1994, in 2003 became the first writer to win the award twice.[1] Not since the nineteenth century have so many of the major English Canadian writers been born outside the country. Writing in French has *never* had as many authors born outside Canada as it does now.

For English Canadians, multiculturalism, officially encouraged by the state since 1971, ratified by an act of parliament in 1988, and accepted as part of the definition of Canada by all popular and academic discourse, even by those who object to it most strenuously, has overtaken the French fact as the source of the nation's proud difference from the United States. English Canada commonly imagines itself as a virtuous mean between two undesirable poles: the assimilation of cultural others and the rejection of others in the name of cultural purity, poles supposedly represented by the melting pot of the United States and by French Quebec respectively. Quebec nationalists, in turn, have sometimes feared that state multiculturalism will reduce the Québécois to one among many minorities defined by their relation to English Canada. Writing by minority writers *in French*, however, is as welcome in Quebec as multicultural writing in English Canada and for the same reason: it is taken as a sign of the strength and cosmopolitanism of the national culture.

The two national literatures and their many internal others all obey a modern moral imperative: every people needs a literary representation of

---

[1] The Giller Prize (now the Scotiabank Giller Prize) honors the best novel published in English in Canada each year.

itself lest it remain, in Charles Taylor's terms, unrecognized.[2] The imperative to represent a collective has registered on the literary imagination as a goad, sometimes resented, even resisted, but undeniable. By outsiders, a writer is read as representative of the group; within the group, writing is judged for the adequacy of its representation. The absence until recently of, say, Chinese Canadian writing from the literary canon was seen not merely as a reflection of the racist exclusion of Chinese Canadians from full participation in the economy and the state but as a further aspect of that exclusion.

As Lien Chao notes, Chinese Canadian writing began with anthologies that founded the literature they claimed to be documenting.[3] So, too, anthologies of Italian Canadian, Japanese Canadian, Black Canadian, and Italo Québecois writing,[4] edited by writers seeking traditions to enable their own writing, successfully brought whole literatures into being. Anthologies bringing together writers of diverse backgrounds as representatives of Canadian multiculturalism appeared a decade or so later,[5] part of a larger trend that saw the literary imagination both in the world and within Western nations shift considerably (but far from completely) toward what had been the margins. This shift is not simply because every people has a literary culture. Before 1960 or so, not every people *had* one, and there are still groups unrepresented in Canadian literature. Italian and Ukrainian Canadian literatures warrant entries in the second edition of the *Oxford Companion to Canadian Literature* (1997) but not Greek Canadian literature. Writers of Sri Lankan origin figure prominently in Canadian literature but none of Korean origin. There is, however, a space waiting to be filled by Korean Canadian writing, and a recent anthology heralds the belated emergence of Greek Canadian literature.[6]

---

2 Charles Taylor, *Multiculturalism and "The Politics of Recognition"* (Princeton, NJ: Princeton University Press, 1992).
3 Lien Chao, "Anthologizing the Collective: The Epic Struggles to Establish Chinese Canadian Literature in English," in *Writing Ethnicity: Cross-Cultural Consciousness in Canadian and Québécois Literature*, ed. Winfried Siemerling (Toronto: ECW, 1996), pp. 145–70.
4 Pier Giorgio Di Cicco, *Roman Candles: An Anthology of Poems by Seventeen Italo-Canadian Poets* (Toronto: Hounslow Press, 1978); Chinese Canadian Writers Workshop, *Inalienable Rice: A Chinese and Japanese Canadian Anthology* (Vancouver: Powell Street Revue, 1979); Harold Head, *Canada in Us Now: The First Anthology of Black Poetry and Prose in Canada* (Toronto: NC Press, 1976); Fulvio Caccia and Antonio D'Alfonso, *Quêtes: Textes d'auteurs italo-québécois* (Montreal: Guernica, 1983).
5 Linda Hutcheon and Marion Richmond, eds., *Other Solitudes: Canadian Multicultural Fictions* (Toronto: Oxford University Press, 1990); Smaro Kamboureli, *Making a Difference* (Toronto: Oxford University Press, 2007 [1996]).
6 Tess Fragoulis, *Musings: An Anthology of Greek Canadian Literature* (Montreal: Véhicule Press, 2004).

One might expect multiculturalism to take under its umbrella all writing in Canada, including writing by English and French Canadians, now potentially just two cultural groups among many. However, it does not work that way: George Elliott Clarke and Ying Chen write multicultural literature; Margaret Atwood does not and neither does Claude Jasmin. "We are all immigrants to this place even if we were born here," writes Atwood,[7] but a distinction must be made between settlers and immigrants. The French and British and their descendants had the capacity to make nations and the state in their own image and speaking their own tongues. Immigrants, by contrast, are always reminded that they have come to a country made in the image of others. By this definition, immigrants were not among the explorers, the founding fathers, or the lawmakers. They were, of course, among the pioneers, the workers, and the builders, but as such, their experience often left little trace in the official records and less in the national imagination and has had to be reconstructed after the fact.

There are not many national literatures in Canada; there are two, distinguished by language, which other writers must join even to be accepted as multicultural. Because Stephan Stephansson wrote in Icelandic, and Sadhu Binning writes in Punjabi, Yehuda Elberg and Chava Rosenfarb in Yiddish, and György Vitéz in Hungarian, they are not writing English Canadian or Québécois literature. In the definitions of both national literatures, language is as important as citizenship and more important than residence. The term "other solitudes," coined by Linda Hutcheon and Marion Richmond in 1990, no longer fairly characterizes ethnic Canadian writing in English and French, given the centrality it has achieved, but can still be applied with justice to writing in other languages. Only Josef Škvorecký, who writes in a Czech influenced by English that developed in North America, has come close to having translations of his novels accepted as Canadian literature

In anthologies and literature courses, contemporary multiculturalism includes Aboriginal writing, which came to prominence at the same time and obeys the same imperative of representation. However, there is an important political distinction to be made between Indigenous and immigrant. A further distinction should be made between immigrants and Canadians of African descent, who have always been a disavowed part first of the colonies, French and British, and then of the settler state. Africans, like Aboriginals, are what European settlers in the Americas defined themselves against. Marlene

---

7 Margaret Atwood, "Afterword," in *Journals of Susannah Moodie* (Toronto: Oxford University Press, 1970) p. 62.

NourbeSe Philip, for one, argues that multiculturalism, by treating all ethnic groups as the same kind of entity, deflects attention from those who suffer most grievously from racism.

People of African origin came from the United States in numbers sufficient to sustain a population at the time of the Revolution and in the decade before the Civil War, but African Canadians entered the national literary consciousness only with the influx of immigrants from the Caribbean in the 1960s. George Elliott Clarke, the poet and critic from a Black Loyalist Nova Scotia family, occasionally expresses his discomfort that authors who came as adults are received as the voice of Black Canada by readers conveniently unaware of the nation's history. As he readily acknowledges, however, the current prominence of writers such as Dionne Brand and Austin Clarke has made possible his own efforts to recover an African Canadian literary tradition. Caribbean writers themselves have worked to recover the untold stories of Black Canadians from earlier periods: Brand has collected narratives of Black working women in Ontario,[8] and Afua Cooper has written the history of a Black female slave in New France.[9] The centrality of Caribbean writers to Black literature in both English Canada and Quebec is the converse of what one sees in the United States, where writing by West Indians such as Paule Marshall and Jamaica Kincaid maintains its distinctness from African American writing and is, of all American ethnic writing, probably the most concerned with the land of the writers', or their parents', birth.

Two waves of migrant writing

To understand why the experience of cultural minorities was slow to figure in both national literatures but has since become so central, we must further distinguish between two kinds of migration, that of people speaking languages other than English or French and that of people who are not white, which correspond roughly to the periods of literary history before and after the triumph of multiculturalism. Immigrants in the late nineteenth century and the first sixty years of the twentieth came predominantly from Southern and Eastern Europe, but also from Northern Europe, China, and Japan. They were marginalized by many things, but especially by language. In general, they were working class and did not have literary aspirations even in their own

---

[8] Dionne Brand, *No Burden to Carry: Narratives of Black Working Women in Ontario, 1920s–1950s* (Toronto: Women's Press, 1991).

[9] Afua Cooper, *The Hanging of Angélique: The Untold Story of Canadian Slavery and the Burning of Old Montréal* (Toronto: HarperCollins, 2006).

languages. The experience of these groups figured in literature only when the children and grandchildren wrote about it. What I am calling the *first wave* of ethnic writing is by people born or at least raised in Canada. For these authors, English, and not their mother tongue was the language in which they wrote most comfortably. *The Viking Heart* (1923), by Laura Goodman Salverson, born in Winnipeg of Icelandic parents, was the first Canadian ethnic novel in English. The most prominent groups represented in this first wave are Jews (A. M. Klein, Irving Layton, Richler, Adele Wiseman, Leonard Cohen, Norman Levine, Matt Cohen, and Anne Michaels); Mennonites (Wiebe, Patrick Friesen, Sandra Birdsell, Miriam Toews, and Di Brandt); Italians (Pier Giorgio di Cicco, Frank Paci, Mary di Michele, and Nino Ricci); and Ukrainians (Vera Lysenko, Andrew Suknaski, George Ryga, and Janice Kulyk Keefer). By my definition, the first wave also includes writers of Japanese (Roy Kiyooka, Joy Kogawa, Roy Miki, Gerry Shikatani, Hiromi Goto, Rui Umezawa, and Kerri Sakamoto) and Chinese descent (Fred Wah, Jim Wong-Chu, SKY Lee, Wayson Choy, and Judy Fong Bates) for they, too, grew up in Canada. The equivalent in Quebec would be Italians such as Antonio D'Alfonso, Fulvio Caccia, and Marco Micone. However, the first wave of ethnic writing appeared later and had less impact on Québécois literature.

In the 1950s, Europe itself began importing labor to replace a naturally declining population. A decade or so after Britain and France, Canada eased its racist immigration policies and opened the doors to immigrants from areas perceived as racially distinct. The primary sources of immigrants shifted to Asia and the Caribbean, to what is now commonly called the global South. The majority of the new Canadians continued to be people willing to do cheap labor and to sacrifice themselves for the sake of their children, and we can expect to wait a full generation for substantial writing by Korean, Vietnamese, or Somali Canadians.

New immigration rules explicitly welcome people with skills or with money, but many Asian and African professionals have been unable to have their qualifications recognized or to find work commensurate with their training. More fortunate are those middle-class or potentially middle-class people who already know English or French and who come to study and receive Canadian qualifications. To this latter group, distinguished by race but not by language or education, belong the writers who have made literature in English Canada and Quebec so resoundingly multicultural. They include Mistry, Bharati Mukherjee, Anita Rau Badami, Suniti Namjoshi, Shauna Singh Baldwin, and Rahul Varma from India; Rienzi Crusz, Ondaatje, and Shyam

Selvadurai from Sri Lanka; Vassanji and George Seremba from East Africa; Claire Harris, Rabindranath Maharaj, Brand, Shani Mootoo, Neil Bissoondath, and Ramabai Espinet from Trinidad; Philip from Tobago; Lillian Allen, Olive Senior, and Cooper from Jamaica; Austin Clarke and Cecil Foster from Barbados; Cyril Dabydeen from Guyana; Djanet Sears from the Afro-Caribbean diaspora in Britain; and Nalo Hopkinson, who grew up in several Caribbean nations. The first of these authors to come to Canada was Clarke in 1955, the most recent Badami in 1991. The majority came in the 1960s and 70s.

In Quebec the equivalent of this *second wave*, writers who came as adults and already had French, include the Haitians Émile Ollivier, Gérard Étienne, Marie-Célie Agnant, and Dany Laferrière; Anne-Marie Alonzo and Mona Latif-Ghattas from Egypt; Nadine Ltaif and Wajdi Mouawad from Lebanon; Naïm Kattan from Iraq; and Mary Abécassis Obadia and David Bendayan, Sephardic Jews from Morocco. My distinction between first and second waves becomes blurred, however, when applied to Québécois literature: I have classified Micone as a child of immigrants and Alonzo as an immigrant, even though he came at age thirteen and she at twelve. Whereas Jewish writers in English were all born in Canada, Jews writing in French, like those writing in Yiddish, came to the country as adults. The Haïtians are distinct because most came as involuntary exiles in the 1960s, fleeing the Duvalier dictatorship. They form an unusually coherent cohort – the members of the literary movement Haïti Littéraire came *en bloc* – and the myth of return is more prominent in their work than in that of any other group. And, as we shall see below, in Quebec there is a category of migrant writer that does not fit my two waves: the writer who writes in a second language learned as an adult.

What I am calling the second wave of migrant writers came from the former British and French empires, and have ancestral ties to South or West Asia or to Africa, even when they came from the Caribbean. In contrast, first-wave writers were from Europe, Japan, or China, areas that had not fallen under British or French colonialism. Multiculturalism, in literature at least, must therefore be understood in conjunction with postcolonialism, the creative and critical movement which emphasizes the ways that European imperialism has shaped the world. The colonization of Africa and Asia created native élites who spoke and wrote English or French. In the Caribbean, there is no language that is not European in origin. Since decolonization, which occurred in India in 1947, in Sri Lanka in 1948, and in most of the Caribbean and Africa in the 1960s (though Haïti has been independent since 1804), many people left conditions of economic or political instability along routes defined by language and colonial history. The journeys of Ondaatje, Vassanji, and Laferrière to Toronto and Montreal are thus related to the journeys by V. S. Naipaul, Salman Rushdie, Jamaica Kincaid, and Tahar Ben Jelloun to the cultural metropoles of London, New York, and Paris.

The shared experience of colonialism explains why writers from Sri Lanka, Guyana, and Nova Scotia have read the same literature and have similar literary ambitions. The emphasis that critical postcolonialism places on European imperialism may however obscure the rapid spread of English around the globe *since* the end of the British Empire. Other languages are under more threat from English now than at the height of the British Empire, partly as a result of American cultural imperialism, but also of the centrality of English in the fields of technology, electronic communication, and business. Multiculturalism in literature cannot be thought apart from the penetration of English into every corner of the earth.

The migrant writers who chose Canada did so primarily because it was North America. In Laferrière's first and best-known novel, scandalously entitled *Comment faire l'amour avec un nègre sans se fatiguer* (1985), a Haïtian living in Montreal cruises for English-speaking white girls because, he explains, "I want America." When Brand came to Toronto, she says the "plane landed in Canada, but I was in America." Canada, of course, is not the metropolitan center but a former colony, itself arguably postcolonial.[10] Québécois literature has a long tradition of identifying itself as colonized, not so much by France as by Britain and English Canada. Pierre Vallières wrote *Nègres blancs d'Amérique* (1968) and Michèle Lalonde the poem "Speak White" (to which Micone wrote the immigrant's reply: "Speak What?").[11] The Ivorian Ahmadou Kourouma was able to publish his novel *Les Soleils des indépendances* (1968) in Montreal, after it had been refused in Paris, because in Quebec they could appreciate the literary value of his non-standard French.

Given the country's status as both First World and periphery, many migrations ending in Canada have involved intermediate waystations. My list of writers and their origins obscures how many came by way of England (Rienzi Crusz, Ondaatje), the US (Bharati Mukherjee, Lillian Allen, Vassanji, Shauna Singh Baldwin), or elsewhere (Claire Harris had been in Nigeria). Most migrant writers in Quebec have come through France first. The younger generation have inherited migratory patterns from their parents: Mootoo,

---

10 Laura Moss, ed., *Is Canada Postcolonial?: Unsettling Canadian Literature* (Waterloo, ON: Wilfrid Laurier University Press, 2003).
11 Marco Micone, "Speak What," in *Lectures plurielles*, ed. Norma López-Therrien (Montreal: Éditions Logiques, 1991), pp. 63–5.

who grew up in Trinidad, was born in Ireland; Baldwin, born in Montreal, grew up in India. Canada has also proven a waystation for migrants bound for elsewhere. Embittered by her experience of racism in Montreal and Toronto, Bharati Mukherjee denounced Canadian multiculturalism and left for the United States. Brian Moore, the author of *The Luck of Ginger Coffey* (1960), about an Irish immigrant in Montreal, continued his career in California. Namjoshi now lives in Devon, D'Alfonso in Toronto, Caccia in Paris, Baldwin in Milwaukee. Laferrière has lived most of the last fifteen years in Miami.

Almost all the writers belonging to my second wave have studied in Canada; the few exceptions – Vassanji, Baldwin, and Mukherjee – studied in the United States. All published their first work in Canada. Several have founded publishing houses, like TSAR, established by Vassanji and his wife, Nurjehan Aziz; Sister Vision, co-founded by Makeda Silvera, or Naaman, the project of Antoine Naaman, in order to foster multicultural writing. All these writers born elsewhere are touted by the Canadian media, awarded government grants, and eligible for Canadian prizes. English Canadian and Québécois readers read them with the pleasure of recognition and the sense of fulfilling a responsibility with which they read their own. These second-wave writers enjoy more success than Canadian residents who established literary careers elsewhere, like poets Louise Bennett and Lorna Goodison from Jamaica, and novelists Jan Carew from Guyana and Sam Selvon from Trinidad, who are not taught in Canadian literature courses nor included in anthologies.

Second-wave writing and transnationalism

The experience of studying and then publishing in Canada has affected how second-wave writers pitch their voice and how they imagine their audience. Those, like Selvadurai or Sergio Kokis, who set works entirely elsewhere are nonetheless writing for Canadian readers. So are Brand, who writes that she has only "diplomatic relations" with the country she lives in,[12] and Mootoo, who pledges loyalty to the State of Migrancy.[13] Their connections to Canada explain why the second wave of migrant authors are accepted as Canadian literature, but their success in finding readers is also attributable

---

12 Dionne Brand, *A Map to the Door of No Return: Notes to Belonging* (Toronto: Doubleday Canada, 2001), p. 83.
13 Shani Mootoo, *The Predicament of Or* (Vancouver: Polestar, 2001), p. 81.

to their membership in other national literatures. Espinet, originally from Trinidad, and Vassanji, from East Africa, are published in India, the land of their ancestors, and the latter also features in the influential Heinemann African Writers Series. Even Bissoondath, outspoken in making his choice of Canada a rejection of Trinidad, appears in every anthology of Caribbean fiction. Canadians value this transnationalism. They read Ondaatje, Selvadurai, Mistry, or Vassanji for news of the rest of the world, as they do not read authors living in Asia or Africa north of South Africa, or novels in translation. Mistry's three novels are set entirely in Bombay or a city like Bombay and constitute a survey of Indian history since 1971 as it might have made itself felt in the lives of ordinary citizens, yet he is received by Canadians as one of theirs, and a Canadian director, Sturla Gunnarsson, made a film of *Such a Long Journey* in 1998. Vassanji's *The Book of Secrets* (1994) and *The In-Between World of Vikram Lall* (2003), both set in Africa, have won much more acclaim than his novels about immigrants, *No New Land* (1991), set in Toronto, or *Amriika* (1999), set in the US.

A reverse principle holds for white British, American, Australian, or South African writers who came to Canada as adults. Carol Shields, Daphne Marlatt, or Janette Turner Hospital are not usually considered multicultural or even immigrants. In their case, citizenship and language are not sufficient to qualify as Canadian writers: they must also write about Canada. Lewis DeSoto's novel *A Blade of Grass* (2003), because it is set entirely in South Africa, is not received as Canadian. And Thomas King, who came from the US, might not occupy the position he does in Aboriginal Canadian writing if he did not set his books in Canada. Writers who came as adults from France, Belgium, and Switzerland to Quebec, unlike British or American writers in English Canada, *are* treated as immigrants with an outsider's perspective.[14] The narrator of Flora Balzano's *Soigne ta chute* (1991), like the author born in Algeria of European stock and raised in France, calls people like herself "la minorité audible."[15] Nevertheless, the same qualification holds true: such authors are assimilable as long as they write about Quebec. The Canadian content criterion is waived, however, for Kokis or Chen, who can write about Brazil, China, or places not on the map and still write Québécois literature.

The career of Austin Clarke, the doyen of second-wave writers, is instructive because it largely predates the boom in multiculturalism. Clarke, who

---

14 See Clément Moisan and Renate Hildebrand, *Ces Étrangers du dedans: Une histoire de l'écriture migrante au Québec 1937–1997* (Quebec: Nota Bene, 2001).
15 Flora Balzano, *Soigne ta chute* (Montreal: XYZ, 1992), p. 38.

came from Barbados to study in Toronto, began his writing career in 1964 with *Survivors of the Crossing* and has since published more than eighteen titles, yet it was not until 2002, when his novel *The Polished Hoe* received the Giller Prize, that he finally, at the age of sixty-eight, won a firm position in the national canon. The ambivalence was mutual: Clarke took twenty-six years to decide to become a citizen. His slow acceptance in Canada is in part a function of the tardiness with which he established his place in Caribbean literature, where he never received the recognition accorded fellow West Indians, Selvon and George Lamming, who had written about migration to Britain a decade or so before. Toronto did not occupy the space that London did in the imagination of West Indian readers; Clarke's use of literary creole in narrative, while a stylistic breakthrough, came after Selvon's; and his accounts of growing up in Barbados followed Lamming's. Clarke's originality lay elsewhere: while Selvon wrote about young men circulating in the metropolis, Clarke was the first to explore the experience of women largely confined to rooms in other people's houses. *The Meeting Point* (1967), the first volume of his Toronto trilogy, concerns women who came under the West Indian Domestic Worker Scheme, started in 1955. Clarke secured a place alongside Mistry and Vassanji only when, thirty-five years after that novel, he once again wrote from the point of view of a woman living at close quarters with her boss in the 1950s, but this time he set the story entirely in the land of his birth (fictionalized as Bimshire). The point I am making – that Canadian readers prefer the transnational, set elsewhere, to the subnational – relates to literary reception, but also to the literary imagination, what it is possible to write: *The Polished Hoe* is, by any measure, Clarke's most realized novel.

Whereas an important part of the second wave's appeal is that the authors speak for groups larger than or outside the nation, first-wave writers represent groups smaller than the nation and enter Canadian literature without foreign currency to exchange. They do not bring "news from a foreign country," to echo the title of Alberto Manguel's novel (*News From a Foreign Country Came*, 1991), but merely from Canada's own margins. It is because he is not writing Italian literature that Micone belongs to the first wave. The same restriction will face Arab, Latin American, or Vietnamese Canadians who write in English or French in the future.

The second wave of writers understandably prefer not to be called *immigrant* or *ethnic*, terms that have acquired stigma as a result of the enforced marginalization of the first wave of immigrants. Ethnics are defined by their relation to another group presumed to be "non-ethnic." As a character in a Mistry story puts it, "If you ask me, mosaic and melting pot are both nonsense, and ethnic is a polite way of saying bloody foreigner."[16] Writers of the second wave tend to define themselves by their experience of travel rather than arrival, and to write about cultural exchange rather than the drama of cultural loss, about métissage or hybridity rather than synthesis or cultural convergence. They are *migrants* when they emphasize their displacement and *transcultural* when they stress their position as cultural mediators. (D'Alfonso, Caccia, and Lamberto Tassinari, who came as an adult from Italy in 1980, introduced Fernando Ortiz's term *transculturalism* to Canada in their trilingual cultural magazine *Vice Versa*.) The frequently used term *écriture migrante* means not just writing by migrants but writing that is itself "on the move." In order to avoid the connotations of value carried by the words *ethnic*, *migrant*, and *transcultural*, I will retain the terms *first* and *second* wave, even though the two waves overlap and the distinction will break down in the near future.

In the last two decades first-wave writers, born in Canada, have learned that, to match the success of Mistry and Ondaatje, they, too, must imagine an elsewhere. Sakamoto and Keefer have written about Canadians who "return" to the lands their parents left. Ricci's first novel, *Lives of the Saints*, set entirely in the rural Italy from which his parents came, won the Governor General's Award in 1990 and was a bestseller. The author wanted "to give readers a sense of people within a community where they are not marginalized as ethnic."[17] The two sequels, however, *bildungsromane* about growing up in southern Ontario, were inevitably less successful.

Quebec's difference

This is the moment to note an important difference between multicultural writing in Quebec and that in English Canada. Immigrant writers in Quebec come from all over the world, not just from *la francophonie*. Alice Parizeau was a Pole, Régine Robin and Monique Bosco Ashkenazi Jews whose families had fled Eastern Europe, Kokis a Brazilian whose parents came from Latvia. All these writers passed through France first. Two who did not are Chen from Shanghai and Aki Shimazaki from Japan. Chen's first novel, *La Mémoire de l'eau* (1992), fits into a new and unusual movement of Chinese writers writing about China in languages other than Chinese, a movement that includes Ha Jin in

---

16 Rohinton Mistry, *Tales from Firozsha Baag* (Markham: Penguin, 1987) p. 160.
17 Kamboureli, *Making a Difference*, p. 484.

the United States and Dai Sijie and Shan Sa in France. After *Les Lettres chinoises* (1993), an epistolary novel featuring correspondents in Shanghai and Montreal, Chen has moved away from China or Quebec as settings. *L'Ingratitude* (1995), although nominally set in China, is a dead daughter's bitter account of her relation to her mother. Its interest is in psychology, its mode irony.

Because they write in French, Kokis, Chen, and Shimazaki are not writing Brazilian, Chinese, or Japanese literature. They are not in the position of Mistry or Ollivier, who write Indian or Haïtian, diasporan, and postcolonial literature as well as Canadian or Québécois literature. They are also unlike Kogawa or Micone in that they do not have communities for which they speak. It is tempting to locate them in the great twentieth-century tradition of foreigners writing French literature, from Beckett and Ionesco to Cioran and Kundera. Nancy Huston, who moved from Alberta to Paris and married Tzvetan Todorov, the French literary critic originally from Bulgaria, is a prime example. When *Cantique des Plaines*, Huston's own translation of her novel *Plainsong*, won the Governor General's Award for the best novel in French in 1993, a group of Quebec publishers objected strenuously to her eligibility. That dispute was short-lived, however, and today Huston is more read in Quebec than in English Canada.

Writers who write in their second (or third) language are rarer in recent English Canadian literature – Manguel from Argentina and Rawi Hage from Lebanon (*De Niro's Game*, 2006) are examples – but a related phenomenon is the refugee writer. *Notes from the Hyena's Belly* (2000), Nega Mezlekia's memoir of growing up in Ethiopia and fleeing the Red Terror, and Nelofer Pazira's *A Bed of Red Flowers* (2005), about escaping the communists in Afghanistan only to discover that the mujahidin who replaced them were as oppressive, both address a Western audience in the world language, English, as part of their appeal to universal notions of dignity and human rights.

In order to understand contemporary multicultural writing, we must compare it to that by first-wave writers who entered the canon without transnational connections. Klein, Layton, Richler, and Leonard Cohen were all from Montreal. Montreal has always attracted newcomers because it was bilingual and distinct from rural Quebec, and therefore felt more cosmopolitan than Toronto, which until the 1960s shared values with rural and small-town Ontario. Montreal's Jews have, however, an ambivalent relation to Quebec. The expectations and values that had brought them to the New World were associated with English rather than with French. Before the Quiet Revolution, Jews from Eastern Europe were wary of Quebec's distinctly unmodern Catholic Church. In essays which appeared first in

American magazines,[18] Richler claimed that the origins of Quebec nationalism lay in Catholic anti-Semitism, a charge that produced greater cries of wounded outrage in Quebec than any of the denunciations of Canadian racism by Brand or Philip have done in English Canada. Jews set a pattern for subsequent immigrants to Quebec, the so-called allophones (neither anglo- nor francophones), who tended to learn English instead of French until provincial laws culminating in Bill 101 in 1977 forced the children of immigrants to attend French-language schools. The gravitation of immigrants to English explains why there is less first-wave writing in Québécois literature. (Micone, by contrast, not only writes in French but has supported Quebec independence because, when he was young, his father wanted him to learn English as the language of the "bosses," and he felt solidarity for the workers instead.)

Jacques Parizeau, the Parti Québécois Premier whose wife, Alice, was a novelist of Polish origins, notoriously attributed the defeat of the referendum on Quebec independence in 1995 to money and "the ethnic vote."[19] Taylor explains that, when ethnic minorities do not assimilate to French or to Quebec, the assumption is that they are captured by Canada or by English, and it is forgotten that immigrants may remain distinct from both host cultures.[20] Quebec nationalism, however, is less concerned with ethnicity than with language, and, where language is concerned, the story of the second generation of immigrants is always of assimilation, usually to English. The presence of other cultures and languages poses no threat to English, which all the children of immigrants outside Quebec will learn, but does threaten French.

In a 1996 essay, *L'Arpenteur et le navigateur*, Monique LaRue made a distinction between a land surveyor, who marks out a territory in order to claim it, and a navigator, who moves without regard to borders. Typical of the former was a friend and fellow writer who resented the neo-Québécois writers for remaining outside, and indifferent to, the national literature. LaRue herself supports the navigator's position and looks forward to a literature free of ethnicity, more cosmopolitan or more Montréalais than Québécois. Nevertheless, because it took seriously the recriminations of the *arpenteur*, her essay aroused accusations of xenophobia by Ghila B. Sroka,

18 Mordecai Richler, "OH! CANADA! Lament for a Divided Country," *The Atlantic Monthly* (December 1977), p. 34, and "O QUEBEC," *The New Yorker* (May 30, 1994), p. 50, and *Oh Canada! Oh Quebec!: Requiem for a Divided Country* (New York: Knopf, 1992).
19 Stanley Gordon, "Jacques Parizeau," in *Canadian Encyclopedia* (Historica Foundation, 2007), http://www.thecanadianencyclopedia.com, accessed August 24, 2007.
20 Charles Taylor, "Le PQ responsable de son malheur," *La Presse* (November 22, 1995), p. B3.

editor of *La Tribune Juive*, and the dispute was continued in the pages of *Le Devoir* by Gary Klang, originally from Haïti, and Jasmin.[21]

The only strategy possible for Quebec and its literature is, of course, to welcome all writing in French. Robin's *La Québécoite* (1983) is a meditation on identity ranging from the Ukrainian shtetl to Montreal by way of the Holocaust, Paris, and New York. The book levels criticisms similar to Richler's: that the Church and therefore the largest part of Quebec history were anti-Semitic and that ethnic-based nationalism is inevitably exclusionist. Robin's sympathies are with Montreal's English-speaking Jews. She even expresses a metropolitan distaste for the French spoken in Quebec and for the prevalence of American popular culture. Robin, however, is welcomed as the new face of Québécois literature because she writes in French for Québécois readers. Although she writes as one who feels a perpetual exile, the socialist in her recognizes how much of the experience of exclusion she shares with the Québécois.

Relations between the first and second waves

Jewish writers have as large a place in English Canadian literature as they do in American, and Jews provide a touchstone against which other minority cultures define themselves: the domestic servants in Clarke's Toronto trilogy live with and work for Jews, who represent both the wealthy establishment and a fellow minority that has known discrimination. Canada must be, however, the only country in the world where Mennonite writing is so salient. Mennonites, as central to rural Prairie literature as Jews to Montreal, never became a cultural touchstone themselves but did much to establish Aboriginal experience as such. As an outsider who did not identify with the British imperial project, Wiebe forged a solidarity between immigrant and Aboriginal that has taken hold in non-Native literature: Margaret Laurence draws a connection between Scottish settlers and the Métis in Manitoba, based on a shared experience of forced displacement by the English; in Latif-Ghattas's *Le Double Conte de l'exil* (1990), Manitakawa, an Aboriginal, and Fève, from Anatolia, live together in Montreal; and in Kattan's *L'Anniversaire* (2000), the protagonist, a Syrian Jew, identifies with other "tribes" such as the Hurons, Algonquins, and Inuit. In Kogawa's *Obasan* (1981), the narrator remarks that

---

21 Gary Klang, "Trop, c'est trop," *Le Devoir* (July 3, 1997), p. A7; Claude Jasmin and Monique Larue, "L'Arpenteur et le navigateur (suite): La Bonne Foi et la déformation: À qui le Québec fait-il peur?" *Le Devoir* (July 15, 1997), p. A7; Gary Klang, "Réplique à Claude Jasmin: Bas les masques," *Le Devoir* (July 29, 1997), p. A7.

her "Uncle could be Chief Sitting Bull squatting here ... All he needs is a feather headdress, and he would be perfect for a picture postcard – 'Indian Chief from Canadian Prairies' – souvenir of Alberta, made in Japan."[22]

The literary prominence of Jews and Mennonites may be attributable to the fact that, unlike most immigrants, they were already minorities in the Old World with long traditions of cultural and religious distinctiveness, both self-chosen and painfully imposed. The most celebrated of the second-wave novelists also come from minority contexts in their lands of origin: Ondaatje is a Burgher, Mistry a Parsi, Vassanji an Ismaili, three groups that earned status as cultural mediators during the British Empire. Migration allowed these writers to turn their ethnic particularity into representativeness and meaning.

From the moment Ondaatje came to study at Bishop's University in 1962 at the age of eighteen, he has been more conscious than other migrant authors of the Canadian literary canon and more determined to win a place in it. Yet he began his career as a cosmopolitan writer, ignoring his Sri Lankan origins and Canadian location and writing about American topics. He first wrote about Sri Lanka in *Running in the Family* (1982), a memoir of a return visit. The aspects of the text that have received most critical attention – the distance that it maintains from the experience of the Sri Lankan majority and its sly balance between fiction and memoir – are related to the same cause: the problem of writing about Burghers, heirs of the Dutch who colonized Sri Lanka before the British and who preserved their distinctness in terms of religion, race, language, and class from Singhalese and Tamil. Any attempt by Ondaatje to answer the question "where are you from?" required a lengthy and qualified explanation. Some distance from the dominant culture serves the literary imagination, but too much detachment from all familiar coordinates risks making it difficult to tell a story at all.

Ondaatje made his problem his solution. He belongs, he says, to the generation that "was the first of the real migrant tradition,"[23] writers like Rushdie, Kazuo Ishiguro, and Mistry, who do not write out of minority experience but make their status as migrants the basis for claims to cosmopolitanism. In spite of Ondaatje's identification with the transnational, his only novel set in Canada, *In the Skin of a Lion* (1987), seeks precursors in first-wave immigrants, those from Southern Europe who built the great public works projects in Toronto in the first four decades of the twentieth century. We can compare his archival research here to the histories by Brand and Cooper

---

22 Joy Kogawa, *Obasan* (Toronto: Penguin, 1983), p. 2.
23 Kamboureli, *Making a Difference*, p. 241.

of Black Canada before their arrival. The characters in *In the Skin of a Lion* are, however, unlike most first-wave immigrants. Reflecting Ondaatje's own immigrant experience, the novel presents crossing water as an existential adventure in which the migrant must make a leap of faith, swing through the void, and risk colliding with a stranger. The central perspective belongs to an English-speaker from rural Ontario, who finds himself "an immigrant to the city."[24] Patrick Lewis's "Canada" is but one of many places from which people have come to the capital of "Upper America." *In the Skin of a Lion* reinvents Toronto in the image of its author's own ideal, a cosmopolitan city built by immigrants. As we have seen, first-wave writing in English was predominantly from Montreal and from small-town or rural Canada. Remarkably, only five of my list of first-wave authors grew up in Toronto (Mary di Michele, Janice Kulyk Keefer, Gerry Shikatani, Anne Michaels, and Kerri Sakamoto), and they are several years younger than Ondaatje and their careers overlap with the second wave. Yet Toronto is now the undisputed capital of English Canadian multicultural writing, where far more than half of my list of second-wave writers live.

A paradox arising from my distinction between two waves of migrants is that Japanese and Chinese Canadian writing in English belong to the first, distinguished by language, rather than the second, distinguished by race. Japanese Canadian writers are all *nisei* or *sansei* (second- or third-generation). Umezawa and Goto, who came to North America as infants after the Second World War, are "new *nisei*." Roy Kiyooka, the *nisei* poet and artist, has described himself as "to all intents and purposes, a white anglo-saxon protestant, with a cleft tongue."[25] Chinese and Japanese Canadians share with second-wave immigrants the experience of racism, including that sponsored by the state. Chinese immigrants had to pay a head tax not levied against other immigrants, and the 1923 Chinese Exclusion Act banned them altogether. Asian Canadians were disenfranchised in British Columbia, and, during the Second World War, the Mackenzie King government responded to racist agitation by dispossessing the *nisei* on the Pacific coast, interning them and forcibly removing them inland.

Kogawa and Miki, a *sansei* poet, played prominent roles in the successful campaign to force the government of Brian Mulroney to apologize and compensate the sufferers in 1988. Miki describes "redress" as a gift by the nation to its victims and, equally important, a gift by Japanese Canadians to the nation.

---

24 Michael Ondaatje, *In the Skin of a Lion* (Toronto: Vintage, 1996), p. 53
25 Kamboureli, *Making a Difference*, p. 91.

In 1994 Miki coordinated a Writers' Union of Canada conference entitled "Writing Thru Race" in Vancouver, bringing together Aboriginal, Chinese- and Japanese-Canadians, and second-wave writers. The conference attracted charges that it was itself racist because only writers of color were invited, and the federal Department of Heritage withdrew its funding. That conference successfully marked a new self-asserted visibility of writers belonging to what are called *visible minorities*.

To clarify the distinction I make between the first wave (all second-generation or later) and the second (who are first-generation Canadians) it is worth comparing Japanese and Chinese Canadian writing with that by West Indians and South Asians. At one point in the early 1990s, *Obasan*, about the relocation of Japanese-Canadians and its aftermath, had attracted more critical attention than any other literary work by a Canadian. This indicates how central multiculturalism had become to the literary canon, but another factor is that Kogawa, the only Canadian to have entered the ethnic American literary canon,[26] is the most resolutely Canadian of authors. Canada is the only home and identity that the narrator, Naomi Nakane, has, which is why her exclusion by the state and other Canadians is so traumatic. Naomi cannot see the actions of the Canadian government as what "they" did to "us" because that would be to accept the distinction at the heart of her family's trauma. Instead she feels the betrayal and mistreatment of the *nisei* and *sansei* as what "we" Canadians did to "ourselves." No wonder Naomi is so paralyzed and numb. Second-wave writers, no strangers to racism, just do not locate Canada in the center in the same way.

Of childhood and ancestors

Like *Obasan*, Goto's *Chorus of Mushrooms* (1994), set in Alberta, Choy's *The Jade Peony* (1995), set in Vancouver's China Town in the 1930s and 1940s, and Bates's *Midnight at the Dragon Cafe* (2003), set in 1950s small-town Ontario, present the child's point of view. Childhood also figures prominently in second-wave memoirs and autobiographical novels, particularly those from the Caribbean, such as Clarke's *Amongst Thorns and Thistles* (1965) and *Growing Up Stupid Under the Union Jack* (1980), Foster's *No Man in the House* (1991), Laferrière's *L'Odeur du café* (1991), and Rachel Manley's two memoirs about growing up in Jamaica's

---

26 See King-Kok Cheung's *An Interethnic Companion to Asian American Literature* (New York: Cambridge University Press, 1997), and Sau-ling Cynthia Wong's *Reading Asian American Literature: From Necessity to Extravagance* (Princeton: Princeton University Press, 1993).

leading political family, *Drumblair* (1996) and *Slipstream* (2000), but there is an important difference. In the work of first-wave authors, family is at once the source of difference and the repository of identity. Family members embody the full range of attitudes to identity on which a child may model herself. Children seek to penetrate secrets from the past kept from them by adults, secrets that carry the powerful charge of sex and death but always reveal the truth of the self. (Ricci's *Lives of the Saints*, centered on young Vittorio's mother's adulterous affair with a German soldier, relies on similar paradigms.) There is no sense in Choy's novel that his narrators ever grow up, and Kogawa's Naomi, emotionally stunted, never leaves behind the small fearful girl that she was.

For second-wave novelists, by contrast, for whom the act of migration marks an irrevocable break, childhood is set resolutely in the past, and the tone tends to the nostalgic. In Kokis's *Le Pavillon des miroirs* (1994) the contrast afforded by exile in a land of winter makes childhood in Brazil appear more vivid, even as it accentuates the poverty and violence. In tropical childhoods, it would seem, the senses were sharper, and life was lived more outdoors and in public. Family provides a warm shelter but, since it is not marked as different from the society around it, does not function as an allegory for identity.

In some other second-wave writers, migration appears to have thoroughly erased childhood. A reader may well doubt whether Ondaatje, Mistry, or Brand have ever been children. That does not mean, however, they are not interested in family. The focus of writers of South Asian origin on intra-family dynamics is part of what makes them feel so accessible to readers who do not share their ethnicity. Mistry's first novel, *Such a Long Journey* (1991), and the later *Family Matters* (2002), the title of which can be read as a pun, both imagine the paternal point of view. Ondaatje's *Running in the Family* is about an adult son traveling to the land of his birth in order to recover his dead father. Badami's *Tamarind Mem* (1996) juxtaposes a daughter's memoirs with a mother's stories, and her novel *The Hero's Walk* (2001) explores the dynamics of four generations living together (reversing convention by having a young girl leave Canada to join her grandparents in India). Once again, however, family does not function allegorically.

Second-wave writers from Africa or the Caribbean for whom migration is not just their own experience but also part of their *ancestral* heritage have sometimes more in common with first-wave writers than with their South Asian counterparts. Vassanji's novels, *The Gunny Sack* (1989) and *The Book of Secrets*, both trace several generations of an Indian family who came to British East Africa. The titular gunny sack and book of secrets are like Choy's jade peony, objects embodying a cultural inheritance from the past. In both novels, ancestry (including adultery and miscegenation) serves as an allegory of history and identity. Vikram Lall of *The In-Between World*, an Asian born in Kenya, recalls with guilt and shame how he, his sister, and their English and Kikuyu childhood friends acted out the tragic tensions between the groups in the period before and after Kenyan independence. That novel is usefully read alongside David Odhiambo's *Kipligat's Chance* (also 2003), where another eponymous narrator, like the author a Luo from Kenya, makes his peace with a Punjabi friend and rival after both have fled Africa and come to Vancouver.

The African and South Asian diasporas in the Caribbean have fostered a second, less coercive, properly *Caribbean* diaspora to Britain, France, the Netherlands, the United States, and Canada. Mootoo, for instance, looks back to Trinidad, not to India. Other Trinidadians, however, such as Philip, Brand, and Espinet, are haunted by the ancestral homelands of Africa and India. In *A Map to the Door of No Return* (2001) Brand describes how, as a descendant of New World Africans whom slavery had deliberately left without any knowledge of Africa, she can feel no belonging anywhere. As a girl she was frustrated with her grandfather who claimed once to know but no longer to remember what African language group her family came from. The desire for a single point of origin that would anchor identity is a desire for a genealogy-based identity such as first-wave immigrants have.

While second-wave writing often includes a map in the prefatory material, first-wave writers are more likely to feature a family tree. Lee's *Disappearing Moon Café* (1990) is a good example; *The Gunny Sack* features a map *and* a family tree. Brand has written a multigenerational family saga, *At the Full and Change of the Moon* (1999), tracing the descendants of a Trinidadian slave who have spread to both sides of the Atlantic. Although it, too, includes a family tree, it is an antigenealogy that begins with what is, in effect, an end: the original ancestor leads a mass suicide of slaves at the beginning of the nineteenth century. None of her descendants remembers Marie Ursule, but they are doomed to repeat her despair. Migration to North America or Europe is merely another version of the Middle Passage, the transportation in chains from Africa across the ocean.

Haïtian Québécois writers appear less concerned than Brand or Philip, author of *Looking for Livingstone: An Odyssey of Silence* (1991), with Africa. Perhaps because Haïti had a successful revolution and 200 years of independence or because of the compulsory nature of their exile, when Haïtians imagine an "odyssey home," to borrow G. E. Clarke's phrase,[27] it is Haïti

---

27 George Elliott Clarke, *Odysseys Home: Mapping African-Canadian Literature* (Toronto: University of Toronto Press, 2002).

not Africa they dream of, and the obstacles to a return are not ontological but political and economic. Brand's volume of poetry *Land to Light On* (1997) points to the absence of any such land, while the title of Phelps's *Mon pays que voici* (1968) refers to Haïti (both titles, of course, also proclaim that the poets' home is the poetry itself). However, if they do not always look back to a common point of origin, Caribbean writers share a restlessness. Brand's first novel, *In Another Place Not Here* (1996), traces two mirror journeys, both desperately unhappy: that of a young political radical to a West Indian island, and after her suicide, that of her peasant lover to the radical's home in Toronto. In Ollivier's *Passages* (1991), two journeys intersect in Miami and death: that of desperate people fleeing Haïti in boats and that of a lonely exile from Montreal forever seeking a better place. Ollivier's posthumous novel, *La Brûlerie* (2004), concerns aging Haïtian exiles ("ex-îles") whose tragedy is that, having defined their lives by an elsewhere, they never appreciated Montreal as the setting of their lives.

New directions in multicultural writing

The unsettled in-between state of the migrant, often terrible, can sometimes be redefined as liminality, hybridity, and fluidity, postmodern values that trouble fixed identities and provide some room for liberation. Instability can be transgression. There are, for instance, more migrant authors in Canada writing frankly about homosexuality than there are among Caribbean or South Asian authors who stay at home. Examples from the Caribbean include Brand, Silvera, Nigel Thomas, and Mootoo. Selvadurai's *Funny Boy* (1994) was a Canadian bestseller. Canada provides these authors with a more hospitable environment, but all regard the struggle against discrimination by sexual orientation as part of the larger struggle against racial and gendered oppression.

Philip and Brand were vocal in two Toronto controversies concerning racism in the arts: the "Into the Heart of Africa" exhibit at the Royal Ontario Museum in 1989 that highlighted Canada's extensive involvement in British imperialism; and the production of the musical "Showboat" in 1993. Women writers, it would seem, are more radical and politically consistent than male writers. In *In the Skin of a Lion* Ondaatje admires his anarchist immigrants for their determination to light a bomb under the status quo, but their radicalism feels like the author's artistic manifesto, at best politically confused. Complaints of political confusion have also been levelled against his *Anil's Ghost* (2000), set in Sri Lanka.

If Canadian readers who do not share the writers' ethnicity appear to show more interest in South Asia than in the Caribbean, it may be because of South Asian writers' perceived accessibility and blunted politics. Instead of asking why South Asian writers are the most read, however, we could ask why the three best second-wave novelists are from South Asia or of South Asian origin. Mistry, Ondaatje and Vassanji's success has undoubtedly something to do with the capacity of their novels to create a complete world the reader can enter. It is not always clear what language people are speaking in their novels, nor is it an issue. Caribbean texts, by contrast, inevitably foreground the problem of language. That concern with language explains why most West Indian Canadian writers in English and French are poets and why the bulk of multicultural poetry in Canada is written by West Indians.

We have been discussing the ways that multiculturalism is also globalization, but what of Canadians' relations to places that are not lands of origin? A long tradition of Canadian writing is inspired by experience abroad: Laurence, David Godfrey, and Audrey Thomas have all written about Africa, as has Gil Courtemanche, whose *Un dimanche à la piscine à Kigali* (2000) concerns a Québécois journalist in Rwanda at the time of the 1994 genocide. A new phenomenon, however, is the white English-speaking Canadian who writes novels without Canadian characters. In *Sweetness in the Belly* (2005), Camilla Gibb is able to render her anthropological research in Muslim Ethiopia in compelling fictional form by eliminating the ethnographer and making the protagonist a white Muslim, the orphaned child of British hippies born in North Africa. Karen Connelly's *The Lizard Cage* (2005) brings the oppression of the Burmese to distant readers by telling the story of a political prisoner in solitary confinement in the 1980s.

The bulk of Yann Martel's Booker-Prize-winning *Life of Pi* (2001) is set on a lifeboat in the Pacific. Yara El-Ghadban, writing in *Le Devoir*, reads the Montrealer's novel as an allegory of contemporary Quebec.[28] Religion, no longer a social constraint, has become an element of individual self-definition and inherently pluralist: Pi, born in the former French colony of Pondicherry in India, is at once Hindu, Muslim, and Christian. Lost at sea with a fierce tiger with the English name of Richard Parker (think of colonization as shipwreck), Pi successfully learns to manage the threat. El-Ghadban's allegorical reading breaks down, however, because Martel's novel is written in English. According to the terms of the allegory, the novel, if not Pi himself,

---

28 Yara El-Ghadban, "Le Nouveau Québec: La Société des multiples présences," *Le Devoir* (August 30, 2006), p. B5.

has been swallowed by the tiger. Quebec experiences an ambivalence that English Canada does not, related to the two meanings of the term "globalization" mentioned at the beginning of this essay. In ways that feel paradoxical, multiculturalism both diversifies Canadian society and its literatures and contributes to the triumph of English.

For the first time, anonymous and pseudonymous countries, long common in Caribbean and African literature, are appearing in English Canadian and Québécois literature. The land of exile from which Kokis and Shimazaki's novels look back on Brazil and Japan is an *hors-lieu* (non-space) that goes unnamed. In Mootoo's *Cereus Blooms at Night* (1996), missionaries resembling the Canadian Presbyterians who proselytized among Trinidad's East Indians have come to a Caribbean island called Lantanacamara from a place whose only name is the Shivering Northern Wetlands.

Ironically, the mixing of races and cultures in Toronto, Montreal, and Vancouver has been slow to figure in literature. Works that do imagine the intersection of immigrant cultures not just with the host culture but with each other include Dominique Blondeau's *Les Feux de l'exil* (1991), which features *récits* by three women from Marrakesh, Guadeloupe, and Shanghai; Monique Proulx's *Les Aurores montréales* (1996), which includes the perspectives of a Mexican student, a young Chinese from Shanghai, an Italo-Québécoise, a Haitian, and an Aboriginal; and Brand's *What We All Long For* (2005), in which four friends, of Vietnamese, West Indian, Black Nova Scotian, and Italian ancestry, a generation younger than the author and born in Canada, make Toronto their home. In Rawi Hage's *Cockroach* (2008), the narrator, a Christian Arab thief from a country like Lebanon, has almost nothing to do with the "Anglos" and the "French" of Montreal, whom he scorns and resents. Instead, the unsavory Montreal underworld he inhabits is filled with migrants from all over the Muslim world, but especially Iran. He himself is half-cockroach as befits the setting, but in this immigrant rewriting of Kafka, the insect is a greedy and resourceful trickster and, above all, a survivor.

Muslim writing has not had the prominence in English Canadian or Québécois literature that it has in Britain and France. Vassanji has mostly written about Shamsis, a fictionalized version of Ismailis in East Africa, a minority sect largely defined by their difference from other Muslims. But his novel *The Assassin's Song* (2007), significantly his first set in India, announces a new interest in religion. It depicts a syncretic Sufism whose spiritual vision combined Islam and Hinduism but which breaks down into deadly modern fundamentalisms.

The distinction I have made between two waves will soon no longer be able to account for English Canadian and Québécois literature. We can expect to see more writers of Asian, African, and Caribbean origin *raised in Canada*, like Joël Des Rosiers and Stanley Péan (of Haitian ancestry), Abla Farhoud (Lebanese), Priscilla Uppal (South Asian), or André Alexis and Tessa McWatt (Afro-Caribbean); and more who resist the demand that they write out of ethnic experience, like Evelyn Lau and Alexis. We can expect a breaking down of groups based on lands of origin and the emergence of new formulations of race and belonging. The term *African Canadian*, for instance, is being redefined by Lawrence Hill, born in Toronto to American parents, a Black father and a white mother; by Odhiambo, who came from Kenya at age twelve; and by Esi Edugyan, born in Calgary of Ghanaian parents. Des Rosiers proclaims he is "Québécois pure laine crépue" (a pun on "pure wool," meaning of ancestry stretching back to New France, and "woolly hair").[29]

Hill's 2007 historical novel *The Book of Negroes* recreates the story of the Black Loyalists, the freed American slaves who sailed for Nova Scotia with the British in 1783 and whose names were recorded in the original book of that name. Like Brand and Cooper, Hill recovers an African-Canadian history that predates his parents' arrival, and, like Brand in *At the Full and Change of the Moon*, he locates Canada in a larger Black Atlantic, but Hill is also able to imagine the Africa that his narrator comes from and, just as important, that she returns to. The novel traces the Middle Passage, plantation slavery in the American South, and the journey to freedom, but then returns across the Atlantic with the many Black Loyalists who, disillusioned with the hostility and deprivation meted out to them in Nova Scotia, accepted the British offer to resettle them in the new colony of Sierra Leone. Aminata Diallo, the narrator, herself ends up in London, reminding readers that the relations between Canada and Britain have been neither one-way nor monochromatic.

The only thing one can predict about the future of multicultural literature in Canada is that this history will need not just to be supplemented but rewritten, as new forms emerge to alter the picture.[30]

---

29 Joël Des Rosiers, *Théories caraïbes: Poétique du déracinement* (Montreal: Triptyque, 1996), p 181

30 This essay owes much to advice from Pascal Riendeau, Russell Brown, Marlene Goldman, Jody Mason, and Corinne Beauquis. They are in no way responsible for the opinions expressed.

PART FIVE

*

WRITING IN FRENCH

29

Poetry

ROBERT YERGEAU (TRANSLATION JENNIFER HIGGINS)

While poetry would eventually enable Québécois literature, and subsequently Acadian, Franco-Ontarian, and Franco-Manitoban writing, to make the transition to modernity, it had first to pass through a long period of uncertainty and obscurity. Even in 1981, Laurent Mailhot and Pierre Nepveu maintained that up until the end of the nineteenth century, "les rimeurs français d'Amérique imitent, racontent, prêchent, se plaignent, décrivent, chantent mais n'*écrivent* guère."[1] Nonetheless, the sheer bulk of the *Textes poétiques du Canada français* (*TPCF*)[2] remains striking: twelve volumes covering the period from 1606 to 1867 (10,000 pages, 3,857 poems, 227,175 lines), published between 1987 and 2000.[3] Furthermore, the prefaces accompanying the poetry identify and define the development of two and a half centuries of a literary life which had, so far, never been considered as autonomous, but rather as a tributary of other historical, political, and social domains. Who would have thought that French Canada produced so many poems? While the *TPCF* may not represent a fundamental shift of the milestones in the

---

1 "The French versifiers of America imitated, recounted, preached, complained, described and sang, but never *wrote*," Laurent Mailhot and Pierre Nepveu, eds., "Introduction," in *La Poésie québécoise des origines à nos jours* (Montreal: Typo, 1986 [1981]), p. 3. Authors' italics.
2 *French-Canadian Poetical Texts*. Unlike drama or fiction, it is rare for whole volumes of poetry to be translated. However, in order to assist the anglophone reader, we have in the following provided translations of the original French titles of the volumes as well as of the poems.
3 Jeanne d'Arc Lortie, s.c.o., ed., with the collaboration of Pierre Savard and Paul Wyczynski, *TPCF*, vol. I: *1606–1806* (Montreal: Fides, 1987); Jeanne d'Arc Lortie, s.c.o., ed., with the collaboration of Yolande Grisé, Pierre Savard, and Paul Wyczynski, vol. II: *1806–1826* (Montreal: Fides, 1989); Yolande Grisé and Jeanne d'Arc Lortie, s.c.o., eds., with the collaboration of Pierre Savard and Paul Wyczynski, vol. III: *1827–1837* (Montreal: Fides, 1990); vol. IV: *1838–1849* (Montreal: Fides, 1991); vol. V: *1850–1855* (Montreal: Fides, 1992); vol. VI: *1856–1858* (Montreal: Fides, 1993); vol. VII: *1859* (Montreal: Fides, 1994); vol. VIII: *1860* (Montreal: Fides, 1995); vol. IX: *1861–1862* (Montreal: Fides, 1996); vol. X: *1863–1864* (Montreal: Fides, 1997); vol. XI: *1865–1866* (Montreal: Fides, 1999); vol. XII: *1866–1867* (Montreal: Fides, 2000).

history of French-Canadian poetry that have been established over the course of several centuries, the collection is a vitally important achievement. Functioning within both synchronic and diachronic perspectives, it uncovers, classifies, and puts into context thousands of compositions in verse.

The nineteenth century: where it all began

The embryonic seventeenth and eighteenth centuries may be passed over swiftly, with only one poet, Marc Lescarbot (1570–1642), meriting a brief mention. Lescarbot, who can justly be termed the first "poet" of New France, published his *Histoire de la Nouvelle-France* in Paris in 1609, and followed it with the collection *Les Muses de la Nouvelle-France*.[4] The seventeenth and eighteenth centuries may be termed "embryonic": according to the compilers of the *TPCF*, only 281 poems appeared between 1606 and 1806, whereas 3,576 were published between 1806 and 1867. This considerable growth in poetic activity in French Canada is partly explained by the appearance of a number of new literary magazines and journals. By contrast, however, only five collections of poetry were published during this period.[5] We should avoid making the mistake of attributing contemporary literary aspirations to poets whose aims were seldom primarily literary. Even so, certain themes and subjects, anchored in reality or perhaps in the French Canadian psyche, have crossed the centuries and reached ours intact. Michel Bibaud, for example, took it upon himself to warn his compatriots of potential literary pitfalls that awaited them, notably the misuse of the French language: "Très-souvent [sic] à côté d'une phrase Française [sic], / Nous plaçons sans façon une tournure Anglaise [sic]."[6] Gaston Miron, Gérald Godin, and many others were to raise the multi-faceted question of language to the level of poetics, even of politics.

The three dominant figures of the nineteenth century were François-Xavier Garneau (1809–66), Octave Crémazie (1827–79) and Louis Fréchette

---

4 *A History of New France*, *The Muses of New France*.
5 Michel Bibaud (1782–1857), *Epîtres, Satires, Chansons, Epigrammes et autres pièces de vers* (1830); Louis-Thomas Groulx (1819–71), *Mes loisirs: Publication mensuelle en vers* (1848); Adolphe Marsais (1803–after 1879), *Romances et Chansons* (1854); Louis Fiset (1825–98), *Jude et Grazia ou Les malheurs de l'émigration canadienne* (1861); Louis Fréchette, *Mes loisirs* (1863).
6 "We frequently place an English phrase / In the middle of a French sentence" (author's note: there are several mistakes in the French of the citation), Michel Bibaud, "Satire III. Contre la paresse," in *La Poésie québécoise avant Nelligan*, ed. Yolande Grisé (Montreal: Bibliothèque québécoise, 1998), p. 93.

(1839–1908). Their poetry was famous at the time – especially that of Crémazie and Fréchette – but now the first is remembered for his work as a "national historian," the second for his remarkable correspondence, and the third for his short stories.

Has Garneau's prestige as a historian served to promote his poetry or has it, on the contrary, pushed it into the shadows? Given that, according to John Hare, Garneau was the author of twenty-seven poems, it would be rash to suggest that these alone would have sufficed to guarantee that he be remembered as a poet. His work is characterized by its romantico-political flavour, and his poem "Le Voyageur,"[7] with its daring thematic combinations, attests to this. Written during a stay in Europe in 1832, the poem juxtaposes lamentation for his separation from his home country ("Mais errant aujourd'hui sur la terre étrangère, / Sans parents, sans patrie, oublié des humains")[8] with undisguised sensuality ("L'amour guidait mes doigts, et la timide Hélène / En rougissant sentait gonfler son sein").[9] In 1840 Garneau published "Le Dernier huron,"[10] a resolutely patriotic work, before abandoning poetry altogether in order to devote himself to work on his *Histoire du Canada depuis sa découverte jusqu'à nos jours.*[11]

Octave Crémazie founded a bookshop in 1844, with the collaboration of his brother Joseph, but in November 1862 the business went bankrupt and Crémazie was obliged to leave Canada suddenly and under questionable circumstances in order to avoid a likely prison sentence for fraud. He went into exile in France, where he was to lead an extremely impoverished existence. His correspondence with the Abbé Raymond Casgrain, which gradually overshadowed his poetry during the twentieth century, bears witness to solid and pragmatic opinions on the lot of writers, literary life in general, and the situation in his home country. Thus, in a letter, dated August 10, 1866, he pronounces Canada to be a "société d'*épiciers*,"[12] while on January 29, 1867, he expresses the opinion that "si nous parlions iroquois ou huron,

---

7   "The Traveller."
8   "But wandering today on the unfamiliar earth / Without parents, without a country, forgotten by humanity."
9   "Love guided my fingers, and the shy Hélène / Blushing, felt her bosom swell," François-Xavier Garneau, "Le Voyageur. Élégie," in *Anthologie de la poésie québécoise du XIXe siècle (1790–1890)*, ed. John Hare (Montreal: Cahiers du Québec / Hurtubise HMH 1979), pp. 91 and 93.
10 "The Last Huron."
11 *A History of Canada from Its Discovery to the Present Day.*
12 "A nation of *grocers*," Octave Crémazie, *Poèmes et proses*, ed. Odette Condemine (Montreal: Bibliothèque québécoise, 2006), p. 119.

notre littérature vivrait. Malheureusement, nous parlons et écrivons d'une assez piteuse façon, il est vrai, la langue de Bossuet et de Racine.""[13]

To return to his poetry, it could be said that there are two Crémazies: the first is the poet celebrated by his contemporaries for his patriotic verse ("Le Vieux Soldat canadien," 1856, and "Le Drapeau de Carillon," 1858),[14] which he himself would later judge harshly. The second is the more intimate poet, haunted by death, who appears in such poems as "Les Morts" and especially the "Promenade de trois morts,"[15] of which only the first of three projected sections was published in 1862, shortly before the beginning of his European exile. In this latter poem, three dead men return to earth to implore the living to pity them. But the central character is "Le Ver"[16] (with its sanctifying capital letter), the "maître," the "Roi" du "sombre empire sépulcral,"[17] who speaks ill of humanity ("Les vivants n'ont d'oreilles / Que pour ce qui peut les servir"),[18] in order to crush the last remaining illusions of these living dead. This poem, in which personification of the dead extends over hundreds of lines, contains several images, notably "Le flot du Saint-Laurent semble une voix qui pleure,"[19] which anticipate certain Québécois poets of the 1950s and 1960s, such as Gatien Lapointe, author of the famous *Ode au Saint Laurent* (1963).[20]

In his first collection (*Mes Loisirs*, 1863),[21] the young Louis Fréchette gives pride of place to love poetry. Disappointed by his contemporaries' reactions to the two journals that he founded, and to his poetry, Fréchette left Canada for Chicago, from 1866 to 1871, where he published *La Voix de l'exilé*[22] in three parts (1866, 1868, and 1869), a verse lampoon denouncing the 1867 Confederation, which sparked lively debate between partisans and adversaries of the Confederation pact. His greatest work, *La Légende d'un peuple*[23] (published in

---

13 "If we spoke Iroquois or Huron, our literature would come to life. Unfortunately, we write and speak the language of Bossuet and Racine very badly, it must be said," ibid., p. 130.
14 "The Old Canadian Soldier" and "The Flag of Carillon."
15 "The Dead" and "Three Dead Men Walking."
16 "The Worm."
17 The "master," the "King" of the "solemn sepulchral empire."
18 "The living only hear / That which they choose to hear."
19 "The flowing of the Saint Lawrence River, like a human voice crying," Octave Crémazie, "Promenade de trois morts. Fantaisie. I. Le Ver," in Grisé, ed., *La Poésie québecoise*; the verse and text in quotation marks are taken from pp. 247–9.
20 *Ode to the Saint Lawrence River.*
21 *My Pastimes.*
22 *The Voice of the Exile.*
23 *The Legend of the People.*

Paris in 1887), owes much to *La Légende des siècles*[24] by Fréchette's literary idol, Victor Hugo. This legend of a North American people is recounted in around fifty poems which cover more than 300 pages and attain high summits of exaltation. Contemporary criticism accords no merit whatsoever to this epic poem. Nonetheless, a number of critically acclaimed poets of the "Hexagone generation" (named after the publishing house founded in 1953) were eventually to draw upon elements of this poem. They employed, *mutatis mutandis*, elements of its imagery and emphatic lyricism in their own celebrations of Quebec and its cultural heritage, contemporary avatars of the original legend of the people.

Today, Alfred Garneau (1836–1904), recognized for his mastery of the sonnet, and Eudore Évanturel (1852–1919) are generally considered to have made the most important contribution to nineteenth-century poetry. Évanturel's *Premières poésies* (1878)[25] depict nature and the changing seasons, as well as private spaces (such as the bedroom, "un beau salon chez des gens riches"),[26] public scenes (with descriptions of schools, museums, and orphans making their way home from church) and love. The collection is greatly indebted to Romantic and Parnassian poets, particularly Musset (to whom, incidentally, Évanturel pays tribute) and, as such, is filled with subtle and evocative shifts between impression and description. This collection was vehemently attacked by the conservative establishment, who maintained that poetry should serve greater and nobler ends and retain traditional forms. This controversy led Évanturel to publish an expurgated version of his collection in 1888. Did he, by so doing, excuse his critics? Was there, perhaps, an ulterior motive for this backdown given that, the previous year, Évanturel had begun a career as a local government archivist? Whatever the reason, the exponents of ideological and patriotic orthodoxy had once more carried the day. Nevertheless, many of Évanturel's poems retain an impressive sobriety of enunciation and restrained melancholy.

The nineteenth century was one of significant firsts in French-Canadian poetry: the publication of the first collections of poetry (see note 3), including the first by a woman;[27] the first anthologies;[28] and the first prose poems, by Charles Lévesque (1817–59). However, only those poems that tackled

---

24 *The Legend of the Centuries.*
25 *First Poems.*
26 "A beautiful room in a prosperous home."
27 Anne-Marie Duval-Thibault (1862–1958), *Fleurs du printemps*, Preface by Benjamin Sulte (Fall River: Société de Publication de l'Indépendant, 1892).
28 Antonin Nantel, ed., *Les Fleurs de la poésie canadienne* (Montreal: Beauchemin, 1869).

"important" questions (history, national identity, religion) were recognized and accepted in the public domain. A small number of poets did produce work that would today be described as intimist (concerned with changing moods, the turmoil of love or daily life), but these poems were, at best, ignored by the dominant conservative commentators of the day. All in all, the *TPCF* catalogues a total of 422 "identified authors" (including those whose identity was initially obscured by pseudonyms), 487 "unidentified pseudonyms" and 594 "anonymous" authors.[29] Thus, between 1606 and 1867, the identity of 71.9 percent of verse writers remains hidden. There are several possible explanations for this prevalent desire for anonymity, including fear of social stigma and of jeopardizing current or future social status.

And then there was Nelligan …

The oeuvre of Émile Nelligan (1879–1941) marks an epistemological break in the history of Québécois literature. All of his poetry was written between 1896 and 1899, at which point he was interned in a mental hospital, where he remained until his death. His friend Louis Dantin collected and published 107 of his poems as early as 1904, in *Émile Nelligan et son œuvre*,[30] thus helping to establish the reputation of the young poet. Nelligan's oeuvre and life story have fascinated and inspired numerous writers, critics, and literary historians, among whom one of the most significant is Paul Wyczynski, who wrote several books about him.[31] Some of his poems ("Le Vaisseau d'or," "La Romance du vin," and "Soir d'hiver" among others)[32] have become classics, and he remains the only really legendary figure of Québécois literature.

Nelligan, who described himself as aspiring to the "règne de l'Art"[33] is, indisputably, an accomplished poet.[34] In his most successful poems, the form is far from being an amalgamation of semi-assimilated influences; rather, he transcends form to reveal a series of sensations, motifs, desires, dreams, regrets, and anguish, all of which combine and result in a compelling musicality. Here,

---

29 Grisé and Lortie, and eds., *TPCF*, vol. XII, p. 10.
30 *Émile Nelligan's Life and Work.*
31 See, for example, Paul Wyczynski, *Nelligan 1879–1941* (Montreal: Fides, 1987), and l'*Album Nelligan: Une biographie en images* (Montreal: Fides, 2002).
32 "The Golden Boat," "The Wine Romance," and "Winter Evening."
33 "Throne of Art."
34 Émile Nelligan, "Rêve d'artiste," in *Œuvres complètes*, vol. I: *Poésies complètes 1896–1941*, ed. Réjean Robidoux and Paul Wyczynski (Montreal: Fides, 1991), p. 157.

for example, is the first of the five quintets that make up "Soir d'hiver,"[35] a quintessentially Nelliganian poem:

> Ah! comme la neige a neigé!
> Ma vitre est un jardin de givre.
> Ah! comme la neige a neigé!
> Qu'est-ce que le spasme de vivre
> À la douleur que j'ai, que j'ai![36]

Acoustic harmonies and structures are created by alliteration, and an effect of insistence is created by the echo of the first line of each quintet ("Ah ! comme la neige a neigé!" "Tous les étangs gisent gelés," "Pleurez, oiseau de février")[37] in the third line of each. This occurs in every stanza except the second, in which "les étangs"[38] is replaced by "ses espoirs,"[39] the use of the third-person possessive pronoun creating a distance between the poet and his narrative, and accentuating the drama of this narrative. Nelligan magnifies the effect of his imagery with pleonasm and inversion of grammatical symmetry ("la neige a neigé,""pleurez mes pleurs").[40] These brief examples indicate a wealth of formal effects that is all the more admirable for being the work of a young poet only just out of adolescence.

One of Nelligan's contemporaries, Albert Lozeau (1878–1924), wrote two poems about him (the first in July 1905 and the second in January 1910) as well as an article, published in 1904. Lozeau also published his own collections of poetry, L'Âme solitaire (1907) and Le Miroir des jours (1912),[41] which frequently achieve a subtle juxtaposition of conventional form with individual expression. In Lozeau's own words, "J'ai dit ce que j'ai vu d'une voix simple et franche."[42] While the desire for frankness and simplicity does not constitute the sole criterion for successful poetry, it is proof of Lozeau's decision to distance himself from grandiloquence and pathos.

During the first three decades of the twentieth century, the regionalist debate resulted in conflict between those who aimed to promote a certain

---

35 "Winter Evening."
36 "Oh! How the snow has snowed! / My window is a garden of frost. / Oh! How the snow has snowed! / What is life's brief spasm / To this pain of mine, of mine?," Nelligan, "Soir d'hiver," in Œuvres complètes, vol. I, p. 299.
37 "Oh! How the snow has snowed!," "All the ponds lie frozen," "Weep, bird of February."
38 "the ponds."
39 "his/her hopes."
40 "The snow has snowed," "cry, my tears."
41 The Solitary Soul and The Mirror of the Days.
42 "I said what I saw, in a frank and simple voice," Albert Lozeau, "Épilogue," "Les images du pays," Œuvres poétiques complètes, ed. Michel Lemaire (Montreal: Presses de l'Université de Montréal, 2002), p. 344.

set of Canadian values (respect for tradition, rural life, and religion) and young, so-called "exotic," poets who revolted against what they perceived to be indoctrination, preferring to promote a poetic production the aims of which were solely artistic. The multiple and complex machinations of this debate have been described by Annette Hayward, who notes the impossibility of dissociating these tensions from differing ideas related to the burgeoning of nationalism in Quebec around 1900.[43] Among those regionalist poets favored at the time by the critical establishment, the most memorable are Pamphile Lemay, Nérée Beauchemin, Albert Ferland, and Blanche Lamontagne-Beauregard, author of *Par nos champs et nos rives* (1917).[44] The younger, less conventional, school included Marcel Dugas, René Chopin, Guy Delahaye, and Paul Morin. Today, two poets, one from each of these currents, continue to be critically acclaimed: Jean Aubert Loranger (1896–1942), of the "exotic" movement, and Alfred DesRochers (1901–78), a regionalist. The former published his *Les Atmosphères*[45] in 1920; here, he abandons the sacrosanct convention of rhyme and breaks with regular line-lengths, as demonstrated in the collection's introductory piece, in which the poet "appuie des deux mains et du front sur la vitre / Ainsi, je touche le paysage," saying, "je suis énorme, Énorme ... / Monstrueusement énorme."[46]

While the poetry of Albert Lozeau had constituted, at least in formal terms, a continuation of the nineteenth century, Loranger's work paved the way towards Québécois poetic modernity. This repetition of the word "énorme" preceded, on its third occurrence, by an adverb so alien to poetic expression of the time, prefigures a certain prosaic approach that Saint-Denys Garneau would later exploit in his own poetics. Similarly, several metaphorical and thematic elements (the tension between interiority and exteriority, the images of the window and of the countryside, and the concept of balance) anticipate Garneau's *Regards et jeux dans l'espace*.[47] However, alongside this innovative work, Loranger was also to publish, in 1925, *À la recherche du régionalisme: Le village: Contes et nouvelles du terroir*[48] just as Lozeau had published, in 1916,

---

43 Annette Hayward, *La Querelle du régionalisme au Québec (1904–1931): Vers l'autonomisation de la littérature québécoise*, Preface by Dominique Garand (Ottawa: Le Nordir, 2006), pp. 560–1.
44 *By Our Fields and Rivers*.
45 *Atmospheres*.
46 "Lean my hands and forehead against the window / Thus, I touch the landscape beyond," "I am enormous, Enormous ... / Grotesquely enormous," Jean Aubert Loranger, "Je regarde dehors par la fenêtre," in *Les atmosphères* (Montreal: Imprimeur L. Ad. Morissette, 1920), p. 38.
47 *Games and Gazes in Space*.
48 *In Search of Regionalism: The Village: Stories and Tales From Our Country*.

Lauriers et feuilles d'érable,[49] further proof of the ambivalent stance of many writers with regard to regionalism.

By contrast, Alfred DesRochers does not view the rural landscape through a pane of glass, but immerses himself in it. He idealizes the lives of lumberjacks and trappers "[q]ui sont morts en rêvant d'asservir la nature."[50] This line appears in the introductory poem of his most important collection, *À l'ombre de l'Orford* (1929),[51] named after a mountain in the Eastern Townships, the region where DesRochers was born. The poem is a French Canadian epic, the opening line of which runs: "Je suis un fils déchu de race surhumaine / Race de violents, de forts, de hasardeux."[52] This initial antithesis, the series of dramatic images that culminates in the second line of the third quatrain ("J'entends pleurer en moi les grands espaces blancs"),[53] and the alexandrines the cadences of which are shaped by the gusts of wind that blow through the poem all conspire to make DesRochers' poem a resounding proof that conventional versification was not a spent force. Furthermore, as several critics have observed, the juxtaposition of conventional versification with elements of the Canadian vernacular, especially anglicisms, succeeded to some extent in pleasing both the regionalists and the "exotics." This appeasement only applied with regard to form, however, because ideologically speaking, DesRochers remained resolutely regionalist.

Québécois modernity

The contrast between the poetry of *À l'ombre de l'Orford* and that of *Regards et jeux dans l'espace*, by Saint-Denys Garneau (1912–43) is arresting. Although only eight years separate the two collections, the rupture is absolute: regular verse and grandiose expression have given way to disordered lines and fractured rhythms. The absence of rhyme, irregular line-length, and prosaic lexis constitute a brusque departure from the conventions of versification that had thus far been venerated and perpetuated by Québécois poets. This new formal freedom is associated with images in the poetry of a child creating

---

49 *Laurels and Maple Leaves*.
50 "Who died dreaming of subjugating nature," Alfred DesRochers, "Le Cycle des bois et des champs: Liminaire," in *À l'ombre de l'Orford*, ed. Richard Giguère (Montreal: Presses de l'Université de Montréal, 1993 [1929]), p. 156.
51 *In The Shadow of Mount Orford*.
52 "I am a failed son of a superhuman race / A race of violent, strong, daring men," DesRochers, "Le Cycle," p. 155.
53 "I hear the great white spaces crying within me," ibid., p. 155.

imaginary worlds: in the first piece in the collection, "Le Jeu,"[54] the poet proclaims "Voici ma boîte à jouets / Pleine de mots pour faire de merveilleux enlacements."[55] As the collection progresses, however, the horizon darkens as the initial enchanted young creator gives way to a disenchanted subject, alone in his "réduit,"[56] in which he hopes to discover "matière / Pour vivre et l'art."[57] With *Regards et jeux dans l'espace*, Saint-Denys Garneau brings the subject, and poetry itself, into the arena of modernity, albeit a dysphoric modernity.

Alain Grandbois (1900–75) represents the opposing pole of Québécois poetic modernity, most notably with *Les Îles de la nuit*,[58] published seven years after Saint-Denys Garneau's collection. The work (and the lives) of these two poets have assumed opposing positions within contemporary literary history: on one side stands Saint-Denys Garneau's fractured and interrupted poetry, combined with a tortured spiritual progress; on the other is the song of Grandbois, driven by a powerful lyricism celebrating physical love, and in harmony with the breath of freedom that was blowing through 1960s Quebec. (This opposition was an important catalyst of many of the ideological debates of contemporary literary history.)[59] These two collections are set apart by their contrasting form and versification, but are united by shared semantic elements, the last poem of *Les Îles de la nuit* recalling the end of all "games and gazes in space": "Fermons l'armoire aux sortilèges / Il est trop tard pour tous les jeux."[60]

Saint-Denys Garneau and Alain Grandbois were part of what would come to be known as the "generation of solitude" or the "great elders" ("grands aînés"), a generation that also included Rina Lasnier (1915–97) and Anne Hébert (1916–2000). Rina Lasnier's work extends over fifty years – from *Images et Proses* (1941) to a new and revised edition of *Présence de l'absence* (1992)[61] – and includes over twenty collections. These are characterized by an impressively

---

54 "The Game."
55 "Here is my toybox / Full of words to weave together in wonderful patterns," St-Denys-Garneau (sic), "Le Jeu," *Regards et jeux dans l'espace*, ed. Réjean Beaudoin (Montreal: Boréal, 1993 [1937]), p. 12.
56 "Hideout."
57 "Material / For art and life," St-Denys Garneau (sic), "[Autrefois]," in *Regards*, p. 56.
58 *Islands of the Night*.
59 For further discussion of this, see Pierre Nepveu's essay, "Un trou dans notre monde," *L'Écologie du réel: Mort et naissance de la littérature québécoise contemporaine* (Montreal: Boréal, 1988), pp. 63–77.
60 "Let us close the box of magic tricks / It is too late now for all these toys," Alain Grandbois, "Fermons l'armoire ..., " in *Les Îles de la nuit: Poèmes* (Montreal: l'Hexagone, 1963 [1944]), pp. 93–4.
61 *Images and Prose* and *Presence of Absence*.

wide-ranging lyricism and by the sensual and spiritual celebration of life lived to the fullest, always within the context of awareness of personal and national origins. Lasnier frames her work within a variety of different verse forms, most notably the versicle. Anne Hébert, Saint-Denys Garneau's cousin, produced one of the richest and most accomplished collections in all of contemporary Québécois poetry, *Le Tombeau des rois* (1953).[62] Here, inner turmoil and outer menace interweave in a spellbinding symbolism that culminates in the eponymous final poem. From the opening distich ("J'ai mon cœur au poing / Comme un faucon aveugle")[63] to the interrogatory cadence of the closing septet ("D'où vient donc que cet oiseau frémit / Et tourne vers le matin / Ses prunelles crevées?")[64] of *Le Tombeau des rois*, the narrator is at once Euripides and Orpheus, subject and object of both a transfiguring death and a failed resurrection, in which fantasy and mysticism mingle with eroticism. The precision with which bold, incisive imagery exposes this hermetic, devastated world for our inspection bears witness to Hébert's expert handling of the poetic scalpel.

Let us now return to the 1940s, a decade during which poetic language and versification, brought so decisively into modernity by Saint-Denys Garneau and Grandbois, were subject to still more upheavals. In 1948 Paul-Marie Lapointe (1929–) produced *Le Vierge incendié*,[65] an exploration of surrealism and automatism. Here, verse and prose compositions denounce religion ("les églises de faux sentiments")[66] and individual alienation from society, while proclaiming the transcendent power of free love. This collection was published in the same year and by the same publisher (Mytramythe) as *Refus global*,[67] a manifesto by the painter Paul-Émile Borduas denouncing all forms of alienation, particularly that caused by the excessive power of the clergy. *Le Vierge incendié* did not attract much critical attention or acclaim until the 1960s, or even the 1970s, when it was reissued in *Le Réel absolu*.[68]

Paul-Marie Lapointe, herald of a society on the brink of catastrophe ("Quand le marteau se lève / quand les bûchers vont flamber noir / sur le

---

62 *The Tomb of the Kings.*
63 "I hold my heart in my hand / Like a blind falcon," Anne Hébert, "Le tombeau des rois," in *Le Tombeau des rois: Poèmes* (Paris: Seuil, 1960 [1953]), pp. 59 and 61.
64 "Why then does this bird quiver / And turn towards the morning / His blinded eyes?"
65 *The Burned Virgin.*
66 "Churches of false sentiment," Paul-Marie Lapointe, "Untitled," in *"Le Vierge incendié": Le Réel absolu 1948–1965* (Montreal: l'Hexagone, 1971 [1948]), p. 15.
67 *Total Refusal.*
68 *The Absolute Real.*

peuple déterminé"),[69] was the contemporary of another young poet who, in 1949, was to begin work on a work of major importance. This poet was Roland Giguère (1929–2003) and the small volume of verse was *Faire naître*,[70] produced by Erta (the name was obtained by aphaeresis, taking away the first syllable, from "Alberta"), the publishing house that Giguère founded especially for this purpose. In 1965, the first of his three retrospective collections (the two others being *La Main au feu* in 1973 and *Forêt vierge folle* in 1978)[71] appeared with the emblematic title *L'Âge de la parole*:[72] "L'âge de la parole – comme on dit l'âge du bronze – se situe, pour moi, dans ces années 1949–1960, au cours desquelles j'écrivais pour nommer, appeler, exorciser, ouvrir, mais appeler surtout. J'appelais. Et à force d'appeler, ce que l'on appelle finit par arriver."[73] On his return to Quebec after a prolonged stay in France (1957–63), Giguère observed that the province was experiencing a period of cultural and social effervescence, where one could breathe more freely. Roland Giguère's poetic and pictorial oeuvre, seen as a whole, succeeds in its aim to "donner à voir,"[74] to use the title of a collection of poems by Paul Éluard, a formative influence on Giguère.

The landscape of Québécois poetry at the end of the 1940s and in the 1950s is rich and varied. It is marked by the presence of several varied groups: the "aînés," Alain Grandbois, Rina Lasnier, and Anne Hébert; young surrealist poets (Thérèse Renaud; Gilles Hénault, author of *Théâtre en plein air*;[75] Paul-Marie Lapointe; Claude Gauvreau, and Roland Giguère) and those grouped around the new publishing house, the Hexagone, which was inaugurated in 1953 with *Deux sangs*,[76] a collection by Olivier Marchand and Gaston Miron. The Hexagone was to establish the reputation of several new poets in the years that followed (most notably Jean-Guy Pilon, Fernand Ouellette, and Michel van Schendel), and also took on poets of the previous generation (Rina Lasnier and Alain Grandbois) as well as poets with varied poetic backgrounds

---

69 "When the hammer is lifted / when the funeral pyres will blaze black / over the stubborn people," Lapointe, *Le Vierge incendié*, p. 15.
70 *Bringing Into Being*.
71 *The Hand in the Flames* and *Mad and Virgin Forest*.
72 *The Word Age*.
73 "I perceive the word age – rather as one would say 'the bronze age' – as being between 1949 and 1960, years during which I wrote in order to name, to call, to exorcize, to open, but above all to call. I was calling. And thanks to this calling, that which we were calling for finally happened," Roland Giguère, "De l'âge de la parole à l'âge de l'image," *Forêt vierge folle* (Montreal: l'Hexagone, 1978), p. 110.
74 "Give to see."
75 *Open-Air Theatre*.
76 *Two Bloods*.

(such as Paul-Marie Lapointe and Roland Giguère). This publishing house brought an end to the social isolation of many poets by creating an arena for literary exchange and by organizing meetings and readings, so much so that it gave its name to the generation of poets born in the late 1920s and early 1930s (Pierre Perrault, Gaston Miron, Roland Giguère, Paul-Marie Lapointe, Michel van Schendel, Fernand Ouellette, and Jean-Guy Pilon, among others). However, the most intransigent poet of these years, Claude Gauvreau (1925–71), never identified himself with this "Hexagone generation." Gauvreau's virulent, even vulgar and scatological, imagery denounces the clergy, the bourgeoisie, and society as a whole, as in the vitriolic "Ode à l'ennemi,"[77] which, after a torrent of impassioned images, concludes with the threatening distich: "Vous êtes des incolores / Pas de pitié!"[78] The poet is merciless towards all those who obstruct his "liberté libre,"[79] to use a Rimbaldian phrase.

This frenzied quest for liberty is bound up with the climate of Québécois society at the time, which was felt to be stifling and alienating. It could also be linked, despite the circumspection with which such an argument must always be approached, to Gauvreau's personal life: he was confined to a mental hospital on several occasions. It was, in fact, during one such confinement that he composed a series of poems with the revealing title *Poèmes de détention* (1961).[80] This collection contains examples of linguistic transgression carried to the point of disorder (or perhaps of the creation of a new order), which had its beginnings in the late 1940s and which is inseparable from his dedication to the quest for liberty:

> Je suis dieu pour mes sourires secrets
> Et en vérité je suis moi-même
> Franc noble et plein de liberté
> Draggammalamalatha birbouchel
> Ostrumaplivi tigaudô umô transi LI[81]

It was not until the publication of the *Œuvres créatrices complètes*[82] in 1977, six years after Gauvreau's suicide, that his protean oeuvre (consisting of poetry, novels, dramas, and texts written for the radio) could be assessed in

---

77 "Ode to the Enemy."
78 "You are all insipid / No one will have pity on you!," Claude Gauvreau, "Ode à l'ennemi," in *État mixte (1950–1951)*, in *Œuvres créatrices complètes* (Montréal: Parti-pris, 1977), p. 261.
79 "Free freedom."
80 *Poems of Detention.*
81 "I am god for my secret smiles / And in truth I am myself / Frank, noble and full of liberty / Draggammalamalatha birboushell / Ostrumaplivi tigodo umo transi LI," Claude Gauvreau, "Recul," in *Poèmes de détention (1961)*, in *Œuvres créatrices*, p. 871.
82 *Complete Creative Works.*

its entirety. Even if it had been better known in the 1960s, it is likely that it would have received a lukewarm reception, such was the preeminence of poetry concerned with issues of nationality (national origins, cultural, and geographical heritage and language, for example) at that time.

The work falling into this bracket of "national" poetry included *Recours au pays*[83] (1961) by Jean-Guy Pilon, *Sémaphore* followed by *Voyage au pays de mémoire* (1962) by Gilles Hénault,[84] *Ode au Saint-Laurent* (1963) by Gatien Lapointe,[85] *Terre Québec* (1964) by Paul Chamberland,[86] *Mémoire* (1965) by Jacques Brault,[87] *Cantouques: Poèmes en langue verte, populaire et quelquefois française* (1967) by Gérald Godin,[88] *Pays sans parole* (1967) by Yves Préfontaine,[89] *En désespoir de cause* (1971) by Pierre Perrault,[90] and, finally, the "poster-poem" ("poème-affiche") by Michèle Lalonde (1937–), "Speak White," which was presented at poetry readings from the late 1960s and finally published in 1974. The one hundred or so stanzas of this poem denounce Anglo-Saxon socio-economic dominance and call for solidarity among oppressed peoples. While this poem is the best-remembered protest piece written during this period of unrest and upheaval, the most famous and fêted collection is *L'Homme rapaillé*[91] by Gaston Miron (1928–96), a figurehead of contemporary Québécois literature. This collection condenses, exalts, and reintegrates "national" poetry, drawing together (as in the verb in the title, "rapailler")[92] several "poetic cycles," including "La marche à l'amour," and "L'amour et le militant,"[93] titles that encapsulate the two main axes of the work, love and political conviction.

This juxtaposition of ethics and aesthetics creates a poetry which simultaneously perpetuates the great French lyric tradition and reaches into the heart of Québécois identity. Thus, poems such as "L'Octobre" could be said to continue the epic that began in the opening poem of *À l'ombre de l'Orford*: from the "fils déchu de race surhumaine"[94] to the poet who proclaims "je suis né ton fils par en haut là-bas."[95] The difference, however, is that, while DesRochers

---

83 *Turn Back to the Homeland.*
84 *Semaphore* and *Journey to a Land of Memory.*
85 *Ode to the Saint Lawrence River.*
86 *Quebec Soil.*
87 *Memory.*
88 *Cantouques: Verses Written in Colourful, Popular and Occasionally French, Language.*
89 *Wordless Country.*
90 *Last Resort.*
91 *The Rag Man.*
92 "Rapailler" means "to bundle together" or "to assemble."
93 "The March of Love" and "Love and the Militant."
94 "Failed son of a superhuman race."
95 "I was born your son, up high over there," Gaston Miron, "L'Octobre," in *L'homme rapaillé: Les poèmes*, ed. Marie-Andrée Beaudet (Paris: Gallimard, 1999 [1970]), p. 103.

idealized a past that he wanted to see perpetuated, Miron evokes the past in order to create a background against which he sets out his hopes for the future ("Nous te ferons, Terre de Québec"),[96] a vision of "l'avenir dégagé / l'avenir engagé."[97] The pugnacious and incantatory power of the grandiloquent poems of *L'Homme rapaillé* embodies a living language which finds form and meaning at the source of Miron's vision of individual and public life.

The French Canadian adventure

Quebec in the 1960s was not the only Canadian province experiencing extensive cultural, social, and political transformation, all imbued with a sense of the need to affirm national identity. Three publishing houses, Éditions d'Acadie (Moncton, New Brunswick), Éditions Prise de parole (Sudbury, Ontario) and Éditions du Blé (Winnipeg, Manitoba) were founded in 1972, 1973, and 1974 respectively. Athough Acadian, Franco-Ontarian, and Franco-Manitoban literatures were active before the 1970s, it is nonetheless true that these three publishing houses were responsible for creating French-Canadian literature with a "pan-Canadian scope."[98]

The first book published by Éditions d'Acadie (1972–99) was a collection of poems by Raymond Guy LeBlanc (1945–), *Cri de terre*: "Je suis acadien / Ce qui signifie / Multiplié fourré dispersé acheté aliéné vendu révolté / Homme déchiré vers l'avenir."[99] The poet is torn, but nonetheless turns to the future, as LeBlanc's subsequent collections confirm, and as is confirmed by the title of his 1988 collection, *Chants d'amour et d'espoir*.[100]

While Raymond Guy LeBlanc engendered the Acadian creative renaissance, the poet, playwright, cinéaste, and visual artist Herménégilde Chiasson (1946–) was its most forceful and polyvalent incarnation: "Comment arriver à dire que nous ne voulons plus être folkloriques …"[101] This rejection sets the tone for

---

96 "We will create you, Land of Quebec."
97 "A future of freedom / a future of commitment."
98 J. R. Léveillé, "Préface," in *Les Éditions du Blé: 25 ans d'édition* (Saint-Boniface: les Éditions du Blé, 1999), p. 8.
99 *Cry of the Land*, "I am Acadian / Which means / Multiple multi-layered dispersed bought alienated sold revolted / Man torn towards the future," Raymond Guy LeBlanc, "Je suis acadien," in *Cri de terre*, ed. Pierre l'Hérault (Moncton: Éditions d'Acadie, 1992 [1972]), p. 65.
100 *Songs of Love and Hope*.
101 "How can we articulate the fact that we don't want to be 'folksy' any more …" Herménégilde Chiasson, "Quand je deviens patriote," in *"Mourir à Scoudouc": Émergences* (Ottawa: L'Interligne, 2003 [1974]), p. 47.

Chiasson's creative trajectory and highlights the inevitable tensions between the search for identity and artistic freedom which is evident in the plural titles of such collections as *Prophéties* (1986), *Existences* (1991), *Miniatures* (1995), *Climats* (1996), *Conversations* (1999), *Actions* (2000), *Légendes* (2000) and *Parcours* (2005).[102]

In *Géographie de la nuit rouge*[103] (1984), Gérald Leblanc (1945–2005) "travaille à une géographie d'errances, en essayant d'aller plus loin. d'aller [sic] voir ailleurs et partout."[104] He made Moncton, no less, the radiant and painful focal point of all departures and all returns: "qu'est-ce que ça veut dire, venir de Moncton? ... Moncton est une prière américaine, un long cri de coyote dans le désert de cette fin de siècle. ... qu'est-ce que ça veut dire, venir de nulle part?"[105] This question is posed in the last piece in a book, the title of which summarizes Leblanc's poetics and his personal quest: *L'extrême frontière*[106] (1988). From orality to textuality, from quests for identity to linguistic transgression, from "la Main de Moncton qui rote le chiac"[107] to "l'horizon [qui] est une longue phrase aux rythmes déployés,"[108] the most important Acadian poets (from Raymond Guy LeBlanc to Serge Patrice Thibodeau, from Gérald Leblanc to Christian Brun, from Herménégilde Chiasson to Jean-Philippe Raîche, from Hélène Harbec to Fredric Gary Comeau, from Dyane Léger to France Daigle) have molded and situated their real and fantastical spaces within a dialectic of foreignness and familiarity. The same could be said, to some extent, of all literatures, but it is especially true of those produced within minority groups, such as Acadian, Franco-Ontarian, Franco-Manitoban and, on another level, Québécois, literatures.

Éditions Prise de parole, like Éditions de l'Hexagone and Éditions d'Acadie, played a vital role in the birth and success of Franco-Ontarian poetry, one of the leading lights of which was Patrice Desbiens (1948–). His early collections, especially *L'Espace qui reste*,[109] *L'Homme invisible / The Invisible Man* and *Poèmes*

---

102 *Prophets, Existences, Miniatures, Climates, Conversations, Actions, Legends* and *Journeys*.
103 *Geography of the Red Night*.
104 "Works on a geography of wanderings, trying to go further. to [sic] see elsewhere and everywhere," Gérald Leblanc, "Sur le sentier du rouge," in "*Géographie de la nuit rouge*": *Géomancie* (Ottawa: L'Interligne, 2003 [1984]), p. 59.
105 "What does it mean, to come from Moncton? ... Moncton is an American prayer, the lingering cry of a coyote heard in this *fin-de-siècle* desert ... what does it mean, to come from nowhere?" Gérald Leblanc, "untitled," in "*L'expérience du pacifique (1986–1987)*," in *L'extrême Frontière, poèmes 1972–1988*, (Moncton: Éditions d'Acadie, 1988), p. 161.
106 *The Final Frontier*.
107 "Moncton Main Street, which belches out Chiac," (Chiac is a dialect of Acadian French), Gérald Leblanc, "Vivre icitte," in "*Pour vivre icitte (1972–1980)*," in *L'extrême frontière*, p. 29.
108 "The horizon, which is a long sentence with undulating rhythms," Jean-Philippe Raîche, *Une lettre au bout du monde* (Moncton: Éditions Perce-neige, 2001), p. 71.
109 *The Remaining Space*.

anglais,[110] articulate his perception of a threat to his identity in the form of the imposition of an Other language upon him, namely, English. At that stage, Desbiens was like a rat biting its own tail within the maze of bilingualism. He was trapped, but fought back with the well-chosen and powerful weapons of flippancy and self-mockery. In his later collections (*Rouleaux de printemps*, in 1999 and *Hennissements*, in 2002),[111] questions of identity fade into the background: now, hyper-reality verging on the absurd has the upper hand. By caricaturing his own persona of disillusioned poet, dandy of mundane reality, and bard of the profound superficiality of love, Desbiens attains a certain grandeur, exploiting a disconcerting combination of the prosaic and the banal.

Robert Dickson (1944–2007) was another poet with a long-standing association with Éditions Prise de parole. The poetry of his 1997 collection, *Grand ciel bleu par ici*,[112] rejects metaphorical excess, the rhetorical overtones of which would interrupt the moments of abandon, and of terror at the proximity of objects and of beings. His next collection was *Humains paysages en temps de paix relative*,[113] which articulates a move to "aller vers l'autre voyager vers soi."[114] The work of Patrice Desbiens and Robert Dickson has influenced the writing of several poets born or living in northern Ontario, including Michel Dallaire, Pierre Albert, Guy Lizotte and, the most original, Jacques Poirier (1959–). Poirier's *Parfois, en certains jours de lumière parfaite*[115] (2006) is a dialogue with the work of the Portuguese poet Fernando Pessoa, which develops its poetics through a process of borrowing and grafting.

Since the 1960s, four generations of poets based around the Canadian capital, Ottawa, have made their mark alongside those of the so-called "northern school." These include the "aînés," Gabrielle Poulin (1929–) and Jacques Flamand (1935–), followed by those born in the 1940s (Pierre Raphaël Pelletier, Gilles Lacombe, and Andrée Lacelle) and the 1960s (André Leduc, Margaret Michèle Cook, and Stefan Psenak). In general, issues of Franco-Ontarian identity have no place in their poetry, which is above all concerned with articulating, whether it be through a feminist, spiritual, intimist, or humanist lens, human needs and desires in the context of the contemporary world. However, the first of four collections by Éric Charlebois (*Faux-fuyants*,

---

110 *English Poems*.
111 *Spring Rolls* and *Whinnyings*.
112 *Clear Blue Sky Over Here*.
113 *Human Landscapes in a Time of Relative Peace*.
114 "Move towards another travel towards oneself," Robert Dickson, "Sudbury II," in *Humains paysages en temps de paix relative* (Sudbury: Prise de parole, 2002), p. 58.
115 *Sometimes, on Certain Days of Perfect Light*.

2002),[116] and several poems in two collections by Tina Charlebois (*Tatouages et testaments*, 2002 and *Poils lisses*, 2006)[117] present a striking contrast to this turn away from "national" concerns.

These works, by two poets born in the 1970s, question aspects of Franco-Ontarian identity. In *Poils lisses*, Tina Charlebois writes: "Je suis Franco-Ontarienne seulement en Ontario. Traître si je change de province,"[118] highlighting ambivalent attitudes towards identity prevalent in Ontario. Still more questions of identity are raised by Angèle Bassolé-Ouédraogo (1967–), born in Burkina Faso but living in Ottawa since 1992. She has published three collections, *Burkina Blues* (2000), *Avec tes mots* (2003), and *Sahéliennes* (2006),[119] and her poems return to and prolong African "mémoire des femmes,"[120] paying homage to "mères-courages"[121] and posing a painful question: "Comment comprendre / Que nous soyons devenus / Nos propres ennemis?"[122] The roots of this self-interrogation are African, but its scope extends all the way to Ontario.

In 1974, Paul Savoie (1946–) inaugurated the publishing house Éditions du Blé (Manitoba) with his collection *Salamandre*.[123] The strength of this first collection lies in the acute contrast between the (apparently) lyrical imagery and depictions of a universe comprising both beauty and vast emptiness. Rather like Herménégilde Chiasson in Acadia and Patrick Desbiens in Ontario, J. R. Léveillé (1945–) represents Franco-Manitoban modernity. His work explores a wide variety of forms, the most radical of which are to be found in *Montréal poésie* (1987) and *Pièces à conviction* (1999).[124] *Montréal poésie* weaves together a heterogeneous montage of texts, images, collages, and advertisements to form a whole in which conflicting elements ultimately create a level space for art and commerce, aesthetics, and advertising. *Pièces à conviction* carries the aesthetic of collage still further, as words are placed in linear, vertical, and horizontal arrangements, sometimes alone and sometimes in blocks of text, in a variety of fonts and lengths of text, thus multiplying the possible sources of meaning in "poems" the focal points of which are

---

116 *Evasions*.
117 *Tattoos and Testaments* and *Smooth Fur*.
118 "I am Franco-Ontarian only in Ontario. I would be a traitor if I were to change provinces," Tina Charlebois, "untitled," in *Poils lisses* (Ottawa: L'Interligne, 2006), p. 23.
119 *With Your Words* and *Women of Sahelia*.
120 "Women's memory," Angèle Bassolé-Ouédraogo, "untitled," in *Sahéliennes* (Ottawa: L'Interligne, 2006), p. 64.
121 "Courageous mothers," ibid., p. 13.
122 "How can we accept / That we have become / Our own enemies?" ibid., p. 35.
123 *Salamander*.
124 *Montreal Poetry* and *Conviction Pieces*.

everywhere and nowhere, each source being both a part and the whole. In his first collection, *Œuvre de la première mort*,[125] Léveillé announced that "le monde est mon lieu de fiction,"[126] and he was to go on to develop the ideas of this collection in around twenty books, comprising novels, poetry, short stories, and other texts.

Contemporary Quebec

From 1965 onwards, three new strands of poetry began to flourish on the margins of Quebec's major poetical movements: formalism, counter-culture, and feminism. Formalism (as practiced by André Roy, André Gervais, Normand de Bellefeuille, and Roger Des Roches) rejects lyricism and explores the materiality of the text. Counter-culture poetry can be divided into two groups: the first is playful and exuberant but nonetheless voices dissent (Claude Péloquin and Raoul Duguay); the second is more polemical, and characterized by depictions of extreme sexuality, urban wandering, and general tawdriness (Louis Geoffroy, Lucien Francoeur, Josée Yvon, and Denis Vanier). The feminist poets include Nicole Brossard, Madeleine Gagnon, Geneviève Amyot, France Théoret, and Louise Dupré. The placing of all of these poets within such groups serves not to enclose their work within reductive paradigms but to highlight certain aspects of their work. Any "pigeonholing" would be especially reductive given that several among them have explored more than one of these poetical currents, have experimented with them and used them to refine and renew their work from one collection to the next. This tendency is typified in the poetic trajectories of Paul Chamberland (1939–) and François Charron (1952–): during the 1960s and the 1970s, Chamberland moved from "national" poetry (in *Terre Québec* and *L'Afficheur hurle*)[127] to a utopian humanism (in *Demain les dieux naîtront*);[128] Charron moved, between *Littérature-obscénité* (1974) and *La fragilité des choses* (1987),[129] from a persistent critique of poetry and society to metaphysical questionings.

Despite all these polemics, evolutions from poem to text, from word to writing, from polymorphous experimentation to scriptural polyphony,

---

125 *Work of the First Death*.
126 "The world is the setting for my fiction," J. R. Léveillé, *Œuvre de la première mort* (Saint-Boniface: Les Éditions du Blé, 1977), p. 87.
127 *Quebec Soil* and *The Billposter Yells*.
128 *Tomorrow the Gods will be Born*.
129 *Literature-Obscenity* and *The Fragility of Things*.

meant that transgression and subversion gradually established themselves, in the 1970s, as a new incarnation of self-conscious academicism. However, away from this obligatory rebelliousness, certain poets of the 1960s (Jacques Brault, Michel Garneau, Gilbert Langevin, Pierre Morency, and Michel Beaulieu) and the 1970s (Alexis Lefrançois, Marie Uguay, and Robert Melançon) produced works that have come to be recognized as the most interesting of our generation.

Among the most remarkable of these poets is Jacques Brault (1933–). In his first collection, *Mémoire* (1965),[130] exploration of familial and collective memory is communicated in forms that develop from short stanzas to paragraphs featuring a concentration of paratactic syntax, most notably in "Suite fraternelle,"[131] a lengthy and accomplished song, shot through with memories of a brother who died in the war. His later collections gradually break with this elegiac poetry and give way to a more sparse verse which captures "moments fragiles"[132] (also the title of one of his collections, published in 1984), suspended between feelings of communion with, and detachment from, nature, humanity, and the whole of existence: "Si on me demande par ici / dites que je m'éloigne sur la route."[133] This collection belongs to the intimist movement, which was prominent in Québécois poetry during the 1980s and 1990s. This intimism is linked to a "new" lyricism, more concise and pared down than its predecessor, within which the subject defines its relationship with itself and with its surroundings.

This is apparent in the poetry of Hélène Dorion. Even in 1976, Marie Uguay (1955–81) had put forward, in her first collection, *Signes et rumeurs*,[134] alternatives to the formalist and feminist poetry prevalent at the time. The "intimes sollicitudes"[135] described in the first poem are thus emblematic of the whole collection.[136] This was followed by *L'Outre-vie* and, in the year after her death, *Autoportraits*,[137] a subtle and exacting depiction of the modality of love and desire. Two more works by Uguay were published posthumously in 2005, the first of which was her journal (*Journal*), a powerful evocation of the last

---

130 *Memory.*
131 "Fraternal suite."
132 "Fragile moments."
133 "If they ask for me here / say that I am walking away down the road," Jacques Brault, "untitled", in *Moments fragiles* (Saint-Lambert: Le Noroît, 1984), p. 65.
134 *Signs and Sounds.*
135 "Intimate Sollicitudes."
136 Marie Uguay, "Untitled," in *"Signe et rumeur,"* in *Poèmes* (Montreal: Boréal, 2005 [1976]), p. 17.
137 *The After-Life* and *Self-Portraits.*

years of her life and a lucid, intense reflection on the nature of poetry. The second was *Poèmes*, which united previously published work with the hitherto unpublished *Poèmes en marge* and *Poèmes en prose*:[138] "mes mots n'atteignent pas la surface de l'eau / rien ne bouge au fond des yeux."[139] This impotence and immobility do not, however, overshadow the overall achievement of the work. Until her very last poems, Marie Uguay's oeuvre was first and foremost that of a poet, despite the anguish and suffering recorded in her journal: she maintained, and even refined, her mastery of images, their nuanced progression and their subtle unfolding. The two lines of poetry quoted above were written on September 6, 1980, and on February 25, 1980 she was to write "maintenant je suis seule à jamais."[140] From immobility to vertiginous solitude, Marie Uguay had passed through the looking glass of the poem. In the space and time of her poetry, she is no longer alone.

The process of writing this chapter has resulted in a desk piled high with collections of poetry. One pile is made up of collections written by women in the 1920s and 1930s, depicting desire and love in astonishingly free terms for the time. These are *Les Masques déchirés* (1932) by Jovette Bernier, *L'Immortel Adolescent* (1928) by Simone Routier, *La Course dans l'aurore* (1929) by Éva Senécal, and *Chaque heure a son visage* (1934) by Medjé Vézina.[141] Another pile contains *Signaux pour les voyants* by Gilles Hénault, *Mahler et autres matières* by Pierre Nepveu, *Les Heures* by Fernand Ouellette, *La Terre est ici* by Élise Turcotte and *L'Oiseau respirable* by José Acquelin.[142] Yet another pile reveals André Roy's *L'Accélérateur d'intensité* (1987) and Normand de Bellefeuille's *Un visage pour commencer* (2001),[143] tangible proof that intimism and the new lyricism also attract poets generally associated with formalism.

New publishing houses (Le Quartanier, Poètes de brousse, Marchand de feuilles, Le Lézard amoureux, L'Oie de Cravan, and others) and new literary magazines (*Exit, Steak haché, Le Quartanier, Contre-jour, Entrelacs*, and so on) rub shoulders (and compete) with older publishing houses (L'Hexagone, Les Herbes rouges, Le Noroît, Les Écrits des Forges, Triptyque) and established magazines (*Les Écrits, Liberté, Estuaire, Mœbius*). These forums, and many others, promote a burgeoning and immensely varied literary production.

---

138 *Poetry in the Margin* and *Poetry in Prose*.
139 "My words do not rise to the surface of the water / nothing moves in the depths of the eyes," Marie Uguay, "Untitled," in *Poèmes en marge*, in *Poèmes*, p. 161.
140 "Now I am alone for ever," Ibid., p. 165.
141 *Torn Masks, The Immortal Adolescent, The Race at Dawn* and *Each Hour has a Different Face*.
142 *Signals for Seers, Mahler and Other Materials, The Hours, The Earth Is Here*, and *The Breathable Bird*.
143 *The Intensity Accelerator* and *A Face to Begin With*.

Despite all this activity, contemporary poetry has problems and grievances that have become clichés, such as the perennial problem of the overabundance of collections produced for an extremely limited readership. We should, however, resist the temptation to believe in the existence of some bygone golden age of Québécois, Acadian, or Franco-Ontarian poetry which would reflect unfavourably on the quality of poetry in our own generation. Poetry steers its own course of progress, enriched by each new generation of poets, some of whom pay a high price for their explorations.

One painful example is *Nombreux seront nos ennemis*[144] by Geneviève Desrosiers (1970–96), a posthumous collection first published in 1999 and reissued in 2006. This poetry has the imperfections that might be expected of work that explores beyond the pale of hackneyed words and images. In search of the "inespéré vacarme," the narrator traversed "l'aube des abattoirs," then the "jour où tout bascule"[145] and finally the terrible deliverance: "Ça y est, je me déleste. / ... / Ce soir, je dormirai dans un lit d'acier."[146] Such was the poetry of one who "ne ressen[tait] plus le besoin de chercher car je suis à jamais égarée."[147] In the light of Roland Giguère's aphorism, "Pour aller loin: ne jamais demander son chemin à qui ne sait pas s'égarer,"[148] this last quotation acquires a paradoxical meaning: in order to travel as far as possible, must we lose ourselves for ever?

The answer is clear: no theme, however shattering it may be, can form the basis of poetry; only images can do this, such as those in *Nombreux seront nos ennemis*, which appear remarkable now for their insolence, now for their gravity, now for their fresh resonance. "Ne m'oubliez pas,"[149] Geneviève Desrosiers insists. Her poetry is the best guarantee of remembrance. It is also proof, painful but admirable, that today's poets have accepted (or even grasped eagerly) the baton of responsibility from their predecessors, and that their poetry responds not only to questions that today's world asks, but also to those that it is loath to ask.

---

144 *Many Are Our Enemies.*
145 "unimaginable din," "abattoir dawn," and "the day when everything collapses."
146 "This is it, I'm letting go. / Tonight I will sleep on a steel bed," Geneviève Desrosiers, "Ça y est," *Nombreux seront nos ennemis* (Montreal: L'Oie de Cravan, 2006, [1999]), p. 54.
147 "No longer felt the need to search, because I am forever lost," Geneviève Desrosiers, "Untitled," in ibid., p. 90.
148 "In order to travel far: never ask the way unless the one you ask knows how to lose himself."
149 "Don't forget me."

30
Drama
JANE MOSS

The history of francophone theater reflects the complexity of French Canada's political and social evolution over the past four centuries. During the period of French colonial rule, most theatrical activity can be described as amateur performances of French plays staged in salons, military barracks, or *collèges classiques*. In response to Lord Durham's *Report* following the Patriots' Rebellion of 1837–8, native-born French Canadians began building a national theatrical repertoire by writing patriotic historical dramas. With urbanization in the late nineteenth century came the construction of permanent playhouses in Montreal and Quebec City and the founding of professional theater companies. This institutionalization led to the growth of popular entertainment that took the form of burlesque variety shows in Quebec French during the 1920–40 period.

Reacting to calls for change beginning with the 1948 *Refus global* manifesto and continuing through the Quiet Revolution, Quebec drama became part of the collective project of social and cultural transformation. The nationalist or identitary drama of the 1960s and 1970s, which has been labeled *le nouveau théâtre québécois*, is characterized by the use of vernacular language, experimental techniques, and political subject matter. The growing consensus on the need for a distinctly Québécois culture provoked an identity crisis in Canada's other francophone communities, leading to the creation of multiple provincial repertoires of francophone drama. In the aftermath of the defeat of the 1980 referendum on sovereignty-association, Quebec theater turned from dramatizing collective political aspirations to issues more personal and aesthetic. The 1980s are marked by several trends: the continued development of feminist and gay theater, the beginnings of immigrant and Native drama, and growing experimentation with theatrical forms and language which can be labeled postmodern. Since the 1990s, the dramaturgy of Quebec and francophone Canada has explored subjects and artistic concerns that transcend the nationalist and identitary concerns of its regional origins.

Colonial theater

The first theatrical production in French Canada was *Le Théâtre de Neptune*,[1] an allegorical spectacle written by Marc Lescarbot and staged at Port Royal d'Acadie in 1606. The Jesuit *Relations* of 1640 describe an unnamed tragicomedy and mystery play performed by lay colonists in Quebec City to celebrate the birth of the future King Louis XIV. According to theater historian Leonard E. Doucette, French classical plays and edifying works were frequently performed in St. Lawrence River towns beginning in the mid-seventeenth century.[2] But always suspicious of theater's potential for undermining dominant ideologies and promoting immoral behavior, the Catholic Church often issued official condemnations and banned plays during the colonial period. In 1694, the Bishop of Quebec City, Monseigneur de Saint-Vallier, decided to take more serious measures when Governor Frontenac proposed a performance of *Le Tartuffe*, Molière's satire of religious hypocrisy. Threatened with excommunication, Frontenac cancelled the play. What has become known as *L'Affaire Tartuffe* effectively led to the banning of public performances from 1699 until the end of French colonial rule, limiting dramatic activity to didactic and pedagogical plays in Church-run institutions of learning.

After the Conquest, amateur theater returned with performances of French classical plays, performed by English officers in their barracks or by French-Canadian amateurs. The Théâtre de Société was established in Montreal in 1789 as an informal playhouse for French-language productions. Original operettas and social comedies modeled on eighteenth-century French salon comedy or vaudeville were presented there, for example *Colas et Colinette* (1790) and *L'Anglomanie ou, Le diner à l'anglaise* (1802) by a French-born naturalized Canadian named Joseph Quesnel. Later on in Quebec City, the first native-born playwright, Pierre Petitclair, staged comedies of intrigue. *Griphon, ou la vengeance d'un valet* (1837), *La Donation* (1842), and *Une partie de campagne* (1842; 1856)[3] were influenced by both French classicism and melodrama.

---

[1] *Neptune's Theatre*, ed. Edna B. Holman (New York and London: Samuel French, 1927); *The Theatre of Neptune in New France*, ed. Harriet Taber Richardson (Cambridge: Riverside Press, 1927). Where available, translations (both published and unpublished) will be footnoted in the following.

[2] Leonard E. Doucette, *The Drama of Our Past: Major Plays from Nineteenth-Century Quebec* (Toronto: University of Toronto Press, 1997), p. viii.

[3] Here, as elsewhere in the chapter, the two dates indicate first performance of the play and first publication of the text.

Building a national theater

Responding to Lord Durham's comment on the lack of a French Canadian national theater, Antoine Gérin-Lajoie inaugurated the tradition of patriotic historical plays with *Le Jeune Latour* (1844), based on a 1629 incident recounted by Michel Bibaud's *Histoire du Canada sous la domination française* (1837). Since then, in Quebec and other francophone communities, scores of amateur and professional playwrights have dramatized important events in the history of French Canada and glorified the heroes who led the struggle to perpetuate the "French fact" in North America. Theater historians including Jacques Cotnam, John Hare, Étienne-F. Duval, Leonard E. Doucette, and Jane Moss have catalogued plays that depict the "discovery" of Canada, the founding and defense of colonial settlements, Jesuit missionaries, the Acadian Deportation, the Conquest, the Patriots' Rebellion, Métis leader Louis Riel's rebellion and hanging, and threats to close French schools outside of Quebec. The Catholic Church approved of these historical dramas because they reinforced the ideology of *survivance* by preaching conservative religious, social, and patriotic values. In general, nineteenth- and early twentieth-century historical plays defined heroism in terms of religious inspiration, aspirations toward freedom, fidelity to the race, and martyrdom. In the post-Conquest and post-Confederation period, these edifying scenes of past exploits were intended to ease collective French-Canadian anxiety about minority status and discourage emigration to the United States.

The plays of poet Louis-Honoré Fréchette are typical of the genre. *Félix Poutré* (1862; 1871), based on the memoirs of a man claiming to have been a *patriote* who escaped the gallows by feigning madness, was perhaps the most popular French-Canadian play of the nineteenth century. *Papineau* (1880) and *Le Retour de l'exilé* (1880) also present the political events of the 1837–8 Patriots' Rebellion along with idealized portraits of French Canadians who possess the Corneillian virtues of patriotism, piety, honor, generosity, and loyalty to family. *Papineau* is a typical historical melodrama, complete with a sentimental subplot, comic relief provided by colorful *habitants*, a "good" Indian loyal to his French-Canadian benefactors, a villainous spy, stirring political harangues, crowd scenes, and battle scenes with martial music.

In the late nineteenth century, historical plays appealed to growing numbers of urban francophones who also flocked to theaters to see the famous French tragedienne Sarah Bernhardt perform French repertory pieces during her numerous Canadian tours. The demand for more popular entertainment spurred an explosion of theatrical activity of various sorts. During the 1894–1914 period, a number of permanent playhouses were constructed and professional companies founded, leading historians to label this period the Golden Age of theater in Quebec.[4] For three seasons beginning in 1898, the Monument National staged regular "Soirées de famille," amateur productions that offered edifying patriotic plays to the francophone middle class. The first professional francophone troupe was founded in 1898 and housed at the Théâtre des Variétés; the first French theater constructed in Montreal, the Théâtre National, opened its doors in 1900. With a new production and eight performances every week, the Théâtre National was enormously successful staging French versions of Broadway shows under the management of a Frenchman named Paul Cazeneuve. The American model followed a melodramatic formula: a handsome and sensitive hero, a romantic plot, fights, and spectacular explosions or shipwrecks. The first major hit with a more Canadian flavor, Louis Guyon's *Montferrand* (1903; 1923), ran for three weeks and was reprised three times.

In the first decade of the twentieth century, new dramatic forms appeared such as the religious productions and melodramas promoted by Julien Daoust and the topical musical comedy reviews conceived by Cazeneuve. The first big religious hit for Daoust was *La Passion*, written by Germain Beaulieu (1902), which drew 35,000 spectators to the Monument National in the space of three weeks, despite official Church disapproval. During the Easter season of following years, Daoust wrote and produced other religious dramas with titles such as *Le Triomphe de la Croix*, *Pour le Christ*, *Le Défenseur de la Foi*, and *Le Rédempteur*. When he sensed the public's craving for something new, Daoust offered them melodramas, including the enduring Québécois classic of the genre, *Aurore, l'enfant martyre* (1921; film versions 1952 and 2005) by Léon Petitjean and Henri Rollin. At the Théâtre National, Cazeneuve created the end-of-the-year satirical review, beginning with *Ohé! Ohé! Françoise!*, which drew 40,000 spectators in January 1909. The plot was simple: a drunken bum falls asleep on the Place d'Armes and dreams that Maisonneuve comes down from his statue to visit his city. The "revues d'actualité" in subsequent years always included commentary on local people and events, caricatures, musical numbers, and comic dialogues.

Outside of the province of Quebec, there were other signs of theatrical activity. Amateur and school drama groups mounted plays from the French

---

4 See Jean-Marc Larrue, "Entrée en scène des professionnels 1825–1930," in *Le Théâtre au Québec 1825–1980*, ed. Renée Legris, Jean-Marc Larrue, André-G. Bourassa, and Gilbert David (Montreal: VLB éditeur, 1988), pp. 46–59.

classical and boulevard repertoires in the Ottawa-Hull area and in the francophone communities of the maritime and western provinces. Soon, more serious efforts were undertaken. At the Institut canadien-français d'Ottawa and the Cercle dramatique de Hull, as well as in parish halls throughout Franco-Ontario, amateur and school groups were active beginning in the late nineteenth century. While many of the productions were French plays put on for educational purposes, there were some original works by French Canadian authors such as Louis Fréchette, Augustin Laperrière, Régis Roy, and Rodolphe Girard.[5] The oldest company still active in francophone Canada, Le Cercle Molière, was founded to perform plays from the French repertoire in 1925 in Saint-Boniface by three men: André Castelein de la Lande, a Belgian-born French professor, Louis-Philippe Gagnon, a Quebec-born bookstore owner, and Raymond Bernier, a native-born federal employee. Among its early members, the Cercle Molière counted elite French-speakers from the Franco-Manitoban community, including francophone and francophile immigrants, a fact that explains its penchant for plays with universal themes in the European dramatic tradition and its insistence on linguistic correctness. In the older and more homogeneous community of New Brunswick, Father James Branch reinforced historical memory and collective identity in the wake of the Acadian Renaissance with plays entitled *L'émigrant acadien* (1929), *Jusqu'à la mort! ... pour nos écoles!* (1929), and *Vivent nos écoles catholiques! ou la Résistance de Caraquet* (1932). The first true Acadian playwright, Branch wrote these didactic plays to discourage Acadians from emigrating to the United States and to defend the right to maintain French Catholic schools.

In Montreal during the period between the two world wars, professional troupes were attracting increasingly large audiences to variety shows that were in the tradition of the Théâtre National topical musical reviews. Using the language of working-class Quebeckers, these shows were usually improvised comedies based on simple plot lines that incorporated songs, dances, and humorous sketches. The best examples of this type of performance were the annual satiric reviews called *Fridolinades*, created by Gratien Gélinas in 1938. His character Fridolin was a witty, street-smart kid who poked fun at contemporary society. This combination of vernacular (rather than Parisian) French and local subject matter would be essential to building an authentic

---

5 On the origins of Franco-Ontarian theater see Mariel O'Neill Karch and Pierre Karch, "Présentation," in *Augustin Laperrière (1829–1903)* (Ottawa: Les Éditions David, 2002), pp. 23–62.

Québécois dramaturgy. When Gélinas turned from satiric comedy to dramatic realism with *Tit-Coq* (1948; 1950), he found a public ready for major artistic changes and serious social commentary.

At the same time that Fridolin was bringing contemporary French-Canadian life to the stage, the Compagnons de Saint-Laurent founded by Father Émile Legault in 1937 were producing classical and avant-garde continental plays with the double aim of improving professional production standards and giving the audience an aesthetic and spiritual experience. After the Second World War, a number of professional companies including the Théâtre du Rideau Vert (1949), Théâtre du Nouveau Monde (1952), the Apprentis-Sorciers (1955), the Egrégore (1959), and others were formed on the model of Les Compagnons de Saint-Laurent, laying the groundwork for introducing technically and artistically sophisticated avant-garde and classical drama in Montreal. The enthusiasm for creating new art forms in the post-war period inspired writers whose experimental plays were influenced by the *Refus global* manifesto, surrealism, *automatisme*, and the French theater of the absurd. The plays of Claude Gauvreau (*La Charge de l'orignal épormyable*[6] [written in 1956, first performed in 1974], *Les oranges sont vertes* [1958; 1972]), Jacques Languirand (*Les insolites* [1956; 1962],[7] *Les grands départs* [1957; 1958]),[8] Jacques Ferron (*Les grands soleils* [1958]), and others are important for their rejection of the conventions of dramatic realism and rationalism, and for their experimentation with language and Brechtian techniques.

During this initial period of antinaturalistic experimentation, social realism still dominated mainstream drama. Gélinas's *Tit-Coq*[9] exemplifies the genre with its representation of the alienation of the average French Canadian, the oppressive institutions of conservative Quebec society, and the poverty of language that frustrates the expression of ideas and passion. The play is the sad story of a soldier who dreams of romantic love and being part of a family, but is denied happiness because of his illegitimate birth and upbringing in an orphanage. While Tit-Coq is off at war, his girlfriend gives in to family pressure and marries someone else. When he returns, he tries to persuade her to run away with him, only to be disappointed again when a priest convinces them that society would label them adulterers and their children

---

6 Claude Gauvreau, *The Charge of the Expormidable Moose*, tr. Ray Ellenwood (Toronto: Exile Editions, 1996).
7 Jacques Languirand, *The Eccentrics*, tr. Albert Bermel (unpublished).
8 Jacques Languirand, "The Departures," tr. Albert Bermel, in *Gambit: An International Drama Quarterly* 5 (London, 1964), pp. 41–74.
9 Gratien Gélinas, *Tit-Coq*, tr. Kenneth Johnstone (Toronto: Clarke, Irwin, 1967).

bastards. *Tit-Coq*, often considered a turning point in French Canadian drama, was well received in Quebec and on tour in the rest of Canada where it was performed in both official languages. The 1953 film version by director René Delacroix and starring the playwright himself won numerous awards. In 1959, Gélinas satirized the hypocrisy of the bourgeoisie and the corruption of the judicial system in *Bousille et les justes* (first published in 1960),[10] a play about a simple-minded young man who commits suicide after being pressured to perjure himself to protect an acquaintance accused of murder.

Another playwright who used the stage to critique Quebec society during this period of intense introspection leading up to the Quiet Revolution was Marcel Dubé. His first hit, *Zone* (1953; 1968),[11] focuses on an east Montreal teenage gang that turns to cigarette smuggling as a way out of poverty. Inevitably, the charismatic gang leader meets a tragic fate: he accidentally kills a customs agent, is denounced by a fellow gang member, and dies in a failed prison escape. *Zone* rises above lower-class melodrama through Dubé's use of scenic spaces that symbolize imprisonment and through his creation of sympathetic (if misguided) antiheroes. Like Gélinas, he soon switched his focus from working-class to middle-class characters and wrote a series of plays that examine the mediocrity, boredom, and stifling conservative environment of Quebec society. Plays such as *Un simple soldat* (1957; 1958) and *Florence* (1957; 1970) examined personal quests for happiness doomed to failure, while *Bilan* (teleplay 1960; 1968)[12] and *Au retour des oies blanches* (1966; 1969)[13] dramatized the revelation of dark family secrets. Like Dubé's bourgeois protagonists, those of Françoise Loranger's *Une maison ... un jour ...* (1963; 1965) and *Encore cinq minutes* (1966; 1967) come to recognize their *mal d'être*, the existential anguish and spiritual emptiness of their lives. The bourgeois psychological dramas of the 1960s suggest that the problem lies in the moral vacuum of a society that has lost its sense of collective identity.

---

10 Gratien Gélinas, *Bousille and the Just*, tr. Kenneth Johnston (Toronto: Clarke, Irwin, 1961).
11 Marcel Dubé, *Zone*, tr. Aviva Ravel (Toronto: Playwrights Canada, 1982).
12 It is worth noting that the works of many prominent playwrights mentioned in this study were produced as radio or television plays by CKAC, CBF, CBF-FM, and Radio Canada, including plays by Marcel Dubé, Jacques Languirand, Françoise Lornager, Michel Tremblay, Antonine Maillet, Marie-Claire Blais, Elizabeth Bourget, Carole Fréchette, and Jean Marc Dalpé. From their beginnings, radio and television played important roles in supporting the performing arts in francophone Canada by introducing serious drama to a wide audience and by giving financial support to theater professionals. See Pierre Pagé, *Histoire de la radio au Québec: Information, education, culture* (Montreal: Fides, 2007).
13 Marcel Dubé, *The White Geese*, tr. Jean Remple (Toronto: New Press, 1972).

Growing nationalist sentiment soon found expression in political dramas that underscored the historical enmity between anglophones and francophones while dramatizing the federalist-separatist debates dominating public discourse in Quebec. In Ferron's *La Tête du roi* (1963), Dubé's *Les Beaux Dimanches* (1965; 1968),[14] Gélinas's *Hier, les enfants dansaient* (1966),[15] the debates over sovereignty often divide families and force characters to put collective political goals ahead of personal concerns. The tone of political theater sharpened in the late 1960s as debates gave way to attacks on politicians and those opposed to the sovereigntist agenda. Robert Gurik's *Hamlet, prince du Québec* (1968)[16] and Loranger's *Le Chemin du roy* (written with Claude Levac, 1968; 1969) and *Médium saignant* (1970) are examples of how political parody and polemics were acted out on stage during a period when Bill 63 (1969) and the October Crisis (1970) transformed the chambers of government and the streets of Quebec into theaters of high political drama.

Nationalist and identitary theaters

When the trends toward cultural and linguistic specificity, psychological liberation, artistic innovation, and political expression came together at the end of the 1960s, theater took on a key role in affirming ethnolinguistic identities, combating assimilation, and creating a distinctive francophone Canadian literary corpus. As it had always been, the stage was a privileged site for preserving historical memories and reflecting community values, but now it started taking a more critical look at the condition of minority communities and the need for change. At the same time, an expanded corps of theater amateurs and professionals was adopting more sophisticated strategies for self-expression.

Michel Tremblay's *Les Belles-Sœurs* (1968; 1972)[17] is the play that marks the beginning of the new era of francophone dramaturgy in Quebec, usually referred to as *le nouveau théâtre québécois*. When it premiered at Montreal's Théâtre du Rideau Vert, it provoked a huge public debate over the use of

---

14 Marcel Dubé, *O Day of Rest and Gladness!*, tr. Edward Jolliffe and Marcelle Leclerc (unpublished).
15 Gratien Gélinas, *Yesterday the Children Were Dancing*, tr. Mavor Moore (Toronto: Clarke, Irwin, 1967).
16 Robert Gurik, *Hamlet, Prince of Quebec*, tr. Marc F. Gélinas (Toronto: Playwrights Canada, 1981).
17 Michel Tremblay, *Les Belles-Sœurs*, tr. John Van Burek and Bill Glassco, rev. edn. (Vancouver: Talonbooks, 1992 [1974]).

joual (the popular language of east Montreal) and its grimly humorous representation of the lives of working-class Quebeckers. Today, it is considered a classic of Quebec literature (often translated and performed in Europe and the Americas) because of Tremblay's blending of *joual* and lyricism, realistic subject matter and antirealistic stage techniques. In *Les Belles-Sœurs*, Tremblay introduced the neighborhood and some of the characters that would reappear in future plays of his *Cycle des Belles-Sœurs* and in the novels of *Chroniques du Plateau Mont-Royal*. Tremblay's world is peopled by unhappy housewives, pious spinsters, sleazy nightclub entertainers, drag queens, dysfunctional families, drunks, and madmen. The portrayal of Quebec's lower and under classes goes beyond miserablist social realism, seeking explanations without political rhetoric. His daring treatment of sexuality made a blunt statement about the Catholic Church's responsibility for conjugal problems and led the way to creating gay theater in Quebec.

Tremblay's appeal to audiences and critics is due not only to what his characters have to say, but also to the innovative structures of his plays, which often combine elements of classical Greek tragedy, Brechtian dramaturgy, musical composition, burlesque, and avant-garde antirealism. In *Les Belles-Sœurs*, for example, the complaints and petty disputes that pass for normal conversation among the cast of fourteen women is frequently interrupted by intimate revelations in spotlighted monologues and dialogues and by choral recitations composed like musical comedy numbers. Working with the brilliant director André Brassard, Tremblay produced a stream of original plays following his first hit. *La Duchesse de Langeais* (1970; 1973)[18] is the monologue, filled with comedy and pathos, of an aging drag queen. In *À toi, pour toujours, ta Marie-Lou* (1971),[19] the contrapuntal dialogues of two pairs of characters (husband-wife, sisters) span a ten-year period and dramatize the tragic effects of sexual ignorance, excessive piety, and alcoholism. The musical composition of another play on family dysfunction, *Bonjour, là, bonjour* (1974),[20] includes solos, duets, trios, quartets, sextets, and octets. *Damnée Manon, sacrée Sandra* (1977)[21] is composed of the parallel monologues of an outrageous drag queen and a spinster obsessed with rosary beads and religion, while *Albertine, en cinq*

18 Michel Tremblay, *La Duchesse of Langeais and Other Plays*, tr. John Van Burek (Vancouver: Talonbooks, 1976).
19 Michel Tremblay, *Forever Yours, Marie-Lou*, tr. John Van Burek and Bill Glassco (Vancouver: Talonbooks, 1975).
20 Michel Tremblay, *Bonjour, là, bonjour*, tr. John Van Burek and Bill Glassco (Vancouver: Talonbooks, 1975).
21 Michel Tremblay, *Damnée Manon, Sacrée Sandra*, tr. John Van Burek (Vancouver: Talonbooks, 1981).

temps (1984)[22] uses five actresses who simultaneously portray one character at five stages of her life. In *Le Vrai Monde?* (1987)[23] Tremblay raises questions about the artist's right to expose family secrets by presenting his "real" family members and the unflattering caricatural stage versions he created of them. Still writing plays as well as fiction and memoirs, Michel Tremblay continues to dramatize the people and experiences that marked his childhood as well as issues related to sexual identity and artistic production.

Another playwright identified with the *nouveau théâtre québécois* of the 1970s is Jean Barbeau, who used vernacular speech, elements of popular culture, and antirealistic techniques to explore how political and cultural questions affect average Quebeckers. His plays show how social and economic injustice and cultural elitism deprive working-class francophones of dignity and a sense of identity. *Le Chemin de Lacroix* (1970; 1971)[24] spotlights the humiliation of a man mistakenly arrested during the protests against Bill 63 (which gave Quebec anglophones the right to send their children to English-speaking schools), and then interrogated and beaten by the police. Treated as inferior and ignorant, he is finally reduced to silence by a Frenchman who ridicules the way he speaks. Barbeau treats the linguistic question with humor in two one-act plays, *Manon Lastcall* (1970; 1972) and *Joualez-moi d'amour* (1970; 1972), which present *joual* as a sign of the vitality and virility of Quebeckers in contrast to the effeminate pretentiousness of Parisian French. The positive representation of Quebec's linguistic and cultural specificity in Barbeau's early theater is the flip side of satirical attacks on the influences from the United States and France. The antihero of *Ben-Ur* (1971) has consumed so much American popular culture through television and comic books that he is psychologically stunted and alienated, while the would-be playwright of *Le Chant du sink* (1973) suffers a breakdown because his creativity is stifled by the conflicting forces of traditional French Catholic elitism, US materialism, and revolutionary rhetoric.

The mixture of humor, Brechtian and absurdist stage techniques, and cultural nationalist sentiments that characterizes Jean Barbeau's plays is also present in the work of Jean-Claude Germain, another key figure in the drive to build an authentic Québécois drama in the 1970s. As artistic director and

---

22 Michel Tremblay, *Albertine in Five Times*, tr. John Van Burek and Bill Glassco (Vancouver: Talonbooks, 1986).
23 Michel Tremblay, *The Real World?*, tr. Bill Glassco and John Van Burek (Vancouver: Talonbooks, 1988).
24 Jean Barbeau, *The Way of Lacross*, tr. Laurence R. Berard and Philip W. London (Toronto: Playwrights Co-op, 1973).

resident playwright of the Théâtre d'Aujourd'hui (founded as the Théâtre du Même Nom in 1969), his goals were to banish the classical French repertoire and conventional realistic performance styles, to create accessible theater that speaks the language of the people, to create dramatic forms that expressed Quebec's national culture and anticolonial historical consciousness. Germain's early plays were carnivalesque spectacles, using grotesque farce and absurdist strategies to demystify and denounce conservative social institutions (especially the family) and elitist culture, while calling for personal liberation and national independence. Turning his satirical eye on Quebec history, he wrote three plays that reinterpret the past in the light of the present. *Un pays dont la devise est je m'oublie* (1976), *Mamours et conjugat* (1978; 1979), and *A Canadian Play / une plaie canadienne* (1979; 1983) are all attempts at collective exorcism meant to lay blame for present problems and correct the negative image of Quebec. After the satirical attacks on social institutions and history, Germain turned his attention to the alienating effect of European cultural models. *Les hauts et les bas de la vie d'une diva: Sarah Ménard par eux-mêmes* (1974; 1976) and *Les nuits de l'indiva* (1980; 1983) illustrate the need for musical and dramatic forms that affirm Quebec identity and history.

The extraordinary burst of artistic energy that transformed francophone Canadian culture also included the creation of educational and promotional institutions, alternative theater groups, and a women's theater movement. A number of important organizations helped to expand and institutionalize francophone theater between 1960 and 1980. In Montreal, for instance, the École Nationale de théâtre opened in 1960, joining the Conservatoire d'art dramatique, which had been training theater professionals in Montreal since 1954 and in Quebec City since 1958. The Centre d'essai des auteurs dramatiques (CEAD), which changed its name to Centre des auteurs dramatiques in 1991, was created in 1965 to support the creation of a distinctive Québécois dramaturgy. In Ottawa, the National Arts Centre/Centre National des Arts opened in 1969 and frequently showcased Quebec artists and playwrights. Many of the counter-culture or alternative theater groups founded in this period formed the Association Québécoise du Jeune Théâtre (AQJT) in 1972, including the Grand Cirque Ordinaire, the Eskabel, the Pichous, the Grande Réplique, the Théâtre ... Euh!, the Théâtre Parminou, the Théâtre Expérimental de Montréal, and others influenced by the avant-garde theories of Artaud, Brecht, and Piscator.

The theater collectives of the *jeune théâtre* movement shared the sociopolitical goals of the *nouveau théâtre québécois* playwrights, but took their inspiration from leftist cultural politics in insisting on non-hierarchical collective creation based on improvisation techniques, experimentation, and research. The women's theater movement grew naturally out of this alternative theater as newly formed feminist groups such as the Théâtre des Cuisines, the Organisation ô, the Commune à Marie, the Théâtre Expérimental des Femmes, the Folles Alliées, and others took to the stage to dramatize the feminist sociopolitical agenda and to create a sexually liberated *discours au féminin*.

Women's theater joined the ongoing critique of Quebec's social and religious institutions by adding women's voices to the call for change. For the Théâtre des Cuisines, the call was for control over reproduction (*Nous aurons les enfants que nous voulons* [1974; 1975]) and an end to economic exploitation (*Môman travaille pas, a trop d'ouvrage!* [1975; 1976], *As-tu vu? Les maisons s'emportent!* [1980; 1981]). The seven women who composed the monologues of *La nef des sorcières* (1976)[25] were calling for a *prise de parole* and a *prise de conscience* to free themselves and other women from their fear, silence, and solitude. By articulating the desire for self-possession, independence, and sexual liberation, the writers of *La nef* performed a political act, claiming a place for women in Quebec history and society.

Since rejection of traditional female roles was seen as the first step toward liberation Denise Boucher wrote *Les Fées ont soif* (1978)[26] to exorcize the Catholic Church's repressive female archetypes: virgin, mother, whore. In *À ma mère, à ma mère, à ma mère, à ma voisine* (1978; 1979), the four women from the Théâtre experimental de Montréal who would go on to found the Théâtre expérimental des femmes staged an assault on the patriarchal mother figure and called for demystifying, rehabilitating, and reclaiming the female body. These and other plays by women denounced the negative effect of fairytales on young girls, the isolation of housewives, the psychological damage of unrealistic ideals of feminine beauty, and other aspects of patriarchal oppression. In opening up a dramatic space for redefining gender roles and sexuality, women's theater made it easier for gay playwrights to follow Michel Tremblay's lead in theatricalizing homosexuality.

The political and creative energy propelling Quebec theater inspired the growth of regional and identitary theater elsewhere in Canada. Responding to the shift from *French-Canadian* to *Québécois* identity that excluded them, Franco-Ontarian theater activists organized the Coopérative des Artistes du

---

25 *A Clash of Symbols*, tr. Linda Gaboriau (Toronto: Coach House Press, 1979). Also in *Anthology of Québec Women's Plays in English Translation*, vol. I: *1966–1986*, ed. Louise H. Forsyth (Toronto: Playwrights Canada Press, 2006), pp. 277–329.

26 Denise Boucher, *The Fairies Are Thirsty*, tr. Alan Brown (Toronto: Talonbooks, 1982). Also in Forsyth, ed., *Anthology*, vol. I, pp. 331–73.

Nouvel-Ontario (CANO) in 1975 and Théâtre Action in 1972 for the purpose of building a corpus of plays that would represent the daily reality of the French-speaking minority of Ontario. The Théâtre du P'tit Bonheur (now the Théâtre français de Toronto), which had been staging French and Quebec plays in Toronto since 1967, was joined by companies committed to producing regionalist drama – the Théâtre du Nouvel-Ontario (1971) of Sudbury and the Théâtre D'la Corvée (1975, now the Théâtre du Trillium) and the Théâtre de la Vieille 17 (1979) in the Ottawa region.

To create a distinctive Acadian drama, the Théâtre Populaire de l'Acadie (1974) of Caraquet and the Théâtre l'Escaouette (1978) of Moncton joined Antonine Maillet, who had shown Montreal audiences the unique language and culture of her native New Brunswick with plays such as *La Sagouine* (1970; 1971)[27] and *Évangéline Deusse* (1976; 1975).[28] Even the tiny Franco-Columbian community of Vancouver formed a francophone troupe, the Théâtre la Seizième (1974). Together with groups formed since the 1980s in Alberta, Saskatchewan, Ontario, and New Brunswick, these companies became part of the Association des théâtres francophones du Canada (ATFC, founded in 1984 as the Association nationale des théâtres francophones hors Québec).

Outside of Quebec, the identitary phase of drama lasted well beyond the 1980 referendum on sovereignty-association that seemed to put an end to Quebec's politically inspired theater. Beginning in the 1970s and lasting through the 1990s, francophone Canadian playwrights dramatized their regional histories, linguistic situation, economic and social conditions, and prospects for survival. In Ontario, plays such as André Paiement's *Moé, je viens du Nord, s'tie* (1970), Jean Marc Dalpé and Brigitte Haentjens's *Hawkesbury Blues* (1982) and *Nickel* (1984), Dalpé's *Le Chien* (1987),[29] and Michel Ouellette's *Corbeaux en exil* (1991; 1992) and *French Town* (1993; 1994) depicted the precarious status of francophone communities. Materially poor, physically isolated, and under-educated, the Franco-Ontarian characters of these works frequently share a collective experience of dispossession, exile, disglossia, and shame that leads to angry expressions of violence and despair.

But it would be wrong to conclude that all Franco-Ontarian theater presents a dismal portrait of isolated minority communities in decline and threatened with assimilation. Paiement's *Lavalléville* (1974; 1975) and collective creations

---

27 Antonine Maillet, *La Sagouine*, tr. Luis de Céspedes (Toronto: Simon and Pierre, 1979).
28 Antonine Maillet, *Evangeline the Second*, tr. Luis de Céspedes (Toronto: Simon and Pierre, 1987).
29 Jean Marc Dalpé, *Le Chien*, tr. Jean Marc Dalpé and Maureen LaBonté (unpublished, 1988).

such as La Vieille 17's *Les murs de nos villages* (1979; 1983) and La Corvée's *La parole et la loi* (1979; 1980) valorize the vitality and distinctive culture of Franco-Ontario, underscoring the creative possibilities of bilingualism. Beginning with the urbane and sophisticated plays of Robert Marinier in the 1980s and continuing in the 1990s with the postmodern experimentation of Louis Patrick Leroux (founder of Théâtre la Catapulte), Franco-Ontarian theater has moved beyond its origins as a collective quest for identity toward more individual quests for happiness and artistic expression.

In the west, Franco-Manitoban theater continued to present historical plays but also began to deal with contemporary social issues. Claude Dorge took a revisionist view of Louis Riel in *Le Roitelet* (1976; 1980) and focused on the closing of French schools in *L'Article 23* (1985, written with David Arnason). The same subjects were treated in more conventional style by Marcien Ferland, who celebrated the resistance to the closing of French schools in *Les Batteux* (1982; 1983). Roger Auger's *Je m'en vais à Régina* (1975; 1976) marked the beginning of a new Franco-Manitoban dramaturgy. Auger presented the Ducharme family of Saint-Boniface as typical western francophones, facing pressures to assimilate and feeling betrayed by Quebec sovereignists. Since the 1980s Le Cercle Molière has taken up the challenge of building a distinctive Franco-Manitoban repertoire that depicts the situation of the minority community, staging plays by Claude Dorge and Irène Mahé (*La Trilogie des Tremblay* [1986–9]), Mahé and Jean-Guy Roy (*Frenchie* [1986]), and Marc Prescott (*Sex, lies, et les Franco-Manitobains* [1993; 2001]). Recently, Manitoban playwrights have begun to look beyond their community. Prescott's *Encore* (2003) is an amusing romantic comedy in the Neil Simon tradition and his *L'Année du Big-Mac* (1999; 2004) is a wild satire of American politics and commercialism. For his part, Rhéal Cenerini has focused on issues of faith, conscience, and morality in dramas set against the backdrop of European political and historical conflicts – Nazi death camps in the case of *Kolbe* (1990; 1996) and a country torn by ethnic divisions in *Laxton* (2002; 2004).

In the small and dispersed francophone communities of Saskatchewan and Alberta, the development of regional dramaturgies was slower. Founded in 1985, Saskatoon's Troupe du Jour worked to create a theater that reflected the Fransaskois community and reinforced its identity. This was the goal of Laurier Gareau, the father of Fransaskois dramaturgy, who wrote *Pas de problèmes* (1975) to dramatize the reality and language of Regina's francophone community. In *The Betrayal / La Trahison* (English stage version 1982; bilingual edition 1995), Gareau revisited the history of Louis Riel, accusing the Curé of

Batoche of betraying the Métis. Lorraine Archambault's *De blé d'inde et des pissenlits* (1993; 2006) was also a historical play, but here the focus was on the experiences of Québécois, Belgian, and French settlers over a fifty-year period. More recently, the Troupe du Jour has encouraged Fransaskois writers to expand beyond identitary subject matter.

Original plays by Franco-Albertan authors began to appear in the early 1990s. *Il était une fois Delmas, Sask … mais pas deux fois!* (1990; 2006), André Roy and Claude Binet's monologue about the assimilation of francophones in small towns, was staged by Edmonton's Boîte à Popicos (founded in 1978). The Théâtre français d'Edmonton (founded in 1967) performed France Levasseur-Ouimet's comic allegory on linguistic politics *La guerre des mots* (1991; 2004), as well as Jocelyne Verret's *Voulez-vous danser?* (1991; 1996) and *Comme on est différente, comme on se ressemble* (1992). In 1992, the Théâtre français d'Edmonton merged with the Boîte à Popicos, the Théâtre du Coyote (founded in 1985), and other local troupes to become the UniThéâtre. Since then the UniThéâtre has worked to create a distinctive Franco-Albertan drama, staging Levasseur-Ouimet's political comedy, *Bureau de la minorité, bonjour!* (1992; 2004) and two series of *Contes albertains* (2000; 2001). Other francophone Canadian plays and French translations of English-Canadian dramas have also been produced by the UniThéâtre.

While in recent years francophone theater outside of Quebec has been able to transcend its status as regionalist drama focused on the history and community problems, Acadian drama has found it more difficult to let go of a collective memory traumatized by the Deportation of 1755 and subsequent experiences of oppression at the hands of the anglophone majority. In 1975, Jules Boudreau and Calixte Duguay again dramatized the active resistance against the 1875 law closing French schools in a musical spectacle entitled *Louis Mailloux*. The distrust and hostility that have historically characterized relations with anglophones were also staged by Jules Boudreau in *Cochu et le soleil* (1978; 1979), which tells the story of an Acadian family twice dispossessed by the American colonists in the eighteenth century.

In the plays of Acadia's two most prominent authors, Antonine Maillet and Herménégilde Chiasson, collective memory and identity have been constant themes. Maillet has brought to life Acadian history, culture, language, and identity for Montreal audiences in plays such as *La Sagouine*, *Évangéline Deusse*, *Gapi et Sullivan* (1973),[30] *La Veuve enragée* (1977), and *Margot la folle* (1987), but

---

30 Antonine Maillet, *Evangeline the Second*, tr. Luis de Céspedes (Toronto: Simon and Pierre, 1987); *Gapi and Sullivan*, tr. Luis de Céspedes (Toronto: Simon and Pierre, 1987).

she has often been criticized by fellow Acadians for perpetuating a folkloric image of a people untouched by modernity. The need to explore the weight of the past on the Acadian psyche in order to enter modernity has inspired Chiasson to write a cycle of plays: *Histoire en histoire* (1980), *Évangéline, mythe ou réalité* (1982), *Renaissance* (1984), *L'Exil d'Alexa* (1993), *La Vie est un rêve* (1994),[31] *Aliénor* (1997; 1998), *Laurie ou la vie de galerie* (1998; 2002), *Pour une fois* (1999), and *Le cœur de la tempête* (2001). Acadian theater's compulsive use of history and its constant complaint about minority status has created something of an impasse, but there are signs of moving beyond regionalism and identitary drama.

Beyond nationalism, regionalism, and identity

While regionalist theater was growing in minority francophone communities across Canada, much of the theatrical activity fired by the energy of nationalist sentiments dissipated in Quebec after the defeat of the 1980 referendum on sovereignty-association. Questions of personal happiness and minority identities (both sexual and ethnic) replaced collective concerns for subject matter; counter-cultural leftist theater strategies and popular language gave way to postmodern performance and writing pratices and self-consciously literary language. Since the early 1980s, Quebec theater has become increasingly heterogeneous, intimist, experimental, and literary.[32]

Women's theater gradually abandoned its militant feminist stance in the 1980s and *spectacles de femmes* were replaced by plays dramatizing the roles of women in Quebec history and exploring issues such as female creativity, sexuality, and family dynamics. Michèle Lalonde's *Dernier Recours de Baptiste à Catherine* (1977) was one of the first revisionist historical plays in its determination to create dramatic space for portraying women's active roles at key moments in Quebec's past. It was followed in the 1980s by numerous plays that recreated historical periods to dramatize the lives of ordinary women. Marie Laberge's *Ils étaient venus pour …* (1981) and *C'était avant la guerre à l'Anse à Gilles* (1981),[33] Elizabeth Bourget's *En ville* (1982; 1984), Maryse Pelletier's

---

31 Herménégilde Chiasson, *Lifedream*, tr. Jo-Ann Elder (Toronto: Guernica, 2006).
32 See Joseph I. Donohoe, Jr. and Jonathan M. Weiss, *Essays on Modern Quebec Theater* (East Lansing: Michigan State University Press, 1995); Jean Cléo Godin et Dominique Lafon, *Dramaturgies québécoises des années quatre-vingt* (Montreal: Leméac, 1999); Chantal Hébert et Irène Perelli-Contos, eds., *Le Théâtre et ses nouvelles dynamiques narratives* (Quebec: Les Presses de l'Université de Laval, 2004).
33 Marie Laberge, *It Was Before the War at L'Anse-à Gilles*, tr. John Murrell (unpublished).

À qui le p'tit cœur après neuf heures et demie (1980; 1984) and *Du poil aux pattes comme des cwac's* (1982; 1983),[34] and Marthe Mercure's *Tu faisais comme un appel* (1989; 1991)[35] are good examples of this effort to stage the historical experiences of ordinary Quebec women. Jovette Marchessault took a different approach in *La Saga des poules mouillées* (1981),[36] a dramatized biography of four famous French-Canadian women authors which focused on the social stigmas they had to overcome in order to express themselves. Anne Hébert rewrote the Corriveau legend in *La Cage* (1989), acquitting her heroine of murder charges and finding the judicial system guilty of misogyny.

The work of Marie Laberge, Quebec's most prominent woman playwright, illustrates the evolution of women's theater. In her first plays, her female characters are often victims of the conservative, patriarchal Catholic ideology of the past: the raped maid of *C'était avant la guerre*, the sterile woman of *Ils étaient venus pour...*, the suicidal daughter of *Jocelyne Trudelle trouvée morte dans ses larmes* (1983), the depressed wife, of *Deux tangos pour toute une vie* (1984; 1985), the abused anorexic of *L'homme gris* (1984; 1986),[37] and the four unhappy daughters of *Oublier* (1987).[38] When Laberge's female protagonists begin to acknowledge the harm done by idealizing marriage and the family, they can make themselves happier by assuming their sexuality and independence as do the sisters of *Aurélie, ma sœur* (1988)[39] and *Charlotte, ma sœur* (2005).

Once they had dealt with sociopolitical demands for change and created a liberated discourse *au féminin*, women playwrights explored a variety of issues that affect their personal lives. Maternity and motherhood were topics in Pol Pelletier's *La Lumière blanche* (1981; 1989), Louisette Dussault's *Moman* (1979; 1981),[40] Carole Fréchette's *Baby blues* (1989), and Maryse Pelletier's *La Rupture des eaux* (1989). The importance of sexuality and personal happiness were spotlighted in plays such as Maryse Pelletier's *Duo pour voix obstinées* (1985),[41] Elizabeth Bourget's *Appelle-moi* (1995; 1996), Carole Fréchette's *La Peau d'Élisa*

---

34 Maryse Pelletier, *And When the CWAC's Go Marching On*, tr. Louise Ringuet (unpublished).
35 Marthe Mercure, *Blood Sisters*, tr. Maureen LaBonté (unpublished).
36 Jovette Marchessault, *Saga of the Wet Hens*, tr. Linda Gaboriau (Vancouver: Talonbooks, 1983).
37 Marie Laberge, *Night*, tr. Rina Fraticelli (London: Methuen, 1988). Also see Forsyth, ed., *Anthology*, vol. I, pp. 481–513.
38 Marie Laberge, *Take Care*, tr. Rina Fraticelli (unpublished).
39 Marie Laberge, *Aurelie, My Sister*, tr. Rina Fraticelli (unpublished).
40 Louisette Dussault, *Mommy*, tr. Linda Gaboriau, in Forsyth, ed., *Anthology*, vol. I, pp. 375–418.
41 Maryse Pelletier, *Duo for Obstinate Voices*, tr. Louise Ringuet (Montreal: Guernica, 1990).

(1998),[42] and *Jean et Béatrice* (2002).[43] The problematic mother–daughter relationship, a major focus for early feminist theater, continued to generate interest, for example Anne-Marie Alonzo's *Une lettre rouge orange et ocre* (1984), Hélène Pedneault's *La Déposition* (1988),[44] Dominick Parenteau-Lebeuf's *Dévoilement devant notaire* (2002),[45] and Louise Dupré's *Tout comme elle* (2006).

A new generation of women playwrights has now emerged, the daughters of 1970s feminism who focus on social issues that are less gender specific. Following the lead of Fréchette's *Les Quatre Morts de Marie* (1998; 1995)[46] and *Les Sept Jours de Simon Labrosse* (1997; 1999),[47] Geneviève Billette's *Crime contre l'humanité* (1999)[48] and *Le Pays des genoux* (2005; 2004), as well as Evelyne de la Chenelière's *Des fraises en janvier* (1999; 2003)[49] and *Henri & Margaux* (2002; 2003) deal with universal issues such as social justice, friendship, and love.

The staging of gender difference and sexuality begun by Michel Tremblay and expanded by women's theater in the 1970s reflected rapidly changing social attitudes, so it should come as no surprise that gay playwrights would emerge in the 1980s. Leading the way were Normand Chaurette, René-Daniel Dubois, and Michel Marc Bouchard, three brilliant and innovative young authors whose work critiqued the repressiveness of socially constructed gender roles and sexual norms, disrupted the heterosexual male gaze, and created a liberated discourse of homoerotic desire. Tremblay's drag queens had highlighted the performativity and artificiality of gender roles, and gay theater continued to problematize the notion of the natural as well as dramatizing the difficulty of being gay.

Three plays in particular illustrate the aesthetic and theatrical strategies of gay theater. Chaurette's *Provincetown Playhouse, juillet 1919, j'avais 19 ans* (1982;

---

42 Carole Fréchette, *Élisa's Skin*, tr. John Murrell, in *Carole Fréchette: Three Plays* (Toronto: Playwrights Canada, 2002), pp. 73–103.
43 Carole Fréchette, *John and Beatrice*, tr. John Murrell, in *Carole Fréchette: Two Plays* (Toronto: Playwrights Canada, 2007), pp. 5–56.
44 Hélène Pedneault, *Evidence to the Contrary*, tr. Linda Gaboriau (Montreal: NuAge Editions, 1993).
45 Dominick Parenteau-Lebeuf, *The Feminist's Daughter*, tr. David J. Eshelman (unpublished).
46 Carole Fréchette, *The Four Lives of Marie*, tr. John Murrell in *Carole Fréchette: Three Plays*, pp. 1–71.
47 Carole Fréchette, *Seven Days in the Life of Simon Labrosse*, tr. John Murrell, in *Carole Fréchette: Three Plays*, pp. 105–18.
48 Geneviève Billette, *Crime Against Humanity*, tr. Bobby Theodore (Toronto: Playwrights Canada, 2004).
49 Eveline de la Chenelière, *Strawberries in January*, tr. Morwyn Brebner (Toronto: Playwrights Guild of Canada, 2003; Playwrights Canada, 2004).

1981),[50] Dubois's *26 bis, impasse du Colonel Foisy* (1982), and Bouchard's *Les Feluettes ou la répétition d'un drame romantique* (1987)[51] use role-playing and *mise-en-abyme* techniques to blur distinctions between masculine and feminine, illusion and reality, art and life, madness and sanity. The gay characters prefer stylized and exaggeratedly theatrical gestures; they deconstruct and rescript past traumas in ways that create therapeutic narrative distance and point to their own artifice. Not all gay-themed plays are marked by excessive theatricality, but many do share a disturbingly dark view of being gay. For example, Dubois's *Being at Home with Claude* (1985; 1986) and Larry Tremblay's *The Dragonfly of Chicoutimi* (1994) and *La hache* (2006) probe the homicidal psychology of their protagonists. The gay characters of Michel Tremblay's *La Maison suspendue* (1990),[52] however, do seem to have evolved in positive directions, overcoming their *mal d'être* and finding self-acceptance.

Another kind of politically engaged theater emerged in Montreal in the 1980s, one that gave voice to immigrants and Native peoples who spoke other languages, shared different collective memories, and viewed the world from the perspective of their marginalized ethnic communities. As immigration, Native rights, and multiculturalism increasingly became topics of debate, theater became a public forum for portraying cultural differences, alterity, and *métissage*. Marco Micone led the way toward the creation of a theater of heterogeneity with a trilogy of plays depicting the experience of Italian immigrants: *Gens du silence* (1980; 1982), *Addolorata* (1983; 1984),[53] and *Déjà l'agonie* (1988).[54] Following three generations of one family, Micone depicts the pain of departure, the linguistic and cultural difficulties of integration, the impossibility of return, the need for intercultural hybridity. Pan Bouyoucas's *Le cerf-volant* (1993; 2000)[55] focuses on the problems of Greek immigrants, marginalized by their inability to speak French well and by Québécois xenophobia. Like Micone's Italian immigrants, Bouyoucas's Greeks came to Canada for economic opportunities and still daydream about returning to their homeland.

50 Normand Chaurette, *Provincetown Playhouse, July 1919*, tr. William Boulet. In *Quebec Voices: Three Plays* (Toronto: Coach House Press, 1986), pp. 17–51.
51 Michel Marc Bouchard, *Lilies or The Revival of a Romantic Drama*, tr. Linda Gaboriau (Toronto: Coach House Press, 1990).
52 Michel Tremblay, *La Maison suspendue*, tr. John Van Burek (Vancouver: Talonbooks, 1991).
53 Marco Micone, *Two Plays: Voiceless People, Addolorata*, tr. Maurizia Binda (Montreal: Guernica, 1988).
54 Marco Micone, *Beyond the Ruins*, tr. Jill MacDougall (Toronto: Guernica, 1995).
55 Pan Bouyoucas, *The Paper Eagle*, tr. Linda Gaboriau (Toronto: Playwrights Canada, 2006).

For immigrants who left their native countries to escape political violence, memories of home are less nostalgic. Abla Farhoud's plays dramatized the experiences of female Lebanese immigrants, traumatized by memories of patriarchal violence and civil war in their homeland and isolated in their new country. In *Quand j'étais grande* (1983; 1994),[56] *Les filles du 5-10-15c* (1986; 1993),[57] and *Jeux de patience* (1993; 1997),[58] Farhoud forced audiences to acknowledge the diversity of memories in contemporary Quebec. More concerned with Lebanon's national tragedy than with the immigration experience, Wajdi Mouawad has dramatized the absurdity of war, the disruption of normal life, the devastation of cities, the decimation of the population, and the forced departure of people caught in the middle of ethnic and religious conflicts in a series of strikingly original plays: *Journée de noces chez les Cromagnons* (1994),[59] *Les Mains d'Edwige au moment de la naissance* (1999), *Littoral* (1999),[60] *Incendies* (2003),[61] and *Willy Protagoras enfermé dans les toilettes* (1998; 2004).

The staging of Quebec's cultural diversity has encouraged Native peoples to add their voices to those of immigrant playwrights. In 1985, Yves Sioui Durand, Catherine Joncas, and John Blondin founded the Compagnie Ondinnok, whose mission is to use traditional mythology and rituals to create a Native theater. Durand's vision is for a "théâtre de guérison" that retrieves the culture, identity, and spirituality of Native people who have suffered greatly since the arrival of European colonists. Ondinnok established a program to train Native actors in association with the École Nationale de Théâtre, and since 1985 it has produced more than thirteen plays that chronicle the historical experience of Native peoples throughout the Americas and stage their beliefs and ceremonies. *La Conquête de Mexico* (1991), for example, which was staged with Jean-Pierre Ronfard's Nouveau Théâtre Expérimental, presented the Spanish conquest from an Aztec perspective. Durand's *Le Porteur des peines du monde* (1985; 1992) was a ritual reenactment of the mistreatment inflicted upon Indigenous peoples while representing the spiritual belief

---

56 Abla Farhoud, *When I Was Grown Up*, tr. Jill MacDougall, *Women and Performance* 9 (1990).
57 Abla Farhoud, *The Girls from the Five and Ten*, tr. Jill MacDougall, in *Plays by Women*, vol. I (New York: Ubu Repertory Theater Publications, 1988), pp. 111–59.
58 Abla Farhoud, *Game of Patience*, tr. Jill MacDougall, in *Plays By Women*, vol. II (New York: Ubu Repertory Theater Publications, 1994), pp. 37–84.
59 Wajdi Mouawad, *Wedding Day At the Cro-Magnons'*, tr. Shelley Tepperman (Toronto: Playwrights Canada, 2001).
60 Wajdi Mouawad, *Tideline*, tr. Shelley Tepperman (Toronto: Playwrights Canada, 2002).
61 Wajdi Mouawad, *Scorched*, tr. Linda Gaboriau (Toronto: Playwrights Canada, 2005).

system that helps them to survive. The title refers to the Native myth that the sun sweeps away suffering as it moves from east to west and purifies humanity when it rises at dawn. *Ukuamaq* (1993) by Joncas was based on an Inuit legend.

More recent productions of Ondinnok have been aimed at fulfilling its mission to create a bridge between the archaic rituals of Native peoples and their new identities in contemporary society. In *Hamlet le Malécite* (2004), Durand and Jean-Frédéric Messier have rewritten Shakespeare's tragedy to dramatize a young Native man's loss of identity and culture in the corrupt and racist environment of the city. *Contes d'un Indien urbain* (2006), Olivier Choinière's translation of British Columbian author Darrell Denis's *Tales of an Urban Indian*, staged the disillusionment of the younger generation and the false stereotypes that limit self-fulfillment. By reaching out to Indigenous peoples throughout the Americas, Ondinnok plays an important role on Canada's multicultural literary scene.

This diversity being staged makes it clear that francophone theater, once the site of French-Canadian ethnic homogeneity and memory, was increasingly becoming a site of heterogeneity and multiple memories in the 1980s. Francophone drama was also moving away from its origins as conventional naturalist theater – popular entertainment in the mimetic, socio-cultural tradition – toward more avant-garde experimentation on the European high-art model. Among the artists and companies leading this trend were Jean-Pierre Ronfard's Nouveau Théâtre Expérimental (formerly the Théâtre Expérimental de Montréal), Gilles Maheu's Carbone 14, Robert Lepage's Le Théâtre Repère and Ex Machina.[62] Rejecting the realist aesthetic of bourgeois drama, the works of these artists are generated by body gesture and movement, by images and signs, by space and objects. This experimental theater is an exploded form of art that violates spatio-temporal boundaries, destabilizes the logical relation between cause and effect, depsychologizes characters, and thematizes itself with metatheatrical discourse and self-referentiality. Often, canonical texts and historical figures inspire innovative reinterpretations, such as Ronfard's *Don Quichotte* (1984; 1985) and *Les Mille et une nuits* (1985), Maheu's *Marat-Sade* (1984) and *Hamlet-Machine* (1987), Lepage's *Vinci* (1986), *Elseneur* (1995), and *Le Projet Andersen* (2006; 2007).

---

62 See Gilles Girard, "Experimental Theater in Quebec: Some Descriptive Terms," *Essays on Modern Quebec Theater*, ed. Joseph I. Donohoe Jr. and Jonathan M. Weiss (East Lansing: Michigan State University Press, 1995), pp. 151–63; Joseph I. Donohoe Jr. and Jane M. Koustas, eds., *Theater sans frontières: Essays on the Dramatic Universe of Robert Lepage* (East Lansing: Michigan State University Press, 2000).

A new language of the stage has been created in which lighting replaces stage sets, gesture replaces speech, objects metamorphose to create webs of meaning, the unconscious and oneiric replace logic, performance replaces text. Attempting to characterize the many forms that theatrical experimention has taken since the 1980s, critics have used the terms polyphonic, multilingual, multidisciplinary, kaleidoscopic, ludic, disorienting. Because this form of experimentation is committed to theatricality rather than text, many artists refuse the closure implied by publication so, for example, even critically acclaimed works such as Lepage's *Les Plaques tectoniques* (1988) and Maheu's *Le Rail* (1984) and *Le Dortoir* (1988) remain unpublished. Ronfard, on the other hand, usually published his work soon after production, for example *Vie et Mort du Roi Boiteux* (1981) and *Le Titanic* (1986). Some of Lepage's pieces have been published in French and English, for instance *Les Sept branches de la rivière Ota* (1988) / *The Seven Streams of the River Ota* (1997), *Polygraphe* (1988) / *Polygraph* (1994), and *La Trilogie des dragons* (2006) / *The Dragons' Trilogy* (2006).

In addition to acting, writing, and directing, the multi-talented Lepage also makes films and produces operas and rock music shows. From his base in Quebec City, he has mounted productions in Europe, Japan, the United States, and all over Canada, making him an internationally recognized artist. He has even created a Las Vegas show for the Cirque du Soleil, *KÀ* (2005). Lepage appeals to an international audience because he transcends the boundaries of Quebec. His work is marked by bilingualism (trilingualism in the case of *La Trilogie des dragons*, first produced in 1985, which is in English, French, and Chinese), multimedia experimentation, and his exploration of homosexuality, artistic genius, and the creative process. In addition to plays on Leonardo da Vinci and Hans Christian Andersen, Lepage has dramatized Jean Cocteau and Miles Davis (*Les Aiguilles et l'opium* [1991]) and Frank Lloyd Wright (*La Géométrie des miracles* [1998]). His productions of Shakespearean plays have often startled audiences and critics alike. For his work, he has received major awards and honors in Quebec, Canada, and Europe.

At the same time that directors and experimental theater companies were creating new performance styles, new forms of dramatic writing that played with language and narrativity were also emerging.[63] René-Daniel Dubois and Normand Chaurette led the way in creating dramatic discourses that experimented with levels of language and monologue. They were followed by

---

63 See Chantal Hébert and Irène Perelli-Contos, eds., *La Narrativité contemporaine au Québec: Le Théâtre et ses nouvelles dynamiques narratives* (Quebec: Les Presses de l'Université Laval, 2004).

Daniel Danis, Larry Tremblay, and Yvan Bienvenue, to name a few of the playwrights who have been inventing a contemporary poetic language for the theater. The experimentation with language and monologue infuses drama with an emotional charge while avoiding melodrama and leads to cathartic transcendence of the tragic events which often constitute the subject matter of their works. In plays such as *Cendres de cailloux* (1993; 1992)[64] and *Celle-là* (1993)[65] by Danis, *La Leçon d'anatomie* (1992)[66] and *The Dragonfly of Chicoutimi* (1995)[67] by Larry Tremblay, *Règlements de contes* (1995)[68] and *Dits et inédits* (1997) by Bienvenue, the subject is often illness, crime, violence, and death, but instead of staging traumatic acts, they stage the narration of them. Dialogue and action are replaced by monologues and narratives that allow the playwrights to give their characters psychological depth, to poeticize their inner thoughts, and to recount events with the perspective that comes with temporal distance.

The language of these plays is self-consciously literary and used for a variety of effects: sometimes it is lushly and verbosely lyrical, sometimes sexually graphic and vulgar, sometimes an expression of existential anguish. This new theater of language and narrativity, which could be called postdramatic theater for the expression of the postmodern condition, raises serious questions about human nature, spiritual and emotional emptiness, the relationship between language and identity. Other authors are also writing plays in this manner, most notably Carole Fréchette. The protagonists of her *Violette sur la terre* (2002) and *Le collier d'Hélène* (2002)[69] join those of Dubois, Chaurette, Danis, L. Tremblay, and Bienvenue in the struggle against meaninglessness and loneliness.

Two other important forms of dramatic narrativity have also appeared in Québécois and Franco-Canadian theater: the urban tale and the autobiographical drama. In the early 1990s, Yvan Bienvenue and Stéphane Jacques (co-founders of the Montreal Théâtre Urbi et Orbi) began staging annual collective shows of short monologues they called *contes urbains*. The concept is simple: the storyteller recounts a story of city life using a poeticized form of contemporary orality. The stories are often filled with the sort of sex

---

[64] Daniel Danis, *Stone and Ashes*, tr. Linda Gaboriau (Toronto: Coach House Press, 1994).
[65] Daniel Danis, *That Woman*, tr. Linda Gaboriau (Burnaby: Talonbooks, 1998).
[66] Larry Tremblay, *Anatomy Lesson*, in *Talking Bodies*, tr. Sheila Fischman (Vancouver: Talonbooks, 2001), pp. 55–107.
[67] The play was written in English.
[68] Yvan Bienvenue, *Unsettling Accounts*, tr. Shelley Tepperman (unpublished).
[69] Carole Fréchette, *Helen's Necklace*, tr. John Murrell, in *Carole Fréchette: Two Plays*, pp. 61–89.

and violence sensationalized by the tabloid press but dramatized in language that is a literary transposition of popular speech. The stories reflect the alienation and moral vacuum of modern cities, yet in the tradition of the French-Canadian folktale, the *conte urbain* carries a message about social values and warns against moral anarchy. Bienvenue and his collaborators have staged a series of *contes urbains* in Montreal (some published by Dramaturges éditeurs) and inspired local versions in Sudbury, Ottawa, Toronto, Edmonton, and Vancouver. In addition to the *conte urbain*, the autobiographical monologue has also expanded the practice of dramatic narrativity in Quebec theater, the most notable examples being Pol Pelletier's trilogy *Joie* (1992),[70] *Océan* (1996), and *Or* (1997) and Marcel Pomerlo's *L'Inoublié ou Marcel-Pomme-dans-l'eau* (2002).

Conclusion

From its colonial beginnings in Acadie, francophone theater eventually spread across Canada and developed into an important part of francophone Canadian cultural life. Today, theater companies from New Brunswick to British Columbia create highly visible public spaces for the literary expression of dramatists, the creative performance of actors, and the collective social and intellectual experience of spectators. More than just providing entertainment for audiences, Québécois and francophone Canadian drama acts out historical memories, reaffirms distinctive identities, valorizes linguistic differences, and proves the vitality of French-language culture in Canada.

---

70 Pol Pelletier, *Joy*, tr. Linda Gaboriau, in Forsyth, ed. *Anthology of Quebec Women's Plays in English Translation*, vol. II: *1987–2003* (Toronto: Playwrights Canada Press, 2008), pp. 127–71.

31
Fiction

RÉJEAN BEAUDOIN AND ANDRÉ LAMONTAGNE
(TRANSLATION SUSANNA GOLDSCHMIDT)

The origins of the French-Canadian novel and the construction of a national identity (1837–94)

If the first novels published in Canada were adventure stories with romantic overtones, the influence of the Catholic Church soon prevailed in reanchoring novelists' inspiration in patriotism and landownership, ideologies rather more conducive to the production of historical novels and rural *tableaux de mœurs*. The principal concern of the clerical authorities was to encourage literary works that were completely distinct from the French novel of the era, perceived to be decadent and therefore threatening to the Christian faith of its French Canadian readers.

The year 1837 saw the near simultaneous publication of the first two novels published in French Canada, at a time when patriotic rebellions erupted against British colonial power. *L'Influence d'un livre*, by Philippe Aubert de Gaspé fils, recounts the misadventures of a naive pair who seek the path to fortune in a popular alchemy handbook. News items, legends, and local customs, depicted in the manner of Walter Scott, make up this flamboyant tale, which ironically suggests "l'extrême pauvreté intellectuelle de cette société anachronique."[1] Probably written under the guidance of the author's erudite father, the *seigneur* of Saint-Jean-Port-Joli, the novel was not particularly well received, perhaps due to the confusion resulting from the unrest that marked 1837. The "Canadian chronicles" by François-Réal Angers, which were published in the summer of the same year under the title *Les Révélations du crime ou Cambray et ses complices*, take as their theme a spate of thefts, an act of sacrilege

---

1 "The extreme intellectual poverty of this anachronistic society," Philippe Aubert de Gaspé *fils*, *Le Chercheur de Trésors ou l'Influence d'un Livre*, présenté par Léopold LeBlanc (Montreal: Réédition Québec, 1968), p. v. *The Influence of a Book*, tr. Claire Rothman (Montreal: R. Davies, 1993). In the following, English translations of the books discussed will be listed where they exist.

and a murder, all of which were perpetrated in the region of Quebec City. The novelist exploits the news story's sordid appeal by writing in the Gothic manner of the day, while simultaneously criticizing the judicial and prison systems.

La Terre paternelle (1846), by the notary Patrice Lacombe, points to a new direction in French-Canadian literature: to the literature preoccupied with the land, which would dominate the French-Canadian literary landscape for close to a century. This fable was the prototype of what would soon be called the *roman de la terre*.[2] It approvingly relates the misfortune which befalls a family in which both the father and one of the sons have succumbed to the respective temptations of commerce and nomadism, betraying their duty to remain rooted to the soil and thus the ideals of the pioneers who originally settled there. In the same year, Pierre-Joseph-Olivier Chauveau published *Charles Guérin*, a *roman de mœurs canadiennes* centered upon the social ascent of a young lawyer. Above all, the novel stands as an account of the economic and demographic changes taking place in Lower Canada at the beginning of the nineteenth century. Chauveau's novel was warmly received by Canadian and French critics, although the Abbé Henri-Raymond Casgrain would later describe it as a "pastiche des romans français,"[3] and fellow writer Joseph Marmette would judge it to be "sans couleur locale."[4]

Antoine Gérin-Lajoie's novel, *Jean Rivard, le défricheur*, appeared in French Canada's first literary magazine, *Les Soirées canadiennes*, in 1862. Given the overpopulation of cultivated land in the Laurentian region, Jean Rivard chooses an audaciously different path from his educated contemporaries and clears a wooded plot on which he intends to establish an agricultural estate. Gérin-Lajoie gave sequel to his hero's exploits two years later in *Jean Rivard, économiste*, which celebrates the success of Rivard, now the uncontested leader of a whole prosperous canton called Rivardville. Maurice Lemire rightly observes that this book represents "une des expressions les plus complètes d'une idéologie qui, pendant longtemps, a servi de support à l'idéal de survivance"[5] of

---

2 "Novel of the land."
3 "A pastiche of French novels."
4 "Lacking in local color." Abbé Henri–Raymond Casgrain and Joseph Marmette, writing under the joint pseudonym of "Placide Lépine," in *L'Opinion publique* 3.11 (March 14, 1872), p. 122, quoted in David Hayne, "Charles Guérin," in Maurice Lemire, ed., *Dictionnaire des œuvres littéraires du Québec*, 2nd edn. (Montreal: Fides, 1980 [1978]), vol. I, p. 104.
5 "One of the most complete expressions of an ideology which, for a long time, served to underpin the ideal of *survivance*" ("la *survivance*" refers to the survival of the French-Canadian cultural identity). Maurice Lemire, "Jean Rivard," in *Dictionnaire des œuvres littéraires du Québec*, vol. I, p. 414.

French Canada. However, the idea of cultural survival here goes hand in hand with the promotion of education and of economic skill.

In 1863, Philippe Aubert de Gaspé père's novel, *Les Anciens Canadiens*,[6] was published, also in *Les Soirées canadiennes*. The author, then seventy-six years old, had penned a collection of his personal and family memories, half-way between the historical novel à la Walter Scott and the Romantic evocations of medieval France in Charles Nodier or Victor Hugo. The narrative is loosely organized around the historical framework of the famous Battle of the Plains of Abraham of 1759 and the British conquest of Canada. The heroes are two youths of noble extraction: Jules d'Haberville, heir to the seigniory of Saint-Jean-Port-Joli, and Archibald de Locheill, a Scottish orphan exiled after the defeat at Culloden. The two former classmates are forced to face each other on the battlefield when the Seven Years' War calls them to arms. The Corneillian duel between enemy brothers continues after the end of the conflict in the relationship between the Scot and Blanche d'Haberville, Jules's sister, who proudly refuses the offer of marriage from the victor, whereas her brother marries a "daughter of Albion."

The novelist writes openly in favour of the coexistence and intermixture of different ethnic groups. The book propounds a conciliatory memory of past events, a refusal of resentment on the part of the conquered people, and what Jacques Cardinal suggests be read as an endeavor to construct a national Canadian identity.[7] This founding text was an instant bestseller and was immediately translated into English. We should also note the importance of *Forestiers et voyageurs* (1894 [1863]) by Joseph-Charles Taché, a novel midway between a collection of legends and a romantic confabulation. This rough *tableau de mœurs* of the woodsmen of the past inaugurated a tradition later followed by certain twentieth-century writers.

Under the pseudonym of Félicité Angers, Laure Conan published her first novel, *Angéline de Montbrun*, in 1881.[8] This austere young woman was the first of her gender to pursue a career as a writer in French Canada. Many of her works were inspired by historic and patriotic causes which owed much to the programmatic objectives of her mentor, the Abbé Henri-Raymond Casgrain,

---

6 Philippe Aubert de Gaspé, *Canadians of Old*, tr. Jane Brierly (Montreal: Véhicule Press, 1996). First translated in 1864 by Georgiana Pennée, and again in 1890 by Charles G. D. Roberts.
7 See Jacques Cardinal in *La Paix des braves: Une lecture politique des* Anciens Canadiens *de Philippe Aubert de Gaspé* (Montreal: XYZ, 2005).
8 Félicité Angers, *Angéline de Montbrun*, tr. Yves Brunelle (Toronto and Buffalo: University of Toronto Press, 1974).

but it is *Angéline de Montbrun*, that best represents the force and originality of her style as the analysis of love takes center stage. Diary entries, letters and narration are interwoven in this freely autobiographical novel which ends in mystical contemplation. Charles de Montbrun, the heroine's father, is the embodiment of the somewhat distant perfection of the *Ancien Régime*, while Maurice Darville, Angéline's suitor, embraces the republican mores of the age. Patricia Smart perceives in the novel the uneasy protestations of the first feminine voice in a patriarchal literary tradition.[9]

Renewal and continuity (1895–1938)

Published in 1895, *Pour la patrie*[10] is set in 1945 against the backdrop of an anti-Catholic political plot, a conspiracy born in anglophone Masonic lodges. Its author, Jules-Paul Tardivel, was one of the most ardent propagandists of the idea of French Canada's providential vocation, which he conceives in increasingly exalted terms towards the end of the century, as liberalism spreads. He believed that the establishment of a Catholic state in Quebec would create a bastion against the emergent laicism of the modern world. Dr. Joseph Lamirande, the hero of *Pour la patrie*, personifies heaven's design to thwart the instruments of the devil, who are hatching a plot for an atheist Canadian constitution. The idea will finally be foiled thanks to Lamirande's clairvoyance, guided by supernatural apparitions and assisted by the miraculous conversion of an English-speaking member of parliament. Tardivel, the hardened parliamentary columnist, succeeded in sketching certain public figures in a number of his characters, occasionally giving his *roman à thèse* the guise of a *roman à clef*. This book has the distinction of being the first "independentist" novel in French-Canadian literature. Opinions were strongly polarized between the opponents and allies of the polemicist, and the reception of the novel was, predictably, divided between liberal and ultramontanist readers.

Lionel Groulx's novel, *L'Appel de la race* (1922),[11] continued in the politico-religious vein of Tardivel, a Canadian follower of Louis Veuillot, a French journalist and editor of the Catholic newspaper *L'Univers* in Paris. The novel is set in Ottawa in the highly emotional context of the quarrel of Catholic schools over the restrictions to their rights imposed by Regulation 17, which

---

9 Patricia Smart, *Écrire dans la maison du père: L'Émergence du féminin dans la tradition littéraire du Québec* (Montreal: Québec/Amérique, 1988), p. 81.
10 Jules-Paul Tardivel, *For My Country*, tr. Sheila Fishman (Toronto and Buffalo: University of Toronto Press, 1975).
11 Lionel Groulx, *The Iron Wedge*, tr. J. S. Wood (Ottawa: Carleton University Press, 1989).

banned French education in Ontario in 1912. The member of parliament Jules de Lantagnac, who has married an English-speaking girl from the capital's bourgeoisie for reasons of professional advancement, decides to take up the defence of his fellow French speakers. This desire costs him his peaceable home life, as his wife then decides to leave him. The novelist, in addition to touching the nationalist chord, openly attacks the practice of mixed marriages, which he judges to go against the superior cause of the endangered survival of the French-Canadian people.

In 1914, eight years before *L'Appel de la race*, Arsène Bessette wrote, with *Le Débutant*, a "roman de mœurs du journalisme et de la politique dans la province de Québec,"[12] as the subtitle indicates. This urban novel set in Montreal centers on an initiation into the profession of journalism and into love in a society still profoundly bound by religious rituals. The muted reception of the novel was notable for the strict reserve maintained by the Episcopal authorities, and for the conspiracy of silence of professional critics. Until then editor-in-chief of the newspaper *Le Canada français*, the author lost his job, a sanction which spoke all too clearly of the situation he denounced in his novel. Twenty years later, Jean-Charles Harvey, also the editor-in-chief of a daily newspaper, *Le Soleil*, suffered a similar fate after the publication of *Les Demi-Civilisés*,[13] which provoked the wrath of Mgr. Villeneuve, the archbishop of Quebec City. The prelate obtained the journalist's dismissal. Max Hubert, in *Les Demi-Civilisés*, protests against the inertia of a society held together by the union of the Church, the State and rapidly dominating capitalist values.

Notwithstanding these rare examples of urbanism, the French-Canadian novel, from the beginning of the century, never ceased to celebrate the sedentary, agrarian life of its brave inhabitants, the descendants of "une race qui ne sait pas mourir,"[14] as the Breton novelist Louis Hémon proclaimed in *Maria Chapdelaine*,[15] the French edition of which, in 1921, promoted an edifying image of French Canada to the rest of the world. The bestseller follows the predictable model of the Québécois *roman de la terre*, but at the same time it deepens the misunderstandings surrounding the legendary "Canadian cabin": too many trees hide the exotic forest where the regionalist idyll prospers.

---

12 "A novel describing social behaviour in the journalistic and political circles of the province of Quebec."
13 Jean-Charles Harvey, *Fear's Folly*, tr. John Glassco (Ottawa: Carleton University Press, 1982).
14 "A race that does not know how to die out."
15 Louis Hémon, *Maria Chapdelaine*, tr. Alan Brown (Montreal: Tundra Books, 1989). Also see tr. W. H. Blake (Toronto: Macmillan, 1921).

Right up until the end of the 1930s, such eloquent titles as *Restons chez nous* (1908) and *L'Appel de la terre* (1919) by Damase Potvin, *La Terre vivante* (1925) by Harry Bernard and *La Voie des sillons* (1932) continued to be produced.[16]

The dominant voice in literary criticism at the beginning of the twentieth century was the Abbé Camille Roy, one of the main proponents of what was soon to become known as regionalism. This current of ideas made the survival of French Canada into the crux of literary expression centered upon the theme of agricultural life. There were a number of dissenting voices which transgressed this monological discourse, among them that of Albert Laberge, author of *La Scouine* (1918),[17] a novel which was immediately censured. It was not until fifty years later, at the start of the Quiet Revolution, that the work was rehabilitated. In his short series of tableaux, loosely linked like so many different slices of rural life, Laberge belatedly wrote a French-Canadian naturalist novel in robust style.

Un homme et son péché (1933)[18] by Claude-Henri Grignon owes a greater debt to Balzac and Léon Bloy, uniting realism with the melodramatic tone of his account of the tribulations of a young woman who timidly submits to a husband who sacrifices her basely to his all-consuming greed. In the usurer Séraphin Poudrier, complex hero of the novel who is analyzed at length, Grignon creates a mythical character who elicits the fascination of a collective imagination torn between admiration for the power of money and terror for the ravages which it permits in the age of industrial capitalism. It is the advance of capitalism into the ancient forest domain of the hunters and timber drivers that *Menaud, maître-draveur* (1937),[19] by Félix-Antoine Savard, tragically contests. This novel of epic proportions employs a style that is both scholarly and spare, highly polished, inviting a quasi-liturgical reading of the words of *Maria Chapdelaine* (when Menaud listens to his daughter reading excerpts from this novel) in order to avert the pitiless advance of foreign capital. The eponymous hero, after waging a single-handed struggle against the enemy who is both invisible and incapable of capture, descends into madness, having failed to rally the sparse community of migrants to his cause.

---

16 No translations appear to have been published, but the meaning of these titles is as follows: *Restons chez nous*: Let's Stay at Home; *L'Appel de la terre*: The Call of the Land; *La Terre vivante*: The Living Land; *La Voie des sillons*: The Path of the Furrows.
17 Albert Laberge, *Bitter Bread*, tr. Conrad Dion (Montreal: Harvest House, 1977).
18 Claude Henri Grignon, *The Woman and the Miser*, tr. Yves Brunelle (Montreal: Harvest House, 1978).
19 Félix-Antoine Savard, *Master of the River*, tr. Richard Howard (Montreal: Harvest House, 1976).

Towards the end of the 1930s, regionalism reached both its apogee and its swansong in *Trente arpents* (1938) by Ringuet,[20] the pseudonym employed by Dr. Philippe Panneton. The fast-paced story covers four generations of farmers, from the final decades of the nineteenth century up to the eve of the Second World War, and illustrates how rural life was no longer sheltered from the radical changes of modern life. The hero, Euchariste Moisan, will live to see his children gradually desert the countryside for the city and, worse still, follow the path of emigration to the United States. Dispossessed of all his property, Euchariste ends his days at White Falls, Massachusetts, in the house of his son, whose wife and children cannot communicate with him in his own language. The novel captures admirably the fate of traditional country people caught up in the great currents of money and population sweeping across America.

The affirmation of difference (1939–79)

The first resolutely urban novels which appeared towards the end of the Second World War not only transport the action from the countryside to the city, but also attest to a paradigmatic change in fiction writing. In Roger Lemelin's *Au pied de la pente douce*,[21] the still rustic customs of a neighborhood in Quebec City provide the backdrop for the social ascension of the leader of a street gang, Denis Boucher. It is, paradoxically, through literature that the hero will find success, even though the role of writer better suits his romantic and sophisticated friend, Jean Colin. This novel serves as a fine illustration of the notion of "conflit des codes" proposed by the critic André Belleau.[22] In his opinion, this is one of the defining characteristics of the Québécois novel, as it attempts to cater both to French literary norms and to North American popular culture. *Bonheur d'occasion* (1945)[23] establishes the genre of the Montreal novel by setting the difficulties experienced by the Lacasse family in a working-class Montreal community that, though living cheek by jowl with the abundance of goods displayed in the shop windows, is

---

20 Ringuet, *Thirty Acres*, tr. Felix and Dorothea Walter (Toronto: Macmillan Canada, 1940).
21 Roger Lemelin, *The Town Below*, tr. Samuel Putnam (Toronto: McClelland and Stewart, 1948).
22 "Conflict of codes," see André Belleau, "Le Conflit des codes dans l'institution littéraire québécoise," and "Code social et code littéraire dans le roman québécois," both in his *Surprendre les voix* (Montreal: Boréal, 1986) pp. 167–74, 175–92.
23 Gabrielle Roy, *The Tin Flute*, tr. Alan Brown (Toronto: McClelland and Stewart, 1980). See also tr. Hanna Josephson (Toronto: McClelland and Stewart, 1958).

wracked by all manner of privations. The main plot revolves around the unhappy love story of the waitress Florentine Lacasse and the machinist-electrician Jean Lévesque. It is war propaganda that, ironically, offers the urban proletariat hope of escape from their narrow circumstances. The ambitious Jean Lévesque's rival is the young Emmanuel Létourneau. Létourneau, moved by socialist and universalist ideals, vainly deplores the cynicism of capitalism, the true face of which is being revealed in the worldwide conflict.

Aside from the unforgettable tableau of the topography of Montreal and the socio-historical forces at play in the design of its districts, this first novel by Gabrielle Roy, who was born in Manitoba, also marks the beginning of a fertile literary career. The English translation of the novel, brought out by a New York publishing house, ensured the international success of the work. *Bonheur d'occasion* also voices an early feminist message in the heroine's refusal to accept her mother's subservient lot.

The year 1945 also saw the publication of another classic novel written by a woman, *Le Survenant* by Germaine Guèvremont.[24] This accomplished regionalist masterpiece is set in the Sorel Islands and tells the tale of a mysterious stranger's arrival in an old rural community which is profoundly affected by his appearance. The presence of the "grand dieu des routes,"[25] as the character is referred to throughout the narrative, introduces alterity and opens up a doorway into the "wide world" for this microsociety which has been frozen in time and into which the mercantile winds of modern city life and its customs suddenly start to penetrate.

The juvenile revolt of the protagonist of *Poussière sur la ville* (1953) by André Langevin[26] is shorter and more radical than that of Florentine Lacasse. The young novelist paints a harsh picture of a small mining town of the mid-twentieth century. A doctor at the beginning of his career and a free-thinker, Alain Dubois succeeds only in setting everyone against him and his wife, Madeleine. Caught half-way between *Madame Bovary* and *L'Étranger*, this brilliant novel illustrates once again the "conflit des codes" identified by André Belleau, and also shows daring technical innovations both in narrative technique – the relation of events from the character's perspective, the multiplicity of viewpoints, internal monologue – and in style.

---

24 Germaine Guèvremont, *The Outlander*, tr. Eric Sutton (Toronto: McGraw-Hill, 1950).
25 "The great god of the roads," Germaine Guèvremont, *Le Survenant* (Montreal: Fides, 1974), p. 63.
26 André Langevin, *Dust Over the City*, tr. John Latrobe and Robert Gottlieb (Toronto: McClelland and Stewart, 1974).

La Bagarre (1958) by Gérard Bessette[27] draws on several techniques that were key to the novels foreshadowing the Quiet Revolution: plurilingualism, heterogeneity, autoreflexivity, the conflict of linguistic codes resulting from colonialism, and Montreal's cosmospolitanism, the decentered nature of which challenges the expressive powers of the two fictional writers the novel depicts. Jules Lebeuf and Ken Weston, two literature students, one of old French stock and the other American, heatedly debate their sociological positions on the problematic identity of French Canadians. This identity is thrown in sharp relief by the so-called "urban laboratory" of the Montreal quarter in which the novel is set, in which the conditions of working-class life, ethnic and sentimental rivalries all react against each other. In 1960, the novel *Le Libraire*[28] tackles the damaging effects of "la grande noirceur"[29] of the "Index" (a list compiled by the Catholic Church banning books deemed to be dangerous) and of the clergy's stranglehold on public opinion. Initially dismissed from the *collège classique* where he is employed as a proctor, the hero and narrator of the novel, Hervé Jodoin, arrives at Saint-Joachim to take up the post of bookseller, which he performs with the casual and detached air of an outsider. The story takes the form of a diary and employs a laconic tone and a devastating irony which are directed against the narrow-mindedness and simplicity of the villagers.

Yves Thériault deserves recognition as one of the most important writers to address the "symptômes du colonialisme et [les] signes de libération,"[30] as the title of one study has it, yet, in *Agaguk* (1958)[31] the author also tackles the as yet undiscussed issue of Canada's Native populations. The novel, which is the first volume of a trilogy set in the northern territory of the Nunavuk Inuits, tells the story of a couple who break with the tradition of their community and go to live in isolation in the tundra. There, they establish their own system of values, which includes reciprocity in gender roles and the egalitarian division of tasks between them. Aside from the exoticism and local color, the novel

---

27 Gérard Bessette, *The Brawl*, tr. Marc Lebel and Ronald Sutherland (Montreal. Harvest House, 1976).
28 Gérard Bessette, *Not For Every Eye*, tr. Glen Shortliffe (Toronto: Macmillan, 1962).
29 "The great blackness."
30 "Symptoms of colonialism and [the] signs of liberation," Maurice Arguin, *Le Roman québécois de 1944 à 1965: Symptômes du colonialisme et signes de libération* (Montreal: l'Hexagone, 1985).
31 Yves Thériault, *Agaguk*, tr. W. Donald Aaron Wilson and Paul Socken (Waterloo: Wilfrid Laurier University Press, 2007). See also *Shadow of the Wolf: Agaguk*, tr. Miriam Chapin (Toronto: Ryerson, 1963).

can also be read as the tale of the northward movement of Québécois society into the fictional space of a far north dominated by the Royal Canadian Mounted Police and the all-powerful Hudson's Bay Company.

With the start of the new decade of the 1960s, the Quiet Revolution finally began: a period of rapid transformation and of catching up, both in the social and economic order, and in the political and aesthetic. Books such as *L'Aquarium* (1962) by Jacques Godbout, *Le Cassé* (1964) by Jacques Renaud,[32] and *Le Cabochon* (1964) by André Major introduce the theme of revolt by combining national issues with an attack on economic inequalities. In 1965, Hubert Aquin penned a revolutionary novel, *Prochain épisode*,[33] an apology for the armed struggle for the independence of Quebec. Aquin's first novel also agitates for a formal revolution, which caused an immediate stir in Quebec's intellectual circles. But it was the year 1966 which marked the real explosion of the Québécois novel onto the international scene with the publication of two major works: *Une saison dans la vie d'Emmanuel* by Marie-Claire Blais[34] and *L'Avalée des avalés* by Réjean Ducharme,[35] the first of which won the Prix Médicis, while the second was nominated for the Prix Goncourt. Using the intertext of the *roman de la terre*, Marie-Claire Blais's novel effects a carnavalesque reversal by describing the social customs of a society ridden with incest, pedophilia, prostitution, and delinquency. The Rimbauldian and messianic figure of the young poet, Jean-le-Maigre, is the focal point of this narrative of the decline of the family. This decline is also evident in his sister Héloïse, who has gone strangely off the rails, and above all in the innocent frolics of his young brother Emmanuel. Gilles Marcotte sees in that work an example of what he calls the novel in the imperfect, the narrative form of "[une] expérience de langage jamais terminée, interminable."[36]

A similar consciousness of language and of its anxieties finds full expression in the writings of Réjean Ducharme, whose first novel, published by Gallimard in Paris in 1966, caused a stir. The identity of the young, unknown writer was the subject of the wildest hypotheses until it was finally discovered that the

---

32 Jacques Renaud, *Broke City*, tr. David Homel (Montreal: Guernica, 1984).
33 Hubert Aquin, *Prochain épisode*, tr. Penny Williams (Toronto: McClelland and Stewart, 1967).
34 Marie-Claire Blais, *A Season in the Life of Emmanuel*, tr. Derek Coltman (New York: Farrar, Straus, and Giroux, 1966).
35 Réjean Ducharme, *The Swallower Swallowed*, tr. Barbara Bray (London, ON: Hamilton, 1968).
36 "An experience of language which is never completed, which cannot be completed," Gilles Marcotte, *Le Roman à l'imparfait: Essais sur le roman québécois d'aujourd'hui* (Montreal: La Presse, 1976), p. 18.

author did exist in the flesh, but that he absolutely refused to play the media game. The adventures of Bérénice Einberg, the narrator and heroine of *L'Avalée des avalés*, offers a fantasized representation of childhood in the form of a *bildungsroman*. The quest of the young girl, whose age increases from eight to eighteen over the course of the tale, leads her first to an island in the Saint Lawrence River, then to New York, and finally on to Israel, which is in the midst of the Six Day War. The episodes in Bérénice's evolution run from revolt against her parents, through testing friendship, via philosophical questioning to linguistic revolt. In *Le Nez qui voque* (1967), Mille Milles and Chateaugué, two teenagers who have run away from home, take teenage rebellion to the extreme of a suicide pact which they establish after ecstatically reading tales of the adventurous explorers of a bygone age and poems by Émile Nelligan.

Two novels published a year apart, *Salut Galarneau!* (1967) by Jacques Godbout[37] and *La Guerre, yes Sir!* (1968) by Roch Carrier,[38] explore the new horizon of popular humor and the folkloric meeting with the Other, whether he be American or British. François Galarneau is the owner of a hotdog stand, whereas his brother Jacques, who is currently on his way back from a trip to Paris, is making a career for himself as a television scriptwriter. The narrator, François, exploits the stereotypes that he weaves into his tale to depict "the beautiful province" as a mere offshoot of the United States. The hero of *La Guerre, yes Sir!* is no great talker, given that his first appearance in the novel is in a coffin, but his return to his native village serves to loosen tongues and unites around him "the two solitudes" – the French-speaking and the English-speaking Canadians – in a strange ceremony where mourning and festivity combine. The diegetic space of the young soldier killed in action recalls the Canadian Conscription Crisis during the Second World War, and underlines the ideological conflict which it created between English- and French-speakers. This book makes extensive use of exaggerated clichés and surreal confabulations which, ironically, met the expectations of English-speaking Canada, where the work was hailed as a national treasure, and all too often taken at face value.

Turning to a totally different genre, the troubling alterity of the English-speaker takes on a much more violent character in *Trou de mémoire* (1968) by Hubert Aquin[39] and in *Kamouraska* (1970) by Anne Hébert.[40] Skillfully constructed around a strange aesthetic, the second novel by Hubert Aquin concerns the

---

37 Jacques Godbout, *Hail Galarneau!*, tr. Alan Brown (Don Mills: Longman, 1970).
38 Roch Carrier, *La Guerre, yes sir!*, tr. Sheila Fischman (Toronto: Anansi, 1970).
39 Hubert Aquin, *Blackout*, tr. Alan Brown (Toronto: Anansi, 1974).
40 Anne Hébert, *Kamouraska*, tr. Norman Shapiro (New York: Crown, 1973).

historical amnesia of colonized nations. It opens with the murder of Joan Ruskin, the lover of pharmacist and revolutionary Pierre-X. Magnant. The novelist draws on techniques ranging from the French *nouveau roman* to detective fiction to elucidate the motives for a crime whose political consequences seem to align the Québécois cause with the struggles for independence in African countries. Passion and historical drama also mix in *Kamouraska*. The story is set in the nineteenth century, in conquered territory, and revolves around the love triangle between the *Seigneur* of Kamouraska, his wife, a member of the French Canadian bourgeoisie, and an American doctor. The innovative narrative technique employed incorporates changes of voice, the workings of an obsessive memory which confuses temporal reference points, and the kinaesthetic aspect of the protagonist's conscious perception. A work which is emblematic of the emergence of women's writing in Canada, *Kamouraska* also offers a striking description of the epic rigors of the Canadian winter.

The Québécois novels of the 1970s rearticulate in all their fragmented diversity the ideological and aesthetic issues at stake in Québécois society: the "national text" (as defined by Jacques Godbout)[41] and foundation myth, feminism, modernism and postmodernism, the popular novel, and formalism.

Already well known for his short stories, Jacques Ferron made his mark as a novelist with *L'Amélanchier*, his remarkable reinterpretation of the foundation myth. A true work of the intermixture of origins, the tale of Tinamer de Portanqueu, the young heroine of this identity fable, borrows as much from the brief history of Quebec as it does from English and children's literature, notably *Alice in Wonderland*. The chronotype skillfully intertwines personal memory and spatial organization with a quest to discover the position of the self and the collectivity in history (familial, social, and national). The novels of Victor-Lévy Beaulieu reveal their debt to Ferron in the tale of "the Great Tribe," finally published as *La Grande Tribu* in 2008, and culminating in *Don Quichotte de la Démanche* (1974). The concentrated timescale of the book, which covers a day and two nights in the life of the writer Abel Beauchemin, embraces the family saga as an avatar of the history of the Québécois people. This degraded epic constantly, even in its title, draws attention to the frustrated fate of the nation and of the literary forms in which the hero, haunted by the works of James Joyce, seeks to write about it.

---

41 See Jacques Godbout, *Le Réformiste* (Montreal: Quinze, 1975), pp. 147–57. Reprinted from Godbout, "Écrire," *Liberté* 13.4 (November 1971), pp. 135–47.

Proofreaders by profession, André and Nicole Ferron, the faintly incestuous couple from Ducharme's *L'Hiver de force* (1973),[42] frequent the artistic Montreal milieu, towards which they feel a disgust bordering on nausea, all the while reeling off a complete *Who's Who?* of it in their never-ending, disillusioned chatter. A perfect mirror of collective alienation, the Ferrons virtuously practice their own self-negation through sheer inability to escape from the microsociety which imprisons them and which they abhor. In *Les Enfantômes* (1976), the narrator, Vincent Falardeau, is in the process of writing up his memoirs, which cover the period of the post-war years up to the end of the 1960s. The chronicler creates a refracted image of his ruined married life and of the troubled relationship which links him to his sister, Fériée, sinking "alors dans le débris, l'éclat d'un monde déjà explosé."[43]

Feminism finally entered fiction – and modified it profoundly – in the decade of the 1970s. In parallel with the struggle for national liberation, the writings of Nicole Brossard, Hélène Ouvrard, and Louky Bersianik demonstrate the emancipation of the feminine subject that was already emerging in the prose of Claire Martin (*Avec et sans amour*, 1958;[44] *Doux-amer*, 1960), in *Amadou* (1963) by Louise Maheux-Fortier,[45] the first novel to transgress the taboo of lesbianism, and in *Manuscrits de Pauline Archange* (1968)[46] and its sequels *Vivre! Vivre!* (1969) and *Les Apparences* (1970) by Marie-Claire Blais. In 1974, Nicole Brossard published *French Kiss*,[47] a novel of "embrace and exploration" of the body and of language which gives voice to a gendered speech. *L'Amèr ou le chapitre effrité* (1977)[48] is a theoretical reflection as well as the transgressive tale of a mother–daughter relationship. *L'Euguélionne* (1976) by Louky Bersianik[49] takes on myth and the biblical text in order to turn them against their own misogynist logic and extract a new discourse purged of patriarchal essentialism.

---

42 Réjean Ducharme, *Wild to Mild*, tr. Robert Guy Scully (Saint-Lambert, QC: Héritage, 1980).
43 "Into the debris, into the fragments of an already exploded world," Élisabeth Nardout-Lafarge, *Réjean Ducharme: Une poétique du débris* (Saint-Laurent: Fides, 2001), p. 16.
44 Claire Martin, *Love Me, Love Me Not*, tr. David Lobdell (Ottawa: Oberon Press, 1987).
45 Louise Maheux-Fortier, *Amadou*, tr. David Lobdell (Ottawa: Oberon, 1987).
46 Marie-Claire Blais, *The Manuscripts of Pauline Archange*, tr. Derek Coltman (Toronto: McClelland and Stewart, 1982).
47 Nicole Brossard, *French Kiss or A Pang's Progress*, tr. Patricia Claxton (Toronto: Coach House Quebec Translations, 1986).
48 Nicole Brossard, *These Our Mothers, or, The Disintegrating Chapter*, tr. Barbara Godard (Toronto: Coach House Press, 1983).
49 Louky Bersianik, *The Euguelion*, tr. Howard Scott (Montreal: Alter Ego Editions, 1996).

Neither should one overlook the influence of *la nouvelle écriture* (especially in the magazines *La Nouvelle Barre du jour* and *Les Herbes rouges*) on women's writing, as demonstrated by Yolande Villemaire's work. Her novel, *La Vie en prose* (1980), draws together a kaleidoscope of styles in the web of narrative plots which entangle protagonists, styles and genres alike. Spoken language crosses the boundary between private and public, with the heroines' single or conflicting voices launching an attack on the borders. The book and its reception mark the transition from modern to postmodern in the return of the subject, the relativization of all truths and the challenging of hegemonic metanarratives.

In addition to the examples of formalist writing that we have just discussed, the emerging phenomenon of the mass-produced, popular novel is also characteristic of the decade of the 1970s. Following his exceptionally successful career as a playwright, inaugurated by the triumph of his play *Les Belles-Sœurs* (first performed in 1968, published in 1972), Michel Tremblay begins his novelistic cycle, *Chroniques du Plateau Mont-Royal* with *La Grosse Femme d'à-côté est enceinte* (1978),[50] a novel of the Balzacian mold which revives several characters (Albertine, Gabriel, Édouard, Marcel, and Thérèse) from his earlier theatrical cycle and analyzes the extended network of a complex family within the no less sprawling topography of the metropolis. *Thérèse et Pierrette à l'école des Saints-Anges* (1980)[51] examines early childhood and school education, which were then the exclusive province of religious institutions.

Twenty years after the Quiet Revolution had swept this era under the carpet, Gilles Marcotte remarks pertinently that, in 1980, one could still publish Québécois narratives fashioned according to the literary codes of the nineteenth century precisely, he implies, in order to justify the mismanaged historical continuity from 1960 onwards.[52] Laurent Mailhot, on the other hand, describes fiction of this nature as *romans de la parole*, which he distinguishes from *romans de l'écriture*.[53] According to Mailhot, such fictions update the epic tales of former times, since become mythical, under the banner of a realism derived from the oral tradition.[54] Such is the case of the novels of Michel Tremblay and Yves Beauchemin.

---

50 Michel Tremblay, *The Fat Woman Next Door is Pregnant*, tr. Sheila Fischman (Vancouver: Talonbooks, 1981).
51 Michel Tremblay, *Thérèse and Pierrette and the Little Hanging Angel*, tr. Sheila Fischman (Toronto: McClelland and Stewart, 1984).
52 See Gilles Marcotte, "Histoire du temps," *Canadian Literature* 86 (Autumn 1980), pp. 93–9.
53 "Novels of the spoken word," "novels of the written word."
54 Laurent Mailhot, "Romans de la parole (et du mythe)," *Canadian Literature* 88 (Spring 1981), pp. 84–90.

In 1981, Beauchemin published *Le Matou*,[55] which sold several hundreds of thousands of copies in France and Quebec, and was translated into a dozen different languages. The novel, which tells the tale of the commercial misadventures of Florent and Élise Boissoneault, as well as a boy's wanderings along with those of his inseparable alleycat, problematizes both access to wealth for French-speakers in the business arena and their relationships with foreigners and English-speakers. The popular success of *Le Matou* cannot but draw attention to what Simon Harel has read as the syndrome of the French-speaking Québécois clinging to their identity,[56] but one should probably also attribute it in part to the previously unacknowledged truth of the economically disadvantaged position of the colonized.

Another emblematic attempt at cultural rehabilitation was Louis Caron's trilogy, *Les Fils de la liberté*, comprising *Le Canard de bois* (1981), *La Corne de brume* (1982) and *Le Coup de poing* (1990), which seek to recapture the glory of the patriots sacrificed during the infamous rebellions of 1837 and 1838 against British colonial power. The saga *Les Filles de Caleb* (1985–6) by Arlette Cousture[57] called public attention to the forgotten exploits of the frontier woodsmen in regions soon destined for rapid industrial development, as in Haute Mauricie. Beauchemin, Caron and Cousture's bestsellers have been the object of several film adaptations and have enjoyed a broad media coverage previously unheard of in Québécois literature. *Bonheur d'occasion*, Roy's bestselling novel, was also belatedly adapted for the small and big screen in 1983.

After the referendum: the new polarities in post-1980 fiction

Since the 1980 referendum on the independence of Quebec, Québécois fiction has been exploring new directions. The epistemological deconstruction of the national text and the crisis of its political imperatives opened up to novelists the new field of postmodern fiction, of autofiction and of all the new modes of writing about subjectivity. Anne Hébert's prose narrative bears witness to the impending mutation of the novel in the latter half of the twentieth century,

---

55 Yves Beauchemin, *The Alley Cat*, tr. Sheila Fischman (Toronto: McClelland and Stewart, 1986).
56 Simon Harel, *Le voleur de parcours: Identité et cosmopolitisme dans la littérature québécoise contemporaine* (Longueuil: Le Préambule, 1989), pp. 256–60. Harel draws on psychoanalyst Imre Hermann's notion of "attachment theory."
57 Arlette Cousture, *Emilie*, tr. Käthe Roth (Toronto: Stoddart, 1992).

Le Torrent (1950)[58] recounts the tale of an "enfant dépossédé du monde,"[59] stifled by the moral inheritance of the Catholicism passed down to him by a mother who is as over-possessive as she is guilty. This classic novella heralds the deconstruction of the figure of the mother, so omnipresent in Québécois fiction. *Les Chambres de bois* (1958)[60] is a poetic novel about marital alienation, and thus opens up a new door for the narrative of alienation. *Les Fous de Bassan* (1982)[61] represents one of the first Québécois novels whose postmodern aesthetic asserts itself beyond all question in the extensive polyphony of the narrative discourse, the biblical intertextuality, the imaginary projection of collective marginality in the English-speaking microsociety of Griffin Creek, and the intersection of a news item and History. *Le Premier Jardin* (1988)[62] continues this problematization of history with a genealogical investigation into New France and the fate of the infamous "filles du roi,"[63] the young French women sponsored by the King to marry and start families in New France, to whom the novelist gives a voice.

After several well-received novels in the 1960s and 1970s (*Jimmy, Le Cœur de la baleine bleue, Les Grandes Marées*),[64] Jacques Poulin's success as a novelist was fully established with *Volkswagen Blues* (1984),[65] one of the first road novels of the new Québécois imagination. A writer in search of his brother takes to the road accompanied by a young Métis woman. Their itinerary from Gaspé to San Francisco transects the map of the first explorers of French America and revisits key locations in the history of the Native peoples. The narrative has something of the style of the detective novel and of the quest for identity, playing on ethnic and sexual stereotypes. Jacques Poulin's later novels are still haunted by these questions, but ask them within the restricted context of the city of Quebec and its surroundings, as in *Le Vieux Chagrin* (1989), *La Tournée d'automne* (1993)[66] and *Les Yeux bleus de Mistassini* (2002).[67] The trilogy by Louis Gauthier, collected in 2005 under the title *Voyage en Inde avec un grand détour*, offers a remarkable rereading of the adventure of the journey and search for one's self. *Les Silences du corbeau* (1986) by Yvon Rivard had covered similar

---

58 Anne Hébert, *The Torrent*, tr. Gwendolyn Moore (Montreal: Harvest House, 1973).
59 "A child dispossessed of the world."
60 Anne Hébert, *The Silent Rooms*, tr. Kathy Mezei (Don Mills: Paper Jacks, 1974).
61 Anne Hébert, *In the Shadow of the Wind*, tr. Sheila Fischman (Don Mills: Stoddart, 1983).
62 Anne Hébert, *The First Garden*, tr. Sheila Fischman (Toronto: Anansi, 1990).
63 "King's daughters."
64 Jacques Poulin, *The "Jimmy" Trilogy*, tr. Sheila Fischman (Toronto: Anansi, 1979).
65 Jacques Poulin, *Volkswagen Blues*, tr. Sheila Fischman (Toronto: McClelland and Stewart, 1988).
66 Jacques Poulin, *Autumn Rounds*, tr. Sheila Fischman (Toronto: Cormorant, 2002).
67 Jacques Poulin, *My Sister's Blue Eyes*, tr. Sheila Fischman (Toronto: Cormorant, 2007).

ground in turning a trip to India into a metaphor for writing and the spiritual quest.

Maryse (1983) by Francine Noël also plays on identity codes, but in a very different style, as it tells the ideological saga of the generation born in the wake of the Second World War and of its intellectual development. The academic circles of Montreal are the setting for a reworking of the Pygmalion myth in which both the heroine and her friends are liberated, as much by the integration and emancipation of the trendy views of the Parisian Left as by the assertion of their own vernacular speech. In its subordination of the story to the narrative of initiation, and in the dissolution of the dominant discourse in a carnivalesque subversion, *Maryse* articulates the synthesis of feminism and of postmodernism from a new identitary perspective. In *Copies conformes* (1989) by Monique Larue, reflections on identity are accompanied by a pastiche of *The Maltese Falcon* by Dashiell Hammett in a plot set in San Francisco and focusing on an extramarital affair in the era of new technology. *Copies conformes* gives a new tone to women's writing by opening it up to the paradigms of true and false and of extraterritoriality. Robert Lalonde, meanwhile, reintroduced the Amerindian theme and linked it to homosexuality in his novels *Le Dernier été des Indiens* (1982) and *Le Fou du père* (1988).

All these shifts in the literary imagination owe much to the contributions of the numerous writers who, coming from elsewhere, have made Montreal into a cosmopolitan city, particularly in terms of its literary output. In this "post-Québécois" literature, as Pierre Nepveu terms it,[68] identity always plays an important role, but from this point onwards it spills over into migrant literature. *La Québécoite* (1983), by Régine Robin,[69] explores the rerouting of cultural memories in the face of the confrontation with the "we" of the French-speaking Québécois population, still relatively closed to the virtues of racial intermixture. The novel, which is characteristic of migrant literature, tells the tale of the three attempts to emigrate to Montreal made by a French woman of Jewish origin, and articulates the key concepts of the speech of "those caught in between" and of cultural memory. In *Comment faire l'amour avec un nègre sans se fatiguer?* (1985),[70] Dany Laferrière, born in Port-au-Prince, situates his tale of emigration at the nerve center of a Montreal divided between the bourgeois girls who go to McGill University and a squalid room in the

---

68 See Pierre Nepveu, *L'écologie du réel: Mort et naissance de la littérature québécoise contemporaine* (Montreal: Boréal, 1988), p. 14.
69 Régine Robin, *The Wanderer*, tr. Phyllis Aronoff (Montreal: Alter Ego Editions, 1997).
70 Dany Laferrière, *How To Make Love to a Negro*, tr. David Homel (Toronto: Coach House Press, 1987).

French quarter of rue Saint-Denis. Such is the place where two Haïtians live, busy reading the Koran, listening to jazz music, and chasing after young white women in expiation of the ancient wrongs of colonialism. The protagonists' zeal in promoting "négriture" and orientalism in this way injects alterity into the standard Montreal duality. In *Avril ou l'anti-passion* (1990),[71] the Italo-Québécois writer Antonio d'Alfonso offers a reflection on exile, experienced as mourning, and on the encounter between different cultures.

Ying Chen, born in Shanghai, stunned the Québécois literary scene with her second novel, *Les Lettres chinoises* (1993), an epistolary novel modelled on *Les Lettres persanes* by Montesquieu. The dialogue between two fiancés, one of whom has settled in Montreal while the other stayed behind in Shanghai, offers a novel perspective on Québécois society which is contrasted with the changing face of China. *L'Ingratitude* (1995),[72] the success of which increased the author's reputation in France, expresses revolt against the burden of tradition and the family through the terrible story of a young girl who commits suicide in order to escape from her mother's hold on her.

The Quebec writers born just after or at the beginning of the Quiet Revolution offer a different view on their membership of Québécois society to that of writers of an older generation. Monique Proulx, in *Le Sexe des étoiles* (1987),[73] approaches the questioning of identity from the perspective of transsexuality. *Les Aurores montréales* (1996),[74] by the same author, is a collection of short stories which make up a kaleidoscope of Montrealean modernity and marginality. Gaétan Soucy gained notoriety with *La petite fille qui aimait trop les allumettes* (1998),[75] a tale with mythic overtones which opens with the death of a father in a quasi-medieval setting. Stylistically, the author displays great linguistic inventiveness, sometimes akin to that of Réjean Ducharme, and plays skillfully on the carefully guarded secret of the narrator's sex. In *La Rage* (1989), Louis Hamelin deftly brings together two unrelated historical situations: the requisition of ancestral lands in order to build the Mirabel airport, and the techno-scientific expropriation suffered by Generation X. This first novel, which enjoyed unanimous critical acclaim, polarizes the

---

71 Antonio d'Alfonso, *Fabrizio's Passion*, tr. Antonio d'Alfonso (Toronto: Guernica, 1995).
72 Ying Chen, *Ingratitude*, tr. Carol Volk (Toronto: Douglas and McIntyre, 1998).
73 Monique Proulx, *Sex of the Stars*, tr. Matt Cohen (Vancouver: Douglas and McIntyre, 1996).
74 Monique Proulx, *Aurora Montrealis*, tr. Matt Cohen (Vancouver: Douglas and McIntyre, 1997).
75 Gaétan Soucy, *The Little Girl Who Was Too Fond of Matches*, tr. Sheila Fischman (Toronto: Anansi, 2000).

two disparate discourses of scientificity and animality to give form to the feelings of rage and exclusion experienced by young people. Hamelin's preoccupation with ecology also fed into his other novels, such as *CowBoy* (1992)[76] and *Le Joueur de flûte* (2001).

The themes of dispossession, nomadism, and the identity quest are echoed in the works of those called "the young novelists of despair" by Aurélien Boivin.[77] Christian Mistral, a media figure and young novelist, has published a series of successful autofictions – *Vamp* (1988), *Vautour* (1990), *Valium* (2000) – in a style which is "baroque et hyperréaliste," not to say trashy, thus evoking urban drift.[78] Sylvain Trudel made a name for himself with his first novel, *Le Souffle de l'harmattan* (1986), which concerns the uprooting of an adopted child and his African friend. In *Terre du roi Christian* (1989), Trudel continues his exploration of the fantasmatic universe of childhood. Amongst the names of literary figures of growing importance today, that of Lise Tremblay should be mentioned. Her novel, *L'Hiver de pluie* (1995), invents the narrative voice of a woman walking the streets of Quebec City following in the footsteps of Jacques Poulin and his characters.

The self-referentiality of the Québécois novel is, moreover, becoming an increasingly marked trait, a sure sign of its autonomy and intertextual power. So it is that Pierre Gobeil, in *La Mort de Marlon Brando* (1989) refracts his drama of sexual aggression through the lens of the distorted plot of the infamous novel by Germaine Guèvremont, *Le Survenant*, and of the film *Apocalypse Now* (1979). Guillaume Vigneault, on the other hand, takes up the road motif from *Volkswagen Blues* in *Chercher le vent* (2001),[79] by depicting the migration across America and the encounter with the Other. Catherine Mavrikakis in *Ça va aller* (2002) and Monique Proulx in *Le cœur est un muscle involontaire* (2002)[80] portrayed the quasi-sacred figure of novelist Réjean Ducharme. In *Le Mal de Vienne* (1992), Robert Racine presents the reader with an identificatory frenzy, bringing together Hubert Aquin's characters, a page of *La Flore laurentienne* by Frère Marie-Victorin, and the voice of Jean Le Moyne, the essayist who wrote

---

76 Louis Hamelin, *Cowboy*, tr. Jean-Paul Murray (Toronto: Dundurn Press, 2000).
77 Aurélien Boivin, "Les Romanciers de la désespérance," *Québec français* 89 (Spring 1993), pp. 97–9.
78 "Baroque and hyperrealist," in allusion to the chapter heading "Romans baroques et hyperréalisme," in Michel Biron, François Dumont, and Élisabeth Nardout-Lafarge, *Histoire de la littérature québécoise* (Montreal, Boréal, 2008), p. 552–60.
79 Guillaume Vigneault, *Necessary Betrayals*, tr. Susan Ouriou (Vancouver: Douglas and McIntyre, 2002).
80 Monique Proulx, *The Heart is an Involuntary Muscle*, tr. David Homel and Fred A. Reed (Vancouver: Douglas and McIntyre, 2003).

Convergences, an influential collection of humanist essays published at the beginning of the Quiet Revolution.

In Nelly Arcan's writing, cynicism and despair meet in the freedom of the body which circulates as merchandise in *Putain* (2001),[81] while *Folle* (2004) expresses the extreme closure of a present amputated from any future. The striking diversity which can be observed in recent fiction speaks of new affiliations which, in the post-Québécois view of Pierre Nepveu, demonstrate that traditional memberships have been outgrown. The case of Yann Martel, the bestselling author of *Life of Pi* (2001) – a book which was written and published in English before being translated into French in 2003 – is emblematic of the choice of the young writer in his demand for a transnational ideology. The recent vitality of fantasy and science-fiction writing (André Carpentier, Jean-Pierre April, Esther Rochon, and Élisabeth Vonarburg) is another current in this departure from the national text.

Francophone fiction in Acadia, Manitoba, Ontario and the western provinces

The literature of Canada's francophone communities shares more than one trait in common with the evolution of Québécois literature. The struggle against cultural assimilation initially motivates a messianic ideology; legendary memories of survival give rise, sooner or later, to the foundation of a literary institution which is more or less locally autonomous, and to the establishment of publishing houses ("Prise de parole" is a good example in French Ontario, as is "Éditions de l'Acadie" in New Brunswick), rapidly followed by a rise in literary production and, today, of the post-identity aesthetic.

In New Brunswick, we have observed the succession of novels of the land, such as *Pour la terre* (1918) by Louis-Arthur Melanson, and of folkloric tales and legends preceding the works of Antonine Maillet, the most internationally recognized of all Acadian writers. Winner of the Prix Goncourt in 1979 for *Pélagie-la-charrette*, she is celebrated for her novels, which have a Rabelaisian touch. The eponymous heroine invites the reader to relive the sad historical episode of the deportation of her people in 1755, the founding myth of Acadia and commonly referred to as "Le Grand Dérangement."[82] The novelist makes

---

81 Nelly Arcan, *Whore*, tr. Bruce Benderson (New York: Black Cat, 2005).
82 "The Great Upheaval."

no secret of her desire to correct both the official history and the myth of Evangeline popularized by Henry Longfellow in the nineteenth century. Some readings of this novel tend to focus on the folkloric dimension, while others put more emphasis on the modern and carnivalesque aspects of this "épopée de la remémoration et de la parole."[83]

Acadian novelists of the following generation are concerned with redefining the ideological and identitary stakes and with making their voices heard in a literary landscape long dominated by poetry. Jacques Savoie locates his Acadian heroes all over America from Quebec (*Les Portes tournantes*, 1984)[84] to New York (*Une histoire de cœur*, 1988), updating the secular theme of the dislocated family. In *Un fin passage* (2001) and *Petites difficultés d'existence* (2002),[85] France Daigle explores daily life and the encounter with the other in the migration of characters confronted with heteroglossia – English, French, Chiac – in New Brunswick and in other parts of the world.

Except for some rare exceptions, such as *Le Flambeau sacré* (1944) by Mariline (the pseudonym adopted by Alice Séguin) which takes up the political context described in *L'Appel de la race*, the French Ontarian novel does not share the ideological scope of Acadian literature because the francophone presence in Ontario is the result of relatively recent emigration from Quebec. The exploits and spirit of the pioneers and the theme of the forest form another parallel between north Ontarian fiction and the Québécois novel. *François Duvalet* (1954), by the writer of French origin Maurice de Gourmois, is set in "la forêt septentrionale qui aliène, morcelle et absorbe l'homme tout entier pour enfin le rendre à la vie, transformé."[86] The trilogy *Les Chroniques du Nouvel-Ontario*, by Hélène Brodeur, published between 1981 and 1986, tells, in realist style, of the hopes and dramas of Québécois emigrants who were transplanted into the immensity of the Ontarian northeast at the beginning of the century.

Daniel Poliquin, the most prolific of French Ontarian authors, has been affirming his talent as a storyteller and his status as a "cultural Métis" for the last twenty or so years, in an oeuvre which has pushed back the boundaries of the issue of identity: deconstructing the figure of the father in the context of the Native peoples in *L'Obomsawin* (1987) and the slippage of memory in

---

83 "Epic of the remembrance of speech," James de Finney, "Pélagie-la-Charrette," *Dictionnaire des œuvres littéraires du Québec* (Montreal: Fides, 1994), vol. VI, p. 622.
84 Jacques Savoie, *The Revolving Doors* (Toronto: Lester and Orpen Dennys, 1989).
85 France Daigle, *Life's Little Difficulties*, tr. Robert Majzels (Toronto: Anansi, 2004).
86 "The northern forest which alienates, dices and absorbs a man entirely in order to finally bring him back to life, transformed," Yolande Grisé, "La Thématique de la forêt dans deux romans ontarois," *Voix et images* 41 (Winter 1989), p. 270.

L'Écureuil noir (1994)[87] and La Côte de sable (2000). The voices of migrant writers enrich the heterogeneous poetics which feed into the Ontarian novel, from the German writer Marguerite Andersen and her autofiction De mémoire de femme (1982) to Hédi Bouraoui, born in Tunisia, whose transcultural novelistic practice concerns the encounter with the Other (Bangkok Blues, 1994; La Pharaone, 1998).

The precariousness of cultural survival and the challenges to overcome are the law which prevails west of Ontario, in all the provinces where the near-total absence of francophone literary institutions accentuates the demographic and political fragility of the French-speaking population. Literatures of "exiguïté," to use François Paré's elegant term,[88] bring together authors who have come from elsewhere, often from Quebec and France, and French-Canadian writers. For about the last thirty years, the Manitoban writer J. Roger Léveillé has been building up a remarkable body of work, so far not as much discussed in Québécois criticism as it deserves. Preoccupied with displacement and emblematic of similar novels, Le Soleil du lac qui se couche (2001) is a tale of initiation into beauty and the affair between a young Métis woman, who is an architecture student, and a Japanese poet. The figure of the woman of mixed race is central to the life and work of the writer Maurice Constantin-Weyer and his novel Un homme se penche sur son passé (1928),[89] which chronicles his life as an emigrant in Manitoba and which earned him the Prix Goncourt. In La Métisse (1923), Jean Féron (the pseudonym used by Joseph-Marc-Octave Lebel), a Fransaskois (Franco-Saskatchewanian) by adoption, denounces both the violence suffered by a servant at the hands of a Scottish emigrant and the colonial oppression of Louis Riel's people.

Despite publishing four novels and two collections of short stories since 1960, Marguerite A. Primeau, born in Alberta, is still awaiting the recognition and approval that her original prose, characterized by linguistic heterogeneity and the textualization of tensions between French and English, deserves. Her first novel, Dans le muskeg (1960), tells of the imminent assimilation of a French-speaking community in Alberta ironically called Avenir ("future"), as seen through the eyes of a Québécois primary school teacher who gradually loses his messianic ideals and his illusions concerning the bilingualism of Canada. Twenty-five years earlier, in the evocatively titled novel La Forêt

---

87 Daniel Poliquin, Obomsawin of Sioux Junction, tr. Wayne Grady (Vancouver: Douglas and McIntyre, 1991); Black Squirrel, tr. Wayne Grady (Vancouver: Douglas and McIntyre, 1995).
88 "Scantness," François Paré, Les Littératures de l'exiguïté (Hearst: Le Nordir, 1992).
89 Maurice Constant-Weyer, A Man Scans His Past (Toronto: Macmillan, 1929).

(1935),[90] the French writer Georges Bugnet had described the difficulties of a couple – European colonizers – battling with the harshness of the Albertan winter.

The coastal landscapes of British Colombia have provided inspiration for several francophone writers, of whom the first was probably the anthropologist Marius Barbeau, who published *Le Rêve de Kamalmouk* in 1948, an astonishing tale set amongst the Tsimshians of the Skeena River in the northwest of the province. More recently, Monique Genuist, a writer of Alsatian origin, has written more in the vein of the historical novel, of which *Nootka* (2003) offers the solidly researched prototype. It tells the story of the French-speakers who took part in the foundation of what was to become the city of Victoria after the gold rush of the mid-nineteenth century. After the portrayal of the Métis identity, will we witness the emergence of a Native voice in French? Only time will tell.

Having attempted to sketch out the Canadian evolution of French-language fictional prose over nearly two centuries, we arrive at the conclusion that no single characteristic adequately encapsulates the rich variety of the corpus, other than that of the language in which it is written. If one wanted to amplify this statement, one could observe that it embraces the entire range of dialectical nuances encompassed by the French presence in America from the time of Jacques Cartier's voyages to the continent. From the colorful language of Louis Fréchette's *Originaux et détraqués* (1892–3), via the French-Canadian patois of Michel Tremblay's chronicles, to the subtleties of speech of Daniel Poliquin's urban tales, the diversity of lexis and of accentuated words injects much more than just local color into the plurality of narrative forms which characterizes the francophone Canadian novel: it is its very flesh and blood. Yet it would be going too far to emphasize this point to the exclusion of two other important features which are a common thread in both Québécois literature and in the writings of other French-Canadian authors: the preoccupation with identity and the obsession with survival (linguistic and cultural), both expressions of what Anthony Purdy has called "a certain difficulty of being."[91]

---

90 Georges Bugnet, *The Forest*, tr. David Carpenter (Montreal: Harvest House, 1976).
91 Anthony Purdy, *A Certain Difficulty of Being: Essays on the Quebec Novel* (Montreal and Kingston: McGill-Queen's University Press, 1990).

Bibliography

Note: Although there is important criticism on Canadian literature in other languages, only works in English or French are listed.

Reference works
History and geography (general)

De Brou, Dave, and Bill Waiser, eds. *Documenting Canada: A History of Modern Canada in Documents.* Saskatoon: Fifth House, 1992.

Dufresne, Charles, Jacques Grimard, André Lapierre, Pierre Savard, and Gaétan Vallières, eds. *Dictionnaire de l'Amérique française: Francophonie nord-américaine hors Québec.* Ottawa: Presses de l'Université d'Ottawa, 1988.

Early Canadiana Online. Canadian Institute for Historical Microreproductions in partnership with the National Library of Canada. www.canadiana.org.

Gough, Barry M. *Historical Dictionary of Canada.* Lanham: Scarecrow, 1999.

Green, Rayna, with Melanie Fernandez. *The Encyclopaedia of the First Peoples of North America.* Toronto: Douglas and McIntyre, 1999.

Havard, Gilles, and Cécile Vidal. *Histoire de l'Amérique française.* Rev. edn. Paris: Flammarion, 2008 [2003].

Hayes, Derek. *Historical Atlas of Canada: A Thousand Years of Canada's History in Maps.* Vancouver: Douglas and McIntyre, 2002.

Hoxie, Frederick. *Encyclopedia of North American Indians.* Boston: Houghton, 1996.

Lacoursière, Jacques. *Histoire populaire du Québec.* 5 vols. to date. Sillery: Septentrion, 1995–.

Linteau, Paul-André, René Durocher, Jean-Claude Robert, and François Ricard. *Histoire du Québec contemporain.* Montreal: Boréal, 1989.

Litalien, Raymonde, Jean-François Palomino, and Denis Vaugeois. *La Mesure d'un continent: Atlas historique de l'Amérique du Nord, 1492–1814.* Quebec: Presses de l'Université de Paris-Sorbonne/Septentrion Québec, 2007. English version: *Mapping a Continent: Historical Atlas of North America, 1492–1814.* Tr. Käthe Roth. Sillery: Septentrion, 2007.

Marsh, James H. *The Canadian Encyclopedia.* 2nd edn. 4 vols. Edmonton: Hurtig, 1988 [1985]. Also online www.thecanadianencyclopedia.org.

Matthews, Geoffrey, cartographer/designer, and R. Cole Harris et al., eds. *Historical Atlas of Canada.* 3 vols. Toronto: University of Toronto Press, 1987–93.

Morton, Desmond. *A Short History of Canada*. 5th edn. Toronto: McClelland and Stewart, 2001 [1983].
Morton, W(illiam) L(ewis). *The Kingdom of Canada: A General History from Earliest Times*. Toronto: McClelland and Stewart, 1963.
Nelles, H(enry). V(ivian). *A Little History of Canada*. Don Mills, ON: Oxford University Press, 2004. French version: *Une Brève Histoire du Canada*. Tr. Lori Saint-Martin and Paul Gagné. Saint-Laurent: Fides, 2005.

Bibliographies

Ball, John, and Richard Plant, eds. *Bibliography of Theatre History in Canada: The Beginnings through 1984 / Bibliographie du théâtre au Canada: des débuts – fin 1984*. Toronto: ECW Press, 1993.
Beaudoin, Réjean, Annette Hayward, and André Lamontagne, eds. *Bibliographie de la critique de la littérature québécoise au Canada anglais (1939–1989)*. Quebec: Nota bene, 2004.
Boivin, Aurélien. *Le Conte littéraire québécois au xix siècle: Essai de bibliographie critique et analytique*. Montreal: Fides, 1975.
Bond, Mary E., comp. and ed., and Martine M. Caron, comp. *Canadian Reference Sources: An Annotated Bibliography / Ouvrages de référence canadiens: Une bibliographie annotée*. Vancouver: University of British Columbia Press, 1996.
Ingles, Ernie, comp. and ed. *Bibliography of Canadian Bibliographies*. 3rd edn. Toronto: University of Toronto Press, 1994 [1960].
Jones, Joseph. *Reference Sources for Canadian Literary Studies*. Toronto: University of Toronto Press, 2005.
Lamonde, Yvan. *Je me souviens: La Littérature personnelle au Québec (1860–1980)*. Quebec: Institut québécois sur la culture, 1983.
Lamonde, Yvan, and Marie-Pierre Turcot. *La Littérature personnelle au Québec, 1980–2000*. Montreal: Bibliothèque nationale du Québec, 2000.
Lecker, Robert, and Jack David, eds. *The Annotated Bibliography of Canada's Major Authors*, 8 vols. Toronto: ECW Press, 1979–94.
Lecker, Robert, Colin Hill, and Peter Lipert. *English-Canadian Literary Anthologies: An Enumerative Bibliography*. Teeswater: Reference Press, 1997.
Sirois, Antoine. *Bibliography of Comparative Studies in Canadian, Québec and Foreign Literatures, 1930–1995 / Bibliographie d'études comparées des littératures canadienne, québécois et étrangères, 1930–1995*. Sherbrooke: Université de Sherbrooke, 2001.
Waterston, Elizabeth, with Ian Easterbrook, Bernard Katz, and Kathleen Scott. *The Travellers: Canada to 1900: An Annotated Bibliography of Works Published in English from 1577*. Guelph: University of Guelph, 1989.
Watters, Reginald Eyre. *A Checklist of Canadian Literature and Background Materials, 1628–1960*. 2nd edn., revised and enlarged. Toronto: University of Toronto Press, 1972 [1959].
Weiss, Allan, comp. *A Comprehensive Bibliography of English-Canadian Short Stories, 1950–1983*. Toronto: ECW Press, 1988.

Biographical reference works

Chartier, Daniel. *Dictionnaire des écrivains émigrés au Québec, 1800–1999*. Quebec: Nota bene, 2003.

Cook, Ramsay, et al., eds. *Dictionary of Canadian Biography*. 15 vols. to date. Toronto: University of Toronto Press, 1966–. Also in French: *Dictionnaire biographique du Canada*. Quebec: Presses de l'Université Laval, 1966–. Also online www.biographi.ca.

Hamel, Réginald, John Hare, and Paul Wyczynski. *Dictionnaire des auteurs de langue française en Amérique du Nord*. Montreal: Fides, 1989.

Dictionnaire pratique des auteurs québécois. Montreal: Fides, 1976.

Helly, Denise, and Anne-Fanny Vassal. *Romanciers immigrés: Biographies et œuvres publiées au Québec entre 1970 et 1990*. Quebec: Institut québécois de recherche sur la culture, 1993.

Morgan, Henry J. *Sketches of Celebrated Canadians, and Persons Connected with Canada, from the Earliest Period in the History of the Province Down to the Present Time*. Quebec: Hunter, Rose & Co., 1862.

New, William H., ed. *Dictionary of Literary Biography*. 6 vols. Detroit: Gale, 1986–90. vols. LIII: *Canadian Writers since 1960, First Series*; LX: *Canadian Writers since 1960, Second Series*; LXVIII: *Canadian Writers, 1920–1959, First Series*; LXXXVIII: *Canadian Writers, 1920–1959, Second Series*; XCII: *Canadian Writers, 1890–1920*; XCIX: *Canadian Writers before 1890*.

Sylvestre, Guy, Brandon Conron, and Carl F. Klinck, eds. *Canadian Writers: A Biographical Dictionary / Écrivains canadiens: Un dictionnaire biographique*. Toronto: Ryerson, 1964; new edn., revised and enlarged, 1966.

Literary companions and encyclopedias

Archives des lettres canadiennes, 13 vols. to date. Montreal: Fides: 1961–: vol. I: Paul Wyczynski, Bernard Julien, and Jean Ménard, eds., *Mouvement littéraire de Québec 1860*; vol. II: Paul Wyczynski, Bernard Julien, and Jean Ménard, eds., *L'École littéraire de Montréal*; vol. III: Paul Wyczynski, Bernard Julien, Jean Ménard, and Réjean Robidoux, eds., *Le Roman canadien-français*; vol. IV: Paul Wyczynski, Bernard Julien, Jean Ménard, and Réjean Robidoux, eds., *La Poésie canadienne-française*; vol. V: Paul Wyczynski, Bernard Julien, and Hélène Beauchamp-Rank, eds., *Le Théâtre canadien-français*; vol. VI: Paul Wyczynski, François Gallays, and Sylvain Simard, eds., *L'Essai et la prose d'idées au Québec*; vol. VII: Paul Wyczynski, François Gallays, and Sylvain Simard, eds., *Le Nigog*; vol. VIII: François Gallays, Sylvain Simard, and Robert Vigneault, eds., *Le Roman contemporain au Québec (1960–1985)*; vol. IX: François Gallays and Robert Vigneault, eds., *La Nouvelle au Québec: Aperçus*; vol. X: Dominique Lafon et al., eds., *Le Théâtre québécois 1975–1995*; vol. XI: Françoise Lepage, et al., eds., *La Littérature pour la jeunesse 1970–2000*; Dominique Lafon, Rainier Grutman, Marcel Olscamp, Robert Vigneault, et al., eds., *Approches de la biographie au Québec*; vol. XIII: Stéphane-Albert Boulais, ed., *Le Cinéma au Québec: Tradition et modernité*.

Benson, Eugene, and L. W. Conolly. *English-Canadian Theatre*. Toronto: Oxford University Press, 1987.

  eds. *The Oxford Companion to Canadian Theatre*. Toronto: Oxford University Press, 1989.

  eds. *Encyclopedia of Post-Colonial Literatures in English*. 2 vols. London: Routledge, 1994.

Benson, Eugene, and William Toye, eds. *The Oxford Companion to Canadian Literature*. 2nd edn. Toronto: Oxford University Press, 1997 [1983].

Blain, Virginia Helen, Patricia Clements, and Isobel Grundy, eds. *The Feminist Companion to Literature in English: Women Writers from the Middle Ages to the Present*. London: B. T. Batsford, 1990.

Bibliography

Canadian Theatre Encyclopedia. www.canadiantheatre.com.
Chartier, Daniel. *Guide de culture et de littérature québécoises: Les Grandes Œuvres, les traductions, les études et les addresses culturelles*. Quebec: Nota bene, 1999.
Le Guide de la culture au Québec: Littérature, cinéma, essais, revues. Quebec: Nota bene, 2004.
Davey, Frank. *From There to Here: A Guide to English-Canadian Literature Since 1960*. Erin: Porcépic, 1974.
Fortin, Marcel, Yvan Lamonde, and François Ricard. *Guide de la littérature québécoise*. Montreal: Boréal, 1988.
Groden, Michael, Martin Kreiswirth, and Imre Szeman, eds. *The Johns Hopkins Guide to Literary Theory and Criticism*. 2nd edn. Baltimore: Johns Hopkins University Press, 2005 [1994].
Hébert, Pierre, Yves Lever, and Kenneth Landry, eds. *Dictionnaire de la censure au Québec: littérature et cinéma*. Saint-Laurent: Fides, 2006.
Jansohn, Christa, ed. *Companion to the New Literatures in English*. Berlin: Erich Schmidt, 2002.
Kattan, Naïm. *Écrivains des Amériques*. 3 vols. Montréal: Hurtubise HMH, 1972–80.
Kröller, Eva-Marie, ed. *Cambridge Companion to Canadian Literature*. Cambridge: Cambridge University Press, 2004.
Lecker, Robert, Jack David, and Ellen Quigley, eds. *Canadian Writers and Their Works*. 24 vols. Downsview: ECW, 1983–91.
Lemire, Maurice, ed. *Dictionnaire des œuvres littéraires du Québec*. 7 vols. to date. Montreal: Fides, 1978–. Vol. VI: Gilles Dorion, ed., 1994. Vol. VII: Aurélien Boivin, ed., 2003.
Makaryk, Irena, ed. *Encyclopedia of Contemporary Literary Theory: Approaches, Scholars, Terms*. Toronto: University of Toronto Press, 1993.
Moritz, Alfred, and Theresa Moritz. *The Oxford Illustrated Literary Guide to Canada*. Toronto: Oxford University Press, 1987.
Mulvey-Roberts, Marie. *The Handbook to Gothic Literature*. New York: New York University Press, 1998.
New, William H., ed. *Encyclopedia of Literature in Canada*. Toronto: University of Toronto Press, 2002.
Richler, Noah. *This is My Country, What's Yours? A Literary Atlas of Canada*. Toronto: McClelland and Stewart, 2006.
Rubin, Don, ed. *The World Encyclopedia of Contemporary Theatre*. Vol. 2: Americas. London: Routledge, 1996.
Sage, Lorna, ed. *The Cambridge Guide to Women's Writing in English*. Cambridge: Cambridge University Press, 1999.
Story, Norah, ed. *The Oxford Companion to Canadian History and Literature*. Toronto: Oxford University Press, 1967. Updated by: Toye, William, ed. Supplement to *The Oxford Companion to Canadian History and Literature*. Toronto: Oxford University Press, 1973.
Thomas, Clara. *Our Nature, Our Voices: A Guidebook to English Canadian Literature*. Toronto: NeWest Press, 1972.

Literary histories

Biron, Michel, François Dumont, and Élisabeth Nardout-Lafarge. *Histoire de la littérature québécoise*. Montreal: Boréal, 2007.

Gasquy-Resch, Yannick, ed. *Histoire littéraire de la francophonie: littérature du Québec.* Vanves: EDICEF, 1994.

Grandpré, Pierre de, ed. *Histoire de la littérature française du Québec.* 4 vols. Montreal: Beauchemin, 1967–9.

Keith, W. J. *Canadian Literature in English.* 2nd edn. 2 vols. Erin: Porcupine's Quill, 2006 [1985].

Klinck, Carl F. et al., eds. *Literary History of Canada: Canadian Literature in English.* 2nd edn. 3 vols. Toronto: University of Toronto Press, 1976 [1965]. Vol. IV: William H. New et al., eds., Toronto: University of Toronto Press, 1990. French version of 1965 ed.: *Histoire littéraire du Canada: Littérature canadienne de langue anglaise.* Tr. Maurice Lebel. Quebec: Presses de l'Université Laval, 1970.

New, William H. *A History of Canadian Literature.* 2nd edn. Montreal and Kingston: McGill-Queen's University Press, 2003 [1989].

Nischik, Reingard M. ed. *History of Literature in Canada: English-Canadian and French-Canadian.* Rochester: Camden House, 2008. Revised translation of Konrad Gross, Wolfgang Klooss, Reingard M. Nischik, eds. *Kanadische Literaturgeschichte.* Stuttgart: Metzler, 2005.

Tougas, Gérard. *Histoire de la littérature canadienne-française.* Paris: Presses universitaires de France, 1964. English version: *History of French-Canadian Literature.* Tr. Alta Lind Cook. Toronto: Ryerson, 1966.

La vie littéraire au Québec. 5 vols to date. Sainte-Foy: Presses de l'Université Laval, 1991–. Vol. I (1764–1805): Maurice Lemire, ed., *La Voix française des nouveaux sujets britanniques*; vol. II (1806–1839): Maurice Lemire, ed., *Le projet national des Canadiens*; vol. III (1840–1869): Maurice Lemire and Denis Saint-Jacques, eds., *Un peuple sans histoire ni littérature*; vol. IV (1870–1894): Maurice Lemire and Denis Saint-Jacques, eds., *Je me souviens*; vol. V (1895–1918): Denis Saint-Jacques and Maurice Lemire, eds., *Sois fidèle à ta Laurentie.*

Literary history: special topics

Blair, Jennifer, Daniel Coleman, Kate Higginson, and Lorraine York, eds. *ReCalling Early Canada: Reading the Political in Literary and Cultural Production.* Edmonton: University of Alberta Press, 2005.

Blodgett, E. D. *Five-Part Invention: A History of Literary History in Canada.* Toronto: University of Toronto Press, 2003.

Boivin, Aurélien, Gilles Dorion, and Kenneth Landry, eds. *Questions d'histoire littéraire: Mélanges offerts à Maurice Lemire.* Quebec: Nuit blanche, 1996.

Hutcheon, Linda, and Mario J. Valdés, eds. *Rethinking Literary History: A Dialogue on Theory.* New York: Oxford University Press, 2002.

Kennedy, Brian. *The Baron Bold and the Beauteous Maid: A Compact History of Canadian Theatre.* Toronto: Playwrights Canada, 2004.

Klinck, Carl F. *Giving Canada a Literary History: A Memoir.* Ed. Sandra Djwa. Ottawa: Carleton University Press, 1991.

Moisan, Clément, ed. *Histoire littéraire: théories, méthodes, pratiques.* Quebec: Presses de l'Université Laval, 1989.

Rubin, Don, ed. *Canadian Theatre History: Selected Readings.* Toronto: Copp Clark, 1996.

Saint-Jacques, Denis, ed. *Tendances actuelles en histoire littéraire canadienne.* Montreal: Nota bene, 2003.

History of the book, publishing, the literary institution, literary taste

Beaulieu, Victor-Lévy. *Manuel de la petite littérature du Québec*. Montreal: l'Aurore, 1974.

Chartier, Daniel. *L'Émergence des classiques: La Réception de la littérature québécoise des années 1930*. Quebec: Fides, 2000.

Fleming, Patricia Lockhart, and Yvan Lamonde, eds. *History of the Book in Canada*. Toronto: University of Toronto Press, 2004–7. vol. I: Patricia Lockhart Fleming, Gilles Gallichan, and Yvan Lamonde, eds., *Beginnings to 1840*; vol. II: Yvan Lamonde, Patricia Lockhart Fleming, and Fiona A. Black, eds., *1840–1918*; vol. III: Carole Gerson and Jacques Michon, eds., *1918–1980*. French version: *Histoire du livre et de l'imprimé au Canada*. 3 vols. Montreal: Presses de l'Université de Montréal, 2004–7.

Friskney, Janet B. *New Canadian Library: The Ross-McClelland Years 1952–1978*. Toronto: University of Toronto Press, 2007.

Galarneau, Claude, and Maurice Lemire, eds. *Livre et lecture au Québec, 1800–1850*. Quebec: Institut québécois de recherche sur la culture, 1988.

Garand, Dominique, Liette Gaudreau, Robert Giroux, Jean-Marc Lemelin, and André Marquis. *Le Spectacle de la littérature: Les Aléas et les avatars de l'institution*. Montreal: Triptyque, 1989.

Gerson, Carole. *A Purer Taste: The Writing and Reading of Fiction in English in Nineteenth-Century Canada*. Toronto: University of Toronto Press, 1989.

Huggan, Graham. *The Post-colonial Exotic: Marketing the Margins*. London: Routledge, 2001.

Karr, Clarence. *Authors and Audiences: Popular Canadian Fiction in the Early Twentieth Century*. Montreal and Kingston: McGill-Queen's University Press, 2000.

Lanthier, Pierre, and Guildo Rousseau, eds. *La Culture inventée: Les Stratégies culturelles aux 19e et 20e siècles*. Quebec: Institut québécois de recherche sur la culture, 1992.

Leandoer, Katarina. *From Colonial Expression to Export Commodity: English-Canadian Literature in Canada and Sweden, 1945–1999*. Uppsala: Uppsala University Library, 2002.

Lecker, Robert. *Making it Real: The Canonization of English Canadian Literature*. Concord: Anansi, 1995.

  ed. *Canadian Canons: Essays in Literary Value*. Toronto: University of Toronto Press, 1991.

Lemire, Maurice. *La Littérature québécoise en projet au milieu du XIXe siècle*. Saint-Laurent: Fides, 1993.

Lemire, Maurice, with Pierrette Dionne and Michel Lord. *Le Poids des politiques: Livres, lecture et littérature*. Quebec: Institut québécois de recherche sur la culture, 1987.

Lemire, Maurice, with Michel Lord. *Institution littéraire*. Quebec: Institut québécois de la recherche sur la culture, 1986.

Litt, Paul. *The Muses, the Masses, and the Massey Commission*. Toronto: University of Toronto Press, 1992.

MacSkimming, Roy. *The Perilous Trade: Publishing Canada's Writers*. Toronto: McClelland and Stewart, 2003.

Michon, Jacques, ed. *Histoire de l'édition littéraire au Québec au XXe siècle*. 2 vols. to date. Montréal: Fides, 1999–. Vol. I: *La Naissance de l'éditeur, 1900–1939*; vol. II: *Le Temps des éditeurs, 1940–1959*.

Moisan, Clément. *Comparaison et raison: Essais sur l'histoire et l'institution des littératures canadienne et québécoise*. Quebec: Hurtubise HMH, 1986.

Mount, Nick. *When Canadian Literature Moved to New York.* Toronto: University of Toronto Press, 2005.
Murray, Heather. *Come, Bright Improvement: The Literary Societies of Nineteenth-Century Ontario.* Toronto: University of Toronto Press, 2002.
Working in English: History, Institution, Resources. Toronto: University of Toronto Press, 1996.
Ostry, Bernard. *The Cultural Connection: An Essay on Culture and Government Policy in Canada.* Toronto: McClelland and Stewart, 1978.
Parker, George L. *The Beginnings of the Book Trade in Canada.* Toronto: University of Toronto Press, 1985.
Robert, Lucie. *L'Institution du littéraire au Québec.* Quebec: Presses de l'Université Laval, 1989.
Tippett, Maria. *Making Culture: English-Canadian Institutions and the Arts before the Massey Commission.* Toronto: University of Toronto Press, 1990.
Towards a History of the Literary Institution in Canada / Vers une histoire de l'institution littéraire au Canada. Edmonton: The Research Institute for Comparative Literature, University of Alberta, 1988–92. Vol. I: E. D. Blodgett and A. G. Purdy, eds., *Prefaces and Literary Manifestoes / Préfaces et manifestes littéraires*; vol. II: I. S. MacLaren and C. Potvin, eds., *Questions of Funding, Publishing and Distribution / Questions d'édition et de diffusion*; vol. III: C. Potvin and J. Williamson, eds., *Women's Writing and the Literary Institution / L'Écriture au féminin et l'institution littéraire*; vol. IV: Joseph Pivato, ed., *Literatures of Lesser Diffusion / Les littératures de moindre diffusion*; vol. V: E. D. Blodgett and A. G. Purdy, eds., *Problems of Literary Reception / Problèmes de réception littéraire*; vol. VI: I. S. MacLaren and C. Potvin, eds., *Literary Genres / Les Genres littéraires.*
Yergeau, Robert. *Art, argent, arrangement: Le Mécénat d'Etat.* Montreal: David, 2004.
A tout prix: Les Prix littéraires au Québec. Montreal: Triptyque, 1994.
York, Lorraine. *Literary Celebrity in Canada.* Toronto: University of Toronto Press, 2007.

Literary criticism

Literary criticism: general (English and French)

Allard, Jacques. *Traverses de la critique littéraire au Québec.* Montreal: Boréal, 1991.
Atwood, Margaret. *Curious Pursuits: Occasional Writing 1970–2005.* London: Virago, 2005.
Moving Targets: Writing With Intent, 1982–2004. Toronto: Anansi, 2004.
Negotiating with the Dead: A Writer on Writing. Cambridge: Cambridge University Press, 2002.
Payback: Debt and the Shadow Side of Wealth. Toronto: Anansi, 2008.
Second Words: Selected Critical Prose. Toronto: Anansi, 1982.
Survival: Toronto: McClelland and Stewart, 2004 [1972].
Ballstadt, Carl, ed. *The Search for English-Canadian Literature: An Anthology of Critical Articles from the Nineteenth and Early Twentieth Centuries.* Toronto: University of Toronto Press, 1975.
Beaudoin, Réjean. *Naissance d'une littérature: Essai sur le messianisme et les débuts de la littérature canadienne-française (1850–1890).* Montreal: Boréal, 1989.
Bowering, George. *Imaginary Hand: Essays.* Edmonton: NeWest, 1988.
Brochu, André. *L'Instance critique, 1961–1973.* Montreal: Leméac, 1974.

Bibliography

Davey, Frank. *Canadian Literary Power*. Edmonton: NeWest, 1994.
   Reading Canadian Reading. Winnipeg: Turnstone Press, 1988.
   Surviving the Paraphrase: Eleven Essays on Canadian Literature. Winnipeg: Turnstone Press, 1983.
Daymond, Douglas, and Leslie Monkman, eds. *Towards a Canadian Literature: Essays, Editorials and Manifestoes*. 2 vols. Ottawa: Tecumseh, 1984–5.
Dragland, Stan. *Bees of the Invisible: Essays in Contemporary English Canadian Writing*. Toronto: Coach House Press, 1991.
Frye, Northrop. *The Bush Garden: Essays on the Canadian Imagination*. Toronto: House of Anansi Press, 1971.
   Divisions on a Ground: Essays on Canadian Culture. Ed. James Polk. Toronto: Anansi, 1982.
   Northrop Frye on Canada. Collected Works of Northrop Frye, vol. XII. Ed. Jean O'Grady and David Staines. Toronto: University of Toronto Press, 2004.
Gauvin, Lise. *La Fabrique de la langue: De François Rabelais à Réjean Ducharme*. Paris: Seuil, 2004.
Hammill, Faye. *Canadian Literature*. Edinburgh: Edinburgh University Press, 2007.
Hayward, Annette, and Agnès Whitfield, eds. *Critique et littérature québécoise: Critique de la littérature / littérature de la critique*. Montreal: Triptyque, 1992.
Heble, Ajay, Donna Palmateer Pennee, and J. R. (Tim) Struthers, eds. *New Contexts of Canadian Criticism*. Peterborough: Broadview, 1997.
Henighan, Stephen. *When Words Deny the World: The Reshaping of Canadian Writing*. Erin: Porcupine's Quill, 2002.
   Report on the Afterlife of Culture. Emeryville: Biblioasis, 2008.
Jones. D. G. *Butterfly on Rock: A Study of Themes and Images in Canadian Literature*. Toronto: University of Toronto Press, 1970.
Kertzer, Jonathan. *Worrying the Nation: Imagining a National Literature in English Canada*. Toronto: University of Toronto Press, 1998.
Lee, Dennis. *Savage Fields: An Essay on Literature and Cosmology*. Toronto: House of Anansi, 1977.
MacLulich, T. D. *Between Europe and America: The Canadian Tradition in Fiction*. Toronto: ECW Press, 1988.
Mandel, Eli. *Another Time*. Erin: Porcépic, 1977.
   ed. *Contexts of Canadian Criticism*. Chicago: University of Chicago Press, 1971.
Marchand, Philip. *Ripostes: Reflections on Canadian Literature*. Erin: Porcupine's Quill, 1998.
Marcotte, Gilles. *Littérature et circonstances*. Montreal: l'Hexagone, 1989.
Mathews, Robin. *Canadian Literature: Surrender or Revolution*. Toronto: Steel Rail, 1978.
Moss, John, ed. *Future Indicative: Literary Theory and Canadian Literature*. Ottawa: University of Ottawa Press, 1987.
Moss, John. *The Paradox of Meaning: Cultural Poetics and Critical Fictions*. Winnipeg: Turnstone Press, 1999.
Nepveu, Pierre. *L'Écologie du réel: Mort et naissance de la littérature québécoise contemporaine*. Montreal: Boréal, 1988.
New, William H. *Borderlands: How We Talk About Canada*. Vancouver: University of British Columbia Press, 1998.
New, William H. *Land Sliding: Imagining Space, Presence, and Power in Canadian Writing*. Toronto: University of Toronto Press, 1997.

Rigelhof, T. E. *This Is Our Writing.* Erin: Porcupine's Quill, 2000.
Sarkonak, Ralph, ed. "The Language of Difference: Writing in Quebec(ois)." *Special issue of Yale French Studies* 65 (1983).
Shouldice, Larry, ed. and tr. *Contemporary Quebec Criticism.* Toronto: University of Toronto Press, 1979.
Staines, David, ed. *The Canadian Imagination: Dimensions of a Literary Culture.* Cambridge, MA: Harvard University Press, 1977.
Verduyn, Christl, ed. *Literary Pluralities.* Peterborough: Broadview, 1998.
Wilson, Edmund. *O Canada: An American's Notes on Canadian Culture.* New York: Farrar, Straus and Giroux, 1965.
Woodcock, George. *Northern Spring: The Flowering of Canadian Literature.* Vancouver: Douglas and McIntyre, 1987.
  Odysseus Ever Returning: Essays on Canadian Writers and Writing. Toronto: McClelland and Stewart, 1970.
  The World of Canadian Writing. Vancouver/Seattle: Douglas and McIntyre/University of Washington Press, 1980.

Literary criticism: genres

See also numerous entries under the specialized headings of "Literary criticism: special topics."

Fiction: English

Davey, Frank. *Post-National Arguments: The Politics of the Anglophone-Canadian Novel since 1967.* Toronto: University of Toronto Press, 1993.
Dooley, D. J. *Moral Vision in the Canadian Novel.* Toronto: Clarke, Irwin, 1979.
Goldman, Marlene. *Rewriting Apocalypse in Canadian Fiction.* Montreal and Kingston: McGill-Queen's University Press, 2005.
Helms, Gabriele. *Challenging Canada: Dialogism and Narrative Techniques in Canadian Novels.* Montreal and Kingston: McGill-Queen's University Press, 2003.
Jones, Joseph, and Johanna Jones. *Canadian Fiction.* Boston: Twayne, 1981.
Kramer, Reinhold. *Scatology and Civility in the English-Canadian Novel.* Toronto: University of Toronto Press, 1997.
Moss, John. *Patterns of Isolation in English Canadian Fiction.* Toronto: McClelland and Stewart, 1974.
  Sex and Violence in the Canadian Novel: The Ancestral Present. Toronto: McClelland and Stewart, 1977.
  ed. *The Canadian Novel.* 4 vols. Toronto: NC Press, 1978.
Northey, Margot. *The Haunted Wilderness: The Gothic and Grotesque in Canadian Fiction.* Toronto: University of Toronto Press, 1976.
Quigley, Theresia. *The Child Hero in the Canadian Novel.* Toronto: NC Press, 1991.
Rae, Ian. *From Cohen to Carson: The Poet's Novel in Canada.* Montreal: McGill-Queen's University Press, 2008.
Williams, David. *Confessional Fictions: A Portrait of the Artist in the Canadian Novel.* Toronto: University of Toronto Press, 1991.
  Imagined Nations: Reflections on Media in Canadian Fiction. Montreal and Kingston: McGill-Queen's University Press, 2003.

Woodcock, George, ed. *The Canadian Novel in the Twentieth Century: Essays from Canadian Literature*. Toronto: McClelland and Stewart, 1975.

Smith, A. J. M., ed. *Masks of Fiction: Canadian Critics on Canadian Prose*. Toronto: McClelland and Stewart, 1961.

Fiction: French

Beaudoin, Réjean. *Le Roman québécois*. Montreal: Boréal, 1991.

Belleau, André. *Surprendre les voix*. Montreal: Boréal, 1986.

Harel, Simon. *Le Voleur de parcours: Identité et cosmopolitanisme dans la littérature québécoise contemporaine*. Longueil: le Préambule, 1989.

Lamontagne, André. *Le roman québécois contemporain: Les Voix sous les mots*. Montreal: Fides, 2004.

Mailhot, Laurent. *Ouvrir le livre*. Montreal: l'Hexagone, 1992.

Marcotte, Gilles. *Le Roman à l'imparfait: Essais sur le roman québécois d'aujourd'hui*. Montreal: La Presse, 1976.

Paré, François. *Les Littératures de l'exiguïté*. Hearst: Le Nordir, 1992.

Paterson, Janet M. *Moments postmodernes dans le roman québécois*. Ottawa: Les Presses de l'Université d'Ottawa, 1990. English version: *Postmodernism and the Quebec Novel*. Tr. David Homel and Charles Phillips. Toronto: University of Toronto Press, 1994.

Purdy, Anthony. *A Certain Difficulty of Being: Essays on the Quebec Novel*. Montreal and Kingston: McGill-Queen's University Press, 1990.

Shek, Ben-Zion. *Social Realism in the French-Canadian Novel*. Montreal: Harvest House, 1977.

Sirois, Antoine. *Lectures mythocritiques du roman québécois*. Montréal: Triptyche, 1999.

Short Fiction (English and French)

Bardolph, Jacqueline. *Telling Stories: Postcolonial Short Fiction in English*. Amsterdam and Atlanta: Rodopi, 2001.

ed. *Short Fiction in the New Literatures in English*. Nice: Faculté des Lettres et Sciences Humaines de Nice, 1989.

Boucher, Jean-Pierre. *Le Recueil de nouvelles: Études sur un genre littéraire dit mineur*. Saint-Laurent: Fides, 1992.

Carpentier, André, and Michel Lord. "Lectures de nouvelles québécoises." Special issue of *Tangence* 50 (March 1996).

Davis, Rocío G. *Transcultural Reinventions: Asian American and Asian Canadian Short-Story Cycles*. Toronto: TSAR, 2001.

Dvořák, Marta, and William H. New, eds. *Tropes and Territories: Short Fiction, Postcolonial Readings, Canadian Writing in Context*. Montreal and Kingston: McGill-Queen's University Press, 2007.

Hancock, Geoff, ed. *Magic Realism: An Anthology*. Toronto: Aya, 1980.

Ingram, Forrest L. *Representative Short Story Cycles of the Twentieth Century: Studies in a Literary Genre*. The Hague: Mouton, 1971.

Kennedy, J. Gerald, ed. *Modern American Short Story Sequences*. Cambridge: Cambridge University Press, 1995.

King, Thomas. *The Truth about Stories: A Native Narrative*. Toronto: Anansi, 2003.

Lecker, Robert. *On the Line: Readings in the Short Fiction of Clark Blaise, John Metcalf and Hugh Hood*. Downsview: ECW Press, 1982.

Lynch, Gerald. *The One and the Many: English-Canadian Short Story Cycles*. Toronto: University of Toronto Press, 2001.

Lynch, Gerald, and Angela Arnold Robbeson, eds. *Dominant Impressions: Essays on the Canadian Short Story*. Ottawa: University of Ottawa Press, 1999.

Metcalf, John. *Kicking Against the Pricks*. Downsview: ECW, 1982.

Metcalf, John, and J. R. (Tim) Struthers, eds. *How Stories Mean*. Erin: Porcupine's Quill, 1993.

Morin, Lise. *La Nouvelle fantastique québécoise de 1960 à 1985: Entre le hasard et la fatalité*. Quebec: Nuit blanche, 1996.

Nagel, James. *The Contemporary American Short-Story Cycle: The Ethnic Resonance of Genre*. Baton Rouge: Louisiana State University Press, 2001.

New, W. H. *Dreams of Speech and Violence: The Art of the Short Story in Canada and New Zealand*. Toronto: University of Toronto Press, 1987.

Nischik, Reingard M., ed. *The Canadian Short Story: Interpretations*. Rochester: Camden, 2007.

Pellerin, Gilles. *Nous aurions un petit genre: Publier des nouvelles*. Quebec: L'instant même, 1997.

Struthers, J. R. (Tim), ed. *The Montreal Story Tellers: Memoirs, Photographs, Critical Essays*. Montreal: Véhicule, 1985.

Vauthier, Simone. *Reverberations: Explorations in the Canadian Short Story*. Concord: House of Anansi, 1993.

Whitfield, Agnès, and Jacques Cotnam, eds. *La Nouvelle: Écriture(s) et lecture(s)*. Toronto: GREF, 1993.

Drama: English

Anthony, Geraldine, ed. *Stage Voices: Twelve Canadian Playwrights Talk about Their Lives and Work*. Toronto and Garden City: Doubleday Canada, 1978.

Appleford, Rob, ed. *Aboriginal Drama and Theatre*. Toronto: Playwrights Canada Press, 2005.

Bessai, Diane. *Playwrights of Collective Creation*. Toronto: Simon & Pierre, 1992.

Brask, Per, ed. *Contemporary Issues in Canadian Drama*. Winnipeg: Blizzard, 1995.

Brask, Per, and William Morgan, eds. *Aboriginal Voices: Amerindian, Inuit, and Sami Theatre*. Baltimore: Johns Hopkins University Press, 1992.

Conolly, L. W. *Canadian Drama and the Critics: 1987*. Vancouver: Talonbooks, 1995.

Däwes, Birgit. *Native North American Theater in a Global Age*. Heidelberg: Universitätsverlag Winter, 2006.

Filewood, Alan. *Collective Encounters: Documentary Theatre in English Canada*. Toronto: University of Toronto Press, 1987.

—— *Performing Canada: The Nation Enacted in the Imagined Theatre*. Kamloops: University College of the Cariboo, 2002.

Glaap, Albert-Reiner, and Rolf Althof, eds. *On-Stage and Off-Stage: English Canadian Drama in Discourse*. St. John's: Breakwater, 1996.

Grace, Sherrill. *Regression and Apocalypse: Studies in North American Literary Expressionism*. Toronto: University of Toronto Press, 1989.

Grace, Sherrill, and Albert-Reiner Glaap, eds. *Performing National Identities: International Perspectives on Contemporary Canadian Theatre*. Vancouver: Talonbooks, 2003.

Bibliography

Hodkinson, Yvonne. *Female Parts: The Arts and Politics of Female Playwrights.* Montreal: Black Rose, 1991.

Johnston, Denis W. *Up the Mainstream: The Rise of Toronto's Alternative Theatres, 1968–1975.* Toronto: University of Toronto Press, 1991.

Knowles, Ric. *The Theatre of Form and the Production of Meaning: Contemporary Canadian Dramaturgies.* Toronto: ECW Press, 1999.

Maufort, Marc, and Franca Bellarsi, eds. *Crucible of Cultures: Anglophone Drama at the Dawn of a New Millennium.* Brussels: Peter Lang, 2002.

eds. *Siting the Other: Re-visions of Marginality in Australian and English-Canadian Drama.* Brussels: Peter Lang, 2001.

McKinnie, Michael. *City Stages: Theatre and Urban Space in a Global City.* Toronto: University of Toronto Press, 2007.

Mojica, Monique, with Natalie Rewa, eds. "Native Theatre." Special issue of *Canadian Theatre Review* 68 (1991).

Much, Rita, ed. *Women on the Canadian Stage: The Legacy of Hrotsvit.* Winnipeg: Blizzard, 1992.

Rubin, Don. *Canada on Stage: Canadian Theatre Review Yearbook.* 8 vols. Downsview: CTR Publications, 1974–1982.

Saddlemyer, Ann, and Richard Plant, eds. *Later Stages: Essays in Ontario Theatre from the First World War to the 1970s.* Toronto: University of Toronto Press, 1997.

Stuart, E. Ross. *The History of Prairie Theatre: The Development of Theatre in Alberta, Manitoba and Saskatchewan, 1833–1982.* Toronto: Simon and Pierre, 1984.

Usmiani, Renate. *Second Stage: The Alternative Theatre Movement in Canada.* Vancouver: University of British Columbia Press, 1983.

Wagner, Anton, ed. *Contemporary Canadian Theatre: New World Visions.* Toronto: Simon and Pierre, 1985.

ed. *Establishing Our Boundaries: English-Canadian Theatre Criticism.* Toronto: University of Toronto Press, 1999.

Walker, Craig Stewart. *The Buried Astrolabe: Canadian Dramatic Imagination and Western Tradition.* Montreal and Kingston: McGill-Queen's University Press, 2001.

Wallace, Robert. *Producing Marginality: Theatre and Criticism in Canada.* Saskatoon: Fifth House, 1990.

Drama: French

Beauchamp, Hélène, and Joël Beddows, eds. *Les Théâtres professionels du Canada francophone: entre mémoire et rupture.* Ottawa: le Nordir, 2001.

Beauchamp, Hélène, and Gilbert David, eds. *Théâtres québécois et canadiens-français au XXe siècle: Trajectoires et territoires.* Montreal: Presses de l'Université du Québec, 2003.

Donohoe, Joseph I. Jr., and Jonathan M. Weiss, eds. *Essays on Modern Quebec Theater.* East Lansing: Michigan State University Press, 1995.

Godin, Jean-Cleo, and Laurent Mailhot. *Le Théâtre québécois. Introduction à dix dramaturges contemporains.* Montreal: Hurtubise HMH, 1970.

Théâtre québécois II: Nouveaux auteurs, autres spectacles. Montreal: Hurtubise HMH, 1980.

Godin, Jean Cléo, and Dominique Lafon, eds. *Dramaturgies québécoises des années quatre-vingt.* Montreal: Leméac, 1999.

Hébert, Chantal, and Irène Perelli-Contos, eds. *Le Théâtre et ses nouvelles dynamiques narratives*. Vol. II of *La Narrativité contemporaine au Québec*. Quebec: Les Presses de l'Université Laval, 2004.

Ladouceur, Louise. *Making the Scene: La Traduction du théâtre d'une langue officielle à l'autre au Canada*. Quebec: Nota bene, 2005.

Legris, Renée, Jean-Marc Larrue, André-G. Bourassa, and Gilbert David, eds. *Le Théâtre au Québec, 1825–1980: Repères et perspectives*. Montreal: VLB éditeur, 1988.

O'Neill-Karch, Mariel. *Théâtre franco-ontarien: Espaces ludiques*. Vanier: l'Interligne, 1992.

O'Neill-Karch, Mariel, and Pierre Karch, eds. *Augustin Laperrière (1829–1903)*. Ottawa: David, 2002.

Pagé, Pierre. *Histoire de la radio au Québec: information, éducation, culture*. Montreal: Fides, 2007.

Poetry: English

Bentley, D. M. R. *The Confederation Group of Canadian Poets, 1880–1897*. Toronto: University of Toronto Press, 2004.

Brown, E. K. *On Canadian Poetry*. Ottawa: Tecumseh Press, 1973 [1943].

Camlot, Jason, and Todd Swift, eds. *Language Acts: Anglo-Québec Poetry 1976 to the 21st Century*. Montreal: Véhicule, 2007.

Collin, W. E. *The White Savannahs*. Ed. Douglas Lochhead. Toronto: University of Toronto Press, 1975 [1936].

Dudek, Louis, and Michael Gnarowski, eds. *The Making of Modern Poetry in Canada: Essential Articles on Contemporary Canadian Poetry in English*. Toronto: Ryerson Press, 1967.

Glickman, Susan. *The Picturesque and the Sublime: A Poetics of the Canadian Landscape*. Montreal and Kingston: McGill-Queen's University Press, 1998.

Higgins, Iain, ed. "Contemporary Poetics." Special issue of *Canadian Literature* 155 (Winter 1997).

Hogg, Robert, ed. *An English Canadian Poetics*. Vol. I: *The Confederation Poets*. Vancouver: Talonbooks, 2009.

Hurst, Alexandra. *The War Among the Poets: Issues of Plagiarism and Patronage Among the Confederation Poets*. London: Canadian Poetry Press, 1994.

Irvine, Dean. *Editing Modernity: Women and Little-Magazine Cultures in Canada, 1916–1956*. Toronto: University of Toronto Press, 2008.

Lilburn, Tim, ed. *Thinking and Singing: Poetry and the Practice of Philosophy*. Toronto: Cormorant, 2002.

Mackay, Don. *Vis à vis: Fieldnotes on Poetry and Wilderness*. Wolfville: Gaspereau, 2001.

McNeilly, Kevin, ed. "Women & Poetry." Special issue of *Canadian Literature* 166 (Autumn 2000).

Pacey, Desmond. *Ten Canadian Poets: A Group of Biographical and Critical Essays*. Toronto: Ryerson, 1958.

Smith, A. J. M. *On Poetry and Poets: Selected Essays*. Toronto: McClelland and Stewart, 1977.

    Towards a View of Canadian Letters: Selected Critical Essays, 1928–1971. Vancouver: University of British Columbia Press, 1973.

    ed. *The Book of Canadian Poetry: A Critical and Historical Anthology*. Toronto: W. J. Gage, 1943 [1941].

Stevens, Peter, ed. *The McGill Movement: A. J. M. Smith, F. R. Scott and Leo Kennedy*. Toronto: Ryerson, 1969.

Trehearne, Brian. *Aestheticism and the Canadian Modernists: Aspects of a Poetic Influence.* Montreal and Kingston: McGill-Queen's University Press, 1989.
Trehearne, Brian. *The Montreal Forties: Modernist Poetry in Translation.* Toronto: University of Toronto Press, 1999.
Ware, Tracy, ed. *A Northern Romanticism: Poets of the Confederation.* Ottawa: Tecumseh, 2000.
Woodcock, George, ed. *Colony and Confederation: Early Canadian Poets and Their Background.* Vancouver: University of British Columbia Press, 1974.

Poetry: French

Blais, Jacques. *De l'ordre et de l'aventure: La Poésie au Québec de 1934 à 1944.* Quebec: Presses de l'Université Laval, 1975.
Bonenfant, Luc, and François Dumont, eds. "Situations du poème en prose au Québec." Special issue of *Études françaises* 39.3 (2003).
Dumont, François. *La Poésie québécoise.* Montreal: Boréal, 1999.
Filteau, Claude. *Poétiques de la modernité, 1895–1948.* Montreal: l'Hexagone, 1994.
Leroux, Georges, and Pierre Ouellet, eds. *L'Engagement de la parole: Politique du poème.* Montreal: VPL, 2005.
Lortie, Jeanne d'Arc. *La Poésie nationaliste au Canada français, 1606–1867.* Quebec: Presses de l'Université Laval, 1975.
Marcotte, Gilles. *Le Temps des poètes: Description critique de la poésie actuelle au Canada français.* Montreal: Hurtubise HMH, 1969.
Nepveu, Pierre. *Intérieurs du nouveau monde: Essais sur les littératures du Québec et des Amériques.* Montreal: Boréal, 1998.
Royer, Jean. *Introduction à la poésie québécoise: Les Poètes et les œuvres des origines à nos jours.* Montreal: Bibliothèque québécoise, 1989.
Yergeau, Robert, ed. *Itinéraires de la poésie: enjeux actuels en Acadie, en Ontario et dans l'Ouest canadien.* Ottawa: le Nordir, 2004.

Life-writing, and other non-fiction (English and French)

Baena, Rosalía, ed. *Transculturing Auto/Biography: Forms of Life Writing.* London: Routledge, 2006.
Buss, Helen M. *Mapping Our Selves: Canadian Women's Autobiography in English.* Montreal and Kingston: McGill-Queen's University Press, 1993.
Caumartin, Anne, and Martine-Emmanuelle Lapointe, eds. *Parcours de l'essai québécois (1980–2000).* Montreal: Nota bene, 2004.
Egan, Susanna. *Mirror Talk: Genres of Crisis in Contemporary Autobiography.* Chapel Hill: University of North Carolina Press, 1999.
Egan, Susanna, and Gabriele Helms, eds. "Auto/biography." Special issue of *Canadian Literature* 172 (Spring 2002).
—— eds. "Autobiography and Changing Identities." Special issue of *biography* 24 (Winter 2001).
Hébert, Pierre, with Marilyn Baszczynski. *Le Journal intime au Québec: Structure, évolution, réception.* Montreal: Fides, 1988.
Kadar, Marlene, ed. *Essays on Life Writing: From Genre to Critical Practice.* Toronto: University of Toronto Press, 1992.
Neuman, Shirley, ed. "Reading Canadian Autobiography." Special issue of *Essays on Canadian Writing* 60 (Winter 1996).

Rak, Julie, ed. *Auto/biography in Canada: Critical Directions*. Waterloo: Wilfrid Laurier University Press, 2005.

Raoul, Valerie. *Distinctly Narcissistic: Diary Fiction in Quebec*. Toronto: University of Toronto Press, 1993.

Saul, Joanne. *Writing the Roaming Subject: The Biotext in Canadian Literature*. Toronto: University of Toronto Press, 2006.

Comic books and graphic novels (English and French)

Bell, John. *Invaders from the North: How Canada Conquered the Comic Book Universe*. Toronto: Dundurn, 2006.

   ed. *Canuck Comics*. Montreal: Matrix, 1986.

   ed. *Guardians of the North: The National Superhero in Canadian Comic-Book Art*. Ottawa: National Archives of Canada, 1992.

Carpentier, André, ed. "La Bande dessinée." Special issue of *La Barre du jour* (Winter 1975).

Falardeau, Mira. *La Bande dessinée au Québec*. Montreal: Boréal, 1994.

Hirsh, Michael, and Patrick Loubert, eds. *The Great Canadian Comic Books*. Toronto: Peter Martin Associates, 1971.

Lepage, Françoise. *Histoire de la littérature pour la jeunesse: Québec et francophonies du Canada, suivi d'un Dictionnaire des auteurs et des illustrateurs*. Orléans: David, 2000.

Viau, Michel. *BDQ: Répertoire des publications de bandes dessinées au Québec des origines à nos jours*. Laval: Mille-Îles, 1999.

Literary criticism: special topics (including selected background reading)

Aboriginal writing, literary representation of Aboriginal people

Acoose, Janice. *Iskwewak, Kah 'ki yaw ni Wahkomakanak: Neither Indian Princesses Nor Easy Squaws*. Toronto: Women's Press, 1995.

Armstrong, Jeannette C., ed. *Looking at the Words of Our People: First Nations Analysis of Literature*. Penticton: Theytus, 1993.

Braz, Albert. *The False Traitor: Louis Riel in Canadian Literature*. Toronto: University of Toronto Press, 2003.

David, Jennifer. *Story Keepers: Conversations with Aboriginal Writers*. Owen Sound: Ningwakwe Learning Press, 2004.

Eigenbrod, Renate. *Travelling Knowledges: Positioning the Im/Migrant Reader of Aboriginal Literatures in Canada*. Winnipeg: University of Manitoba Press, 2005.

Eigenbrod, Renate, and Jo-Ann Episkenew, eds. *Creating Community: A Roundtable on Canadian Aboriginal Literature*. Penticton and Brandon: Theytus/Bearpaw Publishing, 2002.

Eigenbrod, Renate, and Renée Hulan, eds. *Aboriginal Oral Traditions: Theory, Practice, Ethics*. Halifax: Fernwood Publishing with the Gorsebrook Research Institute, 2008.

Emberley, Julia. *Defamiliarizing the Aboriginal: Cultural Practices and Decolonization in Canada*. Toronto: University of Toronto Press, 2007.

Francis, Daniel. *The Imaginary Indian: The Image of the Indian in Canadian Culture*. Vancouver: Arsenal Pulp, 1992.

Groening, Laura Smyth. *Listening to Old Woman Speak: Natives and AlterNatives in Canadian Literature*. Montreal and Kingston: McGill-Queen's University Press, 2005.

Hoy, Helen. *How Should I Read These? Native Women Writers in Canada.* Toronto: University of Toronto Press, 2001.
Horne, Dee. *Contemporary American Indian Writing: Unsettling Literature.* New York: Peter Lang, 1999.
Hulan, Renée, ed. *Native North America: Critical and Cultural Perspectives.* Toronto: ECW Press, 1999.
King, Thomas. *The Truth About Stories: A Native Narrative.* Toronto: House of Anansi, 2003.
Lutz, Hartmut, ed. *Contemporary Challenges: Conversations with Canadian Native Authors.* Saskatoon: Fifth House, 1991.
Miller, Mary Jane. *Outside Looking In: Viewing First Nations Peoples in Canadian Dramatic Television Series.* Montreal: McGill-Queen's University Press, 2008.
Monkman, Leslie. *A Native Heritage: Images of the Indian in English-Canadian Literature.* Toronto: University of Toronto Press, 1981.
Moses, Daniel David. *Pursued by a Bear: Talks, Monologues and Tales.* Toronto: Exile Editions, 2005.
New, William H., ed. *Native Writers and Canadian Writing.* Vancouver: University of British Columbia Press, 1990.
Ortiz, Simon J., ed. *Speaking for the Generations: Native Writers on Native Writing.* Tucson: University of Arizona Press, 1998.
Petrone, Penny. *Native Literature in Canada: From the Oral Tradition to the Present.* Toronto: Oxford University Press, 1990.
Ruffo, Armand Garnet, ed. *(Ad)dressing Our Words: Aboriginal Perspectives on Aboriginal Literatures.* Penticton: Theytus, 2001.
Taylor, Drew Hayden, ed. *Me Funny: A Far-reaching Exploration of Humour, Wittiness and Repartee Dominant Among First Nations People of North America, as Witnessed, Experienced and Created Directly by Themselves and with the Inclusion of Outside but Reputable Sources Necessarily Familiar with the Indigenous Sense of Humour as Seen from an Objective Perspective.* Vancouver: Douglas and McIntyre, 2005.
Tehariolina, Marguerite Vincent. *La Nation huronne: Son histoire, sa culture, son esprit.* Quebec: Pélican, 1984.

Comparative literature, international scholarship in Canadian literature, translation

Antor, Heinz, Gordon Bölling, Annette Kern-Stähler, and Klaus Stierstorfer, eds. *Refractions of Canada in European Literature and Culture.* New York: Walter de Gruyter, 2005.
Antor, Heinz, Sylvia Brown, John Considine, and Klaus Stierstorfer, eds. *Refractions of Germany in Canadian Literature and Culture.* Berlin: Walter de Gruyter, 2003.
Bayard, Caroline. *The New Poetics in Canada and Québec: From Concretism to Modernism.* Toronto: University of Toronto Press, 1989.
Bayard, Caroline, and Jack David. *Out-Posts/Avant-Postes.* Erin: Porcépic, 1978.
Beaudoin, Réjean, and André Lamontagne, eds. "Francophone/Anglophone." Special issue of *Canadian Literature* 175 (Winter 2002).
Behounde, Ekitike. *Dialectique de la ville et de la campagne chez Gabrielle Roy et chez Mongo Beti.* Montreal: Éditions Qui, 1983.
Blaber, Ronald. *Roguery: The Picaresque Tradition in Australia, Canadian and Indian Fiction.* Springwood: Butterfly, 1990.

Blodgett, E. D. *Configuration: Essays in the Canadian Literatures.* Downsview: ECW Press, 1982.
Brydon, Diana, and Helen Tiffin. *Decolonising Fictions.* Sydney: Dangaroo, 1993.
Camerlain, Lorraine, Nicole Deschamps, Lise Gauvin, Jean Cléo Godin, Laurent Mailhot, Ginette Michaud, Pierre Nepveu, and Irène Hall-Paquin. *Lectures européennes de la littérature québécoise.* Montreal: Leméac, 1982.
Corse, Sarah M. *Nationalism and Literature: The Politics of Culture in Canada and the United States.* Cambridge: Cambridge University Press, 1997.
Dupuis, Gilles, and Dominique Garand, eds. *Italie-Québec: Croisements et coïncidences littéraires.* Montreal: Nota bene, 2009.
Flotow, Luise von, and Reingard Nischik, eds. *Translating Canada.* Ottawa: University of Ottawa Press, 2007.
Fratta, Carla, and Élisabeth Nardout-Lafarge, eds. *Italies imaginaires du Québec.* Montreal: Fides, 2003.
Gauvin, Lise, and Jean-Marie Klinkenberg, eds. *Littérature et institutions au Québec et en Belgique francophone.* Brussels: Editions Labor, 1985.
Gerols, Jacqueline. *Le Roman québécois en France.* LaSalle: Hurtubise HMH, 1984.
Giguère, Richard. *Exil, révolte et dissidence: Étude comparée des poésies québécoise et canadienne (1925–1955).* Quebec: Les Presses de l'Université Laval, 1984.
Goldie, Terry. *Fear and Temptation: The Image of the Indigene in Canadian, Australian, and New Zealand Literatures.* Kingston: McGill-Queen's University Press, 1989.
Gould, Karen, Joseph T. Jockel, and William Metcalfe. *Northern Exposures: Scholarship on Canada in the United States.* Washington: Association for Canadian Studies in the United States, 1993.
Gross, Konrad, and Wolfgang Klooss, eds. *English Literature of the Dominions: Writings on Australia, Canada and New Zealand.* Würzburg: Königshausen and Neumann, 1981.
Huggan, Graham. *Territorial Disputes: Maps and Mapping Strategies in Contemporary Canadian and Australian Fiction.* Toronto: University of Toronto Press, 1994.
Hughes, Terrance. *Gabrielle Roy et Margaret Laurence: Deux chemins, une recherche.* Saint-Boniface: Éditions du Blé, 1983.
Irvine, Lorna M. *Critical Spaces: Margaret Laurence and Janet Frame.* Columbia: Camden House, 1995.
Khoo, Tseen-Ling. *Banana Bending: Asian-Australian and Asian-Canadian Literatures.* Montreal and Kingston: McGill-Queen's University Press, 2003.
Khoo, Tseen-Ling, and Kam Louie, eds. *Culture, Identity, Commodity: Diasporic Chinese Literatures in English.* Montreal and Kingston: McGill-Queen's University Press, 2005.
Kroetsch, Robert, and Reingard M. Nischik, eds. *Gaining Ground: European Critics on Canadian Literature.* Edmonton: NeWest, 1985.
La Bossière, Camille, ed. *Translation in Canadian Literature.* Ottawa: University of Ottawa Press, 1983.
Lecker, Robert. *Borderlands: Essays in Canadian-American Relations.* Toronto: ECW Press, 1991.
McDougall, Russell, and Gillian Whitlock, eds. *Australian/Canadian Literatures in English: Comparative Perspectives.* Melbourne: Methuen Australia, 1987.
Matthews, John Pengwerne. *Tradition in Exile: A Comparative Study of Social Influences on the Development of Australian and Canadian Poetry in the Nineteenth Century.* Toronto: University of Toronto Press, 1962.

Moisan, Clément. *L'Âge de la littérature canadienne: Essai.* Montreal: Hurtubise HMH, 1969.
  Poésie des frontières: Étude comparée des poésies canadienne et québécoise. Quebec: Hurtubise HMH, 1986. English version: *A Poetry of Frontiers: Comparative Studies in Quebec/Canadian Literature.* Tr. George Lang and Linda Weber. Victoria: Press Porcépic, 1983.
Rousseau, Guildo. *L'Image des États-Unis dans la littérature québécoise (1775-1930).* Sherbrooke: Naaman, 1981.
Savary, Claude, ed. *Les Rapports culturels entre le Québec et les Etats-Unis.* Quebec: Institut québécois de recherche sur la culture, 1984.
Siemerling, Wilfried. *Discoveries of the Other: Alterity in the Work of Leonard Cohen, Hubert Aquin, Michael Ondaatje, and Nicole Brossard.* Toronto: University of Toronto Press, 1994.
Simon, Sherry, ed. *Culture in Transit: Translating the Literature of Quebec.* Montreal: Véhicule Press, 1995.
Söderlind, Sylvia. *Margin/Alias: Language and Colonization in Canadian and Québécois Fiction.* Toronto: University of Toronto Press, 1991.
Sutherland, Ronald. *New Hero: Essays in Comparative Quebec/Canadian Literature.* Toronto: Macmillan, 1977.
  Second Image: Comparative Studies in Quebec/Canadian Literature. Toronto: New Press, 1971.
Tougas, Gerard. *Les Écrivains d'expression française et la France.* Paris: Denoël, 1973.
Waterston, Elizabeth. *Rapt in Plaid: Canadian Literature and Scottish Tradition.* Toronto: University of Toronto Press, 2001.
Whitfield, Agnès, ed. *Writing Between the Lines: Portraits of Canadian Anglophone Translators.* Waterloo: Wilfrid Laurier University Press, 2006.

Cultural history and myths

Aquin, Stéphane, ed. *The Global Village: The 1960s.* Montreal: Museum of Fine Arts, 2003.
Archbold, Rick. *I Stand for Canada: The Story of the Maple Leaf Flag.* Toronto: Macfarlane, Walter and Ross, 2002.
Atwood, Margaret. *Strange Things: The Malevolent North in Canadian Literature.* Oxford: Clarendon, 1995.
Bouchard, Joë, Daniel Chartier, and Amélie Nadeau, eds. *Problématiques de l'imaginaire du Nord en littérature, cinéma et arts visuels.* Montreal: Université du Québec à Montréal, 2004.
Coates, Colin, and Cecilia Morgan. *Heroines and History: Representations of Madeleine de Verchères and Laura Secord.* Toronto: University of Toronto Press, 2002.
Coleman, Daniel. *White Civility: The Literary Project of English Canada.* Toronto: University of Toronto Press, 2006.
Doyle, James. *North of America: Images of Canada in the Literature of the United States, 1775-1900.* Toronto: ECW Press, 1983.
Edwardson, Ryan. *Canadian Content: Culture and the Quest for Nationhood.* Toronto: University of Toronto Press, 2007.
Francis, Daniel. *A Road for Canada: The Illustrated Story of the Trans-Canada Highway.* Vancouver: Stanton Atkins and Dosil Publishers, 2006.

Grace, Sherrill E. *Canada and the Idea of North*. Montreal and Kingston: McGill-Queen's University Press, 2001.
Grant, George. *Lament for a Nation: The Defeat of Canadian Nationalism*. Ottawa: Carleton University Press, 1995 [1970].
— *Technology and Empire: Perspectives on North America*. Toronto: House of Anansi, 1969.
Gray, Charlotte. *The Museum Called Canada: 25 Rooms of Wonder*. Toronto: Random House, 2004.
Gwyn, Sandra. *The Private Capital: Ambition and Love in the Age of Macdonald and Laurier*. Toronto: McClelland and Stewart, 1984.
Heaman, E. A. *The Inglorious Arts of Peace: Exhibitions in Canadian Society during the Nineteenth Century*. Toronto: University of Toronto Press, 1999.
Hulan, Renée. *Northern Experience and the Myths of Canadian Culture*. Montreal: McGill-Queen's University Press, 2002.
Innes, Harold. *A History of the Canadian Pacific Railway*. Toronto: McClelland and Stewart, 1923.
Keneally, Rhona Richman, and Johanne Sloan, eds. *Expo '67: Not Just a Souvenir*. Toronto: University of Toronto Press, 2010 [forthcoming].
Kostash, Myrna. *Long Way from Home: The Story of the Sixties Generation in Canada*. Toronto: Lorimer, 1980.
Kröller, Eva-Marie, Margery Fee, Iain Higgins, and Alain-Michel Rocheleau, eds. "Remembering the Sixties." Special issue of *Canadian Literature* 152/3 (Spring/Summer 1997).
Lemire, Maurice. *Le Mythe de l'Amérique dans l'imaginaire "canadien."* Quebec: Nota bene, 2003.
Lortie, André. *The 60s: Montreal Thinks Big*. Montreal: Centre for Canadian Architecture, 2004.
McDougall, Robert L. *Totems: Essays on the Cultural History of Canada*. Ottawa: Tecumseh, 1990.
McGregor, Gaile. *The Wacousta Syndrome: Explorations in the Canadian Langscape*. Toronto: University of Toronto Press, 1985.
McKillop, A. B. *A Disciplined Intelligence: Critical Inquiry and Canadian Thought in the Victorian Era*. Montreal: McGill-Queen's University Press, 1979.
Miedema, Gary R. *For Canada's Sake: Public Religion, Centennial Celebrations, and the Remaking of Canada in the 1960s*. Montreal and Kingston: McGill-Queen's University Press, 2005.
Nelles, H. V. *The Art of Nation-Building: Pageantry and Spectacle at Quebec's Tercentenary*. Toronto: University of Toronto Press, 1999.
Palmer, Bryan D. *Canada's 1960s: The Ironies of Identity in a Rebellious Era*. Toronto: University of Toronto Press, 2009.
Porter, John. *The Vertical Mosaic: An Analysis of Social Class and Power in Canada*. Toronto: University of Toronto Press, 1965.
Revie, Linda L. *The Niagara Companion: Explorers, Artists, and Writers at the Falls, from Discovery Through the Twentieth Century*. Waterloo: Wilfrid Laurier University Press, 2003.
Trudel, Marcel. *Mythes et réalités du Québec*. Saint-Laurent: Bibliothèque québécoise, 2006 [2001].
Turner, Margaret. *Imagining Culture: New World Narrative and the Writing of Canada*. Montreal: McGill-Queen's University Press, 1995.

Warwick, Jack. *The Long Journey: Literary Themes of French Canada*. Toronto: University of Toronto Press, 1968.
Weinmann, Heinz. *Du Canada au Québec: Généalogie d'une histoire*. Montreal: l'Hexagone, 1987.

Gender, sexuality and women's studies

Bacchi, Carol Lee. *Liberation Deferred? The Ideas of the English-Canadian Suffragists, 1877–1918*. Toronto: University of Toronto Press, 1983.
Boutilier, Beverly, and Alison Prentice, eds. *Creating Historical Memory: English-Canadian Women and the Work of History*. Vancouver: University of British Columbia Press, 1997.
Carrière, Marie J. *Writing in the Feminine in French and English Canada: A Question of Ethics*. Toronto: University of Toronto Press, 2002.
Cavell, Richard, and Peter Dickinson, eds. *Sexing the Maple: A Canadian Sourcebook*. Peterborough: Broadview Press, 2006.
Coleman, Daniel. *Masculine Migrations: Reading the Postcolonial Male in "New Canadian" Narratives*. Toronto: University of Toronto Press, 1999.
Cook, Sharon Ann. *"Through Sunshine and Shadow": The Woman's Christian Temperance Union, Evangelicalism, and Reform in Ontario, 1874–1930*. Montreal and Kingston: McGill-Queen's University Press, 1995.
Danylewycz, Marta. *Taking the Veil: An Alternative to Marriage, Motherhood, and Spinsterhood in Quebec, 1840–1920*. Ed. Paul-André Linteau, Alison Prentice, and William Westfall. Toronto: McClelland and Stewart, 1987.
Darias-Beautell, Eva. *Graphies and Grafts: (Con)Texts and (Inter)Texts in the Fiction of Four Contemporary Canadian Women*. Brussels: Peter Lang, 2001.
Dean, Misao. *Practising Femininity: Domestic Realism and the Performance of Gender in Early Canadian Fiction*. Toronto: University of Toronto Press, 1998.
Dickinson, Peter. *Here is Queer: Nationalisms, Sexualities, and the Literature of Canada*. Toronto: University of Toronto Press, 1999.
— *Screening Gender, Framing Genre: Canadian Literature into Film*. Toronto: University of Toronto Press, 2007.
Dybikowski, Ann, Victoria Freeman, Daphne Marlatt, Barbara Pulling, and Betsy Warland, eds. *In the Feminine: Women and Words / Les femmes et les mots Conference*. Edmonton: Longspoon, 1985.
Fiamengo, Janice. *The Woman's Page: Journalism and Rhetoric in Early Canada*. Toronto: University of Toronto Press, 2008.
Fowler, Marian. *The Embroidered Tent: Five Gentlewomen in Early Canada: Elizabeth Simcoe, Catharine Parr Traill, Susanna Moodie, Anna Jameson, Lady Dufferin*. Toronto: Anansi, 1982.
Goldie, Terry. *Pink Snow: Homotextual Possibilities in Canadian Fiction*. Peterborough: Broadview, 2003.
Goldman, Marlene. *Paths of Desire: Images of Exploration and Mapping in Canadian Women's Writing*. Toronto: University of Toronto Press, 1997.
Gould, Karen. *Writing in the Feminine: Feminism and Experimental Writing in Quebec*. Carbondale: Southern Illinois University Press, 1990.
Gray, Charlotte. *Sisters in the Wilderness: The Lives of Susanna Moodie and Catharine Parr Traill*. Toronto: Penguin, 1999.
Green, Mary Jean. *Women and Narrative Identity: Rewriting the Quebec National Text*. Montreal and Kingston: McGill-Queen's University Press, 2001.

Hammill, Faye. *Literary Culture and Female Authorship in Canada 1760–2000*. Amsterdam and New York: Rodopi, 2003.
Howells, Coral Ann. *Contemporary Canadian Women's Fiction: Refiguring Identities*. New York: Palgrave Macmillan, 2003.
  Private and Fictional Words: Canadian Women Novelists of the 1970s and 1980s. London and New York: Methuen, 1987.
Irvine, Lorna. *Sub/Version: Canadian Fictions by Women*. Toronto: ECW Press, 1986.
Joubert, Lucie, and Annette Hayward, eds. *Vieille fille: Lectures d'un personnage*. Montréal: Triptyque, 2000.
Korinek, Valerie. *Roughing It in the Suburbs: Reading* Chatelaine *Magazine in the Fifties and Sixties*. Toronto: University of Toronto Press, 2000.
Lang, Marjory. *Women Who Made the News: Female Journalists in Canada, 1880–1945*. Montreal and Kingston: McGill-Queen's University Press, 1999.
MacMillan, Carrie, Lorraine McMullen, Elizabeth Waterston, *Silenced Sextet: Six Nineteenth-Century Women Novelists*. Montreal: McGill-Queen's University Press, 1993.
McMullen, Lorraine, ed. *Re(dis)covering Our Foremothers: Nineteenth-Century Canadian Women Writers*. Ottawa: University of Ottawa Press, 1990.
McPherson, Kathryn, Cecilia Morgan, and Nancy M. Forestell, eds. *Gendered Pasts: Historical Essays in Femininity, and Masculinity in Canada*. Toronto: University of Toronto Press, 2003.
Neuman, Shirley, and Smaro Kamboureli, eds. *A Mazing Space: Writing Canadian, Women Writing*. Edmonton: Longspoon/NeWest, 1986.
Paradis, Suzanne. *Femme fictive, femme réelle: Le Personnage féminin dans le roman canadien-français, 1884–1966*. Quebec: Garneau, 1966.
Peterman, Michael. *Sisters in Two Worlds: A Visual Biography of Susanna Moodie and Catharine Parr Traill*. Toronto: Doubleday Canada, 2007.
Prentice, Allison, Paula Bourne, Gail Cuthbert Brant, Beth Light, Wendy Mitchinson, and Naomi Black. *Canadian Women: A History*. 2nd edn. Toronto: Harcourt, Brace & Company, 1996 [1988].
Rayside, David. *Queer Inclusions, Continental Divisons: Public Recognition of Sexual Diversity in Canada and the United States*. Toronto: University of Toronto Press, 2008.
Rimstead, Roxanne. *Remnants of Nation: On Poverty Narratives by Women*. Toronto: University of Toronto Press, 2001.
Scheier, Libby, Sarah Sheard, and Eleanor Wachtel, eds. *Language in Her Eye: Views on Women and Gender by Canadian Women Writing in English*. Toronto: Coach House, 1990.
Smart, Patricia. *Writing in the Father's House: The Emergence of the Feminine in the Quebec Literary Tradition*. Toronto: University of Toronto Press, 1991. English version of *Écrire dans la maison du père: L'Émergence du féminin dans la tradition littéraire du Québec*. Montreal: Québec/Amérique, 1988.
Strong-Boag, Veronica, and Anita Clair Fellman, eds. *Rethinking Canada: The Promise of Women's History*. 3rd edn. Toronto: Oxford University Press, 1997 [1986].
Sturgess, Charlotte, and Martin Kuester, eds. *Reading(s) from a Distance: European Perspectives on Canadian Women's Writing*. Augsburg: Wissner-Verlag, 2008.

Exploration, fur trade, and travel

Allen, John Logan, ed. *North American Exploration*. 3 vols. Lincoln: University of Nebraska Press, 1997.

Bibliography

Bouvet, Rachel, André Carpentier, and Daniel Chartier, eds. *Nomades, voyageurs, explorateurs, déambulateurs: Les Modalités du parcours dans la littérature*. Paris: l'Harmattan, 2006.

Brown, Jennifer S. H. *Strangers in Blood: Fur Trade Company Families in Indian Country*. Vancouver: University of British Columbia Press, 1980.

Cooke, Alan, and Clive Holland. *The Exploration of Northern Canada, 500 to 1920: A Chronology*. Toronto: Arctic History, 1978.

Delâge, Denys. *Le Pays renversé: Amérindiens et Européens en Amérique du Nord-Est, 1600–1664*. Montreal: Boréal, 1985.

Eber, Dorothy Harley. *Encounters on the Passage: Inuit Meet the Explorers*. Toronto: University of Toronto Press, 2008.

Emberly, Julia V. *The Cultural Politics of Fur*. Montreal and Kingston: McGill-Queen's University Press, 1997.

Francis, Daniel, and Toby Morantz. *Partners in Furs: A History of the Fur Trade in Eastern James Bay, 1660–1870*. Kingston: McGill-Queen's University Press, 1982.

Given, Brian J. *A Most Pernicious Thing: Gun Trading and Native Warfare in the Early Contact Period*. Ottawa: Carleton University Press, 1994.

Goetzmann, William H. *Exploration and Empire: The Explorer and the Scientist in the Winning of the American West*. Austin: Texas State Historical Association, 2000.

Greenfield, Bruce. *Narrating Discovery: The Romantic Explorer in American Literature, 1790–1855*. New York: Columbia University Press, 1992.

Havard, Gilles. *Empire et métissages: Français et Indiens dans le pays d'en haut, 1660–1715*. Sillery: Septentrion, 2003.

——— *La Grande Paix de Montréal de 1701: Les Voies de la diplomatie franco-amérindienne*. Montreal: Recherches amérindiennes au Québec, 1992.

Innis, Harold A. *The Fur Trade in Canada: An Introduction to Canadian Economic History*. New Haven: Yale University Press, 1930.

Jacquin, Philippe. *Les Indiens blancs: Français et Indiens en Amérique de Nord, XVIe–XVIIIe siècle*. Paris: Payot, 1987.

Jennings, Francis. *The Ambiguous Iroquois Empire: The Covenant Chain Confederation of Indian Tribes with English Colonies from Its Beginnings to the Lancaster Treaty of 1744*. New York: Norton, 1984.

Jetten, Marc. *Enclaves amérindiennes: Les "Réductions" du Canada, 1637–1701*. Sillery: Septentrion, 1994.

Kröller, Eva-Marie. *Canadian Travellers in Europe, 1851–1900*. Vancouver: University of British Columbia Press, 1987.

Morency, Jean, Jeannette Den Toonder, and Jaap Lintvelt, eds. *Romans de la route et voyages identitaires*. Quebec: Nota bene, 2006.

Morgan, Cecilia. *"A Happy Holiday": English-Canadians and Transatlantic Tourism, 1870–1930*. Toronto: University of Toronto Press, 2008.

Rajotte, Pierre, with Anne-Marie Carle and François Couture. *Le Récit de voyage au XIXe siècle: Aux frontières du littéraire*. Montréal: Triptyque, 1997.

Roy, Wendy. *Maps of Difference: Canada, Women, and Travel*. Montreal and Kingston: McGill-Queen's University Press, 2005.

Ruggles, Richard I. *A Country So Interesting: The Hudson's Bay Company and Two Centuries of Mapping, 1670–1870*. Montreal and Kingston: McGill-Queen's University Press, 1991.

Sleeper-Smith, Susan. *Indian Women and French Men: Rethinking Cultural Encounter in the Western Great Lakes*. Amherst: University of Massachusetts Press, 2001.

Smith, Sidonie. *Moving Lives: Twentieth-Century Women's Travel Writing*. Minneapolis: University of Minnesota Press, 2001.

Van Kirk, Sylvia. *Many Tender Ties: Women in Fur Trade Society in Western Canada, 1670–1870*. Winnipeg: Watson and Dwyer, 1980.

Warkentin, John, ed. *The Western Interior of Canada: A Record of Geographical Discovery, 1612–1917*. Toronto: McClelland and Stewart, 1964.

Warkentin, Germaine, ed. *Canadian Exploration Literature: An Anthology*. Toronto: Dundurn, 2006 [1993].

ed., *Critical Issues in Editing Exploration Texts*. Toronto: University of Toronto Press, 1995.

White, Richard. *The Middle Ground: Indians, Empires, and Republics in the Great Lakes Region, 1650–1815*. Cambridge: Cambridge University Press, 1991.

History and literature

Atwood, Margaret. *In Search of* Alias Grace: *On Writing Canadian Historical Fiction*. Charles R. Bronfman Lecture in Canadian Studies. Ottawa: University of Ottawa Press, 1997.

Berger, Carl. *The Sense of Power: Studies in the Ideas of Canadian Imperialism, 1867–1914*. Toronto: University of Toronto Press, 1970.

The Writing of Canadian History: Aspects of English-Canadian Historical Writing since 1900. 2nd edn. Toronto: University of Toronto Press, 1986 [1976].

Bouchard, Gérard. *Genèse des nations et cultures du Nouveau Monde: Essai d'histoire comparée*. Montreal: Boréal, 2000.

Colavincenzo, Marc. *"Trading Magic for Fact," Fact for Magic: Myth and Mythologizing in Postmodern Canadian Historical Fiction*. Amsterdam and New York: Rodopi, 2003.

Duffy, Dennis. *Sounding the Iceberg: An Essay on Canadian Historical Novels*. Toronto: ECW Press, 1986.

Fenton, William. *Re-writing the Past: History and Origin in Howard O'Hagan, Jack Hodgins, George Bowering and Chris Scott*. Rome: Bulzoni, 1988.

Finlay, J. L., and D. N. Sprague. *The Structure of Canadian History*. 6th edn. Scarborough: Prentice, 2000 [1979].

Friesen, Gerald. *Citizens and Nation: An Essay on History, Communication and Canada*. Toronto: University of Toronto Press, 2000.

Gagnon, Serge. *Le Québec et ses historiens de 1840 à 1920: La Nouvelle France de Garneau à Groulx*. Quebec: Les Presses de l'Université Laval, 1978.

Gwyn, Sandra. *Tapestry of War: A Private View of Canadians in the Great War*. Toronto: HarperCollins, 1992.

Howells, Coral Ann, ed. *Where Are the Voices Coming From? Canadian Culture and the Legacies of History*. Amsterdam and New York: Rodopi, 2004.

Kuester, Martin. *Framing Truths: Parodic Structures in Contemporary English-Canadian Historical Novels*. Toronto: University of Toronto Press, 1992.

Lemire, Maurice. *Les Grands Thèmes nationalistes du roman historique canadien-français*. Quebec: Presses de l'Université Laval, 1970.

Morton, Desmond. *When Your Number's Up: The Canadian Soldier in the First World War*. Toronto: Random House, 1993.

Novak, Dagmar. *Dubious Glory: The Two World Wars and the Canadian Novel.* New York: Peter Lang, 2000.
Taylor, M. Brook. *Promoters, Patriots, and Partisans: Historiography in Nineteenth-Century English Canada.* Toronto: University of Toronto Press, 1989.
Vance, Jonathan. *Death So Noble: Memory, Meaning, and the First World War.* Vancouver: University of British Columbia Press, 1997.
Wyile, Herb. *Speaking in the Past Tense: Canadian Novelists on Writing Historical Fiction.* Waterloo: Wilfrid Laurier University Press, 2007.
— *Speculative Fictions: Contemporary Canadian Novelists and the Writing of History.* Montreal and Kingston: McGill-Queen's University Press, 2002.

Missionaries (New France)

Bruneau, Marie-Florine. *Women Mystics Confront the Modern World: Marie de l'Incarnation (1599–1672) and Madame Guyon (1648–1717).* Albany: State University of New York Press, 1998.
Ferland, Rémi. *Les Relations des Jésuites: Un art de la persuasion, procédés de rhétorique et function conative dans les Relations du Père Paul Lejeune.* Quebec: Les Éditions de la huit, 1994.
Le Bras, Yvon, and Pierre Dostie. *L'Amérindien dans les Relations du père Paul Lejeune, 1632–1641: Le lecteur suborné dans cinq textes missionnaires de la Nouvelle France.* Sainte-Foy: Les Éditions de la huit, 1994.
Leclercq, Jean. *L'Amour des lettres et le désir de Dieu: Initiation aux auteurs monastiques du Moyen Age.* Paris: Cerf, 1957. English version: *The Love of Learning and the Desire for God: A Study of Monastic Culture.* Tr. Catharine Misrahi. New York: Fordham University Press, 1961.
Martin, A. Lynn. *The Jesuit Mind: The Mentality of an Elite in Early Modern France.* London: Cornell University Press, 1988.
Ouellet, Réal, ed. *Rhétorique et conquête missionnaire: Le Jésuite Paul Lejeune.* Sillery: Septentrion, 1993.
Sadlier, Anna T. *Women of Catholicity: Memoirs of Margaret O'Carroll, Isabella of Castile, Margaret Roper, Marie de l'Incarnation, Marguerite Bourgeoys.* New York: Benziger Bros., 1917.

Multiculturalism, migration and globalism

Bailyn, Bernard, and Philip D. Morgan, eds. *Strangers within the Realm: Cultural Margins of the First British Empire.* Chapel Hill: University of North Carolina Press, 1991.
Balan, Jars, ed. *Identifications: Ethnicity and the Writer in Canada.* Edmonton: Canadian Institute of Ukrainian Studies, 1982.
Bannerji, Himani. *The Dark Side of the Nation: Essays on Multiculturalism, Nationalism, and Gender.* Toronto: Canadian Scholars, 2000.
Beauregard, Guy, ed. "Asian Canadian Studies." Special issue of *Canadian Literature* 199 (Winter 2008).
Bissoondath, Neil. *Selling Illusions: The Cult of Multiculturalism in Canada.* Toronto: Penguin, 2002 [1994].
Bisztray, George. *Hungarian-Canadian Literature.* Toronto: University of Toronto Press, 1987.
Chao, Lien. *Beyond Silence: Chinese Canadian Literature in English.* Toronto: TSAR, 1997.
Cheadle, Norman, and Lucien Pelletier, eds. *Canadian Cultural Exchange: Translation and Transculturation / Échanges culturels au Canada: Traduction et transculturation.* Waterloo: Wilfrid Laurier Press, 2007.

Christie, Nancy, ed. *Transatlantic Subjects: Ideas, Institutions, and Social Experience in Post-Revolutionary British North America*. Montreal: McGill-Queen's University Press, 2008.

Clarke, George Elliott. *Odysseys Home: Mapping African-Canadian Literature*. Toronto: University of Toronto Press, 2002.

Davis, Geoffrey V., Peter H. Marsden, Bénédicte Leden, and Marc Delrez, eds. *Towards a Transcultural Future: Literature and Society in a "Post"-Colonial World*. Amsterdam: Rodopi, 2005.

Davis, Rocío G., and Rosalía Baena, eds. *Tricks with a Glass: Writing Ethnicity in Canada*. Amsterdam: Rodopi, 2000.

Day, Richard J. F. *Multiculturalism and the History of Canadian Diversity*. Toronto: University of Toronto Press, 2000.

Deer, Glenn, ed. "Asian Canadian Writing." Special issue of *Canadian Literature* 163 (Winter 1999).

Dorsinville, Max. *Caliban without Prospero: Essays on Quebec and Black Literature*. Erin: Porcépic, 1974.

Ertler, Klaus-Dieter, and Martin Löschnigg, eds. *Canada in the Sign of Migration and Trans-Culturalism: From Multi- to Trans-Culturalism / Le Canada sous le signe de la migration et du transculturalisme: Du multiculturalisme au transnationalisme*. Frankfurt: Peter Lang, 2004.

Faragher, John Mack. *A Great and Noble Scheme: The Tragic Story of the Expulsion of the French Acadians from Their American Homeland*. New York: Norton, 2005.

Ferens, Dominika. *Edith and Winnifred Eaton: Chinatown Missions and Japanese Romances*. Urbana: University of Illinois Press, 2002.

Genetsch, Martin. *The Texture of Identity: The Fiction of MG Vassanji, Neil Bissoondath, and Rohinton Mistry*. Toronto: TSAR, 2007.

Greenstein, Michael. *Third Solitudes: Tradition and Discontinuity in Jewish Canadian Literature*. Kingston: McGill-Queen's University Press, 1989.

Harel, Simon. *Le Voleur de parcours: Identité et cosmopolitanisme dans la littérature québécoise contemporaine*. Montreal: le Préambule, 1989.

Hilf, Susanne. *Writing the Hyphen: The Articulation of Interculturalism in Contemporary Chinese-Canadian Literature*. Frankfurt: Peter Lang, 2002.

Hutcheon, Linda, and Marion Richmond, eds. *Other Solitudes: Canadian Multicultural Fictions*. Toronto: Oxford University Press, 1990.

Kamboureli, Smaro. *Scandalous Bodies: Diasporic Literature in English Canada*. Don Mills: Oxford University Press, 2000.

——— ed. *Making a Difference: Canadian Multicultural Literature*. Toronto: Oxford University Press, 2006 [1996].

Kamboureli, Smaro, and Roy Miki, eds. *Trans.Can.Lit.: Resituating the Study of Canadian Literature*. Waterloo: Wilfrid Laurier University Press, 2007.

Lewis, Paula Gilbert. *Traditionalism, Nationalism and Feminism: Women Writers of Quebec*. Westport: Greenwood Press, 1985.

Mackey, Eva. *The House of Difference: Cultural Politics and National Identity in Canada*. Toronto: University of Toronto Press, 2002.

Massey, Irving. *Identity and Community: Reflections on English, Yiddish and French Literature in Canada*. Detroit: Wayne State University Press, 1994.

Moisan, Clément, and Renate Hildebrand. *Ces étrangers du dedans: Une histoire de l'écriture migrante au Québec, 1937–1997*. Quebec: Nota bene, 2001.
Moss, Laura, ed. "Black Writing in Canada." Special issue of *Canadian Literature* 182 (Autumn 2004).
Peepre-Bordessa, Mari. *Transcultural Travels: Essays in Canadian Literature and Society*. Lund: Lund University Press, 1994.
Pivato, Joseph, ed. *Contrasts: Comparative Essays on Italian Canadian Writing*. Montreal: Guernica, 1985.
Ravvin, Norman. *A House of Words: Jewish Writing, Identity and Memory*. Montreal: McGill-Queen's University Press, 1997.
Riedel, Walter. *The Old World and the New: Literary Perspectives of German-Speaking Canadians*. Toronto: University of Toronto Press, 1984.
Schama, Simon. *Rough Crossings: Britain, the Slaves and the American Revolution*. New York: Ecco, 2006.
Siemerling, Winfried, ed. *Writing Ethnicity: Cross-Cultural Consciousness in Canadian and Québécois Literature*. Toronto: ECW Press, 1996.
Siemerling, Winfried, and Katrin Schwenk, eds. *Cultural Difference and the Literary Text: Pluralism and the Limits of Authenticity in North American Literatures*. Iowa City: University of Iowa Press, 1996.
Vassanji, M. G., ed. *A Meeting of Streams: South Asian Canadian Literature*. Toronto: TSAR, 1985.
Wah, Fred. *Faking It: Poetics and Hybridity*. Edmonton: NeWest, 2000.
Walker, James St. G. *The Black Loyalists: The Search for a Promised Land in Nova Scotia and Sierra Leone, 1783–1870*. Toronto: University of Toronto Press, 1992 [1976].
White-Parks, Annette. *Sui Sin Far / Edith Maude Eaton: A Literary Biography*. Urbana: University of Illinois Press, 1995.
Wickberg, Edgar, ed. *From China to Canada: A History of the Chinese Communities in Canada*. Toronto: McClelland and Stewart, 1982.
Winks, Robin. *The Blacks in Canada: A History*. Montreal and Kingston: McGill-Queen's University Press, 1997 [1971].

Postcolonialism and postmodernism

Adam, Ian, and Helen Tiffin, eds. *Past the Last Post: Theorizing Post-Colonialism and Post-Modernism*. Calgary: University of Calgary Press, 1990.
Banerjee, Mita. *The Chutneyfication of History: Salman Rushdie, Michael Ondaatje, Bharati Mukherjee and the Postcolonial Debate*. Heidelberg: C. Winter, 2002.
Bayard, Caroline, and André Lamontagne, eds. "Postmodernismes: Poïesis des Amériques, ethos des Europes." Special issue of *Études littéraires* 27 1 (Summer 1994).
Brydon, Diana, ed. "Testing the Limits: Postcolonial Theories and Canadian Literature." Special issue of *Essays on Canadian Writing* 56 (Fall 1995).
Deer, Glenn. *Postmodern Canadian Fiction and the Rhetoric of Authority*. Montreal and Kingston: McGill-Queen's University Press, 1994.
Green, Mary Jean, Karen Gould, Micheline Rice-Maximin, Keith L. Walker, and Jack A. Yeager, eds. *Postcolonial Subjects: Francophone Women Writers*. Minneapolis: University of Minnesota Press, 1996.

Hutcheon, Linda. *The Canadian Postmodern: A Study of Contemporary English-Canadian Fiction*. Toronto: Oxford University Press, 1988.
  Irony's Edge: The Theory and Politics of Irony. London and New York: Routledge, 1994.
  Narcissistic Narrative: The Metafictional Paradox. London: Methuen, 1984 [1980].
  A Poetics of Postmodernism: History, Theory, Fiction. New York: Routledge, 1988.
  Splitting Images: Contemporary Canadian Ironies. Toronto: Oxford University Press, 1991.
Moss, Laura, ed. *Is Canada Postcolonial? Unsettling Canadian Literature*. Waterloo: Wilfrid Laurier University Press, 2003.
Mukherjee, Arun. *Postcolonialism: My Living*. Toronto: TSAR, 1998.
Simon, Sherry, and Paul St-Pierre, eds. *Changing the Terms: Translating in the Postcolonial Era*. Ottawa: University of Ottawa Press, 2000.
Sugars, Cynthia, ed. *Home-Work: Postcolonialism, Pedagogy and Canadian Literature*. Ottawa: University of Ottawa Press, 2004.
  ed. *Unhomely States: Theorizing English-Canadian Postcolonialism*. Peterborough: Broadview, 2004.
Vautier, Marie. *New World Myth: Postmodernism and Postcolonialism in Canadian Fiction*. Montreal and Kingston: McGill-Queen's University Press, 1998.

Quiet Revolution and Quebec sovereignty movement

Arguin, Maurice. *Le Roman québécois de 1944 à 1965: Symptômes du colonialisme et signes de libération*. Montreal: l'Hexagone, 1985.
Balthazar, Louis. *Bilan du nationalisme au Québec*. Montreal: l'Hexagone, 1986.
Brunet, Michel. *Quebec-Canada anglais: Deux itinéraires, un affrontement*. Montreal: HMH Hurtubise, 1968.
Cambron, Micheline. *Une société, un récit: Discours culturel au Québec (1967–1976)*. Montreal: l'Hexagone, 1989.
Cameron, David. *Nationalism, Self-Determination and the Quebec Question*. Toronto: Macmillan, 1974.
Ferretti, Andrée, and Gaston Miron, eds. *Les Grands Textes indépendantistes*, vol. I: *Écrits, discours et manifestes québécois, 1774–1992*. Montreal: l'Hexagone, 1992; Ferretti, Andrée, ed. *Les Grands Textes indépendantistes*, vol. II: *Écrits, discours et manifestes québécois, 1992–2003*. Montreal: Typo, 2004.
Handler, Richard. *Nationalism and the Politics of Culture in Quebec*. Madison: The University of Wisconsin Press, 1988.
Ilien, Gildas. *La Place des Arts et la Révolution tranquille: Les Fonctions politiques d'un centre culturel*. Quebec: Presses de l'Université Laval, 1999.
Larose, Jean. *La Petite Noirceur*. Montreal: Boréal, 1987.
Larrue, Jean-Marc. *Le Monument inattendu: Le Monument national de Montréal, 1893–1993*. Montreal: HMH Hurtubise, 1993.
Lemco, Jonathan. *Turmoil in the Peaceable Kingdom: The Quebec Sovereignty Movement and Its Implications for Canada and the United States*. Toronto: University of Toronto Press, 1994.
Marcotte, Gilles. *Le Roman à l'imparfait: Essais sur le roman québécois d'aujourd'hui*. Montreal: la Presse, 1976.
Monière, Denis. *Développement des idéologies au Québec*. Montreal: Québec / Amérique, 1977.

Proulx, Serge, and Pierre Vallières, eds. *Changer de société: Déclin du nationalisme culturel, et alternatives sociales au Québec*. Montreal: Québec / Amérique, 1982.

Reid, Malcolm. *The Shouting Signpainters: A Literary and Political Account of Quebec Revolutionary Nationalism*. Toronto: McClelland and Stewart, 1972.

Thomson, Dale C. *Jean Lesage and the Quiet Revolution*. Toronto: Macmillan, 1984.

Trofimenkoff, Susan Mann. *The Dream of Nation: A Social and Intellectual History of Quebec*. Toronto: Gage, 1983.

Vincenthier, Georges. *Histoire des idées au Québec: Des troubles de 1837 au référendum de 1980*. Montreal: VLB, 1983.

Regionalism, urbanism and eco-criticism

Anctil, Pierre, Norman Ravvin, and Sherry Simon, eds. *New Readings of Yiddish Montreal / Traduire le Montréal Yiddish*. Ottawa: Ottawa University Press, 2007.

Ball, John Clement, Robert Viau, and Linda Warley, eds. "Writing Canadian Space / Écrire l'espace canadien." Special issue of *Studies in Canadian Literature / Études en littérature canadienne* 23.1 (1998).

Beeler, Karin, and Dee Horne, eds. *Diverse Landscapes: Re-Reading Place Across Cultures in Contemporary Canadian Writing*. Prince George: University of Northern British Columbia Press, 1996.

Berger, Carl. *Science, God, and Nature in Victorian Canada*. Toronto: University of Toronto Press, 1983.

Driver, Elizabeth, ed. *Culinary Landmarks: A Bibliography of Canadian Cookbooks, 1825–1949*. Toronto: University of Toronto Press, 2008.

Dupré, Louise, Jaap Lintvelt, and Janet Paterson, eds. *Sexuation, espace, écriture*. Quebec: Nota bene, 2002.

Edwards, Justin D., and Douglas Ivison, eds. *Downtown Canada: Writing Canadian Cities*. Toronto: University of Toronto Press, 2005.

Fiamengo, Janice, ed. *Other Selves: Animals in the Canadian Literary Imagination*. Ottawa: University of Ottawa Press, 2007.

Fuller, Danielle. *Writing the Everyday: Women's Textual Communities in Atlantic Canada*. Montreal and Kingston: McGill-Queen's University Press, 2004.

Garand, Dominique. *Griffe du polémique: Le Conflit entre les régionalistes et les exotiques*. Montreal: l'Hexagone, 1989.

Gates, Barbara T., and Ann B. Shteir, eds. *Natural Eloquence: Women Reinscribe Science*. Madison: University of Wisconsin Press, 1997.

Harrison, Dick. *Unnamed Country: The Struggle for a Canadian Prairie Fiction*. Edmonton: University of Alberta Press, 1977.

Hayward, Annette. *La Querelle du régionalisme au Québec 1904–1931: Vers l'autonomisation de la littérature québécoise*. Ottawa: le Nordir, 2006.

Higgins, Iain, ed. "Nature/Culture." Special issue of *Canadian Literature* 170 / 1 (Autumn / Winter 2001).

Jordan, David M. *New World Regionalism: Literature in the Americas*. Toronto: University of Toronto Press, 1994.

Keahey, Deborah. *Making it Home: Place in Canadian Prairie Literature*. Winnipeg: University of Manitoba Press, 1998.

Keefer, Janice Kulyk. *Under Eastern Eyes: A Critical Reading of Maritime Fiction.* Toronto: University of Toronto Press, 1987.
Keith, W. J. *Literary Images of Ontario.* Toronto: University of Toronto Press, 1992.
Larue, Monique, with Jean-François Chassey. *Promenades littéraires dans Montréal.* Montreal: Québec / Amérique, 1989.
Lemire, Maurice. *Mouvement régionaliste dans la littérature québécoise, 1902–1940.* Quebec: Nota bene, 2007.
Nepveu, Pierre, and Gilles Marcotte, eds. *Montréal imaginaire: Ville et littérature.* Saint-Laurent: Fides, 1992.
Omhovère, Claire. *Sensing Space: The Poetics of Geography in Contemporary English-Canadian Writing.* Brussels: Peter Lang, 2007.
Poirier, Guy, ed. "Montréal et Vancouver: Parcours urbains dans la littérature et le cinéma." Special issue of *Tangence* 48 (October 1995).
Polk, James. *Wilderness Writers: Ernest Thompson Seton, Charles G. D. Roberts, Grey Owl.* Toronto: Clarke, Irwin, 1972.
Ricou, Laurie. *The Arbutus / Madrone Files: Reading the Pacific Northwest.* Edmonton: NeWest, 2001.
  Salal: Listening for the Northwest Understory. Edmonton: NeWest, 2007.
  Vertical Man / Horizontal World: Man and Landscape in Canadian Prairie Fiction. Vancouver: University of British Columbia Press, 1973.
Riegel, Christian, and Herb Wylie, eds. *A Sense of Place: Re-Evaluating Regionalism in Canadian and American Writing.* Edmonton: University of Alberta Press, 1998.
Simon, Sherry. *Translating Montreal: Episodes in the Life of a Divided City.* Montreal: McGill-Queen's University Press, 2006.
Stanton, Victoria, and Vincent Tinguely. *Impure: Reinventing the Word: The Theory, Practice and Oral History of "Spoken Word" in Montreal.* Montreal: Véhicule Press, 2001.
Thacker, Robert, *The Great Prairie Fact and Literary Imagination.* Albuquerque: University of New Mexico Press, 1989.
Von Baeyer, Edwinna. *Rhetoric and Roses: A History of Canadian Gardening, 1900–1930.* Markham: Fitzhenry and Whiteside, 1984.
Von Baeyer, Edwinna, and Pleasance Crawford, eds. *Garden Voices: Two Centuries of Canadian Garden Writing.* Toronto: Random, 1995.
Willmott, Glenn. *Unreal Country: Modernity in the Canadian Novel in English.* Montreal and Kingston: McGill-Queen's University Press, 2002.
Zeller, Suzanne *Inventing Canada: Early Victorian Science and the Idea of a Transcontinental Nation.* Toronto: University of Toronto Press, 1987.

Individual authors (selected): anglophone
Acorn, Milton
Lemm, Richard. *Milton Acorn: In Love and Anger.* Ottawa: Carleton University Press, 1999.
Gudgeon, Chris. *Out of This World: The Natural History of Milton Acorn.* Vancouver: Arsenal Pulp Press, 1996.

Bibliography

Armstrong, Jeannette

Cardinal, Douglas, and Armstrong, Jeannette. *The Native Creative Process: A Collaborative Discourse Between Douglas Cardinal and Jeannette Armstrong*. With Photographs by Greg Young-Ing. Penticton: Theytus Books, 1991.

Atwood, Margaret

Bouson, J. Brooks. *Brutal Choreographies: Oppositional Strategies and Narrative Design in the Novels of Margaret Atwood*. Amherst: University of Massachusetts Press, 1993.
Cooke, Nathalie. *Margaret Atwood: A Biography*. Toronto: ECW Press, 1998.
Davey, Frank. *Margaret Atwood: A Feminist Poetics*. Vancouver: Talonbooks, 1984.
Grace, Sherrill. *Violent Duality: A Study of Margaret Atwood*. Ed. Ken Norris. Montreal: Véhicule, 1980.
Hengen, Shannon, and Ashley Thomson, ed. *Margaret Atwood: A Reference Guide 1988–2005*. Lanham: The Scarecrow Press, 2007.
Howells, Coral Ann, *Margaret Atwood*. 2nd edn. Basingstoke: Palgrave Macmillan, 2005 [1996].
  ed. *The Cambridge Companion to Margaret Atwood*. Cambridge: Cambridge University Press, 2006.
McCombs, Judith, ed. *Critical Essays on Margaret Atwood*. Boston: G. K. Hall, 1988.
Moss, John, and Tobi Kozakewich, eds. *Margaret Atwood: The Open Eye*. Ottawa: Ottawa University Press, 2006.
Nicholson, Colin, ed. *Margaret Atwood: Writing and Subjectivity: New Critical Essays*. Basingstoke: Macmillan, 1994.
Nischik, Reingard, ed. *Margaret Atwood: Works and Impact*. Rochester: Camden House, 2000.
Staels, Hilde. *Margaret Atwood's Novels: A Study of Narrative Discourse*. Tübingen: Francke Verlag, 1995.
Sullivan, Rosemary. *The Red Shoes: Margaret Atwood Starting Out*. Toronto: HarperFlamingo, 1998.
Tolan, Fiona. *Margaret Atwood: Feminism and Fiction*. Amsterdam and New York: Rodopi, 2007.
Wilson, Sharon Rose. *Margaret Atwood's Fairy-Tale Sexual Politics*. Jackson: University Press of Mississippi, 1993.
  ed. *Margaret Atwood's Textual Assassinations: Recent Poetry and Fiction*. Columbus: Ohio State University Press, 2003.
  Myths and Fairy Tales in Contemporary Women's Fiction: From Atwood to Morrison. New York: Palgrave Macmillan, 2008.

Avison, Margaret

Kent, David, ed. *Lighting Up the Terrain: The Poetry of Margaret Avison*. Toronto: ECW, 1987.

Birney, Earle

Aichinger, Peter. *Earle Birney*. Boston: Twayne, 1979.
Cameron, Elspeth. *Earle Birney: A Life*. Toronto: Penguin, 1994.
Nesbitt, Bruce, ed. *Earle Birney*. Toronto: McGraw-Hill Ryerson, 1974.

Bissett, Bill

Pew, Jeff, and Stephen Roxborough, eds. *Radiant danse uv being: a poetic portrait of bill bissett*. Roberts Creek: Nightwood Editions, 2006.
Rogers, Linda, ed. *bill bissett: Essays on His Works*. Toronto: Guernica, 2002.

Blaise, Clarke

Lecker, Robert. *An other I: The Fictions of Clark Blaise*. Toronto: ECW Press, 1988.

Bowering, George

Kröller, Eva-Marie. *George Bowering: Bright Circles of Colour*. Vancouver: Talonbooks, 1992.

Mancini, Donato. *Causal Talk: Interviews with Four Poets: rob mclennan, David W. McFadden, Dorothy Trujillo Lusk & George Bowering*. Ottawa: Above/Ground Press, 2004.

Miki, Roy. *A Record of Writing: An Annotated and Illustrated Bibliography of George Bowering*. Vancouver: Talonbooks, 1989.

Brand, Dionne

Butling, Pauline, and Susan Rudy. *Poets Talk: Conversations with Robert Kroetsch, Daphne Marlatt, Erin Mouré, Dionne Brand, Marie Annharte Baker, Jeff Derksen, and Fred Wah*. Edmonton: University of Alberta Press, 2005.

Brooke, Frances

McMullen, Lorraine. *An Odd Attempt in a Woman: The Literary Life of Frances Brooke*. Vancouver: University of British Columbia Press, 1983.

Buckler, Ernest

Bissell, Claude. *Ernest Buckler Remembered*. Toronto: University of Toronto Press, 1989.

Chambers, Robert D. *Sinclair Ross & Ernest Buckler*. Vancouver and Montreal: Copp Clark and McGill-Queen's University Press, 1975.

Cook, Gregory M., ed. *Ernest Buckler*. Toronto and New York: McGraw-Hill Ryerson, 1972.

Dvořák, Marta. *Ernest Buckler: Rediscovery and Reassessment*. Waterloo: Wilfrid Laurier University Press, 2001.

Young, Alan R. *Ernest Buckler*. Toronto: McClelland and Stewart, 1976.

Callaghan, Morley

Boire, Gary. *Morley Callaghan: Literary Anarchist*. Toronto: ECW Press, 1994.

Conron, Brandon. *Morley Callaghan*. New York: Twayne, 1966.

Pell, Barbara. *Faith and Fiction: A Theological Critique of the Narrative Strategies of Hugh MacLennan and Morley Callaghan*. Waterloo: Wilfrid Laurier University Press, 1998.

Campbell, Wilfred

Klinck, Carl F. *Wilfred Campbell: A Study in Late Provincial Victorianism*. Toronto: Ryerson, 1942.

Carr, Emily

Blanchard, Paula. *The Life of Emily Carr*. Vancouver: Douglas and McIntyre, 1987.

Crean, Susan. *The Laughing One: A Journey to Emily Carr*. Toronto: HarperFlamingoCanada, 2001.

Moray, Gerta. *Unsettling Encounters: First Nations Imagery in the Art of Emily Carr*. Vancouver: University of British Columbia Press, 2006.

Shadbolt, Doris. *The Art of Emily Carr*. Toronto and Vancouver: Clarke, Irwin and Douglas and McIntyre, 1979.

Tippett, Maria. *Emily Carr: A Biography*. Toronto: Oxford University Press, 1979.

Clarke, Austin

Algoo-Baksh, Stella. *Austin C. Clarke: A Biography*. Toronto: ECW Press, 1994.

Cohen, Leonard

Gnarowski, Michael. *Leonard Cohen: The Artist and His Critics*. Toronto and New York: McGraw-Hill Ryerson, 1976.

Morley, Patricia A. *The Immoral Moralists: Hugh MacLennan and Leonard Cohen*. Toronto: Clarke, Irwin, 1972.

Ondaatje, Michael. *Leonard Cohen*. Toronto: McClelland and Stewart, 1970.

Scobie, Stephen. *Intricate Preparations: Writing Leonard Cohen*. Toronto: ECW Press, 2000.

Scobie, Stephen. *Leonard Cohen*. Vancouver: Douglas and McIntyre, 1978.

Cohen, Matt

Gibson, Graeme, Wayne Grady, Dennis Lee, and Priscila Uppal, eds. *Uncommon Ground: A Celebration of Matt Cohen*. Toronto: Knopf Canada, 2002.

Connor, Ralph

Ferré, John P. *A Social Gospel for Millions: The Religious Bestsellers of Charles Sheldon, Charles Gordon, and Harold Bell Wright*. Bowling Green: Bowling Green State University Popular Press, 1988.

Crawford, Isabella Valancy

Farmiloe, Dorothy. *Isabella Valancy Crawford: The Life and the Legends*. Ottawa: Tecumseh Press, 1983.

Galvin, Elizabeth. *Isabella Valancy Crawford: We Scarcely Knew Her*. Toronto: Natural Heritage / Natural History, 1994.

Davies, Robertson

Diamond-Nigh, Lynne. *Robertson Davies: Life, Work, and Criticism*. Toronto: York, 1997.

Grant, Judith Skelton. *Robertson Davies: Man of Myth*. Toronto: Viking, 1994.

La Bossière, Camille R., and Linda Morra, eds. *Robertson Davies: A Mingling of Contrarieties*. Ottawa: University of Ottawa Press, 2001.

DeMille, James

Monk, Patricia. *The Gilded Beaver: An Introduction to the Life and Work of James De Mille*. Toronto: ECW, 1991.

Duncan, Sara Jeannette

Dean, Misao. *A Different Point of View: Sara Jeannette Duncan*. Montreal and Kingston: McGill-Queen's University Press, 1991.

Fowler, Marian. *Redney: A Life of Sara Jeannette Duncan*. Toronto: Anansi, 1983.

Tausky, Thomas E. *Sara Jeannette Duncan: Novelist of Empire*. Port Credit: P. D. Meany, 1980.

Findley, Timothy

Bailey, Anne Geddes. *Timothy Findley and the Aesthetics of Fascism*. Vancouver: Talonbooks, 1998.

Bailey, Anne Geddes, and Karen Grandy, eds. *Paying Attention: Critical Essays on Timothy Findley*. Toronto: ECW, 1998.
Brydon, Diana. *Timothy Findley*. New York: Twayne, 1998.
Krause, Dagmar. *Timothy Findley's Novels between Ethics and Postmodernism*. Würzburg: Königshausen and Neumann, 2005.
Pennee, Donna Palmateer. *Moral Metafiction: Counterdiscourse in the Novels of Timothy Findley*. Toronto: ECW, 1991.
York, Lorraine M. *Front Lines: The Fiction of Timothy Findley*. Toronto: ECW, 1991.
— *"The Other Side of Dailiness": Photography in the Works of Alice Munro, Timothy Findley, Michael Ondaatje, and Margaret Laurence*. Toronto: ECW Press, 1988.

Frye, Northrop

Ayre, John. *Northrop Frye: A Biography*. Toronto: Random House, 1989.
Boyd, David, and Imre Salusinszky, eds. *Rereading Frye: The Published and Unpublished Works*. Toronto: University of Toronto Press, 1999.
Cotrupi, Caterina Nella. *Northrop Frye and the Poetics of Process*. Toronto: University of Toronto Press, 2000.
Gill, Glen Robert. *Northrop Frye and the Phenomenology of Myth*. Toronto: University of Toronto Press, 2006.
O'Grady, Jean, and Wang Ning, eds. *Northrop Frye: Eastern and Western Perspectives*. Toronto: University of Toronto Press, 2003.

Gallant, Mavis

Besner, Neil K. *The Light of Imagination: Mavis Gallant's Fiction*. Vancouver: University of British Columbia Press, 1988.
Clement, Lesley D. *Learning to Look: A Visual Response to Mavis Gallant's Fiction*. Montreal and Kingston: McGill-Queen's University Press, 2000.
Côté, Nicole and Peter Sabor, eds. *Varieties of Exile: New Essays on Mavis Gallant*. New York: Peter Lang, 2002.
Gunnars, Kristjana, ed. *Transient Questions: New Essays on Mavis Gallant*. Amsterdam and New York: Rodopi, 2004.
Keefer, Janice Kulyk. *Reading Mavis Gallant*. Toronto: Oxford University Press, 1989.
Merler, Grazia. *Mavis Gallant: Narrative Patterns and Devices*. Ottawa: Tecumseh, 1978.
Schaub, Danielle. *Mavis Gallant*. New York: Twayne, 1998.
Smythe, Karen E. *Figuring Grief: Gallant, Munro and the Poetics of Elegy*. Montreal and Kingston: McGill-Queen's University Press, 1992.

Glassco, John

Kokotailo, Philip. *John Glassco's Richer World: Memoirs of Montparnasse*. Toronto: ECW Press, 1988.
Sutherland, Fraser. *John Glassco: An Essay and Bibliography*. Downsview: ECW Press, 1984.

Grove, F. P.

Gammel, Irene. *Sexualizing Power in Naturalism: Theodore Dreiser and Frederick Philip Grove*. Calgary: University of Calgary Press, 1994.

Grove, Frederick Philip. *A Stranger to My Time: Essays by and about Frederick Philip Grove*. Ed. Paul Hjartarson. Edmonton: NeWest Press, 1986.

Hjartarson, Paul and Tracy Kulba, eds. *The Politics of Cultural Mediation: Baroness Elsa von Freytag-Loringhoven and Felix Paul Greve*. Edmonton: University of Alberta Press, 2003.

Martens, Klaus. *F. P. Grove in Europe and Canada: Translated Lives*. Tr. Paul Morris. Edmonton: University of Alberta Press, 2001.

Spettigue, Douglas O. *FPG: The European Years*. Ottawa: Oberon Press, 1973.

Gustafson, Ralph

Keitner, Wendy. *Ralph Gustafson*. Boston: Twayne, 1979.

McCarthy, Dermot. *A Poetics of Place: The Poetry of Ralph Gustafson*. Montreal and Kingston: McGill-Queen's University Press, 1991.

Haliburton, T. C.

Davies, Richard A. *Inventing Sam Slick: A Biography of Thomas Chandler Haliburton*. Toronto: University of Toronto Press, 2005.

— ed. *The Haliburton Bi-Centenary Chaplet: Papers Presented at the 1996 Thomas Raddall Symposium*. Wolfville, NS: Gaspereau Press, 1997.

— ed. *On Thomas Chandler Haliburton*. Ottawa: Tecumseh, 1979.

Percy, H. R. *Thomas Chandler Haliburton*. Don Mills: Fitzhenry and Whiteside, 1980.

Tierney, Frank M., ed. *The Thomas Chandler Haliburton Symposium*. Ottawa: University of Ottawa Press, 1985.

Hodgins, Jack

Struthers, J. R. (Tim). *On Coasts of Eternity: Jack Hodgins' Fictional Universe*. Lantzville: Oolichan, 1996.

Hood, Hugh

Copoloff-Mechanic, Susan. *Pilgrim's Progress: A Study of the Short Stories of Hugh Hood*. Toronto: ECW Press, 1988.

Garebian, Keith. *Hugh Hood*. Boston: Twayne, 1983.

Morley, Patricia A. *The Comedians: Hugh Hood and Rudy Wiebe*. Toronto: Clarke, Irwin, 1977.

Huston, Nancy

Dvořák, Marta and Jane Koustas, eds. *Vision / Division: L'Œuvre de Nancy Huston*. Ottawa: Presses de l'Université d'Ottawa, 2004.

Larochelle, Corinne. *Corinne Larochelle présente* Cantique des plaines *de Nancy Huston*. Montréal. Leméac, 2001.

Innis, Harold

Acland, Charles R., and William J. Buxton, eds. *Harold Innis in the New Century: Reflections and Refractions*. Montreal and Kingston: McGill-Queen's University Press, 1999.

Creighton, Donald Grant. *Harold Adams Innis: Portrait of a Scholar*. Toronto: University of Toronto Press, 1957.

Havelock, Eric A. *Harold A. Innis: A Memoir*. Toronto: Harold Innis Foundation, 1982.

Patterson, Graeme H. *History and Communications: Harold Innis, Marshall McLuhan, the Interpretation of History.* University of Toronto Press, 1990.

Watson, Alexander John. *Marginal Man: The Dark Vision of Harold Innis.* Toronto: University of Toronto Press, 2006.

Jameson, Anna

Johnston, Judith. *Anna Jameson: Victorian, Feminist, Woman of Letters.* Aldershot, England and Brookfield: Scolar Press, 1997.

Thomas, Clara. *Love and Work Enough: The Life of Anna Jameson.* Toronto: University of Toronto Press, 1967.

Johnson, Pauline

Gray, Charlotte. *Flint & Feather: The Life and Times of E. Pauline Johnson, Tekahionwake.* Toronto: HarperFlamingo Canada, 2002.

Johnston, Sheila M. F. *Buckskin & Broadcloth: A Celebration of E. Pauline Johnson Tekahionwake, 1861–1913.* Toronto: Natural Heritage/Natural History, 1997.

Keller, Betty. *Pauline Johnson: First Aboriginal Voice of Canada.* Montreal: XYZ, 1999.

Strong-Boag, Veronica, and Carole Gerson. *Paddling Her Own Canoe: The Times and Texts of E. Pauline Johnson (Tekahionwake).* Toronto: University of Toronto Press, 2000.

— eds. *Tekahionwake: Collected Poems and Selected Prose.* Toronto: University of Toronto Press, 2002.

Kennedy, Leo

Stevens, Peter, ed. *The McGill Movement: A. J. M. Smith, F. R. Scott and Leo Kennedy.* Toronto: Ryerson Press, 1969.

King, Thomas

Margery Fee, ed. "On Thomas King," special issue of *Canadian Literature* 161/2 (Summer/Autumn 1999).

Davidson, Arnold E., Priscilla L. Walton, and Jennifer Andrews, eds. *Border Crossings: Thomas King's Cultural Inversions.* Toronto: University of Toronto Press, 2003.

Schorcht, Blanca. *Storied Voices in Native American Texts: Harry Robinson, Thomas King, James Welch, and Leslie Marmon Silko.* New York: Routledge, 2003.

Kinsella, W. P.

Murray, Don. *The Fiction of W. P. Kinsella: Tall Tales in Various Voices.* Fredericton: York Press, 1987.

Kirby, William

Pierce, Lorne. *William Kirby: The Portrait of a Tory Loyalist.* Toronto: Macmillan, 1929.

Kiyooka, Roy

O'Brian, John, Naomi Sawada, and Scott Watson, eds. *All Amazed for Roy Kiyooka.* Vancouver: Arsenal Pulp, 2002.

Klein, A. M.

Caplan, Usher. *Like One that Dreamed: A Portrait of A. M. Klein.* Toronto: McGraw-Hill Ryerson, 1982.
Fischer, G. K. *In Search of Jerusalem: Religion, and Ethics in the Writings of A. M. Klein.* Montreal: McGill-Queen's University Press, 1975.
Kattan, Naïm. *A. M. Klein: La Réconciliation des races et des religions.* Montreal: XYZ, 1994. English version: Kattan, Naïm. *A. M. Klein: Poet and Prophet.* Tr. Edward Baxter. Montreal: XYZ, 2001.
Marshall, Tom, ed. *A. M. Klein.* Toronto: Ryerson, 1970.
Mayne, Seymour, ed. *The A. M. Klein Symposium.* Ottawa: University of Ottawa Press, 1975.
Pollock, Zailig. *A. M. Klein: The Story of the Poet.* Toronto: University of Toronto Press, 1994.
Spiro, Solomon J. *Tapestry for Designs: Judaic Allusions in* The Second Scroll *and* The Collected Poems of A. M. Klein. Vancouver: University of British Columbia Press, 1984.
Waddington, Miriam. *Folklore in the Poetry of A. M. Klein.* St. John's: Memorial University, 1981.

Kogawa, Joy

Cheung, King-Kok. *Articulate Silences: Hisaye Yamamoto, Maxine Hong Kingston, Joy Kogawa.* Ithaca: Cornell University Press, 1993.
Beautell, Eva Darias. *Division, Language, and Doubleness in the Writings of Joy Kogawa.* La Laguna: Universidad de la Laguna, 1998.
Kella, Elizabeth. *Beloved Communities: Solidarity and Difference in Fiction by Michael Ondaatje, Toni Morrison, and Joy Kogawa.* Uppsala: Uppsala University, 2000.

Kreisel, Henry

Kreisel, Henry. *Another Country: Writings by and about Henry Kreisel.* Ed. Shirley Neuman. Edmonton: NeWest, 1985.

Kroetsch, Robert

Dorscht, Susan Rudy. *Women, Reading, Kroetsch: Telling the Difference.* Waterloo: Wilfrid Laurier University Press, 1991.
Florby, Gunilla. *The Margin Speaks: A Study of Margaret Laurence and Robert Kroetsch from a Post-Colonial Point of View.* Lund: Lund University Press, 1997.
Lecker, Robert. *Robert Kroetsch.* Boston: Twayne, 1986.
Thomas, Peter. *Robert Kroetsch.* Vancouver: Douglas and McIntyre, 1980.
Tiefensee, Dianne. *The Old Dualities: Deconstructing Robert Kroetsch and His Critics.* Montreal and Kingston: McGill-Queen's University Press, 1994.

Lampman, Archibald

Connor, Carl Y. *Archibald Lampman: Canadian Poet of Nature.* Ottawa: Borealis, 1977 [1929].
Guthrie, Norman Gregor. *The Poetry of Archibald Lampman.* Toronto: Musson, 1927.
McMullen, Lorraine, ed. *The Lampman Symposium.* Ottawa: University of Ottawa Press, 1976.

Laurence, Margaret

Comeau, Paul. *Margaret Laurence's Epic Imagination*. Edmonton: University of Alberta Press, 2005.

Lucking, David. *Ancestors and Gods: Margaret Laurence and the Dialectics of Identity*. New York: Peter Lang, 2002.

Morley, Patricia. *Margaret Laurence*. Boston: Twayne, 1981. Rev. version: *The Long Journey Home*. Montreal and Kingston: McGill-University Press, 1991.

New, William H., ed. *Margaret Laurence*. Toronto: McGraw-Hill Ryerson, 1977.

Nicholson, Colin, ed. *Critical Approaches to the Fiction of Margaret Laurence*. Houndmills: Macmillan, 1990.

Riegel, Christian. *Writing Grief: Margaret Laurence and the Work of Mourning*. Winnipeg: University of Manitoba Press, 2003.

—— ed. *Challenging Territory: The Writing of Margaret Laurence*. Edmonton: University of Alberta Press, 1997.

Sparrow, Fiona. *Into Africa with Margaret Laurence*. Toronto: ECW Press, 1992.

Staines, David, ed. *Margaret Laurence: Critical Reflections*. Ottawa: University of Ottawa Press, 2001.

Thomas, Clara. *The Manawaka World of Margaret Laurence*. Toronto: McClelland and Stewart, 1975.

Verduyn, Christl, ed. *Margaret Laurence: An Appreciation*. Peterborough: Broadview Press, 1988.

Woodcock, George, ed. *A Place to Stand on: Essays by and about Margaret Laurence*. Edmonton: NeWest, 1983.

Layton, Irving

Beissel, Henry and Joy Bennett, eds. *Raging Like a Fire: A Celebration of Irving Layton*. Montreal: Véhicule, 1993.

Cameron, Elspeth. *Irving Layton: A Portrait*. Don Mills: Stoddart, 1985.

Mansbridge, Francis. *Irving Layton: God's Recording Angel*. Toronto: ECW Press, 1995.

Mayne, Seymour, ed. *Irving Layton: The Poet and his Critics*. Toronto: McGraw-Hill Ryerson, 1978.

Leacock, Stephen

Legate, David M. *Stephen Leacock: A Biography*. Toronto: Doubleday Canada, 1970.

Lynch, Gerald. *Stephen Leacock: Humour and Humanity*. Kingston and Montreal: McGill-Queen's University Press, 1988.

—— ed. *Leacock on Life*. Toronto: University of Toronto Press, 2002.

Moritz, Albert, and Theresa Moritz. *Stephen Leacock: His Remarkable Life*. Markham: Fitzhenry and Whiteside, 2002.

Staines, David, ed., with Barbara Nimmo. *The Letters of Stephen Leacock*. Don Mills: Oxford University Press, 2006.

Livesay, Dorothy

Dorney, Lindsay, Gerald Noonan, and Paul Tiessen, eds. *A Public and Private Voice: Essays on the Life and Work of Dorothy Livesay*. Waterloo: University of Waterloo Press, 1986.

McInnis, Nadine. *Dorothy Livesay's Poetics of Desire*. Winnipeg: Turnstone, 1994.

Lowry, Malcolm

Asals, Frederick and Paul Tiessen, eds. *A Darkness that Murmured: Essays on Malcolm Lowry and the Twentieth Century*. Toronto: University of Toronto Press, 2000.

Cross, Richard K. *Malcolm Lowry: A Preface to His Fiction*. Chicago: University of Chicago Press, 1980.

Grace, Sherrill E. *The Voyage that Never Ends: Malcolm Lowry's Fiction*. Vancouver: University of British Columbia Press, 1982.

   ed. *Swinging the Maelstrom: New Perspectives on Malcolm Lowry*. Montreal and Kingston: McGill-Queen's University Press, 1992.

Porteous, J. Douglas. *Landscapes of the Mind: Worlds of Sense and Metaphor*. Toronto: University of Toronto Press, 1990.

Tiessen, Paul, ed. *Apparently Incongruous Parts: The Worlds of Malcolm Lowry*. Metuchen: Scarecrow, 1990.

Vice, Sue. *Self-Consciousness in the Work of Malcolm Lowry: An Examination of Narrative Voice*. Oxford: Oxford University Press, 1988.

Wood, Barry, ed. *Malcolm Lowry: The Writer and His Critics*. Ottawa: Tecumseh, 1980.

MacLennan, Hugh

Buitenhuis, Peter. *Hugh MacLennan*. Ed. William French. Toronto: Forum, 1969.

Cameron, Elspeth. *Hugh MacLennan: A Writer's Life*. Toronto: University of Toronto Press, 1981.

   ed. *Hugh MacLennan: Proceedings of the MacLennan Conference at University College*. Toronto: Canadian Studies Programme, University College, University of Toronto, 1982.

   ed. *The Other Side of Hugh MacLennan: Selected Essays Old and New*. Toronto: Macmillan, 1978.

Cockburn, Robert H. *The Novels of Hugh MacLennan*. Montreal: Harvest House, 1969.

Goetsch, Paul, ed. *Hugh MacLennan*. Toronto: McGraw-Hill Ryerson, 1973.

Lucas, Alec. *Hugh MacLennan*. Toronto: McClelland and Stewart, 1970.

MacLulich, T. D. *Hugh MacLennan*. Boston: Twayne, 1983.

Tierney, Frank M., ed. *Hugh MacLennan*. Ottawa: University of Ottawa Press, 1994.

Mandel, Eli

Jewinski, Ed, and Andrew Stubbs, eds. *The Politics of Art: Eli Mandel's Poetry and Criticism*. Amsterdam and Atlanta: Rodopi, 1992.

Stubbs, Andrew. *Myth, Origins, Magic: A Study of Form in Eli Mandel's Writing*. Winnipeg: Turnstone, 1993.

Marlatt, Daphne

Knutson, Susan. *Narrative in the Feminine: Daphne Marlatt and Nicole Brossard*. Waterloo: Wilfrid Laurier University Press, 2000.

Rosenthal, Caroline. *Narrative Deconstructions of Gender in Works by Audrey Thomas, Daphne Marlatt, and Louise Erdrich*. Rochester: Camden House, 2003.

McLuhan, Marshall

Cavell, Richard. *McLuhan in Space: A Cultural Geography.* Toronto: University of Toronto Press, 2002.
Day, Barry. *The Message of Marshall McLuhan.* London: Lintas, 1967.
Duffy, Dennis. *Marshall McLuhan.* Toronto: McClelland and Stewart, 1969.
Gordon, W. Terrence. *Marshall McLuhan: Escape into Understanding.* Toronto: Stoddart, 1997.
Marchand, Philip. *Marshall McLuhan: The Medium and the Messenger.* Toronto: Vintage Canada, 1998 [1989].
Moss, John, and Linda M. Morra, eds. *At the Speed of Light There Is Only Illumination: A Reappraisal of Marshall McLuhan.* Ottawa: University of Ottawa Press, 2004.
Theall, Donald F. *The Virtual Marshall McLuhan.* Montreal and Kingston: McGill-Queen's University Press, 2001.

McClung, Nellie

Benham, Mary Lile. *Nellie McClung.* Don Mills: Fitzhenry and Whiteside, 2000 [1975].
Devereux, Cecily. *Growing a Race: Nellie L. McClung and the Fiction of Eugenic Feminism.* Montreal and Kingston: McGill-Queen's University Press, 2005.
Gray, Charlotte. *Nellie McClung.* Toronto: Penguin Books Canada, 2008.
Hallett, Mary, and Marilyn Davis. *Firing the Heather: The Life and Times of Nellie McClung.* Saskatoon: Fifth House, 1993.
Macpherson, Margaret. *Nellie McClung: Voice for the Voiceless.* Montreal: XYZ, 2003.
Warne, Randi R. *Literature as Pulpit: The Christian Social Activism of Nellie L. McClung.* Canadian Corporation for Studies in Religion. Waterloo: Wilfrid Laurier University Press, 1993.
Wright, Helen K. *Nellie McClung and Women's Rights.* Agincourt: Book Society of Canada, 1980.

McCulloch, Thomas

McCulloch, William. *Life of Thomas McCulloch, D. D., Pictou.* Ed. Isabella and Jean McCulloch. Truro: n. p., 1920.
Whitelaw, Marjory. *Thomas McCulloch: His Life and Times.* Halifax: Nova Scotia Museum, 1985.

Mistry, Rohinton

Bharucha, Nilufer E. *Rohinton Mistry: Ethnic Enclosures and Transcultural Spaces.* Jaipur: Rawat, 2003.
Dodiya, Jaydipsinh, ed. *The Fiction of Rohinton Mistry: Critical Studies.* New Delhi: Prestige, 1998.
Morey, Peter. *Rohinton Mistry.* Manchester: Manchester University Press, 2004.

Montgomery, Lucy Maud

Epperly, Elizabeth Rollins. *The Fragrance of Sweet-Grass: L. M. Montgomery's Heroines and the Pursuit of Romance.* Toronto: University of Toronto Press, 1992.

Through Lover's Lane: L. M. Montgomery's Photography and Visual Imagination. Toronto: University of Toronto Press, 2007.

Gammel, Irene. *Looking for Anne: How Lucy Maud Montgomery Dreamed up a Literary Classic*. Toronto: Key Porter, 2008.

—, ed. *The Intimate Life of L. M. Montgomery*. Toronto: University of Toronto Press, 2005.

—, ed. *Making Avonlea: L. M. Montgomery and Popular Culture*. Toronto: University of Toronto Press, 2002.

Gammel, Irene, and Elizabeth Epperly, eds. *L. M. Montgomery and Canadian Culture*. Toronto: University of Toronto Press, 1999.

Montgomery, L. M. *Anne of Green Gables: Authoritative Text, Backgrounds, Criticism*. Ed. Mary Henley Rubio and Elizabeth Waterston. New York: W. W. Norton, 2007.

Reimer, Mavis, ed. *Such a Simple Little Tale: Critical Responses to L. M. Montgomery's Anne of Green Gables*. Metuchen: Scarecrow, 1992.

Rubio, Mary, and Elizabeth Waterston. *Writing a Life: L. M. Montgomery*. Toronto: ECW Press, 1995.

Rubio, Mary. *Lucy Maud Montgomery: The Gift of Wings*. Toronto: Doubleday Canada, 2008.

Waterston, Elizabeth. *Kindling Spirit: L. M. Montgomery's Anne of Green Gables*. Toronto: ECW Press, 1993.

Moodie, Susanna

Gray, Charlotte. *Sisters in the Wilderness: The Lives of Susanna Moodie and Catherine Parr Traill*. Toronto: Viking, 1999.

Peterman, Michael A. *Susanna Moodie: A Life*. Toronto: ECW, 1999.

—. *Sisters in Two Worlds: A Visual Biography of Susanna Moodie and Catharine Parr Traill*. Ed. and comp. Hugh Brewster. Toronto: Doubleday Canada, 2007.

—. *This Great Epoch of Our Lives: Susanna Moodie's* Roughing it in the Bush. Toronto: ECW Press, 1996.

Shields, Carol. *Susanna Moodie: Voice and Vision*. Ottawa: Borealis, 1977.

Thurston, John. *The Work of Words: The Writing of Susanna Strickland Moodie*. Montreal: McGill-Queen's University Press, 1996.

Moore, Brian

Craig, Patricia. *Brian Moore: A Biography*. London: Bloomsbury, 2002.

Flood, Jeanne. *Brian Moore*. Lewisburg: Bucknell University Press, 1974.

Gearon, Liam. *Landscapes of Encounter: The Portrayal of Catholicism in the Novels of Brian Moore*. Calgary: University of Calgary Press, 2002.

O'Donoghue, Jo. *Brian Moore: A Critical Study*. Dublin: Gill and Macmillan, 1990.

Sampson, Denis. *Brian Moore: The Chameleon Novelist*. Toronto: Doubleday Canada, 1998.

Sullivan, Robert. *A Matter of Faith: The Fiction of Brian Moore*. Westport: Greenwood, 1996.

Mowat, Farley

Lucas, Alec. *Farley Mowat*. Toronto: McClelland and Stewart, 1976.

King, James. *Farley: The Life of Farley Mowat*. Toronto: HarperFlamingoCanada, 2002.

Orange, John. *Farley Mowat: Writing the Squib*. Toronto: ECW Press, 1993.

Mukherjee, Bharati

Alam, Fakrul. *Bharati Mukherjee*. New York and London: Twayne and Prentice Hall, 1996.
Dlaska, Andrea. *Ways of Belonging: The Making of New Americans in the Fiction of Bharati Mukherjee*. Vienna: Braumüller, 1999.
Nelson, Emmanuel S., ed. *Bharati Mukherjee: Critical Perspectives*. New York: Garland, 1993.

Munro, Alice

Blodgett, E. D. *Alice Munro*. Boston: Twayne, 1988.
Carrington, Ildikó de Papp. *Controlling the Uncontrollable: The Fiction of Alice Munro*. DeKalb: Northern Illinois University Press, 1989.
Carscallen, James. *The Other Country: Patterns in the Writing of Alice Munro*. Toronto: ECW Press, 1993.
Heble, Ajay. *The Tumble of Reason: Alice Munro's Discourse of Absence*. Toronto: University of Toronto Press, 1994.
Howells, Coral Ann. *Alice Munro*. Manchester: Manchester University Press, 1998.
MacKendrick, Louis K., ed. *Probable Fictions: Alice Munro's Narrative Acts*. Downsview: ECW Press, 1983.
Martin, W. R. *Alice Munro: Paradox and Parallel*. Edmonton: University of Alberta Press, 1987.
Mazur, Carol, comp. *Alice Munro: An Annotated Bibliography of Works and Criticism*. Cathy Moulder, ed. Lanham: Scarecrow, 2007.
Miller, Judith, ed. *The Art of Alice Munro: Saying the Unsayable: Papers from the Waterloo Conference*. Waterloo: University of Waterloo Press, 1984.
Rasporich, Beverly J. *Dance of the Sexes: Art and Gender in the Fiction of Alice Munro*. Edmonton: University of Alberta Press, 1990.
Redekop, Magdalene. *Mothers and Other Clowns: The Stories of Alice Munro*. London and New York: Routledge, 1992.
Ross, Catherine Sheldrick. *Alice Munro: A Double Life*. Toronto: ECW Press, 1992.
Thacker, Robert. *Alice Munro: Writing Her Lives: A Biography*. Toronto: McClelland and Stewart, 2005.
    ed. *The Rest of the Story: Critical Essays on Alice Munro*. Toronto: ECW Press, 1999.

nichol, bp

Miki, Roy, and Fred Wah, eds. *Beyond the Orchard: Essays on* The Martyrology. Vancouver: West Coast Line, 1997.
Jaeger, Peter. *ABC of Reading TRG*. Vancouver: Talonbooks, 1999.
Scobie, Stephen. *bpNichol: What History Teaches*. Vancouver: Talonbooks, 1984.

O'Hagan, Howard

Fee, Margery, ed. *Silence Made Visible: Howard O'Hagan and Tay John*. Toronto: ECW Press, 1992.
Tanner, Ella. *Tay John and the Cyclical Quest: The Shape of Art and Vision in Howard O'Hagan*. Toronto: ECW Press, 1990.

Ondaatje, Michael

Barbour, Douglas. *Michael Ondaatje*. Boston: Twayne, 1993.

Hillger, Annick. *Not Needing All the Words: Michael Ondaatje's Literature of Silence*. Montreal: McGill-Queen's University Press, 2006.
Lacroix, Jean-Michel, ed. *Re-Constructing the Fragments of Michael Ondaatje's Works / La Diversité déconstruite et reconstruite de l'œuvre de Michael Ondaatje*. Paris: Presses de la Sorbonne Nouvelle, 1999.
Lee, Dennis. *Savage Fields: An Essay in Literature and Cosmology*. Toronto: Anansi, 1977.
Mundwiler, Leslie. *Michael Ondaatje: Word, Image, Imagination*. Vancouver: Talonbooks, 1984.
Solecki, Sam, ed. *Spider Blues: Essays on Michael Ondaatje*. Montreal: Véhicule, 1985.
Stanton, Katherine. *Cosmopolitan Fictions: Ethics, Politics, and Global Change in the Works of Kazuo Ishiguro, Michael Ondaatje, Jamaica Kincaid, and J. M. Coetzee*. New York: Routledge, 2006.

Page, P. K.

Rogers, Linda, and Barbara Colebrook Peace, eds. *P. K. Page: Essays on Her Works*. Toronto: Guernica, 2001.

Parker, Gilbert

Adams, John Coldwell. *Seated with the Mighty: A Biography of Sir Gilbert Parker*. Ottawa: Borealis, 1979.
Fridén, Georg. *The Canadian Novels of Sir Gilbert Parker: Historical Elements and Literary Technique*. Copenhagen: Ejnar Munksgaard, 1953.

Pollock, Sharon

Grace, Sherrill. *Making Theatre: A Life of Sharon Pollock*. Vancouver: Talonbooks, 2008.
Nothof, Anne F., ed. *Sharon Pollock: Essays on Her Works*. Toronto: Guernica, 2000.

Pratt, E. J.

Clever, Glenn. *On E. J. Pratt*. Ottawa: Borealis, 1977.
— ed. *The E. J. Pratt Symposium*. Ottawa: University of Ottawa Press, 1977.
Collins, Robert G. *E. J. Pratt*. Boston: Twayne, 1988.
Pitt, David G., ed. *E. J. Pratt*. Toronto: Ryerson, 1969.
— *E. J. Pratt*, vol. I: *The Truant Years, 1882–1927*. Toronto: University of Toronto Press, 1984.
— *E. J. Pratt*, vol. II: *The Master Years, 1927–1964*. Toronto: University of Toronto Press, 1987.
McAuliffe, Angela T. C. *Between the Temple and the Cave: The Religious Dimensions of the Poetry of E. J. Pratt*. Montreal and Kingston: McGill-Queen's University Press, 2000.
Smith, A. J. M. *Some Poems of E. J. Pratt: Aspects of Imagery and Theme*. St. John's: Memorial University, 1969.

Purdy, Al

Lynch, Gerald, Shoshannah Ganz, and Josephene T. Kealey, eds. *The Ivory Thought: Essays on Al Purdy*. Ottawa: University of Ottawa Press, 2008.
Rogers, Linda, ed. *Al Purdy: Essays on His Works*. Toronto: Guernica, 2002.
Solecki, Sam. *The Last Canadian Poet: An Essay on Al Purdy*. Toronto: University of Toronto Press, 1999.

Reaney, James

Dragland, Stan, ed. *Approaches to the Work of James Reaney*. Downsview: ECW Press, 1983.

Lee, Alvin A. *James Reaney*. Boston: Twayne, 1968.
Parker, Gerald D. *How to Play: The Theatre of James Reaney*. Toronto: ECW Press, 1991.

Richardson, John

Ballstadt, Carl, ed. *Major John Richardson: A Selection of Reviews and Criticism*. Montreal: Lawrence M. Lande Foundation for Canadian Historical Research, 1972.
Beasley, David R. *The Canadian Don Quixote: The Life and Works of Major John Richardson, Canada's First Novelist*. Erin: Porcupine's Quill, 1977.
Duffy, Dennis. *A Tale of Sad Reality: John Richardson's* Wacousta. Toronto: ECW Press, 1993.
 A World Under Sentence: John Richardson and the Interior. Toronto: ECW Press, 1996.
Hurley, Michael. *The Borders of Nightmare: The Fiction of John Richardson*. Toronto: University of Toronto Press, 1992.
Ross, Catherine Sheldrick, ed. *Recovering Canada's First Novelist: Proceedings from the John Richardson Conference, University of Waterloo, 1977*. Erin: Porcupine's Quill, 1984.

Richler, Mordecai

Boulay, Claude. *L'Impérialisme "Canadian": Chevalier servant: Mordecai Richler*. Trois-Rivières: Bien public, 1995.
Darling, Michael, ed. *Perspectives on Mordecai Richler*. Toronto: ECW Press, 1986.
Davidson, Arnold E. *Mordecai Richler*. New York: Frederick Ungar, 1983.
Kramer, Reinhold. *Mordecai Richler: Leaving St. Urbain*. Montreal: McGill-Queen's University Press, 2008.
Ramraj, Victor J. *Mordecai Richler*. Boston: Twayne, 1983.
Richler, Mordecai. *Un Certain Sens du ridicule*. Ed. Nadine Bismuth. Tr. Dominique Fortier. Montreal: Boréal, 2007.
Sheps, G. David, ed. *Mordecai Richler*. Toronto: Ryerson, 1971.
Woodcock, George. *Mordecai Richler*. Toronto: McClelland and Stewart, 1970.

Roberts, Charles G. D.

Adams, John Coldwell. *Sir Charles God Damn: The Life of Sir Charles G. D. Roberts*. Toronto: University of Toronto Press, 1986.
Boone, Laurel, ed. *The Collected Letters of Charles G. D. Roberts*. Fredericton: Goose Lane, 1989.
Cappon, James. *Charles G. D. Roberts*. Toronto: Ryerson, 1923.
 Roberts and the Influences of His Time. Toronto: William Briggs, 1905.
Pomeroy, E. M. *Sir Charles G. D. Roberts: A Biography*. Toronto: Ryerson, 1943.

Ross, Sinclair

Fraser, Keath. *As for Me and My Body: A Memoir of Sinclair Ross*. Toronto: ECW Press, 1997.
McMullen, Lorraine. *Sinclair Ross*. Ottawa: Tecumseh, 1991 [1979].
Moss, John, ed. *From the Heart of the Heartland: The Fiction of Sinclair Ross*. Ottawa: University of Ottawa Press, 1992.
Stouck, David. *As For Sinclair Ross*. Toronto: University of Toronto Press, 2005.

Ryga, George

Hoffman, James. *The Ecstasy of Resistance: A Biography of George Ryga*. Toronto: ECW Press, 1995.

Innes, Christopher. *Politics and the Playwright: George Ryga*. Toronto: Simon and Pierre, 1985.

Sangster, Charles

Hamilton, W. D. *Charles Sangster*. New York: Twayne, 1971.

Tierney, Frank M. *The Journeys of Charles Sangster: A Biographical and Critical Investigation*. Ottawa: Tecumseh, 2000.

Scott, D. C.

Dragland, Stan. *Floating Voice: Duncan Campbell Scott and the Literature of Treaty 9*. Concord: Anansi, 1994.

——— ed. *Duncan Campbell Scott: A Book of Criticism*. Ottawa: Tecumseh, 1974.

Stich, K. P., ed. *The Duncan Campbell Scott Symposium*. Ottawa: University of Ottawa Press, 1980.

Titley, E. Brian. *A Narrow Vision: Duncan Campbell Scott and the Administration of Indian Affairs in Canada*. Vancouver: University of British Columbia Press, 1986.

Scott, F. R.

Djwa, Sandra. *The Politics of the Imagination: A Life of F. R. Scott*. Toronto: McClelland and Stewart, 1987.

Djwa, Sandra, and R. St. J. Macdonald, eds. *On F. R. Scott: Essays on His Contributions to Law, Literature, and Politics*. Kingston and Montreal: McGill-Queen's University Press, 1983.

Selvon, Sam

Forbes, Curdella. *From Nation to Diaspora: Samuel Selvon, George Lamming and the Cultural Performance of Gender*. Mona: University of West Indies Press, 2005.

Nasta, Susheila, ed. and comp. *Critical Perspectives on Sam Selvon*. Washington: Three Continents, 1988.

Looker, Mark. *Atlantic Passages: History, Community, and Language in the Fiction of Sam Selvon*. New York: Peter Lang, 1996.

Salick, Roydon. *The Novels of Samuel Selvon: A Critical Study*. Westport: Greenwood, 2001.

Wyke, Clement H. *Sam Selvon's Dialectal Style and Fictional Strategy*. Vancouver: University of British Columbia Press, 1991.

Service, Robert

Klinck, Carl F. *Robert Service: A Biography*. Toronto: McGraw-Hill Ryerson, 1976.

Seton, Ernest Thompson

Keller, Betty. *Black Wolf: The Life of Ernest Thompson Seton*. Vancouver: Douglas and McIntyre, 1984.

Redekop, Magdalene. *Ernest Thompson Seton*. Don Mills: Fitzhenry and Whiteside, 1979.

Shields, Carol

Besner, Neil K., ed. *Carol Shields: The Arts of a Writing Life*. Winnipeg: Prairie Fire, 2003.
Dvořak, Marta, and Manina Jones, eds. *Carol Shields and the Extra-Ordinary*. Montreal and Kingston: McGill-Queen's University Press, 2007.
Eden, Edward, and Dee Goertz, eds. *Carol Shields, Narrative Hunger, and the Possibilities of Fiction*. Toronto: University of Toronto Press, 2003.
Trozzi, Adriana. *Carol Shields' Magic Wand: Turning the Ordinary into the Extraordinary*. Roma: Bulzoni, 2001.

Smart, Elizabeth

Echlin, Kim. *Elizabeth Smart: A Fugue Essay on Women and Creativity*. Toronto: Women's Press, 2004.
Sullivan, Rosemary. *By Heart: Elizabeth Smart, A Life*. Toronto and London: Penguin, 1991.

Smith, A. J. M.

Compton, Anne. *A. J. M. Smith: Canadian Metaphysical*. Toronto: ECW Press, 1994.

George F. Walker

Johnson, Chris. *Essays on George F. Walker: Playing With Anxiety*. Winnipeg: Blizzard, 1999.

Thomas, Audrey

Sarbadhikary, Krishna. *Dis-membering / Re-membering: Fictions by Audrey Thomas*. New Delhi: Books Plus, 1999.

Thompson, Judith

Knowles, Ric, ed. *Judith Thompson*. Toronto: Playwrights Canada, 2005.
———. ed. *The Masks of Judith Thompson*. Toronto: Playwrights Canada, 2006.

Traill, Catharine Parr

Eaton, Sara. *Lady of the Backwoods: Biography of Catharine Parr Traill*. Toronto: McClelland and Stewart, 1969.

Urquhart, Jane

Ferri, Laura, ed. *Jane Urquhart: Essays on Her Works*. Toronto: Guernica, 2005.

Van Herk, Aritha

Verduyn, Christl, ed. *Aritha van Herk: Essays on Her Works*. Toronto: Guernica, 2001.

Watson, Sheila

Bowering, George, ed. *Sheila Watson and* The Double Hook. Kemptville: Golden Dog Press, 1985.
Flahiff, F. T. *Always Someone to Kill the Doves: A Life of Sheila Watson*. Edmonton: NeWest, 2005.

Webb, Phyllis

Butling, Pauline. *Seeing in the Dark: The Poetry of Phyllis Webb*. Waterloo: Wilfrid Laurier University Press, 1997.

Collis, Stephen. *Phyllis Webb and the Common Good: Poetry/Anarchy/Abstraction*. Vancouver: Talonbooks, 2007.

Wiebe, Rudy

Keith, W. J. *Epic Fiction: The Art of Rudy Wiebe*. Edmonton: University of Alberta Press, 1981.

ed. *A Voice in the Land: Essays by and about Rudy Wiebe*. Edmonton: NeWest Press, 1981.

Van Toorn, Penny. *Rudy Wiebe and the Historicity of the Word*. Edmonton: University of Alberta Press, 1995 [1991].

Wilson, Ethel

McAlpine, Mary. *The Other Side of Silence: A Life of Ethel Wilson*. Madeira Park: Harbour, 1988.

McMullen, Lorraine, ed. *The Ethel Wilson Symposium*. Ottawa: University of Ottawa Press, 1982.

Pacey, Desmond. *Ethel Wilson*. New York: Twayne, 1967.

Stouck, David. *Ethel Wilson: A Critical Biography*. Toronto: University of Toronto Press, 2003.

Wiseman, Adele

Panofsky, Ruth. *The Force of Vocation: The Literary Career of Adele Wiseman*. Winnipeg: University of Manitoba Press, 2006.

ed. *Adele Wiseman: Essays on her Works*. Toronto: Guernica, 2001.

Individual authors (selected): francophone

Aquin, Hubert

Beaudry, Jacques. *Hubert Aquin: La Course contre la vie*. Montreal: Hurtubise HMH, 2006.

Cliche, Anne Elaine. *Le Désir du roman: Hubert Aquin, Réjean Ducharme*. Montreal: XYZ, 1992.

Dubois, Richard. *Hubert Aquin Blues: Essai*. Montreal: Boréal, 2003.

La Fontaine, Gilles de. *Hubert Aquin et le Québec*. Montreal: Parti pris, 1977.

Lamontagne, André. *Les Mots des autres: La Poétique intertextuelle des œuvres romanesques de Hubert Aquin*. Sainte-Foy: Presses de l'Université Laval, 1992.

Lapierre, René. *L'Imaginaire captif: Hubert Aquin*. Montreal: Quinze, 1981.

Legris, Renée. *Hubert Aquin et la radio: Une quête d'écriture (1954–1977)*. Montreal: Médiaspaul, 2004.

Maccabée Iqbal, Françoise. *Hubert Aquin romancier*. Quebec: Presses de l'Université Laval, 1978.

Martel, Jacinthe, and Jean-Christian Pleau, eds. *Hubert Aquin en revue*. Quebec: Presses de l'Université du Québec, 2006.

Mocquais, Pierre-Yves. *Hubert Aquin, ou, La quête interrompue*. Montreal: Pierre Tisseyre, 1985.

Randall, Marilyn. *Le Contexte littéraire: Lecture pragmatique de Hubert Aquin et de Réjean Ducharme*. Longueuil: le Préambule, 1990.
Richard, Robert. *Le Corps logique de la fiction: Le Code romanesque chez Hubert Aquin*. Montreal: l'Hexagone, 1990.
Wall, Anthony. *Hubert Aquin: Entre référence et métaphore*. Candiac: Balzac, 1991.

Aubert de Gaspé fils

Lasnier, Louis. *Philippe Aubert de Gaspé et l'influence d'un livre*. Montreal: l'Île de la Tortue, 2001.

Beauchemin, Yves

Piccione, Marie-Lyne. *Rencontre autour d'Yves Beauchemin: Actes du colloque de Bordeaux, Centre d'études canadiennes, Université Michel Montaigne, Bordeaux III*. Paris: l'Harmattan, 2001.

Beaulieu, Victor-Lévy

Pelletier, Jacques. *L'Écriture mythologique: Essai sur l'œuvre de Victor-Lévy Beaulieu*. Montreal: Nuit blanche, 1996.

Blais, Marie-Claire

Fabi, Thérèse. *Marie-Claire Blais: Le Monde perturbé des jeunes dans l'œuvre de Marie-Claire Blais: Sa vie, son œuvre, la critique*. Montreal: Éditions Agence d'Arc, 1973.
Green, Mary Jean. *Marie-Claire Blais*. New York: Twayne, 1995.
Stratford, Philip. *Marie-Claire Blais*. Toronto: Forum, 1971.
Laurent, Françoise. *L'Œuvre romanesque de Marie-Claire Blais*. Montreal: Fides, 1986.
Verreault, Robert. *L'Autre Côté du monde: Le Passage à l'âge adulte chez Michel Tremblay, Réjean Ducharme, Anne Hébert et Marie-Claire Blais*. Montreal: Liber, 1998.

Brossard, Nicole

Dupré, Louise. *Stratégies du vertige: Trois poètes: Nicole Brossard, Madeleine Gagnon, France Théoret*. Montreal: Remue-ménage, 1989.
Forsyth, Louise H., ed. *Nicole Brossard: Essays on her Works*. Toronto: Guernica, 2005.

Roch Carrier

Dorion, Gilles. *Roch Carrier: Aimer la vie, conjurer la mort*. Ottawa: Presses de l'Université d'Ottawa, 2004.

Crémazie, Octave

Casgrain, Henri Raymond. *Octave Crémazie*. Montreal: Beauchemin, 1912.
Codemine, Odette. *Octave Crémazie*. Montreal: Fides, 1980.

Ducharme, Réjean

Amrit, Hélène. *Les Stratégies paratextuelles dans l'œuvre de Réjean Ducharme*. Paris: Les Belles Lettres, 1995.
Nardout-Lafarge, Élisabeth. *Réjean Ducharme: Une poétique du débris*. Saint-Laurent: Fides, 2001.

Haghebaert, Elisabeth, and Élisabeth Nardout-Lafarge. *Réjean Ducharme en revue*. Quebec: Presses de l'Université du Québec, 2006.
Laurent, Françoise. *L'Œuvre romanesque de Réjean Ducharme*. Montreal: Fides, 1988.
Leduc-Park, Renée. *Réjean Ducharme: Nietzsche et Dionysos*. Quebec: Presses de l'Université Laval, 1982.
McMillan, Gilles. *L'Ode et le désode: Essai de sociocritique sur* Les enfantômes *de Réjean Ducharme*. Montreal: l'Hexagone, 1995.
Roy, Paul-Émile. *Études littéraires: Germaine Guèvremont, Réjean Ducharme, Gabrielle Roy*. Montreal: Meridien, 1989.
Seyfrid-Bommertz, Brigitte. *La Rhétorique des passions dans les romans de Réjean Ducharme*. Sainte-Foy: Presses de l'Université Laval, 1999.
Vaillancourt, Pierre-Louis. *Réjean Ducharme: De la pie-grièche à l'oiseau-moqueur*. Montreal: l'Harmattan, 2000.
— ed. *Paysages de Réjean Ducharme*. Saint-Laurent: Fides, 1994.

Ferron, Jacques

Biron, Michel. *L'Absence du maitre: Saint-Denys Garneau, Ferron, Ducharme*. Montreal: Presses de l'Université de Montréal, 2000.
— *Jacques Ferron au pays des amélanchiers*. Montreal: Presses de l'Université de Montréal, 1973.
Cantin, Pierre. *Jacques Ferron, polygraphe: Essai de bibliographie suivi d'une chronologie*. Montreal: Bellarmin, 1984.
Faivre-Duboz, Brigitte, and Patrick Poirier, eds. *Jacques Ferron: Le Palimpseste infini*. Outremont: Lanctôt, 2002.
L'Hérault, Pierre. *Jacques Ferron: Cartographe de l'imaginaire*. Montreal: Presses de l'Université de Montréal, 1980.
Marcel, Jean. *Jacques Ferron: Malgré lui*. Montreal: Éditions du jour, 1970.
Mercier, Andrée. *L'Incertitude narrative dans quatre contes de Jacques Ferron: Étude sémiotique*. Quebec: Nota bene, 1998.
Michaud, Ginette. *Ferron post-scriptum*. Outremont: Lanctôt, 2005.
Olscamp, Marcel. *Le Fils du notaire: Jacques Ferron, 1921–1949: Genèse intellectuelle d'un écrivain*. Saint-Laurent: Fides, 1997.
Sing, Pamela V. *Villages imaginaires: Edouard Montpetit, Jacques Ferron et Jacques Poulin*. Saint-Laurent: Fides, 1995.
Poirier, Patrick, ed. *Jacques Ferron: Autour des commencements*. Outremont: Lanctôt, 2000.

Fréchette, Louis

d'Arles, Henri. *Louis Fréchette*. Toronto: Ryerson, 1924.
Blais, Jacques, Hélène Marcotte, and Roger Saumur. *Louis Fréchette, épistolier*. Quebec: Nuit blanche, 1992.
Dugas, Marcel. *Un Romantique canadien: Louis Fréchette, 1839–1908*. Paris: Editions de la "Revue Mondiale," 1934.
Klinck, George A. *Louis Fréchette, prosateur: Une réestimation de son œuvre*. Lévis: Le Quotidien, 1955.
Rinfret, Fernand. *Louis Fréchette*. Saint-Jérôme: Librairie J.-E. Prévost, 1906.

Garneau, Hector de Saint-Denys

Blais, Jacques. *Saint-Denys Garneau et le mythe d'Icare*. Sherbrooke: Cosmos, 1973.
Bourneuf, Roland. *Saint-Denys Garneau et ses lectures européennes*. Quebec: Presses de l'Université Laval, 1969.
Brochu, André. *Saint-Denys Garneau: Le Poète en sursis*. Montreal: XYZ, 1999.
— *La Part incertaine: Poésie et expérience intérieure chez de Saint-Denys Garneau: Essai*. Montreal: Les herbes rouges, 2005.
Durand-Lutzy, Nicole. *Saint-Denys Garneau: La Couleur de Dieu*. Montreal: Fides, 1981.
Gascon, France. *L'Univers de Saint-Denys Garneau: Le Peintre, le critique*. Montreal: Boréal, 2001.
Melançon, Benoît, and Pierre Popovic, eds. *Saint-Denys Garneau et La Relève*. Montreal: Fides, 1995.
Riser, Georges. *Conjonction et disjonction dans la poésie de Saint-Denys Garneau: Étude du fonctionnement des phénomènes de cohésion et de rupture dans des textes poétiques*. Ottawa: Editions de l'Université d'Ottawa, 1984.
Vigneault, Robert. *Saint-Denys Garneau à travers* Regards et jeux dans l'espace. Montreal: Presses de l'Université de Montreal, 1973.
Wyczynski, Paul. *Poésie et symbole: Perspectives du symbolisme: Emile Nelligan, Saint-Denys Garneau, Anne Hébert, et le langage des arbres*. Montreal: Déom, 1965.

Gauvreau, Claude

Chamberland, Roger. *Claude Gauvreau: La Libération du regard*. Quebec: Centre de recherche en littérature québécoise, 1986.
Marchand, Jacques. *Claude Gauvreau, poète et mythocrate*. Montreal: VLB, 1979.
Saint-Denis, Janou. *Claude Gauvreau, le cygne*. Montreal: Presses de l'Université du Quebec, 1978.

Godin, Gérald

Beaudry, Lucille, Robert Comeau, and Guy Lachapelle, eds. *Gérald Godin: Un poète en politique: Essai*. Montreal: l'Hexagone, 2000.
Gervais, André. *Petit glossaire des "Cantouques" de Gérald Godin*. Quebec: Nota bene, 2000.

Grandbois, Alain

Bolduc, Yves. *Alain Grandbois: Le Douloureux Destin*. Montreal: Presses de l'Université de Montréal, 1982.
Gallays, François, and Yves Laliberté. *Alain Grandbois, prosateur et poète*. Orléans: David, 1997.
Greffard, Madeleine. *Alain Grandbois*. Montreal: Fides, 1975.

Guèvremont, Germaine

Cimon, Renée. *Germaine Guèvremont*. Montreal: Fides, 1969.
Duquette, Jean Pierre. *Germaine Guèvremont: Une route, une maison*. Montreal: Presses de l'Université de Montréal, 1973.
Leclerc, Rita. *Germaine Guèvremont*. Montreal: Fides, 1963.

Lepage, Yvan G. *Germaine Guèvremont: La Tentation autobiographique*. Ottawa: Presses de l'Université d'Ottawa, 1998.

Hébert, Anne

Bishop, Neil B. *Anne Hébert, son œuvre, leurs exils: Essai*. Talence: Presses universitaires de Bordeaux, 1993.
Bouchard, Denis. *Une lecture d'Anne Hébert: La Recherche d'une mythologie*. Montreal: Hurtubise HMH, 1977.
Brochu, André. *Anne Hébert: Le Secret de vie et de mort*. Ottawa: Presses de l'Université d'Ottawa, 2000.
Émond, Maurice. *La Femme à la fenêtre: L'Univers symbolique d'Anne Hébert dans* Les Chambres de bois, Kamouraska *et* Les Enfants du sabbat. Sainte-Foy: Presses de l'Université Laval, 1984.
Hébert, Pierre, and Christiane Lahaie. *Anne Hébert et la modernité*. Montreal: Fides, 2000.
Major, Jean-Louis. *Anne Hébert et le miracle de la parole*. Montreal: Presses de l'Université de Montréal, 1976.
Paterson, Janet M. *Anne Hébert: Architexture romanesque*. Ottawa: Presses de l'Université d'Ottawa, 1985.
Paterson, Janet M. and Lori Saint-Martin, eds. *Anne Hébert en revue*. Quebec: Presses de l'Université du Quebec, 2006.
Thériault, Serge A. *La Quête d'équilibre dans l'œuvre romanesque d'Anne Hébert*. Hull: Editions Asticou, 1980.

Hémon, Louis

Ayotte, Alfred, and Victor Tremblay. *L'Aventure Louis Hémon*. Montreal: Fides, 1974.
Bleton, Paul, and Mario Poirier. *Le Vagabond stoïque: Louis Hémon*. Montreal: Presses de l'Université de Montréal, 2004.
Boivin, Aurélien, and Jean-Marc Bourgeois. *Le Saguenay-Lac-Saint-Jean célèbre Louis Hémon: Introduction à l'écrivain et à son œuvre à l'occasion du centenaire de sa naissance*. Alma: Editions du Royaume, 1980.
Bourdeau, Nicole. *Une étude de* Maria Chapdelaine *de Louis Hémon*. Montreal: Boréal, 1997.
Chovrelat, Geneviève. *Louis Hémon, la vie à écrire*. Leuven: Peeters, 2003.
Demers, Patricia. *A Seasonal Romance: Louis Hémon's* Maria Chapdelaine. Toronto: ECW, 1993.
Lévesque, Gilbert. *Louis Hémon: Aventurier ou philosophe?* Montreal: Fides, 1980.
Sauvé, Mathieu-Robert. *Louis Hémon: Le Fou du lac*. Montreal: XYZ, 2000.
Vígh, Árpád. *L'Écriture* Maria Chapdelaine: *Le Style de Louis Hémon et l'explication des québécismes*. Sillery: Septentrion, 2002.

Laberge, Albert

Brunet, Jacques. *Albert Laberge, sa vie et son œuvre*. Ottawa: Éditions de l'Université d'Ottawa, 1969.

Langevin, André

Bond, David J. *The Temptation of Despair: A Study of the Quebec Novelist André Langevin*. Fredericton: York, 1982.

Brochu, André. *L'Évasion tragique: Essai sur les romans d'André Langevin*. LaSalle: Hurtubise HMH, 1985.
Pascal, Gabrielle. *La Quête de l'identité chez André Langevin*. Montreal: Aquila, 1976.

Lasnier, Rina

Alonzo, Anne-Marie. *Rina Lasnier, ou, Le langage des sources: Essais*. Trois-Rivières: Écrits des Forges, 1988.
Kushner, Eva. *Rina Lasnier et son temps: Une étude*. Paris: Seghers, 1969.
Sicotte, Sylvie. *L'Arbre dans la poésie de Rina Lasnier*. Sherbrooke: Cosmos, 1977.

Lemelin, Roger

Bertrand, Daniel. *Roger Lemelin: L'Enchanteur*. Montreal: Stanké, 2000.
Bertrand, Réal. *Roger Lemelin: Le Magnifique*. Laval: Editions FM, 1989.

Lepage, Robert

Charest, Rémy. *Robert Lepage: Quelques zones de liberté*. Quebec: l'instant même, 1995.
Donohoe, Joseph I. Jr., and Jane M. Koustas, eds. *Theater sans frontières: Essays on the Dramatic Universe of Robert Lepage*. East Lansing: Michigan State University Press, 2000.
Dundjerović, Aleksander Saša. *The Cinema of Robert Lepage: The Poetics of Memory*. London: Wallflower, 2003.
— *The Theatricality of Robert Lepage*. Montreal and Kingston: McGill-Queen's University Press, 2007.
Fouquet, Ludovic. *Robert Lepage, l'horizon en images: Essai*. Quebec: l'instant même, 2005.
Hébert, Chantal, and Irène Perelli-Contos. *La Face cachée du théâtre de l'image*. Paris: l'Harmattan, 2001.

Loranger, Françoise

Crête, Jean-Pierre. *Françoise Loranger: La Recherche d'une identité*. Montreal: Leméac, 1974.

Maillet, Antonine

Drolet, Bruno. *Entre dune et aboiteaux ... un peuple: Étude critique des œuvres d'Antonine Maillet*. Montreal: Éditions Pleins bords, 1975.

Marie de l'Incarnation

Brodeur, Raymond, ed. *Marie de l'Incarnation: Entre mère et fils: Le Dialogue des vocations*. Quebec: Presses de l'Université Laval, 2000.
Deroy-Pineau, Françoise. *Marie de l'Incarnation: Marie Guyart, femme d'affaires, mystique, mère de la Nouvelle France, 1599–1672*. Paris: R. Laffont, 1989.
— ed. *Marie Guyard de l'Incarnation, un destin transocéanique, Tours, 1599–Québec, 1672*. Paris and Montreal: l'Harmattan, 2000.
Gourdeau, Claire. *Les Délices de nos cœurs: Marie de l'Incarnation et ses pensionnaires amérindiennes, 1639–1672*. Sillery: Septentrion, 1994.
Mali, Anya. *Mystic in the New World: Marie de l'Incarnation (1599–1672)*. Leiden: E. J. Brill, 1996.
Oury, Guy Marie. *Marie de l'Incarnation (1599–1672)*. 2 vols. Quebec: Presses de l'Université Laval, 1973.

Martin, Claire

Vigneault, Robert. *Claire Martin: Son œuvre, les réactions de la critique*. Montreal: Pierre Tisseyre, 1975.

Miron, Gaston

Filteau, Claude. *L'Homme rapaillé de Gaston Miron*. Montreal: Trécarré, 1984.
Gasquy-Resch, Yannick. *Gaston Miron: Le Forcené magnifique*. Montreal: Hurtubise HMH, 2003.
Maugey, Axel. *Gaston Miron: Une passion québécoise*. Brossard: Humanitas, 1999.
Nepveu, Pierre. *Les Mots à l'écoute: Poésie et silence chez Fernand Ouellette, Gaston Miron et Paul-Marie Lapointe*. Quebec: Nota bene, 2002 [1979].
Royer, Jean. *Voyage en Mironie: Une vie littéraire avec Gaston Miron: Récit*. Saint-Laurent: Fides, 2004.

Nelligan, Émile

Grisé, Yolande, Réjean Robidoux, and Paul Wyczynski, eds. *Émile Nelligan, 1879–1941: Cinquante ans après sa mort*. Saint-Laurent: Fides, 1993.
Michon, Jacques. *Émile Nelligan: Les Racines du rêve*. Montreal: Presses de l'Université de Montréal, 1983.
Orion, Nicétas. *Émile Nelligan, prophète d'un âge nouveau*. Montreal: Phôtismos, 1996.
Samson, Jean-Noël. *Émile Nelligan*. Montreal: Fides, 1968.
Vanasse, André. *Émile Nelligan: Le Spasme de vivre*. Montreal: XYZ, 1996.
Wyczynski, Paul. *Émile Nelligan: Sources et originalité de son œuvre*. Ottawa: Éditions de l'Université d'Ottawa, 1960.

Ouellette, Fernand

Malenfant, Paul Chanel. *La Partie et le tout: Lecture de Fernand Ouellette et Roland Giguère*. Quebec: Presses de l'Université Laval, 1983.

Paradis, Suzanne

Turcotte, Jeanne. *Entre l'Ondine et la vestale: Analyse des* Hauts cris *de Suzanne Paradis*. Quebec: Centre de recherche en littérature québécoise, Université Laval, 1988.

Parizeau, Alice

Berthelot, Anne and Mary Dunn Haymann. *Alice Parizeau: l'épopée d'une œuvre*. Saint-Laurent: Éditions Pierre Tisseyre, 2001.

Poulin, Jacques

Hébert, Pierre. *Jacques Poulin: La Création d'un espace amoureux*. Ottawa: Presses de l'Universite d'Ottawa, 1997.
Miraglia, Anne Marie. *L'Écriture de l'Autre chez Jacques Poulin*. Candiac: Balzac, 1993.
Socken, Paul G. *The Myth of the Lost Paradise in the Novels of Jacques Poulin*. Rutherford: Fairleigh Dickinson University Press, 1993.

Ringuet (pseudonym for Panneton, Philippe)

Viens, Jacques. *La Terre de Zola et* Trente arpents *de Ringuet: Étude comparée*. Montreal: Cosmos, 1970

Lamy, Jean-Paul, and Guildo Rousseau, eds. *Ringuet en mémoire: 50 ans après* Trente arpents. Sillery: Septentrion, 1989.

Routier, Simone

Brosseau, Marie-Claude. *Trois écrivaines de l'entre-deux-guerres: Alice Lemieux, Eva Sénécal et Simone Routier*. Quebec: Nota bene, 1998.

Pageau, René. *Rencontres avec Simone Routier, suivies des lettres d'Alain Grandbois*. Joliette: Parabole, 1978.

Roy, Gabrielle

Daviau, Pierrette. *Passion et désenchantement: Une étude sémiotique de l'amour et des couples dans l'œuvre de Gabrielle Roy*. Montreal: Fides, 1993.

Everett, Jane and Nathalie Cooke, eds. "Gabrielle Roy contemporaine / The Contemporary Gabrielle Roy." Special issue of *Canadian Literature* 192 (Spring 2007).

Everett, Jane and François Ricard, eds. *Gabrielle Roy réécrite*. Quebec: Nota bene, 2003.

Francis, Cécilia W. *Gabrielle Roy: Autobiographe: subjectivité, passions et discours*. Quebec: Presses de l'Université Laval, 2006.

Ricard, François. *Gabrielle Roy, une vie*. Montreal: Boréal, 1996. English version: *Gabrielle Roy: A Life*. Tr. Patricia Claxton. Toronto: McClelland and Stewart, 1999.

Romney, Claude and Estelle Dansereau, eds. *Portes de communications: Études discursives et stylistiques de l'œuvre de Gabrielle Roy*. Sainte-Foy: Presses de l'Université Laval, 1995.

Roy, Alain. *Gabrielle Roy: L'Idylle et le désir fantôme*. Montreal: Boréal, 2004.

Saint-Martin, Lori. *La voyageuse et la prisonnière: Gabrielle Roy et la question des femmes*. Montreal: Boréal, 2002.

Saint-Pierre, Annette. *Au pays de Gabrielle Roy*. Saint-Boniface: Plaines, 2005.

Socken, Paul G. *Myth and Morality in* Alexandre Chenevert *by Gabrielle Roy*. New York: Peter Lang, 1987.

Thériault, Yves

Beaulieu, Victor-Lévy. *Un loup nommé Yves Thériault*. Trois-Pistoles: Éditions Trois-Pistoles, 1999.

Emond, Maurice. *Yves Thériault et le combat de l'homme*. Montreal: Hurtubise HMH, 1973.

Hesse, M. G. *Yves Thériault: Master Storyteller*. New York: Peter Lang, 1993.

Perron, Paul. *Semiotics and the Modern Quebec Novel: A Greimassian Analysis of Theriault's* Agaguk. Toronto: University of Toronto Press, 1996.

Simard, Jean Paul. *Rituel et langage chez Yves Thériault*. Montreal: Fides, 1979.

Tremblay, Michel

Boulanger, Luc. *Pièces à conviction: Entretiens avec Michel Tremblay*. Montreal: Leméac, 2001.

Brochu, André. *Rêver la lune: L'Imaginaire de Michel Tremblay dans les* Chroniques du Plateau Mont-Royal. Montreal: Hurtubise HMH, 2002.

Dargnat, Mathilde. *Michel Tremblay: Le "Joual" dans* Les belles-sœurs. Paris: l'Harmattan, 2002.
David, Gilbert, and Pierre Lavoie, eds. *Le Monde de Michel Tremblay: Des Belles-sœurs à Marcel poursuivi par les chiens*. Montreal: Cahiers de théâtre Jeu / Éditions Lansman, 1993.
Duchaine, Richard. *L'Écriture d'une naissance, naissance d'une écriture: La grosse femme d'à côté est enceinte de Michel Tremblay*. Quebec: Nuit Blanche, 1994.
Gervais, André, dir. *Emblématiques de "l'époque du joual": Jacques Renaud, Gérald Godin, Michel Tremblay, Yvon Deschamps*. Outremont: Lanctôt, 2000.
Jubinville, Yves. *Une Étude de* Les Belles-Sœurs *de Michel Tremblay*. Montreal: Boréal, 1998.
Piccione, Marie-Lyne. *Michel Tremblay, l'enfant multiple*. Talence: Presses universitaires de Bordeaux, 1999.
Usmiani, Renate. *Michel Tremblay*. Vancouver: Douglas and McIntyre, 1982.
   The Theatre of Frustration: Super Realism in the Dramatic Work of F. X. Kroetz and Michel Tremblay. New York: Garland, 1990.
Vigeant, Louise. *Une étude de* A toi, pour toujours, ta Marie-Lou, *de Michel Tremblay*. Montreal: Boréal, 1998.

Index

Aboriginal drama 518–35, 624–5
  beginnings of 520
  community theater 534
  playwrights 520, 521–30, 532–4 (French) 533–4, 535, 624, 625
  white theater presentations of Aboriginal themes 519–20
  see also Métis
Aboriginal peoples
  Algonquins 15, 119
  Beothuks 10, 484
  and Centennial debates 319–20
  Chipewyans 70, 75, 92, 96
  Cree 74, 439, 503, 506, 508, 511, 516, 528, 534
  European representations of: (C17) 10–28, *21* (Illustration)
  see also exploration narratives (French); *Jesuit Relations*
  European representations of: (C18) 51, 68, 70, 71, 72, 74; (C19) 75, 82, 85, 86, 92–3, 118–19, 121, 139, 142; (C20) 4, 296–7, 307, 403, 440, 442, 445, 485, 487, 489, 496, 519–20, 637–8, 644, 649, 651
  first contact 10–11
  French colonization and early European alliances 11–12, 14, 23–8
  Hurons 14, 16, 24, 26, 51
  Inuit 534
  Iroquois 24, 25, 26, 27, 33, 35, 37, 525
  Mi'kmaqs 10, 11, 12, 21, 502, 512, 520, 532
  Mohawk 56, 57–62, 508, 515
  Montagnais 10, 15, 16, 18, 35, 520
  Ojibwa 19, 72, 501, 503, 504, 505, 506, 509, 511, 514, 525, 528

  Okanagan 499, 508, 509
  Oneida 21, *22* (Illustration)
  oral traditions, oratory and early graphic forms 16–20, 27, 508–9
  Pan-Aboriginality 526–7, 533, 534
  protests and activism since 1960s 499, 500, 501, 505, 512, 526–7
  residential schools and abuse 500, 502, 512–13, 527, 531, 532
  Royal Commission on Aboriginal Peoples 509
Aboriginal writing (poetry and prose)
  anthologies 500, 501, 504, 507–8, 515
  En'owkin Center 507, 508
  fiction 238–9, 396–7, 398, 505–6, 510, 512–14, 515, 516
  life-writing 502–3, 504, 512, 513, 551–2, 553–4
  poetry 439–40, 479, 499, 501–2, 503, 506–7, 511, 515, 516
  post-1960 499–517
  pre-1960 57–62, 93, 139, 168, 206, 215, 305, 511
  publishers/publishing 503–4, 505
  Trickster figures 506, 514, 516, 521, 522, 529, 535
  see also Métis
Acadians and Acadia 105, 111–12, 114, 597–8
  drama 609, 617, 619–20
  Evangeline 111–12
  fiction 648–9
  poetry 597–8
Achebe, Chinua 390
Acklom, George 140
Acland, Peregrine 232
  WORKS: *All Else Is Folly* 232, 233
Acoose, Janice 503

Index

Acorn, Milton 426, 429
  WORKS: *The Brain's the Target* 426; *I've Tasted My Blood* 426
Acquelin, José 603
  WORKS: *L'Oiseau respirable* 603
Acta Victoriana 347
Adam, G. Mercer (and A. Ethelwyn Wetherald) 119, 195
  WORKS: *An Algonquin Maiden: A Romance of the Early Days of Upper Canada* 119
Adams, Graham Mercer 190
Adams, Howard 503
  WORKS: *Prisons of Grass: Canada from the Native Point of View* 503
Adderson, Caroline 399
  WORKS: *Bad Imaginings* 398
Adorno, Theodor 450
Agnant, Marie-Célie 562
Ahenakew, Edward 239
Akiwenzie-Damm, Kateri 515
Albert, Lyle Victor 408
  WORKS: *Scraping the Surface* 408
Albert, Pierre 599
Aldrich, Thomas Bailey 134
Alexie, Robert Arthur 512–13
  on residential school abuse 512
  on Native struggle for survival 512
  subversive humor 513
  WORKS: *Porcupines and China Dolls* 512
Alexis, André 395, 579
  WORKS: *Despair and Other Stories* 395
Alford, Edna 398
  WORKS: *The Garden of Eloise Loon* 398
Allen, Lillian 562, 563
Alonzo, Anne-Marie 562, 622
  WORKS: *Une lettre rouge orange et ocre* 622
ALPHABET 311, 424
American War (1812–14) 105, 116, 117, 118, 119, 121
Amiel, Henri Frédéric 134
Amyot, Geneviève 601
Anansi, House of 329, 360, 385, 387, 436
Andersen, Marguerite 650
  WORKS: *De mémoire de femme* 650
Anderson, Ho Che 477
  WORKS: *King* 477; *Pop Life* 477
Anderson, Patrick 287, 302, 305, 307
  WORKS: *A Tent for April* 307
Anderson-Dargatz, Gail 395
  WORKS: *The Miss Hereford Stories* 395
Angers, François-Réal 107, 629–30
  WORKS: *Les Révélations du crime or Combray et ses accomplices* 107

Annharte (Marie Annharte Baker) 507, 516
  WORKS: *Being on the Moon* 516; *Coyote Columbus Café* 516
Appelbaum, Louis 320
Appignanesi, Lisa 539–40, 541–2
  WORKS: *Losing the Dead* 539, 555
April, Jean-Pierre 648
Aquin, Hubert 314, 315, 316, 333, 638, 639, 647
  on historical amnesia 639
  literary influences on 640
  WORKS: *Prochain épisode* 314, 638; *Trou de mémoire* 639–40
Arcan, Nelly 648
  WORKS: *Folle* 648; *Putain* 648
Archambault, Lorraine 619
  WORKS: *De blé d'inde et des pissenlits* 619
Armitage, Simon 437
Armstrong, Jeannette 499, 505, 507, 508
  on Aboriginal rights 505
  co-founder of En'owkin International School of Writing 507
  on effects of colonialism 505
  on environmentalism 516
  WORKS: "Land Speaking" 517; (co-ed.) *Looking At the Words of Our People: A First Nations Analysis of Literature* 508; *Slash* 505; *Whispering in Shadows* 516
Armstrong, Kevin 393
  WORKS: *Night Watch* 393
Arnason, David 398, 618
  WORKS: *The Circus Performers' Bar* 398
Arnold, Matthew 132
Arnott, Joanne 515
Artaud, Antonin 615
Asselin, Oliver 230
Association des théâtres francophones du Canada (ATFC) 617
Association for Native Development in the Performing and Visual Arts 520
Association Québécoise du Jeune Théâtre (AQJT) 615–16
Astor, John Jacob 76
Atlantic Monthly, The 134, 136, 171, 241, 389
Atwood, Margaret 59, 148, 307, 310, 314, 352, 357, 358–65, 376, 385, 397, 424, 426, 429, 432, 453, 454, 497, 559
  and Canada–US relations 362
  and celebrity 359, 360, 362
  as cultural critic 358, 359–60
  and cultural nationalism 360
  dystopian fictions by 359, 362–3
  and environmentalism, wilderness 361, 363, 364

707

Atwood, Margaret (cont.)
  and feminism 361
  and feminist myth revisions 364
  generic range of 362
  as graphic artist (Bart Gerrard) 470–1, 470 (Illustration)
  and history 363, 497
  on human rights 360, 364
  on writer's role 358, 360, 380
  WORKS: criticism and literary essays: "Canadian-American Relations" 362; *In Search of* Alias Grace 497; Introduction to *Alice Munro's Best* 376; *Moving Targets: Writing with Intent 1982–2004* (British title *Curious Pursuits: Occasional Writing 1970-2005*) 359; *Negotiating with the Dead* 358–9, 360, 380; *Payback: Debt and the Shadow Side of Wealth* 365; *Survival* 334, 359, 360, 361; *Second Words* 359; fiction: *Alias Grace* 363–4; *The Blind Assassin* 363, 364; *The Edible Woman* 362; *The Handmaid's Tale* 359, 362–3; *Lady Oracle* 361; *Life Before Man* 362; *Oryx and Crake* 359, 363; *The Penelopiad* 364; *The Robber Bride* 329, 330; *Surfacing* 359, 360, 361, 362, 363; *The Year of the Flood* 365; poetry: *The Animals in That Country* 360–1, 429; *The Circle Game* 359, 429; *The Door* 364; *Good Bones* 399; *The Journals of Susanna Moodie* 94, 361, 429; *Power Politics* 360; "Progressive Insanities of a Pioneer" 361; *The Tent* 364, 399; "You Fit Into Me" 360; short fiction: "The Art of Cooking and Serving" 358; "The Bad News" 365; *Bluebeard's Egg* 399; *Moral Disorder* 358, 359, 364, 365, 397; *Wilderness Tips* 399
Audubon, John James 154, 156
  WORKS: *Viviparous Quadrupeds of North America* 156
Auger, Roger 618
  WORKS: *Je m'en vais à Régina* 618
Austen, Jane 377–8
Avison, Margaret 128, 302, 305, 306, 310, 423, 432
  American influences on 423
  conversion to Christianity 423
  Governor General's Award 423
  WORKS: *Always Now* 423; *Concrete and Wild Carrot* 431; *The Dumbfounding* 423; *Winter Sun* 310, 423

Babstock, Ken 436–7
  on characteristics of his poetry 437
  as establisher of American and British poetic connections 437
  as poetry editor 437
  WORKS: *Airstream Land Yacht* 436; *Days into Flatspin* 436; *Mean* 436
Back, George 85
  WORKS: *Narrative of the Arctic Land Expedition to the Mountains of the Great Fish River* 85
Badami, Anita Rau 561, 562
  WORKS: *The Hero's Walk* 574; *Tamarind Mem* 574
Bailey, Jacob 52–4
  WORKS: "Journal of a Voyage from Pownalboro" 53–4
Baird, Irene 291, 291 n. 8
Baldwin, Shauna Singh 561, 563, 564
Ballantyne, Robert Michael 81–2
  WORKS: *Hudson Bay* 81–2
Balzac, Honoré de 634
Balzano, Flora 565
Bambrick, Winifred 294
  WORKS: *Continental Revue* 294
Bancroft, George 111
Banks, Russell 365
Barbeau, Jean 614
  and *joual* 614
  political and cultural debates 614
  and satire 614
  WORKS: *Ben-Ur* 614; *Le Chant du sink* 614; *Le Chemin de Lacroix* 614; *Joualez-moi d'amour* 614; *Manon Lastcall* 614
Barbeau, Marius 651
  WORKS: *Le Rêve de Kamalmouk* 651
Barbour, Douglas 429
Barfoot, Joan 374
  WORKS: *Dancing in the Dark* 374
Barker, George 267
Barnes, Julian 490
  WORKS: *A History of the World in 10½ Chapters* 490
Barr, Robert 121, 171, 195
Barreto-Rivera, Rafael 430
Barthe, Ulric 230–1
  WORKS: *Similia Similibus* 230–1
Barthes, Roland 112
Bartleman, James 553–4, 555
  on Aboriginal identity 554
  on mixed race family history 553
  WORKS: *Raisin Wine: A Boyhood in a Different Muskoka* 553–4

Bashō, Matsuo 449
Bassolé-Ouédraogo, Angele 564
   WORKS: *Avec tes mots* 600; *Burkina Blues* 600; *Sahaliennes* 600
Bates, Judy Fong 561, 573
Battle of the Plains of Abraham 105, 494, 631
Beadle, Delos White 157–8
   aesthetics of 157
   on connection between horticulture and Canadian identity 158
   editor of *Canadian Horticulturalist* 158
   environmental warnings 158
   horticultural advice 157–8
   WORKS: *Canadian Fruit, Flower, and Kitchen Gardener* 157
Beagan, Tara
   WORKS: *Dreary and Izzy* 535; *The Fort at York* 535
Bealby, John Thomas 159–61
   British Columbia fruit grower 159
   horticultural visionary 159
   (Illustration) 161
   scientific and commercial interests 160
   as translator 160
Beard, George Miller 135
Beattie, Jessie L. 331
   WORKS: *Strength for the Bridge* 331
Beauchemin, Nerée 590
Beauchemin, Yves 642–3
   WORKS: *Le Matou* 642–3
Beaulieu, Germain 608
   WORKS: *La Passion* 608
Beaulieu, Michel 602
Beaulieu, Victor-Lévy 640
   WORKS: *Don Quichotte de la Démanche* 640
Beckett, Samuel 568
Beckwith, John 424
Begamudré, Ven 395
   WORKS: *A Planet of Eccentrics* 395; *Laterna Magika* 396
Bégon, Élisabeth 43–6
   on domestic life in New France 44
   on maternal love 45–6
   rediscovery of archive 43–6
   WORKS: *Correspondance d'Élisabeth Begon avec son gendre* 43–6
Beissel, Henry 519
   WORKS: *Inook and the Sun* 519
Belleau, André 635, 636
Bellefeuille, Normand de 601, 603
   WORKS: *Un visage pour commencer* 603
Beller, Jacob 327
   WORKS: *Jews in Latin America* 327

Belloc, Hilaire 340
Bendayan, David 562
Benedict, Nona 520
   WORKS: *The Dress* 520
Bengough, John Wilson 461
Bennett, Arnold 333
Bennett, Avie 432
Bennett, Louise, 564
Bentley, Richard 99, 100–1
   Haliburton connection 101
   Moodie connection 100–1
Bernard, Harry 634
   WORKS: *La Voie des sillons* 634
Bernhardt, Sarah 607
Bernier, Jovette 603
   WORKS: *Les Masques déchirés* 603
Bersianik, Louky 641
   WORKS: *L'Euguélionne* 641
Berthelot, Hector 461
Bessette, Arsène 633
   WORKS: *Le Débutant* 633
Bessette, Gérard 637
   and anti-Catholicism 637
   on French Canadian identity 637
   on Montreal as urban laboratory 637
   WORKS: *La Bagarre* 637; *Le Librarie* 637
Beynon, Francis Marion 221–2, 410
   anti-conscription 221
   journalism 221
   on women's political rights 221
   WORKS: *Aleta Day* 221–2, 229
Bezmozgis, David 393
   WORKS: *Natasha and Other Stories* 393
Bibaud, Michel 584, 607
Bienvenue, Yvan 627–8
   and "contes urbains" 627
   and French Canadian folk-tale tradition 628
   influence of 628
   WORKS: *Dits et inédits* 627; *Règlements de contes* 627
Big Bear, Chief 399, 488
Billette, Geneviève 622
   WORKS: *Crime contre l'humanité* 622
Binet, Claude 619
Binnie-Clark, Georgina 248, 259–60
   women's homesteader movement 259
   WORKS: *Wheat and Woman* 259, 260; *A Summer on a Canadian Prairie* 259
Binning, Sadhu 559
Bird, Louis 508
Bird, Will 233–4, 243
   WORKS: *And We Go On (Ghosts Have Warm Hands)* 233–4

Birdsell, Sandra 398, 488, 561
  WORKS: *Night Travellers* 398; *The Russländer* 488
Birney, Earle 91, 286, 302, 304, 306–7, 427
  academic career 306, 309, 426
  and *Canadian Poetry Magazine* 304–5
  contribution to west coast poetry scene 427
  and environmentalism 307
  as essayist and radio broadcaster 304, 306
  as influence on poets of 1970s and 1980s 427
  as landscape poet 306–7, 427
  and Second World War writing 307
  WORKS: "ALASKA PASSAGE" 307; *David and Other Poems* 306; *Ghost in the Wheels: Selected Poems, 1977* 433; "The Road to Nijmegen" 307; *Spreading Time* 307; *Trial of a City* 307; *Turvey* 294, 307; "Vancouver Lights" 307
bissett, bill 424, 502
Bissoondath, Neil 395, 562, 565
  WORKS: *Digging Up the Mountains* 395
Bjørnson, Bjørnstjerne 134
Black Canadian writing
  Africadian 439, 457–8, 560
  African Canadian terminology 579
  Black Loyalists 54, 57, 560, 579
  contemporary drama 418–19
  contemporary poetry and prose 439, 550, 559–60, 579
  woman's settlement narrative 88
  see also Ethnic diversity: Caribbean
Black Theatre Workshop, Montreal 418
Blais, Marie-Claire 638
  carnivalesque reversals 638
  on decline of family values 638
  WORKS: *Les Apparences* 641; *Une saison dans la vie d'Emmanuel* 638; *Les Manuscrits de Pauline Archange* 641
Blaise, Clark 385, 386, 388, 389, 546, 548, 550, 552–3
  WORKS: *Days and Nights in Calcutta* (co-authored with Mukherjee) 548; *A North American Education* 388; *The Sorrow and the Terror* (co-authored with Bharati Mukherjee) 552–3
Blake, William 346, 348
Blewett, Jean 228
  WORKS: "The Little Refugee" 228
Blodgett, E. D. 438, 479
  as poet 424
  as translator 438
  WORKS: *Apostrophes: Woman at a Piano* 438

Blondeau, Dominique 578
Blondin, George 508
Bloy, Léon 634
Boates, Brent 469
Bock, Dennis 385
  WORKS: *Olympia* 385
Bök, Christian 436, 483
  WORKS: *Eunoia* 436
Bolduc, Sylvain 473
Bolster, Stephanie 437, 438
Bolt, Carol 405
  WORKS: *Buffalo Jump* 405
Borduas, Paul-Émile 593
  WORKS: *Refus global* 593, 605, 610
Borges, Jorge Luis 480
Borksy, Mary 398
  WORKS: *Influence of the Moon* 398
Borson, Roo 434
Bosco, Monique 567
Bossuet, Jacques-Bénigne 586
Boswell, David 472
Bouchard, Michel Marc 416, 622, 623
Boucher, Denise 616
Boucherville, Georges Boucher de 113
  WORKS: *Une de perdue, deux de trouvées* 113
Boudreau, Jules 619
  WORKS: *Cochu et le soleil* 619; *Louis Mailloux* 619 (with Calixte Duguay)
Bouraoui, Hédi 650
  WORKS: *Bangkok Blues* 650; *La Pharaone* 650
Bourassa, Napoléon 114–15
  WORKS: *Jacques et Marie: Souvenir d'un peuple dispersé* 114–15
Bourgeois, Albéric 4
Bourget, Élizabeth 620, 621
  WORKS: *En ville* 620; *Appelle-moi* 621
Bourinot, John G. 117
Bouyoucas, Pan 623
  WORKS: *Le cerf-volant* 623
Bowering, George 384, 387, 424, 428, 432, 445–6
  Canada's inaugural poet laureate 446
  on heroic masculinity 428
  as historical novelist 446
  intertextuality 445
  parody in 445
  on regional geography and history 428, 445
  WORKS: fiction: *A Short Sad Book* 445; *Burning Water* 445–6; *Shoot!* 445; poetry: *George, Vancouver: A Discovery Poem* 428, 445–6; *Kerrisdale Elegies* 424; short fiction: *Standing on Richards* 387; anthology (ed.): *And Other Stories* 384

Bowering, Marilyn 242, 504
  WORKS: "My Grandfather Was a
    Soldier" 242
Boyd, George Elroy 419
  WORKS: *Consecrated Ground* 419; *Gideon's
    Blues* 419; *Wade in the Water* 419
Boyden, Joseph 381, 396–7, 512
  on Cree First World War soldiers 238, 512
  on cross-generational relations 512
  WORKS: *Born with a Tooth* 396; *Three Day
    Road* 238–9, 512; *Through Black Spruce*
    239, 512
Branch, Father James 609
  WORKS: *L'Émigrant acadien* 609; *Jusqu'a la
    mort! ... pour nos écoles!* 609; *Vivent nos
    écoles catholiques!* 609
Brand, Dionne 432, 439, 552, 560, 562, 563, 564,
    571, 574, 575, 576
  on denunciations of Canadian racism
    569, 576
  on multicultural Toronto 578
  on Trinidadian slave history 575
  WORKS: *At the Full and Change of the Moon*
    575, 579; *In Another Place Not Here* 576;
    Inventory 439; *Land to Light On* 576; *A
    Map to the Door of No Return* 552, 575; *No
    Language Is Neutral* 439; *What We All
    Long For* 578
Brandt, Di 561
Brant, Beth 508, 515
Brant, Joseph (Thayendanegea) 54, 55
  and Mohawk Bible translation, 55, 56
    (Illustration)
Brant, Molly (Koñwatsiàtsiaiéñni) 54, 55
Brassard, André 613
Brault, Jacques 596, 602
  WORKS: *Mémoire* 602; *Moments Fragiles* 602
Brébeuf, Fr. Jean de 35–6, 38, 39, 525
Brebner, Diana 437
  WORKS: *The Ishtar Gate* 437
Brecht, Bertolt 615
Brewster, Elisabeth 381
Brick Books 431–2
Brick magazine 385
Bringhurst, Robert 432, 434, 440, 508
  as pre-eminent poet translator of Haida oral
    narratives 440
  WORKS: *The Beauty of the Weapons* 434; *The
    Calling* 434; *Masterworks of the Classical
    Haida Mythtellers* 440; *Nine Visits to the
    Myth World* 440
British North America Act. 115, 127 *see*
    Confederation

Broadfoot, Barry 405
  WORKS: *Ten Lost Years* 405
Brodeur, Hélene 649
  WORKS: *Les Chroniques du Nouvel-Ontario*
    649
Bronfman, Charles R. 492, 497
Brooke, Frances 47, 93, 106
  on Canadian-British relations 48
  on climate 50
  didactic intentions of 49
  early career in Britain 47
  egalitarian opinions of 51
  on English-French relations in Quebec
    47, 49
  as epistolary novelist 48
  European-Huron comparison in 50–1
  as first English novelist in North America 47
  intertextuality in 49, 51
  as political novelist 48
  Protestant ethic of 49
  satire 49, 52
  as sentimental novelist 47–52
  as travel writer 47
  on women and education 50
  WORKS: *The History of Emily Montague*
    47–52; *The History of Lady Julia
    Mandeville* 47
Brossard, Nicole 3, 315, 398, 601, 641
  francophone feminist theorist, poet,
    novelist, short story writer 398
  WORKS: *L'Amer or le chapitre effrité* 641;
    French Kiss 641
Brown, Chester 472, 476–7, 551
  WORKS: *Ed the Happy Clown* 476; *Gospels*
    adaptation 477; *I Never Liked You* 477;
    Louis Riel: A Comic-Strip Biography 477,
    551; *The Playboy* 477; *Underwater* 477;
    Yummy Fur 476
Brown, E. K. 274, 302, 304, 359
  WORKS: *On Canadian Poetry* 304
Browne, Colin 430
Browning, Robert 495
Brun, Christine 598
Buckler, Ernest 299, 386
  on failed artist as hero 299
  on Maritime landscape 299
  and tall tale 299
  WORKS: *The Mountain and the
    Valley* 299
Bugnet, Georges 650
  WORKS: *La Forêt* 650
Bunyan, John 58, 60
Burdak, Leo 469

Burnard, Bonnie 385
Burney, Frances 47
Burnham, Clint 400
  WORKS: *Airborne Photo* 400
Burroughs, John 135
  WORKS: *Birds and Poets, with Other Papers* 135
Burton, Jean 280
Burwell, Adam Hood 88
  WORKS: *Talbot Road* 88
Bush, Douglas 275
Butler, William 83
  WORKS: *The Great Lone Land* 83

Caccia, Fulvio 561, 564, 567
Cahoots Theatre Projects 417–18
Caitlin, George 82
Call, Frank Oliver 273–4
  WORKS: (ed.) *Acanthus and Wild Grape* 273–4
Callaghan, Barry and Bruce Meyer 241, 359
Callaghan, Morley 248, 268–9, 295, 302, 329, 382, 386
  fiction of the 1920s and 1930s 295
  and Hemingway 268, 269
  on post-war urban Canada 295
  WORKS: *The Lost and Found Stories of Morley Callaghan* 382; *The Loved and the Lost* 295; *That Summer in Paris* 267, 268–9
Callières, Louis Hector de 24, 25, 26
Calvino, Italo 480
Cameron, Anne 398
  WORKS: *Daughters of Copper Woman* 398
Cameron, D. A. 333
Cameron, George Frederick 138
  WORKS: *Lyrics of Freedom, Love, and Death* 138
Campbell, Maria 502–3, 509
  as cultural mediator 510
  Métis history 502
  Métis identity 502
  on Métis and Indian women 503
  as political organizer 503
  WORKS: *Achimoona* 508; *The Book of Jessica* (co-authored with Linda Griffiths) 509; *Halfbreed* 502–3, 521; *Jessica* (drama) 520–1; *Stories of the Road Allowance People* 510
Campbell, William Wilfred 130, 133, 135, 137, 140, 142, 272
  WORKS: *At the Mermaid Inn* 140; *Lake Lyrics and Other Poems* 131; (ed.) *The Oxford Book of Canadian Verse* 272; *Sagas of Vaster Britain* 142; *Snowflakes and Sunbeams* 131

Camus, Albert 636
Canada Council 334, 404, 405
Canada First Movement 167
Canadian Authors Association 142, 260, 262, 278, 282, 286, 304–5, 334
Canadian Broadcasting Commission / Radio Canada (CBC) 296, 297, 303, 306, 357, 366, 370, 382, 394, 403, 427, 454, 499, 547, 553, 555
Canadian Citizenship Act 290, 299
Canadian Fiction Magazine 384
Canadian Forum 357
Canadian Horticulturalist, The 145, 158
Canadian literary history 2, 4
  Cambridge History of English Literature (1917) 1
  Canadian Literature in English (Keith) 4
  Dictionnaire des œuvres du Québec 3
  Histoire de la littérature française du Québec (Grandpré) 3
  A History of Canadian Literature (New) 4
  A Literary History of Canada (Klinck) 187, 348
  new dimensions 5
  in twenty-first century 4, 5
Canadian Literature 331, 333, 427, 439
Canadian Mercury 280–1
Canadian Pacific Railway (CPR) 336
Canadian Poetry Magazine 286, 304–5
Canadian University Services Organization (CUSO) 331, 332
Canadian-American relations 53–4, 63, 64–5, 116–17, 117–18, 120, 329–30, 345, 349, 352, 362, 414
Cardinal, Harold 500
  WORKS: *The Unjust Society* 500
Carew, Jan 564
Cariou, Warren 384, 516
  WORKS: *The Exalted Company of Roadside Martyrs* 384
Carlyle, Thomas 132, 387
Carman, Bliss 130, 133, 135, 136, 137, 141, 142, 171, 191, 200, 225, 273, 276
  WORKS: "Low Tide at Grand Pré" 133; *Low Tide at Grand Pré* 131, 137; "The Man of the Marne" 225; *The Pipes of Pan* 136, 141; *Sappho: One Hundred Lyrics* 141; *Vagabondia* 134, 136, 141
Caron, Louis 237, 643
  WORKS: *L'Emmitouflé* 237; *Les Fils de la liberté* 643
Carpentier, André 648

Index

Carr, Emily 296, 297
  on landscape and Native culture in British Columbia 297
  as visual artist 290
  WORKS: *Klee Wyck* 296, 297
Carr-Harris, Bertha 209–10
  Christian evangelist 209–10
  Temperance activist 209
  WORKS: *Lights and Shades of Mission Work; or Leaves from a Worker's Notebook* 209–10
Carrier, Roch 326–8, 395, 639
  WORKS: *Le Deux-millième étage* 326; *La Guerre, Yes Sir!* 639; *The Hockey Sweater* 395, 422
Carrington, Leonora 308
Carroll, Lewis 640
Carson, Anne 440, 451
  challenge to realist fiction 451
  cross-generic narrative forms in 451–2
  on diaspora and polyglossia 451–2
  international recognition of 440
  intertextuality in 451
  long poems by 451
  WORKS: *Autobiography of Red: A Novel in Verse* 451–2; *Eros the Bittersweet* 451; *Glass, Irony and God* 451; *Plainwater* 451
Cartier, Jacques 10–11, 421, 422, 651
  on Aboriginal people 11
  authorship 11
  on French intentions in New World 11–12
  on religion 12
  WORKS: *Relations* 10–12
cartography 22
  Aboriginal 19–20, 22
  English 72
  French 13
Carver, Raymond 399
Casgrain, Abbé Henri-Raymond 110, 585, 630, 631
Cather, Willa 259
  WORKS: *My Antonia* 259; *O Pioneers!* 259
Cattermole, William 87
  WORKS: *Emigration: The Advantages of Emigration to Canada* 87
Cazeneuve, Paul 608
Cenerini, Rhéal 618
  WORKS: *Kolbe* 618; *Laxton* 618
Centennial 1, 3, 312–34, 359, 405, 426, 478, 501
  see also Expo 67
Cercle Molière, Le 618
Chamberland, Paul 596, 601
  WORKS: *L'Afficheur hurle* 601, *Demain les dieux naîtront* 601, *Terre Québec* 601

Champagne, Dominic 421
Champlain, Samuel de 13, 14, 16
  WORKS: *Carte géographique de la Nouvelle France* 13; *Œuvres de Samuel Champlain* 14
Chan, Marty 417–18
  WORKS: *Mom, Dad, I'm Living with a White Girl* 417–18
Chaput-Rolland, Solange 314
  WORKS: *Mon pays, le Québec or le Canada?* 314
Charlebois, Eric 599
  WORKS: *Faux-fuyants* 599
Charlebois, Tina 600
  WORKS: *Poils lisses* 600; *Tatouages et testaments* 600
Charlevoix, Pierre-François-Xavier de 11, 13, 17, 19, 109, 116
  WORKS: *Histoire de la Nouvelle France* 16; *Journal d'un voyage ... dans l'Amérique* 11, 13
Charron, François 601
  WORKS: *La Fragilité des choses* 601; *Littérature-obscenité* 601
Chartier, Albert 468–9
Châtelaine 313, 317, 322
Chauchetière, Claude 31, 38
Chaurette, Normand 622, 626
  WORKS: *Provincetown Playhouse, juillet 1919, j'avais 19 ans* 622
Chauveau, Joseph Olivier 630
  WORKS: *Charles Guérin* 630
Cheadle, Walter Butler 82–3
  WORKS: *The North West Passage by Land* (co-authored with Viscount Milton) 82–3
Cheechoo, Shirley 528
  WORKS: *Path With No Moccasins* 528
Chekhov, Anton 533
Chen, Ying 559, 565, 567–8, 646
  WORKS: *L'Ingratitude* 568, 646; *Les Lettres chinoises* 568, 646; *La Mémoire de l'eau* 567
Chenelière, Evelyne de la 622
  WORKS: *Des fraises en janvier* 622
Chesterton, G. K. 340
Chiasson, Herménégilde 597–8, 600, 619, 620
  WORKS: (drama) *Aliénor* 620; *Le Cœur de la tempête* 620; *Evangéline, mythe ou réalité* 620; *L'Éxil d'Alexa* 620; *Histoire en histoire* 620; *Laurie ou la vie de galerie* 620; *Pour une fois* 620; *Renaissance* 620; *La Vie est un rêve* 620

713

Chiasson, Herménégilde (cont.)
  (poetry) *Actions, Climats, Conversations, Existences, Legendes, Miniatures, Parcours, Prophéties* 598
Chief Buffalo Child Long Lance (Sylvester C. Long) 249
Child, Philip 232, 233, 294
  WORKS: *The Day of Wrath* 294; *God's Sparrows* 232
children's literature 94, 96, 194, 241, 242, 313, 362, 433–4, 462–3
Chislett, Anne 241
Choinière, Olivier 625
  WORKS: *Contes d'un Indien urbain* (Translation) 625
Chopin, Henri 430
Chopin, René 590
Choquette, Ernest 123
  WORKS: *Les Ribaud: une idylle de 37* 123
Chouart de Groseilliers, Médard 14
Choy, Wayson 393, 544–5, 550, 561
  WORKS: *All That Matters* 545; *The Jade Peony* 393, 545, 573, 574; *Paper Shadows: A Chinatown Childhood* 544; *Searching for Confucius* 545; *Wayson Choy: Unfolding the Butterfly* (Video biography) 545
Choyce, Leslie 438
Cicco, Piero Giorgio di 561
CIV/n 305
Clark, Sally 415
  WORKS: *Life without Instruction* 415; *Moo* 415
Clarke, Austin 331, 381, 562, 565–6
  ambivalence towards Canada 566
  on Caribbean women's experience 566, 570
  as Caribbean writer pre-multiculturalism 565
  slow acceptance of 559
  use of creole in 566
  WORKS: *Amongst Thorns and Thistles* 573; *The Austin Clarke Reader* 395; *Growing Up Stupid Under the Union Jack* 573; *The Meeting Point* 331, 566; *The Polished Hoe* 566; *Survivors of the Crossing* 566
Clarke, George Elliott 333, 419, 439, 457–8, 559, 560, 575
  on Africadian cultural community 457, 458
  cross-generic experimentation 457–8
  intertextuality in 457–8
  on mixing African-Canadian orality with Eurocentric poetic tradition 458
  on politics of race 439, 458
  use of song cycles 458
  WORKS: *Beatrice Chancy* 419, 458; *Black* 458; *Execution Poems: The Black Acadian Tragedy of "George and Rue"* 439, 458; *Québécité: A Jazz Fantasia in Three Cantos* 458; *Whylah Falls* 419, 439, 457–8
Clément, Caroline 265
Clements, Marie 531–2
  crossovers between genres 531
  environmentalism 532
  fusion of myth and realism 531
  on residential schools 531, 532
  use of Aboriginal myths 531, 532
  use of Greek myths 531
  on violence against Aboriginal women 531
  WORKS: *Age of Iron* 531; *Burning Vision* 532; *Copper Thunderbird* 532; *The Girl Who Swam Forever* 532; *Look What You Made Me Do* 532; *The Unnatural and Accidental Women* 531–2; *Urban Tattoo* 532
Clutesi, George 319
Coach House Press 429, 430, 468, 473
Cobbing, Bob 430
Cocking, Matthew 68
Cogswell, Fred 305, 438
  interest in natural maritime world 438
  as translator of Québécois poetry 438
Cohen, Leonard 4, 29, 38, 302, 305, 306, 309, 310, 314, 315, 328, 329, 429, 432, 441–2, 444, 450, 561, 568
  cross-generic narrative forms of 442
  importance of games theory 442
  influences on 441, 442
  as poet-novelist 441
  as songwriter and performer 429
  subversions of epic in 442
  WORKS: Novels: *Beautiful Losers* 429, 442, 450, 459; *The Favourite Game* 429, 441–2; Poems: *Let Us Compare Mythologies* 310; *Selected Poems* 429; *Songs of Leonard Cohen* 429; *The Spice-Box of Earth* 429
Cohen, Matt 387, 561
  WORKS: *Night Flights* 387
Coleman, Helena 131
Coleman, Kathleen Blake (Kit Coleman) 214–15
  first woman war correspondent 214
  journalism 214–15
Coleridge, Samuel Taylor 340, 445
Colette, 325

Collier, Dave 477
    WORKS: *Just the Facts* 477; *Portraits from Life* 477; *Surviving Saskatoon* 469, 477
Collins, Joseph Edward 129
Collins, W. E. 285
    WORKS: *The White Savannahs* 285, 286
colonialism and colonization 332, 333, 345, 487, 501, 505, 512, 518, 522, 523, 525, 526, 528, 531, 535, 563, 637, 642–3, 646
Combe, William 71
Comeau, Gary 598
comics 460–77
    C19–early C20
        graphic artists: (English) 461; (French) 461
        major characters in 461
        political and satirical cartoons 460–1
        publishers/publishing: (English) 460, 461 (French) 461
    early C20
        foreign competition 461, 462
        graphic artists (English) 462; (French) 462
        major characters in 462
        newspaper comic strips 461–2
        publishers/publishing (English) 462; (French) 462
    1919–40
        Comic strip broadsheets (French) 462
        foreign competition 463
        graphic artists (French) 463
        publishers/publishing (French) 462–3
    1941–5
        Canadian "Whites" (English) 463
        graphic artists (English) 464, 465; (French) 463, 464
        humorous and adventure magazines 464
        publishers/publishing (English) 464; (French) 463
        superheroes and heroines 464, 465 (Illustration)
    1950s
        ongoing tradition of educational comic books (English) 464, 467, 474; (French) 463
    1960–mid 1970s
        counter-culture and comic avant-gardism 467, 469
        graphic artists (English) 467, 468, 469, 470–1, 472; (French) 468–9
        major characters in 468, 469
        political and satirical cartoons (English) 469–71; (French) 468
        publishers/publishing (English) 468, 469–71; (French) 468, 469
    mid 1970s–early C21
        Aboriginal artists 467
        comic albums and comic books 429, 471, 472, 473
        foreign competition 471
        graphic artists (English) 4, 460, 471, 472, 474, 475, 475–7; (French) 473, 474, 475, 476, 477
        graphic novels 467, 474
        publishers/publishing (English) 471–2, 475, 477; (French) 472–3, 474, 477
        superheroes 460, 470, 471
        terminology 474
Compagnons de Saint-Laurent 610
Compton, Anne 438
Compton, Wayde 439
Conan, Laure (Marie-Louise-Félicité Angers) 30, 36, 115, 121, 631–2
    affinity with Jesuit ideology 121
    first French Canadian woman writer 631
    as historical novelist 121
    WORKS: *À l'œuvre et à l'épreuve* 121; *Angéline de Montbrun* 121, 631
Confederation 104, 115, 127, 186, 204, 289, 336, 461, 494, 586
    Anglo-French divisions pre-Confederation 104–5
Confederation poets (*see* Post-Confederation poets)
Connelly, Karen 577
Connolly, Kevin 437
Connor, Ralph (Rev. Charles William Gordon) 191, 195, 198–200, 201, 206
    bestsellers 199
    and Canadian nationalism 199
    Christian adventure narratives 198
    relations with publishers 200
    WORKS: *Black Rock* 199; *Corporal Cameron of the North West Mounted Police* 200; *The Foreigner* 200; *Glengarry Schooldays* 199; *The Man from Glengarry* 199, 206, 215; *The Sky Pilot* 199, 206, 215; *The Sky Pilot in No Man's Land* 227
Conquest 114, 120, 122, 123, 201
Constantin-Weyer, Maurice 650
    WORKS: *Un homme se penche sur son passé* 650
Contact 305
Contemporary Verse 287, 305
Cook, James 67, 84
Cook, Margaret Michele 599
Cook, Meira 431

Cook, Michael 408
  WORKS: *The Head, Guts and Soundbone Dance* 408; *Jacob's Wake* 408
cookbooks 161-2
  domestic dimension of nature writing 162
  emphasis on Canadian produce 162
  The Galt Cook Book 161-2
  herbal remedies 162
Cooper, Afua 560, 562, 571, 579
Cooper, Dave 477
  WORKS: *Crumple* 477; *Ripple* 477; *Suckle* 477
Cooper, James Fenimore 113
Copeland, Ann 397
  WORKS: *At Peace* 397
Corneloup, Cornelius 234
  WORKS: *La Coccinelle de 22e* 234-5
Costain, Thomas B. 291
  WORKS: *The Black Rose* 291; *The Silver Chalice* 291
Coulter, John 403, 404
  WORKS: *Riel* 403, 404
Coupland, Douglas 472
  "Generation X" comic strip 472
coureurs de bois 14, 23, 324
Courtemanche, Gil 577
  WORKS: *Un dimanche à la piscine à Kigali* 577
Cousture, Arlette 643
  WORKS: *Les Filles de Caleb* 643
Cox, Palmer 191, 195, 461
Cox, Ross 77
  WORKS: *Adventures on the Columbia River* 77
Crate, Joan 511
  WORKS: *Pale as Real Ladies: Poems for Pauline Johnson* 511
Crawford, Isabella Valancy 88, 139, 168-9, 187-9
  cross-border publishing 169, 187, 189
  poetry 169
  short stories and serial fiction 169, 187
  WORKS: *Malcolm's Katie* 169; *Winona; or, The Foster Sisters* 187; *Wrecked! or, The Rosclerras of Mistree* 187
Crawley, Alan 287, 305
Creeley, Robert 305, 423, 427
Crémazie, Octave 110-11, 584, 585-6
  as letter writer 585-6
  as poet 586
  WORKS: "Le Vieux Soldat canadien"; "Le Drapeau de Carillon" 110, 586; "Promenade de trois morts" 586; "Le Ver" 586
Cross-Canada collaborative projects 408

Crozier, Lorna 432
Crummey, Michael 431, 432, 439
  WORKS: *Hard Light* 439; *River Thieves* 504
Crusz, Rienzi 561, 563
Culleton Mosionier, Beatrice 504-5
  WORKS: *In Search of April Raintree* 504; *Night of the Trickster* 528
cummings, e.e. 285
Cumyn, Alan 240-1
  WORKS: *The Famished Lover* 240; *The Sojourner* 240-1
Currie, Sheldon 386-7
  WORKS: "The Glace Bay Miners' Museum" 386-7
Curzon, Sarah Anne 119

D'Alfonso, Antonio 561, 564, 567, 646
  WORKS: *Avril ou l'anti-passion* 646
Dabydeen, Cyril 562
Daigle, France 598, 649
Dale, Arch 462
Dallaire, Michel 599
Dalpé, Jean Marc 617
  WORKS: *Le Chien* 617; *Hawkesbury Blues* 617; *Nickel* 617
Daniells, Roy 305
Danis, Daniel 626, 627
  WORKS: *Celle-là* 627; *Cendres de cailloux* 627
Daoust, Julien 608
  WORKS: *Le Défenseur de la foi* 608; *Pour le Christ* 608; *Le Rédempteur* 608; *Le Triomphe de la Croix* 608
Davey, Frank 334, 428-9
  founding editor of *Open Letter* 428
  interest in L=A=N=G=U=A=G=E poetry 428
  interest in popular culture 428
  WORKS: "Surviving the Paraphrase" 334
Davidson, Craig 400
  WORKS: *Rust and Bone* 400
Davies, Robertson 291, 295, 403, 452-4
  Centennial participation 320
  colonial ambivalence in 452, 453
  crossovers between fiction and drama in 452-3, 454
  early comic fictions 295
  interest in Jungian psychoanalysis 295, 453
  intertextuality 452
  as newspaper editor 295
  as playwright 295, 453
  postmodern elements in 453, 454

WORKS: *At My Heart's Core* 403; *Cornish Trilogy* 454; *Deptford Trilogy* 454; *Fifth Business* 236, 453–4; *Leaven of Malice* 295, 453; *A Mixture of Frailties* 295; *Tempest-Tost* 295, 453; *What's Bred in the Bone* 453
Dawson, William 144, 145
Day, David 504
Dearing, Ramona 388
  WORKS: *So Beautiful* 388
De Gaulle, Gen. Charles 316, 330, 368
De la Roche, Mazo 248, 265–6
  and autobiography 265
  portrait photos of 265
  relation with Caroline Clement 265
  WORKS: *Jalna* series 265; *Ringing the Changes: An Autobiography* 265
De Mille, James 191, 192, 193–5
  boys' adventure stories by 194
  cross-border and transatlantic publishing of 194
  historical romances by 194
  WORKS: *The B.O.W.C. A Book for Boys* 194; *The Dodge Club or, Italy in 1859* 194; *The Elements of Rhetoric* 194; *The Martyr of the Catacombs: A Tale of Ancient Rome* 194; *A Strange Manuscript Found in a Copper Cylinder* 194
De Soto, Lewis 565
De Vries, Maggie 551–2
Dease, Peter Warren 86
Defoe, Daniel 58
Delahaye, Guy 590
Delisle, Guy 477
  WORKS: *Pyongyang: A Journey in North Korea* 477; *Shenzhen: A Travelogue from China* 477
Delta 305
Demerson, Velma 551
  WORKS: *Incorrigible* 551
Dempster, Barry 382, 432
Denison, Flora MacDonald 218–19
  social salvation fiction by 218
  as suffragist 218
  WORKS: *Mary Melville: The Psychic* 211
Denison, Merrill 403
  WORKS: *Marsh Hay* 403
Dennis, Darrell 535, 625
  WORKS: *Tales of an Urban Indian* 535, 625; *Trickster of Third Avenue East* 535
Dent, Charles 122
Dentin, Louis 588
Derkson, Jeff 430

Des Roches, Roger 417–18
Des Rosiers, Joël 579
Desbarats, George-Édouard 187, 188–9
Desbarats, Peter 314
  WORKS: *The State of Quebec* 314
Desbiens, Jean-Paul 323
  WORKS: *Les Insolences du Frère Untel / Letters of Brother Anonymous* 322, 323
Desbiens, Patrice 598–9, 600
  WORKS: *L'Espace qui reste* 598; *Hénnissements* 599; *L'Homme invisible / The Invisible Man* 598; *Poèmes anglais* 598; *Rouleaux de printemps* 599
Descartes, René 29
DesRochers, Alfred 590, 591, 596
  WORKS: *À l'ombre de l'Orford* 591, 596
Desrosiers, Geneviève 604
Devoir, Le 234, 323, 570, 577
Dewart, Edward Hartley 114, 127
  on colonial literature 114
  editor of first anglophone poetry anthology 114
  WORKS: *Selections from Canadian Poets* 114, 127
Dewdney, Christopher 145, 430–1
  WORKS: *A Palaeozoic Geology of London, Ontario: Poems and Collages* 430; *Predators of the Adoration: Selected Poems, 1972–82* 430; *Signal Fires* 431
Dickens, Charles 65, 178, 192
Dickinson, Adam 431
Dickinson, Emily 156
Dickson, Robert 599
  WORKS: *Grand ciel bleu par ici* 599; *Humains paysages en temps de paix relative* 599
Diefenbaker, John (Prime Minister) 351
Dilworth, Ira 296, 297
Dingle, Adrian 464
Dion, Joseph 503
  WORKS: *My Tribe, The Crees* 503
Dobozy, Tamas 381, 385, 399
  WORKS: *Last Notes* 399
Donlan, John 431
Donnacona 12
Donnell, David 395
  WORKS: *The Blue Ontario Hemingway Boat Race* 395
Dorge, Claude 618
  WORKS: *L'Article 23* 618; *Le Roitelet* 618; *La Trilogie des Tremblay* (with Irène Mahé) 618
Dorion, Hélène 602
Dorn, Edward 445

Dorsey, Candas Jane 384
Doucet, Julie 475, 476
　WORKS: *Dirty Plotte* 475, 476; *Journal* 475, 476; *The Madame Paul Affair* 476; *My New York Diary* 476
Doucette, Leonard E. 606
Dougall, Lily 217–18
　WORKS: *The Madonna of a Day* 217–18
Doutré, Joseph 108–9
　WORKS: *Les Fiancés de 1812* 108–9
Doyle, James 170
Dragland, Stan 431, 434
drama festivals
　AfriCanadian Playwrights Festival 418
　Blyth Festival 404
　Dominion Drama Festival 403
　Edmonton International Fringe Festival 419, 420
　Festival de Théâtre des Amériques (Festival TransAmériques) 520, 532, 533
　Magnetic North Theatre Festival 404
　Shaw Festival, Niagara-on-the-Lake 416
　Stratford Festival 403–4, 452, 454
　summer fringe festivals 419
　World Indigenous Theatre Festival 520
Dubé, Marcel 324, 611
　WORKS: *Au retour des oies blanches* 611; *Les Beaux Dimanches* 612; *Bilan* 611; *Florence* 611; *Un simple soldat* 611; *Zone* 611
Dubois, René-Daniel 622, 626
　WORKS: *26 bis, impasse de Colonel Foisy* 623; *Being at Home with Claude* 623
Duchamp, Marcel 252
Ducharme, Réjean 638–9, 646, 647
　WORKS: *L'Avalée des avalés* 638, 639; *Les Enfantômes* 641; *L'Hiver de force* 641; *Le Nez qui voque* 639
Dudek, Louis 302, 305, 307, 308, 427
　WORKS: *East of the City* 307
Dudoward, Valerie 520
　WORKS: *Teach Me the Ways of the Sacred Circle* 520
Dugas, Marcel 590
Duguay, Calixte 619
Duguay, Raoul 601
Dumont, Marilyn 423, 507, 514
　WORKS: *A Really Good Brown Girl* 514
Duncan, Norman 172, 195
　WORKS: *The Soul of the Street: Correlated Stories of the New York Syrian Quarter* 172; *The Way of the Sea* 172
Duncan, Robert 428

Duncan, Sara Jeannette 52, 139, 169–70, 191, 195, 196, 198, 211, 212
　on copyright law 211
　cross-border and transatlantic publishing 170
　female artist 170
　journalism 191, 211
　on her life in India 212
　on lives of girls and women 166, 170
　novels as social critique 212
　socio-political themes in 172, 211–12
　support for woman suffrage 211
　travel writing by 212
　WORKS: *The Burnt Offering* 212; *A Daughter of Today* 212; "The Heir Apparent" 170; *The Imperialist* 52, 170, 198, 212; "A Mother in India" 170, 171; *The Pool in the Desert* 170; *Set in Authority* 198, 212; *Simple Adventures of a Memsahib* 212; *A Social Departure: How Orthodocia and I Went Round the World By Ourselves* 212; *Those Delightful Americans* 198
Dunlop, William 87
　WORKS: *Statistical Sketches of Upper Canada for the Use of Emigrants* 87
Dupré, Louise 601, 622
Durand, Yves Sioui 533–4, 624
　co-founder of Ondinnok 533
　collaboration with Robert Lepage 533
　Pan-American Indigenous myths 533, 534
　WORKS: *Hamlet le Malécite* 625; *Le Porteur des peines du monde* 533, 624
Durham Report 104, 107–8, 115, 314, 605, 607
Durkin, Douglas 255
Dussault, Louisette 621
　WORKS: *Moman* 621
Dutton, Paul 430
Duval-Thibault, Anne-Marie 587

Edel, Leon 281
Edgar, Pelham 1, 286, 288
Éditions d'Acadie 597–8, 648
Éditions de Blé 597, 600
Éditions Prise de parole 597, 598, 599, 648
Edugyan, Esi 579
Eksteins, Modris 537, 540, 541, 542
　WORKS: *Walking since Daybreak* 537, 538, 540–1
Elberg, Yehuda 559
Eliot, T. S. 252, 262, 271, 278, 285, 297, 300, 340, 344
Elliott, George 391
　WORKS: *The Kissing Man* 391
Éluard, Paul 594

Emerson, Ralph Waldo 134
Engel, Marian 482
  WORKS: *Bear* 482
Engels, Friedrich 51
English, Sharon 388
  WORKS: *Zero Gravity* 388
environmentalism/ecology 74, 76, 96, 158, 164, 206, 253–4, 307, 316, 319, 361, 363, 364, 434, 435, 480, 517, 528, 532, 534, 546, 555, 647
Epic of Gilgamesh 443
Ermatinger, Francis 78
Espinet, Ramabai 562, 565, 575
essays (English) 219, 289, 304, 344–5, 346, 347–9, 352, 359, 362, 367, 377, 378–9, 390, 424, 426, 432, 433, 486, 492, 517; (French) 314, 321–2, 323–4, 569–70, 635, 648
ethnic diversity 252, 262, 290, 299–300, 326, 330–1, 451–2, 491, 543, 561–4, 566–7, 575, 623–4, 645–6, 650
  writers of divers ethnic origins (English)
    Afghan 568
    Africadian 424, 457–8
    anthologies of 558
    Argentinian 568
    Caribbean 331, 395, 552, 560, 562, 577, 579
    Chinese 290, 393, 395, 544–5, 546, 561, 572; Scottish-Chinese-Swedish 449
    Czech 540
    Ethiopian 568
    German 248–50, 540
    Hungarian 300, 479
    Icelandic 395, 561
    Italian 333, 561
    Japanese 290, 331, 428, 448–9, 545–6, 552, 561, 572–3
    Jewish 294, 300–1, 309, 326–8, 393, 441–2, 449–51, 491–2, 539–40, 561, 568–9
    Korean 546, 547–8
    Latvian 538
    Lebanese 568, 579; Scottish-Lebanese 479
    Mennonite 554, 561, 570
    South Asian 392, 395, 443–4, 452, 479, 548, 549–50, 552, 561, 577, 579
    Ukrainian 300, 538, 561
  writers of divers ethnic origins (French)
    African 600
    Brazilian 567
    Caribbean 645–6
    Chinese 567–8, 646
    Egyptian 562

    German 650
    Haïtian 562, 575–6, 579
    Iraqi 562
    Italian 561, 646
    Japanese 567–8
    Jewish 567, 645
    Lebanese 562
    Moroccan 562
    Polish 567
    Tunisian 650
  see also Black Canadians; transculturalism; multiculturalism
ethnic drama (English) 417
  Africadian 419
  African Canadian 418, 419, 458
  Chinese 417–18
  Latin American 418
  multicultural 417–18
  South Asian 417
ethnic drama (French)
  Greek 623
  Italian 623
  Lebanese 624
  see also Aboriginal drama; Métis
Evans, Hubert 232
  WORKS: *The New Front Line* 232
Évanturel, Eudore 587
exploration narratives (English) 70–2, 73–6, 83–5, 86; (French) 10–11, 13, 14
Expo 67, Montreal 312
  and Arctic North 318, 319
  canoe pageant 319
  Christian pavilion 330
  controversies 315–16
  cultural significance of 312, 318–19
  Dutch pavilion 334
  English-French debates on national identity 314, 315–16
  French pavilion 313
  Pavilion of Canada 313
  Pavilion of Canada's Indians 315, 319–20
  Pavilion of Quebec 314
  and popular culture 312, 317–18
  translation problems 314, 322
  writers' participation in 313, 320–2

Factory Theatre 406–7
Faessler, Shirley 395
Fairley, Barker 274, 278, 282
Farhoud, Abla 579, 624
  WORKS: *Les Filles du 5-10-15c* 624; *Jeux de patience* 624; *Quand j'étais grande* 624

719

Faribault, Marcel 314
  WORKS: *Some Thoughts on the Mounting Crisis in Quebec* 314
Faulkner, William 493
Favel, Floyd 527, 532–3
  importance of Aboriginal elements in 533
  revisions of Western genres 533
  WORKS: *All My Relatives* 533; *Artaud and the Tarahumaras* 533; *Governor of the Dew* 533; *House of Sonya* 533; *Lady of Silences* 533
Fawcett, Brian 387
  WORKS: *My Career with the Leafs* 387; *Capital Tales* 387, 641–2
feminism 204, 211, 213, 216, 221–2, 260, 397, 434, 469, 477, 616, 620, 641
  and criticism (English) 310; (French) 599
  and drama (English) 455, 531–2; (French) 616, 620–2
  Famous Five 220
  feminist history 641
  and fiction (English) 361, 364, 378, 379, 380, 448, 456, 489–90, 492; (French) 398, 636, 641–2, 644, 645
  lesbian 415, 455, 492
  maternalist 213, 216, 219
  and poetry (English) 310, 364, 428, 434; (French) 601, 602
Fenian raids 122
Fennario, David 408
  bilingual plays 408
  on English-French tensions in Montreal 408
  on racial and homophobic tensions in Montreal 408
  WORKS: *Balconville* 408; *Condoville* 408
Ferland, Albert 590
Ferland, Jean-Baptiste-Antoine 29, 116, 120
Ferland, Marcien 618
  WORKS: *Les Batteux* 618; *Au temps de la Prairie* 618
Ferne, Doris 287, 305
Féron, Jean (Joseph-Marc-Octave Lebel) 650
  WORKS: *La Métisse* 650
Ferron, Jacques 324, 383, 610, 612, 640
  influences on 640
  reinterpretation of foundation myth 640
  WORKS: *L'Amélanchier* 640; *Contes du pays incertain* 383; *Les grands soleils* 610; *La Tête du roi* 612
Fiddlehead, The 394, 426
Filion, Laetitia 234
  WORKS: *Yolande, la fiancée* 234
Finch, Robert 278, 320, 425

  WORKS: *Dover Beach Revisited* 425; *Poems* 286; *Silverthorn Bush* 425
Findley, Timothy 381, 386, 454–5, 483, 490
  crossovers between fiction and drama in 453–4
  early dramatic career 454
  on history, fiction, and myth 490
  intertextuality and parody 455, 490
  pioneering gay writer 455
  WORKS: drama: *Elizabeth Rex* 455; *The Trials of Ezra Pound* 455; fiction: *The Butterfly Plague* 455; *Famous Last Words* 455, 490; *The Last of the Crazy People* 490; *Not Wanted on the Voyage* 454, 490; *The Piano Man's Daughter* 456; *Spadework* 455; *The Telling of Lies* 490; *The Wars* 237, 455, 482, 490
Finnigan, Joan 386
First Nations (*see* Aboriginal peoples)
First Statement 287, 290, 291, 305, 308
Fitzgerald, F. Scott 268, 409, 475
Fitzgibbon, Agnes 148
  aesthetics of 148–50
  collaboration with C. P. Traill 148
  Illustration by 149
Flamand, Jacques 599
Flaubert, Gustave 636
Fleming, Anne 398
  WORKS: *Pool-Hopping* 398
Fleming, May Agnes 168, 191, 192
  bestsellers by 193
  cross-border publishing 192–3
  migration to New York 193
  short stories and serial novels by 192–3
  WORKS: *The Baronet's Bride* 193; *Eulalie; or, A Wife's Tragedy* 193; *Sybil Campbell; or, The Queen of the Isle* 193
Ford, Ford Madox 264
Ford, R. A. D. 425
  WORKS: *Coming from Afar* 425
Foster, Cecil 562, 573
Foster, Harold 462
Fournier, Pierre 468, 473
Franchers, Gabriel 76–7
Francis, Marvin 516
Francœur, Lucien 601
Franco-Albertan writing 619, 650–1
Franco-Manitoban writing
  drama 609, 618
  fiction 650
  poetry 600–1
Franco-Ontarian writing
  drama 609, 616–18

fiction 649–50
poetry 598–600
Frank, Anne 538
Franklin, Sir John 67, 83–5
    accounts of travel ordeals by 84, 85
    Franklin myth 84
    officers' journals 85
    popularity of travel narratives 83
    on stories of Aboriginal life 85
    WORKS: *Narrative of a Journey to the Shores of the Polar Sea* 83–5
Fransaskois writing 618–19, 650
Franzen, Jonathan 375
Fraser, Brad 416
    WORKS: *Martin Yesterday* 416; *Poor Super Man* 416; *Snake in Fridge* 416; *Unidentified Human Remains and the True Nature of Love* 416
Fraser, D. M. 387
    WORKS: *Class Warfare* 387
Fraser, Keith *Telling My Love Lies* 388
Fraser, Raymond *Rum River* 388
Fraser, Simon 71–2
    landscape descriptions 71–2
    relations with Aboriginal people 72
Fréchette, Carole 621
    WORKS: *Le Collier d'Hélène* 627; *Jean et Béatrice* 622; *La Peau d'Élisa* 621; *Les Quatre Morts de Marie* 622; *Les Sept Jours de Simon Labrosse* 622; *Violette sur la terre* 627
Fréchette, Louis-Honoré 119–20, 127–8, 584, 586–7, 607, 609, 651
    French Canada's first national poet 127–8
    WORKS: *Félix Poutré* 607; *Les Fleurs boréales* 127–8; *La Légende d'un peuple* 119–20, 586; *La Voix de l'exilé* 586; *Mes Loisirs* 586; *Originaux et détraqués* 651
Freeman, Alice Fenton (Faith Fenton) 213–14
    journalism 213
    on position of women 213
    travel writing 213–14
Freeman, David 406, 407
    WORKS: *Battering Ram* 406, 407; *Creeps* 406, 407
French, David 241, 406–7
    WORKS: *Leaving Home* 406, 407; *Of the Fields, Lately* 406–7; *Salt-Water Moon* 406, 407; *1949* 406, 407; *Soldier's Heart* 406, 407
Freud, Vera 359
Freytag-Loringhoven, Baroness Elsa von (Elsa Plotz) 249–50, 251
    Portrait 250
    WORKS: "Love-Chemical Relationship" 252
Friesen, Patrick 431, 561
Frost, Robert 494
Frutkin, Mark 382
Frye, Northrop 3, 139, 145, 151, 274, 302, 306, 309, 311, 313, 321, 325, 333, 339, 340, 343, 344, 345–50, 352, 353, 423, 424, 425, 501
    academic career of 345–6
    on Bible 346, 347, 348, 349, 432
    on Blake 346
    on Canadian-American relations 349
    on Canadian culture 346, 347, 348, 349
    as critic and theorist 346, 423
    on garrison mentality 349
    on myths and archetypes 313, 346, 347
    on Shakespeare, Milton, and Eliot 346
    UTQ annual surveys of Canadian poetry 294, 309, 311, 347–8, 424
    WORKS: *Anatomy of Criticism* 346; *The Bush Garden*; *Conclusion to A Literary History of Canada* 3, 348–9, 350, 501; *T. S. Eliot* 346; *Fearful Symmetry* 346; *Fools of Time: Studies in Shakespearean Tragedy* 346; *The Great Code: The Bible and Literature* 346; *A Natural Perspective: The Development of Shakespearean Comedy and Romance* 346; *The Return of Eden: Five Essays on Milton's Epics* 346; *The Secular Scripture: A Study of the Structure of Romance* 346; *Words with Power: Being a Secondary Study of "The Bible and Literature"* 346, 347
Fuller, Buckminster 318
fur trade
    Aboriginal women's roles in 511
    French fur trade 23, 24
fur traders' journals 67–9, 75–7, 86
    letters (male) 78
    letters (female) 68, 79–80
    logistics of 80
    observations 69
    undelivered letters 80–1
Fussell, Paul 226, 240
Fytche, Maria Amelia 216–17
    New Woman novel by 216
    WORKS: *Kerchiefs to Hunt Souls* 216–17

Gagnon, Charles 317, 330
Gagnon, Madeleine 601
Gale, Lorena 419
    WORKS: *Angélique* 419

Gallant, Mavis 301, 357, 359, 360, 365–9, 380, 381, 384, 394
  comic satires 394
  expatriate writer in Paris 301, 365, 366, 367–8
  first *New Yorker* story 357, 366–7, 394
  on Montreal 369
  on narrative technique 367, 368, 383
  and *The New Yorker* 366
  on outsiders 368, 369
  on post-war Europe 301, 368–9
  reputation in Canada 365–6
  WORKS: *Across the Bridge* 369; *The End of the World and Other Stories* 365; "The Events in May: A Paris Notebook" 367–8; *A Fairly Good Time* 366; *From the Fifteenth District* 366; *Going Ashore* 366; *Green Water, Green Sky* 301, 366; *Home Truths: Selected Stories* 365, 369, 393; Linnet Muir stories 369; "Madeline's Birthday" 357, 359; *Montreal Stories* 365; *Overhead in a Balloon* 368; *Paris Stories* 365; *The Pegnitz Junction* 368; *Selected Stories* 357, 365, 394; "What Is Style?" 367, 368
Galt, John 87
  WORKS: *Bogle Corbet* 87; *Laurie Todd: or, The Settlers in the Woods* 87
Gandhi, Indira 479, 489
Gareau, Laurier 618–19
  WORKS: *The Betrayal /La Trahison* 618; *Pas de problèmes* 618
Garneau, Alfred 587
Garneau, François-Xavier 29, 106, 109–10, 115, 116, 584–5
  celebrator of heroic past 109–10
  francophone response to Durham Report 109
  French Canada's national historian 109, 585
  on Iroquois 109
  liberal ideology of 110
  as poet 585
  WORKS: "Le Dernier Huron" 585; *Histoire du Canada depuis sa découverte jusqu'à nos jours* (3 vols.) 109–10, 585; "Le Voyageur" 585
Garneau, Michel 602
Garneau, Saint-Denys Hector de 329, 590, 591–2
  WORKS: *Regards et jeux dans l'espace* 590, 591
Garner, Hugh 295, 382–3
  WORKS: *Cabbagetown* 295; *Hugh Garner's Best Stories* 382–3

Garnier, Charles 36
Gartner, Zsuzsi 383, 398
Garvin, John W.
  WORKS: (ed.) *Canadian Poets* 272
Gaspé, Philippe Aubert de (fils) 629
  WORKS: *L'Influence d'un livre* 629
Gaspé, Philippe Aubert de (père) 112–13, 127
  construction of national identity in 631
  English translations of 631
  on fiction and history 112, 631
  ideology of 631
  influences on 631
  on "la petite histoire" 112
  reference to Garneau 112
  WORKS: *Les Anciens Canadiens* 112–13, 120, 123, 480, 631
Gaspereau Press 439
Gass, Ken 406, 407
Gaston, Bill 381, 399
  WORKS: *Mount Appetite* 399
Gault, Connie 413
  WORKS: *Sky* 413
Gauthier, Louis 644
  WORKS: *Voyage en Inde avec un grand détour* 644
Gauvreau, Claude 594, 595–6, 610
  WORKS: drama: *La Charge de l'orignal epormyable* 610; *Les Oranges sont vertes* 610; poetry: "Ode à l'ennemi" 596; *Œuvres créatrices complètes* 595; *Poèmes de détention* 595
Geary, Dave 469
Geertz, Clifford 9
Gélinas, Gratien 320, 609–10
  WORKS: *Bousille et les justes* 611; *Fridolinades* 609; *Hier, les enfants dansaient* 612; *Tit-Coq* 610–11
Genet, Jean 533
Genuist, Monique 651
  WORKS: *Nootka* 651
Geoffroy, Louis 601
George, Chief Dan 319, 323, 501
  as orator 501
  as stage and film actor 519
  WORKS: "A Lament for Confederation" 319, 501; *My Heart Soars* 501; "Words to a Grandchild" 501
George, David 54
Gérard, Étienne 562
Gérin-Lajoie, Antoine 607, 630
  WORKS: *Jean Rivard, le défricheur* 630; *Jean Rivard, l'économiste* 630

Germain, Jean-Claude 614–15
  and affirmation of Quebec identity 615
  and carnivalesque 615
  as director of Théâtre d'Aujourd'hui 615
  and historical drama and satire 615
  and nationalistic aims 615
  WORKS: *A Canadian Play / Une plaie canadienne* 615; *Les hauts et les bas de la vie d'une diva* 615; *Mamours et conjugat* 615; *Les nuits de l'indiva* 615; *Un pays dont la devise est je m'oublie* 615
Gervais, André 601
Gibb, Camilla 577
  WORKS: *Sweetness in the Belly* 577
Gibbon, John Murray 228
  WORKS: *The Conquering Hero* 228
Gibson, Graeme 359
  WORKS: *The Bedside Book of Birds: An Avian Miscellany* 359
Gibson, Margaret 398
Gide, André 325
Giguère, Roland 324, 594, 595, 604
  WORKS: *L'Âge de la parole* 594; *Faire naître* 594; *Forêt vierge folle* 594; *La Main au feu* 594
Gilbert, Sky 416
  director of Buddies in Bad Times theater company 415
  plays influenced by Hébert and Tremblay 416
  WORKS: *Drag Queens on Trial* 416
Gill, Charlotte 386
  WORKS: *Ladykiller* 386
Girard, Rodolphe 609
Glass, Joanna McClelland 413
  on Canadian-American relations 413
  on familial emotional violence 413
  WORKS: *Canadian Gothic* 413; *If We Are Women* 413; *Trying* 413
Glassco, Bill 406, 407
Glassco, John 248, 269–71
  and queer culture 269, 271
  as translator 269, 303
  WORKS: *Memoirs of Montparnasse* 270–1
Glennon, Paul 400
  WORKS: *How Did You Sleep?* 400
globalization 369, 434, 536, 556, 577, 578
  migration 537, 543
Globe, The / Globe and Mail, The (Toronto) 136, 137, 138, 169, 177, 206, 211, 213, 215, 509
Glover, Douglas 381, 387–8
  WORKS: *Dog Attempts to Drown Man in Saskatoon* 387; *Notes Home from a Prodigal Son* 387

Gobeil, Pierre 647
  WORKS: *La Mort de Marlon Brando* 647
Godbout, Jacques 638, 639, 640
  WORKS: *L'Aquarium* 638; *Salut Galarneau!* 639
Godfrey, Dave 329, 331–2, 387, 436, 577
  WORKS: *Dark Must Yield* 387; *Death Goes Better with Coca-Cola* 387; *The New Ancestors* 331–2
Godin, Gerald 584, 596
  WORKS: *Cantouques. Poèmes en langue verte* 596
Godwin, William 51
  WORKS: *Political Justice* 51
Goethe, Johann Wolfgang von 134
Goethe, Ottilie von 90
Gogol, Nikolai 178
Goldsmith, Oliver 88
  WORKS: *The Rising Village* 88
Goodison, Lorna 564
Gosse, Philip Henry 146–7
  anti-Darwinism of 147
  entomologist 146, 147
  life and career 146, 147
  narrative style of 146–7
  WORKS: *The Canadian Naturalist* 146–7; *Entomologica Terra Novae* 146
Gothic 117, 193, 295–6, 325, 365, 374, 382, 383, 386–7, 413–14, 456, 480, 495, 515, 630
Goto, Hiromi 561, 572, 573
  WORKS: *Chorus of Mushrooms* 573
Gould, John 399
  WORKS: *Kilter* 399
Goupil, René 37
Gourmois, Maurice de 649
Gowan, Elsie Park 403
Gowdy, Barbara 495
  parodic elements in 480
  on southern Ontario Gothic 495
  as writer of ecological fable 480
  WORKS: *Falling Angels* 495; *Helpless* 495; *Mister Sandman* 495; *The Romantic* 495; *We So Seldom Look on Love* 495; *The White Bone* 480
Grady, Wayne 384
  WORKS: (ed.) *The Penguin Book of Canadian Stories* 384
Graham, Andrew 69
Graham, Gwethalyn 291, 291 n. 8, 294, 318
  WORKS: *Earth and High Heaven* 294; *Swiss Sonata* 294
Grandbois, Alain 592, 594
  WORKS: *Les Îles de la nuit* 592

Grandpré, Pierre de 3
  WORKS: (ed.) *Histoire de la littérature française du Québec* 3
Grant, George 317–18, 319, 350–3, 433
  academic career of 350
  anti-technology 351
  on Canadian-American relations 352
  Christian conservative ideology of 351
  influence on cultural nationalists 352, 353
  as philosopher 350, 351
  WORKS: *English-Speaking Justice* 352; *Lament for a Nation: The Defeat of Canadian Nationalism* 319, 351–2; *Philosophy in the Mass Age* 351; *Technology and Empire: Perspectives on North America* 352; *Time as History* 352
Grass, Günter 316
  WORKS: *The Tin Drum* 327
Graves, Robert 333
Gray, John 241
  WORKS: *Billy Bishop Goes to War* 241, 405
Grey Owl (Archibald Stansfeld Belaney) 249, 489, 511
Griffin, Scott 436
  and Griffin Poetry Prize 436, 440
Griffiths, Buss 474
  WORKS: *Now You're Logging* 474
Griffiths, Linda 405, 509, 521
  WORKS: *Maggie and Pierre* 405
Grignon, Claude-Henri 324, 634
Grip magazine 172, 181, 187, 191, 461
Gross, Paul 242
Groulx, Lionel 632–3
  WORKS: *L'Appel de la race* 632–3
Group of Seven 262, 283
Grove, Frederick Philip 248–55
  autobiography of 248
  double identity of 248–9, 251
  and Elsa Plotz 249–50
  immigrant perspective of 251
  nature writing by 253–4
  portraits of 254
  WORKS: *Fanny Essler* 249; *Fruits of the Earth* 256; *In Search of Myself* 248, 262; *Master of the Mill* 254–5; *Maurermeister Ihles Haus* 249; *Our Daily Bread* 256; *Over Prairie Trails* 248, 252, 253, 263; *A Search for America* 248, 251; *Settlers of the Marsh* 248, 251–2, 256; *The Turn of the Year* 248, 254
Guèvremont, Germaine 293, 314, 636
  WORKS: *Marie-Didace* 293; *Le Survenant / The Outlander* 293, 314, 636, 647

Guilemay, J. 468
Gummerson, Penny 535
  WORKS: *Wawatay* 535
Gunn, Genni 386
  WORKS: *Hungers* 386
Gunners, Kristjana 381
Guppy, Stephen 384
Gurik, Robert 612
Gustafson, Ralph 302, 305, 307, 333, 433
  WORKS: *Configurations at Midnight* 433; *Fire on Stone* 433; *Flight into Darkness* 307; *The Golden Chalice* 307; *Selected Poems* 433
Guyon, Louis 608

Haeffely, Claude 468
Haentjens, Brigitte 617
Hage, Rawi 568
  WORKS: *Cockroach* 578; *De Niro's Game* 568
Hakluyt, Richard 11
Hale, Katherine 228
  WORKS: "Grey Knitting" 228
Halfe, Louise Bernice 439, 507, 511
  on women in the fur trade 511
  WORKS: *Bear Bones and Feathers* 511; *Blue Marrow* 511
Haliburton, Thomas Chandler 52, 55, 60, 61, 100, 111, 178
  on Canadian relations with Britain and America 64–5
  as humorist 63 (Illustration)
  as satirist 63–5
  on slavery and race 64
  as writer of Canada's first bestseller 63
  WORKS: *The Clockmaker* 63–5; *Nature and Human Nature* 65; *The Old Judge* 65; "Recollections of Nova Scotia" 62–3; *Sam Slick's Wise Saws* 65
Hall, Phil 431
Hamelin, Louis 646–7
  WORKS: *Cow Boy* 647; *Le Joueur de flûte* 647; *La Rage* 646
Hammett, Dashiel 645
Hancock, Geoff 384
Harbec, Hélène 598
Hardin, Herschel 519
  WORKS: *Esker Mike and His Wife, Agiluk* 519
Hare, John 585
Harel, Simon 643
Hargrave, James 78, 79, 80

Hargrave, Letitia McTavish 79–80
  on "country marriages" 79–80
  on domestic details of fur trade life 79
  on Hudson's Bay Company 79
  on logistics of letter writing 81
  WORKS: *The Letters of Letitia Hargrave* 79–80
Harmon, Daniel 75
Harper, Stephen (Prime Minister) 224
Harper's magazines 136, 170, 171, 173–7
HarperCollins 385
Harris, Claire 562, 563
Harrison, Charles Yale 232
  WORKS: *Generals Die in Bed* 232
Harrison, Susie Frances 139, 168, 169
  WORKS: *Crowded Out! And Other Sketches* 169
Hart, Julia Catherine Beckwith 106
  WORKS: *St. Ursula's Convent; or, The Nun of Canada* 106
Harvey, Charles 633
  WORKS: *Le Soleil* 633
Hay, Elizabeth 319, 398
  WORKS: *Late Nights on Air* 319
Haynes, Vadney 419
  WORKS: *Blacks Don't Bowl* 419
Hayward, Annette 590
Healey, Michael 405–6
  comic reassessment of *The Farm Show* 405
  interrogation of social and cultural values 405
  political analysis by 406
  WORKS: *The Drawer Boy* 405–6; *Generous* 406; *Plan B* 406
Hearne, Samuel 70, 83, 84, 435
  WORKS: *A Journey from Prince of Wales Fort, in Hudson's Bay* 70
Hébert, Anne 592, 593, 594, 640, 643–4
  deconstruction of mother figure in 644
  and early Québécois postmodern aesthetic 644
  and historical fiction 644
  and narratives of alienation 644
  WORKS: (drama): *La Cage* 621; (poetry): *Le Tombeau des rois* 593; (fiction): *Les Chambres du bois* 644; *Les Fous de Bassan* 644; *Kamouraska* 639, 640; *Le Premier Jardin* 644; *Le Torrent* 643
Hébert, Philippe 111
Hegel, Georg Wilhelm Friedrich 351
Heighton, Steven 388, 432
  WORKS: *Flight Paths of the Emperor* 388; *On Earth As It Is* 388
Hemingway, Ernest 252, 267, 268–9, 301–2, 475
  WORKS: *A Moveable Feast* 268, 269

Hémon, Louis 324, 367, 633
  WORKS: *Maria Chapdelaine* 367, 633, 634
Hempel, Amy 399
Hénault, Gilles 594, 596, 603
  WORKS: *Sémaphore* 596; *Signaux pour les voyants* 603; *Voyage au pays de mémoire* 596; *Théâtre en plein air* 594
Henday, Anthony 68, 69
Henderson, Lee 400
  WORKS: *The Broken Record Technique* 400
Hendry, Tom 407
Henry, Alexander (the elder) 72
  WORKS: *Travels and Adventures in Canada and the Indian Territories* 72
Henry, Alexander (the younger) 75–6
Herbert, John 415
  WORKS: *Fortune and Men's Eyes* 415
Herbes rouges, Les 642
Hexagone Press 322, 594–5, 603
  first publication by 594
  Hexagone generation 587, 595
  significance of 595
Highway, René 523
Highway, Thomson 506, 507, 521–3, 528
  on Aboriginal women 521–2, 523
  collaboration with brother René 523
  Indian reservation plays 522
  on Nanabush, Cree Trickster 521, 522, 534
  on social realism and myth 521, 522
  WORKS: drama: *Aria* 523; *Dry Lips Oughta Move to Kapuskasing* 522; *Ernestine Shuswap Gets Her Trout* 523; *New Song ... New Dance* 523; *The Rez Sisters* 521–2; *Rose* 522–3; *The Sage, The Dancer and the Fool* 523; fiction: *Kiss of the Fur Queen* 506
Hill, Lawrence 550, 579
  on African Canadian history 579
  on Black Canadian identity 550
  on mixed-race relations 550
  WORKS: *Black Berry, Sweet Juice: On Being Black and White in Canada* 550; *The Book of Negroes* 579
Hind, E. Cora 222
  agricultural journalism of 222
  as crop forecaster 222
  suffragist 222
Hind, Henry Youle 81
Hine, Daryl 425
historical drama (English) 118–19, 120, 403, 405, 408–9, 410, 419–20, 479, 525–6; (French) 607, 615, 618, 619, 620–1

725

historical fiction
  C19 (English) 106–7, 108, 113–14, 116–17, 117–18, 119, 121, 122, 194, 201; (French) 107, 108–9, 110, 112–13, 114–15, 115–16, 120, 121, 123, 631
  1900–70 (English) 236, 237–8, 265, 296–7
  post-1970 (English) 363–4, 374, 399, 443–4, 445–6, 447, 448, 449–50, 480–1, 482, 484–6, 487, 488, 489, 490–1, 492–3, 493–7, 579; (French) 631, 640, 643, 644, 646, 648, 649, 651
  fiction and history 105, 106–7, 108–9, 112–13, 483–4
  fiction, history, and myth 457–8, 482–3, 485–6, 489, 490, 493, 495–6, 497, 640, 643, 644, 648
  ghost stories 478–9, 494, 495, 524, 525
  historiographic metafiction 364, 479, 481
  see also Canadian literary history
historical poetry (English) 111, 114, 120–1, 286, 361, 433, 435–6, 457–8, 479, 511; (French) 110–11, 119–20, 586
historical writing (non-fiction) 105–7; (English) 111, 112, 114, 115, 118, 120, 122, 495; (French): 109–10, 116, 117, 584, 585
  C20 335, 336–7, 338, 339, 402–4, 478, 486, 492
Hodgins, Jack 239–40, 374, 381, 382, 385, 386, 496–7
  and British Columbia landscape 496
  magic realism in 496
  myth parody in 497
  use of oral traditions and history 497
  WORKS: *The Barclay Family Theatre* 391; *Broken Ground* 239–40, 497; *The Invention of the World* 482, 497; *The Resurrection of Joseph Bourne* 497; *Spit Delaney's Island* 392
Hodgson, Heather 508
Hoffmann, E. T. A. 480
Hogarth, William 58
Hollingshead, Greg 400
  WORKS: *The Roaring Girl* 400
Hollingsworth, Margaret 415
  WORKS: *Endangered Species* 415
Holmes, Rand 472
Holocaust (Shoah) 444, 450, 491, 539, 540, 546, 570
Hood, Hugh 315, 386, 388
  WORKS: *Around the Mountain: Scenes from Montreal Life* 388; *Flying a Red Kite* 388
Hood, Peter 85
Hopkinson, Nalo 385, 562
Hospital, Janette Turner 565
Hovey, Richard 134
Howard, Richard 425

Howe, Joseph 52, 55–7, 66, 88
  attitude to Black Canadians 57
  as newspaper editor 55, 62
  as politician 55
  as satirist 56–7
  as travel writer 55
  WORKS: *Acadia* 88; *Eastern Rambles* 55; *Poems and Essays* 127; *Western Rambles* 55
Howells, William Dean 136
Howison, John 87
  WORKS: *Sketches of Upper Canada* 87
Hudson's Bay Company 67, 68–70, 78–9, 81, 82, 85, 86, 333, 337, 637–8
Huggan, Isabel 543
  WORKS: *Belonging: Home Away from Home* 543
Hugo, Victor 119, 587, 631
Hunter-Duvar, John 120
Hurtubise, Jacques 473
Huston, James 110
  WORKS: *Le Répertoire national, ou le recueil de littérature canadienne* 110
Huston, Nancy 561, 568
  WORKS: *Plainsong / Cantique des Plaines* 568
Hutcheon, Linda 445
  WORKS: *The Canadian Postmodern* 445; *A Poetics of Postmodernism* 445

Ibsen, Henrik 134
Indigenous peoples (*see* Aboriginal peoples)
Ingram, Forrest 178
Innis, Harold Adams 335–9, 342–3, 352, 353
  on Canadian identity 335, 336–8, 339
  career post-First World War 339
  Chicago doctoral thesis 335
  as communications theorist 338
  as economic historian 335, 336–7
  prose style of 338–9
  theory of staples and raw materials 337
  WORKS: *The Bias of Communication* 338; *Changing Concepts of Time* 338; *The Cod Fisheries* 337–8; *Empire and Communications* 338; *The Fur Trade in Canada* 336–7; *A History of the Canadian Pacific Railway* 336, 338
Ionesco, Eugène 568
Irving, Washington 178
Ishiguro, Kazuo 571
Isham, James 69
Israel, Charles E. 331
  WORKS: *Shadows on a Wall* 331
Itani, Frances 240
  WORKS: *Deafening* 240

Index

Jacques, Stéphane 627
Jameson, Anna Brownell 89, 90
  and Aboriginal North Americans 92–3
  criticism of Aboriginal policy 93
  epistolary narrative form of 91
  and German literature 91
  London literary career 90, 91, 92
  sketchbook 92
  sublime and picturesque 89, 91, 92
  visit to Canada 90, 91
  WORKS: *Winter Studies and Summer Rambles* 90–3
Jameson, Fredric 441
Jarman, Mark Anthony 381, 386, 400
  WORKS: *New Orleans Is Sinking* 399; *19 Knives* 399
Jasmin, Claude 314, 559
  WORKS: *Ethel et le terroriste* 314
Jefferson, Thomas 64
Jelloun, Tahar Ben 563
Jennings, Francis 118
Jesuit Relations
  biblical typologies in 39
  Brébeuf 36 (Illustration)
  chronicle style of 606
  conversion theme in 30, 32, 33–4
  discursive practices in 30
  intertextuality in 31, 38–9
  landscape description in 40
  literary influence of 29–30
  Manitou figure in 34
  narrating martyrdom in 32, 35–8
  narrative construction of 30, 31, 40
  origins of 30
  theology of 30, 31–2, 40–1
Jesuits 29–41
  and Aboriginal languages 30, 33
  and Aboriginal spirituality 33–4
  and ethnography 33, 34–5
  eviction of 40
  martyrdom 35–8
  missionary work of 32–3
  see also Jesuit Relations; Brébeuf
Joe, Rita 501, 502
  WORKS: *Poems of Rita Joe* 502
Jogues, Isaac 37
Johnson, E. Pauline (Tekahionwake) 131, 139, 168, 215, 511
  journalism 215
  Native Canadian material 168, 215
  performance poetry 168, 215
  WORKS: "Canadian Born" 206, 213, 215; "The Cattle Thief" 215; *Legends of Vancouver* 168; "Mothers of a Great Red Race" 206, 215; "My Mother" 206, 215; *The Shagganappi* 168
Johnson, Samuel 47
Johnston, Basil 385, 396, 503, 508, 512, 513
  WORKS: *Indian School Days* 512; *Moose Meat & Wild Rice* 396, 503; *Ojibway Heritage* 396; *The Star-Man* 396
Johnston, Wayne 483, 494–5
  on fiction and Newfoundland history 484, 494
  and "ghost history" 494
  on landscape in fiction 494
  on Newfoundland history 494
  use of postmodern and postcolonial modes 494
  WORKS: *Baltimore's Mansion* 494; *The Colony of Unrequited Dreams* 494; *The Custodian of Paradise* 495; *The Divine Ryans* 494; *Human Amusements* 494; *The Story of Bobby O'Malley* 494; *The Time of Their Lives* 494
Joncas, Catherine 625
  WORKS: *Ukuamaq* 625
Jones, D. G. 425
  WORKS: *Butterfly on Rock: A Study of Themes and Images in Canadian Literature* 425
Jones, Richard 314
  WORKS: *Community in Crisis* 314
Joyce, James 267, 268, 269, 299, 300, 340, 472, 475, 640
Julien, Henri 461

Kady, Vivette 388
  WORKS: *Most Wanted* 388
Kafka, Franz 399, 578
Kane, Margo 519, 526, 527–8
  on Aboriginal women's experience 527
  actress and founder of Native performance groups 527
  and environmentalism 528
  on Métis subjectivity 528
  WORKS: *Confessions of an Indian Cowboy* 528; *Moonlodge* 527–8; *The River Home* 528
Kane, Paul 82
  WORKS: *Wanderings of an Artist among the Indians of North America* 82
Karafilly, Irena F. 539, 541
  WORKS: *The Stranger in the Plumed Hat* 539
Kareda, Urjo 406
Kattan, Naïm 333, 562, 570

Kearns, Lionel 428
Keats, John 132, 340
Keefer, Janice Kulyk 385, 537, 541, 542, 543, 561, 567, 572
  WORKS: *Honey and Ashes: A Story of a Family* 537, 538; *The Paris-Napoli Express* 397
Keeshig-Tobias, Lenore 506, 509
Keith, William J. 4
Kelsey, Henry 68, 69
Kennedy, Leo 280, 281, 282, 286
  WORKS: *The Shrouding* 282
Kenny George 520
  WORKS: *Indians Don't Cry* 520; *October Stranger* 520
Keon, Wayne 501-2
  WORKS: (ed.) *Sweetgrass* 501
Kerr, David 241
Kinch, Martin 407
King, Boston 54
King, Thomas 381, 385, 396-7, 439, 507, 508, 513-14, 565
  Coyote figure 397, 514
  crossovers between Western and Native creation stories 513
  fables of cultural encounter and Native survival 396
  on Native stereotypes 513
  subversive humor in 513
  WORKS: (ed.) *All My Relations* 508; "A Coyote Columbus Story" 397; *Green Grass, Running Water* 510, 513-14; *One Good Story, That One* 396, 510; *A Short History of Indians in Canada* 396; *The Truth about Stories* 396, 509
King, William Lyon Mackenzie (Prime Minister) 299, 305, 572
King, William Ross 153-4
  illustration by 154, 155
  narrative style of 153-4
  wildlife recipes of 153
  woodcraftsman 153-4
  WORKS: *The Sportsman and Naturalist in Canada* 153
Kinkaid, Jamaica 560, 563, 571
Kinsella, W. P. 384, 386, 396
  WORKS: *The Miss Hobbema Pageant* 397; *The Moccasin Telegraph* 396
Kirby, William 117, 127
  historical fiction as Gothic romance 117
  on life in New France 117
  popularity in French translations 117
  promotion by Francis Parkman 117
  WORKS: *The Golden Dog (Le Chien d'or)* 117, 127; *The UE: A Tale of Upper Canada in XII Cantos* 127
Kiyooka, Roy 561, 572
Klein, A. M. 281, 285, 286, 300, 302, 305, 309, 326, 382, 383, 441, 444, 450, 451, 561, 568
  as founder of Jewish Canadian literary tradition 300
  WORKS: *Hath Not a Jew* 286; "Out of the Pulver and the Polished Lens" 285; *The Second Scroll* 300, 458; *Short Stories* 382
Klinck, Carl F. 3-4, 48, 87, 501
  on Canada's bicultural traditions 3-4
  editor of first comprehensive Canadian literary history 3
  on the function of literary history 3
  recognition of Canada's multiethnicity 5
  references to Aboriginal storytelling 4
  WORKS: (ed.) *A Literary History of Canada: Canadian Literature in English* 3, 348, 381
Knight, Ann Cuthbert 88
  WORKS: *A Year in Canada* 88
Knight, Charles 95
Knister, Raymond 177, 178-9, 383
Kogawa, Joy 331, 448-9, 561, 568, 572, 573
  on Canadian identity 573
  cross-generic narrative forms of 448, 449
  in ethnic American literary canon 573
  importance of memory in 449
  influence of Japanese literary traditions on 449
  on Japanese Canadian Second World War history 448, 573
  metafictional strategies of 448
  WORKS: fiction: *Itsuka* 448; *Obasan* 448, 570, 573, 574; poetry: *A Choice of Dreams* 448
Kokis, Sergio 564, 565, 567, 568, 578
  WORKS: *Le Pavillon des miroirs* 567, 574
Kokotailo, Philip 271
Kourouma, Ahmadou 563
  WORKS: *Les Soleils des indépendances*
Kreiner, Philip 395
Kreisel, Henry 294, 382, 383
  WORKS: *The Almost Meeting* 382; *The Rich Man* 294
Kroetsch, Robert 256, 271, 316, 431, 436, 486, 487, 489
  as creator of historical palimpsests 436
  on history, fiction, and myth 489
  long poems of 436
  magic realism in 489
  parody in 489
  and postcolonialism 489

and postmodernism 436, 489
    WORKS: essays: "The Moment of the
        Discovery of America Continues" 486;
        The Crow Journals 489; fiction: *Badlands*
        489; *Gone Indian* 489; *The Studhorse*
        Man 316, 489; *What the Crow Said* 489;
        poetry: *Field Notes* 436; *The Ledger* 436;
        Seed Catalogue 292, 306, 436
Kuester, Martin 446
Kundera, Milan 568
Kuper, Jack 539, 540
    WORKS: *Child of the Holocaust* 540
Kwan, Michael David 544, 550
    WORKS: *Things That Must Not Be Forgotten* 544

L'Abbé, Sonnet 432
La Fayette, Mme de 41
La Potherie, Baqueville de 18, 19, 25–7
La Salle, René Robert Cavalier de 14
La Vérendrye, Pierre Gaultier de Varennes de
    13, 20
    WORKS: *Journals and Letters* 13
Laberge, Albert 634
    WORKS: *La Scouine* 634
Laberge, Marie 620, 621
    and evolution of women's theatre 621
    and female protagonists 621
    WORKS: *Aurélie, ma sœur* 621; *C'était avant*
        la guerre à l'Anse à Gilles 620, 621;
        Charlotte, ma sœur 621; *Deux tangos pour*
        toute une vie 621; *L'Homme gris* 621; *Ils*
        étaient venus pour ... 620, 621; *Jocelyne*
        Trudelle 621; *Oublier* 621
Labillois-Williams, Ida 520
Lacelle, Andrée 599
Lacombe, Gilles 599
Lacombe, Patrice 110, 630
    WORKS: *La Terre paternelle* 630
Laferrière, Dany 562, 563, 564, 645–6
    WORKS: *Comment faire l'amour avec un*
        nègre sans se fatiguer? 563, 645–6;
        L'Odeur du café 573
Lahontan, Louis-Armand de Lom d'Arce 13, 20
Lalonde, Michèle 314, 315, 333, 563, 596
    and revisionist historical drama 620
    WORKS: *Dernier recours de Baptiste à*
        Catherine 620; "Speak White" 315,
        563, 596
Lalonde, Robert 645
    WORKS: *Le Dernier Été des Indiens* 645; *Le*
        Fou du Père 645
Lam, Vincent 395
Lamming, George 566

Lamontagne-Beauregard, Blanche 590
Lampman, Archibald 30, 128–9
    international recognition of 136, 137
    nationalist aspirations of 130
    poetry 135
    premature death of 142
    relationship with Roberts 129
    WORKS: *Among the Millet and Other Poems* 131,
        133, 136; "To Chicago" 135; "The City at
        the End of Things" 141; "The Frogs,"
        "Heat," "In November" 135; *The Land*
        of Pallas 141; *The Story of an Affinity* 134;
        "Two Canadian Poets" 128, 130
Lane, Patrick 432
Langevin, André 636
Langevin, Gilbert 602
Langton, Anne 89
    WORKS: *A Gentlewoman in Upper Canada*
        89; *Langton Records: Journals and Letters*
        89; *The Story of Our Family* 89, 91
Languirand, Jacques 610
Laperrière, Augustin 609
Lapointe, Gatien 586, 596
    WORKS: *Ode au Saint-Laurent* 586, 596
Lapointe, Nicole 463
Lapointe, Paul-Marie 593–4, 595, 596
    WORKS: *La Vièrge incendie* 593
Laronde, Sandra 534
LaRoque, Emma 500, 507
    WORKS: (ed.) *Writing the Circle: Native*
        Women of Western Canada 507
Larue, Monique 569–70, 645
    WORKS: *L'Arpenteur et le navigateur* 569–70;
        Copies conformes 645
Lasnier, Rita 592–3, 594
    WORKS: *Images et Proses* 592; *Présence de*
        l'absence 592
Latif-Ghattas, Mona 562, 570
    WORKS: *Le Double Conte de l'exil* 570
Lau, Evelyn 579
Laurence, Margaret 329, 357, 382, 385, 389, 486,
    543, 570, 577
    Manitoba novels of 487
    Scottish and Métis prairie histories in 487
    theme of colonialism in 487
    writings about Africa by 332, 389–90
    WORKS: "Books That Mattered to Me" 486;
        A Bird in the House 236, 390; *The Diviners*
        236, 487; *Heart of a Stranger* 332; *Long*
        Drums and Cannons 332; *The Prophet's*
        Camel Bell 332; *This Side Jordan* 332; *The*
        Tomorrow-Tamer 332, 389–90; *A Tree for*
        Poverty 332

Index

Laurier, Wilfrid 214
Laut, Agnes 195
Lavaill, Robert 468
Lawrence, D. H. 252
Layton, Irving 302, 308–9, 426, 432, 433, 561, 568
  European sensibility of 309
  Montreal Jewish background 309
  on poet's role 308–9
  range of poetic craft in 309
  WORKS: *Collected Poems* 426; *The Darkening Fire* 433; *Here and Now* 307, 308; *A Red Carpet for the Sun* 308, 309, 423; *The Unwavering Eye* 433; *Waiting for the Messiah* 309; *A Wild Peculiar Joy* 433
Le Moine, James MacPherson 112
LeMoyne, Jean 46, 647
  WORKS: *Convergences* 648
Le Sueur, W. S. 207
Leacock, Stephen 61, 166, 181–4, 276
  conservative humanist values of 183, 184
  cross-border and transatlantic publishing 171, 181
  humor in 166, 172, 177, 182
  satire in 182, 183–4
  short story cycle form of 181
  WORKS: "A, B, and C: The Human Element in Mathematics" 172; *Arcadian Adventures* 181, 183–4; "L'Envoie" 182; "The Flight of College Time" 276; *Literary Lapses* 181; "Marine Excursion of the Knights of Pythias" 182; "My Financial Career" 181; "'The National Literature Problem in Canada" 280; *Sunshine Sketches of a Little Town* 171–2, 178, 181, 182–3
Leblanc, Gerald 598
  WORKS: *L'Extrême Frontière* 598; *Géographie de la nuit rouge* 598
LeBlanc, Raymond Guy 597, 598
  WORKS: *Chants d'amour et d'espoir* 597; *Cri de terre* 597
Leckie, Ross 431
Leduc, Andre 599
Lee, Dennis 329, 352, 425, 431, 432, 433, 436
  children's literature by 433–4
  civic poetics of 433
  as essayist 433
  as founder of Anansi Press 432–3
  influence of 434
  as poetry editor 433
  WORKS: *Alligator Pie* 433; *Body Music: Essays* 433; "Cadence, Country, Silence: Writing in Colonial Space" 433; *Civil Elegies* 433; *Fraggle Rock* 433–4; "Polyphony: Enacting a Meditation" 433
Lee, Nancy 381, 398
  WORKS: *Dead Girls* 398
Lee, SKY 561, 575
  WORKS: *Disappearing Moon Café* 575
Lefrançois, Alexis 602
Léger, Dyane 598
Lejeune, Fr. Paul 15, 17, 18, 21–3, 34, 35, 40
Le May, Pamphile 111, 117, 590
Lemelin, Roger 294, 303
  WORKS: *Au pied de la pente douce* 635; *Les Plouffe / The Plouffe Family* 294, 303
Lemire, Maurice 630
Lemoine, Stewart 419–20
  WORKS: *At the Zenith of the Empire* 420
Leonowens, Anna 210
  missionary zeal of 210
  as suffragist 210
  WORKS: *An English Governess at the Siamese Court* 210
Lepage, Robert 420–1, 625, 626
  imaginative theatricality of 421, 626
  international acclaim of 626
  linguistically polyphonic plays of 421, 626
  transcultural themes in 421
  variety of dramatic productions by 626
  WORKS: *Les Aiguilles et l'opium* 626; *The Dragon's Trilogy / La Trilogie des dragons* 421, 626; *Elseneur* 625; *La Géométrie des miracles* 626; *Polygraph / Polygraphe* 420, 626; *Le Projet Anderson* 625; *Les Sept branches de la rivière Ota / The Seven Streams of the River Ota* 626; *Tectonic Plates / Les Plaques tectoniques* 421, 626; *Vinci* 625
Leprohon, Rosanna Mullins 113–14, 139, 168
  WORKS: *Antoinette de Mirecourt* 113–14
Leroux, Louis Patrick 618
Lescarbot, Marc 15, 38, 402, 584, 606
  WORKS: *Histoire de la Nouvelle France* 584; *Les Muses de la Nouvelle France* 584; *Théâtre de Neptune* 15–16, 402, 606
Leslie, Frank 186, 187, 188, 190
Lesperance, John Talon 116–17
  WORKS: *The Bastonnais: Tale of the American Invasion* 116–17
LeSueur 207, 217
Levasseur-Ouimet, France 619
  WORKS: *Bureau de la minorité, bonjour* 619; *Contes albertains* 619; *La Guerre des mots* 619

Léveillé, J. Roger 600–1, 650
  WORKS: *Montréal poésie* 600; *Œuvre de la première mort* 601; *Pièces à conviction* 600; *Le Soleil du lac se couche* 650
Levertov, Denise 423, 427
Levesque, Charles 587
Levine, Norman 301–2, 382, 388, 561
  WORKS: *Canada Made Me* 301–2; *Thin Ice* 388
Lewis, Lily 191, 204, 212–13
  comic satire 212–13
  journalism 212
life-writing 536–55
  autobiography 208, 213–14, 233–4, 248, 265, 296, 297, 413, 502–3, 527–8, 537, 539, 540–1, 544–5, 546–7, 549–50, 552, 555, 602, 628
  biography 206, 236, 376, 377, 378, 429, 545, 551–2
  family history 241, 242, 537–8, 539–40, 541–2, 553
  fictional and semi-fictional autobiography 210, 217, 221, 251, 263, 266–7, 369, 371, 377, 378, 397, 476, 477
  journals 263–5, 267, 548, 602
  letters 43–4, 77, 86, 89, 94
  memoirs 208, 219, 235, 259–62, 264, 267, 270–1, 300, 303, 308, 323–5, 332, 371, 373, 433, 443, 487, 543, 547–8, 551, 554–5, 573–4
  portrait photography 250, 253, 265, 266, 270
  war memoirs 233–4, 241
  see also Aboriginal life-writing; Métis life-writing
Lighthall, William Douw 120–1, 127, 231
  WORKS: *Songs of the Great Dominion* 120–1, 127
Lilburn, Tom 432, 434, 435
  WORKS: *Kill-site* 435; (ed.) *Poetry and Knowing* 434; (ed.) *Thinking and Singing* 434
Lill, Wendy 241, 410
  on Aboriginal issues 4, 410
  on community social issues 410
  on suffrage issues 410
  WORKS: *All Fall Down* 410; *Chimera* 410; *Glace Bay Miners' Museum* 410; *The Fighting Days* 410; *The Occupation of Heather Rose* 410; *Sisters* 410
literary awards
  Atlantic Monthly Prize 265, 389
  Booker Prize (Man Booker Prize, 2002) 364, 376, 557, 577
  Chalmers Award 521, 522
  Commonwealth Writers' Prize 456
  Dora Mavor Moore Award 521
  Giller Prize 557, 566
  Governor General's Award 235, 248, 286, 290, 291, 291 n. 6, 292, 294, 296, 297, 298, 299, 300, 303, 304, 306, 307, 308, 309, 310, 312, 325, 343, 365, 370, 371, 376, 423, 426, 511, 515, 524, 530, 557, 567, 568
  Griffin Poetry Prize 435, 436, 439, 440
  Jessie Richardson Award for Outstanding New Play 535
  Milton Acorn People's Poetry Award 426
  Prix Américanité 533
  Prix Athanase David 365
  Prix Médicis 638
  Prix Goncourt 638, 648, 650
  Pulitzer Prize 376
  Ryerson Fiction Prize 235
  T. S. Eliot Prize 440
Literary Garland, The 90, 98, 100, 102, 190
Littlewood, Joan 404–5
Livesay, Dorothy 273, 281, 282, 287, 302, 305, 306, 426, 427
  and *Contemporary Verse* 306
  as influence on poets of the 1970s and 1980s 427
  and *New Frontier* 306
  and *New Provinces* 283–4, 306
  as political poet 306, 426
  radio verse dramas of 306
  as woman-centered poet 306
  WORKS: *Call My People Home* 306; *Day and Night* 306; "Day and Night" 306, 436; *The Documentaries* 426; "Fantasia, for Helena Coleman" 306; *The Green Pitcher* 282, 306; *Plainsongs* 426; *Poems for People* 306; *The Self-Completing Tree* 306, 434; *Signpost* 282; *The Unquiet Bed* 306, 426
Lizotte, Guy 599
Logan, William 144
Longfellow, Henry Wadsworth 111, 134, 135, 649
Loranger, Françoise 611
  WORKS: *Le Chemin du roy* 612; *Encore cinq minutes* 611; *Une maison …un jour* 611; *Medium saignant* 612
Loranger, Jean Aubert 590
  WORKS: *À la recherche du régionalisme* 590, *Les Atmosphères* 590

Index

Lord, John Keast 151–2
  British specimen collector 151, 152
  narrative style 151–2
  WORKS: *At Home in the Wilderness* 151; *The Naturalist in Vancouver Island and British Columbia* 145, 151
Lovell, John 186, 190
Lowry, Malcolm 296, 298, 303, 305, 310, 399
  modernist waste land in 298
  wilderness writing of 298
  WORKS: *Hear Us O Lord from Heaven Thy Dwelling Place* 382; *October Ferry to Gabriola* 296, 298–9; *Under the Volcano* 298
Lozeau, Albert 589, 590
  WORKS: *L'Âme solitaire* 589; *Le Miroir des jours* 589
Ltaif, Nadine 562
Lyon, Annabel 399
  WORKS: *Oxygen* 398
Lyotard, Jean-François 442
Lysenko, Vera 300, 561
  WORKS: *Yellow Boots* 300

MacDonald, Ann-Marie 415, 455–7, 479, 495
  on cross-generic narrative experiment in 456–7
  Gothic sensibility in 456, 495
  lesbian perspective of 455, 456
  on Maritime multicultural heritage 456
  on memory and trauma 456
  WORKS: drama: *The Arab's Mouth* 456; *Goodnight Desdemona (Good Morning Juliet)* 415, 456; fiction: *Fall on Your Knees* 456–7, 495
Macdonald, Daniel 413
  WORKS: *MacGregor's Hard Ice Cream and Gas* 413
MacDonald, Sir John A. (Prime Minister) 213–14, 479, 488
MacEwen, Gwendolyn 435
  feminist revisions of Greek and Egyptian myths 435
  influence of Jungian psychology on 435
  WORKS: *Afterworlds* 435
Macfarlane, David 241
  WORKS: *The Danger Tree* 241
Machar, Agnes Maule 116, 139, 168, 205–8
  on Canadian-American relations 116
  Christian ethic of 206
  ecological concerns of 206
  Loyalist ideology of 116
  social reformism of 206–7
  WORKS: *Christie Redfern's Troubles: An American Story* 206, 211; "The Divine Law of Prayer" 207, 219; *Faithful unto Death: A Memorial of John Anderson, Late Janitor of Queen's College* 206, 211; *For King and Country: A Story of 1812* 116, 207; *Katie Johnstone's Cross: A Canadian Tale* 206, 211; *Lays of the North* 139; *Marjorie's Canadian Winter* 208; "Our Lady of the Slums" 207; "Prayer and Modern Doubt" 207, 218; "Quebec to Ontario, A Plea for the life of Riel, September 1885" 208; *Roland Graeme: Knight* 207; *Shenac's Work at Home: A Story of Canadian Life* 206, 213, 215; (co-ed. with Thomas G. Marquis) *Stories of New France* 121; "Unhealthy Conditions of Women's Work in Factories" 207; "Voices Crying in the Wilderness" 207
MacIvor, Daniel 416–17
  WORKS: *A Beautiful View* 417; *In on It* 417; *Monster* 417; *Never Swim Alone* 417
Mackenzie, Alexander 70–1, 83, 84
  connections with North West Company 71
  editorial interventions 71
  landscape description 71
  popularity of *Voyages* 71
  relations with Aboriginal peoples 71
  WORKS: *Voyages* 70–1
Mackenzie Valley Pipeline Inquiry (Berger Inquiry) 319, 509
MacLennan, Hugh 289, 292, 441, 557
  on Anglo-French relations 292
  on Canadian nationalism and importance of history 289–90, 292, 303, 311
  Expo 67 participation by 320
  and First World War 235
  realist fiction of 292
  winner of five Governor General's Awards 292
  WORKS: *Barometer Rising* 235, 292; "Boy Meets Girl in Winnipeg and Who Cares?" 318; *Return of the Sphinx* 320; *Scotchman's Return and Other Essays* 289–90; *Two Solitudes* 235, 292, 456, 458; *Voices in Time* 292; *The Watch That Ends the Night* 292, 297; "Where Is My Potted Palm" 289
MacLeod, Alistair 381, 385, 386, 394, 493–4
  on Cape Breton fishing communities 394, 494
  on memory and cultural history 394

WORKS: *As Birds Bring Forth the Sun* 394; *Island* 394–5; *The Lost Salt Gift of Blood* 394; *No Great Mischief* 494; "The Road to Rankin's Point" 395
MacLeod, Joan 406, 414
 on consumer society 414
 on family dynamics 414
 political resonance of 414
 on power of imagination 414
 WORKS: *Amigo's Blue Guitar* 414; *The Hope Slide* 414; *Jewel* 414; *The Shape of a Girl* 414; *Toronto Mississipi* 414
MacLeod, John 472
Macmillan publishers 283, 286, 331, 385
MacMullen, John 106, 119
 WORKS: *The History of Canada: from its First Discovery to the Present Time* 115
Macpherson, Jay 302, 305, 310, 311, 424
 and female mythic poetry 310
 Frye's influence on 310, 424
 as illustrator 310
 Jonah libretto in ALPHABET 424
 WORKS: *The Boatman* 310, 424; *O Earth Return* 310; *Poems Twice Told* 310; *Welcoming Disaster* 310, 424
Maeterlinck, Maurice 134
magic realism *see* realism
Magrath, T. W. 87
 WORKS: *Authentic Letters from Upper Canada* 87
Maharaj, Rabindranath 562
Mahé, Irene 618
 WORKS: *Frenchie* 618; (with Jean-Guy Roy); *La Trilogie des Tremblay* 618; (with Claude Dorge)
Maheu, Gilles 625
 WORKS: *Le Dortoir* 626; *Hamlet-Machine* 625; *Marat-Sade* 625; *Le Rail* 626
Maheux-Fortier, Louise 641
 WORKS: *Amadou* 641
Mailhot, Laurent 583
Maillet, Antonine 617, 619–20, 648–9
 on collective Acadian memory, history, and identity 619, 648
 critiques of 620, 649
 and Evangeline myth 649
 WORKS: *Évangéline* 617; *Évangéline Deusse* 619; *Gapi et Sullivan* 619; *Margot la folle* 619; *Pélagie-la-charrette* 648; *La Sagouine* 617, 619; *La Veuve enragée* 619
Mair, Charles 118–19, 128
 WORKS: *Dreamland and Other Poems* 128; *Tecumseh: A Drama* 118–19

Major, André 324, 638
 WORKS: *Le Cabochon* 638
Major, Kevin 239
 WORKS: *No Man's Land* 239
Majzels, Robert 316–17
 WORKS: *Hellman's Scrapbook* 316–17
Mallarmé, Stéphane 134
Maltman, Kim 434
Mandel, Eli 426, 427, 432
 WORKS: (ed.) *Contexts of Canadian Criticism* 426; (ed.) *Poets of Contemporary Canada 1960–1970* 432
Manguel, Alberto, 566, 568
 WORKS: *News from a Foreign Country Came* 566, 568
Manley, Rachel 573
 WORKS: *Drumblair* 574; *Slipstream* 574
Mannoni, Ottavo 332
Maracle, Lee 503, 507, 512
 Aboriginal activist protests 512
 on effects of colonialism 512
 WORKS: *Bobby Lee: Indian Rebel* 503; *Ravensong* 512; *Sundogs* 512
Marchand, Olivier 594
Marchessault, Jovette 621
 WORKS: *La Saga des poules mouillées* 621
Marcotte, Gilles 638
Marie de l'Incarnation 29, 35, 37, 41–3
 affinity with Jesuits 42–3
 on Divine love 41, 42–3
 letters to her son 41–2
 as Mother Superior of Quebec Ursulines 41, 42
 on worldliness 41–2
Marie-Victorin, Frère 647
 WORKS: *La Flore laurentienne* 647
Marinier, Robert 618
Marks, Bill 472
 WORKS: *Mister X* 472
Marlatt, Daphne 428, 446–8, 492, 497, 565
 as influence on 1980s and 1990s avant-garde women's poetry 428
 on lesbian identity 447, 492
 poetics of geographical and historical space in 428
 resistance to generic conventions by 447
 significance on queer poetry scene 428, 447
 and TISH 447
 as translator 447
 women's perspectives on Second World War 447, 492

Marlatt, Daphne (cont.)
    WORKS: fiction: *Ana Historic* 447, 492; *Taken* 447, 492; *Zócalo* 447; poetry: *Ghost Works* 447; *Steveston* 428; *Touch to My Tongue* 428
Marlowe, Christopher 390
Marlyn, John 300
    WORKS: *Under the Ribs of Death* 300
Marmette, Joseph 115–16, 630
    WORKS: *Charles et Éva* 115; *François de Bienville* 115–16
Márquez, Gabriel García 489
Marrant, John 54
Marriott, Anne 287, 305
    WORKS: *Calling Adventurers* 307; "The Wind Our Enemy" 307
Marshall, Joyce 321, 382, 383
    WORKS: *Any Time at All* 382
Marshall, Paule 560
Martel, Yann 648
    WORKS: *The History of Pi / L'Histoire de Pi* 577–8, 648
Martens, Klaus 249
Martin, Claire 324–6, 641
    challenge to Royal Society of Canada 325
    critique of Quebec society 325
    as first feminist memoirist in Quebec 324, 325
    on patriarchal abuse 324
    WORKS: *Avec et sans amour* 641; *Dans un gant de fer* 324–5; *Doux-Amer* 641; *In an Iron Glove* (translation) 325
Massey Commission (Royal Commission on National Development in the Arts, Letters and Social Sciences) 290, 293, 304, 443, 452
Massicotte, Stephen 241
Massing, Conni 413
    WORKS: *Gravel Run* 413
Mathews, Robin and James Steele 330
    WORKS: *The Struggle for Canadian Universities: A Dossier* 330
Mavrikakis, Catherine 647
    WORKS: *Ça va aller* 647
McAlmon, Robert 269
McArthur, Peter 171, 195
McCaffery, Steve 430
McCarroll, James 173, 187
McClelland and Stewart 314, 331, 359, 366, 384, 385, 423, 429, 432–3, 435, 503
    New Canadian Library 432
McClung, Nellie 168, 191, 195, 198, 209, 219–20, 229
    campaign speeches of 219–20
    and Christian reformist movement 168
    as prairie fiction writer 198
    as suffragist 219
    WORKS: *The Black Creek Stopping-House* 168; *In Times like These* 219; *Next of Kin* 229; *Purple Springs* 219; *Sowing Seeds in Danny* 198, 219
McCormack, Derek 400
    WORKS: *Dark Rides* 400
McCormack, Eric 384
    WORKS: *Inspecting the Vaults* 384
McCormack, Robert 333
McCrae, John 142, 226
    WORKS: "In Flanders Fields" 226, 422
McCulloch, Thomas, 52, 55, 57–62, 65, 66, 178
    conservative values of 59, 60
    didacticism of 58–9
    as epistolary novelist 57–8
    humor in 60–1
    initial serial publication of 57
    as satirist 58–62
    and tall tales 61, 66
    on women's education 62
    WORKS: *Letters of Mephibosheth Stepsure (The Stepsure Letters)* 56, 57–62
McDonald, Archibald 78
McDougall, Colin
    WORKS: *Execution* 294
McGee, Thomas D'Arcy 127, 189
    WORKS: *Canadian Ballads* 127
McGill Fortnightly Review 275–80
McGrath, Charles 370, 371
McIlwraith, Thomas 162–5
    as environmentalist 164
    as ornithologist 163–5
    poetic style of 164–5
    WORKS: *Birds of Ontario* 163, 164–5
McKay, Don 424, 431, 432, 434, 435
    WORKS: *Camber* 435; *Lependu* 431; *Strike/Slip* 435
McKay, Leo 393
    WORKS: *Like This* 393
McLachlan, Alexander 88, 127
    WORKS: *The Emigrant and Other Poems* 127; *Poems and Songs* 127
McLaren, Floris Clark 287, 305
mclennan, rob 436
    WORKS: *harvest, a book of signifiers* 436
McLeod, Mary 79
McLuhan, Herbert Marshall 313, 335, 338–45, 349, 352, 353
    academic career of 339–40
    and advertising 341
    and the artist 343–4

on Canadian identity and borderlines 344, 345
and co-authors 344
on communications theory, print culture, electronic age 342, 343
early essays on English literature by 340
interest in popular culture 340-2
methodology of 341, 344
on USA 345
WORKS: "Canada, the Borderline Case" 344, 345; "Defrosting Canadian Culture" 344; *From Cliché to Archetype* 344; *The Gutenberg Galaxy* 313, 342-3; *The Interior Landscape* 344; *The Mechanical Bride* 340-2; *Through the Vanishing Point* 344; *Understanding Media* 343
McNamara, Eugene 344
McNaught, Frances 161
WORKS: (co-ed.) *The Galt Cook Book* 161
McTavish, Catherine Turner 79
McWatt, Tessa 579
McWhirter, George 386
Melançon, Robert 602
Melanson, Louis-Arthur 648
WORKS: *Pour la terre* 648
Melville, Herman 445
Mercure, Marthe 621
WORKS: *Tu faisais comme un appel* 621
Merrill, James 425
Merrill, Judith 385
Metcalf, John 382, 384, 388
WORKS: *Girl in Gingham* 384; *Sixteen by Twelve* 384
Métis 80, 83, 445, 482, 487, 488, 503, 533, 644, 651
criticism 500
drama 417, 528, 531-2, 535
fiction 504-5, 510, 512, 650
film 80
life-writing 502-3, 504, 509, 510, 512, 514
poetry 439, 503, 514-15
Metzger, George 469
Mezlekia, Nega 568
WORKS: *Notes from the Hyena's Belly* 568
Michaels, Anne 449-51, 561, 572
on interrelation between history, poetry, and fiction 450
post-Holocaust fiction of 450
use of kabbalistic tradition in 450
WORKS: *Fugitive Pieces* 449-50; *Miner's Pond* 450; *The Weight of Oranges* 450
Michele, Mary di 561, 572
Michelet, Jules 109

Micone, Marco 333, 561, 562, 563, 566, 568, 569, 623
WORKS: *Addolorata* 623; *Déjà l'agonie* 623; *Gens du silence* 623
Mighton, John 420
WORKS: *Possible Worlds* 420
Miki, Roy 428, 448, 561, 572-3
co-ordinator of "Writing Thru Race" conference 573
Japanese Canadian poet and political activist 572
WORKS: *Surrender* 428
Miller, K. D. 386
WORKS: *A Litany in Time of Plague* 386
Miller, Vernon 464
Milton, John 274-5, 547
Milton, William Fitzwilliam (Viscount) 82
WORKS: *The North-West Passage by Land* (co-authored with William Butler Cheadle) 82-3
Miron, Gaston 324, 584, 594, 596-7
WORKS: *L'Homme rapaillé* 596
Miskouensa, Chief 27, 28
Mistral, Christian 647
WORKS: *Valium* 647; *Vamp* 647; *Vautour* 647
Mistry, Rohinton 381, 385, 479, 557, 561, 565, 566, 567, 568, 571, 574, 577
fictions set in India 392
on immigrant sensibilities 393
WORKS: *Family Matters* 574; *A Fine Balance* 557; *Such a Long Journey* 565, 574; *Tales from Firozsha Baag* 392
Mitchell, Ken 382
Mitchell, S. Weir 135
Mitchell, W. O. 295, 296, 383
bildungsroman, fictional forms of 296
as radio broadcaster of short stories 382
as television scriptwriter and playwright 296, 403
WORKS: *Jake and the Kid* 382; *Who Has Seen the Wind* 296
modernism 231, 247-71, 272, 290, 362
and cosmopolitanism 267-8
European influences on 247
and female pioneer figures 261-2
and life-writing 247-8, 271
and portrait photography 250, 254, 261, 265, 266, 268, 270
and queer writing 270-1
and romance 271
see also modernist poetry; modernist fiction
modernist fiction (English) 290, 295, 296-9, 300-2

modernist poetry (English) 231, 272–88, 303–4, 426, 427–8
  American influences 305, 308
  Anglo-French literary relations 302–3
  belatedness 272–3
  controversies 283–4, 287, 290
  cultural context and legacy of 287
  European poetic influences on 278–9, 280, 310
  Little magazines 275–81, 287, 302, 304–6
  McGill poets 275–81, 282, 286
  New Provinces 282–6
  signs of change 273–4
modernist poetry (French) 591–3
modernity
  ambivalence towards 177, 179, 180–1, 196, 620
  and industrialization 254–5, 292–3, 306
  and technological progress 257, 261, 263–4, 342, 343, 351, 353
  and urbanism 222, 267–8, 293–4, 646
  and women 256
Moher, Frank 408
  WORKS: *Odd Jobs* 408
Moiseiwitsch, Carol 472
Mojica, Monique 521, 526–7
  actor and performance artist 526
  deconstructing Indigenous female stereotypes in 526
  Pan-Aboriginality 526–7
  on residential schools 527
  woman-centered storyweaving in 526, 527
  WORKS: *Birdwoman and the Suffragettes* 526; *Princess Pocahontas and the Blue Spots* 526; *The Scrubbing Project* 527
Molière, Jean-Baptiste Poquelin 403, 606
Monroe, Harriet 273
Montcalm, Louis-Joseph de, Marquis de Montcalm 110
Montesquieu, Michel de 50, 646
Montgomery, Lucy Maud 169, 191, 195, 197–8, 248, 262–5
  bestsellers by 197
  cross-border publishing ventures by 168, 197
  and modernity 263–4
  poetry of 228
  portrait photo of 266
  short stories of 168
  WORKS: *The Alpine Path: The Story of My Career* 264; *Anne of Green Gables* 197, 207, 219, 263; *Emily* series 263; *Journals* 263–5; "Our Women" 228; *Rilla of Ingleside* 229

Montreal Society of Natural History 144–5
  nineteenth-century scientific enthusiasm 144
  specimen collections of 144–5
Montreal Star 171–2, 182, 206, 211, 461
Montreal Story Tellers, The 387, 389
Monument National Theatre 608
Moodie, Andrew 418
  WORKS: *Riot* 418
Moodie, John Dunbar 94, 101
  WORKS: *Scenes and Adventures, as a Soldier and Settler during Half a Century* 100; *Ten Years in South Africa* 100
Moodie, Susanna (née Strickland) 47, 48, 62, 87, 89, 98, 99–100, 103
  connection with Bentley, publisher 100–1
  dual readership of 102–3
  early London career 89
  early publication in Canada 90, 98, 103
  emigration and settlement in Canada 89, 94
  Literary Garland connection 90, 98, 100, 102
  periodical publication by 102
  posthumous fame 94
  "Susanna Strickland" 101
  Victoria Magazine 98–9, 102
  woman's pioneer narrative by 101
  WORKS: "Canadians Will You Join the Band" 98; "The Canadian Woodsman" 98; *Life in the Clearings* 100; *Roughing It in the Bush* 94, 98, 99, 100, 101–3, 158, 190, 361; "The Sleigh-Bells: A Canadian Song" 98
Moore, Brian 30, 301, 386, 564
  WORKS: *Black Robe* 30; *The Luck of Ginger Coffey* 564
Moore, Lisa 381, 399
  WORKS: *Open* 399
Mootoo, Shani 562, 563, 564, 575, 576
  WORKS: *Cereus Blooms at Night* 578
More, Sir Thomas 50
Morency, Pierre 602
Morin, Paul 590
Moritz, A. F. 431
  WORKS: *Rest on the Flight into Egypt* 431
Morley, Alan 492
  WORKS: *Vancouver: From Milltown to Metropolis* 510
Morrison, Toni 457
Morrisseau, Norval 319
Morton, W. L. 478, 486
  WORKS: *Manitoba: A History* 486

Moses, Daniel David 30, 417, 439, 479, 503, 506–7, 523–6
  Christian nativity myth in 524
  cultural influences on 506, 524
  deconstruction of native stereotypes by 523
  ghost stories in 524
  historical dramas by 525–6
  on hybridity 525
  and science fiction 524
  on Trickster figure 506, 524
  WORKS: drama: *Almighty Voice and His Wife* 525; *Angel of the Medicine Show* 525; *The Ballad of Burnt Ella* 526; *Big Buck City* 524; *Brébeuf's Ghost* 30, 479, 525; *City of Shadows* 524; *Coyote City* 506, 524; *The Indian Medicine Shows* 507, 525; *Kyotopolis* 524–5; *The Moon and Dead Indians* 417, 525; *Songs of Love and Medicine* 526; *Songs of the Tall Grass* 526; poetry: *Delicate Bodies* 439, 506; *The White Line* 506–7
Mosionier *see* Culleton Mosionier
Mouawad, Wajdi 562, 624
  WORKS: *Incendies* 624; *Journée de noces chez les Cromagnons* 624; *Littoral* 624; *Les Mains d'Edwige au moment de la naissance* 624; *Willy Protagoras* 624
Mouré, Erin 436
  WORKS: *The Green Word* 436; *O Cadoiro* 437
Mowat, Farley 296, 297
  WORKS: *The People of the Deer* 296
Mukherjee, Arun 546, 549, 550
  on postcolonial condition 549
  on transnationalism 549
  WORKS: *Postcolonialism: My Living* 549
Mukherjee, Bharati 395, 546, 548, 550, 561, 563, 564
  on Air India disaster, 1985 548
  critique of multiculturalism by 548, 553, 564
  and transcultural position 548
  WORKS: *Days and Nights in Calcutta* (co-authored with Clarke Blaise) 548; *The Sorrow and the Terror* (co-authored with Blaise) 552–3
multiculturalism 4, 262, 290, 293, 333, 428, 430, 491, 536, 537, 541, 542, 546, 548, 553, 555, 556–7, 559, 560, 562–3, 565, 567, 572, 573, 578, 623
  criticism of 548, 553, 557
  official policy 4, 290, 293, 422, 459, 518, 536, 553, 562–3
  see also ethnic diversity; transculturalism

Munro, Alice 178, 357, 358–65, 368, 370–5, 376, 380, 381, 382, 384, 385, 386, 397
  on ageing and death 374
  and historical fiction 374
  on life-writing and fiction 371, 373
  multidimensional narratives of 375
  and myth revisions 375
  and *The New Yorker* 370, 371
  reputation as short story writer 375
  and Southwestern Ontario 370
  and storytelling 372, 374
  and Virginia Barber 370
  on women's romance fiction 373, 374
  WORKS: *Alice Munro's Best: Selected Stories* 375; *Dance of the Happy Shades* 563; *Friend of My Youth* 374; *Hateship, Friendship, Courtship, Loveship, Marriage* 3, 374; *Lives of Girls and Women* 370, 374; *The Love of a Good Woman* 397; *The Moons of Jupiter* 371; *Open Secrets* 374, 375; *The Progress of Love* 372–4; "The Progress of Love" 372–3; *Runaway* 374; *Something I've Been Meaning to Tell You* 370; *The View from Castle Rock* ("Home," "Working for a Living," "Hired Girl") 371, 374, 397; "White Dump" 358, 372, 373–4, 375; *Who Do You Think You Are? / The Beggar Maid: Stories of Flo and Rose* 371, 391
Murphy, Emily 220
  Famous Five 220
  as social reformer 220
  WORKS: *Janey Canuck in the West* 220
Murray, Laura Ann 99
Murray, Louisa 168
Murrell, John 404, 408–9
  WORKS: *Farther West* 408–9; *Filumena* 408–9; *Waiting for the Parade* 404, 408–9
Musset, Alfred de 587
myths
  Aboriginal myths 95, 177, 297, 440, 506, 513, 521, 522, 531, 532–3, 624, 625
  Frye's influence 310, 313, 346, 347
  modernist mythmaking 296–9, 310
  myth revisions 310, 323–4, 364, 375, 435, 445, 451, 454, 457–8, 479, 482–3, 486, 489–90, 491, 493, 496, 513, 524, 525, 531, 641, 645, 646

Naaman, Antoine 564
Naipaul, V. S. 563

Namjoshi, Suniti 561, 564
National Arts Centre / Centre National des
   Arts, Ottawa 404, 454, 615
National Film Board 313, 386
National identity (English) 2, 54, 66, 106,
   107–8, 114, 115, 116–17, 118, 119–21, 122,
   123, 127, 158, 166–7, 231, 262, 289–90,
   292, 302, 303, 315–16, 320–1, 334, 336,
   338, 339, 345, 351–2, 353, 359, 360, 370,
   422, 440, 478
National identity (French) 109–10, 114–15,
   119–20, 123, 127–8, 314, 468–9, 569, 590,
   596–7, 605, 614–15, 620, 631, 632
   see also Expo 67
Native Earth Performing Arts 520, 521,
   523, 532
Native writing (see Aboriginal writing)
nature writing 5, 134, 145–65, 481–2
   animal stories 167, 173–7, 197, 217
   botanical 96, 148–50
   entomological 146–7
   horticultural 157–61
   ornithological 162–3
   visual documentation 149, 155, 160, 161
   wildlife description 74, 76, 151–7
   see also cookbooks; environmentalism and
   ecological concerns
Nelligan, Émile 314, 588–9, 639
   most important Quebec poet 588
   WORKS: Émile Nelligan et son œuvre 588;
   Poésies 314; "Soir d'hiver" 589
Nepveu, Pierre 583, 603, 645, 648
   WORKS: Mahler et autres matières 603
New, William H. 3, 4, 48, 173, 209, 384, 438
   as Canadian literary critic, editor, and
   historian 438, 439
   as poet 438
   WORKS: (ed.) Canadian Short Fiction 384; A
   History of Canadian Literature 4; (ed.) A
   Literary History of Canada vol. IV 3;
   Science Lessons 438
New France 13–28, 29–46, 110, 112, 117, 120, 644
New Provinces 231, 282–6, 434
   controversies 283–4
   modernist poems in 284–5
   Smith's Preface 284
New Woman 212, 252, 256, 259, 261
New Yorker 357, 359, 366, 367, 368, 370, 372, 476
Newlove, John 435
   anti-nationalist ideology in 435–6
   poetic treatment of historical figures 435
   WORKS: The Fat Man 435; Lies 435
Newton, John 88

nichol, bp 424, 428, 429–30, 467
   American and European connections
   of 430
   deconstructive approach to language and
   culture 430
   experiments with graphic representation
   429, 430, 467
   interest in pop culture 429, 467
   precursor of L=A=N=G=U=A=G=E
   poets 429
   sound poetry 430
   WORKS: Allegory series 467; "Captain
   Poetry" poems 467; The Martyrology
   430, 467; Scraptures sequences 467
Nickel, Barbara 437
   WORKS Domain 437
Nietzsche, Friedrich 352, 445
Nightwood Theatre 415, 526
Nodier, Charles 631
Noël, Francine 645
   WORKS: Maryse 645
Nolan, Yvette 532
   WORKS: Annie Mae's Movement 532; Blade
   532; Job's Wife 532; Video 532
North West Company 67, 70
north, the far 83–6, 307, 318, 319, 363, 403, 404,
   464, 485, 490, 519, 534, 535, 638
   see also Franklin Sir John; travel writing
Northern Review 287, 305
Nouvelle Barre du jour, La 642
Nowlan, Alden 242, 426, 438
   WORKS: Bread, Wine and Salt 426; "Ypres:
   1915" 242

Oates, Joyce Carol 329
   WORKS: Crossing the Borders 329; Valerie
   Miner's Movement 329
Obadia, Mary Abécassis 562
Obama, Barack Hussein 550, 553
   WORKS: Dreams From My Father
   550, 553
Oberle, Frank 540, 541
   WORKS: Finding Home: A War Child's
   Journey to Peace 540
Oberon press 384
Odell, Jonathan 52
   WORKS: "The Agonizing Dilemma" 53;
   The American Times 53
Odhiambo, David 575, 579
   WORKS: Kipligat's Chance 575
Odyssey, The 364, 489
Ogden, Peter Skene 75, 76
O'Grady, Standish 88

O'Hagan, Howard 296–7, 382
  WORKS: Tay John 295, 296–7; The Woman
    Who Got On at Jasper Station 382
O'Hagan, Thomas 141
Oliveros, Chris 475
Ollivier, Émile 562, 568, 576
  WORKS: La Brûlerie 568, 576; Passages 576
Olson, Charles 305, 427, 428
O'Meara, Robert 437
  WORKS: Storm Still 437
Ondaatje, Michael 5, 291, 357, 365, 384, 431,
    432, 443–5, 457, 483, 490–1, 546, 549–50,
    557, 561, 563, 565, 567, 571–2, 574, 577
  cross-generic narrative forms of 443, 444
  cultural displacement and diaspora in 431,
    443, 444, 491
  fascination with adultery in 444
  importance of games in 444
  Leonard Cohen's influence on 443
  resistance to ethnic categorization 491, 571
  subversions of epic in 443
  on Toronto as cosmopolitan city 491, 572
  on transculturalism, transnationalism
    550, 571
  women's roles in 444
  WORKS: essays: Leonard Cohen 443;
    fiction: Anil's Ghost 444, 491, 576;
    Coming Through Slaughter 431, 443;
    Divisadero 444–5, 557; The English
    Patient 298, 431, 444, 490, 557; In the
    Skin of a Lion 443–4, 482, 483, 491,
    571–2, 576; life-writing: Running in the
    Family 443, 491, 549–50, 571, 574;
    poetry: The Cinnamon Peeler 431; The
    Collected Works of Billy the Kid 431, 516;
    Handwriting 431; Secular Love 431
Ondinnok theatre company 533, 624–5
Ormsby, Eric 437
Ortiz, Fernando, 567
Orwell, George 363
Ostenso, Martha 248, 255–6, 262
  WORKS: Wild Geese 256–7
Ouellette, Fernand 594, 603
  WORKS: Les Heures 603
Ouellette, Michel 617
  WORKS: Corbeaux en exil 617
Ouvrard, Hélène 641
Ovid 390
Oxford Companion to Canadian Literature
  (1967) 334; (1997) 558

Paci, Frank 561
Page, Louis Coues 197

Page, P. K. (P. K. Irwin, Judith Cape) 287, 305,
    306, 308, 423, 425, 437
  cosmopolitan sensibility of 437
  cross-overs between poetry and painting 308
  imagery of 308
  intersection of the visual and the visionary
    in 437
  modernist influences on 308
  as visual artist (P. K. Irwin) 308
  WORKS: As Ten, as Twenty 307; Brazilian
    Journal 308; Cry Ararat! 308, 425; The
    Glass Air 308; The Hidden Room 437;
    Hologram: A Book of Glosas 431; The
    Metal and the Flower ("The Bands and
    the Beautiful Children," "Portrait of
    Marina," "The Stenographers," "Stories
    of Snow") 308; The Sun and the Moon 308
Page, Rhoda Ann 99
Paiement, André 617
  WORKS: Lavalléville 617; Moé, je viens du
    Nord, s'tie 617
Palliser, John 81
Palmer, John 407
Panych, Morris 410, 411–12
  affinities with Samuel Beckett 411
  theater of the absurd 411
  references to T. S. Eliot in 411
  WORKS: Girl in the Goldfish Bowl 412;
    Lawrence & Holloman 411–12; 7 stories
    411; Vigil 411
Parameswaran, Uma 417
Paré, François 650
Parenteau-Lebeuf, Dominick 622
  WORKS: Dévoilement devant notaire 622
Parizeau, Alice 567
Parizeau, Jacques 569
Parker, Gilbert 122, 169, 191, 195, 200–2
  British MP 201
  early career of 200
  historical romances by 201
  short stories by 200
  WORKS: Pierre and His People: Tales of the
    Far North 169, 201; Round the Compass
    in Australia 200; The Seats of the Mighty
    122, 201; The Trail of the Sword 201;
    When Valmond Came to Pontiac 201
Parker, Harley 344
Parkinson, Frances 35
Parkman, Francis 118
  Anglo-centered ideology 118
  attitudes to French 118
  as historian 118, 201
  representation of Aboriginals in 118

Parkman, Francis (cont.)
    WORKS *History of the Conspiracy of Pontiac* 118; *The Jesuits in North America in the Seventeenth Century* 35; *Montcalm and Wolfe* 118; *The Oregon Trail* 118
Parti Pris 322, 323
Partridge, Elise 437
Pater, Walter 132
Paterson, Don 437
Patterson, Kevin 393
    WORKS: *Country of Cold* 393
Pazira, Nelofer 568
    WORKS: *A Bed of Red Flowers* 568
Péan, Stanley 579
Peat, Harold R. 227–8
    WORKS: *Private Peat* 227–8
Pedneault, Hélène 622
    WORKS: *La Déposition* 622
Pelletier, Maryse 621
    WORKS: *A qui le p'tit cœur après neuf heures et demie* 621; *Du poil aux pattes come des cwac's* 621; *Duo pour les voix obstinés* 621; *La Rupture des eaux* 621
Pelletier, Pierre Raphael 599
Pelletier, Pol 621, 628
    WORKS: *Joie* 628; *La Lumière blanche* 621; *Océan* 628; *Or* 628
Pelletier, Wilfred 503
    WORKS: *No Foreign Land* 503
Peloquin, Claude 601
Pemmican Publications 504, 505
Perec, Georges 436
Perrault, Pierre 596
    WORKS: *En désespoir de cause* 596
Pessoa, Fernando 599
Peterson, Len 403
Petitclair, Pierre 606
    WORKS: *La Donation* 615; *Griphon, or la vengeance d'un valet* 606; *Une partie de campagne* 615
Petitdidier, Maurice 463
Petitjean, Léon 608
    WORKS: *Aurore, l'enfant martyre* (co-authored with Henri Rollin) 608
Petrone, Penny 507
    WORKS: (ed.) *First People, First Voices* 507; *Native Literature in Canada: From the Oral Tradition to the Present* 508; *Northern Voices* 508
Philibert, André 474
    WORKS: *Oror 70* 474

Philip, Marlene NourbeSe 439, 559, 562, 569, 575
    WORKS: *Looking for Livingstone: An Odyssey of Silence* 575, 576
Pickthall, Marjorie 225, 274, 278, 282
    WORKS: "Marching Man" 225
Pilon, Jean-Guy 594, 596
    WORKS: *Recours au pays* 596
Piscator, Erwin 615
Plamondon, Aimé 230
Planchon, Roger 405
Plantos, Ted 242
    WORKS: *Passchendaele* 242
Poe, Edgar Allan 134, 135, 323, 383
Poirier, Jacques 599
    WORKS: *Parfois, en certains jours de lumière parfaite* 599
Poliquin, Daniel 649–50, 651
    and Aboriginal peoples 649
    as "cultural Métis" 649
    and memory 650
    WORKS: *La Côté de sable* 644; *L'Écureuil noir* 649; *L'Obomsawin* 649
Polley, Sarah 375
Pollock, Sharon 409, 519
    emphasis on social injustices 409
    on familial emotional violence 413
    historical plays of 409
    radio plays of 409
    on women in patriarchal society 409
    WORKS: *Angel's Trumpet* 409; *Blood Relations* 413; *Doc* 413; *Fair Liberty's Call* 409; *Getting it Straight* 409; *The Komagata Maru Incident* 409; *The Making of Warriors* 409; *Man Out of Joint* 409; *Moving Pictures* 409; *One Tiger to a Hill* 409; *Walsh* 409, 519; *Whiskey Six Cadenza* 409
Pomerlo, Marcel 628
    WORKS: *L'Inoublié ou Marcel-Pomme-dans-l'eau* 628
Pond, Peter 72–3
Pontiac 92, 118
Pope, Alexander 50, 51, 58
popular culture 188, 189–90, 340, 341, 428, 429
    bestsellers 185, 192, 193, 195–7, 198–202, 291, 293, 294, 318, 605, 643
    CBC "Canada Reads" 366
    Cirque du Soleil 421, 626
    community theater culture 404
    Expo 67 312, 317–18
    films 80, 83, 242, 313, 314, 317, 330, 508, 608, 611

film and TV script writing 203, 296, 301, 320, 394, 454
influence on contemporary short fiction 399, 400
novels and short stories into film 255–6, 291, 301, 303, 363, 375, 386–7, 395, 557, 565, 608, 611, 643
popular fiction 169, 192, 193, 202–3, 384, 385, 634, 642
radio and TV drama 303, 306, 307, 403, 409, 446, 456, 526, 527, 611
TV environmental programs 546, 555
see also comics
Porcupine's Quill 385, 388
Porter, Anna 537, 541, 542
  WORKS: *The Storyteller: Memory, Secrets, Magic and Lies* 537–8
postcolonialism 331, 332, 433, 448, 529, 532, 549, 562–3, 568
postcolonial critical perspectives 332, 402, 404–5, 408
Post-Confederation poets 121, 131, 438
  American influences on 134–6
  classical and Romantic-Victorian influences on 131–2
  controversies between 140–1
  cross-border migrations by 141
  European influences on 134
  and First World War 142
  formation of group 130–1
  international recognition of 131, 136–7
  Lampman and Scott in Ottawa 141–2
  and landscape 133–4
  Later Canadian Poems 138–9
  later reputations of 142–3
  national recognition of 131, 137–8
  and nature writing 135–6
  Northern Romanticism 132–4
  women poets marginalized by 139
postmodernism 323, 324, 362, 364, 375, 379, 387, 436, 441–59, 536, 541, 549, 576, 605, 640, 642, 643, 644, 645
  Canadian postmodernist aesthetic 436, 481, 482–3
  carnivalesque 379, 454, 615, 645, 649
  cross-genre experimentation 379, 423, 441, 443, 445–6, 447, 448, 450, 451, 452–3, 454–5, 456–8, 480, 484, 485–6, 494, 531
  historiographic metafiction 479, 481
  Hutcheon, Linda 445, 479, 559
  hybridity, formal and cultural 458
  importance of games theory, language games, and play 387, 399, 442, 482

intertextuality 443, 445, 449, 450, 452, 455, 456, 457–8, 485, 486, 489, 490, 492, 494, 495–6, 636, 644, 645
metafictional strategies 323, 324, 448, 479
parody 445, 446, 455, 480, 485, 489, 490, 497
performance 620, 627
Potvin, Damase 634
  WORKS: *L'Appel de la terre* 634; *Restons chez nous* 634
Poulin, Gabriel 599
Poulin, Jacques 644, 647
  on history of Aboriginal peoples 644
  on quest for identity 644
  WORKS: *Le Cœur de la baleine bleue* 644; *Les Grandes marées* 644; *Jimmy* 644; *La Tournée d'automne* 644; *Le Vieux Chagrin* 644; *Volkswagen Blues* 644, 647; *Les Yeux bleus de Mistassini* 644
Pound, Ezra 340, 343
Pratt, E. J. 30, 35, 226, 273, 281–2, 285, 286, 305, 425, 432
  Canadianness of 281
  epic poetry and documentary realism in 281
  Governor General Awards 286
  interest in science and technology 281
  as mythmaker 288
  and *New Provinces* 282–3, 285
  war poems of 226
  WORKS: "Before a Bulletin Board" 226; *Behind the Log* 286; *Brébeuf and His Brethren* 30, 286; *Dunkirk* 286; *The Fable of the Goats* 286; *Newfoundland Verse* 226, 274; *The Roosevelt and the Antinoe* 281–2; "Text of the Oath" 231; *The Titanic* 286; *The Titans* 275; *Towards the Last Spike* 302; *The Witches' Brew* 275
Pratt, Mary Louise 67
Préfontaine, Yves 596
  WORKS: *Pays sans parole* 596
Pre-Raphaelites 333, 618
Prescott, Marc 333, 618
  WORKS: *L'Année Big-Mac* 618; *Encore* 618; *Sex, Lies, et les Franco-Manitobains* 618
Preview 287, 303, 305
Primeau, Marguerite A. 650
  WORKS: *Dans le muskeg* 650
Proulx, Monique 646
  WORKS: *Les Aurores Montréales* 578, 646; *Le Cœur est un muscle involontaire* 647; *Le Sexe des étoiles* 646
Proust, Marcel 325
Prowse, D. W. 494
  WORKS: *A History of Newfoundland* 494

Index

Psenak, Stefan 599
publishing (English)
  C18
    first printing press 104
    periodicals, newspapers 55, 56, 62
  C19 pre-Confederation
    periodicals, newspapers 90, 96, 98–9, 100, 102
    transatlantic print culture 99, 100
  C19 post-Confederation
    bestseller phenomenon 192, 193, 195–6
    book publishing in Canada 186, 189–90
    copyright law 185, 190, 211
    cross-border publishing and American markets 170–2, 173, 186–7, 191–2, 195
    North American print culture 185–6, 204–5
    periodicals 129, 167–8, 172, 175, 177, 181, 190–1, 207, 212, 213, 460, 461
    religious presses and periodicals 191, 194, 196, 198, 200
    women's role in late nineteenth-century print culture 204–5
  C20
    book publishing and publishers 313, 322, 329, 331, 360, 370, 384, 385, 387, 388, 429, 430, 431–2, 433, 438, 439, 473, 475, 477, 564
    economics and politics of book publishing 385, 397
    new modes of publication and publicity 389
    periodicals and literary journals 231, 313, 331, 357, 384, 385, 386, 387, 394, 396, 428, 429, 464, 467
    see also McClelland and Stewart; modernist poetry: little magazines; post-Confederation poets
publishing (French)
  C19
    French Canada's first literary review 630, 631
  C20
    book publishing and publishers 322, 473, 474, 477, 587, 594–5, 597–8, 598–601, 603, 648
    periodicals and literary journals 322, 323, 472, 473, 475, 642
Purdy, Al 291, 305, 425, 432, 651
  WORKS: *The Cariboo Horses* 425; *Collected Poems* 425, 433; *North of Summer: Poems from Baffin Island* 425; *Poems for All the Annettes* 425
Pushkin, Alexander 458

Quan, Andy 393
  WORKS: *Calendar Boy* 393

queer writing
  gay 270–1, 296, 328–9, 393, 455, 477, 515, 576, 616, 622–3, 626, 645
  lesbian 270, 328–9, 398, 415–17, 428, 447, 455, 456, 576, 605, 641
Quesnel, Joseph 606
Quiet Revolution / *Révolution tranquille* 323–6, 568, 605, 611, 634, 637, 638, 642, 646, 648

Racette, Sherry Farrell 510
Racey, Arthur G. 461
Racine, Jean de 586
Racine, Robert 647
  WORKS: *Le Mal de Vienne* 647
Raddall, Thomas H. 291, 299
  WORKS: *His Majesty's Yankees* 291; *The Nymph and the Lamp* 299; *The Pied Piper of Dipper Creek* 299
Radisson, Pierre-Esprit 14
Rae, John 86
Raguencau, Fr. Paul 35–6
Raiche, Jean-Philippe 598
Rasmussen, Knud 86
Rawls, John 352
Ray, Carl 510
Reade, John 128
  WORKS: *The Prophecy of Merlin* 128
realism 177, 179–80, 251, 255, 290, 292–3, 295, 296, 298, 299, 382, 384, 393, 479, 492–3, 642, 649
  challenges to realism 290, 384–5, 400, 451, 485, 490, 531–2
  magic realism 384, 496
Reaney, James 291, 302, 305, 310–11, 424, 430, 432
  as *ALPHABET* editor 311, 424
  comic wit and erudition of 310
  Frye's influence on 310, 424
  influence on later poets 424–5
  as playwright 310–11
  as regional poet 310, 424
  WORKS: *The Box Social* 382; *The Donnellys* 310, 408; *The Red Heart* 310; *A Suit of Nettles* 310; *Twelve Letters to a Small Town* 310
Rebellion (1837) 95, 105, 108, 113, 116, 123, 497, 605, 607, 629, 643
Redbird, Duke 314, 315, 319, 499, 501
Redhill, Michael 393, 484–5
  WORKS: *Consolation* 484–5; *Fidelity* 393
regionalism (French) 589–91, 634, 635
Reibetanz, John 431, 432
  WORKS: *Mining for the Sun* 431
Reichs, Kathy 318
  WORKS: *Déjà Dead* 318

Reid, Jamie 428, 429
  WORKS: *Diana Krall: The Language of Love* 429
religion
  Anglicanism 49, 52, 55, 131, 182, 197, 200, 207, 225, 239, 352
  Baptist 193–5, 196, 335, 339, 350, 351
  Catholicism 12, 21, 23, 26, 29–43, 49, 75, 110, 181, 192–3, 235, 323, 340, 388, 435, 446, 456, 496, 607, 608, 609, 610, 613, 629, 632–3
  and censorship 606, 633, 634
  Christian 88, 106–7, 183, 184, 187, 206–7, 209–10, 214, 217, 222, 225, 226, 227, 229–30, 278, 286, 317, 330, 335, 337, 339, 350, 351, 352, 396, 423, 424, 491, 522, 590
  Christian magazines and religious presses 191, 194, 196, 198, 200, 462–3
  critiques of Quebec Catholic institutions 323, 324–5, 568, 570, 593, 595, 613, 614, 616, 633, 637, 642, 643
  fundamentalism 550, 553, 578
  hybridity 177, 506, 513, 524
  Indigenous 33–4, 74, 396, 508–9, 510, 512
  Ismaili 571, 578
  Jesuit missionaries 29–41, 121
  Judaism 300, 441–2, 450, 571, 578; *see also* Ethnic diversity: Jewish
  Mennonite 487, 488, 554
  Methodist 52–3, 54, 117, 131, 198, 224–5
  multifaith 577
  Muslim 571, 577
  Parsi 392, 565
  Presbyterian 58–9, 197, 198–200, 206, 578
  Quaker 215
  Salvation Army 207
  Sikh 550, 553
  Sufism 578
  Theosophy 213, 218
  United Church 346
  Unitrinitarianism 141
  Ursuline order 41–3, 116, 120
  Woman's Christian Temperance Union (WCTU) 208–9
Renaud, Jacques 638
  WORKS: *Le Cassé* 638
Renaud, Thérèse 594
Ricci, Nino 561, 574
  WORKS: *Lives of the Saints* 567, 574
Richards, David Adams 493
  comparison with William Faulkner 493
  and Miramichi Valley fiction 493
  and social realism 493
  WORKS: *Dancers at Night* 395; *Evening Snow Will Bring Such Peace* 493; *For Those Who Hunt the Wounded Down* 493; *Mercy Among the Children* 493; *Nights Below Station Street* 493; *River of the Brokenhearted* 493
Richardson, John 85, 106–7, 108
  on ambivalent relation between Old and New Worlds 106
  national identity theme 106
  shift in later fiction 108
  WORKS: *The Canadian Brothers* 108; *Wacousta* 106–7
Richardson, Samuel 47, 58
Richler, Mordecai 181, 291, 300–1, 326, 329, 333–4, 386, 460, 491–2, 556, 561, 568, 570
  Aboriginal Trickster figure in 485
  as critic of Quebec anti-Semitism 568
  as film script writer 301
  journalism of 492
  modernist fictional techniques in 301
  Montreal Jewish working-class fiction 300, 485, 491
  post-war European novels of 300
  as satirist and parodist 300, 485, 491
  WORKS: *The Acrobats* 300; *The Apprenticeship of Duddy Kravitz* 300, 491; *Barney's Version* 301, 329, 491; *A Choice of Enemies* 300; *Joshua Then and Now* 491; *Oh Canada! Oh Quebec! Requiem for a Divided Country* 492; *Solomon Gursky Was Here* 481, 485; *Son of a Smaller Hero* 300; *The Street* 326; *St Urbain's Horseman* 326, 491
Riel, Louis 83, 207, 208, 435, 488, 497, 607, 618, 650
Rilke, Rainer Maria 372, 424, 433
Ringuet (Philippe Panneton) 230, 292–3, 324
  WORKS: *Trente Arpents / Thirty Acres* 230, 292–3, 635
Ringwood, Gwen 403, 413, 519
  WORKS: *Maya, or Lament for Harmonica* 519; *Still Stands the House* 403, 413
Rivard, Yvon 644
  WORKS: *Les Silences du courbeau* 644
Roberts, Charles G. D. 122, 128, 137, 166, 173–7, 191
  animal stories of 134, 136, 166, 167, 173–7
  cross-border publishing 170, 173
  early career of 129
  and French Canadian translations 122, 134
  historiography in 122
  humanist ethic of 174
  international recognition of 136, 137, 142
  poetry of 133, 135, 141, 226

Roberts, Charles G. D. (cont.)
    and Young Canada literary movement 129–30
    WORKS: *Ave: An Ode for the Shelley Centenary* 131; *The Book of the Rose* 141; *Canadians of Old* (translation) 3, 122, 127; *Divers Tones* 131; "Do Seek Their Meat from God" 176; *Earth's Enigmas: A Volume of Stories* ("Strayed") 134, 166, 169, 173, 175; "Going Over (the Somme 1919)" 226; *A History of Canada* 122; *The Kindred of the Wild* ("The King of the Marmozekel," "The Lord of the Air," "When Twilight Falls on the Stump Lots") 136, 174, 175; "King of Beasts" 175; *New York Nocturnes and other Poems* 141; *Orion and Other Poems* 128, 131–2, 136; "The Outlook for Literature" 130; "The Poet Is Bidden to Manhattan Island" 133; *Songs of the Common Day* 131, 135, 137; "Tantramar Revisited" 133; *The Watchers of the Trails* 174
Robertson, Lisa 436, 437
    WORKS: *Debbie: An Epic* 436; *The Weather* 436
Robertson, Margaret Murray 206
Roberval, Jean-François de La Roque, Sieur de 120
Robin, Régine 567, 645
    WORKS: *La Québécoite* 570
Robinson, Eden 390, 396, 515
    Gothic dimension of 515
    on importance of landscape in Haisla culture 515
    writing against Native stereotypes 515
    WORKS: *Monkey Beach* 515; *Traplines* 398, 515
Robinson, Harry 396, 439, 508, 510, 514
    collaboration with musicologist 510
    Coyote tales 514
    Creation stories 514
    influence on Thomas King 510
    Okanagan storyteller 510
    WORKS: *Write It on Your Heart: The Epic World of an Okanagan Storyteller* 510
Rochon, Esther 648
Rogers, Charles Gordon 140
Rollin, Henri 608
    WORKS: *Aurore, l'enfant martyre* (co-authored with Léon Petitjean) 608; *roman du terroir / roman de la terre* 292, 293, 630, 633–4, 638
romance 48, 52, 63, 106–7, 108–9, 111, 113, 114, 117, 119, 127, 174, 177, 194, 227, 234, 263, 271, 291, 294, 299, 346, 374, 378, 384, 385, 389, 451

Romney, George 55
Ronfard, Jean-Pierre 624
    and Nouveau Théâtre Expérimental 624, 625
    WORKS: *Don Quichotte* 625; *Les Mille et une nuits* 625; *Le Titanic* 626; *Vie et mort du Roi Boiteux* 626
Rooke, Leon 388
    WORKS: *Cry Evil* 388; *Who Do You Love?* 388
Rose, George MacLean 186, 190
Rose, Richard 406
Rosenblatt, Joe 426
Rosenfarb, Chava 300–1, 326, 559
    transnationalism of 327–8
    works in translation by 327
    Yiddish writer 326, 327–8
    WORKS: *Aroys fun gan Eiden* 327; "Edgia's Revenge" 327; "The Greenhorn" 314
Ross, Alex 77
    WORKS: *Adventures of the First Settlers on the Oregon or Columbia River* 77
Ross, Alexander Milton 163
    WORKS: *The Birds of Canada* 163
Ross, Ian 530
    political romantic comedies by 530
    social satire of 530
    WORKS: *fareWel* 530; *The Gap* 530
Ross, Sinclair 291, 295–6
    alienated artist figure 296
    gender ambiguity in 296
    modernist novelist 295
    short stories by 382, 383, 386
    WORKS: *As For Me and My House* 291, 295–6; *The Lamp at Noon and Other Stories* 382; "One's a Heifer" 386; "The Painted Door" 386
Rousseau, Edmond 120
    WORKS: *Les Exploits d'Iberville* 120
Rousseau, Jean-Jacques 50
    WORKS: *Du contrat social* 50; *Émile* 50
Routier, Simone 603
    WORKS: *L'Immortel Adolescent* 603
Rowan, John 154–7
    empathy with wild animals 156
    on Canada–US differences 155
    utilitarianism of 156–7
    WORKS: *The Emigrant and Sportsman in Canada* 154
Roy, André 601, 603, 619
    WORKS: *L'Accélérateur d'intensité* 603
Roy, Camille 325, 634
Roy, Gabrielle 293–4, 303, 324, 636
    Expo participation by 320, 321–2
    feminine perspective of 293

on rural life 294
on Second World War 293, 636
on urban realism 293, 635
WORKS: *Bonheur d'occasion / The Tin Flute* 293–4, 635–6; Introductory Essay to *Terre des hommes / Man and His World* 321–2; *La Petite Poule d'eau* 294; *Rue Deschambault / Street of Riches* 294
Roy, Jean-Guy 618
WORKS: *Frenchie* (co-authored with Irène Mahé) 618
Roy, Régis 609
Royal Commission on Bilingualism and Biculturalism 320, 322
Rubio, Mary 264
Ruders, Poul 363
Ruffo, Armand Garnet 479, 507, 508, 511
on Grey Owl and family history 511
Ojibwa perspective on colonial history of 511
WORKS: *At Geronimo's Grave* 511; *Grey Owl: The Mystery of Archie Belaney* 511; *Opening in the Sky* 511; "Poem for Duncan Campbell Scott" 511
Rule, Jane 328–9
WORKS: *Desert of the Heart* 329; *The Young in One Another's Arms* 329–30
Runeberg, Johan Ludvig 134
Rushdie, Salman 563, 571
Ruskin, John 162
Russell, Henrietta 135
Ryerson Press, 370, 382
Ryga, George 408, 519, 521, 528, 561
WORKS: *The Ecstasy of Rita Joe* 408, 519

Saba, Ann 472
Safdie, Moshe 318
Sagard, Gabriel 11, 16, 18, 20
WORKS: *Grand voyage du pays des Hurons* 11
Sainte Marie, Buffy 502
Sakamoto, Kerri 561, 567, 572
Salinger, J. D. 66
Sallans, G. Herbert 235–6, 294
WORKS: *Little Man* 235–6, 294
Salutin, Rick 405, 470
WORKS: *The Farmers' Revolt* 405
Salverson, Laura Goodman 561
WORKS: *The Viking Heart* 561
Sanderson, Steve Keewatin 466 (illustration), 467
Sangster, Charles 132
Sanguinet, Simon 117
Sarah, Robyn 431, 437
Saskatchewan Native Theatre 534

Satin, Mark 329
WORKS: (ed.) *Manual for Draft-Age Immigrants to Canada* 329
satire 52–3, 56–7, 58–62, 63–5, 166, 181, 191, 212–13, 294, 295, 300–1, 363, 412, 415, 417–18, 434, 468, 469–71, 491, 492, 513, 519, 525, 529, 530, 586, 609, 614, 615, 618
Saunders, Margaret Marshall 191, 195, 196–7, 217
animal stories of 197, 217
WORKS: *Beautiful Joe* 196, 217; *The House of Armour* 217; *Nita: The Story of an Irish Setter* 207, 217; *Princess Sukey: The Story of a Pigeon and Her Human Friends* 207, 217
Savard, Félix-Antoine 314, 634
WORKS: *Menaud, maître draveur* 314
Savoie, Jacques 649
WORKS: *Un fin passage* 649; *Une histoire de cœur* 649; *Petites difficultés d'existence* 649; *Les Portes tournantes* 649
Savoie, Paul 600
WORKS: *Salamandre* 600
Sawyer, Robert 384–5
Schafer, R. Murray 430
Schlöndorff, Volker 363
Schoemperlen, Diane 399
WORKS: *Red Plaid Skirt* 399
Schoolcraft, Henry 91, 92
Schoolcraft, Jane Johnston 91, 92, 93
Schroeder, Adam Lewis 381, 395
WORKS: *Kingdom of Monkeys* 395
science fiction 385, 472, 524, 648
Scofield, Gregory 439, 503, 514–15
on Cree language and song 515
gay writing of 515
on interconnections between poetry and song 514
on Métis identity 514
WORKS: *I Knew Two Métis Women: The Lives of Dorothy Scofield and Georgiana Houle Young* 514; *Love Medicine and One Song* 515; *Thunder Through My Veins* 503
Scott, Agnes (Amaryllis) 211
Scott, Duncan Campbell 130, 166, 177–81, 479, 511
cross-border publishing by 177
international recognition of 136–7
poetry of 130, 142, 226
short fiction of 134, 177
short story cycle 166
on transition to modernity 179
traditional values of 179

Scott, Duncan Campbell (cont.)
  WORKS: "Charcoal" ("Star Blanket") 177; *The Circle of Affection and Other Pieces in Prose and Verse* 142; *The Green Cloister* 142; "The Height of Land" 133; "How Uncle David Rouse Made His Will" 177; *In the Village of Viger* 134, 166, 167, 177, 178, 179–81; *Labor and the Angel* 142; "The Little Milliner" 177, 179–81; *The Magic House and Other Poems* 131; *New World Lyrics and Ballads* 142; "Paul Farlotte" 181; "The Piper of Arll" 137; "The Reed Player" 136; "To a Canadian Aviator" 226; "To a Canadian Lad Killed in the War" 226
Scott, Frank R. 275, 279, 315, 320, 427, 434
  first poetry book 286
  Fortnightly Poems 279, 281
  and McGill group 275, 280–1, 434
  as satiric poet 434
  WORKS: "The Canadian Authors Meet" 279, 285; *Collected Poems* 433; "The Indians Speak at Expo 67" 315; *Overture* 279, 286
Scott, Frederick George 131, 133, 137, 225
  WORKS: "The Crown of Empire" 225; "In the Winter Woods" 133; *My Lattice and Other Poems* 137; "On the Rue du Bois" 225; *The Soul's Quest and Other Poems* 131
Scott, Peter Dale 434
  WORKS: *Coming to Jakarta: A Poem about Terror* 434; *Listening to the Candle: A Poem on Impulse* 434; *Minding the Darkness: A Poem for the Year 2000* 434
Scott, Sir Walter 480, 481, 629, 631
Scribner's Magazine 171, 177, 382
Sears, Djanet 418, 562
  WORKS: *The Adventures of a Black Girl in Search of God* 418; *Afrika Solo* 418
Secord, Laura 119
Séguin, Alice (Mariline) 649
  WORKS: *Le Flambeau sacré* 649
Sellars, Robert 121
  WORKS: *Hemlock: A Tale of the War of 1812* 121
Sellyn, Nathan 400
  WORKS: *Indigenous Beast* 400
Selvadurai, Shyam 561, 564, 565
  WORKS: *Funny Boy* 576
Selvon, Sam 564, 566
Senécal, Eva 603
  WORKS: *La Course dans l'aurore* 603

Senior, Olive 381, 562
Sen'klip Theatre 534
Seremba, George 562
Service, Robert 226
  WORKS: "Pilgrims" 226
Seth (Gregory Gallant) 472, 476
  WORKS: *Bannock, Beans and Black Tea* 476; *Clyde Fans* 476; *It's a Good life, If You Don't Weaken* 476; *Palooka Ville* 476; *Wimbledon Green: The Greatest Comic Book Collector in the World* 476
Seton, Ernest Thompson 163, 173, 195
  WORKS: *Wild Animals I Have Known* 173
settlement narratives 87–103
  colored settlement 87–8
  immigrant handbooks 87–8
  long poems 88
  major women writers of 89–103
  women's diaries and letters 88–9, 94, 98, 103
Seven Years' War 47
Sewell, Anna 196
  WORKS: *Black Beauty* 196
Shadd, Mary Ann 88
  address to Black American slaves 88
  first Black woman author in Upper Canada 88
  influence of William Cattermole on 88
  WORKS: *A Plea for Emigration: or, Notes of Canada West in its Moral, Social, and Political Aspect: with Suggestions Respecting Mexico, West Indies, and Vancouver's Island for the Information of Colored Emigrants* 87–8
Shakespeare, William 340, 346, 375, 403, 451, 452, 456, 458, 479, 525, 526
Shapiro, Lionel 294
  WORKS: *The Sixth of June* 294
Shaw, George Bernard 333
Shawm, William 370, 371, 372
Shelley, Percy Bysshe 132
Sherman, Jason 406
Shields, Carol 357, 359, 360, 376–80, 565
  and biographical genre 376, 377–8, 379
  as essayist and critic 377, 378–9
  as playwright 376
  as poet 376
  postmodern features in 377, 379
  on storytelling 377
  and white middle-class domestic fiction 376, 379
  and women's perspectives 378, 379, 380
  on women's romance fiction 378

WORKS: biography: *Jane Austen* 376, 379;
  Susanna Moodie: Voice and Vision 376;
  essays and anthology: "Arriving Late:
  Starting Over" 378–9; "Narrative
  Hunger and the Overflowing
  Cupboard" 377; co-ed.: *Dropped
  Threads*, 1 and 2 376; fiction: *Larry's
  Party* 376, 377, 378; *The Republic of Love*
  376, 378; *Small Ceremonies* 376, 377, 379,
  380; *The Stone Diaries* 376, 377–8;
  Swann: A Mystery 376, 378, 379; *Unless*
  376, 379–80; poetry: *Intersect* 376; *Others*
  376; short fiction: *Collected Stories*
  (including "Segue") 376–7, 380;
  Dressing Up for the Carnival 379; *The
  Orange Fish* 379; *Various Miracles* 378, 397
Shikatani, Gerry 561, 572
Shimazaki, Aki 567–8, 578
short story cycle 166, 177–8, 181, 385–, 391–3
Shuster, Joseph 460
Silvera, Makeda 564, 576
Sim, Dave 472, 475
  cross-genre experimentation 475, 476
  as graphic storyteller 475
  intertextuality in 475, 476
  WORKS: *Cerebus* 475
Simard, Jean 233
  WORKS: *Mon fils pourtant heureux* 233
Simard, Rémy 473
Simcoe, Elizabeth 88
Simcoe, John Graves 485
Sime, Jessie Georgina 229
  WORKS: "Munitions!" 229
Simic, Charles 437
Simon, Lorne 512
  WORKS: *Stones and Switches* 512
Simon, Sherry 326, 451–2
Simpson, Anne 432, 438
  WORKS: *Loop* 438
Simpson, Frances Ramsay 79
Simpson, Sir George 78, 81
  WORKS: *Fur Trade and Empire: George
  Simpson's Journal* 78; *Journal of
  Occurrences in the Athabasca Department
  1820 and 1821* 78
Simpson, Thomas 86
  WORKS: *Narrative of the Discovery of the
  North Coast of America* 86
Sinclair, Bertrand 232
  WORKS: *Burned Bridges* 232; *The Inverted
  Pyramid* 232
Sister Vision publishing 564
Škvorecký, Josef 559

Sleeper-Smith, Susan 68
Slipperjack, Ruby 505–6, 508, 515
  WORKS: *Honour the Sun* 505; *Silent
  Words* 506
Smallwood, Joe 483, 494
Smart, Elizabeth 248, 266–7
  and George Barker 267
  journals of 267
  and modernist life-writing 266–7
  WORKS: *By Grand Central Station* 266–7,
  299; *Necessary Secrets* 267; *On the Side of
  Angels* 267
Smart, Patricia 632
Smith, Arthur J. M. 275, 302, 305, 333, 423, 427,
  432, 433
  and *The Book of Canadian Poetry* 284, 287,
  303–4
  early essays on modernism by 278
  later essays and editorial work by 287, 432
  on "native" and "cosmopolitan" 287, 303
  and *New Provinces* 303
  poetry of 279–80, 286, 433
  WORKS: (ed.) *The Book of Canadian Poetry:
  A Critical and Historical Anthology* 287;
  The Classic Shade: Selected Poems 433;
  "Contemporary Poetry" 278, 286;
  "Hamlet in Modern Dress" 278; "The
  Lonely Land" 279, 285; (ed.) *Masks of
  Poetry: Canadian Critics on Canadian
  Verse* 432; *News of the Phoenix* 286;
  "Nightfall" 280; "A Note on
  Metaphysical Poetry" 281; "The
  Sorcerer" 279; "Symbolism in Poetry"
  274, 278, 279, 282
Smith, Adam 51
  WORKS: *Inquiry into the Nature and Causes
  of the Wealth of Nations* 51; *The Theory of
  Moral Sentiments* 51
Smith, Goldwin 191
Smith, Ray 388
  WORKS: *Cape Breton Is the Thought Control
  Centre of Canada* 388
Smith, Ron 393
  WORKS: *What Men Know about Women* 393
Smith, Russell 393
  WORKS: *Young Men* 393
Smythe, Albert E. 131
Snow, Michael 430
Solie, Karen 437
  WORKS: *Short Haul Engine* 437
Solway, David 437
Sontag, Susan 490
  WORKS: "Fascinating Fascism" 490

Soucy, Gaétan 646
  WORKS: *La Petite Fille qui aimait trop les allumettes* 646
Souster, Raymond 242, 302, 305, 307, 308
  WORKS: "Vimy Ridge" 242; *When We Were Young* 307
Spencer, Hanna 537, 539, 540
  WORKS: *Hanna's Diary* 537
Spenser, Edmund 296, 303, 310
Spettigue, Douglas 248
Sprung, Guy 407
Staines, David 432
Starnino, Carmine 437
Stead, Robert 225, 228, 248, 255, 295
  cover illustration of novel 258
  on modernity and masculine identity 257–8
  and prairie realism 295
  WORKS: *Grain (A Romance of the True West)* 256, 257–8; "Kitchener of Khartoum" 225
Stefansson, Vilhjalmur 86
Steffler, John 432
Stein, Gertrude 265, 399, 436, 452
Steinfeld J. J. 395
  WORKS: *Dancing at the Club Holocaust* 395
Stenson, Fred 77
  WORKS: *The Trade* 77
Stephansson, Stephan 559
Sterling, Shirley 512
  WORKS: *My Name Is Seepeetza* 512
Stesichoros 451
Stevens, James 508, 510
  WORKS: *Sacred Legends of the Sandy Lake Cree*, revised as *Sacred Legends* 510
Stewart, Alexander Charles 140
Stewart, Frances 89
Stoker, Bram 480
Storey, Raymond 407
  WORKS: *The Last Bus* 407
Story, Gertrude 398
  WORKS: *The Way to Always Dance* 398
Stowe, Harriet Beecher 206
Strange, Kathleen 248, 260–2
  and multiethnicity 262
  photoportrait of 261
  WORKS: *The Story of a Modern Pioneer* 260–2; *With the West in Her Eyes* 260–2
Stratford, Philip 325
Strickland, Agnes 89, 95, 99, 100, 101
Strickland, Samuel 94, 101
  WORKS: *Twenty-Seven Years in Canada West* 100

Stringer, Arthur 191, 195, 196, 202–3, 273
  in America 202
  as Hollywood screenwriter 203
  poetry of 202
  popular fiction of 202–3
  WORKS: *Open Water* 273; *The Prairie Wife* 202; *The Wine of Life* 202; *The Wire Tappers* 202
Suknaski, Andrew 561
Sun-Kyung, Yi 546, 550
  WORKS: *Inside the Hermit Kingdom: A Memoir* 547–8
Sutherland, John 287, 290, 305
  WORKS: (ed.) *Other Canadians: An Anthology of the New Poetry in Canada 1940-46* 287
Suzuki, David 552, 553, 555
  on environmentalism 546, 555
  and First Nations 555
  on Japanese Canadians' relocation in Second World War 545, 546
  and popular TV ecological series 539, 546, 555
  and postethnic position 539
  WORKS: *David Suzuki: The Autobiography* 545, 546, 552; *Metamorphosis* 545, 546, 552
Svendsen, Linda 386, 398
  WORKS: *Marine Life* 398
Swan, Mary 238
  WORKS: *The Deep* 238
Swan, Susan 483
  WORKS: *The Biggest Modern Woman of the World* 481, 483, 484
Swanton, John 440
Sweatman, Margaret 485–6
  and First World War 486
  generic experiments in 486
  historical fiction and myths 486
  WORKS: *Fox* 484; *When Alice Lay Down with Peter* 485–6
Swift, Jonathan 61, 363, 372
Swift, Todd 437
Swinburne, Algernon Charles 133, 216
Symons, Scott 328
  and Expo 67 328
  on gay topography of Montreal 328
  WORKS: *Combat Journal for Place d'Armes: A Personal Narrative* 317, 328

Taché, Joseph-Charles 631
  WORKS: *Foresters et voyageurs* 631
Tallman, Warren 427

Index

Talonbooks 387
Tamarack 394
Tardivel, Jules-Paul 632
  WORKS: *Pour la patrie* 632
Tarragon Theatre 406, 410, 418
Tassinari, Lamberto 567
Tayler, Margaret
  WORKS: (co-ed.) *The Galt Cook Book* 161
Taylor, Charles 558, 569
Taylor, Drew Hayden 396, 513, 528–30
  on comedy in Native storytelling 396, 513
  and comic satire 529
  on hybridity 529
  tragicomedies of 530
  Trickster aesthetics in 529
  youth-centered dramas of 530
  WORKS: drama: *400 Kilometres* 530; *alterNatives* 529; *The Baby Blues* 529; *Berlin Blues* 529; *The Bootlegger Blues* 529; *The Boy in the Treehouse* 530; *Buz'Gem Blues* 529; *Education is Our Right* 530; *Fearless Warriors* 396; *Girl Who Loved Her Horses* 530; *In a World Created by a Drunken God* 530; *Me Funny* 396; *Only Drunks and Children Tell the Truth* 530; *Someday* 530; *Toronto at Dreamer's Rock* 530; life-writing: *Funny, You Don't Look Like One: Observations from a Blue-Eyed Ojibway* 513
Taylor, Graeme 269
Taylor, Timothy 298–9, 384, 400
  WORKS: *Silent Cruiser* 400; *Stanley Park* 298–9
Tecumseh 113, 114, 115–16, 118, 121
Teesri Duniya Theatre 417
Tekakwitha, Catherine (Kateri) 31–2, 38, 442
Templeton, Ty 472
Tennyson, Alfred Lord 131, 340
Tetso, John 502
  WORKS: *Trapping Is My Life* 502
Textes poétiques du Canada français (TPCP) 583–4, 588
Théâtre de Société 606, 630
Théâtre des Cuisines 616
Théâtre du Nouveau Monde 610
Théâtre du Rideau Vert 610, 612
Théâtre Expérimental des Femmes 616
Théâtre National 608
Theatre Network, Edmonton 407–8
Theatre Passe Muraille 405–6, 520, 522, 525, 526
Théoret, France 601

Thériault, Yves 637–8
  on Canada's Native populations 637–8
  on the far north 638
  WORKS: *Agaguk* 637–8
Theytus Books 504, 505, 508
Thibaudeau, Colleen 424, 431
Thibodeau, Serge Patrice 598
Thien, Madeleine 393
  WORKS: *Simple Recipes* 393
Thiessen, Vern 420
Thomas, Audrey 381, 385, 389, 390–1, 543, 577
  African writings of 389
  Atlantic Monthly Prize 389
  fascination with language 390
  on gender and social politics 390–1
  WORKS: *Intertidal Life* 390; *Ladies and Escorts* 391; *Latakia* 390; *Mrs Blood* 390; *The Path of Totality* 391; *Ten Green Bottles* 385, 389, 390
Thomas, Dylan 423
Thomas, Lilian Beynon 221
Thomas, Nigel 576
Thompson, David 73–5
  on Aboriginal people 74
  apprenticeship with Hudson's Bay Company 73
  posthumous publication of 73
  structure of travel narratives 73–5
  transfer to North West Company 73, 74
  wildlife descriptions 74, 76, 82
  WORKS: *David Thompson's Narrative of his Explorations in Western American* 73–5
Thompson, Judith 403, 406, 410
  WORKS: *Capture Me* 410; *The Crackwalker* 410; *I Am Yours* 410; *Lion in the Streets* 410; *Perfect Pie* 410; *Sled* 410; *White Biting Dog* 410
Thompson, Paul 405, 521
Thomson, E. W. 169, 171
  WORKS: *Old Man Savarin* 169
Thomson, R. H. 241
Thoreau, Henry David 58, 134, 253
Thwaites, Reuben Gold 29, 31
Tibo (Gilles Thibault) 474
TISH magazine and TISH poets 428, 429, 447
Todorov, Tzvetan 9–10
Toews, Miriam 561
Toomer, Jean 457
Topping, Earle 370
Toronto Free Theatre 407
Traill, Catharine Parr (née Strickland) 80, 89, 90, 147–50
  attitudes to Aboriginal people 96–7, 150

Traill, Catharine Parr (née Strickland) (cont.)
  children's literature by 94, 96, 97
  collaboration with Fitzgibbon 148
  early London career 89
  emigration to Canada 89
  female settlers' guides by 94–6
  later career of 97
  letters of 94, 98
  literary career in Canada 94
  London publication 95, 96
  and natural history 96, 148, 150
  periodical publications by 96
  WORKS: *The Backwoods of Canada* 90, 94–6; *Canadian Crusoes* 96, 97; *Canadian Wild Flowers* 96, 148–50; *Cot and Cradle Stories* 94; *Female Emigrant's Guide* 96; "Forest Gleanings" 96; *Lady Mary and Her Nurse* 96; *Studies of Plant Life in Canada* 96; *The Young Emigrants* 94
Traill, Thomas 94
transculturalism 421, 536–55, 567, 650
translation
  Aboriginal languages 55, 56, 93, 96, 305, 440
  English-French / French-English 3, 106, 114, 115, 122, 269, 290, 292, 293, 302–3, 314, 321, 322, 323–4, 325, 438, 447, 463, 533, 568, 625, 626, 631, 636, 643, 648
  language politics 302–3, 322
  other languages 197, 327–8, 559
transnationalism 195, 327–8, 447, 450, 527, 549, 552–3, 565, 566, 571, 648
travel writing 10–11, 47, 67–86
  adventure tourism 82–3
  Far North 83–5
  journeys "home" in late C20 and C21 5, 539, 541, 545, 546, 548, 549–50
  visual documentation 82, 85
  women's travel narratives 90–3, 210, 212–14, 332, 577
  see also exploration narratives; fur traders' journals
Tremblay, Larry 623, 627
  WORKS: *The Dragonfly of Chicoutimi* 623; *La Hache* 623
Tremblay, Lise 647
  WORKS: *L'Hiver de pluie* 647
Tremblay, Michel 316, 320–1, 328, 406, 416, 612–14, 642, 651
  and dramatic structure 613
  and *joual* 612
  and *le nouveau théâtre québécois* 612
  on sexuality and the Catholic Church 613

  WORKS: drama: *Albertine, en cinq temps* 613; *Un Ange cornu des ailes de toile* 321; *Les Belles-Sœurs* 521, 612–13, 642; *Bonjour, là, bonjour* 613; *Le Cahier rouge* 316, 330; *Cycle des Belles-Sœurs* 613; *Damnée Manon, sacrée Sandra* 613; *La Duchesse de Langeais* 613; *La Maison suspendue* 623; *À toi, pour toujours, ta Marie-Lou* 613; *Le Vrai Monde?* 614; fiction: *Chroniques du Plateau Mont-Royal* 613, 642; *La Grosse Femme d'à-côté est enceinte* 642; *Thérèse et Pierrette à l'école des St-Anges* 642
Trobriand, Régis de 108, 113
  WORKS: *Le Rebelle: Histoire Canadienne* 108–9
Troupe du Jour, Saskatoon 618, 619
Trudeau, Pierre (Prime Minister) 405, 468, 469, 477, 500
Trudel, Sylvain 647
  WORKS: *Le Souffle de l'harmattan* 647; *Terre du roi Christian* 647
Trussler, Michael 393
  WORKS: *Encounters* 393
TSAR publishing 564
Tunooniq Theatre 534
Turcotte, Élise 603
  WORKS: *La Terre est ici* 603
Turgenev, Ivan 178
Twain, Mark 61, 65
Tyrell, J. B. 73

Uguay, Marie 602–3
  WORKS: *Autoportraits* 602; *Journal* 602; *L'Outre-vie* 602; *Poèmes* 603; *Signes et rumeurs* 602
Umezawa, Rui 561, 572
United Church of Canada 262
United Empire Loyalists 52–4, 62
  Aboriginal Loyalists 54, 55
  Bailey, Jacob 52–4
  Bartlett, W. S. 53
  Black Loyalists 54; *see also* Brant, Joseph
  Kirby, William 54
  Lampman, Archibald 54, 190
  Mohawk Bible 52–3
  Odell, Jonathan 52, 53
  Stansbury, Joseph 52
UniTheatre 619
Universal Declaration of Human Rights 290
University of Toronto Quarterly 302, 309, 311, 347–8, 424
Uppal, Priscila 579
Urquhart, Jane 495–6
  on Aboriginal legends 496

mythopoeic fictional mode of 495, 496
supernatural in 496
WORKS: *Away* 481–2, 496; *A Map of Glass* 496; *The Stone Carvers* 238; *The Underpainter* 238, 496; *The Whirlpool* 495–6

Valgardson, W. D. 395
WORKS: *Bloodflowers* 395
Vallières, Pierre 323–4, 333, 563
WORKS: *Nègres blancs d'Amérique* / *White Niggers of America* 322, 323–4
Van Camp, Richard 515
WORKS: *The Lesser Blessed* 515
Van Herk, Aritha 489–90
cross-over between realism and myth in 490
exploration of prairie and Northern space in 490
feminist revision of Old World myths by 489
WORKS: *Judith* 489; *No Fixed Address* 489; *The Tent Peg* 489
Van Kirk, Sylvia 68, 79
Van Schendel, Michel 594
Van Toorn, Peter 437
Vancouver, George 67, 84
Vanderhaeghe, Guy 381, 386, 393–4, 484, 492–3
and realism 492–3
and Wild West myths 493
WORKS: *The Englishman's Boy* 492–3; *The Last Crossing* 482, 493; *Man Descending* 393; *Things as They Are?* 393; *The Trouble with Heroes* 393
Vanier, Denis 601
Varma, Rahul 417, 561
WORKS: *Counter Offence* 417; *Bhopal* 417
Varo, Remedios 308
Vassanji, M. G. 395, 546, 557, 562, 563, 564, 565, 566, 571, 577, 578
WORKS: *Amriika* 565; *The Assassin's Song* 578; *The Book of Secrets* 565, 574; *The Gunny Sack* 574; *The In-Between World of Vikram Lall* 565, 575; *No New Land* 565; *A Place Within: Rediscovering India* 548
Vaughn-James, Martin 468
WORKS: *The Cage* 468; *Elephanta* 468; *The Park* 468; *The Projector* 468
Verdecchia, Guillermo 406, 418
on border zones 418
collaboration with Marcus Youssef and Camyar Chai 418

WORKS: *The Adventures of Ali and Ali and the Axes of Evil* 418; *Fronteras Americanas* 418–19; *A Line in the Sand* 418
Verret, Jocelyne 619
WORKS: *Comme on est différente, comme on se ressemble* 619
Veuillot, Louis 632
Vézina, Medjé 603
WORKS: *Chaque heure a son visage* 603
Vietnam war 329–30, 469, 477, 502
Vigneault, Gilles 383
WORKS: *Tales sur la pointe des pieds* 383
Vigneault, Guillaume 647
WORKS: *Chercher le vent* 647
Villemaire, Yolande 642
WORKS: *La Vie en prose* 642
Virgo, Sean 400
WORKS: *White Lies and Other Fictions* 400
visual arts
Aboriginal 319, 467, 532
cross-overs between poetry and painting/book illustrations 296, 297, 308, 310, 510
eighteenth- and nineteenth-century landscape sketches 85, 92
experiments with graphic representation 429, 430
First World War artists 231, 240
Group of Seven 283
modernist photographic portraits 266, 270
representations of Aboriginal people 21, 82, 466
see also comics; nature writing: visual documentation
Vitéz, György 559
Voaden, Herman 403
WORKS: *Ascend as the Sun* 403; *Hill-Land* 403; *Rocks* 403
Vonarburg, Elisabeth 648

Waddington, Miriam 302, 303, 305, 307, 331, 422, 432
WORKS: *Apartment Seven: Essays Selected and New* 307; *Green World* 307; "Jacques Cartier in Toronto" 422; *The Last Landscape* 422
Wade, Mason 314
Wagamese, Richard 514
WORKS: *Keeper 'n Me* 514
Wah, Fred 428, 449, 561
WORKS: *Diamond Grill* 449; "This Dendrite Map: Father / Mother Haibun" 449
Walcott, Derek 439

Walker, David 294
  WORKS: *The Pillar* 294
Walker, George F. 406, 407, 410, 412–13
  black comedies of 407
  social satire in 412
  on struggle for psychic survival 412
  WORKS: *Better Living* 412; *East End* trilogy 412; *The Prince of Naples* 406, 407; *Problem Child* 412; *Suburban Motel* 406, 407, 412
Wallace, David Foster 399
Walter, Felix 280
Wangersky, Russell 393
  WORKS: *The Hour of Bad Decisions* 393
War Exchange Conservation Act (1940) 463
War Measures Act (1970) 315, 469
Waterston, Elizabeth 264
Watmough, David 382
Watson, Sheila 296, 297–8
  Coyote figure in 297
  first major modernist prose writer 297
  as mythographer 297
  The Waste Land influence on 297
  WORKS: *Deep Hollow Creek* 297; *The Double Hook* 296, 297, 458; *A Father's Kingdom* 399
Watson, Wilfred 297, 344
  WORKS: *Friday's Child* 297
Waugh, Evelyn 279
  WORKS: *Brideshead Revisited* 279
Wayman, Tom 427
Weaver, Robert 370, 384
  WORKS: (ed.) *Canadian Short Stories* 384
Webb, Phyllis 306, 427–8
  American poetic influences on 427–8
  Montreal influences on 427
  Recovery of women's lost voices in 427
  west coast influences on 427
  WORKS: *Even Your Right Eye* 309; *Naked Poems* 427; *The Sea Is Also a Garden* 427
Weber, Carl 50
Weber, Max 48
Webster, Barry 400
  WORKS *The Sound of All Flesh* 400
Weil, Simone 435
Welsh, Christine 80
  WORKS: *Women in the Shadows* 80
Wetherald, Agnes Ethelwyn 139, 168
Wetherell, J. E. 138
  WORKS (ed.) *Later Canadian Poems* 138–9
Wharton, Thomas 381, 399
  WORKS *Icefields* 482; *The Logogryph* 399; *Salamander* 480–1, 482

Whitaker, Muriel 241
  WORKS: (ed.) *Great Canadian War Stories* 241
White, Hayden 30, 33, 40
White, Portia 458
Whitman, Walt 135, 145
Wickwire, Wendy 510
Wiebe, Rudy 487–9, 553, 554–5, 556, 561
  on Aboriginal peoples and history 487–8, 570
  on fiction and history 488–9
  on Mennonite heritage 487, 488, 554
  on Métis history 488
  on multiple sources for memoir 555
  and relation to Canadian land 537
  WORKS: *The Blue Mountains of China* 488; *A Discovery of Strangers* 487; *First and Vital Candle* 487; *My Lovely Enemy* 488; *Of This Earth: A Mennonite Boyhood in the Boreal Forest* 554; *Peace Shall Destroy Many* 488; *The Scorched-Wood People* 488; 488; *A Stolen Life: The Journey of a Cree Woman* 487; *Sweeter Than All the World* 488; *The Temptations of Big Bear* 488; *Where Is the Voice Coming From?* 399
Wilde, Oscar 475
wilderness 82–3, 95, 98, 102, 144, 150, 151, 152, 166, 167, 171, 172, 174, 175, 176, 177, 206, 232, 296–7, 298–9, 361, 364, 374, 382, 399, 402, 458, 499
Wilkinson, Sheila 302, 305, 309
  WORKS: *The Hangman Ties the Holly* 309
Willard, Frances 209
Williams, William Carlos 269, 423
Willis, Jane 502
  WORKS: *Geniesh: An Indian Girlhood* 502
Wilson, Ethel 298
  on British Columbia landscape 298
  feminine versions of heroic quest 298
  WORKS: *Hetty Dorval* 298; *Mrs Golightly and Other Stories* 382; *Swamp Angel* 298
Wilson, Robert Rawdon 400
  WORKS: *Boundaries* 400
Windley, Carol 399
  WORKS: *Visible Light* 399
Winter, Michael 393
  WORKS: *One Last Good Look* 393
Wiseman, Adele 300, 561
  WORKS: *The Sacrifice* 300
Withrow, W.H. 117–18
  WORKS: *The Pioneer Preacher* 117–18
Wittgenstein, Ludwig 387

Wollstonecraft, Mary 50, 51
  WORKS: *A Vindication of the Rights of Woman* 51
woman suffrage / suffragists 54, 209, 210, 211, 218–19, 220, 221–2, 260, 410
  Woman's Christian Temperance Union (WCTU) 208, 209
women journalists 204–5, 211, 212–15, 218–19, 221–2
  Canadian Women's Press Club 205
  E. Cora Hind as pre-eminent crop forecaster in North America 222
  Kit Coleman as first woman war correspondent 214
  Sara Jeannette Duncan as pioneer woman journalist 211
Wong, Jan 546, 550
  WORKS: *Red China Blues: My Long March from Mao to Now* 546–7
Wong-Chu, Jim 561
Wood, Joanna E. 168, 216
  women's social problem novels by 216
  WORKS: *The Untempered Wind* 216
Woodcock, George 332, 333, 427
Woolverton, Linus 158–9
  on commercial and national significance of apples 159–60
  editor of *The Canadian Horticulturalist* 158, 159, 160, (illustration)
  producer of "Woolverton Apple" 158–9
Wordsworth, William 131, 132, 133
World War, First 5, 224–43, 420, 486, 537–8
  casualties 225
  Conscription Crisis 225, 290
  drama (English) 241
  drama (French) 230
  fiction (English) 227–8, 229–30, 232, 233, 235–6, 242
  fiction (French) 230, 234–5, 236
  Great War historical novels (English) 236, 237, 238–41

  Great War revival in contemporary literature (English) 237, 241–3, 405, 420, 486, 490
  memoirs 233–4, 241
  modernist critiques of 231
  and nation building 224–5, 231
  poetry (English) 225–6, 228, 229, 242, 422
  Quebec attitudes towards 230–1
  Vimy Ridge 224–5, 226, 227, 235, 238, 242
  war artists 231, 240
World War, Second
  Conscription crises 290, 639
  fiction (English) 294, 444, 447, 448, 488, 490, 492
  fiction (French) 294, 307
  and Japanese Canadians 290, 306, 331, 448, 543, 545, 572, 573
  poetry 292
  pre-war novels 294
Wright, Chester Whitney 335
Wright, Richard 374
  WORKS: *Clara Callan* 374
Wyatt, Rachel 381, 398, 403

Yates, J. Michael 387
  WORKS: *The Abstract Beast* 387
Yeats, William Butler 344
Youmans, Letitia 205–6, 208–9
  WORKS: *Campaign Echoes: The Autobiography of Mrs Letitia Youmans* 208
Young, Phyllis Brett 291, 318, 333
  WORKS: *The Torontonians* 318, 333
Young-Ing, Greg 508
Yvon, José 601

Zola, Émile 120
Zwicky, Jan 431, 434, 435
  lyric ecology of 435
  postmodern philosophical texts by 435
  WORKS: *Lyric Philosophy* 435; *Songs for Relinquishing the Earth* 431; *Wisdom and Metaphor* 435

CPSIA information can be obtained at www.ICGtesting.com
Printed in the USA
LVOW06s1247010415

R9455800001B/R94558PG432353LVX4B/4/P